Lecture Notes in Artificial Intelligence 9692

Subseries of Lecture Notes in Computer Science

More information about this series at http://www.springer.com/series/1244

Leszek Rutkowski · Marcin Korytkowski
Rafał Scherer · Ryszard Tadeusiewicz
Lotfi A. Zadeh · Jacek M. Zurada (Eds.)

Artificial Intelligence and Soft Computing

15th International Conference, ICAISC 2016
Zakopane, Poland, June 12–16, 2016
Proceedings, Part I

 Springer

Editors

Leszek Rutkowski
Częstochowa University of Technology
Częstochowa
Poland

Marcin Korytkowski
Częstochowa University of Technology
Częstochowa
Poland

Rafał Scherer
Częstochowa University of Technology
Częstochowa
Poland

Ryszard Tadeusiewicz
AGH University of Science and Technology
Kraków
Poland

Lotfi A. Zadeh
University of California
Berkeley, CA
USA

Jacek M. Zurada
University of Louisville
Louisville, KY
USA

ISSN 0302-9743   ISSN 1611-3349 (electronic)
Lecture Notes in Artificial Intelligence
ISBN 978-3-319-39377-3   ISBN 978-3-319-39378-0 (eBook)
DOI 10.1007/978-3-319-39378-0

Library of Congress Control Number: 2016939934

LNCS Sublibrary: SL7 – Artificial Intelligence

Printed on acid-free paper

This Springer imprint is published by Springer Nature
The registered company is Springer International Publishing AG Switzerland

Preface

This volume constitutes the proceedings of the 15th International Conference on Artificial Intelligence and Soft Computing, ICAISC 2016, held in Zakopane, Poland, during June 12–16, 2016. The conference was organized by the Polish Neural Network Society in cooperation with the University of Social Sciences in Łódź and the Institute of Computational Intelligence at the Częstochowa University of Technology. Previous conferences took place in Kule (1994), Szczyrk (1996), Kule (1997) and Zakopane (1999, 2000, 2002, 2004, 2006, 2008, 2010, 2012, 2013, 2014, and 2015) and attracted a large number of papers and internationally recognized speakers: Lotfi A. Zadeh, Hojjat Adeli, Rafal Angryk, Igor Aizenberg, Shun-ichi Amari, Daniel Amit, Piero P. Bonissone, Jim Bezdek, Zdzisław Bubnicki, Andrzej Cichocki, Ewa Dudek-Dyduch, Włodzisław Duch, Pablo A. Estévez, Jerzy Grzymala-Busse, Martin Hagan, Yoichi Hayashi, Akira Hirose, Kaoru Hirota, Adrian Horzyk, Eyke Hüllermeier, Hisao Ishibuchi, Er Meng Joo, Janusz Kacprzyk, Jim Keller, Laszlo T. Koczy, Tomasz Kopacz, Adam Krzyzak, James Tin-Yau Kwok, Soo-Young Lee, Derong Liu, Robert Marks, Evangelia Micheli-Tzanakou, Kaisa Miettinen, Krystian Mikołajczyk, Henning Müller, Ngoc Thanh Nguyen, Andrzej Obuchowicz, Erkki Oja, Witold Pedrycz, Marios M. Polycarpou, José C. Príncipe, Jagath C. Rajapakse, Šarunas Raudys, Enrique Ruspini, Jörg Siekmann, Roman Słowiński, Igor Spiridonov, Boris Stilman, Ponnuthurai Nagaratnam Suganthan, Ryszard Tadeusiewicz, Ah-Hwee Tan, Shiro Usui, Fei-Yue Wang, Jun Wang, Bogdan M. Wilamowski, Ronald Y. Yager, Syozo Yasui, Gary Yen, and Jacek Zurada. The aim of this conference is to build a bridge between traditional artificial intelligence techniques and so-called soft computing techniques. It was pointed out by Lotfi A. Zadeh that "soft computing (SC) is a coalition of methodologies which are oriented toward the conception and design of information/intelligent systems. The principal members of the coalition are: fuzzy logic (FL), neurocomputing (NC), evolutionary computing (EC), probabilistic computing (PC), chaotic computing (CC), and machine learning (ML). The constituent methodologies of SC are, for the most part, complementary and synergistic rather than competitive." These proceedings present both traditional artificial intelligence methods and soft computing techniques. Our goal is to bring together scientists representing both areas of research. This volume is divided into five parts:

- Neural Networks and Their Applications
- Fuzzy Systems and Their Applications
- Evolutionary Algorithms and Their Applications
- Agent Systems, Robotics and Control
- Pattern Classification

The conference attracted 343 submissions from 35 countries and after the review process, 133 papers were accepted for publication. The ICAISC 2016 hosted the workshop "Visual Information Coding Meets Machine Learning: Large-Scale Challenges" (VICML 2016) organized by:

- Marcin Korytkowski, Częstochowa University of Technology, Poland
- Krystian Mikolajczyk, Imperial College, UK
- Rafał Scherer, Częstochowa University of Technology, Poland
- Sviatoslav Voloshynovskiy, University of Geneva, Switzerland

The workshop was supported by the project "Innovative Methods of Retrieval and Indexing Multimedia Data Using Computational Intelligence Techniques" funded by the National Science Centre. I would like to thank our participants, invited speakers, and reviewers of the papers for their scientific and personal contribution to the conference. I would also like to thank all the additional reviewers for their helpful reviews.

Finally, I thank my co-workers Łukasz Bartczuk, Piotr Dziwiński, Marcin Gabryel, and Marcin Korytkowski and the conference secretary, Rafał Scherer, for their enormous efforts that helped make the conference a very successful event. Moreover, I would like to appreciate the work of Marcin Korytkowski, who designed the Internet submission system.

June 2016   Leszek Rutkowski

Organization

ICAISC 2016 was organized by the Polish Neural Network Society in cooperation with the University of Social Sciences in Łódź and the Institute of Computational Intelligence at Częstochowa University of Technology.

ICAISC Chair

Honorary Chairs

Lotfi Zadeh   University of California, USA
Hojjat Adeli   The Ohio State University, USA
Jacek Żurada   University of Louisville, USA

General Chair

Leszek Rutkowski   Częstochowa University of Technology, Poland

Co-chairs

Włodzisław Duch   Nicolaus Copernicus University, Poland
Janusz Kacprzyk   Polish Academy of Sciences, Poland
Józef Korbicz   University of Zielona Góra, Poland
Ryszard Tadeusiewicz   AGH University of Science and Technology, Poland

ICAISC Program Committee

Rafał Adamczak, Poland
Cesare Alippi, Italy
Shun-ichi Amari, Japan
Rafal A. Angryk, USA
Jarosław Arabas, Poland
Robert Babuska, The Netherlands
Ildar Z. Batyrshin, Russia
James C. Bezdek, Australia
Marco Block-Berlitz, Germany
Leon Bobrowski, Poland
Piero P. Bonissone, USA
Bernadette Bouchon-Meunier, France
Tadeusz Burczynski, Poland
Andrzej Cader, Poland
Juan Luis Castro, Spain
Yen-Wei Chen, Japan
Wojciech Cholewa, Poland
Fahmida N. Chowdhury, USA

Andrzej Cichocki, Japan
Paweł Cichosz, Poland
Krzysztof Cios, USA
Ian Cloete, Germany
Oscar Cordón, Spain
Bernard De Baets, Belgium
Nabil Derbel, Tunisia
Ewa Dudek-Dyduch, Poland
Ludmiła Dymowa, Poland
Andrzej Dzieliński, Poland
David Elizondo, UK
Meng Joo Er, Singapore
Pablo Estevez, Chile
János Fodor, Hungary
David B. Fogel, USA
Roman Galar, Poland
Alexander I. Galushkin, Russia
Adam Gaweda, USA

Sarunas Raudys, Lithuania
Olga Rebrova, Russia
Vladimir Red'ko, Russia
Raúl Rojas, Germany
Imre J. Rudas, Hungary
Enrique H. Ruspini, USA
Khalid Saeed, Poland
Dominik Sankowski, Poland
Norihide Sano, Japan
Robert Schaefer, Poland
Rudy Setiono, Singapore
Paweł Sewastianow, Poland
Jennie Si, USA
Peter Sincak, Slovakia
Andrzej Skowron, Poland
Ewa Skubalska-Rafajłowicz, Poland
Roman Słowiński, Poland
Tomasz G. Smolinski, USA
Czesław Smutnicki, Poland
Pilar Sobrevilla, Spain
Janusz Starzyk, USA
Jerzy Stefanowski, Poland
Vitomir Štruc, Slovenia
Pawel Strumillo, Poland
Ron Sun, USA
Johan Suykens, Belgium
Piotr Szczepaniak, Poland
Eulalia J. Szmidt, Poland
Przemysław Śliwiński, Poland

Adam Słowik, Poland
Jerzy Świątek, Poland
Hideyuki Takagi, Japan
Yury Tiumentsev, Russia
Vicenç Torra, Spain
Burhan Turksen, Canada
Shiro Usui, Japan
Michael Wagenknecht, Germany
Tomasz Walkowiak, Poland
Deliang Wang, USA
Jun Wang, Hong Kong, SAR China
Lipo Wang, Singapore
Zenon Waszczyszyn, Poland
Paul Werbos, USA
Slawo Wesolkowski, Canada
Sławomir Wiak, Poland
Bernard Widrow, USA
Kay C. Wiese, Canada
Bogdan M. Wilamowski, USA
Donald C. Wunsch, USA
Maciej Wygralak, Poland
Roman Wyrzykowski, Poland
Ronald R. Yager, USA
Xin-She Yang, UK
Gary Yen, USA
John Yen, USA
Sławomir Zadrożny, Poland
Ali M.S. Zalzala, UAE

ICAISC Organizing Committee

Rafał Scherer, Secretary
Łukasz Bartczuk, Organizing Committee Member
Piotr Dziwiński, Organizing Committee Member
Marcin Gabryel, Finance Chair
Marcin Korytkowski, Databases and Internet Submissions

Additional Reviewers

R. Adamczak
M. Al-Dhelaan
E. Avila-Melgar
T. Babczyński
M. Białko
M. Blachnik
L. Bobrowski
P. Boguś
G. Boracchi
L. Borzemski
J. Botzheim
W. Bozejko
T. Burczyński
R. Burduk
C. Castro
K. Cetnarowicz
W. Cholewa
P. Cichosz
R. Czabański
I. Czarnowski
J. de la Rosa
J. Dembski
L. Diosan
L. Dutkiewicz
L. Dymowa
S. Ehteram
A. Fanea
I. Fister
M. Gabryel
P. Głomb
Z. Gomółka
M. Gorzałczany
D. Grabowski
E. Grabska
K. Grąbczewski
J. Grzymala-Busse
Y. Hayashi
P. Held
Z. Hendzel
F. Hermann
H. Hikawa
Z. Hippe
K. Hirota

A. Horzyk
E. Hrynkiewicz
R. Hyde
D. Jakóbczak
A. Janczak
T. Jiralerspong
J. Kacprzyk
W. Kamiński
V. Kecman
E. Kerre
P. Klęsk
L. Koczy
A. Kołakowska
J. Konopacki
J. Korbicz
M. Kordos
P. Korohoda
J. Koronacki
J. Kościelny
L. Kotulski
Z. Kowalczuk
M. Kraft
M. Kretowska
R. Kruse
B. Kryzhanovsky
A. Krzyzak
A. Kubiak
E. Kucharska
J. Kulikowski
O. Kurasova
V. Kurkova
M. Kurzyński
J. Kusiak
J. Kwiecień
A. Ligęza
A. Lisowska
M. Ławryńczuk
J. Łęski
B. Macukow
W. Malina
K. Malinowski
J. Mańdziuk
U. Markowska-Kaczmar

A. Martin
A. Materka
J. Mazurkiewicz
J. Mendel
J. Michalkiewicz
Z. Mikrut
S. Misina
W. Mitkowski
W. Moczulski
W. Mokrzycki
O. Mosalov
T. Munakata
G. Nalepa
M. Nashed
F. Neri
M. Nieniewski
S. Osowski
E. Ozcan
W. Palacz
G. Papa
A. Paszyńska
K. Patan
A. Pieczyński
A. Piegat
Z. Pietrzykowski
V. Piuri
P. Prokopowicz
A. Przybył
R. Ptak
A. Radzikowska
E. Rafajłowicz
E. Rakus-Andersson
A. Rataj
Ł. Rauch
L. Rolka
S. Rovetta
I. Rudas
F. Rudziński
S. Sakurai
N. Sano
A. Sashima
R. Scherer
P. Sevastjanov

Contents – Part I

Fuzzy Systems and Their Applications

Evolutionary Algorithms and Their Applications

Pattern Classification

Agent Systems, Robotics and Control

Contents – Part II

Data Mining

Bioinformatics, Biometrics and Medical Applications

Artificial Intelligence in Modeling and Simulation

Various Problems of Artificial Intelligence

Workshop: Visual Information Coding Meets Machine Learning

Neural Networks and Their Applications

Visualizing and Understanding Nonnegativity Constrained Sparse Autoencoder in Deep Learning

Babajide O. Ayinde[1], Ehsan Hosseini-Asl[1], and Jacek M. Zurada[1,2(✉)]

[1] Electrical and Computer Engineering Department,
University of Louisville, Louisville, KY, USA
{babajide.ayinde,ehsan.hosseiniasl,jacek.zurada}@louisville.edu
[2] Information Technology Institute, University of Social Science, 90-113 Lodz, Poland

Abstract. In this paper, we demonstrate how complex deep learning structures can be understood by humans, if likened to isolated but understandable concepts that use the architecture of Nonnegativity Constrained Autoencoder (NCAE). We show that by constraining most of the weights in the network to be nonnegative using both L_1 and L_2 nonnegativity penalization, a more understandable structure can result with minute deterioration in classification accuracy. Also, this proposed approach yields a more sparse feature extraction and additional output layer sparsification. The concept is illustrated using MNIST and the NORB datasets.

Keywords: Deep architecture · Semi-supervised learning · White-box model · Part-based representation

1 Introduction

In challenging recognition tasks, deep neural network architectures have shown unique properties in learning complex distributions of data without losing their generalization capabilities [1]. In addition, the multi-level abstraction involved in deep architectures affords us the fancy to represent data at multiple levels of hierarchies. Although deep architectures are capable of learning highly nonlinear mappings, they are difficult to train, and it is usually hard to interpret what each layer has learnt. In addition, gradient-based optimization with random initialization used in training the network is susceptible to poor local optima [2].

By pre-training each layer separately in an unsupervised manner and then fine-tuning the stacked layers with a supervised learning approach, the greedy layer-wise algorithm came onboard to ameliorate the efficiency of the training phase [2,3]. With an unsupervised pre-training, patterns in high dimensional data can be captured and represented in low dimensional encoding space. The contrastive-divergence trained restricted Boltzmann machines (RBMs) and autoencoders are the two commonly used unsupervised learning paradigms for

© Springer International Publishing Switzerland 2016
L. Rutkowski et al. (Eds.): ICAISC 2016, Part I, LNAI 9692, pp. 3–14, 2016.
DOI: 10.1007/978-3-319-39378-0_1

extracting rich features in deep architecture. In this work, we focus on learning features using autoencoders.

The motivation behind the autoencoding is to reconstruct the input from its encoded representation with desired attributes, in an unsupervised fashion. With layerwise stacking and unsupervised pre-training of autoencoders followed by a supervised fine-tuning phase, an autoencoder-based deep network is unearthed [2]. It must be remarked that one of the key factors that contributes to the success of deep network training is the appropriate initialization, which is generally achieved by pre-training each autoencoding layer with minimum reconstruction error. The conceived representation of the input to each autoencoding layer serves as the input to the succeeding autoencoding layer, and so on. In deep architectures, a learning system that invariably results in lower layerwise reconstruction error will not only create a better representation of the input, but also a better parameter initialization and improved prediction accuracy [4].

One principal way of improving the classification accuracy as well as the robustness to noise in high dimensional space is to enforce sparseness in the autoencoding [5]. The problem we address in this work is in two-fold: (i) we make an attempt to give a better interpretability to autoencoder-based deep layer architecture by encouraging nonnegative weights in the network, and (ii) we demonstrate how to use Nonnegativity Constrained Sparse Autoencoder (NCSA) to extract meaningful representation that unearths the hidden structure of a high dimensional data.

It is a general belief that humans analyze complex interactions by breaking them into isolated and understandable hierarchical concepts. The emergence of part-based representation in human brain has been conceptually tied to the nonnegativity constraints [6]. One way to foster the understandability problem is to constrain the network's weights to be nonnegative, and this will inevitably enable easier human interpretation, since the cancelation of terms in the scalar product summation is eliminated [7]. In this work and in practice, the cancelations are discouraged rather than eliminated. Drawing inspiration from the idea of Nonnegative Matrix Factorization (NMF) and sparse coding [6,8], the hidden structure of data can be unfolded by learning features that have capabilities to model the data in parts. Although NMF enforces the encoding data and features to be nonnegative thereby resulting in additive data representation, however, incorporating sparse coding within NMF for the purpose of encoding test data is computationally expensive, and with autoencoders, this incorporation is learning-based and fast [9]. In addition, the performance of a deep network can be enhanced using NCSA with part-based data representation capability [1].

It must be remarked that weight penalization is a concept that has been employed both in the understandability and generalization context. It is used to suppress magnitude of the weights by reducing the sum of their squares. Enhancement in sparsity can also be achieved by penalizing sum of absolute values of the weights rather than the sum of their squares [10–14]. We extend the work proposed in [1] by adding an extra penalty term to the cost function to encourage nonnegativity of the network weights and enhance the understandability of the data. Other related work is the Nonnegative Sparse Autoencoder (NNSA) trained with an online algorithm and tied weights and linear output activation function to ameliorate the training hassle [15]. To sum up, this adopts the general autoencoder model with trainable weights and nonlinear activation function, and this inevitably enhances the model flexibility.

A multi-layer perceptron network with strictly non-negative weights and softmax output was shown to extract understandable latent features like characteristic parts of handwritten digits as well as extracting semantic features from text categorization data [7]. Although the understandability of the network is enhanced by constraining the weights in the network to be strictly nonnegative, the transparency trades off a bit of the classification accuracy. Besides, the random initialization used in training the network makes it difficult to scale this approach to large deep network. Nonnegative constrained RBMs have been shown to possess the capability of shattering data in distinct parts, and can be used to enhance classification accuracy [16]. Also, in contrast with the deterministic approach used by autoencoders to minimize the reconstruction error, RBMs use stochasticity to minimize the joint probabilities between the hidden and visible units.

In this work, we visualize part-based representation of data in a deep network using stacked nonnegativity constrained autoencoders. The rest of the paper is structured as follows: Section 2 introduces the network configurations and the notation used in the paper. Section 3 discusses the experimental designs and presents the results. Finally, conclusions are drawn in Sect. 4.

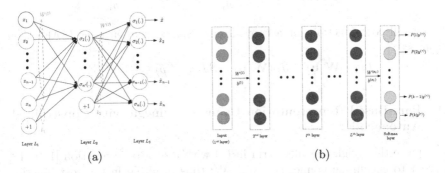

(a)   (b)

Fig. 1. Schematic diagram of (a) a three-layer autoencoder and (b) a deep network

2   Network Details and Notation

The mathematical representation (model) of the neural network autoencoder, which aims to reconstruct its input vector using unsupervised learning, is given in (1) and depicted in Fig. 1(a).

$$\hat{\mathbf{x}} = f_{\mathbf{W},\mathbf{b}}(\mathbf{x}) \approx \mathbf{x} \tag{1}$$

where $\mathbf{x}$ is a normalized input vector, $\mathbf{W} = \{\mathbf{W}_1, \mathbf{W}_2\}$, and $\mathbf{b} = \{\mathbf{b}_1, \mathbf{b}_2\}$ respectively represent the weights and biases of the network

$$\mathbf{h} = g_{\theta_1}(\mathbf{x}) = \sigma(\mathbf{W}_1\mathbf{x} + \mathbf{b}_1) \qquad (2)$$

where $\mathbf{h} \in [0,1]^{n'}$, $\mathbf{W}_1 \in R^{n' \times n}$, $\mathbf{b} \in R^{n' \times 1}$, and $\sigma(x)$ denotes an element-wise application of the logistic sigmoid, $\sigma(x) = 1/(1 + exp(-x))$. The resulting hidden representation, $\mathbf{h}$, is then mapped back to a reconstructed vector, $\hat{\mathbf{x}} \in [0,1]^n$, by a similar mapping function, parameterized by $\theta_2 = \{\mathbf{W}_2, \mathbf{b}_2\}$,

$$\hat{\mathbf{x}} = g_{\theta_2}(\mathbf{h}) = \sigma(\mathbf{W}_2\mathbf{h} + \mathbf{b}_2) \qquad (3)$$

for the purpose of optimizing the parameters in (1), i.e. $\theta = \{\theta_1, \theta_2\}$, the average reconstruction error is the cost of the optimization objective:

$$J_E(\mathbf{W}, \mathbf{b}) = \frac{1}{m} \sum_{i=1}^{m} \frac{1}{2} ||\hat{x}^{(i)} - x^{(i)}|| \qquad (4)$$

where m is the number of examples in the training set.

$$\hat{\rho}_j = \frac{1}{m} \sum_{i=1}^{m} h_j(x^{(i)}) \qquad (5)$$

$$J_{KL}(\rho||\hat{\rho}) = \sum_{j=1}^{n'} \rho \log \frac{\rho}{\hat{\rho}_j} + (1 - \rho) \log \frac{1 - \rho}{1 - \hat{\rho}_j} \qquad (6)$$

The overall cost function for a conventional Sparse Autoencoder (SAE) then becomes:

$$J_{SAE}(\mathbf{W}, \mathbf{b}) = J_E(\mathbf{W}, \mathbf{b}) + \beta J_{KL}(\rho||\hat{\rho}) + \frac{\lambda}{2} ||w^{(l)}||_2^2 \qquad (7)$$

2.1   Part-Based Representation Using a Nonnegativity Constrained Autoencoder

We replace the weight penalty term in (7) with a quadratic function [1,16–18] in order to encourage nonnegativity in $\mathbf{W}$; thus resulting in the cost function expression for L_1/L_2-NCAE as given in (8):

$$J_{L_1/L_2-\mathrm{NCAE}}(\mathbf{W}, \mathbf{b}) = J_\mathrm{E}(\mathbf{W}, \mathbf{b}) + \beta J_{\mathrm{KL}}(p||\hat{\mathbf{p}}) + \frac{\alpha}{2} \sum_{l=1}^{2} \sum_{i=1}^{s_l} \sum_{j=1}^{s_{l+1}} f(w_{ij}^{(l)}) \qquad (8)$$

where

$$f(w_{ij}) = \begin{cases} w_{ij}^2 + |w_{ij}| & w_{ij} < 0 \\ 0 & w_{ij} \geq 0 \end{cases} \qquad (9)$$

and $\alpha \geq 0$. The consequences of minimizing (8) are that: (i) the average reconstruction error is reduced (ii) the sparsity of the hidden layer activation is

increased, and (iii) the number of nonnegative weights is also increased. In order
to encourage negative weights to be positive, the weights are regularized by minimizing their absolute value (L_1 norm) and their Euclidean norm (L_2 norm) [10].
The resultant effect of penalizing the weights with L_1 and L_2 norm is that important connections are selected and their magnitudes are shrunk. The gradient of
(8) is computed in (12) for the purpose of updating the network parameters
using the backpropagation algorithm [19].

$$w_{ij}^{(l)} = w_{ij}^{(l)} - \xi \frac{\partial}{\partial w_{ij}^{(l)}} J_{L_1/L_2-\text{NCAE}}(\mathbf{W}, \mathbf{b}) \tag{10}$$

$$b_i^{(l)} = b_i^{(l)} - \xi \frac{\partial}{\partial b_i^{(l)}} J_{L_1/L_2-\text{NCAE}}(\mathbf{W}, \mathbf{b}) \tag{11}$$

where $\xi > 0$ is the learning rate.

$$\frac{\partial}{\partial w_{ij}^{(l)}} J_{L_1/L_2-\text{NCAE}}(\mathbf{W}, \mathbf{b}) = \frac{\partial}{\partial w_{ij}^{(l)}} J_E(\mathbf{W}, \mathbf{b}) + \beta \frac{\partial}{\partial w_{ij}^{(l)}} J_{\text{KL}}(p \parallel \hat{p})$$
$$+ \alpha g(w_{ij}^{(l)}) \tag{12}$$

where

$$g(w_{ij}) = \begin{cases} w_{ij} + \text{sign}(w_{ij}) & w_{ij} < 0 \\ 0 & w_{ij} \geq 0 \end{cases} \tag{13}$$

2.2   Deep Learning Using L_1/L_2 Nonnegative Constrained Autoencoder (L_1/L_2-NCAE)

In building the deep network, we use a greedy layer-wise training approach with
each layer independently trained with an unsupervised learning technique [20].
Here we stacked several L_1/L_2-NCAE into a deep architecture and we trained
them one after the other, with the input of a layer used as the activation of
its preceding layer. The activation of the last autoencoder is then used as the
input to the softmax layer, a supervised classifier. It must be remarked that the
weights of the softmax layer are also encouraged to be nonnegative using L_1 and
L_2 penalty. We then define the misclassification cost in the softmax layer as:

$$J_{CL}(\mathbf{W}) = -\frac{1}{m} \left[\sum_{r=1}^{m} \sum_{p=1}^{k} 1\left(y^{(r)} = p\right) log \frac{e^{\mathbf{w}_p^T x^{(r)}}}{\sum_{l=1}^{k} e^{\mathbf{w}_l^T x^{(r)}}} \right] \tag{14}$$

where k is the number of classes, $\mathbf{W}$ is the matrix of input weights of all nodes in
the softmax layer, and $\mathbf{w}_p$ is the p-th column of $\mathbf{W}$ referring to the input weights
of the p-th softmax node. The overall cost function of the softmax classifier with
nonnegativity constraint is given as:

$$J_{NC\text{-}Softmax}(\mathbf{W}) = J_{CL}(\mathbf{W}) + \frac{\alpha}{2} \sum_{i=1}^{s_L} \sum_{j=1}^{k} f\left(w_{ij}^{(L)}\right) \tag{15}$$

where s_L denotes the number of hidden nodes of the final autoencoder, $f(\cdot)$ is as in Eq. (9) to penalize the negative weights of the softmax layer. Finally, in the fine-tuning stage, the weights of all the layers are tuned simultaneously in a supervised fashion to improve the accuracy of the classification [20]. It must be noted that only the softmax weights are constrained in the fine-tuning step. The cost function for fine-tuning the Deep Network (DN) is given by

$$J_{DN}\left(\mathbf{W}, \mathbf{b}\right) = J_{CL}\left(\mathbf{W}_{DN}, \mathbf{b}_{DN}\right) + \frac{\alpha}{2} \sum_{i=1}^{s_L} \sum_{j=1}^{k} f\left(w_{ij}^{(L)}\right) \qquad (16)$$

where $\mathbf{W}_{DN}$ contains the input weights of the L_1/L_2-NCAE and softmax layers, and $\mathbf{b}_{DN}$ is the bias input of L_1/L_2-NCAE layers as shown in Fig. 1(b).

3 Experiments

In the first set of experiments, we constructed a deep network using two stacked nonnegativity constrained autoencoders and a softmax layer for classification, and LBFGS in minFunc by Mark Schmidt was used to minimize (8), (15) and (16). In order to understand how the network manipulates and classifies its input, we extracted the subset 1, 2 and 6 from the MNIST handwritten digits. The complete MNIST dataset has 60000 training and 10000 testing set. Each set is a grayscale image of an handwritten digit scaled and centered in a 28×28 pixel box [21]. To have a feel of how the deep network does what it does, we filter an image of digit 2 through the network as shown in Fig. 2.

We also compare the ability of L_1/L_2-NCAE and conventional SAE to discover patterns in high dimensional data. Using t-distributed stochastic neighbor embedding (t-SNE) projection to reduce the 10D representation of digits 1, 2, 6 to 2D space, Fig. 3(a)–(d) visualize the distribution of features encoded by 10 encoding filters of SAE, NCAE, L_1/L_2-NCAE and MNF respectively. It can be observed that the manifold of digits in L_1/L_2-NCAE is obviously more linear than that of SAE. In particular, the manifolds of digits 2, 6 in SAE have more overlap and twists than its L_1/L_2-NCAE counterpart. We also experimented with the full MNIST dataset by training a three-layer L_1/L_2-NCAE network with 196 hidden neurons. The encoding weights $\mathbf{W}_1$, known as receptive field as in the case of image data, are reshaped, scaled, centered in a 28×28 pixel box and visualized. Thus in Fig. 4, we benchmark the receptive field learned by L_1/L_2-NCAE with a three-layer NCAE [1], SAE, and the basis image learned by using NMF [6].

It can be seen from the results in Fig. 4 that L_1/L_2-NCAE learnt receptive field that is more sparse and localized than those of NCAE, SAE, and NMF. We remark that the black pixels in SAE features are a result of the negative weights whose values and frequency are reduced in NCAE with nonnegativity constraints, which are further reduced by imposing an additional L_1 penalty term in L_1/L_2-NCAE as shown in Fig. 6. In the case of L_1/L_2-NCAE, tiny strokes and dots which constitute the basic part of handwritten digits. Figure 5 compares the

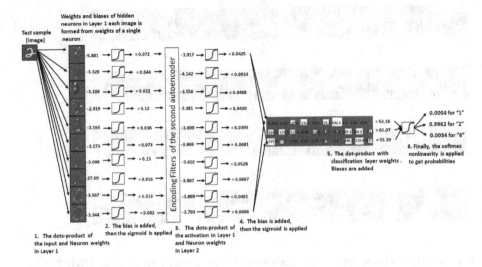

Fig. 2. Filtering the signal through the deep architecture trained using the reduced MNIST data set with class labels 1, 2 and 6. The test image is a 28×28 pixels image unrolled into a vector of 784 values. Both the input test sample and the receptive field of the first autoencoding layer are presented as images. The weights of the output layer are plotted as a diagram with one row for each output neuron and one column for every hidden neuron in $(L-1)^{th}$ layer.

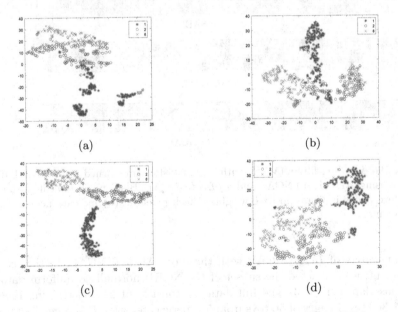

Fig. 3. t-SNE projection [22] of 10D representations of reduced MNIST handwritten digits using (a) SAE (b) NCAE (c) L_1/L_2-NCAE (d) NMF.

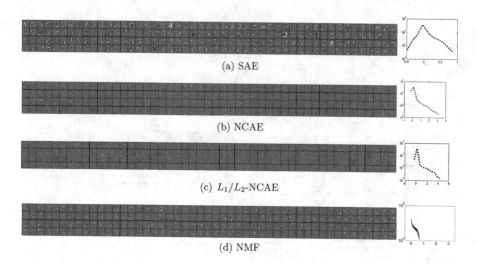

Fig. 4. 196 Receptive fields ($\mathbf{W}^{(1)}$) with weight histogram learned from MNIST digit data set using (a) SAE, (b) NCAE, (c) L_1/L_2-NCAE, and (d) NMF. Black pixels indicate negative, and white pixels indicate positive weights. Black nodes in (b) indicate neurons with zero weights. The range of weights are scaled to $[-1, 1]$ and mapped to the graycolor map. $w <= -1$ is assigned to black, and $w >= 1$ is assigned to white color.

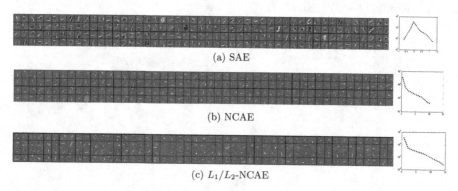

Fig. 5. 196 decoding filters ($\mathbf{W}^{(2)}$) with weight histogram learned from MNIST digit data set using (a) SAE (b) NCAE and (c) L_1/L_2-NCAE. Black pixels indicate negative, and white pixels indicate positive weights. Black pixels in (b) indicate neurons with zero weights.

decoding filters of L_1/L_2-NCAE with those of SAE and NCAE. In the second experiment, we extracted the subset of the NORB normalized-uniform dataset with class labels 1, 2, 3. The full data set consists of 24,300 training images and 24,300 test images of 50 toys from 5 generic categories: four-legged animals, human figures, airplanes, trucks, and cars. The training and testing sets comprise 5 instances of each category. Each image consists of two channels, each of size

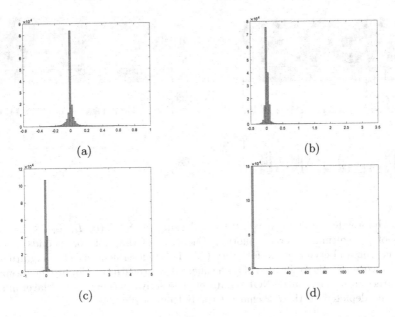

(a)

(b)

(c)

(d)

Fig. 6. Histogram of the 196 encoding filters using (a) SAE (b) NCAE (c) L_1/L_2-NCAE (d) NMF

96×96 pixels. We take the inner 64×64 pixels of each channel and resize it using bicubic interpolation to 32×32 pixels that form a vector with 2048 entries as the input. In this experiment, we trained the network with configuration 2048-10-10-3 on the subset of the NORB data set. Figure 7 shows the randomly sampled test patterns and the weight of the output layer is given in Fig. 8. A deep network constructed using the L_1/L_2-NCAE is contrasted with that constructed with conventional SAE. It can be observed in Fig. 8 that sparsification of the output layer weights is the aftermath of the nonnegativity constraints imposed on the network. In addition, the patterns learned by neurons in each layer are localized, and this allows easy interpretation of what is going on inside the network. This is why we have a sparser, more localized weight distribution of hidden neurons which filters the distinctive part of the input image. Whereas in the case of SAE, the hidden neurons react to the whole image almost equally, and this makes it difficult to have a glimpse of their influence in the classification. The training parameters are given in Table 1.

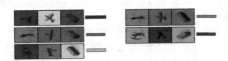

Fig. 7. Exemplary images from NORB data set

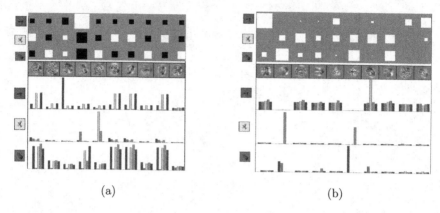

(a) (b)

Fig. 8. The weights of the a network trained using (a) SAE (b) L_1/L_2-NCAE. The weights of the softmax layer are plotted. Each row of the plot corresponds to each output neuron and each column for every $(L-1)^{th}$ hidden neuron. The magnitude of the weight corresponds to the area of each square. Underneath the plot are the receptive fields learned from the reduced NORB dataset. The activations of $(L-1)^{th}$-layer hidden neurons are depicted on the bar chart at the bottom of the plot.

Table 1. Parameter settings for full MNIST and NORB Dataset

Parameters	SAE with Red. dataset	L_1/L_2-NCAE with Red. dataset	SAE with full dataset	L_1/L_2-NCAE with full dataset	NCAE	NMF
Sparsity parameter (p)	0.05	0.05	0.05	0.05	0.05	–
Weight decay penalty (λ)	1e-4	–	0.003	–	–	–
Nonnegativity constraint penalty (α)	–	1e-4	–	0.003	0.003	–
Convergence tolerance	1e-9	1e-9	1e-9	1e-9	1e-9	1e-9
Maximum no. of iterations	400	400	400	400	400	400

Table 2. Classification performance of supervised learning methods on full MNIST dataset.

Model (784-200-20-10)	Before fine-tuning		After fine-tuning		
	Mean ± SD	p-value	Mean ± SD	p-value	# Iterations
Deep L_1/L_2-NCAE*	**86.12± 0.105**		**97.84 ± 0.151**		**124**
Deep NCAE	84.83 ± 0.094	<0.0001	97.91 ± 0.1264	<0.0001	97
Deep SAE	52.81 ± 0.1277	<0.0001	97.29 ± 0.091	<0.0001	400
Deep NNSAE	69.72 ± 0.1007	<0.0001	97.18 ± 0.0648	<0.0001	400
Deep DAE (50 % input dropout)	11.26 ± 0.14	<0.0001	97.11 ± 0.0808	<0.0001	400
Deep NC-DAE (50 % input dropout)	84.37 ± 0.1318	<0.0001	97.42 ± 0.0757	<0.0001	106
Deep DpAE (50 % hidden dropout)	16.77 0.0784	<0.0001	96.73 ± 0.1066	<0.0001	400

In the last set of experiments, we train a deep network on the full MNIST dataset to test if the enhanced ability of the network to shatter data into part could result in improved classification. In order to implement this, we stacked and pretrained two L_1/L_2-NCAEs and the activation of the last autoencoding layer is utilized in training the softmax classifier. Eventually, we finetuned the entire deep network to improve the accuracy of the classification. As shown in Table 2, the classification accuracy and speed of convergence are the figures of merit used to benchmark our results with those of NCAE, NNSAE, DpAE [23], DAE [4] and SAE.

It can be observed from the result in Table 2 that L_1/L_2-NCAE based deep network gives an improved accuracy compared to other methods, especially before finetuning. However, the performance in terms of both the classification accuracy and the speed of convergence is similar to that of the NCAE network. The improved accuracy in both NCAE and L_1/L_2-NCAE based network can be traced to their ability to decompose data more into distinguishable parts. Although the performance of NCAE and L_1/L_2-NCAE are similar and better than other methods (such as NNSAE, DpAE and SAE), L_1/L_2-NCAE improves the understandability of the deep network by constraining more weights to be nonnegative than NCAE. A better insight into the data, in certain scenarios, outweighs the benefits of an accurate but opaque classifier.

4 Conclusion

The notion of interpretability in autoencoder-based deep neural network is addressed in this paper. We analyze the effect of encouraging nonnegativity in a deep architecture on the network performance and its understandability. We also show that by using both L_1 and L_2 penalty factors, most of the weights are forced to be nonnegative, and hence the network becomes more interpretable. In fact, it can be seen that all the weights in the output layer are strictly positive and sparse. In sum, encouraging nonnegativity in NCAE-based deep architecture forces the layers to learn part-based representation of their input leading to a better classification accuracy, and the additional L_1 regularization term improves the network interpretability.

References

1. Hosseini-Asl, E., Zurada, J., Nasraoui, O.: Deep learning of part-based representation of data using sparse autoencoders with nonnegativity constraints. IEEE Trans. Neural Netw. Learn. Syst. **99**, 1–13 (2015)
2. Bengio, Y., Lamblin, P., Popovici, D., Larochelle, H.: Greedy layer-wise training of deep networks. Adv. Neural Inf. Process. Syst. **19**, 153 (2007)
3. Hinton, G., Salakhutdinov, R.: Reducing the dimensionality of data with neural networks. Science **313**(5786), 504–507 (2006)
4. Vincent, P., Larochelle, H., Bengio, Y., Manzagol, P.: Extracting and composing robust features with denoising autoencoders. In: 25th International Conference on Machine learning, pp. 1096–1103. ACM (2008)

5. Lee, H., Ekanadham, C., Ng, A.: Sparse deep belief net model for visual area V2. Adv. Neural Inf. Process. Syst. **7**, 873–880 (2007)
6. Lee, D.D., Seung, H.S.: Learning the parts of objects by non-negative matrix factorization. Nature **401**(6755), 788–791 (1999)
7. Chorowski, J., Zurada, J.M.: Learning understandable neural networks with non-negative weight constraints. IEEE Trans. Neural Netw. Learn. Syst. **26**(1), 62–69 (2015)
8. Olshausen, B.A., et al.: Emergence of simple-cell receptive field properties by learning a sparse code for natural images. Nature **381**(6583), 607–609 (1996)
9. Ranzato, M., Boureau, Y., LeCun, Y.: Sparse feature learning for deep belief networks. Adv. Neural Inf. Process. Syst. **20**, 1185–1192 (2007)
10. Ishikawa, M.: Structural learning with forgetting. Neural Netw. **9**(3), 509–521 (1996)
11. Bartlett, P.L.: The sample complexity of pattern classification with neural networks: the size of the weights is more important than the size of the network. IEEE Trans. Inf. Theory **44**(2), 525–536 (1998)
12. Ayinde, B.O., Barnawi, A.Y.: Differential evolution based deployment of wireless sensor networks. In: 2014 IEEE/ACS 11th International Conference on Computer Systems and Applications (AICCSA), pp. 131–137. IEEE (2014)
13. Gnecco, G., Sanguineti, M.: Regularization techniques and suboptimal solutions to optimization problems in learning from data. Neural Comput. **22**(3), 793–829 (2010)
14. Moody, J., Hanson, S., Krogh, A., Hertz, J.A.: A simple weight decay can improve generalization. Adv. Neural Inf. Process. Syst. **4**, 950–957 (1995)
15. Lemme, A., Reinhart, R., Steil, J.: Online learning and generalization of parts-based image representations by non-negative sparse autoencoders. Neural Netw. **33**, 194–203 (2012)
16. Nguyen, T.D., Tran, T., Phung, D., Venkatesh, S.: Learning partsbased representations with nonnegative restricted Boltzmann machine. In: Asian Conference on Machine Learning, pp. 133–148 (2013)
17. Wright, S.J., Nocedal, J.: Numerical Optimization. Springer, New York (1999)
18. Hashim, H.A., Ayinde, B., Abido, M.: Optimal placement of relay nodes in wireless sensor network using artificial bee colony algorithm. J. Netw. Comput. Appl. **64**, 239–248 (2016)
19. Zurada, J.M.: Introduction to Artificial Neural Systems. West Publishing Co., St. Paul (1992)
20. Hinton, G., Osindero, S., Teh, Y.W.: A fast learning algorithm for deep belief nets. Neural Comput. **18**(7), 1527–1554 (2006)
21. LeCun, Y., Cortes, C., Burges, C.J.: The MNIST database of handwritten digits (1998)
22. der Maaten, L.V., Hinton, G.: Visualizing data using t-SNE. J. Mach. Learn. Res. **9**(11), 2579–2605 (2008)
23. Hinton, G.E., Srivastava, N., Krizhevsky, A., Sutskever, I., Salakhutdinov, R.R.: Improving neural networks by preventing co-adaptation of feature detectors (2012). arXiv preprint arXiv:1207.0580

Experimental Analysis of Forecasting Solar Irradiance with Echo State Networks and Simulating Annealing

Sebastián Basterrech[(✉)]

Department of Computer Science, Faculty of Electrical Engineering
and Computer Science, VŠB–Technical University of Ostrava,
Ostrava, Czech Republic
Sebastian.Basterrech.Tiscordio@vsb.cz

Abstract. The solar energy is a well alternative for covering the high electrical demand, and it starts to be integrated into the energetic grid infrastructure. High forecast accuracy can help in the management of industrial strategies. We present an approach that combines the potential of a Neural Network named *Echo State Networks (ESN)* and a well-known optimisation technique named *Simulating Annealing (SA)*. We use the SA technique for selecting the meteorological variables relevant in the forecasting task and the ESN as forecasting model. We present the results evaluating our approach on a public dataset.

Keywords: Solar irradiance · Echo State Networks · Simulating Annealing · Forecasting · Time-series problems

1 Introduction

Solar energy has received significant attention during last years because is an alternative of renewable resource that can help for reducing the carbon emissions, and it can be used for covering a relevant part of the growing demand of electrical energy. To have accurate solar irradiance predictions help to integrate the energy into the grid, as well as to avoid congestions. Besides, high forecast accuracy helps to mitigate the negative impacts of instable energy sources. In this paper, we present a procedure for forecasting the solar power irradiance using the history of the irradiance and other several meteorological variables. The approach is based on a widely applied metaheuristic technique named *Simulating Annealing (SA)*, which is used for selecting the most significant input features, and the forecasting is done using the *Echo State Networks (ESN)* model. An ESN is a Recurrent Neural Network often used for solving temporal learning problems. We have two main goals in our article, one consists in defining a group of meteorological variables that impact on the solar power. The second one consists in evaluating the accuracy of Echo State Networks for forecasting solar irradiance using the previous information about the solar irradiance and a group

© Springer International Publishing Switzerland 2016
L. Rutkowski et al. (Eds.): ICAISC 2016, Part I, LNAI 9692, pp. 15–24, 2016.
DOI: 10.1007/978-3-319-39378-0_2

of external meteorological variables, such as: wind characteristics, air temperature, etc. Related works of forecasting solar power irradiance has been presented during the last years. Some approaches have been based on classic statistical methods [1], Neural Networks [1–3], and other machine learning techniques have been also studied [4–6]. We evaluate our approach using a well-known public dataset [7], and we present the results for predicting the solar irradiance with a forecasting horizon of three days.

The article is organised as follows. In the next section we define the problem of forecasting a time-series and we present a background on the SA metaheristic and the ESN model. Section 3 introduces our methodology. Section 4 is divided in two parts. First part describes the data set and second part presents the experimental results. The article ends with an outlook and conclusions.

2   Background

In this section we start by formalising the problem of forecasting time-series data. Next, we present a background of the methods used in this article: Echo State Networks and Simulating Annealing.

2.1   Formalization of the Problem

The goal of forecasting a time-series is to predict or estimate future events or trends using the information concerning the past. Given a time-series of real observations $y(1), y(2), \ldots, y(t)$ the problem of forecasting a time-series consists in computing a learning tool $\varphi(\cdot, \mathbf{w})$ with parameters $\mathbf{w}$ that predicts (better as possible) the value of $y(t + \tau)$ with $\tau > 0$ using the precedent points $y(t), y(t - 1), \ldots$. The accuracy of $\varphi(\cdot)$ is assessed using an average over all distances between the target $y(t + \tau)$ and the predicted value that we denoted by $\hat{y}(t + \tau)$. This problem is generalised when we have a set of external features $\mathbf{a}(t)$ in a multidimensional space. In this case the forecast of $y(t + \tau)$ $(\tau > 0)$ is given using the information of $\mathbf{a}(t), \mathbf{a}(t - 1), \ldots, y(t), y(t - 1), \ldots$. The parameters of $\varphi(\cdot, \mathbf{w})$ are computed such that an error measure in an arbitrary range of time $[1, T]$ is minimised, here we consider the widely used *Mean Squared Errors (MSE)*:

$$MSE = \frac{1}{T} \sum_{t=1}^{T} (\hat{y}(t) - y(t))^2. \tag{1}$$

2.2   Simulating Annealing Method

A popular optimisation technique is *Simulating Annealing (SA)*, which is used for continuous and combinatorial optimisation problems on multi-dimensional spaces [8]. The technique is inspired from the thermodynamical process wherein liquids freeze and crystallise or metals cool and anneal. The goal consists in optimising an objective function that in this context is named *energy function*.

The procedure is iterative and stochastic, at each step the method tests as feature solution a random point on the searching space. We replace a current solution s^{curr} (a point on the large space) by a randomly selected *nearby solution* s^{new} that is chosen with a probability p. A *nearby solution* s^{new} is a solution that has a Hamming distance with the current solution s^{curr} less than or equal to d, for an arbitrary d value. The method has a global parameter called *temperature* (T) that decreases in the number of iterations until some arbitrary *frozen* condition T^{end} (following the metal annealing analogy). The model is given by the following selection rule

$$p = \min\{\exp\left(-(E(s^{new}) - E(s^{curr}))/kT\right), 1\}, \tag{2}$$

where k is a constant and p is a probability of selecting a new solution. This rule gives to the model the capacity for exploring new regions that is done jumping from a local minimum to other regions on the searching space. The algorithm has the following input parameters: an initial temperature $T^{(0)}$, a cooling schedule ρ in $[0, 1]$, and a stop condition T^{end}, in next section we specify how we set those parameters.

2.3 Echo State Neural Networks

A Recurrent Neural Network (RNN) is a bio-inspired dynamical system used for solving temporal learning problems. The recurrences allow to the network to learn complex dynamics and to model systems that evolve in time. Besides, the model has been also successfully applied for solving any type of supervised learning problems. Despite the potential of the RNN for solving supervised tasks, they have been seldom applied in real-world applications, due to the fact that often can be hard to set-up the network parameters. First-order methods (optimisation techniques based on the gradient information) have been appropriated for training feedforward networks, although they can fail in the case of recurrent networks [9]. An alternative of the RNN has been introduced at the beginning of the 2000 s with the name of *Echo State Networks (ESN)* [10]. The technique uses the power of RNNs for memorising temporal data and overcomes the drawbacks of training the weights of RNNs, without introducing additional inconveniences. For that reasons, the model is a good alternative for tackling temporal learning tasks.

The network has three layers connected in a forward schema. The first layer typically process the input patterns. The second layer contains recursive connections, and its role is memorising the temporal structure of the patterns and expanding their geometrical information from the input layer in a higher dimensional space. The third layer generates a linear combination of the expansion created by the second layer. The ESN has circuits only in the second layer, which is named *reservoir*. A main characteristic of the model is that the training algorithm only focuses in adjusting a subset of weights, only the weights to the third layer are adjusted. All the rest connections (input and reservoir weights) are random initialized following some algebraic conditions and they are fixed during the learning process. As a consequence, the learning algorithm is fast and robust because the consists in training the parameters of a linear regression. The literature about ESN is very rich, and we can find several applications of the model that show the well performance of ESN for solving temporal learning tasks [11].

We follow by specifying the notation, let N_a, N_x and N_o be the number of input, reservoir and output neurons, respectively. The parameters of the model are the weight matrices, let $\mathbf{w}^{in}$ be a $N_x \times N_a$ matrix collecting input-reservoir weights, let $\mathbf{w}^r$ be a $N_x \times N_x$ matrix collecting hidden-hidden weights, and let $\mathbf{w}^{out}$ a $N_o \times (N_a + N_x)$ matrix with the parameters from input and projected space to the output space. The reservoir is characterized by a multidimensional state $\mathbf{x} = (x_1, \ldots, \mathbf{x}_{N_x})$ given by:

$$x_m(t) = \psi\left(w^{in}_{m0} + \sum_{i=1}^{N_a} w^{in}_{mi} a_i(t) + \sum_{i=1}^{N_x} w^r_{mi} x_i(t-1)\right), \qquad (3)$$

for all $m \in [1, N_x]$ where $\psi(\cdot)$ is the hyperbolic tangent function ($\tanh(\cdot)$). Let $\mathbf{y}(t)$ be the prediction N_o-dimensional vector of the model at time t, which is computed by a linear regression:

$$y_s(t) = w^{out}_{m0} + \sum_{i=1}^{N_a} w^{out}_{mi} a_i(t) + \sum_{i=1}^{N_x} w^{out}_{mi} x_i(t), \quad \forall s \in [1, N_o]. \qquad (4)$$

In our experimental results we use a generalisation of the canonical ESN that computes the reservoir state as follows: firstly, we compute a temporarily vector state $\mathbf{x}'$ using the expression (3). Secondly we compute the state given by:

$$x_m(t) = (1 - \alpha)x'_m(t) + \alpha x_m(t-1), \qquad (5)$$

where the parameter α is called leaky rate and is used for controlling the reservoir state update.

The ESN model has the following global parameters that impact in the model performance: the size of the reservoir (given by the number of reservoir neurons), the input scaling factor (a weighting factor of the input patterns), the spectral radius of the reservoir matrix, the density and topology of the reservoir matrix [11,12]. The reservoir size impacts in the linear separability of the data, there is a tradeoff between the large of the reservoir and overfitting. In our experiments, the training data is normalised. We consider the input scaling factor equal to 1, therefore all the input patterns have equal relevance. The spectral radius controls the stability of the reservoir state and impacts in the memory capacity of the model. An important property of the model is that the stability of the dynamical system $\mathbf{x}(t)$ only depends of the reservoir weight matrix $\mathbf{w}^r$ [11], . The stability is controlled by the spectral radius of $\mathbf{w}^r$, that we denote by $\rho(\mathbf{w}^r)$, if $\rho(\mathbf{w}^r) < 1$ the stability of the ESN can be ensured [11]. An usual practice consists in scaling the initial reservoir, in order to control the spectral radius, the scaling procedure is as follows: $\mathbf{w}^r \leftarrow (\beta/\rho(\mathbf{w}^r))\mathbf{w}^r$, where β is a constant in $(0, 1]$. The sparsity of the reservoir matrix is often set on 20 % non-zero values.

3 Methodology

The section is divided in two parts, the first one present the procedure applied for setting the global parameters of the ESN. The second part contains the used methodology of this article.

3.1 Setting of the Global ESN Parameters

We begin by finding the *best* global parameters of the ESN model. We arbitrary select three parts of the solar global irradiance time-series. The selection was made considering the different trends of the 2015. A first part A has a grown increasing trend in an arbitrary range of time $[a_1, a_2]$ (days in February and March), a second part B doesn't present any evident trend in $[b_1, b_2]$ (days of May and June), and a third part C has a downward trend in $[c_1, c_2]$ (days of October and November). For each period A, B and C we compute ESNs with different global parameters $(N_x, \rho(\mathbf{w}^r), \alpha)$, and we evaluate their accuracy using the MSE (as an averaged error of the three parts). The global parameters of the ESN are computed using the model for forecasting three days ahead. We forecast the solar power using only information of the past of the solar power series, in other words we don't use any other meteorological variables. The evaluated ESN parameter values are defined in a regular spaced-grid points in the following intervals: $\alpha \in [0.5, \ldots, 0.9]$, $N_x \in [30, 35, \ldots, 120, 125]$ and $\rho(\mathbf{w}^r) \in [0.1, 0.15, \ldots, 0.95]$. Let N_x^*, ρ^* and α^* be the *best* global parameters of an ESN according our empirical evaluations. A remark, the evaluations for reservoir matrices with $\rho(\mathbf{w}^r) > 0.55$ were in some cases unstable. This means that the accuracy presented a large variance, therefore we analyse only the results for $\rho(\mathbf{w}^r) \leq 0.55$.

3.2 Feature Selection Using SA Method

We apply the SA method for automatically selecting other meteorological variables for forecasting the solar irradiance. We assume that several external variables impact in the solar irradiance, such as: air temperature, humidity, wind characteristics, etc. Therefore, we use SA as feature selection tool for defining a set of meteorological variables. The selection can not be done in reasonable time using a brute-force strategy or a greedy method due to the large number of variables (in our experiments, we are using more than 20 variables). The procedure for using SA is as follows. Without loss of generality we enumerate the input features by $\{1, \ldots, N\}$, where N is the number of meteorological variables including the solar power. As a consequence, the searching space is $\{0, 1\}^N$, where the solutions have the form $\mathbf{s} = [s_1, s_2, \ldots, s_N]$ where $s_i = 0$ represents that the input feature i is omitted as input of the ESN, and $s_i = 1$ represents that the variable i is an input of the model. For each combination we evaluate the accuracy of an ESN with parameters N_x^*, ρ^* and α^*, the objective is to find $\mathbf{s} \in \{0, 1\}^N$ such that the MSE is minimized. In the SA method, given a current solution $\mathbf{s}^{\text{curr}}$ we must select a *nearby* solution of $\mathbf{s}^{\text{curr}}$ that we denote by $\mathbf{s}^{\text{new}}$. In this step, we random select a set $\mathcal{D}$ of d integer values in $[1, N]$. Next, we define the nearby solution $\mathbf{s}^{\text{new}}$ as $s_j^{\text{new}} = s_j^{\text{curr}}$ for all $j \notin \mathcal{D}$ and $s_j^{\text{new}} = s_j^{\text{curr}} + 1 \bmod 2$ for all $j \in \mathcal{D}$ where mod is the module function.

Our main goal is developing a device for predicting future values in a period Δt using information until a current time. Therefore, given a explanatory variable $\mathbf{a}(t)$ and the target $y(t)$ until time t, we predict the solar irradiance value at time $t + 1$ ($\hat{y}(t + 1)$), we use $\mathbf{a}(t)$, $y(t)$ and $\hat{y}(t + 1)$ for predicting $\hat{y}(t + 2)$, $\mathbf{a}(t)$, $y(t)$, $\hat{y}(t + 1)$ and $\hat{y}(t + 2)$ for predicting $\hat{y}(t + 3)$, and so on. We assume that after a period Δt, we are able to have new measured values for the explanatory variables ($\mathbf{a}$). In other words, we use also other meteorological variables, for instance temperature, at time t for predicting the solar irradiance at time $t + \Delta t$, and so on. We divide the time-series in two parts. The first part (named training) is used for finding the best configuration of the input features and the best global ESN parameters. The second part (named validation) is used for evaluated the adjusted model. We use the fitted model for predicting the values on the validation time-series, and the predicted values of power solar as well as the other meteorological variables are used as input patterns for predicting new values. We set Δt with the value of three days. All codes for data processing have been developed in Matlab (Mathworks Inc. Natick, Ma, USA).

4 Experimental Results

The first part of this section contains a description of the data, the second one presents our experimental results.

4.1 Data Description

We use the meteorological data provided by the National Renewable Energy Laboratory and Solar Technology Acceleration Center (SolarTAC) [7]. The collected data corresponds to the period started in January 1, 2015 till December 5, 2015. The temporal precision of the data is 1 min. The output variable is the global irradiance given by the *Global Horizontal Irradiance* in W/m^2, the input features are: Air Temperature, Wind Chill Temp, Dew Point Temp, Relative Humidity, Wind Speed, Pk Wind Speed, SDev Wind Speed, Wind Direction, Wind Dir at Pk WS, SDev Wind Direction, Station Pressure, Precipitation, Accumulated Precipitation, Zenith Angle, Azimuth Angle, Airmass, CMP22 Temp, CR1000 Temp, CR1000 Battery, and CR1000 Process Time. More information about those variables and the used protocol for collecting the data see is available in [7]. The preprocessing of the data consisted in changing the temporal precision from 1 min to 10 min. Instead of using the variable information each minute, we consider the data each 10 min. The time-series data has 50232 points in this period. All the variables were normalised in $[0, 1]$. Figure 1 presents the three periods used for setting the parameters of the ESN model. Due to the fact that SA is a metaheuristic technique we evaluate our approach of different 30 experiment trials. For each one, we start the SA method by randomly selecting the half part of the input features.

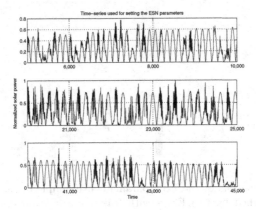

Fig. 1. Training data used for finding the *best* ESN global parameters. The first graphic covers the period since Feb. 3 till Mar. 10, the second graphic covers the period since May 18 till Jun 22, and the third graphics covers the period since Oct. 4 till Nov. 8.

4.2   Results Analysis

As example, we present in Fig. 2 the accuracy of the model when two leaky parameters (α in expression (5)) are evaluated. The graphic shows the MSE on the validation data (three days ahead) for different size of the reservoir and spectral radius. We can see that models with large reservoir size can provoke overfitting on the training data, as a consequence they can have low accuracy for modelling the validation data. According to the results, we set the parameters as follows: $\alpha^* = 0.8$, $N_x^* = 40$ and $\rho^* = 0.25$. A large leaky parameter (0.8) means that a better accuracy is reached when the reservoir state is gradually updated, that is weighting only with 0.2 the new information at each step given by expression (3). Figure 3 illustrates how SA improves the model by selecting a better configuration of input features. The vertical axis shows the $log(MSE)$ and the horizontal axis represents the first 80 iterations. The different curves of Fig. 3 represent different SA experiments. We can see for all cases how the error decreases with the number of iterations. We set the Hamming distance between the current solution and the near solution with $d = 3$. The maximum number of iterations of the SA was 400. A remark, in the SA algorithm we guarantee that the solar power data is always an input feature of the ESN model. Figure 4 presents the evolution of the number of input features by the model over the first 400 iterations. For a better visibility we present as example only 5 random selected SA trials. For instance, the blue curve of Fig. 4 shows how at the iteration 51 of the SA method, the best ESN solution has 12 input features, and at the next step (iteration 52) the best solution has only 6 input features. Table 1 presents the performance on the validation dataset for forecasting 3 days ahead, according to different number of iterations of the SA method. The first column is the number of iterations, the second column shows the best reached accuracy among the 30 SA trials. The next two columns are the mean and the variance of the MSE among the 30 SA experiments. In addition the table shows the number

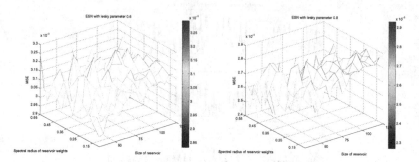

Fig. 2. Sensitivity analysis of the ESN parameters. Example of the accuracy on the validation data reached by two ESNs with leaky rate 0.6 and 0.8 and parameters $N_x \in [30, 125]$ and $\rho(\mathbf{w}^r) \in [0.1, 0.55]$.

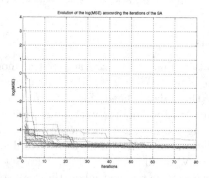

Fig. 3. Evolution of the model accuracy (log(MSE)) over the first 80 iterations of the SA algorithm. Each curve represents the evolution for different initial points of the SA technique

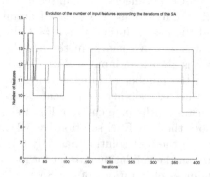

Fig. 4. Example of the evolution of the number of variables used by the SA method in the first 400 iterations.

Table 1. Accuracy of the proposed method when is forecasted three days ahead. The accuracy is presented according the number of iterations in SA algorithm. The columns 2, 3 and 4 are presented using scientific notation.

Iteration	Min (10^{-4})	Mean (10^{-4})	Var (10^{-8})	Number of features
50	5.2612	6.1036	1.0421	12
100	5.1195	5.7287	0.2834	10
150	4.9987	5.5482	0.0891	12
200	4.9986	5.4859	0.08349	10

of input features used by the best configuration at the iterations 50, 100, 150, 200. The lowest reached MSE was 4.9986633×10^{-4} computed using free running prediction over three days. The best combination of input features reached with 400 iterations of SA was composed by the variables: global horizontal irradiance, air temperature, wind chill temp, dew point temp, relative humidity, Pk wind speed, standard deviation of wind speed, accumulated precipitation, Zenith angle, Azimuth angle, CR1000 Temp, and CR1000 Process Time. For more information about those variables see [7].

5 Conclusions and Future Work

We present a procedure for forecasting the solar power irradiance using several external meteorological variables. The approach uses the well-known metaheuristic technique *Simulating Annealing (SA)* for selecting the most significant input features, as well as a specific type of Recurrent Neural Network named *Echo State Networks (ESN)* for forecasting the time-series. We evaluate the proposed method over a real meteorological dataset provided by the Solar Technology Acceleration Center (SolarTAC), Colorado, USA. The SA technique automatically finds a good combination of meteorological variables, which affect the solar power estimation. We consider that we obtain promising results for a forecasting horizon of three days. We are interested in the near future to analyse the group of meteorological variables computed by SA, as well as to extend the period used for training the network model.

Acknowledgement. This work was supported by Grant of SGS No. SP2016/97, VŠB-Technical University of Ostrava, Czech Republic.

References

1. Pedro, H.T.C., Coimbra, C.F.M.: Assessment of forecasting techniques for solar power production with no exogenous inputs. Solar Energy **86**(7), 2017–2028 (2012)
2. Basterrech, S., Prokop, L., Burianek, T., Misak, S.: Optimal design of neural tree for solar power prediction. In: 15th International Scientific Conference on Electric Power Engineering (EPE), Proccedings of the 2014, pp. 273–278, May 2014

3. Basterrech, S., Zjavka, L., Prokop, L., Misak, S.: Irradiance prediction using echo state queueing networks and differential polynomial neural networks. In: 13th International Conference on Intelligent Systems Design and Applications (ISDA), 2013, pp. 271–276, December 2013
4. Diagne, M., David, M., Lauret, P., Boland, J., Schmutz, N.: Review of solar irradiance forecasting methods and a proposition for small-scale insular grids. Renew. Sustain. Energy Rev. **27**, 65–76 (2013)
5. Letendre, S., Makhyoun, M., Taylor, M.: Predicting solar power production: irradiance forecasting models, applications and future prospects. Technical report, Solar Electric Power Association, Washington, DC, USA, March 2014. www.solarelectricpower.org
6. Pelland, S., Remund, J., Kleissl, J., Oozeki, T., De Brabandere, K.: Photovoltaic, solar forecasting: state of art. Technical Report IEA-PVPS T14-01: 2013, International Energy Agency Photovoltaic Power Systems Programme (2013). http://www.iea-pvps.org
7. Andreas, A., Wilcox, S.: Aurora, Colorado (data). Technical Report DA-5500-56491, Solar Technology Acceleration Center (SolarTAC), Colorado, USA (2011). doi:10.5439/1052224
8. Press, W.H., Teukolsky, S.A., Vetterling, W.T., Flannery, B.P.: Numerical Recipes in C++: The Art of Scientific Computing. Cambridge University Press, Cambridge (2002)
9. Bengio, Y., Simard, P., Frasconi, P.: Learning long-term dependencies with gradient descent is difficult. IEEE Trans. Neural Networks **5**(2), 157–166 (1994)
10. Jaeger, H.: The "echo state" approach to analysing and training recurrent neural networks. Technical report 148, German National Research Center for Information Technology (2001)
11. Lukoševičius, M., Jaeger, H.: Reservoir computing approaches to recurrent neural network training. Comput. Sci. Rev. **3**, 127–149 (2009)
12. Butcher, J.B., Verstraeten, D., Schrauwen, B., Day, C.R., Haycock, P.W.: Reservoir computing and extreme learning machines for non-linear time-series data analysis. Neural Networks **38**, 76–89 (2013)

Neural System for Power Load Prediction in a Week Time Horizon

Andrzej Bielecki[✉] and Marcin Lenart

Chair of Applied Computer Science, Faculty of Automation,
Electrical Engineering, Computer Science and Biomedical Engineering,
AGH University of Science and Technology,
Al. Mickiewicza 30, 30-059 Kraków, Poland
azbielecki@gmail.com, marcin.lenart@me.com

Abstract. In this paper a neural system for predicting electric power load in Poland in a week time horizon is presented. The system consists of seven multi-layer neural networks that have common input. Each network is dedicated to predict the total load in one of the seven successive days. Various form of input vectors as well as various ways of encoding them were tested. Verification which type of input data are crucial as well as which periodic aspects should be taken into account in data representation in week prediction was studied. Various numbers of neurons in a hidden layer were tested as well. The mean absolute percentage error (MAPE) is equal to 2.6 % for the most effective system.

Keywords: Multilayer neural network · Electric load prediction

1 Introduction

Both the specific character of the electric power which cannot be stored at the industrial level as well as the great dynamics of the energy market causes instant demand on the systems that predict electric power load on a scale of the whole country [1,2,4,5,8,13,20]. Statistical methods, time series and artificial intelligence systems (AI systems), including expert systems, fuzzy systems, artificial neural networks (ANNs) and hybrid systems, are used to forecast power load. The prediction of twenty four hour profile is a well worked out problem - see, for instance, the papers [3,8–11,16,18,20]. For this task the mean-absolute percentage error (MAPE) varies from 1.1 % to 3.5 %. The mid-term prediction that consists in forecasting power load for a few days is a more difficult task and scientific literature concerning this problem is not as rich as for short-term forecasting - the papers [6,7,12,14,15,17,19,21] can be put as examples. The mentioned lack of literature for the mid-term power load forecasting and the fact that such forecasting is crucial for power industry was the reason of conduct the studies described in this paper. Verification which type of input data are crucial

The paper was supported by the National Centre for Research and Development under Grant no. WND-DEM-1-153/01.

L. Rutkowski et al. (Eds.): ICAISC 2016, Part I, LNAI 9692, pp. 25–34, 2016.
DOI: 10.1007/978-3-319-39378-0_3

as well as which periodic aspects should be taken into account in input data representation in week prediction is the main topic of this paper.

In this paper a system for week prediction of electric power load for Poland is presented and its efficiency is studied. The system is based on a set of seven multi-layer neural networks and it predicts a total daily power load for the seven next days. Various form of input vectors as well as various ways of encoding them were tested. Various numbers of neurons in a hidden layer were tested as well.

2   System for Power Load Prediction

2.1   Data Preparation

This paper presents how different ways of delivering learning data to artificial neural network(ANN) will impact results. To do that it was necessary to create an application which can easily manipulate input data and type of neural network. The *Java* language was chosen and *Encog* library (www.encog.org; access: 10 December 2015) was implemented for a more professional approach.

To create working neural network data, real values that includes weather measurements and electricity usage are required. Data are presented hourly, but in this paper daily predictions are measured and consequently we are averaging temperature of 24 hours and summing 24 electricity usage values of every day.

All values are normalized to a real number from closed interval $[0, 1]$. In case of temperature, interval is slightly different as negative values are allowed here: $[-1, 1]$. This research was performed on a national level. As a result we needed more than one temperature measurement. In that case data from four cities was obtained: Cracow, Warsaw, Poznan and Wroclaw. Whole range of gathered data is between 1 January 2010 and 31 July 2014. It gives us 4,5 year of data which was divided between learning and testing set - three fourths of the set, counting from the beginning of the set, was used as the learning set, the rest was used as the testing set. MAPE was calculated for the testing set.

In order to analyze the possibility of lowering MAPE value in electricity prediction we try to optimize data format of input values. In this paper we aim at showing which format of same values gives the best result. A few parameters were examined as described below.

Size of Input Vector. To get a working neural network we need to pass some values known as input vector. In this case our input contains parameters such as temperature, daily electricity usage, a day of the week and a day of the year. The real issue starts with how long this input vector should be. This question can be answered only empirically. Because of that, we prepared various types of input data to perform ANN learning on them. One of the facts to be verified is whether having a larger input corresponds to better outcome, or it is the other way round.

Because of weekly prediction, we encounters incomplete data - predicting usage in later days creates an issue of missing real electricity usage values of previous one to six days, depending on a day to be predicted. In that case instead of missing value we use predicted value of previous day. By doing that we show ANN that some of its data may not be precise and it has got a chance of being taken into consideration by alternate corresponding weights. We can observe the solution in Fig. 1 where algorithm works recursive by gathering previous electricity usage before calculating the current one.

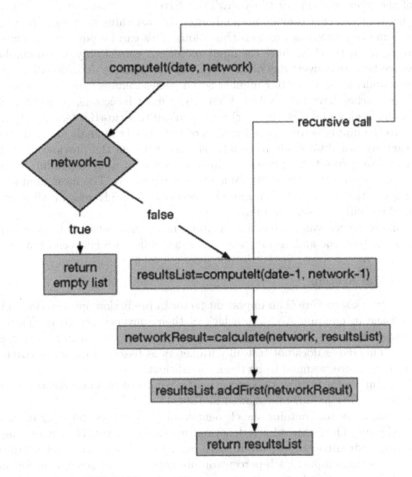

Fig. 1. The algorithm presented as a flowchart

Temperature. In predicting electricity usage we have the two most important factors passing through input vector: previous electricity usage and weather data. In case of weather data a relevant part is mostly temperature. In this research we study two approaches of passing temperature to the input vector. As we have gathered data from four different cities, we can pass those four (normalized) values to ANN or in second approach, average four numbers and pass it to the input vector. In this study we can check whether it is better to pass more data - increasing accuracy or shorten the input vector to give ANN less parameters to proceed.

Periodic Data. Another arguments passing to the input vector of ANN are day of the week and day of the year. They have a common feature: both are periodic. It means that they do not end, after the last value we got the first one on the same conditions as previous transitions. This can become an issue when passing as input to ANN. Since the input vector can consist only of real number values, we have to convert day of the week to some number. Additionally, ANN may not understand why after number seven comes number one. In this paper three approaches have been taken. Firstly, the most basic one, periodic value (day of the week and day of the year) is normalized to a closed interval $[0, 1]$ and passed to the input vector. Secondly, days of the week (and analogously days of the year) are put on a circle in equal distances between the previous and the next day. We access those points by sine and cosine of a corresponding angle. In the third approach we use sine value of the current day. The most significant advantage of that solution is continuity but an obvious disadvantage is that some distant days will have same values.

In this paper we want to test all the above mentioned concepts to determine which is the best one and also if there is relevant difference between them.

2.2   Neural System

Neural network structure is an important factor in prediction optimization. The biggest issue in creating ANNs is a lack of their universal structure. Thus it is necessary to create and investigate the most effective system to resolve each problem. This paper does not test all parameters as based on earlier researches some of them were assumed to be the most efficient.

The input vector in this ANN consists of a couple of previous days that are described by a few parameters showed in Table 1.

The output vector contains one element from $[0, 1]$ interval pointing to daily predicted value. Then, this value is denormalized to show actual electricity usage. The whole system consists of seven multi layer neural networks (perceptrons) that have common input. Each perceptron predicts the total power load for one of the seven successive days.

Table 1. The input vector for the artificial neural network

Parameter	Description
Electricity usage	Usage of electricity by customers throughout 24 h country wide
Temperature	Normalized value in Celsius degree in four cities
Day of the week	Normalized value from interval $[0, 1]$ pointing to a specific day of the week
Day of the year	Normalized value from interval $[0, 1]$ pointing to a specific day of the year

The hidden layer in ANN is very important when it comes to optimizing prediction. A number of layers and neurons in them are parameters that have important influence on the output value. The problem arises when the most optimal settings are varied in respect to the researched problem. Intuitive solutions, like increasing neurons in a hidden layer do not always indicate result optimization. In this paper we study influence that number of neurons in a hidden layer has on predicting output. Previous research showed that changing the number of a hidden layer to more than one gives significant deterioration of predicted value. Therefore in this paper we use only one hidden layer. Three approaches are taken. When number of neurons is: 10, 15 or 20 in one hidden layer. In all cases values are calculated by sigmoid function. We want to check if increasing number of neurons implicates better prediction or vice versa.

When it comes to learning methods, we have a lot of possibilities and techniques. In case of electricity usage prediction non-linear Levenberg-Marquardt optimization method is being used. It was the best one from all that was tested in case of electricity usage prediction. Number of epochs was set to 30. It is suitable to study efficiency provided parameters.

The Research Process. Another step after preparing research is its successful implementation. In the case of ANN, there are a lot of aspects that can be studied effectively such as data and learning. However, testing all of them in one paper is impossible and because of that some of them (like number of epochs) are constant. They were not changed during research whereby results from every approach are comparable.

To summarize all data passing to the input vector are normalized to $[0, 1]$ interval except temperature which is in $[-1, 1]$ interval. There is only one hidden layer with different number of neurons. The output vector contains one element in $[0, 1]$ interval, which points to electricity usage prediction at the national level.

Levenberg-Marquardt algorithm was chosen for a learning method and the epoch number was set to 30. All tested combinations were repeated four times and the best prediction was chosen. All results were put in a few tables to visualize better created dependencies. More accurate results can be seen in the next section.

3 Results

In this section results of previously presented concepts are described and explained. MAPE values are put into a few tables to better visualize differences between specific parameters. All values inside tables are percentages. To have a clearer view, description of the specific set of parameters is moved to another Table 2 and short symbol was created to represent them which takes less space and enables easier table reading.

Table 2. Symbols description

Symbol	Description
ld	number of days before that are passed to the input vector
ln	number of neurons in the hidden layer
n1	four temperatures passed to the input vector, without circle topology of periodic data, without sine continuity of periodic data
n2	four temperatures passed to the input vector, with circle topology of periodic data, without sine continuity of periodic data
n3	one-averaged temperature passed to the input vector, without circle topology of periodic data, without sine continuity of periodic data
n4	one-averaged temperature passed to the input vector, with circle topology of periodic data, without sine continuity of periodic data
n5	four temperatures passed to the input vector, without circle topology of periodic data, with sine continuity of periodic data
n6	one-averaged temperature passed to the input vector, without circle topology of periodic data, with sine continuity of periodic data

3.1 Periodic Data

For the purpose of ensuring proper results verification for periodic data, Table 3 was divided into two sections. The left side presents results of temperature provided as four values to the input vector, contrary to the right side where in all three columns one-average temperature for one day is provided. In both sections there are three identical columns which compare different solutions to the periodic data problem. Respectively from the left side we have a column where data is converted to regular numbers and then normalized, the next one is with circle topology and the last is a case where we use sine values as days representation.

Table 3. Results for periodic data problem

ld	ln	n1	n2	n5	n3	n4	n6
7	10	5,40 %	5,90 %	3,98 %	3,35 %	4,82 %	2,65 %
	15	5,56 %	6,02 %	4,54 %	3,86 %	4,27 %	2,84 %
	20	5,80 %	5,20 %	4,46 %	3,27 %	4,57 %	2,79 %
	25	5,47 %	6,81 %	5,61 %	3,09 %	4,87 %	4,27 %
14	10	6,01 %	5,03 %	4,61 %	3,31 %	5,90 %	2,64 %
	15	5,83 %	5,14 %	4,53 %	3,53 %	6,87 %	2,60 %
	20	5,42 %	5,75 %	4,56 %	3,38 %	5,09 %	2,79 %
	25	5,33 %	5,93 %	4,77 %	4,12 %	5,21 %	2,99 %
21	10	6,04 %	5,60 %	5,57 %	3,28 %	4,98 %	3,41 %
	15	5,67 %	5,44 %	4,96 %	3,41 %	5,37 %	3,40 %
	20	5,04 %	5,66 %	5,96 %	3,34 %	4,21 %	3,40 %
	25	5,44 %	6,02 %	5,53 %	3,84 %	4,61 %	3,43 %

Results here are not very optimistic for circle topology as a successful solution to the periodic data problem. MAPE in their case is definitely worse than other cases, no matter how many neurons hidden layer counts or how many days are passed to the input vector. In that case we can clearly state that it is better to avoid that method for these kind of problems. In the other two approaches we can see that almost all results are better in case of sine, continuous, periodic data interpretation. Only when "number of days before" and "neurons in hidden layer" parameters provided to the input vector are high, basic, non-continuous data interpretation gives slightly better MAPE result. We can conclude that the best approach is to use sine periodic data interpretation, without circle topology.

3.2 Temperature

Here we compare how different provision of temperature to the input vector influences the result. Table 4 was divided into three vertical sections. Each of them compares results when four temperatures are provided to the input vector (left side) or one-averaged (right side). Difference between sections lies in different parameters. It is important that in all sections only temperature parameter is changed and the rest of them stays the same. Because of that comparison, each section is reliable.

Results in this case seem to be clear. In most cases providing one-averaged temperature to the input vector gives a better outcome. Additionally looking at number of days or number of neurons in hidden layer passing to input vector, it is safe to assume that it does not influence outcome in either approach.

Table 4. Results for different temperature approach

ld	ln	n1	n3	n2	n4	n5	n6
7	10	5,40 %	3,35 %	5,90 %	4,82 %	3,98 %	2,65 %
	15	5,56 %	3,86 %	6,02 %	4,27 %	4,54 %	2,84 %
	20	5,80 %	3,27 %	5,20 %	4,57 %	4,46 %	2,79 %
	25	5,47 %	3,09 %	6,81 %	4,87 %	5,61 %	4,27 %
14	10	6,01 %	3,31 %	5,03 %	5,9 %	4,61 %	2,64 %
	15	5,83 %	3,53 %	5,14 %	6,87 %	4,53 %	2,60 %
	20	5,42 %	3,38 %	5,75 %	5,09 %	4,56 %	2,79 %
	25	5,33 %	4,12 %	5,93 %	5,21 %	4,77 %	2,99 %
21	10	6,04 %	3,28 %	5,60 %	4,98 %	5,57 %	3,41 %
	15	5,67 %	3,41 %	5,44 %	5,37 %	4,96 %	3,40 %
	20	5,04 %	3,34 %	5,66 %	4,21 %	5,96 %	3,40 %
	25	5,44 %	3,84 %	6,02 %	4,61 %	5,53 %	3,43 %

3.3   Number of Neurons in Hidden Layer

In this case we are checking if increasing number of neurons in hidden layer optimizes the results. In all cases (n1–n6) we can observe how output MAPE behaves when more neurons are added to the hidden layer. All results can be seen in Table 5. It is divided into three horizontal sections. Each of them represents different "number of days before" parameter provided to the input vector, while in every one of them we have four different combinations of the hidden layer.

Table 5. Results for different numbers of neurons in the hidden layer

ld	ln	n1	n2	n3	n4	n5	n6
7	10	5,40 %	5,90 %	3,35 %	4,82 %	3,98 %	2,65 %
	15	5,56 %	6,02 %	3,86 %	4,27 %	4,54 %	2,84 %
	20	5,80 %	5,20 %	3,27 %	4,57 %	4,46 %	2,79 %
	25	5,47 %	6,81 %	3,09 %	4,87 %	5,61 %	4,27 %
14	10	6,01 %	5,03 %	3,31 %	5,90 %	4,61 %	2,64 %
	15	5,83 %	5,14 %	3,53 %	6,87 %	4,53 %	2,60 %
	20	5,42 %	5,75 %	3,38 %	5,09 %	4,56 %	2,79 %
	25	5,33 %	5,93 %	4,12 %	5,21 %	4,77 %	2,99 %
21	10	6,04 %	5,60 %	3,28 %	4,98 %	5,57 %	3,41 %
	15	5,67 %	5,44 %	3,41 %	5,37 %	4,96 %	3,40 %
	20	5,04 %	5,66 %	3,34 %	4,21 %	5,96 %	3,40 %
	25	5,44 %	6,02 %	3,84 %	4,61 %	5,53 %	3,43 %

Results in this case do not lead to unambiguous conclusions. The general trend is to degrade MAPE values in case of an increase in an amount of neurons, therefore a huge number of exceptions discourages from creating such assumptions. In fact two of the best results occur when the number of neurons are 10 and 15, which are rather low numbers. Also, we cannot conclude that more neurons are better with a bigger input vector (number of days before [ld]) because there are one of the highest MAPE results in this area. To sum up, this case does not give us clear conclusions and we need more research in this area.

3.4   Size of the Input Vector

Size of the input vector is a very interesting parameter to study. It shows the importance of electric usage that had place days before to predict near future. Table 6 is divided, much like in case before, into four sections. All of them contain three different numbers which represent size of input vector. However, each section has different value of neurons in hidden layer.

Interpretation of the results here is difficult, much like in previous cases. General trend does not implicate any conclusions. We can notice that in some

Table 6. Results of different size of the input vector

ln	ld	n1	n2	n3	n4	n5	n6
10	7	5,40 %	5,90 %	3,35 %	4,82 %	3,98 %	2,65 %
	14	6,01 %	5,03 %	3,31 %	5,90 %	4,61 %	2,64 %
	21	6,04 %	5,60 %	3,28 %	4,98 %	5,57 %	3,41 %
15	7	5,56 %	6,02 %	3,86 %	4,27 %	4,54 %	2,84 %
	14	5,83 %	5,14 %	3,53 %	6,87 %	4,53 %	2,60 %
	21	5,67 %	5,44 %	3,41 %	5,37 %	4,96 %	3,40 %
20	7	5,80 %	5,20 %	3,27 %	4,57 %	4,46 %	2,79 %
	14	5,42 %	5,75 %	3,38 %	5,09 %	4,56 %	2,79 %
	21	5,04 %	5,66 %	3,34 %	4,21 %	5,96 %	3,40 %
25	7	5,47 %	6,81 %	3,09 %	4,87 %	5,61 %	4,27 %
	14	5,33 %	5,93 %	4,12 %	5,21 %	4,77 %	2,99 %
	21	5,44 %	6,02 %	3,84 %	4,61 %	5,53 %	3,43 %

cases increasing the input vector causes better MAPE outcome. In other cases we cannot see any dependencies on which we can base our conclusions. It is worth noting, however, that a few of the best results have a lower size of the input vector.

4   Concluding Remarks

The MAPE error for the applied systems of perceptrons depends on the used data and their representation. The MAPE for most effective system is equal to 2.6 %. This result is comparable for results communicated in the papers that refers results for mod-term power load prediction - for instance in [22] MAPE is equal to 2.54 % for monthly prediction. The system of perceptrons that have fifteen neurons in hidden layers turned out to be the most effective one. Furthermore, power load for the last fourteen days was taken into consideration and one-averaged temperature was passed to the input vector. Moreover, the periodic data were encoded without circle topology but with the sine representation.

References

1. Abdel-Aal, R.E., Al-Garni, A.Z.: Forecasting monthly electric energy consumption in eastern Saudi Arabia using univariate time-series analysis. Fuel Energ. Abstr. **38**, 452 (1997)
2. Abdel-Aal, R.E., Al-Garni, A.Z., Al-Nassar, Y.N.: Modelling and forecasting monthly electric energy consumption in eastern Saudi Arabia using abductive networks. Energy **22**, 911–921 (1997)
3. Abdel-Aal, R.E.: Short-term hourly load forecasting using abductive networks. IEEE Trans. Power Syst. **19**, 164–173 (2004)

4. Abdel-Aal, R.E.: Improving electric load forecasts using network committees. Electr. Power Syst. Res. **74**, 83–94 (2005)
5. Abdel-Aal, R.E.: Modeling and forecasting electric daily peak loads using abductive networks. Int. J. Electr. Power Energ. Syst. **28**, 133–141 (2006)
6. Al-Hamadi, H.M., Soliman, S.A.: Long-term, mid-term electric load forecasting based on short-term correlation and annual growth. Electr. Power Syst. Res. **74**, 353–361 (2005)
7. Amjady, N., Keynia, F.: Mid-term load forecasting of power systems by a new prediction method. Energy Convers. Manage. **49**, 2678–2687 (2008)
8. Bartkiewicz, W.: Confidence intervals prediction for the short-term electrical load neural forecasting models. Elektrotechnik und Informationstechnik **117**, 8–12 (2000)
9. Bąk, M., Bielecki, A.: Neural systems for short-term forecasting of electric power load. In: Beliczynski, B., Dzielinski, A., Iwanowski, M., Ribeiro, B. (eds.) ICAN-NGA 2007. LNCS, vol. 4432, pp. 133–142. Springer, Heidelberg (2007)
10. Bielecki, A., Bąk, M.: Methodology of Neural Systems Development. In: Cader, A., Rutkowski, L., Tadeusiewicz, R., Żurada, J. (eds.) Artificial Intelligence and Soft Computing. Challenging Problems of Science - Computer Science, pp. 1–7. Academic Publishing House EXIT, Warszawa (2006)
11. Djukanowic, M., Babic, B., Sobajic, D.J., Pao, Y.H.: Unsupervised/supervised learning concept for 24-hour load forecasting. IEE Proc. **4**, 311–318 (1993)
12. Elattar, E.E., Goulermas, J., Wu, Q.H.: Electric load forecasting based on locally weighted support vector regression. IEEE Trans. Syst. Man Cybern. Part C Appl. Rev. **40**, 438–447 (2010)
13. Espinoza, M., Suykens, J.A.K., Belmans, R., De Moor, B.: Electric load forecasting. IEEE Control Syst. **27**, 43–57 (2007)
14. Geng, G., Qu, R.: Application of fuzzy linear regression to load forecasting. In: Proceeding of China International Conference on Electricity Distribution CICED 2006, pp. 199–205 (2006)
15. Ghiassi, M., Zimbra, D.K., Saidane, H.: Medium term system load forecasting with a dynamic artificial neural network model. Electr. Power Syst. Res. **76**(5), 302–316 (2006)
16. Hsu, Y.Y., Ho, K.L.: Fuzzy expert systems: an application to short-term load forecasting. IEE Proc. **6**, 471–477 (1992)
17. Hu, Z., Bao, Y., Xiong, T.: Electricity load forecasting using support vector regression with memetic algorithms. Scientific World Journal 2013 (2013). Article ID: 292575
18. Kiartzis, S.J., Bakirtzis, A.G., Petridis, V.: Short-term load forecasting using neural networks. Electr. Power Syst. Res. **33**, 1–6 (1995)
19. Mirasgedis, S., Sarafidis, Y., Georgopoulou, E.: Models for mid-term electricity demand forecasting incorporating weather influences. Energy **31**, 208–227 (2006)
20. Peng, T.M., Hubele, N.F., Karady, G.G.: Advancement in the application of neural networks for short-term load forecasting. IEEE Trans. Power Syst. **7**, 250–257 (1992)
21. Singh, A.K., Ibraheem, I., Khatoon, S., Muazzam, M., Chaturvedi, D.K.: Load forecasting techniques and methodologies: a review. In: Proceedinngs of the 2nd Conference on Power, Control and Embedding Systems, pp. 631–640 (2012)
22. Xue, J., Xu, Z., Watada, J.: Building an integrated hybrid model for short-term and mid-term load forecasting with genetic optimization. Int. J. Innovative Comput. Inf. Control **8**, 7381–7391 (2012)

A New Proposition of the Activation Function for Significant Improvement of Neural Networks Performance

Jarosław Bilski[1]([⊠]) and Alexander I. Galushkin[2]

[1] Institute of Computational Intelligence,
Częstochowa University of Technology, Częstochowa, Poland
`Jaroslaw.Bilski@iisi.pcz.pl`
[2] Moscow Institute of Physics and Technology, Dolgoprudny, Russia
`neurocomputer@yandex.ru`

Abstract. An activation function is a very important part of an artificial neuron model. Multilayer neural networks can properly work only when these functions are nonlinear. A simple approximation of an often applied hyperbolic tangent activation function is presented. This proposed function is computationally highly effective. Computational comparisons for two well-known test problems are discussed. The results are very promising in potential applications to FPGA chips designing.

Keywords: Neural networks · Activation function · Transfer function

1 Introduction

In the recent years various soft computing techniques have been developed [13–16, 22–24, 27–31, 34, 40]. Various feedforward multilayer neural networks have been investigated by many scientists, e.g., [2, 3, 18, 19, 25, 26, 35–39]. A large number of networks use non-linear activation functions. These functions are relatively computationally expensive. This is particularly disadvantageous for small networks, for parallel implementation of neural networks and for operating a network which has been already learned. The activation function and its derivative are used in the recall phase and by most learning algorithms in the learning phase, respectively. Thus, efficiency of the activation function is very important for both the working time and learning time of a neural network. This problem has been studied in [1, 17, 20, 21]. Unfortunately, the performance of the presented functions did not prove satisfactory. This necessitates a search for an efficient activation function which will be simple in implementation. This is particularly important in the case of parallel pipelining solutions [4–12, 32, 33]. whose performance may be limited by a slow activation function.

In multilayer or fully connected (FCC) neural networks each neuron can be connected to any input or any previous neuron outputs. After calculating the

© Springer International Publishing Switzerland 2016
L. Rutkowski et al. (Eds.): ICAISC 2016, Part I, LNAI 9692, pp. 35–45, 2016.
DOI: 10.1007/978-3-319-39378-0_4

weighted sum s_i of neuron inputs, the value y_i of the activation function is determined. The Eqs. (1) and (2) describe the recall phase of a network:

$$s_i(n) = \sum_j w_{ij}(n) x_j(n), \tag{1}$$

$$y_i(n) = f(s_i(n)), \tag{2}$$

where $f()$ is the neuron activation function. The hyperbolic tangent (tanh) is very often used as the activation function:

$$y_1 = f_1(s) = \tanh(s) = \frac{e^s - e^{-s}}{e^s + e^{-s}} = \frac{1 - e^{-2s}}{1 + e^{-2s}} = 1 - \frac{2}{1 + e^{2s}} \tag{3}$$

The ability to easily calculate the derivative based on the hyperbolic tangent value is very advantageous:

$$y_1' = \tan h'(s) = 1 - y_1^2 \tag{4}$$

Figure 1 shows the graph of the hyperbolic tangent function and its derivative.

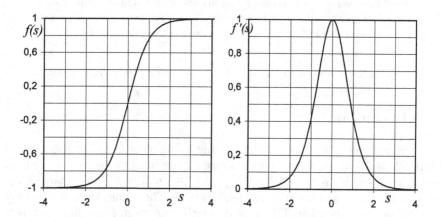

Fig. 1. The graph of the hyperbolic tangent function and its derivative

Unfortunately, calculating the hyperbolic tangent is computationally demanding. To reduce this inconvenience in this paper a linear quadratic (LinQ) activation function is proposed:

$$y_2 = f_2(s) = \begin{cases} as - b; & s \leq -2 + 2a \\ 0.25s(4 - abs(s)); & -2 + 2a < s < 2 - 2a \\ as + b; & s \geq 2 - 2a \end{cases} \tag{5}$$

where a is a slope of function linear part, and b is obtained from:

$$b = 1 - 2s + s^2. \tag{6}$$

The derivative of the LinQ function is given by:

$$y_2' = f_2'(s) = \begin{cases} 1 - 0.5abs(s); & -2 + 2a < x \le 2 - 2a \\ a; & s \le -2 + 2a; s \ge 2 - 2a; \end{cases} \tag{7}$$

In the Fig. 2 the graph of the linear quadratic LinQ function and its derivative is presented. It is easy to see that the proposed function is similar to the hyperbolic tangent, but for larger arguments it does not converge to the values of 1 or -1. The linear quadratic function is a combination of linear and quadratic functions in the appropriate ranges of the s value. There are four ranges: $(-\infty, -2 + 2a)$; $(-2 + 2a, 0)$; $(0, 2 - 2a)$ and $(2 - 2a, \infty)$. In the first and fourth ranges the LinQ function is linear while in the second and third ranges this function is quadratic. In the connection points of these functions their derivatives are equal so that the derivative of the LinQ function is continuous. The slope a and offset b are selected so that the linear functions are tangential to the quadratic functions.

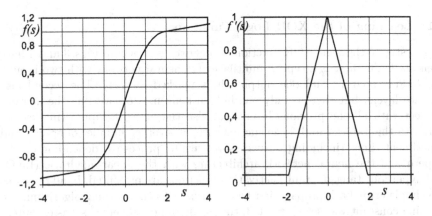

Fig. 2. The graph of the linear quadratic function and its derivative

It is important that the computational load on the linear quadratic function is low. Only one or two multiplications and one addition are needed.

2   Computational Results

First, operation times of LinQ and tanh functions have been investigated. Both functions have been run 10 million times for randomly selected arguments. The results are shown in Table 1. The calculation time of the LinQ function is about four times shorter than the time of the tanh function, while the calculation times of their derivatives are comparable for both functions.

In the next subsections the two learning problems are tested. The first is a simple XOR problem, and the second is the two-spiral problem. For both problems a

Table 1. Times of 10 million computations of the hyperbolic tangent and linear-quadratic activation functions and their ratio.

Function	Function time	Derivative time
tanh	451	88
LinQ	111	90
Speed ratio	0.2461	1.0227

neural network is considered as trained if the error criterion in each iteration of the epoch falls below the set threshold γ:

$$\sum_{i=1}^{N_L} \left[d_i^{(L)}(t) - y_i^{(L)}(t) \right]^2 \leq \gamma. \tag{8}$$

2.1 Learning of the XOR Logic Function

To investigate the logic XOR function two networks shown in Figs. 3 and 4 have been used. The first is a typical multilayer (2) neural network with two inputs, two hidden neurons and one output (it is marked by 221). The second also has two layers, but there is only one hidden neuron. Moreover, all the neurons connect with all the previous layers and also the network inputs (marked by 211f). In the Tables 2 and 3 the success rate, an average number of epochs and experiment times (including unsuccessful learning processes) depending on the slope a and the neural network architecture with the linear-quadratic (LinQ) and hyperbolic tangent (tanh) activation functions are presented. In all the cases the simple error back propagation has been used as the learning algorithm, the learning constant was set to $\eta = 0.3$, the maximum of 200 epochs was executed, and the threshold was set to $\gamma = 0.1$. Each learning process was repeated 100 times.

Table 4 shows the times (without an additional time needed to organize the experiment) of 10 million working/learning epochs depending on the neural net-

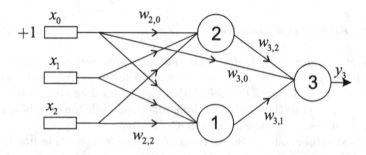

Fig. 3. The two-layer neural networks architecture (221) for learning the XOR problem

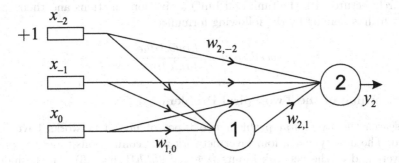

Fig. 4. The two-layer fully connected neural networks architecture (211f) for learning the XOR problem

Table 2. The XOR problem. The success rate, an average number of epochs and experiment times depending on the slope a and the neural network architecture with the **linear-quadratic** activation function.

	slope								
	0.01			0.05			0.1		
Network arch.	Succ. rate	Average epoch	Exper. time	Succ. rate	Average epoch	Exper. time	Succ. rate	Average epoch	Exper. time
221	87	37	0.10	88	34	0.10	88	41	0.11
211f	73	140	0.15	99	54	0.08	98	44	0.08

Table 3. The XOR problem. The success rate, an average number of epochs and experiment times depending on the neural network architecture with the **hyperbolic tangent** activation function and their ratio.

Network arch.	Succ. rate	Average epoch	Exper. time
221	95	35	0.09
211f	94	85	0.14

Table 4. The XOR problem. Times of 10 million learning epochs depending on the neural network architecture with the **hyperbolic tangent** and **linear-quadratic** activation functions and their ratio.

	Working			*Learning*		
Network arch.	tanh time	LinQ time	Speed ratio	tanh time	LinQ time	Speed ratio
221	12	6	0.5000	50	38	0.7600
211f	9	6	0.6667	40	18	0.4500

work architecture with the tanh and LinQ activation functions and their speed ratio, which is defined by the following formula:

$$speed\_ratio = \frac{LinQ\_time}{tanh\_time}.$$ (9)

2.2 Learning of the Two-Spiral Problem

To research the two-spiral problem two types of neural networks have been applied. The first type is a four-layer network with connections to all the previous layers and to the network inputs (marked $2hhh1f$, $h=3..6$). All the hidden layers have h neurons. The second type of network is shown in Fig. 5.

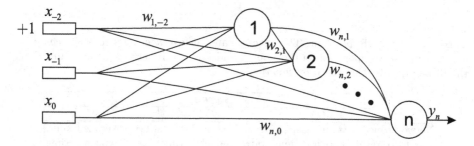

Fig. 5. The fully connected neural networks architecture with n neurons for learning the two-spiral problem

Table 5. The two-spiral problem. The success rate, an average number of epochs and experiment times depending on the slope a and the number of neurons in the fully connected four-layer neural network with the **linear-quadratic** activation function.

| Network arch. | slope | | | | | | | | |
| | 0.001 | | | 0.01 | | | 0.1 | | |
	Succ. rate	Average epoch	Exper. time	Succ. rate	Average epoch	Exper. time	Succ. rate	Average epoch	Exper time
23331f	40	1970	51	27	2519	58	0	-	67
24441f	78	1743	42	72	1795	46	30	2594	73
25551f	93	1353	34	90	1371	37	80	2010	56
26661f	97	1230	36	90	1273	43	95	1386	42

This network is called a fully connected cascade (FCC). Each neuron is connected to all the previous neurons and network inputs. For both network types the error back propagation has been used, the learning factor was set to $\eta = 0.01$, the maximum of 5000 epoch was executed, the threshold was set to $\gamma = 0.1$, and there were 100 trials.

The success rate, an average number of epochs and an experiment times (including unsuccessful learning processes) depending on the slope a and the neural network architecture for the LinQ and tanh activation functions are presented in the Tables 5, 6, 7 and 8 for both types of neural networks respectively.

Table 6. The two-spiral problem. the success rate, an average number of epochs and experiment times depending on the number of neurons in the fully connected four-layer neural network with the **hyperbolic tangent** activation function.

Network of arch.	Succ. rate	Average epoch	Exper. time
23331f	20	2294	75
24441f	81	1741	52
25551f	87	1543	57
26661f	96	1384	52

Table 7. The two-spiral problem. The success rate, an average number of epochs and experiment times depending on the slope s and the number of neurons in the fully connected cascade with the **linear-quadratic** activation function.

	slope								
	0.001			0.01			0.1		
Number of Neurons	Succ. rate	Average epoch	Exper. time	Succ. rate	Average epoch	Exper. time	Succ. rate	Average epoch	Exper time
8	13	2216	72	10	1988	73	0	-	77
10	44	1915	74	41	1993	76	5	3385	99
12	69	1586	74	65	1755	81	39	2352	112
14	76	1660	86	78	1481	79	75	1983	97
16	81	1504	93	88	1509	83	96	1475	70
18	85	1427	101	89	1498	98	99	1238	67

Table 8. The two-spiral problem. The success rate, an average number of epochs and experiment times depending on the number of neurons in the fully connected cascade with the **hyperbolic tangent** activation function.

Number of neurons	Succ. rate	Average epoch	Exper. time
8	12	2093	83
10	38	1861	90
12	73	1580	77
14	81	1597	90
16	90	1570	93
18	92	1598	109

Tables 9 and 10 show the times (without an additional time needed to organize the experiment) of 500 thousand learning epochs depending on the neural network architecture with the tanh and LinQ activation functions and their speed ratio.

Table 9. The two-spiral problem. The times of 500 thousand learning epochs depending on the number of neurons in the fully connected four-layer neural network with the **hyperbolic tangent** and **linear-quadratic** activation functions and their ratio.

Network arch.	*Working*			*Learning*		
	tanh time	LinQ time	Speed ratio	tanh time	LinQ time	Speed ratio
23331f	44	25	0.5682	80	63	0.7875
24441f	57	33	0.5789	104	81	0.7788
25551f	71	42	0.5915	133	102	0.7669
26661f	90	52	0.5778	166	126	0.7590

Table 10. The two-spiral problem. The time of 500 thousand learning epochs depending on the number of neurons in the fully connected cascade with the **hyperbolic tangent** and **linear-quadratic** activation functions and their ratio.

Number of Neurons	*Working*			*Learning*		
	tanh time	LinQ time	Speed ratio	tanh time	LinQ time	Speed ratio
8	38	23	0.6053	86	72	0.8372
10	47	29	0.6170	117	100	0.8547
12	58	36	0.6201	159	135	0.8491
14	68	43	0.6324	201	176	0.8756
16	80	52	0.6500	244	217	0.8893
18	92	61	0.6630	293	261	0.8908

3   Conclusion

In this paper the linear quadratic activation function for a neural network learning algorithm are presented. We have compared computational performance of the linear quadratic activation function with the hyperbolic tangent activation function. Moreover, the time of computations per epoch with the linear quadratic activation function for working/learning process is up to 40 %/30 % shorter than with the hyperbolic tangent function respectively. In most cases the number of epochs needed to learn a neural network is slightly smaller, and success rate is greater. It has been observed that the performance of the proposed solution is promising. Additionally, a parallel approach can be used for calculation of the linear quadratic activation function, which will results in an even greater acceleration. It should be emphasized that the result of acceleration has been only achieved by simple replacing of the activation function without affecting the structure of the network and the learning algorithm. The proposed function can be applied to other learning methods [2,3,18,19,25,37–39].

In future research it might be possible to create a parallel version of the linear quadratic activation function by its implementation in: the SIMD operations, the GPUs accelerators and the FPGAs chips.

References

1. Bilski, J.: The backpropagation learning with logarithmic transfer function. In: Proceedings of 5th Conference On Neural Networks and Soft Computing, Poland, pp. 71–76 (2000)
2. Bilski, J., Rutkowski, L.: A fast training algorithm for neural networks. IEEE Trans. Circuits Syst. II, Analog Digit. Signal Process. **45**(6), 749–753 (1998)
3. Bilski, J.: The UD RLS algorithm for training the feedforward neural networks. Int. J. Appl. Math. Comput. Sci. **15**(1), 101–109 (2005)
4. Bilski, J., Litwiński, S., Smoląg, J.: Parallel realisation of QR algorithm for neural networks learning. In: Rutkowski, L., Siekmann, J.H., Tadeusiewicz, R., Zadeh, L.A. (eds.) ICAISC 2004. LNCS (LNAI), vol. 3070, pp. 158–165. Springer, Heidelberg (2004)
5. Bilski, J., Smoląg, J.: Parallel realisation of the recurrent RTRN neural network learning. In: Rutkowski, L., Tadeusiewicz, R., Zadeh, L.A., Zurada, J.M. (eds.) ICAISC 2008. LNCS (LNAI), vol. 5097, pp. 11–16. Springer, Heidelberg (2008)
6. Bilski, J., Smoląg, J.: Parallel realisation of the recurrent Elman neural network learning. In: Rutkowski, L., Scherer, R., Tadeusiewicz, R., Zadeh, L.A., Zurada, J.M. (eds.) ICAISC 2010, Part II. LNCS(LNAI), vol. 6114, pp. 19–25. Springer, Heidelberg (2010)
7. Bilski, J., Smoląg, J.: Parallel realisation of the recurrent multi layer perceptron learning. In: Rutkowski, L., Korytkowski, M., Scherer, R., Tadeusiewicz, R., Zadeh, L.A., Zurada, J.M. (eds.) ICAISC 2012, Part I. LNCS(LNAI), vol. 7267, pp. 12–20. Springer, Heidelberg (2012)
8. Bilski, J., Smoląg, J.: Parallel approach to learning of the recurrent Jordan neural network. In: Rutkowski, L., Korytkowski, M., Scherer, R., Tadeusiewicz, R., Zadeh, L.A., Zurada, J.M. (eds.) ICAISC 2013, Part I. LNCS(LNAI), vol. 7894, pp. 32–40. Springer, Heidelberg (2013)
9. Bilski, J.: Parallel Structures for Feedforward and Dynamical Neural Networks. AOW EXIT (2013). (in Polish)
10. Bilski, J., Smoląg, J., Galushkin, A.I.: The parallel approach to the conjugate gradient learning algorithm for the feedforward neural networks. In: Rutkowski, L., Korytkowski, M., Scherer, R., Tadeusiewicz, R., Zadeh, L.A., Zurada, J.M. (eds.) ICAISC 2014, Part I. LNCS(LNAI), vol. 8467, pp. 12–21. Springer, Heidelberg (2014)
11. Bilski, J., Smoląg, J.: Parallel architectures for learning the RTRN and Elman dynamic neural networks. IEEE Trans. Parallel Distrib. Syst. **26**(9), 2561–2570 (2015)

12. Bilski, J., Smoląg, J., Żurada, J.M.: Parallel approach to the Levenberg-Marquardt learning algorithm for feedforward neural networks. In: Rutkowski, L., Korytkowski, M., Scherer, R., Tadeusiewicz, R., Zadeh, L.A., Zurada, J.M. (eds.) Artificial Intelligence and Soft Computing. LNCS(LNAI), vol. 9119, pp. 3–14. Springer, Heidelberg (2015)

13. Chu, L.J., Krzyżak, A.: The recognition of partially occluded objects with support vector machines, convolutional neural networks and deep belief networks. J. Artif. Intell. Soft Comput. Res. **4**(1), 5–19 (2014)

14. Cpałka, K., Łapa, K., Przybył, A., Zalasiński, M.: A new method for designing neuro-fuzzy systems for nonlinear modelling with interpretability aspects. Neurocomputing **135**, 203–217 (2014)

15. Cpałka, K., Rebrova, O., Nowicki, R., Rutkowski, L.: On design of flexible neuro-fuzzy systems for nonlinear modelling. Int. J. Gen. Syst. **42**(6), 706–720 (2013)

16. Cpałka, K., Zalasiński, M., Rutkowski, L.: New method for the on-line signature verification based on horizontal partitioning. Pattern Recognit. **47**, 2652–2661 (2014)

17. Duch, W., Jankowski, N.: A survey of neural transfer functions. Neural Comput. Surv. **2**, 163–213 (1999)

18. Fahlman, S.: Faster learning variations on back-propagation: an empirical study. In: Proceedings of Connectionist Models Summer School, Los Atos (1988)

19. Hagan, M.T., Menhaj, M.B.: Training feedforward networks with the Marquardt algorithm. IEEE Trans. Neural Netw. **5**(6), 989–993 (1994)

20. Jankowski, N., Duch, W.: Optimal transfer function neural networks. In: Procedings of the 9th European Symposium on Artificial Neural Networks, Bruges, Belgium, pp. 101–106 (2001)

21. Kamruzzaman, J., Aziz, S.M.: A note on activation function in multilayer feedforward learning. In: Proceedings of International Joint Conference on Neural Networks: IJCNN 2002, vol. 1, pp. 519–523 (2002)

22. Kitajima, R., Kamimura, R.: Accumulative information enhancement in the self-organizing maps and its application to the analysis of mission statements. J. Artif. Intell. Soft Comput. Res. **5**(3), 161–176 (2015)

23. Korytkowski, M., Rutkowski, L., Scherer, R.: Fast image classification by boosting fuzzy classifiers. Inf. Sci. **327**, 175–182 (2016)

24. Łapa, K., Zalasiński, M., Cpałka, K.: A new method for designing and complexity reduction of neuro-fuzzy systems for nonlinear modelling. In: Rutkowski, L., Korytkowski, M., Scherer, R., Tadeusiewicz, R., Zadeh, L.A., Zurada, J.M. (eds.) ICAISC 2013, Part I. LNCS(LNAI), vol. 7894, pp. 329–344. Springer, Heidelberg (2013)

25. Riedmiller, M., Braun, H.: A direct method for faster backpropagation learning: the RPROP algorithm. In: IEEE International Conference on Neural Networks, San Francisco (1993)

26. Rumelhart, D.E., Hinton, G.E., Williams, R.J.: Learning internal representations by error propagation. In: Rumelhart, D.E., McClelland, J.L. (eds.) Parallel Distributed Processing, vol. 1, chap. 8. The MIT Press, Cambridge (1986)

27. Rutkowski, L., Jaworski, M., Pietruczuk, L., Duda, P.: Decision trees for mining data streams based on the Gaussian approximation. IEEE Trans. Knowl. Data Eng. **26**(1), 108–119 (2014)

28. Rutkowski, L., Jaworski, M., Pietruczuk, L., Duda, P.: A new method for data stream mining based on the misclassification error. IEEE Trans. Neural Netw. Learn. Syst. **26**(5), 1048–1059 (2015)

29. Rutkowski, L., Pietruczuk, L., Duda, P., Jaworski, M.: Decision trees for mining data streams based on the McDiarmid's bound. IEEE Trans. Knowl. Data Eng. **25**(6), 1272–1279 (2013)

30. Rutkowski, L., Jaworski, M., Pietruczuk, L., Duda, P.: The CART decision trees for mining data streams. Inf. Sci. **266**, 1–15 (2014)

31. Serdah, A.M., Ashour, W.M.: Clustering large-scale data based on modified affinity propagation algorithm. J. Artif. Intell. Soft Comput. Res. **6**(1), 23–33 (2016)

32. Smoląg, J., Bilski, J.: A systolic array for fast learning of neural networks. In: Proceedings of V Conference Neural Networks and Soft Computing, Zakopane, pp. 754–758 (2000)

33. Smoląg, J., Rutkowski, L., Bilski, J.: Systolic array for neural networks. In: Proceedings of IV Conference Neural Networks and their Applications, Zakopane, pp. 487–497 (1999)

34. Starczewski, A.: A new validity index for crisp clusters. Pattern Anal. Appl. (2015). doi:10.1007/s10044-015-0525-8

35. Tadeusiewicz, R.: Neural Networks. AOW RM (1993). (in Polish)

36. Werbos, J.: Backpropagation through time: what it does and how to do it. Proc. IEEE **78**(10), 1550–1560 (1990)

37. Wilamowski, B.M., Yo, H.: Neural network learning without backpropagation. IEEE Trans. Neural Netw. **21**(11), 1793–1803 (2010)

38. Wilamowski, B.M., Yo, H.: Improved computation for Levenberg-Marquardt training. IEEE Trans. Neural Netw. **21**(6), 930–937 (2010)

39. Yo, H., Reiner, P.D., Xie, T., Bartczak, T., Wilamowski, B.M.: An incremental design of radial basis function networks. IEEE Trans. Neural Netw. Learn. Syst. **25**(10), 1793–1803 (2014)

40. Zalasiński, M., Łapa, K., Cpałka, K.: New algorithm for evolutionary selection of the dynamic signature global features. In: Rutkowski, L., Korytkowski, M., Scherer, R., Tadeusiewicz, R., Zadeh, L.A., Zurada, J.M. (eds.) ICAISC 2013, Part II. LNCS(LNAI), vol. 7895, pp. 113–121. Springer, Heidelberg (2013)

Application of the Givens Rotations
in the Neural Network Learning Algorithm

Jarosław Bilski[1]($^{(\boxtimes)}$), Bartosz Kowalczyk[1], and Jacek M. Żurada[2]

[1] Institute of Computational Intelligence, Częstochowa University of Technology,
Częstochowa, Poland
{Jaroslaw.Bilski,Bartosz.Kowalczyk}@iisi.pcz.pl
[2] Department Electrical and Computer Engineering, University of Louisville,
Louisville, KY 40292, USA
jacek.zurada@louisville.edu

Abstract. This paper presents application of Givens rotations in the process of learning feedforward artificial neural network. This approach is based on QR decomposition. The paper describes mathematical background that needs to be considered during the application of the Givens rotations. The paper concludes with results of example simulations.

Keywords: Neural network training algorithm · QR decomposition · Givens rotation

1 Introduction

Artificial Neural Networks nowadays are broadly used in many areas of human everyday life. They can be found in many areas of forecasting e.g. weather, market tendencies, prices, etc [16,17,22–24,26]. Artificial Neural Networks can also be applied in the scope of various process optimizations, signal filtrations and much more [1,13,14,18,21,27]. Before an ANN is ready to be used, it needs to be trained for solving a demanded task. One of the best known and rudimentary learning algorithms for a feedforward Artificial Neural Network is the Error Back Propagation [8]. Unfortunately this algorithm requires a lot of time and effort to train a network [4,12,18,20]. During the researches aimed at improving teaching process of neural networks many algorithms have been developed [3,9,11,15,25,29]. Many of them require less epoch count than the Back Propagation algorithm but consume more resources, e.g. the Levenberg-Marquardt method [25]. The purpose of this paper is to formulate the Givens algorithm based on QR decomposition and apply it to learning a neural network. The goal is to prove that this approach can achieve desired error value in a significantly shorter time than the Back Propagation method.

2 Givens Rotations Basics

The Givens rotations is one of a few elementary orthogonal transformation methods. The most common practice is to limit rotation around a single plain,

© Springer International Publishing Switzerland 2016
L. Rutkowski et al. (Eds.): ICAISC 2016, Part I, LNAI 9692, pp. 46–56, 2016.
DOI: 10.1007/978-3-319-39378-0_5

stretched between two unit vectors $span\{e_p, e_q\}(1 \leq p < q \leq n)$. Each rotation is described by the following matrix [2].

$$
\mathbf{G}_{pq} = \begin{bmatrix} 1 & & & \cdots & & 0 \\ & \ddots & & & & \\ & & c & \cdots & s & \\ \vdots & & \vdots & \ddots & \vdots & \vdots \\ & & -s & \cdots & c & \\ & & & & & \ddots & \\ 0 & & & \cdots & & 1 \end{bmatrix} \begin{matrix} \\ \\ p \\ \\ q \\ \\ \\ \end{matrix} \tag{1}
$$
$$ \quad\quad\quad p \quad q $$

Matrices $\mathbf{G}_{pq}$ are called rotation matrices or rotations. By definition, those matrices differ from Identity matrix only in terms of four elements

$$
g_{pp} = g_{qq} = c \qquad g_{pq} = -g_{qp} = s, \tag{2}
$$

where

$$
c^2 + s^2 = 1, \tag{3}
$$

which obviously leads to equation $\mathbf{G}_{pq}^T \mathbf{G}_{pq} = \mathbf{I}$ and the proof that matrix $\mathbf{G}_{pq}$ is an orthogonal matrix. The rotation is performed by orthogonal transformation given in Eq. (4)

$$
\mathbf{x} \to \mathbf{y} = \mathbf{G}_{pq}\mathbf{x} \tag{4}
$$

which leads to the following equalities

$$
\begin{aligned}
y_p &= cx_p + sx_q \\
y_q &= -sx_p + cx_q \\
y_i &= x_i \quad (i \neq p, q; i = 1, \dots, n)
\end{aligned} \tag{5}
$$

Let $\mathbf{a} \in \mathbb{R}^n$. From Eq. (5) only two elements of vector $\mathbf{a}$ are being changed during a single rotation. There is a possibility to pick rotation parameters to make one of the elements a_p or a_q equal 0. In order to replace value a_q with 0, Eq. (5) has to be taken under further consideration

$$
\bar{a}_q = -sa_p + ca_q = 0. \tag{6}
$$

Parameters c and s of the rotation matrix have to be calculated according to Eq. (7).

$$
c = \frac{a_p}{\rho}, \qquad s = \frac{a_q}{\rho}, \tag{7}
$$

where

$$
\rho = \begin{cases} a_p\sqrt{1 + (a_q/a_p)^2}, & for \quad |a_p| \geq |a_q| \\ a_q\sqrt{1 + (a_p/a_q)^2}, & for \quad |a_p| < |a_q| \end{cases} \tag{8}
$$

3   The Givens Rotation in a QR Decomposition

The QR decomposition method assumes that any non-singular matrix regular by columns can be depicted by the product of the upper triangle and orthogonal matrices.

$$\mathbf{A} = \mathbf{QR}, \tag{9}$$

where

$$\mathbf{Q}^T\mathbf{Q} = \mathbf{I}, \tag{10}$$

$$\mathbf{Q}^T = \mathbf{Q}^{-1}, \tag{11}$$

$$r_{ij} = 0 \quad for \ i > j. \tag{12}$$

The presented process of the QR decomposition is called the Givens orthogonalization [2]. According to Eqs. 6 and 7, for any vector $\mathbf{a} \in \mathbb{R}^m$, there exists a sequence of Givens rotations $\mathbf{G}_{12}, \mathbf{G}_{13}, \ldots, \mathbf{G}_{1m}$ that can be given as a product of each other

$$\mathbf{G}_1 = \mathbf{G}_{12} \ldots \mathbf{G}_{1,m-1}\mathbf{G}_{1m}. \tag{13}$$

Matrix $\mathbf{G}_1$ is able to perform multiple rotations at once and transform vector $\mathbf{a}$ to the pattern given by the following form

$$\bar{\mathbf{a}} = \mathbf{G}_1\mathbf{a} = e_1\rho = [\rho, 0, \ldots, 0]^T, \rho = \pm\|\mathbf{a}\|_2 \tag{14}$$

Rotation matrix (13) is also able to transform the whole matrix. Let $\mathbf{A}$ be a non-singular matrix regular by columns and let $\mathbf{A} \in \mathbb{R}^{m,n}$. The left-sided multiplication of matrix

$$\mathbf{A} = \mathbf{A}_1 = \mathbf{M}_1 = \begin{bmatrix} \mathbf{a}_1 & \mathbf{B}_1 \end{bmatrix} \tag{15}$$

by matrix (13) results with the pattern shown in Eq. (16)

$$\mathbf{A}_2 = \mathbf{G}_1\mathbf{A}_1 = \bar{\mathbf{G}}_1\mathbf{M}_1 = \begin{bmatrix} \bar{\mathbf{a}}_1 & \bar{\mathbf{B}}_1 \end{bmatrix} = \begin{bmatrix} \rho_1 & \bar{\mathbf{B}}_1 \\ \mathbf{0} & \end{bmatrix} = \begin{bmatrix} r_{11} & r_{12}\cdots r_{1n} \\ \mathbf{0} & \mathbf{M}_2 \end{bmatrix}. \tag{16}$$

At this point, the very left column vector of matrix $\mathbf{A}$ equals as shown in Eq. (14). The top row of matrix $\mathbf{A}$ is also already rotated as desired in the final upper-triangle form. In the next steps new sequences of rotations need to be performed

$$\mathbf{G}_k = \mathbf{G}_{k,k+1} \ldots \mathbf{G}_{k,m-1}\mathbf{G}_{km} \quad (k = 1, \ldots, m - 1). \tag{17}$$

Performing analogous transformations of matrix $\mathbf{M}_k$, each time the input matrix is one step closer to the desired upper-triangle form

$$\mathbf{A}_{k+1} = \bar{\mathbf{G}}_k\mathbf{M}_k = \begin{bmatrix} \bar{\mathbf{a}}_k & \bar{\mathbf{B}}_k \end{bmatrix} = \begin{bmatrix} \rho_k & \bar{\mathbf{B}}_k \\ \mathbf{0} & \end{bmatrix} = \begin{bmatrix} r_{kk} & r_{k,k+1}\cdots r_{k,n} \\ \mathbf{0} & \mathbf{M}_{k+1} \end{bmatrix}, \tag{18}$$

where

$$\mathbf{G}_k = \begin{bmatrix} \mathbf{I}_{k-1} & \mathbf{0} \\ \mathbf{0} & \bar{\mathbf{G}}_k \end{bmatrix}. \tag{19}$$

The algorithm is finished after reaching $m - 1$ steps. Then, the input matrix is fully transformed into the upper-triangle form

$$\mathbf{R} = \mathbf{G}_{m-1} \ldots \mathbf{G}_1 \mathbf{A}_1 = \mathbf{G}_{m-1,m} \ldots \mathbf{G}_{23} \ldots \mathbf{G}_{2m} \mathbf{G}_{12} \ldots \mathbf{G}_{1m} \mathbf{A}_1 = \mathbf{Q}^T \mathbf{A} \quad (20)$$

Orthogonal matrix $\mathbf{Q}$ can be retrieved from respective rotations

$$\mathbf{Q} = \mathbf{G}_1^T \ldots \mathbf{G}_{m-1}^T = \mathbf{G}_{1m}^T \ldots \mathbf{G}_{12}^T \mathbf{G}_{2m}^T \ldots \mathbf{G}_{23}^T \ldots \mathbf{G}_{m-1,m}^T \quad (21)$$

The full QR decomposition has been accomplished by the Givens rotations as given in Eq. (9).

4   Neural Network Learning with a QR Decomposition

The paper assumes learning of a multilayer Neural Network with any differentiable activation function [10]. The purpose of the learning process is to minimize error measure function expressed by the formula given below

$$J(n) = \sum_{t=1}^{n} \lambda^{n-j} \sum_{j=1}^{N_L} \varepsilon_j^{(L)2}(t)$$

$$= \sum_{t=1}^{n} \lambda^{n-t} \sum_{j=1}^{N_L} \left[d_j^{(L)}(t) - f\left(\mathbf{x}^{(L)T}(t) \mathbf{w}_j^{(L)}(n) \right) \right]^2. \quad (22)$$

The following equations show how to formulate an entry point for the Givens algorithm. The first step is to calculate the gradient of error measure function expressed by Eq. (22) and equal it to $\mathbf{0}$.

$$\frac{\partial J(n)}{\partial \mathbf{w}_i^{(l)}(n)} = 2 \sum_{t=1}^{n} \lambda^{n-t} \sum_{j=1}^{N_L} \frac{\partial \varepsilon_j^{(L)}(t)}{\partial \mathbf{w}_i^{(l)}(n)} \varepsilon_j^{(L)}(t)$$

$$= -2 \sum_{t=1}^{n} \lambda^{n-t} \sum_{j=1}^{N_L} \frac{\partial y_j^{(L)}(t)}{\partial \mathbf{w}_i^{(l)}(n)} \varepsilon_j^{(L)}(t) = \mathbf{0}. \quad (23)$$

Equation (23) needs to be transformed further

$$\sum_{t=1}^{n} \lambda^{n-t} \sum_{j=1}^{N_L} \frac{\partial y_j^{(L)}(t)}{\partial s_j^{(L)}(t)} \sum_{p=1}^{N_{L-1}} \frac{\partial s_i^{(L)}(t)}{\partial y_p^{(L-1)}(t)} \frac{\partial y_p^{(L-1)}(t)}{\partial \mathbf{w}_i^{(l)}(n)} \varepsilon_j^{(L)}(t)$$

$$= \sum_{t=1}^{n} \lambda^{n-t} \sum_{p=1}^{N_{L-1}} \frac{\partial y_p^{(L-1)}(t)}{\partial \mathbf{w}_i^{(l)}(n)} \sum_{j=1}^{N_L} \frac{\partial y_j^{(L)}(t)}{\partial s_j^{(L)}(t)} w_{jp}^{(L)} \varepsilon_j^{(L)}(t)$$

$$= \sum_{t=1}^{n} \lambda^{n-t} \sum_{p=1}^{N_{L-1}} \frac{\partial y_p^{(L-1)}(t)}{\partial \mathbf{w}_i^{(l)}(n)} \varepsilon_p^{(L-1)}(t) \quad (24)$$

$$= \sum_{t=1}^{n} \lambda^{n-t} \sum_{q=1}^{N_l} \frac{\partial y_p^{(l)}(t)}{\partial \mathbf{w}_i^{(l)}(n)} \varepsilon_q^{(l)}(t) = \mathbf{0},$$

where $\varepsilon_p^{(l)}(t)$ shows the error value in each layer calculated from the last to the first layer according to Eq. (25)

$$\varepsilon_p^{(l)}(t) = \sum_{j=1}^{N_{l+1}} \frac{\partial y_j^{(l+1)}(t)}{\partial s_j^{(l+1)}(t)} w_{jp}^{(l+1)}(n) \varepsilon_j^{(l+1)}(t). \tag{25}$$

To obtain the desired form, additional transformations need to be performed

$$\sum_{t=1}^{n} \lambda^{n-t} \sum_{q=1}^{N_l} \frac{\partial y_q^{(l)}(t)}{\partial w_i^{(l)}(n)} \varepsilon_q^{(l)}(t)$$

$$= \sum_{t=1}^{n} \lambda^{n-t} \sum_{q=1}^{N_l} \frac{\partial y_q^{(l)}(t)}{\partial s_q^{(l)}(n)} \frac{\partial s_q^{(l)}(t)}{\partial w_i^{(l)}(n)} \varepsilon_q^{(l)}(t)$$

$$= \sum_{j=1}^{n} \lambda^{n-j} \frac{\partial y_i^{(l)}(t)}{\partial s_i^{(l)}(n)} \mathbf{y}^{(l-1)T}(t) \varepsilon_i^{(l)}(t) \tag{26}$$

$$= \sum_{t=1}^{n} \lambda^{n-t} \frac{\partial y_i^{(l)}(t)}{\partial s_i^{(l)}(n)} \mathbf{y}^{(l-1)T}(t) \left[d_i^{(l)}(t) - y_i^{(l)}(t) \right] = \mathbf{0}.$$

At this step the result of transformations (26) is linearized

$$f\left(b_i^{(l)}(t)\right) \approx f\left(s_i^{(l)}(t)\right) + f'\left(s_i^{(l)}(t)\right)\left(b_i^{(l)}(t) - s_i^{(l)}(t)\right) \tag{27}$$

and the following normal equation is given

$$\sum_{t=1}^{n} \lambda^{n-t} f'^2\left(s_i^{(l)}(t)\right) \left[b_i^{(l)}(t) - \mathbf{x}^{(l)T}(t)\mathbf{w}_i^{(l)}(n)\right] \mathbf{x}^{(l)T}(t) = \mathbf{0}. \tag{28}$$

Equation (28) given in a vector form is an entry point for the Givens algorithm

$$\mathbf{A}_i^{(l)}(n)\mathbf{w}_i^{(l)}(n) = \mathbf{h}_i^{(l)}(n), \tag{29}$$

where

$$\mathbf{A}_i^{(l)}(n) = \sum_{t=1}^{n} \lambda^{n-t} f'^2\left(s_i^{(l)}(t)\right) \mathbf{x}^{(l)}(t)\mathbf{x}^{(l)T}(t), \tag{30}$$

$$\mathbf{h}_i^{(l)}(n) = \sum_{t=1}^{n} \lambda^{n-t} f'^2\left(s_i^{(l)}(t)\right) b_i^{(l)}(t)\mathbf{x}^{(l)}(t). \tag{31}$$

To improve equation readability the following substitution is performed

$$\mathbf{z}_i^{(l)}(t) = f'\left(s_i^{(l)}(t)\right)\mathbf{x}^{(l)}(t). \tag{32}$$

Then, Eqs. 30 and 31 are transformed to formulas 33 and 34 respectively

$$\mathbf{A}_i^{(l)}(n) = \sum_{t=1}^{n} \lambda^{n-t} \mathbf{z}_i^{(l)}(t)\, \mathbf{z}_i^{(l)T}(t), \tag{33}$$

$$\mathbf{h}_i^{(l)}(n) = \sum_{t=1}^{n} \lambda^{n-t} f'\left(s_i^{(l)}(t)\right) b_i^{(l)}(t)\, \mathbf{z}_i^{(l)}(t), \tag{34}$$

where

$$b_i^{(l)}(n) = \begin{cases} b_i^{(L)}(n) = f^{-1}\left(d_i^{(L)}(n)\right) & for\ l = L \\ s_i^{(l)}(n) + e_i^{(l)}(n) & for\ l = 1 \dots L-1, \end{cases} \tag{35}$$

$$e_i^{(k)}(n) = \sum_{j=1}^{N_{k+1}} f'\left(s_i^{(k)}(n)\right) w_{ji}^{(k+1)}(n)\, e_j^{(k+1)}(n) \qquad for\ k = 1 \dots L-1. \tag{36}$$

In order to solve Eq. (29), the QR decomposition can be used. After completion, Eq. (29) should be left-sided multiplied by $\mathbf{Q}^T$

$$\mathbf{Q}_i^{(l)T}(n)\, \mathbf{A}_i^{(l)}(n)\, \mathbf{w}_i^{(l)}(n) = \mathbf{Q}_i^{(l)T}(n)\, \mathbf{h}_i^{(l)}(n), \tag{37}$$

$$\mathbf{R}_i^{(l)}(n)\, \mathbf{w}_i^{(l)}(n) = \mathbf{Q}_i^{(l)T}(n)\, \mathbf{h}_i^{(l)}(n). \tag{38}$$

As shown in Eq. (37), vector $\mathbf{h}$ can be rotated along with matrix $\mathbf{A}$. As the result of the QR decomposition, matrix $\mathbf{R}$ is the upper-triangle, so its inversion is not so expensive. Finally, the weights of neurons in each layer can be adjusted according to the following equations

$$\hat{\mathbf{w}}_i^{(l)}(n) = \mathbf{R}_i^{(l)-1}(n)\, \mathbf{Q}_i^{(l)T}(n)\, \mathbf{h}_i^{(l)}(n), \tag{39}$$

$$\mathbf{w}_i^{(l)}(n) = (1-\eta)\, \mathbf{w}_i^{(l)}(n-1) + \eta\, \hat{\mathbf{w}}_i^{(l)}(n). \tag{40}$$

5   Research and Results

The presented Givens QR decomposition algorithm has been tested in two scenarios:

1. learning XOR logic scheme, which is presented in Subsect. 5.1,
2. learning approximation of the logistic curve. More details are presented in Subsect. 5.2.

Both scenarios assume the use of hyperbolic tangent as an activation function. The error criterion of the learning process is formulated by the following equation

$$\sum_{j=1}^{N_L} \left[d_j^{(L)}(t) - y_j^{(L)}(t)\right]^2 \leq \gamma, \tag{41}$$

where γ stands for an acceptable error threshold. During the research two learning parameters have been adjusted to acquire the shortest convergence time: η - learning step and λ - forgetting factor. Each item in Tables 1, 2, 3 and 4 has been produced as average of 100 consecutive runs with constant parameters. At the beginning of every run the network is fully reinitialized. During every iteration, learning samples have been presented in a pseudo-random order. Activation function parameters have been set to 1. As a learning acceptance criterion, an average error epoch has been set to $\gamma = 0.01$. Maximal epoch limit has been set to 600.

5.1   Learning of XOR Logic Scheme

In this scenario of Neural Network consists of two inputs, one output, two layers and one neuron per layer. Each network input is connected to each layer. A single epoch consists of four iterations. Example run results are shown in Fig. 1. In this case an accepted error value is achieved after 6 epochs for the Givens algorithm and after 164 epochs for the Back Propagation algorithm.

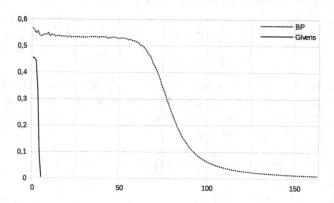

Fig. 1. Example results for learning of XOR logic scheme with the following parameters: Givens algorithm: $\eta = 0.2, \lambda = 0.3$, weight range 2–3. Back Propagation algorithm: $\eta = 0.1$, weight range -0.5–0.5.

Table 1 shows an average success rate of the XOR logic scheme learning process for different values of parameters η and λ. Good results (about 100 % success rate) have been achieved for $\eta \leq 0.4$ and $\lambda > 0.3$. The worst results have been achieved for $\lambda > 0.8$.

Table 2 presents detailed data about an average epoch count for learning the XOR logic scheme by the Givens algorithm depending on values η and λ. As shown in Table 2 the best times have been achieved for $\lambda \leq 0.8$. In this case the value of η significantly affects an average epoch count. Overall good performance (short convergence time) and a high success rate is achievable with parameters in ranges: $0.1 \leq \eta \leq 0.4$ and $0.4 \leq \lambda \leq 0.7$.

Table 1. Success rate depending on η and λ values for learning XOR logic scheme

		λ										
		0.01	0.1	0.2	0.3	0.4	0.5	0.6	0.7	0.8	0.9	0.99
	0.1	0.77	1	1	1	1	1	1	1	1	1	1
	0.2	0.79	0.97	0.98	1	1	1	1	1	1	1	1
	0.3	0.83	0.96	0.98	0.96	1	1	1	1	1	1	1
	0.4	0.73	0.85	0.94	0.95	1	0.99	1	0.99	0.95	0.95	0.91
	0.5	0.69	0.92	0.94	0.89	0.92	0.96	0.98	0.98	0.81	0.7	0.47
η	0.6	0.64	0.86	0.91	0.9	0.88	0.93	0.94	0.94	0.66	0.5	0.35
	0.7	0.62	0.86	0.85	0.77	0.89	0.89	0.92	0.95	0.45	0.27	0.09
	0.8	0.61	0.81	0.78	0.74	0.85	0.87	0.95	0.9	0.33	0.14	0.05
	0.9	0.66	0.58	0.7	0.76	0.94	0.94	0.93	0.86	0.16	0.01	0.04

Table 2. Average convergence epoch count depending on values η and λ for learning the XOR logic scheme

		λ										
		0.01	0.1	0.2	0.3	0.4	0.5	0.6	0.7	0.8	0.9	0.99
	0.1	18.39	8.97	8.77	9.04	9.27	9.57	9.99	10.62	11.77	14.91	43.43
	0.2	9.91	7.29	7.07	6.43	6.86	7.28	7.36	8.56	11.14	17.6	83.34
	0.3	7.16	6.27	7.31	6.55	7.35	9.68	9.96	12.38	16.1	25.98	149.06
	0.4	8.18	6.53	7.37	9.25	10.06	13.81	14.04	25.64	37.42	63.4	189.42
	0.5	8.26	7.47	8.82	12.45	12.37	17.13	24.47	53.86	52.8	84.69	248.47
η	0.6	7.17	8.66	10.22	13.24	15.39	18.77	32.77	72.16	64.26	164.82	281.51
	0.7	7.35	7.73	11.75	13.62	15.97	20.2	40.04	96.76	115.71	160.52	388.11
	0.8	7.03	8.47	12.49	16.42	16.47	21.02	42.15	118.18	118.91	278.36	321.6
	0.9	7.23	9.26	11.6	14.01	18.39	23.39	62.6	136.26	122.25	83	221.75

5.2   Learning a Logistic Curve Approximation

A logistic curve is defined by $x = x(1 - x), 0 \leq x \leq 1$. In this scenario a Neural Network consists of two inputs, one output and two layers. The first layer consists of five neurons. The last layer consists of only one neuron. A network input is connected to each neuron of each layer. A single epoch consists of eleven iterations. The example run results are shown in Fig. 2. In this case an accepted error value is achieved after 4 epochs for the Givens algorithm and after 157 epochs for the Back Propagation algorithm. Table 3 shows an average success rate of the logistic curve approximation learning process for different values of parameters η and λ. In this case, good results (about 100 % success rate) are slightly different from those for the XOR logic scheme learning. A high success rate has been achieved for $\lambda \geq 0.6$. The value of η seems not to have any significant impact on the learning success rate. The worst results have been achieved for $\lambda \leq 0.3$, and no convergence has been met in this case.

Table 4 presents detailed data about an average epoch count for learning the logistic curve approximation by the Givens algorithm depending on values η and λ. As shown in Table 4, the best times have been achieved for $\lambda = 0.9$. Also, in this case the value of η does not affect an average epoch count significantly. Overall good performance (short convergence time) and high success rate is achievable for $0.8 \leq \lambda \leq 0.99$, which is opposite to the XOR logic scheme learning process.

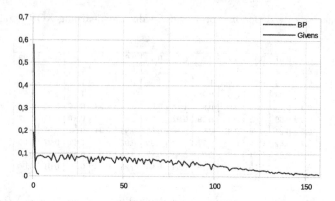

Fig. 2. Example results for learning the logistic curve approximation with the following parameters: Givens algorithm: $\eta = 0.1, \lambda = 0.89$, weight range 0.001–1. Back Propagation algorithm: $\eta = 0.1$, weight range 0.001–1.

Table 3. Success rate depending on values η and λ for learning the logistic curve

		λ										
		0.01	0.1	0.2	0.3	0.4	0.5	0.6	0.7	0.8	0.9	0.99
	0,1	0	0	0,09	0,12	0,47	0,82	0,96	0,99	1	1	1
	0,2	0	0	0,04	0,08	0,3	0,85	0,98	1	1	1	1
	0,3	0	0	0	0,1	0,42	0,89	0,98	1	1	1	0,99
	0,4	0	0	0,01	0,08	0,41	0,89	0,96	1	1	1	1
η	0,5	0	0,01	0,02	0,14	0,44	0,89	0,99	1	1	1	1
	0,6	0	0	0,03	0,18	0,55	0,94	0,99	1	1	1	1
	0,7	0	0	0	0,18	0,62	0,93	0,99	1	1	1	1
	0,8	0	0	0,03	0,2	0,56	0,93	0,99	1	1	1	1
	0,9	0	0	0,01	0,15	0,47	0,92	0,98	1	1	1	1

Table 4. Average convergence epoch count depending on values η and λ for learning the logistic curve

		λ										
		0.01	0.1	0.2	0.3	0.4	0.5	0.6	0.7	0.8	0.9	0.99
	0.1	0	0	31	51	88.83	115.15	85.64	45.81	26.53	14.23	20.32
	0.2	0	0	28.5	30.75	65.33	99.27	62.65	40.57	21.75	12.14	25.73
	0.3	0	0	0	34.6	81	62.31	56.69	34.24	27.44	13.17	27.95
	0.4	0	0	5	33.5	55.59	55.16	46.31	38.48	29.46	14.56	35.77
η	0.5	0	11	9.5	36.79	38	49.04	39.97	37.15	17.28	13.23	46.47
	0.6	0	0	8.33	40.89	40.96	40.89	33.35	29.73	18.32	14.47	46.98
	0.7	0	0	0	33.5	39.4	39.12	27.55	26.88	22.01	11.71	67.63
	0.8	0	0	16.33	27.7	39.55	34.6	35.82	29.09	21.57	13.08	66.36
	0.9	0	0	23	29.53	45	36.55	26.26	22.02	19.99	11.35	76.58

6   Conclusion

The following paper covers the method of learning Neural Network by the QR decomposition performed by the Givens rotations. As shown in Sect. 5 the performance of the presented algorithm is about ten to twenty times faster than the Back Propagation one. The Givens rotations can be applied as a learning method for feedforward Neural Networks. It is very likely that the Givens rotations could be applied in the methods presented in [13,16,19,28]. In the near future a momentum implementation will be taken under consideration as per [3]. Also, a parallel implementation of QR decomposition done by Givens rotations will be attempted as proposed in [4–7,25].

References

1. Chu, L.J., Krzyżak, A.: The recognition of partially occluded objects with support vector machines, convolutional neural networks and deep belief networks. J. Artif. Intell. Soft Comput. Res. **4**(1), 5–19 (2014)
2. Kiełbasiński, A., Schwetlick, H.: Numeryczna Algebra Liniowa. Wydawnictwa Naukowo-Techniczne (1992). (in Polish)
3. Bilski, J.: Momentum modification of the RLS algorithms. In: Rutkowski, L., Siekmann, J.H., Tadeusiewicz, R., Zadeh, L.A. (eds.) ICAISC 2004. LNCS (LNAI), vol. 3070, pp. 151–157. Springer, Heidelberg (2004)
4. Bilski, J.: Struktury równoległe dla jednokierunkowych i dynamicznych sieci neuronowych. Akademicka Oficyna Wydawnicza EXIT (2013). (in Polish)
5. Bilski, J., Smoląg, J.: Parallel realisation of the recurrent multi layer perceptron learning. In: Rutkowski, L., Korytkowski, M., Scherer, R., Tadeusiewicz, R., Zadeh, L.A., Zurada, J.M. (eds.) ICAISC 2012, Part I. LNCS (LNAI), vol. 7267, pp. 12–20. Springer, Heidelberg (2012)
6. Bilski, J., Smoląg, J.: Parallel approach to learning of the recurrent jordan neural network. In: Rutkowski, L., Korytkowski, M., Scherer, R., Tadeusiewicz, R., Zadeh, L.A., Zurada, J.M. (eds.) ICAISC 2013, Part I. LNCS (LNAI), vol. 7894, pp. 32–40. Springer, Heidelberg (2013)
7. Bilski, J., Smoląg, J.: Parallel architectures for learning the RTRN and elman dynamic neural networks. IEEE Trans. Parallel Distrib. Syst. **26**(9), 2561–2570 (2015)
8. Werbos, J.: Beyond Regression: New Tools for Prediction and Analysis in the Behavioral Sciences. Harvard University, Cambridge (1974)
9. Nowicki, R.K., Nowak, B.A., Starczewski, J.T., Cpalka, K.: The learning of neurofuzzy approximator with fuzzy rough sets in case of missing features. In: 2014 International Joint Conference on Neural Networks (IJCNN), pp. 3759–3766, July 2014
10. Bilski, J., Rutkowski, L.: A fast training algorithm for neural networks. IEEE Trans. Circ. Syst. Part II **45**, 749–753 (1998)
11. Bilski, J., Rutkowski, L.: Numerically robust learning algorithms for feed forward neural networks. In: Rutkowski, L., Kacprzyk, J. (eds.) Neural Networks and Soft Computing. Advances in Soft Computing, vol. 19, pp. 149–154. Springer, Heidelberg (2003)
12. Korytkowski, M., Scherer, R., Rutkowski, L.: On combining backpropagation with boosting. In: International Joint Conference on Neural Networks (2006)
13. Sakurai, S., Nishizawa, M.: A new approach for discovering Top-K sequential patterns based on the variety of items. J. Artif. Intell. Soft Comput. Res. **5**(2), 141–153 (2015)
14. Rutkowski, L., Jaworski, M., Pietruczuk, L., Duda, P.: A new method for data stream mining based on the misclassification error. IEEE Trans. Neural Netw. Learn. Syst. **26**(5), 1048–1059 (2015)

15. Kitajima, R., Kamimura, R.: Accumulative information enhancement in the self-organizing maps and its application to the analysis of mission statements. J. Artif. Intell. Soft Comput. Res. **5**(3), 161–176 (2015)
16. Korytkowski, M., Rutkowski, L., Scherer, R.: Fast image classification by boosting fuzzy classifiers. Inform. Sci. **327**, 175–182 (2016)
17. Nowicki, R.K., Korytkowski, M., Nowak, B.A., Scherer, R.: Design methodology for rough neuro-fuzzy classification with missing data. In: 2015 IEEE Symposium Series on Computational Intelligence, pp. 1650–1657, December 2015
18. Tadeusiewicz, R.: Sieci Neuronowe. Akademicka Oficyna Wydawnicza (1993)
19. Mleczko, W.K., Kapuscinski, T., Nowicki, R.K.: Rough deep belief network - application to incomplete handwritten digits pattern classification. In: Dregvaite, G., Damasevicius, R. (eds.) ICIST 2014. CCIS, vol. 538, pp. 400–411. Springer, Heidelberg (2015)
20. Nowak, B.A., Nowicki, R.K.: Learning in rough-neuro-fuzzy system for data with missing values. In: Wyrzykowski, R., Dongarra, J., Karczewski, K., Waśniewski, J. (eds.) PPAM 2011, Part I. LNCS, vol. 7203, pp. 501–510. Springer, Heidelberg (2012)
21. Aghdam, H.M., Heidari, S.: Feature selection using particle swarm optimization in text categorization. J. Artif. Intell. Soft Comput. Res. **5**(4), 231–238 (2015)
22. Hayashi, Y., Tanaka, Y., Takagi, T., Saito, T., Iiduka, H., Kikuchi, H., Bologna, G., Mitra, S.: Recursive-rule extraction algorithm with J48graft and applications to generating credit scores. J. Artif. Intell. Soft Comput. Res. **6**(1), 35–44 (2016)
23. Lee, P., Hsiao, T.: Applying LCS to affective image classification in spatial-frequency domain. J. Artif. Intell. Soft Comput. Res. **4**(2), 99–123 (2014)
24. Chen, Q., Abercrombie, K.R., Sheldon, T.F.: Risk assessment for industrial control systems quantifying availability using mean failure cost (MFC). J. Artif. Intell. Soft Comput. Res. **5**(3), 205–220 (2015)
25. Bilski, J., Smolag, J., Żurada, J.M.: Parallel approach to the Levenberg-Marquardt learning algorithm for feedforward neural networks. In: Rutkowski, L., Korytkowski, M., Scherer, R., Tadeusiewicz, R., Zadeh, L.A., Zurada, J.M. (eds.) Artificial Intelligence and Soft Computing. LNCS, vol. 9119, pp. 3–14. Springer, Heidelberg (2015)
26. El-Samak, F.A., Ashour, W.: Optimization of traveling salesman problem using affinity propagation clustering and genetic algorithm. J. Artif. Intell. Soft Comput. Res. **5**(4), 239–245 (2015)
27. Knop, M., Kapuscinski, T., Mleczko, W.K.: Video key frame detection based on the restricted Boltzmann machine. J. Appl. Math. Comput. Mech. **14**(3), 49–58 (2015)
28. Nowak, B.A., Nowicki, R.K., Mleczko, W.K.: A new method of improving classification accuracy of decision tree in case of incomplete samples. In: Rutkowski, L., Korytkowski, M., Scherer, R., Tadeusiewicz, R., Zadeh, L.A., Zurada, J.M. (eds.) ICAISC 2013, Part I. LNCS, vol. 7894, pp. 448–458. Springer, Heidelberg (2013)
29. Serdah, A.M., Ashour, W.M.: Clustering large-scale data based on modified affinity propagation algorithm. J. Artif. Intell. Soft Comput. Res. **6**(1), 23–33 (2016)

Parallel Learning of Feedforward Neural Networks Without Error Backpropagation

Jarosław Bilski[1]([✉]) and Bogdan M. Wilamowski[2]

[1] Institute of Computational Intelligence, Częstochowa University of Technology,
Częstochowa, Poland
Jaroslaw.Bilski@iisi.pcz.pl
[2] Auburn University, Auburn, AL 36849-5201, USA
wilambm@auburn.edu

Abstract. A parallel architecture of the steepest descent algorithm for training fully connected feedforward neural networks is presented. This solution is based on a new idea of learning neural networks without error backpropagation. The proposed solution is based on completely new parallel structures to effectively reduce high computational load of this algorithm. Detailed parallel 2D and 3D neural network learning structures are explicitly discussed.

Keywords: Forward-only computation · Neural network training · Parallel architectures

1 Introduction

Feedforward neural networks have been investigated by many scientists e.g. [14,19,27,29,30]. The error backpropagation method is relatively simple and has been often used to learn feedforward networks, see e.g. [12,18,28]. Classically there are two phases in the error backpropagation method. In the first phase data are entered into network inputs and calculations are carried forward to network outputs. In the second phase errors at the outputs of network are calculated and they are sent back to all neurons. A new approach to calculate errors in neurons is presented in [29]. In the cited algorithm, all calculations are performed forward in one phase. This eliminates the necessity of transfering the error back and introduces the possibility of using pipelining for learning neural networks. Unfortunately, in the classical approach, neural networks learning algorithms, like other learning algorihms [14,20–23,26], are implemented on a serial computer. Due to a large amount of computational operation of learning algorithms, serial implementation is time consuming and slow. For very large networks computational load of learning algorithms makes it impractical.

An interesting solution to this problem is the use of high performance dedicated parallel structures, see eg. [2–10,24,25]. This paper presents a new concept of parallel realisation of the steepest descent learning without error bacpropagation algorithm. A single iteration/epoch of the parallel architecture requires

L. Rutkowski et al. (Eds.): ICAISC 2016, Part I, LNAI 9692, pp. 57–69, 2016.
DOI: 10.1007/978-3-319-39378-0_6

much fewer computation cycles than a serial implementation. Efficiency of this new architecture seems to be very promising and is explained in the last part of the paper.

In this paper we investigate a parallel structure for [29]. A sample structure of a feedforward fully connected network is shown in Fig. 1. The network has nn (8) neurons and no (2) outputs. The input vector contains ni (2) input signals.

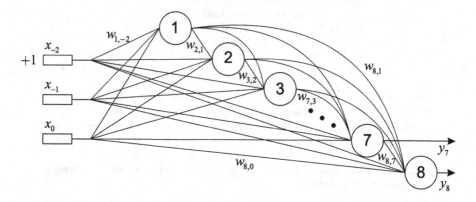

Fig. 1. A fully connected neural network with eight neurons, two inputs and two outputs

The neuron model is shown in Fig. 2. Each neuron connects to all the inputs and all the previous neurons. It should be noted that by leaving out some of the weight connections, a traditional multilayer neural network can be obtained.

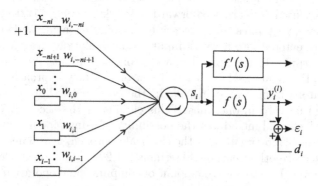

Fig. 2. The neuron model

The input vector to the i-th neuron is given by:

$$[x_{-ni}, \ldots, x_0, \ldots, x_{i-1}]^T \tag{1}$$

where:

$$x_j = \begin{cases} 1 & j = -ni \\ inp_{j+ni} & -ni+1 \le j. \\ y_j & 0 < j < i \end{cases} \qquad (2)$$

The Eqs. (3) and (4) describe the recall phase of the network:

$$s_i(n) = \sum_{j=-ni}^{i-1} w_{ij}(n) x_j(n), \qquad (3)$$

$$y_i(n) = f(s_i(n)), \qquad (4)$$

where $f()$ is the neuron activation function. Correction of network weights is based on the minimization of the error measurement function, which is defined as the sum of squared errors of the network outputs:

$$J(n) = \frac{1}{2} \sum_{p=1}^{np} \sum_{m=1}^{no} \varepsilon_m^{(p)2}(n) = \frac{1}{2} \sum_{p=1}^{np} \sum_{m=1}^{no} \varepsilon_m^{(p)2}(n) \left(d_m^{(p)}(n) - y_m^{(p)}(n) \right)^2. \qquad (5)$$

The steepest descent rule will be used in learning all weights in order to minimize the error measurement function.

$$w_{ij}^{(p)}(n+1) = w_{ij}^{(p)}(n) + \eta \left(-\nabla J_{ij}^{(p)}(n) \right), \qquad (6)$$

where η is the learning factor. It is often determined a priori, but better results are obtained by changing its value during the course of the learning process. The appropriate component of the gradient of the error measurement function takes the form:

$$\nabla J_{ij}^{(p)}(n) = \frac{\partial J(n)}{\partial w_{ij}^{(p)}(n)} = \frac{\partial J(n)}{\partial s_i^{(p)}(n)} \frac{\partial s_i^{(p)}(n)}{\partial w_{ij}^{(p)}(n)} = \frac{\partial J(n)}{\partial s_i^{(p)}(n)} x_j^{(p)}. \qquad (7)$$

By denoted:

$$\delta_i^{(p)}(n) \stackrel{\triangle}{=} -\frac{\partial J(n)}{\partial s_i^{(p)}(n)} \qquad (8)$$

a simpler form of Eq. (7) is obtained:

$$\nabla J_{ij}^{(p)}(n) = \frac{\partial J(n)}{\partial w_{ij}^{(p)}(n)} = -\delta_i^{(p)} x_j^{(p)}. \qquad (9)$$

Therefore, the algorithm (6) takes the form:

$$w_{ij}^{(p)}(n+1) = w_{ij}^{(p)}(n) + \eta \delta_i^{(p)} x_j^{(p)}. \qquad (10)$$

The method of calculation of $\delta_i^{(p)}$ in formula (10) is as follows:

$$\begin{aligned} \delta_i^{(p)}(n) &= -\frac{\partial J(n)}{\partial s_i^{(p)}(n)} = -\frac{\partial y_i^{(p)}(n)}{\partial s_i^{(p)}(n)} \frac{\partial J(n)}{\partial y_i^{(p)}(n)} \\ &= -\frac{\partial y_i^{(p)}(n)}{\partial s_i^{(p)}(n)} \sum_{m=\max(i,nn-no+1)}^{nn} \frac{\partial y_m^{(p)}(n)}{\partial y_i^{(p)}(n)} \frac{\partial J(n)}{\partial y_m^{(p)}(n)} \end{aligned} \qquad (11)$$

By defining

$$f'^{(p)}_i(n) \triangleq \frac{\partial y^{(p)}_i(n)}{\partial s^{(p)}_i(n)}, \tag{12}$$

$$\delta^{(p)}_{ki}(n) \triangleq \frac{\partial y^{(p)}_k(n)}{\partial y^{(p)}_i(n)}, \quad i \leq k \tag{13}$$

a formula is obtained:

$$\delta^{(p)}_i(n) = f'^{(p)}_i(n) \sum_{m=\max(i,nn-no+1)}^{nn} \delta^{(p)}_{mi}(n)\,\varepsilon^{(p)}_m. \tag{14}$$

Of course, the $\delta^{(p)}_{ii}(n)$ assumes the following value

$$\delta^{(p)}_{ii}(n) = \frac{\partial y^{(p)}_i(n)}{\partial y^{(p)}_i(n)} = 1. \tag{15}$$

The $\delta^{(p)}_{ij}(n)$ values are calculated as follows:

$$\begin{aligned}
\delta^{(p)}_{ij}(n) &= \frac{\partial y^{(p)}_i(n)}{\partial y^{(p)}_j(n)} = \frac{\partial y^{(p)}_i(n)}{\partial s^{(p)}_i(n)}\frac{\partial s^{(p)}_i(n)}{\partial y^{(p)}_j(n)} \\
&= f'^{(p)}_i(n) \sum_{k=j}^{i-1} w^{(p)}_{ik}(n) \frac{\partial y^{(p)}_k(n)}{\partial y^{(p)}_j(n)}.
\end{aligned} \tag{16}$$

It leads to:

$$\delta^{(p)}_{ij}(n) = f'^{(p)}_i(n) \sum_{k=j}^{i-1} w^{(p)}_{ik}(n)\,\delta^{(p)}_{kj}(n). \tag{17}$$

As a result, the entire gradient algorithm without backpropagation can be summarized as follows:

$$s_i(n) = \sum_{j=-ni}^{i-1} w_{ij}(n)\,x_j(n), \tag{18}$$

$$y_i(n) = f(s_i(n)), \tag{19}$$

$$\delta^{(p)}_{ii}(n) = 1, \tag{20}$$

$$\delta^{(p)}_{ij}(n) = f'^{(p)}_i(n) \sum_{k=j}^{i-1} w^{(p)}_{ik}(n)\,\delta^{(p)}_{kj}(n), \tag{21}$$

$$\delta^{(p)}_i(n) = f'^{(p)}_i(n) \sum_{m=\max(i,nn-no+1)}^{nn} \delta^{(p)}_{mi}(n)\,\varepsilon^{(p)}_m, \tag{22}$$

$$w^{(p)}_{ij}(n+1) = w^{(p)}_{ij}(n) + \eta\delta^{(p)}_i(n)\,x^{(p)}_j. \tag{23}$$

The initial values of weights within the network are randomly selected (e.g. from the interval $< [-0.5, 0.5 >]$), and the learning coefficient η is usually taken from the range $(0, 1 >$.

The weights w_{ij} (without weights connecting the neurons with the inputs of the network) and the deltas δ_{ij} can be organized in the table (see Table 1) to show the calculation sequence. The calculations of δ_{ij} are performed sequentially row by row from top to bottom of the table. The deltas δ_{ij} in the $i - th$ row can be obtained from the deltas and the weights from the previous rows (21):

Table 1. The computational table contains the weights between neurons and also derivatives δ_{ij} Eqs. (20) and (21)

idx	1	2	$\cdots$	j	$\cdots$	i	$\cdots$	nn
1	δ_{11}	w_{21}	$\cdots$	w_{j1}	$\cdots$	w_{i1}	$\cdots$	w_{nn1}
2	δ_{21}	δ_{22}	$\cdots$	w_{j2}	$\cdots$	w_{i2}	$\cdots$	w_{nn2}
$\cdots$	$\cdots$	$\cdots$	$\cdots$	$\cdots$	$\cdots$	$\cdots$	$\cdots$	$\cdots$
j	δ_{j1}	δ_{j2}	$\cdots$	δ_{jj}	$\cdots$	w_{ij}	$\cdots$	w_{nnj}
$\cdots$	$\cdots$	$\cdots$	$\cdots$	$\cdots$	$\cdots$	$\cdots$	$\cdots$	$\cdots$
i	δ_{i1}	δ_{i2}	$\cdots$	δ_{ij}	$\cdots$	δ_{ii}	$\cdots$	w_{nni}
$\cdots$	$\cdots$	$\cdots$	$\cdots$	$\cdots$	$\cdots$	$\cdots$	$\cdots$	$\cdots$
nn	δ_{nn1}	δ_{nn2}	$\cdots$	δ_{nnj}	$\cdots$	δ_{nni}	$\cdots$	$\delta_{nn,nn}$

2   Parallel Realisation

The parallel two-dimensional structure of the presented algorithm uses the architecture which requires many simple processing elements. Figure 3 shows the two-dimensional parallel structure for learning a neural network, which bases on the above table for a fully connected network (Fig. 1) having two inputs, eight neurons and two outputs. The B and D processing elements correspond to the elements of the main diagonal of the above table. In addition, at the top processing elements connecting neurons with inputs x_i of the network are placed.

Into the structure input signals x_i are entered and the processing is performed row by row. The A processing elements in the appropriate columns calculate sums for the following neurons (18). The B and D processing elements calculate the value of the activation functions f_i and their derivatives f_i'. Sums from the Eq. (21) are calculated in a pipelined manner row by row through the C and E processing elements to determine the δ_{ij} values as a result. Then the structure exposes outputs of the network, and next, after error calculations based on the desired values d_i, the corrections of weights in the network are realized (23). The D and E processing elements differ from the B and C processing elements that are also included in the calculation formulas (22). The cycle is repeated for the next patern.   A few main kinds of functional processing elements are used in the proposed solution (Fig. 4). The A processing elements fulfill three functions: calculate the sum of the formula (18), send the weights to the elements B, C, D and E, also update the weights in accordance with formula (23) based on the δ_i received from the B and D processing elements (in the second version the momentum is included). The B processing elements calculate the values of activation functions and their derivatives, send them respectively to A and C processing elements. In addition, they compute firsts addends from formula (21) and δ_i by multiplying the derivatives by the total sums $sumb$ calculated by the E processing elements. The C processing elements calculate and store δ_{ij} values, then compute the successive partial sums of $sumf$ (21). The D processing elements operate similarly to the B elements, and additionally calculate the

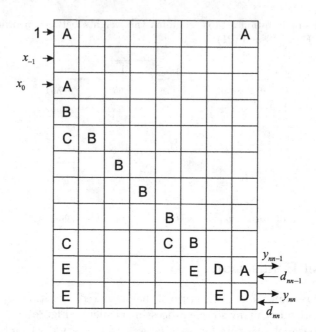

Fig. 3. The parallel two-dimensional structure for learning neural networks

values ε_i and δ_i. The E processing elements additionally calculate the *sumb* sums from formula (22) and send them to the B and D processing elements.

Figure 5 shows a three-dimensional structure. It is based on the modified two-dimensional structure (Fig. 3). The main aim is to obtain a full pipelining during network learning. It is achieved by separating some of the functions of B, D, C and E processing elements and moving them to the T and S processing elements. In this structure weights update is performed after the epoch only. This also necessitates extension of the structure by additional delaying Z elements. The operation of the structure is as follows:

- inputs are given in a pipelined manner;
- successive values are calculated in rows;
- all weights are given simultaneously to the T and S processing elements;
- at the same time known values of δ_{ij} are transmitted to all the S processing elements that are above them;
- the T and S processing elements forming the "staircase" calculate in a pipelined manner the sums *sumf* from the Eq. (21);
- the δ_i are calculated in the B and D processing elements;
- based on the above the cumulative adjustments of weights are obtained after the epoch in the A processing elements.

The modified A - E processing elements are shown in Fig. 6 and the additional S, T and Z processing elements in Fig. 7. The A processing elements have

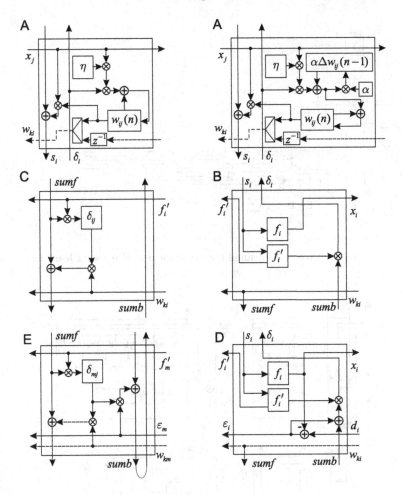

Fig. 4. The processing elements for 2D structure for learning neural networks

been enhanced to support calculating of cumulative network weights adjustments after the epoch. The A processing element is presented in two versions: without and with the momentum component. The B - E processing elements have been simplified, and some of their functions have been taken over to the additional T and S elements.

3   Computational Results

In all the cases, the number of computing cycles has been determined. Tables 2, 3, 4, 5 and 6 show the numbers of computational cycles per one iteration for serial computing, per one epoch for serial computing, per one iteration for 2D parallel computing, per one epoch for 2D parallel computing and per one epoch

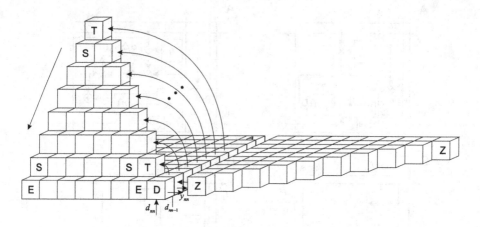

Fig. 5. The three-dimensional structure for neural network learning

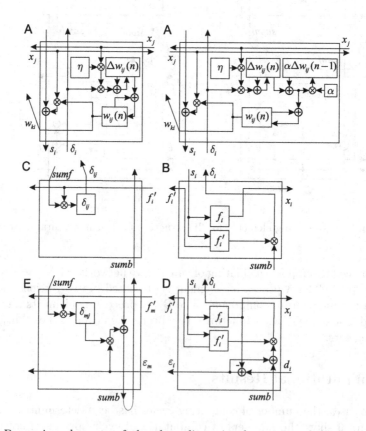

Fig. 6. Processing elements of the three-dimensional structure for neural network learning

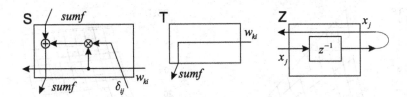

Fig. 7. Additional processing elements of the three-dimensional structure for neural networks learning

Table 2. Number of cycles per one iteration for serial computing

Operation	Number of cycles per one iteration for serial computing
$+/-$	$\frac{n^3}{6} + \frac{n^2}{2} + 2ni + no - \frac{1}{2}o^2 - \frac{2n}{3} + 1\frac{1}{2}o$
$*$	$\frac{n^3}{6} + n^2 + 2ni + no - \frac{1}{2}o^2 - \frac{n}{6} + i + \frac{1}{2}o + 1$
f/f'	$2n$

Table 3. Number of cycles per one epoch for serial computing

Operation	Number of cycles per one epoch for serial computing
$+/-$	$\left(\frac{n^3}{6} + \frac{n^2}{2} + 2ni + no - \frac{1}{2}o^2 - \frac{2n}{3} + 1\frac{1}{2}o\right)p$
$*$	$\left(\frac{n^3}{6} + n^2 + 2ni + no - \frac{1}{2}o^2 - \frac{n}{6} + i + \frac{1}{2}o + 1\right)p$
f/f'	$2np$

Table 4. Number of cycles per one iteration for 2D parallel computing

Operation	Number of cycles per one iteration for 2D parallel computing
$+/-$	$n + i + 2$
$*$	$n + 3$
f/f'	n

Table 5. Number of cycles per one epoch for 2D parallel computing

Operation	Number of cycles per one epoch for 2D parallel computing
$+/-$	$(n + i + 2)p$
$*$	$(n + 3)p$
f/f'	np

for 3D parallel computing, respectively. The formulas for cycles of addition, multiplication and function computation are presented separately. Symbols i, n, o and p denote the numbers of inputs, neurons, outputs and patterns respectively.

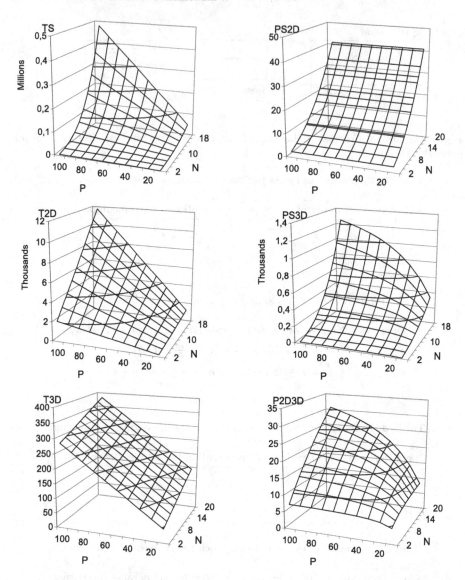

Fig. 8. The number of computing cycles (1 column) for the serial (TS), 2D (T2D) and 3D (T3D) calculations. Charts of performance factors (column 2) for the 2D structure and 3D structure (relative to serial and 2D respectively)

Figure 8 shows the charts of computing cycles number and the charts of performance factors $PS2D = TS/T2D$, $PS3D = TS/T3D$ and $P2D3D = T2D/T3D$ for the neural network with 2 inputs and 1 output. It was assumed that there are 10 to 100 learning patterns in each epoch and 2 to 20 neurons in a network.

Table 6. Number of cycles per one epoch for 3D parallel computing

Operation	Number of cycles per one epoch for 3D parallel computing
$+/-$	$n + i + 3$
$*$	$n + 4$
f/f'	$n + p - 1$

4   Conclusion

In this paper the parallel structures of the steepest descent learning algorithm without error bacpropagation for a fully connected feedforward neural network are presented. We can compare computational performance of the parallel structure of the proposed learning algorithm with a sequential solution for a network with two inputs, one output, up to $N = 20$ neurons and up to $P = 100$ patterns of the learning data. The number of computational cycles of the presented parallel 3D architecture displays only linear growth while in a serial solution this number is of order $\mathcal{O}(n^3 p)$. The performance factor ($PS3D = TS/T3D$) of parallel 3D realisation achieves 1250 for $N = 20$ neurons and $P = 100$ patterns, and it grows fast when these numbers grow, see Fig. 8. It has been observed that the performance of the proposed solution is very promising. A similar parallel approach can be used for other advanced learning algorithms of feedforward neural networks, see eg. [1,7,9]. In future research it might be possible to make an attempt at designing a parallel realisation of learning in other methods [29–31], and structures [20–23] and various fuzzy [15–17], and neuro-fuzzy structures [11,16].

References

1. Bilski, J.: The UD RLS algorithm for training the feedforward neural networks. Int. J. Appl. Math. Comput. Sci. **15**(1), 101–109 (2005)
2. Bilski, J., Litwiński, S., Smoląg, J.: Parallel realisation of QR algorithm for neural networks learning. In: Rutkowski, L., Siekmann, J.H., Tadeusiewicz, R., Zadeh, L.A. (eds.) ICAISC 2004. LNCS (LNAI), vol. 3070, pp. 158–165. Springer, Heidelberg (2004)
3. Bilski, J., Smoląg, J.: Parallel realisation of the recurrent RTRN neural network learning. In: Rutkowski, L., Tadeusiewicz, R., Zadeh, L.A., Zurada, J.M. (eds.) ICAISC 2008. LNCS (LNAI), vol. 5097, pp. 11–16. Springer, Heidelberg (2008)
4. Bilski, J., Smoląg, J.: Parallel realisation of the recurrent Elman neural network learning. In: Rutkowski, L., Scherer, R., Tadeusiewicz, R., Zadeh, L.A., Zurada, J.M. (eds.) ICAISC 2010, Part II. LNCS, vol. 6114, pp. 19–25. Springer, Heidelberg (2010)
5. Bilski, J., Smoląg, J.: Parallel realisation of the recurrent multi layer perceptron learning. In: Rutkowski, L., Korytkowski, M., Scherer, R., Tadeusiewicz, R., Zadeh, L.A., Zurada, J.M. (eds.) ICAISC 2012, Part I. LNCS, vol. 7267, pp. 12–20. Springer, Heidelberg (2012)

6. Bilski, J., Smoląg, J.: Parallel approach to learning of the recurrent Jordan neural network. In: Rutkowski, L., Korytkowski, M., Scherer, R., Tadeusiewicz, R., Zadeh, L.A., Zurada, J.M. (eds.) ICAISC 2013, Part I. LNCS, vol. 7894, pp. 32–40. Springer, Heidelberg (2013)

7. Bilski, J.: Parallel Structures for Feedforward and Dynamical Neural Networks (in Polish). AOW EXIT (2013)

8. Bilski, J., Smolą, J., Galushkin, A.I.: The parallel approach to the conjugate gradient learning algorithm for the feedforward neural networks. In: Rutkowski, L., Korytkowski, M., Scherer, R., Tadeusiewicz, R., Zadeh, L.A., Zurada, J.M. (eds.) ICAISC 2014, Part I. LNCS, vol. 8467, pp. 12–21. Springer, Heidelberg (2014)

9. Bilski, J., Smoląg, J.: Parallel architectures for learning the rtrn and elman dynamic neural networks. IEEE Trans. Parallel Distrib. Syst. 26(9), 2561–2570 (2015)

10. Bilski, J., Smolą, J., Żurada, J.M.: Parallel approach to the levenberg-marquardt learning algorithm for feedforward neural networks. In: Rutkowski, L., Korytkowski, M., Scherer, R., Tadeusiewicz, R., Zadeh, L.A., Zurada, J.M. (eds.) Artificial Intelligence and Soft Computing. LNCS(LNAI), vol. 9119, pp. 3–14. Springer, Heidelberg (2015)

11. Cpałka, K., Łapa, K., Przybył, A., Zalasiński, M.: A new method for designing neuro-fuzzy systems for nonlinear modelling with interpretability aspects. Neurocomputing 135, 203–217 (2014)

12. Fahlman, S.: Faster learning variations on backpropagation: an empirical study. In: Proceedings of Connectionist Models Summer School, Los Atos (1988)

13. Hagan, M.T., Menhaj, M.B.: Training feedforward networks with the Marquardt algorithm. IEEE Trans. Neuralnetworks 5(6), 989–993 (1994)

14. Knop, M., Kapuściński, T., Mleczko, W.: Video key frame detection based on the restricted Boltzmann machine. J. Appl. Math. Comput. Mech. 14(3), 49–58 (2016)

15. Korytkowski, M., Rutkowski, L., Scherer, R.: Fast image classification by boosting fuzzy classifiers. Inf. Sci. 327, 175–182 (2016)

16. Korytkowski, M., Scherer, R., Rutkowski, L.: On Combining backpropagation with boosting. computational collective intelligence. In: 2006 International Joint Conference on Neural Networks, IEEE World Congress on Computational Intelligence, pp. 1274–127. Vancouver, BC, Canada (2006)

17. Nowak, B., Nowicki, R., Starczewski, J.: The learning of neuro-fuzzy classifier with fuzzy rough sets for imprecise datasets. Artifi. Intell. Soft Comput. 8467, 256–266 (2014)

18. Riedmiller, M., Braun, H.: A direct method for faster backpropagation learning: the RPROP algorithm. In: IEEE International Conference on Neural Networks. IEEE, San Francisco (1993)

19. Rumelhart, D.E., Hinton, G.E., Williams, R.J.: Learning internal representations by error propagation. In: Rumelhart, D.E., McCelland, J. (red.) Parallel Distributed Processing, vol. 1, chap. 8. The MIT Press, Cambridge, Massachusetts (1986)

20. Rutkowski, L., Jaworski, M., Pietruczuk, L., Duda, P.: Decision trees for mining data streams based on the gaussian approximation. IEEE Trans. Knowl. Data Eng. 26(1), 108–119 (2014)

21. Rutkowski, L., Jaworski, M., Pietruczuk, L., Duda, P.: A new method for data stream mining based on the misclassification error. IEEE Trans. Neural Netw. Learn. Syst. 26(5), 1048–1059 (2015)

22. Rutkowski, L., Pietruczuk, L., Duda, P., Jaworski, M.: Decision trees for mining data streams based on the McDiarmid's bound. IEEE Trans. Knowl. Data Eng. 25(6), 1272–1279 (2013)

23. Rutkowski, L., Jaworski, M., Pietruczuk, L., Duda, P.: The CART Decision Trees for Mining Data Streams. Inf. Sci. **266**, 1–15 (2014)
24. Smoląg, J., Bilski, J.: A systolic array for fast learning of neural networks. In: Proceedings of Fifth Conference on Neural Networks and Soft Computing, pp. 754–758. Zakopane (2000)
25. Smoląg, J., Rutkowski, L., Bilski, J.: Systolic array for neural networks. In: Proceedings of the fourth Conference on Neural Networks and their Applications, pp. 487–497. Zakopane (1999)
26. Starczewski, A.: A New Validity Index for Crisp Clusters. Pattern Analysis and Applications (2015). doi:10.1007/s10044-015-0525-8
27. Tadeusiewicz, R.: Neural Networks (in Polish). AOW RM (1993)
28. Werbos, J.: Backpropagation through time: what it does and how to do it. Proc. IEEE **78**(10), 1550–1560 (1990)
29. Wilamowski, B.M., Yo, H.: Neural network learning without backpropagation. IEEE Trans Neural Netw. **21**(11), 1793–1803 (2010)
30. Wilamowski, B.M., Yo, H.: Improved Computation For Levenberg–Marquardt Training. IEEE Trans. Neural Netw. **21**(6), 930–937 (2010)
31. Yo, H., Reiner, P.D., Xie, T., Bartczak, T., Wilamowski, B.M.: An incremental design of radial basis function networks. IEEE Trans. Neural Netw. Learn. Syst. **25**(10), 1793–1803 (2014)

Parallelization of Image Encryption Algorithm Based On Chaotic Neural Networks

Dariusz Burak[(✉)]

Faculty of Computer Science and Information Technology,
West Pomeranian University of Technology,
49 Żołnierska St., 71-210 Szczecin, Poland
dburak@wi.zut.edu.pl

Abstract. In this paper the results of parallelizing an image encryption algorithm based on chaotic neural networks are presented. A data dependence analysis of loops is applied in order to parallelize the algorithm. The parallelism of the algorithm is demonstrated in accordance with the OpenMP standard. As a result of this study, it is stated that the most time-consuming loops of the algorithm are suitable for parallelization. The efficiency measurements of a parallel algorithm working in standard modes of operation are shown.

Keywords: Neural network · Chaos · Image encryption · Parallelization · OpenMP

1 Introduction

One of the very important functional features of cryptographic algorithms is cipher speed. This feature is significant in case of block ciphers since they usually work on large data sets. Thus even not much differences of speed may cause the choice of the faster cipher by the user. Therefore, it is all-important to parallelize encryption algorithms in order to achieve faster processing using multi-core processors or multiprocessing systems. In recent years many chaos-based ciphers were proposed. Futhermore neural networks are often introduced to design encryption algorithms considering the complicated and time-varying nature of the structures. Chaotic neural networks (CNNs) are particulary suitable for data protection. Nowadays, there are many descriptions of various ciphers based on chaotic neural networks, for instance [1–10]. The critical issue in such ciphers is program implementation.

Unlike parallel implementations of classical block ciphers, for instance AES [11], IDEA [12], there are only a few parallel implementations of block ciphers based on chaotic neural networks, for example [13–15]. Being seemingly a research gap it is absolutely fundamental to show real functional advantages and disadvantages of the encryption algorithm using software or hardware implementation.

© Springer International Publishing Switzerland 2016
L. Rutkowski et al. (Eds.): ICAISC 2016, Part I, LNAI 9692, pp. 70–80, 2016.
DOI: 10.1007/978-3-319-39378-0_7

The main contribution of the study is developing a parallel algorithm in accordance with OpenMP standard of the image encryption algorithm designed by Bigdeli et al. and presented in [16] based on transformations of a source code written in the C language representing the sequential algorithm.

This paper is organized as follows. The next section briefly describes the image encryption algorithm based on chaotic neural networks. In Sect. 3, parallelization process is fully characterized. In Sect. 4, the experimental results obtained for developed parallel algorithm are presented. Finally, concluding remarks are given in Sect. 5.

2   Description of the Image Encryption Algorithm Based on Chaotic Neural Networks

The image encryption algorithm based on chaotic neural networks [16] is composed of three separate blocks: chaotic neuron layer (CNL), permutation neuron layer (PNL) and a chaotic key generator. Each of the first two layers is 3-input 3-output and includes three neurons. The chaotic key generator block supports these layers by their corresponding weights and biases.

The encryption process consists of the following steps:

1. Select a sequence of 160 bits as the authentication code K, and then split them into five groups, that are further mapped into nine initial parameters $x_1(0)$, $y_1(0)$, $z_1(0)$, $x_2(0)$, $y_2(0)$, $z_2(0)$, $x_3(0)$, $y_3(0)$ and $z_3(0)$. Next, set R as the number of iterations, and N_0 as the complementary secret keys.
2. Iterate three chaotic systems- Chua [17], Lorenz [19] and Lü [18] using a fourth order Runge–Kutta algorithm for N_0 times to obtain $x_1(N_0)$, $y_1(N_0)$, $z_1(N_0)$, $x_2(N_0)$, $y_2(N_0)$, $z_2(N_0)$, $x_3(N_0)$, $y_3(N_0)$ and $z_3(N_0)$. Set the iteration number $r = 1$.
3. Since D is an $N \times N$ pixels image, for $N_0 + i$, $i = (r - 1) \times (N \times N) + 1$, ..., $r \times (N \times N)$ iterate the three chaotic systems, where $i = 1, 2, ...$ represents the i-th iteration of chaotic systems. For each iteration compute W_{dl}, B_{dl} and A_l matrices in the following way:

$$W_{dl,i} = \begin{bmatrix} x_1(N_0 + i) & x_2(N_0 + i) & x_3(N_0 + i) \\ y_1(N_0 + i) & y_2(N_0 + i) & y_3(N_0 + i) \\ z_1(N_0 + i) & z_2(N_0 + i) & z_3(N_0 + i) \end{bmatrix} + \alpha I, \qquad (1)$$

$$a(j, i) = mod(|x_j(N_0 + i)| - floor(x_j(N_0 + i)) \times 10^{14}, 255) + 1, \qquad (2)$$

$(j = 1, 2, 3)$,

$$A_{l,i} = [a(1, i), a(2, i), a(3, i)]^T, \qquad (3)$$

$$b(j, i) = dec2bi(mod(|y_j(N_0 + i)| - floor(y_j(N_0 + i))) \times 10^{14}, 255) + 1, \qquad (4)$$

$(j = 1, 2, 3)$,

$$B_{dl,i} = [b(1, i), b(2, i), b(3, i)]^T, \qquad (5)$$

where $W_{dl,i}$ is the weight matrix, $B_{dl,i}$ and $A_{l,i}$ are the bias matrices of chaotic neuron layer and $dec2bi(x)$ converts decimal number x to a binary value. Besides, I is a 3×3 identity matrix, and the parameter α prevent from occurrence the singularity problem in $W_{dl,i}^{-1}$ matrix (that is necessary in decryption process).

In order to determine the weight matrix of permutation neuron layer W_{cl}, let us define:

$$D_i = [x_1(N_0 + i), y_2(N_0 + i), z_3(N_0 + i)], \tag{6}$$

$$w_{1,i} = arg(max(D_i)), \tag{7}$$

$$w_{2,i} = arg(min(D_i)), \tag{8}$$

where $arg(max(D_i))$ and $arg(min(D_i))$ are the index of the maximum value in the vector D_i and the index of the minimum value in the vector D_i, respectively. Then the non-zero term of the first row and the second row of the matrix $W_{cl,k}$ is determined as:

$$W_{cl,i}(1, w_{1,i}) = W_{cl,i}(2, w_{2,i}) = 1, \tag{9}$$

and, the non-zero term of the third row is determined such that it exists just one $'1'$ in each row/column of the matrix $W_{cl,k}$. Then, the control parameters of the Arnold cat map [21] are derived as [22]:

$$p_i = floor[mod(z_1(N_0 + i) \times 2^{24}), N)], \tag{10}$$

$$q_i = floor[mod(mod(z_1(N_0 + i) \times 2^{48}, 2^{24}), N)], \tag{11}$$

4. Suppose that the P is $N \times N$ pixels plain image. Then, corresponding to each pixel k, there is a vector X_k of order three with the RGB components of the pixel as its entries $X_k = [R_k, G_k, B_k]^T, k = 1, ..., (N \times N)$. Then the total color information of the image will be a $3 \times (N \times N)$ matrix X with columns $X_k, k = 1, ..., (N \times N)$. Compute the matrix X as the input of chaotic neuron layer.

5. In order to generate the secret information, several operations are applied to each column of matrix X, i.e. $X_k, k = 1, ..., (N \times N)$ and $i = (r - 1) \times (N \times N) + 1, ..., r \times (N \times N)$ as:

$$Y_{i,k} = W_{dl,i}X_k, \tag{12}$$

- Normalization (mapping the values of $Y_{1,k}$ into interval $[1,255]$):

$$Y_{2,k} = N(Y_{1,k}), \tag{13}$$

- Manipulation:

$$Y_{3,k} = floor(Y_{2,k}) + mod(Y_{2,k}, floor(Y_{2,k})) = Y_{31,k} + Y_{32,k}, \tag{14}$$

- XOR operation:

$$Y_{4,k} = Y_{31,k} \oplus B_{dl,i}, \tag{15}$$

- Applying chaotic activation function:

$$Y_{5,k} = f(Y_{4,k}, A_{l,i}) + Y_{32,k}, \tag{16}$$

where f() is the chaotic tent map [20].

6. The output of the chaotic neuron layer is the $3 \times (N \times N)$ matrix Y_5 which is then permuted in two stages by permutation neuron layer. At first, each column of Y_5 is linearly permuted as:

$$Y_{6,k} = g(W_{cl,i}Y_{5,k} + B_{cl,i}), \tag{17}$$

where $g(x) = x$, $B_{cl,i} = [0,0,0]^T$ and the calculation of weight matrix $W_{cl,i}$ is as presented in step 3.

7. The output of the linear permutation stage are shuffled. Therefore, each row of matrix Y_6 is arranged in a $N \times N$ matrix and thus three output $N \times N$ matrixes are provided. Then, each matrix is permuted in two-dimensional by Arnold cat map permutation algorithm. Considering the three nonlinearly permuted matrices as three planes of encrypted image(red, green, blue), the output encrypted image is derived, which is called Y_7.

8. If the current round is not the final round of encryption ($r < R$), then set $P = Y_7$. Set $r = r + 1$ and return to step 3. Otherwise, set $P_{final} = Y_7$ is the final cipher image and encryption process is completed.

In the decryption process (symmetric to encryption one), the reverse of encryption process is performed. Therefore, the inverse of PNL and CNL operations should be applied to the cipher image, iteratively. More detailed description of encryption algorithm designed by Bigdeli et al. is given in [16].

3   Parallelization Process of Encryption Algorithm

Given the fact that proposed encryption algorithm can work in block manner it is necessary to prepare a C source code representing the sequential algorithm working in Electronic Codebook (ECB), Cipher Block Chaining (CBC), Cipher Feedback (CFB), Output Feedback (OFB) and Counter (CTR) modes of operation. The source code of the encryption algorithm in the essential ECB mode contains thirty for loops. Twenty two of them include no I/O functions. Some of these loops are time-consuming. Thus their parallelization is critical for reducing the total time of the parallel algorithm execution.

In order to find dependencies in program a research tool for analyzing array data dependencies called Petit was applied. Petit was developed at the University of Maryland under the Omega Project and is freely available for both DOS and UNIX systems [23].

The OpenMP standard was used to present parallelized loops. The OpenMP Application Program Interface (API) [24,25] supports multi-platform shared memory parallel programming in C/C++ and Fortran on all architectures including Unix and Windows platforms. OpenMP is a collection of compiler directives, library routines and environment variables which could be used to specify shared memory parallelism. OpenMP directives extend a sequential programming language with Single Program Multiple Data (SPMD) constructs, work-sharing constructs, synchronization constructs and help to operate on both shared data and private data. An OpenMP program begins execution as a single task (called a master thread). When a parallel construct is encountered, the master thread creates a team of threads. The statements within the parallel construct are executed in parallel by each thread in a team. At the end of the parallel construct, the threads of the team are synchronized. Then only the master thread continues execution until the next parallel construct will be encountered. To build a valid parallel code, it is necessary to preserve all dependencies, data conflicts and requirements regarding parallelism of a program [24,25].

The process of the encryption algorithm parallelization can be divided into the following stages:

- carrying out the dependence analysis of a sequential source code in order to detect parallelizable loops;
- selecting parallelization methods based on source code transformations;
- constructing parallel forms of program loops in accordance with the OpenMP standard.

There are the following basic types of the data dependencies that occur in *for* loops: a Data Flow Dependence, a Data Anti-dependence and an Output Dependence [26,27]. Additionally, control dependence determines the ordering of an instruction i, with respect to a branch instruction so that instruction i is executed in a correct program order.

To find the most time-consuming loops of the algorithm, experiments were carried out for an about 4 megabytes input file.

It appeared that the algorithm has two computational bottlenecks: the first is enclosed in the function bigdeli_enc() and the second is enclosed in the function bigdeli_dec(). The bigdeli_enc() function enables enciphering of the whichever number of data blocks and the bigdeli_dec() does the same for deciphering process (analogically to similar functions of the classic block ciphers like DES-the des_enc(), the des_dec() presented in [28]). Thus the parallelization of *for* loops included in these functions has a unique meaning.

The bodies of the bigdeli_enc() and the bigdeli_dec() functions are as follows:

```
void bigdeli_enc(bigdeli_context *ctx,UINT8 *input,UINT8 *output,
            int input_length){
    for (int i = 0; i<NUMBER_OF_BLOCKS; i++) {
        Encryption(ctx, input, output);
        input+= BLOCKSIZE;
        output+= BLOCKSIZE;
    }
};

void bigdeli_dec(bigdeli_context *ctx,UINT8 *input,UINT8 *output,
            int input_length){
    for (int i = 0; i<NUMBER_OF_BLOCKS; i++) {
        Decryption(ctx, input, output);
        input+= BLOCKSIZE;
```

```
        output+= BLOCKSIZE;
    }
}.
```

Taking into account the strong similarity of the above functions only the first one is examined. Subsequently this analysis is valid in the case of the second one.

In order to apply the data dependencies analysis of the loop included in bigdeli_enc() function the body of the Encryption() function should be put in this loop.

Definitions of the tentMap(), catMap(), ChuaSystem(), LorenzSystem(), LuSystem(), Normalization(), Manipulation(), XOR(), chaoticActivation(), f(), and g() functions included in the body of the Encryption() function are the following:

```
double tentMap(double param,double initial,int iter) {
for (int z = 0; z < NUMBER_OF_ITERATIONS; z++) {
    for (int i=0;i<iter;i++) {
        if ((initial>=0) && (initial<param))
                return (initial/param);
        else
                return((1-initial)/(1-param));
        }
    }
};

void catMap(char output[][N+1], char input[][N+1]){
for(int i = 0; i < N; i++) {
    for(int j = 0; j < N; j++) {
        output[(i + j)
        }
    }
};

void ChuaSystem(double x,double y,double z,
            double *xx,double *yy,double *zz){
    *xx = 10 * y - 20 * x * x * x + 10.0 * x / 7.0;
    *yy = x - y + z;
    *zz = -100.0 * y / 7.0;
};

void LorenzSystem(double x,double y,double z,
            double *xx,double *yy,double *zz){
    *xx = -10 * x + 10 * y;
    *yy =  28 * x - y - z * x;
    *zz = -8.0 / 3.0 * z + x * y;
};
```

```
void LuSystem(double x,double y,double z,
              double *xx,double *yy,double *zz){
   *xx = 36 * y - 36 * x;
   *yy =  - x * z + 20 * x;
   *zz = x * y - 3 * z;
};

void Normalization(double *yy double x,
                   double q1, double q2, double q3){
   *yy = q1 * tanh(q2 * x) * q3);
};

void Manipulation(double y, double *yy){
   *yy = floor(y) + mod(y, floor(y)));
};

void XOR(int y, int b, int *yy){
   *yy = y ^ b;
};

void chaoticActivation(double y, double y2, double a, int iter,
                       double *yy){
   *yy = tentMap(y2,a,iter) + mod(y, floor(y));
};

void g(double x,double *yy) {
   *yy = x;
}.
```

The actual parallelization process of the loop included in the bigdeli_enc() function consists of the five following stages:

- removal of the chaotic key generator operations, construction of matrices W_{dl}, B_{dl}, A_l from the chaotic neuron layer (CNL), construction of matrices W_{cl}, B_{cl} and control parameters p, q from the permutation neuron layer (PNL); all these calculations have to be executed before starting the chaotic neuron layer operations;
- insertion of the following statements in the beginning of the loop body: plaintext = &input[BLOCKSIZE*i]; ciphertext=&output[BLOCKSIZE*i];
- removal from the end of the loop body the following statements: input+= BLOCKSIZE; output+= BLOCKSIZE;
- insertion of the following statements: ChaoticNeuronLayer(ciphertext, plaintext, wdl, bdl, al); PermutationNeuronLayer(ciphertext, wcl, bcl, p, q); the first statement carries out the operations specified in chaotic neuron layer (normalization, manipulation, XOR, chaotic activation), the second one accomplishes the operations included in permutation neuron layer (linear permutation, cat map permutation).

- suitable variables privatization (i, ii, plaintext, ciphertext, wdl, bdl, al, wcl, bcl, p, q, y1, y31, y4, y5, y6) using OpenMP (based on the results of data dependence analysis) for the loop indexing by i;
- adding appropriate OpenMP directive and clauses (#pragma omp parallel for private() shared()) for the loop indexing by i.

The steps above result in the following parallel form of the loop include in the bigdeli_enc() function in accordance with the OpenMP standard:

```
#pragma omp parallel private (i, ii, plaintext, ciphertext,
                              wdl, bdl, al, wcl, bcl, p, q,
                              y1, y31, y4, y5, y6)
#pragma omp for
for (i=0; i<nblocks; i++) {
    plaintext=&input[BLOCKSIZE*i];
    ciphertext = &output[BLOCKSIZE*i];
    for(ii=0; ii<R; ii++) {
        ChaoticNeuronLayer(ciphertext,plaintext, wdl, bdl, al);
        PermutationNeuronLayer(ciphertext, wcl, bcl, p, q);
    }
}.
```

4   Experimental Results

In order to study the efficiency of the presented encryption algorithm eight Quad-Core Intel Xeon Processors 7310 Series - 1.60 GHz and the Intel C++ Compiler (version 13.1.1 20130313 that supports the OpenMP 4.0) were used. The results received for an about 5 megabytes input file (8 bit per pixel image) using two, four, eight, sixteen and thirty-two cores versus the only one have been shown in Tables 1 and 2. The number of threads is equal to the number of processors.

The total running time of the presented encryption algorithm consists of the following operations: data receiving from an input file, data encryption, data decryption and data writing to an output file.

Thus the total speed-up of the parallel encryption algorithm depends heavily on the following four factors:

- the degree of parallelization of the loop included in the bigdeli_enc() function;
- the degree of parallelization of the loop included in the bigdeli_dec() function;
- the method of reading data from an input file;
- the method of writing data to an output file.

The results confirm that the loops included both the bigdeli_enc() and the bigdeli_dec() functions are parallelizable with high speed-up (see Table 1).

The block method of reading data from an input file and writing data to an output file was used. The following C language functions and block sizes

Table 1. Speed-up of the parallel Bigdeli et al. image encryption algorithm in the ECB mode of operation.

Number of threads	Speed-up of the encryption process	Speed-up of the decryption process	Speed-up of the whole algorithm
1	1.00	1.00	1.00
2	1.87	1.95	1.41
4	3.64	3.84	1.82
8	5.81	6.21	2.20
16	6.01	6.33	2.40
32	5.83	6.17	2.20

Table 2. Speed-ups of the parallel Bigdeli et al. image encryption algorithms in the CTR, CBC and CFB mode of operation.

Number of threads	Operation	Speed-up of the CTR mode of operation	Speed-up of the CBC mode of operation	Speed-up of the CFB mode of operation
1	Encryption	1.00	1.00	1.00
1	Decryption	1.00	1.00	1.00
2	Encryption	1.90	1.00	1.00
2	Decryption	1.90	1.90	1.90
4	Encryption	3.50	1.00	1.00
4	Decryption	3.70	3.70	3.70
8	Encryption	5.70	1.00	1.00
8	Decryption	6.00	6.00	6.00
16	Encryption	5.90	1.00	1.00
16	Decryption	6.10	6.10	6.10
32	Encryption	5.70	1.00	1.00
32	Decryption	6.00	6.00	6.00

was applied: fread() with 1024-bytes blocks for data reading and fwrite() with 256-bytes blocks for data writing.

In accordance with Amdahl's Law the maximum speed-up of the encryption algorithm is limited to 4.60, because the fraction of the code that cannot be parallelized is 0.2175.

The encryption algorithm was also parallelized in the following standard modes of operation (CTR, CBC and CFB). The results are presented in Table 2.

When the encryption algorithm operates in the ECB and CTR modes of operation, both the encryption and decryption processes are parallelizable and speed-ups of the whole algorithm are similar (see details- Tables 1 and 2). For the CBC and CFB modes only the decryption process is parallelized so the values of speed-up are lower than for the ECB and CTR modes of operation (see Table 2).

5 Conclusions

In this paper, the parallelization process of the image encryption algorithm designed by Bigdeli et al. has been shown. The time-consuming *for* loops included in the functions responsible for the encryption and decryption processes are parallelizable. The experiments have shown that the application of the parallel encryption algorithm for multiprocessor and multi-core computers would considerably boost the time of the data encryption and decryption. The speed-ups received for these operations can be admitted as satisfactory. Moreover, the developed parallel encryption algorithm can be also helpful for hardware and GPGPU implementations

References

1. Guo, D., Cheng, L., Cheng, L.: A new symmetric probabilistic encryption scheme based on chaotic attractors of neural networks. Appl. Intell. **10**(1), 71–84 (1999)
2. Chan, C., Cheng, L.: The convergence properties of a clipped hopfield network and its application in the design of keystream generator. IEEE Trans. Neural Netw. **12**(2), 340–348 (2001)
3. Rachel, M., Einat, K., Wolfgang, K.: Public channel cryptography by synchronization of neural networks and chaotic maps. Phys. Rev. Lett. **91**(11), 118701/1–118701/4 (2003)
4. Karras, D., Zorkadis, V.: On neural network techniques in the secure management of communication systems through improving and quality assessing pseudorandom stream generators. Neural Netw. **16**(5), 899–905 (2003)
5. Lian, S., Chen, G., Cheung, A., Wang, Z.: A chaotic-neural-network-based encryption algorithm for JPEG2000 encoded images. In: Yin, F.-L., Wang, J., Guo, C. (eds.) ISNN 2004. LNCS, vol. 3174, pp. 627–632. Springer, Heidelberg (2004)
6. Xiao, D., Liao, X.-F.: A combined hash and encryption scheme by chaotic neural network. In: Yin, F.-L., Wang, J., Guo, C. (eds.) ISNN 2004. LNCS, vol. 3174, pp. 633–638. Springer, Heidelberg (2004)
7. Yu, W., Cao, J.: Cryptography based on delayed chaotic neural networks. Phys. Lett. A **356**(4–5), 333–338 (2006)
8. Lian, S.: A block cipher based on chaotic neural networks. Neurocomputing **72**, 1296–1301 (2009)
9. Lian, S., Chen, X.: Traceable content protection based on chaos and neural networks. Appl. Soft Comput. **11**(7), 4293–4301 (2011)
10. Fadil, T.A., Yaakob, S.N., Ahmad, R.B., Yahya, A.: A chaotic neural network-based encryption algorithm for MPEG-2 encoded video signal. Int. J. Artif. Int. Soft Comput. **3**(4), 360–371 (2013)
11. Bielecki, W., Burak, D.: Exploiting loop-level parallelism in the AES algorithm. WSEAS Trans. Comput. **1**(5), 125–133 (2006)
12. Beletskyy, V., Burak, D.: Parallelization of the IDEA algorithm. In: Bubak, M., van Albada, G.D., Sloot, P.M.A., Dongarra, J. (eds.) ICCS 2004. LNCS, vol. 3036, pp. 635–638. Springer, Heidelberg (2004)
13. Burak, D.: Parallelization of encryption algorithm based on chaos system and neural networks. In: Wyrzykowski, R., Dongarra, J., Karczewski, K., Waśniewski, J. (eds.) PPAM 2013, Part II. LNCS, vol. 8385, pp. 364–373. Springer, Heidelberg (2014)

14. Burak, D.: Parallelization of a block cipher based on chaotic neural networks. In: Rutkowski, L., Korytkowski, M., Scherer, R., Tadeusiewicz, R., Zadeh, L.A., Zurada, J.M. (eds.) Artificial Intelligence and Soft Computing. LNCS, vol. 9120, pp. 191–201. Springer, Heidelberg (2015)
15. Burak, D.: Parallelization of an encryption algorithm based on a spatiotemporal chaotic system and a chaotic neural network. In: International Conference On Computational Science, ICCS 2015, Procedia Computer Science, vol. 51, pp. 2888–2892 (2015)
16. Bigdeli, N., Farid, Y., Afshar, K.: A novel image Encryption/Decryption scheme based on chaotic neural networks. Eng. Appl. Artif. Intell. **25**, 753–765 (2012)
17. Botmart, T., Niamsup, P.: Adaptive control and synchronization of the perturbed Chua's system. Math. Comput. Simul. **75**(1–2), 37–55 (2007)
18. Lu, J., Chen, G., Zhang, S.: The compound structure of a new chaotic attractor. Chaos, Solitons Fractals **14**, 669–672 (2002)
19. Li, D., Yin, Z.: Connecting the Lorenz and Chen systems via nonlinear control. Commun. Nonlinear Sci. Numer. Simul. **14**(3), 655–667 (2009)
20. Masuda, N., Aihara, K.: Cryptosystems with discretized chaotic maps. IEEE Trans. Circuits Syst. I: Fundam. Theory Appl. **49**(1), 28–40 (2002)
21. Xiao, D., Liao, X., Wei, P.: Analysis and improvement of a chaos-based image encryption algorithm. Chaos, Solitons Fractals **40**(5), 2191–2199 (2009)
22. Wang, Y., Wong, K., Liao, X., Xiang, T., Chen, G.: A chaos-based image encryption algorithm with variable control parameters. Chaos, Solitons Fractals **41**(4), 1773–1783 (2009)
23. Kelly, W., Maslov, V., Pugh, W., Rosser, E., Shpeisman, T., Wonnacott, D.: New User Interface for Petit and Other Extensions. User Guide (1996)
24. Chapman, B., Jost, G., van der Pas, R.: Using OpenMP - Portable Shared Memory Parallel Programming. The MIT Press, Cambridge (2007)
25. OpenMP Application Program Interface. Version 4.0 (2013)
26. Allen, R., Kennedy, K.: Optimizing Compilers for Modern Architectures: A Dependencebased Approach. Morgan Kaufmann Publishers Inc, San Francisco (2001)
27. Aho, A., Lam, M., Sethi, R., Ullman, J.: Compilers: Principles, Techniques, and Tools, 2nd edn. Prentice Hall, Upper Saddle River (2006)
28. Schneier, B.: Applied Cryptography: Protocols, Algorithms, and Source Code in C, vol. 2. John Wiley & Sons, New York (1995)

Ensemble ANN Classifier for Structural Health Monitoring

Ziemowit Dworakowski[1]([✉]), Tadeusz Stepinski[1], Krzysztof Dragan[1,2],
Adam Jablonski[1], and Tomasz Barszcz[1]

[1] Department of Robotics and Mechatronics, AGH University of Science
and Technology, Krakow, Poland
{zdw,tstepin,tbarszcz}@agh.edu.pl, dragan@itwl.pl
[2] Air Force Institute of Technology, Warsaw, Poland

Abstract. Type and structure of artificial neural network (ANN) have
significant impact on its performance. Furthermore, networks of the same
type and structure often perform differently due to the random distribution of initial weights. These issues cause the practical use of ANNs
a challenging task. Some of the mentioned drawbacks can be eliminated
using ensembles of ANNs. However, relevance of a single ensemble member might be different in different classification or regression tasks. In this
paper we present an autonomous ensemble design method that includes
selection of a subset of ANNs most suitable for solving of a specific task.
The ensemble is able to change its structure by choosing the electors with
respect to their training performance. The proposed method is tested in
practical regression tasks in civil engineering structures monitoring.

Keywords: ANN · Ensemble · SHM

1 Introduction

Structural Health Monitoring (SHM) is a field of growing importance. Autonomous detection and localization of damage in structures allows both significant
increase in their operational safety and reduction of expenses connected with
their operation. SHM is usually performed on a basis of data gathered in periodic or continuous examinations with use of non-destructive techniques. One can
enumerate lots of methods that can provide data for monitoring tasks: ultrasonic
testing [1], vision-based inspection [2], modal analysis [3], operational variables
[4] and many more. SHM is usually based on comparison of structure's behavior
in known, intact state (baseline) with one observed in unknown condition. The
differences are evaluated by autonomous systems and used in order to detect,
localize and quantify the damage. The most simple solution is to quantify the
difference between baseline and unknown state and apply a threshold: If a difference exceeds certain value, the system would interpret corresponding structure's
state as damaged and would raise an alarm. However, in most of the practical
cases, the state of a structure is not only affected by damage, but also by environmental or operational factors (e.g. temperature, changes of loading etc.) which

L. Rutkowski et al. (Eds.): ICAISC 2016, Part I, LNAI 9692, pp. 81–90, 2016.
DOI: 10.1007/978-3-319-39378-0_8

renders the simple threshold-based damage detection a difficult task. Usually, state of a structure can successfully be retrieved only by using many sources of information simultaneously. The multiparametric classification of data require advanced processing algorithms. Artificial Neural Networks (ANNs) are often used in this scope.

Though the field is well-developed, there is still much interest in application of soft computing methods for the purpose of SHM [5]. One can point out many recent implementations of ANNs: mulitlayered perceptron (MLP) networks have been proven to solve the problem of multiparametric classification for the purpose of ultrasonic guided wave based monitoring of aircrafts [6,7], structural optimization [8] or prediction of composite fatigue lifetime [9]. Self organizing maps (SOM) have been successfully implemented for damage detection in composite plates [10]. Radial-basis function networks (RBFs) have been employed for the purpose of monitoring wind turbine blades [11].

Choice of a network structure including both type and number of neurons is usually a challenging task. Each structure has its strengths and weaknesses. The type of structure and its size should be based on distribution of data in data space. Partial overlapping of classes or complicated separation margins require usage of large networks, while small amount of data would require small networks not prone to over-fitting. Clustering of data would increase the effectiveness of non-supervised or RBF networks, while uniform spread of data would cause MLPs to be more efficient. Unfortunately, the distribution of data in classification space is not easily observed. The most commonly used technique of tailoring the network to a task is a trial and error method, based on operator's experience. Another issue that needs to be addressed is the fact that in practice the requirement of uniformity of training and testing datasets is sometimes hard to fulfill, thus the network that is the most effective on training dataset might not provide similar results in operational phase. An illustrative example is the task of fatigue damage detection in a large structure. As damaging a large structure is usually too costly to be executed, classifiers are usually trained on data from limited amount of experiments performed in laboratory conditions, on a subcomponent scale. One can easily observe that data gathered even in the most extensive experimental programme cannot cover all possible damage scenarios that may arise in operational phase. Therefore, should the autonomous data interpretation systems be reliable, they need to be effective even if the data obtained in monitoring are not fully covered by training examples.

Since it was proven that ANN cooperation can show results superior to usage of single ANNs [12], application of different ANN cooperation approaches attracted much attention over recent decades. Out of numerous possibilities, modular and ensemble-based classifiers are arguably the most popular [5,13]. The former rely on ANNs that are experts in specific categories. The data get assigned into category and classified by a proper expert. In SHM such solution have been successfully adapted for gas leakage detection [14]. The latter achieve decision with use of ANNs that each perform independent diagnoses of their own. Weighted average of individual votes is treated as an output of a whole classifier. Ensemble members are usually chosen using *overproduce and choose* strategy that incorporate training of multiple candidate electors and then choice of the most accurate subset [15]. Although many methods were proposed for this task [16], a simple choice of electors that performed best in training phase is still very popular. Ensemble approach found numerous applications in different areas of engineering [17–20].

The aim of research presented in this paper is to design a method that is capable of efficient data classification or regression in various practical applications of SHM. In order to achieve good performance over different datasets it should be able to self-adjust its structure. The robustness of the decision will be achieved through usage of an ensemble of different networks. The method is validated in two distinct experiments regarding practical examples of SHM.

The remainder of this paper is organized as follows: Sect. 2 provides details of ensemble design used by authors. Section 3 provides two distinct experiments in which the ensemble classifier was validated. Finally, Sect. 4 summarizes and concludes the article.

2   Ensemble of ANNs

2.1   Principle of Operation

The procedure includes training a number of networks of three types on a subsets of training data. Evaluation of their performance on a remaining training data allows the classifier to decide whether or not they should be included as electors in final esemble. Following paragraphs provide insight into types of electors that are included in starting pool. The motivation behind the choice of candidate electors was to provide elector pool that is versatile, able to perform both global and local classification and regression tasks and to respond both to training labels and natural clustering of data. Additional requirement was that electors should be well-established in SHM and proven to be effective in practical tasks.

2.2   Candidate Electors

MLP. A network most commonly used in data classification for SHM purpose. Its main advantages include simplicity of implementation and wide availability of software packages that include MLPs. MLP is usually trained in supervised mode with back-propagation algorithm. It divides data space with hypersurfaces. The more neurons in layers, the more hyperplanes can be used for data classification. The performance of the network in training phase is adjusted globally: each neuron performs global classification, the superposition of signals from all neurons is used for output calculation.

RBF. A network similar in the idea to MLP, however here the data space is divided by hyperspheres. The classification is performed locally. Value returned by the classifier is influenced only by neurons placed in close proximity to the data point under evaluation. In cases where data are clustered it can operate in more efficient way than MLP network.

SOM. Self-Organizing Maps trained in non-supervised mode achieve the best performance when the number of classes for separation is unknown or when the data are clustered. SOM networks usually require additional interpretation of result: as they are not provided with target values in training phase, they can not return labels for data that can refer to any physical state of object under monitoring by their own.

2.3   Ensemble Design Algorithm

For each potential ensemble member the training data are divided into subset used for training (A "train" set, 90 % of samples) and subset used for elector evaluation (A "test" set, 10 % of samples). All networks are arranged in order of their performance (measured by MSE metric) on the latter. In the next step, 10 best networks are chosen as final elector set for the classifier. Each of the networks can be assigned a voting weight based on their position in rank, so the best networks have the highest impact on the resulting value. These weights can later be modified based on their performance, provided that additional means of network evaluation are available during their operational phase. However, in case presented in this paper all weights are set to 1. Schematic illustration of training and operation of ensemble is depicted in Figs. 1 and 2.

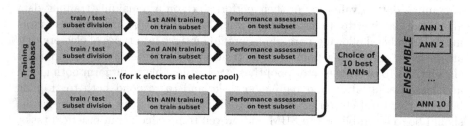

Fig. 1. Training of electors and ensemble design procedure

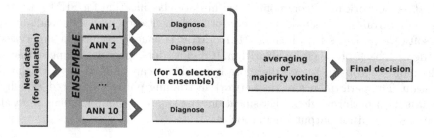

Fig. 2. Operational phase of an ensemble: assessment of new data

3   Experimental Evaluation

3.1   Data Acquisition

In order to evaluate performance of a developed ensemble ANN classifier two experiments have been conducted:

Experiment 1. In aircraft maintenance, detection of fatigue cracks that develop in its structure is an issue of great importance. Several aircraft panels were subjected to a periodic loading to create fatigue damage. One of them was used as source of data for ensemble classifier training and evaluation. The panel was instrumented with piezoelectric transducers that were used for generation and acquisition of ultrasonic signals. Four features that measured the difference between signal and a baseline, were used as an input data for ANN classifier. The purpose was to detect damage on each sensing path and assess its extent. Target values presented to networks in training phase ranged from 0 to 1, where 0 denoted lack of damage in structure and 1 denoted large damage placed directly onto signal propagation path. In a training phase ANN classifier was presented with 110 data samples. Data for evaluation of the ensemble included 46 samples acquired on the same specimen by different sensor pairs. Data were acquired under a LIDER/25/43/L-2/10/NCBiR/2011 project and used thanks to the courtesy of the Polish Air Force Institute of Technology.

Experiment 2. The maintenance and monitoring of wind turbines is often based on Supervisory Control And Data Acquisition (SCADA) systems, which periodically acquire operational and environmental characteristics for the turbine. The damage can be detected indirectly, on a basis of differences between expected and observed performance of a turbine in given environmental conditions. The result predicted by the system can later be compared with acquired values. Differences between prediction and measurement can be used as a damage indicator. Several characteristics (Wind speed, wind direction, rotor speed and generator temperature) were used as inputs for the ANN classifier. The purpose of ANN was to predict power output in given conditions. Training data consisted of 3450 data samples acquired during three consecutive weeks of turbine's operation. New data for ensemble evaluation incorporated 860 samples acquired during fourth week. Target values presented to networks in training phase ranged from 0 to 2000 kW. Data were used thanks to the courtesy of RP GLOBAL Poland.

3.2   Experimental Setup

Main purpose of this work was to create robust classifier applicable in different practical situations. Therefore, initial points for a classifier in both problems were identical. Pool of electors to choose from consisted of 80 networks presented in Table 1. The range of networks' size was determined based on a literature search

Table 1. Electors in initial pool

Type of a network	Number of networks	Range of neuron count
MLP, 1 hidden layer	20	1 – 50
MLP, 2 hidden layers	20	1 – 50
SOM	20	1 – 200
RBF	20	1 – 200

and authors experience - to cover most of typical ANN applications in SHM. Training of the networks and choice of a final elector group for the classifier was performed according to the procedure described in Sect. 2.3. In each case result obtained by voting classifier is compared both to network that obtained highest performance on a training set and averaged performance of all the networks in the electors pool.

3.3   Results

Efficiency of the ANN classifier in fatigue damage assessment and wind turbine power output prediction task can be observed in Table 2. Final sets of electors chosen by a classifier, arranged in order of their training performance, are given in Tables 3 and 4. Ensemble members that obtained better performance than the final ensemble are marked in bold. Visualization of results is given in Figs. 3 and 4.

Results of the first experiment are predictable: networks that scored high on a training data were usually efficient also in "operational phase", but the dependance between training and testing performance is not linear. Some networks relatively weak in the training phase (but still efficient enough to be chosen as final electors) provided high results on testing data.

In the second experiment, however, the networks that scored the best results on new data evaluation set were significantly weaker in a training stage. Overall classifier performance is not only superior to that of first elector, but also better than most of electors treated alone (only the 7th elector scored slightly better than the whole ensemble). Such difference in results of both experiments is caused mainly by non-uniformity of training database and new data obtained in the second example. Turbine happened to produce power almost continuously during training data acquisition. Very small amount of training data acquired

Table 2. Classifier efficiency in both tasks

Classifier	MSE experiment 1	MSE experiment 2
Ensemble classifier	0.0112	0.000211
Network with best performance on a training set	0.0108	0.000589
Average network from the elector pool	0.0309	0.000368

Table 3. Choice of electors in fatigue damage detection experiment. Networks that scored higher than the whole ensemble are marked in bold.

No.	Elector	MSE over test subset	MSE obtained for new data
1	MLP, 2 hidden layers, 7 neurons	0.0116	**0.0108**
2	MLP, 1 hidden layer, 34 neurons	0.0149	0.0743
3	MLP, 2 hidden layers, 22 neurons	0.0167	0.0159
4	MLP, 1 hidden layer, 25 neurons	0.0172	0.0419
5	MLP, 2 hidden layers, 10 neurons	0.0188	0.0254
6	MLP, 2 hidden layers, 19 neurons	0.0219	0.0474
7	MLP, 1 hidden layer, 1 neuron	0.0252	**0.0098**
8	MLP, 1 hidden layer, 7 neurons	0.0255	**0.0104**
9	MLP, 2 hidden layers,34 neurons	0.0290	0.0483
10	SOM, 16 neurons	0.0314	0.0244

Table 4. Choice of electors in power prediction experiment. MSE normalized with respect to maximum power. Networks that scored higher than the whole ensemble are marked in bold.

No	Elector	MSE over test subset	MSE obtained for new data
1	MLP, 1 hidden layer, 35 neurons	0,000168	0,000589
2	MLP, 1 hidden layer, 31 neurons	0,000214	0,000266
3	MLP, 2 hidden layers, 13 neurons	0,000225	0,000244
4	MLP, 2 hidden layers, 39 neurons	0,000240	0,000420
5	MLP, 1 hidden layer, 29 neurons	0,000245	0,000382
6	MLP, 2 hidden layers, 19 neurons	0,000247	0,000235
7	MLP, 2 hidden layers, 35 neurons	0,000248	0,000248
8	MLP, 2 hidden layers, 27 neurons	0,000255	**0,000194**
9	MLP, 1 hidden layer, 37 neurons	0,000260	0,000306
10	MLP, 1 hidden layer, 19 neurons	0,000270	0,000282

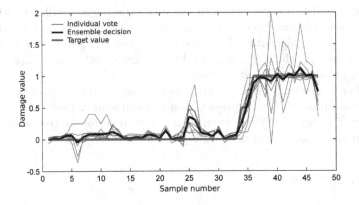

Fig. 3. Experiment 1: extent of damage measured and detected by the ensemble of classifiers.

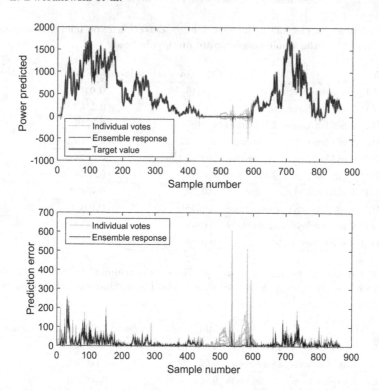

Fig. 4. Experiment 2: power generated and predicted by the ensemble of classifiers.

during standstill turbine caused some networks to return absurd values for analysis of periods out of operation in an ensemble evaluation phase. This is observed in Fig. 4: peaks are clearly visible, especially in error plot. In contrast, regression problem in experiment 1 is relatively simple. The data were not only drawn from similar distribution, but they were also almost linearly separable. The choice of electors reflected this observation: In the first experiment small networks were chosen as ensemble members (See for instance elector no. 1, 7, and 8). In experiment 2, the design algorithm of the ensemble resulted in selection of more complicated networks, which was a good decision from both task complexity and amount of avilable data points of view.

Another interesting remark is that wide range of elector pool is exploited in a selection process: small networks can score in similar tasks just as well as large ones. The impact of training efficiency on final performance is usually more important than influence of network type and size.

4   Conclusions

Two different tasks have been successfully performed by proposed self-adjusting classifier. In each of them, despite same starting point, method resulted in picking different set of electors. In both experiments "first choice", that is - a classifier with the highest performance over a training dataset rendered acceptable result in "operational phase". It is not safe however, to rely only on one network in practical tasks. In case, when training data do not cover all possible states that can happen during classifier's operational phase, response of ANNs can at times be unpredictable. As quality assessment of a training dataset can be a challenging task, usage of a group of different cooperating electors arise as a more reliable choice. This fact is of particular importance from engineering point of view, as in most practical cases of ANN usage, the access to training data of the same distribution and quality as data used further in operational stage is limited.

Acknowledgement. The work presented in this paper was supported by funding from the research project co-fianced by the KIC InnoEnergy Project Agreement number 32_2014_IP110_XSENSOR

References

1. Su, Z., Ye, L., Lu, Y.: Guided Lamb waves for identification of damage in composite structures: a review. J. Sound Vibr. **295**, 753–780 (2006)
2. Uhl, T., Kohut, P., Holak, K., Krupinski, K.: Vision based condition assessment of structures. J. Phys. Conf. Ser. **305**, 012043 (2011)
3. Mendrok, K.: Multiple damage localization using local modal filters. Diagnostyka **15**(3), 15–21 (2014)
4. Korbicz, J., Kowal, M.: Neuro-fuzzy networks and their application to fault detection of dynamical systems. Eng. Appl. Artif. Intell. **20**(5), 609–617 (2007)
5. Worden, K., Staszewski, W.J., Hensman, J.J.: Natural computing for mechanical systems research: a tutorial overview. Mech. Syst. Signal Process. **25**, 4–111 (2011)
6. Worden, K., Manson, G., Denoe, T.: An evidence-based approach to damage location on an aircraft structure. Mech. Syst. Signal Process. **23**, 1792–1804 (2009)
7. Dworakowski, Z., Ambrozinski, L., Packo, P., Dragan, K., Stepinski, T.: Application of artificial neural networks for compounding multiple damage indices in Lamb-wave-based damage detection. Struct. Control Health Monit. **22**, 50–61 (2014)
8. Gomes, H.M., Awruch, A.M., Lopes, P.A.M.: Reliability based optimization of laminated composite structures using genetic algorithms and artificial neural networks. Struct. Saf. **33**, 186–195 (2011)
9. Pierce, S.G., Worden, K., Bezazi, A.: Uncertainty analysis of a neural network used for fatigue lifetime prediction. Mech. Syst. Signal Process. **22**, 1395–1411 (2008)
10. Tibaduiza, D.-A., Torres-Arredondo, M.-A., Mujica, L., Rodellar, J., Fritzen, C.-P.: A study of two unsupervised data driven statistical methodologies for detecting and classifying damages in structural health monitoring. Mech. Syst. Signal Process. **41**, 467–484 (2013)
11. Dervilis, N., Choi, M., Taylor, S., Barthorpe, R., Park, G., Farrar, C., Worden, K.: On damage diagnosis for a wind turbine blade using pattern recognition. J. Sound Vibr. **333**, 1833–1850 (2014)
12. Auda, G., Kamel, M.: CMNN: Cooperative Modular Neural Networks for pattern recognition. Pattern Recogn. Lett. **18**, 1391–1398 (1997)
13. Sharkey, A.J.C. (ed.): Combining Artificial Neural Nets. Springer, London (1999)

14. Kotani, M., Katsura, M., Ozawa, S.: Detection of gas leakage sound using modular neural networks for unknown environments. Neurocomputing **62**, 427–440 (2004)
15. Giacinto, G., Roli, F.: An approach to the automatic design of multiple classifier systems. Pattern Recogn. Lett. **22**, 25–33 (2001)
16. Ruta, D., Gabrys, B.: Classifier selection for majority voting. Inf. Fusion **6**, 63–81 (2005)
17. Zaier, I., Shu, C., Ouarda, T.B.M.J., Seidou, O., Chebana, F.: Estimation of ice thickness on lakes using artificial neural network ensembles. J. Hydrol. **383**(3–4), 330–340 (2010)
18. Abubakar Mas'Ud, A., Stewart, B.G., McMeekin, S.G.: Application of an ensemble neural network for classifying partial discharge patterns. Electr. Power Syst. Res. **110**, 154–162 (2014)
19. Sbarufatti, C., Manson, G., Worden, K.: A numerically-enhanced machine learning approach to damage diagnosis using a Lamb wave sensing network. J. Sound Vibr. **333**(19), 1–27 (2014)
20. Siwek, K., Osowski, S.: Improving the accuracy of prediction of PM 10 pollution by the wavelet transformation and an ensemble of neural predictors. Eng. Appl. Artif. Intell. **25**(6), 1246–1258 (2012)

Characterisation and Modeling of Organic Solar Cells by Using Radial Basis Neural Networks

Dor Gotleyb[1], Grazia Lo Sciuto[2], Christian Napoli[3(✉)], Rafi Shikler[1],
Emiliano Tramontana[3], and Marcin Woźniak[4]

[1] Department of Electrical and Computer Engineering,
Ben-Gurion University of the Negev, Beersheba, Israel
gotleyb@post.bgu.ac.il, rshikler@bgu.ac.il
[2] Department of Engineering, Roma Tre University, Rome, Italy
glosciuto@dii.unict.it
[3] Department of Mathematics and Informatics, University of Catania, Catania, Italy
{napoli,tramontana}@dmi.unict.it
[4] Institute of Mathematics, Silesian University of Technology,
Kaszubska 23, 44-100 Gliwice, Poland
Marcin.Wozniak@polsl.pl

Abstract. Neural network architectures have been proven useful to model the intrinsic characteristics of photovoltaic cells. The possibility to get rid of an a priori model is one of the many advantages of such an approach as well as the resulting accuracy, robustness and speed. Neural networks have been used to model the characteristics of traditional silicon-based photovoltaic modules, and in this work we have investigated a model for new generation organic solar cells. Silicon-based cells were generally prone to be modeled by simple circuital parameter sets, however for organic cells the process is generally impervious. For this reason, we show that the application of Radial Basis Neural Networks has resulted advantageous to modeling. We have used such networks together with an algorithmic solution to automatically parametrize the Voltage-Current characteristics of organic photovoltaic modules.

Keywords: Radial basis neural networks · Parametrical models · Photovoltaic systems · Renewable energy · Organic solar cells

1 Introduction

The fabrication process and the implementation of photovoltaic (PV) cells is a very complex process. In order to enhance the effectiveness of such a process it is often useful to obtain an accurate model of the characteristics of the manufactured cells. However, the study and verification of mathematical models require a huge amount of resources and has a negative impact on the production timetable. Moreover, for the newly developed technology, namely the organic solar cells of last generation, it is very difficult to obtain an analytical model starting from a priori assumptions, due to the complex nature of the material itself. On the

© Springer International Publishing Switzerland 2016
L. Rutkowski et al. (Eds.): ICAISC 2016, Part I, LNAI 9692, pp. 91–103, 2016.
DOI: 10.1007/978-3-319-39378-0_9

contrary, a model-independent technique is paramount to automatically extract model parameters for the characteristics of this new kinds of cells. In this paper, we propose a software system based both on radial basis neural networks and a customised algorithmic approach to accurately model the electrical output behaviour and the voltage-current (I-V) characteristics of organic solar cells. Such parameters suffice to obtain a compact representation of the features of the solar cell and can be extremely important to improve the quality of the device allowing to intervene into the production line, or to enhance the existing predictive models for energy production by means of new generation photovoltaic panels.

It has been shown that the relationship between I-V is nonlinear and cannot be easily expressed by any analytical equation or the equivalent circuit parameters [2]. Therefore, the proposed neural network is used to overcome these difficulties using measured I-V curves.In this work we made use of Artificial Neural Networks for modeling purpose [9,10,14]. A similar approach for segmented silicon based devices [13] and Photovoltaic Thermal collectors (PV/T) has been presented in [16]. A hybrid soft-computing modeling technique uses multi-class [15] or neuro-fuzzy models to predict solar cell short-circuit current and open-circuit voltage, followed by coordinate translation of a measured current-voltage response [1], and other previous approaches have been developed to describe the electrical behaviours of solar cells and the electrical equivalent circuit [3,20], such as gaussian approximation based methods [17,18], fuzzy sets [21], game theory based strategies [22,23], artificial intelligence algorithms [5,8] or other hybrid approaches [6]. Our approach is innovative in that it automatically provides a concise representation (using a few parameters) of the I-V characteristic.

2   Process Chain of the Polymer Solar Cell

In this study we have developed a model for organic photovoltaic devices that are cheap, flexible, lightweight and easy to process, yet typically low in efficiency offering semiconducting properties and the ability of photocurrent generation. Organic materials are thermally evaporated at low temperatures and are processed by printing or spin-coating at room temperature from solution with high absorption coefficients reducing manufacturing costs. The thin layers of organic materials are used to absorb a large fraction of light, generating electron-hole pairs with electro-chemical properties such as charge transport, degradation, mitigation, energy level and solubility [4]. The architecture of organic solar cells consists of an anode in ITO (indium tin-oxide) with a layer of Gold, a Polystyrene sulfonate (PEDOT:PSS), a regioregular poly-3-hexylthiophene (P3HT) and (6,6)-phenyl C61-butyric acid methyl ester (PCBM) bulk heterojunction thin film forming the active layer of the device and an aluminum cathode. A commonly used material as transparent anode is the (ITO)-coated glass substrate offering a satisfactory conductivity, although ITO is expensive. A PEDOT:PSS layer is deposited on top of the device based processing method of simple cheap and spin coating. The photoactive layer, which absorbs incident photons in an organic solar cell, is obtained by mixing equal weight ratios of P3HT and PCBM in a solvent (Fig. 1).

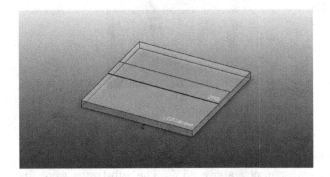

Fig. 1. ITO coated glass in SolidWorks

The procedures for testing organic solar cell devices were carried out in the equipped Dr. Rafi Shiklers laboratory at the Ben-Gurion University of the Negev in Beer-Sheva, Israel. The encapsulation of the solar cells has been processed at low temperature (22°C) compatible with organic materials because they are very sensitive and degrade very fast under normal air conditions. So the electric characterisation of the devices was performed under a dry nitrogen atmosphere (inside glove box) with an O_2 concentration of 1.7 ppm and an H_2O concentration smaller than 0.1 ppm. Isolation glove boxes provide controlled environments that protect contamination-sensitive materials from ambient conditions. Containment glove boxes provide safe processing environments that protect operators from biohazards within the glove box chamber. For controlled atmospheres, nitrogen dry boxes provide an isolated work environment for processing samples or handling air-sensitive materials while maintaining an anaerobic or other gas specific environment within the glove box. The dual glovebox system for polymer electronics fabrication provides an inert atmosphere for spin coating, electrode or counter-electrode deposition and assembly of organic photovoltaic (OPV) and other flexible electronic devices. Integrated into the glovebox system there is a high vacuum chamber with mask transfer system for the thermal evaporative deposition of patterned electrodes and an atomic layer deposition system for counter electrode deposition (Fig. 2).

The architecture of organic solar cells has been realised and investigated with the direct vacuum evaporation of the metal gold on the ITO-Glass substrate. In the first stage it was very important to clean the ITO coated glass. The glass substrate is sized 12 mm × 12 mm × 0.7 mm and is coated in the middle with a rectangular section 6 mm × 12 mm and 90 nm ± 10 nm of transparent thick ITO layer with resistance of 20 Ω/m^2. The ITO is the anode with high transparency, conductivity with high carrier concentration, but it is fragile

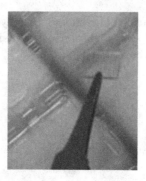

Fig. 2. ITO coated glass

and susceptible to deterioration. At a wavelength of 550 nm the ITO coated glass offers a transparency above 85 %. The substrates were first cleaned in acetone bath, because acetone's powerful solvent for removing organic particles, methanol and isopropanol for 15 min each in an ultrasonic bath (53 kHz at room temperature). The substrates were dipped into distilled water and put into a vacuum oven; afterwards plasma cleaning was used to remove any remaining oxygen molecules. After the cleaning process the glass plate, with upturned ITO layer, was placed on the chuck of the spin coater outside the glove box and aligned by vacuum. The solution of PEDOT:PSS were applied on the samples. Immediately the spin coater was turned on and was rotating with 5000 rpm (revolutions per minute) and an acceleration of 12000 rpm/s for one minute. An annealing on hot plate of an hour at a temperature of 100°C–105°C was necessary, to remove the water that is a solvent for the PEDOT interacting with the active layer and contaminate the glove box. The heater plate ensures even heating across the surface. Thus the cells are transferred into the glove box. Inside the glove box, a solution of photo-active polymer P3HT and PCBM has been prepared. P3HT layers were deposited onto cleaned substrates by spin coating the samples at 1000 rpm for 1 min, resulting in a layer thickness of approximately 100–200 nm Poly(3,4)-ethylenedioxythiophene polystyrenesulfonate (PEDOT:PSS)/ITO/glass substrates using the different types of molds. In the next step the 80 nm thick aluminum cathodes were evaporated on the samples. A mask was used to create the preferred shape of aluminum cathodes. For the thermal evaporation we have used the resistance heated boats and Pieces of aluminum (wire, canes, coils, etc.) are inserted in the boats. After the evaporation of aluminum the devices are put on the heater for 30 min at 140 C inside the glove box. To connect the thin film to electrical wire the Silver Conductive Epoxy was deposited on small part of ITO removed locally and aluminum layer.

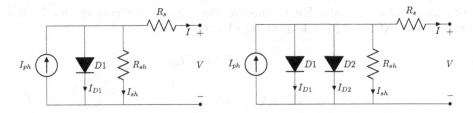

Fig. 3. On the left: the single diode equivalent circuit models of a solar cell. On the Right: the double diode equivalent circuit models of a solar cell.

3   Circuital Models for PV Modules

An accurate model of the photovoltaic cell is paramount to obtain better quality during the fabrication process of PV panels [19]. Commonly several circuital models are adopted in order to parametrize the I-V characteristics of a PV panel or cell. In Fig. 3, left side, a single diode model is represented. Under illumination and normal operating conditions, the single diode model is the most popular model for solar cells. However, the single diode model is particularly inaccurate at low illumination. A more complex model is depicted on the right side of Fig. 3, the double diode model is used to simulate the space-charge recombination effect by incorporating a separate current component with its own exponential voltage dependence. Moreover, the double diode model has been shown to be a more accurate representation of solar cell behavior than the single diode model in some cases. By applying the Kirchoffs current law (KCL) and Kirchoffs voltage law (KVL) to the single diode model we obtain:

$$I = I_{ph} - I_{D1} - I_{sh} \tag{1}$$

$$V_{d_1} = R_s I + V \tag{2}$$

with

$$I_{d_1} = I_{01} \left[\exp\left(\frac{qV_{d_1}}{nkT}\right) - 1 \right] \tag{3}$$

Starting from Eqs. (1), (2) and (3), we can be derive:

$$I = I_{ph} - I_{01} \left[\exp\left(\frac{qV_{d_1}}{nkT}\right) - 1 \right] - \frac{V + R_s I}{R_{sh}} \tag{4}$$

where I_{ph} is photo-current density; I_0 is the saturation current density under reverse bias, R_s is the series resistance, R_{sh} is the shunt resistance, n is the ideality factor, q is the electronic charge, k is Boltzmanns constant and T is the temperature in Kelvin. The current density (I) is current per unit area. From Eq. (5) it is shown that the solar cell parameter extraction problem is reduced to the determination of five parameters (R_s, R_{sh}, I_{ph}, I_{D1}, and n) with a set of experimental I-V data. For the double diode model applying the Kirchoffs current law (KCL) and Kirchoffs voltage law (KVL) we obtain:

$$I = I_{ph} - I_{D1} - I_{D2} - I_{sh} \tag{5}$$

$$V_{d_1} = V_{d_1} = R_s I + V \tag{6}$$

with

$$I_{d_1} = I_{01} \left[\exp \left(\frac{qV_{d_1}}{n_1 kT} \right) - 1 \right] \tag{7}$$

$$I_{d_2} = I_{02} \left[\exp \left(\frac{qV_{d_2}}{n_2 kT} \right) - 1 \right] \tag{8}$$

Starting from Eqs. (5),(6),(7), and (8), we can derive:

$$I = I_{ph} - I_{01} \left[\exp \left(\frac{qV_{d_1}}{n_1 kT} \right) - 1 \right] - I_{02} \left[\exp \left(\frac{qV_{d_1}}{n_2 kT} \right) - 1 \right] - \frac{V + R_s I}{R_{sh}} \tag{9}$$

Equation (9) must be fitted to the experimental I-V curve in order to obtain the seven parameters ($R_s, R_{sh}, I_{ph}, I_{01}, I_{02}, n_1$, and n_2).

4   The RBFNN Based Model

In this work we developed a Radial Basis Neural Network (RBFNN) based approach [24] to obtain a parametrical representation of the I-V characteristics of the presented solar cells. Taking advantage of the universal approximation theorem we trained a RBFNN as in [12] in order to approximate the I-V relation for a given solar cell. RBFNNs consist of three layers: the input, a hidden layer with Radial Basis Function (RBF) neurons and a linear output layers (Fig. 4). This network has been trained using the measured tension V as input and the measured current I as target. Therefore, both the input vector $\mathbf{u}$ and the output vector $\mathbf{y}$ have only one dimension, hence the hidden layer is composed of N fully connected neurons activated by a standard RBF ϕ so that:

$$\phi_k(\mathbf{x}) = e^{-\frac{||\mathbf{Wx} - \mathbf{c}_k||}{\sigma}} \qquad \forall\, k \in [1, N] \cap \mathbb{N} \tag{10}$$

where the input vector $\mathbf{x}$ is multiplied by the input weights matrix $\mathbf{W}$ and $\mathbf{c}_k$ represents the centroid vector. In our implementation we have chosen to adopt a unitary spread by choosing $\sigma = 1$, therefore due to the mono-dimensional nature of the inputs Eq. (10) becomes

$$\phi_k(V) = e^{-(w_{1k}^{(1)} V - c_k)^2} \qquad \forall\, k \in [1, N] \cap \mathbb{N} \tag{11}$$

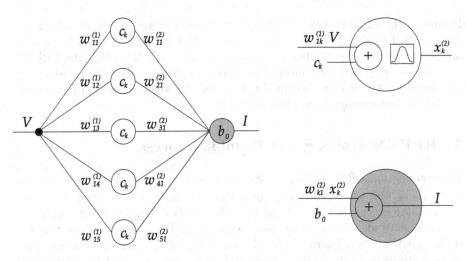

Fig. 4. The implemented radial basis neural network, the related RBF hidden neurons (white) and the output linear neuron (gray).

where x is obtained by multiplying the input (tension) by the corresponding weight in the $N \times 1$ input weights matrix

$$\mathbf{W}^{(1)} = \begin{bmatrix} w_{11}^{(1)} \\ w_{12}^{(1)} \\ \vdots \\ w_{1N}^{(1)} \end{bmatrix} \tag{12}$$

Finally, the overall approximated output (current) $\tilde{I}$ is obtained as linear combination of the outputs $\phi_k(V)$ coming from the hidden RBF neurons:

$$\tilde{I} = b_0 + \sum_{k=1}^{N} w_{k1}^{(2)} \phi_k(V) \tag{13}$$

where b_0 is a simple bias and the linear sum weights are the elements of the $N \times 1$ hidden weights matrix

$$\mathbf{W}^{(2)} = \begin{bmatrix} w_{11}^{(2)} \\ w_{21}^{(2)} \\ \vdots \\ w_{N1}^{(2)} \end{bmatrix} \tag{14}$$

Finally, from Eqs. (11) and (13) it follows that the network approximates the I-V characteristics as

$$\tilde{I}\left(V\Big|\{w_{ij}^{(l)}\}, \{c_k\}, b_0\right) = b_0 + \sum_{i=1}^{N} w_{k1}^{(2)} e^{-(w_{1k}^{(1)}V - c_k)^2} \tag{15}$$

Basing on the expansion in (15) it is then possible to use RBFNNs to obtain a parametrical model of the I-V characteristic. The parameters of such a model are represented by the weights, centroids and biases. It follows that the RBFNN can be trained in order to automatically obtain such parameters, moreover by pruning the network it is also possible to reduce the total number of parameters needed to characterise the photovoltaic cell.

5   RBFNN Training and Pruning Process

The training for a RBFNN is a twofold process in order to determine both the centroids c_k and the weights $w_{ij}^{(l)}$. In a RBFNN the number of neurons of the hidden layer is typically much lower than the number of the training pattern, in facts the centroids, which are the parameters of the RBF, need not be within the training patterns set. Therefore, the determination of the centroids becomes part of the learning process. While, in order to find the weights, the RBFNN must be trained with supervised techniques, for the centroids, there are two strategies: the first uses an unsupervised learning to determine a set of centroids $\{c_k\}$ and use LMS algorithm to train output weights w_{ij}; the second technique trains all parameters together: spread parameters σ_k (which in our case is permanently defined as σ_k), input and output weights $w_{ij}^{(l)}$ and centroids c_k through an supervised learning algorithm such as the backpropagation algorithm. Training methods that separate the tasks of prototype determination and weight optimisation (the first strategy) often do not use the input-output data from the training set for the selection of the prototypes. E.g., the random selection method and the k-means algorithm result in prototypes that are completely independent of the input-output data from the training set. Although this results in fast training, it clearly does not take full advantage of the information contained in the training set. Gradient descent training of RBF networks has proven to be much more effective than more conventional methods [11]. Then, we have obtained the weights and center vectors by iteratively computing the partials and performing the following updates:

$$E(\tau) = \tfrac{1}{2}(\tilde{I} - I)^2$$

$$w_{i,j}^{(l)}(\tau + 1) = w_{i,j}^{(l)}(\tau) - \eta_w \frac{\partial E(\tau)}{\partial w_{i,j}^{(l)}(\tau)}, \tag{16}$$

$$c_k(\tau + 1) = c_k(\tau) - \eta_c \frac{\partial E(\tau)}{\partial c_k(\tau)}$$

where η_w and η_c are learning rate coefficients, and τ represents the training step. After the weights and centroid have been computed, a pruning procedure must be performed in order to shorten the list of parameters to consider for the model. In our simulations we determined that it is possible to preserve a sufficient accuracy while pruning the network to only two neurons. In this manner we obtain a compact analytical model from (15), that is reduced to

$$\tilde{I}(V) = b_0 + w_{\alpha 1}^{(2)} e^{-(w_{1\alpha}^{(1)} V - c_\alpha)^2} + w_{\beta 1}^{(2)} e^{-(w_{1\beta}^{(1)} V - c_\beta)^2} \tag{17}$$

where α and β represent the index of the two remaining neurons after the pruning procedure. The obtained model in (17) represents a model of the I-V characteristics of the examined solar cells based on the seven residual parameters of the neural network after pruning. The said parameters are: $w_{\alpha 1}^{(2)}$, $w_{1\alpha}^{(1)}$, c_α, $w_{\beta 1}^{(2)}$, $w_{1\beta}^{(1)}$, c_β, and b_0.

6   The Experimental Survey and Simulation Results

The Current-voltage measurements took place in the laboratory of organic semiconductor devices at the Ben-Gurion University of the Negev in Beer Sheva. The following equipment has been used to collect the PV cell data used in this work for its characterisation:

- Keithley Model 2420 SourceMeter instrument
- IEEE-488 interface such as the Keithley KPCI-488 3
- Source illumination (also said solar simulator)
- A Stellar Net inc spectrometer

Current and voltage values have been collected with the Keithley SourceMeter (model 2636) and imported with the LabTracer software. The photocurrent is assumed to depend linearly on the light intensity, which is reasonable for the low-light intensities, therefore white-light photocurrent measurements were performed under simulated AM1.5 solar irradiation (100 mW/cm^2) with a K.H. Steuernagel Lichttechnik GmbH Simulator. The emission spectrum has been verified with the spectrometer and is reported in Fig. 5. The simulated light incidence was modulated in order to be comparable to the natural exposition to the sun. The samples were placed at a distance of 7 cm underneath the solar simulator and each cell was tested under the same irradiation conditions. The start, stop, and step values determine the direction and amplitude of the sweep, as well as the number of points that can be collected. In the proposed experimental survey the start and stop voltage are defined in the range 0 to 0.5 or 0 to 0.7 V. The experimental data collected in laboratory have then been used to verify our approach. The proposed RBFNN was trained using the measured tensions as input and the measured currents as targets. The training process and the consequent pruning procedure has been described in Sect. 5. Figure 6 shows the comparison among the measured I-V characteristic and the model represented by the RBFNN after pruning. Additionally, the latter has been analytically obtained in Eq. (17). The overall ensemble of the network parameters is depicted in Fig. 7.

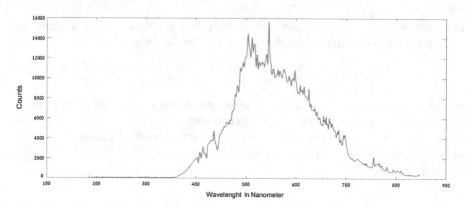

Fig. 5. The spectrum of the solar simulator

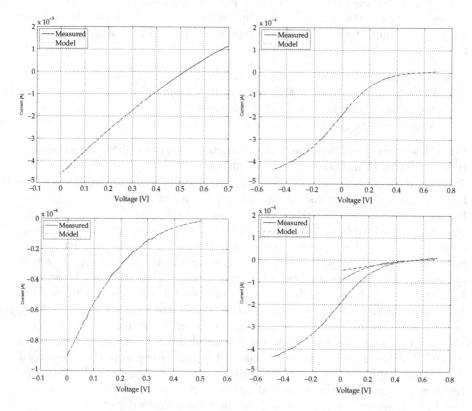

Fig. 6. Several measured I-V relations and the approximation returned by the implemented RBFNN after training and pruning.

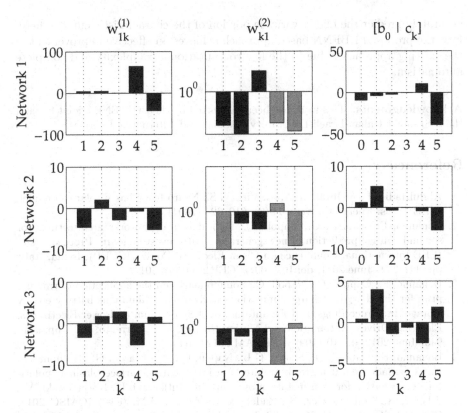

Fig. 7. The RBFNN parameters: the inputs weights $w_{1k}^{(1)}$, the hidden weights $w_{k1}^{(2)}$, the centroids c_k and the bias b_0. The hidden weights $w_{k1}^{(2)}$ are represented in logarithmic scale, for the negative values we represented the absolute logarithm in red color. (Color figure online)

7   Conclusion

This paper proposed a novel technique to model and parametrize the I-V characteristic of an organic solar cell of new generation. The I-V model has been obtained by training a dedicated Radial Basis Neural Network (RBFNN) and giving as output the seven parameters of the cell. The adopted approach is very effective thanks to its independency from the solar radiation values, although requiring its constancy. The RBFNN based model is able to reproduce a parametrical relation of the current for the organic cell as a function of the terminal voltage of the corresponding circuital electrical model. Especially, for the estimation of I-V characteristics, the RBFNN based model perfectly matches the experimental characteristics while giving precise results with a fast and automatic procedure. The relatively small number of parameters has been proven advantageous and suitable for the accurate estimation of the electrical characteristics, therefore outperforming existing models [7] which generally fail to accurately predict the highly variable portion of the characteristic curve. Therefore, the proposed RBFNN based approach achieves an effective improvement of the existing approaches due to the low computational complexity and complete automatism.

Acknowledgments. This work has been supported by the BGU-ENEA joint lab and the ILSE-Joint Italian-Israeli Laboratory on Solar and Alternative Energies.

References

1. AbdulHadi, M., Al-Ibrahim, A.M., Virk, G.S.: Neuro-fuzzy-based solar cell model. IEEE Trans. Energy Convers. **19**(3), 619–624 (2004)
2. Bonanno, F., Capizzi, G., Napoli, C.: Hybrid neural networks architectures for soc and voltage prediction of new generation batteries storage. In: Proceedings of IEEE International Conference on Clean Electrical Power (ICCEP), Ischia, Italy, pp. 341–344, June 2011. doi:10.1109/ICCEP.2011.6036301
3. Bonanno, F., Capizzi, G., Napoli, C.: Some remarks on the application of rnn and prnn for the charge-discharge simulation of advanced lithium-ions battery energy storage. In: Proceedings of IEEE International Symposium on Power Electronics, Electrical Drives, Automation and Motion (SPEEDAM), Sorrento, Italy, pp. 941–945, June 2012. doi:10.1109/SPEEDAM.2012.6264500
4. Bonanno, F., Capizzi, G., Sciuto, G.L., Napoli, C., Pappalardo, G., Tramontana, E.: A cascade neural network architecture investigating surface plasmon polaritons propagation for thin metals in openmp. In: Rutkowski, L., Korytkowski, M., Scherer, R., Tadeusiewicz, R., Zadeh, L.A., Zurada, J.M. (eds.) ICAISC 2014, Part I. LNCS, vol. 8467, pp. 22–33. Springer, Heidelberg (2014). doi:10.1007/978-3-319-07173-2_3
5. Capizzi, G., Bonanno, F., Napoli, C.: Recurrent neural network-based control strategy for battery energy storage in generation systems with intermittent renewable energy sources. In: IEEE International Conference on Clean Electrical Power (ICCEP), pp. 336–340. IEEE (2011)
6. Capizzi, G., Napoli, C., Paternò, L.: An innovative hybrid neuro-wavelet method for reconstruction of missing data in astronomical photometric surveys. In: Rutkowski, L., Korytkowski, M., Scherer, R., Tadeusiewicz, R., Zadeh, L.A., Zurada, J.M. (eds.) ICAISC 2012, Part I. LNCS, vol. 7267, pp. 21–29. Springer, Heidelberg (2012). doi:10.1007/978-3-642-29347-4_3
7. Di Piazza, M.C., Vitale, G.: Photovoltaic field emulation including dynamic and partial shadow conditions. Appl. Energy **87**(3), 814–823 (2010)
8. Dziwiński, P., Bartczuk, Ł., Przybył, A., Avedyan, E.D.: A new algorithm for identification of significant operating points using swarm intelligence. In: Rutkowski, L., Korytkowski, M., Scherer, R., Tadeusiewicz, R., Zadeh, L.A., Zurada, J.M. (eds.) ICAISC 2014, Part II. LNCS, vol. 8468, pp. 349–362. Springer, Heidelberg (2014)
9. Horzyk, A.: Innovative types and abilities of neural networks based on associative mechanisms and a new associative model of neurons. In: Rutkowski, L., Korytkowski, M., Scherer, R., Tadeusiewicz, R., Zadeh, L.A., Zurada, J.M. (eds.) Artificial Intelligence and Soft Computing. LNCS, vol. 9119, pp. 26–38. Springer, Heidelberg (2015). doi:10.1007/978-3-319-19324-3_3

10. Huang, T., Li, C., Duan, S., Starzyk, J.: Robust exponential stability of uncertain delayed neural networks with stochastic perturbation and impulse effects. IEEE Trans. Neural Netw. Learn. Syst. **23**(6), 866–875 (2012). doi:10.1109/TNNLS.2012. 2192135

11. Karayiannis, N.B., Mi, G.W.: Growing radial basis neural networks: merging supervised and unsupervised learning with network growth techniques. IEEE Trans. Neural Netw. **8**(6), 1492–1506 (1997)

12. Napoli, C., Pappalardo, G., Tramontana, E., Nowicki, R.K., Starczewski, J.T., Woźniak, M.: Toward work groups classification based on probabilistic neural network approach. In: Rutkowski, L., Korytkowski, M., Scherer, R., Tadeusiewicz, R., Zadeh, L.A., Zurada, J.M. (eds.) Artificial Intelligence and Soft Computing. LNCS, vol. 9119, pp. 79–89. Springer, Heidelberg (2015). doi:10.1007/978-3-319-19324-3_8

13. Napoli, C., Pappalardo, G., Tramontana, E., Zappalà, G.: A cloud-distributed gpu architecture for pattern identification in segmented detectors big-data surveys. Comput. J. **59**(3), 338–352 (2016). doi:10.1093/comjnl/bxu147

14. Nguyen, V., Starzyk, J., Goh, W., Jachyra, D.: Neural network structure for spatio-temporal long-term memory. IEEE Trans. Neural Netw. Learn. Syst. **23**(6), 971–983 (2012). doi:10.1109/TNNLS.2012.2191419

15. Nowak, B.A., Nowicki, R.K., Woźniak, M., Napoli, C.: Multi-class nearest neighbour classifier for incomplete data handling. In: Rutkowski, L., Korytkowski, M., Scherer, R., Tadeusiewicz, R., Zadeh, L.A., Zurada, J.M. (eds.) Artificial Intelligence and Soft Computing. LNCS, vol. 9119, pp. 469–480. Springer, Heidelberg (2015). doi:10.1007/978-3-319-19324-3_42

16. Ravaee, H., Farahat, S., Sarhaddi, F.: Artificial neural network based model of photovoltaic thermal (pv/t) collector. J. Math. Comput. Sci. **4**(3), 411–417 (2012)

17. Rutkowski, L., Jaworski, M., Pietruczuk, L., Duda, P.: Decision trees for mining data streams based on the gaussian approximation. IEEE Trans. Knowl. Data Eng. **26**(1), 108–119 (2014)

18. Rutkowski, L., Jaworski, M., Pietruczuk, L., Duda, P.: A new method for data stream mining based on the misclassification error. IEEE Trans. Neural Netw. Learn. Syst. **26**(5), 1048–1059 (2015)

19. Sandrolini, L., Artioli, M., Reggiani, U.: Numerical method for the extraction of photovoltaic module double-diode model parameters through cluster analysis. Appl. Energy **87**(2), 442–451 (2010)

20. Singh, K.J., Kho, K.R., Singh, S.J., Devi, Y.C., Singh, N.B., Sarkar, S.: Artificial neural network approach for more accurate solar cell electrical circuit model. Int. J. Comput. Appl. **4**(3), 101–116 (2014)

21. Starczewski, J.T., Nowicki, R.K., Nowak, B.A.: Genetic fuzzy classifier with fuzzy rough sets for imprecise data. In: IEEE International Conference on Fuzzy Systems, FUZZ-IEEE 2014, Beijing, China, pp. 1382–1389, 6–11 July 2014

22. Swiechowski, M., Mandziuk, J.: Self-adaptation of playing strategies in general game playing. IEEE Trans. Comput. Intell. AI Games **6**(4), 367–381 (2014)

23. Waledzik, K., Mandziuk, J.: An automatically generated evaluation function in general game playing. IEEE Trans. Comput. Intell. AI Games **6**(3), 258–270 (2014)

24. Wozniak, M., Polap, D., Nowicki, R.K., Napoli, C., Pappalardo, G., Tramontana, E.: Novel approach toward medical signals classifier. In: International Joint Conference on Neural Networks (IJCNN), pp. 1924–1930. IEEE (2015)

Method Enabling the First Hidden Layer of Multilayer Perceptrons to Make Division of Space with Various Hypercurves

Krzysztof Halawa[✉]

Wrocław University of Technology,
27 Wybrzeże Wyspiańskiego St., 50-370 Wrocław, Poland
krzysztof.halawa@pwr.wroc.pl

Abstract. In this paper, a method for increasing the number of multilayer perceptron inputs has been proposed. Three kinds of additional input variables have been tested. They make it possible to perform data separation by neurons in the first layer of multilayer perceptrons, with the use of hypercurves having various shapes in the two selected dimensions. By using more inputs, single neurons in the first hidden layer are capable of solving some non-linear separable problems, e.g. the XOR function. In dependence of the weight values of these neurons, they may, in some dimensions, realise the similar transformations as neurons in the hidden layer of RBF networks or separated the data with hyperplanes or hyperparabolas. The use of the proposed procedure does not need to implement, from the very beginning, a new network training algorithm. The classification results on the three very popular UCI benchmarks, which contain the real-world data, are presented.

1 Introduction

Multilayer perceptrons (MLPs) are one of the most popular types of artificial neuron networks. They are applied both for fitting and data classification problems. The networks possess many significant advantages [1] including, among other things, the predisposition for multidimensional data processing [1,2]. There exist a very big number of ready-made libraries and toolboxes for work with MLPs. Even a number of training algorithms designed to reduce the influence of outliers have been created [3]. Learning of MLPs is usually significantly faster and easier than training many of various deep learning architectures. Learning of MLPs may be carried out on mobile devices or microcontrollers without large computing power. Such microcontrollers are often used in low cost embedded systems. It seems that due to many important advantages of multilayer perceptrons, they will still be used in numerous applications for many years.

MLPs are feedforward artificial neural networks. They possess one or more hidden layers wherein neurons have a bipolar or unipolar sigmoidal activation function. One hidden layer is sufficient for MLPs to be universal approximators[4].

For fitting problems, MLPs are often applied with one hidden layer and an output layer containing neurons with a linear activation function while, for

© Springer International Publishing Switzerland 2016
L. Rutkowski et al. (Eds.): ICAISC 2016, Part I, LNAI 9692, pp. 104–113, 2016.
DOI: 10.1007/978-3-319-39378-0_10

a classification, networks are used with one hidden layer and an output layer with neurons having sigmoidal activation functions. The number of neurons in the output layer is equal to the number of the network outputs. The gradient algorithms are used for training [5]. Very often, the objective function used during training is the mean squared error

$$\text{MSE} = \frac{1}{Nq} \sum_{i=1}^{N} \sum_{j=1}^{q} \left(y_{j,i}(\mathbf{x}_i) - d_{j,i}\right)^2, \tag{1}$$

where q denotes the number of the network outputs, $y_{j,i}(\mathbf{x}_i)$ denotes the value of the j-th network output, when the network inputs are equal to the elements of the vector $\mathbf{x}_i$, $d_{j,i}$ is the desired value of the j-th network output, N is the number of the pairs in the data set $\{\mathbf{x}_i, \mathbf{d}_i\}_{i=1}^{N}$, $\mathbf{d}_i = [d_{1,i}, d_{2,i}, ..., d_{q,i}]^T$.

The neuron output is described by the formula

$$z = f\left(b + \sum_{k=1}^{n} w_k u_k\right), \tag{2}$$

where f denotes the activation function, n is the number of the neuron inputs, b is the bias, $w_1, ..., w_n$ are the neuron weights, $u_1, ..., u_n$ denote the values of the neuron inputs. The transformation performed by a single neuron with two inputs and a bipolar activation function being hyperbolic tangent is depicted in Fig. 1.

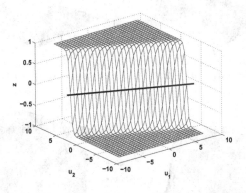

Fig. 1. Transformation performed by the neuron with two inputs and a bipolar activation function.

If the contour lines of the transformation performed by a neuron were drawn, then it would be the straight lines in the n-dimensional space. The centre of the slope was marked, in Fig. 1, by a bold line. For a neuron with n inputs, it is described by the following equation of an n-dimensional straight line $b + \sum_{k=1}^{n} w_k u_k = 0$. The further part of the study is organised as follows. In Sect. 2, the proposed procedure for classification that enables the automatic division of the space with diversified hyper-curves is presented. In Sect. 3, the results of use of the proposed procedure with the three popular benchmarks including real-world data are shown. Analysis of the results and the conclusions are at the end of the paper.

2   The Proposed Procedure

In Fig. 2, some examples of transformations that may be done by a neuron with a sigmoidal activation function being a hyperbolic tangent, when the number of its inputs is increased and, instead of feeding to its inputs the input variables u_1 and u_2 only, one feeds also the signals u_1^2, $u_1 u_2$ and u_2^2 are depicted.

Let us assume that a data set consists two matrices $\mathbf{X}$ and $\mathbf{T}$. The matrix $\mathbf{T}$ is of size $q \times N$ and the size of the matrix $\mathbf{X}$ is $s \times N$, where s denotes the number of the attributes (the number of features, input variables), on the basis of which, the classification is done. The i-th column of the matrix $\mathbf{T}$ includes the desired values of the classifier outputs, when its inputs are equal to the elements of the i-th column of the matrix $\mathbf{X}$. In the further part of the study, it was assumed

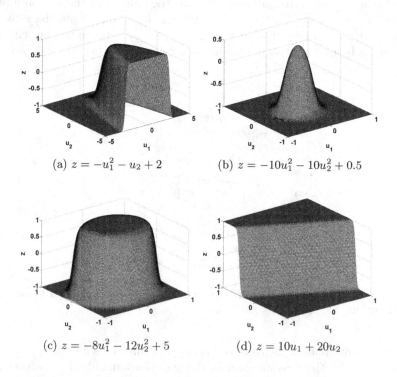

(a) $z = -u_1^2 - u_2 + 2$

(b) $z = -10u_1^2 - 10u_2^2 + 0.5$

(c) $z = -8u_1^2 - 12u_2^2 + 5$

(d) $z = 10u_1 + 20u_2$

Fig. 2. Exemplary transformations made by the neuron which output is equal to $\tanh(w_1 u_1 + w_2 u_2 + w_3 u_1 u_2 + w_4 u_1^2 + w_5 u_2^2 + b)$ for various values of weights $w_1, w_2, ..., w_5$ and b. tanh denotes the hyperbolic tangent

that the signals fed onto the network inputs were rescaled to the interval $[-1, 1]$, i.e. the elements of the matrix $\mathbf{X}$ belong to $[-1, 1]$.

The first stage of the proposed procedure consists in finding the two input variables that are one of the most relevant. Let us denote them by v_1 and v_2. In the papers [6–8], various methods to define the relevance of neuron network inputs are presented and their features have been analysed.

During conducted experiments v_1 and v_2 were chosen in the manner described below; however, many other methods may be used.

In order to find the two very significant inputs, an auxiliary small multilayer perceptron was created, with one hidden layer that contained only 5 sigmoidal neurons. The matrices $\mathbf{X}$ and $\mathbf{T}$ were divided randomly into the training, validating and testing sets in such a way that the training set consists of 60 % columns of the matrices $\mathbf{X}$ and $\mathbf{T}$, the validating one of 15 %, and the testing one of 25 %. The matrices containing 60 % columns of the matrices $\mathbf{X}$ and $\mathbf{T}$ were denoted as $\mathbf{X}_{\text{train}}$ and $\mathbf{T}_{\text{train}}$, respectively, while the matrices for validation were denoted by $\mathbf{X}_{\text{valid}}$ and $\mathbf{T}_{\text{valid}}$. The learning process on the training data was interrupted when the objective function value, calculated on the validating set, increased in 6 successive training epochs.

Next, the medians were calculated of all rows of the matrix $\mathbf{X}_{\text{valtrain}}$ created from a merging of the matrices $\mathbf{X}_{\text{train}}$ and $\mathbf{X}_{\text{valid}}$ in the following way $\mathbf{X}_{\text{valtrain}} = [\mathbf{X}_{\text{train}} \ \mathbf{X}_{\text{valid}}]$. Then, it was investigated how the objective function value (1) calculated on the data not belonging to the test set would change if the signals fed onto individual inputs of the auxiliary network were substituted by their medians. In other words, it was investigated how the value (1) would change after substitution of the given input variable by the median calculated of the row of the matrix $\mathbf{X}_{\text{valtrain}}$, associated with that variable. As the very relevant input variables v_1 and v_2, it was assumed attributes for which the substitution by their medians resulted in the highest increase of the objective function value (1). Obviously, when selecting v_1 and v_2, it should be also borne in mind that they must not be signals that accept binary values only.

The successive step of the proposed procedure consists in calculation of several signals determined on the basis of the values of the input variables v_1 and v_2, and in locating them as additional rows in the matrix $\mathbf{X}$. Each of the signals will formulate one appended row. The matrix extended in such a way has been denoted as $\mathbf{X}_{\text{extended}}$. In the experiments described in Sect. 3, the following additional signals have been applied:

(a) v_1^2, $v_1 \cdot v_2$, v_2^2
(b) combinations of orthogonal not normalised Legendre polynomials of the degrees I and II, i.e. the additional signals were $P_2(v_1)$, $P_2(v_2)$, $P_2(v_1)v_2$, $P_2(v_2)v_1$, v_1v_2, where $P_2(a) = 0.5\left(3a^2 - 1\right)$
(c) several first components of the two-dimensional Fourier series, i.e. the additional signals were $\sin(w_1)$, $\cos(w_1)$, $\sin(w_2)$, $\cos(w_2)$, $\sin(w_1) \cdot \cos(w_2)$, $\sin(w_2) \cdot \cos(w_1)$, $\sin(w_1) \cdot \sin(w_2)$, $\cos(w_1) \cdot \cos(w_2)$, where $w_1 = v_1\pi$, $w_2 = v_2\pi$. In addition to using these components of the Fourier series, the

inputs v_1 and v_2 have been removed and, therefore, the matrix $\mathbf{X}_{\text{extended}}$ had, in this case, the 6 additional rows only (8-2=6).

Legendre polynomials are orthogonal on the interval $[-1, 1]$ whereas, for calculation of the signals specified in the point c of the list shown above, v_1 and v_2 are multiplied by π, since the Fourier series components are orthogonal on the interval $[-\pi, \pi]$. Legendre polynomials of the zero and first degrees are equal to $P_0(a) = 1$ and $P_1(a) = a$; therefore, after addition of the signals specified in point b, the matrix $\mathbf{X}_{\text{extended}}$ with the biases of neurons provided Legendre polynomials of the degrees: 0, 1 and 2.

After constructing the matrix $\mathbf{X}_{\text{extended}}$ according to the point (a) or (b) or (c), the last step of the proposed method consists in use of $\mathbf{X}_{\text{extended}}$ complete with the matrix $\mathbf{T}$ for training of MLPs solving several classification problems that have been described in Sect. 3.

The signals mentioned in points a–c above can be favourably used when the relevancies of v_1 and v_2 do not differ substantially each other. These signals may be applied in problems, for which $MSE1/MSE2 \leq 1.5$, where MSE1 denotes the value of (1) after replacing the most relevant input variable v_1 by its median, MSE2 is the value of (1) after substitution of v_2 by its median. Larger value of the ratio MSE1 to MSE2 indicates that the input v_1 is probably significantly more important than v_2. If a network has a large number of inputs and the relevance of v_1 is substantially higher than v_2 then one may consider to use additional signals that are much more associated with v_1 than with v_2; for example:

(d) v_1^3, v_1^2, $v_1 \cdot v_2$, $v_1^2 \cdot v_2$,

(e) $P_3(v_1)$, $P_2(v_1)$, $P_2(v_1)v_2$, v_1v_2, where $P_3(a) = 0.5\left(5a^3 - 3a\right)$ is the 3rd degree Legendre polynomial.

3   Classification Results on Popular Benchmarks

For the experiments, the free popular benchmarks with real-world data were used that originated from the UC Irvin Repository of machine learning databases [9, 10]. The benchmarks were selected due to their high popularity. Their additional advantage is the accessibility in the standard toolbox Neural Network to the Matlab. Another reason for which the first two of the benchmarks described below were used, was the high number of instances.

The first set was the Thyroid Disease Databases. It included the results of 7200 patients characterised by 21 attributes, of which 15 were binary and 6 continuous. The following 3 classes were considered:

1. Normal, not hyperthyroid
2. Hyper-function
3. Subnormal functioning.

The other dataset was the Brest Cancer Dataset that included the results of 699 biopsies. The classification if the tumour is malignant or benign was conducted on the basis of the following attributes (input variables):

1. Clump Thickness: 1 – 10
2. Uniformity of Cell Size: 1 – 10
3. Uniformity of Cell Shape: 1 – 10
4. Marginal Adhesion: 1 – 10
5. Single Epithelial Cell Size: 1 – 10
6. Bare Nuclei: 1 – 10
7. Bland Chromatin: 1 – 10
8. Normal Nucleoli: 1 – 10
9. Mitoses: 1 – 10.

Another dataset was the Wine dataset that included 178 data of Italian wines derived from three different cultivars. It was recognised which cultivar is the origin of the wine on the basis of measurement of the following parameters:

1. Alcohol
2. Malic acid
3. Ash
4. Alcalinity of ash
5. Magnesium
6. Total phenols
7. Flavanoids
8. Nonflavanoid phenols
9. Proanthocyanins
10. Color intensity
11. Hue
12. OD280/OD315 of diluted wines
13. Proline.

Two series of experiments were carried out. The classification was done with the use of MLPs. In these networks, in the hidden layer and in the output layer, all activation functions were the hyperbolic tangent. The matrix $\mathbf{X}$, in the case of each benchmark, possessed as many rows as many attributes were in a given benchmark. The matrix $\mathbf{T}$ had the number of rows equal to the number of classes. In the conducted experiments, the influence of extension of the matrix $\mathbf{X}$ by appending signals specified on the positions a, b, c of the list from Sect. 2 was investigated. In the case of adding the orthogonal Legendre polynomial, the matrix $\mathbf{X}$ was increased of 5 rows. If the components of two-dimensional Fourier series were appended, then matrix $\mathbf{X}_{extended}$ was bigger by 6 rows (8-2=6), while in the case of addition of the signals v_1^2, $v_1 v_2$, v_2^2, the matrix $\mathbf{X}$ was increased by 3 rows only.

When creating the MLPs, the initial values of their weights are pseudorandom numbers. The training of the networks with the gradient algorithms begins from various starting points and is terminated at various local minima of the objective function, where its values may be highly differentiated. Therefore, in order to obtain reliable results, the following steps were repeated 50 times and the results averaged:

(I) Selection of v_1 and v_2 in accordance with the description of Sect. 2.

(II) Creation of MLPs that have been denoted in the present study as MLP_SMALL, MLP_POLY, MLP_LEG, MLP_F and MLP_BIG.
The networks MLP_SMALL, MLP_POLY, MLP_LEG and
MLP_F had h neurons in their hidden layer, where, in the first experiment series, it was assumed $h = 10$, while in the second series, it was assumed $h = 20$. MLP_BIG had

$$h_{\text{big}} = h + \lceil \frac{6h}{s} \rceil, \tag{3}$$

neurons in the hidden layer, where $\lceil \cdot \rceil$ denotes the ceil function, the value of which is equal to the lowest integer number greater than the function argument.

(III) Training of MLP_SMALL and MLP_BIG on the basis of the matrices $\mathbf{X}$ and $\mathbf{T}$. Training of the network MLP_POLY on the basis of the matrix $\mathbf{T}$ and the matrix $\mathbf{X}$ with appended rows with the signals v_1^2, $v_1 v_2$, v_2^2. Training of the network MLP_LEG on the basis of matrix $\mathbf{T}$ and matrix $\mathbf{X}$ with appended rows containing the orthogonal Legendre polynomials from point b. Training of the network MLP_F on the basis of matrix $\mathbf{T}$ and matrix $\mathbf{X}$ with appended rows with the Fourier series elements and with removed rows of v_1 and v_2. For training of all networks, 60 % of the data was used. The validation set consisted of 15 % of the data and the test set of 25 % of the data. The training process with use of the scaled conjugate gradient backpropagation [11] was interrupted when the objective function value (1) calculated on the validation set increased in 6 successive epochs.

(IV) calculation of the objective function value (1) on the test set and determining of the number of incorrectly classified test data.

After a 50-ple execution of the above procedure, all results determined in its point IV were averaged. The averages are presented in Tables 1, 2, 3, 4, 5 and 6.

It is worthwhile to note that the networks MLP_POLY, MLP_F and MLP_LEG have more inputs and connections from the inputs to the hidden layer neurons than MLP_SMALL. Therefore, the number of neurons in the hidden layer of the networks MLP_BIG was chosen on the basis of the formula (3), so that the network MLP_BIG has at least as many weights as the network MLP_F, which has more connections than MLP_POLY and MLP_LEG. By comparison of the results of MLP_SMALL and MLP_BIG with other networks, one may analyse better the influence of selection of the input signals and the influence of the increase in the weight number. MLP_BIG and MLP_SMALL are the networks, for training of which, no additional input variables (signals) were used. These networks were created only in order to state if the proposed additional signal is the main reason for improved classifications.

In the case of the benchmark Thyroid Disease Databases, when selecting v_1 and v_2, the input variables that had only the binary values were omitted.

It is worth to notice that for all used datasets the ratio $MSE1/MSE2 \leq 1.5$ (Table 7). Therefore, the signals listed in the points a–c were suitable.

On the basis of the results shown in Tables 1, 2, 3, 4, 5 and 6, it is easy to notice that in many cases an increase in the number of neurons deteriorates

Table 1. Objective function (1) calculated on the test set for Cancer Dataset.

h	MLP_SMALL	MLP_BIG	MLP_POLY	MLP_LEG	MLP_F
10	0.030736	0.03731	0.032288	0.031859	0.039463
20	0.031479	0.03143	0.030259	0.030377	0.044535

Table 2. Number of incorrectly classified test data for Cancer Dataset.

h	MLP_SMALL	MLP_BIG	MLP_POLY	MLP_LEG	MLP_F
10	6.52	8.66	6.92	6.84	8.20
20	6.36	6.54	6.16	6.24	9.62

Table 3. Objective function (1) calculated on the test set for Thyroid Dataset.

h	MLP_SMALL	MLP_BIG	MLP_POLY	MLP_LEG	MLP_F
10	0.035195	0.036571	0.022046	0.022985	0.019768
20	0.035627	0.036430	0.024173	0.025380	0.021127

Table 4. Number of incorrectly classified test data for Thyroid Dataset.

h	MLP_SMALL	MLP_BIG	MLP_POLY	MLP_LEG	MLP_F
10	114.32	115.46	75.62	78.50	66.94
20	114.14	117.48	81.90	86.84	71.52

Table 5. Objective function (1) calculated on the test set for Wine Dataset.

h	MLP_SMALL	MLP_BIG	MLP_POLY	MLP_LEG	MLP_F
10	0.029915	0.030966	0.035607	0.030738	0.028828
20	0.055565	0.033308	0.026080	0.033035	0.045060

Table 6. Number of incorrectly classified test data for Wine Dataset.

h	MLP_SMALL	MLP_BIG	MLP_POLY	MLP_LEG	MLP_F
10	2.68	3.16	3.30	2.94	2.38
20	5.26	2.94	2.38	3.12	4.12

Table 7. Mean values of the MSE1/MSE2 ratio.

Dataset	Thyroid Disease	Brest Cancer	Wines
$MSE1/MSE2$	1.120	1.290	1.291

performance instead of making it better although increasing the number of inputs is very likely to improve performance.

The proposed method was tested also on the UCI benchmarks intended for solving of the fitting problems. It proceeded similarly as in the classification investigation case, with the only difference consisting in applications of the networks with the liner activation function in the output layer. For the fitting, the following datasets were used: the abalone dataset, the building data set and the engine dataset. After analysing the results, it was found that the method proposed is good for the classification problems, only, and is not suitable for fitting.

4   Conclusions

In the case of the Cancer dataset, the best qualification was obtained for MLP_LEG and MLP_POLY wherein h was equal to 20. These bigger networks achieved a lower objective function value (1) for the test set as well as a lower number of erroneous classifications. For Thyroid Datasets, MLP_POLY, MLP_LEG and MLP_F always yielded much lower MSE than MLP_SMALL and MLP_BIG. Furthermore, the number of incorrect classified patients was also considerably better. For this datatset, MLP_POLY, MLP_LEG and MLP_F obtained 30 % fewer incorrect classifications than MLP_SMALL and MLP_BIG. When recognising the wine origin for $h = 20$, the best results were obtained with use of MLP_POLY. The wine dataset consisted of a multiply lower number of data than the other datasets. There were only 178 instances in the dataset and, due to that, the bigger networks trained on this set underwent, most probably, overfitting and, in most cases, had a worse generalisation capability. Proposed method went well for the benchmark that had even 21 attributes as well as for the benchmark that had 9 attributes. For Cancer Dataset set, the worst results were obtained for the MLP_F although they were based on the highest number of the additional signals. Therefore, networks MLP_F appear to be useless. On the basis of the analysis of the results obtained, it seems to be worthwhile to consider solutions similar to those used in the network MLP_POLY for classifying large datasets (with a high number of instances in the training dataset) with use of perceptrons having a dozen or more neurons in the hidden layer. The important advantages of the networks of type MLP_POLY are the use of three additional signals only and the very intuitive action as well as division of the hyperspace.

The proposed procedure does not need implementation of any complicated new software. The dimensions where the curve separation takes place with use of more complex shapes than straight lines are only selected automatically. Such a possibility may constitute a useful and interesting alternative with respects to the manual data analysis and arduous selection of its preprocessing way.

In further research, the author intends to test the networks of type MLP_POLY in more detail, on a considerably higher number of the classification problems. More sophisticated ways for selection of the significant inputs, taking in consideration among other things, the correlations will be employed. Methods and hints for automatic selection of additional input variables on the basis of the value of MSE1/MSE2 ratio will be developed. It is worthwhile that the initial values of the weights were chosen with the use of the Nguyen-Windrow algorithm that was designed so that the hyper-slope straight lines are placed possibly uniformly. Small changes of weight values may remarkable change the shape of curves. The development of the weight selection system intended for the curved hyper-slopes may result in a better division of the space and further improvement of the classification results.

References

1. Nelles, O.: Nonlinear System Identification: From Classical Approaches to Neural Networks and Fuzzy Models. Springer Science & Business Media, Berlin (2001)
2. Barron, A.R.: Universal approximation bounds for superpositions of a sigmoidal function. IEEE Trans. Inf. Theory **39**(3), 930–945 (1993)
3. Rusiecki, A., Kordos, M., Kamiński, T., Greń, K.: Training neural networks on noisy data. In: Rutkowski, L., Korytkowski, M., Scherer, R., Tadeusiewicz, R., Zadeh, L.A., Zurada, J.M. (eds.) ICAISC 2014, Part I. LNCS, vol. 8467, pp. 131–142. Springer, Heidelberg (2014)
4. Cybenko, G.: Approximations by superpositions of sigmoidal functions. Math. Control Signals Syst. **2**(4), 303–314 (1989)
5. Rutkowski, L.: Computational Intelligence: Methods and Techniques. Springer Science & Business Media, Heidelberg (2008)
6. Laar, P.V.D., Heskes, T., Gielen, S.: Partial retraining: a new approach to input relevance determination. Int. J. Neural Syst. **9**(1), 75–85 (1999)
7. Olden, J.D., Joy, M.K., Death, R.G.: An accurate comparison of methods for quantifying variable importance in artificial neural networks using simulated data. Ecol. Model. **178**(3), 389–397 (2004)
8. Fock, E.: Global sensitivity analysis approach for input selection and system identification purposes-a new framework for feedforward neural networks. IEEE Trans. Neural Netw. Learn. Syst. **25**(8), 1484–1495 (2014)
9. Murphy, P.M., Aha, D.W.: UCI Repository of machine learning databases, Department of Information and Computer Science, University of California, Irvine, CA (1994). http://www.ics.uci.edu/~mlearn/MLRepository.html
10. Lichman, M.: UCI Machine Learning Repository, School of Information and Computer Science, University of California, Irvine, CA (2013). http://archive.ics.uci.edu/ml
11. Möller, M.F.: A scaled conjugate gradient algorithm for fast supervised learning. Neural Netw. **6**(4), 525–533 (1993)

Rough Restricted Boltzmann Machine – New Architecture for Incomplete Input Data

Wojciech K. Mleczko[1], Robert K. Nowicki[1(✉)], and Rafał Angryk[2]

[1] Institute of Computational Intelligence, Czestochowa University of Technology,
Al. Armii Krajowej 36, 42-200 Czestochowa, Poland
{wojciech.mleczko,robert.nowicki}@iisi.pcz.pl
[2] Department of Computer Science, Georgia State University,
P.O. Box 5060, Atlanta, GA 30302-5060, USA
angryk@cs.gsu.edu
http://www.iisi.pcz.pl
http://grid.cs.gsu.edu/~rangryk

Abstract. In the paper, a rough restricted Boltzmann machine (RRBM) is proposed. It is a hybrid architecture, which extends the restricted Boltzmann machine (RBM) using some elements of the Pawlak rough set theory. The main goal of such hybridization is to allow processing the imperfect input data and expressing the imperfection in the answer of the system. In the paper, one form of the imperfection is considered - missing values. However, the solutions similar to presented one can be designed also to handle e.g. imprecise data. The formal definition of RRBM is illustrated by experimental results on a handwritten digits reconstruction.

Keywords: Restricted Boltzmann machine · Missing data · Rough set theory · Handwritten digits reconstruction

1 Introduction

The original Pawlak rough set theory [41,42] is a tool to analyse data with various detail levels of description. It allows to classifying objects or states observed through abstract classes (atoms). The size and shape of atoms depend on the form of input information, e.g. the set of available features. Moreover, the form of input information can vary for particular objects. It creates an approximation space, which is individual for each observation. According to the theory, the input description (object, state etc.) can be classified to positive, negative and boundary regions of particular classes. The two first cases are interpreted as the input description is sufficient to recognize the object as belonging to the class or not. The third case occurs when the input data is insufficient to made specific decision. The special properties of the rough set theory has been already transferred into fuzzy and neuro-fuzzy classifiers [35–37,49,51], approximators [38], nearest neighbour classificators [34,39] and feedforward neural networks. This paper contains

© Springer International Publishing Switzerland 2016
L. Rutkowski et al. (Eds.): ICAISC 2016, Part I, LNAI 9692, pp. 114–125, 2016.
DOI: 10.1007/978-3-319-39378-0_11

the first proposition of incorporation the rough set theory into the architecture of the restricted Boltzmann machine and results of initial experiments with the new system.

The restricted Boltzmann machine (RBM) [17,50] is a recurrent neural network. In contrast to most artificial neural networks, the values obtained on the non-linear parts of neurons are treated as the probability values and the outputs of the neurons are generated randomly according to this probability. RBMs are applied to filtering, image reconstruction, recognition, and modelling [13]. They are also components of deep belief networks [10,19]. Neural networks are parallel in their nature. Thus, they are often implemented on various physical parallel architectures [3–8,40,52]. Even, the perceptron made by Frank Rosenblatt [43] was implemented as a parallel electro-mechanical device. The author of this paper applied many signal processors connected by dedicated serial bus to realise a fast neural network [2]. Nowadays, artificial neural networks are implemented in structures built from single molecules [29], e.g. distributed in mesoporous silica matrix [27,28].

The paper is organized as follows. Section 2 contains description of RBM and its learning in a nutshell. It is a base for a further consideration. The main contribution is placed in Sect. 3. It is the aforementioned conception of the rough restricted Boltzmann machine (RRBM). The illustration of RRMB working as well as experimental scenario and the results are contained in Sect. 4. The final remarks, conclusions and plans for the future work in the subject are presented in Sect. 5.

2 Introduction to Restricted Boltzmann Machine Learning

The restricted Boltzmann machine is a two layer recurrent neural network. The layers, according to their function, are called 'visible' and 'hidden', and signed by index 'v' and 'h' (e.g. $\mathbf{b}_v$, y_{hj}), respectively. The input values are presented on the outputs of the visible layer as vector $\mathbf{v}_0(t) = [v_{10}(t), \ldots, v_{i0}(t), \ldots, v_{M0}(t)]$, where M is a number of inputs and also a number of neurons in the visible layer, t indicates the specific sample. Then, the data are transmitted to the hidden layer, as it is depicted in Fig. 1. The state of RBM is characterised by the energy function defined as follows [18]

$$E(\mathbf{v}, \mathbf{h}) = \sum_{i=1}^{M} b_{vi} v_i - \sum_{j=1}^{N} b_{hj} h_j - \sum_{i=1}^{M} \sum_{j=1}^{N} v_i h_j w_{ij}, \tag{1}$$

where $\mathbf{v} = [v_1, \ldots, v_i, \ldots, v_M]$ and $\mathbf{h} = [h_1, \ldots, h_j, \ldots, h_N]$ are current states of neurons in the visible and hidden layers, respectively, b_{vi}, b_{hj} are biases in the layers, and w_{ij} is the weight between i-th neuron in the visible layer and j-th neuron in the hidden layer. The network assigns a probability to every possible pair of a visible and a hidden vector

$$p(\mathbf{v}, \mathbf{h}) = \frac{1}{Z} e^{-E(\mathbf{v}, \mathbf{h})}, \tag{2}$$

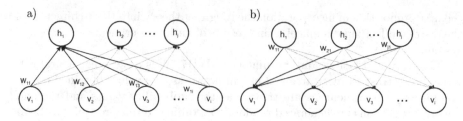

Fig. 1. Directions of data propagation in the restricted Boltzmann machine, (a) from visible layer to hidden, (b) from hidden layer to visible

where Z, is a partition function given by summing over all possible pairs of visible and hidden vectors

$$Z = \sum_{\mathbf{v},\mathbf{h}} e^{-E(\mathbf{v},\mathbf{h})}.\tag{3}$$

The probability which the network assigns to a visible vector $\mathbf{v}$ is given by summing over all possible hidden vectors

$$p(\mathbf{v}) = \frac{1}{Z} \sum_{\mathbf{h}} e^{-E(\mathbf{v},\mathbf{h})}.\tag{4}$$

Given a random input configuration $\mathbf{v}$, the state of the hidden unit j is set to 1 with probability

$$P(h_j = 1|\mathbf{v}) = \sigma\left(b_{hj} + \sum_i v_i w_{ij}\right),\tag{5}$$

where $\sigma(x)$ is the logistic sigmoid function $\frac{1}{1+\exp(-x)}$. Similarly, given a random hidden vector the state of the visible unit i can be set to 1 with probability

$$P(v_i = 1|\mathbf{h}) = \sigma\left(b_{vi} + \sum_i h_j w_{ij}\right).\tag{6}$$

The probability assigned by the network to a training image can be increased by adjusting the weights and the biases to decrease the energy E of that image and to increase the energy of other images, especially those that have low energies and therefore make a big contribution to the partition function. The derivative of the log probability of a training vector with respect to a weight is following

$$\frac{\partial \log p(\mathbf{v})}{\partial w_{ij}} = \langle v_i h_j \rangle_0 - \langle v_i h_j \rangle_\infty,\tag{7}$$

where $\langle \cdot \rangle_0$ denotes the expectations for the data distribution (p_0) and $\langle \cdot \rangle_\infty$ denotes the expectations for the model distribution (p_∞) [30]. It can be done by starting at any random state of the visible units and performing alternating Gibbs sampling for a very long time. One iteration of alternating Gibbs sampling consists of updating all of the hidden units in parallel using (5) followed by updating all of the visible units in parallel using (6) [17]. It is solved by the Contrastive Divergence algorithm [17,18]. Using this procedure can be applied in order to correct the weights and bias of the network

$$\Delta w_{ij} = \eta \left(\langle v_i h_j \rangle_0 - \langle v_i h_j \rangle_\infty \right), \tag{8}$$

$$\Delta b_{vi} = \eta (v_{i0} - v_{i\infty}), \tag{9}$$

$$\Delta b_{hj} = \eta (h_{j0} - h_{j\infty}). \tag{10}$$

The result of reconstruction is given as the vector $\mathbf{v}_\infty(t)$ available on the visible layer. It can be used for further processing as clustering [9,14,22] and pattern recognition [10] using various AI methods e.g. fuzzy systems, neural networks and their hybridization [26].

3 Rough Restricted Boltzmann Machine

The architecture of RBM presented in Sect. 2 works with input vector $\mathbf{v}_0(t)$. It is assumed that all values of the vector are known and initiated the recurrent process of reconstruction. Here we are changing this assumption. Below we propose a new version of RBM architecture — Rough RBM. In this system, the values of the input vector can be presented as real values (as in RBM), as intervals, or can be missing. In the last case the missing values are substituted by the intervals which covers the whole feature space (MCAR) or its parts (MAR, MNAR). It could be treated as a form of multiple imputation [1,48]. Thus, the input values are presented as pair of vectors $\{\underline{\mathbf{v}}_0(t), \overline{\mathbf{v}}_0(t)\}$, where $\underline{\mathbf{v}}_0(t) = [\underline{v}_{10}(t), \ldots, \underline{v}_{i0}(t), \ldots, \underline{v}_{M0}(t)]$ and $\overline{\mathbf{v}}_0(t) = [\overline{v}_{10}(t), \ldots, \overline{v}_{i0}(t), \ldots, \overline{v}_{M0}(t)]$. When the i-th input value is the real value $v_{i0}(t)$ then $\underline{v}_{i0}(t) = \overline{v}_{i0}(t) = v_{i0}(t)$ else it is represented by interval $[\underline{v}_{i0}(t), \overline{v}_{i0}(t)]$. The knowledge of RRBM architecture is stored in the matrix of weights $\mathbf{W} = \{w_{ij}\}$, the same as in RBM. Thus, it can be transferred between both systems. It is dissimilar to the rough neurons proposed by Lingras [31,32]. RBM consists of two layer of neurons — 'visible' and 'hidden'. RRBM consist of four layer — 'visible-lower', 'visible-upper', 'hidden-lower', and 'hidden-upper'. The weight for lower and upper layers are common, i.e. $\mathbf{W}$. Depending on the sign of appropriate weight the information is transmitted from neurons in visible-lower layer to neurons in hidden-lower or hidden-upper layer and from neurons in visible-upper layer to neurons in hidden-upper or hidden-lower layer. It is defined as follows

$$\underline{s}_{hj}(t) = \sum_{\substack{i=0 \\ w_{ij}(t)>0}} w_{ij}(t) \cdot \underline{v}_i(t) + \sum_{\substack{i=0 \\ w_{ij}(t)<0}} w_{ij}(t) \cdot \overline{v}_i(t) + b_{hj}(t) \tag{11}$$

and

$$\overline{s}_{hj}(t) = \sum_{\substack{i=0 \\ w_{ij}(t)>0}}^{N} w_{ij}(t) \cdot \overline{v}_i(t) + \sum_{\substack{i=0 \\ w_{ij}(t)<0}}^{N} w_{ij}(t) \cdot \underline{v}_i(t) + b_{hj}(t). \tag{12}$$

Then, from neurons in hidden-lower layer to neurons in visible-lower or visible-upper layer and from neurons in hidden-upper layer to neurons in visible-upper or visible-lower layer

$$\underline{s}_{vi}(t) = \sum_{\substack{j=0 \\ w_{ij}(t)>0}}^{N} w_{ij}(t) \cdot \underline{h}_j(t) + \sum_{\substack{j=0 \\ w_{ij}(t)<0}}^{N} w_{ij}(t) \cdot \overline{h}_j(t) + b_{vi}(t) \qquad (13)$$

$$\overline{s}_{vi}(t) = \sum_{\substack{i=0 \\ w_{ij}(t)>0}}^{N} w_{ij}(t) \cdot \overline{h}_j(t) + \sum_{\substack{i=0 \\ w_{ij}(t)<0}}^{N} w_{ij}(t) \cdot \underline{h}_j(t) + b_{vi}(t). \qquad (14)$$

There is not direct transmission between visible-lower and visible-upper layers as well as between hidden-lower or hidden-upper layers. The result of the reconstruction is given as the pair of vectors $\{\underline{\mathbf{v}}_\infty(t), \overline{\mathbf{v}}_\infty(t)\}$.

The output of j-th neuron in the hidden-lower layer is signed by $\underline{h}_j(t)$, and $\overline{h}_j(t)$ in the case of hidden-upper layer. They are derived with the probability described by non-linear output of the neurons as follows

$$P\left(\underline{h}_{0j}(t) = 1 | \underline{y}_{\mathrm{h}j}(t)\right) = \underline{y}_{\mathrm{h}j}(t), \qquad (15)$$

$$P\left(\overline{h}_{0j}(t) = 1 | \overline{y}_{\mathrm{h}j}(t)\right) = \overline{y}_{\mathrm{h}j}(t), \qquad (16)$$

where $\underline{y}_{\mathrm{h}j}(t) = \sigma\left(\underline{s}_{vi}(t)\right)$ and $\overline{y}_{\mathrm{h}j}(t) = \sigma\left(\overline{s}_{vi}(t)\right)$, but the following restriction must be meet

$$\underline{h}_{0j}(t) \leq \overline{h}_{0j}(t). \qquad (17)$$

During the learning, the corrections defined in equations (8)–(10) come from both lower and upper layers of the networks. Thus, they are defined as follows

$$\Delta w_{ij}(t) = \eta \frac{\left(\langle \underline{v}_i(t)\underline{h}_j(t)\rangle_0 - \langle \underline{v}_i(t)\underline{h}_j(t)\rangle_\infty\right) + \left(\langle \overline{v}_i(t)\overline{h}_j(t)\rangle_0 - \langle \overline{v}_i(t)\overline{h}_j(t)\rangle_\infty\right)}{2}, \qquad (18)$$

$$\Delta b_{vi}(t) = \eta \frac{(\underline{v}_{i0}(t) - \underline{v}_{i\infty}(t)) + (\overline{v}_{i0}(t) - \overline{v}_{i\infty}(t))}{2}, \qquad (19)$$

$$\Delta b_{\mathrm{h}j}(t) = \eta \frac{(\underline{h}_{j0}(t) - \underline{h}_{j\infty}(t)) + (\overline{h}_{j0}(t) - \overline{h}_{j\infty}(t))}{2}. \qquad (20)$$

4   Experimental Results

The architecture of RRBM presented in Sect. 3 has been implemented in Matlab environment. It allows to comparing the results with implementation of RBM proposed by Karpathy [21]. The investigation has been realised using database, which contains 6000 samples of hand-written digits [20]. The randomly selected 5000 samples has been used for learning, the remaining 1000 samples — for testing. The description of dividing procedure can be found in [33]. The original database is free of missing elements. However, to perform the experiments the specified number of pixels are randomly set as missing. In such case, the input data are substituted by minimum and maximum values of pixel brightness. Algorithm 1 and Fig. 2 illustrate this process.

The experiments are carried out for various level of missing pixels, between 1 % and 14 %. However, it is realised in two scenarios. In the first one the RBM architecture has been learned using complete data. Then, the matrix of weights $\mathbf{W}$ has been transferred to RRBM architecture. The obtained RRBM has been tested using patterns with missing pixels. The second scenario is more time-consuming. The same levels of missing pixels is have been set for learning and testing phase. Obviously, both learning and testing phases are realised on RRBM architecture. For full picture of research, various sizes of the networks have been tested.

a)   b)

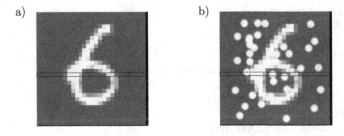

Fig. 2. Example of pattern '6' with marked single line, (a) original, (b) with some pixels set as missing

4.1   Experiment 1

This experiment has been realised with the first scenario. Thus, we have only single RRBM with single matrix of weights $\mathbf{W}$. To illustrate the effect of rough reconstruction we focused on a single line of digit '6' pattern. The line is marked in Fig. 2. As we can see, there are two bright regions on the dark background in this line. In Fig. 3 this two bright parts of pattern, described as 'original', are compared with its rough reconstruction for various level of missing pixels in whole pattern. The rough reconstruction contains the lower part $\underline{\mathbf{v}}_\infty$ obtained on the visible-lower layer and the upper part $\overline{\mathbf{v}}_\infty$ obtained on the visible-upper layer.

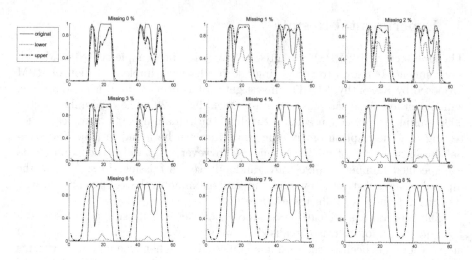

Fig. 3. Rough reconstruction of single line of pattern '6' for various level of missing pixels — the first scenario

---

Algorithm 1. Input data preparation for RRBM

1: **procedure** CREATESYSTEMLT
2:    $numSamples \leftarrow$ number of $sample$
3:    $i \leftarrow sample$
4:    $DATA \leftarrow$ data learning
5:    $dataL \leftarrow$ lower system
6:    $dataT \leftarrow$ top system
7:    **while** $(i < numSample)$ **do**
8:       **if** $(DATA(i) == isIncompleteData)$ **then**
9:          $dataL(i) := min(DATA)$
10:         $dataT(i) := max(DATA)$
11:       **else**
12:         $dataL(i) := DATA(i)$
13:         $dataT(i) := DATA(i)$
14:       **end if**
15:    **end while**
16: **end procedure**

The difference between these two parts of reconstruction is the result of missing pixels appearance. When the state of all pixels are known, both parts are equal as in the first graph (Missing 0 %) in Fig. 3. The rest graphs in the figure illustrate the lower and upper reconstructions for increasing level of missing pixels. When the level is enough high the lower reconstruction obtains the minimum values of brightness, i.e. zero and the upper reconstruction obtains the maximum value, i.e. 1 around the bright areas in pattern. In the case of the pixels located far from bright areas, both lower and upper obtain values close to zero.

The lower and upper reconstruction can be compared to a mould. They limited the space in which we expect the values of brightness. The distance between the reconstructions depend on the level of missing pixels in input patterns. It change from 0 when all pixels are available to 1 when all input pixels are missing. In the last case, the reconstruction covers all possible patterns.

4.2 Experiment 2

This experiment has been realised according to the second scenario. The learning was performed for various level of missing pixels. Thus, it created many rough restricted Boltzmann machines, as we expect, dedicated for work with various level of missing pixels. Figure 4 presents the result of rough reconstruction of selected line of pattern '6' realised by nine of above-mentioned network for input data with the same level of missing pixels. Generally, the results are similar to obtained in Experiment 1. However, comparing to result presented in Fig. 3 (Experiment 1) we can see that for high level of missing pixels the lower reconstruction obtains higher values when there are missing pixels also in learning set. It means that RRBM created in second scenario has higher ability of reconstruction in the case of missing features.

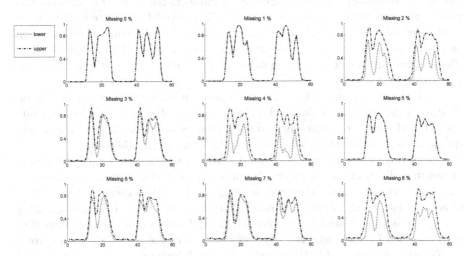

Fig. 4. Rough reconstruction of single line of pattern '6' for various level of missing pixels — the second scenario

4.3 Experiment 3

The aim of this experiment is to test the influence of the hidden layers size and the number of learning steps for the quality of rough reconstruction. The investigation was processed for various level of missing pixels and the average results have been placed in Table 1. As we can see, the number of learning steps is more important than the size of the network. Of course, when the size is sufficient.

Table 1. Error of reconstruction

Number of hidden neurons	epochs			
	100	200	500	1000
100	0.322	0.307	0.291	**0.288**
200	0,323	0.307	0.296	0,291
500	0.327	0.311	0.300	0.294

5   Conclusions and Future Work

In the paper, the new architecture of recurrent neural network has been proposed. It is a hybrid of the restricted Boltzmann machine and some elements of the rough set theory. Thus, the new network has been named rough restricted Boltzmann machine. The architecture and learning procedure of RBM has been extended and adapted to processing data in the form of the interval. In addition, the results of reconstruction are intervals, which cover infinite number of similar patterns. This property of RRMB has been presented in the graphs obtained during the experiments — reconstruction of handwritten digits. The experiments were performed according to two scenarios. It allowed to test the architectures built using data with missing information and the complete one. Both scenarios assumed the use of testing data with various level of missing input information. The various number of learning epochs and the various size of the architecture was also tested.

To know all the properties of the proposed architecture the further investigation is needed. Particularly, the other sets of patterns should be used and the detailed tests for various set and its sequences of missing input information should be done. Moreover, the proposed architecture of RRBM contains the same representation of knowledge as classic RBM, i.e. a single matrix of weights. It allows to easily transfer the knowledge between the systems. However, there are also known other models of rough neurons, e.g. [31]. We expect that such type of neurons can be also applied to build RRBM architectures. It is also tempting to apply the idea of flexible systems [11,12] and connect the level of flexibility with the size of output interval. They will be ones of the next steps in our work.

The aim of RBM and RRBM applications is different than fuzzy systems and feedforward neural networks. However, we think also about a specific form of ensembles of RRBMs modelled on already proposed ensembles contained other rough subsystems [23,24]. The RRBMs can be used as the element of CBIR systems [15,16,25]. Future work can be also devoted to application of RRBM to stream data mining [44–47].

Acknowledgment. The project was funded by the Polish National Science Center under decision number DEC-2012/05/B/ST6/03620.

References

1. Barnard, J., Rubin, D.: Small-sample degrees of freedom with multiple imputation. Biometrika **86**(4), 948–955 (1999)
2. Bilski, J., Nowicki, R., Scherer, R., Litwiski, S.: Application of signal processor TMS320C30 to neural networks realisation. In: Proceedings of the Second Conference Neural Networks and Their Applications, Czestochowa 53–59 (1996)
3. Bilski, J., Litwiński, S., Smolag, J.: Parallel realisation of QR algorithm for neural networks learning. In: Rutkowski, L., Siekmann, J.H., Tadeusiewicz, R., Zadeh, L.A. (eds.) ICAISC 2004. LNCS (LNAI), vol. 3070, pp. 158–165. Springer, Heidelberg (2004)
4. Bilski, J., Smolag, J., Galushkin, A.I.: The parallel approach to the conjugate gradient learning algorithm for the feedforward neural networks. In: Rutkowski, L., Korytkowski, M., Scherer, R., Tadeusiewicz, R., Zadeh, L.A., Zurada, J.M. (eds.) ICAISC 2014, Part I. LNCS, vol. 8467, pp. 12–21. Springer, Heidelberg (2014)
5. Bilski, J., Smolag, J.: Parallel realisation of the recurrent RTRN neural network learning. In: Rutkowski, L., Tadeusiewicz, R., Zadeh, L.A., Zurada, J.M. (eds.) ICAISC 2008. LNCS (LNAI), vol. 5097, pp. 11–16. Springer, Heidelberg (2008)
6. Bilski, J., Smolag, J.: Parallel realisation of the recurrent Elman neural network learning. In: Rutkowski, L., Scherer, R., Tadeusiewicz, R., Zadeh, L.A., Zurada, J.M. (eds.) ICAISC 2010, Part II. LNCS, vol. 6114, pp. 19–25. Springer, Heidelberg (2010)
7. Bilski, J., Smolag, J.: Parallel realisation of the recurrent multi layer perceptron learning. In: Rutkowski, L., Korytkowski, M., Scherer, R., Tadeusiewicz, R., Zadeh, L.A., Zurada, J.M. (eds.) ICAISC 2012, Part I. LNCS, vol. 7267, pp. 12–20. Springer, Heidelberg (2012)
8. Bilski, J., Smolag, J.: Parallel approach to learning of the recurrent jordan neural network. In: Rutkowski, L., Korytkowski, M., Scherer, R., Tadeusiewicz, R., Zadeh, L.A., Zurada, J.M. (eds.) ICAISC 2013, Part I. LNCS, vol. 7894, pp. 32–40. Springer, Heidelberg (2013)
9. Chen, M., Ludwig, S.A.: Particle swarm optimization based fuzzy clustering approach to identify optimal number of clusters. J. Artif. Intell. Soft Comput. Res. **4**(1), 43–56 (2014)
10. Chu, J.L., Krzyzak, A.: The recognition of partially occluded objects with support vector machines and convolutional neural networks and deep belief networks. J. Artif. Intell. Soft Comput. Res. **4**(1), 5–19 (2014)
11. Cpalka, K., Rutkowski, L.: Flexible Takagi-Sugeno fuzzy systems. In: IEEE International Joint Conference on Neural Networks, IJCNN 2005. Proceedings, vol. 3, pp 1764–1769, July 2005
12. Cpalka, K., Rutkowski, L.: Evolutionary learning of flexible neuro-fuzzy systems. In: IEEE International Conference on Fuzzy Systems, FUZZ-IEEE 2008, (IEEE World Congress on Computational Intelligence), pp. 969–975, June 2008
13. Dourlens, S., Ramdane-Cherif, A.: Modeling & understanding environment using semantic agents. J. Artif. Intell. Soft Comput. Res. **1**(4), 301–314 (2011)
14. El-Samak, A.F., Ashour, W.: Optimization of traveling salesman problem using affinity propagation clustering and genetic algorithm. J. Artif. Intell. Soft Comput. Res. **5**(4), 239–245 (2015)
15. Grycuk, R., Gabryel, M., Korytkowski, M., Scherer, R.: Content-based image indexing by data clustering and inverse document frequency. In: Kozielski, S., Mrozek, D., Kasprowski, P., Malysiak-Mrozek, B. (eds.) BDAS 2014. CCIS, vol. 424, pp. 374–383. Springer, Heidelberg (2014)

16. Grycuk, R., Gabryel, M., Korytkowski, M., Scherer, R., Voloshynovskiy, S.: From single image to list of objects based on edge and blob detection. In: Rutkowski, L., Korytkowski, M., Scherer, R., Tadeusiewicz, R., Zadeh, L.A., Zurada, J.M. (eds.) ICAISC 2014, Part II. LNCS, vol. 8468, pp. 605–615. Springer, Heidelberg (2014)
17. Hinton, G.: Training products of experts by minimizing contrastive divergence. Neural Comput. **14**(8), 1771–1800 (2002)
18. Hinton, G.: A practical guide to training restricted Boltzmann machines. Momentum **9**(1), 926 (2010)
19. Hinton, G., Osindero, S., Teh, Y.W.: A fast learning algorithm for deep belief nets. Neural comput. **18**(7), 1527–1554 (2006)
20. The mnist database of handwritten digits. http://yann.lecun.com/exdb/mnist/
21. Karpathy, A.: Code for training restricted Boltzmann machines (RBM) and deep belief networks in MATLAB. https://code.google.com/p/matrbm/
22. Kitajima, R., Kamimura, R.: Accumulative information enhancement in the self-organizing maps and its application to the analysis of mission statements. J. Artif. Intell. Soft Comput. Res. **5**(3), 161–176 (2015)
23. Korytkowski, M., Nowicki, R., Rutkowski, L., Scherer, R.: AdaBoost ensemble of DCOG rough–neuro–fuzzy systems. In: Jdrzejowicz, P., Nguyen, N.T., Hoang, K. (eds.) ICCCI 2011, Part I. LNCS, vol. 6922, pp. 62–71. Springer, Heidelberg (2011)
24. Korytkowski, M., Nowicki, R., Scherer, R.: Neuro-fuzzy rough classifier ensemble. In: Alippi, C., Polycarpou, M., Panayiotou, C., Ellinas, G. (eds.) ICANN 2009, Part I. LNCS, vol. 5768, pp. 817–823. Springer, Heidelberg (2009)
25. Korytkowski, M., Rutkowski, L., Scherer, R.: Fast image classification by boosting fuzzy classifiers. Inform. Sci. **327**, 175–182 (2016)
26. Koshiyama, A.S., Vellasco, M.M.B.R., Tanscheit, R.: GPFIS-control: a genetic fuzzy system for control tasks. J. Artif. Intell. Soft Comput. Res. **4**(3), 167–179 (2014)
27. Laskowski, L., Laskowska, M.: Functionalization of SBA-15 mesoporous silica by Cu-phosphonate units: probing of synthesis route. J. Solid State Chem. **220**, 221–226 (2014)
28. Laskowski, L., Laskowska, M., Balanda, M., Fitta, M., Kwiatkowska, J., Dzilinski, K., Karczmarska, A.: Mesoporous silica SBA-15 functionalized by nickel-phosphonic units: Raman and magnetic analysis. Microporous Mesoporous Mater. **200**, 253–259 (2014)
29. Laskowski, L., Laskowska, M., Jelonkiewicz, J., Boullanger, A.: Spin-glass implementation of a Hopfield neural structure. In: Rutkowski, L., Korytkowski, M., Scherer, R., Tadeusiewicz, R., Zadeh, L.A., Zurada, J.M. (eds.) ICAISC 2014, Part I. LNCS, vol. 8467, pp. 89–96. Springer, Heidelberg (2014)
30. Le Roux, N., Bengio, Y.: Representational power of restricted boltzmann machines and deep belief networks. Neural Comput. **20**(6), 1631–1649 (2008)
31. Lingras, P.: Comparison of neofuzzy and rough neural networks. Inf. Sci. **110**(3–4), 207–215 (1998)
32. Lingras, P.: Fuzzy-rough and rough-fuzzy serial combinations in neurocomputing. Neurocomput. **36**(1–4), 29–44 (2001)
33. Mleczko, W.K., Kapuscinski, T., Nowicki, R.K.: Rough deep belief network - application to incomplete handwritten digits pattern classification. In: Proceedings Information and Software Technologies - 21st International Conference, ICIST 2015, Druskininkai, Lithuania, 15–16 October 2015, pp. 400–411 (2015)
34. Nowak, B.A., Nowicki, R.K., Woźniak, M., Napoli, C.: Multi-class nearest neighbour classifier for incomplete data handling. In: Rutkowski, L., Korytkowski, M., Scherer, R., Tadeusiewicz, R., Zadeh, L.A., Zurada, J.M. (eds.) Artificial Intelligence and Soft Computing. LNCS, vol. 9119, pp. 469–480. Springer, Heidelberg (2015)

35. Nowicki, R.: Rough neuro-fuzzy structures for classification with missing data. IEEE Trans. Syst. Man Cybern. B Cybern. **39**(6), 1334–1347 (2009)
36. Nowicki, R.: On classification with missing data using rough-neuro-fuzzy systems. Int. J. Appl. Math. Comput. Sci. **20**(1), 55–67 (2010)
37. Nowicki, R.: On combining neuro-fuzzy architectures with the rough set theory to solve classification problems with incomplete data. IEEE Trans. on Knowledge and Data. Engineering **20**(9), 1239–1253 (2008)
38. Nowicki, R., Nowak, B., Starczewski, J., Cpalka, K.: The learning of neuro-fuzzy approximator with fuzzy rough sets in case of missing features. In: International Joint Conference on Neural Networks (IJCNN), 2014, pp. 3759–3766, July 2014
39. Nowicki, R.K., Nowak, B.A., Wozniak, M.: Rough k-nearest neighbours for classification in the case of missing input data. In: Proceedings of the 9th International Conference on Knowledge, Information and Creativity Support Systems, Limassol, pp. 196–207, November 2014
40. Patan, K., Patan, M.: Optimal training strategies for locally recurrent neural networks. J. Artif. Intell. Soft Comput. Res. **1**(2), 103–114 (2011)
41. Pawlak, Z.: Rough classification. Int. J. Man Mach. Stud. **20**, 469–485 (1984)
42. Pawlak, Z.: Rough Sets: Theoretical Aspects of Reasoning About Data. Kluwer, Dordrecht (1991)
43. Rosenblatt, F.: The perceptron: a probabilistic model for information storage and organization in the brain. Psychol. Sci. **65**(65), 386–408 (1958)
44. Rutkowski, L., Jaworski, M., Pietruczuk, L., Duda, P.: Decision trees for mining data streams based on the Gaussian approximation. IEEE Trans. Knowl. Data Eng. **26**(1), 108–119 (2014)
45. Rutkowski, L., Jaworski, M., Pietruczuk, L., Duda, P.: A new method for data stream mining based on the misclassification error. IEEE Trans. Neural Networks Learn. Syst. **26**(5), 1048–1059 (2015)
46. Rutkowski, L., Pietruczuk, L., Duda, P., Jaworski, M.: Decision trees for mining data streams based on the McDiarmid's bound. IEEE Trans. Knowl. Data Eng. **25**(6), 1272–1279 (2013)
47. Rutkowski, L., Jaworski, M., Pietruczuk, L., Duda, P.: The CART decision tree for mining data streams. Inf. Sci. **266**, 1–15 (2014)
48. Sartori, N., Salvan, A., Thomaseth, K.: Multiple imputation of missing values in a cancer mortality analysis with estimated exposure dose. Comput. Stat. Data Anal. **49**(3), 937–953 (2005)
49. Scherer, R., Rutkowski, L.: Relational equations initializing neuro-fuzzy system. In: Proceeding of the 10th Zittau Fuzzy Colloquium, Zittau, Germany, pp. 18–22 (2002)
50. Smolensky, P.: Information processing in dynamical systems: foundations of harmony theory. In: Rumelhart, D.E., McLelland, J.L., (eds.) Parallel Distributed Processing: Explorations in the Microstructure of Cognition, vol. 1 Fundations, pp. 194–281. MIT (1986)
51. Starczewski, J., Nowicki, R., Nowak, B.: Genetic fuzzy classifier with fuzzy rough sets for imprecise data. In: IEEE International Conference on Fuzzy Systems (FUZZ-IEEE), 2014, pp. 1382–1389, July 2014
52. Tambouratzis, T., Chernikova, D., Pázsit, I.: Pulse shape discrimination of neutrons and gamma rays using kohonen artificial neural networks. J. Artif. Intell. Soft Comput. Res. **3**(2), 77–88 (2013)

Word Embeddings for the Polish Language

Marek Rogalski[✉] and Piotr S. Szczepaniak

Institute of Computer Science, Lodz University of Technology,
Wolczanska 215, 90-924 Lodz, Poland
800670@edu.p.lodz.pl

Abstract. We present a dataset of word embeddings for the Polish language. Presented embeddings can be used as an input for Artificial Intelligence methods as an alternative for one-hot representation. Spatial relations between embeddings reflect relations such as alternatives and analogies. This improves generalization of methods using presented embeddings. Data from Wikipedia has been used together with skip-gram and contitous-bag-of-words methods introduced originally for English language by Mikolov et al. Current version of embeddings can be downloaded from http://publications.ics.p.lodz.pl/2016/word_embeddings/.

1 Introduction

Representation of text can improve efficiency of artificial intelligence systems that predict most likely word sequences (i.e. language modelling), a vital subtask for spell checking, optical character recognition, speech recognition, machine translation and spam detection.

A common representation for linguistic data is the *one-hot* representation. In this representation each word w is represented as a vector $\boldsymbol{V}(w)$:

$$\boldsymbol{V}(w) = \left[\delta_{ij} \mid i \in \mathbb{Z}_{|D|} \text{ and } j = \text{ind}(w)\right], \tag{1}$$

where $\text{ind}(w)$ is index of the word in ordered dictionary $\boldsymbol{D}$ and δ_{ij} is the Kronecker delta (Table 1).

Representations where almost all elements of $\boldsymbol{V}(w)$ are equal to 0, in particular the one-hot representation, are called *sparse*. For efficiency, sparse representations are usually encoded in compressed form. In the case of one-hot this can be a single integer[1].

The biggest advantages of one-hot representation are its simplicity and low memory overhead. Many classic methods from language processing have been based on the assumption that words can be treated like *symbols* – being either equal or not. This is what the one-hot representation boils down to in practice.

The main drawback of this representation is lack of similarity grading. Highly similar words will be as different from each other as any other random words (Fig. 1).

---

[1] Even though sparse representations are encoded in the compact form all the operations are performed as if they still were full-size vectors.

L. Rutkowski et al. (Eds.): ICAISC 2016, Part I, LNAI 9692, pp. 126–135, 2016.
DOI: 10.1007/978-3-319-39378-0_12

Table 1. Examples of words and their one-hot vectors

w	$\text{ind}(w)$	$V(w)$
abakus	1	$[1,0\ldots0]$
leśnikom	820543	$[0\ldots1\ldots0]$
żyźniejszymi	3624472	$[0\ldots0,1]$

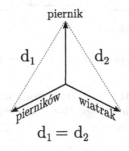

$$d_1 = d_2$$

Fig. 1. Distances of all words in one-hot representation are equal

From the point of view of language processing system this means that each word is a unique – and its usage has to be learned from scratch based on contents of available text corpora. Words which occur rarely are seen in very few contexts. Lack of sufficient number of context examples makes it difficult for artificial intelligence systems to learn usage of a word. When learning process is over, the trained system uses rare words only in the contexts it has seen (overfitting errors) or risk errors and use them in contexts it hasn't seen (underfitting errors).

Stemming and *morphosyntactic annotations* are a major improvement of this representation. Stemming joins all variants of a given word (called jointly - *lexeme*) under the name of its stem – greatly reducing size of dictionary and increasing number of contexts where usage of the stem can be observed.

This is the case especially in heavily inflected languages - like Polish. Online dictionary maintained at `sjp.pl` lists 3 839 346 words composing 196 619 different lexemes (state as of Nov 15th 2015). On average this gives 20 different forms for each lexeme. Some lexemes have a lot more forms: e.g. verb *wkalkulować* (meaning *account for*) has 178 different forms.

Stemming loses information about the exact word that the stem came from. To keep this information in the training data and make it accessible to Artificial Intelligence technique being trained, stems are often enriched with morphosyntactic annotations. Morphosyntactic annotations are indicators that for each stem indicate cases of all grammatical categories that the original word used. Using these annotations it's possible to recover original word that the stem came from.

Stemmed and annotated corpus still can be written in a compressed form – albeit not as a single integer. Instead a set of integers can be used: first one indicates position of the stem of the word in the ordered list of all stems.

Successive integers indicate all morphosyntactic categories that stemmed word belonged to e.g. in [9] the word *morfologicznej* is represented as colon-separated list: `morfologiczny:adj:sg:gen.dat.loc:f:pos` (Fig. 2).

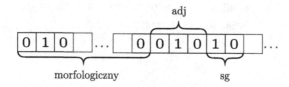

Fig. 2. *Many-hot* representation of the word *morfologicznej*.

Further improvements of this representations include spell correction, synonym detection, word-sense disambiguation and extraction of additional, sometimes hand-crafted features, out of words [5] (Fig. 3).

Dense Representations. Alternative for sparse representations are *dense* representations. Those are relatively small vectors, usually ranging from tens to hundreds dimensions. Main difference between dense and sparse word vectors is that all of the elements of dense vectors carry some information about the represented word. The information about the word identity and its relations with other words is distributed throughout the vector.

In the field of language processing the dense word vectors are called *word embeddings*. This name comes from the fact that the word vectors place or *embed* words at some positions of their word-space.

Word embeddings are natural input for many Artificial Intelligence methods - like neural networks or support vector machines. The embeddings can be fed directly as an input to such systems. Space induced by word embeddings is also well-structured - words which can be used interchangeably often can be found in close proximity, while completely unrelated words are located in remote regions of this space.

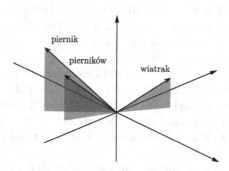

Fig. 3. Distances between word embeddings correspond to their syntactic and semantic similarities. Actual word embeddings have tens or hundreds of dimensions.

Creating word word embeddings in practice is done automatically using some text corpora and a word embedding algorithm. The algorithm and corpora used to embed the words are key factors for their final utility.

1.1 Techniques for Generating Word Embeddings

There are many techniques for generating word embeddings described in the literature. First chronologically was the one described in [1]. It relies on training an auxiliary neural network to predict a one-hot vector of a following word based on one-hot vectors of a few previous words. Key element of this network is the first hidden layer which is shared by all previous words and transforms them from sparse, one-hot representation (roughly $100\,000$ dimensions) into a dense representation (roughly 100 dimensions). Second hidden layer takes concatenation of dense representations of the words and outputs a probability distribution for the following word. The network is trained to minimize prediction error. When training is over the parameter matrix of first hidden layer is retained as an *embedding layer*. Remaining part of the network is discarded. Multiplying one-hot vector of any word by the embedding layer (operation which can be reduced to matrix row lookup) produces word embedding.

Let's denote $\boldsymbol{W}_i$ as the embedding of word w_i using embedding matrix $\boldsymbol{C}$:

$$\boldsymbol{W}_i = \boldsymbol{V}(w_i) \times \boldsymbol{C}. \tag{2}$$

Let's also denote σ to be the activation function of the neural network. Various authors used sigmoid, tanh or a rectified linear unit but the basic structure of the training is the same.

The process of training is an optimization that minimizes error E by modifying embedding matrix $\boldsymbol{C}$ and prediction matrix $\boldsymbol{P}$:

$$E = \left\| \boldsymbol{V}(w_n) - \mathrm{softmax}\Big(\sigma\big(\boldsymbol{W}_{n-1}, \boldsymbol{W}_{n-2}, \cdots\big) \times \boldsymbol{P}\Big) \right\|. \tag{3}$$

This technique was developed and improved upon by other researchers. With some modifications, this basic idea is still the foundation of leading word embedding techniques.

Idea introduced in [8] improved this by slightly changing the objective function of the network. Instead of predicting one-hot vector of the next word it tries to predict its embedding (taken from the embedding layer). Although this seems like a simple change, conceptually it's a significant leap forward. Using this modification the word embeddings that are being trained (by refining parameters of embedding layer) are at the same time used as a reference output for computing error of last layer of the neural network. Using this objective causes training process to gradually move word embeddings closer or further apart while at the same time changing the linear transformation that is responsible for prediction. Again, the process of training can be described as a minimization of the error E in terms of embedding and prediction matrices $\boldsymbol{C}$ and $\boldsymbol{P}$, same as in Eq. (3). The difference is that multiplication by matrix $\boldsymbol{P}$ produces predicted word embeddings (instead of distribution over all the words from dictionary). The probability function used by softmax is changed to rely dot-product as a vector-similarity measure to accommodate this change:

$$p(w_i|\boldsymbol{X}) = \frac{\exp(\boldsymbol{W}_i \cdot \boldsymbol{X})}{\sum_{j \in D} \exp(\boldsymbol{W}_j \cdot \boldsymbol{X})}. \tag{4}$$

Another modification is presented in [10] where the network is trained on two concatenations of word embeddings - one real - created by concatenating word embeddings based on the text corpus - and one corrupted - by choosing different word embedding. Then the network learns a scoring function that scores corrupted concatenations lower than original ones. This modification, although also seemingly simple causes the training process to more effectively shift words in space - by creating bigger pressure to push unrelated word embeddings apart.

In [3] a very similar approach is used - but instead of corrupting last word, the word in the middle is altered. This makes the word embeddings take into account not only the following but also preceding words. It's also shows that word embeddings can benefit from being trained on a task different than just a next word prediction.

Another important development of word embeddings can be found in [4] - where the problem of multiple word meanings is tackled by introducing multiple vectors for each word. If we try to associate some neighbourhood of a word vector with each word then classical word embeddings would divide whole word-space into something which could be conceptually similar to a Vornoi diagram. Each word in this space would occupy a single convex region. Introducing multiple vectors for each word makes it possible to represent more complex areas of this space, even disjoint areas in the case of homonyms. This change is closely related to the notion of word-sense disambiguation, a common theme in statistical language processing.

Work presented in [6] brings a significant quality improvement by inverting the structure of auxiliary neural network. In this approach, called *skip-gram* method, a single word embedding is given as an input to the neural network. Then the network is trained to predict concatenation of word vectors of several neighbouring words. Additionally a *negative sampling* is used, where a random word embedding is used in place of original one and the objective function is changed to minimize the probability of random word. This has effect similar to scoring objective from [10] - it creates a pressure that pushes word embeddings apart.

During training the error is defined here as a sum of errors coming from predicting several nearby words:

$$E(w_n) = E_{-2}(w_n) + E_{-1}(w_n) + E_{+1}(w_n) + E_{+2}(w_n), \tag{5}$$

$$E_t(w_n) = \left\| \boldsymbol{V}(w_{n+t}) - \mathrm{softmax}\big(\sigma(\boldsymbol{W}_n) \times \boldsymbol{P}_t\big) \right\|. \tag{6}$$

During negative sampling the error is defined as:

$$\tilde{E}(w_n) = \tilde{E}_{(-2)}(w_n) + \tilde{E}_{(-1)}(w_n) + \tilde{E}_1(w_n) + \tilde{E}_2(w_n), \qquad (7)$$

$$\tilde{E}_t(w_n) = 1 - \left\| V(w_{n+t}) - \text{softmax}\left(\sigma\left(W_{x \neq n}\right) \times P_t\right) \right\|. \qquad (8)$$

1.2 Properties of Word Embeddings

Main advantage of word embeddings is their organization in the induced word-space. It has been shown in [2,7] that spatial relationships between word embeddings correspond to their semantic and syntactic properties.

Contexts which are used to train word embeddings are still valid when a word such as *dobry* (good) is replaced by *lepszy* (better) or *kiepski* (feeble). This interchangeability makes the training process place them in close proximity.

Similar behaviour can be seen in contexts where some words frequently co-occur. Changing one of them in such context makes it necessary to change the other e.g. "*prezydentem **Stanów Zjednoczonych** jest **Barack Obama**"* (Barack Obama is the president of the United States) and "*prezydentem **Rzecz-pospolitej Polski** jest **Andrzej Duda**"* (Andrzej Duda is the president of the Republic of Poland). Presence of *analogies* makes the training process place their word embeddings in a analogously located areas of the space.

These relations can be exploited. Neighbourhood of word embeddings can be used to find their alternatives (both synonyms and antonyms). Differences between word embeddings can be transferred to new words in order to find their analogies. Word embeddings found by averaging other word embeddings usually show syntactic and semantic properties of their averaged components.

Interesting relations between word embeddings are the main reason of their recent popularity among researchers, which can be seen in the variety of modifications being published.

From the practical perspective, word embeddings used as an input for Artificial Intelligence system lowers number of dimensions (hundreds of dimensions instead of hundreds of thousands) and arranges words in semantically and syntactically organized word-space where small perturbations end up finding closely related words.

Introduction of word embeddings often comes with improved generalization. Artificial Intelligence system trained by classifying words such as *słaby, kiepski, nienajlepszy, dobry, lepszy* as positive/negative has a chance to learn that some region of word-space can be treated as positive or negative decision region. New word, which wasn't observed during training, such as *tragiczny* has a chance to find itself in correct decision region and to be classified correctly. For most real systems the generalization to new words is a very desired property.

2 Published Word Embeddings

2.1 Training Procedure

Training Corpus. As a training corpus we used preprocessed data of article content from Wikipedia. Exact date of database and additional comments can be found in the README file published alongside word embeddings.

Contents of Wikipedia article database was cleaned by removing HTML and Wiki markup. Tables, citations, timelines and URLs have been removed from the corpus. Image captions and link text have been retained. Numbers have been broken down into separate digits. All upper-case letters have been replaced with lower-case. Additionally all words occuring less than 5 times in the corpus have been replaced by a special *rare-word* token. This cleaning process resulted in final vocabulary having 933 198 entries.

Training Algorithm. Training was performed by running 500 iterations of *continous-bag-of-words* and *skip-gram* algorithms as described in [6] over the training corpus. Learning rate was gradually changed from 0.05 to 0. The choice of training schedule was influenced by the need to minimize oscillations of the network around the found minimum.

No testing or validation sets have been used and the network was trained to fit the training data as closely as possible. This choice was justified by high bias of the model (a single layer of 100 sigmoid neurons), unable to learn the much larger training corpus.

Context width was set at five words on each side of the input/predicted word for both algorithms. This was chosen as the average of context widths that tend to produce reasonable outputs (context widths at two or one didn't produce good embeddings; similarly context widths at more than ten).

The *continous-bag-of-words* and *skip-gram* algorithms are characterized by varying efficiency in semantic and syntactic analogies. Both variants have been published in separate files. For higher overall accuracy a concatenation of both word embeddings should be used.

Examples of word-space neighbourhoods can be seen in Tables 2, 3, 4, 5 and 6.

2.2 Using Word Embeddings

The embeddings have been published at http://publications.ics.p.lodz.pl/2016/word_embeddings/.

Word embeddings are organized into lexicographically sorted text files where each line starts with a word and is followed by 100 space-separated real numbers ranging between 0 and 1. Two variants of vectors have been published in separate files - according to algorithm that was used to generate them - *skip-gram* and *continous-bag-of-words* [6].

Table 2. Example word-space neighbourhoods, according to cosine distance of *skip-gram* embeddings.

krokodyl		japonia		szczecinek		pasuje		pasuję	
hipopotam	0.286	korea	0.140	białogard	0.172	pasują	0.212	zadałem	0.358
słoń	0.289	chiny	0.169	wałcz	0.175	pasowało	0.265	pytałem	0.367
goryl	0.309	tajlandia	0.194	stargard	0.182	linkuje	0.280	pzdr	0.385
rekin	0.313	filipiny	0.219	świdwin	0.196	wygląda	0.283	spróbuj	0.394
neolit		marek		brwi		anna		herbata	
neolitu	0.174	policzki	0.176	dariusz	0.162	katarzyna	0.070	kawa	0.226
paleolit	0.190	włosy	0.203	mariusz	0.185	krystyna	0.092	herbaty	0.245
paleolitu	0.194	uszy	0.206	sławomir	0.188	elżbieta	0.098	wanilia	0.258
mezolitu	0.216	karku	0.219	krzysztof	0.197	małgorzata	0.098	cytryny	0.273

Table 3. Example word-space neighbourhoods, according to cosine distance of *continous-bag-of-words* embeddings.

krokodyl		japonia		szczecinek		pasuje		pasuję	
słoń	0.349	tajlandia	0.250	wałcz	0.255	pasowało	0.203	zastosują	0.490
tygrys	0.371	hongkong	0.319	białogard	0.333	pasują	0.217	wyjaśnię	0.492
hipopotam	0.372	rosja	0.330	świdwin	0.344	pasował	0.242	dałem	0.494
żółw	0.372	singapur	0.334	goleniów	0.348	pasowałaby	0.253	podeślę	0.495
neolit		brwi		marek		anna		herbata	
paleolit	0.268	policzki	0.263	jerzy	0.249	barbara	0.099	papryka	0.253
neolitu	0.315	uszu	0.268	andrzej	0.258	joanna	0.112	zupa	0.304
mezolit	0.338	uszy	0.275	sławomir	0.258	katarzyna	0.117	kapusta	0.331
paleolitu	0.344	policzków	0.302	jacek	0.258	agnieszka	0.125	kawa	0.336

Table 4. Example word-space neighbourhoods of analogies, according to cosine distance of *skip-gram* embeddings. Emphasized words are valid analogies.

barbara		pies		berlin		szekspir	
+(ania − anna)		+(kotek − kot)		+(francja − niemcy)		+(polski − angielski)	
ania	0.026	*kotek*	0.095	*berlin*	0.128	**wyspiański**	0.178
kasia	0.275	*pies*	0.128	*bruksela*	0.136	**konwicki**	0.231
andrzejewska	0.277	**piesek**	0.245	paryż	0.166	witkiewicz	0.238
majka	0.290	użytkowość	0.267	tuluza	0.166	**baczyński**	0.241
basia	0.291	misi	0.278	strasburg	0.181	**żeromski**	0.248
blythe	0.299	psem	0.297	antwerpia	0.197	wokulski	0.250

To improve visibility of published word embeddings we kindly request authors that base their work upon them to point it out by referencing this article or including link to the place where they were downloaded.

Table 5. Example word-space neighbourhoods of analogies, according to cosine distance of *continous-bag-of-words* embeddings. Emphasized words are valid analogies.

barbara		pies		berlin		szekspir	
+(ania − anna)		+(kotek − kot)		+(francja − niemcy)		+(polski − angielski)	
ania	0.078	*kotek*	0.021	*francja*	0.038	twardowski	0.312
basia	0.355	*pies*	0.060	*berlin*	0.045	mocarski	0.322
dorotka	0.384	**piesek**	0.243	**paryż**	0.050	wokulski	0.340
barbara	0.386	miś	0.308	bruksela	0.069	**wyspiański**	0.358
marta	0.393	chłopiec	0.337	lozanna	0.078	odludki	0.361
iza	0.399	**szczeniak**	0.345	tuluza	0.138	jakóbczyk	0.363

Table 6. Example word-space neighbourhoods of averages, according to cosine distance of *skip-gram* embeddings. Emphasized words are valid intermediate words.

$\frac{1}{2}$ (pierwszy + piąty)		$\frac{1}{2}$ (poniedziałek + niedziela)		$\frac{1}{2}$ (jezus + mahomet)	
trzeci	0.150	*niedziela*	0.073	*jezus*	0.191
czwarty	0.158	*poniedziałek*	0.073	*mahomet*	0.191
pierwszy	0.164	**czwartek**	0.111	**prorok**	0.239
piąty	0.164	sobota	0.166	chrystus	0.278
drugi	0.172	piątek	0.191	jahwe	0.307
szósty	0.209	wtorek	0.194	jezusa	0.318

3   Summary

We present a dataset of word embeddings for the Polish language. Reimplementing state-of-the-art algorithm is a time-consuming and error-prone task. By publishing an off-the-shelf word embeddings we hope to lower the entry barrier and reduce time spent by other researchers on building their own embeddings.

We hope to create a baseline word embeddings to compare efficiency of other Artificial Intelligence systems. Taking the word embedding quality out of the equation and will allow more direct competition between language processing systems.

References

1. Bengio, Y., Ducharme, R., Vincent, P., Janvin, C.: A neural probabilistic language model. J. Mach. Learn. Res. **3**, 1137–1155 (2003)
2. Chen, Y., Perozzi, B., Al-Rfou, R., Skiena, S.: The expressive power of word embeddings. arXiv preprint (2013). arXiv:1301.3226
3. Collobert, R., Weston, J., Bottou, L., Karlen, M., Kavukcuoglu, K., Kuksa, P.: Natural language processing (almost) from scratch. J. Mach. Learn. Res. **12**, 2493–2537 (2011)

4. Huang, E.H., Socher, R., Manning, C.D., Ng, A.Y.: Improving word representations via global context and multiple word prototypes. In: Annual Meeting of the Association for Computational Linguistics (ACL) (2012)
5. Manning, C.D., Schütze, H.: Foundations of Statistical Natural Language Processing. MIT press, Cambridge (1999)
6. Mikolov, T., Sutskever, I., Chen, K., Corrado, G.S., Dean, J.: Distributed representations of words and phrases and their compositionality. In: Burges, C., Bottou, L., Welling, M., Ghahramani, Z., Weinberger, K. (eds.) Advances in Neural Information Processing Systems 26, pp. 3111–3119. Curran Associates, Inc. (2013)
7. Mikolov, T., Yih, W.t., Zweig, G.: Linguistic regularities in continuous space word representations. In: HLT-NAACL, pp. 746–751 (2013)
8. Mnih, A., Hinton, G.: Three new graphical models for statistical language modelling. In: Proceedings of the 24th International Conference on Machine learning. pp. 641–648. ACM (2007)
9. Przepiórkowski, A.: A comparison of two morphosyntactic tagsets of polish. In: Representing Semantics in Digital Lexicography: Proceedings of MONDILEX Fourth Open Workshop. pp. 138–144. Warsaw (2009)
10. Turian, J., Ratinov, L., Bengio, Y.: Word representations: a simple and general method for semi-supervised learning. In: Proceedings of The 48th Annual Meeting of The Association for Computational Linguistics. pp. 384–394. Association for Computational Linguistics (2010)

Estimation of Deep Neural Networks Capabilities Using Polynomial Approach

Pawel Rozycki[1]([✉]), Janusz Kolbusz[1], Roman Korostenskyi[1], and Bogdan M. Wilamowski[2]

[1] University of Information Technology and Management in Rzeszow,
Sucharskiego 2, 35-225 Rzeszow, Poland
{prozycki,jkolbusz,rkorostenskyi}@wsiz.rzeszow.pl
[2] Auburn University, Auburn, AL 36849-5201, USA
wilambm@auburn.edu
http://wsiz.rzeszow.pl

Abstract. Currently very popular trend in artificial intelligence is the use of deep neural networks. The power of such networks are very large, but the main difficulty is learning these networks. The article presents an analysis of deep neural network nonlinearity with polynomial approximation of neuron activation functions. It is shown that nonlinearity grows exponentially with the depth of the neural network. The effectiveness of the approach is demonstrated by several experiments.

Keywords: Deep neural networks · Activation function · Nonlinearity

1 Introduction

Our civilization encounters increasingly complex problems that often exceeds human capabilities. Until recently, the aim was to create artificial intelligence systems, as perfect as a man. Currently, we are able to create intelligent learning systems exceeding the human intelligent. For example, we can create a model and predict the behavior of complexity of natural processes, which cannot be described mathematically. In order to efficiently model complex multidimensional nonlinear systems it must be used unconventional methods. Due to multidimensionality and nonlinearity algorithmic or statistical methods are not able to provide satisfactory solutions. Methods based on computational intelligence allow for more effective solving of complex problems, such as predict of economic trends, modeling natural phenomena, etc. Among the many methods based on different types of neural networks (SLP, MLP, FCC), fuzzy systems, RBF network, LVQ, PCA and SVM the special attention should be placed on neural networks with deep architecture. These networks contain-ing multiple hidden layers have high computation potential, and thus seem to be a perfect tool for

This work was supported by the National Science Centre, Cracow, Poland under Grant No. 2013/11/B/ST6/01337.

L. Rutkowski et al. (Eds.): ICAISC 2016, Part I, LNAI 9692, pp. 136–147, 2016.
DOI: 10.1007/978-3-319-39378-0_13

modeling complex multidimensional nonlinear systems. Research shows that the process of learning this type of network is very difficult and time-consuming, which makes difficult to use of their potential. These deep neural networks have a much more power that allow to solve much more complex problems. There are currently different methods that can be divided into two main types that can be also used jointly [1,2]: (a) discriminative or supervised such as multi-layer supervised gradient-based method, Convolutional Neural Networks (CNN) or Recurrent Neural Network (RNN); (b) generative or unsupervised such as Restricted Boltzmann Machine (RBM), Deep Belief Networks (DBN) or autoencoders. To use this power this is required to understand the architecture of the neural network and its impact on the functioning of the system and the training process and to find an effective training algorithms that will more quickly and effectively train such networks using its properties. Both of these problems are closely connected. Commonly used network MLP (Multi Layer Perception) have a relatively limited capacity [3] and difficult to train effectively due to vanishing gradient problem that make layers near input less trainable [5,6]. The way to solve this issue could be new training methods such as based on pre-training or segmentation frequently jointly with GPU/HPC accelerated computation techniques [7–10]. It turns out, however, that the new neural networks such as BMLP (Bridged MLP) [3,4] or DNN (Dual Neutral Networks) [4] with the same number of neurons are able to solve the problems of 10 or 100 times more complex [4,11].

2 Nonlinearity Capabilities of Deep Neural Networks

As mentioned in previous chapter the deep neural networks despite of problems with training are able to solve much complex and more nonlinear problem than shallow networks [12–18]. The power of given architecture depends on nonlinearity that can be mod-eled by network configured in this architecture. Question is how nonlinearity of network depends on its architecture. Answer could be key for proper dimensioning of network for given class of problem. This is a complex problem and it probably will not be possible to solve it in general way. However, below we will attempt to attack this issue using three different approaches by approximating nonlinearities by polynomial and trigonometric functions and using digital approach.

Let us assume that neural activation function is approximated by Taylor series expansion, which is polynomial given by

$$f = k_0 + k_1 x + k_2 x^2 + k_3 x^3 + \cdots = \sum_{n=0}^{m} k_n x^n \tag{1}$$

As a example we can consider sigmoid function $\frac{1}{1+e^{-x}}$ that can be expanded into odd polynomial terms:

$$\frac{1}{2} + \frac{x}{4} - \frac{x^3}{48} + \frac{x^5}{480} - \frac{17x^7}{80640} + \cdots \tag{2}$$

Another example is Gaussian function $e^{-\frac{(x-b)^2}{a}}$ used in RBF units can be expanded into:

$$e^{-\frac{b^2}{a}} + \frac{2be^{-\frac{b^2}{a}}x}{a} - \frac{(a-2b^2)e^{-\frac{b^2}{a}}x^2}{a^2} - \frac{2(b(3a-2b^2)e^{-\frac{b^2}{a}})x^3}{3a^3}$$
$$+ \frac{(3a^2-12ab^2+4b^4)e^{-\frac{b^2}{a}}x^4}{6a^4} + \dots$$

That for b=0 gives even polynomial terms:

$$1 - \frac{x^2}{a} + \frac{x^4}{2a^2} + \dots \tag{3}$$

For simplicity let us consider first four terms of (1):

$$f = k_0 + k_1 x + k_2 x^2 + k_3 x^3 \tag{4}$$

Let us now consider N neurons in shallow architecture, shown in Fig. 1a, then the nonlinearities given by (4) are able to produce a nonlinear function given by:

$$F = \sum_{i=1}^{N} \left(k_{0i} + k_{1i}x + k_{2i}x + k_{3i}x^3\right) = a_0 + a_1 x + a_2 x + a_3 x^3 \tag{5}$$

where $a_n = \sum_{i=1}^{N} k_{ni}$

Maximal polynomial degree of such expression is equal to maximal polynomial degree of activation function and is independent from the number of neurons N. One may notice that in shallow architecture the order of polynomial does not increase. In other words nonlinearity does not increase.

In the case of deep architecture shown in Fig. 1b, the output of previous layer n-1 neuron is the input of the next layer n and the nonlinear function for layer n in given by:

$$f_n(x) = k_{0n} + k_{1n}f_{n-1}(x) + k_{2n}f_{n-1}(x)^2 + k_{3n}f_{n-1}(x)^3 \tag{6}$$

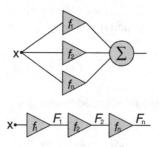

Fig. 1. Two general types of ANN architectures: (a) shallow, (b) deep.

For $N=2$ it gives:

$$F_2(x) = k_{02} + k_{12}(F_1(x)) + k_{22}(F_1(x))^2 + k_{32}(F_1(x))^3 \qquad (7)$$
$$F_2(x) = k_{02} + k_{12}(k_{01} + k_{11}x + k_{21}x^2 + k_{31}x^3)$$
$$+k_{22}(k_{01} + k_{11}x + k_{21}x^2 + k_{31}x^3)^2$$
$$+k_{32}(k_{01} + k_{11}x + k_{21}x^2 + k_{31}x^3)^3$$

It means that maximal polynomial degree is 9.
For $N = 3$

$$F_3(x) = k_{03} + k_{13}(F_2(x)) + k_{23}(F_2(x))^2 + k_{33}(F_2(x))^3 \qquad (8)$$

the maximal polynomial degree is determined by last term where:

$$k_{33}\left(k_{32}\left(k_{01} + k_{11}x + k_{21}x^2 + k_{31}x^3\right)^3\right)^3$$

gives highest polynomial degree equals 27. As can be observed in the deep architecture the order of polynomial describing output function increases rapidly with the number of layers. It means that such deep system has better ability to correctly classify patterns because separation surface can be more nonlinear. The detailed analysis was done only for $N \leq 3$ where the largest order of output polynomial is 9 for $N=2$ and 27 for $N=3$ but it can be concluded that the maximal polynomial degree of nonlinearity depends exponentially on the number of layers and for activation functions expansion with maximal polynomial degree m is given by m^N.

The cases shown in Fig. 1 have only one input but for multiple inputs similar conclusions can be withdrawn that deeper networks produce more nonlinear surfaces that shallow networks.

The power grid increases linearly with the width and exponentially with the depth. Therefore, it can be concluded that in order to solve complicated problems should use deep architecture.

3   Experimental Results

To confirm better capability of deep neural network in solving complex problems three experiments with well-known benchmarks have been prepared: two-spiral classification problem, Shwefel function approximation problem and Parity-9 problem. All problems have been tried to resolve with neural networks with different architectures form single-layer SLP shallow network to multilayer BMLP deep network and second-order NBN algorithm [19]. In all experiments NBN 2.08 software [20] have used.

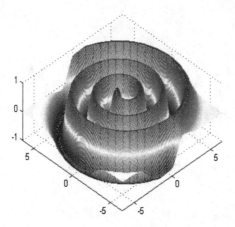

Fig. 2. Visualization of the two-spiral problem

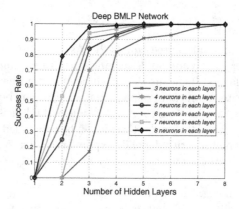

Fig. 3. Two-spiral problem training success rate with different architectures

3.1 Two-Spiral Problem

First experiment has been done for classical classification two-spiral problem described in [21] and shown in Fig. 2.

Figure 3 and Table 1 shows training success rates achieved with NBN algorithm for BMLP architectures. For each network used in experiments, all the hidden layers (from 1 to 5) consist the same number of neurons, from 3 to 8. Due to randomness of NBN algorithm all experiments have been repeated 100 times (trials). The success rate is defined as ratio of the number of success trials to the number of all trials.

The shallow architecture networks with one hidden layer were not able to train successfully while with deeper networks training success rate is growing very fast. Note that the network with 12 neurons in two-layer architecture (6-6) achieve 0.37 success rate while the same 12 neurons in three-later architecture

Table 1. Success rate of two-spiral classification problem for different SLP and BMLP architectures with NBN algorithm

Number of hidden layers	Number of neurons per hidden layer	Number of hidden neurons	Success Rate
SLP			
1	3	3	0
1	4	4	0
1	5	5	0
1	6	6	0
1	7	7	0
1	8	8	0
BMLP			
2	3	6	0
2	4	8	0
2	5	10	0.25
2	6	12	0.37
2	7	14	0.53
2	8	16	0.79
3	3	9	0.17
3	4	12	0.70
3	5	15	0.84
3	6	18	0.91
3	7	21	0.94
3	8	24	0.98
4	3	12	0.82
4	4	16	0.91
4	5	20	0.93
4	6	24	0.94
4	7	28	0.97
4	8	32	0.99
5	3	15	0.91
5	4	20	0.98
5	5	25	0.99
5	6	30	1
5	7	35	1
5	8	40	1

(4-4-4) gives 0.70 success rate and in four-layer architecture (3-3-3-3) reaches 0.82. Similar, 16 neurons in two layers achieves 0.79 success rate while four layer architecture with 4 neurons in each layer allow to achieve 0.91 result.

3.2 Shwefel Function

Second experiment was prepared for Shwefel function given by

$$z\left(x,y\right) = 2 * 418.9829 - x sin\left(\sqrt{|x|}\right) - y sin\left(\sqrt{|y|}\right)$$

shown in Fig. 4.

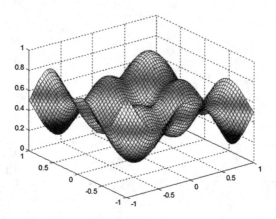

Fig. 4. Surface of normalized Shwefel function.

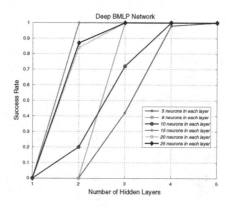

Fig. 5. Shwefel function training success rate for different architectures.

Results achieved for approximation of Shwefel function with different architectures have been shown in Fig. 5 and Table 2. As can be observed for all networks with shallow architectures the success rate is equals 0, while with deeper architectures reach much better results. Similar to the two-spiral experiment

Table 2. Success rates for Shwefel function approximation with SLP and BMLP architectures and NBN algorithm

Number of hidden layers	Number of neurons per hidden layer	Number of hidden neurons	Success rate
SLP			
1	5	5	0
1	8	8	0
1	10	10	0
1	15	15	0
1	20	20	0
1	25	25	0
1	50	50	0
1	100	100	0
BMLP			
2	5	10	0
2	8	16	0
2	10	20	0.20
2	15	30	1
2	20	40	0.84
2	25	50	0.87
3	5	15	0.42
3	8	24	1
3	10	30	0.72
3	15	45	1
3	20	60	1
3	25	75	1
4	5	20	0.98
4	8	32	1
4	10	40	1
4	15	60	1
4	20	89	1
4	25	100	1

given number of neurons in deeper architecture allows to achieve better result than the same number of neurons in shallower architecture. As an example 20 neurons in single hidden layer architecture ware not able to train with success while the same 20 neurons in two hidden layers architecture (10-10) achieved 0.20 success rate and in four hidden layer architecture (5-5-5-5) reached 0.98.

Table 3. Success rate of Parity-9 problem for different architectures with NBN algorithm

Number of hidden layers	Number of neurons per hidden layer	Number of hidden neurons	Success rate
SLP			
1	2	2	0
1	3	3	0
1	4	4	0
1	5	5	0.32
1	6	6	0.68
1	7	7	0.84
1	8	8	0.98
1	9	9	1
1	10	10	1
BMLP			
1	1	1	0
1	2	2	0
1	3	3	0
1	4	4	0.48
1	5	5	0.82
1	6	6	0.96
1	7	7	1
2	1	2	0.04
2	2	4	0.66
2	3	6	1
2	4	8	1
2	5	10	1
3	1	3	0.48
3	2	6	1
3	3	9	1
4	1	4	0.88
4	2	8	1
5	1	5	0.99
5	2	10	1
6	1	6	1
6	2	12	1

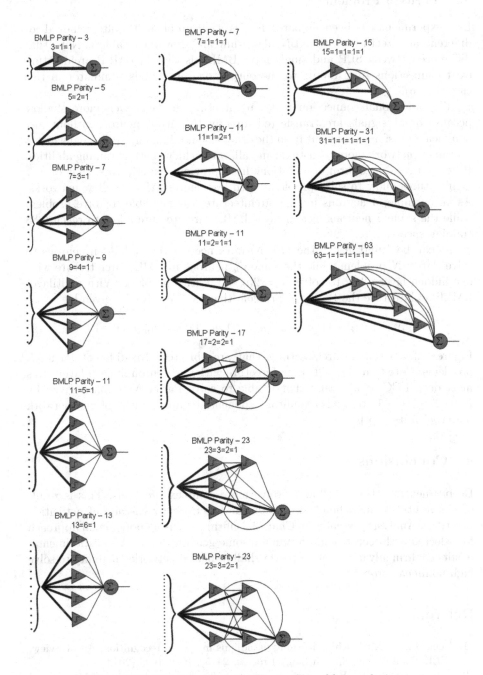

Fig. 6. BMLP architectures for Parity-N problems solution

3.3 Parity-9 Problem

Last experiment has been prepared for Parity-9 problem. Results achieved for different architectures with NBN algorithm are shown in Table 3. Note that difference between SLP and single layer BMLP is that in BMLP architecture exist connections from inputs to the output neuron that is summator in this case (Fig. 6).

This additional connection make architecture, in fact, even more shallow because input signals are transferred directly to output neuron without any nonlinear transformations but from the other side it add many additional weights that make network more adjustable and allow to achieve better training abilities. Presented results confirm observations from previous experiments, that deeper architectures allow to solve problems with less neurons than shallow networks. As an example, 4 neurons in SLP architecture was not able to solve problem while the same 4 neurons in four-layer BMLP architecture allow to reach 0.88 training success rate.

As can be found in [22] the SLP network needs $n_h = N$ hidden neurons to solve Parity-N problem while the same n_h neurons in BMLP architecture with one hidden layer allow to solve $N = 2n_h + 1$ Parity problem. With multilayer BMLP architecture the Parity-N problem that can be solved is given by

$$N = 2\,(n_1 + 1)\,(n_2 + 1)\,(n_3 + 1)\,(n_4 + 1)\,...\,(n_n + 1) - 1 \qquad (9)$$

Figure 6 shows sample architectures that are able to solve different Parity-N problems. Note that the BMLP architecture with one neuron in each layer gives most deep FCC architecture that is able to solve Parity-N problem given by $N = 2^{(n_h+1)} - 1$, that also confirm exponential improvement of the network power with its depth.

4   Conclusions

Deeper neural networks allow to solve more complex problems. This is result of possibility for modeling more nonlinear functions by cascade of activation functions. Analysis presented in Chap. 2 confirm that using polynomial approach for selected architectures and formulate some generalization. Also experimental results confirm advantage of deep over shallow neural networks in ability to solve high nonlinear problems.

References

1. Deng, L., Li, X.: Machine learning paradigms in speech recognition: An overview. IEEE Trans. Audio Speech Lang. Process. **21**(5), 1060–1089 (2013)
2. Lee, H., Grosse, R., Ranganath, R., Ng, A.: Unsupervised learning of hierarchical representations with convolutional deep belief networks. Commun. Assoc. Comput. Mach. (ACM) **54**(10), 95–103 (2011)

3. Wilamowski, B.M.: Neural network architectures and learning algorithms - how not to be frustrated with neural networks. IEEE Ind. Electron. Mag. **3**(4), 56–63 (2009)

4. Hunter, D., Yu, H., Pukish, M.S., Kolbusz, J., Wilamowski, B.M.: Selection of proper neural network sizes and architectures–A comparative study. IEEE Trans. Industr. Inf. **8**, 228–240 (2012)

5. Bengio, Y.: Learning deep architectures for AI. Found. Trends Mach. Learn. **2**(1), 1–127 (2009)

6. Hochreiter, S.: The vanishing gradient problem during learning recurrent neural nets and problem solutions. Int. J. Unc. Fuzz. Knowl. Based Syst. **06**, 107 (1998)

7. Erhan, D., Bengio, Y., Courvelle, A., Manzagol, P., Vencent, P., Bengio, S.: Why does unsupervised pre-training help deep learning? J. Mach. Learn. Res. **9**, 201–208 (2010)

8. Schmidhuber, J.: Deep learning in neural networks: An overview. Neural Netw. **61**, 85–117 (2015)

9. LeCun, Y., Bengio, Y., Hinton, G.: Deep learning. Nature **521**(7553), 436–444 (2015)

10. Olas, T., Mleczko, W.K., Nowicki, R.K., Wyrzykowski, R., Krzyzak, A.: Adaptation of RBM learning for intel MIC architecture. In: Rutkowski, L., Korytkowski, M., Scherer, R., Tadeusiewicz, R., Zadeh, L.A., Zurada, J.M. (eds.) Artificial Intelligence and Soft Computing. LNCS, vol. 9119, pp. 90–101. Springer, Heidelberg (2015)

11. Wilamowski, B.M., Hunter, D., Malinowski, A.: Solving parity-N problems with feedforward neural networks. In: Proceedings of the 2003 IEEE IJCNN, pp. 2546–2551. IEEE Press (2003)

12. Xu, Y.: An experimental study on speech enhancement based on deep neural networks. IEEE Signal Process. Lett. **21**(1), 65–68 (2011)

13. Gao, J., et al.: Modeling interestingness with deep neural networks. U.S. Patent No. 20,150,363,688, 17 December 2015

14. Erhan, D., et al.: Scalable object detection using deep neural networks. In: Proceedings of the IEEE Conference on Computer Vision and Pattern Recognition (2014)

15. Zhang, X., et al.: Improving deep neural network acoustic models using generalized maxout networks. In: 2014 IEEE International Conference on Acoustics, Speech and Signal Processing (ICASSP). IEEE (2014)

16. Montufar, G.F., et al.: On the number of linear regions of deep neural networks. In: Advances in Neural Information Processing Systems (2014)

17. Oquab, M., et al.: Learning and transferring mid-level image representations using convolutional neural networks. In: Proceedings of the IEEE Conference on Computer Vision and Pattern Recognition (2014)

18. Szegedy, C., Toshev, A., Erhan, D.: Deep neural networks for object detection. In: Advances in Neural Information Processing Systems (2013)

19. Wilamowski, B.M., Yu, H.: Neural network learning without backpropagation. IEEE Trans. Neural Netw. **21**(11), 1793–1803 (2010)

20. Wilamowski, B.M., Yu, H.: NNT - Neural Networks Trainer. http://www.eng.auburn.edu/wilambm/nnt/. Accessed 15 January 2016

21. Alvarez-Sanchez, J.R.: Injecting knowledge into the solution of the two-spiral problem. Neural Comput. Appl. **8**, 265–272 (1999)

22. Różycki, P., Kolbusz, J., Bartczak, T., Wilamowski, B.M.: Using parity-N problems as a way to compare abilities of shallow, very shallow and very deep architectures. In: Rutkowski, L., Korytkowski, M., Scherer, R., Tadeusiewicz, R., Zadeh, L.A., Zurada, J.M. (eds.) Artificial Intelligence and Soft Computing. LNCS, vol. 9119, pp. 112–122. Springer, Heidelberg (2015)

Training Neural Networks by Optimizing Random Subspaces of the Weight Space

Ewa Skubalska-Rafajłowicz[✉]

Department of Computer Engineering, Faculty of Electronics,
Wrocław University of Science and Technology, Wrocław, Poland
ewa.rafajlowicz@pwr.wroc.pl

Abstract. This paper describes a new approach to feed-forward neural networks learning based on a random choice of a set of neurons which are temporally active in the process of neural network weight adaptation. The rest of the network weights is locked out (frozen). In contrast to the "dropout" method introduced by Hinton et al. [15], the neurons (along with their connections) are not removed from the neural network during training, only their weights are not modified, i.e. stay constant. This means that in every epoch of training only the random part of the neural networks (a chosen set of neurons and its connections) adapts. Freezing of neurons suppresses overfitting and prevents drastic increment of weights during the learning process, since the overall structure of the neural networks does not change. In many cases the approach based on training only some parts of the neural network (subspaces of the weight space) shortens the time of training. Experimental results for medium size neural networks used for modeling regression are also provided.

Keywords: Neural network training · Stochastic gradient decent · Random subspace optimization · Over-fitting · Deep learning

1 Introduction

In this paper we propose a new strategy of optimization based methods of neural networks learning. In this strategy only a randomly chosen part of neurons along with their connections, i.e., in-going and out-going weights is adjusted in every epoch. The rest of the network remains temporarily unchanged. We will say that the neurons not chosen for training are temporarily frozen. Changing at once only a part of the decision variables is applied in many optimization (and other numerical) methods starting from the coordinate descent (Gauss-Seidel) strategy or alternating direction method of multipliers [6,19]. However, these methods are based on fixed partition of optimized variables. On the other hand, random selection of neurons, when only one unit is updated at a time is performed in asynchronous learning of the Hopfield network [13]. The approach proposed here introduces an additional level of variability to the process of neural network learning similarly as stochastic gradient does, enlarging exploration capability of

© Springer International Publishing Switzerland 2016
L. Rutkowski et al. (Eds.): ICAISC 2016, Part I, LNAI 9692, pp. 148–157, 2016.
DOI: 10.1007/978-3-319-39378-0_14

the neuron weight space. Furthermore, this strategy allows neurons to be more evenly exploited, since only some neurons, i.e., a randomly selected subspace of weights will be updated in the actual epoch of training. As a consequence, it will result in more evenly distributed network weights and better neural network generalization possibility [2].

From this point of view, one can see some similarities between freezing randomly chosen parts of the learned neural network that is proposed here and the Dropout method [15]. Dropout is a random procedure in which only randomly chosen neural network neurons (hidden units) are trained, whereas the rest of the neural net neurons and their incoming and outcoming connections are temporarily removed from the neural network during a small period time of training. Stochastic gradient decent (SGD) training is lately often combined with the dropout method [1,15,21]. It is known that dropout gives visible improvements on many benchmark data sets for speech and image classification [1,8,21,24]. Dropout is used for preventing a trained neural network from overfitting and it usually improves the performance of SGD training of deep neural nets [5,8,14,20,23].

Although the freezing strategy can be applied not only to learn feed-forward neural nets (FFNN), in this paper we restrict ourselves to FFNN architecture with one hidden layer of sigmoid neurons and a linear output neuron, i.e., the simplest structure which is known to be the universal approximator [7,16] and SGD learning algorithm. Nevertheless, it should be noted, that the freezing strategy can be used also with many other popular optimization based FFNN training methods, such as Levenberg-Marquardt, conjugate gradient methods, BFSG [10,12], among many others.

This paper is structured as follows. The next section describes the structure of our FFNN and the problems of training it in the context of overfitting in nonlinear regression neural network models training. Section 3 presents details of the learning strategy proposed here with randomly frozen neurons. Section 4 shows some simulation results which explain and confirm proposals and conclusions developed in the previous sections. In Sect. 5 we summarize the provided simulation results and indicate possible further developments.

2   Network Structure, Learning Optimal Weights and the Problem of Overfitting

We assume that the neural network is a usually used FFNN with one or more hidden layers. The output of the network is given by:

$$y_{net}(X) = \sum_{j=1}^{M} w_j^{(0)} \phi_j^{(0)}(X),$$
(1)

where $X \in R^n$ ($X = (x_1, \ldots, x_n)^T$) is an input vector, M is the number of neurons in the hidden layer (the last hidden layer), and $w_j^{(0)}$ is a weight joining j-th neuron to the output of the network. For the network with exactly one hidden layer we have

$$\phi_j^{(0)}(X) = f_{act}\left(\sum_{i=1}^{n} w_{ij}^{(-1)} x_i + b_j\right), \, j = 1, \ldots, M, \tag{2}$$

where f_{act} is an activation function. In general, for the network with $K > 1$ hidden layers,

$$\phi_j^{(0)}(X) = f_{act}\left(\sum_{i=1}^{M^{(-1)}} w_{ij}^{(-1)} \phi_i^{(-1)}(X) + b_j^{(-1)}\right), \, j = 1, \ldots, M, \tag{3}$$

where $\phi_j^{(0)}(X)$ is an ouput of j-th neuron in the last hidden layer and consecutively

$$\phi_j^{(-k)}(X) = f_{act}\left(\sum_{i=1}^{M^{(-k-1)}} w_{ij}^{(-k-1)} \phi_i^{(-k-1)}(X) + b_j^{(-k-1)}\right), \tag{4}$$

where $j = 1, \ldots, M^{(-k)}$, $k = 1, \ldots, K-1$, $M^{(-K)} = n$ and $\phi_i^{(-K)}(X) = x_i$, $i = 1, \ldots, n$ and $M^{(0)} = M$.

Usually the problem of neural network training is over-parameterized. It means that the number of data points in the learning sequence $(X_j, y_j), j = 1, \ldots, N$, i.e., N is often smaller than the number of the neural network parameters.

From the theoretical point of view, if $N \leq M$ and matrix

$$\chi = \begin{bmatrix} \phi_1^{(0)}(X_1), & \phi_2^{(0)}(X_1), & \ldots, & \phi_M^{(0)}(X_1) \\ \cdots & \cdots & \\ \phi_1^{(0)}(X_N), & \phi_2^{(0)}(X_N), & \ldots, & \phi_M^{(0)}(X_N) \end{bmatrix} \tag{5}$$

is a matrix of a full rank (i.e., has a rank N), then there exist weights in the last hidden layer $W^{(0)} = (w_1^{(0)}, \ldots, w_M^{(0)})^T$ such that neural networks (1–3) interpolates the learning sequence.

It is well known that the least mean square errors minimization leads in such a case to the partial solution $W^{(0)} = (\chi^T \chi)^{-1} \chi^T Y$, where $Y = (y_1, y_2, \ldots, y_N)^T$. A similar approach is often used when training small RBF networks [12]. Also, extreme learning machines [17] utilize such kinds of ideas. Unfortunately, matrix χ is usually badly conditioned and may lead to significant numerical errors. Although the rest of the neural network weights can be used for preconditioning, the perfect solutions are also undesirable, since interpolating or almost interpolating networks behave poorly on test data (other than training ones).

3   Description of the Algorithm

We will use for FFNN training the Stochastic Gradient Descent (SGD) algorithm with mini-batches of the size MB and additional momentum term [12,21,22].

Traditional SGD picks at random a small set of training examples (i.e., random mini-batch) at each iteration and updates all network weights on the basis of this set only. In random weight subspace optimization we will randomly select (uniformly, but without repetitions) L neurons among all M neurons forming the hidden layer. If the network contains more hidden layers the similar random selection will be repeated on every hidden layer. The weights of all in-going and out-going connections of the selected neurons will be updated. The rest of the neural networks weights will be unchanged. We say that this part of the networks is temporarily frozen. Here we assume that the same weight subspace selection will be used during the whole epoch. Furthermore, we fix that each epoch consists of N/MB iterations. As a consequence, every epoch consists of the same number of learning example presentations, independently of mini-batch size N.

Thus, in every epoch the set of neurons is randomly divided onto two complementary sets: neurons which remain frozen, i.e., are not updated in this epoch, and the rest of the neural network neurons which will be trained in this epoch. More precisely, only their in-going and out-going connections which are not connected to the frozen neurons will be updated.

$$w(t + 1) := w(t) + \Delta w(t + 1) \tag{6}$$

$$\Delta w(t + 1) := \mu \, \Delta w(t) - \alpha \, \nabla E_{MB}/MB, \tag{7}$$

where t is the number of iteration, and $w(t)$ symbolizes weight of any non-frozen network connection at time t. μ stands for the momentum coefficient and α is the learning rate. ∇E_{MB} denotes the stochastic gradient obtained with respect to a randomly selected mini-batch of training samples. It is possible to use momentum in two different ways - the global and the local. In the global momentum regime only $\Delta w(0) = 0$. In the local momentum regime Δw is set to zero at the beginning of each epoch. The last approach allows us to additionally stabilize training.

It may be useful to start with a full neuron set training (without frozen neurons), however it was not necessary in our experiments. It should be noted that in general, stochastic gradient ∇E_{MB} is computed for the whole network. In contrary, the number of the weight updates is strongly reduced depending only on L.

3.1 Learning Rate and Other Training Parameters

We have used a small constant learning rate α during all the training. We established the learning rate value on the basis of experiments. Namely, we have used the learning rate that gives stable convergence in the 10 initial epochs.

3.2 Some Comments About Dropout

The dropout method can be implemented in different ways (see [8, 11, 15, 21, 25]) and is usually used for classification (logistic regression). We have applied this method for comparison reasons during training FFNN for regression. It was important to have similar circumstances when we are freezing some neurons instead of dropping them out. Thus, we have chosen the dropout strategy without any regularization, but accompanied by a larger momentum term, i.e., $\mu = 0.99$ (according to indications given in [21]). To stabilize the training process we have to reset the momentum term at the beginning of every epoch. Otherwise the learning rate should be much smaller than that used by the freezing approach. At test time one single neural network without dropout was used. The outgoing weights of every neuron were scaled down according to the probability $1 - p$, where p is a probability that a given neuron will be temporarily removed from the network. In our experiments $p = 0.5$.

4   Numerical Experiments Results

We have performed SGD training of neural networks with one hidden layer of 100 neurons as a model of the following regression problem.

$$Y = f(X_1, X_2) + \varepsilon = \exp\left[-5X_1 + 1\right] + 0.5\exp\left[-0.25(11X_2 - 2)^2\right] + \varepsilon, \quad (8)$$

where $X_1, X_2 \in [0,1]$ are independent uniformly distributed random variables and ε is a Gaussian white noise with variance $\sigma^2 = 0.01$, i.e., $\varepsilon \sim \mathcal{N}(0, 0.1)$. The training sequence consists of 100 independent and identically distributed (i.i.d.) data points. Similarly, the testing set contains also a hundred i.i.d. elements.

We have used stochastic gradient descent with 5 and 10 -sized mini-batches and a traditional mean squared error as a criterion function. Furthermore, apart from MSE for the learning and the testing set also a mean absolute error (MAE) was also monitored. It is easy to check that if we know the true regression function $f(X_1, X_2)$, the expected value of MAE is

$$E\{|Y - f(X_1, X_2)|\} \approx 0.799 \quad (9)$$

and the expected value of MSE is 0.01.

Although it seems that regression model (8) is relatively easy to approximate by a small size FFNN with one hidden layer, in our learning experiments we have have used a neural network equipped with 100 neurons in its hidden layer.

The initial weights are taken uniformly from $[0, 1]$ interval. All experiments shown in Tables 1 and 2 were performed, starting from the same initial point. The columns labeled by (DR 50) contain errors obtained for droput of 50 neurons. Training all 100 neurons was performed without freezing. Monte Carlo errors given in these Tables were computed on the basis of the 100000 random samples. Tables 1 and 2 contain final errors obtained after 5000 epochs of training. The training process details from the first 1000 epochs are depicted in Fig. 1.

The theoretical analysis and many experiments [3,4,9,20] indicate, that that local minima are not a problem for larger size FFNN. Instead of local minima, an extremely large number of saddle points where the gradient is zero is observed. So, regardless of the initial weights, the neural network nearly always

Table 1. Training and testing errors for mini-batch of size 5 after 5000 epochs of training with local momentum $\mu = 0.9$ (0.99 for dropout) and constant learning rate $\alpha = 0.05$

Number of trained neurons	100	10	20	30	40	50	DR 50
Training errors							
MAE_{train}	0.093	0.091	0.091	0.083	0.088	0.091	0.108
MSE_{train}	0.013	0.014	0.013	0.010	0.012	0.013	0.019
Testing errors							
MAE_{test}	0.120	0.128	0.121	0.103	0.117	0.120	0.139
MSE_{test}	0.023	0.025	0.023	0.016	0.021	0.023	0.030
Monte Carlo errors							
MAE_{MC}	0.121	0.123	0.121	0.106	0.112	0.117	0.135
MSE_{MC}	0.023	0.024	0.024	0.018	0.20	0.022	0.030

arrives at solutions of very similar quality, especially if the size of the network is large. Thus, we have performed some additional experiments: for the full network learned without freezing and for the network with $L = 30$, i.e., when 70 neurons from one hundred were frozen in every epoch. In all the cases the size of mini-batch was equal to 5 and each experiment was repeated five times. The averaged results of training after 5000 epochs are given in Table 3. One can see, that the mean errors are very close to that presented in Table 1. According to these facts we restrict further experiments to the one common starting point. Tables 4 and 5 provide the training and testing errors after 10000 epochs of training for mini-batches of size 5 and 10, respectively.

Table 2. Training and testing errors for mini-batch of size 10 after 5000 epochs of training with local momentum $\mu = 0.9$ (0.99 for dropout) and the constant learning rate $\alpha = 0.05$

Number of trained neurons	100	10	20	30	40	50	DR 50
Training errors							
MAE_{train}	0.098	0.100	0.096	0.089	0.089	0.092	0.118
MSE_{train}	0.014	0.015	0.014	0.013	0.012	0.013	0.023
Testing errors							
MAE_{test}	0.123	0.127	0.122	0.113	0.117	0.120	0.149
MSE_{test}	0.024	0.026	0.025	0.021	0.022	0.023	0.035
Monte Carlo errors							
MAE_{MC}	0.118	0.127	0.117	0.107	0.113	0.117	0.146
MSE_{MC}	0.028	0.026	0.022	0.018	0.021	0.022	0.036

Table 3. Averaged training and testing errors for mini-batch of size 5 after 5000 epochs of training with local momentum $\mu = 0.9$ and the constant learning rate $\alpha = 0.05$

Number of trained neurons	MAE training	MSE training	MAE testing	MSE testing
100	0.094	0.014	0.125	0.025
30	0.084	0.011	0.106	0.017

Table 4. Training and testing errors for mini-batch of size 5 after 10000 epochs of training with local momentum $\mu = 0.9$ and the constant learning rate $\alpha = 0.05$

Number of trained neurons	100	10	30	DR 50
Training errors				
MAE_{train}	0.093	0.090	0.089	0.103
MSE_{train}	0.013	0.012	0.012	0.017
Testing errors				
MAE_{test}	0.121	0.121	0.114	0.134
MSE_{test}	0.023	0.024	0.020	0.027
Monte Carlo errors				
MAE_{MC}	0.116	0.115	0.107	0.131
MSE_{MC}	0.022	0.022	0.019	0.028

Table 5. Training and testing errors for mini-batch of size 10 after 10000 epochs of training with local momentum $\mu = 0.9$ (0.99 for dropout) and the constant learning rate $\alpha = 0.05$

Number of trained neurons	100	10	50	DR 50
Training errors				
MAE_{train}	0.096	0.097	0.092	0.103
MSE_{train}	0.013	0.015	0.013	0.018
Testing errors				
MAE_{test}	0.121	0.127	0.120	0.136
MSE_{test}	0.023	0.026	0.023	0.029
Monte Carlo errors				
MAE_{MC}	0.116	0.127	0.115	0.128
MSE_{MC}	0.022	0.026	0.021	0.027

It can be once more observed that SGD is a very slowly convergent method, especially for regression problems. The best results we have obtained for $L = 30$ and a very long training time. It was $MSE_{learn} = 0.0084$, $MAE_{learn} = 0.074$ for the learning sequence and $MSE_{test} = 0.0107$, $MAE_{test} = 0.085$ for testing. The number of epochs was about 23500 for local momentum and 13500 for global momentum. Validity of the solution was confirmed by Monte Carlo simulations

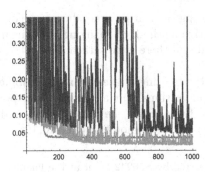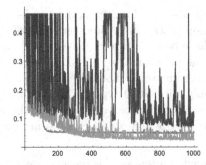

Fig. 1. Results of first 1000 epochs of the training. Left panel: MSE for the learning set. Right panel: MSE for the testing set. Blue – traditional FFNN, yellow – the network with freezing $L = 30$, green – dropout for 50 neurons left. (Color figure online)

using 100000 random observations, namely $MSE_{MC} = 0.011$ and $MAE_{MC} = 0.084$. It was a slightly better result than that obtained for the testing set.

5   Discussion and Conclusions

In this paper we have presented a new neural network training strategy, when in every epoch of training only a randomly chosen and structurally connected network weights are updated. The learning algorithm temporarily keeps constant the rest of the neuron weights. We say that these weights are frozen. We have shown experimentally, that for SGD method of learning this approach can provide better and faster solutions than the classical strategy of the whole network training. It occurred that the proposed method provides a very good generalization and – in contrast to the dropout – it is much more stable and it does not need a regularization.

We have decided to use a testing set of the same size as the learning set. Both of them were relatively small, i.e., the number of samples N was equal to the number of neurons in the hidden layer. This assumption allows us to trustworthy control of the training process. Errors obtained by the Monte Carlo method confirm credibility of the solutions.

It should be noted that in our example the smaller size mini-batches accelerate the training. Furthermore, too large learning rates, even if they do not destabilize the training process, result in larger finally obtainable values of MSE_{train} and MSE_{test}.

In our experiments (without any regularization) freezing gave better results than the dropout method. Nevertheless, further comparisons are needed.

The performed experiments suggest that over-parametrized (with respect to the number of data samples) FFNN models can be learned efficiently without over-fitting symptoms. We claim that the random subspace selection is efficient, although slow in combination with SGD, for large scale multivariate optimization problem. From the stochastic optimization point of view it is important to provide a safe and trusty method of decreasing the learning rate during the optimization process [18]. However some adaptive methods of changing the learning rate have been known for decades [12], and still there is no satisfactory solution from the point of view of SGD.

Furthermore, it should be noted, that the freezing strategy can be combined not only with SGD type FFNN training algorithms, but also with other popular optimization based training methods, for example, Levenberg-Marquardt, conjugate gradient, quasi-Newton methods and their modifications [10,12].

Acknowledgments. This research was supported by $S50242$ grant at the Faculty of Electronics, Wrocław University of Science and Technology.

References

1. Ba, J., Frey, B.: Adaptive dropout for training deep neural networks. In: Advances in Neural Information Processing Systems (NIPS), pp. 3084–3092 (2013)
2. Bartlett, P.L.: The sample complexity of pattern classification with neural networks: the size of the weights is more important than the size of the network. IEEE Trans. Inf. Theor. **4**(2), 525–536 (1998)
3. Baldi, P., Hornik, K.: Learning from examples without local minima. Neural Netw. **2**(1), 53–58 (1989)
4. Choromanska, A., Henaff, M., Mathieu, M., Arous, G.B., LeCun, Y.: The loss surface of multilayer networks. In: Proceedings of the Conference on AI and Statistics (2014). http://arxiv.org/abs/1412.0233
5. Bengio, Y.: Learning deep architectures for AI. Found. Trends Mach. Learn. **2**(1), 1–127 (2009)
6. Boyd, S., Parikh, N., Chu, E., Peleato, B., Eckstein, J.: Distributed optimization and statistical learning via the alternating direction method of multipliers. Found. Trends Mach. Learn. **3**(1), 1–122 (2011)
7. Cybenko, G.: Approximation by superpositions of a sigmoidal function. Math. Control, Signals Syst. **2**(4), 303–314 (1989)
8. Dahl, G.E., Sainath, T.N., Hinton, G.E.: Improving deep neural networks for LVCSR using rectified linear units and dropout. In: IEEE International Conference on Acoustic Speech and Signal Processing (ICASSP 2013), Vancouver (2013)
9. Dauphin, Y., Pascanu, R., Gulcehre, C., Cho, K.: Identifying and attacking the saddle point problem in highdimensional non-convex optimization. In: Proceedings of Advances in Neural Information Processing Systems, vol. 27, pp. 2933–2941 (2014)
10. Fine, T.: Feedforward Neural Network Methodology. Statistics for Engineering and Information Science. Springer, New York, Inc (1999)
11. Goodfellow, I.J., Warde-Farley, D., Mirza, M., Courville, A., Bengio, Y.: Maxout networks. In: Proceedings of the 30th International Conference on Machine Learning, pp. 1319–1327. ACM (2013)
12. Haykin, S.: Neural Networks: A Comprehensive Foundation, 2nd edn. Prentice Hall PTR, Upper Saddle River (1998)
13. Hertz, J., Krogh, A., Palmer, R.G.: Introduction to the Theory of Neural Computation. Addison-Wesley, Redwood City (1991)

14. Hinton, G.E., Osindero, S., Teh, Y.: A fast learning algorithm for deep belief nets. Neural Comput. **18**, 1527–1554 (2006)
15. Hinton, G.E., Srivastava, N., Krizhevsky, A., Sutskever, I., Salakhutdinov, R.R.: Improving neural networks by preventing co-adaptation of feature detectors (2012). http://arxiv.org/abs/1207.0580
16. Hornik, K.: Approximation capabilities of multilayer feedforward networks. Neural Netw. **4**, 251–257 (1991)
17. Huang, G.-B., Zhu, Q.-Y., Siew, C.-K.: Extreme learning machine: theory and applications. Neurocomputing **70**(1), 489–501 (2006)
18. Kushner, H., Yin, G.: Stochastic Approximation and Recursive Algorithms and Applications, II edn. Springer-Verlag, New York, Inc (2003)
19. Nocedal, J., Wright, S.J.: Numerical Optimization, 2nd edn. Springer, New York (2006)
20. LeCun, Y., Bengio, Y., Hinton, G.: Deep learning (Review). Nature **521**, 436–444 (2015)
21. Srivastava, N., Hinton, G., Krizhevsky, A., Sutskever, I., Salakhutdinov, R.: Dropout: a simple way to prevent neural networks from overfitting. J. Mach. Learn. Res. **15**, 1929–1958 (2014)
22. Sutskever, I., Martens, J., Dahl, G., Hinton, G.: On the importance of initialization and momentum in deep learning. In: Proceedings of the 30th International Conference on Machine Learning, Atlanta, Georgia, USA (2013)
23. Schmidhuber, J.: Deep Learning and Neural Networks: An Overview. arXiv:1404.7828 (2014)
24. Qiu, X., Zhang, L., Ren, Y., Suganthan, P., Amaratunga, G.: Ensemble deep learning for regression and time series forecasting. 2014 IEEE Symposium on Computational Intelligence in Ensemble Learning (CIEL), pp. 1–6 (2014). doi:10.1109/CIEL.2014.7015739
25. Wang, S.I., Manning, C.D.: Fast dropout training. In: Proceedings of the 30th International Conference on Machine Learning, Atlanta, Georgia, USA (2013)

Single Layer Feedforward Networks Construction Based on Orthogonal Least Square and Particle Swarm Optimization

Xing Wu[1], Pawel Rozycki[2(✉)], and Bogdan M. Wilamowski[1]

[1] Auburn University, Auburn, AL 36849-5201, USA
xzw0015@tigermail.auburn.edu, wilambm@auburn.edu
[2] University of Information Technology and Management in Rzeszow,
Sucharskiego 2, 35-225 Rzeszow, Poland
prozycki@wsiz.rzeszow.pl

Abstract. According to the simplicity and universal approximation capability, single layer feedforward networks (SLFN) are widely used in classification and regression problems. The paper presents a new OLS-PSO constructive algorithm based on Orthogonal Least Square (OLS) method and Particle Swarm Optimization (PSO) algorithm. Instead of evaluating the orthogonal components of each neuron as the conventional OLS method, a new recursive formulation is derived. Then based on the new evaluation of each neuron's contribution, the PSO algorithm is used to seek the optimal parameters of the new neuron in continuous space. The proposed algorithm is experimented on some practical regression problems and compared with other constructive algorithms. Results show that proposed OLS-PSO algorithm could achieve a compact SLFN with good generalization ability.

Keywords: Single Layer Feedforward Networks (SLFN) · Constructive algorithm · Orthogonal Least Square (OLS) · Particle Swarm Optimization (PSO)

1 Introduction

Because of the universal approximation capability [1], single layer feedforward network (SLFN) became a popular model for classification and regression problems. Due to its simple structure and good supervised learning performance, SLFNs are widely used in different application fields, such as signal processing, time-series prediction and control, etc [2,3].

The architecture of SLFN consists of three layers: an input layer, a hidden layer with nonlinear activation function and an output summator. Popular investigated activation functions for hidden layer include sigmoid function and Radial Basis Function (RBF).

This work was partially supported by the National Science Centre, Cracow, Poland under Grant No. 2013/11/B/ST6/01337.

L. Rutkowski et al. (Eds.): ICAISC 2016, Part I, LNAI 9692, pp. 158–169, 2016.
DOI: 10.1007/978-3-319-39378-0_15

The tunable parameters of the SLFN include the hidden parameters and the output weights that connecting the hidden nodes to the output summator. For SLFN with sigmoid hidden layer, hidden parameters are input weights (including bias); for SLFN with RBF hidden layer, hidden parameters are center and width of each hidden node.

The SLFN learning consists two main tasks: determining the optimal network size and searching the optimal parameters. Though many gradient based algorithms and evolutionary methods for fixed size SLFN training worked well [15,20,21], it is still difficult to determine the optimal network size. In order to extend these algorithms to construction, trial and error approach is popularly used, which leads to heavy computation.

To simplify the construction process, different methods were investigated to involve the alteration of the network size into the parameters tuning process. There are two main strategies to alter the SLFN architecture: constructive strategy and pruning strategy [4]. The constructive algorithms start from a small SLFN and then add additional hidden neurons until satisfactory solution is found. The pruning algorithms do it in the opposite way, that start with a large SLFN and then remove the least important neurons. As shown by T.Y. Kwok and D.Y. Yeung [5], the constructive algorithms are more computationally economical and likely to find smaller-size solutions than pruning algorithms. In this paper, we will focus on the constructive algorithm.

Another important issue for SLFN construction is the parameters tuning strategy after altering the network structure. For constructive algorithms, it means how to tune the parameters after adding new hidden neurons. Since tuning all the parameters each time will slow down the computational efficiency, many researchers only tune part of the parameters and freeze the rest [4–8].

In this paper, a new constructive algorithm based on Orthogonal Least Square (OLS) and Particle Swarm Optimization (PSO) is proposed for SLFN learning. Each time adding a new neuron, freeze previous hidden parameters, a reformulated OLS is derived to update the least square optimal solution of the output weights recursively. The hidden parameters of the new added neuron are tuned with PSO algorithm by using the contribution of the hidden neuron defined in the reformulated OLS algorithm.

The rest of the paper is organized as following. In Sect. 2, conventional OLS algorithm is reformulated into a recursive way. Section 3 introduces PSO algorithm for optimization of the hidden parameters of the new neuron. In Sect. 4, several popular benchmarks are given to validate the effectiveness of the proposed OLS-PSO algorithm. Experiment results are compared with the other constructive algorithms. Section 5 gives the conclusion.

2   Reformulation of OLS Algorithm

The Orthogonal Least Square (OLS) algorithm was originally proposed for model selection [9]. Then it is popular used in RBF networks training for center selection [10,11]. While the conventional OLS algorithm mainly focused on the selection and only determined the least square solutions in the last step, in this section, a new formulation of OLS algorithm is derived that could update all the parameters recursively, which will be more suitable for dynamic construction of SLFN.

The conventional OLS algorithm is a stepwise forward selection method. In the SLFN construction scheme, a candidate parameters pool is initially generated for the $(K+1)_{th}$ neuron selection,

$$W_{K+1}^{pool} = \{\mathbf{w}_{K+1}^{(1)}, \mathbf{w}_{K+1}^{(2)}, ..., \mathbf{w}_{K+1}^{(N)}\} \tag{1}$$

whose corresponding outputs are,

$$H_{K+1}^{pool} = \{\mathbf{h}_{K+1}^{(1)}, \mathbf{h}_{K+1}^{(2)}, ..., \mathbf{h}_{K+1}^{(N)}\} \tag{2}$$

The core idea of the OLS algorithm is to convert each component of the model (each column of $\mathbf{H}_K$) into a set of orthogonal basis vectors by using QR decomposition.

$$\mathbf{H}_K = \mathbf{O}_K \mathbf{\Delta}_K \tag{3}$$

in which, $\mathbf{\Delta}_K$ is a $(K+1) \times (K+1)$ upper triangle matrix with 1s on the diagonal.

$$\mathbf{\Delta}_K = \begin{bmatrix} 1 & a_{01} & a_{02} & \cdots & a_{0K} \\ 0 & 1 & a_{12} & \cdots & a_{1K} \\ 0 & 0 & \ddots & \ddots & \vdots \\ \vdots & \ddots & \ddots & 1 & a_{K-1K} \\ 0 & \cdots & \cdots & 0 & 1 \end{bmatrix}$$

$\mathbf{O}_K$ is an $N \times (K+1)$ matrix with orthogonal columns ($\mathbf{o}_0$ is for bias),

$$\mathbf{O}_K = [\mathbf{o}_0, \mathbf{o}_1, ..., \mathbf{o}_K] \qquad \mathbf{o}_i \mathbf{o}_j = 0, \quad \text{for all} \quad i \neq j \tag{4}$$

With the storage of above decomposition for previous SLFN, for each candidate in the pool (2), Gram-Schmidt process is carried out to expand $\mathbf{O}_K$, $\mathbf{\Delta}_K$ to $\mathbf{O}_{K+1}$, $\mathbf{\Delta}_{K+1}$ by simply adding a new column. The detail of the process is described as below,

For i from 1 to N (every candidate in the pool),

1. Expanding new column to $\mathbf{\Delta}_K$.

For j from 0 to K, $a_{jK+1}^{(i)} = \dfrac{\mathbf{o}_j^T \mathbf{h}_{K+1}^{(i)}}{\mathbf{o}_j^T \mathbf{o}_j}$

2. Expanding new column to $\mathbf{O}_K$.
$\mathbf{o}_{K+1}^{(i)} = \mathbf{h}_{K+1}^{(i)} - \sum_{j=0}^{K} a_{jK+1}^{(i)} \mathbf{o}_j$

The advantage of the OLS algorithm is that by converting each component into an orthogonal vector, the cost function (SSE) of SLFN with K hidden neurons can be presented as,

$$C = \mathbf{y}^T \mathbf{y} - \sum_{j=0}^{K} \frac{(\mathbf{o}_j^T \mathbf{y})^2}{\mathbf{o}_j^T \mathbf{o}_j} \tag{5}$$

which means, every hidden neuron's contribution to the total error reduction can be described independent to each other.

As a result, for the $(K + 1)_{th}$ neuron, one just select the candidate with the biggest contribution,

$$\arg \max_i \{[err]_{K+1}^{(i)} = \frac{(\mathbf{o}_{K+1}^{(i)}{}^T \mathbf{y})^2}{\mathbf{o}_{K+1}^{(i)}{}^T \mathbf{o}_{K+1}^{(i)}}\} \tag{6}$$

While one finished the selection process (assume K_m neurons are selected), the least square solutions of output weights can be simply achieved by solving the following equation,

$$\mathbf{\Delta}_{K_m} \theta = \mathbf{g}_{K_m} \tag{7}$$

in which,

$$\mathbf{g}_{K_m} = [\frac{\mathbf{o}_1^T \mathbf{y}}{\mathbf{o}_1^T \mathbf{o}_1}, \frac{\mathbf{o}_2^T \mathbf{y}}{\mathbf{o}_2^T \mathbf{o}_2}, ..., \frac{\mathbf{o}_{K_m}^T \mathbf{y}}{\mathbf{o}_{K_m}^T \mathbf{o}_{K_m}}]^T \tag{8}$$

2.1 Reformulated OLS Algorithm

In this section, the conventional OLS algorithm is reformulated in a recursive way that is more suitable for dynamic construction.

Given a SLFN with K hidden neurons, whose hidden matrix is $\mathbf{H}_K$. While $\mathbf{H}_K^T \mathbf{H}_K$ is non-singular, the global optimal solution for the output weights θ_K can be simply computed as,

$$\hat{\theta}_K = \mathbf{H}_K^\dagger \mathbf{y} \tag{9}$$

where $\mathbf{H}_K^\dagger$ is the Moore-Penrose generalized inverse [12] of the hidden matrix $\mathbf{H}_K$.

$$\mathbf{H}_K^\dagger = (\mathbf{H}_K^T \mathbf{H}_K)^{-1} \mathbf{H}_K^T \tag{10}$$

For a guess of the $(K+1)_{th}$ hidden neuron with hidden parameters $\mathbf{w}_{K+1}^{(i)}$ and outputs $\mathbf{h}_{K+1}^{(i)}$, do a temporary linear regression to the target $\mathbf{h}_{K+1}^{(i)}$ with current SLFN (with K hidden neurons). Denote the optimal solution and residual error of this regression as $\hat{\theta}_t^{(i)}$ and $\mathbf{e}_t^{(i)}$.

$$\hat{\theta}_t^{(i)} = \mathbf{H}_K^\dagger \mathbf{h}_{K+1}^{(i)} \tag{11}$$

$$\mathbf{e}_t^{(i)} = \mathbf{h}_{K+1}^{(i)} - \mathbf{H}_K \hat{\theta}_t^{(i)} \tag{12}$$

Denote the errors for current SLFN as $\mathbf{e}_K = \mathbf{y} - \tilde{\mathbf{y}}_K$, and the new errors after adding $(K + 1)_{th}$ neuron as $\mathbf{e}_{K+1}$. Then we have the following conclusions. The contribution of this guess $(\mathbf{w}_{K+1}^{(i)})$ can be described as,

$$[err]_{K+1}^{(i)} = \frac{(\mathbf{h}_{K+1}^{(i)}{}^T \mathbf{e}_K)^2}{\mathbf{h}_{K+1}^{(i)}{}^T \mathbf{e}_t^{(i)}} \tag{13}$$

which can replace (6) to evaluate the error reduction contribution of the new neuron with any possible hidden parameters.

While one find the optimal neuron with maximum contribution, denote its outputs are $\mathbf{h}_{K+1}$, the corresponding variables in the temporary regression are $\boldsymbol{\theta}_t$ and $\mathbf{e}_t$. Then the parameters can be updated recursively as following,

$$
\mathbf{H}^\dagger_{K+1} =
\begin{bmatrix}
\mathbf{H}^\dagger_K - \dfrac{\hat{\boldsymbol{\theta}}_t \mathbf{e}_t^T}{\mathbf{h}_{K+1}^T \mathbf{e}_t} \\
\dfrac{\mathbf{e}_t^T}{\mathbf{h}_{K+1}^T \mathbf{e}_t}
\end{bmatrix}
\tag{14}
$$

$$
\hat{\boldsymbol{\theta}}_{K+1} =
\begin{bmatrix}
\hat{\boldsymbol{\theta}}_K - \dfrac{\mathbf{h}_{K+1}^T \mathbf{e}_K}{\mathbf{h}_{K+1}^T \mathbf{e}_t} \hat{\boldsymbol{\theta}}_t \\
\dfrac{\mathbf{h}_{K+1}^T \mathbf{e}_K}{\mathbf{h}_{K+1}^T \mathbf{e}_t}
\end{bmatrix}
\tag{15}
$$

$$
\mathbf{e}_{K+1} = \mathbf{e}_K - \dfrac{\mathbf{h}_{K+1}^T \mathbf{e}_K}{\mathbf{h}_{K+1}^T \mathbf{e}_t} \mathbf{e}_t
\tag{16}
$$

2.2   Relation to Conventional OLS Algorithm

While the conventional OLS algorithm used the orthogonal vectors as space basis vectors, each new neuron was decomposed as a representation of the previous basis vectors and a new orthogonal vector,

$$
\mathbf{h}_{K+1} = \sum_{j=0}^{K} a_{jK+1} \mathbf{o}_j + \mathbf{o}_{K+1}
\tag{17}
$$

Instead, the reformulated OLS algorithm regarded the orthogonal vectors as latent variables, and used the previous components as basis vectors directly.

$$
\mathbf{h}_{K+1} = \sum_{j=0}^{K} \theta_{t,j} \mathbf{h}_j + \mathbf{e}_t
\tag{18}
$$

in which, $\theta_{t,j}$ is the j_{th} element of $\boldsymbol{\theta}_t$.

Since $\{\mathbf{o}_0, \mathbf{o}_1, ..., \mathbf{o}_K\}$ are the orthogonal basis vectors of $\{1, \mathbf{h}_1, ..., \mathbf{h}_K\}$, we can conclude that the residual error of the temporary regression ($\mathbf{e}_t$) in (18) is actually the decomposed orthogonal vector of the new neuron ($\mathbf{o}_{K+1}$) in (17).

By reformulated the conventional OLS algorithm, all the parameters could be updated recursively. Therefore, the proposed reformulated OLS algorithm is more suitable for dynamic construction of SLFN.

3   Particle Swarm Optimization

The conventional OLS algorithm mainly worked as a selection method, which used the error reduction contribution criterion to pick the best component from a candidate pool. However, the parameters of the SLFN are not necessary limit in the discrete space, like the candidate pool. In this paper, the hidden parameters of the new added neuron are optimized in the continuous space to maximize the new derived contribution function (13). Considering the multimodal characteristic and the existence of the plateaus, in this paper, instead of the gradient based methods, Particle Swarm Optimization (PSO) is used to tune the new added neuron's hidden parameters.

The PSO algorithm is a population based stochastic optimization technique developed by Kennedy and Eberhart [13] in 1995, inspired by social behavior of bird flocking and fish schooling. Unlike genetic algorithm (GA), the PSO algorithm doesn't have the complicated operators, such as crossover and mutation [14], therefore it has less parameters to set. Due to the efficiency and simplicity, PSO is popular used for neural networks learning alternative to back propagation (BP) algorithm [15–17].

The PSO algorithm optimizes an objective function by having a population of candidate solutions, called particles, which are initialized randomly in the searching space. Each particle has a position and velocity. These particles are moved around the searching space to seek the global optima by updating their positions and velocities iteratively according to simple formula. The movement of each particle is influenced by its individual best known position (**pbest**) and the best known position in the swarm (**gbest**). Assume a population with N particles, for the i_{th} particle, denote its position and velocity are $\mathbf{x}^{(i)}, \mathbf{v}^{(i)} \in R^m$. Then each dimension of $\mathbf{x}^{(i)}$ and $\mathbf{v}^{(i)}$ are updated as,

$$v_j^{(i)} = c_0 \times v_j^{(i)} + c_1 \times rand() \times (pbest_j^{(i)} - x_j^{(i)}) + c_2 \times rand() \times (gbest_j - x_j^{(i)}) \quad (19)$$

$$w_j^{(i)} = w_j^{(i)} + v_j^{(i)} \quad (20)$$

in which, $x_j^{(i)}, v_j^{(i)}$ are the j_{th} dimension of $\mathbf{x}^{(i)}$ and $\mathbf{v}^{(i)}$ $(j = 1, 2, ..., D)$. c_1, c_2 are the acceleration constants with positive values set by user. $rand()$ is randomly generated number in the range [0,1]. $pbest_j^{(i)}$ is the j_{th} dimension of the best known position (**pbest**$^{(i)}$) in the i_{th} particle's searching history. $gbest_j$ is the j_{th} dimension of the best known position (**gbest**) in the entire swarm. c_0 is called inertia weight introduced by Shi and Eberhart [18], which plays a key role in balancing the exploration and exploitation process of the swarm. Many researches have been done on the parameters setting of the PSO algorithm [22]. In this paper, we will use the suggested setting in [22]: $c_1 = c_2 = 2$; a linearly decreasing inertia weight c_0 starts at 0.9 and ends at 0.4. The extensive experiments have been done to verify the appropriateness of c_0, c_1 and c_2 and the recommended values gave the best result.

It has been shown that the neural networks with smaller size tend to produce smoother functions, which could generalize better [19]. Inspired by this, we have a bound for the searching space of those hidden parameters. Assume the maximum amplitude of the input data is $r > 0$, which means the input range $\subseteq [-r, r]$. Then the hidden parameters of each neuron is bounded as 10 times of this range, which is $[-10r, 10r]$. In particular for the width σ of the RBF node, we bounded it as $\sigma \in (0, 10r]$. The velocity corresponding to each parameter is bounded in the same range $[10r, 10r]$ to constrain the exploration of the swarm. As a result, in each iteration as the PSO proceeds, after the velocity is updated with (19), it is determined as,

$$
v_j^{(i)} = \begin{cases} -10r & \text{if } v_j^{(i)} \leq -10r \\ v_j^{(i)} & \text{if } -10r < v_j^{(i)} < 10r \\ 10r & \text{if } v_j^{(i)} \geq 10r \end{cases} \tag{21}
$$

after the parameters are updated with (20), for all the parameters of sigmoid SLFN and centers of RBF network, they are determined as,

$$
x_j^{(i)} = \begin{cases} -10r & \text{if } x_j^{(i)} \leq -10r \\ x_j^{(i)} & \text{if } -10r < x_j^{(i)} < 10r \\ 10r & \text{if } x_j^{(i)} \geq 10r \end{cases} \tag{22}
$$

for the width of RBF network, they are determined as,

$$
x_j^{(i)} = \begin{cases} \epsilon & \text{if } x_j^{(i)} \leq \epsilon \\ x_j^{(i)} & \text{if } \epsilon < x_j^{(i)} < 10r \\ 10r & \text{if } x_j^{(i)} \geq 10r \end{cases} \tag{23}
$$

in which, ϵ is a small positive value set by user.

3.1   Process Description

The PSO procedure in the proposed OLS-PSO algorithm is shown in Fig. 1. Each time after this procedure, the optimal parameters of the new hidden neuron is stored in **gbest**. The variables $\hat{\theta}_t$, e_t corresponding to this best particle will be reused for the update of $\mathbf{H}_{K+1}^{\dagger}$, $\hat{\theta}_{K+1}$ and e_{K+1} according to (14–16). The construction process will continue until the desired error arrives, or the number of hidden neurons arrives the maximum preset number, or the greatest contribution of the new neuron is smaller than some threshold set by user, which means the construction saturates.

4   Experiments

In this section, the proposed OLS-PSO algorithm is experimented on several 2-D function approximation benchmarks. The experiment results are compared with other constructive algorithms introduced in Sect. 1.

All the experiments are carried out on Windows 7 Enterprise 64-bit operating system, Intel®Core™2 Quad CPU Q8400 2.67 GHz process, 4.00 GB RAM, MATLAB R2012a platform.

1: Assume current SLFN has K hidden neurons, whose hidden matrix is $\mathbf{H}_K$, the Moore-Penrose generalized inverse of the hidden matrix is $\mathbf{H}_K^\dagger$, the optimal output weights of current SLFN is $\hat{\boldsymbol{\theta}}_K$, the error is $\mathbf{e}_K$. One is trying to add the $(K+1)_{th}$ hidden neuron.

2: Initialize a population of N particles with random positions $\{\mathbf{x}_{K+1}^{(1)}, \mathbf{x}_{K+1}^{(2)}, ..., \mathbf{x}_{K+1}^{(N)}\}$ and random velocities $\{\mathbf{v}_{K+1}^{(1)}, \mathbf{v}_{K+1}^{(2)}, ..., \mathbf{v}_{K+1}^{(N)}\}$. Each position is initialized as $\mathbf{pbest}^{(i)}$, whose fitness calculated by (11-13) is f_i. Pick the maximum fitness as f_g and the corresponding particle position as $\mathbf{gbest}$.

3: **for** $t \leftarrow 1$ to T **do**   ▷ Iteration number

4:    **for** $i \leftarrow 1$ to N **do**   ▷ Each particle

5:       **for** $j \leftarrow 1$ to D **do**   ▷ Each dimension

6:          update each velocity with (19)(21)

7:          udpate each parameter with (20)(22)(23)

8:       **end for**

9:       Calculate fitness $[err]_{K+1}^{(i)}$ of current parameters using (11-13)

10:       **if** $[err]_{K+1}^{(i)} > f_i$ **then**

11:          $\mathbf{pbest}^{(i)} \leftarrow \mathbf{x}_{K+1}^{(i)}$

12:          $f_i \leftarrow [err]_{K+1}^{(i)}$

13:       **end if**

14:       **if** $[err]_{K+1}^{(i)} > f_g$ **then**

15:          $\mathbf{gbest} \leftarrow \mathbf{x}_{K+1}^{(i)}$

16:          Store $\hat{\boldsymbol{\theta}}_t$ and $\mathbf{e}_t$

17:          $f_g \leftarrow [err]_{K+1}^{(i)}$

18:       **end if**

19:    **end for**

20: **end for**

Fig. 1. Tuning hidden parameters with PSO

4.1 2-D Function Approximation

In this experiment, the proposed OLS-PSO algorithm is compared with the algorithms by T.Y. Kwok and D.Y. Yeung in [4] on eight 2-dimensional benchmarks. In [4], several objective functions had been proposed to optimize the hidden parameters of each new neuron and quickprop [23] was used for the optimization task. Mesh plots of these benchmark functions are shown in Fig. 2.

The SLFNs with sigmoid activation function are constructed to approximate the above eight functions. For each function, both noiseless and noisy training sets are generated for the SLFN learning. The noiseless training set has 225 patterns, which are generated randomly by the uniform distribution in each corresponding input range. Based on the noiseless training set, independent and identically distributed (i.i.d.) Gaussian noise with mean zero and standard deviations 0.1 are added as the noisy training set. The testing data set is 100×100 patterns generated from a regular spaced grid in the input range of each function.

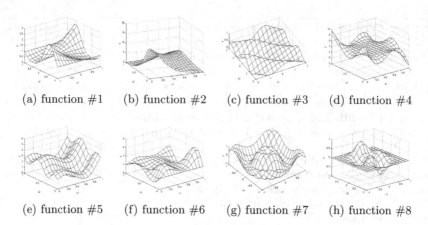

(a) function #1   (b) function #2   (c) function #3   (d) function #4

(e) function #5   (f) function #6   (g) function #7   (h) function #8

Fig. 2. Meshplot of the eight functions for approximation

Table 1. Comparison of testing FVU in average for 20 trials while approximating the 2-D functions with noiseless training set

Function #	S_1	S_2	S_3	$\sqrt{S_1}$	$\sqrt{S_2}$	$\sqrt{S_3}$	S_{cascor}	$OLS - PSO$
1	0.0594	0.0970	0.0559	0.0705	0.0969	0.0508	0.0901	**0.0271**
	(0.0065)	(0.0124)	(0.0086)	(0.0167)	(0.0124)	(0.0094)	(0.0093)	**(0.0073)**
2	0.0132	0.0246	0.0216	0.0119	0.0227	0.0172	0.0235	**0.0011**
	(0.0073)	(0.0046)	(0.0097)	(0.0079)	(0.0054)	(0.0091)	(0.0072)	**(0.0005)**
3	0.2108	0.1523	0.1404	0.2255	0.1563	0.1337	0.1549	**0.0708**
	(0.0735)	(0.0395)	(0.0654)	(0.0590)	(0.0389)	(0.0718)	(0.0391)	**(0.0228)**
4	0.3472	0.2851	0.2040	0.4398	0.2646	0.2103	0.2674	**0.1692**
	(0.0951)	(0.0363)	(0.1055)	(0.3965)	(0.0402)	(0.0746)	(0.0291)	**(0.0553)**
5	0.0585	0.0290	0.0521	0.0537	0.0293	0.0633	0.0271	**0.0093**
	(0.0227)	(0.0059)	(0.0289)	(0.0162)	(0.0054)	(0.0407)	(0.0037)	**(0.0039)**
6	0.2057	0.1634	0.2927	0.2253	0.1676	0.2963	0.1693	**0.1393**
	(0.0334)	(0.0159)	(0.0986)	(0.0457)	(0.0189)	(0.0780)	(0.0194)	**(0.0852)**
7	0.5479	0.3063	0.3904	0.6235	0.3142	0.4352	0.3024	**0.2417**
	(0.1170)	(0.0379)	(0.0991)	(0.1973)	(0.0353)	(0.1543)	(0.0218)	**(0.0536)**
8	0.2591	0.2454	0.2191	0.2493	0.2321	0.2167	0.2401	**0.2120**
	(0.0379)	(0.0264)	(0.0322)	(0.0357)	(0.0156)	(0.0386)	(0.0174)	**(0.0361)**

* In each cell, the above value is the averaged RMSE while the value in the bracket is the standard deviation.

The performances of these algorithms are evaluated on the prediction accuracy of the testing data set by calculating the fraction of variance unexplained (FVU) [4].

$$\text{FVU} = \frac{(\mathbf{y} - \tilde{\mathbf{y}})^T (\mathbf{y} - \tilde{\mathbf{y}})}{\sum_{p=1}^{P} (y_p - \bar{y})^2} \tag{24}$$

Table 2. Comparison of testing FVU in average for 20 trials while approximating the 2-D functions with noisy training set

Function #	S_1	S_2	S_3	$\sqrt{S_1}$	$\sqrt{S_2}$	$\sqrt{S_3}$	S_{cascor}	$OLS - PSO$
1	0.0717	0.0949	0.0600	0.0731	0.0961	0.0580	0.0953	**0.0327**
	(0.0130)	(0.0085)	(0.0123)	(0.0145)	(0.0130)	(0.0148)	(0.0106)	**(0.0071)**
2	0.0111	0.0237	0.0190	0.0139	0.0227	0.0209	0.0222	**0.0013**
	(0.0066)	(0.0047)	(0.0200)	(0.0104)	(0.0060)	(0.0136)	(0.0046)	**(0.0005)**
3	0.1811	0.2264	0.1854	0.2094	0.2092	0.1517	0.1993	**0.0971**
	(0.0462)	(0.0678)	(0.0611)	(0.0484)	(0.0545)	(0.0545)	(0.0480)	**(0.0184)**
4	0.3160	0.2805	0.2308	0.3746	0.2725	0.2085	0.2797	**0.1509**
	(0.0641)	(0.0374)	(0.0737)	(0.0931)	(0.0281)	(0.0916)	(0.0280)	**(0.0586)**
5	0.0572	0.0287	0.0656	0.0538	0.0276	0.0615	0.0286	**0.0100**
	(0.0200)	(0.0060)	(0.0301)	(0.0221)	(0.0035)	(0.0350)	(0.0058)	**(0.0046)**
6	0.2240	0.1654	0.2520	0.2250	0.1685	0.3017	0.1690	**0.1594**
	(0.0473)	(0.0226)	(0.0882)	(0.0428)	(0.0248)	(0.0812)	(0.0206)	**(0.0819)**
7	0.5860	0.3273	0.4280	0.6166	0.3141	0.4519	0.3244	**0.2529**
	(0.1269)	(0.0363)	(0.1171)	(0.1741)	(0.0280)	(0.1327)	(0.0306)	**(0.0435)**
8	0.2969	0.2941	**0.2595**	0.2886	0.2970	0.2696	0.3024	0.2931
	(0.0374)	(0.0466)	**(0.0344)**	(0.0354)	(0.0291)	(0.0353)	(0.0358)	(0.0658)

* In each cell, the above value is the averaged RMSE while the value in the bracket is the standard deviation.

in which, $\mathbf{y} = [y_1, y_2, ..., y_P]^T \in R^P$ are the desired outputs for the testing patterns. $\tilde{\mathbf{y}}$ are the actual outputs with the trained SLFN. $\bar{y}$ is the average value of the desired outputs for all the testing patterns.

$$\bar{y} = \frac{1}{P} \sum_{p=1}^{P} y_p \tag{25}$$

All the algorithms constructed a SLFN with sigmoid activation function by adding hidden neurons from 1 to 15. All the objective functions in [4] are optimized by quickprop [23], in which 100 is set as the maximum iteration number. To increase the probability to find the global optimal parameters of the new neuron, 4 candidates are trained together in each stage. While using the proposed OLS-PSO algorithm, after many experiments, the population size have been set as 20 and the maximum iteration number of the PSO have been set as 20.

Since all the algorithms has randomness involved, each construction is repeated 20 times. The averaged FVU and corresponding standard deviation for the testing data set among the 20 times are recorded. Table 1 shows the results while training with noiseless data set, Table 2 shows the results while training with noisy data set. For each approximated function, the best result is highlighted with bold in the table. From the comparisons, one can observe that for most functions, while constructing SLFN with the same number of hidden neurons, the proposed OLS-PSO algorithm could achieve better accuracy with both noiseless and noisy training data set. Note that The OLS-PSO algorithm converged faster than other objective functions, which also demonstrated that a more compact SLFN could be constructed to arrive a similar generalization accuracy. All the other objective functions are optimized 4×100 epochs by quickprop while the OLS-PSO algorithm had 20×20 evaluations of the error contribution. Because of the simplicity of the PSO, that no gradient information is required and only forward computation is performed, the proposed OLS-PSO algorithm constructed the SLFN slightly faster than the other algorithms.

5 Conclusion

In this paper, a new constructive algorithm for SLFN construction is proposed based on Orthogonal Least Square (OLS) and Particle Swarm Optimization (PSO). As the other constructive algorithms, the proposed OLS-PSO algorithm constructs the SLFN by adding hidden neurons one by one. Each time adding a new neuron, all the hidden parameters of previous SLFN are frozen. With the error reduction contribution defined in the OLS, the PSO algorithm is used to search the optimal parameters of the new added neuron. All the output weights of the SLFN keep to be least square optimal. Unlike the conventional OLS used in model selection, which needs to evaluate the orthogonal components of each neuron, a new formulation is derived that is more efficient and suitable for dynamic construction of SLFN.

The proposed OLS-PSO algorithm is compared with other popular constructive algorithms, the comparison results demonstrated that the OLS-PSO algorithm could achieve very compact SLFN with good generalization ability. The PSO algorithm works well to search the global optimal parameters of the hidden neuron based on the multimodal contribution function. However, it was shown much slower than those constructive ELMs. In fact, the PSO algorithm was criticized with slow convergence in the vicinity of the global minimum. Further work will focused on the combination of the PSO and gradient method to speed up the optimization process.

References

1. Hornik, K.: Approximation capabilities of multilayer feedforward networks. Neural Netw. **4**, 251–257 (1991)
2. Lin, B., Lin, B., Chong, F., Lai, F.: Higher-order-statistics-based radial basis function networks for signal enhancement. IEEE Trans. Neural Netw. **18**(3), 823–832 (2007)
3. Min, C.C., Srinivasan, D., Cheu, R.: Neural networks for continuous online learning and control. IEEE Trans. Neural Netw. **17**(5), 1511–1531 (2006)
4. Kwok, T.Y., Yeung, D.Y.: Objective functions for training new hidden units in constructive neural networks. IEEE Trans. Neural Netw. **8**(5), 1131–1148 (1997)
5. Kwok, T.Y., Yeung, D.Y.: Constructive algorithms for structure learning in feedforward neural networks for regression problems. IEEE Trans. Neural Netw. **8**(3), 630–645 (1997)
6. Huang, G.-B., Zhu, Q.-Y., Siew, C.-K.: Extreme learning machine: a new learning scheme of feedforward neural networks. In: 2004 International Joint Conference on Neural Networks (IJCNN-2004), (Budapest, Hungary), July 25–29 (2004)

7. Huang, G.-B., Chen, L.: Enhanced random search based incremental extreme learning machine. Neurocomputing **71**(16–18), 3460–3468 (2008)
8. Feng, G., Huang, G.B., Lin, Q., Gay, R.: Error minimized extreme learning machine with growth of hidden nodes and incremental learning. IEEE Trans. Neural Netw. **20**(8), 1352–1357 (2009)
9. Chen, S., Billings, S.A., Luo, W.: Orthogonal least squares methods and their applications to non-linear system identification. Int. J. Control **50**, 1873–1896 (1989)
10. Chen, S., Hong, X., Luk, B.L., Harris, C.J.: Construction of tunable radial basis function networks using orthogonal forward selection. IEEE Trans. Syst. Man Cybern. B **39**(2), 457–466 (2009)
11. Zhang, L., Li, K., He, H., Irwin, G.W.: A new discrete-continuous algorithm for radial basis function networks construction. IEEE Trans. Neural Netw. Learn. Syst. **24**(11), 1785–1798 (2013)
12. Rao, C.R., Mitra, S.K.: Generalized Inverse of Matrices and Its Applications. Wiley, New York (1971)
13. Kennedy, J., Eberhart, R.C.: Particle swarm optimization. In: Proceedings of IEEE International Conference on Neural Network, Perth, Australia, pp. 1942–1948 (1995)
14. Langdon, W.B., Poli, R.: Evolving problems to learn about particle swarm optimizers and other search algorithms. IEEE Trans. Evol. Comput. **11**(5), 561–578 (2007)
15. Zhang, C., Shao, H., Li, Y.: Particle swam optimisation for evolving artificial neural network. In: Proceedings of the IEEE Intemational Conference on Systems, Man, and Cybernetics, pp. 2487–2490 (2000)
16. Han, F., Yao, H.-F., Ling, Q.-H.: An improved extreme learning machine based on particle swarm optimization. In: Huang, D.-S., Gan, Y., Premaratne, P., Han, K. (eds.) ICIC 2011. LNCS, vol. 6840, pp. 699–704. Springer, Heidelberg (2012)
17. Mendes, R., Cortez, P., Rocha, M., Neves, J.: Particle swarms for feedforward neural network training. In: Proceedings International Joint Conference on Neural Networks, pp. 1895–1899 (2002)
18. Shi, Y., Eberhart, R.C.: A modied particle swarm optimizer. In: Proceedings of IEEE World Conference on Computation Intelligence, pp. 69–73 (1998)
19. Bartlett, P.L.: The sample complexity of pattern classification with neural networks: the size of the weights is more important than the size of the network. IEEE Trans. Inf. Theory **44**, 525–536 (1998)
20. Wilamowski, B.M., Yu, H.: Improved computation for Levenberg Marquardt training. IEEE Trans. Neural Netw. **21**(6), 930–937 (2010)
21. Xie, T., Yu, H., Hewlett, J., Rozycki, P., Wilamowski, B.: Fast and efficient second order method for training radial basis function networks. IEEE Trans. Neural Netw. **24**(4), 609–619 (2012)
22. Shi, Y., Eberhart, R.C.: Empirical study of particle swarm optimization. In: Proceeding of the 1999 Congress on Evolutionary Computation, Piscataway, pp. 1945–1950 (1999)
23. Fahlman, S.E.: Faster learning variations on backpropagation: an empirical study. In: Proceedings of 1988 Connectionist Models Summer School, pp. 38–51 (1988)

Fuzzy Systems and Their Applications

Problems of Identification of Cloud-Based Fuzzy Evolving Systems

Sašo Blažič[(✉)] and Igor Škrjanc

Faculty of Electrical Engineering, University of Ljubljana,
Tržaška 25, 1000 Ljubljana, Slovenia
{saso.blazic,igor.skrjanc}@fe.uni-lj.si

Abstract. In this paper some problems that arise in identification of nonlinear systems described by the cloud-based fuzzy rule-based model are shown. These models do not assume fixed partitioning of the space of antecedent variables. The Mahalanobis distance among the data samples is proposed for local density calculation which is more suitable when the data are scattered around the input-output surface. The identification algorithms are given in a recursive form which is necessary for the implementation of an evolving system. The proposed algorithms are illustrated on a simple simulation model of a static system.

1 Introduction

In this paper we deal with nonlinear systems which are modelled by fuzzy rule-based (FRB) models. The paper is focused on the identification issues of the FRB models. Traditionally, FRB systems often assumed fixed partitioning of the space of antecedent variables. This means that only the consequent models' parameters need to be estimated. Identification of the Takagi-Sugeno fuzzy model is the one that arguably received the most attention; the early works date to the 1980s [12]. Later many works followed and the area is still alive. When the model needs to be estimated on line, recursive algorithms are needed. Often a version of recursive least squares algorithm has been applied. Global and local approaches to estimate consequent models' parameters were presented in [2]. The problem of identification of dynamic systems is that with the local approach the local models have more appropriate local behaviour while the fuzzy model is less accurate globally [11]. Nevertheless, different local identification approaches are presented by [6], [3], [9], [4] etc.

The second problem in nonlinear system identification is to properly partition the space of antecedent variables. The methods are based on learning algorithms for neural networks [15], evolving clustering [8], subtractive clustering [2], fuzzy c-means clustering [6], Gustafson-Kessel clustering [5] and others [7,10,14].

Recently, a special type of fuzzy FRB systems with non-parametric antecedents has been proposed in [1]. Unlike traditional Mamdani and Takagi-Sugeno FRB systems, the approach does not require an explicit definition of fuzzy sets (and their corresponding membership functions) for each input variable. Data clouds are subsets of previous data samples with common properties.

© Springer International Publishing Switzerland 2016
L. Rutkowski et al. (Eds.): ICAISC 2016, Part I, LNAI 9692, pp. 173–182, 2016.
DOI: 10.1007/978-3-319-39378-0_16

In the original works [1] data closeness has been used as a similarity measure. The approach itself is not limited to any particular similarity measure to classify data into clouds. In identification of dynamical systems it is very important to distinguish among the operating regions that demonstrate different system dynamics. Those regions could be seen as natural clouds. Even if we choose to select the framework of cloud based system identification, there are still a number of subtasks that have to executed. There are also some possible changes that can be introduced to the original method while still keeping the general methodology.

The relative density in the original papers [1] was based on Euclidean distance among the data samples in the cloud although it was stated that any other distance could be used. In the current paper two distance metrics are compared: the original Euclidean distance and Mahalanobis distance where we introduced some versions for calculating actual density.

We limit ourselves to static systems that map the multi-dimensional input space to the real numbers in this work. This simplifies the problem of identification because the problems related to identification of dynamic systems are omitted.

2   Takagi-Sugeno Fuzzy Model of a Nonlinear System

A typical Takagi-Sugeno fuzzy model [13] is given in the form of rules:

$$\text{if } z_1 \text{ is } \mathbf{A}_{1,k_1} \ \ldots \ \text{and } z_q \text{ is } \mathbf{A}_{q,k_q} \text{ then } y = \phi_j(\mathbf{x})$$
$$j = 1, \ldots, m \quad k_1 = 1, \ldots, f_1 \quad k_q = 1, \ldots, f_q \tag{1}$$

The q-element vector $\mathbf{z}^T = [z_1, ..., z_q]$ denotes the input or variables in the antecedent part of the rules, and variable y is the output of the model. With each variable in the antecedent z_i $(i = 1, \ldots, q)$, f_i fuzzy sets $(\mathbf{A}_{i,1}, \ldots, \mathbf{A}_{i,f_i})$ are associated, and each fuzzy set $\mathbf{A}_{i,k_i}$ $(k_i = 1, \ldots, f_i)$ is associated with a real-valued function $\mu_{A_{i,k_i}}(z_i) : \mathbb{R} \to [0, 1]$, that produces membership grade of the variable z_i with respect to the fuzzy set $\mathbf{A}_{i,k_i}$. To make the list of fuzzy rules complete, all possible variations of fuzzy sets are given in Eq. (1), yielding the number of fuzzy rules $m = f_1 \times f_2 \times \cdots \times f_q$. The variables z_i are not the only inputs of the fuzzy system. Implicitly, the n-element vector $\mathbf{x}^T = [x_1, ..., x_n]$ also represents the input to the system. It is usually referred to as the consequence vector. The functions $\phi_j(\cdot)$ can be arbitrary smooth functions in general, although linear or affine functions are usually used.

The system in Eq. (1) is easily described in the closed form in the case of a product-sum Takagi-Sugeno fuzzy model

$$y = \frac{\sum_{k_1=1}^{f_1} \cdots \sum_{k_q=1}^{f_q} \mu_{A_{1,k_1}}(z_1) \ldots \mu_{A_{q,k_q}}(z_q) \, \phi_j(\mathbf{x})}{\sum_{k_1=1}^{f_1} \cdots \sum_{k_q=1}^{f_q} \mu_{A_{1,k_1}}(z_1) \ldots \mu_{A_{q,k_q}}(z_q)} \tag{2}$$

Note a slight abuse of notation in Eq. (2) since j is not explicitly defined as a running index. From Eq. (1) it is evident that each j corresponds to a specific variation of indexes k_i, $i = 1, \ldots, q$.

To simplify Eq. (2), a partition of unity is considered where functions $\beta_j(\mathbf{z})$ defined as

$$\beta_j(\mathbf{z}) = \frac{\mu_{A_{1,k_1}}(z_1)\cdots\mu_{A_{q,k_q}}(z_q)}{\sum_{k_1=1}^{f_1}\cdots\sum_{k_q=1}^{f_q}\mu_{A_{1,k_1}}(z_1)\cdots\mu_{A_{q,k_q}}(z_q)} \qquad j = 1,\ldots,m \qquad (3)$$

give information about the fulfilment of the respective fuzzy rule in the normalized form. It is obvious that $\sum_{j=1}^{m}\beta_j(\mathbf{z}) = 1$ irrespective of $\mathbf{z}$ as long as the denominator of $\beta_j(\mathbf{z})$ is not equal to zero (this can be easily prevented by stretching the membership functions over the whole potential area of $\mathbf{z}$). Combining Eqs. (2) and (3) and changing summation over k_i by summation over j we arrive to the following equation:

$$y = \sum_{j=1}^{m}\beta_j(\mathbf{z})\phi_j(\mathbf{x}) \qquad (4)$$

From Eq. (4) it is evident that the output of a fuzzy system is a function of the antecedent vector $\mathbf{z}$ (q-dimensional) and the consequence vector $\mathbf{x}$ (n-dimensional). The dimension of the input space d may be and usually is lower than $(q + n)$ since it is usual to have the same variables present in $\mathbf{z}$ and $\mathbf{x}$.

The class of fuzzy models have the form of linear models, this refers to $\{\beta_j\}$ as a set of basis functions. The use of membership functions in input space with overlapping receptive fields provides interpolation and extrapolation. It is very common to define the output value as a linear combination of consequence variables $\mathbf{x}$

$$\phi_j(\mathbf{x}) = \boldsymbol{\theta}_j^T\mathbf{x}, \quad j = 1,\ldots,m, \quad \boldsymbol{\theta}_j^T = [\theta_{j1},\ldots,\theta_{jn}] \qquad (5)$$

If the matrix of the coefficients for the whole set of rules is denoted as $\boldsymbol{\Theta}^T = [\boldsymbol{\theta}_1,\ldots,\boldsymbol{\theta}_m]$ and the vector of membership values as $\boldsymbol{\beta}^T(\mathbf{z}) = [\beta_1(\mathbf{z}),\ldots,\beta_m(\mathbf{z})]$, then Eq. (4) can be rewritten in the matrix form

$$y = \boldsymbol{\beta}^T(\mathbf{z})\boldsymbol{\Theta}\mathbf{x} = \sum_{j=1}^{m}\beta_j(\mathbf{z})\boldsymbol{\theta}_j^T\mathbf{x} \qquad (6)$$

A fuzzy model in the form given in Eq. (6) is referred to as an affine Takagi-Sugeno model and can be used to approximate any arbitrary function that maps any compact set $\mathbf{C} \subset \mathbb{R}^d$ from the input space (the input space is the space of the union of variables in $\mathbf{x}$ and $\mathbf{z}$) to $\mathbb{R}$ with any desired degree of accuracy.

3   Identification of the Antecedent Part

The local density γ_k^j is defined by a suitable kernel over the distances between the current sample $\mathbf{z}(k)$ and all the previous samples that have already been classified to a particular cloud (j-th in this case) [1]:

$$\gamma_k^j = \frac{1}{1 + \rho\frac{\sum_{i=1}^{M^j}d_{ki}^j}{M^j}} \qquad j = 1,\ldots,m \qquad (7)$$

where d^j_{ki} denotes the square of the (Euclidean) distance between the current data sample $\mathbf{z}(k)$ and the i-th sample of the j-th cloud $\mathbf{z}^j_i$, while M^j is the number of input data samples associated with the j-th cloud. Note the factor ρ which is not present in [1] and will be discussed later.

3.1 Density Based on Mahalanobis Distance

Mahalanobis distance is conceptually different from the Euclidean one. It is defined between an observation and a group of observations. The latter is characterised with its mean and the corresponding covariance matrix. In our case the distance will be calculated between two samples but taking into account the covariance matrix of the cloud data samples. The cloud is characterised by the mean value of the samples in the j-th cloud $\boldsymbol{\mu}^j$ and the associated covariance matrix $\boldsymbol{\Sigma}^j$. The square of the distance between the current data sample $\mathbf{z}(k)$ and the i-th sample of the j-th cloud $(\mathbf{z}^j_i)$ can therefore be computed as

$$d^j_{ki} = (\mathbf{z}(k) - \mathbf{z}^j_i)^T (\boldsymbol{\Sigma}^j_{M^j})^{-1}(\mathbf{z}(k) - \mathbf{z}^j_i) \tag{8}$$

with $\boldsymbol{\mu}^j(k)$ and $\boldsymbol{\Sigma}^j(k)$ given by

$$\boldsymbol{\mu}^j_{M^j} = \frac{1}{M^j} \sum_{i=1}^{M^j} \mathbf{z}^j_i$$

$$\boldsymbol{\Sigma}^j_{M^j} = \frac{1}{M^j - 1} \sum_{i=1}^{M^j} (\mathbf{z}^j_i - \boldsymbol{\mu}^j_{M^j})(\mathbf{z}^j_i - \boldsymbol{\mu}^j_{M^j})^T \tag{9}$$

where the lower index in $\boldsymbol{\mu}^j(k)$ and $\boldsymbol{\Sigma}^j(k)$ gives the number of data samples taken into account during the calculation of the corresponding variable.

By introducing (8) into (7) we obtain the non-recursive formula for density calculation:

$$\gamma^j_k = \frac{1}{1 + \rho \dfrac{\sum_{i=1}^{M^j} (\mathbf{z}(k) - \mathbf{z}^j_i)^T (\boldsymbol{\Sigma}^j_{M^j})^{-1}(\mathbf{z}(k) - \mathbf{z}^j_i)}{M^j}} \tag{10}$$

Eq. (10) can be transformed into the recursive form by further developing the summation in it:

$$\sum_{i=1}^{M^j} (\mathbf{z}(k) - \mathbf{z}^j_i)^T (\boldsymbol{\Sigma}^j_{M^j})^{-1}(\mathbf{z}(k) - \mathbf{z}^j_i) = \sum_{i=1}^{M^j} ((\mathbf{z}(k) - \boldsymbol{\mu}^j_{M^j}) - (\mathbf{z}^j_i - \boldsymbol{\mu}^j_{M^j}))^T (\boldsymbol{\Sigma}^j_{M^j})^{-1} \times$$

$$\times ((\mathbf{z}(k) - \boldsymbol{\mu}^j_{M^j}) - (\mathbf{z}^j_i - \boldsymbol{\mu}^j_{M^j})) = \underbrace{M^j (\mathbf{z}(k) - \boldsymbol{\mu}^j_{M^j})^T (\boldsymbol{\Sigma}^j_{M^j})^{-1}(\mathbf{z}(k) - \boldsymbol{\mu}^j_{M^j})}_{T_1} -$$

$$\underbrace{- 2 \sum_{i=1}^{M^j} (\mathbf{z}^j_i - \boldsymbol{\mu}^j_{M^j})^T (\boldsymbol{\Sigma}^j_{M^j})^{-1}(\mathbf{z}(k) - \boldsymbol{\mu}^j_{M^j})}_{T_2} + \underbrace{\sum_{i=1}^{M^j} (\mathbf{z}^j_i - \boldsymbol{\mu}^j_{M^j})^T (\boldsymbol{\Sigma}^j_{M^j})^{-1}(\mathbf{z}^j_i - \boldsymbol{\mu}^j_{M^j})}_{T_3} \tag{11}$$

To try to simplify the expression further we need to fulfill the conditions for the covariance matrix inversion. First denote the matrix of all the vectors $(\mathbf{z}_i^j - \boldsymbol{\mu}_{M^j}^j)$ of the j-th cloud in its columns by $\boldsymbol{\Xi}_j$ (dimension $q \times M^j$). The matrix $\boldsymbol{\Sigma}_{M^j}^j$ from (9) is non-singular if and only if $\boldsymbol{\Xi}_j$ has rank q. Since all the rows in $\boldsymbol{\Xi}_j$ have zero mean, at least $q+1$ columns are needed for the matrix $\boldsymbol{\Xi}_j$ to achieve full rank. If $M^j \geq q+1$ and all the measurements are independent, the matrix $\boldsymbol{\Sigma}_{M^j}^j$ can be inverted (its inverse is $(M^j - 1)(\boldsymbol{\Xi}_j\boldsymbol{\Xi}_j^T)^{-1}$). Then it is easy to see that the term T_3 in (11) is identical to $(M^j - 1)\,\mathrm{trace}(\boldsymbol{\Xi}_j^T(\boldsymbol{\Xi}_j\boldsymbol{\Xi}_j^T)^{-1}\boldsymbol{\Xi}_j)$ which is in turn equal to $(M^j - 1)q$ (q is the dimension of the antecedent vector). The term T_2 is identical to 0 due to the definition of $\boldsymbol{\mu}_{M^j}^j$ in (9). The formula for the relative density (10) therefore takes the form suitable for the recursive implementation:

$$\gamma_k^j = \frac{1}{1 + \rho\left[(\mathbf{z}(k) - \boldsymbol{\mu}_{M^j}^j)^T(\boldsymbol{\Sigma}_{M^j}^j)^{-1}(\mathbf{z}(k) - \boldsymbol{\mu}_{M^j}^j) + \frac{(M^j-1)q}{M^j}\right]} \tag{12}$$

The expression in square brackets in Eq. (12) is equivalent to the quadratic form in Eq. (10) and therefore always positive. Now it is properly to discuss the parameter ρ. This parameter directly influences "overlapping" of local densities which is analogous to overlapping of membership functions in the context of fuzzy systems. Small values of ρ have similar effect as wide membership functions. By increasing ρ, the analogous membership functions become narrower.

The benefit of using Mahalanobis distance is to describe the ellipsoidally shaped clouds. In fact any cloud stretched in a certain direction can be described easier. The size and the shape of the ellipsoid depends on the covariance matrix of the data in the cloud. While the idea of having such clouds is appealing, it holds a caveat. If a cloud is based on some measurements in a small region of space, the covariance matrix $\boldsymbol{\Sigma}_{M^j}^j$ becomes small and a relatively close measurement may have low density with respect to this particular cloud. The problem lies in the fact that the volume of the cloud (or better of the ellipsoid defined by its covariance matrix) is too small. To prevent this phenomenon, the inverse of the covariance matrix in Eq. (12) is replaced by its normalised version:

$$\gamma_k^j = \frac{1}{1 + \rho\left[\dfrac{(\mathbf{z}(k) - \boldsymbol{\mu}_{M^j}^j)^T(\boldsymbol{\Sigma}_{M^j}^j)^{-1}(\mathbf{z}(k) - \boldsymbol{\mu}_{M^j}^j)}{\sqrt{\det\left((\boldsymbol{\Sigma}_{M^j}^j)^{-1}\right)}} + \dfrac{(M^j-1)q}{M^j}\right]} \tag{13}$$

The normalising factor is the square root of the determinant of the matrix which is proportional to the volume of the ellipsoid. In some cases (e.g. when $\boldsymbol{\Sigma}_{M^j}^j$ is not of a full rank) it is possible to use multiplication with $(\det \boldsymbol{\Sigma}_{M^j}^j)^{\frac{1}{2}}$ instead of division with the square root given in (13).

There exist other possibilities of coping with the aforementioned problem of "small" clouds. One approach is to only perform normalisation (13) if $(\det \boldsymbol{\Sigma}_{M^j}^j)^{\frac{1}{2}}$ falls below a certain threshold (typically 1), otherwise unnormalised algorithm (12) is used. Thus, automatic normalisation of "big" signals is still achieved via the Mahalanobis metric while over-shrinking of clouds is prevented.

Equation (9) is not suitable for implementation in the recursive identification algorithm because it needs to have all the past data stored. This algorithm can be adapted for our purpose as follows. If a new data sample (say $\mathbf{z}$) is assigned to the j-th cloud, the update of the mean and the covariance matrix can be calculated using the Algorithm 1:

$$
\begin{aligned}
M^j &\leftarrow M^j + 1 \\
\mathbf{d} &\leftarrow \mathbf{z} - \boldsymbol{\mu}^j \\
\boldsymbol{\mu}^j &\leftarrow \boldsymbol{\mu}^j + \tfrac{1}{M^j}\mathbf{d} \\
\mathbf{S}^j &\leftarrow \mathbf{S}^j + \mathbf{d}(\mathbf{z} - \boldsymbol{\mu}^j)^T \\
\boldsymbol{\Sigma}^j &\leftarrow \tfrac{1}{M^j-1}\mathbf{S}^j
\end{aligned}
$$

All the states $(M^j,\ \boldsymbol{\mu}^j,\ \mathbf{S}^j)$ of this algorithm are initialised with zeros. Note that the lower indexes are omitted in the algorithms.

In order to calculate the relative density (12) or (13), one needs the inverse of the covariance matrix. To avoid inverting the matrix in each sampling instant, Woodbury matrix identity is used to obtain the recursive form for the matrix inversion. Last two steps of Algorithm 1 therefore change in Algorithm 2:

$$
\begin{aligned}
\bar{\mathbf{S}}^j &\leftarrow \bar{\mathbf{S}}^j - \bar{\mathbf{S}}^j\mathbf{d}\left[1 + (\mathbf{z} - \boldsymbol{\mu}^j)^T\bar{\mathbf{S}}^j\mathbf{d}\right]^{-1}(\mathbf{z} - \boldsymbol{\mu}^j)^T\bar{\mathbf{S}}^j \\
(\boldsymbol{\Sigma}^j)^{-1} &\leftarrow (M^j - 1)\bar{\mathbf{S}}^j
\end{aligned}
$$

Algorithm 2 introduces a new state $\bar{\mathbf{S}}^j$ as an inverse of $\mathbf{S}^j$ from Algorithm 1. It is initialised with a large positive definite matrix, usually a diagonal one. Note that the inverse in Algorithm 2 applies to a (positive) scalar and is not problematic. Note also that Algorithm 1 exactly reproduces the mean and the covariance matrix from (9) while Algorithm 2 also achieves this but there is a slight difference in the initialisation phase. After the full rank of the covariance matrix is achieved, all three algorithms become identical.

But since starting a new cloud with enough initial data is extremely important for robust operation, the above mentioned small difference is irrelevant. Enough initial data means that data are kept in a buffer before a decision for starting a new cloud is taken. Usually, this means that more than $q+1$ measurements are kept. Then, there is no need of initialising the inverse of the covariance matrix with a big positive matrix. Instead, real data from the buffer are used.

3.2 The Determination of the Input-Output Mapping

Any nonlinear mapping that maps a compact set from the input space to $\mathbb{R}$ can be approximated by a number of general approximators. One possibility is to use a Takagi-Sugeno model given in Eq. (6). The problem of identifying the model is a very well-known one and has been treated by many authors in the last decades. Most traditional approach is to somehow estimate the parameters $\boldsymbol{\theta}_j$ while simultaneous identification of parameters $\boldsymbol{\theta}_j$ and functions $\beta_j(\cdot)$ has also received quite some attention in the literature.

Here we will try to obtain a very simple and also not so accurate model by only analysing the covariance matrices of the clouds. We will assume that measurement vectors are composed of the input vector $\mathbf{x}$ and the corresponding output y:

$$\mathbf{z}^T = \begin{bmatrix} \mathbf{x}^T & y \end{bmatrix} \tag{14}$$

One possibility to obtain input-output mapping is to deduce it solely by analysing the input part of the FRB. For this purpose, the following idea is used. The data in the input-output space lie along the hyper-surface representing the input-output mapping. Due to disturbances, measurement noise, parasitic disturbances and other sources of errors, the data do not lie exactly on the surface, but are spread in the vicinity of the hyper-surface. Analysing the data in the cloud it turns out that the eigenvectors associated with the dominant eigenvalues lie along the hyper-surface while the smallest eigenvalue is associated with the eigenvector that is perpendicular to the hyper-surface. For the j-th cloud, this normal vector is denoted by $\mathbf{n}_j$. This vector determines the tangential hyper-plane in the centre of the cloud. In the context of nonlinear systems, the normal vector to the hyper-plane changes from one operating point to another. The normal vector in a certain operating can be obtain by linear combination of individual normal vectors associated with individual clouds. Here we will use normalised densities associated with the clouds as the factors of the linear combination. This leads to the following estimate of the normal vector:

$$\mathbf{n}_k = \frac{\sum_{j=1}^{m} \gamma_k^j \mathbf{n}_j}{\sum_{j=1}^{m} \gamma_k^j} \tag{15}$$

When a measurement $\mathbf{z}_k^T = \begin{bmatrix} \mathbf{x}_k^T & y_k \end{bmatrix}$ is obtained, a local linearised model can be obtained:

$$\begin{bmatrix} \mathbf{x}^T - \mathbf{x}_k^T & y - y_k \end{bmatrix} \mathbf{n}_k = 0 \tag{16}$$

Equation (16) describes the hyper-plane with the normal vector $\mathbf{n}_k$ through the point $\begin{bmatrix} \mathbf{x}^T & y \end{bmatrix}^T$. This method enables obtaining the local linear model without the need for performing the identification of the consequent part of the FRB. The method also has some drawbacks due to the fact that the data inside a cloud usually do not lie along a hyper-plane and the required normal direction to the surface is contaminated with the direction of the nonlinearity in a certain direction.

4   Simulation Examples

First a static system

$$y = u^3 \tag{17}$$

will be treated. The data collected from the system are depicted in Fig. 1. In the left part of Fig. 1 the data clouds obtained by calculating the densities using Euclidean distance are shown in different colours. The right part of Fig. 1 shows the results of the example where the density is calculated by the second version of the Mahalanobis distance (Eq. 13). The ellipses show the one standard deviation

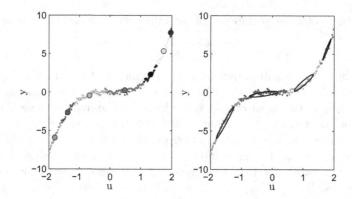

Fig. 1. The clouds obtained with the density calculation based on the Euclidean distance (left) and the corrected Mahalanobis distance (13) (right)

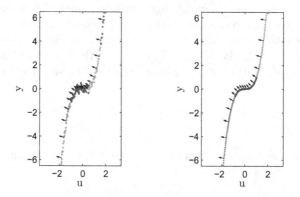

Fig. 2. The data in the clouds and the normal vector calculated from the eigenvectors by Eq. (15)

boundary. All other parameters are the same in both approaches: new cloud is started when the local density falls below 0.4, $\rho = \frac{1}{n} = \frac{1}{2}$. The first thing to note is that lower number of clouds is obtained in the latter case which is understandable because the clouds adapt their shape to the data to a certain extent.

In Fig. 2 the data clouds are depicted together with the normal vectors given by Eq. (13). The left part of the figure shows the case with high noise (the same data as in Fig. 1 while in the right part the case with low noise is analysed. As expected, normal vectors are estimated very well when the data lie almost along the hyper-plane. Around nonlinearities and/or in the case of higher noise the estimated normal to the surface becomes less accurate leading to the wrong linearised model.

The input partition of the two models (illustrated in Fig. 1) was used to design two fuzzy models where the consequent parameters were estimated by the classical least squares method (global optimum of the parameters is searched

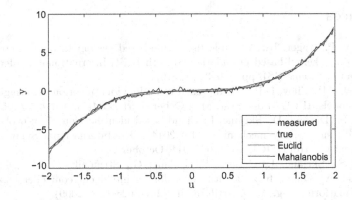

Fig. 3. The comparison of the two simulated outputs with the original one (Color figure online)

for in a non-recursive way). Figure 3 shows the true output of the system with a green colour and the measured one with the black colour. Both outputs of the fuzzy models are also shown. The model that is based on Euclidean distance is shown in red, the one based on Mahalanobis distance is shown in blue. The comparison of errors shows that the proposed method results in the mean square error (MSE) of 0.0172 among the model output and the true output while the MSE of 0.0232 is achieved in the case of Euclidean-distance-based model. This means that the lower error is achieved while lower number of parameters is tuned (4 clouds instead of 7).

5   Conclusions

In this paper we focused only on the identification of static mappings although the approach is suitable also for dynamic systems. By static we refer to the property that the output of the system only depends on the current inputs and not on internal states. Having said that we do not assume that the nonlinearity is time invariant. On the contrary, the model with (slowly) varying system parameters is one of the main targets when speaking about the evolving systems in general.

In this paper an alternative way of describing local density in the cloud-based evolving systems is discussed. The Mahalanobis distance among the data samples is used which leads to the density that is more suitable when the data are scattered around the input-output surface. All the algorithms for the identification of the cloud parameters are given in a recursive form which is necessary for the implementation of the evolving systems. It is also shown that a simple linearised model can be obtained without identification of the consequent parameters. All the proposed algorithms are illustrated on a simple simulation model of a static system.

References

1. Angelov, P., Yager, R.: A simple fuzzy rule-based system through vector membership and kernel-based granulation. In: 5th IEEE International Conference on Intelligent Systems (IS), pp. 349–354 (2010)
2. Angelov, P.P., Filev, D.P.: An approach to on-line identification of Takagi-Sugeno fuzzy models. IEEE Trans. Syst. Man Cyber. Part B **34**(1), 484–497 (2004)
3. Blažič, S., Dovžan, D., Škrjanc, I.: Cloud-based identification of an evolving system with supervisory mechanisms. In: 2014 IEEE International Symposium on Intelligent Control (ISIC), pp. 1906–1911, October 2014
4. Blažič, S., Škrjanc, I., Gerkšič, S., Dolanc, G., Strmčnik, S., Hadjiski, M.B., Stathaki, A.: Online fuzzy identification for an intelligent controller based on a simple platform. Eng. Appl. Artifi.Intell. **22**(4), 628–638 (2009)
5. Dovžan, D., Škrjanc, I.: Recursive clustering based on a gustafsonkessel algorithm. Evolving Syst. **2**, 15–24 (2011)
6. Dovžan, D., Škrjanc, I.: Recursive fuzzy c-means clustering for recursive fuzzy identification of time-varying processes. ISA Trans. **50**(2), 159–169 (2011)
7. Johanyák, Z.C., Papp, O.: A hybrid algorithm for parameter tuning in fuzzy model identification. Acta Polytech. Hung. **9**(6), 153–165 (2012)
8. Kasabov, N.K., Song, Q.: DENFIS: dynamic evolving neural-fuzzy inference system and its application for time-series prediction. IEEE Trans. Fuzzy Syst. **10**(2), 144–154 (2002)
9. Precup, R.E., Preitl, S.: PI and PID controllers tuning for integral-type servo systems to ensure robust stability and controller robustness. Electr. Eng. **88**(2), 149–156 (2006)
10. Rădac, M., Precup, R., Petriu, E., Preitl, S.: Application of IFT and SPSA to servo system control. IEEE Trans. Neural Netw. **22**(12), 2363–2375 (2011)
11. Sorensen, O.: Neural networks performing system identification for control applications. In: Third International Conference on Artificial Neural Networks, 25–27, pp. 172–177. Institution of Engineering and Technology, Brighton, May 1993
12. Sugeno, M., Kang, G.: Structure identification of fuzzy model. Fuzzy Sets Syst. **28**(1), 15–33 (1988)
13. Takagi, T., Sugeno, M.: Fuzzy identification of systems and its applications to modelling and control. IEEE Trans. Syst. Man, Cybern. **15**, 116–132 (1985)
14. Vaščák, J.: Adaptation of fuzzy cognitive maps by migration algorithms. Kybernetes **41**(3/4), 429–443 (2012)
15. Werbos, P.: Beyond regression: New tools for prediction and analysis in the behavioral sciences. Ph.D. dissertation, Harvard University, Cambridge (1974)

Uncertainty Measurement for the Interval Type-2 Fuzzy Set

Sarah Greenfield$^{(\boxtimes)}$

De Montfort University, Leicester LE1 9BH, UK
s.greenfield@dmu.ac.uk
http://www.tech.dmu.ac.uk/~sarahg/

Abstract. In this paper, two measures of uncertainty for interval type-2 fuzzy sets are presented, evaluated, compared and contrasted. Wu and Mendel regard the length of the type-reduced set as a measure of the uncertainty in an interval set. Greenfield and John argue that the volume under the surface of the type-2 fuzzy set is a measure of the uncertainty relating to the set. For an interval type-2 fuzzy set, the volume measure is equivalent to the area of the footprint of uncertainty of the set. Experiments show that though the two measures give different results, there is considerable commonality between them. The concept of *invariance under vertical translation* is introduced; the uncertainty measure of a fuzzy set has the property of invariance under vertical translation if the value it generates remains constant under any vertical translation of the fuzzy set. It is left unresolved whether invariance under vertical translation is an essential property of a type-2 uncertainty measure.

Keywords: Interval type-2 fuzzy set · Uncertainty · Uncertainty bounds · Volume measure of uncertainty · Invariance under vertical translation

1 Introduction

In 1965 Zadeh introduced the concept of the (type-1) fuzzy set [26]. Type-1 membership functions are of questionable accuracy as their derivation tends to be subjective or reliant on large sets of data. The practical application of fuzzy sets is within a Fuzzy Inferencing System (FIS). Uncertainty in type-1 FISs derives from various sources, e.g. "The meanings of the words that are used in the antecedents and consequents of rules can be uncertain" and "Measurements that activate a type-1 FLS may be noisy and therefore uncertain." [19, p. 117]. It is therefore very difficult, if not impossible, to determine a type-1 membership function, and consequently it seems somewhat inappropriate to use crisp numbers, possibly expressed to several decimal places, to represent degrees of membership. Klir and Folger [16, p. 12] comment:

"... it may seem problematical, if not paradoxical, that a representation of fuzziness is made using membership grades that are themselves precise real

L. Rutkowski et al. (Eds.): ICAISC 2016, Part I, LNAI 9692, pp. 183–194, 2016.
DOI: 10.1007/978-3-319-39378-0_17

numbers. Although this does not pose a serious problem for many applications, it is nevertheless possible to extend the concept of the fuzzy set to allow the distinction between grades of membership to become blurred. Sets described in this way are known as *type 2 fuzzy sets*."

One might argue that the type-1 membership function *does* reflect the certainty of a proposition. Does not a membership grade of 1 imply certain truth, a grade of 0 certain falsehood, and a grade of 0.5 total uncertainty? But really what is being quantified here is not so much uncertainty as *vagueness*. This is what lies behind the common use of *fuzziness* as a so-called measure of uncertainty for type-1 fuzzy sets [23, p. 5384].

Zadeh's 1975 innovation of the *type-2 fuzzy set* [27–29] provides an intuitive model of uncertainty. A type-2 fuzzy set (defined in Subsect. 2.2) may be thought of as an adaptation of a type-1 fuzzy set [19, p. 118]:

"Imagine blurring the type-1 membership function ... Then, at a specific value of x, say x', there no longer is a single value for the membership function (u'); instead the membership function takes on values wherever the vertical line intersects the blur. Those values need not all be weighted the same; hence, we can assign an amplitude distribution to all of those points. Doing this for all $x \in X$, we create a three-dimensional membership function — a type-2 membership function — that characterizes a type-2 fuzzy set."

Type-2 fuzzy sets take two forms, *generalised*, with variable secondary membership grades (Subsect. 2.2) between 0 and 1, and the simpler *interval*, where all secondary membership grades are 1. The specific concern of this paper is the interval type-2 fuzzy set. These are increasingly used in applications [3,5,6,11,13,15,17,20,21], since interval type-2 fuzzy inferencing is less computationally complex than its generalised counterpart [12,19].

The concept of a fuzzy uncertainty measure is analogous to that of error bars in statistics. Therefore such a measure has the potential to provide valuable information. By quantifying the uncertainty associated with the aggregated fuzzy set [7, p. 1015], one is in effect *measuring the uncertainty of the inference generating the aggregated set*. In fuzzy image processing [5,6,13], for example, an uncertainty measure would indicate the reliability of the processed outputs.

In [23] five measures of uncertainty for interval type-2 fuzzy sets are surveyed, most notably the *centroid length* measure. A measure not considered in this survey is that of the area of the interval set's Footprint Of Uncertainty (FOU). In this report the centroid length and the FOU area measures are compared and contrasted.

The next section covers preliminaries such as assumptions and definitions. Following that, in Sect. 3, the two uncertainty measures are presented, after which, in Sect. 4, the experiments by which the methods are compared and contrasted are described and their implications assessed. Finally Sect. 5 concludes the paper.

2   Preliminaries

2.1   Assumptions

The following assumptions relate to fuzzy sets:

1. The type-1 fuzzy set is contained within a unit square and may be viewed as a curve represented by (x, u) co-ordinates.
2. The type-2 fuzzy set is contained within a unit cube and may be viewed as a surface represented by (x, u, z) co-ordinates.
3. The domain (x-axis) is discretised.

2.2   Definitions

Let X be a universe of discourse. A type-1 fuzzy set A on X is characterised by a membership function $\mu_A : X \to [0,1]$ and can be expressed as follows [26]:

$$A = \{(x, \mu_A(x)) |\ \mu_A(x) \in [0,1]\ \forall x \in X\}. \tag{1}$$

In the following the notation $U = [0,1]$ is employed.

Let $\tilde{P}(U)$ be the set of fuzzy sets in U. A type-2 fuzzy set $\tilde{A}$ in X is a fuzzy set whose membership grades are themselves fuzzy [27–29]. This implies that $\mu_{\tilde{A}}(x)$ is a fuzzy set in U for all x, i.e. $\mu_{\tilde{A}} : X \to \tilde{P}(U)$ and

$$\tilde{A} = \{(x, \mu_{\tilde{A}}(x)) |\ \mu_{\tilde{A}}(x) \in \tilde{P}(U)\ \forall x \in X\}. \tag{2}$$

It follows that $\forall x \in X\ \exists J_x \subseteq U$ such that $\mu_{\tilde{A}}(x) : J_x \to U$. Applying (1), we obtain:

$$\mu_{\tilde{A}}(x) = \{(u, \mu_{\tilde{A}}(x)(u)) |\ \mu_{\tilde{A}}(x)(u) \in U\ \forall u \in J_x \subseteq U\}. \tag{3}$$

X is called the primary domain and J_x the primary membership of x while U is known as the secondary domain and $\mu_{\tilde{A}}(x)$ the secondary membership of x.

Putting (2) and (3) together, we obtain the definition of a *generalised type-2 fuzzy set*:

$$\tilde{A} = \{(x, (u, \mu_{\tilde{A}}(x)(u))) |\ \mu_{\tilde{A}}(x)(u) \in U,\ \forall x \in X \wedge \forall u \in J_x \subseteq U\}. \tag{4}$$

Definition 1 (Interval Type-2 Fuzzy Set). *An* interval type-2 fuzzy set *is a type-2 fuzzy set whose secondary membership grades are all 1.*

In the interval case, Eq. 4 reduces to:

$$\tilde{A} = \{(x, (u, 1)),\ \forall x \in X \wedge \forall u \in J_x \subseteq U\}. \tag{5}$$

Definition 2 (Footprint Of Uncertainty [19]). *The* Footprint Of Uncertainty (FOU) *is the projection of the type-2 fuzzy set onto the $x - u$ plane.*

The FOU defines the interval set, as all its secondary membership grades are 1.

Definition 3 (Lower Membership Function). *The* Lower Membership Function (LMF) *of a type-2 fuzzy set is the type-1 membership function associated with the lower bound of the FOU.*

Definition 4 (Upper Membership Function). *The* Upper Membership Function (UMF) *of a type-2 fuzzy set is the type-1 membership function associated with the upper bound of the FOU.*

Discretisation is the process by which a continuous set is converted into a discrete set through a process of slicing.

Definition 5 (Vertical Slice [19]). *A vertical slice of a type-2 fuzzy set is a plane through the x-axis, parallel to the u − z plane.*

Definition 6 (Degree of Discretisation). *The* degree of discretisation *is the separation of the slices.*

Definition 7 (Rectangular Type-2 Fuzzy Set). *A* rectangular type-2 fuzzy set *is an interval type-2 fuzzy set whose FOU extends between the lines $x = 0$ and $x = 1$, with LMF and UMF both running parallel to the x-axis.*

Figure 1 depicts two rectangular type-2 fuzzy sets.

Definition 8 (Blank Type-2 Fuzzy Set). *The* blank type-2 fuzzy set *is a rectangular type-2 fuzzy set whose LMF is the line $u = 0$ and UMF is the line $u = 1$.*

Definition 9 (Invariance under Vertical Translation). *An attribute of a fuzzy set has the property of* Invariance under Vertical Translation (IVT) *if it remains constant under any vertical translation of the fuzzy set.*

Definition 10 (Embedded Set). *An embedded set is a special kind of type-2 fuzzy set, which relates to the type-2 fuzzy set in which it is embedded in this way: For every primary domain value, x, there is a unique secondary domain value, u, plus the associated secondary membership grade that is determined by the primary and secondary domain values, $\mu_{\tilde{A}}(x)(u)$.*

The centroid length uncertainty measure is inextricably linked with the defuzzification process of a type-2 fuzzy set. Type-reduction, the first stage of type-2 defuzzification, creates a type-1 fuzzy set know as the Type-Reduced Set (TRS). Assuming that the primary domain X has been discretised, the TRS of a type-2 fuzzy set may be defined thus [19, p. 121], [27]:

Definition 11. *The TRS associated with a type-2 fuzzy set $\tilde{A}$ with primary domain X discretised into N points $X = \{x_1, x_2, \ldots, x_N\}$, is*

$$C_{\tilde{A}} = \left\{ \left(\frac{\sum_{i=1}^{N} x_i \cdot u_{k_i}}{\sum_{i=1}^{N} u_{k_i}}, \mu_{\tilde{A}}(x_1)(u_{k_1}) * \ldots * \mu_{\tilde{A}}(x_N)(u_{k_N}) \right) \middle| \forall (u_{k_1}, u_{k_2}, \ldots, u_{k_N}) \right.$$

$$\left. \in J_{x_1} \times J_{x_2} \times \ldots \times J_{x_N} \subseteq U^N \right\}.$$

$$(6)$$

For the TRS of an interval type-2 fuzzy set, Definition 11 reduces to:

Definition 12 (TRS of an Interval Type-2 Set). *The TRS associated with an interval type-2 fuzzy set $\tilde{A}$ with primary domain X discretised into N points $X = \{x_1, x_2, \ldots, x_N\}$, is*

$$C_{\tilde{A}} = \left\{ \left(\frac{\sum_{i=1}^{N} x_i \cdot u_{k_i}}{\sum_{i=1}^{N} u_{k_i}}, 1 \right) \middle| \forall (u_{k_1}, u_{k_2}, \ldots, u_{k_N}) \in J_{x_1} \times J_{x_2} \times \ldots \times J_{x_N} \subseteq U^N \right\}.$$

(7)

Mendel and John's Representation Theorem [19, p. 121] provides a precise method for defuzzification of type-2 fuzzy sets. Though Definitions 11 and 12 do not explicitly mention embedded sets, they appear implicitly in Eqs. 6 and 7. When these equations are presented in algorithmic form (Algorithm 1), they are explicitly referred to. Exhaustive type-reduction (Algorithm 1) processes *every* embedded set in turn, hence the term *'exhaustive method'* [8,9]. Each embedded set is defuzzified as a type-1 fuzzy set. The defuzzified value is paired with the minimum secondary membership grade of the embedded set, which in the interval case is 1, as all the secondary membership grades are 1. The set of ordered pairs constitutes the TRS, which is then defuzzified as a type-1 fuzzy set to give the defuzzified value of the type-2 fuzzy set.

Input: a discretised interval type-2 fuzzy set
Output: a discrete type-1 fuzzy set (the TRS)

1 **forall the** *embedded sets* **do**
2   calculate the primary domain value (x) of the type-1 centroid of the type-2 embedded set ;
3   pair the secondary grade (1) with the primary domain value (x) to give set of ordered pairs ($x, 1$) {these points lie on a line} ;
4 **end**

Algorithm 1: Type-reduction of an interval discretised type-2 fuzzy set to a type-1 fuzzy set, adapted from Mendel [18].

2.3 Principle of Type-2 Uncertainty Measurement

Mendel [18, p. 11] advocates the *fundamental design requirement* with regard to type-2 uncertainty measurement: "When all sources of uncertainty disappear, a type-2 FLS must reduce to a comparable type-1 FLS." This principle is patently valid.

It follows from this requirement that there is no uncertainty associated with a type-1 fuzzy set, and hence so called measures of uncertainty for type-1 fuzzy sets [1,2,4,22] *cannot be measuring uncertainty*; perhaps they are measuring another characteristic of the type-1 set such as vagueness (Sect. 1).

3 Type-2 Uncertainty Measures

In this section the two interval type-2 uncertainty measures of TRS length and FOU area are presented; these measures contrast strongly in their rationales and derivations.

3.1 Length of the TRS as a Measure of Uncertainty

Wu and Mendel propose that the *length* of the TRS of an interval set provides a measure of the uncertainty of the set [25]. The most widely adopted method for type-reducing an interval type-2 fuzzy set is the *Karnik-Mendel Iterative Procedure (KMIP)* [14]. The result of type-reduction of an interval type-2 fuzzy set is an interval (a particular case of a type-1 fuzzy set), with the defuzzified value at the midpoint. The endpoints of the interval are termed *uncertainty bounds* [25, p. 622]. The iterative procedure is an efficient search method for locating these endpoints. It is an approximate technique [7, 14, p. 203]. Since the publication of the KMIP, various more efficient versions have been proposed [24], which differ somewhat in their search strategy whilst giving the same result. However, in this paper the absolutely accurate Exhaustive Method [7] is used. Though it has relatively high computational complexity, in the experiments described below the discretisation employed is coarse enough for defuzzification to be accomplished relatively speedily.

3.2 Area of the FOU as a Measure of Uncertainty

How type-2 fuzzy sets model uncertainty is the subject of [10]. In this book chapter it is proposed that the third dimension reflects the uncertainty arising out of a deficit in information. From this premise it is argued that the volume under the surface of the type-2 fuzzy set is a measure of the uncertainty relating to the set. For an interval type-2 fuzzy set, since the secondary membership grades all take the value of 1, the area of the FOU is equivalent to the volume under the surface of the type-2 fuzzy set. The measure is applied to the aggregated fuzzy set [7, p. 1015]; this in effect measures the uncertainty of the inference from which the aggregated set is generated (Sect. 1).

Minimum Uncertainty. The least amount of uncertainty possible is 0. This corresponds to a type-2 fuzzy set in which every secondary membership function is a vertical line of height 1, with 0 area, originating from an FOU that is a line. Such a type-2 fuzzy set is equivalent to, and reducible to, a type-1 fuzzy set.

Maximum Uncertainty. At the other extreme, the greatest amount of uncertainty possible is 1. There is only one type-2 fuzzy set having uncertainty of 1, an interval set for which the support for each vertical slice's secondary membership function is the complete interval [0, 1]. The area of the FOU is 1. This type-2 fuzzy set may be described as a unit cube (of volume 1). It is fitting that it has an uncertainty of 1, as, being essentially formless, like a blank sheet of paper, it is devoid of information. For this reason it is termed the *blank type-2 fuzzy set*.

4 Experiments

4.1 Methodology

The two uncertainty measures are compared and contrasted experimentally, using specially constructed test sets. There are four experimental test runs. For three of the test runs rectangular interval type-2 fuzzy sets (Fig. 2) are employed. For the fourth test run, the underlying test set has no specific symmetry or form (Fig. 1). The strategy adopted is to either alter the distance between the LMF and the UMF, or keep this distance constant whilst translating the test set vertically, in each instance applying both the centroid length and the FOU area measures. The accurate Exhaustive Method [7] is used to generate the TRS, as opposed to the KMIP [14], which is an approximation. For all the test sets the domain has a degree of discretisation of 0.1, so engendering 11 evenly spaced vertical slices.

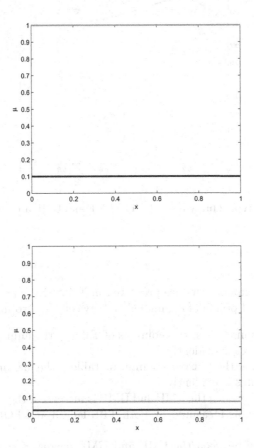

Fig. 1. Rectangular type-2 fuzzy test sets. The LMF and UMF are shown as bold lines.

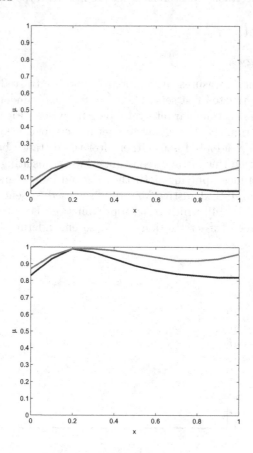

Fig. 2. Asymmetric type-2 fuzzy test sets. The LMF and UMF are shown as bold lines.

4.2   Results

The results of the experiments are presented in Tables 1, 2, 3 and 4.

There are several points of commonality between the two measures:

1. From the trend in the last two columns of Table 2, the minimum uncertainty for both measures is evidently 0.
2. From the trend in the last two columns of Table 1, the maximum uncertainty for both measures is evidently 1.
3. If the distance between the LMF and UMF is increased, the amount of uncertainty increases, as measured by both TRS length and FOU area (Tables 1 and 2).
4. As the distance between the LMF and UMF decreases to 0 (Table 2), the TRS length and FOU area both decrease to 0. Both measures tend to the value 0 as representing no uncertainty i.e. total certainty, as for a type-1 fuzzy set.

Table 1. Rectangular test sets with defuzzified values of 0.5000000000. The UMF is constant at 1, and the LMF decreases from 0.1 towards 0.

LMF	UMF	Left Uncert. bound	Right Uncert. bound	Length of TRS	Area of FOU
0.1	1	0.2157894737	0.7842105263	0.5684210526	0.9000000000
0.01	1	0.0500000000	0.9500000000	0.9000000000	0.9900000000
0.001	1	0.0054455446	0.9945544554	0.9891089109	0.9990000000
0.0001	1	0.0005494505	0.9994505495	0.9989010989	0.9999000000
0.00001	1	0.0000549945	0.9999450055	0.9998900110	0.9999900000
0.000001	1	0.0000054999	0.9999945001	0.9999890001	0.9999990000
0.0000001	1	0.0000005500	0.9999994500	0.9999989000	0.9999999000
0.00000001	1	0.0000000550	0.9999999450	0.9999998900	0.9999999900
0.000000001	1	0.0000000055	0.9999999945	0.9999999890	0.9999999990
0.0000000001	1	0.0000000005	0.9999999994	0.9999999989	0.9999999999

Table 2. Rectangular test sets with defuzzified values of 0.5000000000. The UMF is constant at 1, and the LMF increases from 0.9 towards 1.

LMF	UMF	Left Uncert. bound	Right Uncert. bound	Length of TRS	Area of FOU
0.9	1	0.4855769231	0.5144230769	0.0288461538	0.1000000000
0.99	1	0.4986288848	0.5013711152	0.0027422303	0.0100000000
0.999	1	0.4998635619	0.5001364381	0.0002728761	0.0010000000
0.9999	1	0.4999863629	0.5000136371	0.0000272742	0.0001000000
0.99999	1	0.4999986364	0.5000013636	0.0000027273	0.0000100000
0.999999	1	0.4999998636	0.5000001364	0.0000002727	0.0000010000
0.9999999	1	0.4999999864	0.5000000136	0.0000000273	0.0000001000
0.99999999	1	0.4999999986	0.5000000014	0.0000000027	0.0000000100
0.999999999	1	0.4999999999	0.5000000001	0.0000000003	0.0000000010

Table 3. Rectangular test sets with defuzzified values of 0.5000000000. The distance between the LMF and UMF is constant at 0.05, but the height of the test set increases.

LMF	UMF	Left Uncert. bound	Right Uncert. bound	Length of TRS	Area of FOU
0.025	0.075	0.3526315789	0.6473684211	0.2947368421	0.0500000000
0.125	0.175	0.4538461538	0.5461538462	0.0923076923	0.0500000000
0.225	0.275	0.4724770642	0.5275229358	0.0550458716	0.0500000000
0.325	0.375	0.4803921569	0.5196078431	0.0392156863	0.0500000000
0.425	0.475	0.4847715736	0.5152284264	0.0304568528	0.0500000000
0.525	0.575	0.4875518672	0.5124481328	0.0248962656	0.0500000000
0.625	0.675	0.4894736842	0.5105263158	0.0210526316	0.0500000000
0.725	0.775	0.4908814590	0.5091185410	0.0182370821	0.0500000000
0.825	0.875	0.4919571046	0.5080428954	0.0160857909	0.0500000000
0.925	0.975	0.4928057554	0.5071942446	0.0143884892	0.0500000000

Table 4. Asymmetric test sets with variable defuzzified values. The shape and size of the test set is constant, but the height of the test set increases.

Min. LMF	Max. UMF	Left Uncert. bound	Right Uncert. bound	Defuzzified value	Length of TRS	Area of FOU
0.02	0.19	0.3363636364	0.5248226950	0.4442324244	0.1884590587	0.0610000000
0.22	0.39	0.4484567901	0.5096952909	0.4805290824	0.0612385007	0.0610000000
0.42	0.59	0.4693014706	0.5060240964	0.4881952415	0.0367226258	0.0610000000
0.62	0.79	0.4781413613	0.5043695381	0.4915292610	0.0262281768	0.0610000000
0.82	0.99	0.4830284553	0.5034280118	0.4933946116	0.0203995565	0.0610000000

5. As the distance between the LMF and UMF increases to 1 (Table 1), the TRS length and FOU area both increase to 1. Both measures tend to the value 1 as indicating maximum uncertainty, as for a blank fuzzy set.

Nonetheless there are clear discrepancies in the values reached by the two measures; they are not equivalent. If an interval set is translated in the $x - u$ plane so that its u co-ordinate is increased, its uncertainty *decreases*, as measured by TRS length, yet the FOU area measure remains constant. There is thus an extreme contrast between the two measures in regard to IVT (Definition 9), as the FOU area measure adheres absolutely to IVT, whereas the TRS length measure does not. Is IVT an essential characteristic for a type-2 fuzzy uncertainty measure? In other words, should IVT be a design requirement? If so, then TRS length is unacceptable as an uncertainty measure; if not TRS length is a valid measure of uncertainty.

5   Conclusion

Two measures for the uncertainty relating to an interval type-2 fuzzy set are examined in this paper. Though as techniques they totally contrast, the experiments presented show that similarities are nonetheless apparent in their behaviour.

The most telling difference in the outcomes of the two measurement techniques is in relation to invariance under vertical translation, a characteristic which the FOU area measure adheres to, but the TRS length measure does not. Whether IVT is an essential characteristic for a type-2 fuzzy uncertainty measure is left unresolved, a suitable topic for further work.

References

1. Bonissone, P.P.: A pattern recognition approach to the problem of linguistic approximation. In: Proceedings of the IEEE International Conference on Cybernetics and Society, Denver, Colorado, USA, pp. 793–798 (1979)

2. Bonissone, P.P.: A fuzzy sets based linguistic approach: theory and applications. In: Proceedings of the 12th Winter Simulation Conference, Orlando, Florida, USA, pp. 99–111 (1980)
3. Boumella, N., Djouani, K., Boulemden, M.: On an interval type-2 TSK FLS A1–C1 consequent parameters tuning. In: Proceedings of the IEEE Symposium on Advances in Type-2 Fuzzy Logic Systems 2011, Paris, April 2011
4. Dubois, D., Prade, H.: Fuzzy cardinality and the modeling of imprecise quantification. Fuzzy Sets Syst. **16**, 199–230 (1985)
5. Fisher, P.F.: Remote sensing of land cover classes as type 2 fuzzy sets. Remote Sens. Environ. **114**(2), 309–321 (2010)
6. Galar, M., Barrenechea, E., Fernandez, J., Bustince, H., Beliakov, G.: Representing images by means of interval-valued fuzzy sets. Application to stereo matching. In: Proceedings of the IEEE Symposium on Advances in Type-2 Fuzzy Logic Systems 2011, Paris, April 2011
7. Greenfield, S., Chiclana, F.: Accuracy and complexity evaluation of defuzzification strategies for the discretised interval type-2 fuzzy set. Int. J. Approximate Reasoning **54**(8), 1013–1033 (2013). doi:10.1016/j.ijar.2013.04.013
8. Greenfield, S., Chiclana, F.: Defuzzification of the discretised generalised type-2 fuzzy set: experimental evaluation. Inf. Sci. **244**, 1–25 (2013). doi:10.1016/j.ins.2013.04.032
9. Greenfield, S., Chiclana, F., John, R.I.: Type-reduction of the discretised interval type-2 fuzzy set. In: Proceedings of FUZZ-IEEE 2009, Jeju Island, Korea, pp. 738–743, August 2009
10. Greenfield, S., John, R.I.: The uncertainty associated with a type-2 fuzzy set. In: Seising, R. (ed.) Views on Fuzzy Sets and Systems from Different Perspectives. STUDFUZZ, vol. 243, pp. 471–483. Springer, Heidelberg (2009). doi:10.1007/978-3-540-93802-6_23
11. Hagras, H., Wagner, C.: Introduction to interval type-2 fuzzy logic controllers – towards better uncertainty handling in real world applications. IEEE Syst. Man Cybern. eNewsletter (2009). (issue 27)
12. John, R.I., Coupland, S.: Type-2 fuzzy logic: a historical view. IEEE Comput. Intell. Mag. **2**(1), 57–62 (2007). doi:10.1109/MCI.2007.357194
13. Jurio, A., Paternain, D., Lopez-Molina, C., Bustince, H., Mesiar, R., Beliakov, G.: A construction method of interval-valued fuzzy sets for image processing. In: Proceedings of the IEEE Symposium on Advances in Type-2 Fuzzy Logic Systems 2011, Paris, April 2011
14. Karnik, N.N., Mendel, J.M.: Centroid of a type-2 fuzzy set. Inf. Sci. **132**, 195–220 (2001)
15. Kayacan, E., Cigdem, O., Kaynak, O.: On novel training method based on variable structure systems approach for interval type-2 fuzzy neural networks. In: Proceedings of the IEEE Symposium on Advances in Type-2 Fuzzy Logic Systems 2011, Paris, April 2011
16. Klir, G.J., Folger, T.A.: Fuzzy Sets, Uncertainty, and Information. Prentice-Hall International, Englewood Cliffs (1992)
17. Leottau, L., Melgarejo, M.: Implementing an interval type-2 fuzzy processor onto a DSC 56F8013. In: Proceedings of FUZZ-IEEE 2010, Barcelona, Spain, pp. 1939–1942 (2010)
18. Mendel, J.M.: Uncertain Rule-Based Fuzzy Logic Systems: Introduction and New Directions. Prentice-Hall PTR, Upper Saddle River (2001)
19. Mendel, J.M., John, R.I.: Type-2 fuzzy sets made simple. IEEE Trans. Fuzzy Syst. **10**(2), 117–127 (2002). doi:10.1109/91.995115

20. Sanz, J.A., Fernández, A., Bustince, H., Herrera, F.: A genetic tuning to improve the performance of fuzzy rule-based classification systems with interval-valued fuzzy sets: degree of ignorance and lateral position. Int. J. Approximate Reasoning **52**, 751–766 (2011)

21. Tellez-Velazquez, A., Molina-Lozano, H., Moreno-Armendariz, M.A., Rubio-Espino, E., Villa-Vargas, L.A., Batyrshin, I.: Parametric type-2 fuzzy control design for the ball and plate system. In: Proceedings of the IEEE Symposium on Advances in Type-2 Fuzzy Logic Systems 2011, Paris, April 2011

22. Wenstøp, F.: Quantitative analysis with linguistic values. Fuzzy Sets Syst. **4**, 99–115 (1980)

23. Wu, D., Mendel, J.M.: Uncertainty measures for interval type-2 fuzzy sets. Inf. Sci. **177**, 5378–5393 (2007)

24. Wu, D., Mendel, J.M.: Enhanced Karnik-Mendel algorithms. IEEE Trans. Fuzzy Syst. **17**(4), 923–934 (2009)

25. Wu, H., Mendel, J.M.: Uncertainty bounds and their use in the design of interval type-2 fuzzy logic systems. IEEE Trans. Fuzzy Syst. **10**(5), 622–639 (2002)

26. Zadeh, L.A.: Fuzzy Sets. Inf. Control **8**, 338–353 (1965)

27. Zadeh, L.A.: The concept of a linguistic variable and its application to approximate reasoning. Inf. Sci. **8**, 199–249 (1975)

28. Zadeh, L.A.: The concept of a linguistic variable and its application to approximate reasoning - II. Inf. Sci. **8**, 301–357 (1975)

29. Zadeh, L.A.: The concept of a linguistic variable and its application to approximate reasoning - III. Inf. Sci. **9**, 43–80 (1975)

Slicing Strategies for the Generalised Type-2 Mamdani Fuzzy Inferencing System

Sarah Greenfield[(✉)] and Francisco Chiclana

De Montfort University, Leicester LE1 9BH, UK
s.greenfield@dmu.ac.uk
http://www.tech.dmu.ac.uk/~sarahg/

Abstract. As a three-dimensional object, there are a number of ways of slicing a generalised type-2 fuzzy set. In the context of the Mamdani Fuzzy Inferencing System, this paper concerns three accepted slicing strategies, the vertical slice, the wavy slice, and the horizontal slice or α-plane. Two ways of defining the generalised type-2 fuzzy set, vertical slices and wavy slices, are presented. Fuzzification and inferencing is presented in terms of vertical slices. After that, the application of all three slicing strategies to defuzzification is described, and their strengths and weaknesses assessed.

Keywords: Type-2 fuzzy set · Defuzzification · Type-reduction · Mamdani Fuzzy Inferencing System

1 Introduction

Type-2 fuzzy sets are an extension of type-1 fuzzy sets in which the sets' membership grades are type-1 fuzzy sets. The concept dates back to Zadeh's seminal paper of 1975 [1]. They take two forms, the interval, for which all secondary membership grades are 1, and the generalised, where the secondary membership grade may take any value between 0 and 1. For the computationally simpler interval type-2 Fuzzy Inferencing System (FIS) [2] applications in areas such as control, simulation and optimisation have been developed [3–8]. So far, generalised type-2 fuzzy applications are few in number [2,9,10]. This is attributable to the enormous computational complexity of generalised type-2 fuzzy inferencing. Strategies have been developed that reduce the computational complexity of all stages of the generalised type-2 FIS [11–14], and of particular relevance to this paper, [15]. In [16] three of these strategies are evaluated.

Uncertainty is ineradicably present in the factors upon which decisions are made. The ability to deal with uncertainty is desirable in an FIS because better uncertainty handling gives more accurate outputs. The interval type-2 fuzzy set, an enhancement of the ubiquitous type-1 fuzzy set, has an inbuilt facility to handle uncertain inputs. However the generalised type-2 fuzzy set, an augmentation of the interval type-2 fuzzy set, provides uncertainty handling that is subtle and sophisticated [17]. More generalised type-2 applications are desirable, since at

© Springer International Publishing Switzerland 2016
L. Rutkowski et al. (Eds.): ICAISC 2016, Part I, LNAI 9692, pp. 195–205, 2016.
DOI: 10.1007/978-3-319-39378-0_18

present the generalised type-2 fuzzy set's remarkable facility for dealing with uncertainty is not being fully exploited (Subsect. 5.1).

The focus of this paper is the Mamdani FIS[1] (Fig. 1), in which a crisp numerical input passes through three stages of processing: fuzzification, inferencing, and lastly, the crucial stage of defuzzification. Through defuzzification, the *aggregated set* produced during the inferencing stage is converted into a crisp number which is the output of the FIS. For discretised type-1 fuzzy sets, defuzzification is a simple procedure, with several defuzzification techniques available including the centroid, centre of maxima and mean of maxima [18]. In contrast, defuzzification of a discretised type-2 fuzzy set (as formed in a type-2 FIS) is a process consisting of two stages [19]:

1. Type-reduction, which converts a type-2 fuzzy set to a type-1 fuzzy set known as the Type-Reduced Set (TRS), and
2. defuzzification of the type-1 TRS.

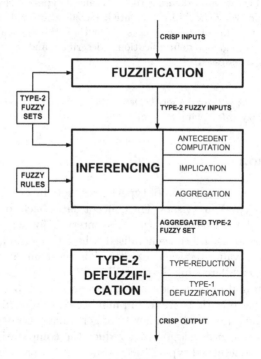

Fig. 1. The Mamdani type-2 FIS.

The paper is structured as follows: The next section presents two ways of defining the generalised type-2 fuzzy set (vertical slices and wavy slices).

---

[1] The alternative is the Takagi-Sugeno-Kang FIS for which the output membership functions are either linear or constant; defuzzification is superfluous as the outputs may be aggregated via a simple weighted sum.

Section 3 describes the join and meet inferencing algorithms which employ vertical slices. Section 4 concerns type-2 defuzzification approaches based on wavy slices, vertical slices and horizontal slices (α-planes). Lastly, Sect. 5 concludes the paper.

2 Defining the Type-2 Fuzzy Set

This section describes how the type-2 fuzzy set may be defined through either vertical slices or wavy slices.

2.1 The Vertical Representation

Let X be a universe of discourse. A type-1 fuzzy set A on X is characterised by a membership function $\mu_A : X \to [0,1]$ and can be expressed as follows [20]:

$$A = \{(x, \mu_A(x))|\ \mu_A(x) \in [0,1]\ \forall x \in X\}. \tag{1}$$

Let $\tilde{P}(U)$ be the set of fuzzy sets in $U=[0,1]$. A type-2 fuzzy set $\tilde{A}$ in X is a fuzzy set whose membership grades are themselves fuzzy [1,21,22]. This implies that $\mu_{\tilde{A}}(x)$ is a fuzzy set in U for all x, i.e. $\mu_{\tilde{A}} : X \to \tilde{P}(U)$ and

$$\tilde{A} = \{(x, \mu_{\tilde{A}}(x))|\ \mu_{\tilde{A}}(x) \in \tilde{P}(U)\ \forall x \in X\}. \tag{2}$$

It follows that $\forall x \in X\ \exists J_x \subseteq U$ such that $\mu_{\tilde{A}}(x) : J_x \to U$. Applying (1) gives:

$$\mu_{\tilde{A}}(x) = \{(u, \mu_{\tilde{A}}(x)(u))|\ \mu_{\tilde{A}}(x)(u) \in U,\ \forall u \in J_x \subseteq U\}. \tag{3}$$

X is called the primary domain and J_x the primary membership of x while U is known as the secondary domain and $\mu_{\tilde{A}}(x)$ the secondary membership of x. Putting (2) and (3) together we obtain

$$\tilde{A} = \{(x, (u, \mu_{\tilde{A}}(x)(u)))|\ \mu_{\tilde{A}}(x)(u) \in U,\ \forall x \in X \wedge \forall u \in J_x \subseteq U\}. \tag{4}$$

Definition 1 (Vertical Slice [2]). *A vertical slice of a type-2 fuzzy set is a plane through the x-axis, parallel to the $u-z$ plane.*

2.2 The Wavy Slice Representation Theorem

An *embedded type-2 fuzzy set (embedded set)* or *wavy slice* [2,16] (Fig. 2) is a special kind of type-2 fuzzy set, which relates to the type-2 fuzzy set in which it is embedded in this way: For every primary domain value, x, there is a unique secondary domain value, u, plus the associated secondary membership grade that is determined by the primary and secondary domain values, $\mu_{\tilde{A}}(x)(u)$.

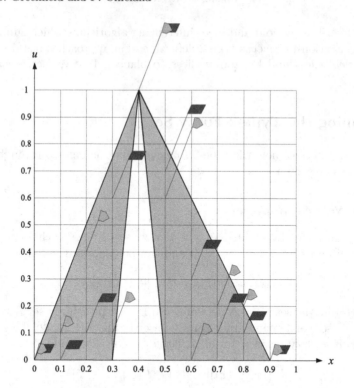

Fig. 2. Two embedded type-2 fuzzy sets, indicated by different flag styles. The flag position in the $x - u$ plane shows the primary membership grade. The flag height indicates the secondary membership grade.

Definition 2 (Embedded Set). *Let $\tilde{A}$ be a type-2 fuzzy set in X. For discrete universes of discourse X and U, an embedded set $\tilde{A}_e$ of $\tilde{A}$ is defined as the following type-2 fuzzy set*

$$\tilde{A}_e = \{(x_i, (u_i, \mu_{\tilde{A}}(x_i)(u_i)))| \ \forall i \in \{1, \dots, N\} : x_i \in X \ \ u_i \in J_{x_i} \subseteq U\}. \quad (5)$$

$\tilde{A}_e$ contains exactly one element from J_{x_1}, J_{x_2}, $\dots$, J_{x_N}, namely u_1, u_2, $\dots$, u_N, each with its associated secondary grade, namely $\mu_{\tilde{A}}(x_1)(u_1)$, $\mu_{\tilde{A}}(x_2)(u_2), \dots, \mu_{\tilde{A}}(x_N)(u_N)$.

Mendel and John have demonstrated that a type-2 fuzzy set is definable as the union of its embedded type-2 fuzzy sets [2,16]. This result is known as the type-2 fuzzy set *Representation Theorem* or *wavy slice Representation Theorem*, and is formally stated thus [2, Page 121]:

Let $\tilde{A}_e^j$ denote the jth embedded set for type-2 fuzzy set $\tilde{A}$, i.e.,

$$\tilde{A}_e^j \equiv \left\{ \left(x_i, \left(u_i^j, \mu_{\tilde{A}}(x_i)(u_i^j) \right) \right), i = 1, \dots, N \right\}$$

where $\{u_i^j, \ldots, u_N^j\} \in J_{x_i}$. Then $\tilde{A}$ may be represented as the union of its embedded sets, i.e.,

$$\tilde{A} = \sum_{j=1}^{n} \tilde{A}_e^j, \text{ where } n \equiv \prod_{i=1}^{N} M_i.$$

3   Type-2 Fuzzy Inferencing Using Vertical Slices

In this section the join and meet algorithms for fuzzification of, and inferencing with, discretised generalised type-2 fuzzy sets are presented [19].

The formula for the join operation of two discretised type-2 fuzzy sets $\tilde{A}$ and $\tilde{B}$ is

$$\mu_{\tilde{A} \cup \tilde{B}}(x) = \sum_{u \in J_x^u} \sum_{w \in J_x^w} f_x(u) \star g_x(w)/(u \vee w) \quad x \in X, \tag{6}$$

and the formula for the meet operation is

$$\mu_{\tilde{A} \cap \tilde{B}}(x) = \sum_{u \in J_x^u} \sum_{w \in J_x^w} f_x(u) \star g_x(w)/(u \wedge w) \quad x \in X, \tag{7}$$

where $\vee$ is the maximum operator, $\wedge$ is the minimum operator, $\star$ signifies a t-norm, and $\sum\sum$ represents union over $J_x^u \times J_x^w$.

Join and meet operations proceed vertical slice by vertical slice[2], so it is sufficient to specify how these operations may be applied to two slices. Let $\tilde{A}$ and $\tilde{B}$ be two type-2 fuzzy sets, in which the co-domains are discretised into N slices, and the domains sliced vertically at the points $x_{\tilde{A}}$ and $x_{\tilde{B}}$ respectively. Two type-1 fuzzy sets,

$$S_{\tilde{A}} = \{z_{A_1}/u_{A_1} + z_{A_2}/u_{A_2} + \cdots + z_{A_N}/u_{A_N}\},$$

$$S_{\tilde{B}} = \{z_{B_1}/u_{B_1} + z_{B_2}/u_{B_2} + \cdots + z_{B_N}/u_{B_N}\},$$

are generated. To join these two slices necessitates that all N^2 possible min / max pairings of $S_{\tilde{A}}$ and $S_{\tilde{B}}$ be created: $\min(z_{A_1}, z_{B_1})/\max(u_{A_1}, u_{B_1}) + \min(z_{A_1}, z_{B_2})/\max(u_{A_1}, u_{B_2}) + \cdots + \min(z_{A_N}, z_{B_N})/\max(u_{A_N}, u_{B_N})$. Similarly, for meet, pairings are generated as follows: $\min(z_{A_1}, z_{B_1})/\min(u_{A_1}, u_{B_1}) + \min(z_{A_1}, z_{B_2})/\min(u_{A_1}, u_{B_2}) + \cdots + \min(z_{A_N}, z_{B_N})/\min(u_{A_N}, u_{B_N})$.

The next stage is the same for join and meet. For every resultant domain value ('denominator') generated, the maximum membership grade ('numerator') is selected. The resultant set of pairs is the join or meet of the two slices.

4   Approaches to Type-2 Defuzzification

This section summarises and evaluates generalised type-2 defuzzification approaches based on wavy slices, vertical slices and horizontal slices.

---

[2] The optimised inferencing algorithms described in [11] employ vertical slices.

4.1   Exhaustive Defuzzification

The strategy known as *Exhaustive Defuzzification*, (so called because every embedded set is processed in turn), is built upon the foundation of the wavy slice Representation Theorem [2] and is therefore precise[3] [2]. However it is a very inefficient method owing to its high computational complexity deriving from the large number of embedded sets. Its first and main stage consists of type-reduction of the type-2 fuzzy set to form the TRS [16], defined thus:

Definition 3. *The TRS associated with a type-2 fuzzy set $\tilde{A}$ with primary domain X discretised into N points $X = \{x_1, x_2, \ldots, x_N\}$, is*

$$C_{\tilde{A}} = \left\{ \left(\frac{\sum_{i=1}^{N} x_i \cdot u_{k_i}}{\sum_{i=1}^{N} u_{k_i}}, \mu_{\tilde{A}}(x_1)(u_{k_1}) * \ldots * \mu_{\tilde{A}}(x_N)(u_{k_N}) \right) \middle| \right. \tag{8}$$
$$\left. \forall (u_{k_1}, u_{k_2}, \ldots, u_{k_N}) \in J_{x_1} \times J_{x_2} \times \ldots \times J_{x_N} \subseteq U^N \right\},$$

where $*$ is a t-norm.

Embedded sets (Fig. 2) are referred to implicitly in 8 and explicitly in Algorithm 1.

Input: a discretised generalised type-2 fuzzy set
Output: a discrete type-1 fuzzy set (the TRS)

1   **forall the** *embedded sets* **do**
2 | find the minimum secondary membership grade (z) ;
3 | calculate the primary domain value (x) of the type-1 centroid of the embedded type-2 fuzzy set ;
4 | pair the secondary grade (z) with the primary domain value (x) to give set of ordered pairs (x, z) {x-values may correspond to multiple z-values} ;
5   **end**
6   **forall the** *primary domain (x) values* **do**
7 | select the maximum secondary grade {make each x correspond to a unique value} ;
8   **end**

Algorithm 1. Exhaustive type-reduction of a discretised type-2 fuzzy set to a type-1 fuzzy set, adapted from Mendel [19].

4.2   Vertical Slice Centroid Type-Reduction (VSCTR)

VSCTR is a highly intuitive method employed by John [23]; the paper of Lucas et al. [12] renewed interest in this strategy. In this approach each vertical slice of

---

[3] Discretisation in itself brings an unavoidable element of approximation. However the exhaustive method does not subsequently introduce further inaccuracies.

the type-2 fuzzy set is defuzzified as a type-1 fuzzy set. By pairing the domain value with the defuzzified value of the vertical slice, a type-1 fuzzy set is formed, which is easily defuzzified to give the defuzzified value of the type-2 fuzzy set. Though chronologically preceding it, this method is a generalisation of the Nie-Tan Method for interval type-2 fuzzy sets.

Input: a discretised generalised type-2 fuzzy set
Output: a discrete type-1 fuzzy set (the TRS)

1 **forall the** *vertical slices* **do**
2   find the defuzzified value using the centroid method ;
3   pair the domain value of the vertical slice with the defuzzified value to give set of ordered pairs (i.e. a type-1 fuzzy set) ;
4 **end**

Algorithm 2. VSCTR of a discretised type-2 fuzzy set to a type-1 fuzzy set.

In [24], VSCTR performed well for both efficiency and accuracy when compared experimentally with other generalised type-2 defuzzification techniques against benchmark values generated by exhaustive defuzzification. The experiments reported in [25] demonstrate that the Nie-Tan defuzzified value (of the interval type-2 fuzzy set) approximates to the exhaustive defuzzified value more closely as domain discretisation becomes finer.

4.3 The α-Plane Representation

Another recognised technique for the defuzzification of generalised type-2 fuzzy sets employs the α-Planes Representation, proposed by Liu in 2008, [15,26][4]. In this strategy a generalised type-2 fuzzy set is decomposed into a set of α-planes, which are horizontal slices equivalent to interval type-2 fuzzy sets. Each α-plane is then defuzzified via the Karnik-Mendel Iterative Procedure (KMIP) [15], so forming an approximation to the TRS. Defuzzifying the resultant type-1 fuzzy set gives a defuzzified value for the generalised type-2 fuzzy set. Below this method is presented algorithmically (Algorithm 3), and diagrammatically (Fig. 3).

Though the α-Planes Method was envisaged by Liu as being used in conjunction with the KMIP [15], any interval defuzzification method may be used. Any variation on the KMIP, such as the Enhanced Iterative Algorithm with Stop Condition (EIASC) [28] will locate the endpoints of the TRS interval. Other interval methods, such as the Greenfield-Chiclana Collapsing Defuzzifier [29,30], or the Nie-Tan Method [31], will defuzzify the α-plane [32]; their defuzzified values (located in the vicinity of the centre of the interval) may then be formed into a type-1 fuzzy set equivalent to the TRS.

---

[4] Independently of Liu, and at about the same time, Wagner and Hagras introduced the notion of zSlices [27], a concept very similar to that of α-planes.

Input: a discretised generalised type-2 fuzzy set **Output**: a discrete type-1 fuzzy set 1   decompose the type-2 fuzzy set into α-planes ; 2   **forall the** α-*planes* **do** 3   find the left and right endpoints using the KMIP ; 4   pair each endpoint with the α-plane height to give set of ordered pairs,   i.e. a type-1 fuzzy set {each α-plane is paired with two endpoints } ; 5   **end**

Algorithm 3. Type-reduction of a type-2 fuzzy set to a type-1 fuzzy set using the α-Plane Method.

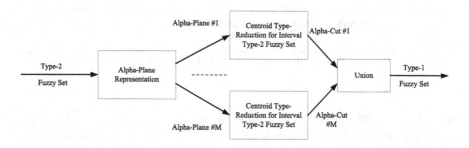

Fig. 3. Type-reduction using the α-planes representation (from Liu [15]).

In [24] the α-Planes Method has been shown to be inferior to two generalised defuzzification techniques, the Sampling Defuzzifier [13] and VSCTR [12], in relation to both accuracy and efficiency. The concept of the *truncated generalised type-2 fuzzy set* is introduced in [33], where it is shown that applying the α-planes strategy to the truncated type-2 fuzzy set makes for more efficient defuzzification, since there are fewer α-planes to process. Intuitive, one might expect that accuracy would also be improved, as irrelevant α-planes (between the maximum secondary membership grade and the truncation grade) would be eliminated and therefore not be able to distort the defuzzified value. However experiments show this not to be the case; in 22 out of 25 instances truncation worsens accuracy [34]. This points to deeply entrenched issues with the method's accuracy.

5   Conclusion

Generalised type-2 fuzzy sets may be defined through vertical slices, or equivalently, through wavy slices. The join and meet algorithms which drive the fuzzification and inferencing stages of the FIS are always implemented via vertical slices. Regarding defuzzification, approaches have been derived from each of the three slicing techniques. Exhaustive defuzzification, based on the wavy slice representation, is absolutely precise but prohibitively inefficient. VSCTR has been shown experimentally to provide an excellent approximation to the exhaustive method, and to be the fastest of the three techniques. Experiments have shown the α-Planes Method to be inferior to VSCTR as regards both speed and accuracy [24].

5.1 Further Work

In order to exploit the generalised type-2 fuzzy set's particular ability for uncertainty handling, more generalised type-2 applications need to be created. This requires the development of optimised algorithms to overcome the problem of computational complexity in generalised type-2 fuzzy inferencing. The research reported in [11,24] shows the progress already made towards this objective. However further efficiencies are feasible in both inferencing and defuzzification.

ExpressJAM: The *FastJAM (Fast Join and Meet)* optimisation [11] reduces computational complexity in the FIS inferencing stages. Initial work has begun on *ExpressJAM (Express Join and Meet)*, a further optimisation of FastJAM that applies to the particularly complex aggregation substage of the inferencing stage, and is optimisable yet further in software via parallel processing.

Generalised Greenfield-Chiclana Collapsing Defuzzifier: The *Greenfield-Chiclana Collapsing Defuzzifier* is an interval type-2 method whose superiority over other interval methods is demonstrated in [24]. Generalisation of this interval technique to the generalised type-2 fuzzy set will result in the *Generalised Greenfield-Chiclana Collapsing Defuzzifier*.

References

1. Zadeh, L.A.: The concept of a linguistic variable and its application to approximate reasoning. Inf. Sci. **8**, 199–249 (1975)
2. Mendel, J.M., John, R.I.: Type-2 fuzzy sets made simple. IEEE Trans. Fuzzy Syst. **10**(2), 117–127 (2002). http://dx.doi.org/10.1109/91.995115
3. Castillo, O., Melin, P.: A review on the design and optimization of interval type-2 fuzzy controllers. Appl. Soft Comput. **12**, 1267–1278 (2012). http://dx.doi.org/10.1016/j.asoc.2011.12.010
4. Celik, E., Bilisik, O.N., Erdogan, M., Gumus, A.T., Baracli, H.: An integrated novel interval type-2 fuzzy MCDM method to improve customer satisfaction in public transportation for Istanbul. Transp. Res. Part E Logist. Transp. Rev. **58**, 28–51 (2013)
5. Dereli, T., Altun, K.: Technology evaluation through the use of interval type-2 fuzzy sets and systems. Comput. Ind. Eng. **65**(4), 624–633 (2013)
6. Abbadi, A., Nezli, L., Boukhetala, D.: A nonlinear voltage controller based on interval type 2 fuzzy logic control system for multimachine power systems. Int. J. Electr. Power Energy Syst. **45**(1), 456–467 (2013)
7. Esposito, M., Pietro, G.D.: Interval type-2 fuzzy logic for encoding clinical practice guidelines. Knowl.-Based Syst. **54**, 329–341 (2013). http://dx.doi.org/10.1016/j.knosys.2013.10.001

8. Castillo, O., Melin, P.: A review on interval type-2 fuzzy logic applications in intelligent control. Inf. Sci. **279**, 615–631 (2014)
9. John, R.I., Coupland, S.: Type-2 fuzzy logic: a historical view. IEEE Comput. Intell. Mag. **2**(1), 57–62 (2007). doi:10.1109/MCI.2007.357194
10. Linda, O., Manic, M.: General type-2 fuzzy C-means algorithm for uncertain fuzzy clustering. IEEE Trans. Fuzzy Syst. **20**(5), 883–897 (2012). doi:10.1109/TFUZZ. 2012.2187453
11. Greenfield, S., John, R.I.: Optimised generalised type-2 join and meet operations. In: Proceedings of FUZZ-IEEE 2007, pp. 141–146. London, July 2007
12. Lucas, L.A., Centeno, T.M., Delgado, M.R.: General type-2 fuzzy inference systems: analysis, design and computational aspects. In: Proceedings of FUZZ-IEEE 2007, pp. 1743–1747. London (2007)
13. Greenfield, S., Chiclana, F., John, R.I., Coupland, S.: The sampling method of defuzzification for type-2 fuzzy sets: experimental evaluation. Inf. Sci. **189**, 77–92 (2012). http://dx.doi.org/10.1016/j.ins.2011.11.042
14. Zhou, S.M., Chiclana, F., John, R.I., Garibaldi, J.M.: Type-1 OWA operators for aggregating uncertain information with uncertain weights induced by type-2 linguistic quantifiers. Fuzzy Sets Syst. **159**(24), 3281–3296 (2008). ISSN:0165-0114. http://dx.doi.org/10.1016/j.fss.2008.06.018
15. Liu, F.: An efficient centroid type-reduction strategy for general type-2 fuzzy logic system. Inf. Sci. **178**(9), 2224–2236 (2008). doi:10.1016/j.ins.2007.11.014
16. Greenfield, S., Chiclana, F.: Defuzzification of the discretised generalised type-2 fuzzy set: experimental evaluation. Inf. Sci. **244**, 1–25 (2013). http://dx.doi.org/10.1016/j.ins.2013.04.032
17. Greenfield, S., John, R.I.: The uncertainty associated with a type-2 fuzzy set. In: Seising, R. (ed.) Views on Fuzzy Sets and Systems from Different Perspectives. Studies in Fuzziness and Soft Computing, vol. 243, pp. 471–483. Springer, Heidelberg (2009). http://dx.doi.org/10.1007/978-3-540-93802-6_23
18. Leekwijck, W.V., Kerre, E.E.: Defuzzification: criteria and classification. Fuzzy Sets Syst. **108**, 159–178 (1999). doi:10.1016/j.fss.2008.06.018
19. Mendel, J.M.: Uncertain Rule-Based Fuzzy Logic Systems: Introduction and New Directions. Prentice-Hall, PTR, Upper Saddle River (2001)
20. Zadeh, L.A.: Fuzzy sets. Inf. Control **8**, 338–353 (1965)
21. Zadeh, L.A.: The concept of a linguistic variable and its application to approximate reasoning - II. Inf. Sci. **8**, 301–357 (1975)
22. Zadeh, L.A.: The concept of a linguistic variable and its application to approximate reasoning - III. Inf. Sci. **9**, 43–80 (1975)
23. John, R.I.: Perception modelling using type-2 fuzzy sets. PhD thesis, De Montfort University (2000)
24. Greenfield, S., Chiclana, F.: Accuracy and complexity evaluation of defuzzification strategies for the discretised interval type-2 fuzzy set. Int. J. Approx. Reason. **54**(8), 1013–1033 (2013). http://dx.doi.org/10.1016/j.ijar.2013.04.013
25. Greenfield, S., Chiclana, F.: Type-reduction of the discretised interval type-2 fuzzy set: approaching the continuous case through progressively finer discretisation. J. Artif. Intell. Soft Comput. Res. **1**, 183–193 (2011)
26. Mendel, J.M., Liu, F., Zhai, D.: α-plane representation for type-2 fuzzy sets: theory and applications. IEEE Trans. Fuzzy Syst. **17**(5), 1189–1207 (2009)
27. Wagner, C., Hagras, H.: Toward general type-2 fuzzy logic systems based on zSlices. IEEE Trans. Fuzzy Syst. **18**(4), 637–660 (2010)

28. Wu, D., Nie, M.: Comparison and practical implementation of type-reduction algorithms for type-2 fuzzy sets and systems. In: Proceedings of FUZZ-IEEE 2011, pp. 2131–2138. Taiwan (2011)

29. Greenfield, S., Chiclana, F., Coupland, S., John, R.I.: The collapsing method of defuzzification for discretised interval type-2 fuzzy sets. Inf. Sci. **179**(13), 2055–2069 (2009). http://dx.doi.org/10.1016/j.ins.2008.07.011

30. Greenfield, S., Chiclana, F., John, R.I.: Type-reduction of the discretised interval type-2 fuzzy set. In: Proceedings of FUZZ-IEEE 2009, pp. 738–743. Jeju Island, Korea, August 2009

31. Nie, M., Tan, W.W.: Towards an efficient type-reduction method for interval type-2 fuzzy logic systems. In: Proceedings of FUZZ-IEEE 2008, pp. 1425–1432, Hong Kong, June 2008

32. Greenfield, S., Chiclana, F.: Combining the α-plane representation with an interval defuzzification method. In: Proceedings of EUSFLAT-LFA 2011, pp. 920–927, Aix-les-Bains, July 2011

33. Greenfield, S., Chiclana, F.: The structure of the type-reduced set of a continuous type-2 fuzzy set. In: Proceedings of EUSFLAT 2013, Milan, September 2013. http://dx.doi.org/10.2991/eusflat.2013.102

34. Greenfield, S., Chiclana, F.: Type-reduced set structure and the truncated type-2 fuzzy set. Technical Report, DMU

On the Sensitivity of Weighted General Mean Based Type-2 Fuzzy Signatures

István Á. Harmati[1(✉)] and László T. Kóczy[2,3]

[1] Department of Mathematics and Computational Sciences,
Széchenyi István University, Győr, Hungary
`harmati@sze.hu`
[2] Department of Automation, Széchenyi István University, Győr, Hungary
`koczy@sze.hu`
[3] Department of Telecommunications and Mediainformatics,
Budapest University of Technology and Economics, Győr, Hungary

Abstract. Fuzzy signatures offer a possible way of describing, modeling and analysing of complex systems, when the exact mathematical model is not known or too difficult to handle. In these cases the input values have uncertainties, due to lack of knowledge or human activities. These uncertainties have influence on the final decision about the system. The uncertainties are taken into consideration as fuzzy sets, for example representing the uncertainty of a linguistic variable. In this paper we discuss the input sensitivity of type-2 weighted general mean aggregation operator and fuzzy signatures which are equipped with general means as aggregation operators.

Keywords: Fuzzy signatures · Fuzzy model · Weighted general mean · Aggregation operators · Sensitivity

1 Introduction

In science and technology often arise problems of describing, modeling and analysing complex systems, but usually the exact mathematical model is not known or too difficult to deal with, due to lack of detailed knowledge of the parameters or the behaviour of the system. Human activities, lack of reproducibility and not well-defined interdependencies between the variables are also common features.

One of the possible ways of modeling such systems is the fuzzy signature based approach. In this modeling technique the complex systems is described by a set of qualitative measures, which are also arranged into a hierarchical framework expressing interconnections and dependencies, and modeling the human approach to the problem. There is a wide variety of applications, for example in economy, in the medical field [1], and in several fields of engineering and informatics, for example robotics [2], data mining [3] and civil engineering [4,5].

© Springer International Publishing Switzerland 2016
L. Rutkowski et al. (Eds.): ICAISC 2016, Part I, LNAI 9692, pp. 206–218, 2016.
DOI: 10.1007/978-3-319-39378-0_19

In mathematical point of view, fuzzy signatures are hierarchical representations of data structuring into vectors of fuzzy values [6]. A fuzzy signature is defined as a special multidimensional fuzzy data structure, which is a generalization of vector valued fuzzy sets [8]. Vector valued fuzzy sets are special cases of L-fuzzy sets which were introduced in [7]. A fuzzy signature is defined by

$$A\colon X \to S^{(n)}, \tag{1}$$

where X is the universe of discourse, $1 \leq n$ and

$$S^{(n)} = \times_{i=1}^{n} S_i \qquad S_i = \begin{cases} [0,1] \\ S^{(m)} \end{cases} \tag{2}$$

A fuzzy signature can be represented by a nested vector value fuzzy sets and by a tree graph also (see Fig. 1), the latter one is more expressive [8].

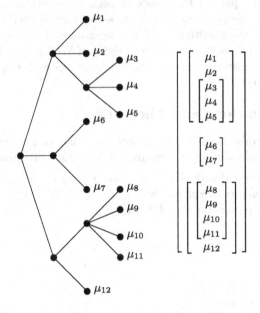

Fig. 1. A fuzzy signature graph and the corresponding nested vectors.

Values at the leaves or input values (μ-s) are usually depend on the opinion of human experts or determined by estimation methods. The final conclusion, the output of the fuzzy signature is computed from the inputs applying suitable aggregation functions, this is the membership value of the whole fuzzy signature. If the input values are not crisp numbers but fuzzy sets then the output is a fuzzy set also. Due to the built-in uncertainty or lack of detailed information of the complex system that we are going to model, different human experts or different kind of estimation methods may give different scores to the same situation.

In real applications a fuzzy signature based model should have some robustness, so the output should not change *too* much if the input values change a *little*.

We mean by sensitivity of fuzzy signatures that the change of the input fuzzy sets (measured by an appropriate distance) how influence the change of the output fuzzy set. In the following we discuss the issue how the membership value or membership function of the whole fuzzy signature changes if the membership values in the nested vectors change. In other words, if we think of the tree graph representation, how the membership value of the root changes if the membership values of leaves change. For answering this question we have to know the structure of the signature tree and the applied aggregation operators. We examine the case when all the operators applied on membership values and membership functions in the signature are from the class of weighted generalized mean aggregation operators (WGMs). The case when the inputs are crisp membership values (not fuzzy sets) was discussed in [9–11], while the type-2 case was firstly introduced in [12], but the question was discussed using different approach.

In the remaining part of the paper in Sect. 2 we review some mathematical definitions and theorems, in Sect. 3 the sensitivity of WGM is discussed, in Sect. 4 we examine the sensitivity of fuzzy signatures in general and in special cases, finally in Sect. 5 we discuss the sensitivity of WGM if the inputs are fuzzy numbers, and the sensitivity of type-2 fuzzy signatures with respect to a kind of Minkowski-type metric.

2   Basic Definitions and Theorems

The weighted generalized mean form a very large class of aggregation operators. Their various special cases often arise also in theoretical and practical problems.

Definition 1 (Generalized Mean). *(see for example [13] or [14]) Let* $x_1, \ldots, x_n$ *be nonnegative real numbers and* $p \in \mathbb{R}$ *($p \neq 0$). Then their generalized mean with parameter* p *is defined by:*

$$M_p(x_1, \ldots, x_n) = \left[\frac{1}{n} \sum_{k=1}^{n} x_k^p \right]^{\frac{1}{p}} \tag{3}$$

Some special cases in p:

- $p = 1$ arithmetic mean
- $p = 2$ quadratic mean
- $p = -1$ harmonic mean

Definition 2 (Weighted generalized mean; WGM). *Let* $x_1, \ldots, x_n$ *and* $w_1, \ldots, w_n$ *be nonnegative real numbers,* $w_i \geq 0, \sum_{i=1}^{n} w_i = 1$ *and* $p \in \mathbb{R}$ *($p \neq 0$). Then the weighted generalized mean of* $x_1, \ldots, x_n$ *with weights* $w_1, \ldots, w_n$ *and with parameter* p *is defined by:*

$$M_p^w(x_1, \ldots, x_n) = \left[\sum_{k=1}^{n} w_k x_k^p \right]^{\frac{1}{p}} \tag{4}$$

We note here that the weighted generalized mean is sometimes called *'scaled norm'*. We do not use this terminology because of the possible misunderstanding: the properties of the norm are fulfilled only when $p \geq 1$, but the WGM is defined for every $p \in \mathbb{R}$.

The generalized mean is a special case of the weighted generalized mean with weights $w_k = \frac{1}{n}$. The limits at $\pm\infty$ regardless to the weights (see for example [13]):

$$\lim_{p\to\infty} \left[\sum_{k=1}^{n} w_k x_k^p\right]^{\frac{1}{p}} = \max(x_i) \qquad \lim_{p\to-\infty} \left[\sum_{k=1}^{n} w_k x_k^p\right]^{\frac{1}{p}} = \min(x_i) \qquad (5)$$

The limit if $p \to 0$ is the weighted geometric mean:

$$\lim_{p\to 0} \left[\sum_{k=1}^{n} w_k x_k^p\right]^{\frac{1}{p}} = \prod_{i=1}^{n} x_i^{w_i} \qquad (6)$$

Our aim is to discuss how the membership function of the whole fuzzy signature changes if the input values change. Since in our case the aggregation operators in the signature are weighted general mean operators, we have to examine the sensitivity of this kind of operator w.r.t. the change of its input vector. The change of the input vector is measured by a p-norm, so first we recall its definition (see for example [15]).

Definition 3 (p-norm). *Let $p \geq 1$ a real number and $\mathbf{x} = (x_1, \ldots, x_n) \in \mathbb{R}^n$. Then the p-norm of $\mathbf{x}$ is defined by*

$$\|\mathbf{x}\|_p = \left(\sum_{k=1}^{n} |x_k|^p\right)^{\frac{1}{p}} \qquad (7)$$

Some widely used p-norms:

- $p = 1$ (taxicab norm) $\|\mathbf{x}\|_1 = |x_1| + \ldots + |x_n|$
- $p = 2$ (euclidean norm) $\|\mathbf{x}\|_2 = \sqrt{x_1^2 + \ldots + x_n^2}$
- $p = \infty$ (maximum norm) $\|\mathbf{x}\|_\infty = \max(|x_1|, \ldots, |x_n|)$

Two important properties of the p-norm:

- If $1 \leq p \leq q \leq \infty$ then $\|\mathbf{x}\|_q \leq \|\mathbf{x}\|_p$.
- If $1 \leq p \leq q \leq \infty$ then $\|\mathbf{x}\|_p \leq \|\mathbf{x}\|_q \cdot n^{1/p-1/q}$.

We will use the generalization of the triangular inequality, the so called Minkowski's inequality.

Theorem 1 (Minkowski's Inequality). *(see for example [13] or [14]). Let $\mathbf{a}, \mathbf{b} \in \mathbb{R}^n$, $p \geq 1$, then the following inequality holds:*

$$\|\mathbf{a} + \mathbf{b}\|_p \leq \|\mathbf{a}\|_p + \|\mathbf{b}\|_p \qquad (8)$$

The generalization of the reverse triangular inequality also holds:

Corollary 1. *If* $\mathbf{a}$, $\mathbf{b} \in \mathbb{R}^n$, $p \geq 1$, *then*

$$\left| \|\mathbf{a}\|_p - \|\mathbf{b}\|_p \right| \leq \|\mathbf{a} - \mathbf{b}\|_p \tag{9}$$

Theorem 2 (Hölder's Inequality). *(see for example [13] or [14]). Let* $\mathbf{a}$, $\mathbf{b} \in \mathbb{R}^n$, $r, s, t \geq 1$ *and* $1/r = 1/t + 1/s$. *Then the following inequality holds:*

$$\left[\sum_{i=1}^{n} |a_i \cdot b_i|^r \right]^{1/r} \leq \left[\sum_{i=1}^{n} |a_i|^t \right]^{1/t} \cdot \left[\sum_{i=1}^{n} |b_i|^s \right]^{1/s} \tag{10}$$

or in terms of p-norms:

$$\|\mathbf{a} \circ \mathbf{b}\|_r \leq \|\mathbf{a}\|_t \cdot \|\mathbf{b}\|_s \tag{11}$$

where '∘' denotes the elementwise product (also known as Hadamard- or Schur-product).

Theorem 3 (Zadeh's Extension Principle). *Let* $f\colon X_1 \times X_2 \times \ldots \times X_n \to Y$ *be a mapping. Let* $A_1, A_2, \ldots, A_n$ *be fuzzy subsets of* $X_1, X_2, \ldots, X_n$, *respectively. Then* $f(A_1, A_2, \ldots, A_n) = B$, *where* B *is a fuzzy subset of* Y *such that*

$$B(y) = \begin{cases} \sup \left\{ \min \left\{ A_1(x_1), \ldots, A_n(x_n) \right\} \mid (x_1, \ldots, x_n) \in f^{-1}(y) \right\} & \text{if } f^{-1}(y) \neq \emptyset \\ 0 & \text{otherwise.} \end{cases}$$

Theorem 4 (Nguyen's Theorem). *(see in [17]) Let* $f\colon X \times X \times \ldots \times X \to X$ *be a continuous function and let* $A_1, A_2, \ldots, A_n$ *be fuzzy numbers. Then*

$$[f(A_1, A_2, \ldots, A_n)]^\alpha = f([A_1]^\alpha, [A_2]^\alpha, \ldots, [A_n]^\alpha)$$

where $f(A_1, A_2, \ldots, A_n)$ *is defined by the extension principle and*

$$f([A_1]^\alpha, [A_2]^\alpha, \ldots, [A_n]^\alpha) = \{ f(x_1, x_2, \ldots, x_n) \mid x_i \in [A_i]^\alpha \}.$$

3   Sensitivity of the Weighted General Mean

In this section we analyse the change of the WGM under the change of its input vector. Note that we examine the case $p \geq 1$. Let we use the following notations:

$$\mathbf{w}^{1/p} = \left(w_1^{1/p}, \ldots, w_n^{1/p} \right) \tag{12}$$

$$\mathbf{w}^{1/p} \circ \mathbf{x} = \left(w_1^{1/p} \cdot x_1, \ldots, w_n^{1/p} \cdot x_n \right) \tag{13}$$

If the input vector is $\mathbf{x} = (x_1, \ldots, x_n)$, the vector of the weights is $\mathbf{w} = (w_1, \ldots, w_n)$, then the weighted generalized mean with parameter p is

$$M = \left[\sum_{i=1}^{n} w_i x_i^p \right]^{\frac{1}{p}} = \left[\sum_{i=1}^{n} \left(w_i^{1/p} x_i \right)^p \right]^{\frac{1}{p}} = \left\| \mathbf{w}^{1/p} \circ \mathbf{x} \right\|_p \tag{14}$$

If the new (maybe perturbed) input vector is $\mathbf{x}^* = (x_1^*, \ldots, x_n^*)$, then the new output is $M^* = \left\|\mathbf{w}^{1/p} \circ \mathbf{x}^*\right\|_p$. So the change of the input is $\Delta\mathbf{x} = \mathbf{x}^* - \mathbf{x}$, the change of the output is $\Delta M = M^* - M$. The upper estimations for $|\Delta M|$:

$$|\Delta M| = \left| \left\|\mathbf{w}^{1/p} \circ \mathbf{x}^*\right\|_p - \left\|\mathbf{w}^{1/p} \circ \mathbf{x}\right\|_p \right| \leq \left\|\mathbf{w}^{1/p} \circ \mathbf{x}^* - \mathbf{w}^{1/p} \circ \mathbf{x}\right\|_p \quad (15)$$

$$= \left\|\mathbf{w}^{1/p} \circ (\mathbf{x}^* - \mathbf{x})\right\|_p = \left\|\mathbf{w}^{1/p} \circ \Delta\mathbf{x}\right\|_p \quad (16)$$

Applying Hölder's inequality we get that

$$|\Delta M| \leq \left\|\mathbf{w}^{1/p} \circ \Delta\mathbf{x}\right\|_p \leq \left\|\mathbf{w}^{1/p}\right\|_r \cdot \|\Delta\mathbf{x}\|_s \quad (17)$$

where $1/p = 1/r + 1/s$. If we use the convention $1/\infty = 0$ then we get

$$|\Delta M| \leq \left\|\mathbf{w}^{1/p}\right\|_p \cdot \|\Delta\mathbf{x}\|_\infty = \|\Delta\mathbf{x}\|_\infty \quad (18)$$

since $\left\|\mathbf{w}^{1/p}\right\|_p = \left[\sum\limits_{i=1}^n \left(w_i^{1/p}\right)^p\right]^{1/p} = 1$.

4 Sensitivity of a Fuzzy Signature

4.1 General Case

Applying the results of the previous section we can analyse the sensitivity of fuzzy signatures in which the values are determined by a WGM operator in every nodes. The sensitivity bound of the whole fuzzy signature can be derived from the bounds of the WGM-s, according to the graph structure of the signature. The whole computation can be carried out from the leaves of the signature to the root (see [11]). In general a WGM has WGMs as inputs:

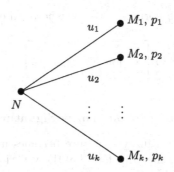

Fig. 2. A part of a fuzzy signature.

Let we denote the inputs of M_i by x_{ij}, $j = 1, \ldots, n_i$, and the weights of the inputs by w_{ij}, $j = 1, \ldots, n_i$, so we have

$$M_i = \left[\sum_{j=1}^{n_i} w_{ij} \cdot x_{ij}^{p_i} \right]^{1/p_i} \tag{19}$$

Then the upper estimation of the change of M_i is given by the previous section:

$$|\Delta M_i| \leq \left[\sum_{j=1}^{n_i} w_{ij} \cdot \Delta x_{ij}^{p_i} \right]^{1/p_i} = \|\mathbf{w_i}^{1/p_i} \circ \Delta \mathbf{x_i}\|_{p_i} \tag{20}$$

Let we denote the minimum of $p_1, p_2, \ldots, p_k$ by p_*. Then because of the properties of the p-norm the following holds for any $i = 1, 2, \ldots, k$:

$$\|\mathbf{w_i}^{1/p_i} \circ \Delta \mathbf{x_i}\|_{p_i} \leq \|\mathbf{w_i}^{1/p_i} \circ \Delta \mathbf{x_i}\|_{p_*} \leq \|\mathbf{w_i}^{1/p_i}\|_{p_*} \cdot \|\Delta \mathbf{x_i}\|_{p_*} \tag{21}$$

Moreover

$$\|\mathbf{w_i}^{1/p_i} \circ \Delta \mathbf{x_i}\|_{p_*} \leq \|\mathbf{w_i}^{1/p_i}\|_{p_*} \cdot \|\Delta \mathbf{x_i}\|_{p_*} \tag{22}$$

Using the above upper estimations we get an upper estimation for the change of the next stage (N, see Fig. 2), where

$$\mathbf{u}^{1/q} = (u_1^{1/q}, \ldots, u_k^{1/q}) \tag{23}$$
$$\Delta \mathbf{M} = (\Delta M_1, \ldots, \Delta M_k) \tag{24}$$

The upper bound is (see [11]):

$$|\Delta N| \leq \|\mathbf{u}^{1/q} \circ \Delta \mathbf{M}\|_q = \left[\sum_{i=1}^{k} u_i \cdot |\Delta M_i|^q \right]^{1/q} \tag{25}$$

$$\leq \left\| \mathbf{u}^{1/q} \circ \|\mathbf{w}^{1/p_i} \circ \Delta \mathbf{x}\|_{p_*} \right\|_q \tag{26}$$

Here the last term is the q-norm of a vector whose ith element is

$$u_i^{1/q} \cdot \left[\sum_{j=1}^{n_i} \left(w_{ij}^{1/p_i} \cdot \Delta x_{ij} \right)^{p_*} \right]^{1/p_*} \tag{27}$$

4.2   Special Case: Homogeneous Fuzzy Signatures

The sensitivity analysis of a fuzzy signature becomes much more simple if the value of the parameter p is the same for all of the WGM operators applied in the nodes. If this condition holds, the output value of the signature is the weighted generalized mean of the input values with parameter p, where the weights are the product of the weights form the root to the leaves.

Definition 4. *A fuzzy signature is called homogeneous if all of the aggregation operators in the nodes are weighted generalized mean operators with the same value of p.*

Lemma 1. *The WGM of $y_1, \ldots, y_k$ with weights $v_1, \ldots, v_k$ and with parameter p where all of the y_i-s are WGM's of x_{ji}-s with weights $w_{1i}, \ldots, w_{n_i i}$ and with the same parameter of p, is the WGM of the x-s with weights $v_i \cdot w_{ji}$*

Proof.

$$
\left[\sum_{i=1}^{k} v_i \cdot y_i^p \right]^{\frac{1}{p}} = \left[\sum_{i=1}^{k} v_i \cdot \left[\left[\sum_{j=1}^{n_i} w_{ji} \cdot x_{ji}^p \right]^{\frac{1}{p}} \right]^p \right]^{\frac{1}{p}} \tag{28}
$$

$$
= \left[\sum_{i=1}^{k} \sum_{j=1}^{n_i} v_i \cdot w_{ji} \cdot x_{ji}^p \right]^{\frac{1}{p}} = \left[\sum_{l=1}^{\sum n_i} c_l \cdot x_l^p \right]^{\frac{1}{p}} \tag{29}
$$

In this case the sensitivity analysis of the fuzzy signature is nothing else but the simple sensitivity analysis of only one weighted generalized mean aggregation operator, which was discussed in Sect. 3.

5   Sensitivity of Type-2 Fuzzy Signatures with Weighted General Mean Aggregation Operators

In this section we analyse the case when the inputs of the weighted general mean are fuzzy sets. For simplicity, and because of practical reasons we assume that all of them are fuzzy numbers (normal, fuzzy convex sets with bounded support and with continuous membership function). Moreover, we handle these fuzzy sets as fuzzy ratings or fuzzy scores given by human experts, because we examine the sensitivity of the operator as the sensitivity of a decision support tool. Here the fuzziness represents the uncertainty (lack of detailed knowledge about the system, lower expertise, etc.) of the given score, or the uncertainty of the given linguistic value.

Remember the sensitivity means how the whole system (in our case: a decision support system) behaves under small perturbations of the input values. As in the case of real or complex values, we have to choose a suitable measure (metric) to give numerical value to the change of the input fuzzy sets and to the output fuzzy set.

There are several distance measures in the field of mathematics of fuzzy sets, see for example [16]. In the following we define a distance metric based on α-cuts and on the Minkowski-type distance. This metric takes into consideration all of the α-cuts, not only the largest deviations. Moreover, this approach give us the possibility the give less importance to lower membership levels by a suitable weighting function, because in decision support methods the lower membership values usually have less importance.

Definition 5. *Let A and B be fuzzy numbers (convex, normal fuzzy sets with bounded support and with continuous membership function) and $q \geq 1$. We define the distance of A and B by*

$$d(A, B) = \int_0^1 \left(|\Delta L(\alpha)|^q + |\Delta R(\alpha)|^q \right)^{1/q} d\alpha \tag{30}$$

where $\Delta L(\alpha) = L_A(\alpha) - L_B(\alpha)$ and $\Delta R(\alpha) = R_A(\alpha) - R_B(\alpha)$, and $L(\alpha)$ and $R(\alpha)$ denote the left and right endpoints of the α-cut intervals, respectively.

Theorem 5. *The distance defined above has distance properties, i.e.:*

1. $d(A, B) \geq 0$;
2. $d(A, B) = 0$ *iff $A = B$ excluding countable set of points;*
3. $d(A, B) = d(B, A)$;
4. $d(A, C) \leq d(A, B) + d(B, C)$.

Proof. Properties 1 and 3 follow immediately form the definition.
Property 3: If $d(A, B) = 0$, then $\left(|\Delta L(\alpha)|^q + |\Delta R(\alpha)|^q \right)^{1/q}$ equals zero excluding countable set of points of the interval $[0, 1]$, so $A = B$ excluding countable set of points. The other direction is straightforward.
Property 4: This inequality follows form the fact that

$$\left(|\Delta L_{AB}(\alpha)|^q + |\Delta R_{AB}(\alpha)|^q \right)^{1/q} \leq$$
$$\leq \left(|\Delta L_{AC}(\alpha)|^q + |\Delta R_{AC}(\alpha)|^q \right)^{1/q} + \left(|\Delta L_{CB}(\alpha)|^q + |\Delta R_{CB}(\alpha)|^q \right)^{1/q}$$

which is the corollary of Minkowski's inequality.

In our case the input fuzzy sets are fuzzy scores form the $[0, 1]$ interval, so their support is that interval. So we deal with nonnegative, convex, normal fuzzy sets. There exist many methods to generalize a usual multivariable real function to fuzzy sets, in our approach we use the most popular (and the oldest) one, Zadeh's extension principle.

Due to the well-known Nguyen's theorem [17] for nonnegative fuzzy numbers, the α-cut of the function is given by the function of the α-cuts. If the input fuzzy sets are $A_1, \ldots, A_n$, then their weighted general mean (M) is given by its α-cuts:

$$M_\alpha = \left[\left[\sum_{i=1}^n w_i L_{A_i}^p(\alpha) \right]^{1/p}, \left[\sum_{i=1}^n w_i R_{A_i}^p(\alpha) \right]^{1/p} \right] \tag{31}$$

where $L_{A_i}(\alpha)$ and $R_{A_i}(\alpha)$ denote the left and right endpoints of the α-cut of input A_i.

If the new (perturbated) inputs are $A_1^*, \ldots, A_n^*$, then the distance of the new (M^*) and the former (M) output fuzzy sets is

$$d(M, M^*) = \int_0^1 \left(|\Delta L_M(\alpha)|^q + |\Delta R_M(\alpha)|^q \right)^{1/q} d\alpha \tag{32}$$

where

$$\Delta L_M(\alpha) = L_M(\alpha) - L_{M^*}(\alpha) = \left[\sum_{i=1}^{n} w_i L_{A_i}^p(\alpha)\right]^{1/p} - \left[\sum_{i=1}^{n} w_i L_{A_i^*}^p(\alpha)\right]^{1/p}$$

(33)

$$\Delta R_M(\alpha) = R_M(\alpha) - R_{M^*}(\alpha) = \left[\sum_{i=1}^{n} w_i R_{A_i}^p(\alpha)\right]^{1/p} - \left[\sum_{i=1}^{n} w_i R_{A_i^*}^p(\alpha)\right]^{1/p}$$

(34)

An upper estimation of $|\Delta L_M(\alpha)|$ and $|\Delta R_M(\alpha)|$ can be given by the reverse triangle inequality:

$$|\Delta L_M(\alpha)| = \left|\left[\sum_{i=1}^{n} w_i L_{A_i}^p(\alpha)\right]^{1/p} - \left[\sum_{i=1}^{n} w_i L_{A_i^*}^p(\alpha)\right]^{1/p}\right|$$

(35)

$$\leq \left[\sum_{i=1}^{n} w_i \left|L_{A_i}(\alpha) - L_{A_i^*}(\alpha)\right|^p\right]^{1/p}$$

(36)

$$= \left[\sum_{i=1}^{n} \left(w_i^{1/p}\left|L_{A_i}(\alpha) - L_{A_i^*}(\alpha)\right|\right)^p\right]^{1/p}$$

(37)

$$= \|\mathbf{w}^{1/p} \circ |\mathbf{L}_A(\alpha) - \mathbf{L}_A^*(\alpha)| \|_p = \|\mathbf{w}^{1/p} \circ |\Delta\mathbf{L}_A(\alpha)| \|_p$$

(38)

where $\mathbf{L}_A(\alpha) = (L_{A_1}, \ldots, L_{A_n})$ and $\circ$ denotes the elementwise product. We get a similar upper bound for $|\Delta R_M(\alpha)|$, of course.

If $|\Delta L_{A_i}(\alpha)| < \varepsilon$ and $|\Delta R_{A_i}(\alpha)| < \varepsilon$ for all $i = 1, 2, \ldots, n$ then we get the following upper estimation of the distance of M and M^*:

$$d(M, M^*) \leq \int_0^1 \left(\|\mathbf{w}^{1/p} \circ |\Delta\mathbf{L}_A(\alpha)| \|_p^q + \|\mathbf{w}^{1/p} \circ |\Delta\mathbf{R}_A(\alpha)| \|_p^q\right)^{1/q} d\alpha$$

(39)

$$\leq \int_0^1 \left(\left[\left(\sum_{i=1}^{n} w_i \cdot \varepsilon^p\right)^{1/p}\right]^q + \left[\left(\sum_{i=1}^{n} w_i \cdot \varepsilon^p\right)^{1/p}\right]^q\right)^{1/q} d\alpha$$

(40)

$$= \varepsilon \cdot 2^{1/q}.$$

(41)

By Hölder's inequality we can give an upper estimation in terms of the norm of the changing of the α-cuts. As we have seen,

$$|\Delta L_M(\alpha)| \leq \|\mathbf{w}^{1/p} \circ |\Delta\mathbf{L}_A(\alpha)| \|_p$$

(42)

Applying Hölder's inequality we get that

$$\|\mathbf{w}^{1/p} \circ |\Delta\mathbf{L}_A(\alpha)| \|_p \leq \|\mathbf{w}^{1/p}\|_s \cdot \|\Delta\mathbf{L}_A(\alpha)\|_t$$

(43)

where $p, s, t \geq 1$ and $1/p = 1/s + 1/t$ ($1/\infty = 0$ by convention). The upper estimation of the distance of M and M^* by the above inequality is the following:

$$d(M, M^*) \leq \int_0^1 \left(\left[\|\mathbf{w}^{1/p}\|_s \cdot \|\Delta\mathbf{L}_A(\alpha)\|_t \right]^q + \left[\|\mathbf{w}^{1/p}\|_s \cdot \|\Delta\mathbf{R}_A(\alpha)\|_t \right]^q \right)^{1/q} d\alpha \tag{44}$$

$$= \|\mathbf{w}^{1/p}\|_s \cdot \int_0^1 \left(\|\Delta\mathbf{L}_A(\alpha)\|_t^q + \|\Delta\mathbf{R}_A(\alpha)\|_t^q \right)^{1/q} d\alpha \tag{45}$$

If $|\Delta L_{A_i}(\alpha)| < \varepsilon$ and $|\Delta R_{A_i}(\alpha)| < \varepsilon$ for all $i = 1, 2, \ldots, n$ then we get the following upper estimation of the distance of M and M^*:

$$d(M, M^*) \leq \|\mathbf{w}^{1/p}\|_s \cdot \int_0^1 \left(\|\Delta\mathbf{L}_A(\alpha)\|_t^q + \|\Delta\mathbf{R}_A(\alpha)\|_t^q \right)^{1/q} d\alpha \tag{46}$$

$$\leq \|\mathbf{w}^{1/p}\|_s \cdot \int_0^1 \left(\left(\varepsilon \cdot n^{1/t} \right)^q + \left(\varepsilon \cdot n^{1/t} \right)^q \right)^{1/q} d\alpha \tag{47}$$

$$= \|\mathbf{w}^{1/p}\|_s \cdot \varepsilon \cdot n^{1/t} \cdot 2^{1/q}. \tag{48}$$

Note that if $w_i = 1/n$ for $i = 1, 2, \ldots, n$ then $\|\mathbf{w}^{1/p}\|_s = n^{-1/t}$, so in this case the upper estimation is simplified to $\varepsilon \cdot 2^{1/q}$.

The sensitivity of a type-2 fuzzy signature can be given similarly to the case of type-1 signatures. Since we deal with nonnegative fuzzy numbers, and we use Zadeh's extension principle to extend the weighted general mean to fuzzy numbers, we only have to determine the endpoints of the α-cuts according to Nguyen's theorem. These endpoints are crisp numbers, so we can apply the results of Sect. 4 estimating the absolute difference on α-levels. In a special case, when all of the weighted general mean aggregation operators have the same parameter (i.e. the signature is homogeneous), then the computation is simplified to only one weighted general mean of fuzzy numbers.

6   Conclusion

The sensitivity of type-2 fuzzy signatures was discussed in the case when all of the aggregation operators are weighted general means with parameter $p \geq 1$. In general case a recursive estimation can be given, but in a special case (when the WGMs have the same parameter) the sensitivity analysis of a fuzzy signature simplified to a sensitivity analysis of WGM on fuzzy numbers.

We note that the sensitivity depends on the choosen distance metric between fuzzy numbers and on the extension of real functions to fuzzy numbers. Zadeh's extension principle and Nguyen's theorem offer an easy way to handle the α-cuts of the result, but usually it has a large support, the membership function is too wide. A possible way to moderate this kind of uncertainty propagation is the t-norm based extension of real functions with a suitable t-norm.

Acknowledgment. This research was supported by National Research, Development and Innovation Office (NKFIH) K105529 and K108405.

References

1. Wong, K.W., Gedeon, T.D., Kóczy, L.T.: Construction of fuzzy signature from data: an example of SARS pre-clinical diagnosis system. In: Proceedings of the IEEE International Conference on Fuzzy Systems (FUZZ-IEEE 2004), pp. 1649–1654. Budapest (2004)
2. Ballagi, Á., Kóczy, L.T., Gedeon, T.D.: Robot cooperation without explicit communication by fuzzy signatures, decision trees. In: Proceedings of the Joint 2009 International Fuzzy Systems Association World Congress and 2009 European Society of Fuzzy Logic and Technology Conference (IFSA-EUSFLAT2009), pp. 1468–1473. Lisbon (2009)
3. Vámos, T., Kóczy, L.T., Biró, G.: Fuzzy signatures in datamining. In: Proceedings of the Joint 9th IFSA World Congress and 20th NAFIPS International Conference, pp. 2842–2846. Vancouver (2001)
4. Molnárka, G., Kóczy, L.T.: Decision support system for evaluating existing apartment buildings based on fuzzy signatures. Int. J. Comput. Commun. Control **6**(3), 442–457 (2011)
5. Bukovics, Á., Kóczy, L.T.: Fuzzy signature-based model for qualification and ranking of residential buildings, XXXVIII. IAHS World Congress on Housing, pp. 290–297. Istanbul (2012)
6. Pozna, C., Minculete, N., Precup, R.E., Kóczy, L.T., Ballagi, Á.: Signatures: definitions, operators and applications to fuzzy modelling. Fuzzy Sets Syst. **201**, 86–104 (2012)
7. Goguen, J.A.: L-fuzzy sets. J. Math. Anal. Appl. **18**(1), 145–174 (1967)
8. Kóczy, L.T., Vámos, T., Biró, G.: Fuzzy signatures. In: Proceedings of the 4th Meeting of the Euro Working Group on Fuzzy Sets and the 2nd International Conference on Soft and Intelligent Computing (EUROPUSE-SIC99), pp. 210–217. Budapest (1999)
9. Harmati, I.Á., Bukovics, Á., Kóczy, L.T.: Sensitivity analysis of the weighted generalized mean aggregation operator, its application to fuzzy signatures. In: IEEE World Congress on Computational Intelligence (WCCI 2014 - FUZZ-IEEE 2014). Peking, China, 06.07.2014–11.07.2014, pp. 1327–1332. IEEE, New York (2014)
10. Harmati, I.Á., Bukovics, Á., Kóczy, L.T.: Sensitivity analysis of fuzzy signatures using Minkowski's inequality. In: Handa, H., Ishibuchi, H., Ong, Y.-S., Tan, K.C. (eds.) Proceedings of the 18th Asia Pacific Symposium on Intelligent and Evolutionary Systems. Proceedings in Adaptation, Learning, Optimization, vol. 1, pp. 587–596. Springer, Switzerland (2014)
11. Harmati, I.Á., Bukovics, Á., Kóczy, L.T.: Minkowski's inequality based sensitivity analysis of fuzzy signatures. J. Artif. Intell. Soft Comput. Res. (Accepted article, in press)
12. Harmati, I.Á., Kóczy, L.T.: On the sensitivity of a special class of type-2 fuzzy signatures. In: Proceedings of the Congress on Information Technology, Computational and Experimental Physics, CITCEP 2015, pp. 219–224. Krakow, Poland, 18–20 December 2015
13. Hardy, G.H., Littlewood, J.E., Pólya, G.: Inequalities. Cambridge University Press, Cambridge (1952)

14. Bullen, P.S.: Handbook of Means and Their Inequalities. Kluwer Academic Publishers, Dordrecht (2003)
15. Golub, G.H., van Loane, C.F.: Matrix Computations. John Hopkins University Press, Baltimore (1996)
16. Bloch, I.: On fuzzy distances and their use in image processing under imprecision. Pattern Recognit. **32**(11), 1873–1895 (1999)
17. Nguyen, H.T.: A note on the extension principle on fuzzy sets. J. Math. Anal. Appl. **64**, 369–380 (1978)

Selected Temporal Logic Systems: An Attempt at Engineering Evaluation

Krystian Jobczyk[1,2(✉)], Antoni Ligęza[2], and Krzysztof Kluza[2]

[1] University of Caen, Caen, France
krystian.jobczyk@unicaen.fr
[2] AGH University of Science and Technology, Kraków, Poland
{ligeza,kluza}@agh.edu.pl

Abstract. This paper is aimed at the engineering evaluating of 3 well-known temporal logic systems: of the Linear Temporal Logic (LTL), of a Fuzzy Linear Temporal Logic (FLTL) and some alternative fuzzy extension of LTL – called a Fuzzy-Time Temporal Logic as a system suitable for an explicit rendering of a fuzzy nature of time. We intend to formulate and defend the thesis – on a base of a behavior of robot in the block world – that chosen systems are only partially capable of satisfying typical requirements of engineers.

Keywords: Linear Temporal Logic · Fuzzy-time tempora logic · Fuzzy Linear Temporal Logic · Engineering evaluation

1 Introduction

The practical utility of the commonly known temporal modal system: Linear Temporal Logic (LTL) or Intervals Allen's algebra ($\mathcal{A}$ll-13) seems to be indisputable, independently of their theoretical – or even philosophical provenance (see: [16]). In fact, temporal logic forms an essential component of many temporal planning tasks such as: generating of robot trajectories satisfying LTL formulas or temporal logic planning with using of model checking machinery. On the other hand, a precise specification of a capability of temporal systems (like their expressive power) appears to be relatively difficult – even from a 'purely' theoretical point of view. For example, it was demonstrated by L. Maximova in [14] that LTL with operator 'next' does not respect the so-called Beth property, what means that not all implicit definitions of this system can be explicitly rendered in its language. This fact seems to justify that the expressive power of LTL is (at least partially) elusive. Additionally, some difficulties with the expressive power evaluation stem from the more practical considerations concerning temporal systems. In fact, it is not clear, which properties of the robot's activity and its work space in temporal logic motion planning can be expressed in known temporal systems.

Objectives of the Paper. According to this, we intend to propose a kind of retrospective evaluation of three temporal systems from the point of view

© Springer International Publishing Switzerland 2016
L. Rutkowski et al. (Eds.): ICAISC 2016, Part I, LNAI 9692, pp. 219–229, 2016.
DOI: 10.1007/978-3-319-39378-0_20

of their 'engineering' utility. We venture to formulate and defend a thesis that neither LTL, nor the so-called Fuzzy Linear Temporal Logic – as some promising LTL-extension from [7], nor some alternative LTL-extension in a form of the Fuzzy-Time Linear are completely capable of expressing the common engineering requirements imposed on (even typical) robot activity in temporal- logic-based motion planning. In order to justify this conjecture we distinguish a handful of such requirements concerning the system's specification, robot actions and a nature of time. This issue forms a main purpose of this paper.

Paper's Motivation and State of Art. The main motivation factor of this paper research is inspired by a lack of a broader comparative discussion on a real expressive power of well- known systems of temporal logics from the point of view of engineering requirements. The considerations of the paper stem from the earlier approaches to the time representation in the framework of LTL – introduced in 1977 in [15] by Amir Pnueli (a point-wise way), of the Allen's All-13 algebra of 13 intervals relations – introduced by J. Allen in [1] – and of the Halpern-Shoham interval temporal logic introduced in [10]. These systems were widely discussed from the meta-logical point of view in a seminal monograph [8]. The optimistic thesis about an utility of LTL in temporal logic motion planning for mobile robots was expressed in [5,6] and in search control knowledge for planning in [3]. The role of LTL as a support of the discrete event-based-model was discussed by Antonniotti in [2]. Temporality in some scheduling contexts was also considered in [9]. A comparative monograph of Emerson [4] gives a broad outlook at the nature of the mutual relationships between modal logic and temporal logic. It forms a kind of inspiration for the authors of the paper to grasp and elucidate the mutual relationships and natural connotations between temporal systems and fuzzy logic systems. An expressive power of some fuzzy logic system with implicitly given temporal component was discussed with respect to some aspects of temporal planning in [12]. In order to preserve some coherence in the material presentation, only these fuzzy logic systems will be discussed, which extend the initial system of Linear Temporal Logic – earlier discussed (in a comparison with Allen's algebra and the Halper-Shoham logic) in the same context in [11]. Some capability of the Halpern-Shoham logic with respect to modelling of some problems of temporal reasoning with preferences was presented in [13].

This attitude determines a subject of our analysis: LTL, FLTL and FTL. For that reason, we omit a description of a well-known Temporal Logic of Action of L. Lamport as a non-fuzzy system, although actions in temporal framework will be a subject of our interest. It also appears that an evaluation of the Lamport's system requires some analysis, which essentially exceeds the thematic scope of this paper.

Paper's Organization. The rest of the paper is organized as follows. In Sect. 2 we formulate our initial problem in a form of some paradigmatic example pf temporal planning with a robot per- forming tasks in block's world. The main paper's body forms Sect. 3, where we present three systems of temporal logic: LTL, FLTL and FTL in order to evaluate their ability to express the requirements imposed on the robot task and its materialization. In Sect. 4 some concluding remarks and a brief outline of future research were formulated.

2   The Problem Formulation and Its Justification

It has been said that a main paper's objective is to evaluate an ability of chosen modal-temporal systems to express the several engineering requirements in examples of temporal planning. In order to realize this goal, we firstly extract a handful of such requirements from a paradigmatic example of the temporal planning with a robot performing the task to relocate the blocks in a given workspace P. Secondly, we check which of the extracted engineering requirements (referring to the robot environments, robot tasks and their temporal requirements) can be captured by *Linear Temporal Logic*, the *Halpern-Shoham temporal logic* and *Allen's interval algebra*.

Problem: We formulate the problem-example that will be addressed in this paper as follows: Consider a robot R that is able to move in a square environment with k-rooms $P_1, P_2, \ldots, P_k$ and a corridor *Corr* for some natural $k > 3$ with blocks A, B, C located somewhere in rooms $P_1, P_2, \ldots, P_k$. Consider that R performs the task: carry all the blocks and put them together in a corridor in an alphabetic order (firstly A, secondly B, finally C). Consider that the robot's activity has the following temporal constraints:

- Take a block B not earlier than $t_0 > 0$ after putting the block A in a corridor;
- Do not take two blocks in the same time;
- The room searching cannot be automatically finished by the robot;
- Visit the rooms $P_1, P_2, \ldots, P_k$ in any order;
- Since a moment t_A visit the rooms in the order: P_1, P_2, P_3.

It easy to see that our problem seems to be a paradigmatic one for all class of similar problems and can be a convenient "bridgehead" for further analysis and attempt of a new system construction. In fact, it contains typical commonly considered commands, tasks, actions concerning robot's activity and its admissible environment. Secondly, such a particularity degree corresponds well with a particularity degree of typical engineering requirements imposed on similar systems.

3   Engineering Requirements of the Problem-Situation

The above example allows us to distinguish the following engineering requirements imposed on the environment of the robot activity, its temporal constraints for its activity and the system specification.

System Specification.

1. *Sequencing:* Carry the blocks in alphabetical order: A, B, C.
2. *Coverage:* Go to rooms: $P_1, P_2, \ldots, P_k$.

3. *Conditions:* If you find a block A, B or C, take it; otherwise stay where you are.
4. *Conceptualization of the robot's activity:* Point-wise events (block A in P_k etc.) and actions on events as processes in time-intervals (the room searching by a robot R, the carrying of the blocks etc.)
5. *Nature of actions:* Some actions finish in the last action event, but some of them can last further automatically in a future (see: the room searching by a robot).

Temporal Requirements.

1. *Temporal sequencing:* Take a block B not earlier than $t_0 > 0$ after putting the block A in a corridor; Since the moment t_A firstly visit the room P_1, after that P_2 and finally P_3.
2. *Temporal coverage:* Do not take two blocks in the same time;
3. *Action duration:* The duration time of some actions (like a room searching) can be longer than some time-interval I_1, but shorter than a time-interval I_2.
4. *Nature of time:* The states should be accessible from the earlier states in a discrete linear time, but potentially – also in a continuous time.

3.1   Linear Temporal Logic (LTL) and Engineering Requirements

In order to evaluate whether LTL is capable of expressing all of the desired engineering requirements, above extracted from the above problem-situation of the robot's activity, we will describe the syntax and semantics of LTL and distinguish the special class of LTL-formulas that could be especially useful for expressing of the above problem-situation.

Syntax. Bi-modal language of LTL is obtained from standard propositional language (with the Boolean constant $\top$) by adding temporal-modal operators such as: *always in a past* (H), *always in a future* (G), *eventually in the past* (P), *eventually in the future* (F), *next and until* ($\mathcal{U}$) and *since* ($\mathcal{S}$) – co-definable with "until". The set FOR of LTL-formulas is given as follows:

$$\phi := \phi|\neg\phi|\phi \vee \psi|\phi\mathcal{U}\psi|\phi\mathcal{S}\psi|H\phi|P\phi|F\phi|Next(\phi) \tag{1}$$

Some of the above operators of temporal-modal types are together co-definable as follows: $F\phi = \top\mathcal{U}$, $P\phi = \top\mathcal{S}\phi$ and classically: $F\phi = \neg G\phi$ and $P\phi = \neg H\phi$.

Semantics. LTL is traditionally interpreted in models based on the pointwise time-flow frames $\mathcal{F} = \langle T, < \rangle$ and dependently on a set of states S. In result, we consider pairs (t, s) (for $t \in T$ representing a time point and $s \in S$) as states of LTL- models. Anyhow, we often consider a function $f : T \mapsto S$ that associates a time-point $t \in T$ with some state $s \in S$ and we deal with pairs (t, f) instead of (t, s). Hence the satisfaction relation $\models$ is defined as follows:

- $(t, f) \models G\phi \iff (\forall t' > t)t' \models \phi$, $(t, f) \models H\phi \iff (\forall t < t')t' \models \phi$.
- $(t, f) \models F\phi \iff (\exists t' > t)t' \models \phi$, $(t, f) \models P\phi \iff (\exists t < t')t' \models \phi$.

- $(t_1, f) \models \phi S \psi \iff$ there is $t_2 < t_1$ such that $t_2, f \models \psi$ and $t, f \models \phi$ for all $t \in (t_1, t_2)$.
- $(t_1, f) \models \phi \mathcal{U} \psi \iff$ there is $t_2 > t_1$ such that $t_2, f \models \psi$ and $t, f \models \phi$ for all $t \in (t_1, t_2)$.
- $(t_k, f) \models Next(\phi) \iff (t_{k+1}, f) \models \phi, k \in \mathbb{N}$.

Specific Set of Formulas of LTL. Due to the observation from [6], we distinguish a class of special formulas of $\mathcal{L}(LTL)$ of two sorts. The first class $X = \{object--names : \psi_1^c, \psi_2^c, \ldots, P_1, \ldots, P_k, Corr, A, B, C; events : A^{P_1}, B^{P_2}, etc.\}$ will describe the robot's environments and its evolution; the second one – $Y = \{actions : see(), move(), \ldots, go(), take(), a_1, a_2, \ldots etc.\}$ – the robot's 'behavior' and activity.

In accordance with our intentions, object-names will be denoted by concrete objects in a considered situations, the events-names by 'real' events such as that "block A is located in a room P_1" etc. In a similar way we encode actions as propositions. It not difficult to observe that LTL, enriched as above, is (at least partially) capable of describing the situation of the robot's activity and partially express desired requirements as follows.

System Specification.

1. *Sequencing:* Carry the blocks in alphabetical order: A, B, C.
   $F(Go(P_1)) \wedge F(Go(P_2)) \wedge \ldots F(Go(P_k))$.
2. *Coverage:* Go to rooms: $P_1, P_2, \ldots, P_k$.
   $Go(P_1) \wedge Go(P_2) \wedge \ldots Go(P_k)$
3. *Conditions:* If you find a block A, B or C, take it; otherwise stay where you are.
   $(See(A) \rightarrow take(A)) \wedge (See(B) \rightarrow take(B)) \wedge (See(C) \rightarrow take(C))$.

Environments of Robot.

1. The blocks A, B, C initially located somewhere in rooms $P_1, \ldots P_k$ but not in a corridor Corr.
   $A^{P_i} \wedge B^{P_j} \wedge C^{P_l} \wedge \neg(A^{Corr} \wedge B^{Corr} \wedge C^{Corr})$
2. The corridor as a final place of the location of blocks A, B, C.

Temporal Requirements.

1. Temporal coverage: Do not take two blocks in the same time:
   $\neg G(take(A) \wedge take(B) \wedge take(C))$
2. *Nature of time:* The states should be accessible from the 'earlier' states in a discrete linear time, but potentially– also in a continuous time.

Independently of such a (relative big) expressive power of LTL, we can observe a difficulty with the expressing of such temporal requirements as delays and move of actions in time (after t_o, longer than t_1, but not shorten than t_2 etc.).

3.2 The Plan Construction and LTL

At the end of the paragraph we shall briefly evaluate how the LTL-formalism can support the plan constructions. We will refer to planning operators classically understood as a sequence of the appropriate actions (expressed in terms of its preconditions and effects). We will focus our attention on the robot's actions that we distinguished in the above engineering requirements. In our case we can approximate a plan construction as follows.

$go(r, P_1, P_2, \ldots P_k)$:
  robot r goes to the room P_1 and-after that – to the adjacent rooms $P_2, \ldots P_k$
  preconditions: • adjacent(P_1, P_2) ... adjacent (P_{k-1}, P_k)
    • blocks are initially located somewhere in rooms $P_1, P_2 \ldots P_k$, but not in a corridor $Corr$:
    $A^{P_i} \wedge B^{P_j} \wedge C^{P_l} \wedge \neq (A^{Corr} \wedge B^{Corr} \wedge C^{Corr})$
  effects: $see(r, A^{P_i}) \wedge see(r, B^{P_j}) \wedge see(r, C^{P_l})$ for $i, j, l \in \{1, 2 \ldots k\}$

$take(r, A, Corr)$
  robot r takes a block A from P_i to the corridor $Corr$
  preconditions: • non-empty(P_i), empty(Corr): $A^{P_j}, \neg Corr^A \wedge \neg Corr^B \wedge \neg Corr^C$
  effects: empty(A^{P_i}), non-empty(corridor):
  $\neg A^{P_i}, Corr^A$

$take(r, B, Corr)$
  robot r takes a block B from P_j to the corridor $Corr$
  preconditions: • non-empty(P_i), empty(Corr): $B^{P_j}, \neg Corr^A \wedge \neg Corr^B \wedge \neg Corr^C$
  effects: empty(A^{P_i}), non-empty(corridor):
  $\neg B^{P_i}, Corr^B$

$take(r, C, Corr)$
  robot r takes a block C from P_j to the corridor $Corr$
  preconditions: • non-empty(P_i), empty(Corr): $C^{P_j}, \neg Corr^A \wedge \neg Corr^B \wedge \neg Corr^C$
  effects: empty(A^{P_i}), non-empty(corridor):
  $\neg C^{P_i}, Corr^B$

4 Some Fuzzy Extension of LTL and Its Expressive Power

This section is aimed at presenting some fuzzy extension of Linear Temporal Logic (LTL), described earlier, in order to capture its expressive power w.r.t. the considered problems. We will denote this new system by FLTL.

Syntax. FLTL has the same syntax of LTL. In particular, let Q be the set of well formed formulas and *Prop* the set of propositional letters, then $\phi \in Q$ if and only if

$$\phi := p | \neg \phi | \phi \wedge \phi | X\phi | G\phi | \phi U \psi, \tag{2}$$

where $p \in Prop$.

Semantics. Semantics of FLTL of Q is defined w.r.t. a linear time structure $\Pi = (S, s_0, s, Lab)$, where S is a non-empty a set of states, s_0 is the initial state, $s \in s_0 \ldots s_\omega$ is an infinite path in Π, and $Lab : S \mapsto [0,1]^{Prop}$ is a fuzzy labeling function. The evaluation Val is defined on Π for set of formulas Q as follows:

(1) $Val(p, s) = Lab(s)(p)$, for $p \in Prop$
(2) $Val(\neg p, s) = 1 - Val(p, s)$
(3) $Val(\phi \wedge \psi, s) = min\{Val(\phi, s), Val(\psi, s)\}$
(4) $Val(\phi \vee \psi, s) = max\{(\phi, s), (\psi, s)\}$
(5) $Val(X\phi, s) = Val(\phi, Next(s))$
(6) $Val(G\phi, s) = min\{Val(\phi, s), Val(G\phi, Next(s)\}$,
(7) $Val(\phi U\psi, s) = max\{Val(\psi, s), min\{Val(\psi, s), Val(\psi U\psi, Next(s))\}\}$.

The condition (1) asserts that a valuation Val in a state s is identified with a labeling function Lab for propositional variables. (3) asserts that a valuation of a conjunction forms a min-norm for valuations for atomic formulas. Valuation for a formula $\psi = X\phi$ in a state s is equal to a valuation of the atomic ϕ in the next state, in $Next(s)$ etc.

In order to evaluate the expressive power of FLTL with respect to the engineering requirements, defined earlier, let us note that this system has the same syntax of LTL. Therefore, it is capable of expressing the features for the robot's motion and environment expressible in LTL. In particular this formalism is suitable to render the same robot motion coverage, action sequencing or its activity plan as LTL. Therefore, no additional portion of information can be extracted in the purely syntactic way.

In order to grasp this (eventual) excessive power of FLTL (w. r. t. the LTL alone), consider against the following robot environment specification:

The blocks A, B, C initially located somewhere in rooms
$P_1, \ldots P_k$ but not in a corridor Corr.
$A^{P_i} \wedge B^{P_j} \wedge C^{P_l} \wedge \neg(A^{Corr} \wedge B^{Corr} \wedge C^{Corr})$.

In LTL, there is a unique way of valuation of such sentences: only 0 and 1 can be associated to atomic formulas. In FLTL, as depicted above, there is a broad spectrum of fuzzy [0,1]-values at our disposal. In order to illustrate this difference in details, let us consider the following simple action sequencing of our robot and our polygonal environment:

$Go(R_1) \rightarrow Move(A)$.

It is clear that this action sequencing can be performed (takes value 1) by valuations associated to atomic LTL-formulas as follows:

$Go(R_1)$	$Move(A)$	$Go(R_1) \rightarrow Move(A)$
1	1	1
0	1	1
0	0	1

In FLTL-case, we have an infinite spectrum of valuation – dependently on a valuation of atomic formulas – computed in accordance with the valuation definition (for simplicity we demonstrate it only for three pairs of values).

$Go(R_1)$	Move(A)	$Go(R_1) \to Move(A)$
0,3	0,4,	0,7
....	....	....
$\frac{1}{10}$	$\frac{1}{10}$	$\frac{9}{10}$
$\frac{3}{75}$	$\frac{2}{25}$	$\frac{24}{25}$

The above values can be obtained as follows: $Val(Go(R_1 \to Move(A)) = Val(\neg Go(R_1) \vee Move(A)) = max\{\neg Go(R_1, Move(A)\} = max\{1 - 0, 3; 0, 4\} = max\{0, 7; 0, 4\} = 0, 7$. These arrangements seem to through a new light for FLTL-expressiveness with respect to the plan representation. In order to elucidate this fact, consider the fragment of LTL-expressible plan conditions for the robot activity with a valuation associated to atomic formulas as depicted:

$take(r, A, Corr)$

  robot r takes a block A from P_i to the corridor $Corr$

  preconditions: • non-empty(P_i), empty(Corr): $A^{P_j}, \neg Corr^A \wedge \neg Corr^B \wedge \neg Corr^C$

$$\qquad\qquad\qquad\qquad\qquad 0,5 \qquad 0,4 \qquad\quad 0,7 \qquad\qquad 0,356$$

  effects: empty(A^{P_i}), non-empty(corridor): $\neg A^{P_i}, Corr^A$

$$\qquad\qquad\qquad\qquad\qquad 0,5 \qquad 0,6$$

These plan conditions with associated truth values can be interpreted as partially executable or – if atomic values represent observability of the plan execution – as partially observable.

5   Fuzzy-Time Temporal Logic

In last section the Fuzzy Linear Temporal Logic without explicit fuzzy-time operators was discussed. In this section some extension of LTL with fuzzy-time operators is investigated and denoted as FTL.

Syntax of FTL. FLT extends the LTL in order to render an explicitly given fuzziness on time. For that reason some fuzzy-operators of called also "almost operators" such as: "almost until" $\mathcal{AU}$, "almost always" $\mathcal{AG}$ etc. These operators and their semantics is often introduced by its bounded versions.

We say that a formula ϕ belongs to the set Q of well-formed FTL-formulas (from now on, simply formulas) if it is defined by a grammar:

$$\phi := p | \neg \phi | \phi \wedge \phi | X\phi | \mathbf{G}\phi | \phi \mathcal{U}\psi | \phi \mathcal{A}\mathcal{U}\psi | \phi \mathcal{A}\mathcal{U}_t\psi | \mathbf{F}\phi | \mathcal{F}_t\phi | \phi \mathcal{F}\psi, \qquad (3)$$

where $p \in Prop$.

It easy to see that[1] the LTL-operator $\mathcal{U}$ ("until") is fibring to a new operator $\mathcal{AU}$ ("almost until") and to its bounded version $\mathcal{AU}_t$. An operator $\mathbf{F}$ constitutes a new class consisting also in a new operator $\mathcal{F}$ (eventually) and $\mathcal{F}_t$ (eventually in the next t instants).

---

[1] Sometimes, further operators such as $\mathcal{AG}$ ("almost always") and $\mathcal{AG}_t$ read as "almost always in the next t instances" are considered. We omit them for a simplicity of the semantics presentations.

Semantics. Semantics of all LTL-operators of FTL was given earlier. The semantics of FLT-formulas is defined w.r.t. a linear time structure $\Pi = (S, s_0, \pi, Lab)$, where S is the set of states, s_0 is the initial state, $\pi = s_0 s_1 \ldots$ is an infinite path in S^ω, and $Lab : S \mapsto [0, 1]^{Prop}$ is the (fuzzy) labeling function that associates to each state some atomic proposition from $Prop$. Additionally π^i indicates the suffix of π, by starting from the i-th position. In such a framework, the semantics for new fuzzy operators can be given as follows (most of them are defined inductively):

- **Almost eventually.**
  $$\pi^i \models \mathcal{F}_t\phi \iff \bigoplus_{j=1}^{i+t}(\pi^j \models \phi), \qquad \pi^i \models \mathcal{F}\phi \iff \bigoplus_{j\leq 1}(\pi^j \models \phi)$$
- **Almost until.** This functor is defined inductively. In the second step, a satisfiability of a formula $\mathcal{AU}_t\phi$ in a suffix π^i is understood as a situation when until j-prefix always ϕ is satisfied; after that ψ is satisfied. Satisfaction condition for $\phi\mathcal{AU}\psi$ is understood as a limit case of the satisfaction condition for $\mathcal{AU}_t\phi$.
  $$\pi^i \models \phi\mathcal{AU}_0\psi \iff \phi^i \models \psi,$$
  $$\pi^i \models \phi\mathcal{AU}_t\psi \iff max_{i\leq j\leq i+t}(\pi^j \models \psi) \otimes (\pi^i \models \mathcal{G}_{j-1}\phi),$$
  $$\pi^i \models \phi\mathcal{AU}\psi \iff limes_{t\to\infty}(\pi^j \models \mathcal{AU}_t\phi)$$

where $\pi^i \models G_t\phi \iff \bigotimes_{j=1}^{i+t}(\pi^j \models \phi)$.

It easy to observe that the newly introduced operators essentially reinforce the expressive power of our FTL w.r.t. the initial LTL. In order to illustrate this fact let us return to the robot motion and environment specification, which can be more realistically specified.

System Specification.

1. *Sequencing:* Carry the blocks in alphabetical order: A, B, C from some t-instance:
   $F_t(Go(P_1)) \wedge F(Go(P_2)) \wedge \ldots F(Go(P_k))$.
2. *Coverage:* Go to rooms: $P_1, P_2, \ldots, P_k$.
   $Go(P_1) \wedge Go(P_2) \wedge \ldots Go(P_k)$
3. *Conditions:* Almost until you take blocks: A, B, C find them; otherwise stay where you are.
   $(See(A))\mathcal{AU}(take(A)) \wedge (See(B))\mathcal{AU}(take(B)) \wedge (See(C))\mathcal{AU}(take(C))$.

Robot's Environments.

1. From some t-point, the blocks A, B, C will be always located as follows: initially – somewhere in rooms $P_1, \ldots P_k$ but not in a corridor Corr.
   $G_t(A^{P_i} \wedge B^{P_j} \wedge C^{P_l} \wedge \neg(A^{Corr} \wedge B^{Corr} \wedge C^{Corr}))$

5.1   Short Juxtaposition

In order to finish our comparative evaluation of the chosen systems of temporal logic, let us compare the detected features of all systems in the table below.

Th considered criteria refer to a time nature, a possibility of the action rendering and to some capability of rendering of fuzziness by all these systems.

Properties	LTL	FLTL	FTL
• time linearity	yes	yes	yes
• time fuzziness	no	no	yes
• way of time representation	pointwise	pointwise/interval	pointwise/interval
• distinction between events and actions	partial	partial	partial
• different actions types	no	no	no
• possibility to express fuzziness of actions	no	partial	yes
• possibility to express the processes	partial	partial	partial
• possibility to express the moves and delays in time	no	no	no
• representation of events in time	non-concrete	non-concrete	non-concrete

6   Conclusions and Future Works

In this paper, three important types of temporal modal logic: Linear Temporal Logic, Allen's interval algebra and Halpern-Shoham logic have been evaluated. We formulated and defended a thesis that these formalisms only partially satisfy typical engineer's requirements imposed on robot's activity in a block's world. We find this attempt promising for further extensions. The natural direction of the current investigation can be an evaluation of the expressive power of well-known temporal logic of action of L. Lamport – not only from the practical, but also from a theoretical point of view. It seems to be also promising to compare LTL with other powerful systems such as Transparent Intensional Logic (TIL).

Nevertheless, it appears that the most important common shortcoming of all these systems is their non-sensibility for different types of actions, processes and events. For example, these systems are not capable of capturing a difference between actions and events. In addition, it sometime arises a need of a sharp distinguishing between actions that can last in a future independently of their initiator and its intentions and actions, which do not have such a property. This issue seems to be a promising subject of future research.

References

1. Allen, J.: Maintaining knowledge about temporal intervals. Commun. ACM **26**(11), 832–843 (1983)
2. Antonniotti, M., Mishra, B.: Discrete event models + temporal logic = supervisory controller: automatic synthesis of locomotion controllers. In: Proceedings of IEEE International Conference on Robotics and Automation (1999)
3. Bacchus, F., Kabanza, F.: Using temporal logic to express search control knowledge for planning. Artif. Intell. **116**, 123–191 (2000)
4. Emerson, A.: Temporal and modal logic. Handbook of Theoretical Computer, vol. B, pp. 995–1072. Elsevier, Amsterdam (1990)
5. Fainekos, G., Kress-Gazit, H., Pappas, G.: Hybrid controllers for path planning: a temporal logic approach. In: Proceeding of the IEEE International Conference on Decision and Control, Sevilla, pp. 4885–4890, December 2005
6. Fainekos, G., Kress-Gazit, H., Pappas, G.: Temporal logic moton planning for mobile robots. In: Proceeding of the IEEE International Conference on Robotics and Automaton, pp. 2032–2037 (2005)
7. Frigeri, A., Pasquale, L., Spoletini, P.: Fuzzy Time in LTL. In: Logic in Computer Science (2012)
8. Gabbay, D., Kurucz, A., Wolter, F., Zakharyaschev, M.: Logics, Many-Dimentional Modal: Theory and Application. Elsevier, Amsterdam (2003)
9. Grobler-Debska, A., Kucharska, E., Dudek-Dyduch, E.: Idea of switching algebraic-logical models in flow-shop scheduling problem with defects. In: Methods and Models in Automaton and Robotics (MMAR), pp. 532–537 (2013)
10. Halpern, J., Shoham, Y.: A propositional modal logic of time intervals. J. ACM **38**, 935–962 (1991)
11. Jobczyk, K., Ligeza, A.: Systems of temporal logic for a use of engineering. towards a more practical approach. In: Stýskala, V., Kolosov, D., Snášel, V., Karakeyev, T., Abraham, A. (eds.) EMACOM 2015. Advances in Intelligent Systems and Computing, vol. 423, pp. 147–157. Springer, Switzerland (2016)
12. Jobczyk, K., Ligeza, A.: Temporal planning in terms of a fuzzy integral logic (FLI) versus temporal planning in PDDL. In: Proceedings of INISTA, pp. 1–8 (2015)
13. Jobczyk, K., Ligeza, A., Karczmarczuk, J.: Fuzzy temporal approach to the handling of temporal interval relations and preferences. In: Proceedings of INISTA (2015)
14. Maximova, L.: Temporal logics with operator 'the next' do not have interpolation or Beth property. Sibirskii Matematicheskii Zhurnal **32**(6), 109–113 (1991)
15. Pnueli, A.: The temporal logic of programs. In: Proceedings of the 18th Annual Symposium on Foundation of Computer Science, pp. 46-57 (1977)
16. van Benthem, J., Bezhanishvili, G.: Modal logic of space. In: Aiello, M., Pratt-Hartmann, I., Van Benthem, J. (eds.) Handbook of Spatial Logics. Springer, Netherlands (2007)

New Approach for Nonlinear Modelling Based on Online Designing of the Fuzzy Rule Base

Krystian Lapa[1(✉)], Krzysztof Cpałka[1], and Yoichi Hayashi[2]

[1] Institute of Computational Intelligence,
Częstochowa University of Technology, Częstochowa, Poland
{krystian.lapa,krzysztof.cpalka}@iisi.pcz.pl
[2] Department of Computer Science, Meiji University, Tokyo, Japan
hayashiy@cs.meiji.ac.jp

Abstract. The problem of online nonlinear modelling emerges among others from limitations of memory. This problem is often solved by using evolving systems. Evolving fuzzy systems play significant role as they are distinguishable by clear representation of knowledge (by fuzzy rules) which allows an interpretation of their behavior. The structure and the parameters of those systems can be selected online. Moreover, the fuzzy rules can represent operating points of modeled object, which can also be identified online. Then, the data from identification can be used for learning. In this paper we proposed an evolving fuzzy system for nonlinear modelling with endless number of steady states and negligible time of non-steady states. It is based on analysis of firing level of the fuzzy rules with possibilities of background learning.

Keywords: Nonlinear modeling · Genetic programming · Fuzzy system · Rules selection online

1 Introduction

The online processing of the data is an important issue often discussed in the literature [52]. For online processing of the data evolving systems (ES) can be used. These systems can adapt to newly incoming data samples (by modifying their parameters and the structure, which allows to obtain best possible results). These systems can be used for a classification, modelling and control problems (see e.g. [11,22,44–46]). The standard systems (not evolving ones) have limitations due to limit of memory for storing data samples and time needed for iterative processing of data [36]. The key element of processing data online is to find appropriate compromise between complexity and stability (possibilities of life-long learning) [85]. It is worth to note that many computational intelligence methods (see e.g. [1,3,5–7,14,18–20,27–31,33,34,37,39,49,54–58,61–63,69–73,82,87]) are successfully used in pattern recognition (see e.g. [15–17,88–93]), modelling (see e.g. [4,12,13]) and optimization (see e.g. [21,23–25,32,40,41,81]) issues. Neuro-fuzzy systems (see e.g.

© Springer International Publishing Switzerland 2016
L. Rutkowski et al. (Eds.): ICAISC 2016, Part I, LNAI 9692, pp. 230–247, 2016.
DOI: 10.1007/978-3-319-39378-0_21

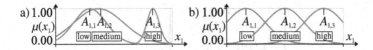

Fig. 1. Interpretability emerged from parameters of fuzzy sets: (a) low, (b) high.

[9,10,65–68,74,75]) combine the natural language description of fuzzy systems (see e.g. [38,45,46]) and the learning properties of neural networks (see e.g. [76,77,79,80,83,84]).

In case of evolving systems, evolving fuzzy systems (EFS) [50] play significant role. Those systems are based on interpretable fuzzy rules [64]. Fuzzy rules take form of 'IF ... THEN ...' and they are based on fuzzy sets. EFS are designed step by step, on the basis of incoming data samples. The purpose of systems design is to provide high accuracy and low complexity (resulting from for example low number of fuzzy rules [26]). To obtain such systems, a few approaches can be found in the literature: approaches based on merging similarity fuzzy rules [47, 53,59], approaches based on adding fuzzy rules into system only when specified conditions are met [48,51,60] or approaches based on modification of currently existing fuzzy rules [2,50,78].

The fuzzy systems (see e.g. [9,10,12,13,15,16,24,88,89]) interpretability can result not only from the low number of fuzzy rules and fuzzy sets, but also from the semantic of appropriate selected parameters of fuzzy sets [26] (Fig. 1). The semantic simplifies (clarifies) understanding of how models [26] (Fig. 1), classifiers [2,42] and control systems [43] work. It is worth to mention that the interpretability of the online designed models is an important issue. It emerges from possibilities of understanding how the current object works, and it allows us to model the typical states of the object. Those states in the further part of this paper will be called operation points. In the fuzzy systems each operation point can be represented by single fuzzy rule.

In this paper, the evolving fuzzy system based on analyzing of firing level of the rules is proposed. Moreover, a few approaches were tested, including modification of parameters of fuzzy sets and possibilities of background learning with using prepared (auxiliary) data samples.

This paper is divided as follows: in Sect. 2 the proposed system is described, in Sect. 3 an idea of designing of the proposed system is presented, in Sect. 4 simulation results are shown, whereas in Sect. 5 the conclusions are drawn.

2   Neuro-fuzzy System for Online Nonlinear Modelling

The proposed approach uses neuro-fuzzy system of Mamdani type [64]. This system was designed in a way to allow online flexible build of fuzzy rules. This process is based on creating and modifying fuzzy rules. The fuzzy rules are based on dynamical base of fuzzy sets defined as follows:

$$\mathbf{C} = \left\{ \begin{array}{l} A_{1,1}, ..., A_{1,L_1^A}, ..., \\ A_{n,1}, ..., A_{n,L_n^A}, \\ B_{1,1}, ..., B_{1,L_1^B}, ..., \\ B_{m,1}, ..., B_{m,L_m^B} \end{array} \right\} = \{C_1, ..., C_{L^c}\}, \tag{1}$$

where $A_{i,l}$ stands for input fuzzy sets, $i = 1, ..., n$ stands for input index, n stands for number of inputs, $l = 1, ..., L_i^A$ stands for index of fuzzy set, L_i^A stands for number of input fuzzy sets from base (1) related to input i. $B_{j,l}$ stands for output fuzzy sets, $j = 1, ..., m$ stands for output index, m stands for number of outputs, $l = 1, ..., L_j^B$ stands for index of fuzzy set, L_j^B stands for number of output fuzzy sets from base (1) related to output j, $L^C = \sum_{i=1}^n L_i^A + \sum_{j=1}^m L_j^B$ stands for, changing in the learning process, total number of fuzzy sets. This approach allows to work with elastic number of fuzzy sets. Each fuzzy set $A_{i,l}$ is represented by membership function $\mu_{A_{i,l}}(x)$, while each fuzzy set $B_{j,l}$ is represented by membership function $\mu_{B_{j,k}}(y)$. In the proposed approach a Gaussian-type membership functions were used. Therefore, for the fuzzy sets the following parameters were assigned:

$$\begin{cases} A_{i,l} = \{x_{i,l}^A, \sigma_{i,l}^A, c_{i,l}^A\} & \text{for input fuzzy set} \\ B_{j,l} = \{y_{j,l}^B, \sigma_{j,l}^B, c_{j,l}^B\} & \text{for output fuzzy set,} \end{cases} \tag{2}$$

where $x_{i,l}^A$ and $y_{j,l}^B$ stands for centers of fuzzy sets, $\sigma_{i,l}^A$ and $\sigma_{j,l}^B$ stands for widths of fuzzy sets, $c_{i,l}^A$ i $c_{j,l}^B$ stands for counters of using fuzzy sets, treat as heaviness.

The fuzzy rules base contains fuzzy rules $\mathbf{R}_k$, where $k = 1, ..., N$ stands for fuzzy rule index, N stands for actual number of fuzzy sets. The number of fuzzy rules can change in a learning process (Sect. 3). In the proposed approach fuzzy rules are connected with the fuzzy sets by indexes $I_{i,k}^A$ and $I_{j,k}^B$:

$$\mathbf{R}_k = \{I_{1,k}^A, ..., I_{n,k}^A, I_{1,k}^B, ..., I_{m,k}^B\}, \tag{3}$$

where each index $I_{i,k}^A$ refers to one input fuzzy set from base $\mathbf{C}$ and each index $I_{j,k}^B$ refers to one output fuzzy set from base $\mathbf{C}$. This approach allows sharing of single fuzzy sets by many fuzzy rules, which notation is defined as:

$$R_k : \text{IF} \begin{pmatrix} x_1 \text{ is } A_{1,I_{1,k}^A} \text{ AND} \\ x_2 \text{ is } A_{2,I_{2,k}^A} \text{ AND} \\ ... \\ x_n \text{ is } A_{n,I_{n,k}^A} \end{pmatrix} \text{THEN} \begin{pmatrix} y_1 \text{ is } B_{1,I_{1,k}^B} \text{ AND} \\ y_2 \text{ is } B_{2,I_{2,k}^B} \text{ AND} \\ ... \\ y_m \text{ is } B_{m,I_{m,k}^B} \end{pmatrix}. \tag{4}$$

The firing level (activation level) of fuzzy rule $\mathbf{R}_k$ is calculated as:

$$\tau_k(\bar{\mathbf{x}}) = \mathop{T}_{i=1}^n \left\{ \mu_{A_{i,I_{i,k}^A}}(\bar{x}_i) \right\} = T\left\{ \mu_{A_{1,I_{1,k}^A}}(\bar{x}_1), ..., \mu_{A_{n,I_{n,k}^A}}(\bar{x}_n) \right\}, \tag{5}$$

where $T(\cdot)$ is any triangular t-norm [64]. In case of using product type of t-norm the Eq. (5) is defined as:

$$\tau_k(\bar{\mathbf{x}}) = \prod_{i=1}^n \mu_{A_{i,I_{i,k}^A}}(\bar{x}_i). \tag{6}$$

In case of singleton defuzzification, the interferences from k-th rule are calculated independently for each j-th output by triangular t-norm (which is an interference operator in the Mamdani type of fuzzy system) (see e.g. [64]):

$$\mu_{\bar{B}_{j,k}}\left(\bar{\mathbf{x}}, y\right) = \mu_{\mathbf{A}_k \to B_{j,k}}\left(\bar{\mathbf{x}}, y\right) = T\left\{\tau_k\left(\bar{\mathbf{x}}\right), \mu_{B_{I_{j,k}^{B}}}\left(y\right)\right\}. \tag{7}$$

The aggregation of interference of fuzzy rules is calculated as follows:

$$\mu_{B_j'}\left(\bar{\mathbf{x}}, y\right) = \mathop{S}_{k=1}^{N}\left\{\mu_{\bar{B}_{j,k}}\left(\bar{\mathbf{x}}, y\right)\right\} = S\left\{\mu_{\bar{B}_{j,1}}\left(\bar{\mathbf{x}}, y\right), ..., \mu_{\bar{B}_{j,N}}\left(\bar{\mathbf{x}}, y\right)\right\}, \tag{8}$$

where $S\left(\cdot\right)$ is triangular t-conorm. In case of use of product t-conorm, the Eq. (8) is defined as:

$$\mu_{B_j'}\left(\bar{\mathbf{x}}, y\right) = 1 - \prod_{k=1}^{N}\left(1 - \mu_{\bar{B}_{j,k}}\left(\bar{\mathbf{x}}, y\right)\right). \tag{9}$$

The defuzzificated values of fuzzy system of its j-th output can be calculated with for example center of area method:

$$\bar{y}_j\left(\bar{\mathbf{x}}\right) = \frac{\sum\limits_{l=1}^{L_j^{B}} y_{j,l}^{B} \cdot \mu_{B_j'}\left(\bar{\mathbf{x}}, y_{j,l}^{B}\right)}{\sum\limits_{l=1}^{L_j^{B}} \mu_{B_j'}\left(\bar{\mathbf{x}}, y_{j,l}^{B}\right)}, \tag{10}$$

where $y_{j,l}^{B}$ are values equal to maximum (isolated) points of the functions $\mu_{B_{j,k}}\left(y\right)$ (which are centers of used in simulations Gaussian-type fuzzy sets) (Sect. 4).

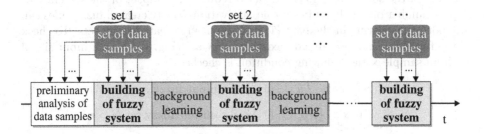

Fig. 2. The idea of proposed evolving fuzzy system.

3   Description of Proposed Method

In this paper three cases were presented (their details are included in next part of this Section):

- In **Case 1** fuzzy rules and fuzzy sets are added into the system on the basis of analysis of firing level of fuzzy rules (5).
- In **Case 2** additional modification of fuzzy system parameters based on heaviness of fuzzy sets is performed.
- In **Case 3** additional background learning on the basis of auxiliary data samples is performed.

3.1   Preliminary Analysis of Data Samples

The purpose of preliminary analysis of data samples (Fig. 2) is to estimate initialization values of widths of fuzzy sets. Each sample $\bar{\mathbf{x}}$ consist of n input signals and m output signals : $\bar{\mathbf{x}} = \{\bar{x}_1, ..., \bar{x}_n, \bar{x}_{n+1}, ..., \bar{x}_{n+m}\} = \{\bar{x}_1, ..., \bar{x}_h\}$, for which a minims $\mathbf{x}^{\min}$ and maxims $\mathbf{x}^{\max}$ are determined. The minims and maxims allows to determine widths of fuzzy sets in the following way:

$$\sigma_i = \sigma^{\mathrm{par}} \cdot \left(x_i^{\max} - x_i^{\min}\right), \tag{11}$$

where $\sigma^{\mathrm{par}} \in [0, 1]$ stands for parameter specifying the initial width of fuzzy sets (lower value stands for narrower fuzzy sets).

3.2   Building of Fuzzy System

In the proposed method new fuzzy rules are added into system when the actual sample $\bar{\mathbf{x}}$ do not active with (specified by parameter $\tau^{\mathrm{akt}} \in [0,1]$) level any of existed fuzzy rules in form of (4). This condition can be write as:

$$\tau^{\mathrm{akt}} > \max_{k=1,...,N} \left\{ \sqrt[n]{\tau_k(\bar{\mathbf{x}})} \right\}. \tag{12}$$

The use of the square root in the Eq. (12) reduces the impact of the system (10) inputs number on results of fuzzy rules activation. Newly created fuzzy rules can use both the existing in the base (1) and the newly created fuzzy sets. To check if the fuzzy rule can use already existing fuzzy set (Fig. 3) for each input signal $\bar{x}_i$ from sample $\bar{\mathbf{x}}$ the following condition is checked:

$$\begin{cases} \mu^{\mathrm{akt}} > \max\limits_{l=1,...,L_i^A} \left\{\mu_{A_{h,l}}(\bar{x}_i)\right\} & \text{for input fuzzy set } (i \le n) \\ \mu^{\mathrm{akt}} > \max\limits_{l=1,...,L_{i-n}^B} \left\{\mu_{B_{h-n,l}}(\bar{x}_i)\right\} & \text{for output fuzzy set } (i > n), \end{cases} \tag{13}$$

where $\mu^{\mathrm{akt}} \in [0, 1]$ stands for threshold value specifying when existing fuzzy set might be used (it acts similar to a function parameter τ^{akt} of fuzzy rules). If the condition (13) is met, a fuzzy rules can use existing fuzzy set (with highest value of membership function) and the index I_i^A or I_{i-n}^B is set on index of this fuzzy set. In the other case, a new fuzzy set is inserted into fuzzy sets base (2) with parameters initialized as follows:

$$\begin{cases} x_{i,l}^A = \bar{x}_i; \sigma_{i,l}^A = \sigma_i; c_{i,l}^A = 1 & \text{for input fuzzy set } (i \le n) \\ y_{j,l}^B = \bar{x}_{n+j}; \sigma_{j,l}^B = \sigma_{n+j}; c_{j,l}^B = 1 & \text{for output fuzzy set } (i > n). \end{cases} \tag{14}$$

In the proposed approach we assumed that every data sample can represent important operation point for modelled object, which means that every data sample has to be included in the modelling process. Due to this, proposed algorithm can be used mostly for modelling objects with endless number of steady states and negligible time of non-steady states. It is not directly suitable for modelling oscillating objects.

If the sample has not met the condition (12) for **Case 2** and **Case 3** the parameters of the fuzzy sets existing in the base **C** with higher value of membership function are additionally modified. Due to using heaviness of fuzzy sets in this modification, the insensitivity of changes slowly decreases. Thanks to that the fuzzy sets retain in clear (interpretable) positions (they do not overlap each other). Moreover, the information about operation points is also kept. The modification of fuzzy sets is carried out as follows:

$$
\begin{cases}
x_{i,l}^A = \frac{c_{i,l}^A \cdot x_{i,l}^A + 1 \cdot \bar{x}_i}{c_{i,l}^A + 1}; \; c_{i,l}^A = c_{i,l}^A + 1 & \text{for input fuzzy set } (i \le n) \\
y_{i-n,l}^B = \frac{c_{i-n,l}^B \cdot y_{i-n,l}^B + 1 \cdot \bar{x}_i}{c_{i-n,l}^B + 1}; \; c_{i-n,l}^B = c_{i-n,l}^B + 1 & \text{for output fuzzy set } (i > n),
\end{cases}
\tag{15}
$$

which is based on the idea of moving clusters from the Ward method [86]. In case of creating new rule the parameters of existing fuzzy sets connected to this rule are also modified according to Eq. (15). Therefore, the building of fuzzy system is based on standard fuzzy system mechanisms: the analysis of firing (activation) of fuzzy rules and analysis of the values of fuzzy sets membership functions. This approach is new in the literature.

3.3 Background Learning

EFS are by default system parameters which cannot be tuned. It results from theoretically infinite number of incoming online data samples. However, in **Case 3**

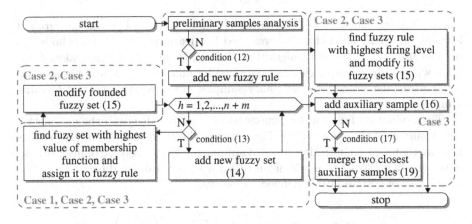

Fig. 3. The block schema of proposed approach (Case 1, 2 and 3).

a method of background learning (tuning) of parameters of fuzzy sets is presented. It was achieved by creating and storing maximum of $R^{\max}$ auxiliary samples for each fuzzy rule. The process of tuning (Fig. 2) can be executed for example in additional thread. Each auxiliary sample of k-th rule is stored in the form of cluster as in Ward's method [86]. Each cluster is represented by centers $x^R_{h,k,d}$ and heaviness $c^R_{k,d}$ where $d = 1, ..., R^{\max}$ is an index of auxiliary sample, $k = 1, ..., N$, and $h = 1, ..., n + m$.

The process of creating auxiliary samples is connected to the process of creating and modifying fuzzy rules. Each of incoming data samples becomes an auxiliary sample for those rules for with highest value of firing (activation) level:

$$x^R_{h,k,d} = \bar{x}_h; c^R_{k,d} = 1. \tag{16}$$

When the number of auxiliary samples for specified rule is higher than maximum number of data samples $R^{\max}$:

$$d > R^{\max}, \tag{17}$$

then, two closest auxiliary samples are merged. The distance between auxiliary samples (with taking into account heaviness) is calculated as follows:

$$dist_{d1,d2} = \frac{c^R_{k,d1} \cdot c^R_{k,d2}}{c^R_{k,d1} + c^R_{k,d2}} \cdot \sum_{h=1}^{n+m} \left| \frac{x^R_{h,k,d1} - x^R_{h,k,d2}}{x^{\max}_h - x^{\min}_h} \right|, \tag{18}$$

where $d1$, $d2$ are indexes of two comparing auxiliary samples. It is worth to mention that the comparison (18) is executed $R^{\max} / (2! \cdot (R^{\max} - 2)!)$ times. Therefore, the number $R^{\max}$ cannot be very high. The merging of two closest auxiliary samples is performed as follows:

$$x^R_{h,k,d3} = \frac{c^R_{k,d1} \cdot x^R_{h,k,d1} + c^R_{k,d2} \cdot x^R_{h,k,d2}}{c^R_{k,d1} + c^R_{k,d2}}; c^R_{k,d3} = c^R_{k,d1} + c^R_{k,d2}, \tag{19}$$

where $d3$ is an index of newly created auxiliary sample. For the background learning, a genetic algorithm [64] was used (for learning any other methods can be also used, i. a.: gradient algorithms [65,66,68] or evolutionary algorithms [67]), which aims to minimize error obtained for all auxiliary samples in all rules (in the learning process the auxiliary samples are treated as normal learning samples).

The evaluation function for genetic algorithm includes both the complexity and accuracy of the system (10). The interpretability of the system (10) results from mechanisms included in proposed approach (slowly decrease of insensitivity of moving fuzzy sets and mechanisms of adding fuzzy rules and fuzzy sets). The complexity of system (10) is defined as follows:

$$CMPL = w^{\text{rule}} \cdot N + w^{\text{fset}} \cdot \left(\sum_{i=1}^{n} L^A_i + \sum_{j=1}^{m} L^B_j \right), \tag{20}$$

where $w^{rule} \in [0,1]$ stands for weight of fuzzy rules (set experimentally to 1.0), $w^{fset} \in [0,1]$ stands for weight of fuzzy sets (set experimentally to 0.5). The accuracy of the system (10) is determined by $RMSE$:

$$RMSE = \frac{1}{Z \cdot m} \sum_{i=1}^{Z} \sum_{j=1}^{m} \sqrt{\left(\bar{y}_j\left(\bar{\mathbf{x}}_z\right) - x_{z,n+j}\right)^2}. \tag{21}$$

4   Simulations

4.1   Simulation Problems

In our paper a following nonlinear modelling problems were used: plant (marked as #1) [35], chemical plant [10] (marked as #2), Box & Jenkins gas furnace problem (marked as #3) [10]. The data used for building of fuzzy system was modified in a way to allow an online creation of fuzzy system: (a) from data a 10 % randomly chosen samples are selected and delivered into fuzzy system (approaches like that can be found in the literature), (b) those samples are used to create auxiliary samples (Case 3), (c) the 100 % of data is used for testing the system (10). This procedure was repeated 20 times. Each simulation for each problem was repeated 50 times and results were averaged.

4.2   Selection of Parameters

The parameters σ^{par}, τ^{akt} and μ^{akt} have decisive impact on accuracy and complexity of the system (10). The parameter σ^{par} (responsible for initial widths of fuzzy sets) was set experimentally to value 0.15 to obtain appropriate (interpretable) number of fuzzy sets (Fig. 4a)) and fuzzy rules (Fig. 4b)). The parameter τ^{akt} (threshold value specifying when to add new fuzzy rule) was set experimentally to value 0.25, the parameter μ^{akt} (threshold value specifying when existing fuzzy set might be used) was set experimentally to value 0.20. To choose those parameters both the good accuracy (Fig. 5a)) and good complexity

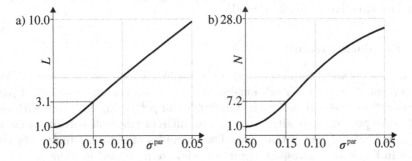

Fig. 4. Dependences between parameter σ^{par} and: (a) average number of fuzzy sets of each input and output (L), (b) average number of fuzzy rules (N).

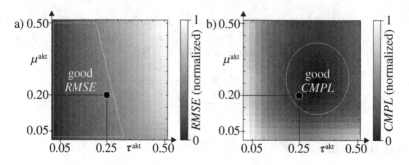

Fig. 5. Averaged for all problems dependences between parameters τ^{akt} and u^{akt} and: (a) *RMSE*, (b) *CMPL*. The dots stand for optimal set of parameters founded by experimental method.

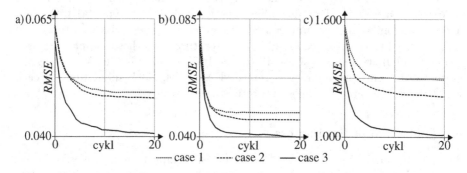

Fig. 6. Process of building of fuzzy system for considered problem: (a) #1, (b) #2, (c) #3.

(Fig. 5b)) were considered. The parameters of background learning were chosen experimentally: mutation probability $p_m = 0.15$, crossover probability $p_c = 0.75$, number of maximum auxiliary samples $R^{max} = 3$. In equations that define firing level of rules (5), interference of rules (7) and aggregation of interference (8) the product triangular norms were used.

4.3   Simulation Results

The results obtained for considered problems for all cases were shown in Fig. 6 and presented in Table 2. Additionally, in Fig. 7 results of combinations of parameters $\tau^{par} \in [0.025, 0.500]$ with step 0.025 and $\mu^{akt} \in [0.025, 0.500]$ with step 0.025 were presented. It allows to achieve different trade-off between accuracy and complexity of the system (10). The examples of obtained fuzzy sets were shown in Fig. 8 and corresponding fuzzy rules are presented in Table 1.

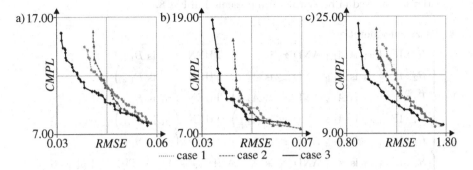

Fig. 7. Pareto fronts [8] obtained due to testing different values of parameter τ^{akt} and u^{akt} for considered problem: (a) #1, (b) #2, (c) #3.

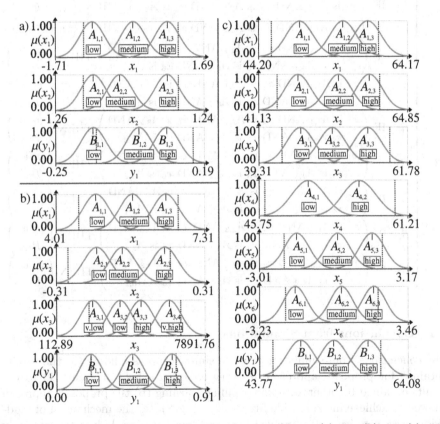

Fig. 8. The examples of fuzzy sets for considered problems: (a) #1, (b) #2, (c) #3. Dotted lines stands for minims (left line) and maxims (right line) of learning data.

Table 1. The example notations of fuzzy rules obtained for considered problems. The linguistics labels used in fuzzy rules are presented in Fig. 8.

#	Fuzzy rules notation
1	R_1 : IF $\left(x_1 \text{ is } A_{1,1} \text{ AND } x_2 \text{ is } A_{2,1} \right)$ THEN $\left(y_1 \text{ is } B_{1,2} \right)$ R_2 : IF $\left(x_1 \text{ is } A_{1,2} \text{ AND } x_2 \text{ is } A_{2,2} \right)$ THEN $\left(y_1 \text{ is } B_{1,2} \right)$ R_3 : IF $\left(x_1 \text{ is } A_{1,2} \text{ AND } x_2 \text{ is } A_{2,3} \right)$ THEN $\left(y_1 \text{ is } B_{1,3} \right)$ R_4 : IF $\left(x_1 \text{ is } A_{1,2} \text{ AND } x_2 \text{ is } A_{2,1} \right)$ THEN $\left(y_1 \text{ is } B_{1,1} \right)$ R_5 : IF $\left(x_1 \text{ is } A_{1,3} \text{ AND } x_2 \text{ is } A_{2,3} \right)$ THEN $\left(y_1 \text{ is } B_{1,3} \right)$
2	R_1 : IF $\left(x_1 \text{ is } A_{1,1} \text{ AND } x_2 \text{ is } A_{2,2} \text{ AND } x_3 \text{ is } A_{3,4} \right)$ THEN $\left(y_1 \text{ is } B_{1,3} \right)$ R_2 : IF $\left(x_1 \text{ is } A_{1,1} \text{ AND } x_2 \text{ is } A_{2,3} \text{ AND } x_3 \text{ is } A_{3,4} \right)$ THEN $\left(y_1 \text{ is } B_{1,3} \right)$ R_3 : IF $\left(x_1 \text{ is } A_{1,2} \text{ AND } x_2 \text{ is } A_{2,1} \text{ AND } x_3 \text{ is } A_{3,3} \right)$ THEN $\left(y_1 \text{ is } B_{1,2} \right)$ R_4 : IF $\left(x_1 \text{ is } A_{1,2} \text{ AND } x_2 \text{ is } A_{2,1} \text{ AND } x_3 \text{ is } A_{3,1} \right)$ THEN $\left(y_1 \text{ is } B_{1,1} \right)$ R_5 : IF $\left(x_1 \text{ is } A_{1,2} \text{ AND } x_2 \text{ is } A_{2,2} \text{ AND } x_3 \text{ is } A_{3,2} \right)$ THEN $\left(y_1 \text{ is } B_{1,2} \right)$ R_6 : IF $\left(x_1 \text{ is } A_{1,3} \text{ AND } x_2 \text{ is } A_{2,3} \text{ AND } x_3 \text{ is } A_{3,2} \right)$ THEN $\left(y_1 \text{ is } B_{1,3} \right)$
3	R_1 : IF $\left(\begin{array}{l} x_1 \text{ is } A_{1,1} \text{ AND } x_2 \text{ is } A_{2,1} \text{ AND } x_3 \text{ is } A_{3,1} \text{ AND} \\ x_4 \text{ is } A_{4,1} \text{ AND } x_5 \text{ is } A_{5,2} \text{ AND } x_6 \text{ is } A_{6,2} \end{array} \right)$ THEN $\left(\begin{array}{l} y_1 \text{ is} \\ B_{1,1} \end{array} \right)$ R_2 : IF $\left(\begin{array}{l} x_1 \text{ is } A_{1,1} \text{ AND } x_2 \text{ is } A_{2,1} \text{ AND } x_3 \text{ is } A_{3,1} \text{ AND} \\ x_4 \text{ is } A_{4,1} \text{ AND } x_5 \text{ is } A_{5,1} \text{ AND } x_6 \text{ is } A_{6,1} \end{array} \right)$ THEN $\left(\begin{array}{l} y_1 \text{ is} \\ B_{1,2} \end{array} \right)$ R_3 : IF $\left(\begin{array}{l} x_1 \text{ is } A_{1,1} \text{ AND } x_2 \text{ is } A_{2,1} \text{ AND } x_3 \text{ is } A_{3,2} \text{ AND} \\ x_4 \text{ is } A_{4,1} \text{ AND } x_5 \text{ is } A_{5,3} \text{ AND } x_6 \text{ is } A_{6,3} \end{array} \right)$ THEN $\left(\begin{array}{l} y_1 \text{ is} \\ B_{1,1} \end{array} \right)$ R_4 : IF $\left(\begin{array}{l} x_1 \text{ is } A_{1,2} \text{ AND } x_2 \text{ is } A_{2,2} \text{ AND } x_3 \text{ is } A_{3,2} \text{ AND} \\ x_4 \text{ is } A_{4,1} \text{ AND } x_5 \text{ is } A_{5,2} \text{ AND } x_6 \text{ is } A_{6,2} \end{array} \right)$ THEN $\left(\begin{array}{l} y_1 \text{ is} \\ B_{1,2} \end{array} \right)$ R_5 : IF $\left(\begin{array}{l} x_1 \text{ is } A_{1,2} \text{ AND } x_2 \text{ is } A_{2,2} \text{ AND } x_3 \text{ is } A_{3,2} \text{ AND} \\ x_4 \text{ is } A_{4,2} \text{ AND } x_5 \text{ is } A_{5,1} \text{ AND } x_6 \text{ is } A_{6,1} \end{array} \right)$ THEN $\left(\begin{array}{l} y_1 \text{ is} \\ B_{1,2} \end{array} \right)$ R_6 : IF $\left(\begin{array}{l} x_1 \text{ is } A_{1,3} \text{ AND } x_2 \text{ is } A_{2,3} \text{ AND } x_3 \text{ is } A_{3,3} \text{ AND} \\ x_4 \text{ is } A_{4,2} \text{ AND } x_5 \text{ is } A_{5,1} \text{ AND } x_6 \text{ is } A_{6,1} \end{array} \right)$ THEN $\left(\begin{array}{l} y_1 \text{ is} \\ B_{1,3} \end{array} \right)$ R_7 : IF $\left(\begin{array}{l} x_1 \text{ is } A_{1,3} \text{ AND } x_2 \text{ is } A_{2,3} \text{ AND } x_3 \text{ is } A_{3,3} \text{ AND} \\ x_4 \text{ is } A_{4,2} \text{ AND } x_5 \text{ is } A_{5,1} \text{ AND } x_6 \text{ is } A_{6,1} \end{array} \right)$ THEN $\left(\begin{array}{l} y_1 \text{ is} \\ B_{1,3} \end{array} \right)$

4.4 Conclusions from Simulations

The conclusions from simulations can be summed up as follows: (a) the results obtained for proposed approach are very close (in a field of accuracy) to the results obtained by other authors for offline learning (b) the proposed approach allowed to achieve interpretable fuzzy rules (Fig. 8), (c) the mechanism of modifying fuzzy sets (case 2) improved proposed method (case 1) by approximately 5 % (see Table 2), (d) the mechanism of background learning (case 3) improved proposed method (case 1) by additional approximately 15 % (Table 2), (e) the

Table 2. Summary results of $RMSE$ and $CMPL$ (*best $CMPL$* stands for $CMPL$ obtained for *best $RMSE$*).

Problem	Case	Avg. $RMSE$	Avg. $CMPL$	Best $RMSE$	Best $CMPL$	Avg. N	Avg. Fuzzy sets	Others authors $RMSE$ (offline)
#1	1	0.049	10.733	0.029	11.500	5.710	10.045	0.013-0.054 [35]
	2	0.048	10.845	0.029	13.000	5.730	10.230	
	3	**0.040**	11.505	**0.013**	14.000	6.220	10.570	
#2	1	0.049	14.070	0.025	14.000	7.390	13.360	0.006-0.009 [10]
	2	0.045	13.783	0.026	12.000	7.110	13.345	
	3	**0.040**	14.253	**0.015**	16.000	7.560	13.385	
#3	1	1.305	18.700	0.884	18.000	7.035	23.330	0.296–0.450 [10]
	2	1.203	18.813	0.845	21.000	7.310	23.005	
	3	**1.036**	19.690	**0.648**	20.000	7.885	23.610	

low number of obtained fuzzy rules allows to effectively identify operation points, (f) the background learning allows to obtain significant improvement in a field of accuracy (Fig. 7 and Table 2), (g) the proposed method allows to build fuzzy rules for data samples which represent sporadic existing operation points.

5 Conclusions

The proposed approach to online build of fuzzy systems allows us to obtain good results in both accuracy and complexity fields. The mechanism of background learning significantly improved proposed approach. It can be also used in other online learning methods. In the future, authors consider i.a.: including additional interpretability criteria, the use of *don't care* type of fuzzy sets and use of weights of rules resulting from frequency of their use. The proposed method is actually tested on real data obtained from non-invasive online identification of engine.

Acknowledgments. The project was financed by the National Science Centre (Poland) on the basis of the decision number DEC-2012/05/B/ST7/02138.

References

1. Abbas, J.: The bipolar choquet integrals based on ternary-element sets. J. Artif. Intell. Soft Comput. Res. **6**(1), 13–21 (2016)
2. Angelov, P.P., Lughofer, E., Zhou, X.: Evolving fuzzy classifiers using different model architectures. Fuzzy Sets Syst. **159**(23), 3160–3182 (2008)
3. Bartczuk, Ł.: Gene expression programming in correction modelling of nonlinear dynamic objects. In: Borzemski, L., Grzech, A., Świątek, J., Wilimowska, Z. (eds.) ISAT 2015, Part I. AISC, vol. 429, pp. 125–134. Springer, Heidelberg (2016)

4. Bartczuk, Ł., Przybył, A., Koprinkova-Hristova, P.: New method for nonlinear fuzzy correction modelling of dynamic objects. In: Rutkowski, L., Korytkowski, M., Scherer, R., Tadeusiewicz, R., Zadeh, L.A., Zurada, J.M. (eds.) ICAISC 2014, Part I. LNCS (LNAI), vol. 8467, pp. 169–180. Springer, Heidelberg (2014)
5. Bartczuk, Ł., Rutkowska, D.: Medical diagnosis with type-2 fuzzy decision trees. In: Kacki, E., Rudnicki, M., Stempczyńska, J. (eds.) Computers in Medical Activity. AISC, vol. 65, pp. 11–21. Springer, Heidelberg (2008)
6. Bartczuk, Ł., Rutkowska, D.: Type-2 fuzzy decision trees. In: Rutkowski, L., Tadeusiewicz, R., Zadeh, L.A., Zurada, J.M. (eds.) ICAISC 2008. LNCS (LNAI), vol. 5097, pp. 197–206. Springer, Heidelberg (2008)
7. Bruździński, T., Krzyżak, A., Fevens, T., Jeleń, Ł.: Web-based framework for breast cancer classification. J. Artif. Intell. Soft Comput. Res. 4(2), 149–162 (2014)
8. Cococcioni, M., Ducange, P., Lazzerini, B., Marcelloni, F.: A Pareto-based multi-objective evolutionary approach to the identification of Mamdani fuzzy systems. Soft. Comput. 11, 1013–1031 (2007)
9. Cpalka, K.: A method for designing flexible neuro-fuzzy systems. In: Rutkowski, L., Tadeusiewicz, R., Zadeh, L.A., Żurada, J.M. (eds.) ICAISC 2006. LNCS (LNAI), vol. 4029, pp. 212–219. Springer, Heidelberg (2006)
10. Cpałka, K., Łapa, K., Przybył, A., Zalasiński, M.: A new method for designing neuro-fuzzy systems for nonlinear modelling with interpretability aspects. Neuro-computing 135, 203–217 (2014)
11. Cpałka, K., Łapa, K., Przybył, A.: A new approach to design of control systems using genetic programming. Inf. Technol. Control 44(4), 433–442 (2015)
12. Cpałka, K., Rebrova, O., Nowicki, R., Rutkowski, L.: On design of flexible neuro-fuzzy systems for nonlinear modelling. Int. J. Gen. Syst. 42(6), 706–720 (2013)
13. Cpałka, K., Rutkowski, L.: Flexible Takagi-Sugeno neuro-fuzzy structures for nonlinear approximation. WSEAS Trans. Syst. 4(9), 1450–1458 (2005)
14. Cpałka, K., Rutkowski, L.: Flexible Takagi-Sugeno fuzzy systems. In: Proceedings of the 2005 IEEE International Joint Conference on Neural Networks, IJCNN 2005, vol. 3, pp. 1764–1769 (2005)
15. Cpałka, K., Zalasiński, M.: On-line signature verification using vertical signature partitioning. Expert Syst. Appl. 41(9), 4170–4180 (2014)
16. Cpałka, K., Zalasiński, M., Rutkowski, L.: New method for the on-line signature verification based on horizontal partitioning. Pattern Recogn. 47, 2652–2661 (2014)
17. Cpałka, K., Zalasiński, M., Rutkowski, L.: A new algorithm for identity verification based on the analysis of a handwritten dynamic signature. Appl. Soft Comput. 43, 47–56 (2016)
18. Das, S., Kar, S., Pal, T.: Group decision making using interval-valued intuitionistic fuzzy soft matrix and confident weight of experts. J. Artif. Intell. Soft Comput. Res. 4(1), 57–77 (2014)
19. Duda, P., Hayashi, Y., Jaworski, M.: On the strong convergence of the orthogonal series-type kernel regression neural networks in a non-stationary environment. In: Rutkowski, L., Korytkowski, M., Scherer, R., Tadeusiewicz, R., Zadeh, L.A., Zurada, J.M. (eds.) ICAISC 2012, Part I. LNCS (LNAI), vol. 7267, pp. 47–54. Springer, Heidelberg (2012)
20. Duda, P., Jaworski, M., Pietruczuk, L.: On pre-processing algorithms for data stream. In: Rutkowski, L., Korytkowski, M., Scherer, R., Tadeusiewicz, R., Zadeh, L.A., Zurada, J.M. (eds.) ICAISC 2012, Part II. LNCS (LNAI), vol. 7268, pp. 56–63. Springer, Heidelberg (2012)

21. Dziwiński, P., Avedyan, E.D.: A new approach to nonlinear modeling based on significant operating points detection. In: Rutkowski, L., Korytkowski, M., Scherer, R., Tadeusiewicz, R., Zadeh, L.A., Zurada, J.M. (eds.) ICAISC 2015, Part II. LNCS (LNAI), vol. 9120, pp. 364–378. Springer, Heidelberg (2015)
22. Dziwiński, P., Bartczuk, Ł., Przybył, A., Avedyan, E.D.: A new algorithm for identification of significant operating points using swarm intelligence. In: Rutkowski, L., Korytkowski, M., Scherer, R., Tadeusiewicz, R., Zadeh, L.A., Zurada, J.M. (eds.) ICAISC 2014, Part II. LNCS (LNAI), vol. 8468, pp. 349–362. Springer, Heidelberg (2014)
23. Er, M.J., Duda, P.: On the weak convergence of the orthogonal series-type kernel regresion neural networks in a non-stationary environment. In: Wyrzykowski, R., Dongarra, J., Karczewski, K., Waśniewski, J. (eds.) PPAM 2011, Part I. LNCS, vol. 7203, pp. 443–450. Springer, Heidelberg (2012)
24. Gabryel, M., Cpałka, K., Rutkowski, L.: Evolutionary strategies for learning of neuro-fuzzy systems. In: Proceedings of the I Workshop on Genetic Fuzzy Systems, Granada, pp. 119–123 (2005)
25. Gabryel, M., Korytkowski, M., Scherer, R., Rutkowski, L.: Object detection by simple fuzzy classifiers generated by boosting. In: Rutkowski, L., Korytkowski, M., Scherer, R., Tadeusiewicz, R., Zadeh, L.A., Zurada, J.M. (eds.) ICAISC 2013, Part I. LNCS (LNAI), vol. 7894, pp. 540–547. Springer, Heidelberg (2013)
26. Gacto, M.J., Alcalá, R., Herrera, F.: Interpretability of linguistic fuzzy rule-based systems: an overview of interpretability measures. Inf. Sci. 181(20), 4340–4360 (2011)
27. Galkowski, T., Pawlak, M.: Nonparametric function fitting in the presence of nonstationary noise. In: Rutkowski, L., Korytkowski, M., Scherer, R., Tadeusiewicz, R., Zadeh, L.A., Zurada, J.M. (eds.) ICAISC 2014, Part I. LNCS (LNAI), vol. 8467, pp. 531–538. Springer, Heidelberg (2014)
28. Galkowski, T., Pawlak, M.: Orthogonal series estimation of regression functions in nonstationary conditions. In: Rutkowski, L., Korytkowski, M., Scherer, R., Tadeusiewicz, R., Zadeh, L.A., Zurada, J.M. (eds.) ICAISC 2015, Part I. LNCS (LNAI), vol. 9119, pp. 427–435. Springer, Heidelberg (2015)
29. Gałkowski, T., Rutkowski, L.: Nonparametric fitting of multivariate functions. IEEE Trans. Autom. Control 31(8), 785–787 (1986)
30. Galkowski, T., Starczewski, A., Fu, X.: Improvement of the multiple-view learning based on the self-organizing maps. In: Rutkowski, L., Korytkowski, M., Scherer, R., Tadeusiewicz, R., Zadeh, L.A., Zurada, J.M. (eds.) ICAISC 2015, Part II. LNCS (LNAI), vol. 9120, pp. 3–12. Springer, Heidelberg (2015)
31. Gręblicki, W., Rutkowski, L.: Density-free Bayes risk consistency of nonparametric pattern recognition procedures. Proc. IEEE 69(4), 482–483 (1981)
32. Grycuk, R., Gabryel, M., Korytkowski, M., Scherer, R., Voloshynovskiy, S.: From single image to list of objects based on edge and blob detection. In: Rutkowski, L., Korytkowski, M., Scherer, R., Tadeusiewicz, R., Zadeh, L.A., Zurada, J.M. (eds.) ICAISC 2014, Part II. LNCS (LNAI), vol. 8468, pp. 605–615. Springer, Heidelberg (2014)
33. Jaworski, M., Er, M.J., Pietruczuk, L.: On the Application of the Parzen-Type Kernel Regression Neural Network and Order Statistics for Learning in a Non-stationary Environment. In: Rutkowski, L., Korytkowski, M., Scherer, R., Tadeusiewicz, R., Zadeh, L.A., Zurada, J.M. (eds.) ICAISC 2012, Part I. LNCS (LNAI), vol. 7267, pp. 90–98. Springer, Heidelberg (2012)

34. Jaworski, M., Pietruczuk, L., Duda, P.: On resources optimization in fuzzy clustering of data streams. In: Rutkowski, L., Korytkowski, M., Scherer, R., Tadeusiewicz, R., Zadeh, L.A., Zurada, J.M. (eds.) ICAISC 2012, Part II. LNCS (LNAI), vol. 7268, pp. 92–99. Springer, Heidelberg (2012)

35. Juang, C.F., Lin, C.T.: An on-line self-constructing neural fuzzy inference network and its applications. IEEE Trans. Fuzzy Syst. **6**, 12–31 (1998)

36. Kaisler, S., Armour, F., Espinosa, J.A., Money, W.: Big data: issues and challenges moving forward. In: Proceedings of the 46th Hawaii International Conference on System Sciences (HICSS), pp. 995–1004. IEEE (2013)

37. Kitajima, R., Kamimura, R.: Accumulative information enhancement in the self-organizing maps and its application to the analysis of mission statements. J. Artif. Intell. Soft Comput. Res. **5**(3), 161–176 (2015)

38. Korytkowski, M., Nowicki, R., Scherer, R.: Neuro-fuzzy rough classifier ensemble. In: Alippi, C., Polycarpou, M., Panayiotou, C., Ellinas, G. (eds.) ICANN 2009, Part I. LNCS, vol. 5768, pp. 817–823. Springer, Heidelberg (2009)

39. Korytkowski, M., Rutkowski, L., Scherer, R.: Fast image classification by boosting fuzzy classifiers. Inf. Sci. **327**, 175–182 (2016)

40. Laskowski, Ł., Laskowska, M.: Functionalization of SBA-15 mesoporous silica by Cu-phosphonate units: probing of synthesis route. J. Solid State Chem. **220**, 221–226 (2014)

41. Laskowski, Ł., Laskowska, M., Bałanda, M., Fitta, M., Kwiatkowska, J., Dziliński, K., Karczmarska, A.: Mesoporous silica SBA-15 functionalized by nickel-phosphonic units: Raman and magnetic analysis. Microporous Mesoporous Mater. **200**, 253–259 (2014)

42. Łapa, K., Cpałka, K., Galushkin, A.I.: A new interpretability criteria for neuro-fuzzy systems for nonlinear classification. In: Rutkowski, L., Korytkowski, M., Scherer, R., Tadeusiewicz, R., Zadeh, L.A., Zurada, J.M. (eds.) ICAISC 2015, Part I. LNCS(LNAI), vol. 9119, pp. 448–468. Springer, Heidelberg (2015)

43. Łapa K., Cpałka K., Aspects of structure and parameters selection of control systems using firework algorithm. Advances in Intelligent Systems and Computing (in print) (2015)

44. Łapa, K., Cpałka, K., Wang, L.: New method for design of fuzzy systems for nonlinear modelling using different criteria of interpretability. In: Rutkowski, L., Korytkowski, M., Scherer, R., Tadeusiewicz, R., Zadeh, L.A., Zurada, J.M. (eds.) ICAISC 2014, Part I. LNCS, vol. 8467, pp. 217–232. Springer, Heidelberg (2014)

45. Łapa, K., Przybył, A., Cpałka, K.: A new approach to designing interpretable models of dynamic systems. In: Rutkowski, L., Korytkowski, M., Scherer, R., Tadeusiewicz, R., Zadeh, L.A., Zurada, J.M. (eds.) ICAISC 2013, Part II. LNCS(LNAI), vol. 7895, pp. 523–534. Springer, Heidelberg (2013)

46. Łapa, K., Zalasiński, M., Cpałka, K.: A new method for designing and complexity reduction of neuro-fuzzy systems for nonlinear modelling. In: Rutkowski, L., Korytkowski, M., Scherer, R., Tadeusiewicz, R., Zadeh, L.A., Zurada, J.M. (eds.) ICAISC 2013, Part I. LNCS(LNAI), vol. 7894, pp. 329–344. Springer, Heidelberg (2013)

47. Leng, G.: A hybrid learning algorithm with a similarity-based pruning strategy for self-adaptive neuro-fuzzy systems. Appl. Soft Comput. **9**(4), 1354–1366 (2009)

48. Lima, E., Hell, M., Ballini, R., Gomide, F.: Evolving fuzzy modelling using participatory learning. In: Angelov, P., Filev, D., Kasabov, N. (eds.) Evolving Intelligent Systems: Methodology and Applications, pp. 67–86. Wiley, New York (2010)

49. Ludwig, S.A.: Repulsive self-adaptive acceleration particle swarm optimization approach. J. Artif. Intell. Soft Comput. Res. **4**(3), 189–204 (2014)

50. Lughofer, E.: Evolving Fuzzy Systems - Methodologies. Advanced Concepts and Applications. Springer, Heidelberg (2011)
51. Lughofer, E., Hüllermeier, E.: On-line redundancy elimination in evolving fuzzy regression models using a fuzzy inclusion measure. In: Proceedings of the EUSFLAT 2011 Conference, pp. 380–387. Elsevier, Aix-Les-Bains, France (2011)
52. Lughofer, E.: On-line assurance of interpretability criteria in evolving fuzzy systems - achievements, new concepts and open issues. Inf. Sci. **251**, 22–46 (2013)
53. Maciel, L., Lemos, A., Gomide, F., Ballini, R.: Evolving fuzzy systems for pricing fixed income options. Evolving Syst. **3**(1), 5–18 (2012)
54. Nobukawa, S., Nishimura, H., Yamanishi, T., Liu, J.-Q.: haotic states induced by resetting process in izhikevich neuron model. J. Artif. Intell. Soft Comput. Res. **5**(2), 109–119 (2015)
55. Patgiri, C., Sarma, M., Sarma, K.K.: A class of neuro-computational methods for assamese fricative classification. J. Artif. Intell. Soft Comput. Res. **5**(1), 59–70 (2015)
56. Pietruczuk, L., Duda, P., Jaworski, M.: A new fuzzy classifier for data streams. In: Rutkowski, L., Korytkowski, M., Scherer, R., Tadeusiewicz, R., Zadeh, L.A., Zurada, J.M. (eds.) ICAISC 2012, Part I. LNCS(LNAI), vol. 7267, pp. 318–324. Springer, Heidelberg (2012)
57. Pietruczuk, L., Duda, P., Jaworski, M.: Adaptation of decision trees for handling concept drift. In: Rutkowski, L., Korytkowski, M., Scherer, R., Tadeusiewicz, R., Zadeh, L.A., Zurada, J.M. (eds.) ICAISC 2013, Part I. LNCS (LNAI), vol. 7894, pp. 459–473. Springer, Heidelberg (2013)
58. Pietruczuk, L., Zurada, J.M.: Weak convergence of the recursive parzen-type probabilistic neural network in a non-stationary environment. In: Wyrzykowski, R., Dongarra, J., Karczewski, K., Waśniewski, J. (eds.) PPAM 2011, Part I. LNCS, vol. 7203, pp. 521–529. Springer, Heidelberg (2012)
59. Ramos, J.V., Pereira, C., Dourado, A.: The building of interpretable systems in real-time. In: Angelov, P., Filev, D., Kasabov, N. (eds.) Evolving Intelligent Systems: Methodology and Applications, pp. 127–150. Wiley, New York (2010)
60. Rubio, J.J.: Stability analysis for an on-line evolving neuro-fuzzy recurrent network. In: Angelov, P., Filev, D., Kasabov, N. (eds.) Evolving Intelligent Systems: Methodology and Applications, pp. 173–199. Wiley, New York (2010)
61. Rutkowska, A.: Influence of membership functions shape on portfolio optimization results. J. Artif. Intell. Soft Comput. Res. **6**(1), 45–54 (2016)
62. Rutkowski, L.: Sequential pattern-recognition procedures derived from multiple Fourier-series. Pattern Recogn. Lett. **8**(4), 213–216 (1988)
63. Rutkowski, L.: Adaptive probabilistic neural networks for pattern classification in time-varying environment. IEEE Trans. Neural Netw. **15**(4), 811–827 (2004)
64. Rutkowski, L.: Computational Intelligence. Springer, New York (2008)
65. Rutkowski, L., Cpałka, K.: Compromise approach to neuro-fuzzy systems. In: Sincak, P., Vascak, J., Kvasnicka, V., Pospichal, J. (eds.) Intelligent Technologies - Theory and Applications, vol. 76, pp. 85–90. IOS Press (2002)
66. Rutkowski, L., Cpałka, K.: Flexible structures of neuro-fuzzy systems. In: Quo Vadis Computational Intelligence. Studies in Fuzziness and Soft Computing, vol 54, pp. 479–484. Springer (2000)
67. Rutkowski, L., Cpałka, K.: Flexible weighted neuro-fuzzy systems. In: Proceedings of the 9th International Conference on Neural Information Processing (ICONIP 2002), Orchid Country Club, Singapore, 18–22 November, 2002 CD

68. Rutkowski, L., Cpałka, K.: Neuro-fuzzy systems derived from quasi-triangular norms. In: Proceedings of the IEEE International Conference on Fuzzy Systems, Budapest, 26–29 July, vol. 2, pp. 1031–1036 (2004)
69. Rutkowski, L., Jaworski, M., Pietruczuk, L., Duda, P.: Decision trees for mining data streams based on the Gaussian approximation. IEEE Trans. Knowl. Data Eng. **26**(1), 108–119 (2014)
70. Rutkowski, L., Jaworski, M., Pietruczuk, L., Duda, P.: The CART decision tree for mining data streams. Inf. Sci. **266**, 1–15 (2014)
71. Rutkowski, L., Pietruczuk, L., Duda, P., Jaworski, M.: Decision trees for mining data streams based on the McDiarmid's bound. IEEE Trans. Knowl. Data Eng. **25**(6), 1272–1279 (2013)
72. Rutkowski, L., Przybył, A., Cpałka, K., Er, M.J.: Online speed profile generation for industrial machine tool based on neuro-fuzzy approach. In: Rutkowski, L., Scherer, R., Tadeusiewicz, R., Zadeh, L.A., Zurada, J.M. (eds.) ICAISC 2010, Part II. LNCS (LNAI), vol. 6114, pp. 645–650. Springer, Heidelberg (2010)
73. Rutkowski, L., Rafajłowicz, E.: On optimal global rate of convergence of some non-parametric identification procedures. IEEE Trans. Autom. Control **34**(10), 1089–1091 (1989)
74. Scherer, R.: Neuro-fuzzy systems with relation matrix. In: Rutkowski, L., Scherer, R., Tadeusiewicz, R., Zadeh, L.A., Zurada, J.M. (eds.) ICAISC 2010, Part I. LNCS (LNAI), vol. 6113, pp. 210–215. Springer, Heidelberg (2010)
75. Scherer, R., Rutkowski, L.: Relational equations initializing neuro-fuzzy system. In: Proceedings of the 10th Zittau Fuzzy Colloquium, Zittau, Germany, pp. 18–22 (2002)
76. Smyczyńska, J., Hilczer, M., Smyczyńska, U., Stawerska, R., Tadeusiewicz, R., Lewiński, A.: Artificial neural models - a novel tool for predictying the efficacy of growth hormone (GH) therapy in children with short stature. Neuroendocrinol. Lett. **36**(4), 348–353 (2015). ISSN: 0172–780X, ISSN-L: 0172–780X
77. Smyczyńska, U., Smyczyńska, J., Hilczer, M., Stawerska, R., Lewiński, A., Tadeusiewicz, R.: Artificial neural networks - a novel tool in modelling the effectiveness of growth hormone (GH) therapy in children with GH deficiency. Pediatric Endocrinology **14**(2(51)), 9–18 (2015)
78. Soleimani, H., Lucas, K., Araabi, B.N.: Recursive Gath-Geva clustering as a basis for evolving neuro-fuzzy modelling. Evolving Syst. **1**(1), 59–71 (2010)
79. Starczewski, J.T., Bartczuk, Ł., Dziwiński, P., Marvuglia, A.: Learning methods for type-2 FLS based on FCM. In: Rutkowski, L., Scherer, R., Tadeusiewicz, R., Zadeh, L.A., Zurada, J.M. (eds.) ICAISC 2010, Part I. LNCS (LNAI), vol. 6113, pp. 224–231. Springer, Heidelberg (2010)
80. Szarek, A., Korytkowski, M., Rutkowski, L., Scherer, R., Szyprowski, J.: Application of neural networks in assessing changes around implant after total hip arthroplasty. In: Rutkowski, L., Korytkowski, M., Scherer, R., Tadeusiewicz, R., Zadeh, L.A., Zurada, J.M. (eds.) ICAISC 2012, Part II. LNCS, vol. 7268, pp. 335–340. Springer, Heidelberg (2012)
81. Szarek, A., Korytkowski, M., Rutkowski, L., Scherer, R., Szyprowski, J.: Forecasting wear of head and acetabulum in hip joint implant. In: Rutkowski, L., Korytkowski, M., Scherer, R., Tadeusiewicz, R., Zadeh, L.A., Zurada, J.M. (eds.) ICAISC 2012, Part II. LNCS, vol. 7268, pp. 341–346. Springer, Heidelberg (2012)
82. Szczypta, J., Przybył, A., Wang, L.: Evolutionary approach with multiple quality criteria for controller design. In: Rutkowski, L., Korytkowski, M., Scherer, R., Tadeusiewicz, R., Zadeh, L.A., Zurada, J.M. (eds.) ICAISC 2014, Part I. LNCS (LNAI), vol. 8467, pp. 455–467. Springer, Heidelberg (2014)

83. Tadeusiewicz, R.: Neural networks as a tool for modeling of biological systems. Bio-Algorithms Med-Syst. **11**(3), 135–144 (2015)
84. Tadeusiewicz, R.: Neural networks in mining sciences - general overview and some representative examples. Arch. Min. Sci. **60**(4), 971–984 (2015)
85. Thrun, S.: Explanation-Based Neural Network Learning: A Lifelong Learning Approach. Kluwer Academic Publishers, Boston (1996)
86. Ward, J.H.: Hierarchical grouping to optimize an objective function. J. Am. Stat. Assoc. **58**, 236–244 (1963)
87. Yamamoto, Y., Yoshikawa, T., Furuhashi, T.: Improvement of performance of Japanese P300 speller by using second display. J. Artif. Intell. Soft Comput. Res. **5**(3), 221–226 (2015)
88. Zalasiński, M., Cpałka, K.: A new method of on-line signature verification using a flexible fuzzy one-class classifier, pp. 38–53. Academic Publishing House EXIT (2011)
89. Zalasiński, M., Cpałka, K.: New approach for the on-line signature verification based on method of horizontal partitioning. In: Rutkowski, L., Korytkowski, M., Scherer, R., Tadeusiewicz, R., Zadeh, L.A., Zurada, J.M. (eds.) ICAISC 2013, Part II. LNCS (LNAI), vol. 7895, pp. 342–350. Springer, Heidelberg (2013)
90. Zalasiński, M., Cpałka, K., Er, M.J.: New method for dynamic signature verification using hybrid partitioning. In: Rutkowski, L., Korytkowski, M., Scherer, R., Tadeusiewicz, R., Zadeh, L.A., Zurada, J.M. (eds.) ICAISC 2014, Part II. LNCS (LNAI), vol. 8468, pp. 216–230. Springer, Heidelberg (2014)
91. Zalasiński, M., Cpałka, K., Er, M.J.: A new method for the dynamic signature verification based on the stable partitions of the signature. In: Rutkowski, L., Korytkowski, M., Scherer, R., Tadeusiewicz, R., Zadeh, L.A., Zurada, J.M. (eds.) ICAISC 2015, Patr II. LNCS (LNAI), vol. 9120, pp. 161–174. Springer, Heidelberg (2015)
92. Zalasiński, M., Cpałka, K., Hayashi, Y.: New method for dynamic signature verification based on global features. In: Rutkowski, L., Korytkowski, M., Scherer, R., Tadeusiewicz, R., Zadeh, L.A., Zurada, J.M. (eds.) ICAISC 2014, Part II. LNCS (LNAI), vol. 8468, pp. 231–245. Springer, Heidelberg (2014)
93. Zalasiński, M., Cpałka, K., Hayashi, Y.: New fast algorithm for the dynamic signature verification using global features values. In: Rutkowski, L., Korytkowski, M., Scherer, R., Tadeusiewicz, R., Zadeh, L.A., Zurada, J.M. (eds.) ICAISC 2015, Part II. LNCS (LNAI), vol. 9120, pp. 175–188. Springer, Heidelberg (2015)

New Approach for Interpretability
of Neuro-Fuzzy Systems
with Parametrized Triangular Norms

Krystian Łapa[1]($\boxtimes$), Krzysztof Cpałka[1], and Lipo Wang[2]

[1] Institute of Computational Intelligence,
Częstochowa University of Technology, Częstochowa, Poland
{krystian.lapa,krzysztof.cpalka}@iisi.pcz.pl
[2] Nanyang Technological University Singapore, Singapore, Singapore
elpwang@ntu.edu.sg

Abstract. In this paper we proposed a new approach for interpretability of the neuro-fuzzy systems. It is based on appropriate use of parametric triangular norms with weights of arguments, which shape depends on values of their parameters and weights. The use of those norms as aggregation and inference operators increases precision of fuzzy system. Due to that, the rule base can be simpler and easier to interpretation. However, interpretation of parametric triangular norms is not that obvious as interpretation of nonparametric triangular norms such as algebraic or minimal norms. Proposed approach is based on choosing values of parameters from a set of values, where each value have its own interpretation. Additionally, a modified tuning algorithm for selection both the structure and structure parameters of fuzzy system with interpretability criteria under consideration is proposed. Proposed approach were tested on well-known nonlinear simulation problems.

Keywords: Nonlinear modeling · Fuzzy system · Interpretability criteria · Accuracy

1 Introduction

The fuzzy systems (see e.g. [12,15–21,29,30,34,42,43,48,80,81,85,94–99]) are based on fuzzy rules. In the past researchers paid attention to the accuracy of fuzzy systems while ignoring issues of their interpretability. However, in the 1990 s they started to notice the fact that a large number of rules or fuzzy sets in those rules is not conducive to the readability of the rule base. Nowadays fuzzy system designers are trying to reach an acceptable compromise between accuracy and interpretability [31,38,54]. In the literature a number of papers on the subject of interpretability of fuzzy systems can be found. Their authors have proposed among the others: (a) solutions aimed at reducing the number of fuzzy rules [2,4,31,38,54], reducing the number of fuzzy sets [35], reducing the number of system inputs [4,92] and reducing fuzzy system elements by merging [13,36], (b) solutions related to correct

© Springer International Publishing Switzerland 2016
L. Rutkowski et al. (Eds.): ICAISC 2016, Part I, LNAI 9692, pp. 248–265, 2016.
DOI: 10.1007/978-3-319-39378-0_22

notation of fuzzy rules [4,49], correct activation of fuzzy rules [54] and distinguishability and interdependence of fuzzy sets [55,56,64], (c) solutions related to fuzzy systems construction aimed at interpretability, based on additional weights of importance of the rules, antecedences, consequences and system inputs [13,65,71], parameterized triangular norms [13,28,68] and precise defuzzification mechanism [13]. The literature abounds in numerous attempts to systematize solutions for interpretability (e.g. [3,32,82]).

The solutions proposed in this paper can be summarized as follows: (a) it is based on a use of parametric triangular norms with weights of arguments and on appropriate use of values of weights of fuzzy system elements. Proposed idea concerns choosing parameters values from a set of values, where each value have its own interpretation; (b) in this paper a new algorithm for selection the structure and parameters of a fuzzy system, constructed on the basis of the golden ball [60] algorithm is proposed. Moreover, the proposed algorithm takes into account all the interpretability criteria and it belongs to the methods based on populations [71]. The use of the learning algorithm also creates a good opportunity to find an appropriate trade-off between interpretability and accuracy. It is worth to note that many computational intelligence methods (see e.g. [1,5–9,22–27,33,39–41,44,50,58,61–63,66,67,69,76–79,83,86,87,93]) are successfully used in pattern recognition, modelling and optimization issues.

This paper is divided into following sections: in Sect. 2 a description of a fuzzy system is presented. In Sect. 3 a description of proposed learning algorithm is shown. The results of simulations are presented in Sect. 4, finally the conclusions are described in Sect. 5.

2   Description of a Neuro-Fuzzy System

In this paper a typical multi-input, multi-output flexible fuzzy system of the Mamdani-type is considered [13,14,70,71]. Neuro-fuzzy systems combine the natural language description of fuzzy systems and the learning properties of neural networks (see e.g. [11,46,47,84,88–91]). This system performs mapping $\mathbf{X} \rightarrow \mathbf{Y}$, where $\mathbf{X} \subset \mathbf{R}^n$ and $\mathbf{Y} \subset \mathbf{R}^m$. The rule base of this system consists of a collection of N fuzzy rules R^k, $k = 1, \ldots, N$. Each rule R^k takes the following form:

$$R^k : \left[\left(\text{IF } (x_1 \text{ is } A_1^k) \left| w_{1,k}^A \text{ AND } \ldots \text{ AND } (x_n \text{ is } A_n^k) \left| w_{n,k}^A \right. \right) \left| w_k^{\text{rule}} \right. \right], \quad (1)$$

$$\text{THEN } (y_1 \text{ is } B_1^k) \left| w_{1,k}^B , \ldots, (y_m \text{ is } B_m^k) \left| w_{m,k}^B \right. \right.$$

where n is the number of inputs, m is the number of outputs, $\bar{\mathbf{x}} = [\bar{x}_1, \ldots, \bar{x}_n] \in \mathbf{X}$ is a vector of input signals, $\mathbf{y} = [y_1, \ldots, y_m] \in \mathbf{Y}$ is a vector of output linguistic variables, $A_1^k, \ldots, A_n^k$ are input fuzzy sets characterized by membership functions $\mu_{A_i^k}(x_i)$ $(i = 1, \ldots, n)$, $B_1^k, \ldots, B_m^k$ are output fuzzy sets characterized by membership functions $\mu_{B_j^k}(y_j)$ $(j = 1, \ldots, m)$, $w_{k,i}^A \in [0, 1]$ are weights of antecedents, $w_{j,k}^B \in [0, 1]$ are weights of consequences, and $w_k^{\text{rule}} \in [0, 1]$

are weights of rules. Fuzzy sets A_i^k and B_j^k represent linguistic variables (e.g. *'very low'*, *'low'*, *'medium'*, *'high'*, *'very high'*, *'near* [value]*'*). In this paper we consider system based on Gaussian membership functions, which reflects well the industrial, natural, medical and social processes; however, our solutions may be related to any other membership function. The flexibility of the system is a result of using: (a) weights in the rule base, (b) precise aggregation operators of antecedences and rules (Sect. 2.2), (c) precise inference operators (Sect. 2.2), and (d) a precise defuzzification process (Sect. 2.1).

2.1   Defuzzification Process

Defuzzification is used to determine output signals $\bar{y}_j$ of fuzzy system for given input signals. This is carried out as follows (with center of area method):

$$
\bar{y}_j = \frac{\sum_{r=1}^{R_j} \bar{y}_{j,r}^{\text{def}} \cdot \overset{N}{\underset{k=1}{\overset{\leftrightarrow}{S^*}}} \left\{ \overset{\leftrightarrow}{T^*} \left\{ \tau_k\left(\bar{\mathbf{x}}\right), \mu_{B_j^k}\left(\bar{y}_{j,r}^{\text{def}}\right); 1, w_{j,k}^B, p^{\text{imp}} \right\}; w_k^{\text{rule}}, p^{\text{agr}} \right\}}{\sum_{r=1}^{R_j} \overset{N}{\underset{k=1}{\overset{\leftrightarrow}{S^*}}} \left\{ \overset{\leftrightarrow}{T^*} \left\{ \tau_k\left(\bar{\mathbf{x}}\right), \mu_{B_j^k}\left(\bar{y}_{j,r}^{\text{def}}\right); 1, w_{j,k}^B, p^{\text{imp}} \right\}; w_k^{\text{rule}}, p^{\text{agr}} \right\}}, \tag{2}
$$

where $\overset{\leftrightarrow}{T^*}$ and $\overset{\leftrightarrow}{S^*}$ are Aczél-Alsina parameterized triangular norms with weights of arguments (Sect. 2.2), $\tau_k\left(\bar{\mathbf{x}}\right)$ is the activation level of the rule k, p^{imp} is a shape parameter of t-norm used for inference, p^{agr} is a shape parameter of t-conorm used for aggregation of inferences from rules, and $\bar{y}_{j,r}^{\text{def}}$ $(r = 1, \ldots, R_j)$ are discretization points. In the system considered in this paper the number of discretization points R_j for any output j does not have to be equal to the number of rules N. It is creating a good opportunities for increasing the interpretability and accuracy of the fuzzy system. This issue was discussed in detail in our previous papers [13,14,51]. The activation level of the k-th rule $\tau_k\left(\bar{\mathbf{x}}\right)$ in the formula (2) is determined for the input signals vector $\bar{\mathbf{x}}$ and it is defined as follows:

$$
\tau_k\left(\bar{\mathbf{x}}\right) = \overset{n}{\underset{i=1}{\overset{\leftrightarrow}{T^*}}} \left\{ \mu_{A_i^k}\left(\bar{x}_i\right); w_{k,i}^A, p^\tau \right\}, \tag{3}
$$

where p^τ is a shape parameter of t-norm used for aggregation of antecedences.

2.2   Aggregation and Inference Operators

Use of parametrized-type triangular norms with weights of arguments considered in this paper contributes indirectly to an increase of the interpretability of the system (2). It results from high working precision of these operators, which allows for achieving the expected accuracy of the system (2) with a smaller number of rules N. In this paper a parametrized triangular norms with weights of arguments of Aczél-Alsina type are used. They are defined as follows:

$$
\begin{cases}
\overset{*}{\vec{T}}\{\mathbf{a};\mathbf{w},p\} = \begin{cases}
\text{drastic t} - \text{norm} & \text{for} \quad p = 0 \\
\text{minimum t} - \text{norm} & \text{for} \quad p = \infty \\
\exp\left(-\left(\sum\limits_{i=1}^{n}(-\ln(1 - w_1 \cdot (1 - a_1)))^p\right)^{\frac{1}{p}}\right) & \text{for } p \in (0,\infty)
\end{cases} \\
\overset{*}{\vec{S}}\{\mathbf{a};\mathbf{w},p\} = \begin{cases}
\text{drastic t} - \text{conorm} & \text{for} \quad p = 0 \\
\text{maximum t} - \text{conorm} & \text{for} \quad p = \infty \\
1 - \exp\left(-\left(\sum\limits_{i=1}^{n}(-\ln(1 - w_i \cdot a_i))^p\right)^{\frac{1}{p}}\right) & \text{for } p \in (0,\infty)
\end{cases}
\end{cases}
\tag{4}
$$

where p is a shape parameter of norm, $w_1 \ldots, w_n \in [0,1]$ are weights of arguments $a_1, \ldots, a_n \in [0,1]$.

3   Description of a Learning Algorithm

The proposed learning algorithm belongs to so-called population-based algorithms ([74]) and its purpose is to select the structure and the parameters of the fuzzy system (2). Population-based algorithms can be defined as search procedures based on the mechanisms of natural selection and inheritance and they use the evolutionary principle of survival of the fittest individuals. What differs population algorithms from traditional optimization methods, among others, is that they do not process task parameters directly, but their encoded form, they do not conduct a search starting from a single point, but from a population of points, they use only the objective function and not its derivatives, and they use probabilistic selection rules. It is worth to notice that, the gradient algorithms (see e.g. [72,73,75]) can also be applied to proposed interpretability criteria.

3.1   Encoding of Potential Solutions

Encoding of population of potential solutions used in the algorithm refers to the Pittsburgh approach [37]. A single individual of the population ($\mathbf{X}_{ch}$) is therefore an object that encodes the complete structure $\mathbf{X}_{ch}^{\text{str}}$ of the fuzzy system (2), its set parameters $\mathbf{X}_{ch}^{\text{set}}$ and real parameters $\mathbf{X}_{ch}^{\text{par}}$:

$$
\mathbf{X}_{ch} = \left\{\mathbf{X}_{ch}^{\text{str}}, \mathbf{X}_{ch}^{\text{set}}, \mathbf{X}_{ch}^{\text{par}}\right\}.
\tag{5}
$$

Part $\mathbf{X}_{ch}^{\text{str}}$ of the individual $\mathbf{X}_{ch}$ encodes in a binary form the whole structure of the fuzzy system (2):

$$
\mathbf{X}_{ch}^{\text{str}} = \left\{
\begin{array}{c}
x_1, \ldots, x_n, \\
A_1^1, \ldots, A_n^1, \ldots, A_1^{Nmax}, \ldots, A_n^{Nmax}, \\
B_1^1, \ldots, B_m^1, \ldots, B_1^{Nmax}, \ldots, B_m^{Nmax}, \\
\text{rule}_1, \ldots, \text{rule}_{Nmax}, \\
\bar{y}_{1,1}^{\text{def}}, \ldots, \bar{y}_{1,Rmax}^{\text{def}}, \ldots, \bar{y}_{m,1}^{\text{def}}, \ldots, \bar{y}_{m,Rmax}^{\text{def}}
\end{array}
\right\} = \left\{X_{ch,1}^{\text{str}}, \ldots, X_{ch,L^{\text{str}}}^{\text{str}}\right\},
\tag{6}
$$

where $ch = 1, ..., Npop$ is the index of an individual in a population, $Npop$ is the number of individuals in a population, $Nmax$ is the maximum number of rules in the system (2), $Rmax$ is the maximum number of discretization points in the system (2) and L^{str} is the number of the individual components $\mathbf{X}_{ch}^{\text{str}}$ (referred as genes from now on) is determined as $L^{\text{str}} = Nmax \cdot (n + m + 1) + n + Rmax \cdot m$. The principle adopted in the encoding genes of $\mathbf{X}_{ch}^{\text{str}}$ is such that the gene with value 0 of the individual $\mathbf{X}_{ch}^{\text{str}}$ excludes the associated element from the system structure (2) and vice versa.

Part $\mathbf{X}_{ch}^{\text{set}}$ of the individual $\mathbf{X}_{ch}$ encodes the set parameters, which values have direct impact on interpretability. $\mathbf{X}_{ch}^{\text{set}}$ contains: (a) weights of antecedences, consequences and rules, and (b) parameters of triangular norms used for aggregation of antecedences (p^{agr}), inference of rules (p^{imp}) and aggregation of inference of rules (p^{τ}). Each of those parameters is chosen from a set of values. Each value from set have its own interpretation. Part $\mathbf{X}_{ch}^{\text{set}}$ takes the following form:

$$\mathbf{X}_{ch}^{\text{set}} = \left\{ \begin{array}{c} w_{1,1}^{A}, \ldots, w_{1,n}^{A}, \ldots, w_{Nmax,1}^{A}, \ldots, w_{Nmax,n}^{A}, \\ w_{1,1}^{B}, \ldots, w_{m,1}^{B}, \ldots, w_{1,Nmax}^{B}, \ldots, w_{m,Nmax}^{B}, \\ w_{1}^{\text{rule}}, \ldots, w_{Nmax}^{\text{rule}}, \\ p^{\tau}, p^{\text{imp}}, p^{\text{agr}}, \end{array} \right\} = \left\{ X_{ch,1}^{\text{set}}, \ldots, X_{ch,L^{\text{set}}}^{\text{set}} \right\},$$

(7)

where $L^{\text{set}} = Nmax \cdot (n + m + 1) + 3$ is the number of components of individual $\mathbf{X}_{ch}^{\text{set}}$. The set of possible values for weights is defined as follows:

$$\text{set}^{w} = \{0.0, 0.5, 1.0\}, \tag{8}$$

where value 0.0 can be interpretable as not important, values 0.5 as important, and value 1.0 as very important. Additionally, when value 0.0 is chosen for an element, it its treat as reduced from a system (2). For parametrized triangular norms (4) the set of possible values was chosen to obtain similar behavior to the non-parametrized norms (see Table 1). The set of possible values is defined as follows:

$$\text{set}^{p} = \{0.00, 0.63, 1.00, 1.51, 10.00\}. \tag{9}$$

Table 1. The parameters that close behavior of triangular norm Aczél-Alsina to non-parametrical norms.

Triangular norm	Drastic	Łukasiewicz	Algebraic	Hamacher	Minimum
Similarity parameter	0.00	0.63	1.00	1.51	10.00
Similarity level	Identical	Close	Identical	Close	Close

Part $\mathbf{X}_{ch}^{\text{par}}$ of the individual $\mathbf{X}_{ch}$ encodes the real parameters of the fuzzy system and it has the following form:

$$\mathbf{X}_{ch}^{par} = \left\{ \begin{array}{c} \bar{x}_{1,1}^A, \sigma_{1,1}^A, \ldots, \bar{x}_{n,1}^A, \sigma_{n,1}^A, \ldots \\ \bar{x}_{1,Nmax}^A, \sigma_{1,Nmax}^A, \cdots, \bar{x}_{n,Nmax}^A, \sigma_{n,Nmax}^A, \\ \bar{y}_{1,1}^B, \sigma_{1,1}^B, \ldots, \bar{y}_{m,1}^B, \sigma_{m,1}^B, \cdots \\ \bar{y}_{1,Nmax}^B, \sigma_{1,Nmax}^B, \cdots, \bar{y}_{m,Nmax}^B, \sigma_{m,Nmax}^B, \\ \bar{y}_{1,1}^{def}, \ldots, \bar{y}_{1,Rmax}^{def}, \cdots, \bar{y}_{m,1}^{def}, \ldots, \bar{y}_{m,Rmax}^{def} \end{array} \right\} = \left\{ X_{ch,1}^{par}, \ldots, X_{ch,L^{par}}^{par} \right\},$$

(10)

where $\bar{x}_{i,k}^A, \sigma_{i,k}^A$ are membership function parameters of input fuzzy sets A_i^k, $\bar{y}_{j,k}^B, \sigma_{j,k}^B$ are membership function parameters of output fuzzy sets B_j^k, and $L^{par} = Nmax \cdot (2 \cdot n + 2 \cdot m + 1) + Rmax \cdot m$ is the number of components of individual $\mathbf{X}_{ch}^{par}$. Those parameters are significantly affecting interpretability of system (2), but there is no possibility to choose values of them from a set. In this case, the interpretability criteria presented in our previous paper [51] can be used.

3.2 Evaluation of Potential Solutions

The purpose of proposed algorithm is to minimize the value of the evaluation function specified for the individual $\mathbf{X}_{ch}$ in the following way:

$$\text{ff}\left(\mathbf{X}_{ch}\right) = T^* \left\{ \begin{array}{c} \text{ffacc}\left(\mathbf{X}_{ch}\right), \text{ffint}\left(\mathbf{X}_{ch}\right); \\ w_{\text{ffacc}}, w_{\text{ffint}} \end{array} \right\},$$

(11)

where component ffacc $(\mathbf{X}_{ch})$ specifies the accuracy of the system (2), component ffint $(\mathbf{X}_{ch})$ specifies interpretability of the system (2) according to the adopted interpretability criteria, $w_{\text{ffacc}} \in [0,1]$ represents weight of the component ffacc $(\mathbf{X}_{ch})$, $w_{\text{ffint}} \in [0,1]$ represents weight of the component ffint $(\mathbf{X}_{ch})$ (values of weights w_{ffacc} and w_{ffint} result from expectations of the user regarding the ratio between the accuracy of the system (2) and its interpretability), and $T^* \{\cdot\}$ is algebraic triangular norm with weights of arguments defined as:

$$T^* \{\mathbf{a}; \mathbf{w}\} = \prod_{i=1}^{n} \left(1 + (a_i - 1) \cdot w_i\right).$$

(12)

Component ffacc $(\mathbf{X}_{ch})$ in formula (11) is determined as follows:

$$\text{ffacc}\left(\mathbf{X}\right) = \frac{1}{m} \sum_{j=1}^{m} \frac{\frac{1}{Z} \sum_{z=1}^{Z} |d_{z,j} - \bar{y}_{z,j}|}{\max\limits_{z=1,\ldots,Z} \{d_{z,j}\} - \min\limits_{z=1,\ldots,Z} \{d_{z,j}\}},$$

(13)

where Z is the number of rows of a learning sequence, $d_{z,j}$ is the desired output value of output j for input vector z $(z = 1, \ldots, Z)$, $\bar{y}_{z,j}$ is the real output value j calculated by the system for the input vector $\bar{x}_z$. Equation (13) takes into account the normalization of errors at different outputs of the system (2) in order to eliminate significant differences between them.

The component ffint $(\mathbf{X}_{ch})$ represent the interpretability criteria, which apply mostly to the component $\mathbf{X}_{ch}^{\mathrm{par}}$. Those criteria allows to obtain: (a) correct arrangement of fuzzy sets, (b) correct firing of the fuzzy rules, (c) cohesion of fuzzy set shapes, (d) appropriate fitting of fuzzy rules to data etc. The examples of interpretability criteria was considered in our previous papers (see e.g. [51]).

3.3   Processing of Potential Solutions

For selection the structure and parameters of the system (2) a modified golden ball algorithm (GB) [60] is proposed. The GB algorithm was chosen due to following advantages: (a) it allows for precise local search of the search space (due to using multiple populations), (b) it allows for precise global search of the search space (due to migration mechanism between populations), (c) it allows obtain high performance (it is achieved thanks to separate learning parameters of each population, which can be modified in case of giving bad results), (d) it allows to obtain good diversity of solutions (due to competition mechanism between populations).

The proposed algorithm works according to the following steps:

Step 1. Initialization. In this step a $Npop$ individuals (players) of population are randomly initiated and randomly assigned to $Nteam$ populations (teams). Each team obtains $Npla = Npop/Nteam$ players ($Npop$ should be multiplicity of $Nteam$). Each player is evaluated using fitness function (11). Moreover, each team gets randomly initiated set of parameters:

$$\mathbf{TEAM}_e = \{p_m, p_c, m_r\}, \tag{14}$$

where $p_m \in (0,1)$ is team mutation probability, $p_c \in (0,1)$ is team crossover probability, $m_r \in (0,1)$ is team mutation insensitivity, $e = 1, ..., Nteam$ stands for index of team.

Step 2. Teams traning. This step is carried out $Nstep$ times for each team separately. In the beginning, for each team a time variable t is set to 0.

Step 2.1. New players creation. In this step a $Npla$ new players are created for each team, according to evolutionary strategy $(\mu + \lambda)$ [71]. Those players are created by cloning the players chosen via roulette wheel method [71] from actual players of the team. If the condition $\mathbf{TEAM}_e\{p_c\} < \mathrm{U}_r(0,1)$ (where $\mathrm{U}_r(a,b)$ stands for random value from range [a,b]) is met, those genes are additionally crossovered with genes randomly chosen via roulette wheel method players from players of the team. $\mathbf{TEAM}_e\{p_c\}$ stands for using field p_c of team $\mathbf{TEAM}_e$.

Step 2.2. New players modification. In this step each gene $X_{ch,g}^{\mathrm{par}}$ of newly created players is mutated (when condition $\mathbf{TEAM_e}\{p_m\} < \mathrm{U}_r(0,1)$ is met) according to following equation:

$$X_{ch,g}^{\mathrm{par}} := X_{ch,g}^{\mathrm{par}} + \left(\bar{X}_{ch,g}^{\mathrm{par}} - \underline{X}_{ch,g}^{\mathrm{par}} \right) \cdot \mathrm{U}_r(-1,1) \cdot \mathbf{TEAM}_e\{m_r\} \cdot \frac{Nstep - t}{Nstep}, \tag{15}$$

where range $[\underline{X}^{\text{par}}_{ch,g}, \overline{X}^{\text{par}}_{ch,g}]$ stands for minimum and maximum allowed value of gene $X^{\text{par}}_{ch,g}$, $Nstep$ stands for maximum number of steps of teams training. It is easy to notice that, the range of mutation is decreasing with each step of teams training (due to increasing value t). In turn, for each gene $X^{\text{str}}_{ch,g}$ (when condition $X^{\text{str}}_{ch,g}$ is $\mathbf{TEAM}_e\{p_m\} < \mathrm{U}_r(0,1)$ is met) a random value from set $\{0,1\}$ is assigned. Genes $X^{\text{set}}_{ch,g}$ are modified analogically to genes $X^{\text{str}}_{ch,g}$. The new values of genes coding weights are randomly chosen from set (8), and the new values of triangular norms parameters (4) are randomly chosen from set (9).

Step 2.3. New players evaluation. After modification of genes from Step 2.2, all new players are evaluated according to fitness function (11).

Step 2.4. Selection of team players. The selection of team players is independent for each team and it lies on choosing $Npla$ best players from both the actual teams players and the newly created players from Step 2.1.

Step 2.5. Stop condition of teams traning. In this step a value t is incremented. After that, the condition $t < Nstep$ is checked. If this condition is met, algorithm goes back to step 2.1, otherwise algorithm goes to next step (Step 3).

Step 3. League competition. In this step each $\mathbf{TEAM}_e$ compete (playing matches) $Nmatch$ times with all teams. Each match consist of $Natt$ attacks. Each attack relies on comparing values of fitness function of randomly chosen players from both teams. The player with better value of fitness function scores one point for its team. The team with more (or equal) points gets a league point. On the basis of league points the teams are sorted (from best to worst). It is worth to mention that, the results of competition are determined by random factor, which ensure appropriate migration between teams from next step.

Step 4. Players transfer. Players migration (transfer) between teems is based on moving players between better and worst teams. Best team from best half of the teams is transferring $Nrep$ ($Nrep < Npla$) worst players with $Nrep$ best players from best team from worst half of the teams, etc. Thus, the last part of this step will concern transfer between worst team from best half of the teams with worst team from worst half of the teams.

Step 5. Changing training plans. In this step, a parameters (14) of worst half of the teams are changed by averaging them with parameters from better half of the teams (the parameters of best team from worst half of the teams are averaged with parameters of best team from best half of teams, etc.).

Step 6. Stop condition. In this step a number of iterations of the algorithm is checked. If this number reached value of $Niter$ algorithm stops and best found solution is presented, otherwise algorithm goes back to Step 2.

4   Simulations

The set of nonlinear issues (see e.g. [52,53]) examined in the simulations is shown in Table 2. The purpose of the simulations was to obtain systems of the forms (2) characterized by the lowest values of elements of the form (13). In this paper the following interpretability criteria were considered: (a) complexity criterium, (b) reducing overlapping of fuzzy sets criterium, (c) increasing integrity of shape criterium, and (d) increases complementarity criterium (for details see our previous paper [51]). In the simulations the algorithm described in Sect. 3 to select its structure and parameters were used. The simulations were performed for five different variants of weights of the evaluation function (11): from the one focused on accuracy (W1) to the one focused on interpretability (W5) (see Table 3). A set of the proposed algorithm parameters was selected experimentally as following: number of iterations $Niter = 50$, number of individual training steps $Nstep = 20$, number of players $Npop = 100$, number of teams $Nteam = 10$, number of matches $Nmatch = 2$, number of attacks $Natt = 20$ and number of transfered players $Nrep = 2$. A set of parameters of the fuzzy system was selected as following: maximum number of rules $Nmax = 7$, and maximum number of discretization points $Rmax = 21$.

Each simulation (for each variant W1...W5) was repeated 100 times. The obtained results were averaged and presented in Table 4 and in Fig. 1. The learn-

Table 2. Simulation problems discussed.

No	Test set name	Number of input attributes	Number of output attributes	Number of sets	Problem label
1	Nelson function [57]	2	1	128	NF
2	Yacht Hydro-dynamics [59]	5	1	308	YH
3	Concrete Slump [10]	7	3	103	CS

Table 3. A set of variants of the weights of the evaluation function (11).

Variant	w_{ffacc}	w_{ffint}	Description
W1	0.90	0.10	focused on high accuracy
W2	0.70	0.30	focused on accuracy
W3	0.50	0.70	intermediate between W2 and W4
W4	0.30	0.70	focused on interpretability
W5	0.10	0.90	focused on high interpretability

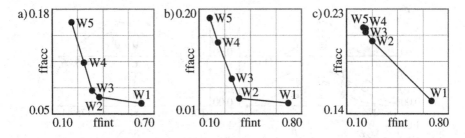

Fig. 1. Obtained trade-off between accuracy and interpretability for problem: (a) NF, (b) YH, (c) CS.

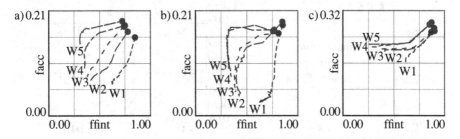

Fig. 2. Averaged learning process for problem: (a) NF, (b) YH, (c) CS. Filled circles stands for best solutions from first iteration of proposed algorithm.

Table 4. Averaged simulation results for considered problems.

Simulation problem	Evaluation function	case					Other authors results [45,51]
		W1	W2	W3	W4	W5	
NF	ffacc $(\cdot)$	0.063	0.069	0.078	0.095	0.144	n/a
	ffint $(\cdot)$	0.643	0.386	0.360	0.322	0.270	n/a
	RMSE	1.348	1.446	1.636	2.046	3.263	1.104 - 2.653
YH	ffacc $(\cdot)$	0.027	0.040	0.049	0.076	0.095	n/a
	ffint $(\cdot)$	0.652	0.416	0.365	0.321	0.287	n/a
	RMSE	2.614	3.617	4.281	6.996	8.629	0.820 - 2.236
CS	ffacc $(\cdot)$	0.153	0.183	0.190	0.198	0.202	n/a
	ffint $(\cdot)$	0.646	0.346	0.310	0.288	0.268	n/a
	RMSE	14.563	16.864	18.104	19.152	19.302	11.941 - 16.668

ing process was presented in Fig. 2. Typical examples of rules obtained for case W3 (which represent balanced trade-off between accuracy and interpretability) were presented in Fig. 3 and in Table 5. The notation of fuzzy rules examples obtained for case W3 and shown in Fig. 3 were presented in Table 5.

The conclusions from the simulations can be summarized as follows: (a) choosing specified values from set allow to obtain interpretable values of weights and values of parameters of triangular norms, (b) obtained results are similar (in a field of accuracy) to results presented by other authors, (c) use of variants

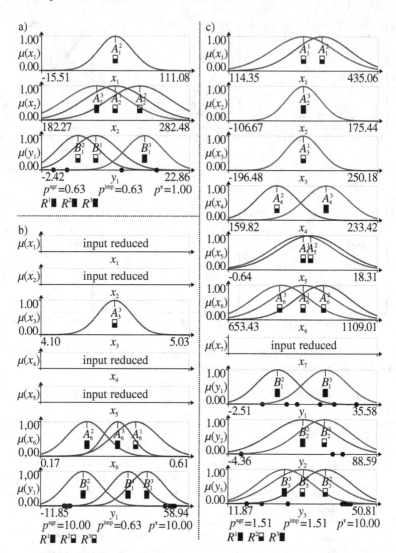

Fig. 3. Examples of obtained fuzzy sets (case W3) for problem: (a) NF, (b) YH, (c) CS. Rectangles stands for weights of fuzzy sets and rules (filled rectangle - very important value, half-filled rectangle - important value, empty rectangle - not important value). Circles stands for discretization points.

W1-W5 allows to obtain diversified solutions (in a field of expected trade-off between accuracy and interpretability).

Table 5. Summary with examples of fuzzy rules in the form of (1) of the fuzzy system (2) for variant W3 (Fig. 3).

NF	R^1 : IF $(x_2$ is $medium\,\lvert m\,)$ THEN $(y$ is $medium\,\lvert m\,)\,\lvert h$ R^2 : IF $(x_1$ is $near\,(47.78)\,\lvert m$ ANDx_2 is $high\,\lvert m\,)$ THEN $(y$ is $low\,\lvert m\,)\,\lvert h$ R^3 : IF $(x_2$ is $low\,\lvert h\,)$ THEN $(y$ is $high\,\lvert h\,)\,\lvert h$
YH	R^1 : IF $\left(froude\ number\ \text{is}\ high\,\lvert m\,\right)$ THEN $\left(resistance\ \text{is}\ medium\,\lvert h\,\right)\,\lvert h$ R^2 : IF $\left(froude\ number\ \text{is}\ low\,\lvert h\,\right)$ THEN $\left(resistance\ \text{is}\ low\,\lvert h\,\right)\,\lvert m$ R^3 : IF $\left(\begin{array}{l} l.displ.\ \text{is}\ near\,(7.57)\,\lvert m\ \text{AND} \\ froude\ number\ \text{is}\ medium\,\lvert h \end{array}\right)$ THEN $\left(resistance\ \text{is}\ high\,\lvert h\,\right)\,\lvert m$
CS	R^1 : IF $\left(\begin{array}{c} cement\ \text{is}\ low\,\lvert m\ \text{AND} \\ fly\ ash\ \text{is}\ near\,(26.85)\,\lvert m\ \text{AND} \\ sp\ \text{is}\ low\,\lvert m\ \text{AND} \\ coarse\ aggr.\ \text{is}\ medium\,\lvert m \end{array}\right)$ THEN $\left(str.\ \text{is}\ medium\,\lvert m\,\right)\,\lvert h$ R^2 : IF $\left(\begin{array}{c} cement\ \text{is}\ high\,\lvert m\ \text{AND} \\ water\ \text{is}\ low\,\lvert m\ \text{AND} \\ sp\ \text{is}\ high\,\lvert m\ \text{AND} \\ coarse\ aggr.\ \text{is}\ high\,\lvert m \end{array}\right)$ THEN $\left(\begin{array}{c} slump\ \text{is}\ low\,\lvert h\ \text{AND} \\ flow\ \text{is}\ low\,\lvert h\ \text{AND} \\ str.\ \text{is}\ high\,\lvert m \end{array}\right)\,\lvert m$ R^3 : IF $\left(\begin{array}{c} slag\ \text{is}\ near\,(34.38)\,\lvert h\ \text{AND} \\ water\ \text{is}\ high\,\lvert h\ \text{AND} \\ coarse\ aggr.\ \text{is}\ low\,\lvert m \end{array}\right)$ THEN $\left(\begin{array}{c} slump\ \text{is}\ high\,\lvert h\ \text{AND} \\ flow\ \text{is}\ high\,\lvert m\ \text{AND} \\ str.\ \text{is}\ low\,\lvert h \end{array}\right)\,\lvert h$

5   Conclusions

In this paper a new approach for interpretability of neuro-fuzzy systems with parametrized triangular norms was presented. In this approach, it is assumed that, a part of parameters are selected from set of defined values, where each of those values have its own interpretation. Those sets concerns weights (of antecedences, consequences and rules) and parameters of parametrized triangular norms with weights of arguments. This approach required use of proper learning algorithm. Therefore, we proposed modified golden ball algorithm, which allows to select parameters from set of values, select real values of parameters, and select binary parameters. Proposed learning algorithm can be used to learning all types of systems, where both the parameters and the structure have to be found. Obtained simulations results can be considered as good in a both fields of accuracy and interpretability.

Acknowledgment. The project was financed by the National Science Centre (Poland) on the basis of the decision number DEC-2012/05/B/ST7/02138.

References

1. Abbas, J.: The bipolar Choquet integrals based on ternary-element sets. J. Artif. Intell. Soft Comput. Res. **6**(1), 13–21 (2016)
2. Alcal, R., Ducange, P., Herrera, F., Lazzerini, B., Marcelloni, F.: A multi-objective evolutionary approach to concurrently learn rule and data base sof linguistic fuzzy rule-based systems. IEEE Trans. Fuzzy Syst. **17**, 1106–1122 (2009)
3. Alonso J. M.: Modeling Highly Interpretable Fuzzy Systems, European Centre for Soft Computing (2010)
4. Alonso, J.M., Magdalena, L.: HILK++: an interpretability-guided fuzzy modeling methodology for learning readable and comprehensible fuzzy rule-based classifiers. Soft Computing **15**(10), 1959–1980 (2011)
5. Bartczuk, Ł.: Gene expression programming in correction modelling of nonlinear dynamic objects. Adv. Intell. Syst. Comput. **429**, 125–134 (2016)
6. Bartczuk, Ł., Przybył, A., Koprinkova-Hristova, P.: New method for nonlinear fuzzy correction modelling of dynamic objects. In: Rutkowski, L., Korytkowski, M., Scherer, R., Tadeusiewicz, R., Zadeh, L.A., Zurada, J.M. (eds.) ICAISC 2014, Part I. LNCS, vol. 8467, pp. 169–180. Springer, Heidelberg (2014)
7. Bartczuk, Ł., Rutkowska, D.: Type-2 fuzzy decision trees. In: Rutkowski, L., Tadeusiewicz, R., Zadeh, L.A., Zurada, J.M. (eds.) ICAISC 2008. LNCS (LNAI), vol. 5097, pp. 197–206. Springer, Heidelberg (2008)
8. Bartczuk, Ł., Rutkowska, D.: Medical diagnosis with type-2 fuzzy decision trees, computers in medical activity. Adv. Intell. Soft Comput. **65**, 11–21 (2009)
9. Bruździński, T., Krzyżak, A., Fevens, T., Jeleń, Ł.: Web-based framework for breast cancer classification. J. Artif. Intell. Soft Comput. Res. **4**(2), 149–162 (2014)
10. Cheng, Y.I.: Modeling slump flow of concrete using second-order regressions and artificial neural networks. CCC **29**(6), 474–480 (2007)
11. Cierniak, R., Rutkowski, L.: On image compression by competitive neural networks and optimal linear predictors. Signal Process. Image Commun. **156**, 559–565 (2000)
12. Cpalka, K.: A method for designing flexible neuro-fuzzy systems. In: Rutkowski, L., Tadeusiewicz, R., Zadeh, L.A., Żurada, J.M. (eds.) ICAISC 2006. LNCS (LNAI), vol. 4029, pp. 212–219. Springer, Heidelberg (2006)
13. Cpalka, K.: A new method for design and reduction of neuro-fuzzy classification systems. IEEE Trans. Neural Networks **20**, 701–714 (2009)
14. Cpalka, K.: On evolutionary designing and learning of flexible neuro-fuzzy structures for nonlinear classification. Nonlinear Anal. Series A. Theor. Methods Appl. **71**(2009), e1659–e1672 (2009). Elsevier
15. Cpałka, K., Łapa, K., Przybył, A., Zalasiński, M.: A new method for designing neuro-fuzzy systems for nonlinear modelling with interpretability aspects. Neurocomput. **135**, 203–217 (2014)
16. Cpałka, K., Rebrova, O., Nowicki, R., Rutkowski, L.: On design of flexible neuro-fuzzy systems for nonlinear modelling. Int. J. General Syst. **42**(6), 706–720 (2013)
17. Cpałka, K., Rutkowski, L.: Flexible Takagi-Sugeno neuro-fuzzy structures for nonlinear approximation. WSEAS Trans. Syst. **4**(9), 1450–1458 (2005)
18. Cpałka K., Rutkowski L.: Flexible Takagi-Sugeno fuzzy systems, Neural Networks. In: Proceedings of the 2005 IEEE International Joint Conference on IJCNN 2005, vol. 3, pp. 1764–1769 (2005)
19. Cpałka, K., Zalasiński, M.: On-line signature verification using vertical signature partitioning. Expert Syst. Appl. **41**(9), 4170–4180 (2014)

20. Cpałka, K., Zalasiński, M., Rutkowski, L.: New method for the on-line signature verification based on horizontal partitioning. Pattern Recogn. **47**, 2652–2661 (2014)
21. Cpałka, K., Zalasiński, M., Rutkowski, L.: A new algorithm for identity verification based on the analysis of a handwritten dynamic signature. Appl. Soft Comput. **43**, 47–56 (2016)
22. Das, S., Kar, S., Pal, T.: Group decision making using interval-valued intuitionistic fuzzy soft matrix and confident weight of experts. J. Artif. Intell. Soft Comput. Res. **4**(1), 57–77 (2014)
23. Duda, P., Hayashi, Y., Jaworski, M.: On the Strong convergence of the orthogonal series-type kernel regression neural networks in a non-stationary environment. In: Korytkowski, M., Scherer, R., Tadeusiewicz, R., Zadeh, L.A., Zurada, J.M., Rutkowski, L. (eds.) ICAISC 2012, Part I. LNCS, vol. 7267, pp. 47–54. Springer, Heidelberg (2012)
24. Duda, P., Jaworski, M., Pietruczuk, L.: On pre-processing algorithms for data stream. In: Rutkowski, L., Korytkowski, M., Scherer, R., Tadeusiewicz, R., Zadeh, L.A., Zurada, J.M. (eds.) ICAISC 2012, Part II. LNCS, vol. 7268, pp. 56–63. Springer, Heidelberg (2012)
25. Dziwiński, P., Avedyan, E.D.: A new approach to nonlinear modeling based on significant operating points detection. In: Rutkowski, L., Korytkowski, M., Scherer, R., Tadeusiewicz, R., Zadeh, L.A., Zurada, J.M. (eds.) ICAISC 2015. LNCS, vol. 9120, pp. 364–378. Springer, Heidelberg (2015)
26. Dziwiński, P., Bartczuk, Ł., Przybył, A., Avedyan, E.D.: A new algorithm for identification of significant operating points using swarm intelligence. In: Rutkowski, L., Korytkowski, M., Scherer, R., Tadeusiewicz, R., Zadeh, L.A., Zurada, J.M. (eds.) ICAISC 2014, Part II. LNCS, vol. 8468, pp. 349–362. Springer, Heidelberg (2014)
27. Er, M.J., Duda, P.: On the weak convergence of the orthogonal series-type kernel regresion neural networks in a non-stationary environment. In: Wyrzykowski, R., Dongarra, J., Karczewski, K., Waśniewski, J. (eds.) PPAM 2011, Part I. LNCS, vol. 7203, pp. 443–450. Springer, Heidelberg (2012)
28. Farahbod, F., Eftekhari, M.: Comparsion of different T-norm operators in classification problems. Int. J. Fuzzy Logic Syst. **2**(3), 33–41 (2012)
29. Gabryel, M., Cpałka, K., Rutkowski, L.: Evolutionary strategies for learning of neuro-fuzzy systems. In: Proceeding of the I Workshop on Genetic Fuzzy Systems, Granada, pp. 119–123 (2005)
30. Gabryel, M., Korytkowski, M., Scherer, R., Rutkowski, L.: Object detection by simple fuzzy classifiers generated by boosting. In: Korytkowski, M., Scherer, R., Tadeusiewicz, R., Zadeh, L.A., Zurada, J.M., Rutkowski, L. (eds.) ICAISC 2013, Part I. LNCS, vol. 7894, pp. 540–547. Springer, Heidelberg (2013)
31. Gacto, M.J., Alcal, R., Herrera, F.: Integration of an index to preserve the semantic interpretability in the multi-objective evolutionary rule selection and tuning of linguistic fuzzy systems. IEEE Trans. Fuzzy Syst. **18**, 515–531 (2010)
32. Gacto, M.J., Alcal, R., Herrera, F.: Interpretability of linguistic fuzzy rule-based systems: an overview of interpretability measures. Inf. Sci. **181**(20), 4340–4360 (2011)
33. Gałkowski, T., Rutkowski, L.: Nonparametric recovery of multivariate functions with applications to system identification. Proc. IEEE **73**(5), 942–943 (1985)
34. Grycuk, R., Gabryel, M., Korytkowski, M., Scherer, R., Voloshynovskiy, S.: From single image to list of objects based on edge and blob detection. In: Korytkowski, M., Scherer, R., Tadeusiewicz, R., Zadeh, L.A., Zurada, J.M., Rutkowski, L. (eds.) ICAISC 2014, Part II. LNCS, vol. 8468, pp. 605–615. Springer, Heidelberg (2014)

35. Guillaume, S., Charnomordic, B.: Generating an interpretable family of fuzzy partitions from data. IEEE Trans. Fuzzy Syst. **12**(3), 324–335 (2004)

36. Icke, I., Rosenberg, A.: Multi-objective genetic programming for visual analytics. In: Silva, S., Foster, J.A., Nicolau, M., Machado, P., Giacobini, M. (eds.) EuroGP 2011. LNCS, vol. 6621, pp. 322–334. Springer, Heidelberg (2011)

37. Ishibuchi, H., Nakashima, T., Murata, T.: Comparsion of the Michigan and Pittsburgh approaches to the design of fuzzy classification systems. Electr. Commun. Japan, Part 3 **80**(12), 379–387 (1997)

38. Ishibuchi, H., Nojima, Y.: Analysis of interpretability-accuracy tradeoff of fuzzy systems by multiobjective fuzzy genetics-based machine learning. Int. J. Approximate Reasoning **44**, 4–31 (2007)

39. Jaworski, M., Er, M.J., Pietruczuk, L.: On the application of the parzen-type kernel regression neural network and order statistics for learning in a non-stationary environment. In: Rutkowski, L., Korytkowski, M., Scherer, R., Tadeusiewicz, R., Zadeh, L.A., Zurada, J.M. (eds.) ICAISC 2012, Part I. LNCS, vol. 7267, pp. 90–98. Springer, Heidelberg (2012)

40. Jaworski, M., Pietruczuk, L., Duda, P.: On resources optimization in fuzzy clustering of data streams. In: Rutkowski, L., Korytkowski, M., Scherer, R., Tadeusiewicz, R., Zadeh, L.A., Zurada, J.M. (eds.) ICAISC 2012, Part II. LNCS, vol. 7268, pp. 92–99. Springer, Heidelberg (2012)

41. Kitajima, R., Kamimura, R.: Accumulative information enhancement in the self-organizing maps and its application to the analysis of mission statements. J. Artif. Intell. Soft Comput. Res. **5**(3), 161–176 (2015)

42. Korytkowski, M., Nowicki, R., Scherer, R.: Neuro-fuzzy rough classifier ensemble. In: Alippi, C., Polycarpou, M., Panayiotou, C., Ellinas, G. (eds.) ICANN 2009, Part I. LNCS, vol. 5768, pp. 817–823. Springer, Heidelberg (2009)

43. Korytkowski, M., Rutkowski, L., Scherer, R.: From ensemble of fuzzy classifiers to single fuzzy rule base classifier. In: Rutkowski, L., Tadeusiewicz, R., Zadeh, L.A., Zurada, J.M. (eds.) ICAISC 2008. LNCS (LNAI), vol. 5097, pp. 265–272. Springer, Heidelberg (2008)

44. Korytkowski, M., Rutkowski, L., Scherer, R.: Fast image classification by boosting fuzzy classifiers. Inf. Sci. **327**, 175–182 (2016)

45. Kummer, N., Najjaran, H.: Adaboost.MRT: boosting regression for multivariate estimation. Artif. Intell. Res. **3**(4), 64–76 (2014)

46. Laskowski, Ł., Laskowska, M.: Probing of synthesis route. J. Solid State Chem. **220**, 221–226 (2014)

47. Laskowski, Ł., Laskowska, M., Bałanda, M., Fitta, M., Kwiatkowska, J., Dziliński, K., Karczmarska, A.: Raman and magnetic analysis. Microporous Mesoporous Mater. **200**, 253–259 (2014)

48. Li, X., Er, M.J., Lim, B.S., Zhou, J.H., Gan, O.P., Rutkowski, L.: Fuzzy regression modeling for tool performance prediction and degradation detection. Int. J. Neural Syst. **2005**, 405–419 (2010)

49. Liu, F., Quek, C., Ng, G.S.: A novel generic hebbian ordering-based fuzzy rule base reduction approach to Mamdani neuro-fuzzy system. Neural Comput. **19**, 1656–1680 (2007)

50. Ludwig, S.A.: Repulsive self-adaptive acceleration particle swarm optimization approach. J. Artif. Intell. Soft Comput. Res. **4**(3), 189–204 (2014)

51. Lapa K.: Algorithms for extracting interpretable expert knowledge in nonlinear modeling issues, PhD Thesis (in polish), Czestochowa University of Technology (2015)

52. Łapa, K., Przybył, A., Cpałka, K.: A new approach to designing interpretable models of dynamic systems. In: Rutkowski, L., Korytkowski, M., Scherer, R., Tadeusiewicz, R., Zadeh, L.A., Zurada, J.M. (eds.) ICAISC 2013, Part II. LNCS, vol. 7895, pp. 523–534. Springer, Heidelberg (2013)

53. Łapa, K., Zalasiński, M., Cpałka, K.: A new method for designing and complexity reduction of neuro-fuzzy systems for nonlinear modelling. In: Rutkowski, L., Korytkowski, M., Scherer, R., Tadeusiewicz, R., Zadeh, L.A., Zurada, J.M. (eds.) ICAISC 2013, Part I. LNCS, vol. 7894, pp. 329–344. Springer, Heidelberg (2013)

54. Marquez A. A., Marquez F. A., Peregrin A.: A multi-objective evolutionary algorithm with an interpretability improvement mechanism for linguistic fuzzy systems with adaptive defuzzification. In: IEEE International Conference on Fuzzy Systems, pp. 1–7 (2010)

55. Mencar, C., Castellano, G., Fanelli, A.M.: On the role of interpretability in fuzzy data mining. Int. J. Uncertainty Fuzziness Knowl. Based Syst. 15(5), 521–537 (2007)

56. Mencar, C., Castiello, C., Cannone, R., Fanelli, A.M.: Interpretability assessment of fuzzy knowledge bases: a cointension based approach. Int. J. Approximate Reasoning 52(4), 501–518 (2011)

57. Nelson, W.: Analysis of performance-degradation data. IEEE Trans. Reliab. 2(2), 149–155 (1981)

58. Nobukawa, S., Nishimura, H., Yamanishi, T., Liu, J.-Q.: Chaotic states induced by resetting process in Izhikevich Neuron Model. J. Artif. Intell. Soft Comput. Res. 5(2), 109–119 (2015)

59. Ortigosa I., Lopez R., Garcia J.: A neural networks approach to residuary resistance of sailing yachts prediction. In: Proceedings of the International Conference on Marine Engineering MARINE 2007 (2007)

60. Osaba, E.: Golden Ball: a novel meta-heuristic to solve combinatorial optimization problems based on soccer concepts. Appl. Intell. 12(2013), 145–166 (2013)

61. Patgiri, C., Sarma, M., Sarma, K.K.: A class of neuro-computational methods for assamese fricative classification. J. Artif. Intell. Soft Comput. Res. 5(1), 59–70 (2015)

62. Pietruczuk, L., Duda, P., Jaworski, M.: A new fuzzy classifier for data streams. In: Rutkowski, L., Korytkowski, M., Scherer, R., Tadeusiewicz, R., Zadeh, L.A., Zurada, J.M. (eds.) ICAISC 2012, Part I. LNCS, vol. 7267, pp. 318–324. Springer, Heidelberg (2012)

63. Pietruczuk, L., Duda, P., Jaworski, M.: Adaptation of decision trees for handling concept drift. In: Rutkowski, L., Korytkowski, M., Scherer, R., Tadeusiewicz, R., Zadeh, L.A., Zurada, J.M. (eds.) ICAISC 2013, Part I. LNCS, vol. 7894, pp. 459–473. Springer, Heidelberg (2013)

64. Pulkkinen, P., Koivisto, H.: A dynamically constrained multiobjective genetic fuzzy system for regression problems. IEEE Trans. Fuzzy Syst. 18(1), 161–177 (2010)

65. Riid, A., Rüstern, E.: Interpretability, interpolation and rule weights in linguistic fuzzy modeling. In: Fanelli, A.M., Pedrycz, W., Petrosino, A. (eds.) WILF 2011. LNCS, vol. 6857, pp. 91–98. Springer, Heidelberg (2011)

66. Rutkowska, A.: Influence of membership functions shape on portfolio optimization results. J. Artif. Intell. Soft Comput. Res. 6(1), 45–54 (2016)

67. Rutkowski, L.: Identification of MISO nonlinear regressions in the presence of a wide class of disturbances. IEEE Trans. Inform. Theory 37(1), 214–216 (1997)

68. Rutkowski, L., Cpaka, K.: Flexible neuro fuzzy systems. IEEE Trans. Neural Networks 14, 554–574 (2003)

69. Rutkowski, L.: Adaptive probabilistic neural networks for pattern classification in time-varying environment. IEEE Trans. Neural Networks **15**(4), 811–827 (2004)
70. Rutkowski, L.: Flexible Neuro-Fuzzy Systems. Kluwer Academic Publishers, Dordrecht (2004)
71. Rutkowski, L.: Computational Intelligence. Springer, Heidelberg (2008)
72. Rutkowski, L., Cpałka, K.: Flexible structures of neuro-fuzzy systems. In: Sincak, P., Vascak, J. (eds.) Quo Vadis Computational Intelligence. Studies in Fuzziness and Soft Computing, vol. 54, pp. 479–484. Springer, Heidelberg (2000)
73. Rutkowski, L., Cpałka, K.: Compromise approach to neuro-fuzzy systems. In: Sincak, P., Vascak, J., Kvasnicka, V., Pospichal, J. (eds.) Intelligent Technologies - Theory and Applications, vol. 76, pp. 85–90. IOS Press (2002)
74. Rutkowski L., Cpałka K.: Flexible weighted neuro-fuzzy systems. In: Proceedings of the 9th Internationa; Conference on Neural Information Processing (ICONIP-02), Orchid Country Club, Singapore, 18–22 November 2002. CD
75. Rutkowski L., Cpałka K.: Neuro-fuzzy systems derived from quasi-triangular norms. In: Proceedings of the IEEE International Conference on Fuzzy Systems, Budapest, 26–29 July 2004, vol. 2, pp. 1031–1036 (2004)
76. Rutkowski, L., Jaworski, M., Pietruczuk, L., Duda, P.: Decision trees for mining data streams based on the gaussian approximation. IEEE Trans. Knowl. Data Eng. **26**(1), 108–119 (2014)
77. Rutkowski, L., Jaworski, M., Pietruczuk, L., Duda, P.: The CART decision tree for mining data streams. Inf. Sci. **266**, 1–15 (2014)
78. Rutkowski, L., Pietruczuk, L., Duda, P., Jaworski, M.: Decision Trees for mining data streams based on the McDiarmid's bound. IEEE Trans. Knowl. Data Eng. **25**(6), 1272–1279 (2013)
79. Rutkowski, L., Przybył, A., Cpałka, K., Er, M.J.: Online speed profile generation for industrial machine tool based on neuro-fuzzy approach. In: Rutkowski, L., Scherer, R., Tadeusiewicz, R., Zadeh, L.A., Zurada, J.M. (eds.) ICAISC 2010, Part II. LNCS, vol. 6114, pp. 645–650. Springer, Heidelberg (2010)
80. Scherer, R.: Neuro-fuzzy systems with relation matrix. In: Rutkowski, L., Scherer, R., Tadeusiewicz, R., Zadeh, L.A., Zurada, J.M. (eds.) ICAISC 2010, Part I. LNCS, vol. 6113, pp. 210–215. Springer, Heidelberg (2010)
81. Scherer R., Rutkowski L.: Relational equations initializing neuro-fuzzy system. In: Proceeding of the 10th Zittau Fuzzy Colloquium, Zittau, Germany, pp. 18–22 (2002)
82. Shukla, P.K., Tripathi, S.P.: A new approach for tuning interval type-2 fuzzy knowledge bases using genetic algorithms. J. Uncertainty Anal. Appl. **2**(4), 1–15 (2014)
83. Starczewski, J.T., Bartczuk, Ł., Dziwiński, P., Marvuglia, A.: Learning methods for type-2 FLS based on FCM. In: Rutkowski, L., Scherer, R., Tadeusiewicz, R., Zadeh, L.A., Zurada, J.M. (eds.) ICAISC 2010, Part I. LNCS, vol. 6113, pp. 224–231. Springer, Heidelberg (2010)
84. Szarek, A., Korytkowski, M., Rutkowski, L., Scherer, R., Szyprowski, J.: Application of neural networks in assessing changes around implant after total hip arthroplasty. In: Rutkowski, L., Korytkowski, M., Scherer, R., Tadeusiewicz, R., Zadeh, L.A., Zurada, J.M. (eds.) ICAISC 2012, Part II. LNCS, vol. 7268, pp. 335–340. Springer, Heidelberg (2012)
85. Szarek, A., Korytkowski, M., Rutkowski, L., Scherer, R., Szyprowski, J.: Forecasting wear of head and acetabulum in hip joint implant. In: Rutkowski, L., Korytkowski, M., Scherer, R., Tadeusiewicz, R., Zadeh, L.A., Zurada, J.M. (eds.) ICAISC 2012, Part II. LNCS, vol. 7268, pp. 341–346. Springer, Heidelberg (2012)

86. Szczypta, J., Przybył, A., Cpałka, K.: Some aspects of evolutionary designing optimal controllers. In: Rutkowski, L., Korytkowski, M., Scherer, R., Tadeusiewicz, R., Zadeh, L.A., Zurada, J.M. (eds.) ICAISC 2013, Part II. LNCS, vol. 7895, pp. 91–100. Springer, Heidelberg (2013)

87. Szczypta, J., Przybył, A., Wang, L.: Evolutionary approach with multiple quality criteria for controller design. In: Rutkowski, L., Korytkowski, M., Scherer, R., Tadeusiewicz, R., Zadeh, L.A., Zurada, J.M. (eds.) ICAISC 2014, Part I. LNCS, vol. 8467, pp. 455–467. Springer, Heidelberg (2014)

88. Smyczyńska, J., Hilczer, M., Smyczyńska, U., Stawerska, R., Tadeusiewicz, R., Lewiński, A.: Artificial neural models - a novel tool for predictying the efficacy of growth hormone (GH) therapy in children with short stature. Neuroendocrinology Lett. 36(4), 348–353 (2015). (ISSN: 0172-780X, ISSN-L: 0172-780X)

89. Smyczyńska, U., Smyczyńska, J., Hilczer, M., Stawerska, R., Lewiński, A.: Artificial neural networks - a novel tool in modelling the effectiveness of growth hormone (GH) therapy in children with GH deficiency. Pediatric Endocrinology 14(2(51)), 9–18 (2015)

90. Tadeusiewicz, R.: Neural networks as a tool for modeling of biological systems. Bio-Algorithms Med-Syst. 11(3), 135–144 (2015)

91. Tadeusiewicz, R.: Neural networks in mining sciences - general overview and some representative examples. Archivum Min. Sci. 60(4), 971–984 (2015)

92. Vanhoucke, V., Silipo, R.: Interpretability in multidimensional classification. In: Casillas, J., Cordón, O., Herrera, F., Magdalena, L. (eds.) Interpretability Issues in Fuzzy Modeling. Studies in Fuzziness and Soft Computing, vol. 128, pp. 193–217. Springer, Heidelberg (2003)

93. Yamamoto, Y., Yoshikawa, T., Furuhashi, T.: Improvement of performance of Japanese P300 speller by using second display. J. Artif. Intell. Soft Comput. Res. 5(3), 221–226 (2015)

94. Zalasiński M., Cpałka K.: A new method of on-line signature verification using a flexible fuzzy one-class classifier, pp. 38–53. Academic Publishing House EXIT (2011)

95. Zalasiński, M., Cpałka, K.: New approach for the on-line signature verification based on method of horizontal partitioning. In: Rutkowski, L., Korytkowski, M., Scherer, R., Tadeusiewicz, R., Zadeh, L.A., Zurada, J.M. (eds.) ICAISC 2013, Part II. LNCS, vol. 7895, pp. 342–350. Springer, Heidelberg (2013)

96. Zalasiński, M., Cpałka, K., Er, M.J.: New method for dynamic signature verification using hybrid partitioning. In: Rutkowski, L., Korytkowski, M., Scherer, R., Tadeusiewicz, R., Zadeh, L.A., Zurada, J.M. (eds.) ICAISC 2014, Part II. LNCS, vol. 8468, pp. 216–230. Springer, Heidelberg (2014)

97. Zalasiński, M., Cpałka, K., Er, M.J.: A new method for the dynamic signature verification based on the stable partitions of the signature. In: Rutkowski, L., Korytkowski, M., Scherer, R., Tadeusiewicz, R., Zadeh, L.A., Zurada, J.M. (eds.) ICAISC 2015. LNCS, vol. 9120, pp. 161–174. Springer, Heidelberg (2015)

98. Zalasiński, M., Cpałka, K., Hayashi, Y.: New method for dynamic signature verification based on global features. In: Rutkowski, L., Korytkowski, M., Scherer, R., Tadeusiewicz, R., Zadeh, L.A., Zurada, J.M. (eds.) ICAISC 2014, Part II. LNCS, vol. 8468, pp. 231–245. Springer, Heidelberg (2014)

99. Zalasiński, M., Cpałka, K., Hayashi, Y.: New fast algorithm for the dynamic signature verification using global features values. In: Rutkowski, L., Korytkowski, M., Scherer, R., Tadeusiewicz, R., Zadeh, L.A., Zurada, J.M. (eds.) ICAISC 2015. LNCS, vol. 9120, pp. 175–188. Springer, Heidelberg (2015)

An Application of Fuzzy Logic to Traffic Lights Control and Simulation in Real Time

Bartosz Poletajew and Adam Slowik[✉]

Department of Electronics and Computer Science,
Koszalin University of Technology, Sniadeckich 2 Street, 75-453 Koszalin, Poland
bartoszpoletajew@o2.pl, aslowik@ie.tu.koszalin.pl

Abstract. In this paper, the fuzzy system for traffic lights control and simulation in real time is presented. The main advantages of the proposed system are as follows: adaptation of the green light activity time to the conditions which occur on the given roads intersection; shorter reduction time (in relation to the other state-of-the-art fuzzy system) of vehicle numbers on the particular roads. Due to these two advantages, the road infrastructure is less congested and the traffic participants possesses the possibility of faster movement. The fuzzy system presented in this paper was tested on the traffic scenario taken from literature. The results obtained using proposed approach were compared to the results obtained using other state-of-the-art fuzzy system chosen from literature. Due to our approach, the number of vehicles in given crossroads is reduced in shorter time.

1 Introduction

Fuzzy systems [1,2] which are based on fuzzy logic [3–6] possesses many practical applications [7–9,12]. One of them is control of traffic lights [10,11]. The traffic lights control problem is based on perform of appropriate control of vehicles movement in urban area. Nowadays, the city functioning without appropriate traffic control is more and more difficult. The speed of life and city residents mobility are increasing, therefore the number of vehicles in the city is increasing too. The higher number of vehicles in the city influences the movement comfort of vehicles in the city area, public safety, road infrastructure condition, environments pollution, and human healthiness. One of the possible way to solve these problems is adaptation of the road infrastructure to the constantly changing of the road conditions. The excellent example is an appropriate using of the traffic lights control. This solution is the cheapest one and the reorganization of the traffic lights is least burdensome for road users. In the literature, we can find some applications of the fuzzy systems to the traffic lights control. In the paper [11], the Mamdani fuzzy system for traffic lights control is presented. This system is based on linguistic variables such as: number of vehicles and the total length of these vehicles. In the paper [10], the adaptive fuzzy system for traffic lights control is presented. This system is based on linguistic variables such as: number of vehicles, total length of these vehicles (together with the space

© Springer International Publishing Switzerland 2016
L. Rutkowski et al. (Eds.): ICAISC 2016, Part I, LNAI 9692, pp. 266–275, 2016.
DOI: 10.1007/978-3-319-39378-0_23

between particular vehicles), and the average velocity of these vehicles. In the fuzzy systems [10,11] the value of the maximal green light activity time is longer than one minute. Also, we must remember about the human factor which exists in this problem besides the economic criteria such as: time of vehicle movement, fuel cost, maintenance cost of road infrastructure. As, we know the speed of life is more and more intensive. Therefore, also the human stress level is higher. This human stress expression is often enough visible in drivers road aggression. So, if the green activity time is too longer in one road (of course the vehicle movement is stopped in the second road) then the human stress level can be rapidly increased in particular drivers. Therefore, the suggested solution is connected with the shortening of the maximal value of the green activity time. Due to this, the traffic lights will be toggle more often, and the number of vehicles will be faster reduced in given road intersection. In this paper, the fuzzy system for traffic lights control and simulation in real time is presented. The proposed system was named FS-TLC (Fuzzy System for Traffic Lights Control). The main advantages of the proposed fuzzy system are: adaptation of the green activity time to the traffic conditions in given road intersection, and the shorter time which is needed for number of vehicles reduction in particular roads. Due to these advantages, the road infrastructure is less overburden by the vehicles, and the vehicles have the possibility for faster movement. The presented fuzzy system was tested on the traffic scenario which was taken from literature. The results obtained using proposed FS-TLC system were compared with the results obtained using fuzzy system presented in the paper [10]. Using FS-TLC system, the shorter times (which are required for number of vehicles reduction in given intersection) were obtained than in the case of the fuzzy system presented in paper [10]. This paper consists of the following sections: in Sect. 2, the problem of traffic lights control is shortly described; in Sect. 3, the proposed fuzzy system (FS-TLC) is presented; in Sect. 4, the traffic scenario is presented in detail, and the results obtained during experiments are shown; and finally in Sect. 5, the conclusions are presented.

2   Problem of Traffic Lights Control

The problem of appropriate traffic lights control is based on the streamline of vehicles movement in given road intersection [10]. It is directly connected with the effective vehicles ride through the city, but have also an enormous influence on road infrastructure condition and environments pollution. If the traffic will be faster reduced on the crowded road intersection then the efficiency of the public transport will be straightened in the whole city. The appropriate control of the traffic lights can affect on less discomfort and stress level of car drivers. Of course the other rational advantages are: reduction of environments pollution, and reduction of financial expenses connected with improvement of the road conditions.

3   Proposed Fuzzy System for Traffic Lights Control

Let's assume that, our crossroads consists of two roads (which intersect each other): the north-south (NS) road, and east-west (EW) road. The fuzzy system (which is proposed in this paper) is based on four input linguistic variables, and two output linguistic variables. The input linguistic variables are as follows: number of vehicles in the north-south road (VNS), number of vehicles in the east-west road (VEW), the total weight of vehicles in the north-south road (WNS), and the total weight of vehicles in the east-west road (WEW). The output linguistic variables are represented by: green light activity time in the north-south road (GNS) and green light activity time in the east-west road (GEW). The input linguistic variables such as: VNS and VEW consists of three linguistic values: small (SM), medium (ME), large (LA). These linguistic variables (VNS and VEW) are described by the fuzzy set which is presented in the Fig. 1a. The input linguistic variables such as: WNS and WEW consists of two linguistic values: light (LI) and heavy (HE). These linguistic variables (WNS and WEW) are described by the fuzzy set which is presented in Fig. 1b. The output linguistic variables such as: GNS and GEW consists of five linguistic values: very short (XS), short (SH), average (AV), long (LO), very long (XL). These linguistic variables (GNS and GEW) are described by the fuzzy set which is presented in Fig. 1c. In our fuzzy system (FS-TLC), the fuzzy operators PROD-MAX were applied.

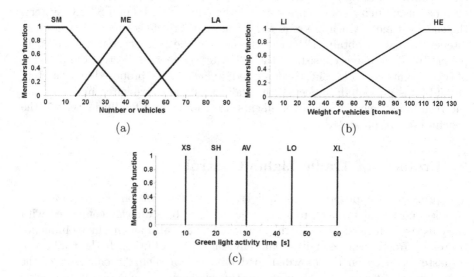

Fig. 1. Graphical representation of fuzzy sets which represent: the input linguistic variables VNS and VEW (a), the input linguistic variables WNS and WEW (b), the output linguistic variables GNS and GEW (c)

The input data for our fuzzy system are randomly generated in accordance to the assumed traffic scenario in given crossroads (the detailed description of the assumed traffic scenario is in the further part of this section). When the input data (VNS, VEW, WNS, WEW) will be inserted into the fuzzy system inputs, the fuzzification process (using PROD operator) is performed. The results obtained from fuzzification goes to the inference block. In the inference block, the rules activation level is checked. The fuzzy system (FS-TLC) consists of 72 fuzzy rules (36 fuzzy rules are assigned to the output GNS, and other 36 fuzzy rules are assigned to the output GEW). The fuzzy rules coding scheme is as follows: for example the encoded fuzzy rule SM, SM, LI, LI, XS which is connected with the output GNS represents the decoded fuzzy rule:

IF VEW=SM AND VNS=SM AND WEW=LI AND WNS=LI THEN GNS=XS

The fuzzy rules for FS-TLC system are presented in Table 1.

Table 1. The fuzzy rules for FS-TLC system

The fuzzy rules for GNS output in FS-TLC system:		
SM, SM, LI, LI, XS	SM, SM, HE, LI, XS	SM, SM, LI, HE, SH
SM, SM, HE, HE, SH	SM, ME, LI, LI, AV	SM, ME, HE, LI, AV
SM, ME, LI, HE, LO	SM, ME, HE, HE, LO	SM, LA, LI, LI, LO
SM, LA, HE, LI, LO	SM, LA, LI, HE, XL	SM, LA, HE, HE, XL
ME, SM, LI LI, XS	ME, SM, HE, LI, XS	ME, SM, LI, HE, SH
ME, SM, HE, HE, SH	ME, ME, LI, LI, AV	ME, ME, HE, LI, AV
ME, ME, LI, HE, LO	ME, ME, HE, HE, LO	ME, LA, LI, LI, LO
ME, LA, HE, LI, LO	ME, LA, LI, HE, XL	ME, LA, HE, HE, XL
LA, SM, LI, LI, XS	LA, SM, HE, LI, XS	LA, MS, LI, HE, SH
LA, SM, HE, HE, SH	LA, ME, LI, LI, AV	LA, ME, HE, LI, AV
LA, ME, LI, HE, LO	LA, ME, HE, HE, LO	LA, LA, LI, LI, LO
LA, LA, HE, LI, LO	LA, LA, LI, HE, XL	LA, LA, HE, HE, XL
The fuzzy rules for GEW output in FS-TLC system:		
SM, SM, LI, LI, XS	SM, SM, HE, LI, SH	SM, SM, LI, HE, XS
SM, SM, HE, HE, SH	SM, ME, LI, LI, XS	SM, ME, HE, LI, SH
SM, ME, LI, HE, XS	SM, ME, HE, HE, SH	SM, LA, LI, LI, XS
SM, LA, HE LI, SH	SM, LA, LI, HE, XS	SM, LA, HE, HE, SH
ME, SM, LI LI, AV	ME, SM, HE, LI, LO	ME, SM, LI, HE, AV
ME, SM, HE, HE, LO	ME, ME, LI, LI, AV	ME, ME, HE, LI, LO
ME, ME, LI, HE, AV	ME, ME, HE, HE, LO	ME, LA, LI, LI, AV
ME, LA, HE, LI, LO	ME, LA, LI, HE, AV	ME, LA, HE, HE, LO
LA, SM, LI, LI, LO	LA, SM, HE, LI, XL	LA, MS, LI, HE, LO
LA, SM, HE, HE, XL	LA, ME, LI, LI, LO	LA, ME, HE, LI, XL
LA, ME, LI, HE, LO	LA, ME, HE, HE, XL	LA, LA, LI, LI, LO
LA, LA, HE, LI, XL	LA, LA, LI, HE, LO	LA, LA, HE, HE, XL

The fire level for each rule was computed using PROD operator. The height method was used for defuzzification of both output linguistic variables: GNS and GEW. After computation of the crisp output value GNS and GEW, the road with higher value of green light activity time (higher value between GNS and GEW) was opened as first. The road with smaller value of green light activity time (smaller value between GNS and GEW) was opened as a second. When, the single cycle of green lights changing for both roads will be finished then the new input data are inserted into the inputs of our fuzzy system. In the case when any vehicle does not exists in the given intersection, then the road with higher priority is opened on the XS time (see Fig. 1c).

4 Description of Experiments

During experiments, the simulation process was performed in order to efficiency comparison between proposed FS-TLC system and fuzzy system presented in paper [10]. In the next part of this paper, the fuzzy system presented in paper [10] is named as AEO. Both fuzzy systems (FS-TLC and AEO) were tested on the situation when the traffic is rapidly growing in the given intersection. The applied traffic scenario was chosen from paper [10]. In the experiments, the vehicles are randomly generated for all roads (in given intersection) in five seconds cycles. The value of weight for each vehicle is randomly generated from the range [3; 8] tonnes. The simulation process was divided into eight stages (the duration for each stage is equal to five minutes). The characteristic of the particular simulation stages is as follows:

Stage 1: The initial number of vehicles on the particular roads is equal to 5. Next, the number of vehicles is randomly generated from the range [0; 3] for each road (north-south road and east-west road) by 30 s time period. After vehicles generation, the traffic lights control process is started off.

Stage 2: The initial number of vehicles for each road is equal to the final value (for given road) obtained at the end of the stage 1. In the second stage, we assumed that the number of vehicles will increase in the east-west road (in relation to the number of vehicles in the north-south road). In this stage, the number of vehicles is randomly generated from the range [0; 5] for the east-west road, and from the range [0; 3] for the north-south road.

Stage 3: In the third stage, we assumed that the number of vehicles will increase in the north-south road (in relation to the number of vehicles in the east-west road). Therefore, the number of vehicles is randomly generated from the range [0; 3] for the east-west road, and from the range [0; 5] for the north-south road.

Stage 4: In this stage, the number of vehicles is rapidly growing in the north-south road. In the east-west road, the number of vehicles is moderate growing. Therefore, the number of vehicles is randomly generated from the range [0; 5] for the east-west road, and from the range [0; 9] for the north-south road.

Stage 5: In the fifth stage, the number of vehicles is increase for the east-west road, but the number of vehicles is not changed for the north-south road. Therefore, the number of vehicles for both roads (east-west road, and north-south road) is randomly generated from the range [0; 9].

Stage 6: In this stage, the reduction process of traffic intensity (in our intersection) is began. The number of vehicles is decreased to the minimal level for the north-south road. The number of vehicles is decreased to the moderate level for the east-west road. Therefore, the number of vehicles is randomly generated from the range [0; 5] for the east-west road, and from the range [0; 3] for the north-south road.

Stage 7: In the seventh stage, the number of vehicles for the both roads is decreased to the minimal level. Therefore, the number of vehicles is randomly generated from the range [0; 3] for the east-west road and for the north-south road.

Stage 8: In this final stage, the new vehicles are not generated. The simulation process is stopped (for both fuzzy systems: FS-TLC and AEO) when the last vehicle left the intersection. The value of time obtained when the last vehicle left the intersection is the result of fuzzy system (FS-TLC and AEO) operation.

The 20 simulation processes were taken during our experiment . The average simulation time (from 20-fold repetition) was equal to: 2504.3 [s] for FS-TLC fuzzy system, and 2545.5 [s] for AEO fuzzy system. The shorter times (in 19 cases on 20 possible) were obtained using proposed FS-TLC fuzzy system. The results obtained in our experiments are presented in Table 2. The symbol "Difference" (see Table 2) represents the difference of simulation time between AEO fuzzy system and FS-TLC fuzzy system.

It is worth to noticed that in only one case, the simulation time obtained by fuzzy system AEO is shorter than the simulation time obtained by fuzzy system FS-TLC. However in this one case, the difference in simulation time is small and equal to 6 s only.

The another difference between fuzzy system FS-TLC and fuzzy system AEO is the average number of vehicles in the particular roads. Using the proposed FS-TLC system we obtained the smaller number of vehicles than the number of vehicles obtained using AEO system for east-west road as well as for the north-south road. The results obtained using FS-TLC system and AEO system are presented in Fig. 2 (for east-west road) and in Fig. 3 (for north-south road). Also, it is worth to notice in accordance to the taken traffic scenario that the east-west road is less crowded. It can be seen when the data presented in Fig. 2 will be compared with the data presented in Fig. 3.

The characteristic of traffic intensity in the north-south road (Fig. 3) is in accordance with taken assumptions. In the north-south road, the higher number of vehicles is taken into account (in all simulation processes) during computation of green light activity time than in the case of east-west road (Fig. 2). The average number of vehicles (from the all 20 simulations) is equal to: 72 (FS-TLC) and 80 (AEO) for the north-south road; 83 (FS-TLC) and 90 (AEO) for the east-west

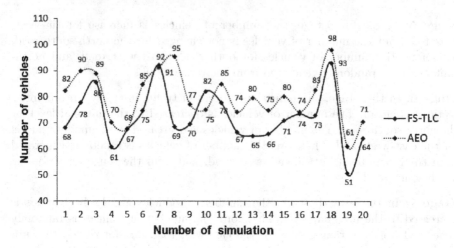

Fig. 2. The average number of vehicles in the east-west road for each fuzzy system

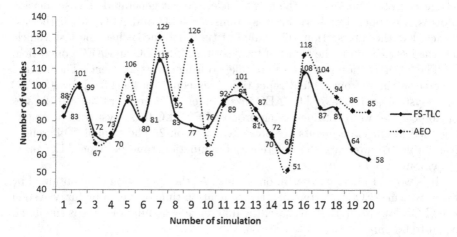

Fig. 3. The average number of vehicles in the north-south road for each fuzzy system

road. It can be seen that due to application of the FS-TLC fuzzy system the average number of vehicles is decreased (in relation to AEO fuzzy system) in the both roads.

If we take into consideration the average values of green light activity time for particular roads, we can see that for the east-west road (Fig. 4) and for the north-south road (Fig. 5) the obtained values are oscillated into the range of long (LO) green light activity time.

Based on the data presented in Fig. 4 and presented in Fig. 5, it can be seen that the average values of green light activity time which are obtained using AEO fuzzy system are higher twice than the average values of green light activity time which are obtained using FS-TLC fuzzy system. The average green light activity

Table 2. The particular simulation times for fuzzy systems: FS-TLC and AEO

Simulation	FS-TLC Simulation time [s]	AEO [10] Simulation time [s]	Difference [s]
1	2599	2635	36
2	2561	2635	74
3	2363	2419	56
4	2403	2517	114
5	2525	2563	38
6	2455	2497	42
7	2595	2589	-6
8	2471	2525	54
9	2559	2589	30
10	2445	2495	50
11	2543	2581	38
12	2535	2559	24
13	2509	2535	26
14	2583	2633	50
15	2305	2371	66
16	2585	2603	18
17	2437	2459	22
18	2689	2725	36
19	2417	2449	32
20	2507	2531	24

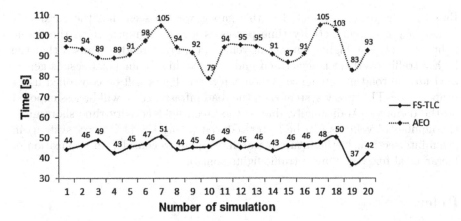

Fig. 4. The average values of green light activity time in the east-west road for each fuzzy system

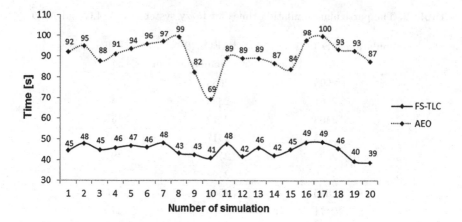

Fig. 5. The average values of green light activity time in the north-south road for each fuzzy system

time (from the all 20 simulations) is equal to: 45 [s] (FS-TLC) and 91 [s] (AEO) for the north-south road; 46 [s] (FS-TLC) and 93 [s] (AEO) for the east-west road. Finally, we can said that due to the shortening of the green light activity time (see the results obtained for FS-TLC fuzzy system), the time required for vehicles movement through the given intersection is shortened too. Also, due to application of FS-TLC system, the smaller traffic overload is generated for all roads.

5 Conclusions

Based on the results presented in this paper, we can seen that the parameter values of green light activity time possesses a huge significance in the traffic lights control. The higher number of vehicles (in given road) is caused that the higher traffic overload is generated and also the higher financial cost is generated for the road maintenance. When the traffic lights will be controlled using proposed FS-TLC fuzzy system then the road infrastructure will be less exposed on the damages. Additionally, due to the green light activity time shortening, the number of vehicles can be faster reduced (using FS-TLC fuzzy system) in given intersection. In the future research, we plan to consider an application of hierarchical fuzzy system to traffic lights control.

References

1. Cox, E.: The Fuzzy Systems Handbook: A Practitioner's Guide to Building, Using, and Maintaining Fuzzy Systems, 2nd edn. Academic Press, London (1999)
2. Pedrycz, W., Gomide, F.: Fuzzy Systems Engineering: Toward Human-Centric Computing. Wiley-IEEE Press, USA (2007)

3. Klir, G.J., Yuan, B.: Fuzzy Sets and Fuzzy Logic: Theory and Applications. Prentice Hall, Upper Saddle River (1995)
4. Mendel, J.M.: Uncertain Rule-Based Fuzzy Logic: Introduction and new directions. Prentice Hall, USA (2000). McCluskey, E.J.: Minimization of boolean function. Bell Syst. Techn. J. **35**(5), 1417–1444 (1956)
5. Zadeh, L.A.: Fuzzy Sets. Inf. Control **8**, 338–353 (1965)
6. Rutkowski, L.: Methods and Techniques of Artificial Intelligence. PWN, Warszawa (2011). (in Polish)
7. Slowik, A.: Fuzzy control of trade-off between exploration and exploitation properties of evolutionary algorithms. In: Corchado, E., Kurzyński, M., Woźniak, M. (eds.) HAIS 2011, Part I. LNCS, vol. 6678, pp. 59–66. Springer, Heidelberg (2011). doi:10.1007/978-3-642-21219-2_9
8. Li, Z., Chun-Yi, S., Guanglin, L., Su, H.: Fuzzy approximation-based adaptive backstepping control of an exoskeleton for human upper limbs. IEEE Trans. Fuzzy Syst. **23**(3), 555–566 (2015)
9. Dianshuang, W., Zhang, G., Jie, L.: A fuzzy preference tree-based recommender system for personalized business-to-business e-services. IEEE Trans. Fuzzy Syst. **23**(1), 29–43 (2015)
10. Aksac, A., Uzun, E., Ozyer, T.: A real time traffic simulator utilizing an adaptive fuzzy inference mechanism by tunning fuzzy parameters. Appl. Intell. **26**, 698–720 (2011). Springer Science+Business Media, LLC
11. Sumiati, Triono Sigit, H., Kapuji, A.: Mamdani fuzzy inference system application setting for traffic lights. Int. J. Appl. Innovation Eng. Manage. **3**(10), 56–62 (2014)
12. Slowik, A.: Type-2 fuzzy logic control of trade-off between exploration and exploitation properties of genetic algorithms. In: Rutkowski, L., Korytkowski, M., Scherer, R., Tadeusiewicz, R., Zadeh, L.A., Zurada, J.M. (eds.) EC 2012 and SIDE 2012. LNCS, vol. 7269, pp. 368–376. Springer, Heidelberg (2012). doi:10.1007/978-3-642-29353-5_43

Implementation of a Parallel Fuzzy System in the FPGA Circuit

Marek Poplawski[✉]

Department of Electronics and Computer Science,
Koszalin University of Technology, Sniadeckich 2 Street, 75-453 Koszalin, Poland
marpop@ie.tu.koszalin.pl

Abstract. This paper describes an implementation of a fuzzy system. For this purpose, a dedicated architecture of a fuzzy logic controller system was elaborated in a FPGA circuit. This system has 3 independent inputs and 2 outputs and is composed of 4 internal blocks: fuzzification, inference, defuzzification and control. The fuzzy inference processes implemented are the techniques of a calculation of a only activated rules and an application of a parallel processing allows for very quick selection of only active rules from the whole rules base. The distribution and shapes of fuzzy sets allow to activate one or two fuzzy rules for one discrete (sharp) value of the input variable. Input and output linguistic variables and corresponding fuzzy sets were defined.

1 Introduction

An objective of this work is a presentation of practical implementation of a digital fuzzy system [1]. For this purpose, a dedicated architecture of the fuzzy system was elaborated [2,3]. The propossed fuzzy system is based on the classical Mamdani model in which one can distinguish the following blocks: fuzzification, inference and defuzzification. In this paper methods of accelerated calculation in a proposed system were presented. An application of calculate only activated rules and an application of parallel processing was applied [4]. The idea of processing only activated rules was presented in the paper [5,6]. The calculate only active rules in fuzzy system from the knowledge base allow to reduce the time of inference processing, also besides elimination of verifying the activation degree of all fuzzy rules allows to accelerate inference process [7,8]. In a hardware realization of fuzzy systems only 2^n rules from L^n rules existing in the rule base are activated (where L - number of input fuzzy sets, n - number of input linguistic variables) [5,6]. For example for values: $L = 5$, $n = 3$, the whole rule base is described by 125 rules and in this case only 8 rules are activated. The parallel processing of activated rules also allows to reduce the time of inference processing [8,9]. The knowledge, based on which rules are activated in the proposed system and parallel processing of the rules presented in this paper [10–12]. Proposed fuzzy system was described using the language of the equipment description VHDL, simulated and implemented on the FPGA circuit [13,14].

© Springer International Publishing Switzerland 2016
L. Rutkowski et al. (Eds.): ICAISC 2016, Part I, LNAI 9692, pp. 276–283, 2016.
DOI: 10.1007/978-3-319-39378-0_24

2   The Propossed Fuzzy System

The propossed fuzzy system was simulated and realized on the FPGA circuit Xilinx Spartan-6 LX16 FPGA [15,16]. This system has 3 independent inputs and 2 outputs, and is composed of 3 internal blocks: fuzzification (b in), inference (b inf) and defuzzification (b out). The main task of the fuzzy system (Fig. 1) is generation of output signals (y0, y1) based on input signals (x0, x1, x2). The block structure of the proposed fuzzy system described using the language of the equipment description VHDL was presented in Fig. 2.

In the proposed fuzzy system the fuzzification process is performed by reading out the values of a membership function of activated sets as well as codes of these sets from system's memory. This process is very quickly realized in a parallel architecture, because reduces reading pairs of values for each channel. The input linguistic variables (x0, x1, x2) are described by 5 terms which are described by 256 samples, with 8 bit resolution (Fig. 3). The input block (b_in) is divided into three independent fuzzy channels composed of blocks "fuzzy_x" (where x = 0, 1, 2), as shown in Fig. 2. An appearance of the high state on the input "enable" of fuzzy_x blocks begins the fuzzification process. A sharp value of the input signal "input(7:0)" indicates the address of memory, which corresponds to the appropriate discreet sample of the point of the rule activation stored in the memory of the block "fuzzy_x". Each input sharp value is mapped (transformed) into 2 pairs of values. This discreet sample contains two 8-bit values of the points of the rule activation ($\mu0, \mu1$) and two 3-bit codes of fuzzy sets (T0, T1). Each sample contains 2 pairs of fuzzy values, such as (T0, $\mu0$) and (T1, $\mu1$) where T0, T1 - activated sets, $\mu0, \mu1$ - activated fuzzy values. In the memory of the block "fuzzy_x" altogether 256 of such samples describing the input linguistic variables are stored. Reading a 3-byte values of the samples (T0, $\mu0$) and (T1, $\mu1$) from the memory and transferring them to the output mi0, mi1 and t of the block "fuzzy_x" finishes operations of the fuzzyfication. The mapping process is very quickly realized in the proposed parallel architecture, because it reduces reading pairs of values for each channel. Next, that data is transferred to the inference block (b_inf). The end of the fuzzification process, starts the inference process.

A fuzzy rule base was created based on relations between input and output variables, which was saved in the system's memory as a look-up table. A single pair of rules (Ra, Rb) consists of three simple premises connected by conjunction

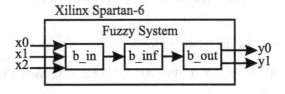

Fig. 1. A general block diagram of a fuzzy system.

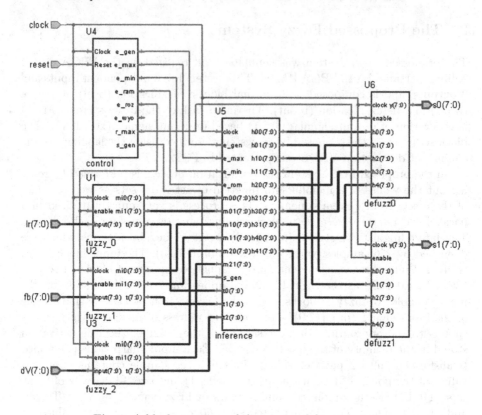

Fig. 2. A block structure of the proposed fuzzy system.

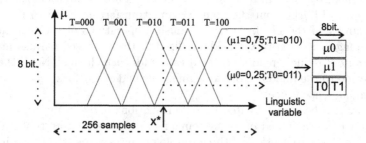

Fig. 3. An example of the input linguistic variable where x* - crisp input value, T - codes sets, T0, T1 - activated sets, $\mu 0, \mu 1$ - activated fuzzy values.

operator AND, and has the following form:

$$Ra := If\ x0 = A0\ AND\ x1 = A1\ AND\ x2 = A2\ then\ Y0 = B0 \qquad (1)$$

$$Rb := If\ x0 = A0\ AND\ x1 = A1\ AND\ x2 = A2\ then\ Y1 = B1 \qquad (2)$$

where: x0, x1, x2 - input linguistic variable, A0, A1, A2 - terms of linguistic variable xi (i = 0, 1, 2), y0, y1 - output linguistic variable, B0, B1 - terms of linguistic variable yi (i = 0, 1).

A possible number of rules describing this system equals to $2 * 5^3 = 250$ rules or 125 pair of rules, but only $2 * 8$ of then are activated for each inference process. In next steps a method of activating fuzzy rules was explained. This method is very important it also explains how an address of activated rule can be calculated. The first step of the fuzzification process, is coding fuzzy input variables into 2 pairs that contain values of the samples $(T0, \mu0)$ and $(T1, \mu1)$ for each input (x2, x1, x0). The second step, started by a high state of the steering line "e_gen" coming from the block "control" begins the inference process.

The inference block shown in Fig. 2 was realized in a parallel inference with a technique of addressing mode. The parallel inference allow to create 8 addresses in memory for each activated rule. The simple example, explain how the address of one rule is generated. A input values (shown in Fig. 4) of block "inference":

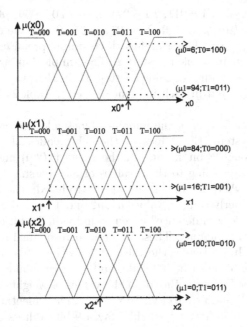

Fig. 4. The examples of the input linguistic variables x0, x1, x2 where x* - crisp input value, T - codes sets, T0, T1 - activated sets, $\mu0, \mu1$ - activated fuzzy values.

Table 1. The example technique of addressing mode for one rule.

Step	Rule 1
1	IF (x0 is 000) AND (x1 is 001) AND (x2 is 010) THEN (y0 is 000)
2	000,001,010
3	000001010

Table 2. The values of state in block the "inference", where example values of input linguistic variable: x0 - $(T0 = 100, \mu0 = 6; T1 = 011, \mu1 = 94)$, x1 - $(T0 = 000, \mu0 = 84; T1 = 001, \mu1 = 16)$, x2 - $(T0 = 010, \mu0 = 100; T1 = 011, \mu1 = 0)$.

Rule	Full rule	Address
1	IF (x0 is 000) AND (x1 is 001) AND (x2 is 010) THEN (y0 is 000)	000001010
2	IF (x0 is 000) AND (x1 is 001) AND (x2 is 001) THEN (y0 is 000)	000001001
3	IF (x0 is 000) AND (x1 is 000) AND (x2 is 010) THEN (y0 is 010)	000000010
4	IF (x0 is 000) AND (x1 is 000) AND (x2 is 001) THEN (y0 is 010)	000000001
5	IF (x0 is 001) AND (x1 is 001) AND (x2 is 010) THEN (y0 is 010)	001001010
6	IF (x0 is 001) AND (x1 is 001) AND (x2 is 001) THEN (y0 is 000)	001001001
7	IF (x0 is 001) AND (x1 is 000) AND (x2 is 010) THEN (y0 is 001)	001000010
8	IF (x0 is 001) AND (x1 is 000) AND (x2 is 001) THEN (y0 is 001)	001000001

x0 - $(T0 = 100, \mu0 = 6; T1 = 011, \mu1 = 94)$, x1 - $(T0 = 000, \mu0 = 84; T1 = 001, \mu1 = 16)$, x2 - $(T0 = 010, \mu0 = 100; T1 = 011, \mu1 = 0)$ and the example rule was shown in Table 1 - step 1. This rule has three simple premises, codes of active fuzzy sets are shown in Table 1 - step 2. The simple linking of these codes, generates the value of address (Table 1 - step 3). In the proposed fuzzy system 8 addresses are generated in each inference process. Table 2 shows 8 activated rules.

The hardware realization of the inference block allow to create 8 addresses. In the proposed system, the values of the 3-bit codes of active fuzzy sets are introduced through 8-bit inputs, in the range tx(2:0) and tx(6:4) (where $x = 0, 1, 2$) and corresponding to them values of membership functions through inputs mix0, mix1 (where $x = 0, 1, 2$) are also introduced. The task of the block "inference" is to properly connect values $\mu1, \mu2$ and T to the outputs of the sub-block "memory" of block "inference" based on individual 3-bit code with weights b2, b1, b0 saved in the memory. These weights corresponded to input linguistic variables x2, x1, x0. In particular the value of the weight '0' corresponds to connection of the value '0' and the T0 code, and '1' corresponds to connection of the value '1' and the T1 code. Based on the values of weights b2, b1, b0 in the range tx(2:0), tx(5:3) and tx(8:6) (where $x = 0, 1, 2$) a sequential linking of codes of active fuzzy sets is performed; in this way a 9-bit address of the conclusion is created. Table 3 shows the values of calculated address and the values of MIN operation.

Each generated address shows rule conclusion. A creation of the 8 address of the conclusion is initiated by the steering signal coming from the block "control" (Fig. 2). The "inference" block contains the conclusion codes of fuzzy rules stored at precisely determined addresses, which values correspond to premises of activated rules. During the reading of indicated codes of rule conclusions, the block "control" initiates an operation "MIN"; which gives as the result the lowest value of the membership function. For example, in Table 3 - rule 1 shows

Table 3. The values of state in the block "inference", where: R - rule number, b2, b1, b0 - state of counter, x2, x1, x0 - inputs values, address - values of calculated address, M - value of MIN operation.

R	b2	b1	b0	x0	x1	x2	address	M
1	0	0	0	$(t0=000; \mu0=0.7)$	$(t0=001; \mu1=0.8)$	$(t0=010; \mu0=0.6)$	000001010	0.6
				$(t1=001; \mu0=0.3)$	$(t1=000; \mu0=0.2)$	$(t1=001; \mu2=0.4)$		
2	0	0	1	$(t0=000; \mu0=0.7)$	$(t0=001; \mu1=0.8)$	$(t0=010; \mu0=0,6)$	000001001	0.4
				$(t1=001; \mu0=0.3)$	$(t1=000; \mu0=0,2)$	$(t1=001; \mu2=0.4)$		
3	0	1	0	$(t0=000; \mu0=0.7)$	$(t0=001; \mu1=0.8)$	$(t0=010; \mu0=0.6)$	000000010	0.2
				$(t1=001; \mu0=0.3)$	$(t1=000; \mu0=0.2)$	$(t1=001; \mu2=0.4)$		
4	0	1	1	$(t0=000; \mu0=0.7)$	$(t0=001; \mu1=0.8)$	$(t0=010; \mu0=0.6)$	000000001	0.2
				$(t1=001; \mu0=0.3)$	$(t1=000; \mu0=0.2)$	$(t1=01; \mu2=0.4)$		
5	1	0	0	$(t0=000; \mu0=0.7)$	$(t0=001; \mu1=0.8)$	$(t0=010; \mu0=0.6)$	001001010	0.3
				$(t1=001; \mu0=0.3)$	$(t1=000; \mu0=0.2)$	$(t1=01; \mu2=0.4)$		
6	1	0	1	$(t0=000; \mu0=0.7)$	$(t0=001; \mu1=0.8)$	$(t0=010; \mu0=0.6)$	001010001	0.3
				$(t1=001; \mu0=0.3)$	$(t1=000; \mu0=0.2)$	$(t1=001; \mu2=0.4)$		
7	1	1	0	$(t0=000; \mu0=0.7)$	$(t0=001; \mu1=0.8)$	$(t0=010; \mu0=0.6)$	001000010	0.2
				$(t1=001; \mu0=0.3)$	$(t1=000; \mu0=0.2)$	$(t1=001; \mu2=0.4)$		
8	1	1	1	$(t0=000; \mu0=0.7)$	$(t0=001; \mu1=0.8)$	$(t0=010; \mu0=0.6)$	001000001	0.2
				$(t1=001; \mu0=0.3)$	$(t1=000; \mu0=0.2)$	$(t1=001; \mu2=0.4)$		

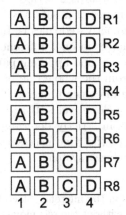

Fig. 5. A collection of state in the propossed parallel inference architecture (an example for system with 2^n inputs, where n = 3) A - generation of address, B - reading fuzzy rule from memory, C- MIN operation, D - MAX operation.

address value (000001010) and "MIN" value (0, 6). In the proposed fuzzy system for each of initial output fuzzy set, the block MAX is assigned. The task of this block is to choose the highest value of the activated output fuzzy set. Figure 5 shows a collection of state in the inference block. That architecture requires to use 8 channels.

In the proposed realization was used as a defuzzification process the CoGS (Center of Gravity for Singletons) This operation is performed parallelly for two output channels in "defuzzx" (where $x = 0, 1$) blocks giving the values of y0 and y1.

3   Simulations and Testing

The proposed digital parallel fuzzy system was described using the language of the equipment description VHDL, and was simulated in the ISE WebPACK environment of the Xilinx company. For this purpose in the first step of testing the values of the input and output membership functions of the fuzzy sets as well as the table of rules were saved in the memory of the system. The input membership functions requires 768 bytes of memory for each channel (x2, x1, x0).

The output membership functions require only 5 bytes of memory for each channel (y1, y0). All rules require to prepare a location in the memory. Next, the test values of input linguistic variables x0, x1, x2 were introduced. In the second step of testing, the proposed fuzzy system was programed in the FPGA circuit Spartan 6. Results of measurements confirmed correct operation of the system.

A collection of number of clock cycles in the inference block is shown in Table 4. The propossed fuzzy system is described by the following parameters: number of fuzzy sets $L = 5$, number of inputs $n = 3$. This table also shows how important the elimination of no activated rules is. In this case for whole number of 125 rules only 8 rules are active in one "inference". Using the techniques of addressing in the inference process and applying parallel processing, very quick selection of only active rules from the whole rule base is possible.

The parallel method of the inference process, allows to calculate the degree of rule activations during only 4 clock cycles. Usage of the addressing techniques requires saved rule conclusions in strictly determined addresses in the system memory. This demand increases the time necessary to create the rule base at the time of constructing of the fuzzy system.

Table 4. Number of clock cycles in the inference block for different types of architectures "serial a" - serial inference without the technique of addressing mode, "serial b" - serial inference with the technique of addressing mode, "parallel" - parallel method of the inference process of fuzzy system, where: n - number of inputs, A - number of fuzzy rules, B - activated rules in the inference process, L - number of fuzzy sets.

$L = 5$	$n = 2$	$n = 3$	$n = 4$	$n = 5$	$n = 6$	$n = 7$
A	25	125	625	3125	15625	78125
B	4	8	16	32	64	128
serial a	100	500	2500	12500	62500	78125
serial b	16	32	64	128	256	512
parallel	4	4	4	4	4	4

References

1. Bosque, G., del Campo, I., Echanobe, J.: Fuzzy systems, neural networks and neuro-fuzzy systems: a vision on their hardware implementation and platforms over two decades. Eng. Appl. Artif. Intell. **32**, 283–331 (2014)
2. Hung, D.: Using FPGA Technique for Design and Implementation of a fuzzy Inference System. In: Fuzzy Logic and Intelligent Systems, pp. 271–288. Kluwer Academic Publishers (1995)
3. Deliparaschos, K.M., Nenedakis, F.I., Tzafestas, S.G.: Design and implementation of a fast digital fuzzy logic controller using FPGA technology. J. Intell. Rob. Syst. **45**(1), 77–96 (2006). Springer, Netherlands
4. Poplawski, M., Bialko, M.: Implementation of parallel fuzzy logic controller in FPGA circuit for guiding electric wheelchair. In: Conference on Human System Interactions - IEEE Xplore, Krakow (2008)
5. Ikeda, H., Kisu, N., Hiramoto, Y., Nakamura, S.: A fuzzy inference coprocessor using a flexible active-rule-driven architecture. In: IEEE International Conference on Fuzzy Systems 1992, vol. 34, pp. 537–544. IEEE (1992)
6. Giuseppe, A., Vincenzo, C., Marco, R., Lorenzo, V.: Rule-driven VLSI fuzzy processor. IEEE Micro **16**(3), 62–74 (1996). IEEE Micro 1996
7. Frías-Martínez, E.: Design of a Lukasiewicz rule-driven fuzzy processor. Soft Comput. **7**(1), 65–71 (2002). Springer
8. Gabrielli, A., Gandolfi, E., Falchieri, D.: Very fast rate 2 input fuzzy processor for high energy physics. Fuzzy Sets Syst. **132**, 261–272 (2002)
9. Watanabe, H., Dettloff, W.D., Yount, K.E.: A VLSI fuzzy logic controller with reconfigurable, cascadable architecture. IEEE J. Solid-State Circuits **25**(2), 376–382 (1990). IEEE
10. Poplawski, M., Bialko, M.: Implementation of fuzzy logic controller in FPGA circuit for guiding electric wheelchair. In: Rutkowski, L., Korytkowski, M., Scherer, R., Tadeusiewicz, R., Zadeh, L.A., Zurada, J.M. (eds.) ICAISC 2012, Part II. LNCS, vol. 7268, pp. 216–222. Springer, Heidelberg (2012)
11. Yager, R.R., Filev, D.P.: Essentials of Fuzzy Modeling and Control. John Wiley and Sons, New York (1994)
12. Patyra, M.J., Grantner, J.L.: Hardware implementaions of digital fuzzy logic controller. Elesiver Inf. Sci. **113**, 19–54 (1999)
13. Patyra, M.J., Grantner, J.L.: Digital fuzzy logic controller: design and implementaions. IEEE Trans. Fuzzy Syst. **4**, 439–459 (1996)
14. Guo, S., Peters, L.: A high-speed fuzzy co-processor implemented in analogue digital technique. Comput. Electr. Eng. **24**, 89–98 (1998)
15. Barriga, A., Sanchez-Solano, S., Brox, P., Cabrera, A., Baturone, I.: Modelling and implementation of fuzzy systems based on VHDL. Int. J. Approximate Reasoning **41**, 164–178 (2006)
16. Spartan-6 design platform board, Complete data sheet

The Method of Hardware Implementation of Fuzzy Systems on FPGA

Andrzej Przybył[1(✉)] and Meng Joo Er[2]

[1] Institute of Computational Intelligence,
Częstochowa University of Technology, Częstochowa, Poland
andrzej.przybyl@iisi.pcz.pl
[2] School of Electrical and Electronic Engineering,
Nanyang Technological University, Singapore, Singapore
emjer@ntu.edu.sg

Abstract. In this paper a method of implementation of fuzzy system on FPGA devices is presented. The method applies to a class of fuzzy systems which are functionally equivalent to a radial basis function networks. In the paper the example fuzzy system was implemented on the FPGA device with the use of the proposed method. The results confirm a high performance of the obtained fuzzy system. This was achieved at a reasonable consumption of the hardware resources of the FPGA.

Keywords: Hardware implementation of fuzzy systems · FPGA · Radial basis function

1 Introduction

Computational intelligence methods (see e.g. [2–4,6–10,13–15,17,29–32,34,38–40,42,48–54,60–64]) offer suitable properties for modeling the nonlinear dynamics of various types of real objects. A different types of neural networks (see e.g. [16,55]) or fuzzy systems (see e.g. [18–27,41,43,56–59,68–74]) have a number of useful features such as the ability to approximate any continuous non-linearity or the ability to interpret the accumulated knowledge. However, from a practical point of view, the other features are also important. For example, the ability to implement in a hardware (e.g. FPGA) to obtain the operation model working in a real time. Moreover, the implementation should be relatively simple and economically justified.

In recent years, a large number of projects have used FPGAs to perform the control and modeling of dynamical systems. In many cases, these projects utilize neural networks [5], fuzzy systems or neuro-fuzzy systems [11,33]. However, in some cases, the degree of complexity of used algorithms is very high and the economy of this solution is questionable.

This is due to the fact that these algorithms are mainly based on arithmetic operations for floating point numbers. In particular floating-point operations such as divide numbers [37], exponential and trigonometric functions are characterized as they have the high complexity and low performance when they are

© Springer International Publishing Switzerland 2016
L. Rutkowski et al. (Eds.): ICAISC 2016, Part I, LNAI 9692, pp. 284–298, 2016.
DOI: 10.1007/978-3-319-39378-0_25

implemented on FPGA devices. FPGA hardware resources are not adapted to the efficient implementation of this type of calculations. FPGAs are well suited for the implementation of fixed-point calculations, such as addition, subtraction and multiplication. Implementation of complex arithmetic operations based on the floating-point numbers consumes a lot of resources of the FPGA hardware. For this reason, in most cases fully parallel implementation of floating-point calculations becomes economically unjustified.

In order to reduce the high consumption of resources a serial or semi-parallel data processing algorithms are used, including the recursive implementations [37]. In this case, the demand for hardware resources significantly decreases. However, computing efficiency drops significantly - which is an obvious drawback of such a solution. It should be noted that in some cases this approach is highly justified. For example, consider the control system whose duty cycle is limited by the limit frequency of operation of actuator, for example about 20 kHz. In this case, the hardware implementation of the complete control algorithm working with the cycle less than 50 µs is pointless, because the generated data are not used earlier than the mentioned time 50 µs elapses. It should be noted that there are a number of applications which drew significant benefits if the processing time is as short as possible. Examples are hardware emulators of various types of real objects used for hardware-in-the-loop (HIL) systems.

As noted in the work [46] there are existing commercial digital real-time HIL simulators that are characterized by 50 µs to 100 µs time steps and computational latency, and therefore they are not able to simulate accurately the very fast dynamics of power electronics systems. The authors suggest that simulation with a time step with value of 1 µ or less is much more appropriate solution. In order to obtain high processing speeds various techniques are used. They cover both the structure of the implemented algorithm and methods of their implementation.

The vast majority of practical implementation on FPGA widely use triangular or trapezoidal fuzzy sets. Such sets are easier to be realized in FPGA than the ones based on a Gaussian functions [1,47]. While many theoretically developed algorithms are based on Gaussian fuzzy sets, which sometimes are considered to be more appropriate to represent fuzzy knowledge. Moreover, if the input variables are represented by complementary membership functions of the fuzzy sets it follows another benefit, namely processing technique is applied only for activated rules. How was indicated in the paper [47], elimination of verification of the activation degree of all fuzzy rules allows to accelerate inference process. One of the possible techniques used in this field is the odd-even method [28].

The results presented in various papers show that in many cases relatively high processing speed is achieved, however, at the expense of low resolution of processed signals. This is due to the applied binary encoding using an average of 6 to 8 bits. Unfortunately, the specificity of many proposed solutions is that increasing resolution of processed words, eg. to 12-bits, causes a significant increase in the consumption of hardware resources.

In this paper we propose a new method for the implementation of fuzzy system on FPGA. This method offers good performance and accuracy with relatively low consumption of hardware resources.

This paper is organized into 4 sections. Section 2 contains an idea of designing the neuro-fuzzy structure to the limitations arising from the implementation in hardware in FPGA devices. Implementation results are presented in Sect. 3. Conclusions are drawn in Sect. 4.

2   The Method of Designing the Fuzzy Structure to the Limitations Arising from the Hardware Implementation

In this work will be considered systems using fuzzy rules of the following form

$$\textbf{IF } (x_1 \textit{ is } \overline{x_1^j}) \textbf{ AND } ... \textbf{ AND } (x_N \textit{ is } \overline{x_N}) \textbf{ THEN}(y \textit{ is } \overline{y}),$$

where x_i indicates the input to the system ($i = 1..N$), y is the output, $\overline{x}_i^j$ are input fuzzy sets for the j-th fuzzy rule ($j = 1..M$) and $\overline{y}^j$ are output fuzzy sets. In the considered systems Gaussian input fuzzy sets are used. The algebraic product is used as a T-norm operator. Rules consequents are a singleton type and the method of centre of gravity for singletons (COGS) is used for defuzzification. For the sake of clarity of description we will present a system with one output. It should be noted that such simplification does not constitute the loss of generality for the general idea presented in this paper.

According to the theory of fuzzy logic and common practice the implementation of fuzzy system is followed in three stages: 1. fuzzification, 2. inference, 3. defuzzification. However, because of the investigated class of fuzzy systems are functionally equivalent to a radial basis function networks [36] (it will be explained in detail in the later in the paper), in the current paper it is proposed a more appropriate method of hardware implementation.

The main features of the proposed method are: 1. operations are implemented in hardware based on fixed-point and simplified floating-point arithmetic, 2. fuzzification and inference is carried out together on the basis of functional similarity to radial basis function networks.

The proposed method is scalable and allows adjustment of the obtained processing speed and the use of hardware resources for a specific application. The next part of the work will present a detailed description of the proposed method of hardware implementation for the considered class of fuzzy structures.

2.1   The Method of Hardware Implementation of the Fuzzification and the Inference Processes

As pointed out in [66] and cited for this statement [35] the most important advantage of using fuzzy basis functions, rather than polynomials or radial basis functions, etc., is that a linguistic fuzzy IF-THEN rule is naturally related to a fuzzy basis function. It should be noted that the way of the design of the system and its implementation not necessarily have to be identical. The design method should be intuitive to the man, while the implementation should be characterized by high efficiency and low cost. Therefore, let's look closer at the class of fuzzy systems presented in the previous section which are functionally equivalent to a radial basis function networks.

In the considered group of systems we assume that we are dealing with a Gaussian input fuzzy sets and every j-th rule uses of separate input fuzzy sets that are unshared with other rules. For each i-th input it exist a degree of membership to the i-th input fuzzy set of j-th fuzzy rule as follows:

$$\mu_i^j = \exp\left(-\left(\frac{x_i - \overline{x}_i^j}{\sigma_i^j}\right)^2\right),\qquad(1)$$

where $\overline{x}_i^j$ and σ_i^j are center and width of input fuzzy set. If we use the product as the T-norm, then the degree of activity of the j-th rule is

$$\mu^j = \mu_1^j \cdot \mu_2^j \cdot \ldots \cdot \mu_N^j = \exp\left(-\left(\frac{x_1 - \overline{x}_1^j}{\sigma_1^j}\right)^2 - \ldots - \left(\frac{x_n - \overline{x}_n^j}{\sigma_N^j}\right)^2\right).\qquad(2)$$

Note that the action outlined above is similar to the way of calculating the values of the radial basis function of the following form

$$\mu^j = \exp\left(-\|\mathbf{x} - \overline{\mathbf{x}}^j\|^2\right),\qquad(3)$$

in which the distance of the input $\mathbf{x}$ from the center of the radial fuzzy set $\overline{\mathbf{x}}^j$ for j-th rule is defined as follows

$$\|\mathbf{x} - \overline{\mathbf{x}}^j\| = \sqrt{\left(\frac{x_1 - \overline{x}_1}{\sigma_1^j}\right)^2 + \ldots + \left(\frac{x_N - \overline{x}_N^j}{\sigma_N^j}\right)^2}.\qquad(4)$$

This phenomenon has been observed and described in the work [36] as a functional equivalence between radial basis function networks and fuzzy inference systems. The specific form, for which each of the inputs has individually defined width σ_i^j of the set is called Hyper Radial Basis Function (HRBF) [45]. In the later part of this work the term fuzzy system (FS) refers to the category of systems that are functionally equivalent to a radial basis function networks.

The Eq. (4) can be rewritten as

$$\|\mathbf{x} - \overline{\mathbf{x}}^j\|^2 = w_0^j + w_{1,1}^j x_1 + w_{1,2}^j (x_1)^2 + \ldots + w_{N,1}^j x_N + w_{N,2}^j (x_N)^2,\qquad(5)$$

where

$$w_0^j = \left(\frac{\overline{x}_1^j}{\sigma_1^j}\right)^2 + \ldots + \left(\frac{\overline{x}_N^j}{\sigma_N^j}\right)^2 ; w_{i,1}^j = -\frac{2\overline{x}_i^j}{\sigma_i^j}; w_{i,2}^j = \left(\frac{1}{\sigma_i^j}\right)^2.\qquad(6)$$

The approach represented by formulas (3) and (5) offers noticeable benefits for the implementation, namely:

1. The Gaussian function is determined only once, in contrast to the classical approach, demanding the use of this function to determine the degree of membership of each input separately (1). The proposed solution is therefore beneficial because the Gaussian function is a troublesome operation in the implementation on FPGA.
2. All other actions necessary to determine the degree of activity of fuzzy rule are based on repetitive and simple activities such as multiplication and addition. These actions are easy to implement on FPGA, they are carried at high speed and consume relatively small hardware resources.

2.2   The Method of Implementation of Defuzzification Process

As it was mentioned earlier in the paper, the singleton membership functions with centers of $\overline{y}^j$ are used on the outputs of the rules. In the defuzzification stage the centre of gravity for singletons (7) is used because of the following features of the method: defuzzified values tend to move smoothly, have good sensitivity to change on inputs and are easy to calculate. According to the paper [12] the centre of gravity for singletons (COGSs) is the most realistic and widely used method of defuzzification in many applications.

$$
y = \frac{\sum_{j=1}^{M} \mu^j \cdot \overline{y}^j}{\sum_{j=1}^{M} \mu^j} = \frac{n}{d} \tag{7}
$$

However, from a practical point of view, it should be noted that this method is difficult to implement, because of used arithmetic division of real numbers. This operation can be avoided if fuzzy system is designed in such a way that the denominator in the formula (7) is equal to one, i.e. $d = 1$. This approach is very comfortable and quite often used in practice. However, in some situations it may be regarded as too restrictive limitation. In the general case (eg. when using Gaussian input fuzzy sets) such a requirement is not met and the operation of real numbers division at the output is required, as shown in Eq. (7).

In many publications this issue was analyzed and various solutions have been proposed. For example, the paper [28] proposes the implementation of a division operation based on method of look-up-table (LUT) and addressing with the 6-bit word. Similarly, in the work [44] it was proposed division in which the divisor was rounded to the 8-bit number. As you can easily guess in both cases this resulted in a very low accuracy of the result.

In another work [37] the implementation of this operation on the basis of single precision floating point arithmetic was used. The result is a high accuracy but achieved at the expense of rather low performance. How it was indicated in the cited reference the obtained floating-point divider needs 26 clock cycles to establish division result. Others floating-point operations like multiplication, addition and subtraction take 5 clock cycles, while similar fixed-point operations takes only one cycle in a typical case. This indicates that the floating-point operations are much less efficient than a fixed-point ones in general. It is also important to note that the floating-point operations consume a lot of hardware resources.

In this paper it is proposed that the division operation required in (7) is performed as in some other works which uses fixed-point arithmetic. In such a case a multiplication by the inverse of the denominator is used instead of the division of two numbers. Determination of the inverse of the denominator is made on the basis of the method of look-up table (LUT). The disadvantage of such a method is that it is necessary to use a large amount of memory to store data in the table with an acceptable accuracy.

In this paper it is proposed to use the simplified 18-bit floating-point numbers to store data in the table. This approach reduces the memory consumption. FPGAs usually have a dedicated Block RAM memory, which are organized as 512 locations of 18-bits words [67]. The proposed simplified floating-point arithmetic is therefore well suited to the optimum utilization of hardware resources.

3   Implementation Results

In our investigation it was considered a problem of hardware implementation of particular parts of a fuzzy structure (FS). Considered structure has four inputs, eight rules and one output. The FS was implemented in the Spartan XC6SLX45-3C FPGA from Xilinx by means of Altium Designer and Xilinx ISE software. To encode the values of the real numbers a 32-bit fixed-point arithmetic were used. Widely known and biggest drawback of fixed-point arithmetic is the limited range and the need for continuous scaling of processed numbers. However, the use of 32-bits width words made it possible to obtain a relatively wide range at the same time fairly good accuracy. Thus, in this case this defect was somewhat minimized. Because of the necessary scaling is closely related to a specific application, this issue will be omitted for the sake of readability of the presentation. It will be presented in detail only in places that are important from the point of view of the presented algorithm.

3.1   Fuzyfication and Inference

According to the method proposed in the previous section operations of fuzzification and inference were carried out in the overall processing of input data. As a result, determination of the output value of the formula (5) requires a series of operations such as multiplication and addition. It is possible to perform these actions both in parallel, series and the in series-parallel mode. Fully parallel implementation of calculations allows us to achieve high performance at the expense of high demand on hardware resources. Serial implementation allows us to reduce the use of hardware resources, but with a significant loss of obtained processing efficiency. While a semi-serial or a semi-parallel implementation allows for compromise.

In the presented example the semi-serial implementation was used. However, the use of high-performance fixed-point calculations made it possible to achieve high-speed processing.

Elementary operations for the input of the rule (5) are executed in parallel as shown in Fig. 1. The elementary function has three 32-bits width inputs. First two inputs (W1 and W2) are the weights coefficients $w^j_{i,1}$ and $w^j_{i,2}$ respectively, the third input (X) is the input to the FS, i.e. x_i as defined in (5). As a result this function performs several operations in one cycle. The register shown in Fig. 1 acts as a component partial sum according to the formula (5). Initial value of the register is equal to weight w^j_0 and it is set in the first clock cycle. Three 32-bit fixed point multipliers (FP_MULTIPLIER_1, 2 and 3) and one 32-bit adder (ADDER_1) generates the output within the second cycle. Using the second 32-bit adder (ADDER_2) and one register the whole squared weighted sum (5) for one rule with four inputs is obtained in the fifth cycle. In the sixth cycle the LUT block indicated as EXP_FUNCTION is used to determine the output value of the nonlinear exponential function. The LUT consists of 1024 words each 12-bits width to store the shape of gausoid function with a reasonable accuracy. Summing up, in the general case the whole process of calculation of rule activation degree requires the following number of clock cycles

$$c_r = 2 + N \tag{8}$$

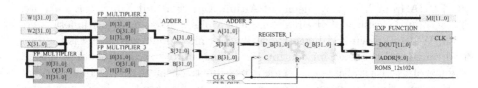

Fig. 1. The hardware implementation of the elementary function.

To calculate the output value y of the FS we need to perform the above described processing for all M rules. This can be done in sequence (serial method) or in parallel (for example with the use of pipelining) to obtain a different speed processing of the implemented system. As mentioned earlier in this paper was carried out the semi-serial implementation method.

3.2   The Defuzification Proces

In the proposed method Fig. 2 shows how all the rules are indicated in order to determine their activation degree μ^j and their consequent $\mu^j \cdot \overline{y}^j$. While, Fig. 3 shows the module used for sequentially processing all rules. Two adders and two registers are used to accumulate values of activation degrees and consequents of

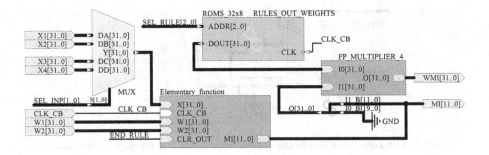

Fig. 2. The hardware implementation of the algorithm used to determine the consequents of fuzzy rules.

all rules. The results, i.e. the nominator and the denominator of the Eq. (7) are obtained within the following number of clock cycles

$$c_{rms} = M \cdot c_r. \tag{9}$$

After the nominator n and denominator d are determined the one extra clock cycle is necessary to calculate the current output value of the FS according to used method of defuzzification (7). First of these two values is multiplied by the reciprocal of the other (Fig. 3) in order to obtain the value of y according to the following formula $y = n \cdot RECIPROCAL\,(d)$.

The RECIPROCAL module used for this purpose has one input and one output which are 12-bits and 27-bits width unsigned words respectively. The input has a fixed point 3.9 bit representation, i.e. three bits for the integer value and nine bits for fraction. This gives the useful range of $d \in (0; 8)$. Since every single rule has the activation degree with a range of $\mu^j \in \langle 0; 1 \rangle$ this allows to store the information about the sum of activation degree values for many rules. The upper limit for the used fixed point representation for the reciprocal input is, for example, when eight rules have activation coefficient close to unity which is rather unrealistic in properly designed system.

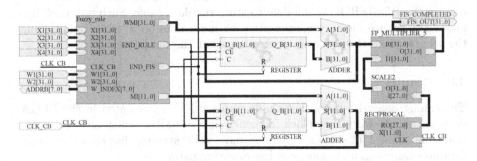

Fig. 3. The block diagram of the implemented fuzzy system with one output.

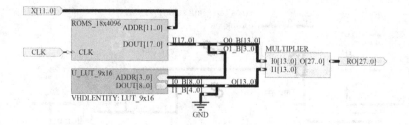

Fig. 4. The method of hardware implementation of the reciprocal function.

The RECIPROCAL module is implemented as an look-up table (LUT) located in a read-only memory and it stories 4096 words (Fig. 4). Value of the input of the module is treated as a 12-bit address, which indexes the table. Each indexed word location stores the result of operation RO = 1/X in a 18-bit simplified floating-point (SFP) format.

The SFP is proposed in this paper a nonstandard format of encoding floating-point numbers. The SFP is an encoding format tailored to a specific application. It allows to reduce the number of bits of a binary word and to simplify their processing. The general idea is derived from the standard IEEE754 but limited to the processing of positive numbers and with a limited range. In the SFP format the 18-bit word is divided into two bitfields: 4-bits for exponent and 14-bits for mantissa. The exponent is a positive number with range of $(0; 15)$. It gives the useful range for floating-point values of $\langle 0; 32768)$ with an acceptable accuracy. For example, the accuracy is about 0.01% for numbers with a value close to unity or larger. In the paper the exponent is limited to the range of $\langle 0; 8)$ for practical reasons.

The detailed method of processing the SFP numbers is shown in Fig. 4. Two LUTs are used. First (ROMS_18x4096) stores the 18-bit words in SFP format. The second one (U_LUT_9x16) together with the fixed-point multiplier is used to change the SFP format to the fixed-point one. The U_LUT_9x16 is a binary decoder which converts the 4-bits binary number (input) to the 1-of-9 output bits. The fixed-point format which is used on the output of the RECIPROCAL module is compatible with the rest of the system. While the SFP format is used only in the RECIPROCAL module to store the data table. Such approach has allowed to reduce memory consumption by more than 50%, while maintaining the accuracy and the processing performance at the same level.

3.3   Results

The timing analysis shows that the exemplary FS implemented in the FPGA device is able to work with clock frequency above 50MHz, which gives the reaction time below $1\,\mu s$. This allows us to build a FS system, that could be useful for some kind of applications, e.g. hardware emulators.

The implementation results presented in the Table 1 are valid for a system with one output. However, for a system with multiple outputs the resource con-

Table 1. Performance and the FPGA resource usage of the exemplary fuzzy system implemented with the use of the proposed method.

Response time	DSP48A1	Registers	Block RAM	LUTs
49 cycles	21	35	10	627
0.98 μs	(36 %)	(0.1 %)	(9 %)	(2 %)

sumption will be almost the same when the serial implementation is used. Obviously, the response time will be many times larger (proportional to the number of outputs) compared to the system with one output.

4   Summary

In this paper a method of implementation of fuzzy system on FPGA devices was presented. The method applies to a class of fuzzy systems which are functionally equivalent to the radial basis function networks. Thanks to this similarity it was possible to propose the effective methods of such fuzzy systems implementation in FPGA-type programmable systems. For a demonstration of the method the results of the implementation of an exemplary fuzzy system in the FPGA was presented. The results show that the FS system with four inputs, eight rules and one output can work with the processing cycle of less than one microsecond. It makes the proposed solution useful in practice.

Presented solution is highly scalable, because depending on the requirements it is possible to shortening response time at the expense of increase the hardware resources. Similarly, it is possible to increase the number of inputs and outputs and the number of rules of the system.

Acknowledgment. The project was financed by the National Science Centre (Poland) on the basis of the decision number DEC-2012/05/B/ST7/02138.

References

1. Antonio-Mendez, R., de la Cruz-Alejo, J., Peñaloza-Mejia, O.: Fuzzy logic control on FPGA for solar tracking system. In: Ceccarelli, M., Ceccarelli, E.E.H. (eds.) Multibody Mechatronic Systems. Mechanisms and Machine Science, vol. 25, pp. 11–21. Springer, Switzerland (2015)
2. Aghdam, M.H., Heidari, S.: Feature selection using particle swarm optimization in text categorization. J. Artif. Intell. Soft Comput. Res. **5**(4), 231–238 (2015)
3. Aissat, K., Oulamara, A.: A priori approach of real-time ridesharing problem with intermediate meeting locations. J. Artif. Intell. Soft Comput. Res. **4**(4), 287–299 (2014)
4. Akhtar, Z., Rattani, A., Foresti, G.L.: Temporal analysis of adaptive face recognition. J. Artif. Intell. Soft Comput. Res. **4**(4), 243–255 (2014)

5. Bahoura, M., Park, C.-W.: FPGA-implementation of dynamic time delay neural network for power amplifier behavioral modeling. Analog Integr. Circuits Signal Process. **73**, 819–828 (2012)
6. Bartczuk, Ł.: Gene expression programming in correction modelling of nonlinear dynamic objects. ISAT 2015 – Part I. AISC, vol. 429, pp. 125–134. Springer, Switzerland (2016)
7. Bartczuk, Ł., Przybył, A., Koprinkova-Hristova, P.: New method for nonlinear fuzzy correction modelling of dynamic objects. In: Rutkowski, L., Korytkowski, M., Scherer, R., Tadeusiewicz, R., Zadeh, L.A., Zurada, J.M. (eds.) ICAISC 2014, Part I. LNCS, vol. 8467, pp. 169–180. Springer, Heidelberg (2014)
8. Bartczuk, Ł., Rutkowska, D.: Medical diagnosis with type-2 fuzzy decision trees. In: Kącki, E., Rudnicki, M., Stempczyńska, J. (eds.) Computers in Medical Activity. AISC, vol. 65, pp. 11–21. Springer, Heidelberg (2009)
9. Bartczuk, Ł., Rutkowska, D.: Type-2 fuzzy decision trees. In: Rutkowski, L., Tadeusiewicz, R., Zadeh, L.A., Zurada, J.M. (eds.) ICAISC 2008. LNCS (LNAI), vol. 5097, pp. 197–206. Springer, Heidelberg (2008)
10. Bas, E.: The training of multiplicative neuron model based artificial neural networks with differential evolution algorithm for forecasting. J. Artif. Intell. Soft Comput. Res. **6**(1), 5–11 (2016)
11. Bosque, G., del Campo, I., Echanobe, J.: Fuzzy systems, neural networks and neuro-fuzzy systems: a vision on their hardware implementation and platforms over two decades. Eng. Appl. Artif. Intell. **32**, 283–331 (2014)
12. Benzekri, A., Azrar, A.: FPGA-based design process of a fuzzy logic controller for a dual-axis sun tracking system. Arab. J. Sci. Eng. **39**, 6109–6123 (2014)
13. Camargo, E., Aguilar, J.: Advanced supervision of oil wells based on soft computing techniques. J. Artif. Intell. Soft Comput. Res. **4**(3), 215–225 (2014)
14. Chen, M., Ludwig, S.A.: Particle swarm optimization based fuzzy clustering approach to identify optimal number of clusters. J. Artif. Intell. Soft Comput. Res. **4**(1), 43–56 (2014)
15. Cheng, S., Shi, Y., Qin, Q., Zhang, Q., Bai, R.: Population diversity maintenance in brain storm optimization algorithm. J. Artif. Intell. Soft Comput. Res. **4**(2), 83–97 (2014)
16. Cierniak, R., Rutkowski, L.: On image compression by competitive neural networks and optimal linear predictors. Signal Process. Image Commun. **156**, 559–565 (2000)
17. Cpałka, K., Łapa, K., Przybył, A.: A new approach to design of control systems using genetic programming. Inf. Technol. Control **44**(4), 433–442 (2015)
18. Cpałka, K., Rutkowski, L.: Flexible Takagi-Sugeno fuzzy systems. In: Proceedings of the International Joint Conference on Neural Networks 2005, Montreal, pp. 1764–1769 (2005)
19. Cpałka, K., Rutkowski, L.: Flexible Takagi-Sugeno neuro-fuzzy structures for nonlinear approximation. WSEAS Trans. Syst. **4**(9), 1450–1458 (2005)
20. Cpałka, K., Rutkowski, L.: A new method for designing and reduction of neuro-fuzzy systems. In: Proceedings of the 2006 IEEE International Conference on Fuzzy Systems (IEEE World Congress on Computational Intelligence, WCCI 2006), Vancouver, pp. 8510–8516 (2006)
21. Cpalka, K.: A method for designing flexible neuro-fuzzy systems. In: Rutkowski, L., Tadeusiewicz, R., Zadeh, L.A., Żurada, J.M. (eds.) ICAISC 2006. LNCS (LNAI), vol. 4029, pp. 212–219. Springer, Heidelberg (2006)
22. Cpałka, K.: On evolutionary designing and learning of flexible neuro-fuzzy structures for nonlinear classification. Nonlinear Anal. Series A Theory Methods Appl. **71**, 1659–1672 (2009). Elsevier

23. Cpałka, K., Rebrova, O., Nowicki, R., Rutkowski, L.: On design of flexible neuro-fuzzy systems for nonlinear modelling. Int. J. Gen. Syst. **42**(6), 706–720 (2013)
24. Cpałka, K., Zalasiński, M.: On-line signature verification using vertical signature partitioning. Expert Syst. Appl. **41**(9), 4170–4180 (2014)
25. Cpałka, K., Zalasiński, M., Rutkowski, L.: New method for the on-line signature verification based on horizontal partitioning. Pattern Recognit. **47**, 2652–2661 (2014)
26. Cpałka, K., Łapa, K., Przybył, A., Zalasiń ski, M.: A new method for designing neuro-fuzzy systems for nonlinear modelling with interpretability aspects. Neurocomputing **135**, 203–217 (2014)
27. Cpałka, K., Zalasiński, M., Rutkowski, L.: A new algorithm for identity verification based on the analysis of a handwritten dynamic signature. Appl. Soft Comput. **43**, 47–56 (2016). http://dx.doi.org/10.1016/j.asoc.2016.02.017
28. Deliparaschos, K.M., Nenedakis, F.I., Tzafestas, S.G.: Design and implementation of a fast digital fuzzy logic controller using FPGA technology. J. Intell. Robot. Syst. **45**, 77–96 (2006)
29. Dziwiński, P., Bartczuk, Ł., Przybył, A., Avedyan, E.D.: A new algorithm for identification of significant operating points using swarm intelligence. In: Rutkowski, L., Korytkowski, M., Scherer, R., Tadeusiewicz, R., Zadeh, L.A., Zurada, J.M. (eds.) ICAISC 2014, Part II. LNCS, vol. 8468, pp. 349–362. Springer, Heidelberg (2014)
30. Dziwiński, P., Avedyan, E.D.: A new approach to nonlinear modeling based on significant operating points detection. In: Rutkowski, L., Korytkowski, M., Scherer, R., Tadeusiewicz, R., Zadeh, L.A., Zurada, J.M. (eds.) Artificial Intelligence and Soft Computing. LNCS, vol. 9120, pp. 364–378. Springer, Heidelberg (2015)
31. Gałkowski, T., Rutkowski, L.: Nonparametric recovery of multivariate functions with applications to system identification. Proc. IEEE **73**(5), 942–943 (1985)
32. Gałkowski, T., Rutkowski, L.: Nonparametric fitting of multivariate functions. IEEE Trans. Autom. Control **31**(8), 785–787 (1986)
33. Gdaim, S., Mtibaa, A., Mimouni, M.F.: Design and experimental implementation of DTC of an induction machine based on fuzzy logic control on FPGA. IEEE Trans. Fuzzy Syst. **23**(3), 644–655 (2015)
34. Gręblicki, W., Rutkowski, L.: Density-free Bayes risk consistency of nonparametric pattern recognition procedures. Proc. IEEE **69**(4), 482–483 (1981)
35. Li, H., Gupta, M.: Fuzzy Logic and Intelligent Systems, pp. 50–55. Kluwer Academic Publishers, Boston (1995)
36. Jang, J.S.R., Sun, C.T.: Functional equivalence between radial basis function networks and fuzzy inference systems. IEEE Trans. Neural Netw. **4**(1), 156–159 (1993)
37. Kluska, J., Hajduk, Z.: Hardware implementation of P1-TS fuzzy rule-based systems on FPGA. In: Rutkowski, L., Korytkowski, M., Scherer, R., Tadeusiewicz, R., Zadeh, L.A., Zurada, J.M. (eds.) ICAISC 2013, Part I. LNCS, vol. 7894, pp. 282–293. Springer, Heidelberg (2013)
38. Korytkowski, M., Rutkowski, L., Scherer, R.: From ensemble of fuzzy classifiers to single fuzzy rule base classifier. In: Rutkowski, L., Tadeusiewicz, R., Zadeh, L.A., Zurada, J.M. (eds.) ICAISC 2008. LNCS (LNAI), vol. 5097, pp. 265–272. Springer, Heidelberg (2008)
39. Korytkowski, M., Rutkowski, L., Scherer, R.: Fast image classification by boosting fuzzy classifiers. Inf. Sci. **327**, 175–182 (2016)
40. Li, X., Er, M.J., Lim, B.S., Zhou, J.H., Gan, O.P., Rutkowski, L.: Fuzzy regression modeling for tool performance prediction and degradation detection. Int. J. Neural Syst. **20**(05), 405–419 (2010)

41. Łapa, K., Cpałka, K., Wang, L.: New method for design of fuzzy systems for nonlinear modelling using different criteria of interpretability. In: Rutkowski, L., Korytkowski, M., Scherer, R., Tadeusiewicz, R., Zadeh, L.A., Zurada, J.M. (eds.) ICAISC 2014, Part I. LNCS, vol. 8467, pp. 217–232. Springer, Heidelberg (2014)

42. Łapa, K., Przybył, A., Cpałka, K.: A new approach to designing interpretable models of dynamic systems. In: Rutkowski, L., Korytkowski, M., Scherer, R., Tadeusiewicz, R., Zadeh, L.A., Zurada, J.M. (eds.) ICAISC 2013, Part II. LNCS, vol. 7895, pp. 523–534. Springer, Heidelberg (2013)

43. Łapa, K., Zalasiński, M., Cpałka, K.: A new method for designing and complexity reduction of neuro-fuzzy systems for nonlinear modelling. In: Rutkowski, L., Korytkowski, M., Scherer, R., Tadeusiewicz, R., Zadeh, L.A., Zurada, J.M. (eds.) ICAISC 2013, Part I. LNCS, vol. 7894, pp. 329–344. Springer, Heidelberg (2013)

44. Hassan, M.Y., Sharif, W.F.: Design of FPGA based PID- like fuzzy controller for industrial applications. IAENG Int. J. Comput. Sci. 34(2), 1–7 (2007)

45. Osowski, S.: Sieci neuronowe w ujeciu algorytmicznym, pp. 160–188. WNT, Warszawa (1996)

46. Poon, J., Haessig, P., Hwang, J., Celanovic, I.: High-speed hardware-in-the loop platform for rapid prototyping of power electronics systems. In: 2010 IEEE Conference on Innovative Technologies for an Efficient and Reliable Electricity Supply (CITRES), pp. 420–424 (2010)

47. Poplawski, M., Bialko, M.: Implementation of fuzzy logic controller in FPGA circuit for guiding electric wheelchair. In: Rutkowski, L., Korytkowski, M., Scherer, R., Tadeusiewicz, R., Zadeh, L.A., Zurada, J.M. (eds.) ICAISC 2012, Part II. LNCS, vol. 7268, pp. 216–222. Springer, Heidelberg (2012)

48. Przybył, A., Cpałka, K.: A new method to construct of interpretable models of dynamic systems. In: Rutkowski, L., Korytkowski, M., Scherer, R., Tadeusiewicz, R., Zadeh, L.A., Zurada, J.M. (eds.) ICAISC 2012, Part II. LNCS, vol. 7268, pp. 697–705. Springer, Heidelberg (2012)

49. Rutkowski, L.: Sequential estimates of probability densities by orthogonal series and their application in pattern classification. IEEE Trans. Syst. Man Cybern. 10(12), 918–920 (1980)

50. Rutkowski, L.: On nonparametric identification with prediction of time-varying systems. IEEE Trans. Autom. Control 29(1), 58–60 (1984)

51. Rutkowski, L.: Nonparametric identification of quasi-stationary systems. Syst. Control Lett. 6(1), 33–35 (1985)

52. Rutkowski, L.: Real-time identification of time-varying systems by non-parametric algorithms based on Parzen kernels. Int. J. Syst. Sci. 16(9), 1123–1130 (1985)

53. Rutkowski, L.: A general approach for nonparametric fitting of functions and their derivatives with applications to linear circuits identification. IEEE Trans. Circuits Syst. 33(8), 812–818 (1986)

54. Rutkowski, L.: Application of multiple Fourier-series to identification of multivariable non-stationary systems. Int. J. Syst. Sci. 20(10), 1993–2002 (1989)

55. Rutkowski, L.: Adaptive probabilistic neural networks for pattern classification in time-varying environment. IEEE Trans. Neural Netw. 15(4), 811–827 (2004)

56. Rutkowski, L., Cpałka, K.: Flexible structures of neuro-fuzzy systems, Quo Vadis Computational Intelligence. Fuzziness and Soft Computing, vol. 54, pp. 479–484. Springer (2000)

57. Rutkowski, L., Cpałka, K.: Compromise approach to neuro-fuzzy systems. In: Sincak, P., Vascak, J., Kvasnicka, V., Pospichal, J. (eds.) Intelligent Technologies - Theory and Applications, vol. 76, pp. 85–90. IOS Press, Amsterdam (2002)

58. Rutkowski, L., Cpałka, K.: A neuro-fuzzy controller with a compromise fuzzy reasoning. Control and Cybern. **31**(2), 297–308 (2002)
59. Rutkowski, L., Przybył, A., Cpałka, K., Er, M.J.: Online speed profile generation for industrial machine tool based on neuro-fuzzy approach. In: Rutkowski, L., Scherer, R., Tadeusiewicz, R., Zadeh, L.A., Zurada, J.M. (eds.) ICAISC 2010, Part II. LNCS, vol. 6114, pp. 645–650. Springer, Heidelberg (2010)
60. Rutkowski, L., Pietruczuk, L., Duda, P., Jaworski, M.: Decision Trees for mining data streams based on the McDiarmid's bound. IEEE Trans. Knowl. Data Eng. **25**(6), 1272–1279 (2013)
61. Rutkowski, L., Jaworski, M., Pietruczuk, L., Duda, P.: Decision trees for mining data streams based on the Gaussian approximation. IEEE Trans. Knowl. Data Eng. **26**(1), 108–119 (2014)
62. Rutkowski, L., Jaworski, M., Pietruczuk, L., Duda, P.: The CART decision tree for mining data streams. Inf. Sci. **266**, 1–15 (2014)
63. Rutkowski, L., Rafajłowicz, E.: On optimal global rate of convergence of some nonparametric identification procedures. IEEE Trans. Autom. Control **34**(10), 1089–1091 (1989)
64. Starczewski, J.T., Bartczuk, Ł., Dziwiński, P., Marvuglia, A.: Learning methods for type-2 FLS based on FCM. In: Rutkowski, L., Scherer, R., Tadeusiewicz, R., Zadeh, L.A., Zurada, J.M. (eds.) ICAISC 2010, Part I. LNCS, vol. 6113, pp. 224–231. Springer, Heidelberg (2010)
65. Tomera, M.: Porównanie jakości pracy trzech algorytmów typu PID: liniowego, rozmytego i neuronowego. Automatyka, Elektryka, Zakłócenia **6**, 59–77 (2011). (in Polish)
66. Wang, L., Mendel, J.M.: Fuzzy basis functions, universal approximation, and orthogonal least-squares learning. IEEE Trans. Neural Netw. **3**(5), 807–814 (1992)
67. Xilinx Spartan-6 FPGA User Guides. UG389 v1.5, UG389 v1.2 (2014). http://www.xilinx.com/support/documentation/user_guides/
68. Zalasiński, M., Cpałka, K.: Novel algorithm for the on-line signature verification. In: Rutkowski, L., Korytkowski, M., Scherer, R., Tadeusiewicz, R., Zadeh, L.A., Zurada, J.M. (eds.) ICAISC 2012, Part II. LNCS, vol. 7268, pp. 362–367. Springer, Heidelberg (2012)
69. Zalasiński, M., Cpałka, K.: Novel algorithm for the on-line signature verification using selected discretization points groups. In: Rutkowski, L., Korytkowski, M., Scherer, R., Tadeusiewicz, R., Zadeh, L.A., Zurada, J.M. (eds.) ICAISC 2013, Part I. LNCS, vol. 7894, pp. 493–502. Springer, Heidelberg (2013)
70. Zalasiński, M., Łapa, K., Cpałka, K.: New algorithm for evolutionary selection of the dynamic signature global features. In: Rutkowski, L., Korytkowski, M., Scherer, R., Tadeusiewicz, R., Zadeh, L.A., Zurada, J.M. (eds.) ICAISC 2013, Part II. LNCS, vol. 7895, pp. 113–121. Springer, Heidelberg (2013)
71. Zalasiński, M., Cpałka, K., Er, M.J.: New method for dynamic signature verification using hybrid partitioning. In: Rutkowski, L., Korytkowski, M., Scherer, R., Tadeusiewicz, R., Zadeh, L.A., Zurada, J.M. (eds.) ICAISC 2014, Part II. LNCS, vol. 8468, pp. 216–230. Springer, Heidelberg (2014)
72. Zalasiński, M., Cpałka, K., Hayashi, Y.: New method for dynamic signature verification based on global features. In: Rutkowski, L., Korytkowski, M., Scherer, R., Tadeusiewicz, R., Zadeh, L.A., Zurada, J.M. (eds.) ICAISC 2014, Part II. LNCS, vol. 8468, pp. 231–245. Springer, Heidelberg (2014)

73. Zalasiński, M., Cpałka, K., Hayashi, Y.: New fast algorithm for the dynamic signature verification using global features values. In: Rutkowski, L., Korytkowski, M., Scherer, R., Tadeusiewicz, R., Zadeh, L.A., Zurada, J.M. (eds.) Artificial Intelligence and Soft Computing. LNCS, vol. 9120, pp. 175–188. Springer, Heidelberg (2015)

74. Zalasiński, M., Cpałka, K., Er, M.J.: A new method for the dynamic signature verification based on the stable partitions of the signature. In: Rutkowski, L., Korytkowski, M., Scherer, R., Tadeusiewicz, R., Zadeh, L.A., Zurada, J.M. (eds.) Artificial Intelligence and Soft Computing. LNCS, vol. 9120, pp. 161–174. Springer, Heidelberg (2015)

Learning Rules for Hierarchical Fuzzy Logic Systems Using Wu & Mendel IF-THEN Rules Quality Measures

Krzysztof Renkas[✉] and Adam Niewiadomski

Institute of Information Technology, Lodz University of Technology,
ul. Wólczańska 215, 90-924 łódz, Poland
800561@edu.p.lodz.pl, adam.niewiadomski@p.lodz.pl

Abstract. This paper focuses on problems related to learning rules using numerical data for the *Hierarchical Fuzzy Logic Systems (HFLS)* described in [12]. Using hierarchical structure of *Fuzzy Logic Systems (FLS)* complex problems could be divided into subproblems with smaller dimensions. "Hierarchical" means that fuzzy sets produced as output of one of fuzzy logic systems are then processed as an input of another one as the sets of auxiliary variables. The main problem is to learn a rulebase with numerical data, which does not contain any data for those auxiliary variables. Learning rules for FLS in short could be accomplished by using many different approaches, building one, complex rulebase using all available input and output variables for complex problems. Our learning method based on the *Wang & Mendel (W&M)* method adopted for the HFLS with selective activation of unit FLS were introduced in [13]. The main scope of this paper is to extend our method applying quality measures of IF-THEN rules in the sense of *Wu & Mendel (Wu&M)* to remove conflicting rules. The proposal presented in this paper operates on a type-1 HFLS, built with the fuzzy logic systems (in the sense of Mamdani). An example of single-player games, i.e. where the "enemy" is controlled by agents is used. Two new problems are briefly introduced.

Keywords: Hierarchical fuzzy logic systems · Learning fuzzy rules · Nonlinear control systems · Selective unit fuzzy logic systems activation · Rules quality measures · IF-THEN rules · Simulation in computer games

1 Introduction

In particular, we are interested in computational intelligence methods based on FLS that make it possible to solve different **complex** problems. In general, fuzzy logic systems are useful in the case when a controlled process is not linear and the use of traditional controllers may appear inefficient. Fuzzy logic system is a control unit based on fuzzy logic [20], which makes decisions based on knowledge containing the rules like *IF ...THEN ...;* with unspecified predicates [19]. Those rules are expressed by natural language using *Linguistic Variables (LV)*.

The new solution proposed here is to learn HFLS rulebase using numerical data and *Wu & Mendel IF-THEN rules quality measures (Wu&M IF-THEN RQM)*. Application

© Springer International Publishing Switzerland 2016
L. Rutkowski et al. (Eds.): ICAISC 2016, Part I, LNAI 9692, pp. 299–310, 2016.
DOI: 10.1007/978-3-319-39378-0_26

of quality measures allows us to discover and evaluate a descriptive model of rules using the knowledge described by the whole training database - not limited to a single sample of training data. The proposed solution is an example of linguistic summarization in the sense of Mendel. Different quality measures take into account different aspects of assessed rules and make it possible to select rules from the point of view of their informativeness. Our proposal is based on the Wang & Mendel learning algorithm created for the traditional FLSs purposes, newly adapted for HFLSs with selective FLS activation (see [13]).

The rest of the paper is organized as follows: Subsect. 1.1 treats about our motivation to develop HFLS and HFLS learning methods; Subsect. 1.2 contains some literature references with description of our former works. Description of some Wu&M IF-THEN rules quality measures is presented in Sect. 2. Section 3 contains our new learning algorithm for HFLS with appliaction of Wu&M IF-THEN rules quality measures. In Sect. 4, tests and the results are described. The last Sect. 5 contains conclusions and some future directions of the research with new problems proposal.

1.1 Motivation

Below we can see the example of one rule that belongs to the FLS rulebase for tank decision making inference process during the battle:

```
RULE 0 : IF TANKS_COUNT IS MEDIUM AND AVERAGE_TANKS_FORCE IS MEDIUM
AND FORCE_DIFFERENCE_TO_THE_NEAREST_OPPONENT IS POSITIVE AND
DISTANCE_TO_THE_NEAREST_OPPONENT IS BIG AND ALLIES_COUNT IS BIG
AND AVERAGE_ALLIES_FORCE IS BIG AND TANK_IS_BEING_ATTACKED IS NO
THEN ACTION IS PATROL;
```

Using FLS for our sample problem we enumerate seven input variables and one output. To solve this problem we have to build 1458 rules using seven antecedents and one consequent. During one inference for battalion of 5 tanks we have to fire 7290 rules performing over $824 \cdot 10^3$ mathematical operations.

Figure 1 shows examples of two FLS: a traditional one (a) and hierarchical (b). HFLS contains many FLSs and outputs of one FLS are then considered as input of another one. The hierarchical structure looks more complicated, but in reality it allows us to simplify a complex problem into several subproblems with smaller dimensions. Our tank problem could be solved using the structure presented on Fig. 2. Moreover, not

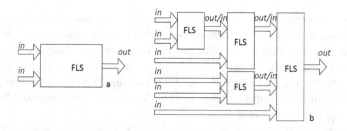

Fig. 1. Examples of two fuzzy logic systems, traditional (a) and hierarchical (b).

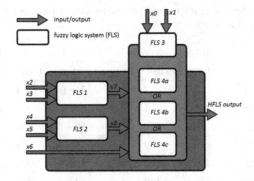

Fig. 2. General diagram of designed HFLS structure.

each of the combined FLSs works during each iteration of inference because of selective activation of unit FLSs mechanism application. The example rules are presented below for strategist, risk, support and offensive strategy action:

```
RULE 0 : IF TANKS_COUNT IS SMALL AND AVERAGE_TANKS_FORCE IS SMALL
THEN STRATEGY IS DEFENSIVE;
RULE 0 : IF FORCE_DIFFERENCE_TO_THE_NEAREST_OPPONENT IS NEGATIVE
AND DISTANCE_TO_THE_NEAREST_OPPONENT IS SMALL THEN RISK IS BIG;
RULE 0 : IF ALLIES_COUNT IS SMALL AND AVERAGE_ALLIES_FORCE IS SMALL
THEN SUPPORT IS ZERO;
RULE 0 : IF RISK IS ZERO AND SUPPORT IS ZERO THEN ACTION IS PATROL;
```

Using HFLS we enumerate nine variables (seven original and two auxiliary). In this case we have to build **only** 78 rules with max two antecedents and one consequent grouped into six rulebases. During one inference for a battalion of 5 tanks we have to fire only 184 rules performing less than $21 \cdot 10^3$ mathematical operations. The full number summaries of fired rules and performed mathematical operations during the inference for different battalions in FLS and HFLS is described in Table 1 and in Fig. 3.

Thus HFLS make it possible to divide complex problems into several subproblems with smaller rulebases and simpler rules which has a possitive impact on performance. This is because of a huge reduction of the number of fired rules and performed mathematical operations during each inference. **So it is worth developing HFLS.**

Learning rules is one of the possible ways to develop HFLS. Building rules using natural language, anyone could be an expert who could create a rulebase to solve some intuitive problems. However, having for example ten rulebases created by different 'experts', we could have ten **different** rulebases despite the simplicity of the problem. Consequently the inference engine using those rulebases could make different decisions for the same input data. Moreover, rulebases prepared by experts represents their subjective opinion and could be designed in a logical way using reasoned decisions giving 'ideal' rulebase - not always consistent with the real decisions. Thus learning rules with a training data is a very important issue.

In [13] we proposed W&M method based learning algorithm adapted to the hierarchical structure of FLS. This method is **very limited** because of using very simple

Table 1. Number of performed mathematical operations during inference for battalions of 1, 5 and 10 tanks in HFLS and FLS.

operation	HFLS					FLS
	strategist	risk	support	action	total	
fuzzification	2	2	2	2 + 1	9	7
rule firing level	1	1	1	1 + 0	4	6
rule output	50	50	50	50 + 50	250	50
number of rules	9	9	9	16 + 1	44	1458
rules aggregation	400	400	400	800	2000	72850
deffuzification	149	149	149	149	596	149
total	1026	1026	1026	1848	4926	164853
number of math operations for battalion of						
1 tank	1026	1026	1026	1848	**4926**	**164853**
5 tanks	1026	513	513	924	**20526**	**824265**
10 tanks	1026	1026	1026	1848	**40026**	**164853**

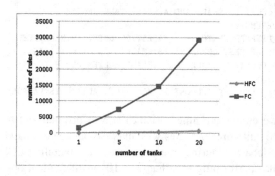

Fig. 3. Number of fired rules during inference for different battalions in HFLS and FLS.

measure during removing conflicting rules process. This measure depends only on the single sample of data, which gets the highest value. This means that finally only limited number of samples have an effect on the learning process. Please see an example of data shown on Fig. 4. This example shows some sample data, which represents chosen tank actions in relation to the tank power.

We can see two main groups of points: dots (that belong mainly to the low power) and stars (that belong to the high power). Rule's degree from the W&M method is performed as algebraic product of membership value of sample data to available fuzzy sets; rule with the best degree of truth is taken into account. Using this degree during learning process we would get two main rules with degree equal to 1:

```
IF POWER IS LOW THEN ACTION IS ATTACK;
IF POWER IS HIGH THEN ACTION IS RUN AWAY;
```

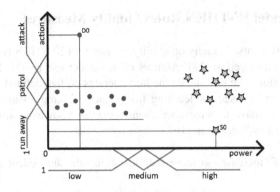

Fig. 4. Sample of data which represents chosen tank actions in relation to the tank power.

However, we can see that those two of learned rules do not make sense. They were chosen because of points D0 and S0 - they get the best rule's degree. Taking into account all the points we would say, that if the power is low we have to run away or to patrol; if the power is high we have to patrol - not run away. So we want to emphasize, that used rule's degree does not fully exploit power of learning process based on numerical data and it is important to develop this method to use more complex measures.

1.2   Literature References and Former Works

Authors in [16] says that using fuzzy models all parameters should be learnt in appropriate way by using experimental data and respective learning algorithms. The Wang & Mendel method which is designed as learning algorithm on numerical data for traditional FLS is described in [17]. Authors of [18] use linguistic summaries to generate fuzzy rules.

Authors of [14] introduce learning a two layer hierarchical fuzzy logic system using cooperative co-evolution. Application of genetic and bacterial programming algorithms for learning hierarchical interpolative fuzzy rules is described in [1]. Fuzzy *Feature Subset Selection (FFS)* for learning purposes is described in [6,7] using Wang & Mendel method, in [9] using fuzzy rough set or genetic algorithm in [3]. Linguistic hedges applied to learning rules combined with genetic algorithm are described in [4,5,10,11]. Authors in [2] presents a tuning based on genetic algorithms by fitting the membership functions changing their basic parameters and fitting the rules using linguistic hedges. Another interesting approach of inducing fuzzy rules using ant colony optimization algorithm and linguistic hedges is presented in [8].

Our HFLS with selective activation of unit FLSs mechanism is described in [12] with comparison to traditional FLS. [13] introduces our new learning method based on the W&M method adopted for HFLS. This paper describes extension for our method of learning rules presented in [13] for the system described in [12].

2   Wu & Mendel IF-THEN Rules Quality Measures

In this paper we are focused chiefly on quality measures of IF-THEN rules in the sense of Wu & Mendel described in [18]. Authors of this paper use IF-THEN rules for linguistic summarization. The introduced method operates on five defined IF-THEN rules quality measures and is used for learning fuzzy rules. Talking about IF-THEN rules quality measures we have to remember about 'general' knowledge quality measures originally described by Traczyk in [15].

Degree of Truth, T increases as more data satisfying the antecedent also satisfy the consequent.

$$T = \frac{\sum_{m=1}^{M} min(\mu_{S_1}(v_1^m), \mu_{S_2}(v_2^m))}{\sum_{m=1}^{M} \mu_{S_1}(v_1^m)}. \tag{1}$$

Degree of Sufficient Coverage, C describes whether a rule is supported by enough data. To compute C firstly we have to compute the *coverage ratio*, which is

$$r_c = \frac{\sum_{m=1}^{M} t_m}{M}. \tag{2}$$

where

$$t_m = \begin{cases} 1, \mu_{S_1}(v_1^m) > 0 \text{ and } \mu_{S_2}(v_2^m) > 0 \\ 0, \quad \text{otherwise} \end{cases} \tag{3}$$

Sufficient coverage is

$$C = f(r_c). \tag{4}$$

where f is a function that maps r_c into C. Function $f(r_c)$ is S-shape function. It is determined by two parameters r_1 and r_2 where $0 \le r_1 \le r_2$ and $r_1 = 0.02$ and $r_2 = 0.15$ are used in this paper.

$$f(r_c) = \begin{cases} 0, & r_c \le r_1 \\ 2(\frac{r_c - r_1}{r_2 - r_1})^2, & r_1 < r_c < \frac{r_1 + r_2}{2} \\ 1 - 2(\frac{r_2 - r_c}{r_2 - r_1})^2, & \frac{r_1 + r_2}{2} \le r_c \le r_2 \\ 1, & r_c \ge r_2 \end{cases} \tag{5}$$

Degree of Usefulness, U describes how useful a summary is. A rule is useful if and only if it has a high degree of truth (T) and it has sufficient coverage.

$$U = min(T, C). \tag{6}$$

Degree of Outlier, O which indicates the possibility that a rule describes only outliers instead of a useful pattern.

$$O = \begin{cases} min(max(T, 1 - T), 1 - C), & T > 0 \\ 0, & T = 0 \end{cases} \tag{7}$$

Degree of Simplicity, S the simplicity of a summary can be measured by its lengh, i.e., how many antecedents and consequents the rule has.

$$S = 2^{2-l}.$$
(8)

where l is the total number of antecedents and consequents of the rule.

Symbols M is the number of training data, y_m is the mth object, v_n is the name of nth attribute, v_n^m is the value of the nth attribute for y_m.

3   Learning Rules Algorithm for Hierarchical Fuzzy Logic Systems Using Wu & Mendel IF-THEN Rules Quality Measures

3.1   Our Rules Learning Algorithm with Wu & Mendel IF-THEN Rules Quality Measures Application

Input. Operating on many input variables and one output we need to have training data as a set of pairs of the input and output values, i.e.:

$$(x_1(t), x_2(t), \ldots, x_n(t); y(t)).$$
(9)

where $t = 1, 2, \ldots T$ is an index of the sample data, T is a number of the training data, $x_i(t)$ is an input value of the input variable x_i for the given sample data t, n is a number of input variables, $y(t)$ is an input value of the output variable y.

Algorithm **STEP 1:** divide input and output domains into fuzzy regions. For each input and output variable (x_i, y) we need to indicate the minimum and the maximum value getting the intervals for each variable using numerical data. For auxiliary variables we need to define these values. We need to divide each of the defined intervals into $2N_i + 1$ regions, where $i = 1..n$. N_i could be different for each variable. For each region we need to define label and membership function to yield FSs of a given variable.
STEP 2: define groups of variables. For each unit FLS of our HFLS we need to define one group denoting input and output variables.
STEP 3: generate a separate rulebase for each group of variables. When the output variable for a given group is not the auxiliary variable, generate fuzzy rules using all combinations of input and output LV. The generated rules contain conflicting rules (different conclusions for the same conditions). Otherwise, the expert should generate rules or define generation process. We should not take into account consequent values during generating rules; the generated rulebase should not contain conflicting rules.
STEP 4: compute the rule's degree denoted by $D(R_k)$ and values of Wu&M IF-THEN rules quality measures presented in Subsect. 2 for each sample data and for each of the generated rules, for all unit rulebases. Degree is an algebraic product of input values membership values to LV fuzzy sets and could be expressed as follows:

$$D(R_k) = \mu_{A_1}(x_1) \cdot \mu_{A_2}(x_2) \cdot \ldots \cdot \mu_{A_n}(x_n) \cdot \mu_B(y) = \mu_B(y) \prod_{i=1}^{n} \mu_{A_i}(x_i).$$
(10)

where R_k is rule expressed as follows:

$$R_k : \text{IF } x_1 \text{ IS } A_1 \text{ AND } \dots \text{ AND } x_n \text{ IS } A_n \text{ THEN } y \text{ IS } B. \tag{11}$$

Equation (10) could be used if the output LV for a given rulebase is not auxiliary variable. Otherwise, we need to assume that membership value for this variable is equal to 1 on the faith of the expert knowledge. In that case we could simplify Eq. (10) to:

$$D(R_k) = \mu_{A_1}(x_1) \cdot \mu_{A_2}(x_2) \cdot \dots \cdot \mu_{A_n}(x_n) = \prod_{i=1}^{n} \mu_{A_i}(x_i). \tag{12}$$

We assume the value obtained using (12) as a membership value for a given value of auxiliary LV during computing degree for another unit rulebases where this LV occurs as an antecedent.

Computing Wu&M rules quality measures iterating the sample of data and then rules, we have to do this in two stages. Firstly, during this step we have to compute separately the nominator and the denominator of degree of truth (T). Also we have to compute nominator of r_c for degree of sufficient coverage (C). Final values of mentioned Wu&M IF-THEN rules quality measures would be computed in the next step after iteration of all sample of data.

STEP 5: Compute the final values of Wu&M rules quality measures for each rule for each of unit rulebases with conflicting rules.

STEP 6: Remove conflicting rules, leaving rules with the highest value of chosen Wu&M IF-THEN rules quality measures. Additionally we could remove rules with the degree less than some α value, where $0 \le \alpha \le 1$.

To fit our proposal to the designed structure we propose two variants of modification to provide selective activation of unit FLS support.

Variant 1. During learning tank action rulebases, method learn each of them using alternative Eq. (13) during computing rule's degree.

$$D(R_k) = D_{Strategist}(t, s)\mu_B(y) \prod_{i=1}^{n} \mu_{A_i}(x_i). \tag{13}$$

$D_{Strategist}(t, s)$ is the best degree for strategist rules whose conclusions are equal to a given strategy s. In short in this case degrees of learned rules using sample data t additionally take into account the best degree for strategist rules, which choose a strategy that is associated with a given rulebase.

Variant 2. Learning tank action rulebases, a method learns only one rulebase strictly associated with the strategy, that is equal to a strategy conclusion of strategist rule with the highest degree. In short, the method learns only one rulebase for a given sample of data.

3.2 Our Basic Rulebase Power Measure

As a basic measure to evaluate a rule's degrees of all learned rulebases we would like to introduce rulebase power:

Definition 1. *Rulebase Power, denoted as RP, is a measure for comparing general degree for the entire rulebase. RP is expressed as a weighted average of obtained number of rules rc_i, whose degrees are in the defined ranges, relative to the total number of rules R. Each range should have associated weight $w_i = 0+(i-1)\cdot\frac{1}{N-1} : w_i \in [0, 1], w_i < w_{i+1}$, where $i = 1..N$, N is the number of all ranges. RP could be expressed as:*

$$RP = \frac{\sum_{i=1}^{N} rc_i \cdot w_i}{R}. \tag{14}$$

$RP \in [0, 1]$. If RP equals 0, that means that degree of all rules include into deprecated range with a zero weight. RP equal to 1 means that degree's of all rules include into the range with the highest degree values.

4 Tests and Results

4.1 Tests

Processing training data using two variants of our new learning method described in Subsect. 3.1 and three Wu&M IF-THEN rules quality measures six rulebases were learned. Also two rulebases were learned using our basic learning method described in [13]. Each of learned rulebases are HFLS rulebases. At the beginning a summary and a comparison of learned rulebases are described. Summary and comparison refers to the different learned rules, the number of learned rules with some specified rule's degrees and power of the whole rulebase expressed by a proposed measure (see Definition 1).

Two variants of each learned rulebase using our basic learning method and new one using only T and C Wu&M IF-THEN RQM were tested. The first test applies to general behaviour of the game. In this test case the game *Tank 1990–2012* was launched 72 times counting losses in subsequent stages taking stage 11 as the last one. The second test includes comparison of the times needed to get victory by battalion controlled by HFLS. The game was run 50 times for each rulebase, player tank could not move or perform any actions.

4.2 Results

Table 2 contains a percentage summary of different rules taken into final rulebase during learning process using different Wu&M IF-THEN rules quality measures in comparison to our basic method. We can notice that rulebases learned using our method with C and U Wu&M rules quality measures have the same values because both rulebases are equal to each other. Table 3 contains comparison of mentioned rulebases taking into account for example rulebase power described in Subsect. 3.2. Table 4 shows the results of the first and the second test.

Table 2. Percentage summary of different rules taken into the final rulebase during learning using our new learning method with different Wu&M rules quality measures application in comparison to the rulebases learned using our basic learning method.

	T	C	U
V1 [%]	22	62	62
V2 [%]	18	62	62

Table 3. Summary of the rulebases learned by our basic learning method and new one using different Wu&M rules quality measures during removing conflicting rules. Rulebases were learned using both variants of our method. During generating linguistic variables different FS types were used (triangular, L, gamma).

	$v1$	$v2$	$v1;T$	$v2;T$	$v1;C$	$v2;C$	$v1;U$	$v2;U$
$D = 0$ [%]	4	6	3.70	6.17	23.46	32.10	23.46	32.10
$0 < D$ [%]	96.30	93.83	96.30	93.83	76.54	67.90	76.54	67.90
$D = 1$ [%]	17	19	17.28	18.52	17.28	18.52	17.28	18.52
RP [%]	51.40	54.66	50.39	53.54	45.34	46.13	45.34	46.13

Table 4. Losses in the following stages (72 tests) and average time necessary to win (50 tests) playing the game *Tank 1990–2012* for different rulebases.

stage number	1	2	3	4	5	6	7	8	9	10	11	defeat	victory	time
Original	3	10	8	12	11	8	9	6	4	1		72 (100 %)	0 (0 %)	29.8 s
Our;v1	3	13	8	15	15	6	10	1	1			72 (100 %)	0 (0 %)	21.6 s
Our;v2	5	9	7	18	13	10	9	0	1			72 (100 %)	0 (0 %)	23.1 s
Our;v1;T	3	10	10	18	16	5	8	2				72 (100 %)	0 (0 %)	**21.0 s**
Our;v2;T	2	14	8	19	12	9	7	1				72 (100 %)	0 (0 %)	22.7 s
Our;v1;C	7	7	12	15	9	15	5	1	0	1		72 (100 %)	0 (0 %)	22.1 s
Our;v2;C	6	5	13	16	10	12	8	1	1			72 (100 %)	0 (0 %)	22.0 s

5 Conclusions and Future Work

The tests run prove correctness of the proposed learning method for HFLSs. Application of IF-THEN rules quality measures is very important, because it allows us to discover some interesting information about our data and learning rules. The basic method using rule's degree tries to construct a predictive model whereas the application of IF-THEN rules quality measures allows us to discover a descriptive model. Moreover, the possibility of using different IF-THEN rules quality measures enables us to obtain different rulebases during learning process on the same sample of data.

The results obtained during test cases show a positive impact on the tank control using learned rulebases, but the differences are not very big.

The summary presented in Table 3 shows a little worse general rulebase power of learned rules using our new method with Wu&M IF-THEN RQM application but this is natural. Rulebase power is predicted by the rule's degree which is the main criterion during choosing rules in our basic method; the application of Wu&M rules quality measures during removing conflicting rules enables choosing rules **seemingly** worse.

Another interesting observation is that in our case the degree of usefulness has no effect on the final rulebase in comparison to the degree of sufficient coverage. That means that in our case the second measure is more restrictive than degree of truth.

Also as we can see in Table 2 and in Table 3 we can say, that application of C measure gives us a rulebase that contains more different rules than T in comparison to our basic method. Also we have to notice that the number of rule's degree equal to 0 is much higher (about 20–30 % in comparison to 3–6 %), but it has no negative impact on the obtained results.

Moreover, analysing the results we could notice that the first modification variant of our method got slightly better results than the second variant, regardless of the IF-THEN rules quality measure used during removing conflicting rules process.

During future research we could apply new IF-THEN rules quality measures and tuning fuzzy sets function using linguistic hedges during learning process. Also it is important to present application of our solution to another class of problems unrelated to the controlling vehicles in computer games, such as controlling autonomous drone and central heating stove.

References

1. Balazs, K., Koczy, L.: Hierarchical-interpolative fuzzy system construction by genetic and bacterial programming algorithms. In: IEEE International Conference on Fuzzy Systems (FUZZ), pp. 2116–2122, June 2011
2. Casillas, J., Cordon, O., Herrera, F., del Jesus, M.: Genetic tuning of fuzzy rule-based systems integrating linguistic hedges. In: Joint 9th IFSA World Congress and 20th NAFIPS International Conference, vol. 3, pp. 1570–1574, July 2001
3. Chakraborty, B.: Genetic algorithm with fuzzy fitness function for feature selection. In: Proceedings of the 2002 IEEE International Symposium on Industrial Electronics, ISIE 2002, vol. 1, pp. 315–319 (2002)
4. Chen, C.Y., Hsieh, Y.T., Liu, B.D.: Circuit implementation of linguistic-hedge fuzzy logic controller in current-mode approach. IEEE Trans. Fuzzy Syst. **11**(5), 624–646 (2003)
5. Chen, C.Y., Liu, B.D., Tsao, J.Y.: Adaptive fuzzy logic controller blending the concepts of linguistic hedges and genetic algorithms. In: IEEE International Fuzzy Systems Conference Proceedings, FUZZ-IEEE 1999, vol. 3, pp. 1299–1304, August 1999
6. Cintra, M., de Arruda, C., Monard, M.: Fuzzy feature subset selection using the Wang & Mendel method. In: Eighth International Conference on Hybrid Intelligent Systems, HIS 2008, pp. 590–595, September 2008
7. Cintra, M., Martin, T., Monard, M., Camargo, H.: Feature subset selection using a fuzzy method. In: International Conference on Intelligent Human-Machine Systems and Cybernetics, IHMSC 2009, vol. 2, pp. 214–217, August 2009
8. Galea, M., Shen, Q.: Linguistic hedges for ant-generated rules. In: IEEE International Conference on Fuzzy Systems, pp. 1973–1980 (2006)

9. Guo, C., Zheng, X.: Feature subset selection approach based on fuzzy rough set for high-dimensional data. In: IEEE International Conference on Granular Computing (GrC), pp. 72–75, October 2014

10. Liu, B.D.: Linguistic hedges and fuzzy rule base systems. In: Proceedings of the 2003 International Conference on Neural Networks and Signal Processing, vol. 2, pp. 1724–1727, December 2003

11. Liu, B.D., Chen, C.Y., Tsao, J.Y.: Design of adaptive fuzzy logic controller based on linguistic-hedge concepts and genetic algorithms. IEEE Trans. Syst. Man Cybern. Part B Cybern. 31(1), 32–53 (2001)

12. Renkas, K., Niewiadomski, A.: Hierarchical fuzzy logic systems and controlling vehicles in computer games. J. Appl. Comput. Sci. (JACS) 22(1), 201–212 (2014). http://it.p.lodz.pl/file.php/12/2014-1/jacs-1-2014-RenkasNiewiadomski.pdf

13. Renkas, K., Niewiadomski, A., Kacprowicz, M.: Learning rules for hierarchical fuzzy logic systems with selective fuzzy controller activation. In: Rutkowski, L., Korytkowski, M., Scherer, R., Tadeusiewicz, R., Zadeh, L.A., Zurada, J.M. (eds.) Artificial Intelligence and Soft Computing. LNCS, vol. 9119, pp. 260–270. Springer, Heidelberg (2015)

14. Stonier, R., Young, N.: Co-evolutionary learning and hierarchical fuzzy control for the inverted pendulum. In: The 2003 Congress on Evolutionary Computation, CEC 2003, vol. 1, pp. 467–473, December 2003

15. Traczyk, W.: Evaluation of knowledge quality. Systems Science 23 (1997)

16. Vachkov, G., Fukuda, T.: Structured learning of fuzzy models for reduction of information dimensionality. In: IEEE International Fuzzy Systems Conference Proceedings, FUZZ-IEEE 1999, vol. 2, pp. 963–968, August 1999

17. Wang, L.X., Mendel, J.: Generating fuzzy rules by learning from examples. IEEE Trans. Syst. Man Cybern. 22(6), 1414–1427 (1992)

18. Wu, D., Mendel, J., Joo, J.: Linguistic summarization using if-then rules. In: IEEE International Conference on Fuzzy Systems (FUZZ), pp. 1–8, July 2010

19. Yager, R.R., Filev, D.P.: Essentials of Fuzzy Modeling and Control. A Wiley-Interscience publication, John Wiley & Sons, New York (1994)

20. Zadeh, L.A.: The concept of a linguistic variable and its applications to approximate reasoning (i). Inf. Sci. 8, 199–249 (1975)

Cyclic Scheduling Line with Uncertain Data

Jarosław Rudy[(✉)]

Department of Control Systems and Mechatronics, Wrocław University of Science
and Technology, Janiszewskiego 11-17, 50-372 Wrocław, Poland
jaroslaw.rudy@pwr.edu.pl

Abstract. In this paper, a cyclic permutation flow shop problem for
a certain production line with uncertain data is considered. The goal is
to minimize the cycle time. The uncertain elements in the system are
identified and modeled as fuzzy numbers. A metaheuristic fuzzy-aware
algorithm is developed and tested against 3 deterministic algorithms.
The fuzzy algorithm significantly outperforms deterministic algorithms
70 % of the time with similar computation time. The fuzzy algorithm is
also more reliable, providing solutions with smaller standard deviation.

Keywords: Flow shop scheduling · Cyclic production · Uncertain
knowledge · Simulated annealing · Fuzzy processing times · Fuzzy cycle
time

1 Introduction

Nowadays, production companies must remaining flexible in order to meet the
requirements of the clients, forcing them to apply Just-In-Time production techniques. In result, the companies are switching production strategy from mass
manufacturing of a single product into manufacturing a mixture of products
(details), commonly referred to as *Minimal Part Set* or MPS. The most common optimization of such systems is minimization of the cycle time – the time
between the beginning of one MPS and the beginning of the next one. Moreover,
many production systems are characterized by uncertain data, especially when
the tasks are performed by human operators. Use of hydraulic and pneumatic
motors coupled with properties of details can result in uncertain processing times
as well.

In this paper, we consider a cyclic scheduling problem with uncertain data
using a miniature production line. Here we present a brief overview of research
considering cyclic job scheduling and fuzzy scheduling problems. We start with
cyclic scheduling, which received considerable attention. In the paper [8], theoretical and numerical properties of methods for obtaining the minimal cycle time
are studied. The cycle time is estimated through several expressions which are
then compared based on their convergence speed. The distribution of the number
of MPS needed to ascertain the cycle time is examined, with 3 to 4 MPS being

This work was co-financed by the Młoda Kadra, grant no. B50298.

© Springer International Publishing Switzerland 2016
L. Rutkowski et al. (Eds.): ICAISC 2016, Part I, LNAI 9692, pp. 311–320, 2016.
DOI: 10.1007/978-3-319-39378-0_27

enough almost 98 % of the time. In the paper [2], graph models of the problem is employed to establish block elimination properties. Conducted research indicate improvement of the efficiency of the search process for cyclic flow shop problem. Solving methods using parallel computing have also appeared, for example, in the paper [1] two parallel techniques – vector processing and multi-walk method – were employed to solve cyclic flexible job shop scheduling problem (CFJSSP). New method of computing the cycle time was also presented.

As for fuzzy scheduling problems, a number of different approaches exist, most of them focused on solving problems with fuzzy processing times or fuzzy duedate. Ishibuchi *et al.* [3] used fuzzy duedate for each job to represent the satisfaction of decision maker for the completion time of that job. Two problems were considered: (1) maximization of the minimum satisfaction over all jobs and (2) maximization of the total satisfaction. Hybrid genetic algorithms (GA) for solving those problems were demonstrated. Genetic algorithms were also employed by Sakawa and Kubota [7] to solve multi-objective job shop scheduling problem with fuzzy processing times and fuzzy duedates. Gantt charts were used to help define similarity between individuals in the GA. The results were compared to the simulated annealing algorithm (SA). Parallel scheduling problems were also considered – in the paper [6], three fuzzy scheduling models for solving such problems were introduced and tested using hybrid intelligent algorithm. Fuzzy scheduling have also been modeled outside of production and manufacturing. In the paper [10], the fuzzy sets theory and integer programming were used to obtain solution for multi-objective nurse scheduling problem. The proposed algorithm was aimed at providing personalized and equitable schedules that were also satisfying for the hospital management. Aside from integer programming other exact algorithms were used. For example, in the paper [4] the branch and bound method was used to solve job shop scheduling problem with fuzzy data. For further reading on using fuzzy techniques for solving production planning and scheduling problems, consider paper [11].

2   System Description

We consider a miniature production line, as shown in Fig. 1, which consists of five separate machines. The flow of every detail through the system can be divided into separate phases called stations.

Station A consists of conveyor belt (step A1) that transports details from the storage to the pneumatic arm. The arm then transports details to the second station (step A2). The duration of this step is fuzzy due to the pneumatic mechanism. Next is station B with four steps from B1 to B4. Step B1 is performed by the human operator (and is thus fuzzy) and consists of transporting the detail to a lift. Step B2 employs that lift to deliver the detail to a measurement station. Step B3 is used to measure the properties of the detail (*e.g.* material, mass, height). Step B4 transports the detail to the next station using an inclined slope (the duration of this step is fuzzy).

Station C is the main station, consisting of a movable plate and two machines used for the treatment of the detail. The plate can set the detail in one of the four positions: (1) starting position, where detail is received, (2) first machine, (3) second machine and (4) detail exit. Moreover, the plate can hold up to four details at the same time. The steps performed on this station are: (1) transport of the detail to the first machine, (2) treatment by the first machine, (3) transport to the second machine, (4) treatment by the second machine and (5) transport to the exit position on the plate.

Station D is used to transport the detail from the plate to the last station, by the use of another pneumatic arm (step D1) and inclined slope (step D2). Duration for both steps is fuzzy. Station E is the last station used for sorting (dividing) details. During step E1 the detail moves along a conveyor belt until it is pushed off the belt at its assigned exit. During step E2 the detail is finally transported to the correct storage.

Fig. 1. Miniature production line

3   Mathematical Model

Described system can be identified as a cyclic permutation flow shop scheduling problem. There is set $\mathcal{M} = \{1, 2, \ldots, m\}$ of m machines and set $\mathcal{J} = \{1, 2, \ldots, n\}$ of n jobs (details) to be processed. $p_{i,j}$ describes the processing time of job j on machine i, while $t_{i,j}$ designates transportation time of job j from machine i to machine $i + 1$. Lastly, $s_{i,j,k}$ is the refitting time of machine i from job j to job k. In all cases $i \in \{1, 2, \ldots, m\}$ and $j, k \in \{1, 2, \ldots, n\}$.

In our production system, we decided to distinguish following processing steps: physical measurement (Step B3), first processing (step C2), second processing (step C4) and sorting of the details (steps E1 and E2). Operation processing times p_i depend on the detail to be processed. Between each pair of subsequent machines i and $i + 1$ exists a non-zero transportation time. Decomposition of the production system can be seen in Table 1. Refitting takes place only before first and second processing (steps C2 and C4) and depends on the details to be processed before and after the fitting.

We have defined a flow shop production system with 4 machines $\mathcal{M} = \{1, 2, 3, 4\}$. Set of operations is defined as $\mathcal{O} = \{1, 2, \ldots, 4n\}$ and each job j consists of 4 operations $(\mathcal{O}_{1,j}, \ldots, \mathcal{O}_{4,j})$ processed on subsequent machines.

Table 1. Machines and transportation times

Action	Times	Steps
Transportation of job j to machine 1	$(t_{0,j})$	A1, A2, B1, B2
Processing of job j on machine 1	$(p_{1,j})$	B3
Transportation of job j to machine 2	$(t_{1,j})$	B4, C1
Processing of job j on machine 2	$(p_{2,j})$	C2
Transportation of job j to machine 3	$(t_{2,j})$	C3
Processing of job j on machine 3	$(p_{3,j})$	C4
Transportation of job j to machine 4	$(t_{3,j})$	C5, D1, D2
Processing of job j on machine 4	$(p_{4,j})$	E1, E2

In each cycle only one MPS (Minimal Part Set) is performed, during which all operations from $\mathcal{O}$ are to be processed. Moreover, this set can be decomposed into non-empty subsets $\mathcal{O}_k$, $k \in \{1, 2, \ldots, m\}$, containing operations from one machine k, thus $\prod_{k \in \mathcal{M}} \mathcal{O}_k = \mathcal{O}$. In our case $|\mathcal{O}_k| = n$ for all k.

Schedule of jobs can be defined as a permutation $\pi = (\pi(1), \pi(2), \ldots, \pi(n))$, where $\pi(i)$ is an i-th job from permutation π. Now, let $[S^x]_{m \times n}$ be a matrix of starting times of jobs on x-th MPS, where $S^x_{i,j}$ is a starting time of job j on machine i. We assume that not only the schedule of jobs is cyclic, but the timetable of the system is fully cyclic. As such, there exists a constant $T(\pi)$ called period, such that $S^{x+1}_{i,\pi(j)} = S^x_{i,\pi(j)} + T(\pi)$, where $i = 1, 2, \ldots, m$, $j = 1, 2, \ldots, n$ and $x \in \mathbb{N}$. Period $T(\pi)$ depends on permutation π and is called *cycle time*. Minimal value of $T(\pi)$ will be called *minimal cycle time* and will be denoted as $T^*(\pi)$. Our goal is to minimize following function:

$$T^*(\pi^*) = \min\{T^*(\pi) : \pi \in \Phi\}, \tag{1}$$

where Φ denotes a set of all feasible permutations. Moreover, following constraints are to be followed:

$$S_{i,\pi(j)} + p_{i,\pi(j)} \leq S_{i+1,\pi(j)}, \quad i = 1, \ldots, m-1, \quad j = 1, \ldots, n, \tag{2}$$

$$S_{i,\pi(j)} + p_{i,\pi(j)} \leq S_{i,\pi(j+1)}, \quad i = 1, \ldots, m, \quad j = 1, \ldots, n-1, \tag{3}$$

$$S_{i,\pi(n)} + p_{i,\pi(n)} \leq S_{i,\pi(1)} + T, \quad i = 1, \ldots, m, \tag{4}$$

$$S_{i+1,\pi(n)} \leq S_{i,\pi(1)} + T, \quad i = 1, \ldots, m-1. \tag{5}$$

Without the loss of generality, we can assume that start and completion times of the first detail on first machine are as follows: $S_{1,\pi(1)} = 0$ and $C_{1,\pi(1)} = p_{1,\pi(1)}$. Completion times of details on the machines are calculated using the following recursive equation:

$$C_{i,\pi(j)} = \max \{C_{i,\pi(j-1)} + s_{i,\pi(j),\pi(k)}, C_{i-1,\pi(j)} \\ + t_{i-1,\pi(j)}\} + p_{i,\pi(j)}, \tag{6}$$

where $i = 1, \ldots, m$, $j = 1, \ldots, n$ and $k = 1, \ldots, n$. The goal is to optimize the following objective function:

$$T(\pi) = \max_{i \in \mathcal{M}} \{C^x_{i,\pi(n)} - S^x_{i,\pi(1)}\}. \tag{7}$$

4   Identification of Fuzzy Data

We will now proceed to identify the uncertain data in our production line. Let us consider step B3 for some job j. The processing time of some operation in j was measured a number of times (11 in this case), creating a vector $\bar{p}_j$ with 11 elements as shown in Table 2. The estimated processing time for step B3 can be now modeled using fuzzy number $B^3 = (B^3_a, B^3_v, B^3_c)$ as follows:

$$b^3_a = \min(p_{1,j}, p_{2,j}, \ldots, p_{11,j}) = 2.32, \tag{8}$$

$$b^3_b = \frac{p_{1,j} + p_{2,j} + \cdots + p_{11,j}}{11} = 2.79, \tag{9}$$

$$b^3_c = \max(p_{1,j}, p_{2,j}, \ldots, p_{11,j}) = 3.44, \tag{10}$$

yielding $B^3 = (2.32, 2.79, 3.44)$.

Table 2. Results of measurement of $\bar{p}$ for step B3 (in seconds)

$p_{1,j}$	$p_{2,j}$	$p_{3,j}$	$p_{4,j}$	$p_{5,j}$	$p_{6,j}$	$p_{7,j}$	$p_{8,j}$	$p_{9,j}$	$p_{10,j}$	$p_{11,j}$
3.44	2.92	3.16	3.12	2.76	2.72	3.08	2.60	2.52	2.32	2.40

The above procedure can be applied to all steps in the production process and then be used to define all processing and transport times through fuzzy numbers. For example, transport time $t_{3,j}$ is the sum of times of steps C5, D1, D2. Thus, it can be represented as a fuzzy number computed as a sum of 3 fuzzy numbers *i.e.* $t_{3,j} = C^5 + D^1 + D^2$. The resulting fuzzy numbers are presented in Table 3. Transport times are identical for all jobs. Fuzzy number $p_{i,j}$ represents fuzzy processing time of job j on machine i. This time is dependent on the scaling parameter γ_j which is different for various jobs. For example, tasks processed on machine 1 can have processing time represented by fuzzy numbers like $(2.32, 2.79, 3.44)$ with $\gamma_j = 1$, $(4.64, 5.58, 6.88)$ with $\gamma_j = 2$ and $(1.16, 1.395, 1, 72)$ for $\gamma_j = 0.5$. Machine 4 has been divided into 3 general versions, depending on the chosen sorting destination. Parameters α_j and β_j represent the actual treatment time (as opposite to the treatment initialization with time of 1.40) for job j. We observe that the uncertainty in the considered system is significant, as the ratio $\frac{c}{a}$ can be as high as 2 or 3 for some of the presented fuzzy numbers. Let us also notice that fuzzy numbers $p_{2,j}$ and $p_{3,j}$ are also real numbers (as $a = b = c$).

Table 3. Fuzzy numbers obtained for the considered production system

Fuzzy number	a	b	c
C^5	3.44	3.44	3.45
D^1	17.52	27.20	47.52
D^2	0.69	1.51	2.92
$t_{0,j}$	13.76	17.61	24.44
$t_{1,j}$	4.64	6.75	10.65
$t_{2,j}$	3.44	3.44	3.45
$t_{3,j}$	21.65	32.15	53.89
$p_{1,j}$	$2.32 \cdot \gamma_j$	$2.79 \cdot \gamma_j$	$3.44 \cdot \gamma_j$
$p_{2,j}$	$1.40 + \alpha_j$	$1.40 + \alpha_j$	$1.40 + \alpha_j$
$p_{3,j}$	$1.40 + \beta_j$	$1.40 + \beta_j$	$1.40 + \beta_j$
$p_{4,j}^A$	1.40	2.71	5.04
$p_{4,j}^B$	2.44	4.03	7.32
$p_{4,j}^C$	3.32	4.36	7.84

5 Computer Experiment

We performed a series of computer tests to research the numerical properties of the proposed algorithm. For the purpose of the experiment a simulated annealing (SA) scheme was implemented and employed. The choice of such a method is dictated by previous numerouos successful uses of SA in job scheduling *e.g.* it has recently been proposed for a multi-objective flowshop scheduling problem in [9]. The algorithm used in this paper is based on SA employed by Pempera *et al.* [5] for solving bi-criteria flow shop scheduling problem. The algorithm was modified to consider single criterion goal function of minimizing the cycle time. The goal function is computed using the fuzzy operations on fuzzy numbers obtained as shown in the previous section. The core of the algorithm produces a final permutation (solution) which is then evaluated as shown in the next part of this section.

First, 3 deterministic algorithms were added for comparison, resulting in 4 algorithms in total. The fuzzy algorithm F is based on fuzzy instances, where processing, refitting and transport times in the form of fuzzy numbers *e.g.* $\{a, b, c\}$. This algorithm uses operations on fuzzy numbers. The deterministic algorithms work on real numbers, which are generated from the fuzzy instances. For algorithm D_{MIN} left value of the fuzzy number is used *i.e* fuzzy number $\{a, b, c\}$ yields real number a. Similarly, the real numbers generated for algorithms D_{MID} and D_{MAX} would be b and c respectively.

Fuzzy algorithm and the deterministic algorithm will be called FA and DA respectively. Each algorithm produces a final permutation of jobs π for a given instance. This permutation is then used to perform 100 simulations. During each simulation the actual processing and transport times are random, based on the previously measured properties of the system. This yields a collection of 100 cycle times from $T_1(\pi)$ to $T_{100}(\pi)$, which can be further transformed into statistic functions like minimum $T_{MIN}(\pi)$, maximum $T_{MAX}(\pi)$ or average $T_{AVG}(\pi)$. Thus, for a given instance a single run of one algorithm yields 3 numbers, meaning 12 numbers for 4 algorithms. Each algorithm was set to run for 10 000 iterations, but can terminate earlier if additional termination conditions are satisfied.

Instances were prepared in 10 size groups with each group having number of jobs n from 5 to 50. 5 different instances were generated for each size group, yielding 50 instances in total. Instance n_i means i-th instance of size n. For each instance each algorithm was run 10 times. The summarized results of 10 runs for instance 10_1 are shown in Table 4.

The table presents the most important data about the 10 runs: (1) the best run, (2) the worst run, (3) the average over all runs and (4) standard deviation over all runs. All data is presented in percents for easy comparison. Thus, value 100 indicates the best cycle time out of 4000 (10 runs × 100 simulations × 4 algorithms) and value of 200 indicates two times worse (higher) cycle time.

The best runs are similar for every algorithm (*e.g.* the T_{MIN} from best run is similar for all algorithms). This means that all algorithms will yield similar results if repeated enough number of times. However, the average runs are different and prove that the FA outperforms the remaining algorithms. T_{MAX} (*worst cycle time in 100 simulations*) for avarage run of the FA is better than T_{MIN} (*best cycle time in 100 simulations*) for avarage runs of any DA. This effect is even more visible for worst runs. Actually, T_{MAX} of worst run of the FA (value 197.8) is better than all bold T_{MIN} values for all DAs with the exception of one case (value 175.8).

The FA is also more stable for the same number of iterations. This can be observed from standard deviation also presented in Table 4. The result indicate deviation from roughly 1.5 to 15 % for the FA, while DAs have deviation ranging

Table 4. Summary of results for instance 10_1 (10 runs, all data in percents)

Algorithm	Cycle data	Best run	Average run	Worst run	Run deviation
F	T_{MIN}	100	105.1	107.9	2.31
	T_{MID}	118.9	121.5	124.6	1.41
	T_{MAX}	138.1	**165.3**	**197.8**	13.00
D_{MIN}	T_{MIN}	103.0	**251.9**	**450**	49.03
	T_{MID}	119.7	281.1	478.7	43.84
	T_{MAX}	139.4	319.7	515.7	40.57
D_{MID}	T_{MIN}	103.3	**208.7**	**448.5**	65.14
	T_{MID}	119.3	235.6	477	58.19
	T_{MAX}	137.7	279.1	518.6	49.82
D_{MAX}	T_{MIN}	100.6	**175.8**	**392.6**	53.85
	T_{MID}	118.2	202.9	416.4	47.02
	T_{MAX}	132.7	243.6	451.7	42.96

from 40 to 65 % (mostly centered around 45 %). Overall, the deviation for the FA is at least 3 times better than for other DAs (10 times better in many cases).

Let us also note that Table 4 presents typical results, as for most other instances the conclusions are similar. Now, we consider the overall performance of the FA for different instances (instance sizes). In Fig. 2a we present the performance of the FA compared with the DA that supplied the worst solution of all DAs. The best observed advantage of the FA is, depending on the instance size, 2 to 5.5 times that of the worst DA (2 to 5.5 times lower values of T_{MID} averaged over all runs of all instances of a given size). The worst observed advantage is 1.3 to 2 times that of the worst DA, while the average advantage is from 1.5 to 3 times the worst DA. The best advantage increases with instance size, while average and worst advantage remain roughly the same for all instance sizes.

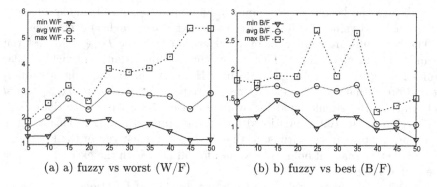

(a) a) fuzzy vs worst (W/F)   (b) b) fuzzy vs best (B/F)

Fig. 2. Performance of the fuzzy algorithm against deterministic algorithms, depending on instance size

Those results are interesting, but it would be more conclusive to compare the FA to the best of the DAs. However, our tests indicate that each DA can be the best, depending on specific instance (or even specific run). That means, we do not know *a priori* which DA to choose. Thus, we need to run all 3 DAs to determine the best of them. In the end, we compare the 3 DAs (run in sequence) with single FA. The results are shown in Fig. 2b.

The best advantage is from 1.4 to 2.7, the average advantage is from 1.1 to 1.7 and those values seem to decrease with the increase in instance size, at least for $n > 30$. The most interesting part is the worst advantage which ranges from 0.8 to 1.4. This would indicate that, while the FA is still better on the average, it can sometimes provide worse solutions than the 3 DAs working together. However, the values in the Figure are below 1.0 for only one instance group ($n = 50$).

Let us also notice that the FA takes only slightly longer to execute than a single DA. In result, the FA executes almost three times faster then 3 DAs working together. This assumes all algorithms complete iterations. However, additional halting conditions can stop the algorithms prematurely (*e.g.* no further improvements observed). This sometimes happen for the DAs, reducing their actual execution time, but such reduced runs are characterised by much worse cycle times

found. This is the source of the high standard deviation observed in the DAs that was mentioned early.

In order to further research the performance of the FA we divided the instances into four groups, based on the results provided by the FA. The groups are as follows:

1. Instances for which the FA was similar to the chosen algorithm with the significance of 2.5 % (cycle time between 97.5 % and 102.5 % that of the other algorithm).
2. Instances for which the FA was worse (cycle time greater than 102.5 % that of the other algorithm).
3. Instances for which the FA was better (cycle time less than 97.5 %, but higher than 80 % that of the other algorithm).
4. Instances for which the FA was significantly better (cycle time less than 80 % that of the other algorithm).

With the above categories defined we can now describe the performance of the FA as shown in Table 5. The second column compares the algorithm to the worst of the 3 DAs. In result, the FA is always better and almost always much better (except one instance). The third column compares the FA with the best DA, showing that the FA is better almost 80 % of the time and is worse only for 2 instances (4 %). For 9 instances the FA provided results approximately equal to that of the best DA.

Table 5. Performance of the fuzzy algorithm

Case	1 (similar)	2 (worse)	3 (better)	4 (much better)
Vs. worst	0 (0 %)	0 (0 %)	1 (2 %)	49 (98 %)
Vs. best	9 (18 %)	2 (4 %)	5 (10 %)	34 (68 %)

Additionally, statistical hypothesis tests, using t-test of the Octave software were performed with significance level $\alpha = 0.05$. Let B_i denote T_{MID} of the best DA divided by T_{MID} of the FA for run $i \in [1, 500]$ (there were 500 runs in total). In result, $B_i = 1.5$ means the FA provided 50 % better average cycle time for that run. Similarly, let W_i denote the same, but with the worst DA instead of the best one. Now we treat B_i (W_i) as samples from B (W) distribution with the unknown mean μ_B (μ_W). We have formulated following 4 hypotheses: $\mu_W = 2.76$, $\mu_W > 2.65$, $\mu_B = 1.21$ and $\mu_B > 1.17$. The hypotheses were accepted using the t-test and the chosen significance level (*i.e.* no statistical rationale for rejecting any of those hypotheses).

An alternative FA using trapezoidal fuzzy numbers was also developed for comparison. Research indicated the performance of both FAs was similar with minor differences: the trapezoidal FA tended to provide better values of T_{MIN}, but worse values of T_{MAX}. The trapezoidal FA wasn't able to achieve superiority in overall solution quality or execution time compared to the triangular FA.

6 Conclusions

In this paper with presented a fuzzy algorithm for a certain cyclic flow shop system with fuzzy data. The algorithm was tested using instances with various number of jobs. The results indicate that the proposed algorithm significantly outperforms the deterministic algorithms 70 % of the time and is worse only 4 % of the time, while taking similar time to execute. Moreover, the fuzzy algorithm provides solutions much more reliably, proved by several times lower standard deviation of obtained results.

References

1. Bożejko, W., Pempera, J., Wodecki, M.: Parallel simulated annealing algorithm for cyclic flexible job shop scheduling problem. In: Rutkowski, L., Korytkowski, M., Scherer, R., Tadeusiewicz, R., Zadeh, L.A., Zurada, J.M. (eds.) Artificial Intelligence and Soft Computing. LNCS, vol. 9120, pp. 603–612. Springer, Heidelberg (2015)
2. Bożejko, W., Uchroński, M., Wodecki, M.: Block approach to the cyclic flow shop scheduling. Comput. Ind. Eng. **81**, 158–166 (2015)
3. Ishibuchi, H., Yamamoto, N., Murata, T., Tanaka, H.: Genetic algorithms and neighborhood search algorithms for fuzzy flowshop scheduling problems. Fuzzy Sets Syst. **67**(1), 81–100 (1994)
4. Kuroda, M., Wang, Z.: Fuzzy job shop scheduling. Int. J. Prod. Econ. **44**(1–2), 45–51 (1996)
5. Pempera, J., Smutnicki, C., Żelazny, D.: Optimizing Bicriteria flow shop scheduling problem by simulated annealing algorithm. Procedia Comput. Sci. **18**, 936–945 (2013)
6. Peng, J., Liu, B.: Parallel machine scheduling models with fuzzy processing times. Inf. Sci. **166**(1–4), 49–66 (2004)
7. Sakawa, M., Kubota, R.: Fuzzy programming for multiobjective job shop scheduling with fuzzy processing time and fuzzy duedate through genetic algorithms. Eur. J. Oper. Res. **120**(2), 393–407 (2000)
8. Smutnicki, C.: An efficient algorithm for finding minimal cycle time in cyclic job shop scheduling problem. In: 16th International Conference on Intelligent Engineering Systems, pp. 381–386 (2012)
9. Smutnicki, C., Pempera, J., Rudy, J., Żelazny, D.: A new approach for multi-criteria scheduling. Comput. Ind. Eng. **90**, 212–220 (2015)
10. Topaloglu, S., Selim, H.: Nurse scheduling using fuzzy modeling approach. Fuzzy Sets Syst. **161**(11), 1543–1563 (2010)
11. Türkşen, I.B., Fazel Zarandi, M.H.: Production planning and scheduling: fuzzy and crisp approaches. Practical Applications of Fuzzy Technologies. The Handbooks of Fuzzy Sets Series, vol. 6, pp. 479–529. Springer, New York (1999)

Identification of a Multi-criteria Model of Location Assessment for Renewable Energy Sources

Wojciech Sałabun$^{(\boxtimes)}$, Jarosław Wątróbski, and Andrzej Piegat

Faculty of Computer Science and Information Technology,
West Pomeranian University of Technology, Szczecin, Poland
{wsalabun,jwatrobski,apiegat}@wi.zut.edu.pl

Abstract. The paper presents an identification method of a multi-criteria model of location assessment for renewable energy sources (RES). Sustainable energy systems have a growing importance for the long-term national strategic planning, which requires multi-facet decision making. The multi-criteria decision-analysis (MCDA) methods are widely used in this field. However, the used methods usually identify discrete values of preferences for selected alternatives. Most of the calculation must be repeated for each set of alternatives. This study is intended to identify the multi-criteria model in the space of the problem, not only for a few selected alternatives. The model should be independent of the considered alternatives and related strictly to the domain of criteria. As the result, a model identified once can be used repeatedly. For this purpose, the COMET method is used in the identification process. It has provided the fuzzy model, which can be used repeatedly for different sets of alternatives. The model is verified by using the set of possible offshore wind farm localization.

Keywords: Multi-criteria decision-making · COMET method · Fuzzy logic · Renewable energy sources

1 Introduction

The renewable energy sources (RES) are the main way to make the national economies more independent from conventional energy sources. However, it requires decision-making in situation of contradictory criteria, i.e., economical, technological, environmental and social [1,2,12,22]. The typical problems include tasks of selecting: technologies, projects, management options, etc. The main problem is selecting the best possible solution for location choosing of a new infrastructure of the renewable energy sources.

The paper is an extension of previous work [23], where the AHP and Promethee methods were used to assess a set of decision-making alternatives. The considered problem presents an assessment of an offshore wind farm location, where a big number of component criteria creates an area for the use the

© Springer International Publishing Switzerland 2016
L. Rutkowski et al. (Eds.): ICAISC 2016, Part I, LNAI 9692, pp. 321–332, 2016.
DOI: 10.1007/978-3-319-39378-0_28

multi-criteria decision-analysis (MCDA) methods [25–27]. However, specificity of the considered problem allows application more than one MCDA method [10,24]. The purpose of this paper is identifying a fuzzy model, which could be used repeatedly for different sets of alternatives. In this way, if the set of alternatives is changed, then the model will further be used to make the assessment. The MCDA method has not to be repeated because instead we can use the identified model. It will be identified with use of the COMET method, and will be verified on the basis of the alternatives set used in [23].

The rest of the paper is organized as follows: First, we give an outline of a literature review for MCDM methods in the field of the renewable energy sources. Then, we describe the COMET method as a tool for identification of the fuzzy model. Then, the location of an offshore wind farm is analyzed for ten criteria to identify the fuzzy model in full space of the problem. Finally, we discuss results and their importance.

2   Literature Review

This section presents selected research papers related to multi-criteria decision-analysis support systems in the RES domain. They are presented in terms of

Table 1. Research related to the use of MCDA methods in problems of RES.

Application area	Method	Criteria number	Ref.
Selecting of renewable energy power plant technologies	Fuzzy DEA	7	[3]
Selecting of suitable electricity generation alternatives	Promethee	5	[21]
Selecting of renewable energy power plant technologies	ELECTRE III	8	[6]
Renewable energy sources project selection	Electre	8	[9]
Deriving wind farm land suitability index and classification	AHP	10	[2]
Deriving wind farm land suitability index and classification	Fuzzy AHP	9	[16]
Assessmnet of land management options	AHP	12	[11]
Selecting site location	Naide	9 or 10	[4,5]
Assessment of the exploitation of a geothermal resource	Promethee II	5	[8]
Evaluation and ranking of alternative energy exploitation schemes of a low temperature geothermal field	Promethee	4	[7]

the method and subject of the research problem in Table 1. It shows a large variety of RES problems that are solved by using MCDA methods, where the most popular one is the AHP and Promethee methods [2,7,8,11,16,21]. The all authors have obtained discrete values of assessed alternatives. Additionally, the real problem of selecting an appropriate method can be observed in [24].

3 The COMET Method

The COMET method is a very effective approach, which is completely fresh in the field of renewable energy sources. The basic concept of the COMET method was proposed by prof. Piegat [14,15]. In previous works, the accuracy of COMET method was verified [13]. The proposed approach is more efficient than MCDM methods (e.g. AHP or TOPSIS methods). The formal notation of the COMET method should be shortly recalled in the five following steps [17–20].

Step 1. Define the space of the problem – the problem expert determines the dimensionality of the problem by selecting the number r of criteria, $C_1, C_2, ..., C_r$. Then, the set of fuzzy numbers for each criterion C_i is selected (1):

$$
\begin{aligned}
C_1 &= \{\tilde{C}_{11}, \tilde{C}_{12}, ..., \tilde{C}_{1c_1}\} \\
C_2 &= \{\tilde{C}_{21}, \tilde{C}_{22}, ..., \tilde{C}_{2c_1}\} \\
&\quad\quad\text{..........................} \\
C_r &= \{\tilde{C}_{r1}, \tilde{C}_{r2}, ..., \tilde{C}_{rc_r}\}
\end{aligned}
\tag{1}
$$

where $c_1, c_2, ..., c_r$ are numbers of the fuzzy numbers for all criteria.

Step 2. Generate characteristic objects – The characteristic objects (CO) are obtained by using the Cartesian Product of fuzzy numbers cores for each criteria as follows (2):

$$
CO = C(C_1) \times C(C_2) \times ... \times C(C_r)
\tag{2}
$$

As the result, the ordered set of all CO is obtained (3):

$$
\begin{aligned}
CO_1 &= \{C(\tilde{C}_{11}), C(\tilde{C}_{21}), ..., C(\tilde{C}_{r1})\} \\
CO_2 &= \{C(\tilde{C}_{11}), C(\tilde{C}_{21}), ..., C(\tilde{C}_{r2})\} \\
&\quad\quad\text{..................................} \\
CO_t &= \{C(\tilde{C}_{1c_1}), C(\tilde{C}_{2c_2}), ..., C(\tilde{C}_{rc_r})\}
\end{aligned}
\tag{3}
$$

where t is the number of CO (4):

$$
t = \prod_{i=1}^{r} c_i
\tag{4}
$$

Step 3. Rank the characteristic objects – the expert determines the Matrix of Expert Judgment (MEJ). It is a result of pairwise comparison of the COs by the problem expert. The MEJ structure is presented (5):

$$MEJ = \begin{pmatrix} \alpha_{11} & \alpha_{12} & \ldots & \alpha_{1t} \\ \alpha_{21} & \alpha_{22} & \ldots & \alpha_{2t} \\ \ldots & \ldots & \ldots & \ldots \\ \alpha_{t1} & \alpha_{t2} & \ldots & \alpha_{tt} \end{pmatrix} \tag{5}$$

where α_{ij} is the result of comparing CO_i and CO_j by the expert. The more preferred characteristic object gets one point and the second object gets zero points. If the preferences are balanced, both objects get a half point. It depends solely on the knowledge of the expert and can be presented as (6):

$$\alpha_{ij} = \begin{cases} 0.0, & f_{exp}(CO_i) < f_{exp}(CO_j) \\ 0.5, & f_{exp}(CO_i) = f_{exp}(CO_j) \\ 1.0, & f_{exp}(CO_i) > f_{exp}(CO_j) \end{cases} \tag{6}$$

where f_{exp} is the expert mental judgment function.

Afterwards, the vertical vector of the Summed Judgments (SJ) is obtained as follows (7):

$$SJ_i = \sum_{j=1}^{t} \alpha_{ij} \tag{7}$$

The last step assigns to each characteristic object an approximate value of preference. As a result, the vertical vector P is obtained, where $i - th$ row contains the approximate value of preference for CO_i. The principle of an insufficient reason and SJ vector are used to this aim. The best CO gets one point, and the worst gets zero points.

Step 4. The rule base – each characteristic object and value of preference is converted to a fuzzy rule as follows (8):

$$IF \ C(\tilde{C}_{1i}) \ AND \ C(\tilde{C}_{2i}) \ AND \ldots THEN \ P_i \tag{8}$$

In this way, the complete fuzzy rule base is obtained.

Step 5. Inference and final ranking – each alternative is presented as a set of crisp numbers (e.g., $A_i = \{a_{1i}, a_{2i}, ..., a_{ri}\}$). This set corresponds to criteria $C_1, C_2, ..., C_r$. Mamdani's fuzzy inference method is used to compute preference of $i - th$ alternative. The obtained results form the final ranking.

4   Use of the COMET Method in Choosing the Location of an Offshore Wind Farm

At the beginning, all criteria should be defined. We use the same criteria as in [23]. Hence, we have ten criteria, which can be divided in three main groups: spatial factors, economic factors, environmental and social risk. Spatial factors include:

- C_1 - average depth of the basin (in meters) determined for each location on the basis of the available bathymetry data, $C_1 \in [20, 70]$.

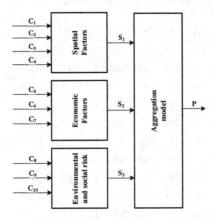

Fig. 1. Detailed hierarchy of the identified model.

Table 2. Geographical coordinates of the considered alternatives

A_i	Approx. Longitude	Approx. Latitude
A_1	$17°15'E$	$55°00'N$
A_2	$17°00'E$	$55°05'N$
A_3	$17°15'E$	$55°35'N$
A_4	$16°55'E$	$55°25'N$
A_5	$16°15'E$	$55°00'N$
A_6	$15°15'E$	$54°30'N$

Table 3. Values of criteria for the alternatives set

C_i	Criterion name	A_1	A_2	A_3	A_4	A_5	A_6
C_1	Average depth of the basin	40	31	29	62	51	35
C_2	Distance from the shoreline	34.7	45.6	86.3	77.1	63.1	44.9
C_3	Distance from the NEN connection	31	45	82	79	61	41
C_4	Type of seabed	vg	g	vg/g	mg	vg	g
C_5	The investment cost	9040	9023	11231	10602	7870	7324
C_6	Payback time	9	10	11	15	14	12
C_7	Annual energy production	2803	2432	3132	3415	2132	1897
C_8	Conflict with fisheries	8	5	9	4	5	6
C_9	Threat to navigation safety	2	1	5	1	5	2
C_{10}	Influence on the protected areas	2	8	1	1	4	1

Table 4. The results of COMET method for spatial factors

CO_i	C_1	C_2	C_3	C_4	SJ	S_1
CO_1	20	30	30	0	11.5	11/15
CO_2	20	30	30	1	15.5	15/15
CO_3	20	30	90	0	6.5	6/15
CO_4	20	30	90	1	13.5	13/15
CO_5	20	90	30	0	7.5	7/15
CO_6	20	90	30	1	14.5	14/15
CO_7	20	90	90	0	3.5	3/15
CO_8	20	90	90	1	10.5	10/15
CO_9	70	30	30	0	5.5	5/15
CO_{10}	70	30	30	1	12.5	12/15
CO_{11}	70	30	90	0	1.5	1/15
CO_{12}	70	30	90	1	8.5	8/15
CO_{13}	70	90	30	0	2.5	2/15
CO_{14}	70	90	30	1	9.5	9/15
CO_{15}	70	90	90	0	0.5	0/15
CO_{16}	70	90	90	1	4.5	4/15

- C_2 - distance from the shoreline (in kilometers) measured in a straight line to the coast. The increase of the distance from the edge causes a significant increase of the cost of building the farm (transport equipment, longer building time, and etc.), $C_2 \in [30, 90]$.
- C_3 - distance from the NEN connection (in kilometers) measured as distance of each farm to the nearest NEN port, $C_3 \in [30, 90]$.
- C_4 - type of seabed is a quality rating of the seabed for marine construction: rocky bottom - the best, grainy - very good, silty-sandy bottom - good, muddy - moderately good, $C_4 \in [0, 1]$.

Economic factors include:

- C_5 - the investment cost (in million PLN). It is estimated assuming a 7 MW turbine power, $C_5 \in [7000, 12000]$.
- C_6 - payback time (in years) is the calculation of payback periods making possible to obtain annual profit. This value is determined using the unit price of electricity, unit price of certificates of origin, and operating costs. They are based on the calculated profit for the year, as well as on taking into account the specified operating baskets payback time, $C_6 \in [5, 15]$.
- C_7 - annual energy production based on the annual average wind speed and wind turbine performance, $C_7 \in [1500, 4000]$.

Finally, environmental and social risk include ($C_8 - C_{10} \in [0, 10]$) :

Table 5. The results of COMET method for economic factors

CO_i	C_5	C_6	C_7	SJ	S_2
CO_1	7000	5	1500	14.5	14/15
CO_2	7000	5	2750	22.5	22/15
CO_3	7000	5	4000	26.5	26/15
CO_4	7000	10	1500	10.5	10/15
CO_5	7000	10	2750	19.5	19/15
CO_6	7000	10	4000	25.5	25/15
CO_7	7000	15	1500	6.5	6/15
CO_8	7000	15	2750	15.5	15/15
CO_9	7000	15	4000	23.5	23/15
CO_{10}	9500	5	1500	8.5	8/15
CO_{11}	9500	5	2750	17.5	17/15
CO_{12}	9500	5	4000	24.5	24/15
CO_{13}	9500	10	1500	5.5	5/15
CO_{14}	9500	10	2750	13.5	13/15
CO_{15}	9500	10	4000	21.5	21/15
CO_{16}	9500	15	1500	2.5	2/15
CO_{17}	9500	15	2750	9.5	9/15
CO_{18}	9500	15	4000	18.5	18/15
CO_{19}	12000	5	1500	3.5	3/15
CO_{20}	12000	5	2750	11.5	11/15
CO_{21}	12000	5	4000	20.5	20/15
CO_{22}	12000	10	1500	1.5	1/15
CO_{23}	12000	10	2750	7.5	7/15
CO_{24}	12000	10	4000	16.5	16/15
CO_{25}	12000	15	1500	0.5	0/15
CO_{26}	12000	15	2750	4.5	4/15
CO_{27}	12000	15	4000	12.5	12/15

- C_8 - conflict with fisheries as the conflict of interests with the marine fisheries sector is estimated at a 10 points scale with 10 as the biggest conflict.
- C_9 - threat to navigation safety based on the traffic map of water, determining how much influence it can have on a location for sailing in terms of possible dangers of ship collisions with wind farms.
- C_{10} - Influence on the protected areas is the proximity of Natura 2000 protected areas of the potential offshore location. Determines the possible impact of investment on the protected are a on ten-element scale, assuming that 0 means the least impact on protected areas, while 10 is the biggest one.

Table 6. The results of COMET method for enviromental and social risk

CO_i	C_8	C_9	C_{10}	SJ	S_3
CO_1	0	0	0	26.5	26/26
CO_2	0	0	5	25.5	25/26
CO_3	0	0	10	22.5	22/26
CO_4	0	5	0	23.5	23/26
CO_5	0	5	5	19.5	19/26
CO_6	0	5	10	14.5	14/26
CO_7	0	10	0	15.5	15/26
CO_8	0	10	5	10.5	10/26
CO_9	0	10	10	6.5	6/26
CO_{10}	5	0	0	24.5	24/26
CO_{11}	5	0	5	21.5	21/26
CO_{12}	5	0	10	17.5	17/26
CO_{13}	5	5	0	18.5	18/26
CO_{14}	5	5	5	13.5	13/26
CO_{26}	5	5	10	8.5	8/26
CO_{16}	5	10	0	9.5	9/26
CO_{17}	5	10	5	5.5	5/26
CO_{18}	5	10	10	2.5	2/26
CO_{19}	10	0	0	20.5	20/26
CO_{20}	10	0	5	16.5	16/26
CO_{21}	10	0	10	11.5	11/26
CO_{22}	10	5	0	12.5	12/26
CO_{23}	10	5	5	7.5	7/26
CO_{24}	10	5	10	3.5	3/26
CO_{25}	10	10	0	4.5	4/26
CO_{26}	10	10	5	1.5	1/26
CO_{27}	10	10	10	0.5	0/26

For the purpose of the reduction of the rules base and of the comparisons number the modular approach will be used. Its structure is presented on Fig. 1.

The set of six assessed alternatives is taken from [23]. Table 2 contains the approximate ghographical coordinates of the concidered alternatives, i.e. $A_1 - A_6$. The detailed values of criteria for each alternative is presented in Table 3.

The first module concerns spatial facors. The criteria $C_1 - C_4$ are evaluated by two fuzzy numbers for each criterion (9):

$$\mu_{C_{11}} = \frac{70-x}{50}, \ \mu_{C_{12}} = \frac{x-20}{50}, \mu_{C_{41}} = 1 - x, \mu_{C_{42}} = x,$$
$$\mu_{C_{21}} = \mu_{C_{31}} = \frac{90-x}{60}, \mu_{C_{22}} = \mu_{C_{32}} = \frac{x-30}{60} \tag{9}$$

Table 7. The results of COMET method for aggregation module

CO_i	S_1	S_2	S_3	SJ	P
CO_1	0	0	0	0.5	0/26
CO_2	0	0	0.5	3.5	3/26
CO_3	0	0	1	6.5	6/26
CO_4	0	0.5	0	9.5	9/26
CO_5	0	0.5	0.5	12.5	12/26
CO_6	0	0.5	1	15.5	15/26
CO_7	0	1	0	18.5	18/26
CO_8	0	1	0.5	21.5	21/26
CO_9	0	1	1	24.5	24/26
CO_{10}	0.5	0	0	7.5	7/26
CO_{11}	0.5	0	0.5	10.5	10/26
CO_{12}	0.5	0	1	5.5	5/26
CO_{13}	0.5	0.5	0	1.5	1/26
CO_{14}	0.5	0.5	0.5	13.5	13/26
CO_{15}	0.5	0.5	1	17.5	17/26
CO_{16}	0.5	1	0	19.5	19/26
CO_{17}	0.5	1	0.5	22.5	22/26
CO_{18}	0.5	1	1	25.5	25/26
CO_{19}	1	0	0	2.5	2/26
CO_{20}	1	0	0.5	4.5	4/26
CO_{21}	1	0	1	8.5	8/26
CO_{22}	1	0.5	0	11.5	11/26
CO_{23}	1	0.5	0.5	14.5	14/26
CO_{24}	1	0.5	1	16.5	16/26
CO_{25}	1	1	0	20.5	20/26
CO_{26}	1	1	0.5	23.5	23/26
CO_{27}	1	1	1	26.5	26/26

Next, we generate the characteristic objects and create the MEJ matrix. The matrix is transformed to vector SJ and subsequently to preference vector S_1. In this way, we identify the first module. There are 16 rules, which are related to characteristic objects. The summary of these steps is presented in Table 4.

The second module concerns economic factors. The criteria $C_5 - C_7$ include three triangular fuzzy numbers for each criterion. The cores of these numbers are as follows: $C(C_{51}) = 7000, C(C_{52}) = 9500, C(C_{53}) = 1200, C(C_{61}) = 5, C(C_{62}) = 10, C(C_{63}) = 15, C(C_{71}) = 1500, C(C_{72}) = 2750, C(C_{73}) = 4000.$

Table 8. The results of preferences from three modules for the considered alternatives

A_i	A_1	A_2	A_3	A_4	A_5	A_6
S_1	0.8477	0.7569	0.5349	0.2630	0.5867	0.7506
S_2	0.5839	0.4639	0.4160	0.4365	0.3682	0.4079
S_3	0.6333	0.6556	0.4556	0.8373	0.5222	0.7222
P	0.6122	0.5341	0.4562	0.5291	0.4670	0.5134

There are 27 rules, which are related with generated characteristic objects. The summary of these steps is presented in Table 5.

The third module concerns environmental and social risk. The criteria $C_8 - C_10$ include three triangular fuzzy numbers for each criterion. The cores of these numbers are as follows: $C(C_{81}) = 0, C(C_{82}) = 5, C(C_{83}) = 10, C(C_{91}) = 0, C(C_{92}) = 5, C(C_{93}) = 10, C(C_{101}) = 0, C(C_{102}) = 5, C(C_{103}) = 10$. There are 27 rules, which are related to generated characteristic objects. The summary of these steps is presented in Table 6.

The last module is aggregation module of the previous three modules. The input signals $S_1 - S_3$ are evaluated with three traingular fuzzy numbers for each criterion. Cores of these numbers are as follows: $C(S_{11}) = 0, C(S_{12}) = 0.5, C(S_{13}) = 1, C(S_{21}) = 0, C(S_{22}) = 0.5, C(S_{23}) = 1, C(S_{31}) = 0, C(S_{32}) = 0.5, C(S_{33}) = 1$. There are 27 rules, which are related to generated characteristic objects. The summary of these steps is presented in Table 7.

Table 8. shows complete results for the considered set of alternatives. The best alternative in respect of spatial factors is the alternative A_1 (0.8477), and the worst is the alternative A_4 (0.2630). The best alternative in respect of economical factors is the alternative A_1 (0.5839), and the worst is the alternative A_5 (0.3682). The best alternative in respect to environmental and social risk is the alternative A_4 (0.8373), and the worst is the alternative A_3 (0.4556).

The final assessment P is fully consistent with the results published in [23]. It means that we got the same ranking as in the previous research for the selected set of alternatives. However, the obtained model can be used repeatably for each set of alternatives from the domain of the space of the problem.

5   Conclusions

The COMET method is a useful tool from the MCDA domain, which can be applied in the RES field. The identified model of location assessment of an offshore wind farm can be used repeatable and it could be applied in the full space of the problem. Any number of alternatives can be evaluated because the values of the alternatives attributes do not affect the parameters of the model. This is the main reason why the COMET method is free of rank reversal phenomenon (change in the rank ordering when the set of alternatives has been changed).

Moreover, fuzzy modeling allows for use of varying levels of significance for each criterion. At the same time, it allows for use of relatively easy computation mechanism. The application of modular approach allows for making a partial analysis of preferences according to the main groups of criteria.

The identified model has been verified in respect of the reference set of alternatives. For this set, the final ranking is fully consistent with reference data. Future studies should be focused on the possibility of determining local significance criteria for different alternatives to enable a more complex analysis.

References

1. Afgan, N.H., Carvalho, M.G.: Multi-criteria assessment of new and renewable energy power plants. Energy **27**(8), 739–755 (2002)
2. Al-Yahyai, S., Charabi, Y., Gastli, A., Al-Badi, A.: Wind farm land suitability indexing using multi-criteria analysis. Renewable Energy **44**, 80–87 (2012)
3. Baysal, M.E., Sarucan, A., Kahraman, C., Engin, O.: The selection of renewable energy power plant technology using fuzzy data envelopment analysis. In: Proceedings of the 2011 World Congress on Engineering, pp. 1140–1143 (2011)
4. Cavallaro, F., Ciraolo, L.: A multicriteria approach to evaluate wind energy plants on an Italian island. Energy Policy **33**(2), 235–244 (2005)
5. Forte, F., Nijkamp, P., Torrieri, F.: Shared choices on local sustainabiiity projects: a decision support framework. Res. Memorandum **2001**, 24 (2001)
6. Georgopoulou, E., Lalas, D., Papagiannakis, L.: A multicriteria decision aid approach for energy planning problems: the case of renewable energy option. Eur. J. Oper. Res. **103**(1), 38–54 (1997)
7. Goumas, M., Lygerou, V.: An extension of the PROMETHEE method for decision making in fuzzy environment: ranking of alternative energy exploitation projects. Eur. J. Oper. Res. **123**(3), 606–613 (2000)
8. Haralambopoulos, D.A., Polatidis, H.: Renewable energy projects: structuring a multi-criteria group decision-making framework. Renewable Energy **28**(6), 961–973 (2003)
9. Haurant, P., Oberti, P., Muselli, M.: Multicriteria selection aiding related to photovoltaic plants on farming fields on Corsica Island: a real case study using the ELECTRE outranking framework. Energy Policy **39**(2), 676–688 (2011)
10. Jankowski, J.: Integration of collective knowledge in fuzzy models supporting web design process. In: Jędrzejowicz, P., Nguyen, N.T., Hoang, K. (eds.) ICCCI 2011, Part II. LNCS, vol. 6923, pp. 395–404. Springer, Heidelberg (2011)
11. Nigim, K., Munier, N., Green, J.: Pre-feasibility MCDM tools to aid communities in prioritizing local viable renewable energy sources. Renewable Energy **29**(11), 1775–1791 (2004)
12. Panwar, N.L., Kaushik, S.C., Kothari, S.: Role of renewable energy sources in environmental protection: a review. Renew. Sustain. Energy Rev. **15**(3), 1513–1524 (2011)
13. Piegat, A., Sałabun, W.: Comparative analysis of MCDM methods for assessing the severity of Chronic Liver Disease. In: Rutkowski, L., Korytkowski, M., Scherer, R., Tadeusiewicz, R., Zadeh, L.A., Zurada, J.M. (eds.) Artificial Intelligence and Soft Computing. LNCS, vol. 9119, pp. 228–238. Springer, Heidelberg (2015)

14. Piegat, A., Sałabun, W.: Identification of a multicriteria decision-making model using the characteristic objects method. Appl. Comput. Intell. Soft Comput. **2014**, 14 (2014)
15. Piegat, A., Sałabun, W.: Nonlinearity of human multi-criteria in decision-making. J. Theor. Appl. Comput. Sci. **6**(3), 36–49 (2012)
16. Sagbas, A., Mazmanoglu, A.: Use of multi-criteria decision analysis to assess alternative wind power plants. J. Eng. Res. **2**(1), 147–161 (2014)
17. Sałabun, W.: Application of the fuzzy multi-criteria decision-making method to identify nonlinear decision models. Int. J. Comput. Appl. **89**(15), 1–6 (2014)
18. Sałabun, W.: Reduction in the number of comparisons required to create matrix of expert judgment in the comet method. Manage. Prod. Eng. Rev. **5**(3), 62–69 (2014)
19. Sałabun, W.: The characteristic objects method: a new distance based approach to multicriteria decisionmaking problems. J. Multi-Criteria Decis. Anal. **22**(1–2), 37–50 (2015)
20. Sałabun, W.: The use of fuzzy logic to evaluate the nonlinearity of human multi-criteria used in decision making. Przeglad Elektrotechniczny (Electr. Rev.) **88**(10b), 235–238 (2012)
21. Topcu, Y.I., Ulengin, F.: Energy for the future: an integrated decision aid for the case of Turkey. Energy **29**(1), 137–154 (2004)
22. Twidell, J., Weir, T.: Renewable Energy Resources. Routledge, London (2015)
23. Wątróbski, J., Ziemba, P., Wolski, W.: Methodological aspects of Decision Support System for the location of renewable energy sources. In: Proceedings of the Federated Conference on Computer Science and Information Systems. Annals of Computer Science and Information Systems, vol. 5, pp. 1451–1459 (2015)
24. Wątróbski, J., Jankowski, J., Piotrowski, Z.: The selection of multicriteria method based on unstructured decision problem description. In: Hwang, D., Jung, J.J., Nguyen, N.-T. (eds.) ICCCI 2014. LNCS(LNAI), vol. 8733, pp. 454–465. Springer, Heidelberg (2014)
25. Ziemba, P., Piwowarski, M., Jankowski, J., Wątróbski, J.: Method of criteria selection and weights calculation in the process of web projects evaluation. In: Hwang, D., Jung, J.J., Nguyen, N.-T. (eds.) ICCCI 2014. LNCS, vol. 8733, pp. 684–693. Springer, Heidelberg (2014)
26. Wątróbski, J., Jankowski, J.: Knowledge management in MCDA domain. In: Proceedings of the Federated Conference on Computer Science and Information Systems. Annals of Computer Science and Information Systems, vol. 5, pp. 1445–1450 (2015)
27. Wątróbski, J., Jankowski, J.: Guideline for MCDA method selection in production management area. In: Rewski, P., Novikov, D., Bakhtadze, N., Zaikin, O. (eds.) New Frontiers in Information and Production Systems Modelling and Analysis. Intelligent Systems Reference Library, vol. 98, pp. 119–138. Springer, Heidelberg (2016)

Integration of Multiple Graph Datasets and Their Linguistic Summaries: An Application to Linked Data

Lukasz Strobin[✉] and Adam Niewiadomski

Institute of Information Technology, Lodz University of Technology,
ul. Wólczańska 215, 90-924 Lodz, Poland
800337@edu.p.lodz.pl, adam.niewiadomski@p.lodz.pl

Abstract. This paper presents a novel method of generating and evaluating linguistic summaries of content stored in distributed graph datasets, like LinkedData. Linguistic summarization is a well known data mining technique, aimed to discover patterns in data and present them in natural language. So far, this method has been researched only for relational databases. In our recent paper we have presented how to adapt this method for graph datasets. We have solved the problems of subject definition (further extended in this paper), retrieval of the attributes for summarization, generalization of summarizers and qualifiers. In this paper we extend that research by adapting proposed method to distributed interlinked graph datasets, which results in obtaining new summaries, and therefore new knowledge. We discuss how to follow different types of equivalence links that may exists between graph datasets. In order to measure characteristics specific for summaries of distributed graph data we propose new truth values (degree of subject appropriateness, degree of summarizer order and degree of linkage), and adapt existing ones (degree of covering). We run several experiments on Linked Data and discuss the results.

1 Introduction

In recent years a significant increase in popularity of graph databases has been observed. This approach to data storage significantly differs from relational databases - there is no rigid schema, data may easily be heterogeneous (information concerning different subjects may be 'tangled' together) and distributed among several 'endpoints' [1]. These characteristics facilitated emerging of Semantic Web, which essentially is a global, distributed and interconnected graph database, whose endpoints are freely available over the Internet [2].

This paper presents a novel method of creating linguistic summaries of such distributed graph datasets, which has not been attempted before. Linguistic summaries, defined by Yager, Kacprzyk and Zadrozny [3,4], are intended for relational databases only. These algorithms provide means of discovering general knowledge and complex patterns in data and presenting it in human-readable

© Springer International Publishing Switzerland 2016
L. Rutkowski et al. (Eds.): ICAISC 2016, Part I, LNAI 9692, pp. 333–343, 2016.
DOI: 10.1007/978-3-319-39378-0_29

quasi-natural sentences. There have been several extensions to this method, for instance to handle time series [5]. Basics are given in Sect. 2.

Our research lies within areas of Semantic Web mining (with subfields like content, structure and usage mining [6,7], see survey on this topic [8]) and graph data mining [9], and more precisely - graph summarization. Most often graph summarization is a problem of extracting frequent patterns (subgraphs) from a large graph [10–12]. A different research area is presented in [13], where elements of fuzzy set theory are used to express fuzzy queries for graph databases (precisely - extending Cypher query language for Noe4j).

Research presented here is a continuation of our previous paper [14], where we have adapted the method of linguistic summaries for graph data scenario, but only considering a single data source. Similar work, that is on linguistic summaries of graph databases, is presented in [15], which was published shortly after our paper. In [15] new concepts, named 'Structure Summaries' and 'DataStructure Summaries' are introduced, which are capturing relations between two types of vertices. Despite new nomenclature these constructs are logically equivalent to 1st and 2nd form of summary (see (1) and (2)), and therefore to our approach, which is based on data extraction from graph to pseudo-relational model.

Most important elements our previous paper are explained in Sect. 2. In Sect. 3 we show how to create linguistic summaries of a distributed graph databases, where graph vertices are interlinked between different datasets. Afterwards, we show that navigating deeper in the graph, that is retrieve graph vertices separated by more than one edge from the subject, results in obtaining new summaries. In Sect. 4 we analyze the problem of truth values (quality measures). We adapt measures 'degree of imprecision' (T_2) and 'degree of covering' (T_3) and propose new ones, that describe the characteristics specific for summaries of graph datasets - 'degree of subject appropriateness', 'degree of summarizer order' and 'degree of linkage'. In Sect. 5 we show the application results - generated summaries for LinkedData, centered around DBPedia.

2   Linguistic Summaries of Relational and Graph Datasets

Linguistic summaries is data mining technique aimed at obtaining high level knowledge from large datasets. The first form of a linguistic summary is presented by Eq. (1), see Example 1. Second form of linguistic summaries is presented in Eq. (2), see Example 2.

$$Q \quad P \quad are/have \quad S \quad [T] \tag{1}$$

$$Q \quad P \quad being/having \quad W \quad are/have \quad S \quad [T] \tag{2}$$

where Q is the *linguistic quantifier*; P is the subject of the summary (set of objects represented by the database tuples d_i); S is a property of interest, the so-called summarizer represented by a fuzzy or a crisp set (discrete set in particular).

Example 1. About quarter (Q) workers (P) have high salary (S) [0.67] (T)

Example 2. Some (Q) young (W) employees (P) have average salary (S) [1.0]

The crucial part of the algorithm in the sense of Yager is the computation of the degree of truth T. The algorithm is strictly based on Zadeh calculus of linguistically quantified statements, and is computed by T_1 $(Q\ P\ are/have\ S)$ = $\mu_Q(\frac{\sum_{i=1}^{m}\mu_S(d_i)}{m})$, where d - tuple, m - number of tuples, $\mu_S(d_i)$ - membership value of tuple d to summarizer S (e.g. S - 'has high salary'), μ_Q is membership value to quantifier Q (e.g. Q - about quarter).

So far this method has been researched mostly for relational databases. However, in a recent work [14] we have presented an approach to using this method on graph datasets. Due to heterogeneity of a graph database source, initially one needs to select a **subject** of a summary, retrieve all vertices that belong to this class, and obtain their **attributes** (graph vertices connected to the subject ones). In case of a relational database this is trivial (each table tuple is a subject), however for a heterogeneous graph dataset this is no longer true. Selecting all vertices for summarization is one approach, however such summary would not be consistent (vertices are interlinked, vertex types have different properties, etc.). We have proposed to use on ontological class as a subject of a summary.

After retrieval of all instances of classes c, one needs to retrieve all connected vertices (see Fig. 1) - ones for which given instance is a *subject* (properties, as indicated in Fig. 1 by a_i), and for which it is an *object* (graph vertices for which given instance is a property of, indicated in Fig. 1 by a_i^{rev}). Hence, for each attribute $a_i \in A$ the set of values X_i is obtained. After this extraction step, we obtain a relational-like structure (see (4)) and generate linguistic summaries according to the known methods.

Attribute values X_i are used for creating of summarizers and qualifiers. Each $x_i^j \in X_j$ is a summarizer. As we have proven in our previous paper, computing the set of *generalizations* for each value $(SUP(x_i^j))$ may create additional summarizers (see Example 3). Generalizations of concept c is the set of broader (generalized, direct and inferred, which means linked with more than one generalizing predicate) concepts (terms) - all levels 'above' c. Broader (generalization) terms are linked using predicates such as: rdf:subClassOf, skos:broader (not transitive, hence only one level above concept c is considered), skos:broaderTransitive, linkedgeodata:parentFeature, and others. Value set of attribute A_i that is used for creating summarizers and qualifiers, augmented by these generalizations, are presented in (3).

$$X_i' = X_i \cup (\forall_{x_i^j \in X_i} SUP(x_i^j)) \tag{3}$$

Example 3. Say we summarize vertices with class 'Person', and one of the properties is 'occupation'. In the dataset direct 'occupations' are 'Painter' and 'Writer', and 'Painter' and 'Writer' are both instances of class 'Artist'. Hence, property value 'Artist' is a **generalization** of both 'occupations', and can be added to set of summarizers.

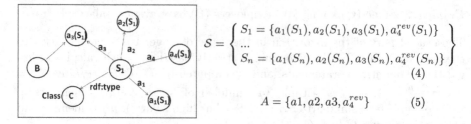

$$S = \left\{ \begin{array}{l} S_1 = \{a_1(S_1), a_2(S_1), a_3(S_1), a_4^{rev}(S_1)\} \\ \cdots \\ S_n = \{a_1(S_n), a_2(S_n), a_3(S_n), a_4^{rev}(S_n)\} \end{array} \right\} \quad (4)$$

$$A = \{a1, a2, a3, a_4^{rev}\} \quad (5)$$

Fig. 1. Gathering vertices that are of given summary class ($S1 \rightarrow rdf : typeOf \rightarrow c \cup SUB(c)$), attributes ($a_1, a_2, a_1^{rev}$), and attribute value sets ($X_{A_1}, X_{A_2}, X_{A_1^{rev}}$). a^{rev} stands for 'reverse' attribute, that is - selected vertex is an object, not a subject of a triple (arrow pointing towards selected summary subject). S in (4) - the set of graph vertices that are selected as subjects of the summary, A in (5) - set of retrieved attributes (graph edges directly connected to subject vertices) that will be used for generating summarizers and qualifiers. Can be compared to columns in a relation (from relational data model).

3 Multi-source Extensions to Linguistic Summaries of Graph Datasets

First considered case of distributed datasets is the situation where information about the same subject (e.g. music) is distributed between different datasets. In case of LinkedData, it is usually the case where two databases concerning the same subject are created independently, and afterwards connected (e.g. DBTune and MusicBrainz). Some examples of equivalent classes are shown in Table 1. In such cases classes and properties are marked as equivalent, using specific links (e.g. for Semantic Web these links are owl:equivalentClass and owl:equivalentPropoerty). Data extraction in such scenario is shown in Fig. 2 - one needs to gather all instances of selected subject from first database (see D_1 in 4) and its properties and equivalent classes from D_2 etc. See Example 4.

Example 4. Say we want to create summaries in musical domain. In Linked-Data there are 3 popular databases in this domain - DBPedia, DBTune and MusicBrainz. However, these databases use different ontologies, hence different classes and properties (DBPedia - DBPedia ontology, MusicBrainz - Music Ontology). Therefore, in order to consistently extract data for summaries one needs to navigate equivalence links between these classes and properties.

$$S = S_1 \cup ... \cup S_n = \left\{ \begin{array}{l} S_1^{D_1} = \{a_1(S_1^{D_1}), a_2(S_1^{D_1}), a_3(S_1^{D_1}), a_4^{rev}(S_1^{D_1})\} \\ \cdots \\ S_2^{D_2} = \{a_1(S_2^{D_2}), a_2(S_2^{D_2}), a_3(S_2^{D_2}), a_4^{rev}(S_2^{D_2})\} \\ \cdots \\ S_n^{D_n} = \{a_1(S_n^{D_n}), a_2(S_n^{D_n}), a_3(S_n^{D_n}), a_4^{rev}(S_n^{D_n})\} \end{array} \right\} \quad (4)$$

Second considered case of interlinked datasets is shown in Fig. 3. In this case equivalence links (in Semantic Web 'owl:sameAs' link) exist between vertices

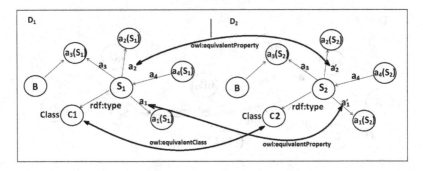

Fig. 2. Gathering vertices that are of given summary class $(S1, S2 \rightarrow rdf : typeOf \rightarrow SUB(c))$, D_1, D_2 - different, distributed datasets

Table 1. Some examples of equivalent classes and properties, within the same ontology and between different ontologies

Class / Property	Equivalent
dbpedia.org/ontology/Film	sw.opencyc.org/concept/Mx..ycA
	umbel.org/umbel/rc/Movie-CW
	yago-knowledge.org/resource/wordnet_movie
	www.freebase.com/film/film
dbpedia.org/ontology/List	www.w3.org/2004/02/skos/core#OrderedCollection
dbpedia.org/ontology/Place	schema.org/Place
	dbpedia.org/ontology/Location

in different datasets, which means that linked vertices are describing the same entity, and data stored in different databases augment (add more information to) each other. Hence, the total attribute set for summarization is a concatenation of the information stored in each database, as shown in (5) (compare to (4) where only a single source is considered). Some statistics about linkage of DBPedia to other datasets is shown in Table 2.

Example 5. Say we want to create summaries in film domain. As a dataset about movies we may use LinkedMDB. By adding the geographical dataset (e.g. GeoNames), and following two sameAs links (LinkedMDB $\rightarrow$ DBPedia $\rightarrow$ GeoNames) one may create new summaries using additional information from other dataset - like 'almost all high rated movies are produced in big cities'.

$$\mathcal{S} = \left\{ \begin{array}{l} S_1 = \{a_1^{D_1}(S_1), a_2^{D_1}(S_1), a_3^{D_1}(S_1), a_4^{D_1}(S_1), a_5^{D_2}(S_1'), a_6^{D_2}(S_1')\} \\ ... \\ S_n = \{a_1^{D_1}(S_n), a_2^{D_1}(S_n), a_3^{D_1}(S_n), a_4^{D_1}(S_n), a_5^{D_2}(S_n'), a_6^{D_2}(S_n')\} \end{array} \right\} \quad (5)$$

Last extension to the data extraction for graph datasets is shown in Fig. 4 - retrieving higher order attributes, that is vertices not directly connected to

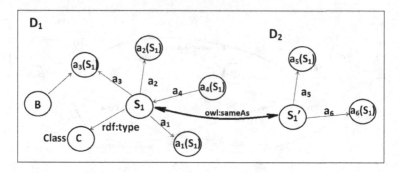

Fig. 3. Following owl:sameAs links to gather additional attributes of a subject, D_1, D_2 - different, distibuted datasets

Table 2. Some example statistics about sameAs linkage from DBPedia to other datasets for selected classes

Class	Count	Linked to	Links count	Linkage %
dbpedia:Book	31172	bookmashup/books	9078	29
dbpedia:Country	1550	eurostat.linkedstatistics.org	253	16
dbpedia:Settlement	475458	sws.geonames.org	85647	18
		linkedgeodata.org	103633	21
dbpedia:MusicalWork + dbpedia:Band	188319	musicbrainz.org	22981	11
dbpedia:Species	279883	lod.geospecies.org	15974	5

the subject vertex, but separated by two or more graph edges - see Example 6. Figure 4 also indicates that following identity links (like $owl:sameAs$) is also required in such cases. Extracted data from graph shown in Fig. 4 is shown in (6) (compare to (4)) - where attribute a_1 comes from database D_1, a_1a_3 is a 2-nd order attribute (also from D_1), and a_1b_1 is a 2-nd order attribute, but obtained from D_2 after following identity link between graph vertex $a_1(S_1)$ in D_1 and vertex B in a different dataset - D_2.

Example 6. Consider summaries for the subject class 'Writer', which is directly connected to edges of type 'Book'. Each 'Book' also has a set of properties, for instance 'Genre'. Adding this as a second-order property of a 'Writer' can create new summaries (E.g. Most writers from Sweden write mystery books).

$$
\mathcal{S} = \begin{cases} S_1 = \{a_1^{D_1}(S_1), a_1a_3^{D_1}(S_1), a_1a_4^{D_1}(S_1), a_1b_1^{D_2}(B), a_1b_2^{D_2}(B)\} \\ \dots \\ S_n = \{a_1^{D_1}(S_n), a_1a_3^{D_1}(S_n), a_1a_4^{D_1}(S_n), a_1b_1^{D_2}(B_n), a_1b_2^{D_2}(B_n)\} \end{cases} \tag{6}
$$

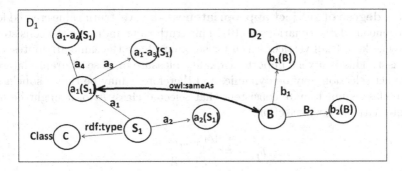

Fig. 4. Gathering n-th order attributes - vertices separated from the root vertex (S_1) by n edges. In such cases following owl:sameAs extracts more information and also leads to new summaries

4   Adapted and New Quality Measures for Linguistic Summaries of Multiple Graph Datasets

Quality measures are means to describe various characteristics of a summary. All quality measures have been developed for relational databases, and some cannot be directly used in graph datasets, hence we have adapted these ones for graph data model - T_2 and T_3. Additionally, we propose three new quality measures that describe features specific to a graph dataset - T_1^G, T_2^G and T_3^G.

T_2 - **degree of imprecision**, see (7), where $in(c)$ is defined by Definition 1. In the context of graph datasets, in which vertices have hierarchical generalization - specialization taxonomy (a clear example of this are class taxonomies), we have proposed a measure of how imprecise a given vertex is. For instance, for DBPedia ontology: $T_2(class : Artist) < T_2(class : Writer) < T_2(class : Poet)$.

$$T_2 = 1 - in(c) \tag{7}$$

Definition 1. *Imprecision of a concept is defined by*

$$in(c) = \frac{height(complete - tree_c)}{height(subtree(c))} \tag{8}$$

where: *concept* - graph vertex (e.g. - an ontological class), *height(x)* - number of levels of a tree of concepts (e.g. ontology, specialization-generalization relations), *complete − tree_c* - tree of specialization-generalization (like class taxonomy) that concept c is a member of, *subtree(c)* - tree of concepts starting with concept c and following all specialization relations downwards

T_3 - **degree of covering** - Quality measure indicating what percentage of the complete dataset is involved in the summary, see (9)

$$T_3 = \frac{|S|}{|D|} \tag{9}$$

where $|S|$ - the number of retrieved subjects, $|D|$ - size of the dataset

T_1^G - **degree of subject appropriateness** - a novel truth value created for a heterogeneous data scenario, see (10). This truth value indicates the consistency of chosen class. If all vertices taken for summary have the same attributes - the value is 1. This is a very important quality measure on case of graph datasets, as subject selection may be dynamic, and therefore it may be that a subclass of chosen class is much more consistent that selected class. Also, it might be used for automatic subject selection.

$$T_1^G = \frac{\sum_{i=1}^{|A|} count(a_i)}{|S| * |A|} \tag{10}$$

where A is the set of all attributes, $count(a_i)$ is the number of retrieved subjects that have this attribute, S - number of retrieved subjects for summary (Table 3)

T_2^G - **degree of summarizer order** - a novel truth value created for a graph data scenario, see (11). This truth value is related to the number of graph edges that separate the subject from an attribute. See Example 7.

$$T_2^G = \frac{1}{|path(S, a_i)|} \tag{11}$$

where $|path(S, a_i)|$ is a length of a path between the subject S and the attribute a_i.

T_3^G - **degree of linkage** - a novel truth value created for a interlinked data scenario, see (12). This truth value is related to the number of datasets involved in creating of the summary, and is increasing proportionally to this number. See Example 7.

$$T_3^G = 1 - 2^{-|n_D|} \tag{12}$$

where $|n_D|$ is the number of datasets involved in the summary.

Example 7. In Fig. 4, $T_2^G(a_1) = 1$, $T_2^G(a_1 b_1) = \frac{1}{2}$.
For $|n_D| = 1$, $T_3^G = 0$, for $|n_D| = 2$, $T_3^G = \frac{1}{2}$ and for $|n_D| = 3$, $T_3^G = \frac{3}{4}$.

Table 3. T_3 and T_1^G for selected classes in the context of DBPedia

Class	Count	T_2	T_3	T_1^G
dbpedia:Agent	2371260	0.5	0.79	0.01
dbpedia:Settlement	442280	0.62	0.147	0.14
dbpedia:Insect	114855	1	0.0383	0.45
dbpedia:Work	396046	0.37	0.13	0.13
dbpedia:WrittenWork	51019	0.5	0.017	0.33
dbpedia:Album	93826	1	0.031	0.6

5 Application - Generating Linguistic Summaries for LinkedData

We have run several experiments of using our method in Linked Data, starting with DBPedia (since it can be considered a 'central' point for Linked Data [16]). The computational cost of our method is the cost of creating normal linguistic summaries for relational databases with the overhead of data retrieval from graph to a relational-like model. In our experiments we have used publicly available SPARQL endpoints and Apache Jena, hence the initial step was downloading the data to a local database using a multi-threaded Java Program. For fuzzy logic related computations we have used jFuzzyLogic library [17]. Table 4 shows some examples of generated summaries, but only those spanning across several endpoints.

Table 4. Linguistic summaries created for integrated multiple graph datasets, which are made possible by methods proposed in this paper - interlinking and retrieving higher order attributes

No.	Summary	Datasets	T_1	T_2	T_3	T_1^G	T_2^G	T_3^G	T_{final}
1	About quarter Scandinavian writers write mystery books	Bookmashup DBPedia	0.31	0.75	0.006	0.08	0.5	0.5	0.23
2	A lot of Oscar-winning actors are of European descent	DBPedia Eurostat	0.34	0.75	0.001	0.61	0.5	0.5	0.45
3	Most of bands have a guitar player	Musicbrainz DBTune DBPedia	0.53	1	0.007	0.04	0.5	0.75	0.47
4	Some airlines are owned by Asian governments	DBPedia YAGO3 Eurostat	0.91	1	0.001	0.07	0.5	0.75	0.53
5	Some mammals are human sources of food	DBPedia Umbel GeoSpecies	0.64	0.3	0.002	0.1	0.5	0.75	0.38

6 Conclusions and Future Work

In this paper we have presented a novel method of generating and evaluating linguistic summaries for distributed graph datasets. We have shown how to extract data for summarization in the basic form, and how to use the fact that vertices are interconnected to each other in order to obtain new information. That is: generalization of summarizer and qualifier (along with proposal of a novel measure of a 'imprecision' of a notion), ways to retrieve information from several datasets interlinked in different ways (equivalence links between properties and vertices), and methods and benefits of using higher order attributes for summarization. Apart of adapting some existing quality measures - degree of imprecision and degree of coverage, we have also proposed new ones, specific for graph datasets - degree of subject appropriateness, degree of linkage and degree of summarizer order.

Proposed method has been thoroughly tested on Linked Data, which is a global distributed graph dataset. We have shown that our proposals result in obtaining new knowledge, with summaries spanning across several datasets, and that proposed quality measures successfully indicate various characteristics of these summaries.

References

1. Angles, R., Gutierrez, C.: Survey of graph database models. ACM Comput. Surv. **40**(1), 1:1–1:39 (2008)
2. Hausenblas, M., Halb, W., Raimond, Y., Heath, T.: What is the size of the semantic web. In: Proceedings of the International Conference on Semantic Systems. ISemantics 2008 (2008)
3. Yager, R.R.: A new approach to the summarization of data. Inf. Sci. **28**(1), 69–86 (1982)
4. Kacprzyk, J., Yager, R.R., Zadrożny, S.: A fuzzy logic based approach to linguistic summaries of databases. Int. J. Appl. Math. Comput. Sci. **10**(4), 813–834 (2000)
5. Kacprzyk, J., Wilbik, A., Zadrozny, S.: An approach to the linguistic summarization of time series using a fuzzy quantifier driven aggregation. Int. J. Intell. Syst. **25**(5), 411–439 (2010)
6. Srivastava, J., Cooley, R., Deshpande, M., Tan, P.N.: Web usage mining: discovery and applications of usage patterns from web data. SIGKDD Explor. Newsl. **1**(2), 12–23 (2000)
7. Kosala, R., Blockeel, H.: Web mining research: a survey. SIGKDD Explor. Newsl. **2**(1), 1–15 (2000)
8. Stumme, G., Hotho, A., Berendt, B.: Semantic web mining: state of the art and future directions. Web Seman. Sci. Serv. Agents World Wide Web **4**(2), 124–143 (2006). Semantic Grid - The Convergence of Technologies
9. Aggarwal, C.C., Wang, H.: Managing and Mining Graph Data, 1st edn. Springer Publishing Company, Incorporated, US (2010)
10. Cook, D.J., Holder, L.B.: Mining Graph Data. John Wiley & Sons, Hoboken (2006)
11. Kuramochi, M., Karypis, G.: Frequent subgraph discovery. In: Proceedings of the 2001 IEEE International Conference on Data Mining. ICDM 2001, Computer Society, pp. 313–320. IEEE, Washington, DC (2001)
12. Yan, X., Han, J.: gspan: graph-based substructure pattern mining. In: Proceedings of the 2002 IEEE International Conference on Data Mining. ICDM 2002, Computer Society 721-724. IEEE, Washington, DC (2002)
13. Castelltort, A., Laurent, A.: Fuzzy queries over NoSQL graph databases: perspectives for extending the cypher language. In: Laurent, A., Strauss, O., Bouchon-Meunier, B., Yager, R.R. (eds.) IPMU 2014, Part III. CCIS, vol. 444, pp. 384–395. Springer, Heidelberg (2014)
14. Strobin, L., Niewiadomski, A.: Linguistic summaries of graph datasets using ontologies: an application to semantic web. In: Núñez, M., Nguyen, N.T., Camacho, D., Trawinski, B. (eds.) ICCCI 2015. LNCS, vol. 9329, pp. 380–389. Springer, Heidelberg (2015). doi:10.1007/978-3-319-24069-5_36

15. Castelltort, A., Laurent, A.: Extracting fuzzy summaries from nosql graph databases. In: Andreasen, T., Christiansen, H., Kacprzyk, J., Larsen, H., Pasi, G., Pivert, O., De Tré, G., Vila, M.A., Yazici, A., Zadrozny, S. (eds.) Flexible Query Answering Systems 2015. Advances in Intelligent Systems and Computing, vol. 400, pp. 189–200. Springer International Publishing, Switzerland (2016)
16. Lehmann, J.: DBpedia - a large-scale, multilingual knowledge base extracted from wikipedia. Semant. Web J. **6**(2), 167–195 (2014)
17. Cingolani, P., Alcalá-Fdez, J.: jfuzzylogic: a robust and flexible fuzzy-logic inference system language implementation. In: FUZZ-IEEE, pp. 1–8. IEEE (2012)

Combining Fuzzy Cognitive Maps and Discrete Random Variables

Piotr Szwed[(⊠)]

AGH University of Science and Technology, Kraków, Poland
pszwed@agh.edu.pl

Abstract. In this paper we propose an extension to the Fuzzy Cognitive Maps (FCMs) that aims at aggregating a number of reasoning tasks into a one parallel run. The described approach consists in replacing real-valued activation levels of concepts (and further influence weights) by random variables. Such extension, followed by the implemented software tool, allows for determining ranges reached by concept activation levels, sensitivity analysis as well as statistical analysis of multiple reasoning results. We replace multiplication and addition operators appearing in the FCM state equation by appropriate convolutions applicable for discrete random variables. To make the model computationally feasible, it is further augmented with aggregation operations for discrete random variables. We discuss four implemented aggregators, as well as we report results of preliminary tests.

Keywords: Fuzzy Cognitive Maps · FCM · Discrete random variable

1 Introduction

Fuzzy Cognitive Maps (FCMs) are a well-known tool for modeling and qualitative analysis of various problems [1–4]. They use a simple representation of knowledge in a form of a directed graph, in which vertexes are interpreted as concepts and edges attributed with weights as causal relationships. FCMs exhibit certain similarity to neural networks as regards structural properties and reasoning techniques. However, they are considered a semantic modeling tool: concepts, which are typically identified by experts, occur in the problem domain, and weights specifying influences can be explained based on experts knowledge or data used in a learning process. Below we provide a short theoretical introduction to FCMs.

Let $C = \{c_1, \dots, c_n\}$ be a set of FCM concepts. A state of the FCM is an n-dimensional vector of concept activation levels ($n = |C|$), which, depending on a setting, are real values from $[0, 1]$ or $[-1, 1]$.

Causal relations between concepts are represented in an FCM by edges and assigned weights. A positive weight of an edge linking two concepts c_j and c_i models a situation, where an increase of the level of c_j results in a growing c_i; a negative weight is used to describe the opposite rapport. Often, during modeling

© Springer International Publishing Switzerland 2016
L. Rutkowski et al. (Eds.): ICAISC 2016, Part I, LNAI 9692, pp. 344–355, 2016.
DOI: 10.1007/978-3-319-39378-0_30

an ordinal scale of linguistic weights is employed. The symbolic names are then mapped onto a set of real values from the interval $[-1, 1]$, e.g. *strong_negative* (-1), *negative* (-0.66), *medium_negative* (-0.33), *neutral* (0), *medium_positive* (0.33), *positive* (0.66), *strong_positive* (1.0).

A representation of FCM, which is used during reasoning, is an $n \times n$ influence matrix $W = [w_{ij}]$. A value of an element w_{ij} corresponds to a weight of the edge linking concepts c_j and c_i (0 values are used, if there is no link). Reasoning with FCM consists in building a sequence of states: $\alpha = A(0), A(1), \ldots, A(k), \ldots$ starting from an initial vector $A(0)$ of concepts activation levels. Successive elements are calculated according to the formula (1). In the $k + 1$ iteration the vector $A(k)$ is multiplied by the influence matrix W, then the resulting activation levels of concepts are mapped onto the assumed range by means of an *activation* (or *squashing*) function S.

$$A_i(k + 1) = S(\sum_{j=1}^{n} w_{ij} A_j(k)) \tag{1}$$

Commonly used activation functions include bivalent or trivalent step functions, a linear function with cutting off values beyond $[-1, 1]$, various sigmoidal functions including the logistic function or the hyperbolic tangent. In our experiments we have also used another S-shaped function S_{exp} defined as $S_{exp}(x) = 1 - \exp(-mx)$ if $x \geq 0$ and $\exp(-mx) - 1$, if $x < 0$. The coefficient m allows to adjust the curve slope.

Basically, a sequence of consecutive states $\alpha = A(0), A(1), \ldots, A(k), \ldots$ is infinite. However, it was shown that after k iterations, where k is a number close to the rank of matrix W, a steady state is reached or a cycle occurs.

The sequence of states α can be interpreted in two ways. Firstly, it can be treated as a representation of a dynamic behavior of the modeled system. In this case there exist implicit temporal relations between consecutive system states and the whole sequence describes an evolution of the system in the form of a *scenario*. Under the second interpretation, the sequence represents a non-monotonic fuzzy inference process, in which selected elements of a steady state are interpreted as reasoning results. In both cases results of reasoning with FCMs can be interpreted only qualitatively, as they strongly depend on granularity of weights and the activation function used. For example, rather a few scenario steps indicating the predicted development tendencies should be considered or, in the case of reasoning, meaningful results can be associated to an ordering of activation levels in a steady state and their proportions.

Both applications of FCMs usually involve executing them for multiple combinations of initial activation levels of concepts: either to test several scenarios starting from various initial states, perform sensitivity analysis or to validate reasoning results for several inputs.

In this paper we propose an extension to the FCM model, named FCM4DRV, that aims at aggregating a number of reasoning tasks into a one parallel run. The described extension was motivated by the problem of qualitative evaluation of reasoning results for an FCM model of risks related to IT security [5–7], however, it is rather a general one, than tailored for a specific purpose. The idea behind FCM4DRV consists in replacing real-valued activation levels of concepts (and further influence weights) by random variables. Such extension, followed by the implemented software tool, allows for statistical analysis of multiple reasoning results. We replace multiplication and addition operators appearing in FCM state equation by appropriate convolutions applicable for discrete random variables. To make the model computationally feasible, we further augment it with aggregation operations for discrete random variables. We discuss four implemented aggregators, as well as we report preliminary test results for an FCM model, which was examined in our previous work [8].

The paper is organized as follows: next Sect. 2 discusses related works and gives a motivation for FCM extension. It is followed by Sect. 3, which introduces FCM4DRV. Next Sect. 4 presents four implemented aggregators. Results of experiments are reported in Sect. 5. Last Sect. 6 provides concluding remarks.

2   Related Works

Fuzzy Cognitive Maps (FCMs) were proposed by Kosko [1] as a method for specification and analysis of causal relations between concepts. A large number of applications of FCMs were reported, e.g. in project risk modeling [9], crisis management and decision making, analysis of development of economic systems and the introduction of new technologies, traffic prediction [10], ecosystem analysis [11], signal processing and decision support in medicine. A survey on Fuzzy Cognitive Maps and their applications can be found in [3].

Over last 15 years a number of FCM extensions have been proposed. Fuzzy Gray Cognitive Maps [12] use gray numbers (pairs defining interval bounds) as weights in influence matrix. In Intuitionistic FCMs [13] weights of influence matrix are also pairs of numbers, the first expresses an impact (μ), the second a hesitation margin (π). Dynamic Random FCMs [14] introduce probabilities of concept activation, as well as a capability of updating weights during execution. Other extensions described in [4] include Rule-based FCMs, Fuzzy Cognitive Networks and Fuzzy Time Cognitive Maps. The model of RFCMs (Relational Fuzzy Cognitive Maps) proposed of in [15] shares to a certain extent features of the discussed FCM4DRV approach. It used fuzzy numbers as concept activation levels and fuzzy relations to define their influences.

In our previous works [5–7] we have proposed to use FCMs for evaluation of risk related to security of IT systems. FCM models were hierarchical structures, in which concepts represented assets, risk factors and countermeasures. The FCM reasoning technique was then applied to perform risk aggregation: at first risk factors and countermeasures were combined, then states of low-level assets and their influences allowed to assign utility values to assets placed at higher levels in the hierarchy. However, the method faced the problem of correct benchmarking for obtained risk levels, e.g. a question can arise: *how to map a value 0.12 determined for a certain asset to an ordinal scale of low, medium and high risk*. Selection of thresholds supporting such scale can be determined by evaluating numerous combinations of countermeasures. Moreover, preferably it should be based on statistical distribution of system features, e.g. according to best practices some security functions are likely to be implemented more often than others. One of the motivating applications of described here extension to the FCM model was to facilitate thresholds selection, based on percentile ranks of concept activation levels.

3 Fuzzy Cognitive Maps for Discrete Random Variables

Random variable $X\colon \Omega \to E$ is a function that maps a sample space Ω into a measurable space E. The sample space represents a set of experiments, measurements or events. A random variable X is called *discrete*, if E is finite or countable, otherwise it is *continuous*. Probability function $p(x) = P(X = x)$, assigns a value from $[0, 1]$ to an outcome of a random variable X. Moreover, it is required for the sum (or integral) of $p(x)$ over $x \in E$ to be equal 1.0.

In the presented model random variables are used as concept activation levels of Fuzzy Cognitive Maps. Although we assume, that their values lay within a certain interval $[min, max] \subseteq \mathbb{R}$, e.g. $min = -1$, $max = 1$, we consider them discrete, i.e. their ranges E are finite. In particular, we represent them as discrete probability mass functions $p\colon E \to [0, 1]$, as well as apply addition and multiplication operators appropriate rather for discrete random variables than continuous. Special cases of random variables are *singletons*, which have a single value $c\colon E_c = \{c\}$ occurring with the probability $p_c(c) = 1$.

3.1 Arithmetic of Discrete Random Variables

Let X and Y be two independent discrete random variables (DRV) with probability distributions $p_x(x)$ and $p_y(z)$. Their sum $Z = X \oplus Y$ is also a random variable with the range $E_z = \{z\colon \exists (x, y) \in E_x \times E_y \land z = x + y\}$ and whose probability distribution $p_z(z)$ is a *convolution* of $p_x(x)$ and $p_y(y)$ (2)[1].

$$p_z(z) = \sum_{\substack{x \in E_x \\ z = x + y}} \sum_{y \in E_y} p_x(x)p_y(y) \tag{2}$$

Similarly, a product $V = X \otimes Y$ is a random variable with the range $E_v = \{v\colon \exists (x, y) \in E_x \times E_y \land v = x \cdot y\}$ and a probability distribution given by (3)

$$p_v(v) = \sum_{\substack{x \in E_x \\ v = x \cdot y}} \sum_{y \in E_y} p_x(x)p_y(y) \tag{3}$$

Let $S : \mathbb{R} \to \mathbb{R}$ be a scalar function. It induces a function $\hat{S}\colon \{X_i\} \to \{X_i\}$ in the domain of DRVs $\{X_i\}$. Variable $Y = \hat{S}(X)$ is defined as:

$$E_y = \bigcup_{x \in E_x} S(x) \quad \text{and} \quad p(y) = \sum_{\substack{x \in E_x \\ y = S(x)}} p(x) \tag{4}$$

---

[1] Convolution is often defined as $p_z(z) = \sum_x p_x(x)p_y(z - x)$. Formula (2) is an equivalent definition.

3.2   Formulation of FCM4DRV

In FCM4DRV, which is an extension to the basic FCM model, concept activation levels are represented by discrete random variables (DRVs), similarly the influence matrix W is an $n \times n$ matrix of DRVs and FCM states are n-dimensional vectors of DRVs. Let us observe, that a classical FCMs can be considered a special case of the extended model, where all DRVs are just singletons (single values with assigned probability 1). Under such assumptions, the FCM state Eq. (1) can be rewritten as in (5) using defined earlier summation $\oplus$ and multiplication $\otimes$ operators, as well as an activation function $\hat{S}$ defined in the domain of DRVs.

$$A_i(k+1) = \hat{S}(w_{i1} \otimes A_1(k) \oplus w_{i2} \otimes A_2(k) \oplus \cdots \oplus w_{in} \otimes A_n(k)) \qquad (5)$$

Analogously to the classical model, execution of FCM4DRV produces a sequence of states $\alpha = A(0), A(1), \ldots, A(k), \ldots$, whose convergence can be checked based on selected distance measure for DRVs.

Unfortunately, in most practical situations calculation of a new FCM state with formula (5) is computationally unfeasible. Let us consider a simple case of $n \times n$ influence matrix F of singletons (i.e. a real-valued matrix) and an initial state vector A_0 of DRVs, each having ranges of k elements. Then, in the worst case the DRV ranges in A_1 will comprise k^n elements, k^{2n} elements for A_2, k^{in} for A_i and so on. If we assume quite a reasonable values $k = 100$ and $n = 10$, then probably the calculation of A_1 with $10 \cdot 100^{10} = 10^{21}$ mapping elements would fail.

To handle this problem we introduce additional *aggregation* operation into the state equation that is applied to partial results obtained during evaluation of expression appearing on the right side of the state Eq. (5). An aggregation function $\hat{G}$ converts an input DRV X into a smaller (i.e. having less numerous mapping) variable $Y = \hat{G}(X)$. It is expected that the number of elements appearing in the range of Y is bounded by a selected positive integer: $|E_Y| < k$ and certain equivalence criteria are satisfied $Y \approx X$.

The FCM state equation extended by aggregation function $\hat{G}$ is given by (6). It reflexes the most natural order of evaluating expressions (from left to right).

$$
\begin{aligned}
A_{i1}(k+1) &= f_{i1} \otimes A_1(k) \\
A_{i2}(k+1) &= \hat{G}(A_{11}(k) \oplus (f_{i2} \otimes A_2(k))) \\
&\vdots \\
A_{in}(k+1) &= \hat{G}(A_{1n-1}(k) \oplus (f_{in} \otimes A_n(k))) \\
\text{and finally:} \\
A_i(k+1) &= \hat{S}(A_{in}(k+1))
\end{aligned}
\qquad (6)
$$

Equivalence relation $Y \approx X$ for random variables can be based on various measures, e.g. equality or expected values $E(X) = E(Y)$ or distances between two distributions. At this point, however, we did not make attempt do qualitatively evaluate aggregation functions and analyze their influence on states reached during reasoning. Instead in the next Sect. 4, we describe a few proto-type aggregation procedures implementing variants of $\hat{G}$ function that were used during experiments.

4   Aggregators

For a discrete random variable X its probability mass function $p_X \colon E_X \to [0,1]$ is actually represented as a set of pairs: $p_X = \{(x,p) \colon x \in E_X \wedge p \in [0,1]\}$. In our experiments E_X was finite and hence bounded: $E_X \subset [x_{min}, x_{max}]$. The basic idea behind at least three aggregators described in this section consists in performing one-dimensional clustering. Values $x \in E_X$ laying close are grouped into clusters $E_{X1}, \ldots, E_{Xi}, \ldots E_{Xk}$ and each cluster E_{Xi} is replaced by a single pair (v_i, p_i). The method of establishing v_i and p_i depends on algorithm. Typically, v_i is obtained by kind of averaging values in E_{Xi} and p_i by summing probabilities.

4.1   Simple k-means

Simple k-means is an adaptation of well-known k-means clustering algorithm. The main difference is that initial centroids are not randomly selected, but evenly distributed within the range $[x_{min}, x_{max}]$. For the resulting representation $p_V = \{(v_i, p_i)\}$ of the output random variable V, elements v_i are cluster centers and p_i is a sum of probabilities assigned to elements $E_{Xi} = \{x_{ij}\}$ forming a cluster: $p_i = \sum_{x \in E_{Xi}} p(x)$. The method does not assure that the mean value of X will be kept by V. In spite of this, during experiments $E(X)$ and $E(V)$ occurred to be quite close.

4.2   DBSCAN

DBSCAN (Density-based spatial clustering of applications with noise) is a widely used clustering algorithm characterized by low complexity $O(n \log n)$. It is controlled by two parameters ϵ – minimal distance between data points forming a neighborhood and λ – minimal cluster size. During algorithm execution points, whose neighborhood size is smaller than λ are rejected as outliers. On the other side, neighborhoods having at least λ elements are converted to clusters and further expanded. Outcome of the algorithm, including the number of clusters, depends on established values of ε and λ.

The discussed aggregator has been based on DBSCAN implementation in JavaML library [16] with the following parameters: $\varepsilon = \frac{x_{max} - x_{min}}{k}$, where k is an upper limit on the number of resulting clusters and $\lambda = 6$. After running the clustering algorithm, values belonging to the clusters E_{Xi} were converted to pairs (v_i, p_i) according to formula (7).

$$p_i = \sum_{x \in E_{Xi}} p_X(x) \text{ and } v_i = \frac{1}{p_i} \sum_{x \in E_{Xi}} x \cdot p_X(x) \qquad (7)$$

4.3 UniBins Aggregator

UniBins aggregator divides the range $[x_{min}, x_{max}]$ of an input variable X into k uniformly distributed bins represented by values $v_0, \ldots, v_{k-1}$. Bins borders are fuzzy and a level, at which an input element x can be assigned to a bin is quantitatively described by a bin's membership function. This concept is illustrated in Fig. 1.

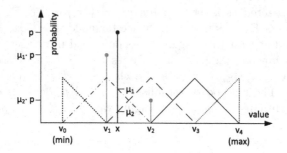

Fig. 1. UniBins aggregator. Value x with the probability p laying between v_1 and v_2 contributes $\mu_1 \cdot p$ to probability of v_1 and $\mu_2 \cdot p$ to probability of v_2. Factors μ_1 and μ_2 are determined according to triangle membership functions around v_1 and v_2 marked with dash-dot and dashed lines.

4.4 Percentile Rank Aggregator

Percentile rank aggregator assigns equal probability $\Delta p = 1/k$ to each output value, while preserving the percentile ranks of input distribution. The assumed granulation level is Δp. The basic algorithm idea is shown in Fig. 2a. Let us analyze the sequence $(x_i, p_i), \ldots, (x_{i+3}, p_{i+3})$. As $p_i + p_{i+1} + p_{i+2} < \Delta p < p_i + p_{i+1} + p_{i+2} + p_{i+3}$ the value v_{k+1} will be placed between x_{i+3} and x_{i+4}. The

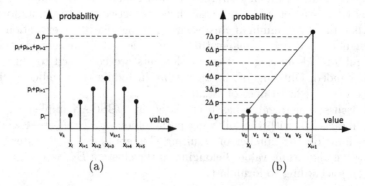

Fig. 2. PercentileRank aggregator: (a) multiple input values aggregated into one (b) significant change of amplitude resulting in multiple output elements

exact position depends on $\Delta p - p_i - p_{i+1} - p_{i+2}$, the smaller the value is, the distance between x_{i+3} and v_{k+1} is smaller.

Another feature of the percentile rank aggregator is its capability to produce multiple output values in case of rapid changes of input PMF. This is illustrated in Fig. 2b: placement of output values $v_1, \ldots, v_6$ correspond to points of intersection of line linking x_i and x_{i+1} with successive percentile ranks: $2\Delta p, 3\Delta p, \ldots, 7\Delta p$.

5   Experiments and Results

In this section we present results of experiments aiming at demonstrating computational feasibility of the proposed FCM4DRV model. We implemented a prototype software tool in Java, which supports operations on DRVs, provides discussed earlier aggregation procedures and allows to conduct FCM reasoning.

Described further experiments were performed on an FCM model that was previously discussed in [8]. The map presented in Fig. 3 specifies concepts and their influences intended to characterize the domain of academic units, e.g. university departments. Although the model accuracy may be disputable, it was

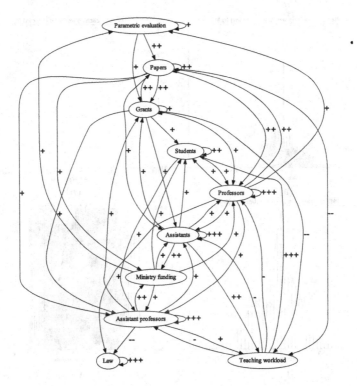

Fig. 3. Fuzzy cognitive map for analysis of academic units development [8]. Linguistic values $(-\,-\,-, \,-\,-, \,-, \,+, \,++, \,+\,+\,+)$ are mapped to numeric weights $(-1, -0.66, -0.33, 0.33, 0.66, 1)$.

selected as a benchmark, because it was previously quite extensively tested. Moreover, it has easy to perceive semantic, what facilitates the analysis.

The influence matrix used during the experiments comprised single real values, i.e. singletons with assigned probability 1. However, all elements of the initial state vector, were random variables of 100 values uniformly distributed in the interval $[-1, 1]$. The only exception was the input concept *Law*, which in each iteration was reset to the single value 1 with probability 1.0. The aggregators were configured to keep sizes of DRVs limited to $k = 100$.

All experiments were conducted using Java 8, run on Intel Core i7-2675QM laptop at 2.20 GHz, 8 GB memory under Windows 7. The number of iterations was limited to 25, as regardless of activation function and aggregator used all calculations converged to steady states within that bound. Execution times (25 iterations) depended on aggregators: for *Simple k-means* execution times ranged at 9 min 41 s, for *DBSCAN* about 6 min 51 s, for *UniBins* about 5.5 s and, finally, 4 s in the case of *PercentileRank*.

Figure 4 shows typical probability distributions obtained by applying previously discussed aggregators. We have selected for comparison the concept *Teaching workload* at iteration 6. Plots (a) and (c) show that observed PMFs are

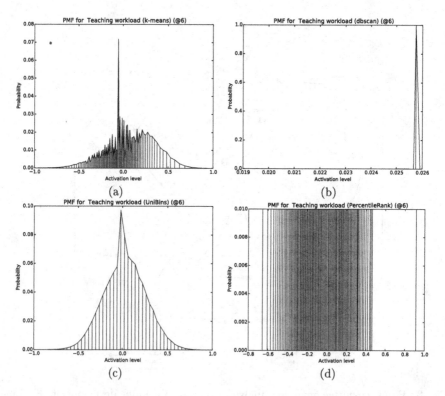

Fig. 4. Comparison of PMFs for four aggregators: (a) simple k-means (b) DBSCAN (c) UniBins (d) PercentileRank

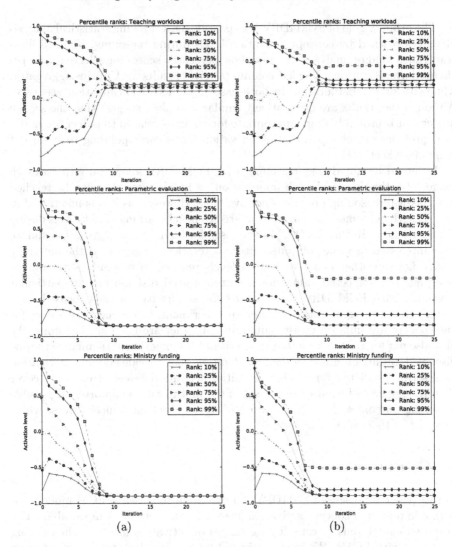

Fig. 5. Comparison of percentile scores obtained (a) UniBins aggregator (b) Percentile Rank aggregator. In both cases exp activation function was used.

mixtures of 3 (simple k-means) or 2 (UniBins) Gaussian distributions. A typical feature of DBSCAN aggregator is a small number of resulting clusters and in consequence a significant reduction of the number of values occurring in a resulting discrete random variable. In this case the input variable comprising 600 elements was converted to 4 clusters. The plot (d) shows results of applying PercentileRank aggregator. High amplitudes in other diagrams, e.g. (a) correspond to high frequencies of values.

The primary goal of FCM4DRV is to provide data enabling statistical analysis of ranges reached by concept activation levels during reasoning. Figure 5 illustrates such kind of analyzes. It shows how percentile scores for selected concepts changed over iterations. The left column (a) gives results for UniBins aggregator, while (b) for PercentileRank. In both cases S_{exp} activation function was used. Although the results are qualitatively similar, the plots suggest that the second aggregator is probably more appropriate for analyses related to percentile ranks, as it provides better separation of activation levels corresponding to $k - 1$ cut points (see Sect. 4.4).

It should be noted that reasoning with FCM4DRV allows only to establish ranges of activation levels, full information on FCM states that can be reached in a classical reasoning process is not available. However, as it was mentioned in Sect. 2, such outcomes fits our needs related to benchmarking of risk levels during risk assessment. In this case FCMs were used for hierarchical aggregation and we were interested in values obtained after m iterations, where m is the hierarchy depth. On the other hand, activation levels reached in a steady state can be interpreted as expected values for a certain initial distribution. In particular reasoning with FCM4DRV can be used for sensitivity analysis focused on a certain concept, e.g. we may consider an experiment, in which initial values for one concept are uniformly distributed and all other are fixed as singletons. We may also put forward a claim that theoretically, for experiments similar to the one discussed, results obtained *in the first iteration* may provide enough information to describe predicted tendencies: as initial activation levels of concepts cover their ranges, sets of values determined in the first iteration comprise all possible reasoning outcomes. However, the use of aggregators introduces errors, which were not at this point analyzed.

6   Conclusions

In this paper we discuss FCM4DRV, an extension to classical FCM model consisting in replacing concept activation levels with discrete random variables. The proposed model aims at establishing ranges of activation levels reached during reasoning with FCMs. We were motivated by a particular problem of selecting accurate thresholds during IT security risk analysis with FCM [5–7], however, the presented here solution is more general and can be applied to a variety of problems. The FCM4DRV extension includes augmenting classical FCM state equation with appropriate operators applicable to DRVs, as well as introducing aggregators, special functions that transform DRVs into similar ones, yet less memory consuming and requiring smaller computational effort. We implemented a prototype software tool supporting the FCM4DRV model and we reported experiments demonstrating its computational feasibility and typical results.

We plan to develop features that are still missing: first of all provide tools for assessing similarity measures between DRVs, errors introduced by aggregators, as well as provide analysis on their influence on reasoning results.

References

1. Kosko, B.: Neural Networks and Fuzzy Systems: A Dynamical Systems Approach to Machine Intelligence. Prentice Hall, Englewood Cliffs (1992)
2. Aguilar, J.: A survey about Fuzzy Cognitive Maps papers (invited paper). Int. J. **3**(2), 27–33 (2005)
3. Papageorgiou, E.: Learning algorithms for fuzzy cognitive maps: a review study. IEEE Trans. Syst. Man Cybernetics, Part C: Appl. Rev. **42**(2), 150–163 (2012)
4. Papageorgiou, E.I., Salmeron, J.L.: Methods and algorithms for fuzzy cognitive map-based modeling. In: Papageorgiou, E.I. (ed.) Fuzzy Cognitive Maps for Applied Sciences and Engineering. ISRL, vol. 54, pp. 1–28. Springer, Heidelberg (2014)
5. Szwed, P., Skrzynski, P., Grodniewicz, P.: Risk assessment for SWOP telemonitoring system based on Fuzzy Cognitive Maps. In: Dziech, A., Czyżewski, A. (eds.) MCSS 2013. CCIS, vol. 368, pp. 233–247. Springer, Heidelberg (2013)
6. Szwed, P., Skrzynski, P.: A new lightweight method for security risk assessment based on Fuzzy Cognitive Maps. Appl. Math. Comput. Sci. **24**(1), 213–225 (2014)
7. Szwed, P., Skrzynski, P., Chmiel, W.: Risk assessment for a video surveillance system based on Fuzzy Cognitive Maps. Multimedia Tools Appl., 1–24 (2014). doi:10.1007/s11042-014-2047-6
8. Szwed, P.: Application of fuzzy cognitive maps to analysis of development scenarios for academic units. Automatyka/Automatics **17**(2), 229–239 (2013)
9. Lazzerini, B., Mkrtchyan, L.: Analyzing risk impact factors using extended fuzzy cognitive maps. IEEE Syst. J. **5**(2), 288–297 (2011)
10. Chmiel, W., Szwed, P.: Learning Fuzzy Cognitive Map for traffic prediction using an evolutionary algorithm. In: Dziech, A., Leszczuk, M., Baran, R. (eds.) MCSS 2015. CCIS, vol. 566, pp. 195–209. Springer, Heidelberg (2015). doi:10.1007/978-3-319-26404-2_16
11. Ozesmi, U., Ozesmi, S.: Ecological models based on people's knowledge: a multistep fuzzy cognitive mapping approach. Ecol. Model. **176**(1–2), 43–64 (2004)
12. Salmeron, J.L., Gutierrez, E.: Fuzzy grey cognitive maps in reliability engineering. Appl. Soft Comput. **12**(12), 3818–3824 (2012). Theoretical issues and advanced applications on Fuzzy Cognitive Maps
13. Iakovidis, D., Papageorgiou, E.: Intuitionistic fuzzy cognitive maps for medical decision making. IEEE Trans. Inf. Technol. Biomed. **15**(1), 100–107 (2011)
14. Aguilar, J.: Dynamic random fuzzy cognitive maps. Computación y Sistemas **7**(4), 260–270 (2004)
15. Słoń, G.: Application of models of relational fuzzy cognitive maps for prediction of work of complex systems. In: Rutkowski, L., Korytkowski, M., Scherer, R., Tadeusiewicz, R., Zadeh, L.A., Zurada, J.M. (eds.) ICAISC 2014, Part I. LNCS, pp. 307–318. Springer, Heidelberg (2014)
16. Abeel, T., Van de Peer, Y., Saeys, Y.: Java-ML: a machine learning library. J. Mach. Learn. Res. **10**, 931–934 (2009)

Evolutionary Algorithms and Their Applications

Natural Computing in Pump-Scheduling Optimization for Water Supply System: Case Study

Maria José de Paula Castanho, Angelita Maria de Ré, Fábio Hernandes,
Emanuel da Costa Luz, Mauro Miazaki[✉], and Sandro Rautenberg

Midwestern State University, UNICENTRO, Guarapuava, PR, Brazil
{zeza,angelita,hernandes,maurom,srautenberg}@unicentro.br,
emanuel.luz@bol.com.br

Abstract. The electrical energy cost represents a significant fraction of the total cost in a water supply system. Any optimization in pumping operational procedures results in a reduction of this cost. The aim of this paper is the optimization of pump operation in a water distribution system, located at Guarapuava, Brazil. For this, we used two techniques of Natural Computing: Genetic Algorithms and Shuffled Frog Leaping Algorithm. Both techniques were effective when comparing with a traditional approach. However, in our experiments, the SFLA achieved lower costs.

Keywords: Water supply · Electrical energy · Genetic Algorithms · Shuffled Frog Leaping Algorithm

1 Introduction

In Brazil, the electrical energy cost of a water supply system varies between 9 % and 24 % of the company's expenses, depending on the country region [20]. In some places, it is the second largest expense. Improving the pumping operational procedures can save energy and, as a consequence, minimize the company's expenses, without any additional investment.

In the domain of water distribution, several studies have been conducted for optimizing the design of Water Distribution Networks (WDN) [15,21,24]. Jowwit and Germanopoulos [11] used Linear Programming to produce optimal pumping schedules. Pasha and Lansey [19] also adopted Linear Programming. However, they considered online data into the model for optimizing the pump operation in real-time. Also in the real-time pumping-scheduling problem, Giacomello et al. [8] applied a hybrid optimization method, based on Linear Programming and Greedy Algorithm. Price and Ostfeld [22] used a skeletonized operational graph. In order to handle with the uncertainty in water demand, Goryashko and Nemirovski [10] employed the Robust Counterpart Methodology in Linear Programming Models. Outeiro et al. [4] dealt with such uncertainty by including

© Springer International Publishing Switzerland 2016
L. Rutkowski et al. (Eds.): ICAISC 2016, Part I, LNAI 9692, pp. 359–369, 2016.
DOI: 10.1007/978-3-319-39378-0_31

fuzzy linear programming to their models. McCormick and Powell [16] derived a simplified model from a standard hydraulic simulator, and used a descent method to produce initial schedules, as well as a two-stage simulated annealing to generate optimal solutions. Fracasso *et al.* [7] used Markov Decision Processes in a framework to optimize the electricity costs, as well as to prevent water demand interruption by minimizing the risk of pipe rupture.

Moreover, several works regarding the use of Natural Computing techniques to solve the optimal design of WDN have also been reported in the scientific literature. The first studies of Natural Computing for reducing the energetic cost of pumping systems appeared in 1994 [17]. Originally, they employed the Genetic Algorithms (GA). Since then, several authors used this approach [2,17,25]. However, according to the authors, in order to obtain better results for pump scheduling, Genetic Algorithms should be hybridized with other techniques. The methodology used by Kurek and Ostfeld [12] combined SPEA2 (an evolutionary multiobjective algorithm) with EPANET (a hydraulic simulation software) for finding a trade-off between pumping costs and water quality. Odan *et al.* [18] generated optimal pump schedules using A MultiALgorithm-Genetically-Adaptive-Method (AMALGAM) and other methodological approaches to enable this scheduling in real-time. López-Ibánez *et al.* [13] developed an application based on the Ant Colony Optimization technique for the optimal scheduling of pumps. Rajabpour *et al.* [23] determined the optimal operation of the pumping stations using a Jumping Particle Swarm Optimization (JPSO) algorithm to achieve the minimum energy cost. Eusuff and Lansey [5] developed the SFLANET, a computer model that uses the Shuffled Frog Leaping Algorithm (SFLA) with the EPANET to determine the optimal discrete pipe measures for new pipe networks.

Since the reduction of expenses in water supply systems is an important problem to solve, with economic impacts, we aim to compare two important techniques of Natural Computing in this work: GA and SFLA. These algorithms were implemented and tested using real data from the water distribution system of Guarapuava, a city in the South of Brazil, with a population of 167,328 in 2010 (souce: IBGE – Brazilian Institute of Geography and Statistics).

The paper is structured as follow: the problem is presented in Sect. 2; Sect. 3 discusses the Materials and Methods used in this work; Sect. 5 describes the results; finally, Sect. 6 outlines the conclusions and some directions for future work.

2   Problem Description

The SANEPAR (Sanitation Company of Paraná) is the company responsible for water supply and water treatment in the city of Guarapuava. The water catchment is done in a river (*Rio das Pedras*) using two pipelines (diameters: 400 mm and 350 mm; length: 1,112 m; elevation: about 100 m). Three pumps compose the water catchment station: two of 447,42 kW and one of 335,56 kW, with respective water flow rate of 594m^3/h and 432m^3/h. Only two pumps can work

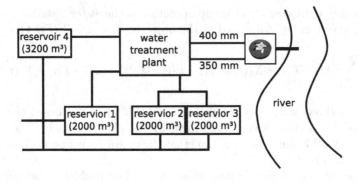

Fig. 1. Guarapuava's water supply system

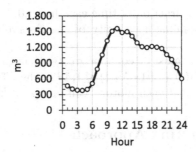

Fig. 2. Average hourly water demand in Guarapuava (January 2013)

together due to the station capacity for producing drinking water (currently, limited to 1,188m³/h). The station has four interconnected reservoirs with 9,200m³ of maximum capacity. In order to avoid cavitation in the water distribution network, as a rule, the minimum volume adopted is 1/3 of the maximum capacity. A simplified scheme of Guarapuava's water supply system is depicted in Fig. 1.

In Brazil, the electricity tariffs are determined by ANEEL (Brazilian Electricity Regulatory Agency), which establishes the charges for each type of company. The water distribution companies pay the tariff called "green horo-sazonal". This means that there are different tariffs for electricity (kWh), according to the periods of the day. The tariff is more expensive in peak hours, between 18 h and 21 h. In the period of the gathered data, the cost in peak hours was R$ 0,59/kWh and in other hours was R$ 0,14/kWh.

The data used in this work are the water demand measurements in Guarapuava, during January 2013. A model was developed from such data, in order to obtain an average water demand behavior for each hour of a day (see Fig. 2). There are 24 data points, corresponding to the 24 h. The first data point is the average water demand from 00:01 am to 01:00 am, considering all the 31 days of January 2013. The second point is the average demand from 01:01 am to 02:00, and so on.

The energy daily cost of the pump operation in the water distribution system of Guarapuava can be formulated as the objective function Z (Eq. 1):

$$Z = \sum_{t=1}^{24} [441 * T(t) * X_1(t) + 331 * T(t) * X_2(t) + 441 * T(t) * X_3(t)] \qquad (1)$$

where 441 and 331 values are the demand in kWh for each motor i ($i = 1, 2, 3$); $T(t)$ is the electricity consumption tariff in R\$/kWh for each period t ($t = 1, 2, ..., 24$); $X_i(t)$ is the amount of time that the motor i must be working (pumping) for each period t.

The formulation of the optimal pump scheduling problem relies on the following set of assumptions:

1. each pump can work a fraction of time each hour: $0 \le X_i(t) \le 60$;
2. the maximum and minimum capacity of the reservoirs must be observed: $3066 \le V(t) \le 9200$;
3. the treatment capacity must be equal or greater than the total pumped water: $594 * X_1(t) + 432 * X_2(t) + 594 * X_3(t) \le 1,188$, where 594 and 432 values are the amount of water that each motor i can pump working an entire hour.

3   Natural Computing Approaches

Natural Computing uses nature as inspiration for the development of new computational techniques that can be used to solve complex problems. Among the developed techniques, there are the bio-inspired algorithms. They are based on populations with two main approaches: (i) evolutionary algorithms (biological evolution) and (ii) swarm algorithms. Genetic Algorithms (GA), Evolutionary Programming, Evolutionary Strategy and Genetic Programming are examples of evolutionary algorithms. Their evolutionary operators change the individual characteristics. Ant Colony Optimization, Particle Swarm Optimization and Shuffled Frog Leaping Algorithm (SFLA) are swarm algorithms. These algorithms are based on the collective behavior of individuals changing their knowledge [3]. In common, these approaches rely on the behavior of population elements, which evolve over time (generations) as a system for solving a certain problem.

In this paper, two Natural Computing approaches are adopted to optimize pumping schedule: (i) the GA, using a computational representation of chromosomes as processing elements; and (ii) the SFLA, adopting virtual frogs as computing units. These techniques are described in this section.

3.1   Genetic Algorithms (GA)

Genetic Algorithms are techniques inspired in the natural evolution, with the purpose of finding solutions for problems that require search, adaptation and optimization [9]. A typical implementation of GA is depicted in Algorithm 1.

Algorithm 1. The Genetic Algorithm

```
1: pop.init()
2: repeat
3:    pop.evaluatePopulation()
4:    pop.getBestIndividuals()
5:    pop.applyEvolutionaryOperators()
6: until stop_criteria = true
```

First, an initial random population is generated (Line 1 in Algorithm 1). Note that the random individuals generated in this step must satisfy all the constraints of the problem. Then, from Line 2 to Line 6, an evolutionary process is executed on the generated population of chromosomes (candidate solutions). During the process, each chromosome is evaluated through fitness (Line 3), which is a measure of how adequate a candidate solution is to solve a given problem. Next, a set of chromosomes (with the best fitness values) are selected (Line 4). The genetic operators, such as crossover and mutation, are applied over the selected chromosomes (Line 4), improving the population and/or introducing diversity. Then, the evolutionary process is repeated, until a stop criteria is satisfied (Line 6).

In our approach, the crossover and mutation operators are implemented as follows: (i) the crossover takes two individuals as parameters and performs crossing in a cutoff point. The cutoff point can be fixed or randomly settled. After making the crossing, the new individuals are evaluated according to the problem constraints. If valid individuals are generated, they replace the parents in the next generation. (ii) In the mutation, once an individual is selected, a variation occurs over a random allele representing a peak hour of power consumption.

3.2 Shuffled Frog Leaping Algorithm (SFLA)

The SFLA algorithm is a memetic metaheuristic [6], designed to search a solution for an optimization problem using a heuristic search. It is based on the evolution of memes, produced by individual interactions (local search) and a global information exchange among individuals in a population. Meme is an intellectual or cultural information unit that is transmitted from an individual to another, analogous to the biological evolution [1].

In SFLA, we have "frogs" that evolve through a memetic evolution. The frogs are hosts for memes, i.e., a vector of memotypes. A memotype represents an idea, similar to a gene in a GA. The SFLA gradually improves ideas contained in each frog within a virtual population. In SFLA, ideas are passed among all individuals in the population, while in GA the interaction is only between parents and siblings.

In order to better understand the dynamics of the algorithm, we must consider the following situation: a group of frogs leaping in a swamp. This swamp has a number of rocks in certain places, where the frogs can jump. The goal of the frogs is to find the stone with the maximum amount of available food, as

---

Algorithm 2. The Shuffled Frog-Leaping Algorithm

1: Input$\{N, im, iN, F\}$;
2: Output$\{The best frog\}$;
3: Generate a random population of F frogs;
4: Calculate the fitness for each frog;
5: **for** $i = 1$ to N **do**
6:     Rank the F frogs in the decreasing order by fitness value;
7:     Select the frog with the best position in the swamp (X_g);
8:     Shuffle the frogs among the Im Memeplexes;
9:     **for** $j = 1$ to Im **do**
10:        **for** $k = 1$ to iN **do**
11:            Define the best (X_b) and the worst (X_w) frogs in Memeplex j;
12:            Generate a new frog (X_{new}) by improving the position of X_w using Eqs. 2 and 3;
13:            **if** the position is improved **then**
14:                $X_w \leftarrow X_{new}$;
15:            **else**
16:                Randomly generate a new frog (X_{rand});
17:                $X_w \leftarrow X_{rand}$;
18:            **end if**
19:        **end for**
20:     **end for**
21: **end for**
22: Output the best solution;

---

soon as possible, thus improving their memes. A more detailed description of SFLA can be seen in Algorithm 2.

The Algorithm 2 shows two main schemes: a global execution flow and a local search, where occurs memetic evolution. In the first the control variables are defined (line 1): number of generations (N) – how many generations will be realized in the execution (the main loop); number of memeplex (Im) – memeplex is a subset of frogs; number of evolution (iN) – iterations executed for each memeplex; number of frogs (F) – population size of frogs, which are possible solutions. The line 2 defines the output: the best frog (i.e., the best solution).

The other variables are: (X_w) is the position of the worst frog in memeplex, that has the greater fitness value in the local search space; (X_b) is the position of best frog in the memeplex, that has the lowest fitness value in the local search space; (X_g) is the position of the best frog in the swamp, that has the lowest fitness value in the global search space.

In the line 3, the first population of frogs is randomly generated and checked whether the created solutions (frogs) are feasible, according to the constraints of the problem. Next, the fitness of each frog is calculated (line 4).

Then, from lines 5 to 20 occurs the global search. N iterations are performed. In line 6, the population of feasible frogs is sorted in descending order by the fitness value. Next, the best global solution in each iteration is selected (the best frog, X_g) in the line 7.

The local search starts in the line 8 and ends in the 18, where each memeplex is improved by cultural evolution (there are Im memeplexes. The loop in the lines 9–17 defines the number of evolution iterations inside each memeplex. Such evolution aims to improve the position of the worst frog (X_w) in memeplex, which is enhanced by the infection process of ideas, using the best frog (X_b) (lines 10 and 11). From lines 12 to 16, if the new generated frog is better than the worst frog (X_w), then substitute X_w. Otherwise, a new frog is randomly generated to substitute X_w.

The new frog is generated using the Eqs. 2 and 3 [14].

$$D = Rand() * (X_b - X_w) \tag{2}$$

$$X_{new} = D + X_w, \qquad D_{Min} \leq D \leq D_{Max} \tag{3}$$

where X_w and X_b are the worst and best frog positions respectively in memeplex; $Rand()$ generates a random number between $(0, 1)$; and D_{Min} and D_{Max} are the minimum and maximum allowed change in the position of a frog, respectively. If X_{New} is better than the original fitness worst X_w, X_w is replaced by X_{New}. Otherwise, the best overall frog X_g is used instead of X_b to carry out the strategic update. If still there is no improvement, a viable solution to replace X_w is generated randomly. The process continues for a predefined number of iterations in each memeplex. Then all the frogs are shuffled to exchange global information. Local search is followed by global, until a predetermined convergence criterion to be satisfied.

The frog shuffling is the distribution of the frogs among the memeplexes. After the sorting, for example, if we have Im = 3 (number of memeplexes), frog ranking 1 goes to memeplex 1, frog ranking 2 goes to memeplex 2, frog ranking 3 goes to memeplex 3, frog ranking 4 goes to memeplex 1, and so on.

4   GA and SFLA Specification

The data structure used for the chromosome and frog instances in GA and SFLA, respectively, is showed in Fig. 3. This specifies 24 items for estimating the use of the three pumps, in discrete minutes, per hours in a day. Highlighted in red, three items represent the peak time interval (from 18 to 20 h). Considering the Natural Computing approaches, each item refers to an allele in AG chromosome and a memes in SFLA frog.

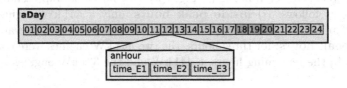

Fig. 3. Data structure representing a daily pumping schedule.

On developing the Natural Computing approaches, we considered the following restrictions of the water supply system: (i) the installed treatment capacity (1188m^3) limits the pumping of water to the supply system; (ii) to avoid cavitation, the amount of water in the reservoirs can not be less than 3066m^3; and (iii) the upper level of water in the reservoirs is limited to 9200m^3.

To find out an intrinsic system behavior, a preliminary analysis on a monthly data set (January 2013) was conducted. The analysis is depicted in Fig. 2.

Such analysis revealed the peaks of water consumption. Regardless a day of the week, the peaks tend to occur from 11 to 15 h and from 18 to 20 h. By relating the identified intervals and the energy tariffs, the following statements were confirmed: (i) the last interval is comprised in the peak hours energy cost; and (ii) it is strongly recommended avoid the use the pumps between 18 to 20 h to minimize the energy expenses.

For implementing the approaches, the formulation discussed in Sect. 2 were used, adding the pump operation rules: (i) only two pumps can work together, i.e., at least one of them must be zero; and (ii) the sum of pump operations cannot exceed 120 min (maximum time of pumps working together).

5   Results and Discussion

GA and SFLA approaches were developed using the JAVA programming language. They were tested by varying the parameters. For GA initial population: {50, 100, 150, 200}; generations: {50, 100, 200, 1000}; mutation: {0.3, 0.5}, high rate for promoting gene exchanging and not content updating; crossover: {0.6, 0.9}, previous tests showed that lower crossover rates do not improve the solutions; and cut-off point: fixed, random. For SFLA initial population: {50, 100}; memeplex subsets: {10, 20}; generations: {5, 10}; and evolution in memeplex: {1, 3}.

In the tests, the best GA individual emerged after 100 generations, among 100 individuals. It was adopted the random cut-off point, using 0.6 and 0.5 for crossover and mutation rates, respectively. Depicted in Fig. 4(a), the individual represents a pump-scheduling as follows: (i) **inside peak hours**: only a 441 kW engine is used for 39 min, minimizing the energy consumption in the critical interval; and (ii) **outside peak hours**: for six hours, the two 441 kW engines were completely activated. In the remaining hours, a 441 kW and the 331 kW engines were fully used.

The best SFLA individual arose after 10 generations, among 50 individuals in 20 memeplex. Depicted in Figure Fig. 4(b), the individual represents a pump-scheduling as follows: (i) **inside peak hours**: only a 441 kW engine is used for 14 min, minimizing the energy consumption in the critical interval; and (ii) **outside peak hours**: for three hours, the two 441 kW engines were completely activated. In the remaining hours, a 441 kW and the 331 kW engines were fully used.

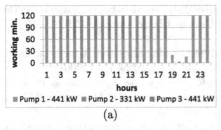 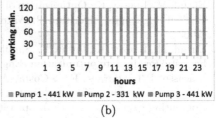

(a)   (b)

Fig. 4. Best individuals for (a) GA and (b) SFLA

6   Conclusion

Managing the energy production and consumption is a crucial issue to any country. It is related to the national policies to better use the available resources and grow in a sustainable way. In Brazil, the total energy consumption is about 10.59 MWh/year. From this amount, approximately, 2.5 % of the energy is taken by the water supply companies for feeding back the economic system with an important element to produce goods and services, the water. In this context, generating savings in water supply companies can represent availability to other purposes.

For reducing operational costs, we investigated the use of Natural Computing approaches for minimizing the pump operations in water supply systems. In a use case, we apply the GA and SFLA approaches. The experiments showed that those approaches can produce substantial reduction of expenditures. The best individuals of GA (R\$ 2,531.20) and SLFA (R\$ 2,376.59) achieved savings of approximately 20 %, when comparing to the real average cost of the company (about R\$ 3,200.00). Also, SLFA saved about 6 % more when compared to GA.

The preliminary results encourage us in a research agenda. As the approaches were developed adopting only one-month data, we aim to advance in this study, considering a large-scale dataset. In such a way, we aim to work on water demand forecasting and water supply system automation.

References

1. Blackmore, S.: The evolution of meme machines. In: Proceedings of the International Congress on Ontopsychology and Memetics, Milan (2002)
2. Boulos, P.F., Wu, Z., Orr, C.H., Moore, M., Hsiund, P., Thomas, D.: Optimal pump operation of water distribution systems using genetic algorithms. The Pennsylvania State University CiteSeerX Archives (2008)
3. de Castro, L.N.: Fundamentals of Natural Computing. Chapman and Hall/CRC, Boca Raton (2006)
4. de P. Castanho, M.J., Outeiro, V.H., Hernandes, F.: Using fuzzy mathematic programming to reduce energy costs. Proceeding Series of the Brazilian Society of Applied and Computational Mathematics, vol. 3(1) (2015). (in Portuguese)

5. Eusuff, M., Lansey, K.: Optimization of water distribution network design using the shuffled frog leaping algorithm. J. Water Resour. Plann. Manage. **129**(3), 210–225 (2003)
6. Eusuff, M., Lansey, K., Pasha, F.: Shuffled frog-leaping algorithm: a memetic meta-heuristic for discrete optimization. Eng. Optim. **38**(2), 129–154 (2006)
7. Fracasso, P.T., Barnes, F.S., Costa, A.H.R.: Energy cost optimization in water distribution systems using markov decision processes. In: 2013 International Green Computing Conference (IGCC), pp. 1–6, June 2013
8. Giacomello, C., Kapelan, Z., Nicolini, M.: Fast hybrid optimization method for effective pump scheduling. J. Water Res. Plann. Manage. **139**(2), 175–183 (2013)
9. Goldberg, D.E.: Genetic Algorithms in Search, Optimization and Machine Learning. Addison-Wesley, Reading (1989)
10. Goryashko, A.P., Nemirovski, A.S.: Robust energy cost optimization of water distribution system with uncertain demand. Autom. Remote Control **75**(10), 1754–1769 (2014)
11. Jowitt, P., Germanopoulos, G.: Optimal pump scheduling in water-supply networks. J. Water Res. Plann. Manage. **118**(4), 406–422 (1992)
12. Kurek, W., Ostfeld, A.: Multiobjective water distribution systems control of pumping cost, water quality, and storage-reliability constraints. J. Water Res. Plann. Manage. **140**(2), 184–193 (2014)
13. Lopez-Ibánez, M., Prasad, T.D., Paechter, B.: Ant colony optimization for optimal control of pumps in water distribution networks. J. Water Res. Plann. Manage. **134**(4), 337–346 (2008)
14. Lu, K., Ting, L., Keming, W., Hanbing, Z., Makoto, T., Bin, Y.: An improved shuffled frog-leaping algorithm for flexible job shop scheduling problem. Algorithms **8**, 19–31 (2015)
15. Maier, H.M., Simpson, A.R., Zecchin, A., Foong, W.K., Phang, K.Y., Seah, H.Y., Tan, C.L.: Ant colony optimization for design of water distribution systems. J. Water Res. Plann. Manage. **129**(3), 200–209 (2003)
16. Mccormick, G., Powell, R.S.: Derivation of near-optimal pump schedules for water distribution by simulated annealing. J. Oper. Res. Soc. **55**, 728–736 (2004)
17. Moreira, D.F., Ramos, H.M.: Energy cost optimization in a water supply system case study. J. Energy (2013)
18. Odan, F., Reis, R., Kapelan, Z.: Real-time multiobjective optimization of operation of water supply systems. J. Water Res. Plann. Manage. **141**(9), 04015011 (2015)
19. Pasha, M., Lansey, K.: Optimal Pump Scheduling by Linear Programming, Chap. 37, pp. 1–10. American Society of Civil Engineers (2009)
20. PMSS: Sanitation sector modernization program: electric power management (2015) (in Portuguese). http://www.pmss.gov.br/index.php/projeto-com-agua/gestao-de-energia-eletrica/
21. Prasad, T., Park, N.: Multiobjective genetic algorithms for design of water distribution networks. J. Water Res. Plann. Manage. **130**(1), 73–82 (2004)
22. Price, E., Ostfeld, A.: Graph theory modeling approach for optimal operation of water distribution systems. J. Hydraul. Eng. **142**(3), 04015061 (2015)

23. Rajabpour, R., Talebbeydokhti, N., Ahmadi, M.H.: Developing new algorithm and its application on optimal control of pumps in water distribution. Int. J. Civil, Environ. Struct. Constr. Architectural Eng. 9(9), 1097–1101 (2015)
24. Savic, D., Walters, G.: Genetic algorithms for least-cost design of water distribution networks. J. Water Res. Plann. Manage. 123(2), 67–77 (1997)
25. van Zyl, J., Savic, D., Walters, G.: Operational optimization of water distribution systems using a hybrid genetic algorithm. J. Water Res. Plann. Manage. 130(2), 160–170 (2004)

Hybrid Parallelization of Evolutionary Model Tree Induction

Marcin Czajkowski$^{(\boxtimes)}$, Krzysztof Jurczuk, and Marek Kretowski

Faculty of Computer Science, Bialystok University of Technology,
Wiejska 45a, 15-351 Bialystok, Poland
{m.czajkowski,k.jurczuk,m.kretowski}@pb.edu.pl

Abstract. This paper illustrates a parallel implementation of evolutionary induction of model trees. An objective is to demonstrate that such evolutionary evolved trees, which are emerging alternatives to the greedy top-down solutions, can be successfully applied to large scale data. The proposed approach combines message passing (MPI) and shared memory (OpenMP) paradigms. This hybrid approach is based on a classical master-slave model in which the individuals from the population are evenly distributed to available nodes and cores. The most time consuming operations like recalculation of the regression models in the leaves as well as the fitness evaluation and genetic operators are executed in parallel on slaves. Experimental validation on artificial and real-life datasets confirms the efficiency of the proposed implementation.

Keywords: Evolutionary algorithms · Decision trees · Parallel computing · MPI · OpenMP

1 Introduction

Decision trees are one of the most known prediction techniques in data mining [13]. Their popularity can be explained by their ease of application, fast operation and effectiveness. Regression and model trees [12] may be considered as a variant of decision trees, designed to approximate real-valued functions instead of being used for classification tasks. Main difference between regression trees and model trees is that, for the latter, constant value in the terminal nodes is replaced by the regression planes.

Despite fifty years of research on the decision trees, a few open issues still remain [16]. To mitigate some of them (e.g. application of heuristics such as greedy algorithms where locally optimal decisions are made in each tree node) evolutionary algorithms (EAs) are applied to the decision tree induction [1]. The strength of such approach lies in global search for splits and predictions, and it results in higher accuracy and smaller output trees in comparison to popular top-down decision tree inducers [19]. However, one of the major drawbacks associated with the application of EAs is relatively high tree induction time, especially for large scale data. In the recent survey [1] on the evolutionary induction of decision

© Springer International Publishing Switzerland 2016
L. Rutkowski et al. (Eds.): ICAISC 2016, Part I, LNAI 9692, pp. 370–379, 2016.
DOI: 10.1007/978-3-319-39378-0_32

trees, authors put on the first place in the future trends the need of speeding up the evolutionary induction.

Fortunately EAs are naturally prone to parallelism and the process of artificial evolution can be implemented in various ways [5]. There are three main strategies that have been studied for the parallelization and/or distribution of the computation effort in EAs:

- master-slave paradigm [3] - parallelization of the most time consuming operations in each evolutionary loop (usually fitness recalculation);
- cellular (fine-grained) algorithm [15] - redistribution of single individuals which can communicate only with the nearest individuals (for the selection and reproduction) based on the defined neighborhood topology;
- island (coarse-grained) model [2] - grouping individuals into sub-populations that are distributed between islands and can evolve independently.

In this paper, a parallelization with a hybrid MPI+OpenMP approach (which is considered as providing better efficiency than e.g. pure MPI version [20]) is proposed to the evolutionary induction of regression and model trees. It is applied to a system called Global Model Tree (GMT) [6] that is used in many real-life applications [7]. The main objectives of this work are to accelerate the GMT system and to enable efficient evolutionary induction of decision trees on large scale data. Previously, we managed to apply similar idea for parallelizing the evolutionary induction of classification trees [8]. To the best of our knowledge, proposed solution is the first research on parallelization the evolutionary induction of regression or model trees, as there have been no such attempts in the literature.

This paper is organized as follows. The next section provides a brief background on the GMT system. Section 3 describes our approach for parallel implementation of evolutionary tree induction in detail. Section 4 presents experimental validation of the proposed solution on artificial and real-life datasets. In the last section, the paper is concluded and possible future works are sketched.

2   Global Model Tree System

The general structure of the GMT system follows a typical EA [17] framework with an unstructured population and a generational selection. Model trees are represented in their actual form as univariate trees, so each split in the internal node is based on a single attribute. If the attribute is nominal, at least one value is associated with each branch (inner disjunction). In case of a continuous-valued attribute, the typical inequality tests are applied. Initial individuals are constructed using greedy strategies [19] on random subsamples of the training data, and the tests in internal nodes are searched on random subsets of attributes. Each tree leaf contains a multivariate linear regression model that is constructed using the standard regression technique [18] with objects associated with that node. A dependent variable (y) is explained by the linear combination of multiple independent variables $\{x_1, x_2, \ldots, x_q\}$:

$$y = \beta_0 + \beta_1 * x_1 + \beta_2 * x_2 + \ldots + \beta_q * x_q, \tag{1}$$

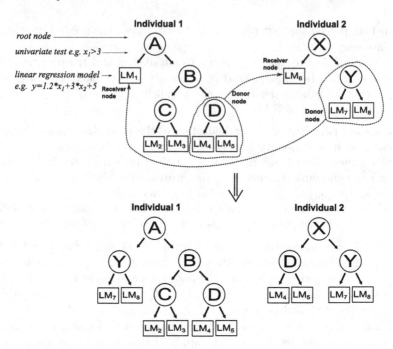

Fig. 1. Crossover between two individuals and the resulting offspring. Each individual has one donor node and one receiver node.

where q is the number of independent variables and β_i $(0 \leq i \leq q)$ are fixed coefficients that minimize the sum of the squared residuals of the model. Additionally, in every node information about training instances associated with the node is stored. This enables the algorithm to perform more efficiently local structure and tests modifications during applications of genetic operators.

Tree-based representation requires developing specialized genetic operators corresponding to classical mutation and crossover. Application of the operators can modify the tree structure, tests in internal nodes, and models in the leaves. The mutation operator makes random changes in some places of the selected individuals. The crossover operator attempts to combine elements of two existing individuals (parents) to create a new solution. The GMT system performs various specialized variants of genetic operators. An example of asymmetric crossover where the subtree of the first/second individual is replaced by a new one that was duplicated from the second/first individual is illustrated in Fig. 1. The replaced subtree starts in the node denoted as a receiver, and the duplicated subtree starts in the node denoted as a donor. It is preferred that the receiver node has a high error per instance and it is replaced by the donor node, which should have a small value of error as it is duplicated. The application of this particular variant is more likely to improve affected individuals because, with higher probability, the good nodes are duplicated and replace the weak nodes. Several variants of crossover and mutations were proposed in [6], e.g.:

- finding a new test or modification of the existing one (shift threshold on continuous attribute, re-grouping nominal attribute values) in the internal node;
- pruning the internal node and transforming it into the leaf with a new multivariate linear regression model;
- expanding the leaf into the internal node;
- replacing one of the following: subtree, branch, node, or test between two affected individuals;
- modification of the linear regression models in the leaves (add, remove, or change attributes).

Successful application of any operator results in a necessity for relocation of the instances between tree parts rooted in the modified nodes.

The selection mechanism is based on the ranking linear selection [17] with the *elitist strategy*, which copies the best individual founded so far to the next population. The fitness function measures the performance of the individuals in terms of meeting the problem objective. In the context of decision trees, a direct minimization of the prediction performance measured on the learning set often leads to the over-fitting problem and poor performance on unseen testing instances. Therefore, efficient fitness function should consider not only the predictive error but also the complexity of the tree. In GMT, the authors adapt the Bayesian Information Criterion (BIC) [21] as a fitness function. The BIC fitness is equal to:

$$Fit_{BIC}(T) = -2 * ln(L(T)) + ln(n) * k(T), \tag{2}$$

where $L(T)$ is the tree (T) maximum of likelihood function, $k(T)$ is the complexity term, and n equals the number of instances. The function $L(T)$ is common for regression models [9] and is defined as:

$$ln(L(T)) = -0.5n * [ln(2\pi) + ln(SS_e(T)/n) + 1]. \tag{3}$$

The term $SS_e(T)$ is the sum of squared residuals of the tree T (on the training set).

3   Parallel Implementation of the GMT System

The proposed parallelization of the model tree evolutionary inducer is based on the sequential GMT algorithm for univariate model trees. The general flowchart of our hybrid MPI+OpenMP approach is illustrated in Fig. 2. One can observe that the evolutionary induction is run in a sequential way on a master node and the most time consuming operations (evaluation of the individuals, recalculation of the regression models and genetic operators) are performed in parallel on the available nodes (slaves). This master-slave parallelization approach, where the master distributes the population among the slaves and, finally, it gathers and merges the results, does not affect the results of the induction. Information

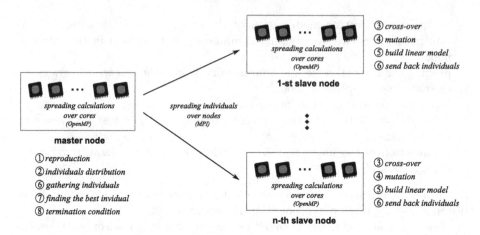

Fig. 2. Hybrid parallel approach of the evolutionary model tree induction

about the location of the training instances is stored in each node of model trees. This way the genetic operators can efficiently obtain the fitness corresponding to the individual [6]. The actual fitness calculation is embedded into the post mutation and crossover processing, when the instances in the affected parts of the tree (or trees) are relocated. This mechanism increases the memory complexity of the induction but significantly reduces its computational complexity. As a consequence, the most time consuming elements of the algorithm are genetic operators and thus are performed in parallel. In addition, each tree node contains information about the regression models. After each successive application of any genetic operator the regression models in the affected leaves are recalculated, which also takes considerable amount of time.

The first level of parallelization the GMT solution (see Fig. 2) applies distributed memory approach where the master node spreads individuals from the population over slave nodes using message-passing strategy [10]. The role of the master node is to perform selection and reproduction (steps (1) and (7)) as well as the verification of termination condition (step (8)). In each evolutionary loop, the master evenly distributes individuals among the slaves (step (2)). To avoid wasting resources, the chunk of population is left on the master which also works as a slave. Migration the individuals between nodes (steps (2) and (6)) is performed with the framework of the message-passing interface (MPI [11]) and requires: packing the tree structures into a flat message; transferring the message between nodes (sending/receiving); and unpacking the message into the corresponding tree. The packed tree structure contains information about its size and the information about each tree node:

- node type (leaf or internal node);
- type and definition of a test (only for internal node);
- definition of the multivariate linear regression model;
- additional statistics (number of instances that reaches the node, prediction error).

To avoid unnecessary unpacking-packing operations (for the trees that will not be selected into the next generation) on the master, the fitness value of the migrated individual is also transferred. However, no information about the objects redistribution in the tree is included in the package. Including such information would strongly increase the size of the package, especially on large scale datasets. Therefore, alike in our previously presented research [8], we recover the redistribution of the instances in those nodes that will be affected by the genetic operators. It is performed on slave nodes which execute the mutation and crossover operations (steps (3) and (4)). If the genetic operator is successful, then there is also a need to reallocate the instances in the sub-trees and rebuild regression models in the leaves (step (5)). Otherwise, the nodes statistics from the received package remain unchanged. It should be emphasis that the GMT system mutates the internal nodes in lower parts of the tree with higher probability. This may enhance a possible speedup of such partial nodes reconstruction as it is expected that the lower parts of the tree held fewer instances that need to be reallocated.

Second level of parallelization that applies shared (OpenMP [4]) memory approach is performed on slave nodes. All the calculations assigned to the slave node are spread over cores which run the algorithm blocks in parallel. Depending on the genetic operator type, each core processes a single individual at a time (in case of mutation) or pairs of affected individuals (in case of crossover) in parallel. All cores within the node operate independently but share the same memory resources. In contrast to the distributed memory approach, no data communication between the cores is required as the access and modification of the same memory space by one core is visible to all other cores. However, additional synchronization during write/read operations is needed in order to insure appropriate access to shared memory. Parallelization with shared memory approach is also applied on the master node for the distribution and gathering population from other nodes. In addition, those individuals that were transformed into leaves after the application of genetic operators are extended into stumps in parallel by cores at each slave node.

4   Experiments

In this section we show the performance of the proposed parallel version of the GMT system. Two sets of experiments were performed on real-life and artificial datasets using evolutionary induced regression and model trees.

4.1   Setup

All presented results were obtained with a default setting of parameters from the sequential version of the GMT system. We have tested one artificially generated dataset called *Armchair* [6] with 4 different number of instances (from 1 000 to 1 000 000) and 4 real-life datasets available in the UCI Machine Learning Repository [14]. In addition, we have compared the time performance between regression and model tree inductions, and provide some detailed time-sharing information of our MPI+OpenMP parallelization.

In the paper we focus only on the time performance of the GMT system, therefore, results for the prediction accuracy are not enclosed. However, for all tested datasets, the proposed hybrid approach achieved very good results - the same as the sequential version [6].

Experiments were performed on a cluster of sixteen SMP servers (nodes) running Ubuntu 12 and connected by an Infiniband network (20 Gb/s). Each server was equipped with 16 GB RAM, 2xXeon X5355 2.66 GHz CPUs with total number of cores equal 8. We used the Intel version 15.1 compiler, MVAPICH version 2.2 and OpenMP version 3.0. Within each node, the shared memory approach (OpenMP) was applied whereas between the nodes the message-passing interface (MPI) was used. For performance measuring we made use of the Multi-Processing Environment (MPE) library with the graphical visualization tool Jumpshot-4 [11].

4.2 Results

In the first experiment, the authors focus on the overall speedup of the proposed hybrid MPI+OpenMP approach. Table 1 presents the obtained mean speedup for different datasets. Only the best combination of nodes and cores is shown and it looked as follows for all tested datasets:

- results for 2 cores: 1 node with 2 OpenMP threads;
- results for 4 cores: 4 nodes with 1 OpenMP thread;
- results for 8, 16, 32, 64 cores: 8 nodes with 1, 2, 4, 8 OpenMP threads per node, respectively.

It should be recalled that the shared memory approach is strongly linked and limited by the available hardware (e.g. 8 cores in one node), whereas within the distributed memory approach it is usually easier to create more numerous configurations.

Results enclosed in Table 1 show that the proposed hybrid parallelization noticeable decreases the tree induction time on artificial and real-life datasets.

Table 1. Mean speedup reported for different number of cores

Dataset	Instances	Attributes	Speedup on different number of cores					
			2	4	8	16	32	64
Armchair	1 000	2	1.91	3.64	6.25	9.81	14.24	20.11
Armchair	10 000	2	1.85	3.38	6.19	9.98	14.99	22.81
Armchair	100 000	2	1.85	3.40	6.04	9.97	14.74	20.85
Armchair	1 000 000	2	1.72	3.31	5.62	9.08	13.52	17.52
Stock	950	9	1.47	3.21	3.92	8.08	11.86	19.49
Pol	15 000	48	1.74	3.23	5.47	9.06	14.95	18.33
Fried	40 768	10	1.80	2.81	5.09	8.54	13.63	23.08
Elnino	178 080	9	1.80	2.82	5.79	7.82	11.82	15.80

The speedup for 64 cores is in range from ×15.8 on the *Elnino* dataset to ×23.1 on the *Fried* dataset. With such speedup, the average tree induction time for GMT on the *Elnino* dataset (the biggest dataset from [6]) decreased from over 10 h to 40 min. The smaller speedup on the largest datasets (*Armchair* with 1 million instances and *Elnino*) may be caused by the necessity of reallocating large number of instances (after unpacking the message) in the affected node on the slaves. However, the algorithm speedup is still higher than for the evolutionary induced classification trees where the maximum speedup did not exceed ×15 [8] on artificially generated datasets. We can observe that the speedup differences between 32 and 64 cores are relatively small considering doubling the number of cores. The possible reason is the size of the population (default: 64 individuals). To achieve effective parallelization, the total number of cores should not exceed half of the population size because for some operations like crossover, each core performs calculations on two individuals.

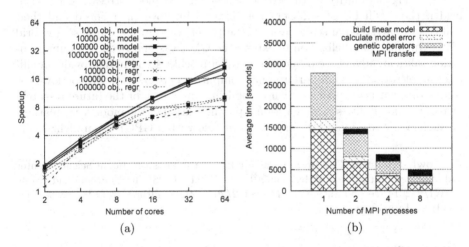

Fig. 3. Performance evaluation: (a) speedup comparison between model and regression (*regr*) tree induction on the *Armchair* dataset with different number of objects, (b) detailed time-sharing information of model tree induction (without OpenMP) with different number of slaves. Evaluation performed on the *Armchair* dataset with 100 000 instances.

Figure 3(a) illustrates the performance of the regression and model tree induction on the *Armchair* dataset with various number of instances. We can observe that with the increase of the number of cores the disproportion between the speedup for both types of tree representations is getting higher (around 2× smaller speedup for 64 cores in favor of model trees). To better understand why the proposed approach performs differently on regression and model trees see Fig. 3(b) which illustrates in details the time-sharing information for the induction of the model trees. In case of the model tree induction, more than 60 % of the evolutionary loop time is spent on building the linear models in the leaves and calculating their errors. We can observe, that this part of the algorithm is well scalable (over 95 %), however, it only exists for the evolutionary induced model trees as the regression trees does not have linear models in the leaves. Other parallelized parts like genetic operators (which include embedded fitness recalculations) are also well scalable (around 95 %), however, due to the overhead (MPI transfer) the speedup improvement on larger number of cores is smaller. For 8 processes the MPI takes almost 30 % of the evolutionary loop time in case of the model trees and approximately 50 % for the regression trees. In addition, as some parts of the algorithm have to run sequentially, the efficiency for the higher number of cores is getting smaller, as expected from the Amdahl's law [10].

5   Conclusion and Future Works

The growing popularity of the evolutionary induced model trees can be withheld if there will be no sufficient solutions to improve their speed and their ability to analyze large scale data. In the paper, the authors propose a hybrid MPI+OpenMP parallelization to extend the GMT system. Proposed implementation takes an advantage of modern parallel machines and may provide an efficient acceleration on high-performance computing clusters as well as on low-cost commodity hardware. We see many promising directions for the future research. One of the possibilities is an additional parallelization of the models calculations in the leaves (with OpenMP) as well as to deal with a GPGPU parallelization.

Acknowledgments. This project was funded by the Polish National Science Center and allocated on the basis of decision 2013/09/N/ST6/04083 (first author) and grants W/WI/2/2014 (second author) and S/WI/2/2013 (third author) from Bialystok University of Technology.

References

1. Barros, R.C., Basgalupp, M.P., Carvalho, A.C., Freitas, A.A.: A survey of evolutionary algorithms for decision-tree induction. IEEE Trans. Syst. Man Cybern. Part C Appl. Rev. **42**(3), 291–312 (2012)
2. Bull, L., Studley, M., Bagnall, A., Whittley, I.: Learning classifier system ensembles with rule-sharing. IEEE Trans. Evol. Comput. **11**, 496–502 (2007)
3. Cantu-Paz, E.: Efficient and Accurate Parallel Genetic Algorithms. Kluwer Academic, Norwell (2000)
4. Chapman, B., Jost, B.G., van der Pas, R., Kuck, D.J.: Using OpenMP: Portable Shared Memory Parallel Programming. MIT Press, Cambridge (2007)
5. Chitty, D.M.: Fast parallel genetic programming: multi-core CPU versus many-core GPU. Soft. Comput. **16**, 1795–1814 (2012)
6. Czajkowski, M., Kretowski, M.: Evolutionary induction of global model trees with specialized operators and memetic extensions. Inf. Sci. **288**, 153–173 (2014)
7. Czajkowski, M., Czerwonka, M., Kretowski, M.: Cost-sensitive global model trees applied to loan charge-off forecasting. Decis. Support Syst. **74**, 55–66 (2015)

8. Czajkowski, M., Jurczuk, K., Kretowski, M.: A parallel approach for evolutionary induced decision trees. MPI+OpenMP implementation. In: Rutkowski, L., Korytkowski, M., Scherer, R., Tadeusiewicz, R., Zadeh, L.A., Zurada, J.M. (eds.) ICAISC 2015. LNCS, vol. 9119, pp. 340–349. Springer, Heidelberg (2015)
9. Gagne, P., Dayton, C.M.: Best regression model using information criteria. J. Mod. Appl. Stat. Methods **1**, 479–488 (2002)
10. Grama, A., Karypis, G., Kumar, V., Gupta, A.: Introduction to Parallel Computing. Addison-Wesley, Boston (2003)
11. Gropp, W., Lusk, E., Skjellum, A.: Using MPI: Portable Parallel Programming with the Message-Passing Interface. The MIT Press, Cambridge (2014)
12. Hastie, T., Tibshirani, R., Friedman, J.: The Elements of Statistical Learning. Data Mining, Inference, and Prediction, 2nd edn. Springer, New York (2009)
13. Kotsiantis, S.B.: Decision trees: a recent overview. Artif. Intell. Rev. **39**, 261–283 (2013)
14. Lichman, M.: UCI Machine Learning Repository. University of California, School of Information and Computer Science, Irvine (2013). http://archive.ics.uci.edu/ml
15. Llora, X.: Genetics-Based Machine Learning using Fine-grained Parallelism for Data Mining. Ph.D. Thesis. Barcelona, Ramon Llull University (2002)
16. Loh, W.: Fifty years of classification and regression trees. Int. Stat. Rev. **83**(3), 329–348 (2014)
17. Michalewicz, Z.: Genetic Algorithms + Data Structures = Evolution Programs, 3rd edn. Springer, New York (1996)
18. Press, W.H., Flannery, B.P., Teukolsky, S.A., Vetterling, W.T.: Numerical Recipes in C. Cambridge University Press, Cambridge (1988)
19. Rokach, L., Maimon, O.Z.: Top-down induction of decision trees classifiers - a survey. IEEE Trans. SMC, Part C **35**(4), 476–487 (2005)
20. Rabenseifner, R., Hager, G., Jost, G.: Hybrid MPI/OpenMP parallel programming on clusters of multi-core SMP nodes. In: Proceedings of PDP'17, pp. 427–436 (2009)
21. Schwarz, G.: Estimating the dimension of a model. Ann. Stat. **6**, 461–464 (1978)

Application of Genetic Algorithms in the Construction of Invertible Substitution Boxes

Tomasz Kapuściński[1], Robert K. Nowicki[1(✉)], and Christian Napoli[2]

[1] Institute of Computational Intelligence, Czestochowa University of Technology,
Al. Armii Krajowej 36, 42-200 Czestochowa, Poland
{tomasz.kapuscinski,robert.nowicki}@iisi.pcz.pl
[2] Department of Mathematics and Informatics, University of Catania,
Viale A. Doria 6, 95125 Catania, Italy
napoli@dmi.unict.it
http://www.iisi.pcz.pl

Abstract. Existing literature shows that genetic algorithms can be successfully used for automated construction of S-boxes. In this paper we show the usage of genetic algorithm, more specifically NSGA-II, as an aid in designing and testing of invertible substitution boxes which are special case of substitution boxes. Many cryptographic properties of S-boxes are often contradicting each other. It is therefore difficult to find an optimal solution. NSGA-II proved to be a valuable tool in finding a range of solutions from which we can later select an appropriate S-box for a cipher. We also show that we can use NSGA-II to test integration of S-boxes with a cipher and automatically reject S-boxes which make the cipher weak.

Keywords: NSGA-II · Substitution box · Invertible · S-box · Cryptography · Genetic algorithm

1 Introduction

Construction of cryptographic primitives such as block ciphers and hash function is an important problem in cryptography. Over time new vulnerabilities are found which means that new cryptosystems need to be designed in order to replace the old ones. As systems become increasingly more complex and new more advanced methods of cryptanalysis are discovered, cryptographers find it more difficult to design new systems that would be immune to all known forms of attacks. For this reason many scientists find it necessary to use automated techniques such as methods used in artificial intelligence. Artificial intelligence has been successfully used in various fields [1,6,12,14,18,21] also related to computer security and cryptography. Neural networks were used as a base for many ciphers and cryptographically secure hash functions [15,16,22]. Some metaheuristic methods such as evolutionary algorithms were used to optimize components of cryptographic primitive. Substitution boxes (S-boxes) are especially important because they

© Springer International Publishing Switzerland 2016
L. Rutkowski et al. (Eds.): ICAISC 2016, Part I, LNAI 9692, pp. 380–391, 2016.
DOI: 10.1007/978-3-319-39378-0_33

are a core component of most modern block ciphers and are responsible for resistance against many cryptanalytic techniques. Genetic algorithms proved to be effective in optimizing cryptographic properties of S-boxes [2,3,13].

In the investigations presented in the paper the process of creating invertible substitution boxes has been defined as multi-objective optimization. The list of objectives expresses the desirable properties of such S-boxes and entire algorithms. To take it into account a well known multi-objective genetic algorithm NSGA-II has been adopted and applied.

The paper is organized as follows. In the remaining part of Introduction the idea of substitution boxes, in particular invertible substitution boxes, and NSGA-II algorithm are presented. Then, Sect. 2 contains the details of proposed solution. It includes a discussion of coding the S-boxes in chromosomes and definitions of objectives. Both issues have been illustrated by appropriate algorithms. Equally important is the Sect. 3. It contains details and results of experimental research. The final section covers conclusions and plans for future works in the subject.

1.1   Substitution Boxes

Substitution boxes, also known as S-boxes, are an important component of modern block ciphers. An S-box is a function that takes m bits of input and transforms it to n bits of output. Good S-box has a highly nonlinear mapping between input and output bits in order to satisfy Shannon's properties of confusion and diffusion [4,19]. Cipher has good confusion if there is a complex relationship between the secret key and the ciphertext. Cipher has good diffusion if the ciphertext bits depends on all plaintext bits, and changing one input bit will change each output bit with probability about 50 %. S-box structure and properties directly affect confusion and diffusion of a cipher.

There is a special type of S-boxes which are commonly used in block ciphers based on the model known as substitution-permutation network. In those ciphers, a substitution box usually represents a bijective boolean function because substitution needs to be reversed in order to ensure that decryption is possible. Such S-boxes are therefore invertible n, n-functions. This means that for every such S-box there exists an inverse S-box which effectively reverses substitution. In order to differentiate them from ordinary S-boxes, in this paper we call them invertible S-boxes. A very well known example of invertible S-box is 8-bit S-box used in AES [7].

Invertible S-boxes have many interesting cryptographic properties that differentiate them from other S-boxes. For example, invertible S-boxes are always balanced. Boolean function is balanced if the number of ones and zeros in its truth table is equal. Invertible S-boxes are essentially permutations of 2^n values, so each bit appears exactly 2^{n-1} times as one and zero [3,8]. This also contributes to difficulty in constructing them.

1.2 NSGA-II

The nondominated sorting genetic algorithm II (NSGA-II) [9] is nowadays commonly known and probably the most popular multi-objective evolutionary algorithm. It is a direct successor of the NSGA [20]. NSGA-II solves the main problems of NSGA, mainly high computational complexity of nondominated sorting. The subsequent Pareto fronts are determined using domination counts assigned for each solution in a population, domination counts stored number of the solutions which dominate the current one and set of solutions dominated by it. The first Pareto front includes the solutions with the count equal to zero. The procedure is repeated for next fronts applying the previously determined sets. Such procedure causes that the NSGA-II outperforms its predecessor as well as other multi-objective evolutionary algorithms.

The decision to use NSGA-II for our research is based on the fact that several S-box properties are contradicting each other. This means that trying to optimize one property often results in degrading other properties. For this reason finding a substitution box with good properties can be a very difficult task. Moreover, in the case of invertible substitution boxes, it is impossible to find an S-box with perfect nonlinearity and several other properties are constrained. Using a single value to represent fitness of all cryptographic properties in single-objective algorithms may be inadequate. Multi-objective algorithms like NSGA-II can use all properties to find Pareto optimal populations and provide a set of solutions with satisfying properties. Cryptographer can later decide which S-box will be the most appropriate for given cipher. In order to use NSGA-II, we need to define the objectives and representation of S-boxes in chromosomes.

2 Implementation of Genetic Algorithm

This section describes implementation details of our research. In order to use NSGA-II we need to define a coding method, objectives and genetic operators. Coding method specifies how genetic material in form of bits is decoded into an S-box. Objectives in multi-objective algorithms define how good a potential solution is relative to other solutions. Unlike fitness function in single-objective genetic algorithms, NSGA-II objectives represent problems we want to minimize, that is the lower objective value the better. Genetic operators are used in the process of selecting next population.

2.1 Coding

One of the problems associated with invertible S-boxes is how to encode them for the purpose of genetic algorithms. Only a very small fraction of all n-bit boolean functions represent valid invertible S-boxes. For example, the number of all valid 8-bit S-boxes is

$$(2^8)^{256} = 2^{2048}$$

The number of all valid invertible 8-bit S-boxes is

$$(2^8)! = 256! \approx 2^{1684}$$

Therefore, the probability that randomly chosen 8-bit S-box will be invertible is approximately

$$\frac{2^{1684}}{2^{2048}} = 2^{-364} \approx 10^{-110}$$

This means that arbitrary coding can not be used because genetic algorithm would be unlikely to find a valid solution. For this reason coding method has to be specifically designed.

The second problem is related to how genetic operators work. In general, mutation of one bit should introduce relatively small changes to the resulting S-box and crossover should create an S-box that is similar to both parent S-boxes. Coding that does not satisfy those criteria would make it more difficult to find the desired solution using genetic algorithm. However, because invertible S-boxes are a type of permutation, there is no trivial way of coding to achieve this.

During our research we created an algorithm that allows proper encoding of invertible S-boxes and minimizes changes performed by genetic operators. This algorithm performs swap operations similarly to how random shuffle algorithms does, however instead of randomly selecting indices they are computed using an array called selection table. Values in the selection table are constrained to specific ranges which depend on position of values within the table. First value is constrained to range $[0, n - 1]$, second value is constrained to range $[0, n - 2]$, and so on. The last value is always 0. An example of a valid selection table is shown below.

6 3 1 3 2 0 0

From the definition of selection tables we can deduce that the number of all possible selection tables of size n is

$$n * (n - 1) * (n - 2) * \ldots * 2 * 1 = n!$$

Values in selection table are used to calculate indices of elements to swap with corresponding value in array. We iterate over all values in selection table in a loop. The element on position i is swapped with element $i + selection[i]$. If i and $i + selection[i]$ are the same, no swap operation is performed. After the swap, element that was originally on position $i + selection[i]$ will be in position i and will not be swapped with any other element in subsequent swaps. The algorithm is presented below. The process realised by the algorithm is illustrated in Fig. 1.

Like random shuffle, our algorithm has computational complexity of $O(n)$ and constant memory requirements. A selection table uniquely represents a valid permutation and since the number of all selection tables of size n is $n!$, they effectively map to all possible permutations of the same size. Therefore, we can use selection tables to encode invertible S-boxes.

Algorithm 1. Algorithm for decoding S-boxes from selection tables

```
function DECODESBOX(selection, n)
    Create an array sbox with length n
    for i = 0; i < n; i ← i + 1 do
        sbox[i] ← i
    end for
    for i = 0; i < n; i ← i + 1 do
        index ← i + selection[i]
        if i ≠ index then
            temp ← sbox[i]
            sbox[i] ← sbox[index]
            sbox[index] ← temp
        end if
    end for
    return sbox
end function
```

$$
\begin{array}{ccccccc}
0 & 1 & 2 & 3 & 4 & 5 & 6 \\
\mathbf{6} & 1 & 2 & 3 & 4 & 5 & \mathbf{0} \\
6 & \mathbf{4} & 2 & 3 & \mathbf{1} & 5 & 0 \\
6 & 4 & \mathbf{3} & \mathbf{2} & 1 & 5 & 0 \\
6 & 4 & 3 & \mathbf{0} & 1 & 5 & \mathbf{2} \\
6 & 4 & 3 & 0 & \mathbf{2} & 5 & \mathbf{1} \\
6 & 4 & 3 & 0 & 2 & \mathbf{5} & 1 \\
6 & 4 & 3 & 0 & 2 & 5 & \mathbf{1}
\end{array}
\qquad
\begin{array}{l}
0 \leftrightarrow 6 = 0 + 6 \\
1 \leftrightarrow 4 = 1 + 3 \\
2 \leftrightarrow 3 = 2 + 1 \\
3 \leftrightarrow 6 = 3 + 3 \\
4 \leftrightarrow 6 = 4 + 2 \\
5 \leftrightarrow 5 = 5 + 0 \\
6 \leftrightarrow 6 = 6 + 0
\end{array}
$$

Fig. 1. Swap operations using selection table 6 3 1 3 2 0 0

Every selection table represents a unique permutation and therefore can be used to encode an invertible S-box. In our implementation, an encoded solution contains 256 integers representing a selection table which is decoded and then used to calculate the S-box.

2.2 Objectives

In this section we describe the objectives defined for NSGA-II. For the purpose of this research we limited the number of objectives to three in order to ensure stability of the algorithm.

Nonlinearity. Nonlinearity is an essential property of good substitution boxes. The higher nonlinearity of an S-box, the more difficult it is to approximate its operation using combination of linear functions, and as a result it is more resistant to linear cryptanalysis. There are many definitions of nonlinearity in existing literature [4]. We decided to use Peak-to-Average Power Ratio (PAR) with respect to Walsh-Hadamard Transform described in [17]. The value of PAR provides an information about how good the best linear approximation of S-box can be. Low value means that S-box has high nonlinearity and is therefore more secure. High value means that an S-box is highly linear and is therefore more susceptible to linear analysis. Completely linear S-boxes have a maximum value of 2^n, where n is the number of output bits. Finding an S-box with good nonlinearity using PAR value is therefore a minimization problem. Because of this, PAR can be used directly as an objective in NSGA-II unlike other nonlinearity indicators. PAR with respect to WHT is shown on Eq. 1.

$$F_k = 2^{-n} \sum_{x \in Z_2^n} (-1)^{f(x)+x\cdot k}$$

$$PAR(f) = 2^n \max_{\forall k}(|F_k|)^2. \tag{1}$$

A tests performed on one million randomly generated 8-bit invertible S-boxes show that an average value of PAR is about 9.5. The minimum was 4.0 and maximum was 33.0625. Standard AES S-box has nonlinearity of 4.0.

Hamming Distance Score. A hamming weight of a binary vector is a number of bits in this vector set to 1. A hamming distance is a Hamming weight of a difference between two binary vectors. Difference is usually defined as an exclusive OR of two vectors. In this case, Hamming distance between two vectors will be a number of differing bits.

Hamming distance can be used to measure the quality of substitution boxes. An S-box should, on average, change half of the input bits. We can calculate Hamming distances between all possible S-box input values and the corresponding output values and analyze them. On average, the number of bits changed by substitution should be about half of the number of output bits. In the case of 8-bit S-boxes, average Hamming distance should be close to 4.0 (Fig. 2).

Calculating Hamming distances between inputs and outputs of an S-box can be used in an objective for NSGA-II. Since NSGA-II seeks to minimize the objectives, we can define a negative score based on Hamming distance counts. The method of calculating the Hamming distance score is shown on Algorithm 2.

The bias 2^{-8} is used to normalize the score to range $[0,1]$. The completely linear identity S-box has a score of 1.0, which is also the highest value possible.

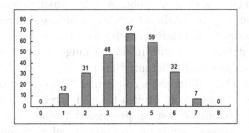

Fig. 2. Counts of Hamming distances for AES S-box

Algorithm 2. Algorithm for calculating score based on Hamming distances in S-box

---

function HAMMINGDISTANCESCORE($sbox$)
    Create an array $count$ with length 9
    for $i = 0;\ i < 9;\ i \leftarrow i + 1$ **do**
        $count[i] \leftarrow 0$
    end for
    for $x \leftarrow 0;\ x < 256;\ x \leftarrow x + 1$ **do**
        $y \leftarrow f(x)$
        $d \leftarrow x + y$
        $c \leftarrow$ number of ones in d
        $count_c \leftarrow count_c + 1$
    end for
    $sum \leftarrow count[0] + 0.1 \times count[1] + 0.01 \times count[2] + 0.01 \times count[6] + 0.1 \times count[7] + count[8]$
    return $sum \times 2^{-8}$
end function

The score of 0.0 is a theoretical minimum. AES S-box has a Hamming distance score of about 0.009883. A test performed on one million randomly generated 8-bit invertible S-boxes show that an average score was about 0.01625, the lowest score was 0.003086 and the highest was 0.05578.

Diffusion Score. Diffusion is a highly desired property of a cipher where a change of any bit of input vector will result in all output bits changed with a probability of 50 %. Even a small probabilistic deviation can result in whole cipher being susceptible to differential cryptanalysis.

In our research we used a modified AES-128 cipher implementation which accepts custom invertible substitution boxes. We used it in order to test integration between S-box and cipher. Testing all possible cases for each potential solution (2^{128} plaintexts, 2^{128} differentials, and 2^{128} secret keys) is impractical due to extreme time needed for all calculations. Instead we decided to perform a probabilistic test using randomly chosen secret keys and plaintexts. The procedure is presented on Algorithm 3.

In the test, we generate random plaintext x_1 and compute ciphertext y_1. We invert specific bit in the plaintext and obtain x_2 for which we calculate ciphertext y_2. Ciphertexts y_1 and y_2 are XORed together to obtain difference Δy. The bias 2^{-13} is chosen in order to normalize results to a range $[0, 1]$. The value of 0 is a case where each difference results in 50 % change of every output bit which means statistical analysis and differential cryptanalysis will be ineffective. The value of 1 is a case where differences result in 100 % change of all output bits which means cipher can be easily broken using differential cryptanalysis. Since diffusion test is a probabilistic test, in practice diffusion score will always be a value above 0. This value depends on the number of performed tests. For 256

Algorithm 3. Algorithm for calculating diffusion score of given S-box

---

function DIFFUSIONSCORE(*sbox*, *tests*)
    Construct *cipher* with *sbox*
    diffusion $\leftarrow$ 0
    for $b \leftarrow 0; b < 128; b \leftarrow t + 1$ **do**
        Initialize *count* to 0
        for $t \leftarrow 0; t < tests; t \leftarrow t + 1$ **do**
            Generate random plaintext x_1
            $y_1 \leftarrow cipher(x_1)$
            Invert bit b in x_1
            $y_2 = cipher(x_2)$
            $\Delta y \leftarrow y_1 + y_2$
            for $i \leftarrow 0; i < 128; i \leftarrow i + 1$ **do**
                if bit i in Δy is set **then**
                    $count[i] \leftarrow count[i] + 1$
                end if
            end for
        end for
        for $i = 0; i < 128; i \leftarrow i + 1$ **do**
            diffusion $\leftarrow$ *diffusion* $+ \frac{|count_i - \frac{1}{2} tests|}{tests}$
        end for
    end for
    return $2^{-13} \times diffusion$
end function

---

tests, original AES has a score about 0.05. Increasing the number of tests results in smaller values of the score but it also increases time needed for calculations.

3 Experimental Research

For our research we used an open source library jMetal version 4.5.2 [10]. It is a library with single- and multi-objective optimization methods using various evolutionary algorithms, including NSGA-II. This library was chosen due to simple design and extensible implementation. For the purpose of our experiment we wrote a customized version of NSGA-II in order to allow evaluation of solutions on multiple threads and enable saving of partial results to a file.

3.1 Scenario

Using our customized NSGA-II implementation, we performed a simulation where randomly chosen population of invertible substitution boxes was subject to evolutionary optimization. We chose a population size of 200, single point crossover operator with probability 0.8 and bit flip mutation operator with probability 0.05. The total number of generations was 10, 000. Every 500 generations, current population was saved with their objectives to a file for later analysis.

Solutions were encoded as 256 variables, 8 bits long each. Variables were decoded to values from 0 to 255 and later scaled to ranges appropriate for values in selection table. Decoded selection table is then used to calculate an S-box.

3.2 Results

The simulation time was 23 h, 24 min and 2 s. The final population was saved to a file and objectives were analyzed in a program. Summary statistics of objectives are presented in Table 1.

Figure 4 shows that majority of S-boxes have nonlinearity below 10. 8 S-boxes have been found with PAR 4.0. The remaining two objectives of those S-boxes are presented in Table 2. Their lowest Hamming distance score is 0.01097656 and the highest score is 0.02328125.

Because their nonlinearity is the highest possible in 8-bit invertible S-boxes, which is also exactly the same as in AES S-box, they are good candidates for use in a new cipher. Analysis of partial results show that these S-boxes were gradually being found during simulation (Fig. 3).

Figure 4 also shows that majority of S-boxes in final population have Hamming distance score below 0.01. The lowest score is 0.005546875, however this S-box has relatively low nonlinearity of 14.0625. The best S-box with nonlinearity of 5.0625 has a score 0.0064453125. A cryptographer can choose to use this S-box if its Hamming distances are more important than a small sacrifice in nonlinearity.

Table 1. Summary statistics of objectives in final population

	Minimum	Average	Maximum
Nonlinearity (PAR)	4.0	7.8084375	18.0625
Hamming distance score	0.00554688	0.00853691	0.02328125
Diffusion score	0.04829216	0.04906658	0.05064440

Table 2. S-boxes with PAR = 4.0

S-box	Hamming distance score	Diffusion score
1	0.01179688	0.04959965
2	0.01164063	0.04976130
3	0.01578125	0.04936028
4	0.01109375	0.04979086
5	0.01097656	0.04992056
6	0.01953125	0.04988623
7	0.02328125	0.04981518
8	0.01390625	0.05005264

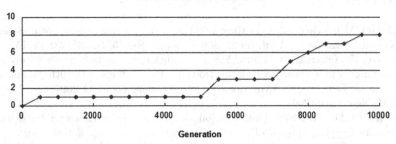

Fig. 3. The number of S-boxes with PAR = 4 after every 500 generations

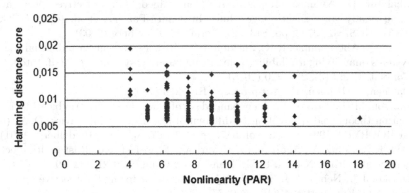

Fig. 4. Distribution of S-boxes based on PAR Nonlinearity and Hamming distance score

Diffusion scores show that all found substitution boxes have acceptable values. Weak S-boxes that resulted in poor diffusion in a cipher were automatically discarded by genetic algorithm because their scores were worse than scores of other S-boxes.

4   Conclusions and Future Work

In our research we showed that multi-objective genetic algorithms can be successfully used as a tool for construction of invertible substitution boxes for cryptographic purposes. With proper coding method, NSGA-II was able to find a set of S-boxes with good cryptographic properties which can be later used as a component of a new block cipher. One of the objectives was used to test integration of S-boxes with AES cipher which means it could eliminate S-boxes that perform poorly when used in a cipher but otherwise has good properties.

In the future, our research will concentrate on gradually adding more objectives based on cryptographic properties of S-boxes as well as testing our approach using new block ciphers. We will also adopt our method to various modifications of NSGA-II such as steady-state NSGA-II [5,11].

References

1. Aghdam, M.H., Heidari, S.: Feature selection using particle swarm optimization in text categorization. J. Artif. Intell. Soft Comput. Res. **5**(4), 231–238 (2015)
2. Aguirre, H., Okazaki, H., Fuwa, Y.: An evolutionary multiobjective approach to design highly non-linear boolean functions. In: Proceedings of the 9th Annual Conference on Genetic and Evolutionary Computation, GECCO 2007, pp. 749–756. ACM, New York (2007)
3. Burnett, L.D.: Heuristic Optimization of Boolean Functions and Substitution Boxes for Cryptography. Ph.D. thesis, Queensland University of Technology (2005)
4. Carlet, C., Ding, C.: Nonlinearities of s-boxes. Finite Fields Appl. **13**(1), 121–135 (2007)
5. Chafekar, D., Xuan, J., Rasheed, K.: Constrained multi-objective optimization using steady state genetic algorithms. In: Cantú-Paz, E., et al. (eds.) GECCO 2003. LNCS, vol. 2723, pp. 813–824. Springer, Heidelberg (2003)
6. Chen, Q., Abercrombie, R.K., Sheldon, F.T.: Risk assessment for industrial control systems quantifying availability using mean failure cost (mfc). J. Artif. Intell. Soft Comput. Res. **5**(3), 205–220 (2015)
7. Daemen, J., Rijmen, V.: Aes proposal: Rijndael (1999)
8. Dawson, M.H., Tavares, S.: An expanded set of s-box design criteria based on information theory and its relation to differential-like attacks. In: Davies, D.W. (ed.) EUROCRYPT 1991. LNCS, vol. 547, pp. 352–367. Springer, Heidelberg (1991)
9. Deb, K., Pratap, A., Agarwal, S., Meyarivan, T.: A fast and elitist multiobjective genetic algorithm: Nsga-ii. IEEE Trans. Evol. Comput. **6**(2), 182–197 (2002)
10. Durillo, J.J., Nebro, A.J.: jmetal: A java framework for multi-objective optimization. Adv. Eng. Softw. **42**(10), 760–771 (2011)
11. Durillo, J.J., Nebro, A.J., Luna, F., Alba, E.: On the effect of the steady-state selection scheme in multi-objective genetic algorithms. In: Ehrgott, M., Fonseca, C.M., Gandibleux, X., Hao, J.-K., Sevaux, M. (eds.) EMO 2009. LNCS, vol. 5467, pp. 183–197. Springer, Heidelberg (2009)
12. Hayashi, Y., Tanaka, Y., Takagi, T., Saito, T., Iiduka, H., Kikuchi, H., Bologna, G., Mitra, S.: Recursive-rule extraction algorithm with J48graft and applications to generating credit scores. J. Artif. Intell. Soft Comput. Res. **6**(1), 35–44 (2016)
13. Ivanov, G., Nikolov, N., Nikova, S.: Reversed genetic algorithms for generation of bijective s-boxes with good cryptographic properties. Crypt. Commun., 1–30 (2016)
14. Korytkowski, M., Gabryel, M., Rutkowski, L., Drozda, S.: Evolutionary methods to create interpretable modular system. In: Rutkowski, L., Tadeusiewicz, R., Zadeh, L.A., Zurada, J.M. (eds.) ICAISC 2008. LNCS (LNAI), vol. 5097, pp. 405–413. Springer, Heidelberg (2008)
15. Li, C., Li, S., Zhang, D., Chen, G.: Cryptanalysis of a chaotic neural network based multimedia encryption scheme. In: Aizawa, K., Nakamura, Y., Satoh, S. (eds.) PCM 2004. LNCS, vol. 3333, pp. 418–425. Springer, Heidelberg (2004)
16. Lian, S.: A block cipher based on chaotic neural networks. Neurocomputing **72**(4–6), 1296–1301 (2009). Brain Inspired Cognitive Systems (BICS 2006)/Interplay Between Natural and Artificial Computation (IWINAC 2007)
17. Parker, M.: Generalised s-box nonlinearity. NESSIE Public Document NES/DOC/UIB/WP5/020/A (2003)
18. Serdah, A.M., Ashour, W.M.: Clustering large-scale data based on modified affinity propagation algorithm. J. Artif. Intell. Soft Comput. Res. **6**(1), 23–33 (2016)

19. Shannon, C.E.: Communication theory of secrecy systems*. Bell Syst. Tech. J. **28**(4), 656–715 (1949)

20. Srinivas, N., Deb, K.: Muiltiobjective optimization using nondominated sorting in genetic algorithms. Evol. Comput. **2**(3), 221–248 (1994)

21. Szarek, A., Korytkowski, M., Rutkowski, L., Scherer, R., Szyprowski, J.: Application of neural networks in assessing changes around implant after total hip arthroplasty. In: Rutkowski, L., Korytkowski, M., Scherer, R., Tadeusiewicz, R., Zadeh, L.A., Zurada, J.M. (eds.) ICAISC 2012, Part II. LNCS, vol. 7268, pp. 335–340. Springer, Heidelberg (2012)

22. Yu, W., Cao, J.: Cryptography based on delayed chaotic neural networks. Phys. Lett. A **356**(4–5), 333–338 (2006)

Grammatical Evolution in a Matrix Factorization Recommender System

Matevž Kunaver(⊠) and Iztok Fajfar

Faculty of Electrical Engineering, Trzaska 25, 1000 Ljubljana, Slovenia
{matevz.kunaver,iztok.fajfar}@fe.uni-lj.si,
http://www.fe.uni-lj.si

Abstract. This paper presents preliminary results of using grammatical evolution to evolve expressions that calculate the user/item features used in the matrix factorization recommendation algorithm. The experiment was performed primarily to determine whether grammatical evolution can be applied to this field, and to compare the results with those of the 'traditional' algorithm. For the purpose of the experiment, we used the CoMoDa dataset, which features realistic data collected over five years. The preliminary results are promising and offer a lot of possible future work, some of which is discussed at the end of the paper.

Keywords: Grammatical evolution · Genetic programming · Recommender systems · Collaborative recommender · Matrix factorization

1 Introduction

In recent years, recommender systems have evolved from obscure and rare computational solutions to fully-fledged software that is omnipresent in almost every aspect of human-computer interaction. Now users can not only get active recommendation in the form of search results and personalized program guides but also get recommendations in a more subtle form such as personalized advertisements, which load while they browse the Internet. Recommender systems (RS) have therefore moved onto the next stage of development and are now addressing issues such as big data analysis, implicit feedback collection, contextualization, and personalization. RS have also become economically viable as demonstrated by companies such as Google, Amazon and Netflix. These companies invest large amounts of resources into development of new technologies. One of such developments was the Matrix Factorization (MF) method [4], which was developed as part of the $1,000,000 Netflix prize [1]. However, there is a problem with the algorithm in that, while it does offer great accuracy, it does not scale well and becomes very slow when faced with more 'realistic' datasets, which can contain millions of users, items, and ratings. A lot of effort is therefore put into either distributing the workload of the algorithm (such as Distributed Nonnegative Matrix Factorization (DNMF) [8] and Scalable Nonnegative Matrix Factorization (ScalableNMF) [2]), or speeding up the feature calculation procedure.

© Springer International Publishing Switzerland 2016
L. Rutkowski et al. (Eds.): ICAISC 2016, Part I, LNAI 9692, pp. 392–400, 2016.
DOI: 10.1007/978-3-319-39378-0_34

This paper presents the preliminary results of experiments aiming to achieve the latter: to increase the algorithm's accuracy using as few iterations over a dataset as possible. We move away from the established principles of feature value calculation such as regularized gradient descent [13] by employing grammatical evolution to evolve expressions for feature value calculation, which—at least to our best knowledge—has not been tried before in the field of matrix factorization recommender systems.

Grammatical evolution (GE) [11] is a relatively new evolutionary computation technique, often classified as a subfield of genetic programming (GP) [6]. GE can evolve programs from linear strings of codons by using a context-free grammar usually written in a Backus–Naur form, and a special mapping procedure, which guarantees the syntactical correctness of the obtained programs.

1.1 Problem Statement

This paper presents preliminary results of using GE as part of the MF Recommender System. Most current MF systems rely on the regularized gradient descent method to calculate the values of user and item features (see Materials and Methods below), which, while providing a steady descent in the overall accuracy of the system, requires a large amount of iterations to achieve the desired level of accuracy (measured with RMSE). For the purposes of our experiment, we fix the number of iterations to 100 and compare the results provided by the original (gradient descent) system with those obtained by employing GE. More details follow in the sections below.

2 Materials and Methods

In this section we provide the details about the used data and algorithms as well as the details about the evaluation measure used to compare the results.

2.1 Matrix Factorization Algorithm

The basic idea of the MF algorithm is that we can use a sparse user-item matrix to calculate latent features of each existing user and item (similar to PCA and Eigenvalue space). These features can then be used to compute (predict) the missing values in the user-item matrix. To compute a rating $r(u_m, i_n)$ for the mth user u_m and the nth item i_n, we simply multiply the latent feature vectors as described in the Feature Calculation Algorithm subsection below.

The main challenge with the MF algorithm lies in finding an efficient way to calculate the latent features. In our experiment, we use a 'classic' MF algorithm, which uses regularized gradient descent as the latent feature calculation method. We use 7 latent features as we have identified this number of features to be sufficient in our previous work [10].

The Algorithm. Our implementation of the whole MF algorithm can be summarized as follows:

> Prepare user (**P**) and item (**Q**) latent feature matrices containing starting latent feature values (0.3 in our example).
> Calculate static biases (see explanation below).
> **For** each feature (7 in this example):
>> **Repeat** 100 times:
>>> **For** each rating in the training set:
>>>> Calculate a predicted rating and compare it with the current 'true' rating.
>>>> Adjust the current user/item latent feature based on the regularized gradient descent algorithm.
>>> **End For**
>> **End Repeat**
> **End For**

Prediction Model. If we wish to calculate a predicted rating r for a user u_m and an item i_n, we need the following values: the global bias b, the user bias b_{u_m}, the item bias b_{i_n}, the user latent feature vector $\mathbf{P}(u_m)$ (the mth row of the user latent feature matrix) and the item feature vector $\mathbf{Q}(i_n)$ (the nth row of the item latent feature matrix). The predicted rating is then calculated using the equation

$$r(u_m, i_n) = b + b_{u_m} + b_{i_n} + \mathbf{P}(u_m) * \mathbf{Q}(i_n). \tag{1}$$

Static Biases. As shown in the section above, the predicted rating depends not only on the user/item latent features but also on the biases of the system. The idea is to remove some of the static variance from the feature space by moving the averaged information about the user, item, and overall rating behavior into separate values (i.e., biases). These biases are calculated as follows:

- The global bias b is the average rating of the whole dataset.
- The user bias b_{u_m} is the mth user average rating minus the global bias.
- The item bias b_{i_n} is the nth item average rating minus the global bias.

Feature Calculation Algorithm. During each iteration of the MF algorithm, the latent feature values of the current user and item are adjusted according to the following two equations:

$$\mathbf{P}(u_m, k) = \mathbf{P}(u_m, k) + (err * \mathbf{Q}(i_n, k) - reg * \mathbf{P}(u_m, k)) * \text{pLR}, \tag{2}$$
$$\mathbf{Q}(i_n, k) = \mathbf{Q}(i_n, k) + (err * \mathbf{P}(u_m, k) - reg * \mathbf{Q}(i_n, k)) * \text{qLR}. \tag{3}$$

$\mathbf{P}(u_m, k)$ and $\mathbf{Q}(i_n, k)$ are the current values of the kth latent features of the selected user and item, respectively, while err is the difference between the calculated and the actual rating in the train set. A constant value reg, which is set to 0.3 in our experiment, is used to prevent the feature values to escape the normal bound. Constant values pLR and qLR determine the step (i.e., learning rate) in the gradient descent method and are set to 0.03 in our case.

2.2 Grammatical Evolution

Equations (2) and (3) were the part of the algorithm that we targeted with GE. We performed two experiments: In the first experiment, we replaced both equations with one and the same GE generated expression. That is to say, we used the same expression for the user and item latent feature calculation except that we swapped the positions of the terms $\mathbf{P}(u_m, k)$ and $\mathbf{Q}(i_n, k)$. In the second experiment, however, we used a different expression for each of the two features. The aim of this was to find out whether the original idea with two equally structured equations is indeed better than using two quite different expressions for both features.

Table 1 shows the settings that we used in our GE.

Table 1. The settings used in GE.

Objective	Find an expression that will successfully predict missing feature values
Terminal operands	err - difference between the true and predicted rating (see the previous subsection), $\mathbf{P}(u_m, k)$ - the kth latent feature value of the mth user, $\mathbf{Q}(i_n, k)$ - the kth latent feature value of the nth item, constants 0.01, 0.02, 0.04, and 0.08
Terminal operators	Binary operators $+$, $-$, $*$, and $\%$ (protected division)
Fitness cases	Context Movie Dataset [5]
Raw fitness	RMSE of differences between 3452 pairs of predicted and actual ratings in the training set.
Standardised fitness	Same as raw fitness
Parameters	Population Size: 300 (sensible initialization [12]), Generations: 200, Prob. Mutation: 0.01, Prob. Crossover: 0.20 (LHS crossover [3]), Tournament Size: 5

Apart from the setting shown in Table 1, we used a grammar with the following three productions:

<expr> ::= <expr><op><expr> |
            (<expr><op><expr>) |
            <var>

<op> ::= + | − | * | %
<var> ::= err | $\mathbf{P}(u_m, k)$ | $\mathbf{Q}(i_n, k)$ | 0.01 | 0.02 | 0.04 | 0.08.

Also, it should be noted that we used an LHS crossover operator [3] rather than a standard one-point crossover, as the former turned out to yield better results.

In order to evaluate the cost of the evolved expressions, we used each of the expressions in a full run of the MF algorithm to act as the feature adjustment expression. The resulting latent feature values were then used to compute the cost of the evolved expression, which was the RMSE between actual ratings and predicted ratings calculated using the latent features from the evolved expression. To prevent bloat, we punished the expressions whose length exceeded 200 characters by setting their cost value to 200 (the typical cost of an expression was below 1). In a similar manner we punished the expressions that produced a latent feature value greater than 50. This was done according to similar logic as used in regularization of the gradient descent method—we wished the latent feature values to remain in the range from -5 to $+5$ to avoid the occurrence of over-fitting [10].

2.3   Computer Set-Up

All experiments were performed on a personal computer with an Intel Xeon 3.3 GHz processor, 16 GB of RAM running 64-bit Windows 7 operating system. The experiments did not require a dedicated database server or any special hardware. All algorithms and evaluations were run in Python 2.7, and the code typed using the Spyder editor.

2.4   CoMoDa Dataset

We performed the evaluation using the Context Movie Dataset [5] as the source of our training and test sets. This dataset was acquired during our previous work using an on-line movie rating application (www.ldos.si/recommender.html) that enabled the users to track their viewed movies and to obtain recommendations from several RS algorithms (the hybrid and content-based RS described above and a matrix factorization RS developed separately). The application also features a questionnaire, whose purpose is the collection of contextual data that describes the situation during the item consumption. The application is still available and in use. Additional information about LDOS-CoMoDa can be found in [5].

At the time of writing this paper, the features of the LDOS-CoMoDa are:

- 189 users
- 3029 items (movies and TV series)
- 4316 submitted ratings
- ratings from 1 (don't like it) to 5 (it is amazing) in steps of one
- overall average rating: 3.7931
- item average rating: 3.6387
- user average rating: 4.1204
- average number of ratings per item: 2.373
- average number of ratings per user: 22.85

Each user is described with basic demographic data (i.e., age, sex, location) provided on a voluntary basis. Each item is described with several attributes: genre(s), director, actor(s), language, country, budget and release year. Also, each rating is annotated with associated contextual variables.

During each run of GE the dataset was randomly divided into two parts: a training set, which contained 80 % of the ratings in the dataset and a test set, which contained the remaining 20 % of the ratings.

2.5   Evalutaion

In order to evaluate the cost of expressions evolved using GE as well as determine the efficiency of the original MF algorithm we used the RMSE measure [9], which is frequently used in articles relating to MF and RS. We calculated the RMSE from the differences between the ratings from the test set (see CoMoDa subsection above) and either the ratings predicted with MF algorithm using GE generated expressions or those gained from the baseline MF algorithm. Note that each time an RMSE value was computed after exactly 100 iterations of the MF algorithm.

2.6   Experiment Sequence

In summary, a single experiment was carried out as follows:

1. Create a training and test set by randomly splitting the dataset to 80 %/20 %.
2. Use the standard MF algorithm to calculate the baseline RMSE.
3. Run GE for the set number of generations, calculating the cost (i.e., the RMSE value) of each individual in the population in each generation.
4. Plot and print the evolved expression with the lowest cost and compare it with the cost of the baseline algorithm.

We preformed 2 runs of 10 experiments each. The first run featured the same expression for user and item features while the second run featured different expressions. Each of the experiments used a different test and training set.

3   Results

Table 2 shows the results of our twenty experiments. The first ten rows present the results where equal expressions were used for calculating the user and item latent features, while for the second ten rows we used a different expression for each of the two features. Apart from the obtained RMSE values, the table also summarizes relative improvements of the GE-enhanced MF algorithm over the baseline MF algorithm.

The results show that, in eighteen of the twenty experiments, the use of GE increased the performance (i.e., produced a lower RMSE value) when compared with the baseline algorithm. Table 3 further lists the best, worst and mean relative improvement in both runs. In addition it also lists the Wilcoxon p-values

Table 2. Results of the experiments.

RMSE		Used expressions	Improvement (%)
Baseline	GE		
0.91	0.78	equal	14.2
0.68	0.61	equal	10.3
1.00	0.92	equal	8.0
1.08	1.07	equal	0.9
1.21	1.13	equal	6.6
1.26	1.16	equal	7.9
1.15	0.83	equal	27.8
1.27	1.27	equal	0
1.19	1.16	equal	2.5
1.20	1.01	equal	8.0
0.76	0.52	different	31.5
0.96	0.92	different	4.2
1.21	1.00	different	16.6
1.30	0.86	different	33.8
1.37	1.16	different	15.3
1.18	1.06	different	10.2
1.18	0.99	different	16.1
1.05	0.95	different	9.6
0.83	0.83	different	0
1.08	1.00	different	7.4

that show that each run featured significantly different values. A quick comparison of the results of the first and second half of Table 2 also seems to indicate that using a different equation for each of the two latent features produces much better results (an average improvement of 14.47 %) than using the same expression for both latent features (an average improvement of 8.62 %).

Table 3. Relative improvement comparison and statistical testing.

Used expressions	Relative improvement				Wilcoxon (p-value)
	Best	Mean	Worst	St. dev.	
Equal	27.80	8.62	0.00	8.02	0.0077
Different	33.80	14.47	0.00	10.95	0.0077

4   Conclusions

The aim of this article was twofold: First, to see whether it is possible to use GE in Recommender Systems, more specifically in the MF algorithm. Second, to evaluate the benefit of GE in this field and see whether it can deliver better results than the currently accepted regularized gradient descent variant of the algorithm.

As can be seen from the results, we successfully implemented GE as part of the MF algorithm and used the expressions generated by the GE as replacement equations for the user/item latent feature calculations. In each of the experiments, we observed an improvement of the overall accuracy of the MF algorithm. The improvement was even better when we used a different expression for each of the latent features. It should be noted that all our experiments were carried out using a 'real' dataset that was collected over many years of our research [5]. Due to time constraints, however, we carried out too few experiments in order to draw statistically significant conclusions. Regardless, we have shown that incorporating GE into the MF algorithm provides a way to increase the accuracy of the system without increasing the number of iterations needed to calculate the latent features. Apart from that, the observed improvements are relatively large, so it is definitely worthwhile to continue the research on this topic.

4.1   Future Work

Here is a short list of research activities that we believe are worth trying in the future:

- To run enough experiments to get statistically significant results.
- To use a different number of iterations to determine whether we can achieve the same accuracy with fewer iterations, or even better accuracy with more iterations.
- To experiment with the GE parameters (e.g., population size, type of grammar, type of crossover) to determine if any combination performs better.
- To implement a 10-fold cross validation of the algorithm.
- To parallelize the algorithm to be able to run GE based recommender system in real time.
- To use several other publicly available datasets such as EachMovie, MovieLens and Netflix in order to determine the scalability of this approach.
- To apply GE to other RS algorithms such as the Genre-Preference Collaborative Recommender, which was developed as part of our previous work [7].

Acknowledgments. This work was supported by the Ministry of Education, Science and Sport of Republic of Slovenia under Research program P2-0246 - Algorithms and optimization methods in telecommunications.

References

1. Bennett, J., Lanning, S.: The netflix prize. In: Proceedings of KDD Cup and Workshop, vol. 2007, p. 35 (2007)
2. Benson, A.R., Lee, J.D., Rajwa, B., Gleich, D.F.: Scalable methods for nonnegative matrix factorizations of near-separable tall-and-skinny matrices. In: Advances in Neural Information Processing Systems, pp. 945–953 (2014)
3. Harper, R., Blair, A.: A structure preserving crossover in grammatical evolution. In: Corne, D., et al. (eds.) Proceedings of the 2005 IEEE Congress on Evolutionary Computation, vol. 3, pp. 2537–2544. IEEE Press (2005)
4. Koren, Y., Bell, R., Volinsky, C.: Matrix factorization techniques for recommender systems. Computer **42**(8), 30–37 (2009)
5. Košir, A., Odic, A., Kunaver, M., Tkalcic, M., Tasic, J.F.: Database for contextual personalization. Elektrotehniški vestnik **78**(5), 270–274 (2011)
6. Koza, J.R.: Genetic Programming: On the Programming of Computers by Means of Natural Selection. MIT Press, Cambridge (1992)
7. Kunaver, M., Košir, A., Tasič, J.F.: Hybrid recommender for multimedia item recommendation: development of a hybrid content-collaborative recommender system for multimedia item recommendation. LAP Lambert Academic Publishing (2011)
8. Liu, C., Yang, H.C., Fan, J., He, L., Wang, Y.M.: Distributed non-negativematrix factorization, 15 January 2013, uS Patent 8,356,086
9. Mnih, A., Salakhutdinov, R.: Probabilistic matrix factorization. In: Advances in Neural Information Processing Systems, pp. 1257–1264 (2007)
10. Odić, A., Tkalčič, M., Tasič, J.F., Košir, A.: Predicting and detecting the relevant contextual information in a movie-recommender system. Interact. Comput. **25**, 74–90 (2013)
11. O'Neill, M., Ryan, C.: Grammatical evolution. IEEE Trans. Evol. Comput. **5**(4), 349–358 (2001)
12. Ryan, C., Azad, R.M.A.: Sensible initialisation in chorus. In: Ryan, C., Soule, T., Keijzer, M., Tsang, E.P.K., Poli, R., Costa, E. (eds.) EuroGP 2003. LNCS, vol. 2610, pp. 394–403. Springer, Heidelberg (2003)
13. Takács, G., Pilászy, I., Németh, B., Tikk, D.: Matrix factorization and neighbor based algorithms for the netflix prize problem. In: Proceedings of the 2008 ACM Conference on Recommender Systems, pp. 267–274. ACM (2008)

Memetic Optimization of Graphene-Like Materials on Intel PHI Coprocessor

Wacław Kuś[1]([✉]), Adam Mrozek[2], and Tadeusz Burczyński[3]

[1] Institute of Computational Mechanics and Engineering,
Silesian University of Technology, Gliwice, Poland
waclaw.kus@polsl.pl
[2] AGH University of Science and Technology, Cracow, Poland
amrozek@agh.edu.pl
[3] Institute of Fundamental Technological Research,
Polish Academy of Sciences, Warsaw, Poland
tburczynski@ippt.pan.pl

Abstract. The paper is devoted to the optimization of energy of carbon based atomic structure with use of the memetic algorithm. The graphene like atoms structure is coded into floating point genes and underwent evolutionary changes. The global optimization algorithm is supported by local gradient based improvement of chromosomes. The optimization problem is solved with the use of Intel PHI (Intel Many Integrated Core Architecture – Intel MIC). The example of optimization and speedup measurement for parallel optimization are given in the paper.

Keywords: Parallel computing · Intel PHI · Optimization · Graphene-like materials

1 Introduction

The optimization of new graphene-like structures allows to obtain new stable structures with unique material properties. The goal of the paper is to describe algorithm which can be used to solve the optimization problem of atoms structure search in a parallel way.

Carbon has many allotropes such as diamond, graphite and amorphous phase, as well as numerous synthetic structures like graphene and nanotubes. This phenomenon is caused by the existence of carbon atoms in various hybridization states i.e. atoms of carbon with different electronic configurations, which determine the types of bondings, angles between them and spatial arrangement of neighboring atoms. In the recent years, graphene and similar two-dimensional materials are the subjects of particular interest of researchers ([1–5]) because of unique electronic, thermal and mechanical properties of such structures. Two-dimensional graphene-like materials can be considered as periodic, flat atomic networks, made of stable configurations of carbon atoms in certain hybridization states. Depending on the arrangement of the considered structure, rectangular or

© Springer International Publishing Switzerland 2016
L. Rutkowski et al. (Eds.): ICAISC 2016, Part I, LNAI 9692, pp. 401–410, 2016.
DOI: 10.1007/978-3-319-39378-0_35

triclinic unit cell of given size and atomic density can be identified. An overview of such well known structures (like graphyne and supergraphene), along with detailed description and investigation of their structural and electronic properties using tight-binding method can be found in the work by [2]. The stress-strain relations and mechanical properties were obtained by [6].

Since the stable configurations of atoms correspond to the global (or local in the case of isomers) minima on the Potential Energy Surface (PES), such a task can be considered as an optimization problem. However, searching for the global minimum on the PES is a non-trivial, NP-hard problem, because the number of local minima increases almost exponentially with the number of atoms in the considered structure.

The first group of the methods is based on searching of the PES, combined with simulation of certain physical processes, e.g. Random Searches and Monte Carlo (MC) Simulated Annealing [7] and Basin Hopping Monte Carlo [8]. The second group of computational intelligence methods is inspired by biological mechanisms, present in natural environment and live organisms. The bioinspired optimization methods of atomic structures, such as Genetic Algorithm [9], Artificial Immune System (AIS) [10] and Particle Swarm Optimization [11] have become very popular in the last years.

The authors of this paper successfully implemented set of bioinspired algorithms: Evolutionary Algorithm [12], AIS and PSO [13] for investigation of small aluminium clusters with pair-wise Morse and Murrell-Mottram potentials. Searching for new two-dimensional, graphene-like structures can be performed in the same manner. However, in this case a more sophisticated interatomic interaction model, so called bond-order potential, should be applied. The bond-order potential is able to handle various hybridization states of carbon atoms, allowing creation of bondings with proper, neighborhood-dependent geometry. Additionally, in contrast to the isolated for environment atomic clusters, new algorithm should impose periodicity of the created structure. The hybrid algorithm proposed in this work hybrid algorithm combines Parallel Evolutionary Algorithm, prepared by the authors, and conjugated-gradient optimization, built-in LAMMPS software package [14,15] which helps to form the new atomic configuration. Behavior and potential energy of carbon atoms is determined using Adaptive Intermolecular Reactive Bond Order (AIREBO) potential, as developed by [16]. The presented algorithm has modular construction, thus each component can be replaced with functional equivalent (e.g. EA with AIS, gradient optimization with molecular dynamics, etc.) or adapted to use on new computer architectures. The proposed method can be extended to optimization of the three-dimensional molecular structures and may be considered as an alternative approach to existing ones such as the ab-initio/PSO algorithm called CALYPSO [17]. The presented work, is a continuation of the authors investigations and modeling of atomic systems [6,18,19] and a developed version of the approach applied to the minimization of energy of atomic clusters [13].

The next chapter describes the modelling of graphene-like material with the use of AIREBO potential. The memetic algorithm based on global evolutionary algorithm and local gradient based search is described in Sect. 3. The parallel platform based on Intel PHI coprocessor is presented in Sect. 4. The optimization problem for graphene-like material optimization is given in Sect. 5, where the parallel memetic algorithm is discussed. The result of the chosen optimisation problem and performance obtained with the use of coprocessor Intel PHI are shown in Sect. 6.

2   Graphene-Like Material Modeling

The graphene material plays important role in research and application of new materials. The properties of graphene are well known. The graphene-like materials which are allotropes of graphene are stable atomic structures with coarser atom distribution than graphene. The numerical simulation of graphene allotropes can be performed with the use of static molecular method. Choosing the proper interaction model is very important in numerical simulation. In the presented case, the potential energy, as well as neighbourhood-dependent behaviour of the carbon atoms is determined on the base of the Adaptive Intermolecular Reactive Empirical Bond Order (AIREBO) potential for hydrocarbons [16]. The bond-order interaction mode is based on a set of neighborhood-dependent, switched, mathematical formulas, parametrized to the properties of hydrocarbons. The AIREBO potential in the following form is used in computations:

$$FF = \sum_i \sum_{j \neq i} \left(E_{ij}^{REBO} + E_{ij}^{LJ} + \sum_{k \neq i,j} \sum_{l \neq i,j,k} E_{kijl}^{TORSION} \right) \quad (1)$$

where the term denoted by E_{ij}^{REBO} corresponds to the short range interactions between covalently bonded pair of atoms. The long range interactions in the AIREBO model are computed in a simplified way, using the Lennard-Jones-like function (term E_{ij}^{LJ}) with additional distance-dependent switching functions, which expand the abilities to form different spatial configurations of carbon atoms. The last, torsional potential ($E_{kijl}^{TORSION}$) depends on the neighbouring atom's dihedral angles. All coefficients in 1 depend on coordinates of atoms. The AIREBO potential is fitted to handle different spatial configurations and hybridizations types of carbon atoms properly and is computationally more effective than the ReaxFF [20] approach, which requires additional equilibration of the atomic charge every certain number of iterations [21,22]. The application of the AIREBO potential to the examination of mechanical properties of various two dimensional graphene-like materials has been already performed in [6] and was in a good agreement with the results obtained by other researchers. The resulting atomic structures can be used in multiscale modeling of composite materials [23,24].

The periodicity of the structure is achieved by proper boundary conditions, imposed on the unit cell. The static molecular analysis is performed using package LAMMPS [14,15]. The equilibration process is performed using the minimization method based on the Polak-Ribiere algorithm [25]. After the conjugated-gradient (CG) minimization of the potential energy, the potential energy of the structure is computed.

3   Memetic Algorithm

The evolutionary based algorithms are a well known global optimization technique [26]. The optimizations is performed using an algorithm based on biological observation of the evolution of species. The description of elements, mechanism used in the algorithm are also bioinspired. The optimization is performed for design vector described as individuals with chromosomes or just chromosomes (if an individual contain one chromosome). The design variables are called genes. The objective function value or objective function with some additional terms is called fitness function and says how the individual or chromosome is fitted to the environment defined by the optimization problem.

The memetic algorithms [27, 28] combine evolutionary, global, population based algorithm with local improvements methods for some individuals or chromosomes. The memetic algorithms are sometimes named hybrid algorithms or hybrid evolutionary algorithms because they are a kind of a hybrid of global and local optimization techniques [29].

The global evolutionary algorithm coupled with local conjugate gradient algorithm is used in the paper. The driving part of the optimization is the evolutionary algorithm with evolving population of potential solutions to the problems. The typical operators like mutation and crossover are used without modifications. The selection is also preserved. The gradient algorithm modifies the genes of all chromosomes before computing fitness functions. The modification leads to modification of evolutionary algorithm process of optimum search. The evolutionary operators moves chromosomes to the new areas of attraction and the gradient based algorithm moves chromosome to the local optimum value. The proposed approach works well for a highly multimodal fitness function for which it is hard to close to local optimum using a typical evolutionary algorithm. The algorithm used in the paper is shown in Fig. 1.

The memetic algorithm used in the paper uses floating point number representation of genes. The chromosome genes are modified with the use of uniform and Gaussian mutation combined with a simple crossover. The uniform mutation changes genes values randomly within the box constraints. The Gaussian mutation combined with a simple crossover uses in the first step a simple crossover creating new offspring on the base of two randomly taken chromosomes. The offspring contains parts of two parents chromosomes determined by randomly chosen cutting line. The offspring is modified with the use of Gaussian mutation, some genes are selected and modified with the use of value obtained from random number generator with normal distribution. The selection of chromosomes which will create a new population is performed with the use of ranking selection with elitism. The best chromosome survive due to elitism. The chromosomes with high fitness have the highest probability of being selected to a new population. The ranking of chromosomes is created on the basis of fitness function value. The new rank value is given for each chromosome on the basis of the rank position and rank function. The selection based on the rank value for each chromosome established with roulette wheel method is used in the algorithm.

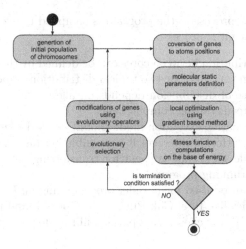

Fig. 1. The memetic algorithm flowchart

4   Intel PHI coprocessor

The Intel PHI coprocessor [30] is a brand name for an Intel Many Integrated Core Architecture (Intel MIC). The coprocessor used in the paper contains a chip with many cores (61 in case of Intel Phi 7120P – code name Knights Corner) connected using a bidirectional ring bus. Each of the cores have 4 threads. The cores are equipped with cache-coherent L2 cache and the coprocessor is equipped with a few (8 in Intel Phi 7120P) memory controllers. The Intel Phi 7120P coprocessor has up to 16 GB of GDDR5 memory with total throughput of 352 GB/sec. The communication between host and coprocessor is based on PCIe bus. The low speed of the PCIe bus should be taken into account during the development of algorithms, the as low as possible communication between host and coprocessor is important factor. One of the cores is used to manage the system operations on the coprocessor. The user can use 60 cores with 4 threads which gives up to 240 threads per coprocessor card.

The programs on the coprocessor can be executed in a few execution modes [30]:

- coprocessor native – the program is compiled for the coprocessor only, cannot be executed on host processor, the special coprocessor instructions like AVX512 can be used to improve the performance of the program,
- offload – the program is compiled for host, but some functions and data are marked and compiled for coprocessor, during execution of the program on the host, some work is offloaded to the coprocessor card, special coprocessor instruction can be used in offloaded part,
- symmetric – the program is executed both on host and coprocessor, the most typical example is MPI usage, where some jobs are executed on host and some on coprocessor, the work should be divided according to performance

of the host and coprocessor, the program is compiled in two versions, one for host and another for coprocessor.

The thread distribution between cores can be defined by the user and threads can be bound to a given core. The two typical distributions types are scatter and compact. The choice of distribution depends on algorithm and communication needed between threads during computations.

The coprocessor native execution mode should be used when comparing performance to other platforms wherever it is possible because in offload execution and symmetric mode some time is spent for transferring data and programs to coprocessor before running program.

The OpenMP can be used for parallel programming on Intel MIC platform, also other approaches like Intel Cilk Plus, MPI, OpenCL and pthreads are supported. The OpenMP was chosen as a parallel library for programs presented in the paper.

5   Optimization of Graphene-Like Material

The graphene-like materials can be optimal which means that for prescribed periodic cell size and given number of atoms one can describe atomic structure with minimal total potential energy of the atomic structure. The memetic algorithm described in Sect. 3 is used to solve the optimization problem. The objective - fitness function was declared with the use of (1). The design variables - genes are positions of atoms in the cell (Fig. 2). The configuration of n atoms have $2n$ design variables (genes).

In the initial population, atoms have randomly generated coordinates and are placed in the area of the unit cell with periodic boundaries. Dimensions, the rectangular or triclinic type of the unit cell, as well as the number of atoms, are part of a set of parameters of the simulation. Such an approach allows to control the value of atomic density of the newly-created structure. The periodicity of the atomic structure significantly reduces the number of design variables. The crucial role in the creation of a new atomic structure is played by the fitness function which is formulated as the total potential energy of the considered atomic system, i.e., the total sum of all potential energies of particular atomic interactions.

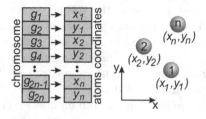

Fig. 2. The example of chromosome and corresponding atoms structure

The local CG method is used for every chromosome in population and is computed by LAMMPS package. The library containing LAMMPS classes is used during the optimization. The main timeconsuming part of the optimization algorithm is local CG method performed by the LAMMPS. The evolutionary algorithms are easily parallelized, the loop with fitness function evaluation is done in parallel way in most approaches [31,32]. The OpenMP [33] library was used in the preparation of numerical results. The parallel algorithm is shown in Fig. 3. The LAMMPS objects for each thread are created and distributed between the cores performing computations.

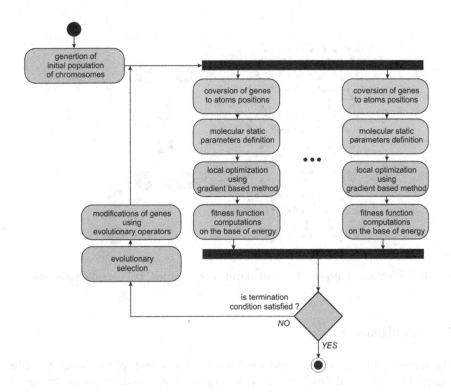

Fig. 3. The parallel memetic algorithm for graphene like materials optimization

6 Results of the Numerical Tests

The problem of optimization of 8 carbon atoms positions in periodic cell was considered. The minimization with the use of memetic algorithm is performed in a parallel way. The optimization was executed several times on coprocessor Intel Phi 7120P in native execution mode. The scatter distribution of threads was used. The obtained speedup for different number of threads are shown in Table 1.

The result of the optimization, the atomic structure is shown in Fig. 4.

Table 1. The speedup obtained during computations in native execution mode

No. of threads	Speedup
1	1.00
2	1.97
4	3.72
8	7.69
16	14.57
32	28.32
48	40.20

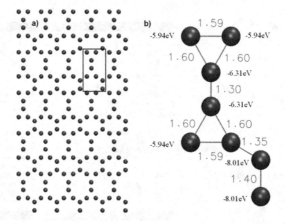

Fig. 4. The obtained atomic structure during optimization, (a) periodic structure, (b) cell

7 Conclusions

The memetic optimization algorithm used for the search of new graphene-like atoms structures scale well on the coprocessor. The speedups above 40 for 48 threads were obtained. The presented algorithm can also be used for the optimization and search for other atoms structures not only the ones based on carbons. The future investigations will be conducted for utilizing the coprocessor in a symmetric mode allowing for the use of two coprocessors and host processors in the same optimization problem solving.

Acknowledgement. The authors are grateful to Czestochowa University of Technology for granting access to Intel CPU and Xeon Phi platforms providing by the MICLAB project No. POIG.02.03.00.24-093/13

References

1. Cranford, S.W., Buehler, M.J.: Mechanical properties of graphyne. Carbon **49**, 4111–4121 (2011)
2. Enyashin, A.N., Ivanovskii, A.L.: Graphene allotropes. Phys. Status Solidi **248**(8), 1879–1883 (2011)
3. Narita, N., Nagai, S., Suzuki, S., Nakao, K.: Electronic structure of three-dimensional graphyne. Phys. Rev. B **62**(16), 11146–11151 (2000)
4. Peng, Q., Ji, W., De, S.: Mechanical properties of graphyne monolayers: a first-principles study. Phys. Chem. Chem. Phys. **14**(38), 13385–13391 (2012)
5. Scarpa, F., Adhikari, S., Phani, A.S.: Effective elastic mechanical properties of single layer graphene sheets. Nanotechnology **20**(6), 065709 (2009)
6. Mrozek, A., Burczyński, T.: Examination of mechanical properties of graphene allotropes by means of computer simulation. Comput. Assist. Methods Eng. Sci. **20**(4), 309–323 (2013)
7. Lloyd, L.D., Johnston, R.L.: Modelling aluminium clusters with an empirical many-body potential. Chem. Phys. **236**, 107–121 (1998)
8. Wales, D.J., Doye, J.P.K.: Global optimization by basin-hopping and the lowest energy structures of Lennard-Jones clusters containing up to 110 atoms. J. Phys. Chem. A **101**, 5111–5116 (1997)
9. Roberts, C., Johnston, R.L., Wilson, N.T.: A genetic algorithm for the structural optimization of morse clusters. Theoret. Chem. Acc. **104**, 123–130 (2000)
10. Shao, X., Cheng, L., Cai, W.: An adaptive immune optimization algorithm for energy minimization problems. J. Chem. Phys. **120**(24), 11401–11406 (2004)
11. Zhou, J.C., Li, W.J., Zhu, J.B.: Particle swarm optimization computer simulation of Ni clusters. Trans. Nonferrous Met. Soc. China **18**, 410–415 (2008)
12. Mrozek, A., Kuś, W., Orantek, P., Burczyński, T.: Prediction of the aluminium atoms distribution using evolutionary algorithm. In: Recent Developments in Artificial Intelligence Methods, vol. 10, pp. 127–130 (2005)
13. Mrozek, A., Kuś, W., Burczyński, T.: Searching of stable configurations of nanostructures using computational intelligence methods. Czasopismo Techniczne **20**(107), 85–97 (2010)
14. Lammps package www: http://lammps.sandia.gov
15. Plimpton, S.: Fast parallel algorithms for short-range molecular dynamics. J. Comp. Phys. **117**, 1–19 (1995)
16. Stuart, S.J., Tutein, A.B., Harrison, J.A.: A reactive potential for hydrocarbons with intermolecular interactions. J. Chem. Phys. **112**(14), 6472–6486 (2000)
17. Wang, Y., Lv, J., Zhu, L., Ma, Y.: Crystal structure prediction via particle-swarm optimization. Phys. Rev. B **82**(9), 094116–0941123 (2010)
18. Mrozek, A., Kuś, W., Burczyński, T.: Nano level optimization of graphene allotropes by means of a hybrid parallel evolutionary algorithm. Comput. Mater. Sci. **106**, 161–169 (2015)
19. Mrozek, A., Kuś, W., Burczyński, T.: Hybrid parallel evolutionary algorithm in optimization of 2D graphene-like materials. Comput. Methods Mater. Sci. **15**(1), 103–110 (2015)
20. Chenoweth, K., van Duin, A.C., Goddard III, W.A.: ReaxFF reactive force field for molecular dynamics simulations of hydrocarbon oxidation. J. Phys. Chem. A **112**, 1040–1053 (2003)
21. Rappe, A.K., Goddard III, W.A.: Charge equilibration for molecular dynamics simulations. J. Chem. Phys. **95**(8), 3358–3363 (1991)

22. Nakano, A.: Parallel multilevel preconditioned conjugate-gradient approach to variable-charge molecular dynamics. Comput. Phys. Commun. **104**, 59–69 (1997)

23. Burczyński, T., Kuś, W.: Optimization of structures using distributed and parallel evolutionary algorithms. In: Wyrzykowski, R., Dongarra, J., Paprzycki, M., Waśniewski, J. (eds.) PPAM 2004. LNCS, vol. 3019, pp. 572–579. Springer, Heidelberg (2004)

24. Ogierman, W., Kokot, G.: Modeling of constitutive behaviour of anisotropic composite material using multiscale approach. Mechanika **2**, 118–122 (2015)

25. Press, W.H., Teukolsky, S.A., Vetterling, W.T., Flanery, B.P.: Numerical Recipes: The Art of Scientific Computing. Cambridge University Press, Cambridge (2007)

26. Michalewicz, Z.: Genetic Algorithms + Data Structures = Evolutionary Algorithms. Springer, Heidelberg (1996)

27. Moscato, P.: On genetic crossover operators for relative order preservation. C3P Report 778, California Institute of Technology, Pasadena, USA (1989)

28. Moscato, P., Cotta, C., Mendes, A.: Memetic algorithms. In: Onwubolu, G.C., Babu, B.V. (eds.) New Optimization Techniques in Engineering. Studies in Fuzziness and Soft Computing, vol. 141, pp. 53–85. Springer, Heidelberg (2004)

29. Orantek, P.: Hybrid evolutionary algorithms in optimization of structures under dynamical loads. In: Burczyński, T., Osyczka, A. (eds.) IUTAM Symposium on Evolutionary Methods in Mechanics. Solid Mechanics and Its Applications, vol. 117, pp. 297–308. Springer, Heidelberg (2004)

30. Ranman, R.: Intel Xeon Phi Coprocessor Architecture and Tools: The Guide for Applications Developers. ApressOpen, New York (2013)

31. Kuś, W.: Grid-enabled evolutionary algorithm application in the mechanical optimization problems. Eng. Appl. Artif. Intell. **20**(5), 629–636 (2007)

32. Kuś, W., Burczyński, T.: Parallel bioinspired algorithms in optimization of structures. In: Wyrzykowski, R., Dongarra, J., Karczewski, K., Wasniewski, J. (eds.) PPAM 2007. LNCS, vol. 4967, pp. 1285–1292. Springer, Heidelberg (2008)

33. OpenMP Architecture Review Board web page. http://openmp.org

On Aggregation of Stages in Multi-criteria Optimization of Chain Structured Processes

Jan Kusiak[1], Paweł Morkisz[2], Piotr Oprocha[2], Wojciech Pietrucha[2],
and Łukasz Sztangret[1(✉)]

[1] Faculty of Metals Engineering and Industrial Computer Science,
AGH University of Science and Technology, Al. Mickiewicza 30,
30-059 Kraków, Poland
{kusiak,szt}@agh.edu.pl
[2] Faculty of Applied Mathematics, AGH University of Science and Technology,
Al. Mickiewicza 30, 30-059 Kraków, Poland
{morkiszp,oprocha}@agh.edu.pl, wojtekpietrucha@gmail.com

Abstract. This work is concerned with complex optimization problems which can be divided into multiple, multi-dimensional problems arranged linearly (as can be observed in the multi-stage industrial processes). The relations between complexity of the problem, level of aggregation of stages into larger groups, and efficiency of search for optimal solution were investigated.

1 Introduction

Typical industrial process (e.g. motivated by metallurgical engineering) can be divided into numerous smaller stages [1,7,9,11]. They are often arranged in a linear manner, along technological path which material (semi-product) have to pass before it reaches its final form. For example, in production of copper from sulfide concentrates, the production line consists of the following stages: copper flash smelting, converting of copper matte to blister copper, fire refining of copper and electrolytic refining [2]. Of course, each stage can be divided even further, since there are real steps (reactions) that have to take place in each stage (and require proper sequence of control parameters, to proceed smoothly).

When choosing a strategy for optimization of such processes, at first an important decision about aggregation of stages must be made. It is possible to consider large number of small (possibly low-dimensional) stages, and try to set control parameters one after another, or look at the process more globally, e.g. aggregate all stages inside one large stage with many control parameters, output parameters etc. (one huge multi-dimensional optimization problem). Performing some partial aggregations and treating them sequentially is another permissible approach.

In the present work an attempt to answer the question which strategy is better was made. As a testing ground a sequence of standard test functions was used and the influence of aggregation on reliability of finding optimal solution was checked. It is continuation of the Authors' previous research undertaken in [6,10].

© Springer International Publishing Switzerland 2016
L. Rutkowski et al. (Eds.): ICAISC 2016, Part I, LNAI 9692, pp. 411–419, 2016.
DOI: 10.1007/978-3-319-39378-0_36

2 Stages, Test Function and Optimization Method

2.1 General Structure of the Problem

In this work a hypothetical industrial process (e.g. metallurgical process) consisting of a few intermediate steps or stages, enumerated by index $i = 1, \ldots, n$ was analysed. In each stage there is the following set of input-output parameters:

(i) vector $\mathbf{x}_i$ of uncontrollable input parameters, e.g. representing initial materials delivered to factory, semi-products from other steps or from other production lines etc.

(ii) vector $\mathbf{p}_i$ of (input) control parameters, ensuring that the reaction/production proceeds properly, effectively, etc.

(iii) vector $\mathbf{y}_i$ of output parameters which represent some parameters of products of this step; usually we keep only these parameters which carry an essential information for further stages of production

(iv) vector $\mathbf{q}_i$ which represents evaluation of the quality of the process at stage i; it may be calculated from $\mathbf{y}_i$, but can be also derivative of some other parameters that we do not keep in $\mathbf{y}_i$.

In practice, in each stage there are two functions Q_i, F_i which bound input-output parameters by the formula:

$$\mathbf{x}_{i+1} = \mathbf{y}_i = F_i(\mathbf{x}_i, \mathbf{p}_i),$$
$$\mathbf{q}_i = Q_i(\mathbf{x}_i, \mathbf{p}_i).$$

Of course, the above dependences define a chain relation between stages. For example, to evaluate quality at stage 3 it is necessary to calculate

$$\mathbf{q}_3 = F_3(\mathbf{x}_3, \mathbf{p}_3) = F_3(\mathbf{y}_2, \mathbf{p}_3) = F_3(F_2(\mathbf{x}_2, \mathbf{p}_2), \mathbf{p}_3)$$
$$= F_3(F_2(F_1(\mathbf{x}_1, \mathbf{p}_1), \mathbf{p}_2), \mathbf{p}_3). \tag{1}$$

For simplicity, in this article an assumption was made that there is only one value describing quality in step i, that is $\mathbf{q}_i = q_i$. The main optimization goal is to find minimum of the function

$$q = w_1 q_1 + w_2 q_2 + \ldots + w_n q_n. \tag{2}$$

where weights $w_i \geq 0$ quantify importance of quality in intermediate step i for the evaluation of quality of the whole process. Again, for simplicity an assumption was made that all quality assessments are equally important, that is $w_i = 1/n$ for each i. Note that in the following approach q is in fact a function $Q(\mathbf{p}_1, \ldots, \mathbf{p}_n)$ because weights $w_1, \ldots, w_n$ as well as materials input vector $\mathbf{x}_1$ are set before the optimization procedure starts.

2.2 Aggregation

Aggregation involves grouping some of stages into one larger stage. For example, if $1 \leq a \leq b \leq n$ then using functions F_i it is possible to define aggregated function F_a^b by composition similar to (1), that is

$$F_a^b(\mathbf{x}_a, \mathbf{p}_a, \mathbf{p}_{a+1}, \dots, \mathbf{p}_b) = F_b(F_{b-1}(\dots(F_a(\mathbf{x}_a, \mathbf{p}_a), \mathbf{p}_{a+1}), \dots), \mathbf{p}_{b-1}), \mathbf{p}_b).$$

This way a single stage, which is a composition of stages from a to b can be achieved. Clearly, similar aggregation of quality function must be performed. It can be done using approach similar to formula (2), that is:

$$q_a^b = \frac{1}{b-a+1}(q_a + q_{a+1} + \dots + q_b) = \frac{1}{b-a+1}\sum_{j=a}^{b} Q_j(\mathbf{x}_j, \mathbf{p}_j)$$

$$= \frac{1}{b-a+1}\sum_{j=a}^{b} Q_j(F_{j-1}(\dots(F_a(\mathbf{x}_a, \mathbf{p}_a), \mathbf{p}_{a+1}), \dots), \mathbf{p}_{j-1}), \mathbf{p}_j)$$

Aggregation for the initial sequence of stages means that a partition of the set $\{1, 2, \dots, n\}$ providing numbers $1 = a_1 < a_2 < \dots < a_s \leq n$ where $1 \leq s \leq n$ is fixed. Then if putting $b_i = a_{i+1} - 1$ for $i = 1, \dots, s-1$ and $b_s = n$ then initial problem consisting of n stages is replaced by problem consisting of s stages, described by functions $F_{a_j}^{b_j}$ and quality functions $q_{a_j}^{b_j}$. By the definition, $F_{a_j}^{b_j}$ has one "materials" input vector $\mathbf{x}_{a_j}$ and vector of control parameters which is a composition of control vectors before aggregations, that is $(\mathbf{p}_{a_j}, \mathbf{p}_{a_j+1}, \dots, \mathbf{p}_{b_j})$. This way a reduction of number of stages is achieved, however the dimensions of the decision problem is increasing as well.

2.3 SIM and SEQ Approaches

The following natural techniques to deal with optimization of chain structured processes will be used [6]:

1. *simultaneous* (SIM),
2. *sequential* (SEQ),

In a simultaneous approach the optimization procedure searches for optimal solutions for all considered stages at once. This approach is equivalent to solving one huge multi-dimensional optimization problem. The SIM approach will be used inside aggregated stages to find their optimal control parameters. If the aggregated stage is described by a function F_a^b then the optimization algorithm modify all control parameters $\mathbf{p}_a, \dots, \mathbf{p}_b$. The opposite to SIM approach is SEQ in which the optimization of each stage is being performed separately from the first to the last stage. Using SEQ approach the optimization procedure solves many low dimensional problems. The SEQ will "transport" solutions between consecutive stages (aggregated or not). Since some stages are aggregated into bigger ones, in fact the optimization procedure will look for optimal values of functions $q_{a_1}^{b_1}, \ldots, q_{a_s}^{b_s}$ sequentially. None of the improvements (e.g. SIMF or SEQC techniques from [6]) will be applied, since it should better reveal influence of aggregation on the whole process, rather than other factors hard to quantify (e.g. effect of credits).

2.4   Measure of Aggregation

Suppose there are some aggregations of stages, that is, the partition $a_1 \leq b_1 < a_2 \leq b_2 < \ldots < a_s \leq b_s$ of the set of indexes $\{1, 2, \ldots, n\}$ as described in Sect. 2.2 is given. Observe that aggregated stage j contains $b_j - a_j + 1$ stages, and therefore it is clear that:

$$\sum_{i=1}^{s} b_i - a_i + 1 = -a_1 + b_s + 1 + \sum_{i=1}^{s-1} b_i + 1 - a_{i+1} = -1 + n + 1 + \sum_{i=1}^{s-1} a_{i+1} - a_{i+1} = n.$$

A measure of the level of aggregation can be expressed by the formula:

$$A = \sum_{i=1}^{k} \frac{(b_i - a_i)^2}{(n-1)^2}. \tag{3}$$

Observe that

$$b_{i+1} - a_i = b_{i+1} - a_{i+1} + a_{i+1} - a_i = (b_{i+1} - a_{i+1}) + (b_i - a_i) + 1$$

and clearly, for any two natural numbers $m^2 + n^2 < (m + n + 1)^2$. Therefore, it is not hard to check that (3) reaches its maximal value when there is only one large aggregated stage, and in this case $A = 1$ because $b_1 = n$ and $a_1 = 1$, while minimal value of A is assigned when there are n single stages (no aggregation), and in such case $a_i = b_i$ for $i = 1, \ldots, n$, hence $A = 0$. In this sense value of A increases when aggregation of stages increases. Note that A is independent on the partition, and only depends on the number of aggregated stages of given length. For example, if $n = 5$ and $a_2 = 3, a_3 = 4$ then there is aggregation of the form $2 - 1 - 2$ that is first aggregated stage is composed of 2 simple stages, next is a single stage, and then again aggregation of two stages appears. Similarly $a_2 = 2, a_3 = 4$ gives structure $1 - 2 - 2$. But in both situations the introduced measure of the level of aggregation will have the same value $A = \frac{1+1}{4^2} = 1/8$.

2.5   Test Function and Optimization Method

The main goal of this paper is to investigate influence of the method of aggregation on the optimization process, rather than influence of complexity of optimized function. When using a more sophisticated function, the effect of aggregation could be highly influenced by the choice of optimization method, starting point, etc. This observation resulted in the decision to choose in each stage the following simple function:

$$q_i = Q_i(\mathbf{x}_i, \mathbf{p}_i) = \sum_{j=1}^{k} (\mathbf{p}_{i,j} - \mathbf{x}_{i,j})^2 \qquad (4)$$

where $\mathbf{p}_{i,j}$ denotes j-th coordinate of the i-th vector $\mathbf{p}_i$. In other words, each Q_i is a simple quadratic function and input vector $\mathbf{x}_i$ is responsible for displacement of the minimum. This way it is easy to check if optimum was reached and at the same time some dependences between consecutive stages in the chain are embedded. In the considerations the input of following stage was equal to the control vector used in previous one $\mathbf{x}_{i+1} = \mathbf{p}_i$, that is $F_i(\mathbf{x}_i, \mathbf{p}_i)$ is simply a projection on the second coordinate. The main ingredient that will change during the tests will be the number of stages (varying between 2 and 10) and the number of dimensions of vectors $\mathbf{x}_i$ and $\mathbf{p}_i$ (varying between 1 and 10).

Since in practice the shape of the graph of Q_i would not be known, an algorithm which allow entire-space search will be used. It would work well with simple function Q_i but also with any other much more complicated function. The decision was made to use Particle Swarm Optimization (PSO) because first of all it has the above features, and second, it will make possible to compare obtained results with those presented in [6]. This method is, similarly to genetic algorithms, motivated by mechanism observed in nature. There is quite large literature on this topic, e.g. see [3–5,8].

Roughly speaking, during optimization position vector $\mathbf{z}_k^i$ of i-th particle in generation k is transformed by the formula

$$\mathbf{z}_{k+1}^i = \mathbf{z}_k^i + \mathbf{v}_{k+1}^i. \qquad (5)$$

where $\mathbf{v}_{k+1}^i$ is a velocity vector modified in consecutive iterations by the formula:

$$\mathbf{v}_{k+1}^i = w\mathbf{v}_k^i + c_1 r_{1,k}^i (\mathbf{p}^g - \mathbf{z}_k^i) + c_2 r_{2,k}^i (\mathbf{p}^i - \mathbf{z}_k^i) \qquad (6)$$

where: $\mathbf{p}^g$ denotes vector of the best position found so far by the whole swarm; vector $\mathbf{p}^i$ represents the best solution found so far by the i-th particle; w is defined as the inertia coefficient; c_1 and c_2 are acceleration coefficients (called also training coefficients); $r_{1,k}^i$ and $r_{2,k}^i$ are numbers from the interval $[0, 1]$ picked at random with the uniform distribution. In each iteration, a leader of the swarm is chosen (the particle with the best value of quality function) and then vectors $\mathbf{p}^g$ and $\mathbf{p}^i$ are updated.

3   Optimization Results

In optimization procedure for a single stage the allowed maximal number of quality function Q_i evaluations was set to $I_{max} = 1000$. When stages are aggregated then this number is multiplied in a sense that the value of Q_a^b can be checked only 1000-times, however, to calculate the value of Q_a^b it is necessary to

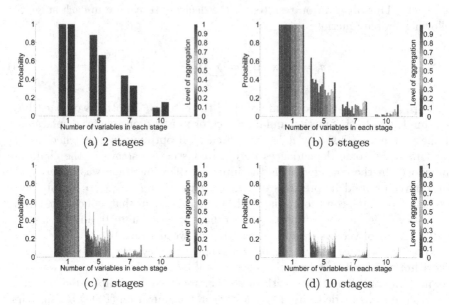

Fig. 1. The probability of finding the global minimum depending on the number of optimization variables and the aggregation level.

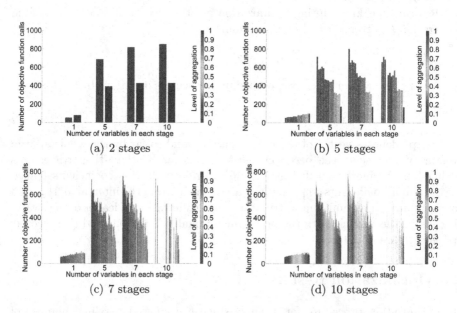

Fig. 2. The average number of objective function calls in successful optimization depending on the number of optimization variables and the aggregation level.

check values of each of the functions $Q_a, \ldots, Q_b$, so in practice $1000 \cdot (b - a + 1)$ checks of basic quality function are preformed. The required accuracy was set to $\varepsilon = 1/1000$, which means that optimization goal is accomplished if value of quality function Q_a^b in each stage is below ε for some sequence of control parameters. The optimization of the whole process was considered as successful if the value of all quality function q was less or equal than assumed accuracy ε.

The computation was made for different number of stages $n = 2, 5, 7, 10$ and for different dimension of test function at each stage $k = 1, 5, 7, 10$ (the same value of k fixed for all stages in the chain). For each combination of the number of stages and the dimension of test function at each stage, optimization procedure was performed 100 times. All possible combinations of aggregations were considered as well

$$1 - 1 - \cdots - 1, 2 - 1 - \ldots - 1, 1 - 2 - 1 - \ldots - 1, \cdots, (n-1) - 1, n.$$

for every fixed number of stages n.

The probability of finding global minimum for different number of stages and for different number of variables in each stage is shown in Fig. 1. Color of each bar on the graph represents value of aggregation A in the optimization procedure calculated according to formula (3). In case of chain composed of only 2 stages, there are only two possible structures $1 - 1$ or 2 and therefore there are only two values of $A = 0$ or $A = 1$, respectively. If there were 5 stages then possible aggregations and possible values of A are presented in Table 1. Figure 2 presents the average number of objective function calls needed in successful optimization to reach required accuracy. When the number of stages increases, the number of possible aggregations increases exponentially.

Table 1. All possible aggregations A for a process with 5 stages.

Number of aggregated stages of given size in the class					No. of elements in the class	Structure of a representant	A
1	2	3	4	5			
5					1	1-1-1-1-1	0
3	1				4	2-1-1-1	0,0625
1	2				3	2-2-1	0,125
2		1			3	3-1-1	0,25
	1	1			2	3-2	0,3125
1			1		2	4-1	0,5625
				1	1	5	1
Total:					**16**		

4 Summary and Conclusions

A problem of optimization of multistage processes was investigated in the present paper. The Authors already developed a few strategies which were presented in [6]. This paper focuses on hybrid approach - a combination of SIM and SEQ approaches. It is evident from the results (see Fig. 1) that if the number of variables is small (5 dimensions) then it is better to use sequential approach. The best results are achieved when there is no aggregation at all. It is interesting that this statement does not change when the number of stages increases.

When the dimension of the problem is high, then SIM approach starts to surpass sequential approach, with the highest probability of finding optimal solution when there is total aggregation (all simple stages aggregated in one stage). The conclusion is that, when the linear process can be divided in large number of small, relatively simple problems, then it may be good idea to keep this splitting. In the case of large optimization problems it seems to be a better choice to use a strategy with measure of aggregation close to one. It is especially visible in Fig. 1(d) where only highly aggregated structures were able to lead to a solution. It is also interesting that average number of function calls was much higher in SEQ approach. It means that this approach needs more computational time to lead to a solution; SIM strategy was giving optimal solution either fast or failed in finding one, see Fig. 2.

Acknowledgements. The research leading to results contained in this paper was supported by National Science Centre in Poland (NCN), Grant no. DEC-2013/11/B/ST8/00352

References

1. Behrens, B.: Integrative process chain optimization using a genetic algorithm. Prod. Eng. **6**, 29–37 (2012)
2. Davenport, W.G., Jones, M.D., King, M.J., Partelpoeg, E.H.: Flash Smelting: Analysis, Control and Optimization. The Minerals, Metals & Materials Society, Warrendale (2001)
3. Eberhart, R.C., Kennedy, J.: A new optimizer using particle swarm theory. In: Proceedings of the Sixth International Symposium on Micro Machine and Human Science, pp. 39–43 (1995)
4. Eberhart, R.C., Kennedy, J.: Particle swarm optimization, vol. 4, pp. 1942–1948 (1995)
5. Helwig, S.: Particle swarms for constrained optimization. Ph.D. thesis, University of Erlangen-Nuremberg (2010)
6. Jarosz, P., Kusiak, J., Małecki, S., Oprocha, P., Sztangret, Ł., Wilkus, M.: A methodology for optimization in multistage industrial processes: a pilot study. Math. Probl. Eng. **2015**, 10 (2015)
7. Kusiak, J., Sztangret, Ł., Pietrzyk, M.: Effective strategies of metamodelling of industrial metallurgical processes. Adv. Eng. Softw. **89**, 90–97 (2015)
8. Ochlak, E., Forouraghi, B.: A particle swarm algorithm for multiobjective design optimization, pp. 765–772. IEEE Computer Society (2006)

9. Shiel, A., Weis, D., Orians, K.: Evaluation of zinc, cadmium and lead isotope fractionation during smelting and refining. Sci. Total Environ. **408**, 2357–2368 (2010)
10. Stanisławczyk, A., Foryś, P., Sztangret, L., Barabasz, B., Kusiak, J.: Optimization of production chains using the nature-inspired techniques. Steel Res. **79**, 617–624 (2008)
11. Wagner, T., Hegels, D., Wiederkehr, T., Peuker, A., Odendahl, S., Rausch, S., Biermann, D., Buchheim, C., Muller, H.: Optimization of the process chain for the efficient manufacturing of forming tools with complex 3d surfaces. In: Tillmann, W., Baumann, S. (eds.) Sonderforschungsbereich 708 Systeme der Blechformteile-fertigung - Erzeugung, Modellierung, Bearbeitung - 6, pp. 213–222 (2013)

A New Differential Evolution Algorithm
with Alopex-Based Local Search

Miguel Leon[(✉)] and Ning Xiong

Mälardalen University, Västerås, Sweden
miguel.leonortiz@mdh.se

Abstract. Differential evolution (DE), as a class of biologically inspired and meta-heuristic techniques, has attained increasing popularity in solving many real world optimization problems. However, DE is not always successful. It can easily get stuck in a local optimum or an undesired stagnation condition. This paper proposes a new DE algorithm Differential Evolution with Alopex-Based Local Search (DEALS), for enhancing DE performance. Alopex uses local correlations between changes in individual parameters and changes in function values to estimate the gradient of the landscape. It also contains the idea of simulated annealing that uses temperature to control the probability of move directions during the search process. The results from experiments demonstrate that the use of Alopex as local search in DE brings substantial performance improvement over the standard DE algorithm. The proposed DEALS algorithm has also been shown to be strongly competitive (best rank) against several other DE variants with local search.

Keywords: Differential evolution · Memetic algorithm · Local search · Alopex · Optimization

1 Introduction

Differential evolution (DE) [1] represents a class of evolutionary algorithms that offer biologically inspired and meta-heuristic techniques to solve many real world optimization problems. As population-based approaches [2], DE performs parallel and beam search thus exhibiting strong ability of exploration in complex and high dimensional spaces. One distinguishing feature of DE is that it utilizes the differences of solutions randomly selected from the population to generate offspring for the new generation. Consequently the search in DE is guided by the distribution of solutions rather than a pre-specified probability function. A deep survey of various DE algorithms and associated operators can be found in [3] and [4]. DE has some attractive properties such as easy programming, simple implementation and relatively low computational expenses while still yielding high performance on complex fitness landscapes. It has become a very competitive alternative among the evolutionary algorithms in engineering optimization applications. In [5] it was indicated that DE algorithms were more efficient and more accurate than several other optimization methods, including controlled random search, simulated annealing and genetic algorithms.

© Springer International Publishing Switzerland 2016
L. Rutkowski et al. (Eds.): ICAISC 2016, Part I, LNAI 9692, pp. 420–431, 2016.
DOI: 10.1007/978-3-319-39378-0_37

However, the performance of DE is not always good. It can easily get stuck in a local optimum or fail to generate better solutions before the population has converged. Recent efforts are made to mitigate this problem with two kinds of countermeasures. The first is to enhance the DE capability by adapting mutation strategies or control parameters of DE during the running of the algorithm, see examples in [6–9] and [10]. The second is to combine DE with local search to increase its convergence speed or the ability to avoid local optima, see the works in [11–13].

This paper proposes a new DE variant Differential Evolution with Alopex-Based Local Search (DEALS), as contribution to the second kind of efforts for enhancing DE performance. Alopex [14] was originally proposed for solving pattern matching and combinatorial optimization problems. It uses local correlations between changes in individual parameter and changes in the function values to estimate the gradient of the landscape. Alopex also contains the idea of simulated annealing that uses the evolving parameter temperature to control the probability of move directions during the search and optimization process. The results from experiments demonstrate that the use of Alopex as local search in DE brings substantial performance improvement over the standard DE algorithm. The proposed DEALS algorithm has also been shown to be strongly competitive (best rank) against several other DE variants with local search.

The remaining of the paper is organized as follows. Section 2 gives a review of the related works. The basic DE is briefly introduced in Sect. 3, which is followed by the explanation of the proposed DEALS algorithm in Sect. 4. Experiment results and evaluation are presented in Sect. 5. Finally we conclude the paper in Sect. 6.

2 Related Work

Since the first proposal of DE in 1997 [15], a lot of works have been done to improve the search ability of this algorithm, resulting in many variants of DE. A brief overview on some of them is given in this section. Ali et al. [12] proposed two different local search algorithms, namely Trigonometric Local Search and Interpolated Local Search, which were applied to refine the best solution and two random solutions in every generation respectively.

Local search differential evolution was developed in [16] where a new local search operator was used on every individual in the population with a probability. The search strategy attempted to find a random better solution between trial vector and the best solution in the generation.

Dai and Zhou [17] combined Orthogonal Local Search with DE in the so-called OLSDE (Orthogonal Local Search Differential Evolution) algorithm. Therein two individuals were randomly selected from the population in each generation and they were used to generate a group of trial solutions with the orthogonal method. Then the best solution from the group of trial solutions replaced the worst individual in the population.

Jia et al. [18] proposed a memetic DE algorithm in combination with chaotic local search (CLS). The adaptive shrinking strategy embedded within CLS enabled the DE optimizer to explore large space in the early search phase and to exploit small regions in the later phase. Moreover, the chaotic iteration produced a higher probability to move into a boundary field, which appeared helpful for avoiding premature convergence to some extent. A similar work of utilizing chaotic principle based local search in DE was presented in [19].

Noman and Iba [11] proposed a crossover-based Local Search (XLS) called DEachSPX. The authors proposed a Lamarckian LS that adapt the length of the search in the crossover step, taking some information from the search. The local search method used by the author is a simple hill-climbing algorithm. This method improve their previous algorithm DEfirSPX [20], which had a fix length of the crossover search. A similar work was proposed in [21] called DExhcSPX. This algorithm also uses a hill climbing crossover approach.

Poikolainen and Neri [22] proposed a DE algorithm employing concurrent fitness based local search (DEcfbLS). The local search was applied to multiple promising solutions in the population, and the selection of individuals for local improvement was based on a fitness-based adaptation rule. Further, the local search operator was realized by making trial moves successively on single dimensions. But there was not much variation in the step sizes of the moves for different variables within an iteration of the search.

3   Differential Evolution

DE is a stochastic algorithm maintaining a population with N_p individuals. Every individual in the population stands for a possible solution to the problem. An individual in the population is represented by vector $X_{i,g}$ with $i = 1, 2, \ldots, N_p$ and g referring to the index of the generation. A cycle in DE consists of three consecutive steps od operations: mutation, crossover and selection which are described as follows:

MUTATION. In this first step, NP mutant vectors are created using individuals randomly selected from the current population. Indeed there are a few mutation strategies which can be used to generate mutant vectors. But only the random mutation strategy will be explained below. The other mutation strategies and their performance are discussed in [23]. The calculation of the mutant vector $V_{i,G}$ using the random mutation strategy is given in Eq. 1.

$$V_{i,g} = X_{r_1,g} + F \times (X_{r_2,g} - X_{r_3,g}) \tag{1}$$

where $V_{i,g}$ represents the mutant vector, i stands for the index of the vector, g stands for the generation, $r_1, r_2, r_3 \in \{1, 2, \ldots, N_p\}$ are random integers and F is the scaling factor in the interval $[0, 2]$.

Figure 1 shows how this mutation strategy works. All the variables in the figure appear in Eq. 1 with the same meaning, and d is the difference vector between $X_{r_2,g}$ and $X_{r_3,g}$.

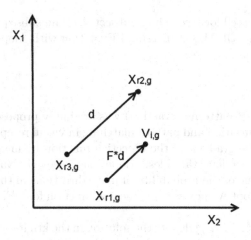

Fig. 1. Random mutation with one difference vector

CROSSOVER. This operation combines every individual in the actual population with the corresponding mutant vector created in the mutation stage. These new solutions created are called trial vectors and we use $T_{i,g}$ to represent the trial vector corresponding to individual i in generation g. Every parameter in the trial vector are decided in terms of Eq. 2

$$T_{i,g}[j] = \begin{cases} V_{i,g}[j] & \text{if } rand[0,1] < CR \quad \text{or} \quad j = j_{rand} \\ X_{i,g}[j] & \text{otherwise} \end{cases} \qquad (2)$$

where j stands for the index of a parameter in the vector, J_{rand} is a randomly selected integer between 1 and N_p to ensure that at least one parameter from the mutant vector will be included in the trial vector and CR is the probability of recombination.

SELECTION. This operation compares a trial vector and its parent solution in the current population to decide the winner to survive in the next generation. Therefore, if the problem of interest is minimization, the individuals in the new generation are chosen using Eq. 3.

$$X_{i,g+1} = \begin{cases} T_{i,g} & \text{if } f(T_{i,g}) < f(X_{i,g}) \\ X_{i,g} & \text{otherwise} \end{cases} \qquad (3)$$

where $X_{i,g}$ is an individual in the population, $X_{i,g+1}$ is the individual in the next generation, $f(T_{i,g})$ represents the objective value of the trial vector and $f(X_{i,g})$ stands for the objective value of the individual in the current population.

4   Differential Evolution with Alopex Local Search

This section discusses the key idea and technical details of utilizing the Alopex method to enhance the search ability of a standard DE algorithm. First we shall introduce Alopex-based local search in Subsect. 4.1, and subsequently we present the new DE variant: DEALS (Differential Evolution with Alopex Local Search) in Subsect. 4.2.

4.1 Alopex

Alopex (algorithm of pattern extraction) was originally proposed by Harth and Tzanakou for optimization and pattern matching in visual receptive fields [14]. It aims to estimate the gradient of the objective function by measuring the effect of changes of independent variables. Alopex also uses the varying parameter Temperature to control the probability of move directions in the search process. In this paper we adopt Alopex as a local search function for DE, which is detailed in the following.

Let $Z^k = (z_1^k, z_2^k, \ldots, z_N^k)$ denote the solution in the kth iteration of the search process. We first calculate the correlation between the variables and objective values for Z^k with respect to a random solution $Z^0 = (z_1^0, z_2^0, \ldots, z_N^0)$ from the population. The correlation is calculated as follows

$$C_j^k = (z_j^k - z_j^0) \times [F(Z^k) - F(Z^0)] \quad for \quad j = 1, 2, \ldots, N \tag{4}$$

Then, considering minimization problem as an example, the probability for a negative move on the jth variable in Z^k is decided using the Bolzmann distribution as

$$P_j^k = \frac{1}{1 + e^{\frac{C_j^k}{T_j^k}}} \tag{5}$$

where T^k is the annealing temperature that is updated in each iteration as the average of the correlations across all variables:

$$T = \frac{1}{N} * \sum_{j=1}^{N} |C_j^k| \tag{6}$$

The calculation of the temperature in (6) enables automatic adjustment of the behavior concerning exploration and exploitation based on condition or progress in the local optimization process. The search will become more randomized when it is far from an optimum with large correlations. In contrast, small correlations will make the search more biased towards a deterministic scheme for better exploitation of a promising region. With the probability of move direction as given in (5), the trial solution $Q^k = (q_1^k, q_2^k, \ldots, q_N^k)$ is generated by

$$q_j^k = z_j^k + \delta_j^k * |z_j^k - z_j^0| * rand(0, 1) \tag{7}$$

where δ_j^k is a sign representing the direction of move as given by

$$\delta_j^k = \begin{cases} 1 & \text{if } P_{h,k} \geq rand(0,1) \\ -1 & \text{otherwise} \end{cases} \tag{8}$$

If Q^k is better than the Z^k, the search moves on to the next iteration with the current solution being updated. Otherwise the trial solution is generated again according to (7) with the hope to find an improved solution in the neighborhood.

As a summary, the Alopex-based local search function ALS (Start, NumEva) can be formulated below, where Start represents the initial solution to which the local search is applied and NumEva is the number of objective evaluations allocated for a single run of local search.

Algorithm 1. function ALS(Start, NumEva)
___
1: $Z^1 = Start$;
2: $k = 1$;
3: **for** i = 1 to NumEva **do**
4:     Z^0=Random individual from population;
5:     **for** j = 1 to N **do**
6:         $q_j^k = z_j^k + \delta_j^k * |z_j^k - z_j^0| * rand(0,1)$;
7:     **end for**
8:     **if** $f(Q^k) < f(Z^k)$ **then**
9:         $Z^{k+1} = Q^k$
10:        $k = k + 1$
11:    **end if**
12: **end for**
___

4.2 DEALS

This subsection describes how the Alopex-based local search can be combined into a DE cycle, giving rise to the new algorithm: DEALS. The basic idea is to apply the Alopex-based search to the most promising individual in the population after completing mutation, crossover, and selection operations in each generation. However, special care has to be taken here to avoid launching the local search from the same location as in the last generation. This entails remembering the solution Xlast in the last generation where local search started (which seems similar to the idea of short memory in tabu search [24]). When the Alopex search is conducted in a new generation, it takes as starting point the best individual from the population but excluding Xlast. The procedure of the proposed DEALS method is outlined in Algorithm 1 .

5 Experiments and Results

This section aims to examine the ability of DEALS to reach the global optimum in both unimodal and multimodal problems. The tests were made on 10 benchmark functions from [25], where functions f1-f5 are unimodal while functions f6-f10 are multimodal. A complete description of these functions can be found in Table 1.

Algorithm 2. DEALS

1: Initialize the population $S(0)$ with randomly created individuals
2: Set Intensity as the number of evaluations used in a single run of local search
3: Set $X_{last}=\{\}$ and t=0;
4: **while** The termination condition is not satisfied **do**
5:     Create mutant vectors using Eq. 1
6:     Create trial vectors by crossover according to Eq. 2
7:     Select winning vectors according to Eq. 3 to obtain population $S(t+1)$
8:     Identify X_{best} as the best from $S(t+1)nX_{last}$
9:     Randomly select solution X' from $S(t+1)nX_{best}$
10:     $Y_{new} = \text{ALS}(X_{best}, \text{Intensity})$
11:     Update $S(t+1)$ by replacing X_{best} by Y_{new}
12:     Set $X_{last} = X_{best}$ and t = t+1
13: **end while**

Table 1. The 10 functions used in the test

FUNCTION
$f1(x) = \sum_{i=1}^{n} z_i^2; z = x - o$
$f2(x) = \sum_{i=1}^{n} (\sum_{j=1}^{i} z_j)^2; z = x - o$
$f3(x) = \sum_{i=1}^{n} (10^6)^{\frac{i-1}{n-1}} z_i^2; z = (x - o) * M$
$f4(x) = (\sum_{i=1}^{n} (\sum_{j=1}^{i} z_j)^2) \times (1 + 0.4|N(0,1)|); z = x - o$
$f5(x) = max\{A_i x - B_i\}; $ *check [25]
$f6(x) = \sum_{i=1}^{n-1} [100 \times (-z_{i+1} + z_i^2)^2 + (z_i - 1)^2]; z = x - o + 1$
$f7(x) = \frac{1}{4000} \times \sum_{i=1}^{n} z_i^2 - \prod_{i=1}^{n} cos(\frac{z_i}{\sqrt{i}})+; z = (x - o) * M$
$f8(x) = -20 \times exp(-0.2 \times \sqrt{\frac{1}{n} \times \sum_{i=1}^{n} z_i^2}) - exp(\frac{1}{n} \times \sum_{i=1}^{n} cos(2\pi z_i)) + 20 + e$ $z = (x - o) * M$
$f9(x) = \sum_{i=1}^{n} [z_i^2 - 10 \times cos(2 \times \pi \times z_i) + 10]; z = x - o$
$f10(x) = \sum_{i=1}^{n} [z_i^2 - 10 \times cos(2 \times \pi \times z_i) + 10]; z = (x - o) * M$

5.1   Experimental Settings

Beside DEALS, the basic DE (DE/rand/1) and other 5 different DE variants were included in the experiments. These DE variants are DENLS [26], OLSDE [17], DEachSPX [11], DEfirSPX [20], DExhcSPX [21]. The results of OLSDE were taken from [17] and the results of DEachSPX, DEfirSPX and DExhcSPX were taken from [11]. The experimental settings for all the algorithms are listed below:

- DE/rand/1: population size $N_P = 60$, $F = 0.9$ and $CR = 0.9$.
- DEALS: population size $N_P = 30/60$, $F = 0.9$, $CR = 0.9$, $n = 10$.
- DENLS: population size $N_P = 60$, $F = 0.9$, $CR = 0.9$ and $p= 0.1$.

- OLSDE: population size $N_P = 30$, $F = 0.9$, $CR = 0.9$, more details can be found in [17].
- DEachSPX: population size $N_P = 30$, $F = 0.9$, $CR = 0.9$, more details can be found in [11].

where p is the percentage that is changing in the individual when we use local search.

All the algorithms were assessed with 30 executions on each of these 10 functions to acquire a fair and reliable results for comparison. The termination condition to finish the execution of these algorithms is that the error of the best result found is below $1.00E - 08$ or the number of evaluations has exceeded 300,000.

5.2   Comparing DEALS with Basic DE and DENLS

First we compare DEALS with basic DE and DENLS. The results from these algorithms on the benchmark functions are summarized in Table 2, in which the numbers in boldface represent the lowest mean errors of the solutions found by the algorithms. The population size used in DEALS was 60, since this population size was used for the other two algorithms. We can see from this table that DEALS was the best in all unimodal functions and in multimodal functions DEALS was the best in 2 functions (f6 and f8) and quite competitive in the other 2 functions (f7 and f10). With pairwise comparison, the observation is that DEALS improved basic DE in almost all the functions (except function f9) and DENLS in all the unimodal functions. On the multimodal functions the results from DEALS and DENLS are generally similar.

Table 2. Results of DEALS, DE and DENLS with population size 60

FUNCTION	DE	DENLS	DEALS
f1	**0.00E+00**	**0.00E+00**	**0.00E+00**
f2	3.39E+01	8.13E−01	**6.02E−04**
f3	6.41E+06	1.23E+06	**1.21E+06**
f4	2.72E+02	4.70E+01	**3.52E+00**
f5	1.36E+02	1.61E+02	**7.76E+01**
f6	3.18E+01	4.61E+01	**7.42E+00**
f7	5.32E−02	**4.60E−03**	1.03E−02
f8	2.10E+01	2.10E+01	**2.09E+01**
f9	**1.22E+01**	1.42E+01	1.75E+01
f10	1.47E+02	**2.70E+01**	2.74E+01

5.3   Comparing DEALS with Others Algorithms

In this subsection, the performance of DEALS is compared with the other algorithms: OLSDE DEachSPX, DEfirSPX, and DExhcSPX. Here the population size was 30 for all the algorithms in comparison. The results from the algorithms are given in Table 3. From this table, we can see that DEALS was the best in 4 of the 5 unimodal functions and the second best in the remaining function. In multimodal cases DEALS can be judged as the best in 3 of the 5 functions (f6, f8 and f10).

Table 4 gives the summarized results of the comparison made above. We compare DEALS with every other algorithm in terms of their errors obtained on all the benchmark functions. The numbers of functions on which DEALS was superior ($\succ$), identical ($=$), or inferior ($\prec$) to another approach are illustrated in this table. The table shows that DEALS outperformed all other approaches in 6–7 functions (at least 60 % of the functions) and this number is much higher than the number of functions where DEALS was outperformed by any other algorithm.

Table 5 shows a rank of the algorithms in relation to their relative errors across all the 10 benchmark functions. The relative error of one algorithm on a certain function is defined as the proportion of the (mean) error of the algorithm

Table 3. Results of DEALS and the other algorithms with population size 30

FUNCTION	DEALS	OLSDE	DEachSPX	DEfirSPX	DExhcSPX
f1	**0.00E+00**	**0.00E+00**	**0.00E+00**	**0.00E+00**	**0.00E+00**
f2	**0.00E+00**	**0.00E+00**	6.60E−05	1.05E−03	9.40E−04
f3	3.72E+05	**2.20E+05**	1.20E+06	1.73E+06	1.54E+06
f4	**8.44E−03**	1.15E+01	4.62E+00	1.04E+01	6.69E+00
f5	**3.85E+02**	8.47E+02	9.00E+02	1.15E+03	1.01E+03
f6	**8.01E−01**	8.81E+00	3.84E+00	1.65E+01	1.41E+01
f7	1.60E−02	4.70E+03	7.39E−03	**4.53E−03**	7.98E−03
f8	**2.09E+01**	2.10E+01	**2.09E+01**	2.10E+01	**2.09E+01**
f9	3.60E+01	3.95E+01	**2.04E+01**	2.47E+01	2.80E+01
f10	**4.61E+01**	5.58E+01	5.27E+01	6.96E+01	6.79E+01

Table 4. Comparison of DEALS against the other algorithms

ALGORITHM	UNIMODAL FUNC.			MULTIMODAL FUNC.			OVERALL		
	$\succ$	$=$	$\prec$	$\succ$	$=$	$\prec$	$\succ$	$=$	$\prec$
OLSDE	2	2	1	5	0	0	7	1	2
DEachSPX	4	1	0	2	1	2	6	2	2
DEfirSPX	4	1	0	3	0	2	7	1	2
DExhcSPX	4	1	0	2	1	2	6	2	2

Table 5. Ranking of the algorithms

ALGORITHM	RANK	SUM OF RELATIVE ERRORS
DEALS	1	**3.17**
OLSDE	3	6.20
DEachSPX	2	4.44
DEfirSPX	5	7.53
DExhcSPX	4	6.78

on that function to the worst error on the function from all the algorithms. It can be observed from the table that DEALS was superior to all the other approaches in terms of the summation of relative errors in all the functions.

6 Conclusion

In this paper we propose the combination of the Alopex-based local search with standard differential evolution, leading to DEALS as a new algorithm for DE. Alopex belongs to a class of search methods that rely on variable perturbation to estimate the gradient information. It also processes the merit of simulated annealing by using the cooling temperature to control the balance between randomized and deterministic searches. The experimental results showed that the use of Alopex as a local search mechanism could substantially enhance the performance of DE in both unimodal and multimodal problems. Besides, our proposed DEALS algorithm obtained the best rank among several DE variants with local search.

More works will be done in future to improve our proposed algorithm. One of the works will be self-adjustment of the intensity of the local search that is used inside a DE cycle. The other interesting attempt will be enhancing DEALS with adaptive mutation strategies and adaptive running parameters. Moreover, DEALS will be tested and possibly further modified in real industrial scenarios.

Acknowledgment. The work is funded by the Swedish Knowledge Foundation (KKS) grant (project no 16317). The authors are also grateful to ABB FACTS, Prevas and VG Power for their co-financing of the project.

References

1. Storn, R., Price, K.: Differential evolution - a simple and efficient heuristic for global optimization over continuous spaces. J. Global Optim. **11**(4), 341–359 (1997)
2. Xiong, N., Molina, D., Leon, M., Herrera, F.: A walk into metaheuristics for engineering optimization: principles, methods, and recent trends. Int. J. Comput. Intell. Syst. **8**(4), 606–636 (2015)
3. Das, S., Suganthan, N.: Differential evolution: a survey of the state-of-the-art. IEEE Trans. Evol. Comput. **15**, 4–31 (2011)

 4. Neri, F., Tirronen, V.: Recent advances in differential evolution: a review and experimental analysis. Artif. Intell. Rev. **33**(1), 61–106 (2010)
 5. Ali, M., Torn, A.: Population set based global optimization algorithms: some modifications and numerical studies. Comput. Oper. Res. **31**, 1703–1725 (2004)
 6. Qin, A., Suganthan, P.: Self-adaptive differential evolution algorithm for numerical optimization. In: The 2005 IEEE Congress on Evolutionary Computation, vol. 2, pp. 1785–1791 (2005)
 7. Zhang, J., Sanderson, A.: Jade: adaptive differential evolution with optional external archive. IEEE Trans. Evol. Comput. **13**, 945–958 (2009)
 8. Leon, M., Xiong, N.: Greedy adaptation of control parameters in differential evolution for global optimization problems. In: IEEE Conference on Evolutionary Computation (CEC2015), Japan, pp. 385–392 (2015)
 9. Tanabe, R., Fukinga, A.: Success-history based parameter adaptation for differential evolution. In: 2013 IEEE Congress on Evolutionary Computation (CEC), Cancun, Mexico, pp. 71–78 (2013)
10. Islam, S.M., Das, S., Ghoshand, S., Roy, S., Suganthan, P.N.: An adaptive differential evolution algorithm with novel mutation and crossover strategies for global numerical optimization. IEEE Trans. Syst. Man Cybern. B Cybern. **42**(2), 482–500 (2012)
11. Noman, N., Iba, H.: Accelerating differential evolution using an adaptative local search. IEEE Trans. Evol. Comput. **12**, 107–125 (2008)
12. Ali, M., Pant, M., Nagar, A.: Two local search strategies for differential evolution. In: Proceedings of 2010 IEEE Fifth International Conference on Bio-Inspired Computing: Theories and Applications (BIC-TA), Changsha, China, pp. 1429–1435 (2010)
13. Xie, W., Yu, W., Zou, X.: Diversity-maintained differential evolution embedded with gradient-based local search. Soft comput. **17**, 1511–1535 (2013)
14. Harth, E., Tzanakou, E.: Alopex: a stochastic method for determining visual receptive fields. Vision Res. **14**, 1475–1482 (1974)
15. Storn, R., Price, K.: Differential evolution - a simple and efficient adaptive scheme for global optimization over continuous spaces. Tech rep. tr-95-012, Comput. Sci. Inst., Berkeley, CA, USA (1995)
16. Jirong, G., Guojun, G.: Differential evolution with a local search operator. In: Proceedings of the 2010 2nd International Asia Conference on Informatics in Control, Automation and Robotics (CAR), Wuhan, China, vol. 2, pp. 480–483 (2010)
17. Dai, Z., Zhou, A.: A diferential ecolution with an orthogonal local search. In: Proceedings of the 2013 IEEE Congress on Evolutionary Computation (CEC), Cancun, Mexico, pp. 2329–2336 (2013)
18. Jia, D., Zheng, G., Khan, M.K.: An effective memetic differential evolution algorithm based on chaotical search. Inf. Sci. **181**, 3175–3187 (2011)
19. Pei-chong, W., Xu, Q., Xiao-hong, H.: A novel differential evolution algorithm based on chaos local search. In: Proceedings of the International Conference on Information Engineering and Computer Science (ICIECS 2009), Wuhan, China, pp. 1–4 (2009)
20. Noman, N., Iba, N.: Enhancing differential evolution performance with local search for high dimensional function optimization. In: Proceedings of the 2005 Conference on Genetic and Evolutionary Computation (GECCO 2005), pp. 967–974 (2005)
21. Lozano, M., Herrera, F., Krasnogor, N., Molina, D.: Real-coded memetic algorithms with crossover hill-climbing. Evol. Comput. **12**(3), 273–302 (2004)

22. Poikolainen, I., Neri, F.: Differential evolution with concurrent fitness based local search. In: Proceedings of the 2013 IEEE Congress on Evolutionary Computation (CEC), Cancun, Mexico, pp. 384–391 (2013)
23. Leon, M., Xiong, N.: Investigation of mutation strategies in differential evolution for solving global optimization problems. In: Rutkowski, L., Korytkowski, M., Scherer, R., Tadeusiewicz, R., Zadeh, L.A., Zurada, J.M. (eds.) ICAISC 2014, Part I. LNCS, vol. 8467, pp. 372–383. Springer, Heidelberg (2014)
24. Glover, F.: Future paths for integer programming and links to artificial intelligence. Comput. Oper. Res. **13**(5), 533–549 (1986)
25. Suganthan, P.N., Hansen, N., Liang, J.J., Deb, K., Chen, Y.P., Auger, A., Tiwari, S.: Problem definitions and evaluation criteria for the cec 2005 special session on real-parameter optimization. Technical report, Technical Report, Nanyang Technological University, Singapore and KanGAL Report Number 2005005 (Kanpur Genetic Algorithms Laboratory, IIT Kanpur), May 2005
26. Leon, M., Xiong, N.: Eager random search for differential evolution in continuous optimization. In: Pereira, F., Machado, P., Costa, E., Cardoso, A. (eds.) EPIA 2015. LNCS, vol. 9273, pp. 286–291. Springer, Heidelberg (2015)

New Method for Fuzzy Nonlinear Modelling Based on Genetic Programming

Krystian Łapa[1(✉)], Krzysztof Cpałka[1], and Petia Koprinkova-Hristova[2]

[1] Institute of Computational Intelligence, Częstochowa University of Technology,
Częstochowa, Poland
{krystian.lapa,krzysztof.cpalka}@iisi.pcz.pl
[2] Institute of Information and Communication Technologies,
Bulgarian Academy of Sciences, Sofia, Bulgaria
pkoprinkova@bas.bg

Abstract. In this paper a new method for fuzzy nonlinear modeling is proposed. This method is a hybridization of genetic algorithm and genetic programming. The innovations in this method concern, among others, using weights of aggregation operators, fitness function criteria and possibilities of automatic creation of fuzzy rules base. The proposed method was tested with use of typical nonlinear modelling benchmarks.

Keywords: Nonlinear modeling · Genetic programming · Genetic algorithm · Fuzzy system · Structure selection

1 Introduction

Computational intelligence (see e.g. [2–4,9,12,14,15,26,28–30,33,48,55,62–65]) is one of the rapidly developing fields. It applies to among others: neural networks (see e.g. [38,39,74,78,79]), fuzzy systems (see e.g. [7,8,16,18,19,57–59,61,67,68]), learning algorithms (see e.g. [17,19,25,73]), etc. These systems can be used in many fields such as: optimization (see e.g. [23,32,36,37,70,71,76]), identification (see e.g. [20–22,52,53,66,82–85]), classification (see e.g. [27,31,34, 50,51,54,80,81]), control systems (see e.g. [44]) and nonlinear modelling (see e.g. [5,6,41,42]). This paper is focused on nonlinear modelling with use of new approach based on genetic programing and genetic algorithm.

One of the mostly used systems for nonlinear modelling are fuzzy systems [56]. These systems can achieve high accuracy and interpretable knowledge in a form of fuzzy rules. Most papers in the literature concerns selecting parameters of fuzzy system with specified amount on fuzzy rules. To achieve that a genetic algorithms [60], population-based algorithms [77], differential evolution [47] etc. are used. The approaches that allows simultaneous selection of system structure and system parameters can be found less often. These approaches are based mainly on hybrid population-based algorithms [17] and on genetic programming [1,13,49,69].

Genetic programming (GP) is an interesting technique. It is an evolutionary algorithm (see e.g. [72]) which makes possible to find computer programs

© Springer International Publishing Switzerland 2016
L. Rutkowski et al. (Eds.): ICAISC 2016, Part I, LNAI 9692, pp. 432–449, 2016.
DOI: 10.1007/978-3-319-39378-0_38

that perform a user-defined task represented as a tree structure. Every leaf of the tree can contain a numeric value (constant or a system input value). In turn, each node of the tree contains mathematical operators which are usually used to obtain results based on child nodes numerical values. Three types of mathematical operators are used: single argument operators (e.g. "cos $(\cdot)$"), two argument operators (e.g. "+") and multi arguments operators (e.g. "avg $(\cdot)$"). GP and other evolutionary algorithms (like evolutionary strategies, evolutionary programming, genetic algorithm etc.) rely on a population of solutions and are mostly used for optimization problems. These methods are based on a natural evolution (using mechanisms like natural selection, inheritance, survival) which gives them an advantage over other methods used for optimization problems like analytic methods, gradient methods and random methods (see e.g. [56]).

The genetic programming can be used as three different approaches in the fuzzy systems. The first approach is based on using GP directly to select consequences functions in Takagi-Sugeno fuzzy systems (see e.g. [44]). The second approach is based on using GP to create new inputs for fuzzy system (it reduces complexity of the system). The third approach (mostly often used) is based on using GP to select antecedences of the fuzzy rules (see e.g. [10]). In this approach mathematical operators from GP are replaced by fuzzy operators. In [13] fuzzy operator AND was used, in [24] additional fuzzy operators OR, 'NOT', 'greater', 'lesser' and 'near' were used. In [43] operators AND, parent operators OR and fuzzy set operator NOT were used.

The proposed method is based on third approach. This method can be distinguished by: (a) use of elastic weighted triangular norms as operators AND and OR, (b) use of operator NOT for fuzzy sets, (c) use of new encoding of the system, (d) use of fitness function with complexity of the system and new criteria of correct notations of fuzzy rules, and (e) use of proposed hybrid learning algorithm which is based on genetic algorithm and genetic programming.

The structure of proposed paper consists of: Sect. 2 with description of the proposed method, Sect. 3 with presentation of simulation results, and Sect. 4 with conclusions.

2 Proposed Method Description

This section contains: description of the proposed fuzzy system, method of its encoding and initialization, definition of fitness function and description of proposed learning algorithm.

2.1 Description of Fuzzy System

This paper is based on Mamdani type fuzzy system [56], where fuzzy rules can be in general defined as:

$$R^k : \left[\begin{pmatrix} \text{IF } (\bar{x}_1 \text{is[NOT]} A_{1,k}) \text{ AND/OR} \ldots \text{AND/OR } (\bar{x}_n \text{is[NOT]} A_{n,k}) \\ \text{THEN } (y_1 \text{is} B_{1,k}) \ldots, (y_m \text{is} B_{m,k}) \end{pmatrix} \right], \quad (1)$$

where n is a number of inputs, m is a number of outputs, $\bar{\mathbf{x}} = [\bar{x}_1, \ldots, \bar{x}_n] \in \mathbf{X}$, $\mathbf{y} = [y_1, \ldots, y_m] \in \mathbf{Y}$, $A_1^k, \ldots, A_n^k$ are input fuzzy sets and $B_1^k, \ldots, B_m^k$ are output fuzzy sets. In the proposed method fuzzy rules (1) are represented by trees obtained from genetic programming (Fig. 1a)). Using these trees creates the need of use of fuzzy sets base, which allow fuzzy sets connect with leaves of trees. Fuzzy sets base is defined as:

$$\mathbf{C} = \left\{ \begin{array}{l} A_{1,1}, \ldots, A_{1,R}, \ldots, \\ A_{n,1}, \ldots, A_{n,R}, \\ B_{1,1}, \ldots, B_{1,R}, \ldots, \\ B_{m,1}, \ldots, B_{m,R} \end{array} \right\} = \{C_1, \ldots, C_{L^c}\}, \qquad (2)$$

where n is number of inputs, m is number of outputs, R is a number of fuzzy sets stored for each input $i = 1, \ldots, n$ or output $j = 1, \ldots, m$ in base (2), $L^c = R \cdot (n+m)$ stands for total number of fuzzy sets. Each input fuzzy set $A_{i,r}$ is represented by membership function $\mu_{A_{i,r}}(\bar{x})$, while each output fuzzy set $B_{j,r}$ is represented by membership function $\mu_{B_{j,r}}(\bar{x})$. It is worth to notice that the second index of fuzzy sets used in Eq. (2) does not stand for index of the rule (as in Eq. (1)) but it stands for index of fuzzy set stored for each input and output. The proposed method is based on Gaussian-type membership function, which is defined by two parameters: center of fuzzy set (x) and width of fuzzy set (σ).

Each element of the tree (see Fig. 1a)) is described by a set of parameters: $l, o, i, r, w_1, w_2, N^L$ i N^P. The parameter l decides if element is treated as a node $(l = 0)$ or leaf $(l = 1)$. The parameter o indicates operator of a given element: $o = 0$ for $l = 1$ stands for 'IS', $o = 1$ for $l = 1$ stands for 'NOT', $o = 0$ for $l = 0$ stands for 'AND' (triangular t-norm with weights of arguments [56]) and $o = 1$ for $l = 0$ stands for 'OR' (triangular s-norm with weights of arguments). The parameter i (for leaf) stands for input index of associated fuzzy set. The parameter r (for leaf) stand for index of associated fuzzy set $A_{i,r}$ (see Fig. 1b)). The parameter w_1 stands for weight of left child node, w_2 stands for weight of right child node (see Fig. 1c)), N^L stands for left child node (for node) and N^P stands for right child node (for node). Taking into consideration mentioned parameters the output of any of the tree element (both nodes and leaves) can be calculated as:

$$\mu_N(\bar{\mathbf{x}}) = \left\{ \begin{array}{ll} \mu_{A_{i,r}}(\bar{x}_i) & \text{for } o = 0 \,\&\, l = 1 \text{ (denoted IS)} \\ 1 - \mu_{A_{i,r}}(\bar{x}_i) & \text{for } o = 1 \,\&\, l = 1 \text{ (denoted NOT)} \\ T^* \{\mu_{N^L}(\bar{\mathbf{x}}), \mu_{N^P}(\bar{\mathbf{x}}); w_1, w_2\} & \text{for } o = 0 \,\&\, l = 0 \text{ (denoted AND)} \\ S^* \{\mu_{N^L}(\bar{\mathbf{x}}), \mu_{N^P}(\bar{\mathbf{x}}); w_1, w_2\} & \text{for } o = 1 \,\&\, l = 0 \text{ (denoted OR)} \end{array} \right. , \quad (3)$$

where $T^*(\cdot)$ stands for triangular t-norm with weights of arguments $S^*(\cdot)$ stands for triangular s-norm with weights of arguments (see e.g. [56]).

The activation (firing) level of fuzzy rule based on structure presented on Fig. 1(a) is calculated as follows:

$$\tau_k(\bar{\mathbf{x}}) = \mu_{N_k^{\text{root}}}(\bar{\mathbf{x}}), \qquad (4)$$

where N_k^{root} stands for root of the tree of k-th fuzzy rule ($k = 1, .., K$) and K stands for number of fuzzy rules. Defuzzificated output values of the system for each output j can be calculated for example with center of area method [56]:

$$\bar{y}_j(\bar{\mathbf{x}}) = \frac{\sum\limits_{r=1}^{R} y_{j,r}^B \cdot \mathop{S}\limits_{k=1}^{K} \left\{ T\left\{ \tau_k(\bar{\mathbf{x}}), \mu_{B_{j,n_{j,k}^B}}\left(y_{j,r}^B\right) \right\} \right\}}{\sum\limits_{r=1}^{R} \mathop{S}\limits_{k=1}^{K} \left\{ T\left\{ \tau_k(\bar{\mathbf{x}}), \mu_{B_{j,n_{j,k}^B}}\left(y_{j,r}^B\right) \right\} \right\}}, \tag{5}$$

where $y_{j,r}^B$ are centers of output fuzzy sets $B_{j,r}$ and $n_{j,k}^B$ stands for index connecting k-th fuzzy rule with j-th output fuzzy set. For example $n_{j=1,k=2}^B = 3$ means that the second fuzzy rule is associated with the third set of the first output $B_{j=1,n_{j=1,k=2}^B=3}$.

2.2   Encoding Description

In the proposed approach encoding of the system (5) is based on encoding tree elements $\mathbf{N}$ (3) (Fig. 1a)) as sets of parameters:

$$\mathbf{N} = \left\{ l, o, i, r, w_1, w_2, \mathbf{N}^{\mathrm{L}}, \mathbf{N}^{\mathrm{P}} \right\}. \tag{6}$$

The encoding of fuzzy system (5) is defined as:

$$\mathbf{X}_{ch} = \left\{ \mathbf{X}_{ch}^{\text{fsets}}, \mathbf{X}_{ch}^{\text{rules}} \right\}. \tag{7}$$

The part $\mathbf{X}_{ch}^{\text{fsets}}$ encodes parameters of fuzzy sets base (2):

$$\mathbf{X}_{ch}^{\text{fsets}} = \left\{ \begin{array}{l} x_{1,1}^A, \sigma_{1,1}^A, ..., x_{1,R}^A, \sigma_{1,R}^A, ..., \\ x_{n,1}^A, \sigma_{n,1}^A, ..., x_{n,R}^A, \sigma_{n,R}^A, \\ y_{1,1}^B, \sigma_{1,1}^B, ..., y_{1,R}^B, \sigma_{1,R}^B, ..., \\ y_{m,1}^B, \sigma_{m,1}^B, ..., y_{m,R}^B, \sigma_{m,R}^B \end{array} \right\}, \tag{8}$$

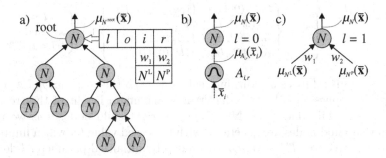

Fig. 1. Structure of: (a) tree representing fuzzy rule with parameters set of each tree element, (b) leaf and its connection with fuzzy set, (c) node and children weights.

thus the part $\mathbf{X}_{ch}^{\text{rules}}$ encodes parameters of fuzzy rules:

$$\mathbf{X}_{ch}^{\text{rules}} = \left\{ \begin{array}{c} \mathbf{N}_1^{\text{root}}, n_{1,1}^B, ..., n_{m,1}^B, \\ \mathbf{N}_2^{\text{root}}, n_{1,2}^B, ..., n_{m,2}^B, \\ ..., \\ \mathbf{N}_K^{\text{root}}, n_{1,K}^B, ..., n_{m,K}^B \end{array} \right\}, \qquad (9)$$

where $\mathbf{N}_k^{\text{root}}$ is a root of the tree of k-th rule, $n_{j,k}^B$ is an index connecting k-th fuzzy rule with fuzzy set of j-th output. In the proposed method the part $\mathbf{X}_{ch}^{\text{fsets}}$ encoding parameters of fuzzy sets is processed by a genetic algorithm and the part $\mathbf{X}_{ch}^{\text{rules}}$ encoding fuzzy rules is processed by a genetic programming.

2.3   System Initialization

The parameters of fuzzy sets encoded in $\mathbf{X}_{ch}^{\text{fsets}}$ are initialized randomly taking into consideration adjustments to the considered simulation problem. Next, the number of fuzzy sets $K \in \left[K^{\min}, K^{\max} \right]$ is chosen randomly. After the number of fuzzy rules is chosen the parameters of part $\mathbf{X}_{ch}^{\text{fsets}}$ are initialized using the following function:

$$\mathbf{X}_{ch}^{\text{rules}} = \left\{ \begin{array}{c} init\left(\mathbf{N}_1^{\text{root}}, 1, 1\right), U_c\left(1, R\right), ..., U_c\left(1, R\right), \\ init\left(\mathbf{N}_2^{\text{root}}, 1, 1\right), U_c\left(1, R\right), ..., U_c\left(1, R\right), \\ ..., \\ init\left(\mathbf{N}_K^{\text{root}}, 1, 1\right), U_c\left(1, R\right), ..., U_c\left(1, R\right), \end{array} \right\}, \qquad (10)$$

where $U_c(a, b)$ is a function returning random integer value from the range $[a, b]$ and $init\left(\mathbf{N}, lvl, l\right)$ is a recursive function that initializes randomly trees from a genetic programming. The function $init\left(\mathbf{N}, lvl, l\right)$ is defined as:

$$init\left(\mathbf{N}, lvl, l\right) = \left\{ \begin{array}{l} \mathbf{N} = \left\{ \begin{array}{l} 1, U_c\left(0, 1\right), U_c\left(1, n\right), U_c\left(1, R\right), \\ U_r\left(0, 1\right), U_r\left(0, 1\right), \\ null, null \end{array} \right\} \text{ for } \left\{ \begin{array}{c} l = 1 \\ \text{or} \\ lvl \geq lvl^{\max} \end{array} \right. \\ \mathbf{N} = \left\{ \begin{array}{l} 0, U_c\left(0, 1\right), U_c\left(1, n\right), U_c\left(1, R\right), \\ U_r\left(0, 1\right), U_r\left(0, 1\right), \\ init(\mathbf{N}^L, lvl + 1, U_c\left(0, 1\right)), \\ init(\mathbf{N}^P, lvl + 1, U_c\left(0, 1\right)) \end{array} \right\} \text{ for } \left\{ \begin{array}{c} l = 0 \\ \text{and} \\ lvl < lvl^{\max} \end{array} \right. \end{array} \right.$$

$$(11)$$

where $U_r(a, b)$ is a function returning real value from the range $[a, b]$, lvl stands for height (deepness) of the tree, $lvl^{\max}$ is a maximum height of the tree, $\mathbf{N}^L$ stands for left child node, and $\mathbf{N}^P$ stands for right child node. It is worth to mention that child nodes are generated with increased value lvl which limits the height of the tree to $lvl^{\max}$. Moreover, randomly initialized parameter l decides if child node will be a leaf or node.

2.4   System Evaluation

For evaluation of the system (5) the following fitness function was used:

$$\text{ff}\left(\mathbf{X}_{ch}\right) = T^* \left\{ \begin{array}{c} \text{ffacc}(\mathbf{X}_{ch}), \text{ffcom}(\mathbf{X}_{ch}), \text{ffsam}(\mathbf{X}_{ch}), \text{ffmul}(\mathbf{X}_{ch}); \\ w_{\text{ffacc}}, w_{\text{ffcom}}, w_{\text{ffsam}}, w_{\text{ffmul}} \end{array} \right\}, \quad (12)$$

where component ffacc $(\mathbf{X}_{ch})$ specifies the accuracy of the system (5), component ffcom $(\mathbf{X}_{ch})$ specifies complexity of the system (5), component ffsam $(\mathbf{X}_{ch})$ stands for a penalty for using the same fuzzy set multiple times by fuzzy rules (which is non-desired), component ffmul $(\mathbf{X}_{ch})$ stands for a penalty for using the same input multiple times by single fuzzy rule (with is non-desired), w_{ffacc}, w_{ffcom}, w_{ffsam}, w_{ffmul} are weights of components, $T^*\{\cdot\}$ is a n-argument extension of algebraic triangular norm with weights of arguments. The components of fitness function are described in detail in the next part of current Section.

The component ffacc $(\mathbf{X}_{ch})$ of function (12) is defined as:

$$\text{ffacc}\left(\mathbf{X}\right) = \frac{1}{m} \sum_{j=1}^{m} \frac{\frac{1}{Z} \sum_{z=1}^{Z} |d_{z,j} - \bar{y}_{z,j}|}{\max\limits_{z=1,\ldots,Z} \{d_{z,j}\} - \min\limits_{z=1,\ldots,Z} \{d_{z,j}\}}, \quad (13)$$

where Z is the number of rows of a learning sequence, $d_{z,j}$ is the desired output value of output j for input vector z $(z = 1, \ldots, Z)$, $\bar{y}_{z,j}$ is the real output value j calculated for the input vector $\bar{\mathbf{x}}_z$. Equation (13) takes into account the normalization of errors at different outputs of the system (5), which allows using function (13) in triangular norm used in function (12).

The component ffcom $(\mathbf{X}_{ch})$ of function (12) is defined as:

$$\text{ffcom}\left(\mathbf{X}_{ch}\right) = \frac{1}{K} \sum_{k=1}^{K} \frac{\text{com}\left(\mathbf{X}_{ch}^{\text{rules}}\{\mathbf{N}_k^{\text{root}}\}\right)}{2^{lvl^{\max}} - 1}, \quad (14)$$

where $\mathbf{X}_{ch}^{\text{rules}}\{\mathbf{N}_k^{\text{root}}\}$ stands for using element $\mathbf{N}_k^{\text{root}}$ of individual $\mathbf{X}_{ch}^{\text{rules}}$, denominator stands for maximum number of tree elements (Mersenne's number), numerator stands for actual number of tree elements calculated as follows:

$$\text{com}\left(\mathbf{N}\right) = \begin{cases} 1 & \text{for } \mathbf{N}\{l\} = 1 \\ 1 + \text{com}\left(\mathbf{N}\{\mathbf{N}^L\}\right) + \text{com}\left(\mathbf{N}\{\mathbf{N}^P\}\right) & \text{for } \mathbf{N}\{l\} = 0 \end{cases}. \quad (15)$$

The component ffsam $(\mathbf{X}_{ch})$ of function (12) is defined as:

$$\text{ffsam}\left(\mathbf{X}_{ch}\right) = \frac{\left(\begin{array}{c} \sum\limits_{i=1}^{n} \sum\limits_{r=1}^{R} \max\left(0, \sum\limits_{k=1}^{K} \text{sm}^A\left(\mathbf{X}_{ch}^{\text{rules}}\{\mathbf{N}_k^{\text{root}}\}, i, r\right) - 1\right) + \\ + \sum\limits_{j=1}^{m} \sum\limits_{r=1}^{R} \max\left(0, \sum\limits_{k=1}^{K} \text{sm}^B\left(\mathbf{X}_{ch}^{\text{rules}}\{n_{j,k}^B\}, j, r\right) - 1\right) \end{array} \right)}{K \cdot \left(2^{lvl^{\max}-1} + m\right)}, \quad (16)$$

where denominator stands for maximum number of leaves and output fuzzy sets m for all K fuzzy rules, numerator stands for penalty for using specified fuzzy set more than 1 time by any fuzzy rule, function $sm^A(\mathbf{N_k}, i, r)$ stands for number of using input fuzzy set $A_{i,r}$ by k-th rule, function $sm^B(n^B, j, r)$ stands for number of using output fuzzy set $B_{j,r}$ by k-th rule. The function $sm^A(\mathbf{N}, i, r)$ from Eq. (16) was defined as follows:

$$
sm^A(\mathbf{N}, i, r) = \begin{cases} 1 & \text{for } \begin{cases} \mathbf{N}\{l\} = 0 \text{ and} \\ (\mathbf{N}\{i\} = i \text{ and } \mathbf{N}\{r\} = r) \end{cases} \\ 0 & \text{for } \begin{cases} \mathbf{N}\{l\} = 0 \text{ and} \\ (\mathbf{N}\{i\} \neq i \text{ or } \mathbf{N}\{r\} \neq r) \end{cases} \\ \begin{pmatrix} sm^A(\mathbf{N}\{\mathbf{N^L}\}, i, r) + \\ +sm^A(\mathbf{N}\{\mathbf{N^P}\}, i, r) \end{pmatrix} & \text{for } \mathbf{N}\{l\} = 1 \end{cases} , \quad (17)
$$

and the function $sm^B(n^B, j, r)$ was defined as follows:

$$
sm^B(n^B, j, r) = \begin{cases} 1 \text{ for } n^B = r \\ 0 \text{ for } n^B \neq r \end{cases} . \quad (18)
$$

The component $\text{ffmul}(\mathbf{X}_{ch})$ of function (12) was defined with assumption that one fuzzy rule cannot use multiple fuzzy sets which are connected to the same input:

$$
\text{ffmul}(\mathbf{X}_{ch}) = \frac{1}{n \cdot K} \left(\sum_{i=1}^{n} \max \left(0, \sum_{k=1}^{K} \text{mul}\left(\mathbf{X}_{ch}^{\text{rules}} \{\mathbf{N}_k^{\text{root}}\}, i \right) - 1 \right) \right), \quad (19)
$$

where function $\text{mul}(\mathbf{N}, i)$ stands for penalty of multiple use of fuzzy sets connected to i-th input by single rule:

$$
\text{mul}(\mathbf{N}, i) = \begin{cases} 0 & \text{for } \mathbf{N}\{l\} = 1 \text{ and } \mathbf{N}\{i\} \neq i \\ 1 & \text{for } \mathbf{N}\{l\} = 1 \text{ and } \mathbf{N}\{i\} = i \\ \begin{pmatrix} \text{mul}(\mathbf{N}\{\mathbf{N^L}\}, i) + \\ +\text{mul}(\mathbf{N}\{\mathbf{N^P}\}, i) \end{pmatrix} & \text{for } \mathbf{N}\{l\} = 0 \text{ and } \mathbf{N}\{o\} = 0 \\ \frac{1}{2} \begin{pmatrix} \text{mul}(\mathbf{N}\{\mathbf{N^L}\}, i) + \\ +\text{mul}(\mathbf{N}\{\mathbf{N^P}\}, i) \end{pmatrix} & \text{for } \mathbf{N}\{l\} = 0 \text{ and } \mathbf{N}\{o\} = 1 \end{cases} . \quad (20)
$$

The penalty resulting from using OR operator in minimization of fitness function (12) is smaller than penalty for using AND operator. Using the OR operator for the same inputs is acceptable (as opposed to AND operator), but it complicates readability of fuzzy rules.

2.5 Description of Learning Algorithm

The proposed learning algorithm purpose is to select parameters of the fuzzy sets stored in base (2) and to select the structure of the fuzzy rules. Proposed algorithm works according to the following steps:

- **Step 1.** In this step a N^{pop} individuals of population **P** are initialized according to description from Sect. 2.3.
- **Step 2.** This step involves evaluation of the individuals of population **P** by fitness function (12).
- **Step 3.** In this step a N^{pop} of child individuals are generated and stored in temporary population **P'**. The genes $\mathbf{X}_{ch}^{\text{fsets}}$ of these individuals are initialized with use of genetic algorithm crossover operator. The individuals for crossover are selected by roulette wheel method from population **P**. The genes $\mathbf{X}_{ch}^{\text{rules}}$ of these individuals are initialized by choosing randomly genes $n^{\mathbf{B}_{\text{j,k}}}$ and root nodes from preselected parents.
- **Step 4.** This step purpose is to mutate individuals (each individual is mutated with probability $p_{m1} \in (0,1)$) from population **P'**. The genes $\mathbf{X}_{ch}^{\text{fsets}}$ are mutated (with probability $p_{m2} \in (0,1)$) with use of standard genetic mutation operator. In turn the genes $\mathbf{X}_{ch}^{\text{rules}}$ are mutated (with probability $p_{m3} \in (0,1)$). This mutation is based on random changes of parameters $\mathbf{N}\{i\}$, $\mathbf{N}\{r\}$ and $n_{j,r}^{B}$. Independent mutation probabilities $p_{m1} \neq p_{m2} \neq p_{m3}$ (where $p_{m1} \gg p_{m2} > p_{m3}$) balance the mutation in a following way: (a) mutation should be processed on the greater part of the population **P'** (p_{m1}) which allows proper diversity of population, (b) from the other hand, genes mutation probability (p_{m2}) cannot be high due to degeneration of the population, (c) changes in connection between leafs and nodes (p_{m3}) should be rarely performed, as too intense changes in relationships between the fuzzy rules and fuzzy sets could hinder the convergence of the algorithm.
- **Step 5.** Next, the individuals from population **P'** are pruned. This process is based on replacing randomly selected node of each genetic programming tree (with probability $p_x \in (0,1)$) by randomly generated leaf (init($\mathbf{N},0,1$)).
- **Step 6.** In this step extension of genetic programming trees from population **P'** is performed. This process is based on replacing randomly selected leaf of each genetic programming tree (with probability $p_l \in (0,1)$) by randomly generated node (init($\mathbf{N}, lvl, 0$)). The lvl stands for actual height of leaf, which prevents excessive growth of the tree.
- **Step 7.** In this step for each individual from population **P'** a new fuzzy rule is added (with probability p_d and only when $K < K^{\max}$) (according to Eq. (11)) or existing randomly chosen fuzzy rule is removed (with probability p_u and only when $K > K^{\min}$).
- **Step 8.** After modification of individuals from population **P'** (Steps 3-7) each individual is evaluated by fitness function (12).
- **Step 9.** Next, the individuals from populations **P** and **P'** are merged and only N^{pop} best individuals are chosen to replace population **P**.
- **Step 10.** In the last step of the algorithm the purpose is to check if stop condition is met (for example if the number of executed iterations of algorithm reaches specified value). If so, the algorithm stops. Otherwise, algorithm goes back to step 3.

2.6   Fuzzy Rules Notation

As it was mentioned earlier, in the proposed system (5) a varied fuzzy operators were used to aggregate antecedences of fuzzy rules and to process the fuzzy sets. Due to that the notation of fuzzy rules is defined as:

$$R_k : \text{IF } \underbrace{\text{zp}\left(\mathbf{X}_{ch}^{\text{rules}}\left\{\mathbf{N}_k^{\text{root}}\right\}\right)}_{\text{definition by function}} \text{THEN} \begin{pmatrix} y_1 \text{ IS } B_{1,\mathbf{X}_{ch}^{\text{rules}}\{n_{1,k}^B\}}, \cdots, \\ y_m \text{ IS } B_{m,\mathbf{X}_{ch}^{\text{rules}}\{n_{m,k}^B\}} \end{pmatrix}, \tag{21}$$

where function zp($\cdot$) defines antecedences of fuzzy rules in the following way:

$$\text{zp}\left(\mathbf{N}\right) = \begin{cases} x_{\mathbf{N}\{i\}} \text{ IS } A_{\mathbf{N}\{i\},\mathbf{N}\{r\}} & \text{for } \mathbf{N}\{l\} = 1 \text{ and } \mathbf{N}\{o\} = 0 \\ x_{\mathbf{N}\{i\}} \text{ IS NOT } A_{\mathbf{N}\{i\},\mathbf{N}\{r\}} & \text{for } \mathbf{N}\{l\} = 1 \text{ and } \mathbf{N}\{o\} = 1 \\ \begin{pmatrix} \text{zp}\left(\mathbf{N}\left\{\mathbf{N}^L\right\}\right)|\mathbf{N}\{w_1\} \\ \text{AND} \\ \text{zp}\left(\mathbf{N}\left\{\mathbf{N}^P\right\}\right)|\mathbf{N}\{w_2\} \end{pmatrix} & \text{for } \mathbf{N}\{l\} = 0 \text{ and } \mathbf{N}\{o\} = 0 \\ \begin{pmatrix} \text{zp}\left(\mathbf{N}\left\{\mathbf{N}^L\right\}\right)|\mathbf{N}\{w_1\} \\ \text{OR} \\ \text{zp}\left(\mathbf{N}\left\{\mathbf{N}^P\right\}\right)|\mathbf{N}\{w_2\} \end{pmatrix} & \text{for } \mathbf{N}\{l\} = 0 \text{ and } \mathbf{N}\{o\} = 1 \end{cases}. \tag{22}$$

It is worth to mention that the values of weights w_1 and w_2 from Eq. (22) can be replaced by their linguistic equivalents: n (not important) for values lower than 0.25, i (important) for values from range [0.25, 0.75] and v (very important) for values higher than 0.75. Then, the fuzzy rule notation may be written as the following example:

$$R_1 : \text{IF } \left(\begin{pmatrix} x_4 \text{ IS NOT } A_{4,5}|v \\ \text{AND} \\ x_6 \text{ IS } A_{6,2}|n \end{pmatrix}|n \\ \text{AND} \\ \begin{pmatrix} x_1 \text{ IS } A_{1,4}|i \\ \text{OR} \\ x_2 \text{ IS } A_{2,2}|n \end{pmatrix}|i \right) \text{ THEN } (y_1 \text{ IS } B_{1,4}). \tag{23}$$

3   Simulation Results

Simulation was performed on the following benchmarks: Box & Jenkins gas furnace problem [11] (BJ), Hang function [75] (HF), Nelson function [45] (NF) and yacht hydrodynamic [46] (YH).

The simulations were executed for three cases: **case 1** which concerns system (5), **case 2** which concerns system (5) with disabled weights (weight values were set to 1: $w_1 = 1$ and $w_2 = 1$), **case 3** which concerns system (5) with disabled weights and disabled operators NOT and OR (o values were set to 0). For all cases a proposed hybrid learning algorithm and proposed fitness criteria were used. This way of testing allowed precise determination of the impact of individual components of the system (5) on the results.

Values of parameters of the algorithm were experimentally selected as follows: number of fuzzy sets in fuzzy sets base (2) for each input and output was set to $R = 5$, minimum number of fuzzy rules was set to $K^{\min} = 3$, maximum number of fuzzy rules was set to $K^{\max} = 5$, maximum height of the tree was set to $lvl^{\max} = 5$, weights of fitness function components were set to (12) $w_{\text{ffacc}} = 1.0$, $w_{\text{ffcom}} = 0.5$, $w_{\text{ffsam}} = 0.2$, $w_{\text{ffmul}} = 0.1$, number of individuals in population $N^{\text{pop}} = 100$, number of algorithm iterations $Nstep = 1000$, individual mutation probability $p_{m1} = 0.7$, genes mutation probability $p_{m2} = 0.2$, rules mutation probability $p_{m3} = 0.1$, pruning of tree probability $p_x = 0.3$, extending of tree probability $p_l = 0.2$, adding new fuzzy rule probability $p_d = 0.2$ and removing fuzzy rule probability to $p_u = 0.3$. For each benchmark and case simulations were repeat 100 times and results were averaged. Obtained results are presented in Table 1, while the example of obtained fuzzy rules and fuzzy sets are presented in Fig. 2 and in the Table 2.

Table 1. Obtained results with comparison with results of other authors ([35,40]).

Problem	Case	Avg. ff	Avg. ffacc	Avg. ffcom	Avg. ffsam	Avg. ffmul	Avg. K	Avg. rmse	Best rmse	Best rmse (other authors)
BJ	1	**0.083**	0.034	**0.089**	**0.006**	0.018	**3.200**	0.505	**0.323**	from 0.219 to 0.449
	2	0.091	0.032	0.110	**0.006**	**0.017**	3.900	0.477	0.405	
	3	0.089	**0.029**	0.107	0.008	0.022	4.100	**0.432**	0.401	
HF	1	**0.100**	0.037	**0.079**	0.012	0.104	**3.167**	**0.137**	0.078	from 0.011 to 0.131
	2	0.107	0.041	0.088	**0.012**	**0.100**	3.467	0.154	0.088	
	3	0.108	0.045	0.080	**0.012**	0.104	3.300	0.167	0.085	
NF	1	**0.064**	0.018	**0.077**	0.004	**0.033**	**3.100**	1.315	1.158	from 1.104 to 2.653
	2	0.068	0.019	0.080	**0.004**	0.038	3.233	1.337	1.189	
	3	0.071	**0.017**	0.085	0.006	0.050	3.433	**1.294**	**1.082**	
YH	1	**0.084**	0.021	**0.092**	0.019	0.053	**3.233**	1.314	**0.690**	from 0.820 to 2.236
	2	0.096	0.022	0.098	0.026	0.075	3.333	1.375	0.993	
	3	0.087	0.028	0.095	**0.013**	**0.036**	3.300	1.747	1.178	

The simulation conclusions are following: (a) best results of fitness function was obtained for case 1 (see Table 1), (b) obtained accuracy for case 1-case 3 is similar (see Table 1), (c) case 1 is characterized by best complexity (for some cases simultaneously with best accuracy), which was possible to obtain due to using weights (see Table 1), (d) obtained results do not differ from the results of other authors (see Table 1). It is worth to mention that other authors results are concentrated mostly on accuracy or on using more complex systems (see e.g. [35,40]), (e) proposed approach is characterized by clear and not-conflicting fuzzy rules (see Fig. 2 and Table 2).

Table 2. Examples of fuzzy rules obtained for case 1.

Problem	Notation of fuzzy rules	Values of fitness function
BJ	R_1 : IF $\left(\begin{array}{c} x_3 \text{ IS } A_{3,4}\|n \\ \text{AND} \\ x_6 \text{ IS } A_{6,4}\|i \end{array} \right)\|v$ AND $x_1 \text{ IS } A_{1,2}\|i$ THEN $(y_1 \text{ IS } B_{1,1})$ R_2 : IF $\begin{array}{c} x_1 \text{ IS } A_{1,5}\|v \\ \text{AND} \\ x_6 \text{ IS } A_{6,1}\|v \end{array}$ THEN $(y_1 \text{ IS } B_{1,5})$ R_3 : IF $\begin{array}{c} x_1 \text{ IS } A_{1,3}\|i \\ \text{OR} \\ x_5 \text{ IS } A_{5,4}\|n \end{array}$ THEN $(y_1 \text{ IS } B_{1,4})$	$ff = 0.067$ $ffacc = 0.031$ $ffcom = 0.073$ $ffsam = 0.000$ $ffmul = 0.000$ $K = 3.000$ $rmse = 0.467$
HF	R_1 : IF $\begin{array}{c} x_2 \text{ IS NOT } A_{2,4}\|n \\ \text{AND} \\ x_1 \text{ IS } A_{1,1}\|v \end{array}$ THEN $(y_1 \text{ IS } B_{1,5})$ R_2 : IF $\begin{array}{c} x_2 \text{ IS } A_{2,4}\|i \\ \text{OR} \\ x_1 \text{ IS } A_{1,5}\|n \end{array}$ THEN $(y_1 \text{ IS } B_{1,2})$ R_3 : IF $\begin{array}{c} x_2 \text{ IS } A_{2,5}\|v \\ \text{OR} \\ x_2 \text{ IS } A_{2,3}\|i \end{array}$ THEN $(y_1 \text{ IS } B_{1,1})$	$ff = 0.102$ $ffacc = 0.037$ $ffcom = 0.073$ $ffsam = 0.015$ $ffmul = 0.125$ $K = 3.000$ $rmse = 0.140$
NF	R_1 : IF $\begin{array}{c} x_1 \text{ IS NOT } A_{1,1}\|i \\ \text{AND} \\ x_2 \text{ IS NOT } A_{2,5}\|n \end{array}$ THEN $(y_1 \text{ IS } B_{1,1})$ R_2 : IF $\begin{array}{c} x_2 \text{ IS } A_{2,3}\|v \\ \text{OR} \\ x_1 \text{ IS } A_{1,1}\|n \end{array}$ THEN $(y_1 \text{ IS } B_{1,3})$ R_3 : IF $\begin{array}{c} x_1 \text{ IS NOT } A_{1,5}\|n \\ \text{OR} \\ \left(\begin{array}{c} x_1 \text{ IS } A_{1,2}\|n \\ \text{OR} \\ x_2 \text{ IS } A_{2,1}\|v \end{array} \right)\|v \end{array}$ THEN $(y_1 \text{ IS } B_{1,5})$	$ff = 0.051$ $ffacc = 0.015$ $ffcom = 0.073$ $ffsam = 0.000$ $ffmul = 0.000$ $K = 3.000$ $rmse = 1.267$
YH	R_1 : IF $\begin{array}{c} x_2 \text{ IS NOT } A_{2,1}\|n \\ \text{AND} \\ x_6 \text{ IS } A_{6,4}\|n \end{array}$ THEN $(y_1 \text{ IS } B_{1,1})$ R_2 : IF $\begin{array}{c} x_1 \text{ IS } A_{1,4}\|n \\ \text{AND} \\ x_6 \text{ IS } A_{6,5}\|v \end{array}$ THEN $(y_1 \text{ IS } B_{1,5})$ R_3 : IF $\left(\begin{array}{c} \left(\begin{array}{c} x_4 \text{ IS } A_{4,2}\|i \\ \text{AND} \\ x_2 \text{ IS } A_{2,4}\|i \end{array} \right)\|n \\ \text{OR} \\ \left(\begin{array}{c} x_5 \text{ IS } A_{5,3}\|n \\ \text{OR} \\ x_6 \text{ IS } A_{6,1}\|v \end{array} \right)\|n \end{array} \right)$ THEN $(y_1 \text{ IS } B_{1,2})$	$ff = 0.072$ $ffacc = 0.021$ $ffcom = 0.105$ $ffsam = 0.015$ $ffmul = 0.125$ $K = 3.000$ $rmse = 1.308$

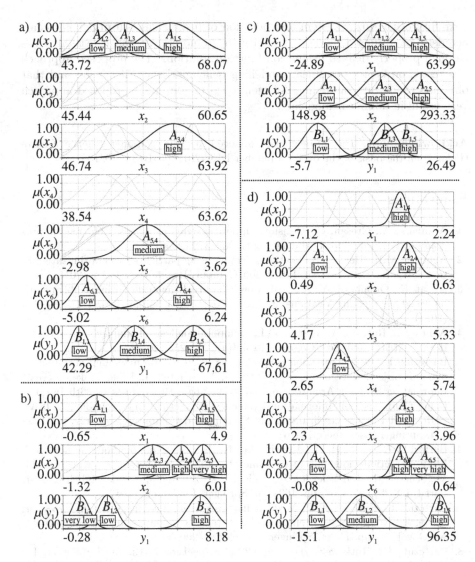

Fig. 2. Examples of fuzzy sets obtained for problems: (a) BJ, (b) HF, (c) NF, (d) YH for fuzzy rules presented in Table 2.

4   Conclusions

In this paper a new hybrid learning algorithm for selection of the structure and the parameters of the fuzzy systems for nonlinear modelling is presented. In presented approach fuzzy rules take form of binary trees. Nodes of these trees decide on aggregation operators (AND/OR) and the leaves of these trees are connected to the input fuzzy sets (with possibilities of using negation operator NOT). Each node contains additional weights of its children which increase flexibility of the fuzzy system and notation of fuzzy rules. An important characteristic of proposed method is ability to promote clear and consistent rules through properly defined evaluation function solutions. The proposed approach was tested on typical nonlinear modelling benchmarks and it can be said that obtained results are satisfying. All mentioned factors make proposed approach very useful in nonlinear modeling.

Acknowledgment. The project was financed by the National Science Centre (Poland) on the basis of the decision number DEC-2012/05/B/ST7/02138.

References

1. Abraham, A., Grosan, C.: Decision support systems using ensemble genetic programming. J. Inf. Knowl. Manage. **5**(4), 303–313 (2006)
2. Aghdam, M.H., Heidari, S.: Feature selection using particle swarm optimization in text categorization. J. Artif. Intell. Soft Comput. Res. **5**(4), 231–238 (2015)
3. Aissat, K., Oulamara, A.: A priori approach of real-time ridesharing problem with intermediate meeting locations. J. Artif. Intell. Soft Comput. Res. **4**(4), 287–299 (2014)
4. Akhtar, Z., Rattani, A., Foresti, G.L.: Temporal analysis of adaptive face recognition. J. Artif. Intell. Soft Comput. Res. **4**(4), 243–255 (2014)
5. Bartczuk, Ł.: Gene expression programming in correction modelling of nonlinear dynamic objects. In: Borzemski, L., Grzech, A., Świątek, J., Wilimowska, Z. (eds.) Information Systems Architecture and Technology: Proceedings of 36th International Conference on Information Systems Architecture and Technology - ISAT 2015 - Part I. Advances in Intelligent Systems and Computing, vol. 429, pp. 125–134. Springer, Heidelberg (2016)
6. Bartczuk, Ł., Przybył, A., Koprinkova-Hristova, P.: New method for nonlinear fuzzy correction modelling of dynamic objects. In: Rutkowski, L., Korytkowski, M., Scherer, R., Tadeusiewicz, R., Zadeh, L.A., Zurada, J.M. (eds.) ICAISC 2014, Part I. LNCS, vol. 8467, pp. 169–180. Springer, Heidelberg (2014)
7. Bartczuk, Ł., Rutkowska, D.: Medical diagnosis with type-2 fuzzy decision trees. In: Kącki, E., Rudnicki, M., Stempczyńska, J. (eds.) Computers in Medical Activity. AISC, vol. 65, pp. 11–21. Springer, Heidelberg (2009)
8. Bartczuk, L., Rutkowska, D.: Type-2 fuzzy decision trees. In: Rutkowski, L., Tadeusiewicz, R., Zadeh, L.A., Zurada, J.M. (eds.) ICAISC 2008. LNCS (LNAI), vol. 5097, pp. 197–206. Springer, Heidelberg (2008)
9. Bas, E.: The training of multiplicative neuron model based artificial neural networks with differential evolution algorithm for forecasting. J. Artif. Intell. Soft Comput. Res. **6**(1), 5–11 (2016)
10. Bastian, A.: Identifying fuzzy models utilizing genetic programming. Fuzzy Sets Syst. **113**, 333–350 (2000)
11. Box, G., Jenkins, G.: Time Series Analysis: Forecasting and Control. Holden-Day, San Francisco (1970)
12. Camargo, E., Aguilar, J.: Advanced supervision of oil wells based on soft computing techniques. J. Artif. Intell. Soft Comput. Res. **4**(3), 215–225 (2014)

13. Carmona, C.J., Ruiz-Rodado, V., del Jesus, M.J., Weber, A., Grootveld, M., González, P., Elizondo, D.: A fuzzy genetic programming-based algorithm for subgroup discovery and the application to one problem of pathogenesis of acute sore throat conditions in humans. Inf. Sci. **298**, 180–197 (2015)
14. Chen, M., Ludwig, S.A.: Swarm optimization based fuzzy clustering approach to identify optimal number of clusters. J. Artif. Intell. Soft Comput. Res. **4**(1), 43–56 (2014)
15. Cheng, S., Shi, Y., Qin, Q., Zhang, Q., Bai, R.: Population diversity maintenance in brain storm optimization algorithm. J. Artif. Intell. Soft Comput. Res. **4**(2), 83–97 (2014)
16. Cpalka, K.: A method for designing flexible neuro-fuzzy systems. In: Rutkowski, L., Tadeusiewicz, R., Zadeh, L.A., Żurada, J.M. (eds.) ICAISC 2006. LNCS (LNAI), vol. 4029, pp. 212–219. Springer, Heidelberg (2006)
17. Cpałka, K., Łapa, K., Przybył, A., Zalasiński, M.: A new method for designing neuro-fuzzy systems for nonlinear modelling with interpretability aspects. Neurocomputing **135**, 203–217 (2014)
18. Cpałka, K., Rebrova, O., Nowicki, R., Rutkowski, L.: On design of flexible neuro-fuzzy systems for nonlinear modelling. Int. J. Gen. Syst. **42**(6), 706–720 (2013)
19. Cpałka, K., Rutkowski, L.: Flexible takagi-sugeno neuro-fuzzy structures for nonlinear approximation. WSEAS Trans. Syst. **4**(9), 1450–1458 (2005)
20. Cpałka, K., Zalasiński, M.: On-line signature verification using vertical signature partitioning. Expert Syst. Appl. **41**(9), 4170–4180 (2014)
21. Cpałka, K., Zalasiński, M., Rutkowski, L.: New method for the on-line signature verification based on horizontal partitioning. Pattern Recognit. **47**, 2652–2661 (2014)
22. Cpałka, K., Zalasiński, M., Rutkowski, L.: A new algorithm for identity verification based on the analysis of a handwritten dynamic signature. In: Applied Soft Computing (2016). http://dx.doi.org/10.1016/j.asoc.2016.02.017
23. Dziwiński, P., Avedyan, E.D.: A new approach to nonlinear modeling based on significant operating points detection. In: Rutkowski, L., Korytkowski, M., Scherer, R., Tadeusiewicz, R., Zadeh, L.A., Zurada, J.M. (eds.) Artificial Intelligence and Soft Computing. LNCS, vol. 9120, pp. 364–378. Springer, Heidelberg (2015)
24. Edmonds, A.N., Kershaw, P.S.: Genetic programming of fuzzy logic production rules with application to financial trading. In: Proceedings of the IEEE World Conference on Computational Intelligence, Orlando, Florida (1994)
25. Gabryel, M., Cpałka, K., Rutkowski, L.: Evolutionary strategies for learning of neuro-fuzzy systems. In: Proceedings of the I Workshop on Genetic Fuzzy Systems, pp. 119–123, Granada (2005)
26. Gabryel, M., Grycuk, R., Korytkowski, M., Holotyak, T.: Image indexing and retrieval using GSOM algorithm. In: Rutkowski, L., Korytkowski, M., Scherer, R., Tadeusiewicz, R., Zadeh, L.A., Zurada, J.M. (eds.) Artificial Intelligence and Soft Computing. LNCS, vol. 9119, pp. 706–714. Springer, Heidelberg (2015)
27. Gabryel, M., Korytkowski, M., Scherer, R., Rutkowski, L.: Object detection by simple fuzzy classifiers generated by boosting. In: Rutkowski, L., Korytkowski, M., Scherer, R., Tadeusiewicz, R., Zadeh, L.A., Zurada, J.M. (eds.) ICAISC 2013, Part I. LNCS, vol. 7894, pp. 540–547. Springer, Heidelberg (2013)
28. Gabryel, M., Woźniak, M., Damaševičius, R.: An application of differential evolution to positioning queueing systems. In: Rutkowski, L., Korytkowski, M., Scherer, R., Tadeusiewicz, R., Zadeh, L.A., Zurada, J.M. (eds.) Artificial Intelligence and Soft Computing. LNCS, vol. 9120, pp. 379–390. Springer, Heidelberg (2015)

29. Gałkowski, T., Rutkowski, L.: Nonparametric recovery of multivariate functions with applications to system identification. Proc. IEEE **73**(5), 942–943 (1985)

30. Gałkowski, T., Rutkowski, L.: Nonparametric fitting of multivariate functions. IEEE Trans. Autom. Control **31**(8), 785–787 (1986)

31. Gręblicki, W., Rutkowski, L.: Density-free Bayes risk consistency of nonparametric pattern recognition procedures. Proc. IEEE **69**(4), 482–483 (1981)

32. Grycuk, R., Gabryel, M., Korytkowski, M., Scherer, R., Voloshynovskiy, S.: From single image to list of objects based on edge and blob detection. In: Rutkowski, L., Korytkowski, M., Scherer, R., Tadeusiewicz, R., Zadeh, L.A., Zurada, J.M. (eds.) ICAISC 2014, Part II. LNCS, vol. 8468, pp. 605–615. Springer, Heidelberg (2014)

33. Grycuk, R., Gabryel, M., Korytkowski, M., Scherer, R.: Content-based image indexing by data clustering and inverse document frequency. In: Kozielski, S., Mrozek, D., Kasprowski, P., Małysiak-Mrozek, B., Kostrzewa, D. (eds.) Beyond Databases, Architectures, and Structures. Communications in Computer and Information Science, vol. 424, pp. 374–383. Springer, Heidelberg (2014)

34. Korytkowski, M., Nowicki, R., Scherer, R.: Neuro-fuzzy rough classifier ensemble. In: Alippi, C., Polycarpou, M., Panayiotou, C., Ellinas, G. (eds.) ICANN 2009, Part I. LNCS, vol. 5768, pp. 817–823. Springer, Heidelberg (2009)

35. Kummer, N., Najjaran, H.: Adaboost.MRT: boosting regression for multivariate estimation. Artif. Intell. Res. **3**(4), 64–76 (2014)

36. Laskowski, Ł., Laskowska, M.: Functionalization of SBA-15 mesoporous silica by Cu-phosphonate units: probing of synthesis route. J. Solid State Chem. **220**, 221–226 (2014)

37. Laskowski, Ł., Laskowska, M., Bałanda, M., Fitta, M., Kwiatkowska, J., Dziliński, K., Karczmarska, A.: Mesoporous silica SBA-15 functionalized by nickel-phosphonic units: Raman and magnetic analysis. Microporous Mesoporous Mater. **200**, 253–259 (2014)

38. Laskowska, M., Laskowski, Ł., Jelonkiewicz, J.: SBA-15 mesoporous silica activated by metal ions-verification of molecular structure on the basis of Raman spectroscopy supported by numerical simulations. J. Mol. Struct. **1100**, 21–26 (2015)

39. Laskowski, Ł., Laskowska, M., Jelonkiewicz, J., Boullanger, A.: Spin-glass implementation of a hopfield neural structure. In: Rutkowski, L., Korytkowski, M., Scherer, R., Tadeusiewicz, R., Zadeh, L.A., Zurada, J.M. (eds.) ICAISC 2014, Part I. LNCS, vol. 8467, pp. 89–96. Springer, Heidelberg (2014)

40. Łapa, K.: Algorithms for extracting interpretable expert knowledge in nonlinear modeling issues, Ph.D. Thesis (in polish), Czestochowa University of Technology (2015)

41. Łapa, K., Przybył, A., Cpałka, K.: A new approach to designing interpretable models of dynamic systems. In: Rutkowski, L., Korytkowski, M., Scherer, R., Tadeusiewicz, R., Zadeh, L.A., Zurada, J.M. (eds.) ICAISC 2013, Part II. LNCS, vol. 7895, pp. 523–534. Springer, Heidelberg (2013)

42. Łapa, K., Zalasiński, M., Cpałka, K.: A new method for designing and complexity reduction of neuro-fuzzy systems for nonlinear modelling. In: Rutkowski, L., Korytkowski, M., Scherer, R., Tadeusiewicz, R., Zadeh, L.A., Zurada, J.M. (eds.) ICAISC 2013, Part I. LNCS, vol. 7894, pp. 329–344. Springer, Heidelberg (2013)

43. Mendes, R.R.F., Voznika, F.B., Freitas, A.A., Nievola, J.C.: Discovering fuzzy classification rules with genetic programming and co-evolution. In: Siebes, A., De Raedt, L. (eds.) PKDD 2001. LNCS (LNAI), vol. 2168, pp. 314–325. Springer, Heidelberg (2001)

44. Nallasamy, K., Ratnavelu, K.: Optimal control for stochastic linear quadratic singular Takagi-Sugeno fuzzy delay system using genetic programming. Appl. Soft Comput. **12**, 2085–2090 (2012)
45. Nelson, W.: Analysis of performance-degradation data. IEEE Trans. on Reliab. **2**(2), 149–155 (1981)
46. Ortigosa, I., Lopez, R., Garcia, J.: A neural networks approach to residuary resistance of sailing yachts prediction. In: Proceedings of the International Conference on Marine Engineering MARINE (2007)
47. Price, K., Storn, R.: Differential evolution - a simple and efficient heuristic for global optimization over continuous spaces. J. Global Optimiz. **11**, 341–359 (1997)
48. Przybył, A., Jelonkiewicz, J.: Genetic algorithm for observer parameters tuning in sensorless induction motor drive. In: Rutkowski, L., Kacprzyk, J. (eds.) Neural Networks and Soft Computing. Advances in Soft Computing, vol. 19, pp. 376–381. Springer, Heidelberg (2003)
49. Maher, R.A., Mohamed, J.M.: An enhanced genetic programming algorithm for optimal controller design. In: Intelligent Control and Automation, vol. 4, pp. 94–101 (2013)
50. Rutkowski, L.: Sequential estimates of probability densities by orthogonal series and their application in pattern classification. IEEE Trans. Syst. Man Cybern. **10**(12), 918–920 (1980)
51. Rutkowski, L.: On nonparametric identification with prediction of time-varying systems. IEEE Trans. Autom. Control **29**(1), 58–60 (1984)
52. Rutkowski, L.: Nonparametric identification of quasi-stationary systems. Syst. Control Lett. **6**(1), 33–35 (1985)
53. Rutkowski, L.: Real-time identification of time-varying systems by non-parametric algorithms based on Parzen kernels. Int. J. Syst. Sci. **16**(9), 1123–1130 (1985)
54. Rutkowski, L.: Sequential pattern-recognition procedures derived from multiple Fourier-series. Pattern Recogn. Lett. **8**(4), 213–216 (1988)
55. Rutkowski, L.: Adaptive probabilistic neural networks for pattern classification in time-varying environment. IEEE Trans. Neural Netw. **15**(4), 811–827 (2004)
56. Rutkowski, L.: Computational Intelligence: Methods and Techniques. Springer, Heidelberg (2008)
57. Rutkowski, L., Cpałka, K.: Flexible structures of neuro-fuzzy systems. Quo Vadis Computational Intelligence, Studies in Fuzziness and Soft Computing, vol. 54, pp. 479–484. Springer (2000)
58. Rutkowski, L., Cpałka, K.: Compromise approach to neuro-fuzzy systems. In: Sincak, P., Vascak, J., Kvasnicka, V., Pospichal, J. (eds.) Intelligent Technologies - Theory and Applications, pp. 85–90. IOS Press, Amsterdam (2002)
59. Rutkowski, L.: Cpałka, K.: Flexible weighted neuro-fuzzy systems. In: Proceedings of the 9th International Conference on Neural Information Processing (ICONIP 2002), Orchid Country Club, Singapore, 18–22 November 2002 (2002)
60. Rutkowski, L., Cpałka, K.: Flexible neuro-fuzzy systems. IEEE Trans. Neural Netw. **14**, 554–574 (2003)
61. Rutkowski, L.: Cpałka, K.: Neuro-fuzzy systems derived from quasi-triangular norms. In: Proceedings of the IEEE International Conference on Fuzzy Systems, Budapest, 26–29 July 2004, vol. 2, pp. 1031–1036 (2004)
62. Rutkowski, L., Jaworski, M., Pietruczuk, L., Duda, P.: Decision trees for mining data streams based on the gaussian approximation. IEEE Trans. Knowl. Data Eng. **26**(1), 108–119 (2014)
63. Rutkowski, L., Jaworski, M., Pietruczuk, L., Duda, P.: The CART decision tree for mining data streams. Inf. Sci. **266**, 1–15 (2014)

64. Rutkowski, L., Pietruczuk, L., Duda, P., Jaworski, M.: Decision trees for mining data streams based on the McDiarmid's bound. IEEE Trans. Knowl. Data Eng. **25**(6), 1272–1279 (2013)
65. Rutkowski, L., Przybył, A., Cpałka, K., Er, M.J.: Online speed profile generation for industrial machine tool based on neuro-fuzzy approach. In: Rutkowski, L., Scherer, R., Tadeusiewicz, R., Zadeh, L.A., Zurada, J.M. (eds.) ICAISC 2010, Part II. LNCS, vol. 6114, pp. 645–650. Springer, Heidelberg (2010)
66. Rutkowski, L., Rafajłowicz, E.: On optimal global rate of convergence of some nonparametric identification procedures. IEEE Trans. Autom. Control **34**(10), 1089–1091 (1989)
67. Scherer, R.: Neuro-fuzzy Systems with relation matrix. In: Rutkowski, L., Scherer, R., Tadeusiewicz, R., Zadeh, L.A., Zurada, J.M. (eds.) ICAISC 2010, Part I. LNCS, vol. 6113, pp. 210–215. Springer, Heidelberg (2010)
68. Scherer, R., Rutkowski, L.: Relational equations initializing neuro-fuzzy system. In: Proceedings of the 10th Zittau Fuzzy Colloquium, Zittau, Germany, pp. 18–22 (2002)
69. Soltoggio, A.: A comparison of genetic programming and genetic algorithms in the design of a robust, saturated control system. In: Deb, K., Tari, Z. (eds.) GECCO 2004. LNCS, vol. 3103, pp. 174–185. Springer, Heidelberg (2004)
70. Smyczyńska, J., Hilczer, M., Smyczyńska, U., Stawerska, R., Tadeusiewicz, R., Lewiński, A.: Artificial neural models - a novel tool for predicting the efficacy of growth hormone (GH) therapy in children with short stature. Neuroendocrinol. Lett. **36**(4), 348–353 (2015). (ISSN: 0172-780X, ISSN-L: 0172-780X)
71. Smyczyńska, U., Smyczyńska, J., Hilczer, M., Stawerska, R., Lewiński, A., Tadeusiewicz, R.: Artificial neural networks - a novel tool in modelling the effectiveness of growth hormone (GH) therapy in children with GH deficienc. Pediatr. Endocrinol. **14**(2(51)), 9–18 (2015)
72. Stanimirovic, Z., Maric, M., Bozovic, S., Stanojevic, P.: An efficient evolutionary algorithm for locating long-term care facilities. Inf. Technol. Control **41**(1), 77–89 (2012)
73. Starczewski, J.T., Bartczuk, Ł., Dziwiński, P., Marvuglia, A.: Learning methods for type-2 FLS based on FCM. In: Rutkowski, L., Scherer, R., Tadeusiewicz, R., Zadeh, L.A., Zurada, J.M. (eds.) ICAISC 2010, Part I. LNCS, vol. 6113, pp. 224–231. Springer, Heidelberg (2010)
74. Szarek, A., Korytkowski, M., Rutkowski, L., Scherer, R., Szyprowski, J.: Application of neural networks in assessing changes around implant after total hip arthroplasty. In: Rutkowski, L., Korytkowski, M., Scherer, R., Tadeusiewicz, R., Zadeh, L.A., Zurada, J.M. (eds.) ICAISC 2012, Part II. LNCS, vol. 7268, pp. 335–340. Springer, Heidelberg (2012)
75. Sugeno, M., Yasukawa, T.: A fuzzy logic based approach to qualitative modeling. IEEE Trans. Fuzzy Syst. **1**, 7–31 (1993)
76. Szarek, A., Korytkowski, M., Rutkowski, L., Scherer, R., Szyprowski, J.: Forecasting wear of head and acetabulum in hip joint implant. In: Rutkowski, L., Korytkowski, M., Scherer, R., Tadeusiewicz, R., Zadeh, L.A., Zurada, J.M. (eds.) ICAISC 2012, Part II. LNCS, vol. 7268, pp. 341–346. Springer, Heidelberg (2012)
77. Szczypta, J., Łapa, K., Shao, Z.: Aspects of the selection of the structure and parameters of controllers using selected population based algorithms. In: Rutkowski, L., Korytkowski, M., Scherer, R., Tadeusiewicz, R., Zadeh, L.A., Zurada, J.M. (eds.) ICAISC 2014, Part I. LNCS, vol. 8467, pp. 440–454. Springer, Heidelberg (2014)
78. Tadeusiewicz, R.: Neural networks as a tool for modeling of biological systems. Bio Algorithms Med Syst. **11**(3), 135–144 (2015)

79. Tadeusiewicz, R.: Neural networks in mining sciences - general overview and some representative examples. Arch. Min. Sci. **60**(4), 971–984 (2015)
80. Zalasiński, M., Cpałka, K.: A new method of on-line signature verification using a flexible fuzzy one-class classifier. Academic Publishing House EXIT, Warsaw (2011)
81. Zalasiński, M., Cpałka, K.: New approach for the on-line signature verification based on method of horizontal partitioning. In: Rutkowski, L., Korytkowski, M., Scherer, R., Tadeusiewicz, R., Zadeh, L.A., Zurada, J.M. (eds.) ICAISC 2013, Part II. LNCS, vol. 7895, pp. 342–350. Springer, Heidelberg (2013)
82. Zalasiński, M., Cpałka, K., Er, M.J.: New method for dynamic signature verification using hybrid partitioning. In: Rutkowski, L., Korytkowski, M., Scherer, R., Tadeusiewicz, R., Zadeh, L.A., Zurada, J.M. (eds.) ICAISC 2014, Part II. LNCS, vol. 8468, pp. 216–230. Springer, Heidelberg (2014)
83. Zalasiński, M., Cpałka, K., Er, M.J.: A new method for the dynamic signature verification based on the stable partitions of the signature. In: Rutkowski, L., Korytkowski, M., Scherer, R., Tadeusiewicz, R., Zadeh, L.A., Zurada, J.M. (eds.) Artificial Intelligence and Soft Computing. LNCS, vol. 9120, pp. 161–174. Springer, Heidelberg (2015)
84. Zalasiński, M., Cpałka, K., Hayashi, Y.: New fast algorithm for the dynamic signature verification using global features values. In: Rutkowski, L., Korytkowski, M., Scherer, R., Tadeusiewicz, R., Zadeh, L.A., Zurada, J.M. (eds.) Artificial Intelligence and Soft Computing. LNCS, vol. 9120, pp. 175–188. Springer, Heidelberg (2015)
85. Zalasiński, M., Cpałka, K., Hayashi, Y.: New method for dynamic signature verification based on global features. In: Rutkowski, L., Korytkowski, M., Scherer, R., Tadeusiewicz, R., Zadeh, L.A., Zurada, J.M. (eds.) ICAISC 2014, Part II. LNCS, vol. 8468, pp. 231–245. Springer, Heidelberg (2014)

Aspects of Evolutionary Construction of New Flexible PID-fuzzy Controller

Krystian Łapa[1(✉)], Jacek Szczypta[1], and Takamichi Saito[2]

[1] Institute of Computational Intelligence,
Częstochowa University of Technology, Częstochowa, Poland
{krystian.lapa,jacek.szczypta}@iisi.pcz.pl
[2] Department of Computer Science, Meiji University, Tokyo, Japan
saito@cs.meiji.ac.jp

Abstract. In this paper a new approach for designing control systems is presented. It is based on ensemble of PID controller and flexible neuro-fuzzy system with dynamic structure. A hybrid population-based algorithm is proposed to select the structure and its parameters. In this hybridization a genetic algorithm is used to select the controller structure and evolutionary strategy is used to simultaneously select the controller parameters. The proposed approach allows design interpretable control systems based on different control criteria and different controlled object. The proposed controller structure and proposed learning algorithm were tested on typical control problem.

Keywords: Evolutionary algorithm · PID algorithm · Fuzzy system · Structure selection

1 Introduction

The problem of designing the structure and selecting the parameters of control systems is an important topic in the literature. For this process different approaches are used: analytical approaches (well-known in the literature) and approaches based on using computational intelligence [3,17–19,21–23,25,27,29,30,36,38,42, 46–51,55–63,66–72]. One of the most commonly used types of controllers are the ones based on the combination of linear correction terms. The structure of these controllers is based on functional blocks of proportional (P), integral (I) and derivative (D) type. In the literature many types of specialized structures are presented (e.g. PI, PID, PI in cascade, PI with feed-forward [7,31], PI or PID with additional low-pass [37], PID with anti-windup and compensation mechanism [45], pseudo-derivative feedback (PDF), pseudo-derivative feedback with feed-forward gain (PDFF) [64] etc.). From the other hand, the control systems based on computational intelligence usually do not have strictly defined structures. Their structure can be based on e.g. neural networks [20], fuzzy systems [4–6,14,15], neuro-fuzzy systems [8,9,12,13,16,32,53,54], etc. Gradient algorithms, population based algorithms [11,65], etc. can be used to select the structure and the parameters of these control systems. The third type of controllers

© Springer International Publishing Switzerland 2016
L. Rutkowski et al. (Eds.): ICAISC 2016, Part I, LNAI 9692, pp. 450–464, 2016.
DOI: 10.1007/978-3-319-39378-0_39

are hybrids of other mentioned types. The hybridization can be based on combined controller structures (see e.g. [1, 26]) or on using computational algorithms to select structure and parameters of typical PID controllers (see e.g. [35]).

Taking into account hybrid approaches, an ensemble of PID controllers and fuzzy systems is worth attention. The advantages of this ensemble was proved in i.a. [1, 26]. The use of fuzzy system can not only affect system accuracy but it also makes possible to obtain interpretable knowledge in a form of fuzzy rules [33, 34, 44, 52]. Initially, the interpretability of fuzzy systems referred only to the number of fuzzy rules, but gradually the interpretability criteria which refer to many aspects of fuzzy systems were introduced. These criteria can concern, among the others, correct notation of fuzzy rules [2], correct activation of fuzzy rules [39], distinguishability of fuzzy sets [41], precise defuzzification mechanism [10] etc. The use of these criteria results in increasing readability of fuzzy rules, fuzzy sets, understanding of deffuzification mechanism etc. The overall summary on interpretability criteria can be found, for example in [2, 24]. Unfortunately, PID-fuzzy controllers presented in the literature usually are characterized by high number of fuzzy rules [40], static structures [26] and statically (or partial statically) distributed fuzzy sets [43].

In this paper a new structure of flexible PID-fuzzy controller is proposed. This structure is based on ensemble of PID controller and fuzzy system and it allows for dynamic reduction of its elements. The flexibility of the controller was achieved by using, among the others, precise defuzzification operator and dynamic number of system inputs. Moreover, the new system encoding and new tuning algorithm based on hybrid genetic-evolutionary algorithm are proposed. The proposed controller structure and the proposed learning algorithm were tested on typical control problem.

This paper is organized into 5 sections. Section 2 contains description of proposed controller, Sect. 3 describes an idea of using evolutionary method for controller optimization. Simulation results are presented in Sect. 4 and conclusions are drawn in Sect. 5.

2 Description of New PID-fuzzy Controller

The PID controller, as mentioned above, consists of the following functional blocks: proportional P with parameter K^P (see Fig. 1 (a)), integral I with parameter K^I (see Fig. 1 (b)) and derivative D with parameter K^D (see Fig. 1 (c)). The typical structure of PID controller is based on control blocks (CB) with single output (see Fig. 1 (d)). These blocks can act as a whole controller or as a part of the controller. In case of PID-fuzzy controllers, CB blocks are modified to a form with number of outputs equal to number of functional blocks (see Fig. 1 (e)).

In this paper we propose a modified CB structure (see Fig. 1 (f)), which allows for reduction of its functional blocks or reduction of whole CB structure from a controller (proposed approach takes assumption that controller consists of multiple CB blocks). The reduction takes place when additional binary parameters C^P, C^I, C^D and C^{CB}) have value equal to 0.

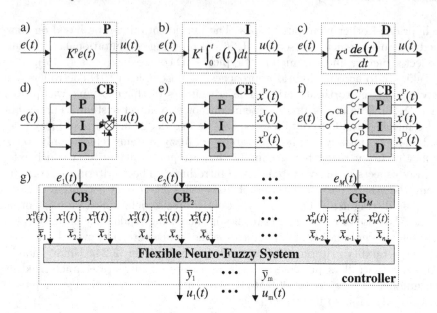

Fig. 1. Structure of: (a) proportional functional block P, (b) integral functional block I, (c) derivative functional block D, (d) typical CB block, (e) fuzzy systems CB block, (f) proposed CB block, (g) proposed flexible PID-fuzzy controller.

Moreover, a new flexible PID-fuzzy controller structure is proposed. This structure is based on proposed CB block and flexible fuzzy system (see Fig. 1 (g)). Proposed structure makes possible, among the others, support of any number of input signals (this number is equal to the number of CB blocks). The output values of proposed CB blocks are calculated as follows:

$$\begin{cases} x_s^P(t) = K_s^P \cdot e_s(t) \cdot C_s^{CB} \cdot C_s^P \\ x_s^P(t) = K_s^I \cdot \int_0^t e_s(t)\,dt \cdot e_s(t) \cdot C_s^{CB} \cdot C_s^I \ , \\ x_s^P(t) = K_s^D \cdot \frac{de_s(t)}{dt} \cdot e_s(t) \cdot C_s^{CB} \cdot C_s^D \end{cases} \tag{1}$$

where $s = 1, ..., M$ stands for index of CB, M stands for number of CB, $e_i(t)$ stands for input of controller, C_s^* stands for reduction parameter, $*$ stands for any CB element (P, I, D or CB). According to Eq. (1) each CB block returns three outputs, which are transformed into fuzzy system input vector $\bar{\mathbf{x}}$ as follows:

$$\bar{\mathbf{x}} = \begin{cases} x_1^P(t), x_1^I(t), x_1^D(t), \\ x_2^P(t), x_2^I(t), x_2^D(t), \\ ..., \\ x_M^P(t), x_M^I(t), x_M^D(t) \end{cases} = \{\bar{x}_1, ..., \bar{x}_n\}, \tag{2}$$

where $n = 3M$ stands for the number of fuzzy system inputs.

In this paper a typical multi-input, multi-output flexible fuzzy system of the Mamdani-type is considered. This system performs mapping $\mathbf{X} \to \mathbf{Y}$, where

$\mathbf{X} \subset \mathbf{R}^n$ and $\mathbf{Y} \subset \mathbf{R}^m$. The rule base of this system consists of a collection of N fuzzy rules R^k, $k = 1, \ldots, N$. Each rule R^k takes the following form:

$$R^k : \left[\begin{pmatrix} \text{IF } (x_1 \text{ is } A_1^k) \text{ AND } \ldots \text{ AND } (x_n \text{ is } A_n^k) \\ \text{THEN } (y_1 \text{ is } B_1^k), \ldots, (y_m \text{ is } B_m^k) \end{pmatrix} \right], \tag{3}$$

where $\bar{\mathbf{x}} = [\bar{x}_1, \ldots, \bar{x}_n] \in \mathbf{X}$ is a vector of input signals, $\bar{\mathbf{y}} = [\bar{y}_1, \ldots, \bar{y}_m] \in \mathbf{Y}$ is a vector of output signals, $A_1^k, \ldots, A_n^k$ are input fuzzy sets characterized by membership functions $\mu_{A_i^k}(\bar{x}_i)$, $i = 1, \ldots, n$, $B_1^k, \ldots, B_m^k$ are output fuzzy sets characterized by membership functions $\mu_{B_j^k}(\bar{y}_j)$, $j = 1, \ldots, m$, m is the number of outputs. The flexibility of the system is a result of using dynamic number of inputs and a precise defuzzification process. Outputs of the system are calculated, for example, by center of area method:

$$u_j(t) = \bar{y}_j = \frac{\sum\limits_{r=1}^{R_j} \bar{y}_{j,r}^{\text{def}} \cdot \underset{k=1}{\overset{N}{S}} \left\{ T \left\{ \tau_k(\bar{\mathbf{x}}), \mu_{B_j^k}(\bar{y}_{j,r}^{\text{def}}) \right\} \right\}}{\sum\limits_{r=1}^{R_j} \underset{k=1}{\overset{N}{S}} \left\{ T \left\{ \tau_k(\bar{\mathbf{x}}), \mu_{B_j^k}(\bar{y}_{j,r}^{\text{def}}) \right\} \right\}}, \tag{4}$$

where $\bar{y}_{j,r}^{\text{def}}$ $(r = 1, \ldots, R_j)$ are discretization points (in the system considered in this paper the number of discretization points R_j for any output j does not have to be equal to the number of rules N, which creates good opportunities for increasing the interpretability and accuracy of the fuzzy system), $\tau_k(\bar{\mathbf{x}})$ is the activation level of the rule k determined for the input signals $\bar{\mathbf{x}}$ as follows:

$$\tau_k(\bar{\mathbf{x}}) = \underset{i=1}{\overset{n}{T}} \left\{ \begin{cases} 1 & \text{for } \bar{x}_i = 0 \\ \mu_{A_i^k}(\bar{x}_i) & \text{for } \bar{x}_i \neq 0 \end{cases} \right\}, \tag{5}$$

where $T\{\cdot\}$ and $S\{\cdot\}$ are triangular norms [52]. In this paper algebraic (product) triangular norms were used. These norms are defined as follows:

$$\begin{cases} T\{\mathbf{a}\} = T\{a_1, \ldots, a_n\} = \underset{i=1}{\overset{n}{T}} \{a_i\} = \prod\limits_{i=1}^{n} a_i \\ S\{\mathbf{a}\} = S\{a_1, \ldots, a_n\} = \underset{i=1}{\overset{n}{S}} \{a_i\} = 1 - \prod\limits_{i=1}^{n} (1 - a_i) \end{cases}. \tag{6}$$

3   Description of New Learning Algorithm

In this paper a new modification of genetic-evolutionary algorithm is proposed. It is based on genetic algorithm (for selection controller structure) and evolutionary algorithm (for selection controller parameters). The process of simultaneously select the structure and the structure parameters is described in detail later in this section. Proposed algorithm was adjusted to the proposed structure of the controller (by proper encoding of the structure) and to the tested simulation problem (by suitable definition of fitness function, which evaluate not only the accuracy of the controller, but also its complexity and interpretability).

3.1 Encoding of Potential Solutions

Encoding of population of potential solutions used in the algorithm refers to the
Pittsburgh approach [28]. A single individual of the population $(\mathbf{X}_{ch})$ is therefore
an object that encodes the complete structure $\mathbf{X}_{ch}^{\mathrm{str}}$ of the controller (4) and its
real number parameters $\mathbf{X}_{ch}^{\mathrm{par}}$:

$$\mathbf{X}_{ch} = \left\{ \mathbf{X}_{ch}^{\mathrm{par}}, \mathbf{X}_{ch}^{\mathrm{str}} \right\}. \tag{7}$$

The part $\mathbf{X}_{ch}^{\mathrm{par}}$ which encodes real number parameters of $\mathbf{X}_{ch}$ is defined as follows:

$$\mathbf{X}_{ch}^{\mathrm{par}} = \left\{ \begin{array}{l} K_1^{\mathrm{P}}, K_1^{\mathrm{I}}, K_1^{\mathrm{D}}, ..., K_M^{\mathrm{P}}, K_M^{\mathrm{I}}, K_M^{\mathrm{D}}, \\ \bar{x}_{1,1}^A, \sigma_{1,1}^A, ..., \bar{x}_{n,1}^A, \sigma_{n,1}^A, ..., \\ \bar{x}_{1,N}^A, \sigma_{1,N}^A, ..., \bar{x}_{n,N}^A, \sigma_{n,N}^A, \\ \bar{x}_{1,1}^B, \sigma_{1,1}^B, ..., \bar{x}_{m,1}^B, \sigma_{m,1}^B, ..., \\ \bar{x}_{1,N}^B, \sigma_{1,N}^B, ..., \bar{x}_{m,N}^B, \sigma_{m,N}^B, \\ \bar{y}_{1,1}^{\mathrm{def}}, ..., \bar{y}_{1,R}^{\mathrm{def}}, ..., \bar{y}_{m,1}^{\mathrm{def}}, ..., \bar{y}_{m,R}^{\mathrm{def}} \end{array} \right\} = \left\{ X_{ch,1}^{\mathrm{par}}, ..., X_{ch,L^{\mathrm{par}}}^{\mathrm{par}} \right\}, \tag{8}$$

where $K_s^{\mathrm{P}}, K_s^{\mathrm{I}}, K_s^{\mathrm{D}}$ stand for parameters of CB_s, $s = 1, ..., M$, $\bar{x}_{i,k}^A, \sigma_{i,k}^A$ stand
for centers and widths of input fuzzy sets, $i = 1, ..., n$ stands for index of fuzzy
system input, $k = 1, ..., N$ stands for index of fuzzy system rule, N stands for
number of fuzzy rules, $\bar{x}_{j,k}^B, \sigma_{j,k}^B$ stand for centers and widths of output fuzzy sets ,
$j = 1, ..., m$ stands for index of fuzzy system output, $\bar{y}_{j,r}^{\mathrm{def}}$ stands for discretization
points, $r = 1, ..., R$ stands for index of discretization points, R stands for number
of discretization points, $L^{\mathrm{par}} = 3M + 2N(n+m) + mR$ stands for number of real
number parameters. In this paper a Gaussian type of fuzzy sets were chosen for
both input and output fuzzy sets.

The part $\mathbf{X}_{ch}^{\mathrm{str}}$, which encodes binary parameters of $\mathbf{X}_{ch}$ is defined as follows:

$$\mathbf{X}_{ch}^{\mathrm{str}} = \left\{ \begin{array}{l} C_1^{\mathrm{CB}}, ..., C_M^{\mathrm{CB}}, \\ C_1^{\mathrm{P}}, C_1^{\mathrm{I}}, C_1^{\mathrm{D}}, ..., C_M^{\mathrm{P}}, C_M^{\mathrm{I}}, C_M^{\mathrm{D}}, \\ \bar{y}_{1,1}^{\mathrm{def}}, ..., \bar{y}_{1,R}^{\mathrm{def}}, ..., \bar{y}_{m,1}^{\mathrm{def}}, ..., \bar{y}_{m,R}^{\mathrm{def}} \end{array} \right\} = \left\{ X_{ch,1}^{\mathrm{str}}, ..., X_{ch,L^{\mathrm{str}}}^{\mathrm{str}} \right\}, \tag{9}$$

where C_s^{CB} stands for reduction of CB_s, $C_s^{\mathrm{P}}, C_s^{\mathrm{I}}, C_s^{\mathrm{D}}$ stand for reduction of CB_s
functional blocks (see Fig. 1 (f)), $\bar{y}_{j,r}^{\mathrm{def}}$ stands for reduction of respectively discretization points encoded in part $\mathbf{X}_{ch}^{\mathrm{par}}$, $L^{\mathrm{str}} = 3(1+M) + mR$ stands for number
of binary parameters. The equation defining outputs of CB blocks (1) with taking
into account proposed encoding is defined as follows:

$$\left\{ \begin{array}{l} x_i^{\mathrm{P}}(t) = \mathbf{X}_{ch}^{\mathrm{par}} \left\{ K_i^{\mathrm{P}} \right\} \cdot e_i(t) \cdot \mathbf{X}_{ch}^{\mathrm{str}} \left\{ C^{\mathrm{CB}} \right\} \cdot \mathbf{X}_{ch}^{\mathrm{str}} \left\{ C^{\mathrm{P}} \right\} \\ x_i^{\mathrm{P}}(t) = \mathbf{X}_{ch}^{\mathrm{par}} \left\{ K_i^{\mathrm{I}} \right\} \cdot \int_0^t e_i(t)\, dt \cdot e_i(t) \cdot \mathbf{X}_{ch}^{\mathrm{str}} \left\{ C^{\mathrm{CB}} \right\} \cdot \mathbf{X}_{ch}^{\mathrm{str}} \left\{ C^{\mathrm{I}} \right\}, \\ x_i^{\mathrm{P}}(t) = \mathbf{X}_{ch}^{\mathrm{par}} \left\{ K_i^{\mathrm{D}} \right\} \cdot \frac{de_i(t)}{dt} \cdot e_i(t) \cdot \mathbf{X}_{ch}^{\mathrm{str}} \left\{ C^{\mathrm{CB}} \right\} \cdot \mathbf{X}_{ch}^{\mathrm{str}} \left\{ C^{\mathrm{D}} \right\} \end{array} \right. \tag{10}$$

where $\mathbf{X}_{ch}^{\mathrm{par}} \{g\}$ stands for referring to g-th gene of part $\mathbf{X}_{ch}^{\mathrm{par}}$. The output of the
proposed system (4) with taking into account proposed encoding is defined as
follows:

$$\bar{y}_j = \frac{\sum_{r=1}^{R_j} \mathbf{X}_{ch}^{str} \left\{ \bar{y}_{j,r}^{def} \right\} \cdot \mathbf{X}_{ch}^{par} \left\{ \bar{y}_{j,r}^{def} \right\} \cdot \underset{k=1}{\overset{N}{S}} \left\{ T \left\{ \tau_k \left(\bar{\mathbf{x}} \right), \mu_{B_j^k} \left(\mathbf{X}_{ch}^{par} \left\{ \bar{y}_{j,r}^{def} \right\} \right) \right\} \right\}}{\sum_{r=1}^{R_j} \mathbf{X}_{ch}^{str} \left\{ \bar{y}_{j,r}^{def} \right\} \cdot \underset{k=1}{\overset{N}{S}} \left\{ T \left\{ \tau_k \left(\bar{\mathbf{x}} \right), \mu_{B_j^k} \left(\mathbf{X}_{ch}^{par} \left\{ \bar{y}_{j,r}^{def} \right\} \right) \right\} \right\}}. \quad (11)$$

The use of binary reduction of discretization points $\mathbf{X}_{ch}^{str} \left\{ \bar{y}_{j,r}^{def} \right\}$ causes using only $\sum_{r=1}^{R} \mathbf{X}_{ch}^{str} \left\{ \bar{y}_{j,r}^{def} \right\}$ discretization points in Eq. (11).

3.2 Genetic-Evolutionary Algorithm

The proposed genetic-evolutionary algorithm works according to the following steps:

- **Step 1. Initialization.** In this step a N^{pop} individuals are randomly initialized (the real number genes are initialized randomly accordingly to simulation problem and the binary genes are initialized randomly) and stored into population **P**.
- **Step 2. Evaluation.** Next, each individual from population **P** is evaluated by the proposed fitness function, designed to evaluate accuracy of the controller, its complexity and interpretability (12). The fitness function definition is described in detail in Sect. 3.3.
- **Step 3. Reproduction.** In this step a new N^{pop} individuals are created and stored into population **P**′. Those individuals are created using typical crossover operator [52] from genetic algorithm. Parents of the individuals are chosen by roulette wheel method [52].
- **Step 4. Mutation.** In this step individuals from population **P**′ are mutated. The genes of individuals encoded in $\mathbf{X}_{ch}^{par}$ are mutated with probability p_m by evolutionary strategy mutation, and the genes encoded in $\mathbf{X}_{ch}^{str}$ are mutated with probability p_s ($p_s < p_m$ due to higher impact on the system output) by genetic algorithm mutation. The proposed distinction in mutation makes possible to keep the correct solution diversity of the population without perversion.
- **Step 5. Evaluation.** This step involves evaluation of individuals from population **P**′ with use of the fitness function (12) .
- **Step 6. Individuals selection.** In this step a N^{pop} best individuals (according to fitness function value) is chosen from **P** ∪ **P**′. Next, these individuals replace population **P**.
- **Step 7. Stopping condition.** In this part of the algorithm the stopping condition is checked (this condition can rely on checking if certain number of iterations is achieved). If this condition is met, then the algorithm stops and the best solution is presented. Otherwise, the algorithm goes back to Step 3.

3.3   Evaluation of Potential Solutions

Each individual $\mathbf{X}_{ch}$ is evaluated by the following fitness function:

$$\text{ff}\left(\mathbf{X}_{ch}\right) = \sum_{f=1}^{F} a_f w_f \text{ffc}_f\left(\mathbf{X}_{ch}\right), \tag{12}$$

where $\text{ffc}_f\left(\mathbf{X}_{ch}\right)$ stands for fitness function component, $f = 1, ..., F$, F stands for number of fitness function components (this number depends, among the others, from simulation problem), w_f stands for weights of fitness function components, a_f stands for normalizations of fitness function components. The function $\text{ffc}_1\left(\mathbf{X}_{ch}\right)$ is responsible for complexity of the controller and it is defined as follows:

$$\text{ffc}_1\left(\mathbf{X}_{ch}\right) = \frac{1}{L^{\text{str}}} \sum_{l=1}^{L^{\text{str}}} X_{ch,l}^{\text{str}}. \tag{13}$$

The function $\text{ffc}_2\left(\mathbf{X}_{ch}\right)$ is responsible for interpretability of fuzzy system rules (by promoting properly distributed fuzzy sets) and it is defined as follows:

$$\text{ffc}_2\left(\mathbf{X}_{ch}\right) = \frac{\sum_{i=1}^{n}\sum_{k=1}^{N-1}\text{ier}^A\left(\overrightarrow{x}_{i,k+1}^{A}, \overrightarrow{x}_{i,k}^{A}\right) + \sum_{j=1}^{m}\sum_{k=1}^{N-1}\text{ier}^B\left(\overrightarrow{x}_{j,k+1}^{B}, \overrightarrow{x}_{j,k}^{B}\right)}{(n+m)\cdot(N-1)}, \tag{14}$$

where $\overrightarrow{x}_i^A = sort\left(\mathbf{X}_{ch}^{\text{par}}\{\bar{x}_{i,1}^A\}, ..., \mathbf{X}_{ch}^{\text{par}}\{\bar{x}_{i,N}^A\}\right)$ and $\overrightarrow{x}_j^B = sort\left(\mathbf{X}_{ch}^{\text{par}}\{\bar{x}_{j,1}^B\}, ..., \mathbf{X}_{ch}^{\text{par}}\{\bar{x}_{j,N}^B\}\right)$ stands for ascended sorted vectors containing centers of fuzzy sets of i-th inputs and j-th outputs. The function $\text{ier}^A(\cdot)$ (and analogically for outputs $\text{ier}^B(\cdot)$) stands for penalty for incorrect distributed fuzzy sets:

$$\text{ier}^A\left(x_1, x_2\right) = \begin{cases} (x_2 - x_1)/b_i^A & \text{for } x_2 - x_1 < b_i^A \\ 0 & \text{for } x_2 - x_1 \geq b_i^A \end{cases}, \tag{15}$$

where b_i^A (and analogically b_j^B for outputs) stands for minimum acceptable distance between center of neighboring fuzzy sets:

$$b_i^A = \frac{1}{N}\left(\max_{k=1,...,N}\left(\mathbf{X}_{ch}^{\text{par}}\{\bar{x}_{i,k}^A\}\right) - \min_{k=1,...,N}\left(\mathbf{X}_{ch}^{\text{par}}\{\bar{x}_{i,k}^A\}\right)\right). \tag{16}$$

The rest fitness function components depend from simulation problem and they are defined in Sect. 4.

4   Simulation Results

4.1   Problem Description

In our simulations a problem of designing controller structure and tuning parameters for double spring-mass-damp object was considered (see Fig. 2). More

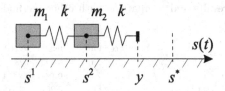

Fig. 2. Simulated spring-mass-damp object. s^* stands for desired position of the mass m_1

details about this model can be found in our previous paper [35]. Object parameters were set as follows: spring constant k was set to $10\,\text{N/m}$, coefficient of friction $\mu = 0.5$, masses $m_1 = m_2 = 0.2$ kg. Initial values of: s^1, v^1, s^2 i v^2 were set to zero, and s^* is a desired position of mass m_1 (see Fig. 2), simulation length T^{all} was set to 10 s, output signal of the controller was limited to the range $y \in (-2, +2)$, quantization resolution for the output signal y of the controller as well as for the position sensor for s^1 and s^2 was set to 10 bit, time step in the simulation was equal to $T = 0.1$ ms, while interval between subsequent controller activations were set to twenty simulation steps (number of iteration of the model is calculated as $Z = T^{\text{all}}/T$). For the considered problem a trapezoidal shape of desired signal s^* was used (see Fig. 4). The input of the controller $e_1(t) = s^*$, $e_2(t) = s^1$, $e_3(t) = s^1 - s^*$ ($M = 3$). Moreover, for considered simulation problem, the following fitness function components (13) were additionally used:

- RMSE standing for accuracy of the controlled object:

$$\text{ffc}_3\left(\mathbf{X_{ch}}\right) = RMSE = \sqrt{\frac{1}{Z} \cdot \sum_{i=1}^{Z} \varepsilon_i^2} = \sqrt{\frac{1}{Z} \cdot \sum_{i=1}^{Z} \left(s_i^* - s_i^1\right)^2}, \quad (17)$$

- Overshooting of the controller:

$$\text{ffc}_4\left(\mathbf{X_{ch}}\right) = \max_{i=1,\dots,Z}\left\{s_i^1\right\}. \quad (18)$$

- Oscillations of the output of the controller:

$$\text{ffc}_5\left(\mathbf{X_{ch}}\right) = \sum_{o=1}^{O-1} |r_o - r_{o+1}|, \quad (19)$$

where r_c stands for each local minims and maxims of the output values of the controller, $c = 1, \dots, O$, O stands for number of minims and maxims of osculations.

4.2 Controller and Algorithm Parameters

The parameters of the controller and learning algorithm were set experimentally to: number of fuzzy rules $N = 3$, number of discretization points $R = 10$, number

Table 1. Simulation results and comparison with other methods, n/a stands for not available data.

Method		ff(·)	ffc₁(·)	ffc₂(·)	ffc₃(·)	ffc₄(·)	ffc₅(·)	PID elements
Passive system		n/a	n/a	n/a	0.822	n/a	n/a	n/a
PID controller [35]	best (by ffc₃(·))	n/a	n/a	n/a	**0.050**	15.374	**1.040**	6.000
	best (by ffc₄(·))	n/a	n/a	n/a	0.051	12.315	1.117	10.000
Proposed approach	best	**1.052**	**0.474**	**0.092**	0.090	2.657	1.256	**4.000**
	average	1.468	0.509	0.148	0.128	**2.450**	1.195	4.544

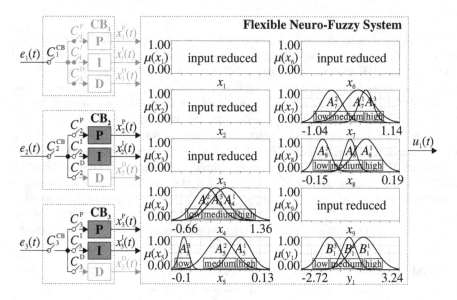

Fig. 3. Structure of best obtained flexible PID-fuzzy controller.

of individuals in population $N^{pop} = 100$, number of iterations = 1000, mutation probability $p_m = 0.25$, binary mutation probability $p_s = 0.15$, normalization parameters of fitness function components $a_1 = 1.0$, $a_2 = 1.0$, $a_3 = 10.0$, $a_4 = 0.01$, $a_5 = 0.1$, weights of fitness function components $w_1 = 0.2$, $w_2 = 0.5$, $w_3 = 1.0$, $w_4 = 0.1$, $w_5 = 0.1$. The simulations were repeated 100 times and results were averaged.

4.3   Obtained Results

The obtained results are presented in Table 1. The best founded controller structure is presented in Fig. 3, the corresponding signals of the controller in Fig. 4 and notation of the corresponding fuzzy rules can is defined as follows:

$$\begin{cases} R^1 : \text{IF} & \left(\begin{array}{c} x_2^{\text{P}}(t) \text{ is high AND } x_2^{\text{I}}(t) \text{ is high AND} \\ x_3^{\text{P}}(t) \text{ is medium AND } x_3^{\text{I}}(t) \text{ is high} \end{array} \right) \text{THEN } u_1(t) \text{ is high} \\ R^2 : \text{IF} & \left(\begin{array}{c} x_2^{\text{P}}(t) \text{ is low AND } x_2^{\text{I}}(t) \text{ is medium AND} \\ x_3^{\text{P}}(t) \text{ is low AND } x_3^{\text{I}}(t) \text{ is medium} \end{array} \right) \text{THEN } u_1(t) \text{ is medium} \\ R^3 : \text{IF} & \left(\begin{array}{c} x_2^{\text{P}}(t) \text{ is medium AND } x_2^{\text{I}}(t) \text{ is low AND} \\ x_3^{\text{P}}(t) \text{ is high AND } x_3^{\text{I}}(t) \text{ is low} \end{array} \right) \text{THEN } u_1(t) \text{ is low} \end{cases}$$

$$(20)$$

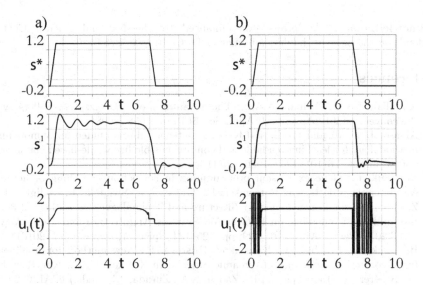

Fig. 4. Signals from: (a) the best obtained flexible PID-fuzzy controller, (b) the best PID controller from [35].

4.4   Simulation Conclusions

Conclusions from the simulations are as follows: **(a)** obtained accuracy of the system (see ffc$_3(\cdot)$ in Table 1) is acceptable and close to results from literature (with lower complexity of the controller); **(b)** the number of used PID functional elements is the best in comparison with other results (see Table 1); **(c)** using ensemble with fuzzy systems allowed us to obtain the smallest oscillations of the controller output (see ffc$_4(\cdot)$ in Table 1 and Fig. 4); **(e)** obtained controller structure is simple and fuzzy sets distribution is correct (see Fig. 3); **(f)** fuzzy rules notation is simple and interpretable (see Eq. 20 and Fig. 3).

5   Summary

The use of ensemble of flexible fuzzy system and PID controller allowed us to obtain non-complex controllers with low number of readable and clear fuzzy rules. Moreover, controller accuracy was acceptable and controller output oscillations, due to using fuzzy logic, were the smallest in comparison to other authors results (it is a big advantage of the proposed ensemble). The proposed algorithm and dynamic structure of the controller allow us to automatically match parameters of the controller, and also its structure, to the considered simulation problem. In the future authors plan to use, among the others, dynamic number of fuzzy rules and fuzzy sets, new interpretability criteria and multi-population algorithms.

Acknowledgment. The project was financed by the National Science Center (Poland) on the basis of the decision number DEC-2012/05/B/ST7/02138.

References

1. Abdullah, I.A.O., Ayman, A.A.L.: The advantages of PID fuzzy controllers over the conventional types. Am. J. Appl. Sci. **5**(6), 653–658 (2008)
2. Alonso, J.M., Magdalena, L.: HILK++: an interpretability-guided fuzzy modeling methodology for learning readable and comprehensible fuzzy rule-based classifiers. Soft. Comput. **15**(10), 1959–1980 (2011)
3. Bartczuk, Ł.: Gene expression programming in correction modelling of nonlinear dynamic objects. In: Borzemski, L., Grzech, A., Świątek, J., Wilimowska, Z. (eds.) Information Systems Architecture and Technology: Proceedings of 36th International Conference on Information Systems Architecture and Technology–ISAT 2015–Part I. AISC, vol. 429, pp. 125–134. Springer, Switzerland (2016)
4. Bartczuk, Ł., Przybył, A., Koprinkova-Hristova, P.: New method for nonlinear fuzzy correction modelling of dynamic objects. In: Rutkowski, L., Korytkowski, M., Scherer, R., Tadeusiewicz, R., Zadeh, L.A., Zurada, J.M. (eds.) ICAISC 2014, Part I. LNCS, vol. 8467, pp. 169–180. Springer, Heidelberg (2014)
5. Bartczuk, Ł., Rutkowska, D.: Medical diagnosis with type-2 fuzzy decision trees. In: Kącki, E., Rudnicki, M., Stempczyńska, J. (eds.) Computers in Medical Activity. AISC, vol. 65, pp. 11–21. Springer, Heidelberg (2009)
6. Bartczuk, Ł., Rutkowska, D.: Type-2 fuzzy decision trees. In: Rutkowski, L., Tadeusiewicz, R., Zadeh, L.A., Zurada, J.M. (eds.) ICAISC 2008. LNCS (LNAI), vol. 5097, pp. 197–206. Springer, Heidelberg (2008)
7. Boiko, I.: Variable-structure PID controller for level process. Control Eng. Pract. **21**(5), 700–707 (2013)
8. Cpalka, K.: A method for designing flexible neuro-fuzzy systems. In: Rutkowski, L., Tadeusiewicz, R., Zadeh, L.A., Żurada, J.M. (eds.) ICAISC 2006. LNCS (LNAI), vol. 4029, pp. 212–219. Springer, Heidelberg (2006)
9. Cpałka, K.: On evolutionary designing and learning of flexible neuro-fuzzy structures for nonlinear classification. Nonlinear Anal. A: Theor. Meth. Appl. **71**, 1659–1672 (2009)
10. Cpałka, K.: A new method for design and reduction of neuro-fuzzy classification systems. IEEE Trans. Neural Netw. **20**, 701–714 (2009)
11. Cpałka, K., Łapa, K., Przybył, A.: A new approach to design of control systems using genetic programming. Inf. Technol. Control **44**(4), 433–442 (2015)
12. Cpałka, K., Łapa, K., Przybył, A., Zalasiński, M.: A new method for designing neuro-fuzzy systems for nonlinear modelling with interpretability aspects. Neurocomputing **135**, 203–217 (2014)

13. Cpałka, K., Rebrova, O., Nowicki, R., Rutkowski, L.: On design of flexible neuro-fuzzy systems for nonlinear modelling. Int. J. Gen. Syst. **42**(6), 706–720 (2013)
14. Cpałka K., Rutkowski L.: Flexible Takagi-Sugeno fuzzy systems. In: Proceedings of the International Joint Conference on Neural Networks, pp. 1764–1769. Montreal (2005)
15. Cpałka, K., Rutkowski, L.: Flexible Takagi-Sugeno neuro-fuzzy structures for nonlinear approximation. WSEAS Trans. Syst. **4**(9), 1450–1458 (2005)
16. Cpałka K., Rutkowski L.: A new method for designing and reduction of neuro-fuzzy systems. In: Proceedings of the 2006 IEEE International Conference on Fuzzy Systems (IEEE World Congress on Computational Intelligence, WCCI 2006), pp. 8510–8516. IEEE, Vancouver (2006)
17. Cpałka, K., Zalasiński, M.: On-line signature verification using vertical signature partitioning. Expert Syst. Appl. **41**(9), 4170–4180 (2014)
18. Cpałka, K., Zalasiński, M., Rutkowski, L.: New method for the on-line signature verification based on horizontal partitioning. Pattern Recogn. **47**, 2652–2661 (2014)
19. Cpałka, K., Zalasiński, M., Rutkowski, L.: A new algorithm for identity verification based on the analysis of a handwritten dynamic signature. Appl. Soft. Comput. **43**, 47–56 (2016). http://dx.doi.org/10.1016/j.asoc.2016.02.017
20. Duch W., Korbicz J., Rutkowski L., Tadeusiewicz R. (eds.), Biocybernetics and Biomedical Engineering 2000. Neural Networks, Akademicka Oficyna Wydawnicza, EXIT, Warsaw 2000, vol. 6 (in Polish) (2000)
21. Dziwiński, P., Avedyan, E.D.: A new approach to nonlinear modeling based on significant operating points detection. In: Rutkowski, L., Korytkowski, M., Scherer, R., Tadeusiewicz, R., Zadeh, L.A., Zurada, J.M. (eds.) ICAISC 2015. LNCS, vol. 9120, pp. 364–378. Springer, Heidelberg (2015)
22. Dziwiński, P., Bartczuk, Ł., Przybył, A., Avedyan, E.D.: A new algorithm for identification of significant operating points using swarm intelligence. In: Rutkowski, L., Korytkowski, M., Scherer, R., Tadeusiewicz, R., Zadeh, L.A., Zurada, J.M. (eds.) ICAISC 2014, Part II. LNCS, vol. 8468, pp. 349–362. Springer, Heidelberg (2014)
23. El-Samak, A.F., Ashour, W.: Optimization of traveling salesman problem using affinity propagation clustering and genetic algorithm. J. Artif. Intell. Soft Comput. Res. **5**(4), 239–245 (2015)
24. Gacto, M.J., Alcalá, R., Herrera, F.: Interpretability of linguistic fuzzy rule-based systems: an overview of interpretability measures. Inf. Sci. **181**(20), 4340–4360 (2011)
25. Gałkowski, T., Rutkowski, L.: Nonparametric recovery of multivariate functions with applications to system identification. Proc. IEEE **73**(5), 942–943 (1985)
26. Radu, V.: Stochastic Modeling of Thermal Fatigue Crack Growth. ACM, vol. 1. Springer, Heidelberg (2015)
27. Hayashi, Y., Tanaka, Y., Takagi, T., Saito, T., Iiduka, H., Kikuchi, H., Bologna, G., Mitra, S.: Recursive-rule extraction algorithm with j48graft and applications to generating credit scores. J. Artif. Intell. Soft Comput. Res. **6**(1), 35–44 (2016)
28. Ishibuchi, H., Nakashima, T., Murata, T.: Comparsion of the Michigan and Pittsburgh approaches to the design of fuzzy classification systems. Electron. Commun. Jpn. **80**(12), 379–387 (1997)
29. Kasthurirathna, D., Piraveenan, M., Uddin, S.: Evolutionary stable strategies in networked games: the influence of topology. J. Artif. Intell. Soft Comput. Res. **5**(2), 83–95 (2015)
30. Korytkowski, M., Rutkowski, L., Scherer, R.: Fast image classification by boosting fuzzy classifiers. Inf. Sci. **327**, 175–182 (2016)

31. Leva, A., Papadopoulos, A.V.: Tuning of event-based industrial controllers with simple stability guarantees. J. Process Control **23**, 1251–1260 (2013)
32. Łapa, K., Cpałka, K., Wang, L.: New method for design of fuzzy systems for nonlinear modelling using different criteria of interpretability. In: Rutkowski, L., Korytkowski, M., Scherer, R., Tadeusiewicz, R., Zadeh, L.A., Zurada, J.M. (eds.) ICAISC 2014, Part I. LNCS, vol. 8467, pp. 217–232. Springer, Heidelberg (2014)
33. Łapa, K., Przybył, A., Cpałka, K.: A new approach to designing interpretable models of dynamic systems. In: Rutkowski, L., Korytkowski, M., Scherer, R., Tadeusiewicz, R., Zadeh, L.A., Zurada, J.M. (eds.) ICAISC 2013, Part II. LNCS, vol. 7895, pp. 523–534. Springer, Heidelberg (2013)
34. Łapa, K., Zalasiński, M., Cpałka, K.: A new method for designing and complexity reduction of neuro-fuzzy systems for nonlinear modelling. In: Rutkowski, L., Korytkowski, M., Scherer, R., Tadeusiewicz, R., Zadeh, L.A., Zurada, J.M. (eds.) ICAISC 2013, Part I. LNCS, vol. 7894, pp. 329–344. Springer, Heidelberg (2013)
35. Łapa, K., Szczypta, J., Venkatesan, R.: Aspects of structure and parameters selection of control systems using selected multi-population algorithms. In: Rutkowski, L., Korytkowski, M., Scherer, R., Tadeusiewicz, R., Zadeh, L.A., Zurada, J.M. (eds.) Artificial Intelligence and Soft Computing. LNCS, vol. 9120, pp. 247–260. Springer, Heidelberg (2015)
36. Li, X., Er, M.J., Lim, B.S.: Fuzzy regression modeling for tool performance prediction and degradation detection. Int. J. Neural Syst. **20**, 405–419 (2010)
37. Maggio, M., Bonvini, M., Leva, A.: The PID+p controller structure and its contextual autotuning. J. Process Control **22**, 1237–1245 (2012)
38. Liu, C., Sun, F.: Lens distortion correction using ELM. In: Cao, J., Mao, K., Cambria, E., Man, Z., Toh, K.-A. (eds.) Proceedings of ELM-2014 Volume 2, PALO, vol. 4, pp. 21–30. Springer, Heidelberg (2014)
39. Marquez A. A., Marquez F. A., Peregrin A.: A multi-objective evolutionary algorithm with an interpretability improvement mechanism for linguistic fuzzy systems with adaptive defuzzification. In: IEEE International Conference on Fuzzy Systems, pp. 1–7 (2010)
40. Malhotra, R., Sodhi, R.: Boiler flow control using PID and fuzzy logic controller. IJCSET **1**(6), 315–319 (2011)
41. Mencar, C., Castiello, C., Cannone, R., Fanelli, A.M.: Interpretability assessment of fuzzy knowledge bases: a cointension based approach. Int. J. Approximate Reasoning **52**(4), 501–518 (2011)
42. Murata, M., Ito, S., Tokuhisa, M., Ma, Q.: Order estimation of japanese paragraphs by supervised machine learning and various textual features. J. Artif. Intell. Soft Comput. Res. **5**(4), 247–255 (2015)
43. Natsheh, E., Buragga, K.A.: Comparison between conventional and fuzzy logic PID controllers for controlling DC motors. IJCSI Int. J. Comput. Sci. Issues **7**(5), 128–134 (2010)
44. Przybył, A., Cpałka, K.: A new method to construct of interpretable models of dynamic systems. In: Rutkowski, L., Korytkowski, M., Scherer, R., Tadeusiewicz, R., Zadeh, L.A., Zurada, J.M. (eds.) ICAISC 2012, Part II. LNCS, vol. 7268, pp. 697–705. Springer, Heidelberg (2012)
45. Ribića, A.I., Mataušek, M.R.: A dead-time compensating PID controller structure and robust tuning. J. Process Control **22**, 1340–1349 (2012)
46. Rutkowski, L.: Sequential estimates of probability densities by orthogonal series and their application in pattern classification. IEEE Trans. Syst. Man Cybern. **10**(12), 918–920 (1980)

47. Rutkowski, L.: Nonparametric identification of quasi-stationary systems. Syst. Control Lett. **6**(1), 33–35 (1985)
48. Rutkowski, L.: Real-time identification of time-varying systems by non-parametric algorithms based on Parzen kernels. Int. J. Syst. Sci. **16**(9), 1123–1130 (1985)
49. Rutkowski, L.: A general approach for nonparametric fitting of functions and their derivatives with applications to linear circuits identification. IEEE Trans. Circuits Syst. **33**(8), 812–818 (1986)
50. Rutkowski, L.: Application of multiple Fourier-series to identification of multivariable non-stationary systems. Int. J. Syst. Sci. **20**(10), 1993–2002 (1989)
51. Rutkowski, L.: Adaptive probabilistic neural networks for pattern classification in time-varying environment. IEEE Trans. Neural Netw. **15**(4), 811–827 (2004)
52. Rutkowski, L.: Computational Intelligence. Springer, Heidelberg (2008)
53. Rutkowski, L., Cpałka, K.: Flexible structures of neuro-fuzzy systems. Quo Vadis Computational Intelligence, Studies in Fuzziness and Soft Computing, Springer **54**, 479–484 (2000)
54. Rutkowski L., Cpałka K.: Compromise approach to neuro-fuzzy systems. In: Proceedings of the 2nd Euro-International Symposium on Computational Intelligence, vol. 76, pp. 85–90. Koszyce (2002)
55. Rutkowski, L., Jaworski, M., Pietruczuk, L., Duda, P.: Decision trees decision trees for mining data streams based on the Gaussian approximation. IEEE Trans. Knowl. Data Eng. **26**(1), 108–119 (2014)
56. Rutkowski, L., Jaworski, M., Pietruczuk, L., Duda, P.: The CART decision tree for mining data streams. Inf. Sci. **266**, 1–15 (2014)
57. Rutkowski, L., Jaworski, M., Pietruczuk, L., Duda, P.: A new method for data stream mining based on the misclassification error. IEEE Trans. Neural Netw. Learn. Syst. **26**(5), 1048–1059 (2015)
58. Rutkowski, L., Pietruczuk, L., Duda, P., Jaworski, M.: Decision Trees for mining data streams based on the McDiarmid's bound. IEEE Trans. Knowl. Data Engi. **25**(6), 1272–1279 (2013)
59. Rutkowski, L., Przybył, A., Cpałka, K.: Novel online speed profile generation for industrial machine tool based on flexible neuro-fuzzy approximation. IEEE Trans. Ind. Electron. **59**(2), 1238–1247 (2012)
60. Rutkowski, Leszek, Przybył, Andrzej, Cpałka, Krzysztof, Er, Meng Joo: Online speed profile generation for industrial machine tool based on neuro-fuzzy approach. In: Rutkowski, Leszek, Scherer, Rafał, Tadeusiewicz, Ryszard, Zadeh, Lotfi A., Zurada, Jacek M. (eds.) ICAISC 2010, Part II. LNCS, vol. 6114, pp. 645–650. Springer, Heidelberg (2010)
61. Starczewski, J.T., Bartczuk, Ł., Dziwiński, P., Marvuglia, A.: Learning methods for type-2 FLS based on FCM. In: Rutkowski, L., Scherer, R., Tadeusiewicz, R., Zadeh, L.A., Zurada, J.M. (eds.) ICAISC 2010, Part I. LNCS, vol. 6113, pp. 224–231. Springer, Heidelberg (2010)
62. Starczewski, J., Rutkowski, L.: Interval type 2 neuro-fuzzy systems based on interval consequents. In: Rutkowski, L., Kacprzyk, J. (eds.) Neural Networks and Soft Computing. Advances in Soft Computing, vol. 19, pp. 570–577. Physica, Verlag (2003)
63. Starczewski, J.T., Rutkowski, L.: Connectionist structures of type 2 fuzzy inference systems. In: Wyrzykowski, R., Dongarra, J., Paprzycki, M., Waśniewski, J. (eds.) Parallel Processing and Applied Mathematics. Lecture Notes in Computer Science, vol. 2328, pp. 634–642. Springer, Heidelberg (2002)
64. Cheng, S., Li, C.-W.: Fuzzy PDFF-IIR controller for PMSM drive systems. Control Eng. Pract. **19**, 828–835 (2011)

65. Yeomans, J.S.: A parametric testing of the firefly algorithm in the determination of the optimal osmotic drying parameters of mushrooms. J. Artif. Intell. Soft Comput. Res. **4**(4), 257–266 (2014)
66. Zalasiński, M., Cpałka, K.: Novel algorithm for the on-line signature verification. In: Rutkowski, L., Korytkowski, M., Scherer, R., Tadeusiewicz, R., Zadeh, L.A., Zurada, J.M. (eds.) ICAISC 2012. LNCS, vol. 7268, pp. 362–367. Springer, Heidelberg (2012)
67. Zalasiński, M., Cpałka, K.: Novel algorithm for the on-line signature verification using selected discretization points groups. In: Rutkowski, L., Korytkowski, M., Scherer, R., Tadeusiewicz, R., Zadeh, L.A., Zurada, J.M. (eds.) ICAISC 2013. LNCS, vol. 7894, pp. 493–502. Springer, Heidelberg (2013)
68. Zalasiński, M., Cpałka, K., Er, M.J.: New method for dynamic signature verification using hybrid partitioning. In: Rutkowski, L., Korytkowski, M., Scherer, R., Tadeusiewicz, R., Zadeh, L.A., Zurada, J.M. (eds.) ICAISC 2014. LNCS, vol. 8468, pp. 216–230. Springer, Heidelberg (2014)
69. Zalasiński, M., Cpałka, K., Er, M.J.: A new method for the dynamic signature verification based on the stable partitions of the signature. In: Rutkowski, L., Korytkowski, M., Scherer, R., Tadeusiewicz, R., Zadeh, L.A., Zurada, J.M. (eds.) ICAISC 2015. LNCS, vol. 9120, pp. 161–174. Springer, Heidelberg (2015)
70. Zalasiński, M., Cpałka, K., Hayashi, Y.: New method for dynamic signature verification based on global features. In: Rutkowski, L., Korytkowski, M., Scherer, R., Tadeusiewicz, R., Zadeh, L.A., Zurada, J.M. (eds.) ICAISC 2014. LNCS, vol. 8468, pp. 231–245. Springer, Heidelberg (2014)
71. Zalasiński, M., Cpałka, K., Hayashi, Y.: New fast algorithm for the dynamic signature verification using global features values. In: Rutkowski, L., Korytkowski, M., Scherer, R., Tadeusiewicz, R., Zadeh, L.A., Zurada, J.M. (eds.) ICAISC 2015. LNCS, vol. 9120, pp. 175–188. Springer, Heidelberg (2015)
72. Zalasiński, M., Łapa, K., Cpałka, K.: New algorithm for evolutionary selection of the dynamic signature global features. In: Rutkowski, L., Korytkowski, M., Scherer, R., Tadeusiewicz, R., Zadeh, L.A., Zurada, J.M. (eds.) ICAISC 2013. LNCS, vol. 7895, pp. 113–121. Springer, Heidelberg (2013)

Chaos Enhanced Repulsive MC-PSO/DE Hybrid

Michal Pluhacek[1]([✉]), Roman Senkerik[1], Adam Viktorin[1], and Ivan Zelinka[2]

[1] Faculty of Applied Informatics, Tomas Bata University in Zlin,
Nam T.G. Masaryka 5555, 760 01 Zlin, Czech Republic
{pluhacek,senkerik}@fai.utb.cz
[2] Faculty of Electrical Engineering and Computer Science,
Technical University of Ostrava, 17. Listopadu 15,
708 33 Ostrava-poruba, Czech Republic
ivan.zelinka@vsb.cz

Abstract. In this paper a previously proposed method is extended with pseudo-random number generator based on chaotic sequences. Several recent approaches for designing the evolutionary computational techniques are merged in the proposed method. The proposed method represents a hybridization of heterogeneous swarm based PSO and differential evolution extended with the chaotic sequences implementation. The performance of the proposed method is tested on IEEE CEC 2013 benchmark set.

Keywords: Particle swarm optimization · PSO · Differential evolution · DE · Chaos · Hybrid method

1 Introduction

The Particle Swarm Optimization (PSO) [1–4] and Differential Evolution (DE) [5,6] are among the most prominent representatives of evolutionary computational techniques (ECTs). Recently it has been shown that using chaotic sequences as pseudorandom number generators (PRNGs) may be very beneficial for various ECTs [7–12].

Popular trend for ECTs design is hybridization. Given the popularity of PSO and DE and the focus of the researching community on the improvement of these methods, the hybridization of PSO and DE was an inevitable step [13,14]. The performance of DE and PSO on certain types of optimization problems is often

Michal Pluhacek—This work was supported by Grant Agency of the Czech Republic GACR P103/15/06700S, by the Programme EEA and Norway Grants for funding via grant on Institutional cooperation project nr. NF-CZ07-ICP-4-345-2016, further by the Ministry of Education, Youth and Sports of the Czech Republic within the National Sustainability Programme Project no. LO1303 (MSMT-7778/2014. Also by the European Regional Development Fund under the Project CEBIA-Tech no. CZ.1.05/2.1.00/03.0089 and by Internal Grant Agency of Tomas Bata University under the Project no. IGA/CebiaTech/2016/007.

© Springer International Publishing Switzerland 2016
L. Rutkowski et al. (Eds.): ICAISC 2016, Part I, LNAI 9692, pp. 465–475, 2016.
DOI: 10.1007/978-3-319-39378-0_40

very different. Thru the process of hybridization it is possible to achieve good results on very broad spectrum of optimization tasks.

In this paper recently proposed hybrid of Multiple-choice strategy for PSO [15–17] and DE (MC-PSO/DE) is further extended with chaotic PRNG. The goal is to show that the performance of such hybrid method can be further improved by implementation of chaotic sequences. The performance of proposed chaotic method is tested using the CEC 13 benchmark set [18] and compared with canonical MC-PSO/DE and state-of art representative for CEC 13 Benchmark the fk-PSO [19].

In the next two sections the original PSO and DE algorithms are shortly described. The used chaotic systems are briefly described in the next sections. Following is the description of proposed hybrid method. The experiment is designed and results presented in following sections.

2   Particle Swarm Optimization Algorithm

Original PSO takes the inspiration from behavior of fish and birds. The knowledge of global best found solution (typically noted $gBest$) is shared among the particles in the swarm. Furthermore each particle has the knowledge of its own (personal) best found solution (noted $pBest$). Last important part of the algorithm is the velocity of each particle that is taken into account during the calculation of the particle movement. The new position of each particle is then given by (1), where x_i^{t+1} is the new particle position; x_i^t refers to current particle position and v_i^{t+1} is the new velocity of the particle.

$$x_i^{t+1} = x_i^t + v_i^{t+1} \tag{1}$$

To calculate the new velocity the distance from $pBest$ and gBest is taken into account alongside with current velocity (2).

$$v_{ij}^{t+1} = w \cdot v_{ij}^t + c_1 \cdot Rand \cdot (pBest_{ij} - x_{ij}^t) + c_2 \cdot Rand \cdot (gBest_j - x_{ij}^t) \tag{2}$$

Where:

v_{ij}^{t+1} - New velocity of the ith particle in iteration $t+1$. (component j of the dimension D).

w – Inertia weight value.

v_{ij}^t - Current velocity of the ith particle in iteration t. (component j of the dimension D).

c_1, $c_2=$ 2- Acceleration constants.

$pBest_{ij}$ – Local (personal) best solution found by the ith particle. (component j of the dimension D).

$gBest_j$ - Best solution found in a population. (component j of the dimension D).

x_{ij}^t - Current position of the ith particle (component j of the dimension D) in iteration t.

$Rand$ – Pseudo random number, interval $(0, 1)$.

Finally the linear decreasing inertia weight [2,4] is used. The dynamic inertia weight is meant to slow the particles over time thus to improve the local search capability in the later phase of the optimization. The inertia weight has two control parameters w_{start} and w_{end}. A new w is given in the iteration by (3), where t stands for current iteration number and n stands for the total number of iterations. The typical values used in this study were $w_{start} = 0.9$ and $w_{end}=0.4$.

$$w = w_{start} - \frac{((w_{start} - w_{end}) \cdot t)}{n} \qquad (3)$$

3   Differential Evolution

Similarly to PSO the DE is a population-based optimization method that works on real-number-coded individuals [5]. For each individual $x_{i,G}$ in the current generation G, DE generates a new trial individual $x'_{i,G}$ by adding the weighted difference between two randomly selected individuals $x_{r1,G}$ and $x_{r2,G}$ to a randomly selected third individual $x_{r3,G}$. The resulting individual $x'_{i,G}$ is crossed-over with the original individual $x_{i,G}$. The fitness of the resulting individual, referred to as a perturbed vector $u_{i,G+1}$, is then compared with the fitness of $x_{i,G}$. If the fitness of $u_{i,G+1}$ is greater than the fitness of $x_{i,G}$, then $x_{i,G}$ is replaced with $u_{i,G+1}$; otherwise, $x_{i,G}$ remains in the population as $x_{i,G+1}$. DE is quite robust, fast, and effective, with global optimization ability. It does

1. Input: $D, G_{max}, NP \geq 4, F \in (0,1+), CR \in [0,1]$, and initial bounds: $\vec{x}^{(lo)}, \vec{x}^{(hi)}$.

2. Initialize: $\begin{cases} \forall i \leq NP \wedge \forall j \leq D : x_{i,j,G=0} = x_j^{(lo)} + rand_j[0,1] \bullet \left(x_j^{(hi)} - x_j^{(lo)} \right) \\ i = \{1,2,...,NP\}, \ j = \{1,2,...,D\}, \ G = 0, \ rand_j[0,1] \in [0,1] \end{cases}$

$\begin{bmatrix} \text{3. While } G < G_{max} \\ \\ \begin{bmatrix} \text{4. Mutate and recombine:} \\ \qquad 4.1 \quad r_1, r_2, r_3 \in \{1,2,....,NP\}, \text{ randomly selected, except: } r_1 \neq r_2 \neq r_3 \neq i \\ \qquad 4.2 \quad j_{rand} \in \{1,2,...,D\}, \text{ randomly selected once each } i \\ \forall i \leq NP \begin{cases} 4.3 \ \ \forall j \leq D, u_{j,i,G+1} = \begin{cases} x_{j,r_3,G} + F \cdot (x_{j,r_1,G} - x_{j,r_2,G}) \\ \qquad \text{if } (rand_j[0,1] < CR \vee j = j_{rand}) \\ x_{j,i,G} \text{ otherwise} \end{cases} \\ \text{5. Select} \\ \vec{x}_{i,G+1} = \begin{cases} \vec{u}_{i,G+1} & \text{if } f(\vec{u}_{i,G+1}) \leq f(\vec{x}_{i,G}) \\ \vec{x}_{i,G} & \text{otherwise} \end{cases} \end{cases} \\ G = G + 1 \end{bmatrix} \end{bmatrix}$

Fig. 1. DE schematic

not require the objective function to be differentiable, and it works well even with noisy and time-dependent objective functions. Please refer to [5,6] for the detailed description of the used DE/rand/1/bin strategy (4) as well as for the complete description of all other strategies.

$$u_{i,G+1} = x_{r1,G} + F \cdot (x_{r2,G} - x_{r3,G}) \tag{4}$$

The full schematic of DE algorithm is given in Fig. 1.

4   Chaotic Maps

In this section four discrete dissipative chaotic systems (maps) are described. These four chaotic maps were used as CPRNGs for the velocity calculation in PSO (See (2)). The choice was based on previous research [10–12].

4.1   Lozi Chaotic Map

The Lozi map is a simple discrete two-dimensional chaotic map. The map equations are given in (5). The typical parameter values are: a = 1.7 and b = 0.5 with respect to [20]. For these values, the system exhibits typical chaotic behavior and with this parameter setting it is used in the most research papers and other literature sources. The x,y plot of Lozi map with the typical setting is depicted in Fig. 2.

$$\begin{aligned} X_{n+1} &= 1 - a\,|X_n| + bY_n \\ Y_{n+1} &= X_n \end{aligned} \tag{5}$$

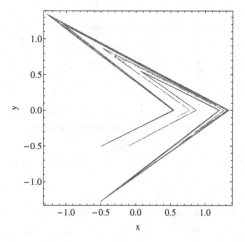

Fig. 2. x,y plot of Lozi map

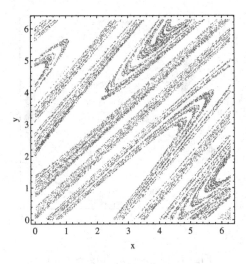

Fig. 3. x,y plot of Dissipative standard map

4.2 Dissipative Standard Map

The Dissipative standard map is a two-dimensional chaotic map [11]. The parameters used in this work are $b = 0.6$ and $k = 8.8$ based on previous experiments [15,16] and suggestions in literature [20]. The x,y plot of Dissipative standard map is given in Fig. 3. The map equations are given in (6).

$$X_{n+1} = X_n + Y_{n+1}(mod2\pi)$$
$$Y_{n+1} = bY_n + k\sin X_n(mod2\pi) \qquad (6)$$

4.3 Burgers Chaotic Map

The Burgers map (See Fig. 4) is a discretization of a pair of coupled differential equations The map equations are given in (7) with control parameters $a = 0.75$ and $b = 1.75$ as suggested in [20].

$$X_{n+1} = aX_n - Y_n^2$$
$$Y_{n+1} = bY_n + X_nY_n \qquad (7)$$

4.4 Tinkerbell Map

The Tinkerbell map is a two-dimensional complex discrete-time dynamical system given by (8) with following control parameters: $a = 0.9$, $b = -0.6$, $c = 2$ and $d = 0.5$ [20]. The x,y plot of the Tinkerbell map is given in Fig. 5.

$$X_{n+1} = X_n^2 - Y_n^2 + aX_n + bY_n$$
$$Y_{n+1} = 2X_nY_n + cX_n + dY_n \qquad (8)$$

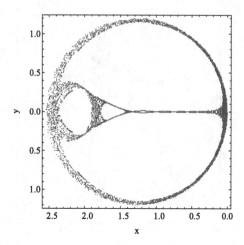

Fig. 4. x,y plot of Burgers map

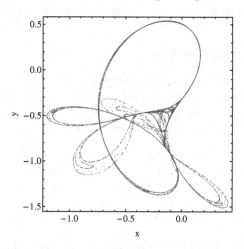

Fig. 5. x,y plot of Tinkerbell map

5   MC-PSO/DE Hybrid with Repulsive Strategy

The hybrid method proposed in this paper is mostly based on the PSO. In the original MC-PSO [15,16] four different velocity calculation formulas are defined. Afterwards each particle is randomly assigned one of the pre-defined formulas in each iteration. The particle can either: stay in its current position, follow randomly chosen particle, follow its own *pBest* or follow the *gBest*. The probability of selection of particular behavior is given by three numbers b_1, b_2 and b_3. These numbers represent border values for different behavior rules and they follow the pattern: $b_1 < b_2 < b_3$. During the calculation of new velocity for each particle a random number r is generated from the interval <0, 1> and it determines the particular behavior rule to apply. For further details (including full pseudocode of the original MC-PSO) please refer to [15].

For the purposes of hybridization [17] two changes were introduced into the original MC-PSO. Firstly the DE/rand/1/bin is performed on stationary particles. Secondly to prevent fast premature convergence the *gBest* is used as a repulsive point. The repulsive strategy was firstly introduced in [21] and it was implemented in the hybrid method [17] in such manner that the *gBest* is repulsing the particles instead of attracting them (See (12)).

For clarity the selection process of new velocity calculation formula and the DE implementation can be described as follows:

During the new velocity and position calculation a random number r is generated:

If $r < b_1$ DE/rand/1/bin is performed for the particle and the new velocity of particle is given by (9):

$$v(t + 1) = 0 \tag{9}$$

If $b_1 < r < b_2$ the new velocity of particle is given by (10):

$$v(t + 1) = w \cdot v(t) + c \cdot Rand \cdot (x_r(t) - x(t)) \tag{10}$$

d If $b_2 < r < b_3$ the new velocity of particle is given by (11):

$$v(t + 1) = w \cdot v(t) + c \cdot Rand \cdot (pBest - x(t)) \tag{11}$$

If $b_3 < r$ the new velocity of particle is given by (12):

$$v(t + 1) = w \cdot v(t) - c \cdot Rand \cdot (gBest - x(t)) \tag{12}$$

Where $x_r(t)$ is the position of randomly chosen particle and $c = 2$.

The chaotic PRNG is used in this paper to generate the random number r and the *Rand* number for Eqs. (10–12) for all other purposes a canonical PRNG is used.

6   Experiment

In this study the performance of the MC-PSO/DE with four different chaotic PRNGs was tested on the IEEE CEC 2013 benchmark set [15] for dimension setting $(dim) = 10$. According to the benchmark rules 51 separate runs were performed for each algorithm and the maximum number of cost function evaluations (CFE) was set to 100000. The population size was set to 40. The border values for MC-PSO were set to following values: $b_1 = 0.5$, $b_2 = 0.7$ and $b_3 = 0.95$. Several tuning experiments were performed to select the combination of border values for general use. It may be possible to achieve better performance on a single problem by tuning these values further.

Other controlling parameters of the PSO and DE were set to typical values as follows:

For PSO:

$c_1, c_2 = 2$; $w_{start}= 0.9$; $w_{end}= 0.4$; $v_{max}= 0.2$;

For DE:

$CR = 0.9$; $F = 0.5$;

These typical settings are based on literature [1–6].

The mean results of canonical MC-PSO/DE and four different chaotic PRNGs (Noted Lozi, Dissipative, Burgers and Tinkerbell) are compared in Table 1 alongside with the state-of art representative for CEC 13 Benchmark the fk-PSO [19]. Only significantly best results are given in bold numbers.

Furthermore as an example the mean history of the best found solution during the optimization in given in Fig. 6.

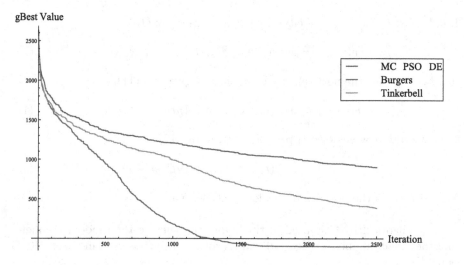

Fig. 6. Mean best value history comparison – f_{22}

In the Table 1 the benchmark functions are divided into unimodal (noted with ^{u}), basic multimodal (noted with ^{m}) and composite functions (noted with ^{c}). The original canonical MC-PSO/DE [17] shows very good performance in many cases and the performance is comparable with the fk-PSO. However it is also clear that by implementing various chaotic PRNGs it is possible to improve the performance of the method significantly in many cases. This is depicted in Fig. 6 where the performance of canonical version and version with PRNG based on Burgers map and Tinkerbell map are compared in the case of f_{22}.

In many other cases the performance of the canonical method seems to be significantly improved when the chaotic PRNG was applied; most notably f_4, f_{11}, f_{14}, f_{15}, f_{22} and f_{23}.

Table 1. Mean results comparison, $dim = 10$, max. CFE $= 100000$

$f(x)$	f_{min}	fk-PSO	MC-PSO-DE	Lozi	Dissipative	Burgers	Tinkerbell
f_1^u	-1400	-1.40E+03	-1.40E+03	-1.40E+03	-1.40E+03	-1.40E+03	-1.40E+03
f_2^u	-1300	1.43E+05	**2.56E+03**	4.38E+04	1.84E+04	1.39E+04	2.62E+04
f_3^u	-1200	6.74E+05	**-1.17E+03**	3.42E+06	1.27E+05	2.44E+04	1.69E+05
f_4^u	-1100	-6.84E+02	-9.28E+02	-6.75E+02	**-1.01E+03**	-6.27E+02	-5.07E+02
f_5^u	-1000	-1.00E+03	-1.00E+03	-1.00E+03	-1.00E+03	-1.00E+03	-1.00E+03
f_6^m	-900	-8.97E+02	-8.97E+02	-8.94E+02	-8.94E+02	-8.97E+02	-8.96E+02
f_7^m	-800	**-7.98E+02**	-8.00E+02	-7.99E+02	-8.00E+02	-8.00E+02	-8.00E+02
f_8^m	-700	-6.80E+02	-6.80E+02	-6.80E+02	-6.80E+02	-6.80E+02	-6.80E+02
f_9^m	-600	-5.97E+02	-5.97E+02	-5.98E+02	-5.99E+02	-5.99E+02	-5.98E+02
f_{10}^m	-500	-4.99E+02	-5.00E+02	-5.00E+02	-5.00E+02	-5.00E+02	-5.00E+02
f_{11}^m	-400	-4.00E+02	-3.90E+02	-3.97E+02	-3.96E+02	-3.99E+02	-3.98E+02
f_{12}^m	-300	-2.93E+02	-2.89E+02	-2.96E+02	-2.95E+02	-2.97E+02	-2.98E+02
f_{13}^m	-200	-1.89E+02	-1.87E+02	-1.95E+02	-1.94E+02	-1.96E+02	**-1.96E+02**
f_{14}^m	-100	-6.22E+01	9.09E+02	7.30E+02	8.52E+02	**-9.77E+01**	3.22E+02
f_{15}^m	100	5.54E+02	1.07E+03	8.75E+02	9.74E+02	**3.67E+02**	1.04E+03
f_{16}^m	200	2.00E+02	2.01E+02	2.01E+02	2.01E+02	2.01E+02	2.01E+02
f_{17}^m	300	**3.11E+02**	3.29E+02	3.24E+02	3.25E+02	3.27E+02	3.27E+02
f_{18}^m	400	4.16E+02	4.32E+02	4.25E+02	4.27E+02	4.32E+02	4.30E+02
f_{19}^m	500	5.01E+02	5.01E+02	5.01E+02	5.01E+02	5.01E+02	5.01E+02
f_{20}^m	600	6.03E+02	6.03E+02	6.03E+02	6.03E+02	6.03E+02	6.02E+02
f_{21}^c	700	1.08E+03	1.10E+03	1.10E+03	1.10E+03	1.10E+03	1.10E+03
f_{22}^c	800	9.22E+02	1.90E+03	1.52E+03	1.82E+03	8.23E+02	**8.23E+02**
f_{23}^c	900	1.42E+03	2.07E+03	1.39E+03	1.70E+03	**9.60E+02**	9.62E+02
f_{24}^c	1000	1.20E+03	1.20E+03	1.20E+03	1.20E+03	1.20E+03	1.20E+03
f_{25}^c	1100	1.31E+03	1.30E+03	1.30E+03	1.30E+03	1.30E+03	1.30E+03
f_{26}^c	1200	1.39E+03	1.32E+03	1.32E+03	1.33E+03	1.31E+03	1.33E+03
f_{27}^c	1300	1.67E+03	1.61E+03	1.62E+03	1.62E+03	1.61E+03	1.61E+03
f_{28}^c	1400	1.73E+03	1.69E+03	1.73E+03	1.70E+03	1.69E+03	1.72E+03

It is therefore safe to say that the implementation of chaotic sequences may not be only beneficial for basic ECTs but also for hybrid methods such as the presented MC-PSO/DE with chaotic PRNG. Also is it shown that the presented chaos enhanced hybrid method can achieve very good results and in some cases excellent performance, in comparison with another state-of-art PSO based method. The proposed hybrid method enhanced with CPRNG based on Burgers chaotic map managed to obtain better or similar results with the fk-PSO in total of 22 from 28 functions.

7   Conclusion

In this study a previously proposed hybrid method called MC-PSO/DE has been enhanced with four different chaotic pseudo-random number generators. Motivation came from previous successful experiments with chaos enhanced metaheuristics. The goal was to investigate whether the chaotic PRNGs can improve the performance of complex hybrid method. As the results indicate it seems that the chaotic sequences may be beneficial for the method in many cases. However the selection of particular chaotic system seems very problem-dependant and this issue will be addressed in further studies. Various adaptive approaches may be designed to resolve the problem of selection among the chaotic systems. The chaotic sequences and their mutual influence with ECTs will also remain the focus of future research. This work should encourage more researchers to use the implementation of chaotic sequences into various ECTs as it is easily usable plug-in method that often brings surprisingly good results as has been shown in this and also previous studies. In the near future the proposed method will be tested for waste transportation network problem solving [22–24].

References

1. Kennedy, J., Eberhart, R.: Particle swarm optimization. In: Proceedings of the IEEE International Conference on Neural Networks, pp. 1942–1948 (1995)
2. Shi, Y., Eberhart, R.: A modified particle swarm optimizer. In: Proceedings of the IEEE International Conference on Evolutionary Computation (IEEE World Congress on Computational Intelligence), pp. 69–73. I. S (1998)
3. Kennedy, J.: The particle swarm: social adaptation of knowledge. In: Proceedings of the IEEE International Conference on Evolutionary Computation, pp. 303–308 (1997)
4. Nickabadi, A., Ebadzadeh, M.M., Safabakhsh, R.: A novel particle swarm optimization algorithm with adaptive inertia weight. Appl. Soft Comput. $11(4)$, 3658–3670 (2011). ISSN 1568–4946
5. Price, K.V.: An introduction to differential evolution. In: Corne, D., Dorigo, M., Glover, F. (eds.) New Ideas in Optimization, pp. 79–108. McGraw-Hill Ltd, Maidenhead (1999)
6. Price, K.V., Storn, R.M., Lampinen, J.A.: Differential Evolution - A Practical Approach to Global Optimization. Natural Computing Series. Springer, Heidelberg (2005)
7. Caponetto, R., Fortuna, L., Fazzino, S., Xibilia, M.G.: Chaotic sequences to improve the per formance of evolutionary algorithms. IEEE Trans. Evol. Comput. $7(3)$, 289–304 (2003)
8. Alatas, B., Akin, E., Ozer, B.A.: Chaos embedded particle swarm optimization algorithms. Chaos, Solitons Fractals $40(4)$, 1715–1734 (2009). ISSN 0960–0779
9. Araujo, E., Coelho, L.: Particle swarm approaches using Lozi map chaotic sequences to fuzzy modelling of an experimental thermalvacuum system. Appl. Soft Comput. $8(4)$, 1354–1364 (2008)
10. Senkerik, R., Pluhacek, M., Kominkova Oplatkova, Z., Davendra, D., Zelinka, I.: Investigation on the differential evolution driven by selected six chaotic systems in the task of reactor geometry optimization. In: 2013 IEEE Congress on Evolutionary Computation (CEC), pp. 3087–3094, 20–23, June 2013

11. Pluhacek, M., Senkerik, R., Davendra, D., Oplatkova, Z.K., Zelinka, I.: On the behavior and performance of chaos driven PSO algorithm with inertia weight. Comput. Math. Appl. **66**, 122–134 (2013)
12. Pluhacek, M., Senkerik, R., Zelinka, I.: Particle swarm optimization algorithm driven by multichaotic number generator. Soft. Comput. **18**, 631–639 (2014)
13. Pant, M., Thangaraj, R., Grosan, C., Abraham, A.: Hybrid differential evolution - particle swarm optimization algorithm for solving global optimization problems. In: Third International Conference on Digital Information Management, ICDIM 2008, pp. 18–24, 13–16, November 2008
14. Xiaobing, Y., Cao, J., Shan, H., Zhu, L., Guo, J.: An adaptive hybrid algorithm based on particle swarm optimization and differential evolution for global optimization. The Sci. World J., vol. 2014, Article ID 215472, p. 16 (2014). doi:10. 1155/2014/215472
15. Pluhacek, M., Senkerik, R., Zelinka, I.: Multiple choice strategy – a novel approach for particle swarm optimization – preliminary study. In: Rutkowski, L., Korytkowski, M., Scherer, R., Tadeusiewicz, R., Zadeh, L.A., Zurada, J.M. (eds.) ICAISC 2013, Part II. LNCS, vol. 7895, pp. 36–45. Springer, Heidelberg (2013)
16. Pluhacek, M., Senkerik, R., Zelinka, I.: Investigation on the performance of a new multiple choice strategy for PSO Algorithm in the task of large scale optimization problems. In: 2013 IEEE Congress on Evolutionary Computation (CEC), pp. 2007–2011, 20–23 June 2013
17. Pluhacek, M., Senkerik, R., Zelinka, I., Davendra, D.: MC-PSO/DE hybrid with repulsive strategy – initial study. In: Onieva, E., Santos, I., Osaba, E., Quintian, H., Corchado, E. (eds.) HAIS 2015. LNCS, vol. 9121, pp. 213–220. Springer, Heidelberg (2015)
18. Liang, J.J., Qu, B.-Y., Suganthan, P.N., Hernendez-Diaz, A.G.: Problem Definitions and Evaluation Criteria for the CEC 2013 Special Session and Competition on Real-Parameter Optimization, Technical Report 201212. Zhengzhou University, Zhengzhou China and Technical Report, Nanyang Technological University, Singapore, Computational Intelligence Laboratory (2013)
19. Nepomuceno, F., Engelbrecht, A.: A self-adaptive heterogeneous pso for real-parameter optimization. In: Proceedings of the IEEE International Conference on Evolutionary Computation (2013)
20. Sprott, J.C.: Chaos and Time-Series Analysis. Oxford University Press, Oxford (2003)
21. Riget, J.: Vestterstrom J S: A Diversity-guided particle swarm optimizer - the ARPSO. University of Aarhus, Denmark, Technical report, EVAlife, Department of Computer Science (2002)
22. Pavlas, M., Nevrl, V., Popela, P., omplk, R.: Heuristic for generation of waste transportation test networks. In: 21st International Conference on Soft Computing, MENDEL 2015, Brno, Czech Republic, pp. 189–194, 23–25 June 2015
23. Roupec, J., Popela, P., Hrabec, D., Novotn, J., Olstad, A., Haugen, K.: Hybrid algorithm for network design problem with uncertain demands. In: Proceedings of the World Congress on Engineering and Computer Science, WCECS 2013. Lecture Notes in Engineering and Computer Science, vol. 1, pp. 554–559 (2013)
24. Hrabec, D., Popela, P., Roupec, J., Mazal, J., Stodola, P.: Two-stage stochastic programming for transportation network design problem. In: Matoušek, R. (ed.) Mendel 2015. Advances in Intelligent Systems and Computing, vol. 378, pp. 17–25. Springer, Switzerland (2015)

The Method of the Evolutionary Designing the Elastic Controller Structure

Andrzej Przybył[1], Krystian Łapa[1(✉)], Jacek Szczypta[1], and Lipo Wang[2]

[1] Institute of Computational Intelligence,
Częstochowa University of Technology, Częstochowa, Poland
{andrzej.przybyl,krystian.lapa,jacek.szczypta}@iisi.pcz.pl
[2] School of Electrical and Electronic Engineering,
Nanyang Technological University, Central Area, Singapore
elpwang@ntu.edu.sg

Abstract. In the paper a method for the design of the control system is presented. With the use of an evolutionary methods an initial structure of the controller is adjusted such that the designed controller fulfills the control objective in the best way possible. This elastic structure consists of basic functional blocks and filters. The proposed method is able to find such the structure and parameters of the controller, which make it immune to measurement noise that could disrupt the work of the control system. As a result, the process of controller design is performed easier and faster.

Keywords: Evolutionary optimization · Elastic controller structure · PID algorithm · Structure selection · Filter selection

1 Introduction

The problem of designing control systems is well known in science [1]. This is due to the fact that the quality of work of individual parts or even of entire machines mainly depends on the characteristics of the used controller. It should be noted that in this context, the design of the control system is not only the selection of parameters for a known controller structure. On the contrary, it is a much broader concept. Namely, the design of the control system consists of the following elements:

- indication of measurable signals, which can be used in a feedback loop,
- selection of the controller structure,
- tuning of controller parameters,
- implementation in target hardware platform with fulfillment of requirements of real-time work.

Usually these steps are performed in the presented order. If this approach does not lead to achieve the desired effect (that is, to obtain a satisfactory quality of work), then the whole procedure must be repeated starting from the second

© Springer International Publishing Switzerland 2016
L. Rutkowski et al. (Eds.): ICAISC 2016, Part I, LNAI 9692, pp. 476–492, 2016.
DOI: 10.1007/978-3-319-39378-0_41

step. The controller structure needs to be modified (or completely changed) and the tuning procedure must be carried out starting from the beginning.

In the literature there are known controller structures which are typically used, they are: controllers structures based on the combination of linear correction terms, e.g. PID controllers (optionally with gain scheduling algorithm, with feed-forward path or with additional low-pass filters [2], state feedback controllers, nonlinear controllers based on computational intelligence and hybrid controllers, in which are combined approaches from other groups. However, in practice PID controllers are used the most often [1]. It is a result of widespread knowledge of how they work and their relatively simple implementation in a microprocessor-based control systems.

It is important to point out that the control system design process is difficult and time consuming. Sometimes, in order to obtain a better quality of control, an engineer, basing on his experience, has to modify the controller structure. Modification of the controller structure, usually performed by means of trial and error method, causes the process of controller design much more difficult.

Among the experimental methods for the design of control systems, methods based on artificial intelligence [17,20–22,25–28,31,38–43,56,63,64] and in particular the methods of evolution [32–34] are becoming more common. The effectiveness of these methods is proven by their diversity. They include, among others, fuzzy systems [8–14,36,53,54], optimization methods [5–7,19,22–24,29,30,37,44–52], decision trees [3,4] and can be used in wide area of problems [15,16,18,57–62,65,67–74]. These methods make the design of the control system easier. However, in many cases the obtained controller is sensitive to interference, which commonly occurs in the real-world conditions. The measurement noise and limited resolution of the digital word used to carry information about the measured values can lead to unstable controller operation.

In this paper it is proposed the use of low-pass finite-impulse-response filters (FIR) with programmable characteristics for each of the measurement signals used in the feedback loop. These filters are designed to suppress interference that could disrupt the work of the control system. So, it is possible to find the structure and parameters of the controller, which makes it immune to this type of interference. We suggest the use of an universal initial structure which in the process of evolution will be adjusted in a way that the designed controller fulfills the control objective in the best way possible. This elastic structure consists of basic functional blocks and filters, both with programmable connections and parameters. Due to this approach the design of the control system can be regarded as one continuous process, unlike the commonly used method of trial and error. As a result, the process of controller design is performed easier and faster. Details of the proposed method are described in Sect. 3.

This paper is organized into 5 sections. Section 2 contains a description of the extended PID controller structure, while Sect. 3 shows the proposed evolutionary algorithm used to design control system. Simulation results are presented in Sect. 4. Conclusions are drawn in Sect. 5.

2 Description of Proposed PID Controller

Proposed controller is based on elastic structure, which among the others, depends from number of controller input signals fb_i, $i = 1, ..., FB$, FB stands for number of feedback signals (see Fig. 1). In proposed structure assumptions that fb_1 stands for desired value of fb_2 and the rest of the feedback signals stand for additional measurable signals were made. Moreover, the control blocks (CB) and finite impulse response filters (FIR) can be dynamically switched off or on by changing controller parameters. Due to that, the design of the controller should not only consider selecting the real parameters of the controller but also integer parameters encoding its structure.

Proposed controller (see Fig. 1) uses typical P, I and D elements (see. respectively Fig. 2(a), (b) and (c)). These elements can be part of typical control block CB (see Fig. 2(d)). The output value of typical control block takes the following form:

$$u(t) = K^P e(t) + K^I \int_0^t e(t)\, dt + K^D \frac{de(t)}{dt}, \tag{1}$$

where K^P, K^I and K^D stand respectively for parameters of P, I and D elements of control block. The proposed CB structure allows for additional reduction of P, I, D elements by using integer values C^P, C^I, C^D and reduction of whole control block by integer value C^{CB}. The reduction takes place if the integer values are set to 0. The output of the proposed CB takes the following form:

$$u(t) = \begin{cases} C^P \cdot K^P e(t) + C^I \cdot K^I \int_0^t e(t)\, dt + C^D \cdot K^D \frac{de(t)}{dt} & \text{for } C^{CB} = 1 \\ e(t) & \text{for } C^{CB} = 0 \end{cases}. \tag{2}$$

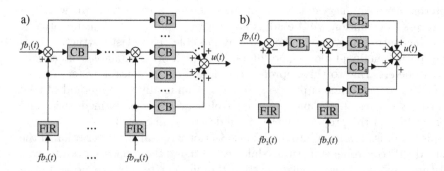

Fig. 1. Proposed controller structure: (a) with any number of FB feedback signals, (b) with 3 feedback signals.

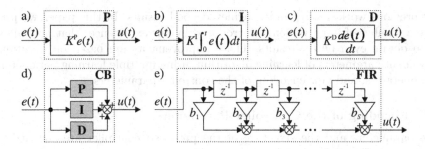

Fig. 2. Typical structure of: (a) element P, (b) element I, (c) element D, (d) control block CB, (e) filter FIR, z^{-1} stands for values from previous time step.

The proposed FIR filters used in controller are based on typical FIR filters (see Fig. 2(e)) with using an additional integer parameter C^F to reduction of the filter (in case of reduction the output of the filter is exact to input of the filter). Thus, the output of the proposed filter takes the following form:

$$u(t) = \begin{cases} \sum_{s=1}^{S} b_s e(t-s-1) \text{ for } C^F = 1 \\ e(t) \qquad\qquad \text{for } C^F = 0 \end{cases} \tag{3}$$

where $e(t)$ stands for input value, $e(t-i)$ stands for input value from $t-i$ time step, b_s stands for weights of filter, $s = 1, ..., S$, S stands for length of the filter (S has to be an odd number). The weights of the filter are calculated using filter parameters: transition frequency ft and lenght of the filter S, which are a part of the elastic structure of the controller and should be selected by learning algorithm as well. The weights values b_s are calculated as follows:

$$b_s = \begin{cases} \frac{\sin\left(2\pi ft\left|s-\frac{1}{2}(S-1)\right|\right)}{\pi\left|s-\frac{1}{2}(S-1)\right|} \text{ for } s = \frac{1}{2}(S-1) \\ 2\,ft \qquad\qquad \text{for } s \neq \frac{1}{2}(S-1) \end{cases} \tag{4}$$

The proposed controller structure is characterized by the following advantages: **(a)** it is able to process any number of feedback signals fb_i, **(b)** it uses cascade control blocks configuration which allows us to obtain good accuracy of the controller, **(c)** the structure is dynamic, each CB block, CB block elements (P,I,D) and filter FR can be switched off or on, **(d)** it has great capabilities of learning due to many selectable parameters **(e)** it is able to minimize the impact of feedback signals noises by use of the FIR filters.

3   Description of the Proposed Algorithm

A new hybrid evolutionary algorithm is presented to select the proposed controller parameters and parameters encoding controller structure. It is based on an ensemble of genetic algorithm (to select controller structure) and evolutionary strategy (to select controller parameters). This ensemble was proposed in our previous work [33,67] and it achieved good results. In this paper we propose a number of improvements (introduced by our experience) that may allow us to obtain even better results. These improvements are based on iteration-dependent parameters of learning algorithm, using multiple learning parameters and operators, and new encoding of the controller parameters.

3.1 Encoding of the Controller Parameters

The parameters and the structure of the proposed controller are encoded in chromosome $\mathbf{X}_{ch}$ defined as follows:

$$\mathbf{X}_{ch} = \left\{ \mathbf{X}_{ch}^{\mathrm{par}}, \mathbf{X}_{ch}^{\mathrm{str}} \right\}, \tag{5}$$

where part $\mathbf{X}_{ch}^{\mathrm{par}}$ encodes the real parameters of the controller and part $\mathbf{X}_{ch}^{\mathrm{str}}$ encodes integer parameters of the controller. The part $\mathbf{X}_{ch}^{\mathrm{par}}$ is defined as follows:

$$\mathbf{X}_{ch}^{\mathrm{par}} = \left\{ \begin{matrix} K_1^{\mathrm{P}}, K_1^{\mathrm{I}}, K_1^{\mathrm{D}}, ..., K_M^{\mathrm{P}}, K_M^{\mathrm{I}}, K_M^{\mathrm{D}}, \\ ft_1, ..., ft_R \end{matrix} \right\} = \left\{ X_{ch,1}^{\mathrm{par}}, ..., X_{ch,L^{\mathrm{par}}}^{\mathrm{par}} \right\}, \tag{6}$$

where $K_m^{\mathrm{P}} \in [0, 20], K_m^{\mathrm{I}} \in [0, 50], K_m^{\mathrm{D}} \in [0, 5]$ stand for CB P, I, D parameters, $m = 1, ..., M$, M stands for number of CB blocks, $ft_r \in [0.1, 0.5]$ stands for transition frequency, $r = 1, ..., R$, R stands for number of filters, $L^{\mathrm{par}} = 3M + R$ stands for number of genes in part $\mathbf{X}_{ch}^{\mathrm{par}}$. The part $\mathbf{X}_{ch}^{\mathrm{str}}$ is defined as follows:

$$\mathbf{X}_{ch}^{\mathrm{str}} = \left\{ \begin{matrix} C_1^{\mathrm{P}}, C_1^{\mathrm{I}}, C_1^{\mathrm{D}}, ..., C_M^{\mathrm{P}}, C_M^{\mathrm{I}}, C_M^{\mathrm{D}}, \\ C_1^{\mathrm{CB}}, ..., C_M^{\mathrm{CB}}, C_1^{\mathrm{F}}, ..., C_R^{\mathrm{F}} \\ F_1, ..., F_R \end{matrix} \right\} = \left\{ X_{ch,1}^{\mathrm{str}}, ..., X_{ch,L^{\mathrm{str}}}^{\mathrm{str}} \right\}, \tag{7}$$

where $C_m^{\mathrm{P}} \in \{0, 1\}, C_m^{\mathrm{I}} \in \{0, 1\}, C_m^{\mathrm{D}} \in \{0, 1\}$ stand for activation of CB PID elements (values equal to 1 stands for active element), $C_m^{\mathrm{CB}} \in \{0, 1\}$ stands for activation of m-th control block, $C_r^{\mathrm{F}} \in \{0, 1\}$ stands for activation of r-th filter (values equal to 1 stands for active element), $F_r \in \{0, ..., 9\}$ stands for lenght of the filter (real lenght of the filter is calculated as $S_r = 5 + 2F_r$), $L^{\mathrm{str}} = 4M + 2R$ stands for number of genes in part $\mathbf{X}_{ch}^{\mathrm{str}}$.

3.2 Proposed Algorithm Description

Proposed algorithm is based on new iteration-dependent mutation and crossover from genetic algorithm and evolutionary strategy. The algorithm works according to the following steps:

- **Step 1. Initialization.** In this step the value *iteration* is set to 0. Next the N individuals (each individual $\mathbf{X}_{ch}$ represents controller encoded by chromosome (5)) are randomly initialized and stored in population $\mathbf{P}$. The initialization of individuals' genes is realized as follows:

$$\begin{cases} X_{ch,g}^{\mathrm{par}} = U^{\mathrm{g}} \left(\underline{X}_{ch,g}^{\mathrm{par}}, \overline{X}_{ch,g}^{\mathrm{par}} \right) \\ X_{ch,h}^{\mathrm{str}} = U^{\mathrm{h}} \left(\underline{X}_{ch,h}^{\mathrm{str}}, \overline{X}_{ch,h}^{\mathrm{str}} \right) \end{cases}, \tag{8}$$

where $U^g(a, b)$ returns a random real value from the range $[a, b]$. $\underline{X}^{par}_{ch,g}$ and $\overline{X}^{par}_{ch,g}$ stand respectively for minims and maxims values of genes $X^{par}_{ch,g}$, $g = 1, ..., L^{par}$, $U^h(a, b)$ returns random integer value from the range $[a, b]$. $\underline{X}^{str}_{ch,h}$ and $\overline{X}^{str}_{ch,h}$ stand respectively for minims and maxims values of genes $X^{str}_{ch,h}$, $h = 1, ..., L^{str}$.

- **Step 2. Evaluation.** In this step each individual is evaluated by fitness function defined as follows:

$$\text{ff}(\mathbf{X}_{ch}) = \sum_{f=1}^{F} w_f \cdot \text{ffcom}_f(\mathbf{X}_{ch}), \tag{9}$$

where $\text{ffcom}_f(\mathbf{X}_{ch})$ stands for fitness function components which depend from simulation problem (see Sect. 4.1), w_f stands for weights of fitness function components, $f = 1, ..., F$, F stands for number of fitness function components.

- **Step 3. Probabilities calculation.** In this step the value *iteration* is incremented. Next, the dynamic parameters for mutation and crossover are calculated as follows:

$$\begin{cases} p_1 = 0.2 + 0.2 \cdot \alpha \\ p_2 = 0.2 \cdot \alpha \\ p_3 = 0.5 \cdot \alpha \\ p_4 = 0.1 \cdot \alpha \\ p_5 = 0.2 \cdot \alpha \cdot \alpha \end{cases}, \tag{10}$$

where p_1 stands for gene mutation probability, p_2 stands for gene mutation range, p_3 stands for chance of select gene directly from one of parents while crossover, p_4 stands for integer gene mutation probability (this value is small due to higher impact on the system), p_5 stands for chance of assign random integer value into integer gene (all parameters p were estimated experimentally on the basis of experience of authors), α stands for iteration-dependent value calculated as:

$$\alpha = 1 - \frac{iteration}{iteration^{max}}. \tag{11}$$

where $iteration^{max}$ stands for maximum number of iteration of the algorithm.

- **Step 4. Reproduction.** In this step a N new individuals are created and stored in population $\mathbf{P}'$. For each individual the condition $U^g(0, 1) < p_c$ is checked (where p_c stands for crossover probability). If this condition is met, new individual is created as a result of crossover between two individuals selected by the roulette wheel method [55] from population $\mathbf{P}$. Otherwise, the individual is created as a result of cloning and mutating of one individual selected by the roulette wheel method [55] from population $\mathbf{P}$. The mutation is performed according to Eq. (13) described in detail in Step 5. The genes obtained from crossover are calculated as:

$$
\begin{cases}
X_{ch,g}^{\mathrm{par}} =
\begin{cases}
X_{ch,g}^{\mathrm{A,par}} & \text{for } U^{\mathrm{g}}(0,1) < 0.5 \text{ and } U^{\mathrm{g}}(0,1) < p_3 \\
X_{ch,g}^{\mathrm{B,par}} & \text{for } U^{\mathrm{g}}(0,1) \geq 0.5 \text{ and } U^{\mathrm{g}}(0,1) < p_3 \\
X_{ch,g}^{\mathrm{A,par}} + U^{\mathrm{g}}(0,1) \cdot \left(X_{ch,g}^{\mathrm{B,par}} - X_{ch,g}^{\mathrm{A,par}} \right) & \text{for } U^{\mathrm{g}}(0,1) \geq p_3
\end{cases} \\
X_{ch,h}^{\mathrm{str}} =
\begin{cases}
X_{ch,h}^{\mathrm{A,str}} & \text{for } U^{\mathrm{g}}(0,1) < 0.5 \text{ and } U^{\mathrm{g}}(0,1) < p_3 \\
X_{ch,h}^{\mathrm{B,str}} & \text{for } U^{\mathrm{g}}(0,1) \geq 0.5 \text{ and } U^{\mathrm{g}}(0,1) < p_3 \\
X_{ch,h}^{\mathrm{A,str}} + U^{h}\left(X_{ch,h}^{\mathrm{A,str}}, X_{ch,h}^{\mathrm{B,str}} \right) & \text{for } U^{\mathrm{g}}(0,1) \geq p_3
\end{cases}
\end{cases}
, \quad (12)
$$

where $X_{ch,*1}^{\mathrm{A},*2}$ and $X_{ch,*}^{\mathrm{B},*}$ stand respectively for genes from the first and second parent, *1 stands for 'par' or 'str', *2 stands for 'g' or 'h'. The purpose of Eq. (12) is to increase chance to select gene values directly from parents or in the other case to select gene values between gene values of parents (if condition $U^{\mathrm{g}}(0,1) \geq p_3$ is met).

– **Step 5. Mutation.** In this step genes of individuals from population $\mathbf{P}'$ are mutated. For each individual the condition $U^{\mathrm{g}}(0,1) < p_m$ is checked (where p_m stands for mutation probability). If this condition is met, genes of the individual are modified as follows:

$$
\begin{cases}
X_{ch,g}^{\mathrm{par}} =
\begin{cases}
X_{ch,g}^{\mathrm{par}} + U^{g}(-1,1) \cdot p_2 \cdot \left(\overline{X}_{ch,g}^{\mathrm{par}} - \underline{X}_{ch,g}^{\mathrm{par}} \right) & \text{for } U^{\mathrm{g}}(0,1) < p_1 \\
X_{ch,g}^{\mathrm{par}} & \text{for } U^{\mathrm{g}}(0,1) \geq p_1
\end{cases} \\
X_{ch,h}^{\mathrm{str}} =
\begin{cases}
X_{ch,h}^{\mathrm{str}} + U^{h}(-1,1) & \text{for } U^{\mathrm{g}}(0,1) < p_4 \\
X_{ch,h}^{\mathrm{str}} & \text{for } U^{\mathrm{g}}(0,1) \geq p_4
\end{cases}
\end{cases}
. \quad (13)
$$

Next, if condition $U^{\mathrm{g}}(0,1) < p_t$ is met (where p_t stands for integer mutation probability, which also depends from the iteration number $p_t = p_o \cdot \alpha$, where p_o stands for integer mutation factor) additional integer mutation is performed:

$$
X_{ch,h}^{\mathrm{str}} =
\begin{cases}
X_{ch,h}^{\mathrm{str}} + U^{h}\left(\underline{X}_{ch,h}^{\mathrm{str}}, \overline{X}_{ch,h}^{\mathrm{str}} \right) & \text{for } U^{\mathrm{g}}(0,1) < p_5 \\
X_{ch,h}^{\mathrm{str}} & \text{for } U^{\mathrm{g}}(0,1) \geq p_5
\end{cases}
. \quad (14)
$$

– **Step 6. Repair.** This step purpose is to repair (cut to specified ranged) gene values of individuals from population $\mathbf{P}'$ which is calculated as follows:

$$
\begin{cases}
X_{ch,g}^{\mathrm{par}} = \min\left(\overline{X}_{ch,g}^{\mathrm{par}}, \max\left(\underline{X}_{ch,g}^{\mathrm{par}}, X_{ch,g}^{\mathrm{par}} \right) \right) \\
X_{ch,h}^{\mathrm{str}} = \min\left(\overline{X}_{ch,h}^{\mathrm{str}}, \max\left(\underline{X}_{ch,h}^{\mathrm{str}}, X_{ch,h}^{\mathrm{str}} \right) \right)
\end{cases}
. \quad (15)
$$

– **Step 7. Evaluation.** In this step all individuals from population $\mathbf{P}'$ are evaluated according to fitness function (9).
– **Step 8. Merging.** This step aim is to select the best N individuals from merged populations $\mathbf{P}$ and $\mathbf{P}'$. Selected individuals replace population $\mathbf{P}$.
– **Step 9. Stopping condition.** In this step the stop condition is checked ($iteration \geq iteration^{\max}$). If this condition is met, algorithm stops and the best individual according to the fitness function value is presented. Otherwise, the algorithm goes back to Step 3.

4 Simulations Results

In our simulations a problem of designing controller structure and tuning parameters for double spring-mass-damp object was considered (see Fig. 3). More details about this model can be found in our previous paper [67]. Object parameters were set as follows: spring constant $k = 10$ N/m, coefficient of friction $\mu = 0.5$, masses $m_1 = m_2 = 0.2$ kg. Initial values of: s^1, v^1, s^2 i v^2 were set to zero, and s^* is a desired position of mass m_1 (see Fig. 3), simulation length T^{all} was set to 10 s, output signal of the controller was limited to the range $u \in (-2, +2)$, quantization resolution for the output signal y of the controller as well as for the position sensor for s^1 and s^2 was set to 8 bit, time step in the simulation was equal to $T = 0.1$ ms, while interval between subsequent controller activations were set to twenty simulation steps, number of model iteration is calculated as $Z = T^{\text{all}}/T$. The feedback signals for the controller was chosen as: $fb_1 = s^*$, $fb_2 = s^1$, $fb_3 = s^2$ ($FB = 3$).

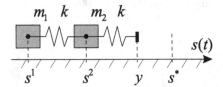

Fig. 3. Simulated spring-mass-damp object.

4.1 Problem Evaluation

For problem under consideration a trapezoidal shape of desired signal s^* was used (see Fig. 4). Moreover, for considered simulation problem, a following fitness function components (9) were used:

- Complexity of the controller:

$$\text{ffcom}_1\left(\mathbf{X}_{ch}\right) = \frac{\sum\limits_{m=1}^{M} \left(\mathbf{X}_{ch}^{\text{str}}\left\{C_m^{\text{P}}\right\} + \mathbf{X}_{ch}^{\text{str}}\left\{C_m^{\text{I}}\right\} + \mathbf{X}_{ch}^{\text{str}}\left\{C_m^{\text{D}}\right\} + \mathbf{X}_{ch}^{\text{str}}\left\{C_m^{\text{CB}}\right\}\right)}{4M}, \quad (16)$$

where notation $\mathbf{X}_{ch}^{\text{str}}\{a\}$ stands for using gene a from chromosome $\mathbf{X}_{ch}$.
- RMSE standing for accuracy of the controlled object:

$$\text{ffcom}_2\left(\mathbf{X_{ch}}\right) = RMSE = \sqrt{\frac{1}{Z} \cdot \sum_{i=1}^{Z} \varepsilon_i^2} = \sqrt{\frac{1}{Z} \cdot \sum_{i=1}^{Z} \left(s_i^* - s_i^1\right)^2}, \quad (17)$$

- Overshooting of the controller:

$$\text{ffcom}_3\left(\mathbf{X_{ch}}\right) = \max_{i=1,\ldots,Z}\left\{s_i^1\right\}. \quad (18)$$

– Oscillations of the output of the controller:

$$\text{ffcom}_4\left(\mathbf{X_{ch}}\right) = \sum_{o=1}^{O-1} \sqrt{|r_o - r_{o+1}|}, \qquad (19)$$

where r_o stands for each local minims and maxims of the output values of the controller (those minims and maxims were selected with ignoring noise influence on the signals), $o = 1, ..., O$, O stands for number of minims and maxims of osculations.

4.2   Simulation Parameters

In the simulations the following values of parameters were set experimentally: fitness function components weights $w_1 = 0.1$, $w_2 = 10$, $w_3 = 0.01$, $w_4 = 0.1$, crossover probability $p_c = 0.75$, mutation probability $p_m = 0.75$, integer mutation factor $p_o = 0.50$, number of algorithm iterations $iteration^{\max} = 1000$, number of individuals in populations $N = 100$.

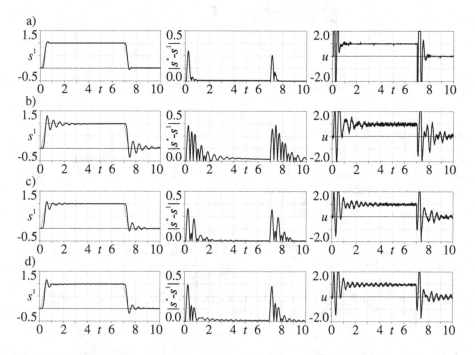

Fig. 4. Best simulations results for: (a) case 0, (b) case 1, (c) case 2, (d) case 3. s^1 stands for position of the mass m_1, $|s^* - s^1|$ stands for difference with desired position of mass m_1 (s^*) and s^1, u stands for output of the controller.

Table 1. Averaged simulation results.

Case	Noise	ff$(\cdot)$	ffcom$_1(\cdot)$ complexity	ffcom$_2(\cdot)$ accuracy	ffcom$_3(\cdot)$ oscilations	ffcom$_4(\cdot)$ over-shoot.	pid$(\cdot)$	fir$(\cdot)$
0	0 %	1.389	0.500	0.057	18.674	1.049	7.500	0.000
1	1 %	3.628	**0.437**	0.162	31.743	1.160	6.550	0.000
2		3.423	0.467	0.153	29.280	**1.137**	7.000	0.700
3		**3.080**	0.502	**0.144**	**13.767**	1.190	7.500	2.000

4.3   Simulation Cases

In the simulations four cases were tested to show the effectiveness of the proposed controller and learning algorithm:

- **Case 0** - case without filters and noise of the feedback signals (to present possibilities of learning algorithm).
- **Case 1** - case without filters and with 1 % of noise of s^1 and s^2 feedback signals (to show how noise of the signals affect the results).
- **Case 2** - case with filters and with 1 % of noise of s^1 and s^2 feedback signals (to show impact of the filters on the results).
- **Case 3** - case with static filters (C^F were set to 1) and with 1 % of noise of s^1 and s^2 feedback signals (to show impact of the filters on the results).

For each case simulations were repeat 100 times and results were averaged.

4.4   Obtained Results

The averaged simulations results are presented in Table 1, the best simulations results are presented in Tables 2, 3, Figs. 4 and 5.

Table 2. The best simulation results (by fitness function value).

Case	Noise	ff$(\cdot)$	ffcom$_1(\cdot)$ complexity	ffcom$_2(\cdot)$ accuracy	ffcom$_3(\cdot)$ oscila-tions	ffcom$_4(\cdot)$ over-shoot.	pid$(\cdot)$	fir$(\cdot)$
0	0 %	1.194	0.467	0.049	15.263	1.038	7.000	0.000
1	1 %	2.438	0.467	0.103	28.572	1.294	7.000	0.000
2		**1.752**	0.667	**0.074**	22.780	1.077	10.000	1.000
3		**1.807**	0.533	**0.076**	21.885	1.157	8.000	2.000

4.5   Simulation Results

Conclusions from the simulation are as follows: **(a)** including noise of feedback signals significantly degrade the performance of controller (see Fig. 4(a) and (b) and ff$(\cdot)$ values in Table 1); **(b)** adding filters allowed us to reduce impact of noise (see Fig. 4(c) and (d) and ff$(\cdot)$ values in Table 1); **(c)** using dynamic reduction

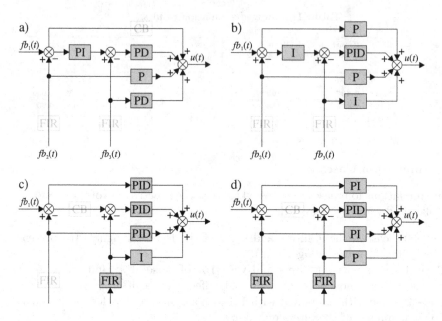

Fig. 5. Best simulations structures obtained for: (a) case 0, (b) case 1, (c) case 2, (d) case 3. Gray rectangles stands for reduced elements of the controller.

of filters in learning process (case 2) led to obtain 0.7 (in average) active filters in the controller, which allowed us to obtain 5.6 % accuracy improvement and 7.8 % oscillations improvement of the system (see Fig. 4(b) and (c) and Table 1); **(d)** using static active filters led to obtain 11.1 % accuracy improvement and 56.6 % oscillations improvement (see Fig. 4(b) and (d) and Table 1); **(e)** obtained structures are simple and the average reduction of controller elements is close to 50 % (see Fig. 5 and Table 3); **(f)** the best obtained accuracy of the controller (see Table 2) without noise of feedback signals is better than accuracy obtained

Table 3. Parameters of controllers obtained for the best simulation results, '-' stands for parameters reduced by the corresponding integer parameters.

Parameters	Values of parameters											
	Case 0			Case 1			Case 2			Case 3		
K_1^P K_1^I K_1^D	2.36	0.03	-	-	0.01	-	-	-	-	-	-	-
K_1^P K_2^I K_2^D	-	-	-	18.57	-	-	12.55	43.97	0.38	15.30	17.87	-
K_1^P K_3^I K_3^D	15.25	-	1.11	7.559	49.94	0.01	6.59	23.67	0.11	10.21	23.80	0.13
K_1^P K_4^I K_4^D	14.08	-	-	7.79	-	-	3.34	23.43	0.39	6.34	23.64	-
K_1^P K_5^I K_5^D	1.907	-	0.60	-	50.00	-	-	0.08	-	3.87	-	-
ft_1 F_1 S_1	-	-	-	-	-	-	-	-	-	0.11	0	5
ft_2 F_2 S_2	-	-	-	-	-	-	0.10	2	9	0.10	2	9

by hybrid multi-population algorithms [35]; **(g)** the best obtained accuracy of the controller (see Table 2) with noise of feedback signals and with use of filters (case 2 and case 3) is close to accuracy obtained by hybrid population algorithms without noise of feedback signals [66].

5 Summary

The proposed elastic structure of the controller containing proposed CB blocks and FIR filters allowed us to obtain accurate and simple controllers, with reduced impact of feedback signals noise on the performance of the controller. Moreover, the proposed training algorithm, which allows reduction of any component of the controller and simultaneously selection of its parameters, allowed us to obtain a very good results in terms of accuracy, superior to the results presented in the literature. In the future, the authors plan to use the proposed controller and learning algorithm in a more complex control problems.

Acknowledgment. The project was financed by the National Science Center (Poland) on the basis of the decision number DEC-2012/05/B/ST7/02138.

References

1. Alia, M.A.K., Younes, T.M., Alsabbah, S.A.: A design of a PID self-tuning controller using LabVIEW. J. Softw. Eng. Appl. **4**, 161–171 (2011)
2. Astrom, K.J., Hagglund, T.: PID Controllers: Theory, Design, and Tuning. Instrument Society of America: Research Triangle Park, North Carolina (1995)
3. Bartczuk, Ł., Rutkowska, D.: Type-2 fuzzy decision trees. In: Rutkowski, L., Tadeusiewicz, R., Zadeh, L.A., Zurada, J.M. (eds.) ICAISC 2008. LNCS (LNAI), vol. 5097, pp. 197–206. Springer, Heidelberg (2008)
4. Bartczuk, Ł., Rutkowska, D.: Medical diagnosis with type-2 fuzzy decision trees. In: Kkacki, E., Rudnicki, M., Stempczyńska, J. (eds.) Computers in Medical Activity. AISC, vol. 65, pp. 11–21. Springer, Heidelberg (2009)
5. Bartczuk, Ł., Przybył, A., Dziwiński, P.: Hybrid state variables - fuzzy logic modelling of nonlinear objects. In: Rutkowski, L., Korytkowski, M., Scherer, R., Tadeusiewicz, R., Zadeh, L.A., Zurada, J.M. (eds.) ICAISC 2013, Part I. LNCS, vol. 7894, pp. 227–234. Springer, Heidelberg (2013)
6. Bartczuk, Ł., Przybył, A., Koprinkova-Hristova, P.: New method for nonlinear fuzzy correction modelling of dynamic objects. In: Rutkowski, L., Korytkowski, M., Scherer, R., Tadeusiewicz, R., Zadeh, L.A., Zurada, J.M. (eds.) ICAISC 2014, Part I. LNCS, vol. 8467, pp. 169–180. Springer, Heidelberg (2014)
7. Bartczuk, Ł.: Gene expression programming in correction modelling of nonlinear dynamic objects. Adv. Intell. Syst. Comput. **429**, 125–134 (2016)
8. Cpałka, K., Rutkowski, L.: Flexible Takagi-Sugeno fuzzy systems. In: Proceedings of the 2005 IEEE International Joint Conference on Neural Networks, IJCNN 2005, vol. 3, pp. 1764–1769 (2005)
9. Cpałka, K., Rutkowski, L.: Flexible Takagi-Sugeno neuro-fuzzy structures for nonlinear approximation. WSEAS Trans. Syst. **4**(9), 1450–1458 (2005)

10. Cpalka, K.: A method for designing flexible neuro-fuzzy systems. In: Rutkowski, L., Tadeusiewicz, R., Zadeh, L.A., Żurada, J.M. (eds.) ICAISC 2006. LNCS (LNAI), vol. 4029, pp. 212–219. Springer, Heidelberg (2006)

11. Cpałka, K., Rutkowski, L.: A new method for designing and reduction of neuro-fuzzy systems. In: Proceedings of the 2006 IEEE International Conference on Fuzzy Systems (IEEE World Congress on Computational Intelligence, WCCI 2006), Vancouver, pp. 8510–8516 (2006)

12. Cpałka, K.: On evolutionary designing and learning of flexible neuro-fuzzy structures for nonlinear classification. In: Nonlinear Analysis Series A: Theory, Methods and Applications, vol. 71, pp. 1659–1672. Elsevier (2009)

13. Cpałka, K., Rebrova, O., Nowicki, R., Rutkowski, L.: On design of flexible neuro-fuzzy systems for nonlinear modelling. Int. J. Gen. Syst. **42**(6), 706–720 (2013)

14. Cpałka, K., Łapa, K., Przybył, A., Zalasiński, M.: A new method for designing neuro-fuzzy systems for nonlinear modelling with interpretability aspects. Neurocomputing **135**, 203–217 (2014)

15. Cpałka, K., Zalasiński, M.: On-line signature verification using vertical signature partitioning. Expert Syst. Appl. **41**(9), 4170–4180 (2014)

16. Cpałka, K., Zalasiński, M., Rutkowski, L.: New method for the on-line signature verification based on horizontal partitioning. Pattern Recogn. **47**, 2652–2661 (2014)

17. Cpałka, K., Łapa, K., Przybył, A.: A new approach to design of control systems using genetic programming. Inf. Technol. Control **44**(4), 433–442 (2015)

18. Cpałka, K., Zalasiński, M., Rutkowski, L.: A new algorithm for identity verification based on the analysis of a handwritten dynamic signature. Appl. Soft Comput. (2016, in press). http://dx.doi.org/10.1016/j.asoc.2016.02.017

19. Duch, W., Korbicz, J., Rutkowski, L., Tadeusiewicz, R. (eds.): Biocybernetics and Biomedical Engineering. Neural Networks, vol. 6. Akademicka Oficyna Wydawnicza EXIT, Warsaw (2000). (in Polish)

20. Duda, P., Jaworski, M., Pietruczuk, L.: On pre-processing algorithms for data stream. In: Rutkowski, L., Korytkowski, M., Scherer, R., Tadeusiewicz, R., Zadeh, L.A., Zurada, J.M. (eds.) ICAISC 2012, Part II. LNCS, vol. 7268, pp. 56–63. Springer, Heidelberg (2012)

21. Duda, P., Hayashi, Y., Jaworski, M.: On the strong convergence of the orthogonal series-type kernel regression neural networks in a non-stationary environment. In: Rutkowski, L., Korytkowski, M., Scherer, R., Tadeusiewicz, R., Zadeh, L.A., Zurada, J.M. (eds.) ICAISC 2012, Part I. LNCS, vol. 7267, pp. 47–54. Springer, Heidelberg (2012)

22. Starczewski, J.T., Bartczuk, Ł., Dziwiński, P., Marvuglia, A.: Learning methods for type-2 FLS based on FCM. In: Rutkowski, L., Scherer, R., Tadeusiewicz, R., Zadeh, L.A., Zurada, J.M. (eds.) ICAISC 2010, Part I. LNCS, vol. 6113, pp. 224–231. Springer, Heidelberg (2010)

23. Dziwiński, P., Bartczuk, Ł., Przybył, A., Avedyan, E.D.: A new algorithm for identification of significant operating points using swarm intelligence. In: Rutkowski, L., Korytkowski, M., Scherer, R., Tadeusiewicz, R., Zadeh, L.A., Zurada, J.M. (eds.) ICAISC 2014, Part II. LNCS, vol. 8468, pp. 349–362. Springer, Heidelberg (2014)

24. Dziwiński, P., Avedyan, E.D.: A new approach to nonlinear modeling based on significant operating points detection. In: Rutkowski, L., Korytkowski, M., Scherer, R., Tadeusiewicz, R., Zadeh, L.A., Zurada, J.M. (eds.) ICAISC 2015. LNCS, vol. 9120, pp. 364–378. Springer, Heidelberg (2015)

25. Er, M.J., Duda, P.: On the weak convergence of the orthogonal series-type kernel regresion neural networks in a non-stationary environment. In: Wyrzykowski, R., Dongarra, J., Karczewski, K., Waśniewski, J. (eds.) PPAM 2011, Part I. LNCS, vol. 7203, pp. 443–450. Springer, Heidelberg (2012)
26. Gałkowski, T., Rutkowski, L.: Nonparametric recovery of multivariate functions with applications to system identification. Proc. IEEE **73**(5), 942–943 (1985)
27. Roger Jang, J.-S., Sun, C.-T.: Functional equivalence between radial basis function networks and fuzzy inference systems. IEEE Trans. Neural Netw. **4**(1), 156–159 (1993)
28. Jaworski, M., Pietruczuk, L., Duda, P.: On resources optimization in fuzzy clustering of data streams. In: Rutkowski, L., Korytkowski, M., Scherer, R., Tadeusiewicz, R., Zadeh, L.A., Zurada, J.M. (eds.) ICAISC 2012, Part II. LNCS, vol. 7268, pp. 92–99. Springer, Heidelberg (2012)
29. Kasthurirathna, D., Piraveenan, M., Uddin, S.: Evolutionary stable strategies in networked games: the influence of topology. J. Artif. Intell. Soft Comput. Res. **5**(2), 83–95 (2015)
30. Kinsy, M.A., Majstorovic, D., Haessig, P., Poon J., Celanovic N., Celanovic I., Devadas, S.: High-speed real-time digital emulation for hardware-in-the-loop testing of power electronics: a new paradigm in the field of electronic design automation (EDA) for power electronics systems. In: emphMesago PCIM GmbH, pp. 1–6 (2011)
31. Korytkowski, M., Rutkowski, L., Scherer, R.: Fast image classification by boosting fuzzy classifiers. Inf. Sci. **327**, 175–182 (2016)
32. Łapa, K., Przybył, A., Cpałka, K.: A new approach to designing interpretable models of dynamic systems. In: Rutkowski, L., Korytkowski, M., Scherer, R., Tadeusiewicz, R., Zadeh, L.A., Zurada, J.M. (eds.) ICAISC 2013, Part II. LNCS, vol. 7895, pp. 523–534. Springer, Heidelberg (2013)
33. Łapa, K., Zalasiński, M., Cpałka, K.: A new method for designing and complexity reduction of neuro-fuzzy systems for nonlinear modelling. In: Rutkowski, L., Korytkowski, M., Scherer, R., Tadeusiewicz, R., Zadeh, L.A., Zurada, J.M. (eds.) ICAISC 2013, Part I. LNCS, vol. 7894, pp. 329–344. Springer, Heidelberg (2013)
34. Łapa, K., Cpałka, K., Wang, L.: New method for design of fuzzy systems for nonlinear modelling using different criteria of interpretability. In: Rutkowski, L., Korytkowski, M., Scherer, R., Tadeusiewicz, R., Zadeh, L.A., Zurada, J.M. (eds.) ICAISC 2014, Part I. LNCS, vol. 8467, pp. 217–232. Springer, Heidelberg (2014)
35. Łapa, K., Szczypta, J., Venkatesan, R.: Aspects of structure and parameters selection of control systems using selected multi-population algorithms. In: Rutkowski, L., Korytkowski, M., Scherer, R., Tadeusiewicz, R., Zadeh, L.A., Zurada, J.M. (eds.) ICAISC 2015. LNCS, vol. 9120, pp. 247–260. Springer, Heidelberg (2015)
36. Li, X., Er, M.J., Lim, B.S.: Fuzzy regression modeling for tool performance prediction and degradation detection. Int. J. Neural Syst. **20**, 405–419 (2010)
37. Makinana, S., Malumedzha, T., Nelwamondo, F.V.: Quality parameter assessment on iris images. J. Artif. Intell. Soft Comput. Res. **4**(1), 21–30 (2014)
38. Murata, M., Ito, S., Tokuhisa, M., Ma, Q.: Order estimation of Japanese paragraphs by supervised machine learning and various textual features. J. Artif. Intell. Soft Comput. Res. **5**(4), 247–255 (2015)
39. Osowski, S.: Sieci neuronowe w ujkeciu algorytmicznym (in Polish), pp. 160–188. WNT, Warszawa (1996)

40. Pietruczuk, L., Duda, P., Jaworski, M.: A new fuzzy classifier for data streams. In: Rutkowski, L., Korytkowski, M., Scherer, R., Tadeusiewicz, R., Zadeh, L.A., Zurada, J.M. (eds.) ICAISC 2012, Part I. LNCS, vol. 7267, pp. 318–324. Springer, Heidelberg (2012)

41. Pietruczuk, L., Zurada, J.M.: Weak convergence of the recursive Parzen-type probabilistic neural network in a non-stationary environment. In: Wyrzykowski, R., Dongarra, J., Karczewski, K., Waśniewski, J. (eds.) PPAM 2011, Part I. LNCS, vol. 7203, pp. 521–529. Springer, Heidelberg (2012)

42. Jaworski, M., Er, M.J., Pietruczuk, L.: On the application of the Parzen-type kernel regression neural network and order statistics for learning in a non-stationary environment. In: Rutkowski, L., Korytkowski, M., Scherer, R., Tadeusiewicz, R., Zadeh, L.A., Zurada, J.M. (eds.) ICAISC 2012, Part I. LNCS, vol. 7267, pp. 90–98. Springer, Heidelberg (2012)

43. Pietruczuk, L., Duda, P., Jaworski, M.: Adaptation of decision trees for handling concept drift. In: Rutkowski, L., Korytkowski, M., Scherer, R., Tadeusiewicz, R., Zadeh, L.A., Zurada, J.M. (eds.) ICAISC 2013, Part I. LNCS, vol. 7894, pp. 459–473. Springer, Heidelberg (2013)

44. Przybyl, A., Smolkag, J., Kimla, P.: Distributed control system based on real time ethernet for computer numerical controlled machine tool (in Polish). Przeglad Elektrotechniczny 86(2), 342–346 (2010)

45. Przybył, A., Cpałka, K.: A new method to construct of interpretable models of dynamic systems. In: Rutkowski, L., Korytkowski, M., Scherer, R., Tadeusiewicz, R., Zadeh, L.A., Zurada, J.M. (eds.) ICAISC 2012, Part II. LNCS, vol. 7268, pp. 697–705. Springer, Heidelberg (2012)

46. Przybył, A., Er, M.J.: The idea for the integration of neuro-fuzzy hardware emulators with real-time network. In: Rutkowski, L., Korytkowski, M., Scherer, R., Tadeusiewicz, R., Zadeh, L.A., Zurada, J.M. (eds.) ICAISC 2014, Part I. LNCS, vol. 8467, pp. 279–294. Springer, Heidelberg (2014)

47. Przybył, A., Szczypta, J., Wang, L.: Optimization of controller structure using evolutionary algorithm. In: Rutkowski, L., Korytkowski, M., Scherer, R., Tadeusiewicz, R., Zadeh, L.A., Zurada, J.M. (eds.) Artificial Intelligence and Soft Computing. LNCS, vol. 9120, pp. 261–271. Springer, Heidelberg (2015)

48. Rutkowski, L.: Sequential estimates of probability densities by orthogonal series and their application in pattern classification. IEEE Trans. Syst. Man Cybern. 10(12), 918–920 (1980)

49. Rutkowski, L.: Nonparametric identification of quasi-stationary systems. Syst. Control Lett. 6(1), 33–35 (1985)

50. Rutkowski, L.: Real-time identification of time-varying systems by non-parametric algorithms based on Parzen kernels. Int. J. Syst. Sci. 16(9), 1123–1130 (1985)

51. Rutkowski, L.: A general approach for nonparametric fitting of functions and their derivatives with applications to linear circuits identification. IEEE Trans. Circ. Syst. 33(8), 812–818 (1986)

52. Rutkowski, L.: Application of multiple Fourier-series to identification of multivariable non-stationary systems. Int. J. Syst. Sci. 20(10), 1993–2002 (1989)

53. Rutkowski, L., Cpałka, K.: Flexible structures of neuro-fuzzy systems. In: Sincak, P., Vascak, J. (eds.) Quo Vadis Computational Intelligence. Studies in Fuzziness and Soft Computing, vol. 54, pp. 479–484. Springer, Heidelberg (2000)

54. Rutkowski, L., Cpałka, K.: Compromise approach to neuro-fuzzy systems. In: Sincak, P., Vascak, J., Kvasnicka, V., Pospichal, J. (eds.) Intelligent Technologies - Theory and Applications, vol. 76, pp. 85–90. IOS Press (2002)

55. Rutkowski, L.: Computational Intelligence. Springer, Heidelberg (2008)
56. Rutkowski, L.: Adaptive probabilistic neural networks for pattern classification in time-varying environment. IEEE Trans. Neural Netw. **15**(4), 811–827 (2004)
57. Rutkowski, L., Przybył, A., Cpałka, K., Er, M.J.: Online speed profile generation for industrial machine tool based on neuro-fuzzy approach. In: Rutkowski, L., Scherer, R., Tadeusiewicz, R., Zadeh, L.A., Zurada, J.M. (eds.) ICAISC 2010, Part II. LNCS, vol. 6114, pp. 645–650. Springer, Heidelberg (2010)
58. Rutkowski, L., Przybył, A., Cpałka, K.: Novel online speed profile generation for industrial machine tool based on flexible neuro-fuzzy approximation. IEEE Trans. Industr. Electron. **59**(2), 1238–1247 (2012)
59. Rutkowski, L., Pietruczuk, L., Duda, P., Jaworski, M.: Decision trees for mining data streams based on the McDiarmid's bound. IEEE Trans. Knowl. Data Eng. **25**(6), 1272–1279 (2013)
60. Rutkowski, L., Jaworski, M., Pietruczuk, L., Duda, P.: Decision trees for mining data streams based on the Gaussian approximation. IEEE Trans. Knowl. Data Eng. **26**(1), 108–119 (2014)
61. Rutkowski, L., Jaworski, M., Pietruczuk, L., Duda, P.: The CART decision tree for mining data streams. Inf. Sci. **266**, 1–15 (2014)
62. Rutkowski, L., Jaworski, M., Pietruczuk, L., Duda, P.: A new method for data stream mining based on the misclassification error. IEEE Trans. Neural Netw. Learn. Syst. **26**(5), 1048–1059 (2015)
63. Starczewski, J.T., Rutkowski, L.: Connectionist structures of type 2 fuzzy inference systems. In: Wyrzykowski, R., Dongarra, J., Paprzycki, M., Waśniewski, J. (eds.) PPAM 2001. LNCS, vol. 2328, pp. 634–642. Springer, Heidelberg (2002)
64. Starczewski, J., Rutkowski, L.: Interval type 2 neuro-fuzzy systems based on interval consequents. In: Rutkowski, L., Kacprzyk, J. (eds.) Neural Networks and Soft Computing, pp. 570–577. Physica-Verlag, New York (2003). A Springer-Verlag Company, Heidelberg
65. Schulte, T., Kiffe, A., Puschmann, F.: HIL simulation of power electronics and electric drives for automotive applications. emphElectronics **16**(2), 130–135 (2012)
66. Szczypta, J., Łapa, K., Shao, Z.: Aspects of the selection of the structure and parameters of controllers using selected population based algorithms. In: Rutkowski, L., Korytkowski, M., Scherer, R., Tadeusiewicz, R., Zadeh, L.A., Zurada, J.M. (eds.) ICAISC 2014, Part I. LNCS, vol. 8467, pp. 440–454. Springer, Heidelberg (2014)
67. Szczypta, J., Przybył, A., Cpałka, K.: Some aspects of evolutionary designing optimal controllers. In: Rutkowski, L., Korytkowski, M., Scherer, R., Tadeusiewicz, R., Zadeh, L.A., Zurada, J.M. (eds.) ICAISC 2013, Part II. LNCS, vol. 7895, pp. 91–100. Springer, Heidelberg (2013)
68. Zalasiński, M., Cpałka, K.: Novel algorithm for the on-line signature verification. In: Rutkowski, L., Korytkowski, M., Scherer, R., Tadeusiewicz, R., Zadeh, L.A., Zurada, J.M. (eds.) ICAISC 2012, Part II. LNCS, vol. 7268, pp. 362–367. Springer, Heidelberg (2012)
69. Zalasiński, M., Cpałka, K.: Novel algorithm for the on-line signature verification using selected discretization points groups. In: Rutkowski, L., Korytkowski, M., Scherer, R., Tadeusiewicz, R., Zadeh, L.A., Zurada, J.M. (eds.) ICAISC 2013, Part I. LNCS, vol. 7894, pp. 493–502. Springer, Heidelberg (2013)
70. Zalasiński, M., Łapa, K., Cpałka, K.: New algorithm for evolutionary selection of the dynamic signature global features. In: Rutkowski, L., Korytkowski, M., Scherer, R., Tadeusiewicz, R., Zadeh, L.A., Zurada, J.M. (eds.) ICAISC 2013, Part II. LNCS, vol. 7895, pp. 113–121. Springer, Heidelberg (2013)

71. Zalasiński, M., Cpałka, K., Er, M.J.: New method for dynamic signature verification using hybrid partitioning. In: Rutkowski, L., Korytkowski, M., Scherer, R., Tadeusiewicz, R., Zadeh, L.A., Zurada, J.M. (eds.) ICAISC 2014, Part II. LNCS, vol. 8468, pp. 216–230. Springer, Heidelberg (2014)

72. Zalasiński, M., Cpałka, K., Hayashi, Y.: New method for dynamic signature verification based on global features. In: Rutkowski, L., Korytkowski, M., Scherer, R., Tadeusiewicz, R., Zadeh, L.A., Zurada, J.M. (eds.) ICAISC 2014, Part II. LNCS, vol. 8468, pp. 231–245. Springer, Heidelberg (2014)

73. Zalasiński, M., Cpałka, K., Er, M.J.: A new method for the dynamic signature verification based on the stable partitions of the signature. In: Rutkowski, L., Korytkowski, M., Scherer, R., Tadeusiewicz, R., Zadeh, L.A., Zurada, J.M. (eds.) ICAISC 2015. LNCS, vol. 9120, pp. 161–174. Springer, Heidelberg (2015)

74. Zalasiński, M., Cpałka, K., Hayashi, Y.: New fast algorithm for the dynamic signature verification using global features values. In: Rutkowski, L., Korytkowski, M., Scherer, R., Tadeusiewicz, R., Zadeh, L.A., Zurada, J.M. (eds.) ICAISC 2015. LNCS, vol. 9120, pp. 175–188. Springer, Heidelberg (2015)

Extended Study on the Randomization and Sequencing for the Chaos Embedded Heuristic

Roman Senkerik[1]([⊠]), Michal Pluhacek[1], Ivan Zelinka[2], Adam Viktorin[1], and Jakub Janostik[1]

[1] Faculty of Applied Informatics, Tomas Bata University in Zlin,
Nam T.G. Masaryka 5555, 760 01 Zlin, Czech Republic
{senkerik,pluhacek,aviktorin,janostik}@fai.utb.cz
[2] Faculty of Electrical Engineering and Computer Science,
Technical University of Ostrava, 17. Listopadu 15,
708 33 Ostrava-poruba, Czech Republic
ivan.zelinka@vsb.cz

Abstract. This research deals with the hybridization of two softcomputing fields, which are chaos theory and evolutionary algorithms. This paper investigates the utilization of the time-continuous chaotic system, which is Ueda oscillator, as the chaotic pseudo random number generator (CPRNG) embedded into the selected heuristics. Through the utilization of time-continuous systems and with different sampling times from very small to bigger, it is possible to fully keep, suppress or remove the hidden complex chaotic dynamics from the generated pseudo random data series. Repeated simulations were performed investigating the influence of the oscillator sampling time to the selected heuristic, which is differential evolution algorithm (DE). Experiments are focused on the extended investigation, whether the different randomization and pseudo random numbers distribution given by particular CPRNG or hidden complex chaotic dynamics providing the unique sequencing are beneficial to the heuristic performance. This research utilizes set of 4 selected benchmark functions, three different sampling rates of Ueda oscillator; further results are compared against canonical DE.

Keywords: Differential evolution · Complex dynamics · Deterministic chaos · Randomization · Ueda oscillator

R.Senkerik—This work was supported by Grant Agency of the Czech Republic - GACR P103/15/06700S, further by This work was supported by the Ministry of Education, Youth and Sports of the Czech Republic within the National Sustainability Programme project No. LO1303 (MSMT-7778/2014) and also by the European Regional Development Fund under the project CEBIA-Tech No. CZ.1.05/2.1.00/03.0089., partially supported by Grant of SGS No. SP2016/175 of VSB - Technical University of Ostrava, Czech Republic and by Internal Grant Agency of Tomas Bata University under the project No. IGA/CebiaTech/2016/007.

L. Rutkowski et al. (Eds.): ICAISC 2016, Part I, LNAI 9692, pp. 493–504, 2016.
DOI: 10.1007/978-3-319-39378-0_42

1   Introduction

This research deals with the hybridization of the two softcomputing fields, which are the complex dynamics given by chaos theory dynamics driving the selection of indices in Differential Evolution (DE) algorithm and evolutionary computation techniques (ECT's). Currently the DE [1] is known as powerful heuristic for many difficult and complex optimization problems.

A number of DE variants have been recently developed with the emphasis on adaptivity/selfadaptivity [2], ensemble approach [3] or utilization for discrete domain problems. The importance of randomization as a compensation of limited amount of search moves is stated in the survey paper [4]. This idea has been carried out in subsequent studies describing various techniques to modify the randomization process [5,6] and especially in [7], where the sampling of the points is tested from modified distribution. The importance and influence of randomization operations was also deeply experimentally tested in jDE strategy [8]. Together with this persistent development in such mainstream research topics, the basic concept of chaos driven DE have been introduced.

Recent research in chaotic approach for heuristics generally uses the chaotic map in the place of a pseudo random number generator. This causes the heuristic to map unique regions, since the chaotic map iterates to new regions. The task is then to select a very good chaotic map (or combination of chaotic maps) as the pseudo random number generator (PRNG).

The focus of this research is the direct embedding of chaotic dynamics in the form of chaos pseudo random number generator (CPRNG) for heuristic. The initial concept of embedding chaotic dynamics into the evolutionary/swarm algorithms is given in [9]. Later, the initial study [10] was focused on the simple embedding of chaotic systems for DE and Self Organizing Migration Algorithm (SOMA) [11]. Also the PSO (Particle Swarm Optimization) algorithm with elements of chaos was introduced as CPSO [12] followed by the introduction of chaos embedded PSO with inertia weigh strategy [13], further PSO strategy driven alternately by two chaotic systems [14] and finally PSO with ensemble of chaotic systems [15]. Recently the chaos driven heuristic concept has been utilized in ABC algorithm [16] and applications with DE [17].

The organization of this paper is following: Firstly, the motivation for this research is proposed. The next sections are focused on the description of the concept of chaos driven DE utilizing Ueda oscillator and the experiment background. Results and conclusion follow afterwards.

2   Motivation

This research is an extension and continuation of the previous successful initial experiment with the single/multi-chaos driven DE (ChaosDE), where the positive influence of hidden complex dynamics for the heuristic performance has been experimentally shown.

Nevertheless, the questions remain, as to why it works, why it may be beneficial to use the correlated chaotic time series for generating pseudo random numbers driving the selection, mutation, crossover or other processes in particular heuristics.

Recently many research studies have been carried out focusing on the utilization of different randomization type, different PRNGs, distributions etc. Thus an experiment has been designed, to show, whether the chaos embedded heuristics concept belongs to the group of either *"utilization of different PRNG with different distribution"* or the unique chaos dynamics providing unique sequencing of pseudo random numbers is the key of performance improvements. The last point was also inspired by recent advances in connection of complexity and heuristic [18] together with the research focused on selection of indices in DE [19] where the indices (solutions) for mutation process were not selected randomly, but based on the complex behavior and neighborhood mechanisms.

Since the sequencing in chaotic series generated by the mostly utilized discrete chaotic systems is given directly by the discrete nature and mathematical notations of the used chaotic map, a different type of experiment was performed and presented here. It is focused on the time-continuous chaotic systems, to be more precise, on the investigating the influence of the oscillator sampling time to the DE performance. In contrast to using discrete chaotic systems as CPRNGs, through the utilization of time-continuous systems and with different sampling times from very small to bigger, it is possible to fully keep, suppress or remove the hidden complex chaotic dynamics from the generated data series used for obtaining the pseudo random numbers.

3   Differential Evolution

DE is a population-based optimization method that works on real-number-coded individuals [1]. DE is quite robust, fast, and effective, with global optimization ability. It does not require the objective function to be differentiable, and it works well even with noisy and time-dependent objective functions. There are essentially five inputs to the heuristic. *Dim* is the size of the problem, *Gmax* is the maximum number of generations, *NP* is the total number of solutions, *F* is the scaling factor of the solution and *CR* is the factor for crossover. *F* and *CR* together make the internal tuning parameters for the heuristic. Due to a limited space and the aims of this paper, the detailed description of well known canonical strategy of differential evolution algorithm basic principles is insignificant and hence omitted. Please refer to [1,20] for the detailed description of the used DERand1Bin strategy (both for ChaosDE and Canonical DE) as well as for the complete description of all other strategies.

4   Ueda Oscillator

Ueda oscillator is the simple example of driven pendulums, which represent some of the most significant examples of chaos and regularity.

The Ueda system can be simply considered as a special case of intensively studied Duffing oscillator that has both a linear and cubic restoring force. Ueda oscillator represents the both biologically and physically important dynamical model exhibiting chaotic motion. It can be used to explore much physical behavior in biological systems [21].

The Ueda chaotic system equations are given in (1). The parameters are: $a = 1.0$ $b = 0.05$, $c = 7.5$ and $\omega = 1.0$ as suggested in [22]. Figure 1 shows x, y parametric plots of the chaotic system.

$$\frac{dx}{dt} = y$$
$$\frac{dy}{dt} = -ax^3 - by + c\sin\omega t \tag{1}$$

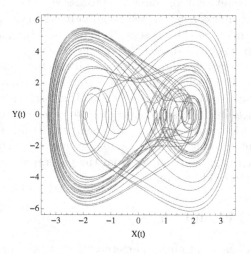

Fig. 1. x, y parametric plot of the UEDA oscillator

5   The Concept of ChaosDE with Time-Continuous Chaotic System as Driving CPRNG

The general idea of CPRNG is to replace the default PRNG with the chaotic system. As the chaotic system is a set of equations with a static start position, we created a random start position of the system, in order to have different start position for different experiments. Thus we are utilizing the typical feature of chaotic systems, which is extreme sensitivity to the initial conditions, popularly known as "butterfly effect". This random position is initialized with the default PRNG, as a one-off randomizer. Once the start position of the chaotic system has been obtained, the system generates the next sequence using its current position.

Generally there exist many other approaches as to how to deal with the negative numbers as well as with the scaling of the wide range of the numbers given by the chaotic systems into the typical range $0 - 1$:

1. Finding of the maximum value of the pre-generated long discrete sequence and dividing of all the values in the sequence with such a maxval number.
2. Shifting of all values to the positive numbers (avoiding of ABS command) and scaling.

Used approach is following: firstly we obtain the simulation (analytic solution) of Ueda oscillator (See Fig. 2 - left), subsequently this simulation output is sampled with selected sampling rate, as in Fig. 2 – right. Finally the scaling into the typical range 0 – 1 for PRNG is performed (Fig. 3) based on the following definition (2):

$$rndreal = mod(abs(rndChaos), 1.0) \tag{2}$$

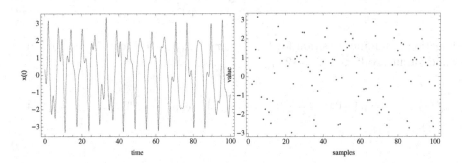

Fig. 2. Simulation outputs – chaotic output of Ueda oscillator (left); Sampled simulation output (sampling rate 0.5 seconds) (right).

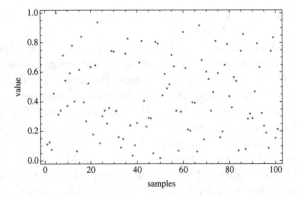

Fig. 3. Detailed sequencing and dynamics of real pseudo-random numbers transferred into the range <0 - 1> generated by means of the chaotic Ueda oscillator

6 Experiment Design

For the purpose of ChaosDE performance comparison within this research, the Schwefel's test function (3), shifted Rastrigin's function (4), shifted 1st De Jong's function (5), and shifted Ackley's original function in the form (6), were selected.

$$f(x) = \sum_{i=1}^{dim} -x_i \sin\left(\sqrt{|x_i|}\right) \tag{3}$$

Function minimum:
Position for E_n: $(x_1, x_2 \ldots x_n) = (420.969, 420.969, \ldots, 420.969)$
Value for E_n: $y = -418.983\,dim$; Function interval: <-500, 500>.

$$f(x) = \sum_{i=1}^{dim} (x_i - s_i)^2 \tag{4}$$

Function minimum: Position for E_n: $(x_1, x_2 \ldots x_n) = s$; Value for E_n: $y = 0$
Function interval: <-5.12, 5.12>.

$$f(x) = -20 \exp\left(-0.02 \sqrt{\tfrac{1}{D}\sum_{i=1}^{dim}(x_i - s_i)^2}\right) - \exp\left(\tfrac{1}{D}\sum_{i=1}^{dim}\cos 2\pi (x_i - s_i)\right) + $$
$$+20 + \exp(1)$$
$$\tag{5}$$

Function minimum: Position for E_n: $(x_1, x_2 \ldots x_n) = s$; Value for E_n: $y = 0$
Function interval: <-30, 30>.

$$f(x) = 10 \dim + \sum_{i=1}^{dim} (x_i - s_i)^2 - 10\cos(2\pi x_i - s_i) \tag{6}$$

Function minimum: Position for E_n: $(x_1, x_2 \ldots x_n) = s$, Value for E_n: $y = 0$
Function interval: <-5.12, 5.12>.
Where s_i is a random number from the 90 % range of function interval; s vector is randomly generated before each run of the optimization process.

The parameter settings for both canonical DE and ChaosDE are following: Population size of 75, dimension $dim = 30$, internal DE parameters $F = 0.5$ and $Cr = 0.9$. Although it was experimentally determined, that ChaosDE requires lower values of Cr parameter, we have used the same settings for canonical DE and ChaosDE to track the changes in distribution and sequencing of pseudo random numbers driving the selection of indices in DE under identical conditions. The maximum number of generations was fixed at 1500 generations. This allowed the possibility to analyze the progress of DE within a limited number of generations and cost function evaluations. Experiments were performed in the environment of *Wolfram Mathematica*; canonical DE therefore has used the built-in *Wolfram Mathematica* pseudo random number generator *Wolfram Cellular Automata* representing traditional pseudorandom number generator in comparisons. All experiments used different initialization, i.e. different initial population was generated within the each run of Canonical or Chaos driven DE.

7 Results

Statistical results of the selected experiments are shown in comprehensive Tables 1, 3, 5 and 7 for all 50 repeated runs of DE/ChaosDE, four different benchmark functions and three settings of sampling time for Ueda oscillator.

Tables 2, 4, 6 and 8 compare the progress of three versions of ChaosDE and Canonical DE. This table contains the average cost function (CF) values for the particular generation No. from all 50 runs. The bold values within the all Tables 1–8 depict the best obtained results. The graphical comparisons of the time evolution of average CF values for all 50 runs and two selected test functions are depicted in Figs. 4 and 5.

Finally Fig. 6 shows the influence of sampling rate to the distribution of pseudo random numbers given by particular CPRNG (left figures) and to the dynamics inside the generated data series (right figures).

Table 1. Results for the Canonical DE and ChaosDE; Schwefel's function

DE Version	Avg CF	Median CF	Max CF	Min CF	StdDev
Canonical DE	−5435.42	−5256.26	−4912.80	−6629.15	550.54
ChaosDE - Sampling 0.1s	**−10238.63**	**−10256.06**	**−9654.24**	−10618.14	**311.47**
ChaosDE - Sampling 0.5s	−9049.66	−8753.35	−7309.98	**−10681.53**	1106.91
ChaosDE - Sampling 1.0s	−9055.76	−9146.33	−7408.15	−10380.80	990.87

Table 2. Comparison of progress towards the minimum for the Schwefel's function

DE Version	Gen. 300	Gen. 600	Gen. 900	Gen. 1200	Gen. 1500
Canonical DE	−4508.42	−4770.18	−5115.39	−5206.44	−5435.42
ChaosDE - Sampling 0.1s	**−5140.43**	**−7232.46**	**−8748.71**	**−9202.15**	**−10238.6**
ChaosDE - Sampling 0.5s	−4359.8	−5165.49	−6407.68	−6908.04	−9049.66
ChaosDE - Sampling 1.0s	−4282.59	−5324.16	−6621.68	−7050.82	−9055.76

Table 3. Results for the Canonical DE and ChaosDE; shifted Rastrigin's func.

DE Version	Avg CF	Median CF	Max CF	Min CF	StdDev
Canonical DE	−40176.4	−37747.8	−30941.2	−52349.8	6854.46
ChaosDE - Sampling 0.1s	−81498.9	−81684.1	−76985.5	−86119.7	2703.62
ChaosDE - Sampling 0.5s	**−84168.1**	**−84552.4**	**−77165**	**−86418.1**	**2655.44**
ChaosDE - Sampling 1.0s	−81549.3	−81665.8	−76269.2	−85821.2	3430.74

Table 4. Comparison of progress towards the minimum for the shifted Rastrigin's function.

DE Version	Gen. 300	Gen. 600	Gen. 900	Gen. 1200	Gen. 1500
Canonical DE	−28227.5	−31457.9	−35281.7	−35363.3	−40176.4
ChaosDE - Sampling 0.1s	**−38232.8**	**−73870.3**	**−81285.0**	**−81451.8**	−81498.9
ChaosDE - Sampling 0.5s	−28698.7	−51134.0	−72439.9	−76859.2	**−84168.1**
ChaosDE - Sampling 1.0s	−27245.2	−39324.4	−58939.3	−66641.8	−81549.3

Table 5. Results for the Canonical DE and ChaosDE; shifted 1st De Jong's func.

DE Version	Avg CF	Median CF	Max CF	Min CF	StdDev
Canonical DE	**5.54E-19**	**5.14E-19**	**1.17E-18**	**1.07E-19**	**2.86E-19**
ChaosDE - Sampling 0.1s	4.3E-14	1.87E-15	2.96E-13	2.26E-16	9.34E-14
ChaosDE - Sampling 0.5s	8.13E-16	1.44E-16	4.95E-15	9.86E-18	1.53E-15
ChaosDE - Sampling 1.0s	2.87E-14	3.92E-17	2.86E-13	1.8E-18	9.03E-14

Table 6. Comparison of progress towards the minimum for the shifted 1st De Jong's function

DE Version	Gen. 300	Gen. 600	Gen. 900	Gen. 1200	Gen. 1500
Canonical DE	**0,009878**	**9,35E-07**	**1,07E-10**	**4,72E-12**	**5,54E-19**
ChaosDE - Sampling 0.1s	0,021934	0,000108	3,71E-08	3,52E-09	4,3E-14
ChaosDE - Sampling 0.5s	0,013758	6,51E-06	1,24E-08	9,6E-10	8,13E-16
ChaosDE - Sampling 1.0s	0,009907	5,09E-06	1,1E-09	4,52E-11	2,87E-14

Table 7. Results for the Canonical DE and ChaosDE; shifted Ackley's function

DE Version	Avg CF	Median CF	Max CF	Min CF	StdDev
Canonical DE	**3.44E-09**	**3.49E-09**	**6.22E-09**	**1.6E-09**	**1.31E-09**
ChaosDE - Sampling 0.1s	1.146266	1.247785	2.013315	5.78E-06	0.661722
ChaosDE - Sampling 0.5s	0.960162	1.155149	1.777997	4.18E-09	0.55887
ChaosDE - Sampling 1.0s	0.461067	2.46E-07	1.777997	2.74E-09	0.751358

Table 8. Comparison of progress towards the minimum for the shifted Ackley's function

DE Version	Gen. 300	Gen. 600	Gen. 900	Gen. 1200	Gen. 1500
Canonical DE	**1.147498**	**0.004668**	**4.04E-05**	**8.35E-06**	**3.44E-09**
ChaosDE - Sampling 0.1s	1.538858	1.222563	1.155629	1.149759	1.146266
ChaosDE - Sampling 0.5s	1.463927	0.962694	0.960186	0.960167	0.960162
ChaosDE - Sampling 1.0s	1.281251	0.532509	0.504672	0.49502	0.461067

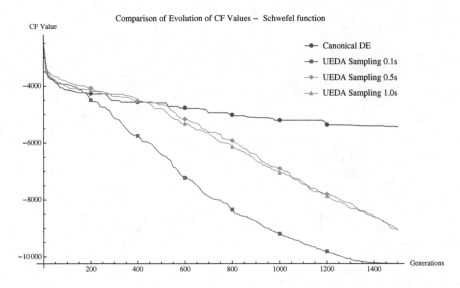

Fig. 4. Comparison of the time evolution of avg. CF values for the all 50 runs of Canonical DE, and three versions of ChaosDE with different sampling rates of Ueda oscillator as CPRNG. Schwefel's function.

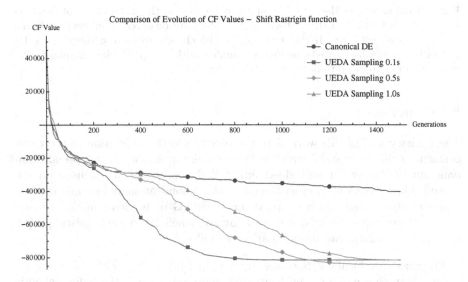

Fig. 5. Comparison of the time evolution of avg. CF values for the all 50 runs of Canonical DE, and three versions of ChaosDE with different samling rates of Ueda oscillator as CPRNG. Shifted Rastrigin's function.

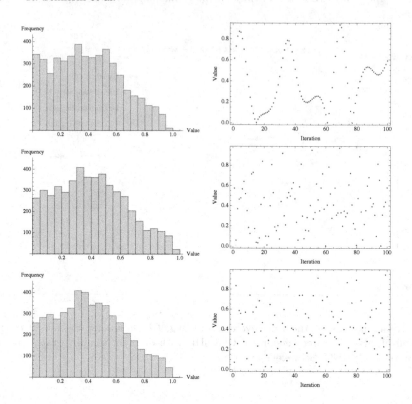

Fig. 6. Comparison of the influence of sampling rate to the distribution of numbers given by Ueda CPRNG; Left: Histogram of the distribution of real numbers transferred into the range <0 - 1>; Right: Example of the chaotic dynamics: range <0 - 1> generated by means of Ueda oscillator sampled with the particular sampling rate; Sampling rates from up to down: 0.1s, 0.5s, 1.0s.

8   Conclusions

The primary aim of this work is to use investigate the utilization of the time-continuous chaotic system, which is Ueda oscillator, as the chaotic pseudo random number generator embedded into DE. Experiments are focused on the extended investigation, whether the different randomization and pseudo random numbers distribution given by particular CPRNG or hidden complex chaotic dynamics providing the unique sequencing are beneficial to the heuristic performance. The findings can be summarized as follows:

- Obtained graphical comparisons and data in Tables 1–8 and Figs. 4–6 support the claim that chaos driven heuristic is more sensitive to the hidden chaotic dynamics driving the selection, mutation, crossover or other processes through CPRNG and less sensitive to the distribution of PRNG/CPRNG.
- Another important phenomenon was discovered – Only sampling rate of 0.1 s keeps the information about the chaotic dynamics (as in Fig. 6 – upper, right)

and by using such chaotic dynamics driving the selection/mutation processes inside heuristic, its performance is significantly different: either the best or the worst against other compared versions.

- In the first two case studies, the performance of ChaosDE was significantly better, and the effect of different CPRNG distribution (versions with sampling rates 0.5 s and 1.0s) became even stronger with the chaotic dynamics kept inside CPRNG sequences (sampling rate 0.1s). Other settings of sampling rates have given comparable performance. Distributions of all three versions of CPRNGs were almost identical (as in Fig. 6 – left parts).
- The third and the fourth case study have given absolutely reversed character of results. The more chaotic dynamics is present (sampling rate 0.1s) or suppressed (sampling rate 0.5s) in the CPRNG sequence, the worse results are obtained with ChaosDE.
- Sequencing of pseudo random numbers and chaotic dynamics hidden inside pseudo random series can be significantly changed by the selection of sampling time in the case of the time-continuous systems. Nevertheless the distributions of CPRNGs with different sampling rates remain almost identical (See Fig. 6 – left parts). In case of discrete systems, the simplest way for changing the influence to the heuristic is to swap currently used chaotic system for different one, or to change the internal parameters of discrete chaotic systems.
- It is clear that (selection of) the best sampling rates are problem-dependent. Similarly to the research focused on the adaptive switching of either discrete chaotic systems or randomization types, it is possible to build the adaptive tuning framework utilizing only one time-continuous system with an automatic adaptation of sampling rate.

References

1. Price, K.V.: An introduction to differential evolution. In: Corne, D., Dorigo, M., Glover, F. (eds.) New Ideas in Optimization, pp. 79–108. McGraw-Hill Ltd, Maidenhead (1999)
2. Brest, J., Greiner, S., Boskovic, B., Mernik, M., Zumer, V.: Self-adapting control parameters in differential evolution: A comparative study on numerical benchmark problems. Evol. Comput. IEEE Trans. 10(6), 646–657 (2006)
3. Mallipeddi, R., Suganthan, P.N., Pan, Q.K., Tasgetiren, M.F.: Differential evolution algorithm with ensemble of parameters and mutation strategies. Appl. Soft Comput. 11(2), 1679–1696 (2011)
4. Neri, F., Tirronen, V.: Recent advances in differential evolution: a survey and experimental analysis. Artif Intell. Rev. 33(1–2), 61–106 (2010)
5. Weber, M., Neri, F., Tirronen, V.: A study on scale factor in distributed differential evolution. Inf. Sci. 181(12), 2488–2511 (2011)
6. Neri, F., Iacca, G., Mininno, E.: Disturbed Exploitation compact Differential Evolution for limited memory optimization problems. Inf. Sci. 181(12), 2469–2487 (2011)
7. Iacca, G., Caraffini, F., Neri, F.: Compact differential evolution light: high performance despite limited memory requirement and modest computational overhead. J. Comput. Sci. Technol. 27(5), 1056–1076 (2012)

8. Zamuda, A., Brest, J.: Self-adaptive control parameters× randomization frequency and propagations in differential evolution. Swarm Evol. Comput. **25**, 72–99 (2015)
9. Caponetto, R., Fortuna, L., Fazzino, S., Xibilia, M.G.: Chaotic sequences to improve the performance of evolutionary algorithms. IEEE Trans. Evol. Comput. **7**(3), 289–304 (2003)
10. Davendra, D., Zelinka, I., Senkerik, R.: Chaos driven evolutionary algorithms for the task of PID control. Comput. Math. Appl. **60**(4), 1088–1104 (2010)
11. Zelinka, I.: SOMA – self-organizing migrating algorithm. New Optimization Techniques in Engineering. Studies in Fuzziness and Soft Computing, vol. 141, pp. 167–217. Springer, Heidelberg (2004)
12. Coelho, L.S., Mariani, V.C.: A novel chaotic particle swarm optimization approach using Henon map and implicit filtering local search for economic load dispatch. Chaos Solitons Fractals **39**(2), 510–518 (2009)
13. Pluhacek, M., Senkerik, R., Davendra, D., Kominkova Oplatkova, Z., Zelinka, I.: On the behavior and performance of chaos driven PSO algorithm with inertia weight. Comput. Math. Appl. **66**(2), 122–134 (2013)
14. Pluhacek, M., Senkerik, R., Zelinka, I., Davendra, D.: New adaptive approach for chaos PSO algorithm driven alternately by two different chaotic maps - an initial study. In: Zelinka, I., Chen, G., Rössler, O.E., Snasel, V., Abraham, A. (eds.) Nostradamus 2013: Prediction, Modeling and Analysis of Complex Systems. AISC, vol. 210, pp. 77–87. Springer, Heidelberg (2013)
15. Pluhacek, M., Senkerik, R., Davendra, D.: Chaos particle swarm optimization with Eensemble of chaotic systems. Swarm Evol. Comput. **25**, 29–35 (2015)
16. Metlicka, M., Davendra, D.: Chaos driven discrete artificial bee algorithm for location and assignment optimisation problems. Swarm Evol. Comput. **25**, 15–28 (2015)
17. Coelho, L.D.S., Ayala, H.V.H., Mariani, V.C.: A self-adaptive chaotic differential evolution algorithm using gamma distribution for unconstrained global optimization. Appl. Math. Comput. **234**, 452–459 (2014)
18. Zelinka, I.: A survey on evolutionary algorithms dynamics and its complexity - Mutual relations, past, present and future. Swarm Evol. Comput. **25**, 2–14 (2015)
19. Das, S., Abraham, A., Chakraborty, U.K., Konar, A.: Differential evolution using a neighborhood-based mutation operator. Evol. Comput. IEEE Trans. **13**(3), 526–553 (2009)
20. Price, K.V., Storn, R.M., Lampinen, J.A.: Differential Evolution - A Practical Approach to Global Optimization. Natural Computing Series. Springer, Berlin Heidelberg (2005)
21. Bharti, L., Yuasa, M., Variability, E., Chaos in Ueda Oscillator. http://www.rist.kindai.ac.jp/no.23/yuasa-EVCUO.pdf
22. Sprott, J.C.: Chaos and Time-Series Analysis. Oxford University Press, Oxford (2003)

Hierarchical and Massively Interactive Approaches for Hybridization of Evolutionary Computations and Agent Systems—Comparison in Financial Application

Leszek Siwik[✉] and Rafal Drezewski

AGH University of Science and Technology, Kraków, Poland
{siwik,drezew}@agh.edu.pl

Abstract. When we think about hybridizing of evolutionary computations and agent systems in fact two approaches are possible: (1) hierarchical one – where agents are used as the management layer and the evolutionary algorithms are executed inside (sub)populations "within" agents and (2) system realized as the population(s) of evolving agents equipped with "DNA" performing life-steps to obtain their life-goals. In this paper we discuss aforementioned approaches and present their sample realization and application for solving a challenging portfolio optimization problem defined as a multi-objective optimization problem with maximization of the investment profit and minimization of the investment risk level.

1 Motivation

One of the promising computational techniques for solving hard and complex optimization problems (both global and local ones especially when the problem is defined as the multi-objective or multi-modal optimization problem) is applying nature-inspired systems and the evolutionary algorithms in particular since they are insensitive to the complexity of the problem to some extent.

The problem however is that evolutionary algorithm works properly (e.g. in terms of searching for a globally optimal solution) if the population consists of fairly different individuals, i.e. the so-called diversity in the population is preserved [2]. Yet many algorithms tend to prematurely loose this useful diversity and, as a result, there is possibility that population gets stuck in some part of the search space (e.g. in the basin of attraction of some local extrema instead of searching for a global one). Loosing the population diversity also limits the possibilities of the application in some areas such as multi-objective optimisation or multi-modal optimisation.

The above-described situation is related to the fact that the model of evolution employed by simple evolutionary algorithms lacks many important features observed in organic evolution [3]. This includes dynamically changing environmental conditions, neither global knowledge nor generational synchronisation

L. Rutkowski et al. (Eds.): ICAISC 2016, Part I, LNAI 9692, pp. 505–516, 2016.
DOI: 10.1007/978-3-319-39378-0_43

assumed, co-evolution of species, evolving genotype-fenotype mapping, etc. That is why many variations of classical evolutionary algorithms were proposed, introducing additional mechanisms following the most important phenomena in evolutionary biology e.g. dedicated cooperation mechanisms [16], coevolutionary mechanisms [8–10], hierarchical approaches [6] or converting problems into multiobjective optimization problems [15]. Yet still obtained results have been not satisfying in many cases.

During the last decades intelligent/autonomous software agents have been gaining more and more applications in various domains. The key concept in multi-agent systems (MAS) constitute intelligent interactions (coordination, cooperation, negotiation). Thus multi-agent systems are ideally suited for representing problems that have many solving methods, involve many perspectives and/or may be solved by many entities [17]. Agents play a key role in the integration of AI sub-disciplines, which often leads to hybrid design of modern intelligent systems.

Since evolutionary algorithms are distributed by nature and since agents are able to perform many complex operations it was then natural that the idea of hybridization of evolutionary computations with (multi)agent systems arouse.

In this paper two fundamental approaches for hybridizing evolutionary computation and agent systems i.e. (1) hierarchical approach (HEAH) with agents used as the management layer and (2) the population of evolving agents (MIEAH) equipped with the "DNA" and performing their "life steps" to obtain their "goals" (i.e. better and better solutions of the problem defined) are discussed, applied for solving challenging, discrete investment portfolio optimization defined as the multi-objective optimization problem, and then compared and concluded.

2   Two Approaches for Hybridization of Evolutionary Computations and Agent Systems

In most approaches for hybridization of evolutionary computations and agent systems reported in the literature (see e.g. [13] or [5] for a review) an evolutionary algorithm is used by an agent to aid realisation of some of its tasks, often connected with learning or reasoning, or to support coordination of some group (team) activity.

But when we think about constituting a new hybrid evolutionary-agent computational paradigm in fact two approaches are possible. In the first one agents constitute a management infrastructure for a distributed realisation of an evolutionary algorithm [14].

In such an approach (see Fig. 1) each agent has the population of individuals inside of it, and this sub-population is evolving according to one of (classical) evolutionary algorithm. Agents themselves can migrate within the computational environment, from one computational node to another, trying to utilize in a best way, free computational resources.

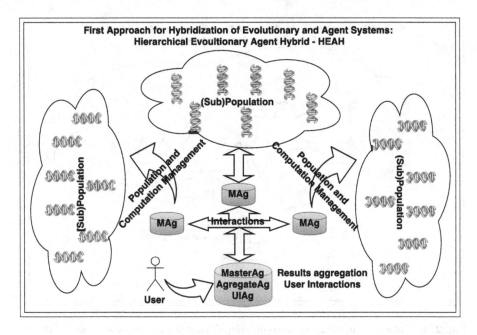

Fig. 1. Agent-based layer used for managing evolutionary computations

In contrary, thinking about the hybridization of evolutionary and agent systems one may imagine the population(s) of evolving agents equipped with "DNA" performing life-steps to obtain their life-goals.

Such an idea with agents located in fixed positions on some lattice (like in a cellular model of parallel evolutionary algorithms) was developed by e.g. [18]. This approach yet interesting was disregarding important, powerful and crucial in facts features of agents i.e. their autonomy and mobility.

The full realization of the idea of incorporating evolutionary processes into a multi-agent systems at a population level regarding full autonomy of agents was the decentralised model of evolution employed by an *evolutionary multi-agent system* – EMAS [12].

Agents of EMAS represent or generate solutions for a given optimisation problem. They are located on islands, which constitute their local environment where direct interactions may take places, and represent a distributed structure of computation. Obviously, agents are able to change their location, which allows for diffusion of information and resources all over the system [12].

In EMAS phenomena of inheritance and selection – the main components of evolutionary processes – are modelled via agent actions of *death* and *reproduction* (see Fig. 2). Inheritance is accomplished by an appropriate definition of reproduction, like in classical evolutionary algorithms. Core properties of the agent are encoded in its genotype and inherited from its parent(s) with the use of variation operators (mutation and recombination). Besides, an agent may possess some knowledge acquired during its life, which is not inherited. Both inherited

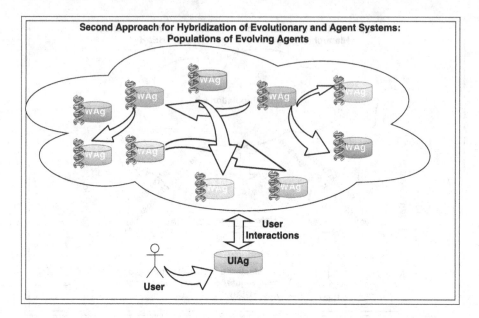

Fig. 2. Evolutionary multi-agent system—population of evolving agents with "DNA" performing life-steps to obtain their life-goals

and acquired information determines the behaviour of an agent in the system (phenotype).

Assuming that no global knowledge is available (which makes it impossible to evaluate all individuals at the same time) and autonomy of the agents (which causes that reproduction is achieved asynchronously), selection is based on the non-renewable resources [4].

In order to realize the selection process "better" (what means that they simply better solve the given problem) agents are given more resources from the environment (or from other agents) and "worse" agents are given less resources (or should give some of its resources to "better" agents). Such mechanisms result in decentralized evolutionary processes in which individuals (agents) make independently all their decisions concerning reproduction, migration, interactions with other agents, etc., taking into consideration conditions of the environment, other agents present within the neighborhood, and resources possessed.

3   Realization of Hierarchical and Interactive Evolutionary-Agent Hybrid Systems

3.1   Realization of Hierarchical Evolutionary-Agent Hybrid System

Hierarchical approach has been implemented using Age—agent-oriented framework [1] (its Java implementation i.e. jAge in fact). The framework supported the authors with implementation of a notion of working agent that was adapted to create an efficient implementation of Master and Slave agents.

Because the representatives of each sub-populations had to be aggregated (in order to form the complete solution) and also because of the necessity of storing the complete non-dominated solutions the system consists of one Master/Aggregate and many slaves/working agents. Master agent is responsible for exchanging information with external world e.g. the user. It is also responsible for forming complete solutions (composed of the representatives of each sub-population and evaluation of the solutions. It also maintains the set of non-dominated solutions found so far (the definition of domination relation and other issues connected with the Pareto approach to multi-objective optimization can be found for example in [7] or [11]). Each sub-population is responsible only for the selected part of solution, and evolved by one working agent.

Master agent has to deal also with typical management tasks i.e. it is responsible for dispatching optimization tasks among Slaves/Working agents. Working agents can manage the populations evolving according to different algorithms. For experiments, working agents managed the (sub)population of individuals being evolved according to NSGA2 evolutionary algorithm for multi-objective optimization [7].

As a result of integration of agent system and NSGA2 [7] algorithm the agent-based co-operative version of NSGA2 was created. Thanks to the computed contribution of the given individual to the quality of the complete solution, the fitness computation in agent-based co-evolutionary NSGA2 is realized with the use of non-dominated sorting and crowding distance metric (see [7]). Additionally, the aggregate agent joins the populations of parents and offspring, and chooses (on the basis of elitist selection and within each sub-population separately) individuals which will form the next generation sub-population used for the creation of complete solutions. The applied schema implies that N best (according to non-dominated sorting and crowding distance metric) individuals survive.

3.2 Predator-Prey Co-Evolutionary Multi-agent System as the Realization of Massively Interactive Approach

As it was stated in Sect. 1 one of two main approaches for hybridization of evolutionary and agents systems is equipping agents with their "DNA" and constructing populations of evolving agents, "living" in their environment, interacting with the other agents realizing their own goals defined (usually) as obtaining the best possible approximations of optimal solutions of single- or multi-objective, local or global optimization problem(s).

Obviously the "live-step" of evolving agents as well as their interaction can be defined in many possible ways—from very simple until complex, respecting many possible species and nations of agents.

One of possible realization is the system of co-evolving (arm-racing in fact) two species of agents: predators and preys which is called the co-evolutionary multi-agent system with predator-prey interactions (*PPCoEMAS*) which is generally discussed in this section (the formal model and detailed presentation of co-evolutionary multi-agent system with predator-prey interactions is given in [11]).

According the general description of evolutionary multi-agent system given in the Sect. 2 the system is composed of environment with graph-like structure, interacting agents and resources. There are two species of agents: predators (their goal is to remove less fitted prey agents) and preys (which represent solutions of multi-objective problem). Agents exist within the environment, they can migrate from node to node (if only there exists connection between nodes and agent has enough resource). Resources (which are possessed only by agents—there is no resource within the environment itself) are used for every activity like migration and reproduction. Agents without resources die and are removed from the system.

Agents of prey species can reproduce when they have sufficient amount of resource. When two ready for reproduction prey agents meet within the same node they reproduce—new agent is created with the use of intermediate recombination and mutation with self-adaptation operators (floating point representation is used). Some amount of resource is transferred from parents to the newly created offspring.

Predators do not reproduce. They can only migrate within the environment and seek for less fitted preys. Each predator has one criteria associated with it (it is encoded within predator's genotype) and it uses this criteria to seek for the worst prey that is located within the same node. Then predator takes all resources from the chosen prey, which dies as a result of this action.

The whole amount of resource within the system is constant—resource is possessed only by predators and preys. As a result of interactions between agents the resource may be transferred from prey to predator (predator-prey interaction) and from prey to another prey (prey-prey interaction).

4   Problem Formulation

As it was stated: the goal of this paper is to compare two approaches for hybridization of evolutionary and agent-based computational paradigms run against the problem of building effective portfolio.

The first question to be answered is how such a problem should be formally defined or which well-known definition should be chosen. Practically, there are some well known models describing building of effective portfolio i.e. Modern Portfolio Theory (MPT), one-factor Sharpe model, CAPM—Capital Asset Pricing Model, APT—Arbitrage Pricing Theory, Post Modern Portfolio Theory (PMPT) etc.

Taking all the pros and cons into consideration—one-factor Sharpe model has been chosen for our experiments so it is discussed below more precisely.

According to one-factor Sharpe model the algorithm of computing the expected risk level and income expectation related to the portfolio of p assets is formulated as in Algorithm 1.

The meanings of the symbols used in Algorithm 1 are as follows:

Algorithm 1. The algorithm (based on the one-factor Sharpe model) of computing the expected risk level and income expectation

---

1 Compute the arithmetic means on the basis of rate of returns;

2 Compute the value of α coefficient $\alpha_i = \overline{R_i} - \beta_i \overline{R_m}$;

3 Compute the value of β coefficient $\beta_i = \frac{\sum_{t=1}^{n}(R_{it}-\overline{R_i})(R_{mt}-\overline{R_m})}{\sum_{t=1}^{n}(R_{mt}-\overline{R_m})^2}$;

4 Compute the expected rate of return of asset i $R_i = \alpha_i + \beta_i R_m + e_i$;

5 Compute the variance of random index $s_{e_i}^2 = \frac{\sum_{t=1}^{n}(R_{it}-\alpha_i-\beta_i R_m)^2}{n-1}$;

6 Compute the variance of market index $s_m^2 = \frac{\sum_{t=1}^{n}(R_{mt}-\overline{R_m})^2}{n-1}$;

7 Compute the risk level of the investing portfolio $\beta_p = \sum_{i=1}^{p}(\omega_i \beta_i)$;

8 $s_{e_p}^2 = \sum_{i=1}^{p}(\omega_i^2 s_{e_i}^2)$;

9 $risk = \beta_p^2 s_m^2 + s_{e_p}^2$;

10 Compute the portfolio rate of return $R_p = \sum_{i=1}^{p}(\omega_i R_i)$;

---

p is the number of assets in the portfolio;

n is the number of periods taken into consideration (the number of rates of return taken to the model);

α_i, β_i are coefficients of the equations;

ω_i is percentage participation of i-th asset in the portfolio;

e_i is random component of the equation;

R_{it} is the rate of return in the period t;

R_{mt} is the rate of return of market index in period t;

R_m is the rate of return of market index;

R_i is the rate of return of the i-th asset;

R_p is the rate of return of the portfolio;

s_i^2 is the variance of the i-th asset;

$s_{e_i}^2$ is the variance of the random index of the i-th asset;

$s_{e_p}^2$ is the variance of the portfolio;

$\overline{R_i}$ is arithmetic mean of rate of return of the i-th asset;

$\overline{R_m}$ is arithmetic mean of rate of return of market index;

The goal of the optimization is to maximize the portfolio rate of return and minimize the portfolio risk level. The task consists in determining values of decision variables $\omega_1 \ldots \omega_p$ forming the vector $\Omega = [\omega_1, \ldots, \omega_p]^T$, where $0\,\% \leq \omega_i \leq 100\,\%$ and $\sum_{i=1}^{p} \omega_i = 100\,\%$ and $i = 1 \ldots p$ and which is the subject of minimization with respect of two criteria $F = [R_p(\Omega) * (-1), risk(\Omega)]^T$.

We gain a classical multiobjective optimization problem the **Multiobjective Optimization of Investing Portfolio Problem (MOIPP)** with two contradictory objectives the risk and expected income which can be formulated as follows:

$$MOIPP \equiv \begin{cases} Max: \; R_p = \sum_{i=1}^{p}(\omega_i R_i) \\ Min: risk = \beta_p^2 s_m^2 + s_{e_p}^2 \\ Taking \; into \; consideration: \\ \quad R \geq 0 \;\; and \; risk \geq 0 \\ \sum_{i=1}^{p} \omega_i = 100\,\% \\ \quad 0\,\% \leq \omega_i \leq 100\,\% \;\; and \;\; i = 1 \ldots p \end{cases}$$

In the course of this paper multi-objective optimization in the Pareto sense is considered, so solving defined MOIPP problem means determining of all feasible and non-dominated alternatives from the set ($\mathcal{D}$). Such defined set is called Pareto set ($\mathcal{P}$) and in objective space it forms so called Pareto frontier ($\mathcal{PF}$).

5 Results

Defined portfolio optimization problem has been solved using the hierarchical evolutionary multi-agent system discussed in Sect. 3.1 and the massively inter- active evolutionary multi-agent system with predator-prey interactions discussed in Sect. 3.2.

Each individual evolved during experiments has been represented as a p-dimensional vector. Each dimension represents the percentage participation of i-th ($i \in 1 \dots p$) share in the whole portfolio.

During presented experiments—Warsaw Stock Exchange quotations from 2003-01-01 until 2005-12-31 were taken into consideration. Simultaneously, the portfolio consists of the following three (experiment I) or seventeen (exper- iment II) stocks quoted on the Warsaw Stock Exchange: in experiment I: RAFAKO, PONARFEH, PKOBP, in experiment II: KREDYTB, COMPLAND, BETACOM, GRAJEWO, KRUK, COMARCH, ATM, HANDLOWY, BZWBK, HYDROBUD, BORYSZEW, ARKSTEEL, BRE, KGHM, GANT, PROKOM, BPHPBK. As the market index, WIG20 has been taken into consideration.

In Fig. 3 the sample approximation of Pareto frontiers (i.e. sets of non- dominated solutions) for both compared evolutionary-agent hybridized systems are presented.

As one may see in first–simpler–experiments consisting in looking for the optimal portfolio consisting of 3 stocks both hybridization approaches have been able to obtain a similar and comparable portfolios taking into consideration defined objectives i.e. expected (maximized) profit and (minimized) investment risk. In particular both compared approaches have been able to obtain portfolios with very similar level of profit and risk in the first one-third part of the Pareto frontier. Also both systems located the majority of final non-dominated individ- uals in this part of the Pareto frontier. The second two-third part of the frontier is visibly worse probed. Also the difference between obtained approximation of the Pareto frontiers is slightly bigger in this part of the frontier.

The model Pareto frontier for the problem defined is evenly dense on its full extent. Since the high-quality solution of the multi-objective optimization problem in the Pareto sense is the set of non-dominated solutions spread over the full extent of the Pareto frontier–concentration of found non-dominated solution in the first one-third part of the frontier observed in Fig. 3 in both cases—it is for sure the space for further improvements. Anyway, since the goal of this paper is to compare hierarchical and massively interactive hybrids of evolutionary and multi-agent computational paradigms, it can be said that both approaches are comparable taking the quality of obtained results into account.

Similar situation can be observed when we look at the Fig. 3(b) presenting pareto frontiers approximation obtained by both systems when the portfolio

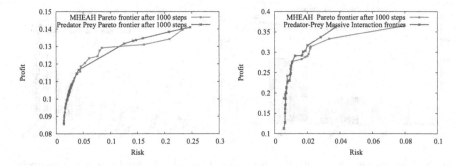

Fig. 3. Pareto frontier approximations after 1000 steps obtained by mixed hierarchical approach and massively interactive approach with predator-prey mechanisms for building effective portfolio consisting of 3 and 17 stocks

consisting of 17 stocks has been optimized. Also in this case both approaches concentrated their solution in the first one-third part of the Pareto frontier. But this time also the model Pareto frontier (not presented here because) is concentrated in this area.

What is interesting, there is as the matter of fact, some slight 'shift' between pareto frontier approximation obtained by compared hybridization approaches and the massively interactive approach has been able to cover slightly better the first half of the frontier whereas the hierarchical approach covered slightly better its second half–what gives for sure the space for further improvements. But again it can be said for sure that both approaches have been able to obtain a really close approximation of the model Pareto frontiers and obtained sets of non-dominated solutions are pretty close and similar.

From the financial point of view it is interesting how (financially) effective is the portfolio proposed by both approaches as the optimal one. Obviously, since we are in the space of multiobjective optimization in the Pareto sense the solution is not the one, single optimal solution but the whole set of non-dominated alternatives. Anyway, in the Fig. 5 the comparison of non-dominated

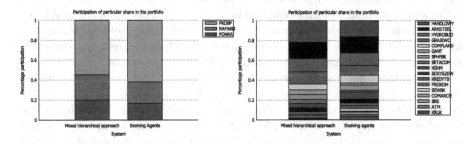

Fig. 4. Effective portfolio consisting of three and seventeen stocks found by hierarchical approach and massively interactive approach i.e. coevolving agents with predator-prey interactions

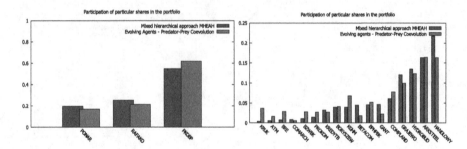

Fig. 5. The histogram of effective portfolios found by hierarchical and massively interactive approach

portfolios found by both systems and located closely on the frontiers diagram are presented.

As one may see obtained portfolios are really close and similar especially in the first–simpler experimental case (optimizing portfolio consisting of 3 stocks). In both cases the main part of proposed portfolio is PKOBP what is the biggest bank in Poland what is absolutely natural and expected. Probably every single human-being investor working without any computational tools would also build his portfolio around stable and profitable banking institution.

Obviously, analyzing the portfolio consisting of 17 stocks the greater variety can be observed nevertheless the general trends are also really close and similar in both cases.

For easier analysis, selected, found, non-dominated portfolios presented in Fig. 5(a) and (b) are presented from different perspective as the percentage share of the portfolio in Fig. 4. Also in this case it is clear that both evolutionary multi-agent hybridized systems have been able to find reasonable and similar (non-dominated) portfolios.

6 Summary and Conclusions

One of the promising computational techniques for solving hard and complex optimization problems (both global and local ones especially when the problem is defined as the multi-objective or multi-modal optimization problem) is applying nature-inspired systems and the evolutionary algorithms in particular since they are insensitive to the complexity of the problem to some extent.

The problem however is the premature loose of population (and solution) diversity and, as a result getting stuck in the basin of attraction of some local extrema instead of searching for a global one. The solution may be the hybridization of evolutionary algorithms with agent systems since the autonomy, mobility and generally saying the "intelligence" of agents may prevent the evolution from getting stuck.

When we think about hybridizing of evolutionary computations and agent systems in fact two approaches are possible: (1) hierarchical one – where agents are used as the management layer and the evolutionary algorithms are executed inside (sub)populations "within" agents and (2) system realized as the population(s) of evolving agents equipped with "DNA" performing life-steps to obtain their life-goals.

The analysis of any economical and financial phenomena is extremely complex and difficult mainly because of many-dimensional relations and dependencies among particular components and participants of the market-game. No wonder so that it is also so difficult to develop really efficient and effective algorithms and computer systems supporting modeling, analyzing and finally—solving market oriented problems. In the consequence the systems for financial or economical modeling and analysis are more and more complex and complicated.

As one may see on presented experimental comparison, there is for sure the space for further improvements, anyway, the general conclusion coming from the comparison is that both systems realizing two different approaches for hybridization of evolutionary computations and agent systems turned out to be comparably effective obtaining similar sets of non-dominated portfolios.

Acknowledgments. The research presented in this paper was partially supported by the AGH University of Science and Technology Statutory Fund no. 11.11.230.124.

References

1. Byrski, A., Oplatková, Z., Carvalho, M., Kisiel-Dorohinicki, M. (eds.): Advances in Intelligent Modelling and Simulation. SCI, vol. 416. Springer, Heidelberg (2012)
2. Bäck, T., Fogel, D., Michalewicz, Z. (eds.): Handbook of Evolutionary Computation. IOP Publishing and Oxford University Press, Bristol (1997)
3. Back, T., Hammel, U., Schwefel, H.-P.: Evolutionary computation: Comments on the history and current state. IEEE Trans. Evol. Comput. **1**(1), 3–17 (1997)
4. Cetnarowicz, K., Kisiel-Dorohinicki, M., Nawarecki, E.: The application of evolution process in multi-agent world (MAW) to the prediction system. In: Tokoro, M. (ed.) Proceedings of the 2nd International Conference on Multi-Agent Systems (ICMAS 1996). AAAI Press (1996)
5. Chen, S.-H., Kambayashi, Y., Sato, H.: Multi-Agent Applications with Evolutionary Computation and Biologically Inspired Technologies. IGI Global, Hershey, New York (2011)
6. Ciepiela, E., Kocot, J., Siwik, L., Dreżewski, R.: Hierarchical approach to evolutionary multi-objective optimization. In: Bubak, M., van Albada, G.D., Dongarra, J., Sloot, P.M.A. (eds.) ICCS 2008, Part III. LNCS, vol. 5103, pp. 740–749. Springer, Heidelberg (2008)
7. Deb, K.: Multi-Objective Optimization using Evolutionary Algorithms. John, Chichester (2001)
8. Dreżewski, R., Siwik, L.: Co-evolutionary multi-agent system with sexual selection mechanism for multi-objective optimization. In: Proceedings of the IEEE World Congress on Computational Intelligence (WCCI 2006) IEEE (2006)
9. Dreżewski, R., Siwik, L.: Multi-objective optimization using co-evolutionary multi-agent system with host-parasite mechanism. In: Alexandrov, V.N., van Albada, G.D., Sloot, P.M.A., Dongarra, J. (eds.) ICCS 2006. LNCS, vol. 3993, pp. 871–878. Springer, Heidelberg (2006)

10. Dreżewski, R., Siwik, L.: The application of agent-based co-evolutionary system with predator-prey interactions to solving multi-objective optimization problems. In: Proceedings of the 2007 IEEE Symposium Series on Computational Intelligence. IEEE (2007)
11. Dreżewski, R., Siwik, L.: Co-evolutionary multi-agent system for portfolio optimization. In: Brabazon, A., O'Neill, M. (eds.) Natural Computation in Computational Finance, pp. 271–299. Springer-Verlag, Berlin, Heidelberg (2008)
12. Kisiel-Dorohinicki, M.: Agent-oriented model of simulated evolution. In: Grosky, W.I., Plášil, F. (eds.) SOFSEM 2002. LNCS, vol. 2540, pp. 253–261. Springer, Heidelberg (2002)
13. Sarker, R., Ray, T.: Agent-Based Evolutionary Search. Springer, Heidelberg (2010)
14. Schaefer, R., Kołodziej, J.: Genetic search reinforced by the population hierarchy. Found. Genet. Algorithms 7, 383–399 (2003)
15. Siwik, L., Dreżewski, R.: Evolutionary multi-modal optimization with the use of multi-objective techniques. In: Rutkowski, L., Korytkowski, M., Scherer, R., Tadeusiewicz, R., Zadeh, L.A., Zurada, J.M. (eds.) ICAISC 2014, Part I. LNCS, vol. 8467, pp. 428–439. Springer, Heidelberg (2014)
16. Wójtowicz, T., Rzecki, K., Pławiak, P., Niedźwiecki, M., Sośnicki, T., Smelcerz, K., Wojtoń, Z.: Tomasz amd Tabor: Emergence of cooperation as a result of mutation and inheritance in pd/pg-like game. Tech. Trans. Fundam. Sci. 18(1–NP/2015), 71–84 (2015)
17. Wooldridge, M.: An Introduction to Multiagent Systems. Wiley, Chichester (2009)
18. Zhong, W., Liu, J., Xue, M., Jiao, L.: A multiagent genetic algorithm for global numerical optimization. IEEE Trans. Syst. Man Cybern. Part B Cybern. 34(2), 1128–1141 (2004)

Multi-chaotic System Induced Success-History Based Adaptive Differential Evolution

Adam Viktorin$^{(\boxtimes)}$, Michal Pluhacek, and Roman Senkerik

Faculty of Applied Informatics, Tomas Bata University in Zlin,
Nam T.G. Masaryka 5555, 760 01 Zlin, Czech Republic
{aviktorin,pluhacek,senkerik}@fai.utb.cz

Abstract. This research paper combines two soft computing fields – chaos theory and evolutionary computing. The proposed multi-chaotic system implements five different chaotic maps as a Pseudo-Random Number Generators (PRNGs) for parent selection process in Differential Evolution (DE) and Success-History based Adaptive Differential Evolution (SHADE) algorithms. The probabilities for selecting chaotic maps are adapted and the adaptation process is based on the previous successful solutions. Therefore, PRNG varies for different test functions. The performance of multi-chaotic system induced DE and SHADE is compared against their canonical versions on CEC2015 benchmark set. Acquired results show that replacing classic PRNG with multi-chaotic PRNG can lead sto improvement in terms of convergence speed and ability to reach the global optimum.

Keywords: Differential Evolution · SHADE · Deterministic chaos · Parent selection · Pseudo-Random Number Generator

1 Introduction

Differential Evolution (DE) and algorithms based on it have been proven to be a simple but effective heuristic methods for solving various optimization problems in many fields and that they can outperform other Evolutionary Algorithms (EAs) [1–5].

Since its discovery in 1995 [6], canonical version of DE algorithm has been thoroughly studied and improved in terms of convergence speed, ability to find the optimal solution and robustness. DE in its canonical form has three main

A. Viktorin—This work was supported by the Programme EEA and Norway Grants for funding via grant on Institutional cooperation project nr. NF-CZ07-ICP-4-345-2016, also by Grant Agency of the Czech Republic – GACR P103/15/06700S, further by the Ministry of Education, Youth and Sports of the Czech Republic within the National Sustainability Programme Project no. LO1303 (MSMT-7778/2014. Also by the European Regional Development Fund under the Project CEBIA-Tech no. CZ.1.05/2.1.00/03.0089 and by Internal Grant Agency of Tomas Bata University under the Projects no. IGA/CebiaTech/2016/007.

L. Rutkowski et al. (Eds.): ICAISC 2016, Part I, LNAI 9692, pp. 517–527, 2016.
DOI: 10.1007/978-3-319-39378-0_44

control parameters (population size NP, scaling factor F and crossover rate CR) and two strategies, mutation strategy and crossover strategy. One of the most powerful directions in performance improvement of DE is adapting its main control parameters in order to avoid the premature convergence to a local optimum. Some of the existing algorithms which adapt control parameters CR and F are jDE [7], SDE [8], SaDE [9] and JADE [10]. The last named algorithm also implements innovative mutation strategy "current-to-$p$best/1" and an optional archive of inferior solutions A. This algorithm formed a base for Success-History based Adaptive Differential Evolution (SHADE) algorithm [11] which additionally extends it by the use of two historical memories M_{CR} and M_F for storing historically successful CR and F values rather than using only one pair of adapted values of CR and F.

Previous research has shown that utilization of Pseudo-Random Number Generators (PRNGs) based on chaotic dissipative maps into various stages of EAs rather than the use of classical PRNGs can be beneficial [12–15]. Additionally, the effect of different chaotic maps used for PRNGs varies and so does the performance of influenced EAs. Research to date has mostly focused on multi-chaotic systems with two different chaotic map PRNGs and switching between them [16,17]. Therefore, this paper proposes a novel multi-chaotic approach which uses five different chaotic dissipative maps for pseudo-random number generation in parent selection process of the DE and SHADE algorithms. The performance is tested on the CEC2015 benchmark set [18] and both algorithms are compared with their canonical versions.

The paper is structured as follows: Next section focuses on chaotic maps and their use as a PRNGs. Section three briefly describes DE, SHADE and multi-chaotic parent selection framework. Sections four and five depict experiment settings and results respectively and sections that follow are result discussion and conclusion.

2   Chaotic Maps

Chaotic maps are systems generated continuously by simple equations from a single initial position. The current position is used for generation of a new position thus creating a sequence which is extremely sensitive to the initial position, which is also known as the "butterfly effect." Sequences generated by chaotic maps have characteristics which are not common in classical random number generation. Therefore, their application in EA can change its behavior and might improve the performance.

The multi-chaotic system presented in this paper uses five different chaotic maps – Burgers, Delayed Logistic, Dissipative, Lozi and Tinkerbell. Each of these maps is generated differently and initial positions also vary. Chaotic maps, their generating equations with specific parameters and initial positions are shown in Table 1. Specific parameter values were set according to [19].

The process of acquiring i-th random integer $rndInt_i$ from chaotic map is depicted in (1).

$$rndInt_i = \text{round}\left(\frac{\text{abs}\,(X_i)}{\max(\text{abs}\,(X_{i \in N}))} * (maxRndInt - 1)\right) + 1 \qquad (1)$$

Where abs(X_i) is an absolute value of i-th X of a chaotic sequence with length of N, max(abs($X_{i \in N}$)) is a maximum of absolute values of X in chaotic sequence and round() is common rounding function. The generated number $rndInt_i$ is from interval [1, $maxRndInt$].

Table 1. Chaotic maps, their specific parameters and initial position.

Chaotic map	Equations	Parameters	Initial position
Burgers map	$X_{n+1} = aX_n - Y_n^2$	$a = 0.75$	$X_0 = [-0.1, -0.01]$
	$Y_{n+1} = bY_n + X_nY_n$	$b = 1.75$	$Y_0 = [0.01, 0.1]$
Delayed logistic map	$X_{n+1} = AX_n(1 - Y_n)$	$A = 2.27$	$X_0 = Y_0 = [0.8, 0.9]$
	$Y_{n+1} = X_n$		
Dissipative map	$X_{n+1} = X_n + Y_{n+1} \;(\text{mod } 2\pi)$	$b = 0.1$	$X_0 = Y_0 = [0, 0.1]$
	$Y_{n+1} = bY_n + k\; sinX_n \;(\text{mod } 2\pi)$	$k = 8.8$	
Lozi map	$X_{n+1} = 1 - a|X_n| - bY_n$	$a = 1.7$	$X_0 = Y_0 = [0, 0.1]$
	$Y_{n+1} = X_n$	$b = 0.5$	
Tinkerbell map	$X_{n+1} = X_n + Y_n + aX_n + bY_n$	$a = 0.9$	$X_0 = [-0.1, -0.01]$
	$Y_{n+1} = 2X_nY_n + cX_n + dY_n$	$b = -0.6$	$Y_0 = [0, 0.1]$
		$c = 2$	
		$d = 0.5$	

3 Differential Evolution, Success-History Based Adaptive Differential Evolution and Multi-Chaotic Parent Selection

DE algorithm as aforementioned has three control parameters – population size NP, crossover rate CR and scaling factor F. In the canonical form of DE, these three parameters are static and set by the user. Other important features of DE algorithm are mutation strategy and crossover strategy. This work uses "rand/1/bin" mutation strategy (2) and binomial crossover (5). SHADE algorithm, on the other hand, uses only two control parameters – population size NP and size of historical memories H. F and CR parameters are automatically adapted based on the evolutionary process and the values for each individual are generated by (4) and (6) respectively. Also, the mutation strategy is different than that of canonical DE. The mutation strategy used in SHADE is called "current-to-$p$best/1" and is depicted in (3). The concept of basic operations in DE and SHADE algorithms is shown in following sections, for a detailed description on feature constraint correction, update of historical memories and external archive handling in SHADE see [11].

3.1   Initialization

The initial population is randomly generated from objective space and has NP individuals in both algorithms. The external archive A in SHADE algorithm is initially empty with a maximum size of NP and historical memories M_{CR} and M_F are both set to the size H where $M_{CR,i} = M_{F,i} = 0.5$ for $(i = 1, \ldots, H)$.

3.2   Mutation Strategies and Parent Selection

In canonical forms of both algorithms, parent vectors are selected by classic PRNG with uniform distribution. Mutation strategy "rand/1/bin" uses three random parent vectors with indexes $r1$, $r2$ and $r3$, where $r1 = U[1, NP]$, $r2 = U[1, NP]$, $r3 = U[1, NP]$ and $r1 \neq r2 \neq r3$. Mutated vector $v_{i,G}$ is obtained from three different vectors x_{r1}, x_{r2}, x_{r3} from current generation G with the help of static scaling factor $F_i = F$ as follows:

$$v_{i,G} = x_{r1,G} + F_i \left(x_{r2,G} - x_{r3,G} \right) \tag{2}$$

Contrarily, SHADEs mutation strategy "current-to-$p$best/1" uses four parent vectors – current i-th vector $x_{i,G}$, vector $x_{pbest,G}$ randomly selected from $NP \times p$ ($p = U[p_{min}, 0.2]$, $p_{min} = 2/NP$) best vectors (in terms of objective function value) from G, randomly selected vector $x_{r1,G}$ from G and randomly selected vector $x_{r2,G}$ from the union of G and external archive A. Where $x_{i,G} \neq x_{r1,G} \neq x_r2, G$.

$$v_{i,G} = x_{i,G} + F_i \left(x_{pbest,G} - x_{i,G} \right) + F_i \left(x_{r1,G} - x_{r2,G} \right) \tag{3}$$

The scaling factor F_i is generated from Cauchy distribution with location parameter value of $M_{F,r}$ which is a randomly selected value from scale factor historical memory M_F, and scale parameter value of 0.1 (4).

$$F_i = C \left[M_{F,r}, 0.1 \right] \tag{4}$$

3.3   Crossover and Elitism

The trial vector $u_{i,G}$ which is compared with the original vector $x_{i,G}$ is completed by crossover operation (5) and this operation is the same for both DE and SHADE algorithms. CR_i value in DE algorithm is again static $CR_i = CR$ whereas with SHADE algorithm its value is generated from a normal distribution with a mean parameter value of $M_{CR,r}$ which is randomly selected value from crossover rate historical memory M_{CR} and with standard deviation value of 0.1 (6).

$$u_{j,i,G} = \begin{cases} v_{j,i,G} & \text{if } U[0,1] \leq CR_i \text{ or } j = j_{rand} \\ x_{j,i,G} & \text{otherwise} \end{cases} \tag{5}$$

Where j_{rand} is randomly selected index of a feature, which has to be updated ($j_{rand} = U[1, D]$), D is the dimensionality of the problem.

$$CR_i = N[M_{CR,r}, 0.1] \tag{6}$$

Individual which will be in the next generation $G+1$ is selected by elitism. When the objective function value of trial vector $\boldsymbol{u}_{i,G}$ is better than that of the original vector $\boldsymbol{x}_{i,G}$, the trial vector will be selected for the next population and the original will be placed into the external archive A. Otherwise, the original will survive and the content of A remains unchanged (7).

$$\boldsymbol{x}_{i,G+1} = \begin{cases} \boldsymbol{u}_{i,G} & \text{if } f(\boldsymbol{u}_{i,G}) < f(\boldsymbol{x}_{i,G}) \\ \boldsymbol{x}_{i,G} & \text{otherwise} \end{cases} \tag{7}$$

3.4   Multi-Chaotic Parent Selection

Multi-chaotic framework for parent selection process is based on ranking selection of Chaotic map based PRNGs (CPRNGs). A list of CPRNGs $Clist$ has to be added to the EA and each CPRNG is initialized with the same probability $pc_{init} = 1/Csize$, where $Csize$ is the size of $Clist$. For example, for five CPRNGs $Csize = 5$ and each of them will have the probability of selection $pc_{init} = 1/5 = 0.2 = 20\%$.

For each individual vector $\boldsymbol{x}_{i,G}$ in generation G, the chaotic generator $CPRNG_k$ is selected from the $Clist$ according to its probability pc_k, where k is the index of selected CPRNG. This selected generator is then used to replace classic PRNG for selection of parent vectors and if the generated trial vector succeeds in elitism, the probabilities are adjusted. There is an upper boundary for the probability of selection $pc_{max} = 0.6 = 60\%$, if the selected CPRNG reach this probability, then no adjustment takes place. Whole process is depicted in (8).

$$\text{if } f(\boldsymbol{u}_{i,G}) < f(\boldsymbol{x}_{i,G}) \text{ and } pc_k < pc_{max} \quad pc_j = \begin{cases} \frac{pc_j + 0.01}{1.01} & \text{if } j = k \\ \\ \frac{pc_j}{1.01} & \text{otherwise} \end{cases} \tag{8}$$

$$\text{otherwise} \qquad\qquad pc_j = pc_j$$

4   Experiment Setting

Canonical DE and SHADE algorithms were compared against their multi-chaotic system induced opposites on the CEC2015 benchmark set functions in 10-dimensional objective space. Control parameters and their values are depicted below. The setting for DE algorithms was based on previous testing and SHADE algorithms were initialized in accordance with [11]. Stopping criterion for all runs was a Maximum number of Test Function Evaluations (MaxTFE). The setting of the multi-chaotic system is shown below as well and each chaotic map was initialized as presented in Table 1.

4.1 Common Setting

- Dimension D: 10
- Runs R: 51
- Maximum number of test function evaluations $MaxTFE$: $10\,000 \times D = 100\,000$

4.2 De Setting

- Population size NP: 100
- Crossover rate CR: 0.8
- Scaling factor F: 0.5

4.3 SHADE Setting

- Population size NP: 100
- External archive A of size H: 100

4.4 Multi-Chaotic System Setting

- List of CPRNGs $Clist$: {Burgers, Delayed Logistic, Dissipative, Lozi, Tinkerbell}
- Size of $Clist$ – $Csize$: 5
- Initial probability pc_{init}: $1/Csize = 1/5 = 0.2$
- Maximal probability $pc_{max} = 0.6$

5 Results

Comparison between statistical characteristics of canonical and multi-chaotic system induced algorithms is depicted in Tables 2 and 3, where the obtained values are differences from the global optimum of a test function from function set. Global optimum for each test function in the CEC2015 benchmark set is equal to $100 \times$ function number (e.g. for function 4 the global optimum value $f(x_0) = 400$). Both tables show median and mean values over 51 independent runs and better value is illustrated by bold. If the mean value obtained by multi-chaotic system induced version of the algorithm is lower than that of canonical version, Wilcoxon signed-rank test p-value is shown in the last column with the null hypothesis that both versions have the same mean ranks and the alternative hypothesis that mean rank value of canonical version is greater than that of multi-chaotic system induced version.

Moreover, the evolution of averaged best obtained value against the Test Function Evaluations (TFE) is shown for two selected functions from CEC2015 benchmark set in Figs. 1 and 2. These figures depict the comparison between all four algorithm versions – canonical DE, multi-chaotic system induced DE, canonical SHADE and multi-chaotic system induced SHADE.

6 Result Discussion

As can be seen in Tables 2 and 3, the performance of both algorithms was improved on the majority of test functions. The p-values obtained from Wilcoxon singed-rank test indicate that with the significance level set to 5 %, DE algorithm induced by multi-chaotic system performs better on 5 functions ($f(1)$, $f(4)$, $f(5)$,$f(6)$ and $f(7)$) and SHADE algorithm induced by multi-chaotic system performs better on 2 functions ($f(4)$ and $f(9)$).

Furthermore, Fig. 1 shows that even when the difference between obtained function values by both versions of the SHADE algorithm is not significant, the convergence of the algorithm is improved and same objective function value is reached in fewer evaluations when using multi-chaotic system CPRNGs instead of PRNG with uniform distribution.

The functions defined in the CEC2015 benchmark set are divided into four categories. First two functions $f(1-2)$ are unimodal functions, functions $f(3-9)$ are simple multimodal functions, functions $f(10-12)$ are hybrid functions and functions $f(13-15)$ are composite functions. As can be seen in Tables 2 and 3, the multi-chaotic versions of algorithms perform better mostly on the simple multimodal functions.

Table 2. Median and mean values of canonical DE and multi-chaotic system induced DE on CEC2015 benchmark set functions, p-values of Wilcoxon signed-rank test between the two versions in the last column.

| f(x) | Canonical DE | | Multi-chaotic system induced DE | | |
	Median	Mean	Median	Mean	p-value
$f(1)$	0.256	0.299	**0.049**	**0.083**	6.90E-09
$f(2)$	**0.000**	**0.000**	**0.000**	**0.000**	-
$f(3)$	20.328	20.321	**20.316**	**20.310**	0.159
$f(4)$	24.563	23.714	**22.150**	**20.676**	0.003
$f(5)$	1101.570	1089.530	**1052.760**	**996.971**	0.021
$f(6)$	5.663	6.551	**1.034**	**2.755**	6.76E-07
$f(7)$	0.556	0.562	**0.409**	**0.407**	2.01E-04
$f(8)$	**0.238**	**0.258**	0.331	0.363	-
$f(9)$	**100.222**	**100.217**	100.230	100.224	-
$f(10)$	216.656	**216.654**	**216.584**	216.690	-
$f(11)$	4.020	131.285	**3.494**	**107.907**	0.146
$f(12)$	**102.022**	**102.007**	102.141	102.093	-
$f(13)$	33.793	33.546	**33.223**	**33.172**	0.072
$f(14)$	2935.540	**3069.170**	**2935.540**	3355.910	-
$f(15)$	**100.000**	**100.000**	**100.000**	**100.000**	-

Table 3. Median and mean values of canonical SHADE and multi-chaotic system induced SHADE on CEC2015 benchmark set functions, p-values of Wilcoxon signed-rank test between the two versions in the last column.

| f(x) | Canonical SHADE | | Multi-chaotic system induced SHADE | | p-value |
	Median	Mean	Median	Mean	
$f(1)$	**0.000**	**0.000**	**0.000**	**0.000**	-
$f(2)$	**0.000**	**0.000**	**0.000**	**0.000**	-
$f(3)$	20.062	18.481	**20.061**	**17.324**	0.096
$f(4)$	3.065	2.784	**2.360**	**2.436**	2.65E-10
$f(5)$	**31.917**	**45.131**	35.296	48.525	-
$f(6)$	0.680	6.039	**0.418**	**5.530**	0.999
$f(7)$	0.178	0.209	**0.166**	**0.196**	0.989
$f(8)$	0.478	0.473	**0.252**	**0.277**	0.370
$f9)$	100.172	100.175	**100.164**	**100.165**	0.005
$f(10)$	**216.537**	216.640	**216.537**	218.455	0.999
$f(11)$	3.343	**119.418**	**3.148**	130.934	-
$f(12)$	101.460	101.445	**101.403**	**101.419**	0.453
$f(13)$	27.853	**27.364**	**27.650**	27.407	-
$f(14)$	**2935.540**	4267.120	**2935.540**	3855.180	0.478
$f(15)$	**100.000**	**100.000**	**100.000**	**100.000**	-

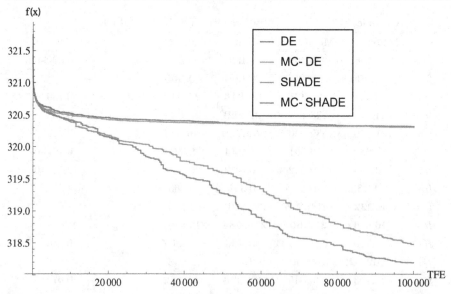

Fig. 1. Average best value development from 51 runs on $f(3)$, $D = 10$. DE – canonical DE, MC – DE – multi-chaotic system induced DE, SHADE – canonical SHADE, MC – SHADE – multi-chaotic system induced SHADE.

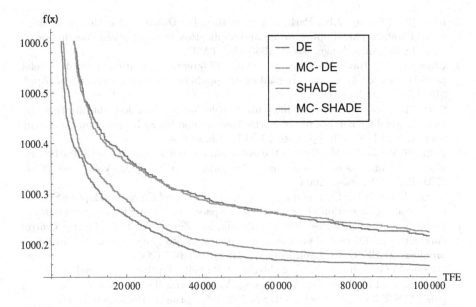

Fig. 2. Average best value development from 51 runs on $f(9)$, $D = 10$. DE – canonical DE, MC – DE – multi-chaotic system induced DE, SHADE – canonical SHADE, MC – SHADE – multi-chaotic system induced SHADE.

7 Conclusion

This research presented a novel multi-chaotic framework and demonstrated its use on a parent selection process in DE and SHADE algorithms. In both cases, the use of the framework was shown to be beneficial in terms of best obtained objective function value and convergence speed on simple multimodal functions from the CEC2015 benchmark set. The results will be examined further and will be extended by different settings for the dimensionality of the problem.

The main goal of this research was to establish, whether the adaptivity of SHADE algorithm will neutralize the valuable characteristics of multi-chaotic system CPNRG which were observed on the canonical DE algorithm. Even when the improvement is not as significant as on DE, it is apparent. Therefore, the proposed framework may be labeled as robust.

The future research will focus on applications of the framework into different parts of evolution process (e.g. crossover and mutation) and on its use in other state-of-art EAs.

References

1. Price, K., Storn, R.M., Lampinen, J.A.: Differential Evolution: A Practical Approach to Global Optimization. Springer Science & Business Media, Heidelberg (2006)

2. Kim, H.K., Chong, J.K., Park, K.Y., Lowther, D.: Differential evolution strategy for constrained global optimization and application to practical engineering problems. IEEE Trans. Magn. **43**(4), 1565–1568 (2007)
3. Chauhan, N., Ravi, V., Chandra, D.K.: Differential evolution trained wavelet neural networks: Application to bankruptcy prediction in banks. Expert Syst. Appl. **36**(4), 7659–7665 (2009)
4. Storn, R.: On the usage of differential evolution for function optimization. In: 1996 Biennial Conference of the North American on Fuzzy Information Processing Society, NAFIPS 1996, pp. 519–523. IEEE, June 1996
5. Babu, B. V., Jehan, M.: Differential evolution for multi-objective optimization. In: The 2003 Congress on Evolutionary Computation, CEC 2003, Vol. 4, pp. 2696–2703. IEEE, December 2003
6. Storn, R., Price, K.: Differential Evolution-a Simple and Efficient Adaptive Scheme for Global Optimization Over Continuous Spaces, vol. 3. ICSI, Berkeley (1995)
7. Brest, J., Greiner, S., Bošković, B., Mernik, M., Zumer, V.: Self-adapting control parameters in differential evolution: a comparative study on numerical benchmark problems. IEEE Trans. Evol. Comput. **10**(6), 646–657 (2006)
8. Omran, M.G., Salman, A., Engelbrecht, A.P.: Self-adaptive differential evolution. In: Hao, Y., Liu, J., Wang, Y., Cheung, Y., Yin, H., Jiao, L., Ma, J., Jiao, Y.C. (eds.) CIS 2005. LNCS, vol. 3801, pp. 192–199. Springer, Heidelberg (2005)
9. Qin, A.K., Huang, V.L., Suganthan, P.N.: Differential evolution algorithm with strategy adaptation for global numerical optimization. IEEE Trans. Evol. Comput. **13**(2), 398–417 (2009)
10. Zhang, J., Sanderson, A.C.: JADE: adaptive differential evolution with optional external archive. IEEE Trans. Evol. Comput. **13**(5), 945–958 (2009)
11. Tanabe, R., Fukunaga, A.: Success-history based parameter adaptation for differential evolution. In: 2013 IEEE Congress on Evolutionary Computation (CEC), pp. 71–78. IEEE, June 2013
12. Skanderova, L., Zelinka, I., Saloun, P.: Chaos Powered Selected Evolutionary Algorithms. In: Zelinka, I., Chen, G., Rössler, O.E., Snasel, V., Abraham, A. (eds.) Nostradamus 2013: Prediction, Modeling and Analysis of Complex Systems. AISC, vol. 210, pp. 111–124. Springer, Heidelberg (2013)
13. Senkerik, R., Pluhacek, M., Kominkova Oplatkova, Z., Davendra, D.: On the parameter settings for the chaotic dynamics embedded differential evolution. In: IEEE Congress on Evolutionary Computation, CEC 2015, pp. 1410–1417. IEEE, May 2015
14. Caponetto, R., Fortuna, L., Fazzino, S., Xibilia, M.G.: Chaotic sequences to improve the performance of evolutionary algorithms. IEEE Trans. Evol. Comput. **7**(3), 289–304 (2003)
15. Davendra, D., Zelinka, I., Senkerik, R.: Chaos driven evolutionary algorithms for the task of PID control. Comput. Math. Appl. **60**(4), 1088–1104 (2010)
16. Pluhacek, M., Senkerik, R., Zelinka, I.: Particle swarm optimization algorithm driven by multichaotic number generator. Soft Comput. **18**(4), 631–639 (2014)
17. Senkerik, R., Pluhacek, M., Oplatkova, Z.K.: An initial study on the new adaptive approach for multi-chaotic differential evolution. In: Silhavy, R., Senkerik, R., Oplatkova, Z.K., Prokopova, Z., Silhavy, P. (eds.) Artificial Intelligence Perspectives and Applications. AISC, vol. 347, pp. 355–362. Springer, Heidelberg (2015)

18. Chen, Q., Liu, B., Zhang, Q., Liang, J.J., Suganthan, P.N., Qu, B.Y.: Problem definition and evaluation criteria for CEC 2015 special session and competition on bound constrained single-objective computationally expensive numerical optimization. In: Computational Intelligence Laboratory, Zhengzhou University, China and Nanyang Technological University, Singapore, Technical report (2014)
19. Sprott, J.C., Sprott, J.C.: Chaos and Time-Series Analysis, vol. 69. Oxford University Press, Oxford (2003)

Pattern Classification

Generalized Shape Language Application to Detection of a Specific Type of Bone Erosion in X-ray Images

Marzena Bielecka[1]([✉]) and Mariusz Korkosz[2]

[1] Chair of Geoinformatics and Applied Computer Science,
Faculty of Geology, Geophysics and Environmental Protection,
AGH University of Science and Technology, Mickiewicza 30, 30-059 Cracow, Poland
bielecka@agh.edu.pl
[2] Division of Rheumatology, Departement of Internal Medicine and Gerontology,
Jagiellonian University Hospital, Śniadeckich 10, 31-531 Cracow, Poland
mariuszk@mp.pl

Abstract. X-ray imaging is crucial in diagnosis of various musculoskeletal diseases. During early disease process, the X-ray changes are often scarce and difficult to capture and the definite localization of osteophytes or erosions is often challenging. Therefore, the attempt to use computer methods to facilitate better diagnosing is of great value. Formal tools for contour description are based on string languages. In Jakubowski's shape languages sixteen primitives are predefined. Finite collection of primitives, however is insufficient for describing natural objects because of irregular character of this type of objects. In this paper the generalized shape language, in which primitives are defined on a higher level of abstraction, is proposed and is used for description and detection of a special type of complex erosions in bone contours.

Keywords: Shape language · Primitives · Contours analysis · Bone contours

1 Introduction

This paper joins two streams of scientific investigations. The first stream concerns the shapes description and recognition. The second one concerns application of artificial intelligence to analysis of medical images.

The problem of shape description and analysis, based on the analysis of contours, have been solved effectively in manufacturing. Theoretical aspects of the Jakubowski's approach were worked out in seventies [17] and then were applied in intelligent manufacturing [18–21]. Recently, this theory has been used in robotic systems for description and recognition building-type objects on the scene on which an autonomous robot operates [8–10]. In Jakubowski's shape languages sixteen primitives are predefined. Finite collection of primitives, however, is insufficient for describing natural objects because of irregular character

© Springer International Publishing Switzerland 2016
L. Rutkowski et al. (Eds.): ICAISC 2016, Part I, LNAI 9692, pp. 531–540, 2016.
DOI: 10.1007/978-3-319-39378-0_45

of this type of objects. In this paper the generalized shape language, in which primitives are defined on a higher level of abstraction, is proposed.

Since the medical imaging has been developed rapidly during last decades, there is a great demand on computer systems for automatic analysis of medical images. X-ray pictures remains a widely used technique of imaging because of its efficiency and low cost. Therefore, systems of their computer analysis are developed intensively - the papers [3,4,13] can be put as examples. The palm pictures analysis is widely used for diagnosis of musculoskeletal diseases [25,26]. The joint width analysis is a well worked out problem [11–14,28] whereas results concerning the bone shape analysis are far from satisfactory [4,5,7]. Attempts that were made to approximate bone contours by given a priori primitives were finished by encoding the contour with a set of extremely short segments, in most cases of line segments [5]. The application of Jakubowski-like primitives in Shaw language to detect such pathological changes like erosions or osteophytes in bones gave efficiency only about 70 % [29]. The problems were caused by the fact that in the mentioned approaches a finite set of predefined primitives were used. As it has been aforementioned, such approach is sufficient to describe artificial objects that are regular.They are insufficient, however, for description of irregular natural objects such as bones. Therefore, a new approach, which consists in using more general primitives, is proposed. The introduced primitives correspond to classical sixteen primitives used by Jabubowski. The proposed formalism has been used effectively for description and detection of a specific type of a complex erosion. It should be mentioned that this paper is a continuation of the previous papers in which the shape language was applied to palm X-ray pictures analysis [4,5,7].

2   X-ray Imaging as the Basis of Musculoskeletal Diseases Diagnosis

X-ray imaging is still considered to be the cornerstone in differential diagnosis of various musculoskeletal diseases. There are several X-ray signs that may help not only to diagnose the disease but also monitor the disease progression and response to treatment.

In musculoskeletal disorders joints and connective tissue are involved and the most important goal is to diagnose the disease as soon as possible since the time from the disease onset to treatment initiation is important for the overall prognosis. Among wide variety of diagnostic tests, imaging is still a very important tool and many diseases in their classification or diagnosis criteria must have X-ray signs included.

The spectrum of rheumatic diseases involves the entities with inflammation and without inflammation. Osteoarthritis (OA) is a primarily degenerative non-inflammatory disease of cartilage, and loss of cartilage is a first triggering mechanism for further changes, including formation of new bone, i.e. osteophytes. Rheumatoid arthritis (RA) in turn is inflammatory arthritis involving the synovial membrane within the joints, which transforms into the pannus invading cartilage and bone. From the clinical point of view the key issue is to distinguish between inflammatory and degenerative diseases because inflammatory entities have worse prognosis and require more aggressive pharmacologic treatment.

X-ray of hands allow to assess the width of joint space, giving the information about the thickness of cartilage, and on the other hand bony outline which tells us about bone damage or bone synthesis. Although OA, which is considered the model for non-inflammatory arthropathy, and RA, being the model of inflammatory arthropathy are both characterized by joint space narrowing, changes within the bone tissue are different. Degenerative joint disease, i.e. OA is responsible for bony overgrowth - osteoproliferation or ostogenesis - in form of osteophytes, which are localized on margins of cortical bone adjacent to the attachment of joint capsule and ligaments. In contrast, RA is a disease where pathologic process within synovial membrane of joints invades and destructs bone, in form of erosions - which in fact represent the bone loss.

During early disease process, both in OA and RA, the X-ray changes are often scarce and difficult to capture, and even for a very experienced radiologist or rheumatologist the definite judgment of certain X-ray signs, eg. osteophytes or erosions, is often challenging. That is why the attempt to use the artificial intelligence methods to facilitate better diagnosing is of great value.

3 Generalized Shape Language

All predefined primitives of Jakubowski's shape language are presented in Fig. 1. They are line segments and circle quadrants.

As it has been aforementioned, these basic segments are improper for the representation of fragments of bone contours because of irregularities of the bone contours. In order to introduce more general primitives let us define a four-component vector $\mathbf{c} = [c', c'', c^x, c^y]$. The first component c' encodes the properties of the tangent line, that can be vertical, horizontal, increasing or decreasing. The second component encodes whether the contour fragment is concave, convex, flat vertical or flat horizontal. The components c^x and c^y encode increase of the x coordinate and the y coordinate, respectively. They can be positive, negative or equal to zero. Let l be a line on the Euclidean plane which has constant values of all four components of the vector $\mathbf{c}$ in all its points i.e. each component of the vector c remains unchanged along the line l. In the set of all such curves let us introduce a relation in the following way: two curves are in relation if they are described by the same vector $\mathbf{c}$. It is an equivalence relation. Let the set of primitives be the set of the equivalence classes - see Fig. 2.

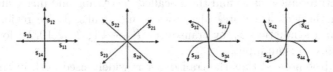

Fig. 1. The classical primitives of the Jakubowski's shape language.

Fig. 2. Examples of primitives p_{31} according to the proposed way; the Jakubowski's primitive p_{31} is marked in bold.

Since the components of vector **c** are mutually dependent, there are only sixteen classes of equivalence relation. They correspond to the Jakubowski's primitives which means that each Jakubowski's primitive is described by one vector **c**. It should be stressed, however, that in the linear Jakubowski's primitives the angle between the primitive and the OX axis can only have values that are multiples of $\frac{\pi}{4}$ and the curvature of curvilinear segments is constant see Fig. 1.

Let us denote the possible vectors **c** by using bi-index as $p_{ij}, i, j \in \{1, 2, 3, 4\}$. Each of these vectors corresponds to one of quadrants of the Cartesian plane - the index i. The vector $\mathbf{c} = [c', c'', c^x, c^y]$, describes the local geometric features of a curve and can be calculated in every point of the curve. Its four components constitute the basis that represents the essential qualitative features of the analyzed contour. The values of the components are traced along the contour. Then, it is segmented into fragments for which the values of the components c', c'', c^x and c^y are constant. As a result the analyzed contour, let it be denoted as k, is described by a string of primitives i.e. the maximal fragments for which the vector **c** is constant. It should be stressed that, in contrast with Jakubowski's approach, in such defined primitives the angle between linear segments and OX axis can have arbitrary values and the curvature of the segment can be variance along the primitive. The contour is characterized by its descriptor that encodes the mentioned string of primitives: $des(k) = p_{i_1j_1}p_{i_2j_2}...p_{i_nj_n}$.

Let us recall briefly the formalism which is used in this paper.

Definition 1. *The l-sinquad is a structure composed of primitives from the l-quadrant, $l = 1, 2, 3, 4$.*

Let $k = k_1 \odot k_2$ denotes concatenation of the contours k_1 and k_2 .

Definition 2. *Let k_1, k_2 be i-sinquad and j-sinquad respectively. Then the contour $k = k_1 \odot k_2$ constitutes ij-biquad.*

These structures allow us to find the so-called decreasing and increasing regions which form the global features like grooves and flanks. These regions can be extracted in a syntactic way by transducer T see Fig. 3, [2,19,24] for which a descriptor $des(k)$ is an input.

It should be noticed that the transducer is widely used both in engineering and medical applications [19,20,27]. The output of the transducer is denoted by $key(k) = a_0b_0w_0 \cdot a_1b_1w_1 \cdots a_{n+1}b_{n+1}w_{n+1}$ where every pair a_ib_j denotes subsequent biquad. Every switch between two sinquads is followed by the $w_i \in \{0,1\}$ which determines whether the biquad is concave (then $w_i = 0$) or convex (then $w_i = 1$) [19]. On the basis of this information it is possibly to find grooves and flanks in the analyzed contour. They are sufficient to detect changes in a bone contour i.e. erosions and osteophytes.

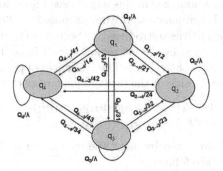

Fig. 3. Transducer where q_i denotes the *ith* state of transducer, $i = 1, 2, 3, 4$ number of sinquad; Q_i/λ denotes that in the *ith* state appears terminal belonging to *ith* sinquad; $Q_{i \to j}/ij$ denotes that in the *ith* state appears terminal belonging to *jth* sinquad and sequence *ij* is written to output.

Definition 3. *If for a given subcontour g of contour k with a description $key(g) = a_0 b_0 w_0 \cdot a_1 b_1 w_1 \cdots a_{n+1} b_{n+1} w_{n+1}$ the conditions $w_0 = w_{n+1} = 0$ and $w_l = 1$ for $1 \leq l \leq n$ are satisfied, then the subcontour constitutes groove - see Fig. 4.*

Definition 4. *If for a given subcontour g of contour k with a description $key(g) = a_0 b_0 w_0 \cdot a_1 b_1 w_1 \cdots a_{n+1} b_{n+1} w_{n+1}$ the conditions $w_0 = w_{n+1} = 1$ and $w_l = 0$ for $1 \leq l \leq n$ are satisfied, then the subcontour constitutes flank - see Fig. 4.*

Definition 5. *The grooves $g_1, ..., g_r$ constitute a cascade of grooves if and only if $hd(g_l) = tl(g_{l+1})$ for $l < r$. The flanks $f_1, ..., f_r$ constitute a cascade of flanks if and only if $hd(g_l) = tl(g_{l+1})$ for $l < r$ - see Fig. 4.*

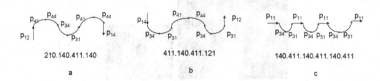

Fig. 4. Examples of a groove, flank and cascade.

4   Complex Erosion Detection

It is assumed that a well-defined bone contour is given as the input of the proposed algorithms. It should be stressed, however, that a preprocessing, in particular contourisation of structures at both X-ray images and other types of medical images is not the trivial task and intensive studies that concern this topic are conducted - [6,15,22]. The contours analyzed in this paper - see Figs. 6 and 9 - were received by using the statistical dominance algorithm proposed in [23].

The generalized primitives, introduced in Sect. 3, were used to generate the description of a finger bone in a joint region - see Fig. 5. The description was done from left to right side of the joint. The sequences of primitives that describe the upper k_1 and lower k_2 side of the healthy joint respectively, are as followed:

$$\mathrm{des}(k_1) = p_{23}p_{34}p_{31}p_{41}p_{44}p_{34}p_{31}p_{22},$$
$$\mathrm{des}(k_2) = p_{22}p_{41}p_{44}p_{33}p_{34}p_{43}.$$

The keys k_1 and k_2 received by using the transducer in Fig. 3 to the $des(k_1)$ and $des(k_2)$ sequences are following:

$$\mathrm{key}(k_1) = 341.411.\mathbf{140}.411.121,$$
$$\mathrm{key}(k_2) = 210.140.\mathbf{430}.341.430.$$

It turns out that the upper side of the healthy joint is a curve with one flank (marked in the $key(k_1)$ in bold) whereas the lower one is a curve with one groove (marked in the $key(k_2)$ in bold). In turn, the pathologies such as erosions and osteophytes that can appear on the bone surface [16] change the shape of the bone contour. As a result it differs significantly from the healthy bone contour. If we analyze the upper side of the finger joint with an erosion then we will receive contour with two flanks. Analogically, for the lower side of the finger joint with an erosion we receive contour with two grooves. Also in the case of the osteophyte the number of flanks and grooves is bigger than one. Therefore it is possible to distinguish immediately the healthy contour from the lesion one only on the basis of the defined primitives and transducer - see Fig. 3 [1,2]. In order to distinguish types of erosions (left, central or right) and osteophytes (left or right) a contex-free

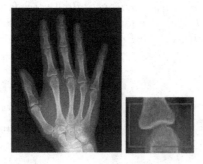

Fig. 5. The example of X-ray picture of a healthy palm with the investigated joint (in the frame).

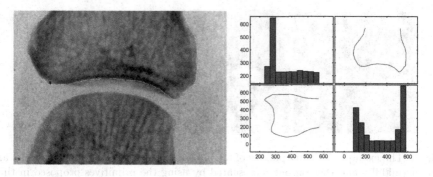

Fig. 6. The healthy joint with an outline made by an expert and with outline received by using the statistical dominance algorithm.

LR(1) grammar can be used. From the medical point of view, however, erosions can be more complex than osteophytes. The simple erosion as in Fig. 7 constitutes two flanks in the upper side or two grooves in the lower side of the bone contour. More complex shapes of erosions can be described by cascades. Let us analyze an upper side of the contour depicted in Fig. 8.

Usually, erosions can be found in the segments of the contour which are described by primitives $p_{23}p_{34}$ or by primitives $p_{31}p_{22}$. These segments are on the left and on the right side of the contour therefore such erosions are called left-side erosion (EL) and right-side erosion (ER). An erosion in the segment described by a primitive p_{31} is called the central erosion (CE). The central erosion is presented in Fig. 8. The sequence of primitives, shown in Fig. 8 (right), is as followed (the primitives that represent pathological changes are marked in bold):

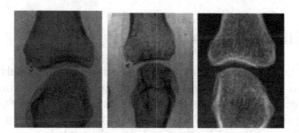

Fig. 7. The example of X-ray pictures with simple erosions - (left and middle), and example of X-ray of a healthy bone (right).

$\mathrm{des}(k) =$

$p_{23}p_{34}p_{31}\mathbf{P_{32}P_{41}P_{11}P_{14}P_{34}P_{41}P_{44}P_{43}P_{14}P_{43}P_{14}P_{34}}p_{31}p_{41}p_{44}p_{34}p_{31}p_{22},$

$\mathrm{key}(k) = 341.411.121.210.140.411.140.430.341.430.341.411.140.411.121,$

In the received contour we can see the cascade of three flanks and one separated flank.

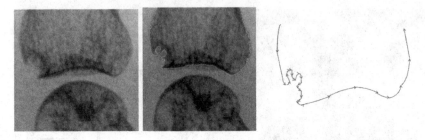

Fig. 8. The example of X-ray picture of a complex erosion (left), outlines made by an expert (middle) and the contour represented by using the primitives proposed in this paper (right).

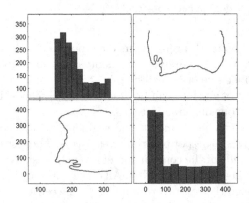

Fig. 9. The complex erosion after preprocessing by using the statistical dominance algorithm.

5   Concluding Remarks

The introduced generalized primitives allow us to analyze effectively the shape of a finger bone in a joint region. In particular, fragments of bone contours can be represented precisely by a proposed primitives. It is impossible by using classical Jakubowski's primitives because of their lack of flexibility - the curvilinear ones have constant curvature and for the linear ones the angle between them and the OX axis can only have values that are multiples of $\frac{\pi}{4}$. Furthermore, the healthy joint can be distinguished quickly from a joint with pathological changes by using proposed primitives and the transducer. Localization of an erosion i.e. whether it is left, right or central, is possible by using a contex-free grammar.

In the case of a complex erosion it can be detected by analyzing complex features of the bone contour like a cascade. The possibility of a description of such pathologies by a cascade is a simple and quick method.

Acknowledgment. This paper was supported by the AGH - University of Science and Technology, Faculty of Geology, Geophysics and Environmental Protection as a part of the statutory project.

References

1. Bielecka, M.: Modified shape language with application to syntactic analysis of contours. Under review
2. Bielecka, M., Bielecki, A., Korkosz, M., Skomorowski, M., Wojciechowski, W., Zieliński, B.: Modified Jakubowski shape transducer for detecting osteophytes and erosions in finger joints. In: Dobnikar, A., Lotrič, U., Šter, B. (eds.) ICANNGA 2011. LNCS, vol. 6594, pp. 147–155. Springer, Heidelberg (2011)
3. Benerjee, S., Bhunia, S., Schaefer, G.: Osteophyte detection for hand osteoarthritis identification in X-ray images using CNNs. In: Proceedings of the Annual International Conference of the IEEE Engineering in Medicine and Biology Society, EMBS 2011, pp. 6196–6199 (2011)
4. Bielecka, M., Bielecki, A., Korkosz, M., Skomorowski, M., Wojciechowski, W., Zieliński, B.: Application of shape description methodology to hand radiographs interpretation. In: Bolc, L., Tadeusiewicz, R., Chmielewski, L.J., Wojciechowski, K. (eds.) ICCVG 2010, Part I. LNCS, vol. 6374, pp. 11–18. Springer, Heidelberg (2010)
5. Bielecka, M., Bielecki, A., Korkosz, M., Skomorowski, M., Wojciechowski, W., Zieliński, B.: Modified Jakubowski shape transducer for detecting osteophytes and erosions in finger joints. In: Dobnikar, A., Lotrič, U., Šter, B. (eds.) ICANNGA 2011, Part II. LNCS, vol. 6594, pp. 147–155. Springer, Heidelberg (2011)
6. Bielecka, M., Piórkowski, A.: Adaptive preprocessing of X-ray hand images. Adv. Intell. Syst. Comput. **283**, 61–70 (2014)
7. Bielecka, M., Skomorowski, M., Zieliński, B.: A fuzzy shape descriptor and inference by fuzzy relaxation with application to description of bones contours at hand radiographs. In: Kolehmainen, M., Toivanen, P., Beliczynski, B. (eds.) ICANNGA 2009. LNCS, vol. 5495, pp. 469–478. Springer, Heidelberg (2009)
8. Bielecki, A., Buratowski, T., Śmigielski, P.: Syntactic algorithm of two-dimensional scene analysis for unmanned flying vehicles. In: Tadeusiewicz, R., Chmielewski, L.J., Wojciechowski, K., Bolc, L. (eds.) ICCVG 2012. LNCS, vol. 7594, pp. 304–312. Springer, Heidelberg (2012)
9. Bielecki, A., Buratowski, T., Śmigielski, P.: Recognition of two-dimensional representation of urban environment for autonomous flying agents. Expert Syst. Appl. **40**, 3623–3633 (2013)
10. Bielecki, A., Buratowski, T., Śmigielski, P.: Three-dimensional urban-type scene representation in vision system of unmanned flying vehicles. In: Rutkowski, L., Korytkowski, M., Scherer, R., Tadeusiewicz, R., Zadeh, L.A., Zurada, J.M. (eds.) ICAISC 2014, Part I. LNCS, vol. 8467, pp. 662–671. Springer, Heidelberg (2014)
11. Bielecki, A., Korkosz, M., Wojciechowski, W., Zieliński, B.: Identifying the borders of the upper and lower metacarpophalangeal joint surfaces on hand radiographs. In: Rutkowski, L., Scherer, R., Tadeusiewicz, R., Zadeh, L.A., Zurada, J.M. (eds.) ICAISC 2010, Part I. LNCS, vol. 6113, pp. 589–596. Springer, Heidelberg (2010)
12. Bielecki, A., Korkosz, M., Zieliński, B.: Hand radiographs preprocessing, image representation in the finger regions and joint space width measurements for image interpretation. Pattern Recogn. **41**, 3786–3798 (2008)

13. Bottcher, J., Pfeil, A., Rosholm, A., Petrovitch, A., Seidl, B.E., Malich, A., Schäfer, M.L., Kramer, A., Mentzel, H.J., Lehmann, G., Hein, G., Kaiser, W.A.: Digital X-ray radiogrammetry combined with semiautomated analysis of joint space widths as a new diagnostic approach in rheumatoid arthritis: a cross-sectional and longitudal study. Arthritis Rheum. **52**, 3850–3859 (2006)

14. Choi, S., Lee, G.J., Hong, S.J., Park, K.H., Urtnasan, T., Park, H.K.: Development of a joint space width measurement method based on radiographic hand images. Comput. Biol. Med. **41**, 987–998 (2011)

15. Davis, L., Theobald, B.J., Lines, J., Toms, A., Bagnall, A.: On the segmentation and classification of hand radiographs. Int. J. Neural Syst. **22**, 1250020 (2012)

16. Jacobson, J.A., Girish, G., Jiang, Y., Resnick, D.: Radiographic evaluation of arthritis: inflammatory conditions. Radiology **248**, 378–389 (2008)

17. Jakubowski, R., Kasprzak, A.: A syntactic description and recognition of rotary machine elements. IEEE Trans. Comput. **C–26**, 1039–1043 (1977)

18. Jakubowski, R.: Syntactic characterization of machine parts shapes. Cybern. Syst. **13**, 1–24 (1982)

19. Jakubowski, R.: Extraction of shape features for syntactic recognition of mechanical parts. IEEE Trans. Syst. Man Cybern. **15**, 642–651 (1985)

20. Jakubowski, R.: A structural representation of shape and its features. Inf. Sci. **39**, 129–151 (1986)

21. Jakubowski, R., Flasiński, M.: Towards a generalized sweeping model for designing with extraction and recognition of 3D solids. J. Des. Manuf. **2**, 239–258 (1992)

22. Piórkowski, A., Gronkowska–Serafin, J.: Towards precise segmentation of corneal endothelial cells. In: Ortuño, F., Rojas, I. (eds.) IWBBIO 2015, Part I. LNCS, vol. 9043, pp. 240–249. Springer, Heidelberg (2015)

23. Piórkowski, A.: Statistical dominance algorithm for edge detection and segmentation of medical images. In: ITiB 2016. Advances in Intelligent and Soft Computing, vol. 471. Springer (2016)

24. Ogiela, M.: Languages of shape feature description and syntactic methods for recognition of morphological changes of organs in analysis of selected X-ray images. Med. Imaging **3338**, 1295–1305 (1998)

25. Ogiela, M., Tadeusiewicz, R.: Picture languages in automatic radiological palm interpretation. Int. J. Appl. Math. Computut. Sci. **15**, 305–312 (2005)

26. Ogiela, M.R., Tadeusiewicz, R., Ogiela, L.: Image languages in intelligent radiological palm diagnostics. Pattern Recogn. **39**, 2157–2165 (2006)

27. Ogiela, M.R., Tadeusiewicz, R.: Syntactic pattern recognition for X-ray diagnosis of pancreatic cancer-algorithms for analyzing the morphologic shape of pancreatic ducts for early diagnosis of changes in the pancreas. IEEE Eng. Med. Biol. Mag. **19**, 94–105 (2000)

28. Sharp, J., Gardner, J., Bennett, E.: Computer-based methods for measuring joint space and estimating erosion volume in the finger and wrist joints of patients with rheumatoid arthritis. Arthritis Rheum. **43**, 1378–1386 (2000)

29. Zieliński, B., Skomorowski, M., Wojciechowski, W., Korkosz, M., Spręźak, K.: Computer aided erosions and osteophytes detection based on hand radiographs. Pattern Recogn. **48**, 2304–2317 (2015)

On the Relation Between kNN Accuracy and Dataset Compression Level

Marcin Blachnik$^{(\boxtimes)}$

Department of Applied Informatics, Silesian University of Technology,
Krasinskiego 8, Katowice, Poland
marcin.blachnik@polsl.pl

Abstract. The paper discusses how instance selection can be used to asses the kNN performance. There exists a strong correlation between the compression level of the dataset obtained by instance selection methods and the prediction accuracy obtained the k-NN classifier trained on full training dataset.

Based on two standard algorithms of instance selection namely CNN and ENN, which belong to two different groups of methods, so called condensation and editing methods, we perform empirical analysis to verify this relation. The obtained results show that this relation is almost linear, so that the level of *compression* is linearly correlated with the *accuracy*. In other words by knowing the compression of instance selection methods we are able to estimate the *accuracy* of the final kNN prediction model.

1 Introduction

In classification problems, which are defined as finding a mapping function $y = f(\mathbf{x})$ that maps each input example $\mathbf{x} \in \Re^m$ into one of c classes $y \in \{s_1, s_2, \ldots s_c\}$ having a training set $\mathbf{T}$ of n tuples $\{\mathbf{x}, y\}$, one of the primary methods to build a prediction model is to use k nearest neighbor algorithm. During the training stage it simply stores the training set $\mathbf{T}$, and than when predicting, the output label is calculated as the majority of k class labels of the nearest examples to the query example $\mathbf{x}$. This simple algorithm works surprisingly well, but it has several serious drawbacks. It is very time consuming during prediction phase as it has to calculate all of the distances between the query example and each example in the training set. Another weakness of the kNN classifier is its noise sensitivity especially for low values of k. A possible solution to overcome these two problems is to use instance selection methods, which could be treated as a preprocessing step of the training phase. So in the preprocessing these methods are used to prune training set by removing undesired examples, i.e. these instances that do not influence the classification process at all and these which have negative impact on the classifier accuracy.

Instance selection methods are often characterized by the performance measure called *compression*, which measures how much data of the original training set $\mathbf{T}$ remains after the selection (denoted as $\mathbf{P}$). This performance measure is evaluated only on the training set and formally is independent of the *prediction*

© Springer International Publishing Switzerland 2016
L. Rutkowski et al. (Eds.): ICAISC 2016, Part I, LNAI 9692, pp. 541–551, 2016.
DOI: 10.1007/978-3-319-39378-0_46

accuracy obtained by the classifier as it simply measures the number of training samples before and after pruning.

$$CMP = \frac{|\mathbf{P}|}{|\mathbf{T}|} \tag{1}$$

where $|\cdot|$ denotes cardinality of given set.

An important question arises what knowledge (if any) can be derived from the value of *compression* and if there is any correlation between this value and some other performance measures. An obvious correlation exists between the *compression* and the execution time; lower values of *compression* lead to the shorter execution time. Interestingly in our research on instance selection methods we have observed a phenomena that the level of *compression* may be related to the value of *prediction accuracy* or shortly *accuracy*. Here we use the standard definition of the *accuracy*, which is defined as

$$ACC = \frac{TP + TN}{TP + TN + FP + FN} \tag{2}$$

where the ACC measures the ratio between all correctly classified examples (the True Positives (TP) and True Negatives (TN), or sum of all diagonal elements of the confusion matrix) and all of the analyzed examples.

In this paper we first describe two basic instance selection methods which were designed to address both problems: reduction of classifier execution time and noise filtering, and then we empirically analyze the earlier mentioned relation between *compression* and *prediction accuracy*.

2   The Instance Selection Algorithms

The instance selection algorithms were developed to improve classifier performance. There are two issues which are addressed by instance selection. The first one is high time complexity during kNN prediction phase and the second one is accuracy improvement. The first problem is a real challenge, as the time complexity during prediction grows linearly with the number of training samples $O(n)$ as it has to calculate all of the distances between each query example and the remaining training examples. This makes kNN very slow. On contrary many other typical machine learning methods such as MLP neural networks or decision trees have much shorter prediction time, as only one query example must be propagated through the model. Although the required size of a neural network or the obtained size of a decision tree depends rather on the complexity of the dataset than on the number of training examples, in practice the complexity also frequently grows with the number of training examples. And thus it also can be noticed that the size of the training dataset frequently influences not only training but also prediction time of other classifiers than kNN.

To alleviate this problem so called condensation instance selection algorithms were developed. These algorithms try to remove as many examples as possible, while preserving the classification accuracy. Usually the accuracy should not change, or can change only within very small limits $acc(kNN(T)) - acc(kNN(condensed(T))) < \epsilon$ where ϵ is near 0. The first condensation algorithm was CNN (condensed nearest neighbor rule) [5] which is presented and discussed in the next subsection.

The second problem - the accuracy of kNN classifier is addressed by so called *editing* methods. The source of accuracy drop in kNN is the noise, which usually is present in the training data. To overcome it, usually larger value of k is used, but this is not always appropriate, so the idea introduced by Wilson in [12] is to remove all noisy examples from the data and then train the 1NN classifier. An example of the second group of algorithms will be discussed in Subsect. 2.2. The literature presents also a third group of instance selection methods, which combines the first two groups, so usually at the first stage the data is cleaned-up and then it is condensed. A nice overview of different instance selection algorithms could be found in [10].

2.1   Condensed Nearest Neighbor Rule

The sketch of CNN algorithm is shown in Algorithm 1. It starts with an empty dataset $\mathbf{P}$ also called set of reference examples or prototypes, then a random

---

Algorithm 1. Schema of the CNN algorithm

Require: T
   $n \leftarrow |\mathbf{T}|$
   $k \leftarrow 1$
   $\mathbf{p}_1 \leftarrow \mathbf{x}_1$
   $flag \leftarrow$ **true**
   while flag **do**
      $flag \leftarrow$ **false**
      for $i = 1 \ldots n$ **do**
         $\bar{y}_i = \text{kNN}(k, \mathbf{P}, \mathbf{x}_i)$
         if $\bar{y}_i \neq y_i$ **then**
            $\mathbf{P} \leftarrow \mathbf{P} \cup \mathbf{x}_i;$
            $\mathbf{T} \leftarrow \mathbf{T} \setminus \mathbf{x}_i$
            $flag \leftarrow$ **true**
         end if
      end for
   end while
   return P

(usually first example) is added as a first prototype and in each iteration new example is added to the set $\mathbf{P}$ if it is misclassified by kNN classifier trained using recent set of reference vectors (here we denote the arguments of $\bar{y} = \text{kNN}(k, \mathbf{P}, \mathbf{x})$ as follows: k - the number of nearest neighbors of kNN, $\mathbf{P}$ - the training set, $\mathbf{x}$ - the example for which we wont to make prediction, $\bar{y}$ - predicted class label).

Finally the set of selected prototypes is returned. This algorithm in the worst case could have complexity of $O(n^3)$ but it happens when the training set is a pure noise, but if there appears any *redundancy* in the data, such that one instance could replace a set of other instances the algorithm starts to work very fast. In real application this algorithm works fast, as usually *redundancy* is present in the data, and compression obtained by this algorithm is on average 33 %.

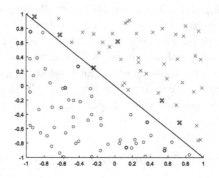

(a) Dataset without noise. Obtained compression=0.12

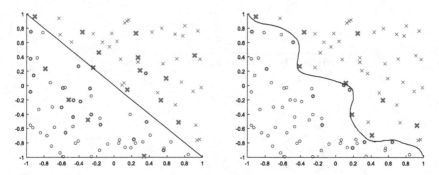

(b) Dataset with noise. Obtained compression=0.34

(c) Dataset with nonlinear decison border. Obtained compression=0.19

Fig. 1. Behavior of CNN algorithm on three simple two class datasets: simple linear classification problem without noise, the same dataset but with 5 % level of noise, and on dataset with more complex (nonlinear) decision border. Solid line represent optimal Bayesian decision border. Instances which remain after selection are marked in bold.

To understand the obtained results it is important to know how the condensation algorithm works and how it influences *compression*. First, when considering a simple linear classification task as presented in Fig. 1(a) only a very small set of examples is required to reconstruct the decision border of the kNN classifier, so the CNN algorithm obtains a very low compression (only a small set of training samples are returned as prototypes). When the decision border gets more complex - more examples are required to reconstruct it (see Fig. 1(c)) and the *compression* increases. Even higher growth of *compression* appears when noise is present as any noisy examples would be stored as reference points together with their neighbor samples, what is presented in Fig. 1(b). In all figures the selected prototypes (after instance selection) are marked in bold.

To summarize, the properties of condensation methods - the value of *compression* reflects both the level of noise and the complexity of the decision border. By default, when the classification task is simple the compression is very low, but when the training data is noisy or the decision border is complex the compression increases. We can also say that in the condensation methods the *compression* reflects redundancy in the data, this is how much clean data do we have to use to train the prediction model.

2.2 Edited Nearest Neighbor Rule

The ENN algorithm is presented in sketch (Algorithm 2). Unlike CNN, it starts with the entry set of examples as a reference set $\mathbf{P} = \mathbf{T}$ and then in each iteration it removes a single instance $\mathbf{x}_i$ which is misclassified by its k nearest neighbors. As a result only noise examples get rejected, so the compression ratio is rather high. It has an $O(n^2)$ complexity, which is independent to the data distribution. However this value can be lowered if the complexity of the nearest neighbor search algorithm gets reduced for example by KD-Tree [2], Ball-Tree [9,11] or Local Sensitive Hashing algorithms [4] leading to $O(n \cdot log(n))$ or even lower.

Algorithm 2. Schema of the ENN algorithm

Require: T, k
   $n \leftarrow |\mathbf{T}|$;
   $\mathbf{P} \leftarrow \mathbf{T}$;
   for $i = 1 \ldots n$ **do**
      $\bar{y}_i =$kNN$(k, (\mathbf{T} \setminus \mathbf{x}_i), \mathbf{x}_i)$;
      if $y_i \neq \bar{y}_i$ **then**
         $\mathbf{P} \leftarrow \mathbf{P} \setminus \mathbf{x}_i$
      end if
   end for
   return P

The *compression* level of the ENN method depends mostly on the number of noisy examples. However, ENN can also remove some border examples, which often are incorrectly classified as presented in Fig. 2(a). So again in contrast to CNN as the decision border gets more complex more samples are removed from the data, because they are treated as noisy samples what is visualized in Fig. 2(c). So the ENN algorithm could be treated as a regularization term for kNN classifier. Its behavior and properties with noise data are shown in Fig. 2(b), where we can observe further decrease of *compression* level.

To summarize the editing methods, in perfect scenario when the decision border is simple the *compression* is very high (almost no samples are rejected

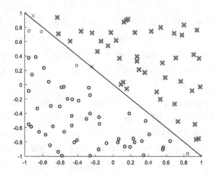

(a) Dataset without noise. Obtained compression=0.94

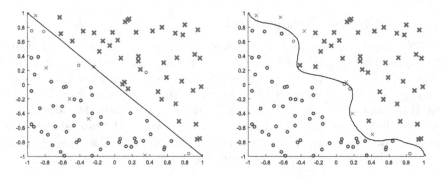

(b) Dataset with noise. Obtained compression=0.89

(c) Dataset with nonlinear decision border. Obtained, compression=0.90

Fig. 2. Behavior of ENN algorithm on three simple two class datasets: simple linear classification problem without noise, the same dataset but with 5 % level of noise, and on dataset with more complex (nonlinear) decision border. Solid line represent optimal Bayesian decision border. Instances which remain after selection are marked in bold.

from the training set), but as the level of noise in the training data increases the value of *compression* decreases, what result in smaller final dataset.

3   Experiments

In order to verify the relation between *prediction accuracy* and *compression* we conducted empirical evaluations. All of the experiments were performed on 42 datasets obtained from Keel Project [6] repository, and most of them are also available from UCI repository [1]. The properties of these datasets are provided in the first four columns of Table 1, these are: name of the dataset, number of attributes and its type (R-real, I - integer, N-nominal), number of examples (in brackets is provided the number of examples with rejected examples containing missing values), and number of classes. In the experiments we used only examples without missing values.

Table 1. Datasets used in the experiments and obtained results which are: accuracy of kNN and compression obtained from CNN and ENN

id	Name	#Attributes (R/I/N)	#Examples	#Classes	kNN accuracy	CNN compression	ENN compression
1	appendicitis	7 (7/0/0)	106	2	0.89	0.36	0.84
2	balance	4 (4/0/0)	625	3	0.90	0.34	0.80
3	banana	2 (2/0/0)	5300	2	0.90	0.23	0.88
4	bands	19 (13/6/0)	365 (539)	2	0.73	0.49	0.72
5	bupa	6 (1/5/0)	345	2	0.66	0.59	0.63
6	cleveland	13 (13/0/0)	297 (303)	5	0.59	0.62	0.56
7	glass	9 (9/0/0)	214	7	0.73	0.46	0.69
8	haberman	3 (0/3/0)	306	2	0.76	0.52	0.69
9	hayes-roth	4 (0/4/0)	160	3	0.72	0.46	0.61
10	heart	13 (1/12/0)	270	2	0.85	0.39	0.78
11	hepatitis	19 (2/17/0)	80 (155)	2	0.90	0.38	0.83
12	ionosphere	33 (32/1/0)	351	2	0.87	0.24	0.86
13	iris	4 (4/0/0)	150	3	0.97	0.15	0.95
14	led7digit	7 (7/0/0)	500	10	0.75	0.48	0.64
15	magic	10 (10/0/0)	19020	2	0.84	0.36	0.83
16	mammographic	5 (0/5/0)	830 (961)	2	0.81	0.44	0.77
17	marketing	13 (0/13/0)	6876 (8993)	9	0.33	0.81	0.29
18	monk-2	6 (0/6/0)	432	2	0.96	0.27	0.97
19	movement libras	90 (90/0/0)	360	15	0.86	0.36	0.81
20	newthyroid	5 (4/1/0)	215	3	0.97	0.10	0.94
21	optdigits	64 (0/64/0)	5620	10	0.99	0.07	0.99
22	page-blocks	10 (4/6/0)	5472	5	0.96	0.10	0.96
23	penbased	16 (0/16/0)	10992	10	0.99	0.04	0.99
24	phoneme	5 (5/0/0)	5404	2	0.90	0.23	0.89
25	pima	8 (8/0/0)	768	2	0.76	0.50	0.74
26	ring	20 (20/0/0)	7400	2	0.81	0.26	0.72
27	satimage	36 (0/36/0)	6435	7	0.91	0.19	0.91
28	segment	19 (19/0/0)	2310	7	0.97	0.11	0.96
29	sonar	60 (60/0/0)	208	2	0.86	0.30	0.83
30	spambase	57 (57/0/0)	4597	2	0.91	0.23	0.90
31	spectfheart	44 (0/44/0)	267	2	0.82	0.49	0.70
32	tae	5 (0/5/0)	151	3	0.61	0.60	0.50
33	texture	40 (40/0/0)	5500	11	0.99	0.07	0.99
34	thyroid	21 (6/15/0)	7200	3	0.94	0.19	0.94
35	titanic	3 (3/0/0)	2201	2	0.79	0.58	0.44
36	twonorm	20 (20/0/0)	7400	2	0.98	0.17	0.97
37	vehicle	18 (0/18/0)	846	4	0.73	0.49	0.71
38	vowel	13 (10/3/0)	990	11	0.99	0.21	0.98
39	wdbc	30 (30/0/0)	569	2	0.97	0.16	0.97
40	wine	13 (13/0/0)	178	3	0.98	0.17	0.97
41	wisconsin	9 (0/9/0)	683 (699)	2	0.98	0.10	0.97
42	yeast	8 (8/0/0)	1484	10	0.60	0.66	0.54

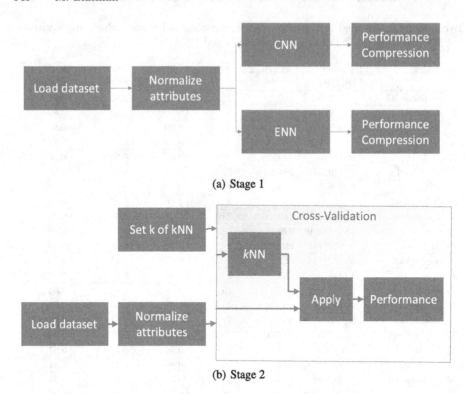

(a) Stage 1

(b) Stage 2

Fig. 3. Processes used to evaluate and validate dataset assessment based on compression.

The experiments were executed in two independent stages presented in Figs. 3(a) and (b). In the first one after loading the data each numerical attribute was normalized in range $[0, 1]$ then both instance selection algorithms were performed and the compression for each of them was calculated. It is important to note that the parameters of this stage (parameters of instance selection methods) were not optimized and the default values were used ($k = 3$ for ENN and $k = 1$ for CNN). As in this experiment we did not train any prediction model we also did not have to perform any cross-validation test. The second stage was dedicated to estimate performance of pure kNN classifier without any instance selection. In this process after loading the data, all numerical attributes were also normalized as in the first step, and then in cross-validation the performance of kNN was estimated for various values of $k = [1, 3, 4, 5, 6, \ldots, 15]$ (in all experiments Euclidean distance was used). Finally only the highest accuracy was reported. The results collected from both experiments are presented in last three columns of Table 1 and plotted in Figs. 4(a) and (b) where the x axis represents compression, and y axis represents accuracy. On both figures we can observe almost linear relation between accuracy and compression. To verify this we calculated Pearson linear correlation coefficient (CC) which for CNN is $CC(CNN, kNN) = -0.9304$ and

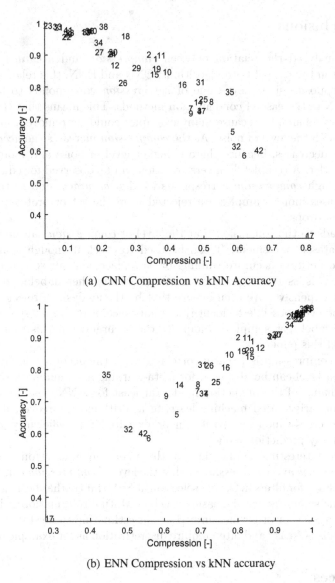

(a) CNN Compression vs kNN Accuracy

(b) ENN Compression vs kNN accuracy

Fig. 4. Relation between compression of CNN and ENN instance selection algorithms vs accuracy of optimized kNN. CNN and ENN were not optimized. Numbers represent *id* of the dataset

respectively for ENN is $CC(ENN, kNN) = 0.9439$. In both cases $|CC|$ suggests very strong correlation between the two variables.

4 Conclusions

We have analyzed the relation between *compression* and *accuracy*. We have shown that in the case of both algorithms, CNN and ENN, this relation is linear but with opposite sign. Low value of *compression* corresponds to high accuracy of kNN in the case of condensation methods. This means that the decision border must be simple because many examples could be removed, moreover it correlates with the level of noise. As the *compression* increases the *accuracy* proportionally decreases, because there is higher level of noise and more complex decision border. A completely inverse relation can be observed for editing methods where high *compression* corresponds to high *accuracy*, and as the level of noise increases more examples are rejected from the set of prototypes, so the *compression* drops.

This leads to the conclusion that the level of *compression* can be effectively used for dataset assessment. It can be used to check if enough samples were collected to perform accurate training or as replacement for so called *learning curve* [14]. This issue is very important for problems where labeling data examples is very expensive. We even believe that by the analysis of rejected samples it should be even possible to identify the subspace of the input space in which we have to label new samples to improve the accuracy, but this topic is out of the scope of this paper.

As the compression is linearly correlated with the accuracy, analysis of the *compression* level can be also used for meta-learning as a landmark to estimate the performance of the prediction model (at least for k-NN classifier and other distance/similarity-based machine learning algorithms). Moreover, it does not require any cross-validation, so it can be executed very efficiently, and much faster than any prediction model.

Another interesting application of the phenomena of strong correlation between *accuracy* and *compression*, is that the level of *compression* can be used as evaluation stage for filters in feature selection [3,8]. So far this has been usually performed using some statistical measures such as Mutual Information or Kullback–Leibler divergence or other measures [13], but estimating these statistics on real valued data is not easy and often require discretization as for example in [7].

References

1. Asuncion, A., Newman, D.: UCI machine learning repository. http://www.ics.uci.edu/~mlearn/MLRepository.html
2. Bentley, J.L.: Multidimensional binary search trees used for associative searching. Commun. ACM **18**(9), 509–517 (1975)
3. Duch, W., Wieczorek, T., Biesiada, J., Blachnik, M.: Comparision of feature ranking methods based on information entropy. In: Proceedings of International Joint Conference on Neural Networks, pp. 1415–1420. IEEE Press, Budapest (2004)
4. Gionis, A., Indyk, P., Motwani, R.: Similarity search in high dimensions via hashing. In: Proceedings of the 25th Very Large Database (VLDB) Conference (1999)

5. Hart, P.: The condensed nearest neighbor rule. IEEE Trans. Inf. Theory **16**, 515–516 (1968)
6. Herrera, F.: Keel, knowledge extraction based on evolutionary learning (2005). http://www.keel.es, spanish National Projects TIC2002-04036-C05, TIN2005-08386-C05 and TIN2008-06681-C06
7. Kachel, A., Biesiada, J., Blachnik, M., Duch, W.: Infosel++: **Inf**ormation based feature **Selection** C++ library. In: Rutkowski, L., Scherer, R., Tadeusiewicz, R., Zadeh, L.A., Zurada, J.M. (eds.) ICAISC 2010, Part I. LNCS, vol. 6113, pp. 388–396. Springer, Heidelberg (2010)
8. Liu, H., Motoda, H.: Feature Selection for Knowledge Discovery and Data Mining. Springer, New York (1998)
9. Omohundro, S.M.: Five balltree construction algorithms. Technical report. TR-89-063, International Computer Science Institute, December 1989
10. Salvador, G., Joaquin, D., Jose, R.C., Francisco, H.: Prototype selection for nearest neighbor classification: taxonomy and empirical study. IEEE Trans. Pattern Anal. Mach. Intell. **34**(3), 417–435 (2012)
11. Uhlmann, J.K.: Satisfying general proximity/similarity queries with metric trees. Inf. Proc. Lett. **40**(4), 175–179 (1991)
12. Wilson, D.: Assymptotic properties of nearest neighbour rules using edited data. IEEE Trans. Syst. Man Cybernetics SMC **2**, 408–421 (1972)
13. Yao, Y.Y.: Information-theoretic measures for knowledge discovery and data mining. In: Karmeshu, P. (ed.) Entropy Measures, Maximum Entropy Principle and Emerging Applications. STUDFUZZ, vol. 119, pp. 115–136. Springer, Heidelberg (2003)
14. Perlich, C.: Learning curves in machine learning. In: Sammut, C., Webb, G.I. (eds.) Encyclopedia of Machine Learning, pp. 577–580. Springer, New York (2011)

Diversity Analysis on Imbalanced Data Using Neighbourhood and Roughly Balanced Bagging Ensembles

Jerzy Błaszczyński and Mateusz Lango[✉]

Institute of Computing Science, Poznań University of Technology,
60-965 Poznań, Poland
{jurek.blaszczynski,mateusz.lango}@cs.put.poznan.pl

Abstract. Bagging ensembles proved to work better than boosting for class imbalanced and noisy data. We compare performance and diversity of the two best performing, in this setting, bagging ensembles: Roughly Balanced Bagging (RBBag) and Neighbourhood Balanced Bagging (NBBag). We show that NBBag makes correct prediction on a higher than RBBag number of difficult to learn minority examples. Then we detect a trade-off between correct recognition of difficult minority examples and majority examples, which makes RBBag better in some cases. We also introduce a simple but effective technique to select parameters for NBBag.

Keywords: Class imbalance · Ensembles · Roughly balanced bagging · Neighbourhood balanced bagging · Diversity · Parametrization

1 Introduction

One of the most important challenges for supervised machine learning is learning from imbalanced data [14]. The data is imbalanced when one of the classes has small number of examples (minority class) in comparison to other classes in the data set (majority classes). Such situation occurs in many important applications e.g. in fraud detection, medical problems, etc. Due to the importance of the problem, many methods to counter class imbalance has been proposed. Following [9] we divide them into two categories: data-level and algorithm-level approaches. By data-level approaches we understand techniques which apply data preprocessing methods, such as re-sampling, to improve classification of imbalanced data without changing the learning algorithm. Typically, these techniques focus on switching class distribution to a more balanced one. The other group of approaches modifies existing algorithms to better model minority class distribution. To this category we assign also specialized ensembles which are usually modifications of bagging or boosting; see their review in [3].

Experiments [6,10] have shown that bagging ensembles work better than extensions of boosting, especially on noisy data sets. Further studies [1,6] demonstrated that Roughly Balanced Bagging (RBBag), which applies specific random under-sampling to create bootstraps, achieves the best results on G-mean

© Springer International Publishing Switzerland 2016
L. Rutkowski et al. (Eds.): ICAISC 2016, Part I, LNAI 9692, pp. 552–562, 2016.
DOI: 10.1007/978-3-319-39378-0_47

and AUC measures among extensions of bagging. However, in the recent work Błaszczyński and Stefanowski have proposed Neighbourhood Balanced Bagging (NBBag), which modifies bootstrap sampling by weighting examples [2]. The weight of an example depends from the class label and the number of examples in the example neighbourhood which belong to the opposite class. The impact of neighbourhood on weights is controlled by parameters: size of the neighbourhood and a scaling factor. It has been shown that NBBag achieves competitive results on G-mean and better results on sensitivity measure than RBBag.

Besides results on G-mean or sensitivity metrics it is unknown how data difficulty factors impact model learned by different specialized extensions of bagging for class imbalance. Since NBBag proved to be better than RBBag on sensitivity measure, it is particularly interesting to analyze on which types of minority examples it performs better then RBBag. Another important issue when comparing two ensembles is the diversity of theirs base classifiers. To the best of our knowledge the diversity of NBBag was never investigated and experimental studies measuring diversity in the context of the minority class are very limited. Furthermore, the authors of NBBag noticed that the results of the classifier significantly depend on the values of parameters [2], which need to be selected after a careful analysis of results produced with different settings. Moreover, they advocate that the best set-up should be elected for a particular data set.

To address these issues, in this paper we propose a method intended to automatically parametrize Neighbourhood Balanced Bagging for imbalanced data sets. We also experimentally study abilities of NBBag to deal with different types of difficult distributions of the minority class and we compare this abilities to its major competitor: RBBag. Additionally, we calculate diversity measure of NBBag and compare the results to the reference algorithms.

2   Related Works

The data set is called imbalanced when one class has substantially less examples then the others. Although the problem of class imbalance relates also to multiclass classification in the majority of the research - and also in this paper - only binary classification is considered. In this case we can define statistics which measure the level of class imbalance: global imbalanced ratio $IR = \frac{N_-}{N_+}$ where N_- and N_+ are the number of majority and minority examples, respectively.

Imbalanced data is causing many problems for standard classifiers. Nevertheless, it has been noticed that the global imbalance ratio is not the only or even not the most important factor which makes learning difficult. Other data difficulty factors such as class overlapping, small disjunct or lack of representativeness significantly deteriorate the quality of induced model even on exactly balanced data. However, adding class imbalance to a data which suffers from these difficulty factors creates a real challenge for machine learning algorithms. It has been shown that in the imbalanced data the deterioration of learner's accuracy caused by other data difficulty factors affects in majority of cases only the recognition of minority class, which usually is a class of particular interest.

In [11] a method for identification of data difficulty factors in real data sets was proposed. The authors distinguish 4 types of examples (enumerated from the easiest to the hardest): safe examples (lying in the region in the feature space dominated by the same class), borderline examples (lying in the class overlapping area), rare examples (a small group of examples in the region of the opposite class) and outlier examples (lying in the area dominated by the opposite class). This types can be identified by checking the distribution of the class labels among k nearest neighbours of the example. For instance, with $k = 5$, if all examples in the neighbourhood are from the opposite class then the example is considered to be an outlier. If there is 4 opposite-class examples it is rare and if there are more than 3 examples from the same class, the example is a safe one. Finally, we assign borderline type to examples with the proportion of the same class examples and the opposite class examples equal 2:3 or 3:2.

However, extensions of bagging for imbalanced data normally do not take into account the types of examples and are just focused on construction of more balanced bootstrap. There are two ways of achieving this goal: by under-sampling majority class or by over-sampling minority class. For their review see e.g. [3].

Exactly Balanced Bagging (EBBag) [7] is the representative of the first group. It copies all minority examples to each bootstrap and then, by random sampling, it adds N_+ majority examples to construct a fully balanced bootstrap. Hido et al. [6] claimed that this sampling strategy does not reflect the true bagging philosophy and they proposed Roughly Balanced Bagging (RBBag). RBBag samples with replacement N_+ examples of the minority class and then the majority examples are sampled in the same way except that the number of examples is taken from binomial distribution ($p = 0.5$, $n = N_+$).

The most known over-sampling extension of bagging is OverBagging (OverBag) [13]. It samples with replacement N_- majority examples to each bootstrap and then the same amount of minority examples is added. This results in bootstraps having multiple copies of some minority examples.

The first bagging extension which uses knowledge of data difficulty factors is Neighbourhood Balanced Bagging (NBBag) [2]. This algorithm has two variants: over-sampling (oNBBag) and under-sampling (uNBBag) both sharing the same idea of modifying sapling probability distribution by assigning weights to examples. NBBag focuses bootstrap sampling toward difficult minority examples. Weight of minority example depends on the analysis of its k nearest neighbours. Minority example is considered the more unsafe the more it has majority examples in its neighbourhood. Hence, the formula for minority example weight is the following: $w(x) = 0.5 \cdot \left(\frac{(N'_-)^\psi}{k} + 1 \right)$ where N'_- is the number of majority examples among k nearest neighbours of the example and ψ is a scaling factor. Setting $\psi = 1$ causes a linear amplification of example weight with an increase of unsafeness and setting ψ to values greater then 1 effects in an exponential amplification. Each majority example is assigned a constant weight $w(x) = 0.5 \cdot \frac{N_+}{N_-}$.

As we mentioned before, both versions of NBBag use the same sampling schema; however, they create bootstrap samples of a different size. uNBBag samples $n = 2N_+$ examples resulting in a sample which is smaller than the entire imbalanced data set. oNBBag creates a bootstrap sample consisting of $n = N_+ + N_-$ elements. Since weights of minority examples are greater then weights of majority examples this results in over-sampling of minority examples.

3   Performance of Bagging Extensions

Most of the extensions of bagging presented in Sect. 2 are non-parametric. They do not introduce any new parameters, which need to be adjusted during construction of an ensemble of classifiers. On the one hand, one can argue that bagging itself is a parametric method since the adequate size of the ensemble for a given problem is not known a priori. The size of the ensemble is an important parameter, which may influence the performance of each of the considered extensions. On the other hand, fixing this parameter enables comparison of ensembles of the same size, which should allow to distinguish ones which perform better than the others under the same conditions.

Another type of parameters are introduced in Neighbourhood Balanced Bagging (NBBag). These are two parameters that control the characteristics of neighbourhood: size of neighbourhood k, and scaling factor ψ. In the experiments comparing NBBag to other bagging extensions [2] these two parameters were carefully selected to provide the best average performance. The selection was made post-hoc, i.e., first results were obtained for a number of promising pairs of parameter values and then the best values were chosen. One down-side of this approach is additional computational cost. The second, more important, one is the robustness of the recommendation. In general, a change in the list of data sets used in experiment may lead to different recommended best values.

Selection of such a type of model parameters is a known problem in machine learning [4]. However, to our best knowledge, this problem has not been yet considered in the context of learning from imbalanced data. Data imbalance may limit application of some more advanced parameter selection techniques. To put it simply, minority class examples are to valuable to spare them for selection purposes only, while majority class examples are not. Following this observation, we investigate application of a basic technique taken from tree learning to this end. In the same way as reduced-error pruning uses training data [12], we divide training data set into two stratified samples. The first sample is used for training NBBag models and the second one to validate the trained models. After the best parameters are selected, NBBag classifier is constructed on the whole training set. Contrary to what was presented in [2], this technique, when construction of a classifier is repeated, as e.g., in cross-validation, does not allow to distinguish best values of parameters for all data sets nor even for one data set. Selection of parameters is performed independently for each constructed classifier.

In the following we present performance of two variants of Neighbourhood Balanced Bagging: under-sampling (uNBBag) and over-sampling (oNBBag) with selection of k and ψ. We consider a limited set of possible values of parameters. In case of k it is: 3, 5, 7, 11. For ψ, it is: 0.25, 0.5, 1, 1.25, 1.5, 1.75, 2, 4. During selection of best parameter phase 1/3 of the training set is used for validation.

The Performance of uNBBag and oNBBag is compared to Exactly Balanced Bagging (EBBag), Over-Bagging (OverBag), and the main competitor: Roughly Balanced Bagging (RBBag). The size of ensembles is fixed to 50 components.

Table 1. Data characteristics

data set	# examples	# attributes	minority class	IR
breast-w	699	9	malignant	1.90
abdominal-pain	723	13	positive	2.58
acl	140	6	1	2.5
new-thyroid	215	5	2	5.14
vehicle	846	18	van	3.25
car	1728	6	good	24.04
scrotal-pain	201	13	positive	2.41
ionosphere	351	34	b	1.79
pima	768	8	1	1.87
credit-g	1000	20	bad	2.33
ecoli	336	7	imU	8.60
hepatitis	155	19	1	3.84
haberman	306	4	2	2.78
breast-cancer	286	9	recurrence-events	2.36
cmc	1473	9	2	3.42
cleveland	303	13	3	7.66
hsv	122	11	4.0	7.71
abalone	4177	8	0-4 16-29	11.47
postoperative	90	8	S	2.75
solar-flare	1066	12	F	23.79
transfusion	748	4	1	3.20
yeast	1484	8	ME2	28.10
balance-scale	625	4	B	11.76

The performance of bagging ensembles is measured using: *sensitivity* of the minority class (the minority class accuracy), its *specificity* (an accuracy of recognizing majority classes), their aggregation to the *geometric mean* (G-mean). For their definitions see, e.g., [5]. These measures are estimated by a stratified 10-fold cross-validation repeated ten times to reduce the variance. The differences between classifiers average results are also analyzed using Friedman and Wilcoxon statistical tests.

The results of G-mean and sensitivity are presented in Tables 2 and 3, respectively. The last row of these tables contains average ranks calculated as in the Friedman test – the lower average rank, the better classifier. Note that, the list

Table 2. G-mean [%] of NBBag and other compared bagging ensembles

data set	EBBag	OverBag	uNBBag	oNBBag	RBBag
breast-w	96.245	96.003	96.472	96.113	96.435
abdominal-pain	79.330	79.398	81.292	80.249	80.099
acl	85.576	80.866	84.359	81.927	85.310
new-thyroid	96.515	96.497	95.867	96.634	96.308
vehicle	95.038	94.934	95.440	95.115	95.417
car	96.668	96.959	96.356	96.851	96.568
scrotal-pain	73.679	74.038	72.923	71.997	75.618
ionosphere	90.540	90.559	90.874	90.568	91.002
pima	74.849	74.358	74.852	74.068	75.626
credit-g	65.737	65.513	67.450	66.628	67.963
ecoli	88.178	83.896	88.435	85.380	88.430
hepatitis	79.137	75.816	78.035	74.762	79.457
haberman	64.144	63.329	63.742	61.779	63.533
breast-cancer	58.175	60.718	58.465	58.795	60.091
cmc	64.191	61.036	65.051	63.787	65.350
cleveland	73.628	51.629	73.260	66.754	71.130
hsv	44.080	20.501	40.957	40.155	37.494
abalone	78.845	69.230	79.517	78.706	79.035
postoperative	35.569	32.657	39.877	39.142	34.847
solar-flare	83.710	64.649	83.149	79.994	83.421
transfusion	66.607	67.748	66.449	66.476	67.143
yeast	84.018	63.167	84.475	79.557	85.016
balance-scale	2.832	23.411	43.285	59.893	54.182
average rank	2.913	4	2.478	3.435	2.174

of data sets in this comparison is the same as in [2]. Data sets in the analyzed tables are ordered from the safest one to the most unsafe one. Characteristics of these data sets are given in Table 1. Looking at both Tables 2 and 3, we can make an outright observation that uNBBag and RBBag stand out as the best performing classifiers. Another observation is that over-sampling extensions of bagging, represented by OverBag and oNBBag, provide worse performance that under-sampling extensions (the rest of classifiers). Detailed comparison on G-mean gives the best average rank to RBBag, however the difference between its rank and ranks of all other classifiers except OverBag is not significant. Friedman test on values of G-mean results in p-value around 0.0002, and according to Nemenyi post-hoc test, critical difference between ranks is around 1.272. An analogous observation is valid only for NBBag and all other classifiers except

Table 3. Sensitivity [%] of NBBag and other compared bagging ensembles

data set	EBBag	OverBag	uNBBag	oNBBag	RBBag
breast-w	96.929	95.851	97.386	96.888	96.846
abdominal-pain	82.178	75.842	84.158	80.050	79.010
acl	87	74.250	87.250	82.500	84.750
new-thyroid	95.714	95.143	95.143	96	95.143
vehicle	97.236	94.523	97.286	95.477	96.935
car	100	95.652	100	95.942	100
scrotal-pain	76.271	70.169	76.441	73.051	75.763
ionosphere	86.032	85.159	87.778	86.984	85.714
pima	80.672	74.925	81.194	79.813	78.396
credit-g	72.933	60.233	73.400	69.867	68.500
ecoli	92	76	92	84	90.571
hepatitis	83.438	67.188	79.062	69.688	77.500
haberman	56.914	59.136	63.827	66.543	55.802
breast-cancer	63.412	54	65.176	59.059	58.471
cmc	70.240	50.721	68.739	63.423	64.685
cleveland	80.286	30.571	79.143	63.429	69.143
hsv	45	7.143	40	35.714	26.429
abalone	80.925	51.224	80.776	75.851	77.045
postoperative	31.250	17.917	44.167	37.917	23.750
solar-flare	88.140	46.977	86.744	81.395	85.581
transfusion	66.517	61.236	72.697	67.753	65.674
yeast	91.765	40.980	90.392	73.529	88.431
balance-scale	99.388	7.347	94.898	79.796	66.327
average rank	1.848	4.870	1.587	3.174	3.522

OverBag. Direct comparison of RBBag and NBBag in Wilcoxon test does not show a significant difference in G-mean (p-value in this test is around 0.247).

When we move to the observed values of sensitivity in Table 3, we can notice considerably better average performance of uNBBag and EBBag than the rest of classifiers. This observation is supported by results of Friedman test (with p-value close to 0) and Nemenyi post-hoc analysis. Wilcoxon tests shows the same result in pairs of classifiers. uNBBag achieves the best average rank in this experiment. Nevertheless, direct comparison of uNBBag and EBBag in Wilcoxon test does not confirm a significant difference in sensitivity (p-value 0.677).

Experimental comparison of performance of bagging extensions leads to conclusions, which are concordant with the ones presented in [2]. RBBag and uNBBag are distinguished as two standing out alternatives. It should be noted that the results presented here are not entirely comparable with these from [2], since the set of compared classifiers has changed. We included EBBag, which proved to be a valuable extension. Another aspect of the presented comparison is the influence of parameter selection on the results. Application of a relatively simple selection technique allowed us to obtain quite satisfying results. The average performance of NBBag has not been observably improved but variability of results for unsafe data sets has decreased (e.g., `balance-scale`). We expect that a technique adapted for imbalanced data should allow to obtain even better results.

4 Measuring Diversity of Ensembles

One of the most important characteristic of an ensemble is diversity of its component classifiers. To put it simple, if all components make the same decision regarding example's classes, the construction of an ensemble is pointless. In [8] authors compare many diversity measures and recommend use of Q-statistics basing on ease of its interpretation. Q-statistics is defined for a pair of components as $Q = \frac{n_{11}n_{00}-n_{01}n_{10}}{n_{11}n_{00}+n_{01}n_{10}}$ where n_{11} is the number of examples on which both classifiers make correct decision, n_{01} and n_{10} are the numbers of examples on which one classifier is wrong and the other makes a correct decision, n_{00} is the number of examples on which both classifiers make incorrect decisions. This formula is calculated for each pair of components and then its averaged for the whole ensemble. $Q = 0$ means independence of component classifiers, positive Q means that classifiers tend to recognize the same elements correctly and negative values signify that components tend to make errors on different examples.

We calculate Q-statistic for NBBag and RBBag on all data sets from previous experiment. Due to space limits, we do not present all the results. We only briefly summarize this analysis. The most diversified classifier according to both median and average of Q-statistic is uNBBag ($Median(Q) = 0.61$). RBBag have a bit less diversified components ($Median(Q) = 0.67$) and oNBBag has the highest averaged results on Q-statistic ($Median(Q) = 0.71$). The biggest differences between algorithms is visible on `haberman` and on `balance-scale`. On these data sets the most diversified classifier has also the highest result on G-mean measure. On other data sets these two factors are not always related.

Further investigation of Q-statistic only for minority examples (Q_{min}) shows that all analyzed algorithms are more diversified on minority class. On some data sets classifiers achieve even negative values of Q_{min}. Likewise the differences between classifiers are a little higher. The ranking of most diversified classifiers remain the same as for over-all Q-statistic: uNBBag ($Median(Q_{min}) = 0.40$), RBBag ($Median(Q_{min}) = 0.47$) and oNBBag ($Median(Q_{min}) = 0.51$).

Another way of investigating diversity is analysis of votes of each component during classification of a particular example. Here, we use a margin measure defined as follows: $margin = \frac{n_{corr}-n_{incorr}}{n_{corr}+n_{incorr}}$, where n_{corr} and n_{incorr} is the number of components which vote for correct and incorrect class, respectively. The margin value equal 1 means completely certain and correct decision, margin -1 means completely certain but incorrect decision. Margin close to 0 indicates uncertainty in making final decision (the number of classifiers voting for the correct class is close to the number of classifiers voting for the opposite class).

We analyze the values of margin calculated for examples with respect to their types. Additionally, we compare margins for examples on which RBBag and uNBBag make different decisions. In Fig. 1 we present histograms of decision margin for minority class on a representative data set (`abalone`). In the first row of the plot one can see decision margins of all examples of a particular type (white bars) achieved by RBBag. Red bars of the histogram indicate margins for examples which are classified incorrectly by RBBag but they are correctly classified by uNBBag. Analogically, green bars demonstrate margin for instances which were classified correctly only by RBBag. The second row of the plot is constructed in the same way but for uNBBag.

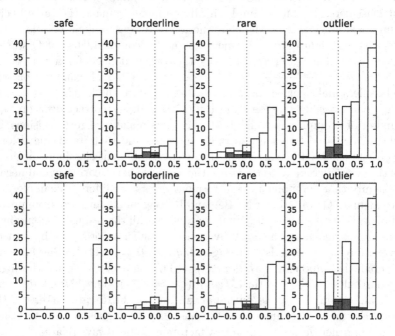

Fig. 1. Histogram of RBBag (top) and uNBBag (down) margins for `abalone` minority examples with respect to their types.

The first impression is that both classifiers work quite similar. Differences are more significant on difficult examples. uNBBag and RBBag do not have problems with correct classification of safe minority examples. Almost all of them are classified with maximal margin. However, with increase of difficulty of examples, both classifiers makes more errors and their confidence goes down. Particularly, a lot of outlier examples are classified incorrectly with high confidence.

Compared algorithms make different final predictions only on more difficult examples and it is clear that uNBBag makes correct decisions on a higher number of minority examples. Unfortunately, there seems to be some kind of trade-off between correct recognition of more difficult minority and majority examples:

this classifier makes more incorrect decisions on majority examples than RBBag. This is the reason why RBBag is sometimes better than uNBBag on G-mean measure. Furthermore, it is worth to notice that when uNBBag makes correct prediction on a minority example and RBBag makes an incorrect one, it is with a rather low confidence. It is quite unlikely to find an example correctly classified by uNBBag and classified incorrectly by RBBag with margin less then -0.5.

5 Conclusions

In this work, we have experimentally compared a number of promising bagging extensions designed to handle class imbalance problem. The best performing extensions in this comparison are: Roughly Balanced Bagging (RBBag) and Neighbourhood Balanced Bagging (NBBag). We have introduced a simple technique for automatic selection of parameters for NBBag during learning from imbalanced data. This technique proved to work well. Nevertheless, we believe that another technique better adapted for the type of learning should allow to obtain even better results. Comparative study of diversity of RBBag and NBBag have shown that NBBag is able to make correct prediction on a higher than RBBag number of difficult to learn minority examples. There is, however, a trade-off between correct recognition of difficult minority examples and majority examples, which allows RBBag to perform better in some cases.

Acknowledgement. The research was supported by NCN grant DEC-2013/11/B/ST6/00963.

References

1. Błaszczyński, J., Stefanowski, J., Idkowiak, L.: Extending bagging for imbalanced data. CORES 2013. Advances in Intelligent Systems and Computing, vol. 226, pp. 269–278. Springer, Switzerland (2013)
2. Błaszczyński, J., Stefanowski, J.: Neighbourhood sampling in bagging for imbalanced data. Neurocomputing **150 A**, 184–203 (2015)
3. Galar, M., Fernandez, A., Barrenechea, E., Bustince, H., Herrera, F.: A review on ensembles for the class imbalance problem: bagging-, boosting-, and hybrid-based approaches. IEEE Trans. Syst. Man Cybern. Part C Appl. Rev. **99**, 1–22 (2011)
4. Guyon, I., Saffari, A., Dror, G., Cawley, G.: Model selection : beyond the Bayesian / Frequentist divide. JMLR **11**, 61–87 (2010)
5. Japkowicz, N., Shah, M.: Evaluating Learning Algorithms: A Classification Perspective. Cambridge University Press, Cambridge (2011)
6. Hido, S., Kashima, H.: Roughly balanced bagging for imbalance data. In: Proceedings of the SIAM International Conference on Data Mining, pp. 143–152 (2008). An extended version in Statistical Analysis and Data Mining, vol. 2 (5–6), pp. 412–426 (2009)
7. Hoens, T.R., Chawla, N.V.: Generating diverse ensembles to counter the problem of class imbalance. In: Zaki, M.J., Yu, J.X., Ravindran, B., Pudi, V. (eds.) PAKDD 2010. LNCS, vol. 6119, pp. 488–499. Springer, Heidelberg (2010)

8. Kuncheva, L., Whitaker, C.: Measures of diversity in classifier ensembles and their relationship with the ensemble accuracy. Machine Learning **51**(2), 181–207 (2003)
9. Kotsiantis, S., Kanellopoulos, D., Pintelas, P.: Handling imbalanced datasets: a review. GESTS Int. Trans. Comput. Sci. Eng. **30**(1), 25–36 (2006)
10. Khoshgoftaar, T., Van Hulse, J., Napolitano, A.: Comparing boosting and bagging techniques with noisy and imbalanced data. IEEE Trans. Syst. Man Cybern. Part A **41**(3), 552–568 (2011)
11. Napierala, K., Stefanowski, J.: Identification of different types of minority class examples in imbalanced data. In: Corchado, E., Snášel, V., Abraham, A., Woźniak, M., Graña, M., Cho, S.-B. (eds.) HAIS 2012, Part II. LNCS, vol. 7209, pp. 139–150. Springer, Heidelberg (2012)
12. Quinlan, R.: C4.5: Programs for Machine Learning. Morgan Kaufmann Publishers, San Mateo (1993)
13. Wang, S., Yao, T.: Diversity analysis on imbalanced data sets by using ensemble models. In: Proceeding IEEE Symposium Computational Intelligence and Data Mining, pp. 324–331 (2009)
14. Yang, Q., Wu, X.: 10 challenging problems in data mining research. Int. J. Inf. Technol. Decis. Making **5**(04), 597–604 (2006)

Dynamic Ensemble Selection Using Discriminant Functions and Normalization Between Class Labels – Approach to Binary Classification

Robert Burduk[✉] and Paulina Baczyńska

Department of Systems and Computer Networks, Wroclaw University of Technology,
Wybrzeze Wyspianskiego 27, 50-370 Wroclaw, Poland
{robert.burduk,paulina.baczynska}@pwr.edu.pl

Abstract. In the classification task, the ensemble selection methods reduce the available pool of the base classifiers. The dynamic ensemble selection methods allow to find the subset of base classifiers for each test sample separately. In finding the best subset of base classifiers many methods used the so-called competence region determined for the validation data set. In this paper, we propose the dynamic ensemble selection in which the validation data set is not necessary and the competence region for the test sample is not determined. Generally, the described method uses only the decision profiles in the selection process. The experiment results based on ten data sets show that the proposed dynamic ensemble selection is a promising method for the development of multiple classifiers systems.

Keywords: Ensemble selection · Multiple classifier system · Binary classification task

1 Introduction

For several years, in the field of supervised learning a number of base classifiers have been used in order to solve one classification task. The use of the multiple base classifier for a decision problem is known as an ensemble of classifiers (EoC) or as multiple classifiers systems (MCSs) [6,12,16]. The building of MCSs consists of three phases: generation, selection and integration [3]. For example, in the third phase the simple majority voting scheme [19] is most popular. Generally, the final decision which is made in the third phase uses the prediction of the base classifiers and it is popular for its ability to fuse together multiple classification outputs for the better accuracy of classification. If the outputs of all base classifiers are used in the third phase then this method is called the classifier fusion.

The second phase of building MCSs is one of the important problems in the creation of these recognition systems [14,20]. This phase is related to the choice of a set of classifiers from the whole available pool of base classifiers. Formally, if we choose one classifier then it is called the classifier selection. But if we

© Springer International Publishing Switzerland 2016
L. Rutkowski et al. (Eds.): ICAISC 2016, Part I, LNAI 9692, pp. 563–570, 2016.
DOI: 10.1007/978-3-319-39378-0_48

choose a subset of base classifiers from the pool then it is called the ensemble selection or ensemble pruning. Generally, in the ensemble selection, there are two approaches: the static ensemble selection and the dynamic ensemble selection [3]. In the static classifier selection one set of classifiers is selected to create EoC. This EoC is used in the classification of all the objects from the testing set. The main problem in this case is to find a pertinent objective function for selecting the classifiers. In the dynamic classifier selection, also called instance-based, for each unknown sample a specific subset of classifiers is selected [5]. It means that we are selecting different EoCs for different objects from the testing set. In this type of the classifier selection, the classifier is chosen and assigned to the sample based on different features [22] or different decision regions [8,15]. The existing methods of the ensemble selection use the validation data set to create the so-called competence region or level of competence. These competencies can be computed by K nearest neighbours from the validation data set.

In this work we will consider the dynamic ensemble selection. The proposed algorithms of the ensemble selection use decision profiles. The paper proposes new conditions for the dynamic ensemble selection that were not presented in our earlier works [1,2]. A common part of the previous studies is the use of decision profiles. In our approaches the validation data set is not used and the competence region for the test sample is not determined.

The remainder of this paper is organized as follows. Section 2 presents the concept of the ensemble of classifiers. Section 3 contains the new method for the dynamic ensemble selection. The experimental evaluation is presented in Sect. 4. The discussion and conclusions from the experiments are presented in Sect. 5.

2   Ensemble of Classifiers

Let us consider the binary classification task. It means that we have two class labels $\Omega = \{0,1\}$. Each pattern is characterized by the feature vector x. The recognition algorithm Ψ maps the feature space x to the set of class labels Ω according to the general formula:

$$\Psi(x) \in \Omega. \tag{1}$$

Let us assume that $k \in \{1, 2, ..., K\}$ different classifiers $\Psi_1, \Psi_2, \ldots, \Psi_K$ are available to solve the classification task. In MCSs these classifiers are called base classifiers. In the binary classification task K is assumed to be an odd number. As a result, of all the classifiers' actions, their K responses are obtained. The output information from all K component classifiers is applied to make the ultimate decision of MCSs. This decision is made based on the predictions of all the base classifiers.

One of the possible methods for integrating the output of the base classifier is the sum rule. In this method the score of MCSs is based on the application of the following sums:

$$s_\omega(x) = \sum_{k=1}^{K} p_k(\omega|x), \qquad \omega \in \Omega, \tag{2}$$

where $p_k(\omega|x)$ is an estimate of the discrimination function (DF) (most often an estimate of the posteriori probability) for class label ω returned by classifier k.

The final decision of MCSs is made following the maximum rule:

$$\Psi_S(x) = \arg\max_\omega s_\omega(x). \tag{3}$$

In the presented method (3) the discrimination functions obtained from the individual classifiers take an equal part in building MCSs. This is the simplest situation in which we do not need additional information on the testing process of the base classifiers except for the models of these classifiers. One of the possible methods in which weights of the base classifier are used is presented in [4].

3   Dynamic Ensemble Selection Algorithm

The proposed algorithm of the ensemble selection uses the decision profiles (DPs) [17]. DP is a matrix containing DFs for each base classifier. In the binary classification task it is as follows:

$$DP(x) = \begin{bmatrix} p_1(0|x) & p_1(1|x) \\ \vdots & \vdots \\ p_K(0|x) & p_K(1|x) \end{bmatrix}. \tag{4}$$

In the first step of the algorithm we change values of DFs which relate to the misclassification on the training set. This set contains N labeled examples $\{(x_1, \overline{\omega}_1), ..., (x_N, \overline{\omega}_N)\}$, where $\overline{\omega}_i$ is true class label of the object described by feature vector x_i. DFs are changed as follows:

$$p'_k(\omega|x) = \begin{cases} p_k(\omega|x), & \text{if} \quad I(\Psi(x), \overline{\omega}) = 1 \\ 0, & \text{if} \quad I(\Psi(x), \overline{\omega}) = 0. \end{cases} \tag{5}$$

where $I(\Psi(x), \overline{\omega})$ is an indicator function having the value 1 in the case of the correct classification of the object described by feature vector x, i.e. when $\Psi(x) = \overline{\omega}$.

In the next step our algorithm, the decision scheme (DS) is calculated according to the formula:

$$DS = \begin{bmatrix} ds_{10} & ds_{11} \\ \vdots & \vdots \\ ds_{K0} & ds_{K1} \end{bmatrix}, \tag{6}$$

where

$$ds_{k\omega} = \overline{ds}_{k\omega} + \beta\sqrt{\frac{\sum_{n=1}^{N}(p'_k(\omega_n|x_n) - \overline{ds}_{k\omega})^2}{N-1}} \tag{7}$$

and

$$\overline{ds}_{k\omega} = \frac{\sum_{n=1}^{N} p'_k(\omega_n|x_n)}{N}. \tag{8}$$

The parameter β in our algorithm determines how we compute DS elements. For example, if $\beta = 0$, then $ds_{k\omega}$ is the average of appropriate DFs received after the condition (5).

For the new object being recognized $\widehat{x}$, the outputs of the base classifiers create $\widehat{DP}$. In the receipt of the $\widehat{DP}$ from the outputs of the base classifiers we propose the process of normalization, which depends on the upper $\overline{p}$ and lower $\underline{p}$ limit of $\widehat{DF}$. We propose the following condition:

$$\text{if} \quad \widehat{p}_\omega^{max} < \overline{p} \quad \text{and} \quad \widehat{p}_\omega^{min} > \underline{p} \quad \text{then} \quad do\,normalization \tag{9}$$

to execute the normalization, where $\widehat{p}_\omega^{max} = \max_k \widehat{p}_k(\omega|x)$, $\widehat{p}_\omega^{min} = \min_k \widehat{p}_k(\omega|x)$, $k \in 1, .., K$. The normalization is executed taking into account $\widehat{p}_\omega^{min}$ of the opposed class label, i.e.:

$$\widehat{p'}_k(0|\widehat{x}) = \frac{\widehat{p}_k(0|\widehat{x}) - \widehat{p}_1^{min}}{\widehat{p}_0^{max} - \widehat{p}_0^{min}} \tag{10}$$

and

$$\widehat{p'}_k(1|\widehat{x}) = \frac{\widehat{p}_k(1|\widehat{x}) - \widehat{p}_0^{min}}{\widehat{p}_1^{max} - \widehat{p}_1^{min}}. \tag{11}$$

for the binary classification with class labels $\{0,1\}$. In the selection phase DS obtained from the learning set (6) is used as follows:

$$\text{if} \quad \widehat{p'}_k(\omega|\widehat{x}) < ds_{k\omega} \quad \text{then} \quad \widehat{p}_k(\omega|\widehat{x}) = 0, k = 1, ..., K, \quad \omega = 0, 1. \tag{12}$$

The obtained decision profile using the formula (12) is applied to make the final decision of the classifiers ensemble. In the experiments the algorithm using the proposed above method is denoted as Ψ_{DS-N}^{β}. Additionally, we use the sum method to make the final decision of the selected classifiers ensemble.

4   Experimental Studies

In the experiential research 10 benchmark data sets were used. Nine of them come from the UCI repository [10] and one is randomly generated - this is the so called Higleyman sets. The details of the data sets are included in Table 1. In the experiment 9 base classifiers were used. Two of them work according to $k - NN$ rule, next two base classifiers use the Support Vector Machines models. The following two base classifiers use the Neutral Network model and the last three base classifiers use the decision trees algorithms, with the various number of branches and the splitting rule. This means that in the experiment we use an ensemble of the heterogonous base classifiers. In our experiments we did not include the impact of the feature selection process on the quality of classifications. Therefore, the feature selection process [13, 18] was not performed. The limitations were established on $\overline{p} = 0.75$ and $\underline{p} = 0.25$.

Table 2 shows the results of the classification for the proposed ensemble selection method Ψ_{DS-N}. We present the classification error and the mean ranks

Table 1. Description of data sets selected for the experiments

Data set	example	attribute	ration (0/1)
Breast Cancer Wisconsin	699	10	1.9
Haberman's Survival	306	3	0.4
Highleyman	400	2	1.0
Ionosphere	351	34	1.8
Indian Liver Patient	583	10	0.4
Mammographic Mass	961	6	1.2
Parkinson	197	23	0.3
Pima Indians Diabetes	768	8	1.9
Sonar	208	60	0.87
Statlog	270	13	1.25

Table 2. Classification error and mean rank positions for the proposed selection algorithm produced by the Friedman test

Data set	Ψ_{DS-N}^{-2}	$\Psi_{DS-N}^{-1.5}$	Ψ_{DS-N}^{-1}	$\Psi_{DS-N}^{-0.5}$	Ψ_{DS-N}^{0}	$\Psi_{DS-N}^{0.5}$	Ψ_{DS-N}^{1}
Cancer	0.042	0.039	0.038	0.038	0.036	0.567	0.683
Haber	0.307	0.293	0.280	0.283	0.277	0.323	0.683
Hig	0.055	0.055	0.055	0.060	0.060	0.245	0.403
Ion	0.071	0.071	0.060	0.069	0.080	0.260	0.589
Liver	0.310	0.309	0.322	0.343	0.355	0.374	0.490
Mam	0.193	0.195	0.191	0.190	0.192	0.214	0.523
Park	0.089	0.084	0.089	0.079	0.095	0.153	0.305
Pima	0.237	0.245	0.243	0.259	0.250	0.261	0.576
Sonar	0.180	0.175	0.175	0.165	0.175	0.260	0.535
Statlog	0.178	0.170	0.167	0.174	0.174	0.189	0.267
Mean Rank	4.40	5.05	**5.80**	5.25	4.50	2	1

obtained by the Friedman test. The presented results are obtained via the 10-fold-cross-validation method. The results in Table 2 demonstrate clearly that the selection the value of the parameter β is important in the proposed ensemble selection method. The performed experiments indicate that the proper value is -1 (the greatest value of the mean rank). Therefore, the algorithm Ψ_{DS}^{-1} was selected for the comparison with other classifiers, i.e. with the base classifiers and the algorithm without the selection used sum method (3).

The classification error with the mean ranks obtained by the Friedman test for these classification methods are presented in Table 3. For the final comparison of results the post-hoc test was used [21]. This test is useful for pairwise comparisons of the considered methods. The critical difference (CD) for this

Table 3. Classification error and mean rank positions for the base classifiers ($\Psi_1, ..., \Psi_9$), algorithm Ψ_S without the selection used sum method (3) and the proposed algorithm Ψ_{DS-N}^{-1} produced by the Friedman test

Data set	Ψ_1	Ψ_2	Ψ_3	Ψ_4	Ψ_5	Ψ_6	Ψ_7	Ψ_8	Ψ_9	Ψ_S	Ψ_{DS-N}^{-1}
Cancer	0.049	0.043	0.026	0.138	0.048	0.052	0.062	0.065	0.059	0.041	0.038
Haber	0.290	0.303	0.327	0.360	0.287	0.297	0.300	0.337	0.297	0.310	0.280
Hig	0.063	0.068	0.168	0.210	0.045	0.048	0.073	0.068	0.070	0.058	0.055
Ion	0.149	0.146	0.234	0.577	0.100	0.103	0.089	0.140	0.106	0.080	0.060
Liver	0.312	0.309	0.271	0.728	0.305	0.302	0.312	0.381	0.357	0.314	0.322
Mam	0.217	0.229	0.225	0.263	0.193	0.196	0.196	0.207	0.200	0.193	0.191
Park	0.142	0.189	0.089	0.553	0.132	0.121	0.089	0.158	0.105	0.079	0.089
Pima	0.279	0.270	0.295	0.366	0.253	0.254	0.261	0.283	0.262	0.236	0.243
Sonar	0.215	0.285	0.220	0.505	0.190	0.190	0.315	0.270	0.295	0.180	0.175
Statlog	0.315	0.311	0.196	0.270	0.196	0.207	0.163	0.319	0.237	0.174	0.167
Mean Rank	5.25	4.65	5.65	1.30	8.45	7.55	6.40	3.35	5.15	8.65	**9.60**

test at $p = 0.05$, $p = 0.1$, is equal to $CD = 4.77$ and $CD = 4.41$ respectively. We can conclude that the post-hoc Nemenyi test detects significant differences between the proposed algorithm Ψ_{DS-N}^{-1} and the three base classifiers Ψ_2, Ψ_4 and Ψ_8 at $p = 0.05$. The ensemble classifier with the sum method Ψ_S is, however, better than the two base classifiers Ψ_4 and Ψ_8. At $p = 0.1$ post-hoc Nemenyi test detects significant differences between 4 base classifiers and the proposed algorithm Ψ_{DS-N}^{-1}. This observation confirms that the proposed in the paper dynamic ensemble selection algorithm can improve the quality of classification compared to the method without the selection.

5   Conclusion

In this paper we have proposed the dynamic ensemble selection methods with using information from decision profiles. The main difference between the proposed in the work algorithm and the existing methods of the dynamic selection is the fact, that the proposed method do not use a validation data set. This set is often used in the dynamic ensemble selection to determine the so-called competence region. In the proposed approach the competence region is not used. The paper proposes new conditions for the dynamic ensemble selection that were not presented in our earlier works [1,2].

The experiments have been carried out on ten benchmark data sets. The aim of the experiments was to compare the proposed dynamic ensemble selection algorithm with nine base classifiers and the ensemble classifiers based on the sum methods. The results demonstrated the correct selection of the parameter β value that is used in the proposed methods. Additionally, the obtained results show an improvement in the quality of the classification with respect to the ensemble method without selection.

Future work might involve the application of the proposed methods for various practical tasks [7,9,11] in which base classifiers are used. Additionally, the advantage of the proposed algorithm, its ability to work in the parallel and distributed environment.

Acknowledgments. This work was supported by the Polish National Science Center under the grant no. DEC-2013/09/B/ST6/02264 and by the statutory funds of the Department of Systems and Computer Networks, Wroclaw University of Technology.

References

1. Baczynska, P., Burduk, R.: Ensemble selection based on discriminant functions in binary classification task. In: Jackowski, K., et al. (eds.) IDEAL 2015. LNCS, vol. 9375, pp. 61–68. Springer, Heidelberg (2015). doi:10.1007/978-3-319-24834-9_8
2. Baczyńska, P., Burduk, R.: Two stage ensemble selection algorithm. J. Theor. Appl. Comput. Sci. **9**, 3–8 (2015)
3. Britto, A.S., Sabourin, R., Oliveira, L.E.: Dynamic selection of classifiers-a comprehensive review. Pattern Recogn. **47**(11), 3665–3680 (2014)
4. Burduk, R.: Classifier fusion with interval-valued weights. Pattern Recogn. Lett. **34**(14), 1623–1629 (2013)
5. Cavalin, P.R., Sabourin, R., Suen, C.Y.: Dynamic selection approaches for multiple classifier systems. Neural Comput. Appl. **22**(3–4), 673–688 (2013)
6. Cyganek, B.: One-class support vector ensembles for image segmentation and classification. J. Math. Imaging Vis. **42**(2–3), 103–117 (2012)
7. Cyganek, B., Woźniak, M.: Vehicle logo recognition with an ensemble of classifiers. In: Nguyen, N.T., Attachoo, B., Trawiński, B., Somboonviwat, K. (eds.) ACIIDS 2014, Part II. LNCS, vol. 8398, pp. 117–126. Springer, Heidelberg (2014)
8. Didaci, L., Giacinto, G., Roli, F., Marcialis, G.L.: A study on the performances of dynamic classifier selection based on local accuracy estimation. Pattern Recogn. **38**, 2188–2191 (2005)
9. Forczmański, P., Łabędź, P.: Recognition of occluded faces based on multi-subspace classification. In: Saeed, K., Chaki, R., Cortesi, A., Wierzchoń, S. (eds.) CISIM 2013. LNCS, vol. 8104, pp. 148–157. Springer, Heidelberg (2013)
10. Frank, A., Asuncion, A.: UCI machine learning epository (2010)
11. Frejlichowski, D.: An algorithm for the automatic analysis of characters located on car license plates. In: Kamel, M., Campilho, A. (eds.) ICIAR 2013. LNCS, vol. 7950, pp. 774–781. Springer, Heidelberg (2013)
12. Giacinto, G., Roli, F.: An approach to the automatic design of multiple classifier systems. Pattern Recogn. Lett. **22**, 25–33 (2001)
13. Guyon, I., Elisseeff, A.: An introduction to variable and feature selection. J. Mach. Learn. Res. **3**, 1157–1182 (2003)
14. Jackowski, K., Krawczyk, B., Woźniak, M.: Improved adaptive splitting, selection: The hybrid training method of a classifier based on a feature space partitioning. Int. J. Neural Syst. **24**(3), 1430007 (2014)
15. Jackowski, K., Woźniak, M.: Method of classifier selection using the genetic approach. Expert Syst. **27**(2), 114–128 (2010)
16. Korytkowski, M., Rutkowski, L., Scherer, R.: From ensemble of fuzzy classifiers to single fuzzy rule base classifier. In: Rutkowski, L., Tadeusiewicz, R., Zadeh, L.A., Zurada, J.M. (eds.) ICAISC 2008. LNCS (LNAI), vol. 5097, pp. 265–272. Springer, Heidelberg (2008)

17. Kuncheva, L.I.: Combining Pattern Classifiers: Methods and Algorithms. Wiley Inc., New York (2004)

18. Rejer, I.: Genetic algorithms in EEG feature selection for the classification of movements of the left and right hand. In: Burduk, R., Jackowski, K., Kurzynski, M., Wozniak, M., Zolnierek, A. (eds.) CORES 2013. AISC, vol. 226, pp. 579–589. Springer, Heidelberg (2013)

19. Ruta, D., Gabrys, B.: Classifier selection for majority voting. Inf. Fusion 6(1), 63–81 (2005)

20. Smętek, M., Trawiński, B.: Selection of heterogeneous fuzzy model ensembles using self-adaptive genetic algorithms. New Gener. Comput. 29(3), 309–327 (2011)

21. Trawiński, B., Smętek, M., Telec, Z., Lasota, T.: Nonparametric statistical analysis for multiple comparison of machine learning regression algorithms. Int. J. Appl. Math. Comput. Sci. 22(4), 867–881 (2012)

22. Woloszyński, T., Kurzyński, M.: A probabilistic model of classifier competence for dynamic ensemble selection. Pattern Recogn. 44(10–11), 2656–2668 (2011)

Towards a Hybrid Learning Approach to Efficient Tone Pattern Recognition

Moses E. Ekpenyong[1]([✉]), Udoinyang G. Inyang[1], and Imeh J. Umoren[2]

[1] Deparment of Computer Science, University of Uyo, Uyo, Nigeria
mosesekpenyong@uniuyo.edu.ng, mosesekpenyong@gmail.com,
udoiinyang@yahoo.com
[2] Department of Computer Science, Akwa Ibom State University,
Mkpat-Enin, Nigeria
hollymehumoren@gmail.com

Abstract. Tone has remained an interesting puzzle to the development of language resources for African languages, mainly because its appearance (within a word) is not segmentally fixed. In this contribution, we begin by proposing a tone marking framework that intelligently tags an input corpus using a close-copy synthesis of tone-tags generated by a Hidden Markov Model (HMM) syllabifier. Next, we investigate the recognition of tone patterns by building a generic architecture that will serve diverse languages. The proposed architecture is a multi-layer feedforward neural network implementing the Levenberg-Marquardt backpropagation algorithm. The network consists of, (i) seventeen inputs describing the tone patterns of Ibibio (ISO 693-3: nic; Ethnologue: IBB), with training data captured from an input corpus of 16,905 phrases; (ii) a target class that learns tone recognition from a combination of the input tone patterns and boundary tone – an important feature used for intonation analysis. Results obtained showed that our tone marking model perfectly tagged the input corpus, except for phonemes with more than one diacritic marks. Concerning the recognition of tone patterns, we deduced from a confusion matrix that 93.1 % of the tone patterns were correctly classified, while the remaining 6.9 % of the patterns were misclassified. A greater chunk of the misclassified cases came from non-boundary tone information, which presence inhibits speech quality. The ROC curve also showed good classification of the training, testing and validation datasets. A future direction of this paper is the introduction of an unsupervised solution and additional tone-bearing information such as syllables and vowels, to improve the learning system; and a comparison of our approach with other methods.

Keywords: Data-driven approach · HMM · Pattern classification · Tone modeling · Speech recognition

1 Introduction

Tone represents one of the most essential features in African languages. Its role ranges from simple pitch/accent type emphasis to elaborate patterns with

© Springer International Publishing Switzerland 2016
L. Rutkowski et al. (Eds.): ICAISC 2016, Part I, LNAI 9692, pp. 571–583, 2016.
DOI: 10.1007/978-3-319-39378-0_49

grammatical meanings. The prediction of this language-dependent feature therefore requires detailed understanding of tone generation patterns. A specific characteristic of tones is that they are non-segmental features, which implies that tones cannot be marked into a lexicon in the way they appear in surface realizations. Despite the central significance of tones, they are not often marked in writing. Although, writing systems do not indicate in any way the behavior of tones in various words, they may not pose difficulties in comprehension. Experimental studies have shown that the absence of tone marks does not significantly affect comprehension, but their presence in text(s) may decrease readability [1]. Even though there is no uniformity in tone marking, its complete absence in any text is even more problematic, and a generic guideline on tone marking is indeed necessary. But the absence of such guideline(s) is not computationally fatal, except when building computational resources that implement tone rates. To non-speakers, the absence of tone marks in texts may be considered as an instance of defective writing, yet most writing systems of tone languages in Africa do not of necessity mark tone. This neglect introduces ambiguity at the contextual level, which can be resolved using a pronunciation dictionary. Nevertheless, the task of correctly inserting tone marks remains a major challenge to language resource development, as tones are not segmentally fixed within a word. To ensure an intelligent tone marking system, knowledge of lexical and structural (or grammatical) ambiguities resolution is important. Also, because neighboring words certainly influence tone realization patterns, the implementation appears inflexible, and requires some form of learning to understand these patterns. In this paper, we identify the data sources relevant for the research. Data were collected from the Ibibio speaking community. Ibibio is a tone language widely spoken by roughly four million (4,000,000) speakers in the south-eastern coastal region of Nigeria, West Africa. The tone system of Ibibio has been classified as a classical terrace tone system [2]; a type of phonetic downdrift, where the high or mid tones (but not the low tone), shift downward in pitch (downstep) after certain other tones. The data used for this research were obtained from existing Ibibio resources [3]. These resources include: (i) a trained Hidden Markov Text-to-Speech Synthesis (HTS) corpus; and (ii) a syllabified corpus. The input, output and processing designs are also given in this paper. The input design specifies the lexicon and corpus formats with appropriate pattern specifications that ensures accurate inference regarding the lexical and structural nature of input words. The specification format is generic and modifiable accross other language structures. The essence of this inference is to guarantee as much as possible, an efficient resolution of lexical and structural ambiguities. Hence, a constraint grammar rule for sentence disambiguation is necessary before processing the inputs.

2   Tone Marking

Until recently, tones were generally not marked in the sub-Saharan African Languages, even though a vast majority of these Languages are tonal [4]. In such languages, the pitch on an individual syllable may be contrastive distinguishing lexical items and grammatical categories such as verb tense. Designers of orthographies were often ignorant about tone and imported many assumptions from the orthographic traditions of European languages [5]. Transporting phonemic contrasts of a colonial language into indigenous languages has led to the over-representation or under-representation of the contrasts, and therefore suggests that the omission of tonal marks from the orthography of many tone languages constitute a barrier to fluent reading. African tone Languages are often written using the IPA-based (Africa) script, which provides diacritic symbols such as an accent for high tone (H) and grave accent for low tone (L). Most of the existing research works on experimenting with orthography include those for languages with established orthography aimed at discovering more about the reading process [6,7]. In the present context, the intention is to discover what kind of tone marking for a given language would best support efficient reading, writing and comprehension.

2.1   Methods of Tone Marking

The two principal schemes for marking tone involve the use of accent diacritics and numbers. The first scheme is mostly employed for representing African corpus. In this method, a high tone vowel is marked with an acute accent (´); a low-toned vowel with a grave accent (`), and a mid toned vowel with a macron (¯) or with a vertical stroke (|), or without tone marking. In the second scheme, a number between 1 and 5 is used to mark the tone level, either with the lowest or highest tone, marked as '1'. In both cases, the tone number(s) may be indicated with a superscript (e.g., $a^2ba^2si^2$ 'God'). Also, rising and falling tones may combine any of these numbers, thus a falling tone for the phoneme ($\hat{a}$), may be marked as, a^{5-3}, or a^{3-5}.

2.2   Minimizing Tone Marking

The most widespread practice has been to omit one of the tone symbols such that a certain tone is simply represented by the symbol of any mark. In some African languages, a low tone is represented by the absence of any tone mark and the symbol omitted could represent the most dominating tone, where the frequency may be determined by a wordlist reference. Although statistics from a large corpus of text would suffice, no such corpus of text exists in the language for selecting a realistic option. A second approach employs a rather ad-hoc way of choosing which tone to omit. The tone(s) to be written are those which change the least. For instance, if a high tone is down-stepped to become a mid or floating low tone, it is better to use low tone because it remains the most stable. This approach requires the determination of which members of the tonal inventory manifest the least contextual variation. Should a low tone undergo few changes than a high tone, then the low tone is marked instead of the high tone. Marking only the stable tones represents an interesting compromise between the ideal of writing tone phonemically. A third approach is to mark the tone of a syllable only when it varies from the tone of the immediately preceding syllable [8].

2.3 Grammatical Tone Marking

In grammatical tone marking, tone melodies are responsible for conveying grammatical information such as verb tense [9]. This concept raises fresh concerns in orthography design. Naturally, grammatical tone is phonemically marked, but this implies that readers must learn to associate complex constellation of tone marks with the grammatical meaning. However the real task lies on reducing the language (not just the phonology) to writing. This broader perspective of putting the language into writing, enables the direct use of morphological or grammatical information [9].

3   System Framework and Methodology

3.1   Automatic Accent Insertion

The automatic accent insertion problem can be informally formulated as follows: Given an unaccented text sequence of words ($w_1w_2w_3 \ldots w_n$), where w_i corresponds to any number of valid words (accented or not), $w_{i1} \ldots w_{im}$. The task is to disambiguate each word, i.e., select the correct words, w_{ik_i}, at every position in the text in order to generate a proper sequence of accented text. In [10], it has been discovered that approximately 85 % of the words in some languages text carry no accent at all, and a greater part of the remaining words can be deduced deterministically on the bases of the unaccented form, and with the use of an exhaustive dictionary, accents can be restored to an unaccented text with a success rate of about 95 %. The remaining challenge at this point mostly revolve around ambiguous unaccented words (words to which more than one valid forms are similar, whether accented or not). Obviously, for many such ambiguities, a simple solution is to systematically select the most frequent alternative from a sequence of hypotheses ($w_{i1} \ldots w_{im}$). The goal can be reformulated as finding a sequence of hypotheses ($w_{1k_1} w_{2k_2} \ldots w_{nk_n}$) that maximizes the overall likelihood of the output sequence. The stochastic model implemented in this paper for word disambiguation implements the hidden Markov modeling principle, within which a text is viewed as the result of two distinct stochastic processes. First is to generate a sequence of abstract symbols; and second, to resolve ambiguous sequence using a language model (LM). In our case, these symbols correspond to the morpho-syntactic tags of a language. To illustrate our HMM approach to automatic accent insertion, a similar description in [11] was adopted. Their algorithm proceeds in two steps: hypothesis generation, which is based on a list of valid words, and candidate selection, and relies on HMMs. The main difference between their method and ours is on how the HMM is used to score competing hypotheses. Candidate selection proceeds by selecting a specific pair (w_{ij}, t_{ij}) at each position. The goal then, is to find the sequence of word/tag pairs whose probability is optimum according to the model,

$$P_i = \prod_{j=1}^{n} P(w_{ij_i}|t_{ij_i})P(t_{ij_i}|t_{i-1j_{i-1}}, t_{i-2j_{i-2}}) \qquad (1)$$

In order to avoid combinatorial problems (computing the product for all possible sequences), the system locates at each position, i, in the sequence, the pair (w_{ij}, t_{ij}) that locally maximizes the global computation of Eq. (1), thus,

$$P_i \times P_{i+1} \times P_{i+2} \qquad (2)$$

where, P_i, is as defined in Eq. (1). The basic components for automatic accent (diacritic) insertion are given in [12]. The system is called DIAC, and consists of a tagger and the language dictionary. The tagger QTAG* is a slightly adapted version of Oliver Masons QTAG trigram tragger, which generic architecture is represented in Fig. 1, to show the process flow for diacritic insertion. Figure 2 shows a modified architecture describing the components of a data-driven tone marking system implemented in this research. We introduce a HMM syllabifier (for the automatic syllabification of words), and a character and tone mapper (to hadle tone mapping). The tone mapper uses a close-copy version of the syllabifier, heavily supervised to ensure tone marking accuracy. These components rely on a knowledgebase (i.e., language model, dictionary, tone pattern-base and Unicode rule-base) to accomplish the tone marking process. The tone marking system was implemented using a NLP script developed in Python with an automatic Unicode rendering of the resultant text. The rendered text is almost 100 % accurate,

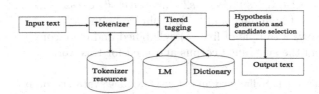

Fig. 1. Generic system architecture of a DIAC. Source [12].

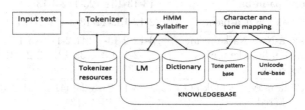

Fig. 2. Modified architecture for a data-driven tone marking system

because of the syllabified close-copy tone synthesis and mapping. This approach is helpful for a preliminary evaluation of the system and for the estimation of the level of exhaustiveness of the trained corpus. Training the corpus/utterances with HMMs is useful because most out-of-vocabulary words are handled with high accuracy. Another advantage of our framework is that the tone-tagging algorithm infers knowledge from the trained corpus, and the syllabified output certainly enhances reading fluency and can be used for pedagogical purposes.

3.2   Database and Corpus Design

The input corpus is a set of utterances used for the HMM training of an Ibibio Text-To-Speech (TTS) system [13]. Two text files served as inputs to the design. The first file is a syllabified form of trainable utterances of the language, generated from a heterogeneous relation graph (HRG), in a speech synthesis experiment [3,14]. The second file is a close-copy tone-tagged version of the same file. The Ibibio tone system is made up of the the following tone marks: High H ('), Low L (`), Down-Step DS (!), Low-High LH (ˇ), High-Low HL (^). The input utterances were tone-tagged according to the following labels: 1-Consonants, 2-H, 3-L, 4-DS, 5-LH, 6-HL. To resolve lexical ambiguity, a constraint grammar rule was employed for words disambiguation to determine its usage in context (within the sentence). However, further research works to perfect the current design would be presented in a future paper.

In a FGN-World Bank Science and Technology Education Post-Basic (STEP-B) project on "Towards Generic Text-To-Speech Technology – Application for African Tone Languages", about two hours of Ibibio speech utterances were tagged (in a supervised manner) for a statistical-parametric speech synthesis research [13], and is adopted in this paper for the purpose of resolving structural ambiguity. Though the corpus does not represent an exhaustive data-set, an exhaustive corpus is expected. The syllabified corpus are the various sentence strings $\{\#s1 - s2 - ... - sn, \#s1 - s2 - ... - sn\#, \#s1 - s2 - ...sn|...\}$, where '#' represents a word boundary and ' |' is a phrase boundary.

Table 1 shows a sample of five (5) syllabified and close-copy tone sequences, generated from the syllabified corpus and used for this work.

Table 1. Syllabified and close-copy tone synthesis corpora

Syllabified Ibibio sentence	Close-copy tone synthesis
bO-Na-kam kuu-kpa-m-ba	13-13-131 123-112-3-13
a-ke-fee-fe-Re a-jak i-kOt a-ba-si	2-12-132-12-13 2-131 2-121 2-13-13
e-Je a-ma-a-nam a-Nwa-Na ke m-me o-wo e-nie n-treu-bOk ke u-sVN Om-mO keed keed	3-12 2-13-2-141 2-112-13 12 3-13 2-12 2-144 3-1133-121 12 2-121 61-15 1331 1331
a-ba-si a-ma-a-siak u-sVN u-bOk-kO O-nO n-di-tO i-sred	3-13-13 2-13-2-1441 2-121 2-131-12 2-13 3-13-13 2-1131
e-jIn O-mO a-di-ben e-Je a-ka i-saN	2-121 2-13 2-14-121 3-12 2-16 2-131

3.3   Tone Feature Extraction

The tone marking problem can be regarded as a pattern recognition problem. Pattern recognition is a branch of machine learning that concentrates on the recognition of patterns and regularities in data. To define the pattern recognition problem, a set of $(16,905 \times 17)$-input vectors specifying the various tones of the Ibibio corpus was setup. Then, a set of one target vector for classifying the tone patterns to which the input vectors are assigned was derived. The approach used to derive the target vectors was to set a scalar value to either 1 or 0, signifying which class a corresponding input pattern belongs to. Our output (target) is a single class that indicates the correctness of the tone pattern prediction. The model architecture on which our pattern prediction framework rests is presented in Fig. 3. As shown in Fig. 3, the architecture is a multi-layer, multi-input and multi-output (MIMO) feed-forward network, useful for function fitting (or regression) problems with sigmoid hidden and softmax output neurons. The number of characters in the longest phrase determines the number of input neurons. In this paper the input layer initially had 17 nodes. The network has one output neuron, since there is only a target value (category) associated with the input vectors; and was trained with the Levenberg-Marquardt algorithm (trainlm) – the fastest backpropagation (network training) function in MATLAB 2015a, that updates weight and bias values according to the Levenberg-Marquardt optimization. The data were partitioned as follows: 70 % (11,833) for training; 15 % (2,536) for validation; and, 15 % (2,536) for testing.

Input-Target Classification. Table 2 shows the Input-Target classification of the first fifteen (15) Ibibio phrases selected from the entire corpus, and used

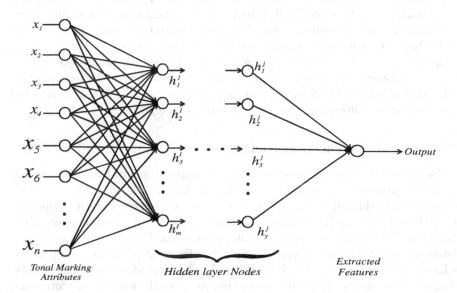

Fig. 3. Pattern recognition neural network architecture

Table 2. Input-Target classification for a set of Ibibio phrases.

Phrase (syllabified)	1	2	3	4	5	6	7	8	9	10	11	12	13	14	15	16	17	Boundary tone	Target
																			1
bO-Na-kam	1	3	1	3	1	3	1	0	0	0	0	0	0	0	0	0	0	1	0
kuu-kpa-m-ba	1	2	3	1	1	2	3	1	3	0	0	0	0	0	0	0	0	3	1
a-ke-fee-fe-Re	2	1	2	1	3	2	1	2	1	3	0	0	0	0	0	0	0	3	1
a-jak	2	1	3	1	0	0	0	0	0	0	0	0	0	0	0	0	0	1	0
i-kOt	2	1	2	1	0	0	0	0	0	0	0	0	0	0	0	0	0	1	0
a-ba-si	2	1	3	1	3	0	0	0	0	0	0	0	0	0	0	0	0	3	1
e-Je	3	1	2	0	0	0	0	0	0	0	0	0	0	0	0	0	0	2	1
a-ma-a-nam	2	1	3	2	1	4	1	0	0	0	0	0	0	0	0	0	0	1	0
a-Nwa-Na	2	1	1	2	1	3	0	0	0	0	0	0	0	0	0	0	0	3	1
ke	1	2	0	0	0	0	0	0	0	0	0	0	0	0	0	0	0	2	1
m-me	3	1	3	0	0	0	0	0	0	0	0	0	0	0	0	0	0	3	1
o-wo	2	1	2	0	0	0	0	0	0	0	0	0	0	0	0	0	0	2	1
e-nie	2	1	4	4	0	0	0	0	0	0	0	0	0	0	0	0	0	4	1
n-treu-bOk	3	1	1	3	3	1	2	1	0	0	0	0	0	0	0	0	0	1	0
ke	1	2	0	0	0	0	0	0	0	0	0	0	0	0	0	0	0	2	1

for the experiment. A total of 16,905 phrases (74,016 phonemes) were classified. A breakdown of the tone statistics for tone bearing units (vowels (41,988)) are distributed as: H (21,980), L (15,739), DH (2,399), LH (1,492), HL (378); while the statistic of non-tone bearing units (consonants) is C (32,028). Each character (phoneme) of the phrase was classified into 17 inputs (the longest phrase), and coded using the tone labels defined in Sect. 3.2. The patterns formed by the input sequences were useful for efficient modeling of the tone pattern.

Aside the tone features, the boundary tones for each phrase (i.e. 1-no tone/ consonant, 2-H, 3-L, 4-DS, 5-LH, 6-HL) – an important feature used for intonation analysis, were also enumerated. Concerning the output, input phrases without a boundary tone were initially marked as bad predictors (i.e., were given a score of 0), and one, otherwise, before learning the system. Hence, the number of inputs now varied between 1 and 18, after the boundary tones were derived. The hidden layer of the network contained 10 neurons. The output considered only one node enumerating the tone correctness (true/false).

3.4   Unicode Character Encoding

Table 3 shows a character encoding table containing standard Unicode combinations that maps to the various graphemes and phonemes (a set of the language's alphabets). In this paper, we employ the Speech Assessment Phonetic Alphabet (SAMPA) [15] – a machine readable format, for representing the phonemes of the language. These characters represent the orthographic form (or grapheme) of the language system and are employed to replace the input phonemes, after knowledge of the tone pattern has been inferred. The Unicode equivalents of these characters are necessary for portability purposes, as the outputs are formatted as Unicode Text Font-8 (UTF-8).

Table 3. Unicode mapping table

Grapheme	Unicode	Phoneme (SAMPA)
High tone		
á	u+00E1	a
é	u+00E9	e
í	u+00ED	i
ó	u+00F3	o
ú	u+00F2	u
ḿ	u+0301u+006D	m
ń	u+0144	n
ɘ́	u+0301u+0259	E
ŋ́	u+0301u+014b	N
ị́	u+0323u+00ED	I
ọ́	u+0323u+00F2	O
ʌ́	u+0301u+028c	V
ụ́	u+0323u+00FA	U
Low tone		
à	u+00E0	a
è	u+00E8	e
ì	u+00EC	i
ò	u+00F2	o
ù	u+00F9	u
m̀	u+0300u+006D	m
ǹ	u+01F9	n
ɘ̀	0300u+0259	E
ŋ̀	u+0300u+014b	N
ị̀	0323u+00EC	I
ọ̀	u+0323u+00F2	O
ʌ̀	u+0300u+028c	V
ụ̀	u+0323u+00F9	U
High-Low tone		
â	u+00E2	a
ê	u+00EA	e
î	u+00EE	i
ô	u+00F4	o
û	u+00FB	u
ɘ̂	u+030cu+0259	E
ộ	u+0323u+00F4	O
Grapheme	Unicode	Phoneme (SAMPA)

Grapheme	Unicode	Phoneme (SAMPA)
Low-High tone		
ǎ	u+01CE	a
ě	u+001B	e
ǐ	u+01D0	i
ǒ	u+01D2	o
ǔ	u+01D4	u
ọ̌	u+0323u+01D2	O
Down-step tone		
!a	u+2193u+00E1	a
!e	u+2193u+00e9	e
!i	u+2193u+00ED	i
!o	u+2193u+00F3	o
!u	u+2193u+00FA	u
!ɘ	u+030cu+0259	E
!ị	u+00EE	I
!ọ	u+0323u+00F4	O
!ʌ	u+0306u+028c	V
!ụ	u+0323u+00FB	U
Consonants		
ŋ	u+014B	N
y	u+0079	j
ɲ	u+0272	J
ʁ	u+0281	R
a	-	a
b	-	b
d	-	d
f	-	f
k	-	k
kp	-	kp
m	-	m
n	-	n
r	-	r
s	-	s
t	-	t
w	-	w

4 Results

4.1 Tone Marking

In this section, the results obtained from an implementation of the data-driven tone processing algorithm are presented. Figure 5 shows a snippet of the result

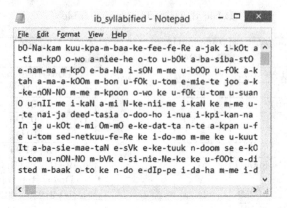

Fig. 4. Input corpus

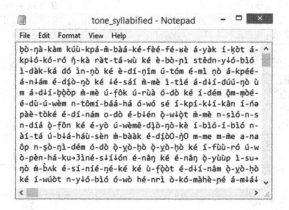

Fig. 5. Tone marked corpus

obtained from the tone marking system. It was observed that the input phrases (words) in the trained corpus (see Fig. 4) were correctly tone marked, thus verifying the correctness of our HMM syllabifier. A possible limitation of this tagger therefore, is the degree of correctness of the tone-tagged sequences (a heavily supervised procedure). One noticeable defect was in the poor rendering of multiple diacritic marks (e.g., the under-dot and H-tone) on the same character, e.g. 'O' in bO-Na-kam, should have been tone marked as bọ̀-ŋà-kàm. Also observed was the ability of the proposed system to handle context-dependency of word derivations that modifies the tone. We are currently investigating ways to ensure a more robust design.

4.2 Tone Pattern Recognition

In this section, we investigate the recognition of tone patterns in the input corpus with patternnet – a feedforward network, using the Levenberg-Marquardt algorithm. Fig. 6 is a confusion matrix showing the various types of errors associated with the final trained network. The diagonal cells represent the number of correctly classified cases, while the off-diagonal cells are the misclassified cases for each class. For Target Class 0 (wrong prediction), 31.2 % instances were correctly classified while Target Class 1 (correct prediction) had 61.9 % correct classification. The last cell of column 3 shows the overall percentage of correctly classified cases. As can be observed from the matrix, the overall performance of the model is 93.1 %, which implies that after training, the network was able to successfully classify the tone patterns with an accuracy of 93.1 %. The remaining 6.9 % of misclassified cases came mainly from target class 0, indicating the negative impact of consonants at word boundaries, on the overall speech quality. Consequently, the introduction of other tone related measurement parameters is necessary to improve the accuracy of the classification system. The Receiver Operating Characteristic (ROC) curve showing the effect of the false positive rate (1-specificity) on the true positive rate (sensitivity) is presented in Fig. 7. As shown in the figure, the curve is closer to the vertical axis indicating a very good classification in all cases (train, test and validation). The present outcome of this work is useful as pedagogical tool (for teaching and learning the syllab-

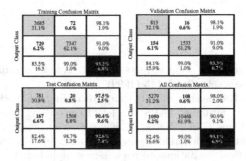

Fig. 6. Confusion matrices for tone pattern experiment

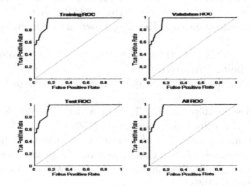

Fig. 7. ROC curve for tone pattern experiment

ification and tone marking of an indegenous language), and in tone verification systems.

5   Conclusion and Future Work

This paper has proposed a hybrid learning methodology in the intelligent extraction and recognition of tone patterns from Ibibio corpus. A MIMO neural network consisting of 18 nodes in the input layer (consisting of a maximum of 17 tone tagged information and a boundary tone vector derived from the tone input class), with one output neuron, was implemented using supervised learning. Most supervised learning techniques have found application in speech processing and the defining characteristic of supervised learning is the availability of annotated training data. A total of 16,905 phrases of test corpus were validated by tone marking the corpus using a data-driven approach. The test corpus was then subjected to a pattern classifier to model the accuracy of tone patterns. Results obtained confirm the correctness of our data-driven tone marking algorithm, and demonstrate the possibility of an efficient tone pattern recognition system for speech corpora. A future direction of this paper is an unsupervised tone recognizer for African languages, and the comparison of our approach with other methods.

References

1. Bird, S.: When marking tone reduces fluency: An orthography experiment in cameroon. Lang. Speech **42**, 83–115 (1999)
2. Urua, E.-A.: The Tone system of Ibibio. In: Proceedings of Workshop on Typology of African Prosodic Systems (TAPS), Bielefeld University, Germany (2001)
3. Ekpenyong, M., Urua, E.-A., Watts, O., King, S., Yamagushi, J.: Statistical parametric speech synthesis for ibibio. Speech Commun. **56**, 243–251 (2014)
4. Nida, E.A.: Practical limitations to a phonemic alphabet. In: Smalley, W. (ed.) Orthography Studies: Articles on New Writing Systems, pp. 22–30 (1964)
5. Baker, P., Bari, A., Dalby, D., Jatta, S., Mann, M., Saeed, J.: Writing African Languages: The Search for a Uniform Script. SOAS, UK (1982)
6. Henderson, L.: Orthographies and Reading. Lawrence Erlbaum Associates, London (1984)
7. Frost, R., Katz, L. (eds.): Orthography, Phonology, Morphology and Meaning. Advances in Psychology, Amsterd (1992)
8. Williamson, K.: Practical Orthography in Nigeria. Heinemann Educational Books, Nigeria (1984)
9. Bird, S.: Strategies for Representing Tone in African Writing Systems: A Critical Review. University of Edinburgh, Edinburgh (1998)
10. Simard, M.: Automatic insertion of accents in french text. In: Ide, N., Voutilainen (ed.) Proceedings of 3rd Conference on Empirical Methods in Natural Language Processing The Association for Computational Linguists, pp. 27–35. ACL/SIGDAT, Spain (1998)
11. EL-Bze, M., Bernard Mrialdo, B., Rozeron, B., Derouault, A.: Accentuation automatique des texts par des methodes probabilistes. Techn. Sci. Inf. **13**(6), 797–815 (1994)

12. Tufis, D., Chitu, A.: Automatic diacritics insertion in romanian texts. In: Proceedings of Complex International Conference on Computational Lexicography (COMPLEX) (1999)
13. Ekpenyong, M.E.: Speech Synthesis for Tone Language Systems. P.hD. Thesis, University of Uyo, Uyo. In: Supervision Collaboration with CSTR, University of Edinburgh, Edinburgh (2013)
14. Ekpenyong, M.: Optimizing speech naturalness in voice uses interface design: a weakly supervised approach. In: Proceedings of IEEE World Congress on Information and Communication Technologies, Mumbai, India, pp. 99–105. IEEE Press, New York (2011)
15. Ekpenyong, M.E.: Agent-based framework for intelligent natural. Telecommun. Syst. J. **52**, 1423–1433 (2013)

Linguistic Descriptors and Analytic Hierarchy Process in Face Recognition Realized by Humans

Paweł Karczmarek[1(✉)], Adam Kiersztyn[1], Witold Pedrycz[2,3,4], and Michał Dolecki[1]

[1] Institute of Mathematics and Computer Science,
The John Paul II Catholic University of Lublin,
ul. Konstantynów 1H, 20-708 Lublin, Poland
{pawelk,adam.kiersztyn,michal.dolecki}@kul.pl
[2] Department of Electrical and Computer Engineering, University of Alberta,
Edmonton, AB T6R 2V4, Canada
wpedrycz@ualberta.ca
[3] Department of Electrical and Computer Engineering, Faculty of Engineering,
King Abdulaziz University, Jeddah 21589, Saudi Arabia
[4] Systems Research Institute, Polish Academy of Sciences, Warsaw, Poland

Abstract. In this paper, we discuss an application of the linguistic descriptions obtained directly from experts' and treated as the votes when characterizing facial images to carry out face classification. Despite various automated face recognition techniques, the expert's opinion plays a pivotal role in making classification decisions when recognizing faces, say in problems of suspect identification. Here, we analyze the impact of critical factors (e.g., a number of experts, voting schemes, distance functions) and their impact on the performance of classification schemes. The well-established Analytic Hierarchy Process (AHP) is used to quantify importance of linguistic descriptors in the process of face recognition by humans. As a result we produce realistic weights improving the accuracy of classification. Experimental results are presented including a number of parametric studies.

Keywords: Linguistic descriptors · Analytic hierarchy process · Face recognition · Voting · Distance functions

1 Introduction

Face recognition has been one of the most visible research pursuits in image analysis. The main reason behind these intensive studies is that the need of biometric identification of people is omnipresent in the current digital society. Among the most evident applications of face recognition are widely understood safety tasks as encountered in border control, passport and driver's license verification, surveillance systems, computer user identification, etc. There have been many methods of facial recognition reported in the literature such as geometric methods [14], Eigenfaces [30], Fisherfaces [2], local descriptors [1,3,4] and Gabor

© Springer International Publishing Switzerland 2016
L. Rutkowski et al. (Eds.): ICAISC 2016, Part I, LNAI 9692, pp. 584–596, 2016.
DOI: 10.1007/978-3-319-39378-0_50

wavelets [25,33], elastic bunch graph matching [31], information fusion and aggregation [20], neural networks [9], sparse representation [32], fuzzy measure [17], etc. Despite of the fact that the methods known in the literature produce good results in experiments conducted in controlled laboratory environments, many of them do not work successfully when applied in practice when one is faced with substantial changes in age, position, illumination, emotion, etc. Here, one of the most appealing factors which may support the accuracies of the algorithms may be an application of the human mechanisms of recognition or the presence of the experienced experts from the fields of cognitive psychology, criminology, or forensic science. Moreover, understanding a way how the people describe other individuals may be of particular relevance. The understanding of this mechanism is crucial from this point of view.

In the literature, there are many studies discussing the complexity of the recognition processes such as eye tracking [6], brain activity regions detection [11], abilities to better recognize familiar than unfamiliar faces, or depth studies on the assessment of particular facial regions saliency [8,13]. Similarly, many authors consider the importance of face areas from the computational and classification point of view, see the works [5,7,12,17,20]. Such studies may help in identifying and quantifying the relevance of parts of faces in the classification processes. For instance, one could assess the relevance of the upper and lower portions of the face, regions of face in the discrimination process. A focused summary of discussion on this topic can be found in [17]. Finally, the problem of utilizing of the manner the people describe other individuals using natural language has been present in the research for more than twenty years. One of the approaches was an application of fuzzy numbers as the vehicles to carry the linguistic descriptions obtained from the pictures [10,21,22]. The authors considered a system where 19 facial features such as the size of eyes were considered. These features were described, for instance, as *small, rather small, medium, rather big,* and *big*. The matching based on a certain measure of overlap was applied to the classification process. In [23] descriptions related to impressions, e.g. *intelligent, childish,* or *cold face,* were added to the system. Other interesting approaches were the use of an Amazon Mechanical Turk service [18] or an attempt to an application of Granular Computing [19]. Finally, in [16] the authors proposed a model of a system where the experts' estimates of facial images are the input to the Analytic Hierarchy Process (AHP, [24,27–29]) which can be used to build a hierarchy of both the abstract facial features according to their saliency and the concrete features associated with the concrete persons according to their shape, length, etc. A comprehensive survey of the works on linguistic descriptors in the context of face recognition is presented in [15].

The main goal of this study is to present a way of classification of faces realized without relying on the use of numeric measurements. We want to examine how the use of Analytic Hierarchy Process involving experts can improve the accuracy of facial recognition process based on the experts' answers regarding particular facial features of a given individual. We establish a novel application of the AHP to the process of ranking the most important and descriptive, in our opinion, facial features. Moreover, our objective is to discuss how to form the description of the face in terms of a collection of fuzzy sets. Furthermore, a particular attention is paid to the process of forming membership functions of the linguistic descriptors so that such functions are reflective of the judgments offered by the experts.

The paper is organized as follows. In Sect. 2 presented is the role of the Analytic Hierarchy Process followed by a description of the general processing scheme. Section 3 covers the experimental results while Sect. 4 delivers the conclusions and the perspectives for the future work.

2   Main Flow of Processing and the Role of AHP

Our objective is to develop a linguistic feature space for face recognition and assess it discriminatory capabilities. The underlying motivation is that faces are described by intuitively appealing and understood features whose quantification is realized in terms of only a few linguistic terms (e.g. *small, medium, large*). Humans do not measure these features but use only the labels. Formally, following this way of description, considering n features and having the quantification carried by c_i, $i = 1, \ldots, n$, linguistic labels, we are concerned with Boolean vectors with total number $c_1 + c_2 + \ldots + c_n$ of 0–1 entries. In contrast, the numeric feature space is formed by n-dimensional vectors. In case of several experts, the Boolean vector can have 0–1 entries built upon the use of the probabilities estimating occurrence of some linguistic labels. Let us consider an example face and its selected set of particular n features (descriptors) $\mathbf{f}_1, \mathbf{f}_2, \ldots, \mathbf{f}_n$ such as eyebrows direction, inter-eye distance, or length of the nose. Each descriptor assumes a finite (small) number of granular values (fuzzy sets) quantified as *small, medium, large*, etc. The descriptors could be concatenated resulting in a single vector delivering a description of a given face, say $\mathbf{f} = [\mathbf{f}_1, \mathbf{f}_2, \ldots, \mathbf{f}_n]$. An overall collection of faces is denoted as Ω. Our goal is to classify any picture (face) as belonging/not belonging to one of the faces present in Ω. The face is characterized by some vector $\mathbf{g}$. The classification is based on the nearest neighbor rule by determining a minimal distance between $\mathbf{g}$ and $\mathbf{f}$ coming from Ω.

To illustrate this issue, we can look for example at the feature eye length. Let us assume that the set of faces were assessed by five experts and that two of them described someone's eyes as *short*, two experts said they are *middle*, while one expert estimated their length to be *long*. In this manner we get the vector of membership values $\mathbf{f} = [0.4, 0.4, 0.2]$. If all the features are estimated, the person is described by the $c_1 + c_2 + \ldots + c_n$-dimensional vector containing the values from the interval $[0, 1]$ and being the result of concatenation of all the n vectors built in the same way as the vector $\mathbf{f}$.

To determine the values of the weights of these features one can apply the well-known Analytic Hierarchy Process. The main idea of the process is that the experts do the pairwise comparisons between the features answering the questions of the form:

To which extent the feature A is preferred over the feature B?

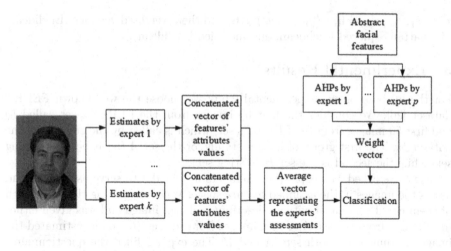

Fig. 1. An overall flow of processing

They can use the nine levels scale and, for instance, the answer 1–1 means that both features A and B are equally preferred while the answer 1–9 means that the feature B is extremely preferred over the feature A. Of course, the experts may choose from the values of $1, 2, \ldots, 9$. This way the so called reciprocal matrix is created. It has the values 1 on the main diagonal and the values $a_{ij} = 1/a_{ji}$, otherwise. The values of the main eigenvector's elements are the weights or priorities of the features compared in the experiment. The details of the AHP process and its comprehensive analysis can be found, for example, in [29].

The main flow of this classification method is presented in Fig. 1. A group of experts evaluate abstract facial features using AHP. These results, after aggregation, form a reference point to be used to weight the evaluations of specific facial parts. Vectors obtained from abstract and real facial features are compared by the Nearest Neighbors (NN) algorithm.

Assuming that p experts took part in the process of pairwise comparisons of the n features one can obtain p vectors of weights, i.e., $w_1, \ldots, w_p$ related with the importance of these facial cues of the form $\mathbf{w}_i = [w_{i1}, w_{i2}, \ldots, w_{in}]$, $i = 1, \ldots, p$. Similarly as in the case of concatenated vectors corresponding to particular facial features we form the weight vectors producing $c_1 + c_2 + \ldots + c_n$ -element vectors $\bar{w}_i$. Of course, if needed weights can be applied in such an obtained form or in the form of their inversions, namely

$$\bar{\mathbf{v}}_i = \max\{\bar{w}_1, \ldots, \bar{w}_n\} - \bar{w}_i. \tag{1}$$

The vectors representing the faces are compared using the distance/similarity functions such as well-known Euclidean, Manhattan, cosine, correlation, modified Euclidean, i.e.,

$$d(x, y) = \frac{\sum_{i=1}^{n}(x_i - y_i)^2}{\sum_{j=1}^{n}(x_j)^2 \sum_{j=1}^{n}(y_j)^2}, \tag{2}$$

$x = (x_1, \ldots, x_n) \neq \mathbf{0}$, $y(y_1, \ldots, y_n) \neq \mathbf{0}$, and their weighted versions (Euclidean, Manhattan, squared Euclidean, and modified Euclidean).

3   Experimental Results

For the purpose of our experimental study we choose the well-known FERET dataset [26]. We consider the first 50 images from the FERET's set called ba and first 50 images from the FERET's set, which is called by the creators of the dataset bk. The first group of images stands for the set A (let it be the training set) while the second is the set B (testing set).

Next, we asked 17 people (lab members or friends) to serve as experts and assess the images in the assumed feature space. When describing the faces, each of them could serve as a witness describing a facial image and was given either fifty images from the set A or fifty images from the set B. No one estimated the images coming from both sets A and B. The experts filled the questionnaires using specially prepared application to make this task easier. In this manner we got 9 questionnaires regarding to the set A and 8 questionnaires regarding to the set B consisting of Boolean values related to the linguistic descriptions of faces.

In this study, we narrow the set of such features to $n = 27$, in our opinion, relatively easy to estimate by people. All these features and possible values they can get are presented in Table 1.

Moreover, we asked 4 experts being (again, lab members or friends) to estimate 27 abstract facial features from Table 1 in the AHP process of pairwise comparisons. The weight values and the average weights obtained by the experts are presented in Fig. 2. One can see that the weights are intuitively appealing since the confidence in the experts' assessments seems to be at a high level except with the case of features related with shapes of the head and forehead and strictly these strictly related with human description and experience such as gender and origin. It probably comes from the fact that a few experts put the weight on the meaning of some features in the process of automatic face recognition while others treated more seriously the features related with human feelings and, more generally, face recognition by humans.

In the first series of numerical experiments we run the tests for all the combinations of 3 experts estimating the images from the training set and all the possible combinations of experts estimating the testing set. The most intuitive approach is majority voting with no weights. We summed the experts' votes regarding to each image and each facial feature, and compared the results increasing the voting result by one point if the results were the same and zero otherwise.

The rank-1, rank-5, and rank-10 recognition rates are included in Tables 2, 3, and 4 for all the combinations of three, five, and seven experts estimating the training and testing sets, respectively. The best distance function itself is the Manhattan one. However, the versions with weights show that the weights obtained from the experts' knowledge about the importance of the facial features in the face recognition process can be very helpful here. It is important that if the weights are introduced then the recognition rates at the level 100 are reached for the lower ranks.

Table 1. Facial features and their linguistic descriptors

Index	Feature	Linguistic descriptors
1	Shape of the face	rectangular, pentagonal, oval, round, triangular, ellipsoidal, trapezoidal, rhomboidal
2	Height of the forehead	low, average, high
3	Width of the forehead	narrow, average, wide
4	Shape of the forehead	rectangular, square, trapezoidal, inversely trapezoidal
5	Length of the eyebrows	short, average, long
6	Direction of the eyebrows	horizontal, turned up, turned down
7	Distance between the eyebrows	merged, narrow, average, wide
8	Position of the eyebrows	low, average, high
9	Shape of the eyebrows	arched, straight, broken-lined, wavy, bushy
10	Thickness of the eyebrows	narrow, average, wide
11	Shape of the lower eyelid	normal, average, saggy
12	Distance between eyelids	narrow, average, wide
13	Eye length	short, average, long
14	Direction of the fissures	horizontal, turned up, turned down
15	Inter-eye distance	narrow, average, wide
16	Length of the nose	short, average, long
17	Width of the nose	narrow, average, wide
18	Length of the nasal bridge	narrow, average, wide
19	Shape of the nasal tip	rounded, spiked, blunt, angular
20	Height of the upper lip	low, average, high
21	Height of the lower lip	low, average, high
22	Width of the mouth	short, average, long
23	Shape of the chin	round, oval, angular, triangular, concave
24	Size of the chin	small, average, big
25	Protrusion of the ears	fitting, average, protruding
26	Gender	female, male
27	Origin	Caucasian, Spanish, Asian, African

Moreover, in Tables 5, 6, 7, and 8 there are shown the recognition rates for the chosen classifiers, i.e. voting, NN with Manhattan distance, NN with modified Euclidean distance and NN with weighted modified Euclidean distance, respectively. All the combinations of experts were considered. It is easy to see that the more experts is involved in the process of estimating the facial features of the particular subjects, the recognition rate is closer to 100 %. Furthermore, one can see that the weights can improve the accuracy of the classifier when are applied for the lower number

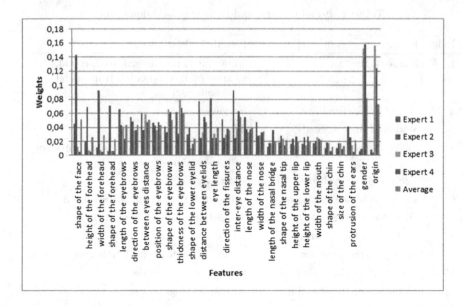

Fig. 2. Average weights of the facial features obtained by four experts taking part in the experiment

Table 2. The recognition rates obtained by majority voting and the comparison of concatenated vectors by using distance functions for all the combinations of three experts estimating the training set and three experts estimating the images from the testing set

Rank	Voting	Euclid.	Manh.	Cosine	Correl.	Mod. Euclid.	W. Euclid.	W. Manh.	W. sq. Euclid.	W. mod. Eucl.
1	56.03	77.96	78.18	77.85	77.70	77.61	76.90	76.64	78.24	78.87
5	85.82	96.97	97.00	97.01	96.90	96.81	97.66	97.20	97.99	97.84
10	93.93	99.21	99.23	99.25	99.20	99.16	99.63	99.46	99.74	99.65
Number of rank for which 100% recognition rate has been reached										
-	48	39	36	36	38	42	32	28	25	27

Table 3. The average recognition rates obtained when five experts estimate the training and five experts estimate the testing set, respectively

Rank	Voting	Euclid.	Manh.	Cosine	Correl.	Mod. Euclid.	W. Euclid.	W. Manh.	W. sq. Euclid.	W. mod. Eucl.
1	71.40	92.36	92.65	92.77	92.64	92.85	91.60	91.28	92.42	92.99
5	93.13	99.86	99.84	99.87	99.86	99.86	99.88	99.85	99.94	99.91
10	97.68	99.99	99.99	99.99	99.99	99.99	100.00	99.99	100.00	100.00
Number of rank for which 100% recognition rate has been reached										
-	47	17	15	17	18	19	11	20	11	11

Table 4. The average recognition rates obtained when seven experts estimate the training and seven experts estimate the testing set, respectively

Rank	Voting	Euclid.	Manh.	Cosine	Correl.	Mod. Euclid.	W. Euclid.	W. Manh.	W. sq. Euclid.	W. mod. Eucl.
1	79.38	97.40	97.80	97.21	97.20	97.40	96.72	97.42	97.28	97.18
5	96.43	100.00	100.00	100.00	100.00	100.00	100.00	100.00	100.00	100.00
10	99.33	100.00	100.00	100.00	100.00	100.00	100.00	100.00	100.00	100.00
Number of rank for which 100% recognition rate has been reached										
-	21	3	4	3	3	4	4	4	4	3

Table 5. Average recognition rates for voting for all the combinations of experts' number

		Number of experts estimating the testing set							
		1	2	3	4	5	6	7	8
Number of experts estimating the training set	1	38.94	36.52	46.16	45.46	50.62	49.10	53.14	52.67
	2	42.23	47.55	50.58	55.57	56.36	57.99	58.45	58.94
	3	46.26	44.18	56.03	55.77	61.79	60.13	64.65	62.95
	4	51.38	53.95	61.60	65.63	68.60	69.62	71.85	71.95
	5	52.92	51.25	64.05	65.02	71.40	70.60	74.55	74.21
	6	55.07	56.56	66.25	69.95	74.10	75.08	77.64	77.88
	7	55.93	54.92	68.33	69.54	75.87	75.55	79.38	77.50
	8	58.06	58.46	70.05	73.24	77.87	78.95	81.81	80.44
	9	56.00	55.86	70.46	71.26	78.68	78.21	82.75	78.00

Table 6. Average recognition rates for comparison of concatenated feature vectors with Manhattan norm for all the combinations of experts' number

		Number of experts estimating the testing set							
		1	2	3	4	5	6	7	8
Number of experts estimating the training set	1	38.94	48.13	53.79	57.47	59.97	61.90	63.00	62.67
	2	47.21	62.75	69.41	74.42	76.93	79.23	80.39	82.56
	3	52.31	69.49	78.18	82.38	85.33	87.70	88.61	89.69
	4	55.78	75.06	82.51	87.41	89.83	91.81	92.76	93.79
	5	58.25	77.58	85.78	89.90	92.65	94.03	95.13	95.94
	6	59.99	80.52	88.23	92.05	94.10	95.76	96.50	97.14
	7	61.40	81.59	89.28	93.02	95.32	96.61	97.80	98.06
	8	62.58	83.24	90.40	94.16	96.19	97.77	98.31	99.11
	9	63.50	83.57	91.43	94.51	96.71	98.64	99.75	100.00

Table 7. Average recognition rates for comparison of concatenated feature vectors with modified Euclidean distance for all the combinations of experts' number

		Number of experts estimating the testing set							
		1	2	3	4	5	6	7	8
Number of experts estimating the training set	1	38.94	48.13	53.79	57.47	59.97	61.90	63.00	62.67
	2	44.38	60.38	69.06	74.35	77.88	80.20	81.94	83.83
	3	50.13	68.48	77.61	82.87	86.11	88.39	89.99	91.29
	4	54.34	73.36	82.45	87.44	90.44	92.42	93.81	94.71
	5	57.08	76.52	85.48	90.11	92.85	94.60	95.73	96.35
	6	59.12	78.65	87.53	91.83	94.29	95.86	96.82	97.55
	7	60.67	80.21	88.94	92.96	95.23	96.69	97.40	97.89
	8	62.39	81.24	89.92	93.83	95.77	96.95	97.47	97.78
	9	62.25	82.43	90.50	94.51	96.21	97.07	97.50	98.00

Table 8. Average recognition rates for comparison of concatenated feature vectors with weighted modified Euclidean distance for all the combinations of experts' number

		Number of experts estimating the testing set							
		1	2	3	4	5	6	7	8
Number of experts estimating the training set	1	38.25	49.26	55.06	59.01	61.66	63.35	64.69	66.22
	2	49.30	63.70	71.06	75.60	78.43	80.35	81.70	83.00
	3	55.54	71.08	78.87	83.41	86.36	88.30	89.70	90.88
	4	59.16	75.57	83.41	87.82	90.50	92.39	93.62	94.57
	5	61.61	78.45	86.33	90.44	92.99	94.62	95.77	96.51
	6	63.25	80.52	88.30	92.19	94.44	95.89	96.69	97.31
	7	64.67	81.96	89.78	93.40	95.36	96.57	97.18	97.44
	8	65.83	82.95	90.75	94.25	95.98	96.93	97.33	97.56
	9	67.50	83.93	91.46	94.80	96.57	97.36	97.00	98.00

of the experts. It can be justified by the fact that the weights can fill the lack of the data coming from the experts' estimation. Note that the weights can be changed depending on the distance function characteristic, i.e. the higher weight obtained the less impact on the classification result. Adding the mentioned weights to the modified Euclidian distance improved average classification result by 1 % point. In cases of the number of experts estimating training set bigger than one and only one expert estimating testing set, the obtained results were better in average by even 5 % points. When the number of experts estimating testing set was 6 and above, the results of weighted modified Euclidian distance were worse by almost one percent point. What is interesting, for only one expert estimating training set, this tendency was reversed and one can note that improvement of classification rate grows with the number of experts estimating testing set from up 3.55 % point.

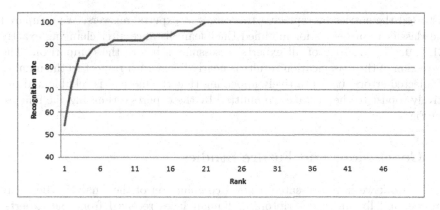

Fig. 3. Percentage recognition rates with regard to rank $n\,(n = 1, \ldots, 50)$ when the normalized lengths of features are considered only

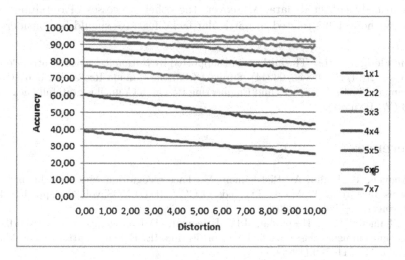

Fig. 4. The recognition rates obtained with distortion (i.e. with injected mistakes to the experts' questionnaires). Here presented are the values of rates obtained when one expert estimates the training set and one expert assesses the testing set (1×1), two experts estimate training and testing set (2×2), etc.

It is worth noting that if we consider only the numeric space of features (15 features which values can be ordered linearly, i.e. *short, medium, long*) and we apply the weighted squared Euclidean distance function for their normalized lengths (i.e. 1 is equal to the longest feature in the dataset), then the recognition rate is 54 % (see Fig. 3) and it easy to see that the presence of experts and an application of the linguistic variables can importantly enhance the accuracy of recognition.

In our last series of experiments we check how the controlled distortion of the experts' assessments can afford the final accuracy of the method. We randomly

distorted the entries by replacing the values of experts' answers. We compared
the classification results for modified Euclidean distance after changing exactly
0.1 %, 0.2 %, ..., 10 % of all experts' assessments before the comparison. The
regression of the classification results is nearly linear with respect to the number
of injected errors. It is intuitively appealing that the method is reliable and relatively robust to the mistakes committed by the experts estimating the images,
see Fig. 4.

4 Conclusions and Future Studies

In this work we have presented a novel combination of the Analytic Hierarchy
Process and linguistic descriptors of human faces received from the experts'
answers. This new approach works great as a complement to standard classifiers.
The most obvious extension of the approach described here can be the use of
automatically collected data. Moreover, the other processes of obtaining and
applying the weights related to particular facial features should be considered.

Acknowledgements. The authors are supported by National Science Centre, Poland
(grant no. 2014/13/D/ST6/03244). Support from the Canada Research Chair (CRC)
program and Natural Sciences and Engineering Research Council is gratefully acknowledged (W. Pedrycz).

References

1. Ahonen, T., Hadid, A., Pietikäinen, M.: Face recognition with local binary patterns. In: Pajdla, T., Matas, J.G. (eds.) ECCV 2004. LNCS, vol. 3021, pp. 469–481.
Springer, Heidelberg (2004)
2. Belhumeur, P.N., Hespanha, J.P., Kriegman, D.J.: Eigenfaces vs. Fisherfaces:
recognition using class specific linear projection. IEEE Trans. Pattern Anal. Mach.
Intell. **19**, 711–720 (1997)
3. Bereta, M., Karczmarek, P., Pedrycz, W., Reformat, M.: Local descriptors in application to the aging problem in face recognition. Pattern Recogn. **46**, 2634–2646
(2013)
4. Bereta, M., Pedrycz, W., Reformat, M.: Local descriptors and similarity measures
for frontal face recognition: a comparative analysis. J. Vis. Commun. Image Represent. **24**, 1213–1231 (2013)
5. Brunelli, R., Poggio, T.: Face recognition: features versus templates. IEEE Trans.
Pattern Anal. Mach. Intell. **15**, 1042–1052 (1993)
6. Duchowski, A.J.: Eye Tracking Methodology. Theory and Practice. Springer,
London (2007)
7. Ekenel, H.K., Stiefelhagen, R.: Generic versus salient region-based partitioning for
local appearance face recognition. In: Tistarelli, M., Nixon, M.S. (eds.) ICB 2009.
LNCS, vol. 5558, pp. 367–375. Springer, Heidelberg (2009)
8. Ellis, H.D., Shepherd, J.W., Davies, G.M.: Identification of familiar and unfamiliar
faces from internal and external features: some implications for theories of face
recognition. Perception **8**, 431–439 (1979)

9. Er, M.J., Wu, S., Lu, J., Toh, H.L.: Face recognition with radial basis function (RBF) neural networks. IEEE Trans. Neural Netw. **13**, 697–710 (2002)
10. Fukushima, S., Ralescu, A.L.: Improved retrieval in a fuzzy database from adjusted user input. J. Intell. Inf. Syst. **5**, 249–274 (1995)
11. Haxby, J.V., Ungerleider, L.G., Horwitz, B., Maisog, J.M., Rapoport, S.I., Grady, C.L.: Face encoding and recognition in the human brain. Proc. Natl. Acad. Sci. USA **93**, 922–927 (1996)
12. Heisele, B., Blanz, V.: Morphable models for training a component-based face recognition system. In: Zhao, W., Chellapa, R. (eds.) Face Processing, Advanced Modeling and Methods, pp. 439–462. Elsevier (2005)
13. Johnston, R.A., Edmonds, A.J.: Familiar and unfamiliar face recognition: a review. Memory **17**, 577–596 (2009)
14. Kanade, T.: Computer Recognition of Human Faces. Birkhauser, Basel (1977)
15. Karczmarek, P., Kiersztyn, A., Rutka, P., Pedrycz, W.: Linguistic descriptors in face recognition: a literature survey and the perspectives of future development. In: SPA 2015 Signal Processing, Algorithms, Architectures, Arrangements, and Applications. Conference Proceedings, Poznan, pp. 98–103 (2015)
16. Karczmarek, P., Pedrycz, W., Kiersztyn, A., Rutka, P.: A study in facial features saliency in face recognition: an analytic hierarchy process approach, unpublished
17. Karczmarek, P., Pedrycz, W., Reformat, M., Akhoundi, E.: A study in facial regions saliency: a fuzzy measure approach. Soft Comput. **18**, 379–391 (2014)
18. Kumar, N., Berg, A.C., Belhumeur, P.N., Nayar, S.K.: Describable visual attributes for face verification and image search. IEEE Trans. Pattern Anal. Mach. Intell. **33**, 1962–1977 (2011)
19. Kurach, D., Rutkowska, D., Rakus-Andersson, E.: Face classification based on linguistic description of facial features. In: Rutkowski, L., Korytkowski, M., Scherer, R., Tadeusiewicz, R., Zadeh, L.A., Zurada, J.M. (eds.) ICAISC 2014, Part II. LNCS, vol. 8468, pp. 155–166. Springer, Heidelberg (2014)
20. Kwak, K.-C., Pedrycz, W.: Face recognition: a study in information fusion using fuzzy integral. Pattern Recogn. Lett. **26**, 719–733 (2005)
21. Nakayama, M., Miyajima, K., Iwamoto, H., Norita, T.: Interactive human face retrieval system based on linguistic expression. In: Proceedings of 2nd International Conference on Fuzzy Logic and Neural Networks, IIZUKA 1992, vol. 2, pp. 683–686 (1992)
22. Nakayama, M., Norita, T., Ralescu, A.: A fuzzy logic based qualitative modeling of image data. In: Proceedings of IPMU 1992, pp. 615–618 (1992)
23. Norita, T.: Fuzzy theory in an image understanding retrieval system. In: Ralescu, A.L. (ed.) Applied Research in Fuzzy Technology, vol. 1, pp. 215–251. Springer Science+Business Media, New York (1994)
24. Pedrycz, W.: Granular Computing: Analysis and Design of Intelligent Systems. CRC Press, Boca Raton (2013)
25. Perez, C.A., Cament, L.A., Castillo, L.E.: Methodological improvement on local gabor face recognition based on feature selection and enhanced borda count. Pattern Recogn. **44**, 951–963 (2011)
26. Phillips, P.J., Wechsler, J., Huang, J., Rauss, P.: The FERET database and evaluation procedure for face recognition algorithms. Image Vis. Comput. **16**, 295–306 (1998)
27. Saaty, T.L.: The Analytic Hierarchy Process. McGraw-Hill, New York (1980)
28. Saaty, T.L.: What is the analytic hierarchy process? In: Mitra, G. (ed.) Mathematical Models for Decision Support. NATO ASI Series, vol. F48, pp. 109–121. Springer, Heidelberg (1988)

29. Saaty, T.L., Vargas, L.G.: Models, Methods, Concepts & Applications of the Analytic Hierarchy Process. Springer, New York (2012)
30. Turk, M., Pentland, A.: Eigenfaces for recognition. J. Cogn. Neurosci. **3**, 71–86 (1991)
31. Wiskott, L., Fellous, J.-M., Krüger, N., von der Malsburg, C.: Face recognition by elastic bunch graph matching. IEEE Trans. Pattern Anal. Mach. Intell. **19**, 775–779 (1997)
32. Wright, J., Yang, A.Y., Ganesh, A., Sastry, S.S., Ma, Y.: Robust face recognition via sparse representation. IEEE Trans. Pattern Anal. Mach. Intell. **31**, 210–227 (2009)
33. Zhang, W., Shan, S., Qing, L., Chen, X., Gao, W.: Are Gabor phases really useless for face recognition? Pattern Anal. Appl. **12**, 301–307 (2009)

Quick Real-Boost with: Weight Trimming, Exponential Impurity, Bins, and Pruning

Przemysław Klęsk[(✉)]

Faculty of Computer Science and Information Technology, West Pomeranian University of Technology, Ul. Żołnierska 49, 71-210 Szczecin, Poland
pklesk@wi.zut.edu.pl

Abstract. The central point of attention for this paper is *weight trimming* — a technique known for speeding up boosted learning procedures. The loss of accuracy introduced by the technique is typically negligible. Recently, an elegant algorithm has been proposed by Appel et al.: it applies weight trimming under AdaBoost, prunes some features using a special error bound, but simultanouesly guarantees the same outcome (ensemble of trees with exactly the same parameters) as if with no trimming. Thus, no loss of training accuracy occurs. In this paper, we supplement the idea by Appel with a suitable extension for *real*-boosting. We prove that this approach gives the same outcome guarantees, both for stumps and trees. Additionally, we analyze the complexity of Appel's idea and we show that in some cases it may lead to computational losses.

1 Introduction

Boosting consists in applying the same learning algorithm over multiple rounds on reweighted data examples. Since the early concepts of weak learnability [6], first, the AdaBoost algorithm with binary $\{-1,1\}$ responses of weak learners has been developed [2,3], then, more conteporary RealBoost [7] and variants (LogitBoost, GentleBoost [4]) have appeared, where responses are real-valued.

The mechanism of examples reweighing is in fact the heart of boosting. In [4], Friedman et al. noted a property that brings out the essence of reweighing and allows for speeding up the procedure. They observed that as the learning progresses the distribution of weights becomes highly skewed towards very small values. A large majority of examples has those tiny weights, whereas only a small fraction of examples has some 'meaningful' weights that contribute to the error measure. One can take advantage of this observation and trim off the 'meaningless' examples before each round. This can be carried out by imposing a certain probability mass, say $1-\alpha = 0.99$, cumuluted by examples with largest weights that one wants to keep. All remaining examples are discarded. Typically, this technique — *weight trimming* — leads to a negligble loss of accuracy.

We like to look at weight trimming the following complementary way. In early rounds, discarding some of the examples can be viewed as a mild subsampling. In later rounds the preserved examples, that concentrate $1 - \alpha$ probability, can be regarded as *support vectors* by an analogy to SVM algorithm. Those are

L. Rutkowski et al. (Eds.): ICAISC 2016, Part I, LNAI 9692, pp. 597–609, 2016.
DOI: 10.1007/978-3-319-39378-0_51

hardest to classify examples, lying closely to the decision boundary, or even on the wrong side of it. Simultaneously, they are the ones that should be shaping the decision boundary being learned the most. Making the procedure focused solely on those examples leads to great computational savings. Figure 1 shows an exemplary illustration of weights distribution on several boosting rounds. We also encourage the reader to look ahead at Fig. 2 (experiments section) depicting 'support vectors under boosting' on both sides of a non-linear decision boundary.

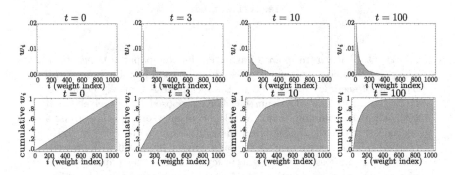

Fig. 1. Weights distribution skewed towards small values as boosting progresses (exemplary experiment); t denotes the round, weights are sorted decreasingly: $w_i \geqslant w_{i+1}$.

Recently, Appel et al. [1] have proposed a very elegant algorithm (named *Quick* stumps or trees) where weight trimming is tailored in a specific fashion. The authors benefit from the speed up only partially but they do not sacrifice the training accuracy. The algorithm looks for best stumps (or splits in a decision tree) and trims off different number of examples for different features using a certain bound on the error measure. Examples are included incrementally in portions and placed in bins (to consider possible splits), and if at a certain point a feature gives no chances to beat the current best, the remaining portions are ignored. Hence, the feature gets pruned. Appel et al. proved their algorithm to *guarantee* the same outcome — the ensemble of stumps (or trees) with exactly the same parameters — as if no weight trimming was applied. The proof pertains to the AdaBoost algorithm (binary responses of weak classifiers) and three possible criterions used for splits selection: zero-one loss, entropy or Gini index.

The contribution of our paper is minor with respect to [1], it includes two elements: (1) we build on the Appel's idea and supplement it with a small extension suitable for *real*-boosting, (2) we indicate the way to analyze the complexity of such 'quick' algorithms. As regards (1), in our real-boosting the responses of weak classifiers are calculated as *half* the *logit transform* and the *exponential error* is used as splits selection criterion. We prove that the above settings also give the same outcome guarantee. We use a similar line of proofs as in [1]. In particular, we point out an interesting connection between the Gini index and the superposition of exponential error with logit transform, useful in the proofs.

As regards (2), we show that the complexity can be viewed as a certain trade-off, which in some cases may lead to computational losses.

2 Notation and Short Review of Appel's Idea [1]

Let $\{(\mathbf{x}_i, y_i)\}_{i=1,\dots,M}$ denote the set of examples, where $\mathbf{x}_i = (x_{i1}, \dots, x_{id}) \in \mathbb{R}^d$ are input vectors of features and $y_i \in \{-1, 1\}$ are corresponding class labels. Let $\{w_i\}_{i=1,\dots,M}$ represent weights of examples on the current boosting round. In many places, we shall use Iverson convention to denote indicator expressions: $[s]$ yields 1 when s is a true statement and 0 otherwise; see e.g. [5].

For classifiers f with binary responses, the weighted error using a zero-one loss function (misclassification probability) is:

$$\varepsilon = \frac{1}{Z} \sum_{1 \leqslant i \leqslant M} w_i [f(\mathbf{x}_i) \neq y_i], \tag{1}$$

where $Z = \sum_{1 \leqslant i \leqslant M} w_i$ can be treated as a normalization constant, and $Z = 1$ if the whole data set is taken into account. When a decision stump is made on the k-th feature at the threshold τ with polarity $p \in \{-1, 1\}$, the error is:

$$\varepsilon^{(k)}(\tau, p) = \frac{1}{Z} \left(\sum_{x_{ik} \leqslant \tau} w_i [p \neq y_i] + \sum_{x_{ik} > \tau} w_i [-p \neq y_i] \right), \tag{2}$$

The learning procedure seeks the best stump $(k^*, \tau^*, p^*) = \arg\min_{(k,\tau,p)} \varepsilon^{(k)}(\tau, p)$.

Suppose that data examples are always sorted (on each boosting round) in order of decreasing weight: $w_i \geqslant w_{i+1}$ for all i. Define Z_m as the mass of the heaviest subset of m examples:

$$Z_m \equiv \sum_{i \leqslant m} w_i. \tag{3}$$

Let us call these examples an m-subset (or subset of size m).

Consider a *preliminary error* calculated with respect to the m-subset for the k-th feature with optimal parameters $\tau_m^{(k)}, p_m^{(k)}$ (minimizers for given m-subset):

$$\varepsilon_m^{(k)}(\tau_m^{(k)}, p_m^{(k)}) = \frac{1}{Z_m} \left(\sum_{\substack{i \leqslant m \\ x_{ik} \leqslant \tau_m^{(k)}}} w_i [p_m^{(k)} \neq y_i] + \sum_{\substack{i \leqslant m \\ x_{ik} > \tau_m^{(k)}}} w_i [-p_m^{(k)} \neq y_i] \right), \tag{4}$$

The crucial observation by Appel et al. [1] is:

$$m < n \quad \Rightarrow \quad Z_m \varepsilon_m^{(k)} \leqslant Z_n \varepsilon_n^{(k)}, \tag{5}$$

which means that the **product of probability mass and error** increases (or stays equal) when larger data subsets are considered for given feature. For the proof of (5) the reader is addressed to [1] or may see an analogous result we prove for the exponential error. Appel benefits from the observation as follows. Suppose ε' stands for the current best (and exact) error attained in the progresses of algorithm by some feature. Then, for another feature (k-th) we have:

$$Z_m \varepsilon_m^{(k)} \geqslant Z\varepsilon' \quad \Rightarrow \quad Z\varepsilon^{(k)} \geqslant Z\varepsilon' \quad \Rightarrow \quad \varepsilon^{(k)} \geqslant \varepsilon', \tag{6}$$

which means that if $Z_m \varepsilon_m^{(k)} \geqslant Z\varepsilon'$ then the k-th feature shall certainly *not* improve the best-so-far error and can be pruned without checking the remaining data. The trick to look at the $Z_m \varepsilon_m^{(k)}$ product rather than $\varepsilon_m^{(k)}$ alone, can be viewed simply as denormalization. It allows us to work with a partial sum of elementary errors rather than error frequency within a given subset.

3   Bound on Exponential Error

We now switch to the real-boosting scenario. Consider half the logit transform as classifier's response on the left and right side of a split (symbolic superscripts):

$$f_m^{(k\leqslant)}(\tau) = \frac{1}{2} \log \frac{\displaystyle\sum_{\substack{i\leqslant m \\ x_{ik}\leqslant \tau}} w_i[y_i = +1]}{\displaystyle\sum_{\substack{i\leqslant m \\ x_{ik}\leqslant \tau}} w_i[y_i = -1]}, \quad f_m^{(k>)}(\tau) = \frac{1}{2} \log \frac{\displaystyle\sum_{\substack{i\leqslant m \\ x_{ik}>\tau}} w_i[y_i = +1]}{\displaystyle\sum_{\substack{i\leqslant m \\ x_{ik}>\tau}} w_i[y_i = -1]}. \tag{7}$$

Given a k-th feature and a split threshold τ, the *preliminary exponential error* (or impurity) for the m-subset is defined as follows:

$$\varepsilon_{\exp\atop m}^{(k)}(\tau) = \frac{1}{Z_m} \left(\sum_{\substack{i\leqslant m \\ x_{ik}\leqslant \tau}} w_i e^{-y_i f_m^{(k\leqslant)}(\tau)} + \sum_{\substack{i\leqslant m \\ x_{ik}>\tau}} w_i e^{-y_i f_m^{(k>)}(\tau)} \right) \tag{8}$$

From now on in the paper we do not refer anymore to the zero-one loss error. Therefore, for simplicity we shall be writing just ε meant as the exponential error, instead of writing $\varepsilon_{\exp}$, unless explicitly needed otherwise.

Let the best split value (the minimizer) be denoted as $\tau_m^{(k)} = \arg\min_\tau \varepsilon_m^{(k)}(\tau)$ and for short let the optimal value of the criterion be written as $\varepsilon_m^{(k)} \equiv \varepsilon_m^{(k)}(\tau_k^{(m)})$.

Theorem 1. *For any $n > m$ the following inequality for the products of probability masses and exponential errors of the subsets holds true:*

$$Z_n \varepsilon_n^{(k)} \geqslant Z_m \varepsilon_m^{(k)}. \tag{9}$$

Proof. First, note that for a fixed $\tau_m^{(k)}$ both $f_m^{(k\leqslant)}(\tau_m^{(k)})$ and $f_m^{(k>)}(\tau_m^{(k)})$, in their forms (7), are miniminizers of respective left and right parts of the error (8) for the m-subset. Let us show it only for the left part (the right is analogous):

$$\frac{\partial}{\partial f_m^{(k\leqslant)}(\tau_m^{(k)})}\left(\sum_{\substack{i\leqslant m \\ x_{ik}\leqslant\tau_m^{(k)}}} w_i e^{-y_i f_m^{(k\leqslant)}(\tau_m^{(k)})}\right) = 0$$

$$\frac{\partial}{\partial f_m^{(k\leqslant)}(\tau_m^{(k)})}\left(e^{-f_m^{(k\leqslant)}(\tau_m^{(k)})}\sum_{\substack{i\leqslant m \\ x_{ik}\leqslant\tau_m^{(k)}}} w_i[y_i{=}{+}1] + e^{f_m^{(k\leqslant)}(\tau_m^{(k)})}\sum_{\substack{i\leqslant m \\ x_{ik}\leqslant\tau_m^{(k)}}} w_i[y_i{=}{-}1]\right) = 0$$

$$-e^{-f_m^{(k\leqslant)}(\tau_m^{(k)})}\sum_{\substack{i\leqslant m \\ x_{ik}\leqslant\tau_m^{(k)}}} w_i[y_i{=}{+}1] = -e^{f_m^{(k\leqslant)}(\tau_m^{(k)})}\sum_{\substack{i\leqslant m \\ x_{ik}\leqslant\tau_m^{(k)}}} w_i[y_i{=}{-}1]. \qquad (10)$$

Taking the logarithm side-wise yields the minimizer, as in formula (7). Now, the following inequalities hold for the product under consideration:

$$Z_m \varepsilon_m^{(k)} = \left(\sum_{\substack{i\leqslant m \\ x_{ik}\leqslant\tau_m^{(k)}}} w_i e^{-y_i f_m^{(k\leqslant)}(\tau_m^{(k)})} + \sum_{\substack{i\leqslant m \\ x_{ik}>\tau_m^{(k)}}} w_i e^{-y_i f_m^{(k>)}(\tau_m^{(k)})}\right)$$

$$\leqslant \sum_{\substack{i\leqslant m \\ x_{ik}\leqslant\tau_n^{(k)}}} w_i e^{-y_i f_n^{(k\leqslant)}(\tau_n^{(k)})} + \sum_{\substack{i\leqslant m \\ x_{ik}>\tau_n^{(k)}}} w_i e^{-y_i f_n^{(k>)}(\tau_n^{(k)})} \qquad (11)$$

$$\leqslant \sum_{\substack{i\leqslant n \\ x_{ik}\leqslant\tau_n^{(k)}}} w_i e^{-y_i f_n^{(k\leqslant)}(\tau_n^{(k)})} + \sum_{\substack{i\leqslant n \\ x_{ik}>\tau_n^{(k)}}} w_i e^{-y_i f_n^{(k>)}(\tau_n^{(k)})} = Z_n \varepsilon_n^{(k)} \qquad (12)$$

The first inequality is true since we have switched from settings: $\tau_m^{(k)}$, $f_m^{(k\leqslant)}$, $f_m^{(k\leqslant)}$ — optimal for the m-subset — to possibly non-optimal ones: $\tau_n^{(k)}$, $f_n^{(k\leqslant)}$, $f_n^{(k\leqslant)}$. The second inequality is true since the summation is taken over a larger set of summands ($i \leqslant n$), which are positive, and thereby the sum may only be increased. Finally, we note that the right-hand-side is now equal to $Z_n \varepsilon_n^{(k)}$. $\square$

4   Quick Tree Growing Algorithm for Real-Boost

In Algorithm 1 we write down the 'quick' tree growing recursion (based on Appel's idea) for the real-boost scenario, where the exponential error works as impurity for splits selection and half the logit transform constitutes responses of tree leafs. The following notation is used: $\mathcal{T}$ stands for the tree built so far and n for the node index for which the current call is made; $\{i\}$ is the set of indexes of examples falling into the current node; α is the probability mass to be trimmed off for the calculation of preliminary errors; q is the number of data portions (within the α mass) for incremental and more accurate error evaluation; s is the number of bins into which weights are placed for split selection. Also, let

Algorithm 1. QuickRealTree

```
 1: procedure QUICKREALTREE(𝒯, n, {i}, α, q, s)
 2:     calculate probability masses: W⁺ := ∑ᵢ wᵢ[yᵢ=+1],  W⁻ := ∑ᵢ wᵢ[yᵢ=−1],  Z:=W⁺+W⁻
 3:     memorize n-th node response as: 1/2 log(W⁺/W⁻)          ▷ take care of W± = 0 cases
 4:     stop recursion if n-th node is pure or maximum depth was reached
 5:     calculate cumulative probability on {wᵢ} and use it to prepare a sequence (m₀, . . . , m_q) such
        that     ∑_{i<m_j} wᵢ/Z < 1 − α + jα/q and ∑_{i≤m_j} wᵢ/Z ⩾ 1 − α + jα/q.
 6:     prepare bins B^{(k),+} = (0, . . . , 0), B^{(k),−} = (0, . . . , 0) of length s for all features 1 ⩽ k ⩽ d
 7:     calculate preliminary errors:
 8:     for 1 ⩽ k ⩽ d do
 9:         width^{(k)} := (max^{(k)} − min^{(k)})/s
10:         for 1 ⩽ i ⩽ m₀ do
11:             b := ⌈(x_{ik} − min^{(k)})/ width^{(k)}⌉          ▷ make bin index bounded to {1,...,s}
12:             if yᵢ = +1 then
13:                 B_b^{(k),+} := B_b^{(k),+} + wᵢ
14:             else
15:                 B_b^{(k),−} := B_b^{(k),−} + wᵢ
16:         (Z_{m₀}ε_{m₀}^{(k)}, τ_{m₀}^{(k)}) :=SELECTBINSPLIT(k, B^{(k),+}, B^{(k),−}, s)
17:     update errors in portions or prune:
18:     Zε' := ∞
19:     order features indexes as (k₁, . . . , k_d) using preliminary errors, so that ε_{m₀}^{(k₁)} ⩽ · · · ⩽ ε_{m₀}^{(k_d)}
20:     for k := k₁, k₂, . . . , k_d do
21:         if Z_{m₀}ε_{m₀}^{(k)} > Zε' then
22:             continue                                        ▷ prune k-th feature (!)
23:         j₀ := [Zε' < ∞] · 1 + [Zε' = ∞] · q
24:         i₀ := m₀
25:         for j₀ ⩽ j ⩽ q do                                  ▷ loop over portions within α mass
26:             for i₀ < i ⩽ m_j do
27:                 b := ⌈(x_{ik} − min^{(k)})/ width^{(k)}⌉      ▷ make bin index bounded to {1,...,s}
28:                 if yᵢ = +1 then
29:                     B_b^{(k),+} := B_b^{(k),+} + wᵢ
30:                 else
31:                     B_b^{(k),−} := B_b^{(k),−} + wᵢ
32:             (Z_{m_j}ε_{m_j}^{(k)}, τ_{m_j}^{(k)}) :=SELECTBINSPLIT(k, B^{(k),+}, B^{(k),−}, s)
33:             if Z_{m_j}ε_{m_j}^{(k)} ⩾ Zε' then
34:                 break                        ▷ jump out from subsets loop to prune k-th feature
35:             i₀ := m_j
36:         if Z_{m_j}ε_{m_j}^{(k)} ⩾ Zε' then
37:             continue                                        ▷ prune k-th feature (!)
38:         else
39:             Zε' := Z_{m_q}ε_{m_q}^{(k)}, k' := k, τ' := τ_{m_q}^{(k)}   ▷ new best feature found, Z_{m_q} ≡ Z
40:     L := {i: x_{ik'} ⩽ τ'}, R := {i: x_{ik'} > τ'}, n_L := #𝒯 + 1, n_R := #𝒯 + 2
41:     memorize within n-th node the best split parameters (k', τ') and children indexes n_L, n_R
42:     𝒯 :=QUICKREALTREE(𝒯, n_L, L, α, q, s)
43:     𝒯 :=QUICKREALTREE(𝒯, n_R, R, α, q, s)
44:     return 𝒯
```

```
 1: procedure SELECTBINSPLIT(k, B⁺, B⁻, s)
 2:     W_L⁺ := B₁⁺, W_L⁻ := B₁⁻, W_R⁺ := ∑_{b=2}^{s} B_b⁺, W_R⁻ := ∑_{b=2}^{s} B_b⁻, Z ≡ ∑_{b=1}^{s} B_b⁺ + ∑_{b=1}^{s} B_b⁻
 3:     Zε*:=W_L⁻ e^{½ log(W_L⁺/W_L⁻)}+W_L⁺ e^{−½ log(W_L⁺/W_L⁻)}+W_R⁻ e^{½ log(W_R⁺/W_R⁻)}+W_R⁺ e^{−½ log(W_R⁺/W_R⁻)}
 4:     width^{(k)} := (max^{(k)} − min^{(k)})/s
 5:     τ* := min^{(k)} +1 width^{(k)}
 6:     for 2 ⩽ b ⩽ s do
 7:         W_L⁺ := W_L⁺ + B_b⁺, W_L⁻ := W_L⁻ + B_b⁻, W_R⁺ := W_R⁺ − B_b⁺, W_R⁻ := W_R⁻ − B_b⁻
 8:         Zε:=W_L⁻ e^{½ log(W_L⁺/W_L⁻)}+W_L⁺ e^{−½ log(W_L⁺/W_L⁻)}+W_R⁻ e^{½ log(W_R⁺/W_R⁻)}+W_R⁺ e^{−½ log(W_R⁺/W_R⁻)}
 9:         if Zε < Zε* then
10:             Zε* := Zε, τ* := min^{(k)} +b width^{(k)}
11:     return (Zε*, τ*)
```

$\min^{(k)}$, $\max^{(k)}$ denote the endpoints of the k-th feature (either actual extremes, or endpoints after outliers have been removed).

We are now going to formulate a theorem which proves, inductively with respect to trimmed subsets, the guarantee of the same outcome for the 'quick' real-tree procedure (Algorithm 1). Suppose a tree has been grown according to the procedure, with weight trimming involved on each recursive stage ($\alpha > 0$). Let $\varepsilon_n^{\exp}$ denote the exponential error committed by the tree trained on the n-subset. This error can be expressed as a weighted average taken over all tree leafs $\{l\}$:

$$\varepsilon_n^{\exp} = \sum_l \frac{Z_{\rho_l}}{Z_n} \varepsilon_{\rho_l}^{\exp}, \tag{13}$$

where ρ_l denotes the set of indexes of data points from the n-subset that fall into the l-th leaf. Think of the optimal tree parameters that led to the smallest value of $\varepsilon_n^{\exp}$ based on the training data within the n-subset. Assume these parameters have been found and fixed. Now, consider a smaller m-subset, $m < n$. Let $\rho_l = u_l \cup \bar{u}_l$, where u_l denotes elements from ρ_l that are in the m-subset, while $\bar{u}_l$ be the elements that are not:

$$u_l = \{i : i \in \rho_l, i \leqslant m\}, \qquad \bar{u}_l = \{i : i \in \rho_l, \ m < i \leqslant n\}. \tag{14}$$

Theorem 2 *For all tree leafs true are the following relations:*

$$Z_{\rho_l} \varepsilon_{\rho_l}^{\exp} = Z_{\rho_l} \sqrt{2 \varepsilon_{\rho_l}^{gini}} \geqslant Z_{u_l} \sqrt{2 \varepsilon_{u_l}^{gini}} = Z_{u_l} \varepsilon_{u_l}^{\exp}, \tag{15}$$

therefore for the whole tree we have:

$$Z_n \varepsilon_n^{\exp} = \sum_l Z_{\rho_l} \varepsilon_{\rho_l}^{\exp} \geqslant \sum_l Z_{u_l} \varepsilon_{u_l}^{\exp} \geqslant Z_m \varepsilon_m^{\exp}. \tag{16}$$

Note that optimal tree parameters for the m-subset may differ from optimal ones for the n-subset, which explains the last inequality. The proof is in Appendix A.

5   Complexity Analysis

Consider the computations needed to populate a single node inside a tree growing recursion. Clearly, a standard procedure, without Appel's modification, requires $\Theta(d(M + s))$ time, since for each feature *all* data examples must be visited, i.e. placed into bins, plus a *single* call to SELECTBINSPLIT must be made with the cost proportional to the number of bins. Let us get rid of $\Theta(\cdot)$ notation and introduce two constants c_1, c_2 representing the costs of bin placement operations (as an example see lines 11–15 or 27–31 of QUICKREALTREE) and split selections (SELECTBINSPLIT) respectively. Then, the total time cost can be written down as: $d(c_1 M + c_2 s)$. Instead, for the 'quick' procedure — with Appel's modification — the total cost becomes[1]:

---

[1] For simplification, assume data indexes mapped to successive integers, so that there are no indexing holes and therefore $m_j - m_{j-1}$ differences reflect sizes of portions.

$$d(c_1 m_0 + c_2 s) + \sum_{k=k_1,k_2,\ldots,k_d} \sum_{j=1}^{q_k} (c_1(m_j - m_{j-1}) + c_2 s), \qquad (17)$$

where $q_k \in \{0, 1, \ldots, q\}$ represents the number of data portions (within α mass) that must be checked for k-th feature before it can be pruned.

Note that $q_1, \ldots, q_d$ quantities are a consequence of the $(k_1, \ldots, k_d)$ permutation, which describes the ordering of features after preliminary error calculation. That permutation is in turn implied by the chosen α. Since at least one of the features has to be later checked in full, then the necessary condition to reach the minimal cost is that the best feature comes first in the permutation: $k_1 = k^*$. Note that this makes $Z_{m_0} \varepsilon_{m_0}^{(k^*)}$ the tightest bound, thereby causing most pruning.

To dispose of the sums from (17) let us introduce an average number $\bar{q}$ of data portions to be checked, instead of $q_1, \ldots, q_d$. More precisely, let $\bar{q}$ be the smallest integer such that the following expression in an upper bound for (17):

$$d(c_1 m_0 + c_2 s) + \sum_{k=k_1,k_2,\ldots,k_d} \sum_{j=1}^{\bar{q}} (c_1(m_j - m_{j-1}) + c_2 s) = dc_1 m_{\bar{q}} + dc_2(1+\bar{q})s. \quad (18)$$

It is now possible to see that (18) can beat the original cost $d(c_1 M + c_2 s)$ when:

$$dc_2 s \bar{q} < dc_1(M - m_{\bar{q}}) \qquad (19)$$

— additional costs paid for split selections must be lower than the gains from non-visited data — a trade off. Obviously, $\bar{q}$ is a quantity dependent on data characteristcs. Hence, we rephrase the gain condition with respect to the number of bins (a parameter we control). It needs to be smaller than the following ratio:

$$s < c_1(M - m_{\bar{q}})/(c_2 \bar{q}). \qquad (20)$$

6 'Ball in Ball' Experiments

Similarly to [4], we construct synthetic data sets according to a 'ball in ball' pattern, where the inner ball represents the positive class. Results show these sets pose difficulties to boosting when the dimension d increases. More specifically, the input vectors are drawn from a standard multidimensional normal distribution, $\mathbf{x}_i \sim N^d(0,1)$, whereas class labels y_i are dependent on radiuses $\|\mathbf{x}_i\|$, obeying the conditional distribution $P(y|\mathbf{x}) = 1/(1 + e^{-\gamma y(\|\mathbf{x}\|^2 - r^2)})$. Hence, in general the problem is non-deterministic, with some overlap of the classes implied by the $\gamma > 0$ parameter. We set up $\gamma = 5$ and for each dimension we choose such r, so that $P(y = +1) \approx 0.4$. The sphere $\|\mathbf{x}\|^2 = r^2$ represents the optimal decision boundary. Knowing all settings, we can accurately estimate the Bayesian error (or so called *true error*) — the best possible for any classifier. Data sets are described in Table 1. The goal of the last data set (D_6) was to simulate a more realistic situation where there are 1 000 features but only 10 % of them

Table 1. Data sets description.

name	dimension d	sample size	Bayesian error	features relevancy
D_1	2	1 000	≈ 0.0860	all
D_2	3	1 000	≈ 0.0590	all
D_3	10	1 000	≈ 0.0258	all

name	dimension d	sample size	Bayesian error	features relevancy
D_4	100	10 000	≈ 0.0081	all
D_5	1000	10 000	≈ 0.0030	all
D_6	1000	10 000	≈ 0.0090	10%

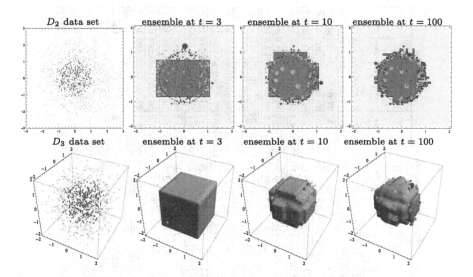

Fig. 2. Ensembles for D_2 and D_3 data sets. Sizes of data points are marked proportional to their current weights under the real-boost procedure.

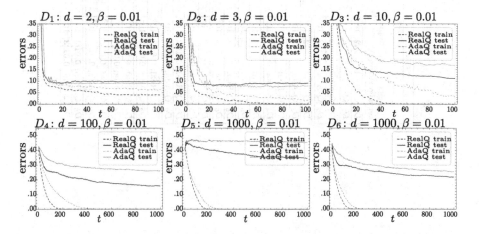

Fig. 3. Errors for ensembles with both internal (α) and external (β) weight trimming.

Table 2. Results of experiments.

data set	algorithm, β	trees max depth, T	test error [%]	α = 0.01 data usage [%]	select split calls [%]	time [s]	time [%]	α = 0.001 data usage [%]	select split calls [%]	time [s]	time [%]	α = 0.0001 data usage [%]	select split calls [%]	time [s]	time [%]
D_1	Q-Real	2, 10^2	.1013	93.30	327.2	0.157	124.8	83.13	229.9	0.159	127.3	81.77	164.5	0.144	**114.3**
D_1	Q-Ada	2, 10^2	.0928	93.38	260.4	0.148	114.5	96.12	214.0	0.154	119.3	98.30	201.6	0.139	**107.2**
D_2	Q-Real	2, 10^2	.0892	75.70	293.5	0.201	121.7	71.73	159.8	0.158	95.28	77.01	136.7	0.150	**90.57**
D_2	Q-Ada	2, 10^2	.0794	91.80	290.9	0.159	**102.0**	96.35	256.5	0.197	126.0	98.66	239.7	0.203	130.0
D_3	Q-Real	2, 10^2	.1122	74.06	268.8	0.404	99.23	79.11	125.0	0.338	**91.95**	85.56	115.8	0.343	93.22
D_3	Q-Ada	2, 10^2	.1736	97.17	332.3	0.410	119.5	99.28	270.1	0.392	**114.1**	99.84	198.7	0.394	115.0
D_4	Q-Real	3, 10^3	.1509	94.24	339.5	522.5	105.4	76.90	143.9	393.8	**79.50**	83.26	104.1	428.4	86.45
D_4	Q-Ada	3, 10^3	.2622	93.79	221.7	490.2	106.3	97.77	164.9	485.1	105.2	99.36	161.2	502.6	**100.9**
D_5	Q-Real	3, 10^3	.3505	96.09	336.6	5 545	116.4	86.70	123.8	4 506	**94.57**	92.71	101.7	4 811	101.0
D_5	Q-Ada	3, 10^3	.4508	90.60	117.4	4 646	**89.64**	97.30	100.5	4 918	94.87	99.27	100.2	5 103	98.46
D_6	Q-Real	3, 10^3	.2037	89.11	312.7	5 189	101.8	81.73	107.5	4 370	**85.74**	88.90	101.5	4 663	91.49
D_6	Q-Ada	3, 10^3	.2633	85.58	107.3	4 361	**87.13**	94.61	100.2	4 922	98.34	97.95	100.1	5 138	102.7
D_1	Q-Real, 0.01	2, 10^2	.0988	99.03	324.8	0.112	180.0	99.61	235.7	0.081	**98.11**	99.89	201.6	0.094	120.0
D_1	Q-Ada, 0.01	2, 10^2	.0905	98.00	163.1	0.137	120.5	99.66	211.9	0.109	106.1	99.94	164.5	0.112	**96.00**
D_2	Q-Real, 0.01	2, 10^2	.0913	95.93	291.3	0.094	125.0	98.77	158.4	0.084	**112.5**	99.76	134.7	0.087	116.7
D_2	Q-Ada, 0.01	2, 10^2	.0793	97.04	289.5	0.170	122.5	99.76	134.7	0.126	**91.01**	99.92	163.1	0.148	106.7
D_3	Q-Real, 0.01	2, 10^2	.1121	94.81	256.4	0.373	135.8	98.85	122.7	0.296	108.8	99.80	111.0	0.289	**106.1**
D_3	Q-Ada, 0.01	2, 10^2	.1682	98.00	309.7	0.396	105.4	99.69	237.7	0.395	**105.1**	99.92	143.5	0.409	108.8
D_4	Q-Real, 0.01	3, 10^3	.1573	98.96	338.4	373.5	112.4	99.03	139.9	337.8	101.7	99.86	103.5	331.1	**99.65**
D_4	Q-Ada, 0.01	3, 10^3	.2623	97.30	224.2	458.1	101.8	99.69	164.7	498.6	110.8	100.1	157.9	470.2	**104.5**
D_5	Q-Real, 0.01	3, 10^3	.3464	99.14	334.1	4 102	111.6	98.59	120.2	3 969	100.8	99.59	101.0	3 956	**100.5**
D_5	Q-Ada, 0.01	3, 10^3	.4524	95.38	117.0	4 462	**93.62**	99.42	100.4	4 748	99.62	99.93	100.1	4 723	99.10
D_6	Q-Real, 0.01	3, 10^3	.2193	98.09	309.9	3 813	107.0	98.70	105.8	3 550	99.58	99.68	101.1	3 506	**98.35**
D_6	Q-Ada, 0.01	3, 10^3	.2575	94.05	107.8	4 125	104.6	99.26	100.2	4 339	99.52	99.91	100.1	4 307	98.78

are relevant (contributing to the decision boundary — being a cylinder in that case).

All experiments were carried out in Wolfram Mathematica 9.0, but with crucial procedures compiled to C language (`CompilationTarget -> C`). Table 2 summarizes the results with the main focus on the speed of execution. In particular, we observe the trade-off between computational gains (less data usage) and losses (more select split calls) for different settings of α parameter. Therefore, percentages reported in each row should be understood as ratios of given quantity for the 'quick' procedure with respect to its 'non-quick' counterpart. The number of bins in all experiments was $s = 64$ and the maximum number of portions for error updates was $q = 5$. In half of experiments the procedure was additionally coupled with a standard (external) weight trimming, where the probability mass to be cut off is represented by $\beta = 0.01$. We group rows in pairs to compare directly 'quick' RealBoost (Q-Real for short) against 'quick' AdaBoost (Q-Ada) procedures. In each row we mark in gray those time cells where a computational gain occured and we bold out the experiments for which the smallest time ratio was attained among different α values. Figure 2 depicts obtained ensembles for small dimensionalities $d = 2, 3$. Figure 3 presents errors of ensembles along training when the additional (external) weight trimming was applied.

7   Conclusions

Following the idea from [1], we have proved that a 'quick' algorithm for *real*-boosted trees can be constructed with a guarantee of the same outcome ensemble. Experimental results show we have set up difficult conditions to test the 'quick' procedures, both in terms of errors and time performance. In 45/72 cases computational losses, rather than gains, were registered. This is due to additional split selections required to incrementally update error bounds. The gains, if appeared at all (for given experiments), were small, of order $\approx 6\,\%$ on average. As regards test errors, RealBoost was better than AdaBoost in majority of cases, especially for higher dimensionalities. Despite a possible scepticism from most of experiments, the case of D_6 data set indicates that in a more realistic setting, where many features exist but most of them are irrelevant, the 'quick' procedures ought to do well computationally, pruning more features.

A   Proof of Outcome Guarantee for 'quick' Tree Growing Procedure with Exponential Impurity

Proof (Theorem 2). First, let us define the Gini error (for the n-subset):

$$\varepsilon_n^{\text{gini}} = \sum_l \frac{Z_{\rho l}}{Z_n} \varepsilon_{\rho l}^{\text{gini}} = \sum_l \frac{Z_{\rho l}}{Z_n} \left(1 - \left(\frac{Z_{\rho l}^+}{Z_{\rho l}} \right)^2 - \left(\frac{Z_{\rho l}^-}{Z_{\rho l}} \right)^2 \right), \tag{21}$$

where $Z_{\rho_l}^+ = \sum_{i \in \rho_l} w_i [y = +1]$, $Z_{\rho_l}^- = \sum_{i \in \rho_l} w_i [y = -1]$ are probability masses for classes. Let us write two representations (22), (23) for the products — mass times Gini error — that will be useful later on:

$$Z_n \varepsilon_{\text{gini}} = \sum_l \left(Z_{\rho_l} - \frac{(Z_{\rho_l}^+)^2}{Z_{\rho_l}} - \frac{(Z_{\rho_l}^-)^2}{Z_{\rho_l}} \right), \tag{22}$$

$$= \sum_l Z_{\rho_l} \left(1 - \left(\frac{Z_{\rho_l}^+}{Z_{\rho_l}} \right)^2 - \left(1 - \frac{Z_{\rho_l}^+}{Z_{\rho_l}} \right)^2 \right) = \sum_l Z_{\rho_l} \underbrace{2 \frac{Z_{\rho_l}^+}{Z_{\rho_l}} \left(1 - \frac{Z_{\rho_l}^+}{Z_{\rho_l}} \right)}_{\varepsilon_{\rho_l}^{\text{gini}}}. \tag{23}$$

We now write out the exponential error and show its connection to Gini error.

$$\varepsilon_n^{\exp} = \sum_l \frac{Z_{\rho_l}}{Z_n} \varepsilon_{\rho_l}^{\exp} = \sum_l \frac{Z_{\rho_l}}{Z_n} \left(\frac{Z_{\rho_l}^+}{Z_{\rho_l}} e^{-\frac{1}{2} \log \frac{Z_{\rho_l}^+}{Z_{\rho_l}^-}} + \frac{Z_{\rho_l}^-}{Z_{\rho_l}} e^{\frac{1}{2} \log \frac{Z_{\rho_l}^+}{Z_{\rho_l}^-}} \right) = \sum_l \frac{Z_{\rho_l}}{Z_n} \left(\frac{Z_{\rho_l}^+}{Z_{\rho_l}} \right)$$

$$\cdot \sqrt{\frac{Z_{\rho_l}^-}{Z_{\rho_l}^+}} + \frac{Z_{\rho_l}^-}{Z_{\rho_l}} \sqrt{\frac{Z_{\rho_l}^+}{Z_{\rho_l}^-}} = \sum_l \frac{Z_{\rho_l}}{Z_n} 2 \sqrt{\frac{Z_{\rho_l}^+}{Z_{\rho_l}} \frac{Z_{\rho_l}^-}{Z_{\rho_l}}} = \sum_l \frac{Z_{\rho_l}}{Z_n} 2 \sqrt{\frac{Z_{\rho_l}^+}{Z_{\rho_l}} \left(1 - \frac{Z_{\rho_l}^+}{Z_{\rho_l}} \right)}. \tag{24}$$

$$Z_n \varepsilon_n^{\exp} = \sum_l Z_{\rho_l} \underbrace{2 \sqrt{\frac{Z_{\rho_l}^+}{Z_{\rho_l}} \left(1 - \frac{Z_{\rho_l}^+}{Z_{\rho_l}} \right)}}_{\varepsilon_{\rho_l}^{\exp}} = \sum_l Z_{\rho_l} 2 \sqrt{\frac{1}{2} \varepsilon_{\rho_l}^{\text{gini}}} = \sum_l Z_{\rho_l} \underbrace{\sqrt{2 \varepsilon_{\rho_l}^{\text{gini}}}}_{\varepsilon_{\rho_l}^{\exp}}. \tag{25}$$

We aim at showing that $Z_{\rho_l} \varepsilon_{\rho_l}^{\exp} \geqslant Z_{u_l} \varepsilon_{u_l}^{\exp}$, which means that if one removes from a leaf the examples that are not in the m-subset but keeps the tree parameters fixed then the mass times error product must decrease or stay unchanged. We remind that $\rho_l = u_l \cup \bar{u}_l$ and $n > m$, see back to definitions (14). Let us observe the square of $Z_{\rho_l} \varepsilon_{\rho_l}^{\exp}$ using a representation from (25) for the leaf error.

$$\left(Z_{\rho_l} \varepsilon_{\rho_l}^{\exp} \right)^2 = (Z_{\rho_l})^2 4 \frac{Z_{\rho_l}^+}{Z_{\rho_l}} \left(1 - \frac{Z_{\rho_l}^+}{Z_{\rho_l}} \right) = (Z_{\rho_l})^2 2 \left(2 \frac{Z_{\rho_l}^+}{Z_{\rho_l}} - 2 \left(\frac{Z_{\rho_l}^+}{Z_{\rho_l}} \right)^2 \right)$$

$$= (Z_{\rho_l})^2 2 \left(1 - \left(\frac{Z_{\rho_l}^+}{Z_{\rho_l}} \right)^2 - 1 + 2 \frac{Z_{\rho_l}^+}{Z_{\rho_l}} - \left(\frac{Z_{\rho_l}^+}{Z_{\rho_l}} \right)^2 \right) = (Z_{\rho_l})^2 2 \left(1 - \left(\frac{Z_{\rho_l}^+}{Z_{\rho_l}} \right)^2 - \left(1 - \frac{Z_{\rho_l}^+}{Z_{\rho_l}} \right)^2 \right)$$

$$= (Z_{\rho_l})^2 2 \left(1 - \left(\frac{Z_{\rho_l}^+}{Z_{\rho_l}} \right)^2 - \left(\frac{Z_{\rho_l}^-}{Z_{\rho_l}} \right)^2 \right) = Z_{\rho_l} 2 \left(Z_{\rho_l} - \frac{(Z_{\rho_l}^+)^2}{Z_{\rho_l}} - \frac{(Z_{\rho_l}^-)^2}{Z_{\rho_l}} \right) \tag{26}$$

Note the similarity of the last expression to a Gini representation (22).

We shall now expand (26) taking advantage of the following lemma (for straightforward algebraic proof see [1]) true for either class label $y \in \{-1, +1\}$:

$$-\frac{(Z_{\rho_l}^y)^2}{Z_{\rho_l}} = -\frac{(Z_{u_l}^y + Z_{\bar{u}_l}^y)^2}{Z_{u_l}^y + Z_{\bar{u}_l}^y} \geqslant -\frac{(Z_{u_l}^y)^2}{Z_{u_l}} - \frac{(Z_{\bar{u}_l}^y)^2}{Z_{\bar{u}_l}}. \tag{27}$$

Therefore, we have:

$$\left(Z_{\rho_l}\varepsilon_{\rho_l}^{\exp}\right)^2 \geqslant Z_{\rho_l}2\left(Z_{u_l}+Z_{\bar{u}_l}-\frac{\left(Z_{u_l}^+\right)^2}{Z_{u_l}}-\frac{\left(Z_{\bar{u}_l}^+\right)^2}{Z_{\bar{u}_l}}-\frac{\left(Z_{u_l}^-\right)^2}{Z_{u_l}}-\frac{\left(Z_{\bar{u}_l}^-\right)^2}{Z_{\bar{u}_l}}\right)$$

$$=Z_{\rho_l}2\left(Z_{u_l}\varepsilon_{u_l}^{\mathrm{gini}}+Z_{\bar{u}_l}\varepsilon_{\bar{u}_l}^{\mathrm{gini}}\right)\geqslant Z_{\rho_l}2Z_{u_l}\varepsilon_{u_l}^{\mathrm{gini}}\geqslant \left(Z_{u_l}\right)^2 2\varepsilon_{u_l}^{\mathrm{gini}}. \quad (28)$$

The equality pass comes from grouping odd and even terms using representations (22). Hence, finally: $Z_{\rho_l}\varepsilon_{\rho_l}^{\exp}\geqslant Z_{u_l}\sqrt{2\varepsilon_{u_l}^{\mathrm{gini}}}=Z_{u_l}\varepsilon_{u_l}^{\exp}.$ $\square$

References

1. Appel, R., et al.: Quickly boosting decision trees – pruning underachieving features early. In: Proceedings of the 30th International Conference on Machine Learning (ICML 2013), vol. 28, pp. 594–602. JMLR Workshop and Conference Proceedings (2013)
2. Freund, Y., Schapire, R.E.: Experiments with a new boosting algorithm. In: Machine Learning: Proceedings of the Thirteenth International Conference, pp. 148–156. Morgan Kaufman, San Francisco (1996)
3. Freund, Y., Schapire, R.E.: A decision-theoretic generalization of on-line learning and an application to boosting. J. Comput. Sci. Syst. Sci. **55**, 119–139 (1997)
4. Friedman, J., Hastie, T., Tibshirani, R.: Additive logistic regression: a statistical view of boosting. Ann. Stat. **28**(2), 337–407 (2000)
5. Graham, R.L., Knuth, D.E., Patashnik, O.: Concrete Mathematics: A Foundation for Computer Science, 2nd edn. Addison-Wesley Longman Publishing Co. Inc, Boston (1994)
6. Schapire, R.E.: The strength of weak learnability. Mach. Learn. **5**, 197–227 (1990)
7. Schapire, R.E., Singer, Y.: Improved boosting using confidence-rated predictions. Mach. Learn. **37**(3), 297–336 (1999)

Instance Selection Optimization for Neural Network Training

Mirosław Kordos[(⊠)]

Department of Computer Science and Engineering,
University of Bielsko-Biala, Willowa 2, Bielsko-Biała, Poland
mkordos@ath.bielsko.pl

Abstract. Performing instance selection prior to the classifier training is always beneficial in terms of computational complexity reduction of the classifier training and sometimes also beneficial in terms of improving prediction accuracy. Removing the noisy instances improves the prediction accuracy and removing redundant and irrelevant instances does not negatively effect it. However, in practice the instance selection methods usually also remove some instances, which should not be removed from the training dataset, what results in decreasing the prediction accuracy. We discuss two methods to deal with the problem. The first method is the parameterization of instance selection algorithms, which allows to choose how aggressively the instances are removed and the second one is to embed the instance selection directly into the prediction model, which in our case is an MLP neural network.

1 Introduction

There are two purposes of instance selection: to decrease noise in the data and to reduce the data size. One of the most popular instance selection methods for noise filtering is ENN (Editted Nearest Neighbor) [21] and for data size reduction is CNN (Condensed Nearest Neighbor) [9]. Although ENN and CNN as single methods are quite simple and there exists methods that perform better both in terms of noise filtering and data compression, when they are applied sequentially ENN followed by CNN they produce exceptionally good results. First ENN removes noise, this is the instances that are wrongly classified by k-NN. Then CNN removes redundant instances in the following way: first it selects one instance and then if the next instance is correctly classified by k-NN using the already selected instances as the training set, it is considered redundant and not selected. If classified incorrectly it is added to the selected instances. Then the process repeats with each remaining instance. The ENN and CNN algorithms are well described in the literature [9,21] and in [12,17,18] the interesting reader can find a detailed comparative study of many instance selection methods.

The standard instance selection methods are rather filters than wrappers and thus have no real-time adjustment to the classifier performance. In practice there are two problems: some of the instances that should be selected do not get selected and some of the instances that should not be selected get selected. That is because ENN and CNN consider only the local neighborhood of each instance

L. Rutkowski et al. (Eds.): ICAISC 2016, Part I, LNAI 9692, pp. 610–620, 2016.
DOI: 10.1007/978-3-319-39378-0_52

and do not take into account how the classification model works. What it means in practice is that there is no guarantee that the set of selected instances will be the optimal one for a given classifier.

Recently there have been several approaches to improve instance selection methods by addressing some of their shortages. In [2] Antoneli et al. presented a genetic approach using a multiobjective evolutionary algorithms for instance selection. In [8] Guillen et al. presented the use of mutual information for instance selection. Their proposition was based on a similar principles as the k-NN based instance selection, but after finding the nearest neighbors of a given example instead of using k-NN to predict its output value, the mutual information (MI) between that example and each of its neighbors was determined. In the next step the loss of mutual information with respect to the neighbors was calculated. If the loss was similar to the example neighbors then this example was selected to the final dataset. The method was experimentally evaluated on artificially generated data with one and two input features. Then in [19] the idea was extended to instance selection in time series prediction.

In [16] a class conditional instance selection (CCIS) was presented. CCIS creates two graphs: one for the nearest neighbors of the same class and one for other class instances than the current example. Next a scoring function, which is based on the distances in graphs, is used to determine the selected instances. In [3] the authors proposed to use ant colony optimization with one classification model used in the instance selection process and another model as the final predictor. In [1] the authors analyzed how instance and feature selection influence neural network performance. In [4] a method to reduce the number of support vectors in SVM training was considered.

From our perspective, very interesting ideas were presented in [20]. The authors designed an instance selection method that took into account the decision boundaries of neural networks like distance from decision boundary, dense regions and class distributions and they proposed an instance selection method adjusted to neural network properties. Their method consisted of two parts: removing far instances and removing dense instances. In the far part they calculated the distance between each instance and the closest instance of the opposite class (the far distance) and removed the instances for which the distance was farther then the average + standard deviation of the far distances. In the dense part they calculated the distance between each instance and the closest instance of the same class (the dense distance) and iteratively removed the instances for which the distance was closer then the average of the dense distances, starting from those with the smallest dense distance and updating the average dense distance at every iteration.

We discuss two methods to deal with the problem. The first method is the parameterization of instance selection algorithms, which allows to choose how aggressively they remove the instances and the second one is to embed the instance selection directly into the prediction model, which in our case is an MLP neural network. To use the MLP neural network for an on-line instance selection no adjustments are required to the error function, neuron transfer functions, to the learning algorithm or to the network architecture.

2 Instance Selection Prior to Neural Network Training

The common problem with instance selection performed before classification is reduction of the classification accuracy. That is true not only for ENN and CNN but also for many other instance selection methods. That may be not of a great concern if the purpose is primary to reduce the dataset size and the accuracy reduction is very little. However, frequently the objective is to obtain high accuracy at the first place and then the possible data size reduction.

As the instance selection method we use a modified ENN (Editted Nearest Neighbor) followed by a modified CNN [9]. The choice of the instance selection algorithms is dictated by their simplicity and by the fact that when whey are both applied in this order, they perform exceptionally well. First ENN removes noise, then CNN removes redundant instances. k-NN can be used as the final prediction algorithm and as the internal CNN and ENN algorithm. In both cases it works best with an optimal k value, which according to our experiments for a broad range of problems can be set to $k = 9$ and moreover this algorithm is not very sensitive to little changes of k. For that reason in all the experiments we will keep $k = 9$ (at the beginning of CNN, when the number of selected instances is fewer than 9 we use all the already selected instances as the neighbors).

However, to address the above mentioned problem we must make some modifications to ENN: we will require that in order for an instance to be rejected by ENN, it must have different class than more as $m=5$ of its neighbors, which will cause only more outlying instances to be removed. If we want to reject even more outlying instances, we can rise the requirement to $m=7$ neighbors of a different class or even 8 or all 9 (which will be the weakest instance selection, preserving most instances in the selected set).

In a similar way, we can apply modifications to CNN to require a different numbers of the instance neighbors to belong to the same class to reject the instance. The more instances of the same class are required the weaker the selection is, resulting in rejecting only the instances situated far from the decision boundaries (and thus very few or none of their neighbors belong to a different class). That is exactly why we need to perform noise reduction first. If some noisy instances, this is instances of a different class surrounded by the current class instances, are still present, they would not allow us to successfully remove the redundant data points, especially when we rise the requirements for the number of the same class neighbors.

All possible values of $m=5$, 6, 7, 8 and 9 for ENN and CNN lead to 25 different combinations. Since there is no place in the paper to show the results of all 25 combinations, we selected four of them in such a way that m for ENN (m_{enn}) equals m for CNN (m_{cnn}) and both m increase from 5 to 8. We found these four combinations to be most representative, well reflecting the general trend and the easiest to interpret.

The modified ENN+CNN algorithm pseudo-code is presented in Algorithm 1, where $\mathbf{T}$ is the original training set, $\mathbf{P}$ is an intermediary set, which is an output in ENN and input to CNN and $\mathbf{S}$ is the selected training set. $\bar{C}(\mathbf{x}_i)$ is the class of a at least m_{ENN} or m_{CNN} nearest neighbors of the instance x_i reduced to

Algorithm 1. The modified ENN+CNN algorithm

Require: $\mathbf{T}, k, m_{ENN}, m_{CNN}$
  $n \leftarrow |\mathbf{T}|$;
  $\mathbf{P} \leftarrow \mathbf{T}$;
  for $i = 1 \ldots n$ **do**
    $\bar{C}(\mathbf{x}_i) = \text{kNN}(k, m_{ENN}, (\mathbf{T} \setminus \mathbf{x}_i), \mathbf{x}_i)$;
    if $C(\mathbf{x}_i) \neq \bar{C}(\mathbf{x}_i)$ **then**
      $\mathbf{P} \leftarrow \mathbf{P} \setminus \mathbf{x}_i$
    end if
  end for
  $\mathbf{S} \leftarrow empty$;
  $\mathbf{S} \leftarrow \mathbf{S} \cup \mathbf{x}_1$;
  $flag \leftarrow$ **true**
  while flag **do**
    $flag \leftarrow$ **false**
    $n \leftarrow |\mathbf{P}|$
    for $i = 1 \ldots n$ **do**
      $k_0 = min(k, sizeof(S))$
      $m_0 = m_{CNN} \cdot k_0/k$
      $\bar{C}(\mathbf{x}_i) = \text{kNN}(k_0, m_0, \mathbf{S}, \mathbf{x}_i)$
      if $\bar{C}(\mathbf{x}_i) \neq C(\mathbf{x}_i)$ **then**
        $\mathbf{S} \leftarrow \mathbf{S} \cup \mathbf{x}_i$;
        $\mathbf{P} \leftarrow \mathbf{P} \setminus \mathbf{x}_i$
        $flag \leftarrow$ **true**
      end if
    end for
  end while
  return $\mathbf{S}$

---

two-class problem: the same class vs. different class, $C(\mathbf{x}_i)$ is the class of the instance x_i, k is the k in k-NN. $\mathbf{S} \leftarrow \mathbf{S} \cup \mathbf{x}_i$ means that the vector x_i is added to the set $\mathbf{S}$ and $\mathbf{P} \leftarrow \mathbf{P} \setminus \mathbf{x}_i$ means that vector x_i is removed from the set $\mathbf{P}$. k_0 and m_0 are used to set k and m_{CNN} to smaller values when the number of already selected instanced in the new training set is less than 9.

3 Instance Selection Embedded in Neural Network Training

It seems reasonable to embed instance selection in the classifier learning process. One advantage is solving the problem of different decision borders of k-NN and a neural network. Another advantage is that in some cases the instance can be not removed totally, but be treated differently in the model learning - as the less liable example and thus less contributing to the model parameters. Still another advantage is the possibility of assessing during the network training how the selection influences the results and adjust the selection accordingly. The drawback of this approach may be in some cases higher computational complexity of the classification process than the joint complexity of the prior instance selection followed by learning the classifier on the reduced set. This is especially evident for large datasets, where k-NN can be efficiently accelerated by methods like k-means clustering and then searching for the nearest neighbors only within one cluster, KD-Tree [5] or Local Sensitive Hashing [11].

We use an MLP neural network with hyperbolic tangent transfer function and we have as many neurons in the output layer as the number of classes. Most of the existing neural network training algorithms can be used. When a vector is given to the trained network inputs, the output neuron associated with this vector class gives signal = 1 and all the other output vectors associated with different classes give the output signal = -1. The error for a single vector $\mathbf{x}_i$ used for instance selection is given by the following formula:

$$Error(\mathbf{x}_i) = \sum_{i=1}^{n}(y_{ai} - y_{ei})^2 \tag{1}$$

where n is the number of classes, which equals the number of output layer neurons, y_{ai} is the actual value of $i - th$ output neuron signal and y_{ei} is the expected value of $i - th$ output neuron signal (which is 1 if the current instance class is represented by the $i - th$ output neuron and 0 otherwise). We assume that a vector is classified correctly if the neuron associated with its class gives a higher signal than any other output neuron. If an instance of the training set is classified incorrectly by a trained neural network, the error that the network gives as a response to that instance is high ($Error(\mathbf{x}_i) > maxError$). On the other hand if an instance is classified correctly and is situated far from a classification boundary (because of the hyperbolic tangent transfer function), the network error obtained for that instance will be very low ($Error(\mathbf{x}_i) < minError$). Thus a solution is to remove from training set $\mathbf{T}$ the instances that produce very high and very low errors. The pseudo-code for the embedded instance selection is shown in Algorithm 2.

Algorithm 2. Instance selection embedded in neural network training

---

Require: T, $minError, maxError$
$\quad n \leftarrow |\mathbf{T}|;$
$\quad$ train the network on **T**
$\quad$ **for** $i = 1 \ldots n$ **do**
$\quad\quad$ **if** $Error(\mathbf{x}_i) > maxError$ or $Error(\mathbf{x}_i) < minError$ **then**
$\quad\quad\quad \mathbf{T} \leftarrow \mathbf{T} \setminus \mathbf{x}_i$
$\quad\quad$ **end if**
$\quad$ **end for**
$\quad$ **if** restart = true **then**
$\quad\quad$ retrain the network on **T** from random weights
$\quad$ **else**
$\quad\quad$ continue training the network on **T** from the current weights
$\quad$ **end if**

There are several parameters in this instance selection. The first two parameters are the *maxError* and the *minError*. The next one is the time point in the network training, when the errors should be calculated and the instances rejected. And the final one is what to do after the instances get removed: train the network further from the current point or start the training anew. For *maxError* we use a value be greater than 1 and smaller than 2 due to the shape of hyperbolic tangent for two class problems, but for multiply classes it may be set to higher values.

The rationale behind using the *maxError* and not simply rejecting all misclassified instances, is that the instances that are situated close to the decision boundaries maybe frequently misclassified, although it is rather due to the neural network properties than due to the instances being noisy. However, if a single instance of one class is in the middle of different class instances then it is surely noise and the error value produced by the network for such an instance will be higher then for the misclassified border instances. However, the *minError* depends more on the neuron weights values and thus a better solution than using a constant value is to use a relative value in relation to the error the network makes on other examples. We use for *minError* some percentage of the average error values of all correctly classified instances of a given class. In the experiments we use four different values of *maxError* and *minError*

While removing irrelevant examples as those, on which the neural network makes the least error, the examples that get removed are those far from the decision border, so those that are not necessary to determine the decision border and thus the decision border remains intact. But while removing them with CNN we have no guarantee that only the irrelevant ones will get removed, because that may depend on the order of the instances being considered. Let us illustrate this in Fig. 2.

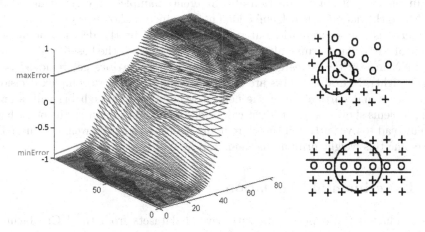

Fig. 1. Left: MLP neural network decision border with *minError* and *MaxEror* shown for the class for which an expected neuron signal is -1. Right: Examples of decision borders that make some instances to be incorrectly classified by k-NN.

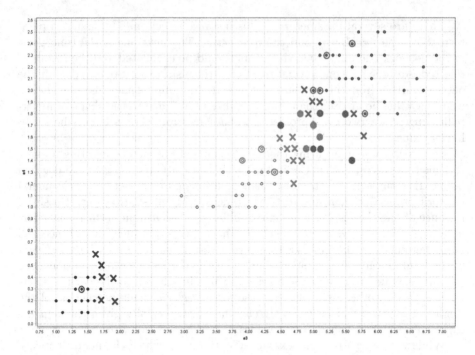

Fig. 2. The instances of Iris dataset selected by CNN (dot inside circle), by neural network (cross) as those with low error values and by both (big solid circle). Neural network selected instances more correctly at the border of red and green class and of blue class, only failed to select border instances of the green class from the blue class side. (Color figure online)

In the case of noise reduction also different examples may get removed by ENN and the neural-network embedded noise reduction, however in this case the difference is not so dramatic, but rather determined by the decision boundary shape of particular learning algorithms. In k-NN, which is the baseline algorithm for ENN mostly the edges get smoothed and narrow stripes get removed (see Fig. 1. right). Neural networks are able to accommodate more complex decision boundaries and particularly if the neuron weights have enough big values and the problems shown in Fig. 1. right can be eliminated, although on the other had it may lead to over-fitting if there are many neurons and large weight values. To overcome this weight pruning methods can be used.

4   Experimental Evaluation

We conducted the experiments with several datasets from the UCI Machine Learning Repository [6]. The datasets were selected to cover different levels of noise, of leaning difficulties (the neural network could achieve the prediction accuracy from 0.6 to 1.0 depending on the dataset) and different number of classes. In this way the approach can be tested for various types of problems. The following dataset were used: Banknote Authentication (4 features, 1372 instances, 2 classes), Climate Simulation Crashes (4 features, 1372 instances, 2 classes), Image Segmentation (19 features, 2310 instances, 7 classes), Satellite Image (36 features, 6435 instances, 7 classes), Vehicle (18 features, 846 instances, 4 classes) and Yeast (8 features, 1484 instances, 10 classes).

We implemented the algorithms in C# language. As the network learning algorithms we use VSS [13], which uses a search-based approach for finding the

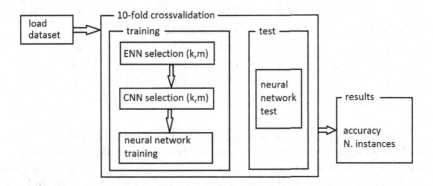

Fig. 3. Processes used to evaluate and validate dataset assessment based on compression. Either ENN and CNN blocks are used or the instance selection embedded in a neural network training.

Table 1. Classification accuracy

method/dataset	Banknote	Climate	ImgSegm	SatImage	Vehicle	Yeast
no selection	99.5	95.1	96.4	90.6	81.6	**60.0**
ENN-CNN 5/9	97.5	94.0	92.3	86.5	81.7	55.7
ENN-CNN 6/9	98.2	94.3	94.6	87.8	**82.0**	55.9
ENN-CNN 7/9	**99.8**	95.1	95.7	90.2	78.4	56.2
ENN-CNN 8/9	98.2	94.5	**96.6**	89.8	80.3	59.0
NN-inc 0.02/1.7	99.4	94.0	94.8	89.3	76.1	59.3
NN-inc 0.05/1.6	99.8	92.2	87.3	91.0	77.2	55.2
NN-inc 0.10/1.5	-	90.8	81.6	91.6	78.1	-
NN-inc 0.20/1.4	-	87.0	70.3	90.2	73.4	-
NN-res 0.02/1.7	99.8	**96.2**	94.8	92.3	81.1	59.0
NN-res 0.05/1.6	99.8	96.0	94.3	**92.4**	80.6	56.5
NN-res 0.10/1.5	-	94.8	93.6	91.6	78.1	-
NN-res 0.20/1.4	-	93.4	80.1	91.3	81.4	-
ENN-CNN std. dev	1.3	2.3	1.2	1.9	2.8	3.5
NN std. dev	1.6	4.0	4.4	2.0	3.5	4.5

Table 2. Ratio of selected instances to all instances

Method/Dataset	Banknote	Climate	ImgSegm	SatImage	Vehicle	Yeast
No selection	100	100	100	100	100	100
ENN-CNN 5/9	3.03	2.80	12.0	10.4	20.7	17.2
ENN-CNN 6/9	3.91	9.18	19.0	11.9	40.4	22.0
ENN-CNN 7/9	5.10	18.5	27.2	18.0	40.3	25.9
ENN-CNN 8/9	7.22	32.9	35.6	35.3	62.4	38.4
NN 0.02/1.7	22.1	11.6	14.8	88.2	77.1	33.3
NN 0.05/1.6	17.8	7.96	9.75	63.7	53.0	24.2
NN 0.10/1.5	–	5.64	7.17	41.7	42.6	–
NN 0.20/1.4	–	2.53	4.37	28.1	34.5	–
ENN-CNN std. dev	1.6	1.5	0.6	1.8	0.9	4.0
NN std. dev	1.6	0.6	0.6	1.9	1.5	4.5

optimal path downwards the error surface [14]. The software can be downloaded from [7]. Also some tests were performed in RapidMiner [10]. We run each test in five 10-fold crossvalidations (50 runs together). Figure 3 shows the diagram representing the experimental setup, where $k=9$ the values m for ENN and CNN are the same and change from 5 to 8. The same setup is used for neural network based instance selection and in this case the ENN and CNN blocks are not used. In this case the instance selection was performed at the final stage of the network learning. Then the network learning was either restarted (**res** in Tables 1 and 2) from random weights or the network trained further "incrementally" (**inc** in Tables 1 and 2) from the point where the selection was done - in both cases using the selected instances only.

The standard deviations of accuracy were relatively constant for each dataset and instance selection parameters, so they are reported once in the bottom row of Tables 1 and 2 as the average standard deviation of the 50 runs (five 10-fold crossvalidations) of each set of instance selection parameters. In ENN+CNN selection the first value is m (here $m = m_{ENN} = m_{CNN}$) and the second k. For neural network based selection the first value is $minError$ and the second is $maxError$. $maxError$ is presented in absolute values and $minError$ in the fraction of the average error value.

5   Conclusions

It was in several cases possible to obtain higher classification accuracy than without instance selection using about 20–30% of the training vectors and always to significantly reduce the dataset size with only a very little accuracy drop - much less then caused by ENN+CNN with standard parameters. However, other experiments showed that ENN with default parameters is very good at removing noise artificially added to the training dataset and thus improving results on such data. However, in the case of the datasets used here, ENN seems to perform too strong instance selection and in particular it removes too many instances situated close to decision boundaries, what shift the decision boundaries causing decrease in the classifier performance. Increasing the required m we can get removed only the instances situated inside other class and thus only noise is removed and the decision borders are left intact. ENN selection does not have much impact on the data size reduction. In the experiments ENN usually reduced the data size about 5% and CNN up to 85%. Also standard CNN selection tends to shift the decision boundaries due to the removal of the instances situated close to the boundaries. And again increasing m from the default 5 to 7 or to 8 helped, but the total number of selected instances at least doubled. However, if decreasing the dataset size is as important as accuracy improvement, the position of the class boundary can be determined first, and then more aggressive elimination can be performed for the instances that are far from the boundary and less aggressive to those that are close. Some of the ideas (the "far" instances) presented in the introduction that were proposed in [20] may be useful. Another good idea is to embed instance selection in the classifier, as was discussed in the paper.

Instance selection performed during the neural network training usually allowed for achieving higher classification accuracies with a comparable number of instances. Thus for the size of datasets presented here it seems to be a good solution. On the other hand, the time of the whole process was significantly longer. It was about 3-4 times faster to perform instance selection first and then to train the network only on about 20% of selected instances. With the increase of the dataset size usually higher percentage of instances can be rejected thus making the difference even bigger. The Yeast dataset is an especially difficult problem with many classes and probably with high noise level. In that case also the $maxError$ parameter did not work as expected. That was, because the network error exceeded the value of 2 for many vectors and probably the $maxError$ should be set to a higher value for such datasets. However, how to determine the optimal value in such cases requires further investigations. The $minError$ already realized the "far" instances idea and it worked quite well. In general a similar solution is used in Support Vector Machines, where vectors that are close to the decision border are of special consideration. In some cases, when one vector is removed as being below the $minError$, another vector that is left in its proximity should be counted with an increased coefficient while calculating the network error in order to prevent shifting of decision borders.

In summary we were able to improve the neural network classifier performance and to observe several interesting properties of the instance selection process. A further research examining all the parameters individually on a large number of datasets is probably going to help develop more effective methods.

References

1. Abroudi, A., Shokouhifar, M., Farokhi, F.: Improving the performance of artificial neural networks via instance selection and feature dimensionality reduction. Int. J. Mach. Learn. Comput. **3**(2), 176–189 (2013)

2. Antonelli, M., Ducange, P., Marcelloni, F.: Genetic training instance selection in multiobjective evolutionary fuzzy systems: A coevolutionary approach. IEEE Trans. Fuzzy Syst. **20**(2), 276–290 (2012)

3. Anwar, I.M., et al.: Instance selection with ant colony optimization. Procedia Comput. Sci. **53**, 248–256 (2015)

4. Blachnik, M., Kordos, M.: Simplifying SVM with weighted LVQ algorithm. In: Yin, H., Wang, W., Rayward-Smith, V. (eds.) IDEAL 2011. LNCS, vol. 6936, pp. 212–219. Springer, Heidelberg (2011)

5. Friedman, J.H., Bentley, J.L., Finkel, R.A.: An algorithm for finding best matches in logarithmic expected time. ACM Trans. Math. Softw. **3**(3), 209–226 (1977)

6. Blake, C., Keogh, E., Merz, C.: UCI Repository of Machine Learning Databases 1998–2015

7. The software used in the paper. http://www.kordos.com/icaisc2016

8. Guillen, A., et al.: New method for instance or prototype selection using mutual information in time series prediction. Neurocomputing **73**(10–12), 2030–2038 (2010)

9. Hart, P.: The condensed nearest neighbor rule. IEEE Trans. Inf. Theory **14**(3), 515–516 (1968)

10. Hofmann, M., Klinkenberg, R.: RapidMiner: Data Mining Use Cases and Business Analytics Applications. CRC Press, Boca Raton (2013)

11. Indyk, P., Motwani, R.: Approximate nearest neighbors: towards removing the curse of dimensionality. In: Proceedings of 30th Symposium on Theory of Computing (1988)

12. Jankowski, N., Grochowski, M.: Comparison of instances seletion Algorithms I. algorithms survey. In: Rutkowski, L., Siekmann, J.H., Tadeusiewicz, R., Zadeh, L.A. (eds.) ICAISC 2004. LNCS (LNAI), vol. 3070, pp. 598–603. Springer, Heidelberg (2004)

13. Kordos, M., Duch, W.: Variable step search algorithm for feedforward networks. Neurocomputing **71**(13–15), 2470–2480 (2008)

14. Kordos, M., Duch, W.: A survey of factors influencing MLP error surface. Control Cybern. **33**(4), 611–631 (2004)

15. Leyva, E., Gonzalez, A., Perez, R.: Three new instance selection methods based on local sets: A comparative study with several approaches from a bi-objective perspective. Pattern Recogn. **48**(4), 1523–1537 (2015)

16. Marchiori, E.: Class conditional nearest neighbor for large margin instance selection. IEEE Trans. Pattern Anal. Mach. Intell. **32**(2), 364–370 (2010)

17. Olvera-López, J.A., Carrasco-Ochoa, J.A., Martínez-Trinidad, J.F., Kittler, J.: A review of instance selection methods. Artif. Intell. Rev. **34**(2), 133–143 (2010)

18. Garcia, S., Derrac, J., Cano, J., Herrera, F.: Prototype selection for nearest neighbor classification: Taxonomy and empirical study. IEEE Trans. Pattern Anal. Mach. Intell. **34**(3), 417–435 (2012)

19. Stojanovic, M., et al.: A methodology for training set instance selection using mutual information in time series prediction. Neurocomputing **141**, 236–245 (2014)

20. Sun, X., Chan, P.K.: An analysis of instance selection for neural networks to improve training speed. In: International Conference on Machine Learning and Applications, pp. 288–293 (2014)

21. Wilson, D.L.: Asymptotic properties of nearest neighbor rules using edited data. IEEE Trans. Syst. Man Cybern. **SMC–2**(3), 408–421 (1972)

Distributed Classification of Text Documents on Apache Spark Platform

Piotr Semberecki and Henryk Maciejewski[✉]

Department of Computer Engineering, Wrocław University of Technology,
Wybrzeże Wyspiańskiego 27, 50-270 Wrocław, Poland
{Piotr.Semberecki,Henryk.Maciejewski}@pwr.edu.pl

Abstract. This paper presents implementation of the system for subject classification of text documents based on the Apache Spark distributed computing framework. Classification of text documents starts with generation of high-dimensional feature vectors from documents; the task realized with methods and tools for natural language processing. The next steps involve reduction of dimensionality of feature vectors and training classifiers. In the paper we show how these consecutive steps can be realized on the Apache Spark platform dedicated to distributed processing of big data. We illustrate the proposed method by a sample classifier aimed to predict subject category of a document in English-language Wikipedia.

Keywords: Text subject classification · Natural Language Processing (NLP) · Machine learning · Apache Spark

1   Introduction

Automatic classification of text documents has recently become an important subfield of text mining. Its popularity and importance is on one hand due to growing availability of large collections of text documents in electronic format and on the other on the need to effectively manage documents in these collections.

Some of the most prominent applications of text classification include subject categorization of scientific papers or news articles, identification of authorship of documents, analysis of sentiment of reviews or comments, recognition of spam e-mail, automatic categorization of customer e-mail messages or tech-support requests, etc. [1–3].

Initial approaches to text categorization were based on expert knowledge encoded in the form of sets of rules on how to assign documents to given predefined classes. Although this approach is still attempted in some real-life applications, recently an alternative methods has emerged based on automatic induction of models/rule sets for text classification given a training collection of documents with known categories. This approach uses methods of natural language processing (NLP) and methods of machine learning (ML), [4,5], and can be broadly outlined in the following steps: (i) Documents in the training collection are represented by vectors of features; this typically yields high-dimensional

© Springer International Publishing Switzerland 2016
L. Rutkowski et al. (Eds.): ICAISC 2016, Part I, LNAI 9692, pp. 621–630, 2016.
DOI: 10.1007/978-3-319-39378-0_53

training data. (ii) Dimensionality of feature vectors needs to be reduced. (iii) Classification models are built based on the training data and evaluated based on independent data. Methods of NLP are commonly used to successfully implement step (i) of this procedure, i.e. to provide relevant document representation, but they can also facilitate dimensionality reduction of the representation which is done in step (ii).

The main objective of this work is to demonstrate how this procedure, i.e., steps (i) through (iii), can be realized using the Apache Spark distributed processing framework [6]. Distributed realizations of various text mining tasks have recently attracted a lot of interest, [7], which is motivated by the fact that collections of documents to be processed are becoming very large, comprising millions of documents, and are often available in distributed environments, such as the Web.

In this work we want to answer the specific questions: how native mechanisms of Apache Spark can be used to distribute NLP-based preprocessing of text documents used to generate feature vectors and, secondly, what library for distributed machine learning tasks can be used to train models for document categorization. To illustrate this, we present a distributed system for subject (topic) classification of text documents obtained from English language Wikipedia [17]. The system is implemented in Python, with the NLP tasks realized with the NLTK toolkit, [8,12], and MLlib library for machine learning on Apache Spark.

The structure of the paper is as follows. In the following section we provide the details on the NLP-based procedure to generate feature vectors representing the text documents. This task is implemented in our system using the NLTK tools for the English language. In Sect. 3, we present the mechanisms of distributed processing in Apache Spark framework that we used in our system. Next in Sect. 4, we present the distributed version of text classifier based on Apache Spark. Finally, in Sect. 5 we report scalability and accuracy of our classifier deployed on a sample cluster on the Amazon MapReduce service.

2   Subject Classification of Text Documents

In this section we outline the supervised-learning approach to subject classification of text documents. The specific challenge related to this task is how to represent documents in the process of training prediction models for text categorization. Generation of effective representations of documents (i.e. feature vectors) can be done with application of NLP methods.

We assume that a collection of m documents is given, $(d_1, c_1), ..., (d_m, c_m)$ as the training set, where each of the documents d_i has a category $c_i \in C$ assigned. The task is to build the classifier $f(d) \rightarrow C$ and to estimate the expected predictive performance of f for the new data.

The task can be solved in the following procedure.

1. Each of the documents is tokenized into sentences and sentences are tokenized into words. This can be done with the NLTK tokenization methods for English (example shown in Sect. 4).

2. Words in each of documents are normalized by identifying base, i.e. the dictionary forms for each of the words. This process is referred to as lemmatization and can be implemented by the NLTK `WordNetLemmmatizer` class. Technically, lemmatization requires that word sense disambiguation is performed, based on probabilistic models encoded in the lemmatizer class, which yields the grammatic class of the word, including its part of speech (POS) designation.

3. List of words included in each of the documents can be reduced by filtering out stopwords (which include such words as conjunctions, pronouns and other common words which are unlikely to be relevant for topic classification). Optionally, further reduction can be tried by filtering by POS tags, leaving only presumably most meaningful words such as nouns, verbs or adjectives.

4. We estimate the vectors of features to represent each of the documents using the bag-of-words approach [4]. Technically, if W denotes the set of n different words (base forms) in the collection D of m documents in the training set, as left by the filtering procedure in the previous step, then a vector of features for a document $d_i, i = 1, ..., m$ is defined as $[f_{ik}], k = 1, ..., n$, where f_{ik} denotes the frequency of word w_k in the i-th document (referred to as term frequency).

5. Elements of the feature vectors are commonly weighed $[v_k f_{ik}], k = 1, ..., n$, where the weight $v_k = \log_2(\frac{1}{P(w_k)}) + 1$, (with $P(w_k)$ denoting the proportion of documents in the training collection D which include the term w_k) is knows as the inverse document frequency. The purpose of this is to strengthen the terms which are likely to be most relevant for classification. The resulting terms are then called term frequency-inverse document frequency, or TF-IDF.

6. Using the feature vectors generated from the m documents, along with the known categories $c_1, ..., c_m$, predictive models are trained. Several approaches to this were reported in literature, ranging from the SVM algorithm to nonparametric methods, see e.g., [9–11].

7. Estimation of predictive performance of the trained classifiers is commonly done empirically, by comparing the actual vs predicted categories as observed on the testing dataset, and is quantified using the following measures of quality of prediction of class c_i: precision $P = \frac{TP}{TP+FP}$, recall $R = \frac{TP}{TP+FN}$ (also referred to as *sensitivity*), specificity $S = \frac{TN}{FP+TN}$, where TP, FP, TN, FN denote the number of true positive, false positive, true negative or false negative events, respectively, when analyzing results of prediction of documents of class c_i by the classifier.

A slightly simplified variant of this procedure was later implemented in Sect. 4 on the Apache Spark distributed processing framework (the simplification was that the orthographic rather than the base forms of words were used to form the set W).

3   Apache Spark Architecture

3.1   Review

Apache Spark is a distributed computing framework which performs operations on working data sets. These data sets are called *resilient distributed datasets* (RDDs).

Apache Spark's programming model is based on processing RDD objects in an acyclic data flow manner, using a set of operators called transformations. This model provides operations derived from functional programming like mapping, filtering, set unification, etc. It gives ability to easily split the computation that would be normally performed in a single thread way over multiple cluster nodes. To gain maximal scalability, at first the data should be placed in distributed file system like Hadoop Distributed File System (HDFS) [15] or Amazon S3.

Apache Spark is written in Scala and is run on Java Virtual Machine. However, it also supports Python which was used for implementing the text classification algorithm presented in this article.

Apache Spark was developed to overcome the issues of Apache Hadoop. Hadoop was a previously developed distributed computing framework, based on the MapReduce paradigm which was introduced by Google [13]. The main drawback of Hadoop is that it always performs hard drive read/write operations for each MapReduce task. On the contrary, Apache Spark can cache the data in the memory and only if data do not fit in memory, it serializes RDD structures and stores them on the hard drive.

It is also problematic that the Apache Hadoop provides only batch mode of processing data, whereas Apache Spark uses micro-batching technique for processing data using internal Spark Streaming library or external Apache Storm framework [16]. This gives the ability to run applications interactively.

In the first phase of data processing Apache Spark creates RDD objects from loaded data. The order of the operations on RDD sets is transformed into direct acyclic graph, scheduled and processed in parallel by the cluster worker nodes. The main program - driver controls the evaluation.

Apache Spark has native libraries that support common Machine Learning algorithms for Clustering, Classification and Data Dimensionality Reduction, which are optimized for RDD datasets processing. Most of them can be used in Python programming language.

3.2   Apache Hadoop Vs Apache Spark in Machine Learning

Apache Spark supports parts of Apache Hadoop environment, for instance the Apache Hive data warehouse solution. It also can use Hadoop Distributed File System (HDFS) and can use Hadoop YARN resource manager.

It is very common in Machine Learning algorithms that the input dataset is read multiple times, for instance when testing different algorithms or providing input data for the model training algorithm. This is called iterative processing. Apache Hadoop has the disadvantage that is not efficient for this type of computations.

In such situations latency is expected to appear due to disk reloading operations. The problem will also occur when performing interactive analytics by Apache Pig and Apache Hive SQL interfaces. All these issues are overcome in Apache Spark as a result of the new approach, based on caching temporary RDD objects in memory.

4 Distributed Text Classifier of Apache Spark

The main idea of this work is to show the scalability of Distributed Text Classifier using Apache Spark and Natural Language Processing Toolkit library (NLTK).

It should be stressed that the approach we show here is very generic, as the user can use in a similar manner virtually any Python libraries, not designed for distributed processing, to achieve processing distribution with Apache Spark. This is possible once the data are stored in *resilient distributed datasets* (RDDs). RDDs are very similar to the distributed memory concept. From the point of view of a Python developer, RDDs resemble lists, however they cannot be directly accessed and modified. This is the main difference between distributed memory and RDDs. Only after performing operations like collect() we can gather the data from distributed datasets. This can be problematic from the debugging perspective, however it provides the high performance for distributed processing on the cluster.

As described in Sect. 2, the text classifier is based on the Bag-of-Words model which is used for representing feature vectors in Machine Learning algorithms. Each number in the vector represents the frequency of occurrence of a word from the Bag-of-Words model. Training and reference vectors include also a value which codes the category of the article. The data used in the process of classifier training and was taken from the English-language Wikipedia. This choice was convenient as the Wikipedia data is free, easy to access and is readily categorized.

Apache Sparks reads the input text files from the HDFS and puts them into the RDD objects. Each line of a file is read as a string an becomes part of a RDD object. For the purpose of simplifying further processing, in our system each article was previously converted into a one-line string. This approach provides an easy way to process the text data and convert the documents into feature vectors. The reason for this is that Apache Spark reads the data from files to RDDs by splitting the input file one-by-line to RDDs elements. To optimize the usage of memory provided for RDDs, all the text files were split into 1 MB chunks containing a few hundred articles each.

Now we explain how distributed processing of data stored in RDDs is realized; to illustrate this we focus on tokenization. The standard (non-distributed) way is to use the NLTK word tokenizer to obtain tokens from text that can be next used as features. In Apache Spark, we can use the same functions and methods to do this in distributed way. However, it is important to keep in mind that the data will be processed on cluster and how the computing will be distributed. It means that there are restrictions depending on the size and settings of the cluster.

The mechanism to provide distributed processing is based on operations like Map(), Filter(), etc. It means that on each of the RDD elements the same operation will be performed. In our text classifier system, each article is tokenized using the Map operation combined with a Python lambda function that takes as an argument the element of RDD and performs the provided operation on it, as illustrated by the following sample code.

Listing 1.1. Example of performing file tokenization using NLTK RegexpTokenizer and RDD object Map() function

```
import pyspark
import nltk

sc = pyspark.SparkContext(appName="MyApplication")
rdd = sc.textFile('path/to/file')
regexp_tokenizer = nltk.RegexpTokenizer("[\w']+")
rdd.map(lambda x: regexp_tokenizer.tokenize(x))
tokens = rdd.collect()
```

Using this mechanism, we can achieve full distribution of the code for generating feature vectors, which is the first phase for document classifier. Exactly in the same way the remaining operations outlined in Sect. 2 were distributed, including [14]:

- sentence tokenization for each articles,
- word tokenization,
- conversion words to lowercase,
- hashing the words,
- calculating TF-IDF statistic and creating Bag-of-Words model,
- converting words hashes into frequency of words appearance vectors,
- split of vectors into training and testing data.

Most of the operations were done directly on RDDs, however during the generation of Bag-of-Words model the collect() operation was performed. It was necessary because only a part of tokens with highest TF-IDF values were stored as intermediate results in a classical, non-distributed form as constants. These words were then compared with tokens in RDDs and the number of occurrences of the words in subsequent documents were recorded as elements of the feature vectors.

To gain the advantage of distributed environment, we used the Apache Spark MLlib library which implements several machine learning algorithms such as Naive Bayes Classifier, Decision Tree and Random Forests for building the classification model.

5   Example

The document classifier was deployed on Amazon MapReduce service. The research was performed on m3.xlarge instance based on Intel Xeon E5-2670 running at 2.6 GHz with 15 GiB Memory and 2×40 GB SSD storage. This instance provided 4 virtual CPU cores for each cluster node. Firstly, the tests were started with 1 Master Node instance and 2 slave nodes. After that, the cluster was extended to 4 slave nodes.

The instance was tested in YARN client cluster mode, because this is the only one that is supported for Python. In tests the number of the executors was changed as well as the number of cores per each executor. Executors are the processes launched on worker nodes. They run tasks on RDD objects and keep data in the memory or disk storage. The number of cores is the number of concurrent tasks that each executor can run.

The classifier was verified using 15 MB of data. In the training data there were three categories: Art, History and Law, with ca. 5 MB of data per category. The categories were split randomly with weights 75 % and 25 % to generate training and testing vectors. The efficiency of classifier was calculated as an average of 14 measurements.

The Naive Bayes algorithm was used with default parameters within MLLib from Apache Spark 1.4.1. The Decision Tree used Gini index for calculating node impurity. The Random Forests algorithm was used to generate 2 sub-trees. Bag-of-Words model used 200 tokens. Predictive performance of the different models is summarized in the following tables.

In terms of accuracy, the best was the Naive Bayes algorithm (Table 1). The worse accuracy was observed for the Decision Tree and Random Forests. The result can be improved by increasing the number of input data and size of the Bag-of-Words vectors. The classifier had problem with History category (Table 2). We can see that there is high misclassification rate in all algorithms and sensitivity below 50 %. The result can be improved by increasing the size of data and length of feature vectors.

Table 1. Accuracy results

Algorithm	Accuracy [%]
Naive Bayes	75.28
Decision Tree	67.90
Random Forests	62.68

Table 2. Classifier parameters for three category classification

Algorithm	Naive Bayes			Decision Tree			Random Forests		
Category	Arts	Hist.	Law	Arts	Hist.	Law	Arts	Hist.	Law
Sensitivity [%]	86.99	49.20	78.94	77.69	47.21	70.40	77.09	8.14	80.15
Specificity [%]	76.48	93.78	90.98	76.78	84.06	90.95	71.48	99.21	68.38
Precision [%]	70.46	70.16	84.41	73.39	57.27	85.70	69.53	71.79	66.31
Miss rate [%]	13.01	50.80	21.06	22.31	52.79	29.60	22.91	91.86	19.85

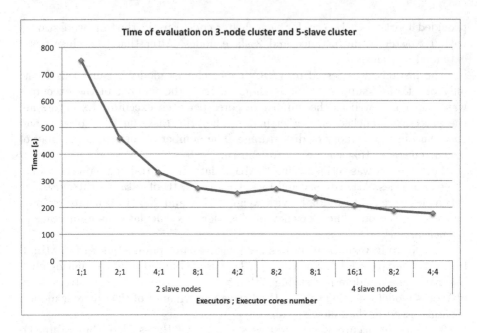

Fig. 1. Total evaluation times in yarn-client mode for 3-node and 5-node cluster.

The scalability performance of the distributed text classifier was tested by changing the combinations of number of Apache Spark's executors and executor cores (Fig. 1). Amazon Elastic MapReduce provides ability to increase the number of slave nodes on the working cluster instance. Therefore, the number of these nodes was changed from 2 to 4. The time of evaluation for the classifier decreased from 750.58 seconds on 1 executor and 1 executor cores to 251.87 seconds 4 executors with 2 cores. Afterwards, the result further improved on 4-slave node cluster as it changed to 177.14 seconds. We can see that the result was almost 3 times better in the 2-node approach and 4 times better in 4-node tests as compared with the single-thread executor evaluation.

As we can see, it is also interesting to realize that to gain the full performance it is important to properly set the cluster and the settings depend on its size.

6   Conclusions

In this work, we demonstrated the distributed version of the text-mining process used to build a model for document topic categorization. Our approach is similar to the previously proposed system based on the Hadoop distributed processing framework [14], however, in our system Apache Spark is used in place of Hadoop. According to our knowledge, it is the first implementation of text categorization system on Apache Spark in Python using the NLTK framework. We showed how NLP tasks for text preprocessing and for generation of feature vectors can be distributed and executed in parallel on subsets of data included in the RDDs by the native mechanism of Apache Spark. In our system we also used the Spark MLLib library for distributed execution of machine learning algorithms. In our simple preliminary study, we showed that the system scales well on a sample Amazon Elastic MapReduce cluster.

There are however several limitations in our study that the reader should be aware of. Firstly, the system was designed for the task of *topic* categorization of text documents, as this is what the simple Bag-of-Words method is commonly used for. This approach does not necessarily guarantee best performance for text classification tasks such as sentiment analysis or authorship attribution. In these cases, more subtle characteristics of the text/its language should be included into the feature vectors (in addition to, or in place of the features generated in steps 4–5 of the process in Sect. 2). Secondly, even for the problem of text topic categorization that we focus on in this work, smarter feature vectors could be constructed, e.g. including collocations in addition to single terms, or using some additional language knowledge on named-entities or on semantic relationships between terms. This could presumably lead to information-heavier features and to further reduction of dimensionality and presumably to better accuracy of classification. Finally, it will be interesting to further test the proposed system on much larger volume of text documents and on a larger-scale cluster.

References

1. Sebastiani, F.: Machine learning in automated text categorization. ACM Comput. Surv. (CSUR) **34**(1), 1–47 (2002)
2. Koppel, M., Schler, J., Argamon, S.: Authorship attribution in the wild. Lang. Resour. Eval. **45**(1), 83–94 (2011)
3. Stamatatos, E.: A survey of modern authorship attribution methods. JASIST **60**(3), 538–556 (2009)
4. Torkkola, K.: Discriminative features for text document classification. Formal Pattern Anal. Appl. **6**(4), 301–308 (2004)
5. Jurafsky, D., Manning, C.: Natural Language Processing. https://www.coursera.org/course/nlp
6. Zaharia, M., Chowdhury, M., Franklin, M.J., Shenker, S., Stoica, I.: Spark: cluster computing with working sets. HotCloud **10**, 10 (2010)
7. Nesi, P., Pantaleo, G., Sanesi, G.: A distributed framework for NLP-based keyword and keyphrase extraction from web pages and documents. In: 21st International Conference on Distributed Multimedia Systems, DMS2015 (2015)
8. Bird, S., Klein, E., Loper, E.: Natural Language Processing with Python - Analyzing Text with the Natural Language Toolkit. O'Reilly, Beijing (2009)
9. Bijalwan, V., et al.: KNN based machine learning approach for text and document mining. Int. J. Database Theo. Appl. **7**(1), 61–70 (2014)
10. Isa, D., et al.: Text document preprocessing with the Bayes formula for classification using the support vector machine. IEEE Trans. Knowl. Data Eng. **20**(9), 1264–1272 (2008)
11. Wang, L., Zhao, X.: Improved KNN classification algorithms research in text categorization. In: 2nd International Conference Consumer Electronics, Communications and Networks (CECNet), IEEE (2012)

12. Perkins, J.: Python 3 Text Processing with NLTK 3 Cookbook. Packt Publishing (2014)
13. Dean, J., Ghemawat, S.: MapReduce: simplified data processing on large clusters. In: OSDI 2004 Sixth Symposium on Operating System Design and Implementation (2004)
14. Rosnova, D.: Practical Natural Language Processing with Hadoop. https:// danrosanova.files.wordpress.com/2014/04/practical-natural-language-processing-with-hadoop.pdf
15. Shvachko, K., Kuang, H., Radia, S., Chansler, R.: The Hadoop Distributed File System. Yahoo!, Sunnyvale, California USA (2010)
16. Zaharia, M., Das, T., Li, H., Hunter, T., Shenker, S., Stoica, I.: Discretized streams: fault-tolerant streaming computation at scale. In: Twenty-Fourth ACM Symposium on Operating Systems Principles, pp. 423–438. ACM New York (2013)
17. De Smedt, T., Marfia, F., Matteucci, M., Daelemans, W.: Using wiktionary to build an italian part-of-speech tagger. In: Métais, E., Roche, M., Teisseire, M. (eds.) NLDB 2014. LNCS, vol. 8455, pp. 1–8. Springer, Heidelberg (2014)

A Hidden Markov Model with Controlled Non-parametric Emissions

Atid Shamaie[(✉)]

Qualcomm Inc., 105 Commerce Valley Drive West, Markham, ON, Canada
ashamaie@qti.qualcomm.com

Abstract. A novel nonparametric model is introduced to model and control emission densities of a non-ergodic hidden Markov model. Having both multiclass and one-class classifications simultaneously, for recognizing the best match between multiple classes and then accepting or rejecting the given input pattern, is the major characteristic of this algorithm. Also, since the proposed method creates independent feature spaces and trains by positive samples only, it allows the vocabulary of trained patterns to grow without any concern about growing into a negative set (which is a problem with algorithms that use negative/garbage sets for binary training).

1 Introduction

Temporal manifolds are used in many applications including speech, hand gesture, and human action recognition. Hidden Markov models (HMM) have been very successful in detecting temporal events in those applications including speech and gesture recognition [1–4]. There have been different versions of HMM including the HMMs with discrete and continuous density emissions [1, 5] used in applications where observations occur with spatial diversity.

Spatially diverse data in a feature space play a major role for applications such as recognition of trajectories for flow detection [6, 7] and gesture recognition [4]. Popular methods used for modelling spatially diverse data include K-means and Gaussian Mixture Models (GMM) [2]. In a vocabulary of words (e.g. spoken words, trajectories, or gestures) individual sequences of symbols from an alphabet create individual words (trajectories, gestures, etc.).

HMMs are particularly good at dealing with temporal variations. A problem with detection of spatio-temporal patterns is, however, controlling the range of acceptable spatial variations. It is of significant value to be able to reject a sequence which is considerably different from the learned patterns. This means that although the HMMs are good at multiclass classifications, they cannot effectively be used for binary classification of accepting/rejecting an input sequence. There have been solutions to this problem in the literature from which creating a garbage model and training a separate HMM for that is popular [8]. However, in those solutions, local range of variations are not controlled and, therefore, there is no way for limiting the acceptable range of deformations. Moreover, in the standard HMM and many variations, having a fixed alphabet for all words cannot model local variations of each word in a high resolution

© Springer International Publishing Switzerland 2016
L. Rutkowski et al. (Eds.): ICAISC 2016, Part I, LNAI 9692, pp. 631–643, 2016.
DOI: 10.1007/978-3-319-39378-0_54

feature space by a set of discrete alphabet codevectors extracted through quantizing the training set.

The continuous density HMM (CDHMM) [1] may seem to be a good candidate for modeling the spatial diversity. However, a problem with this method is that there is no solid way of deciding how to control the range (support) of distributions in the mixture. The mixture density likelihoods used in this model as the probabilities for observations cannot provide a solid way of limiting the range of variations since the likelihoods change smoothly over an area. This is due to the fact that the distance of an observation from the mixtures affects the likelihood. We need to recognize or reject a sequence. Therefore, a clear and strong border for acceptable variations is desirable.

In the next section, we present our motivation for the new method in more detail and some related work in the literature will be discussed. Then the theory of our proposed non-ergodic HMM (on which a left-right topology is imposed) is presented in Sect. 3. At the end an evaluation of the algorithm against a large database of hand-drawn symbols demonstrates advantages and disadvantages of this model against more standard HMMs popular in the literature.

2 Motivation and Recent Related Work

We are interested in rejecting data points in the areas far from the components of a mixture model constituting emissions of a hidden Markov model. In CDHMM, the likelihood of a data point in a given sequence is evaluated through the likelihoods generated by the components in the emission mixture model mixed by a vector of coefficients. This causes a soft passage from high likelihood observations to low likelihoods with a mild slope. Identifying a clear border for accept/reject range of the mixture is, therefore, a problem. We define a more effective range (support) control tool by replacing the popular mixture model with a mixture model controlled by a non-parametric Pitman-Yor process (PYP) in which the discount parameter is controlled by a Gaussian process covariance regression. It is necessary to understand the role of each method in controlling the border of accept/reject regions. The Pitman-Yor process foresees future variations of data points around each component of the mixture model. It allows large deviations from the established components to be included in the acceptable range. We will see in the next section that the border defined through this method alone, when the discount parameter of the PYP is zero, may be too far from the centers of components and may include too much deviations from the training dataset. We use Gaussian processes covariance regression to define a surface of covariance values for adjusting the discount parameter of the Pitman-Yor process throughout the feature space for controlling the borders.

Since both methods of PYP and GP covariance regression significantly depend on the training datasets of each model in a vocabulary individually, it will be inappropriate to allow the components of the emission mixture model to be constructed using the training sets of all models in a vocabulary as is popular in general context of left-right HMM in speech, gesture, and action recognition [2]. For example, if the vocabulary includes five models (words), it is popular in traditional HMM that the training sets of all these words are employed to quantize a set of codevectors as the alphabet of HMMs, therefore, creating a shared alphabet among all the models. However, we want to control the range of the components of the emission mixtures for each of the models in the vocabulary individually. It, therefore, is rational that each component be the best representative of variations of data in the associated area of the feature space for each model separately. We, therefore, allow only the training set of each individual word in the vocabulary to participate in constructing the components of the emission mixture for that model. This makes separate alphabets (set of components) for each word in the vocabulary. In other words, the feature spaces are individualized for the HMMs when we use a separate set of component labels for each HMM's table of emissions. Using the component labels as an alphabet creates a high resolution feature space as the mixtures are continuous. However, it has some limitations that need to be addressed separately. The suggested method is good in supervised contexts meaning the HMMs and their emission densities need to be fully trained. Also, since the HMMs have fixed length left-right state topologies that need to be set a priori, in an unsupervised clustering context, where the number of hidden states may vary depending on the models, this method requires more future work to be suitable.

There are methods reported in the literature that may seem to have some similarities with the method presented in this paper. Hierarchical Dirichlet Process-Hidden Markov Model (HDP-HMM) [9] uses a hierarchical Dirichlet process to control both state changes and emissions of an HMM making it a powerful method for an unsupervised topic modeling where the hidden states represent topics. Topic changing is, therefore, modelled by switching from one hidden state to the next one. Non-markovian behavior of data causes this model to generate unnecessary extra hidden states and rapid switching between the states. This issue has been addressed in the sticky variation of HDP-HMM [11] where a global self-transition bias discourages rapid switching of states. A drawback with this method is the global bias that makes it unsuitable for state-specific duration dynamics to be learned [24]. Moreover, a major issue with all these methods is that each topic needs to be modelled with a single hidden state. Also, in these methods, it is permitted to switch to all other states from an emitting state. These issues make the methods less desirable in applications where a complex pattern in the vocabulary requires more than one hidden state in a strict sequence. It has been demonstrated in [25] that only simple patterns can be modelled with HDP-HMM methods in the context of complex patterns such as action/gesture recognition. On the other hand, since the topics are defined through a common alphabet for the HMMs, variations in each codevector of the alphabet cannot be properly modelled where issues such as co-articulation causes these variations to be different from pattern to pattern. These are major issues in the contexts of gesture, speech, and action recognition. A recent work on dealing with complex words [26] introduces a left-right HDP-HMM in the context of speech recognition where the topology of the sequence of hidden states are set a priori. It addresses the problem of complex patterns but the issues of controlling the range of emissions and rejecting undesirable deviations remain unanswered. Also, each codevector in the alphabet is not necessarily the best representative for the variations of the associated speech unit given that all the models share the same feature space.

3 The Algorithm

In this section we present theoretical details of the proposed algorithm by first explaining a Bayesian nonparametric model (PYP) for learning the mixture model of each word in the vocabulary and inferring from it. Each mixture constitutes the emission density of a hidden Markov model for the associated word. The standard HMM emission table is then modified to accommodate the empty clusters inferred by the PYPs. Finally, the discount parameters of PYPs are modelled by another nonparametric method for controlling the borders of emissions.

3.1 Nonparametric Infinite Emissions for HMM

For controlling the range (support) of each distribution of emission densities of the HMMs a Dirichlet process mixture model (DPM) [10] is imposed on the infinite feature space. If G is distributed according to a Dirichlet process i.e. $G \sim DP(\alpha, H)$, a draw from G is θ_i where $\theta_i | G \sim G$ for $i = 1, 2, \ldots, N$ and the prediction distribution is given by

$$p(\theta_{i+1} = \theta | \theta_1, \theta_2, \ldots, \theta_i, \alpha, H) = \frac{\alpha}{\alpha + N} h(\theta) + \frac{1}{\alpha + N} \Sigma_{k=1}^{K} N_k \delta(\theta, \theta_k). \quad (1)$$

where N_k is the number of observations at partition k, N is the total number of observations, $h(\theta)$ is the base distribution's density, $\delta(\theta, \theta_k)$ is the Kronecker delta function, and α is the parameter of the symmetric Dirichlet distribution.

This Equation indicates that a new observation will be assigned to any of the currently non-empty partitions k with probability $\frac{N_k}{\alpha + N}$ or it will be given a new empty partition with probability $\frac{\alpha}{\alpha + N}$. This is great for learning parameters of a mixture model and allowing a theoretically infinite number of components to be created in order for each component to best represent variations in the training set in the associated region of the feature space. However, when the components of a mixture have many data points assigned to them (large components), they negatively affect the range of the mixture as large components attract large areas around them. The range of the mixture is therefore not controlled.

The Pitman-Yor process (PYP) [13, 14] as a generalization of the Dirichlet process has a discount parameter d, and the prediction probability is characterized by

$$p(\theta_{i+1} = \theta | \theta_1, \theta_2, \ldots, \theta_i, \alpha, H, d) = \frac{\alpha + |\Theta| d}{\alpha + N} h(\theta) + \frac{1}{\alpha + N} \Sigma_{k=1}^{K} (N_k - d) \delta(\theta, \theta_k).$$

$$(2)$$

where $|\Theta|$ is the current number of partitions, and d is defined as the discount parameter in PYP where $0 \leq d < 1$ and $\alpha > -d$. When $d = 0$, Pitman-Yor process becomes Dirichlet process as in Eq. 1.

For learning the emission mixture, we model the training data points of a given pattern (a word in the vocabulary) in the feature space by a Pitman-Yor process mixture model with $d = 0$, which is equivalent to DPM. This is due to the fact that we consider all the data points in the training set of a given model to be representing valid variations, therefore, they should be part of variations included in the components. For prediction, however, the Pitman-Yor process with spatially adjusted d is used for controlling the range of components in the mixture model.

The idea is to partition the feature space of a given model into an infinite number of components (clusters) in the learning phase with some components having training data points assigned to and an unlimited number of empty components. In prediction phase, a data point assigned to an empty component is represented by an extra observation (codevector) added to the emission table of an associated HMM. For a given data point in the prediction phase, PYP assigns the point to either a trained component or initiates an empty component:

$$p(\theta_{i+1} = \theta | \bar{\theta}_1, \bar{\theta}_2, \ldots, \bar{\theta}_i, \alpha, H, d) = \frac{\alpha + |\bar{\Theta}|d}{\alpha + N} h(\theta) + \frac{1}{\alpha + N} \Sigma_{k=1}^{K} (N_k - d)\delta(\theta, \bar{\theta}_k).$$

(3)

where $\bar{\theta}_k$ s are the trained Gaussian components. The PYP of Eq. 3 defines the borders of Gaussian components and considers initiating a new component when the data point $i + 1$ is considerably unlikely to be generated by one of the trained components. The position of a new cluster initiated by the Pitman-Yor process can therefore be anywhere. It should be noted that the mixture model of each word is trained separately and therefore the Gaussian components of each word's mixture are the representation of the variations for that word according to its training data.

The base distribution for the PYP of Eqs. 2 and 3 should be of Gaussian family as the mixture model is Gaussian [19]. Since both mean and covariance of the Gaussians in the mixture model are unknown, the conjugate prior for this case is a Normal-inverse-Wishart distribution [12, 15, 20]. As a proper choice of sampling method for inference from the PYP, we use the Gibbs sampler algorithm for both training and inference [16, 22].

3.2 A Modified Hidden Markov Model

The PYP models the emissions of the hidden Markov models where the component labels are used as alphabet. The PYP likelihood for observing data points not belonging to any of the non-empty components allows for extending the observations into an infinite set of empty components. Let's call this set collectively the complement partition (see Fig. 1). The HMM is thus needed to be modified to accommodate observations from the complement partition. Since there has been no instance of such observations in the clustering process (training) of the PYP mixture model and training of the HMMs, the complement partition is added to each HMM's table of emissions as an extra codevector with a very small probability partially subtracted from other observations (this makes sure that the emission matrix remains stochastic). Assume B_w is the matrix of emissions for the HMM of word w. The probability of an observation from the complement partition is then given by:

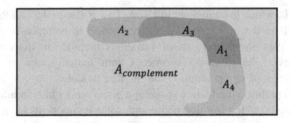

Fig. 1. The partitioned feature space according to the PYP of Eq. 3 with a non-Gaussian base distribution. A1 to A4 are the non-empty components. $A_{complement}$ represents all the empty components.

$$b_{s,w}(o_{K_w+1}) = |K_w| \cdot \varepsilon$$
$$\hat{b}_{s,w}(o_k) = b_{s,w}(o_k) - \varepsilon; \quad k = 1, \ldots, K_w; \quad 0 < \varepsilon \ll 1; \quad \varepsilon \ll \min(B_w) \tag{4}$$

where $\hat{b}_{s,w}(o_k)$ is the adjusted emission probability of observation o_k at state s for the word w; o_{K_w+1} represents observations from the complement partition, and $|K_w|$ denotes the number of occupied partitions in the mixture model for the word w. ε is set to be a very small value (e.g. $\varepsilon = 10^{-16}$). The role of the extra observation is to significantly lower the likelihood for a sequence when there are undesirable deformations. A data point from the complement partition lowers the likelihood of the HMM dramatically. A sequence, therefore, needs to be mainly within the borders of the components of a trained mixture in order for the likelihood to be large. The likelihoods of the HMMs, therefore, is a major factor in accepting/rejecting a sequence.

For training the HMMs, we use the forward-backward algorithm using the component labels as the alphabet [1, 2]. Then the emission matrices of the HMMs are modified to accommodate the extra observation. For evaluation, the Viterbi algorithm is employed. Figure 2 shows a graphical representation of the proposed HMM with PYP emissions.

3.3   Controlling the Border of Emission Densities

Due to the spatial nature of data in a multidimensional feature space, a spatial model is needed to model the discount parameter of the PYP i.e. d. We choose the variance of the training set at all locations in the feature space as a hint for adjusting d. Let's consider the conditional distribution of a multidimensional Gaussian variable given a set of Gaussian variables with the same dimensionality [2].

If x^* is a d-dimensional variable and X represents a set of Gaussian variables, the covariance of the conditional distribution $p(x^*|X)$ is given by:

$$\Sigma_{x^*|X} = \Sigma_{x^*x^*} - \Sigma_{x^*X}^T \Sigma_{XX}^{-1} \Sigma_{x^*X} \tag{5}$$

To avoid the computational burden of a high-dimensional data regression, we can allow the mean and covariance of the data to be modelled by functions sampled from

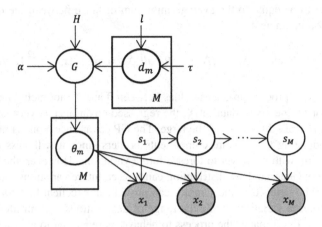

Fig. 2. The graphical representation of the HMM with nonparametric emissions. Note that only emissions are controlled by PYP and not the state changes.

some prior distributions [18]; which is a Gaussian process (GP) [17, 21]. Considering the data to be stationary is reasonable since the shape of patterns are independent of location of observations in the feature space. Therefore, a stationary covariance function such as the squared exponential is suitable:

$$k(x, x^*) = \tau^2 e^{-\frac{|x-x^*|^2}{l^2}} \qquad (6)$$

where τ denotes the magnitude and l is the smoothness of the function. We are interested in the spatial distribution of the data in the space; therefore, we only consider the covariance of the Gaussian process for a given data point:

$$cov(x^*|X) = K(x^*, x^*) - K(x^*, X)^T (K(X, X) + \sigma^2 I)^{-1} K(x^*, X) \qquad (7)$$

The covariance of GP is independent of the outputs and can model the distribution of training data in the feature space. There are two hyper-parameters in the covariance function of Eq. 6 that need to be set in order for the regression to be useful for the Pitman-Yor process. Since we have no output for the data points, we cannot proceed with maximizing the marginal likelihood of the outputs given X and the hyper-parameters. Therefore, we need to use some heuristics. To abide with the constraint $0 \leq d < 1$ for d in Eq. 3, the magnitude τ of the covariance function is accordingly set to a value smaller than but close to 1 (e.g. $\tau = 0.99$). On the other hand, the smoothness parameter l (also called length-scale) need to be set to an appropriate value representing how smoothly the data changes.

Equation 7 can be interpreted as a conditional likelihood of a mixture of basis functions each centered at a data point from the training data set X. The variance of each basis function is then controlled by the length-scale parameter l. In order to set l appropriately so that the mixture of the basis functions do not over fit or under fit the data, we set it to be equal to the average minimum distance between the observations multiplied by a coefficient:

$$l = \eta \, \bar{\Delta}; \quad \bar{\Delta} = \text{mean}(\Delta_1, \ldots, \Delta_N), \quad \textit{for all } \Delta_n = \min\left(|x_i - x_j|^2\right), \ \forall i \neq j \qquad (8)$$

The regression process produces values between 0 and 1 (not including 1). For the points close or on the given data set X, the regressed covariance is very small and for the points away from the set, it will be large. The GP covariance alone is not a suitable method for adjusting the mixture components borders since it will miss areas unobserved in training with no power to foresee future variations. However, the Pitman-Yor process with the Gaussian base distribution can foresee future variations. Setting PYP's d to be the GP covariance of the samples can provide an excellent hint for the PYP to include and foresee variations while the range of distributions is controlled. We recall that a small d in Eq. 3 makes the process to behave more similar to a Dirichlet process with higher probability that a given point is assigned to an already occupied component. A large d causes the process to allow for a new component to be initiated if the point is far away and, therefore, unlikely to have been generated by an occupied component. The GP covariance at a given point x^* is, therefore, used as d i.e. $d = \lambda \, cov(x^*|X)$ for the Pitman-Yor process in order to allow the process to initiate a new component sampled from the base distribution $h(\theta)$ if x^* is far away, or assign one of the trained components if x^* is close to the emission mixture. Figure 3(b, c, d) show the result of applying the PYP to the feature space given the space is modeled by a Pitman-Yor mixture model for the training set presented in Fig. 3(a). In Fig. 3(b), d is set to zero meaning the process is equal to a DPM. In Fig. 3(c), d is set to the GP covariance with length scale $l = 0.0244$ and $\lambda = 1$. The range of the occupied distributions is more limited in this case. In Fig. 3(d), d is multiplied with a coefficient $\lambda > 1$. It should be noted that for prediction purposes only, we set d to the GP covariance multiplied with $\lambda > 1$. Since at this stage, PYP is used for inference only, it is safe to multiply the GP covariance by a coefficient larger than 1 as long as the result d remains smaller than the minimum of number of training data points in all the components.

A necessary step in verifying the completeness of a recognized pattern in a given sequence of data points is to make sure all the trained areas of a pattern are met properly by a given sequence. This requires most of the populous partitions (components) in the trained mixture model to be met throughout the given sequence. Non-populous clusters are of less interest as they probably were not present in all the training samples or they just represent non-significant variations in the training set.

4   Performance Evaluation

The presented algorithm is a method for accepting/rejecting variations. It has the tendency of rejecting unacceptable patterns. High resolution hand-drawn letter recognition is an application for this algorithm (as shown in Fig. 3).

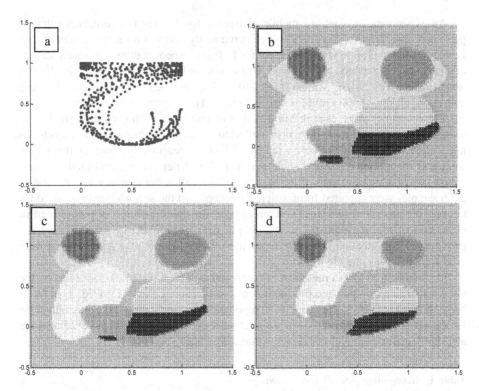

Fig. 3. Classification of space according to the PYP with d set to the GP covariance for the trajectories shown in (a). The classified space with (b) $d = 0$, (c) d set to the GP covariance with length-scale $l = 0.0244$, (d) the space according to PYP with d multiplied with a coefficient larger than 1.

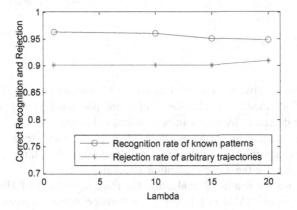

Fig. 4. Recognition rate and true rejection rate of the algorithm vs. coefficient λ. As λ increases the range of clusters decreases meaning more data points are rejected.

An experiment on Android mobile platforms' touch screen hand-drawn letters is presented here. In this experiment, we gathered many samples for seven letters of c, e, L, m, s, v, and z all in lower case except for L, from 70 people drawn on touch screens of each person's personal smart phone. Due to size and model variations of the devices (touch screen resolutions varied from 640×480 to 1920×1080) used for data collection, all the samples were normalized to [0-1].

These samples were captured in a period of one week with each user submitting samples on different days. We also collected a set of arbitrary touch trajectories intended to be none of the seven letters, although occasionally some of them look similar to more simple patterns such as c or L. The latter set was collected for evaluating the false positive rate of the algorithm. We call it the arbitrary set. A total of 2156 samples were captured from which 700 samples of the seven letters were used for training the algorithm. The users' samples used for training were not participated in evaluation of the algorithm. Also the people who participated in training were not participated in evaluation. The rest of samples (1456 including the arbitrary set) were used for evaluating the algorithm.

In classification phase, the range of components in each pattern is controlled by the GP covariance regression and the coefficient λ in addition to the PYP of Eq. 3. In fact λ has a dramatic effect on the range of components. By calculating the GP length-scale for the given data to be about 0.03, we calculated the GP covariance and evaluated the algorithm against different coefficient values. We chose values of 1, 10, 15, and 20 for

Table 1. Recognition rate of hand-drawn letters and rejection rate of arbitrary trajectories

	HMM-GB	HMM-MD	HMM-NPIE
c	0.964	0.958	0.982
e	0.976	0.947	0.990
L	0.923	0.913	0.976
m	0.936	0.931	0.972
s	0.834	0.902	0.927
v	0.890	0.794	0.978
z	0.923	0.913	0.923
arbitrary	0.773	0.886	0.902

Table 2. Performances of the three algorithms

	HMM-GB	HMM-MD	HMM-NPIE
Recognition	0.9222	0.9131	0.9638
Precision	0.9683	0.9734	0.9667
Recall	0.9087	0.9107	0.9581
F1 Score	0.9375	0.9410	0.9624

λ causing ds to be always smaller than the minimum number of members in all components of all models. Evaluation results are presented in Fig. 4. The correct recognition rate decreases by increasing coefficient λ. However, at $\lambda = 20$, the rejection rate of arbitrary sequences shows an increase as is expected. In order to do more evaluation of the algorithm, we compare it with two other algorithms presented in the literature [8, 23] given the same evaluation set, and $\lambda = 1$.

Table 1 shows the results of evaluating the three algorithms of HMM-NPIE presented in this paper, HMM-GB based on a garbage model presented in [8], and HMM-MD based on a state-median model presented in [23]. HMM-GB creates a garbage model using a set of garbage sequences, a set of sequences that are not similar to any pattern in a vocabulary. It then compares the HMM likelihoods of all the models,

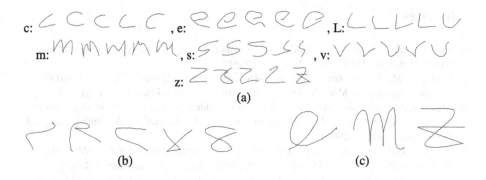

(a)

(b)   (c)

Fig. 5. (a) Samples from the evaluation set showing variations in the captured hand-drawn letters. (b) some samples from the arbitrary set, (c) some of the samples rejected by the algorithm

including the garbage model, for a given sequence and selects the highest likelihood. A sequence for which the garbage model produces the highest likelihood is therefore rejected. HMM-MD creates vectors of medians of state observations in HMMs. For a given sequence, it compares the median of observations in each state with the minimum of the medians of observations in the same state for the training set. Those who are equal or greater than the trained minimums are accepted, and based on the number of accepted states a sequence is accepted or rejected. From Table 1, the HMM-NPIE algorithm shows superior performance both in recognizing the hand-drawn letters and rejecting the trajectories in the arbitrary set. The standard Precision, Recall, and F1 score for the three algorithms are presented in Table 2. The algorithm presented in this paper (HMM-NPIE) has higher recognition, recall, and F1 rates. However, the two other algorithms present a slightly better precision rate. We observed a slightly higher misclassification rate for our algorithm compared to the other two.

A few samples of the captured set of hand-drawn letters and the arbitrary trajectories are presented in Fig. 5(a) and (b). In Fig. 5(c), a few samples which were rejected by the algorithm are presented. The orientation of letter e and extra line drawn in the middle of letter z do not match the boundaries of our models trained with simple drawings of these letters and, therefore, the algorithm has rejected them. For letter m, the extended trajectory at the beginning and end of this sample are beyond the boundaries of the correct trained partitions and, therefore, caused the extra observation we added to the HMM's emission matrix to be experienced many times compared to the HMM of letter m; and therefore the HMM likelihood became very small for this sample and the sample got rejected.

References

1. Rabiner, L.R.: A tutorial on hidden Markov models and selected applications in speech recognition. Proc. IEEE **77**(2), 257–286 (1989)
2. Bishop, C.M.: Pattern Recognition and Machine Learning. Springer, New York (2006)
3. Jelinek, F.: Statistical Methods for Speech Recognition. MIT Press, Cambridge (1997)
4. Shamaie, A., Sutherland, A.: Bayesian fusion of hidden Markov models for understanding bimanual movements. In: Proceedings of 6th IEEE Conference on Automatic Face and Gesture Recognition (2004)
5. Gauvain, J., Lee, C.: Bayesian learning of Gaussian mixture densities for hidden Markov models. In: Proceedings of DARPA Speech Natural Language Workshop, February 1991
6. Ellis, D., Sommerlade, E., Reid, I.: Modelling pedestrian trajectory patterns with Gaussian processes. In: IEEE 12th International Conference on Computer Vision (2009)
7. Kim, K., Lee, D., Essa, I.: Gaussian process regression flow for analysis of motion trajectories. In: Proceedings of IEEE International Conference on Computer Vision (2011)
8. Wilpon, J.G., Rabiner, L.R., Lee, C., Goldman, E.R.: Automatic recognition of keywords in unconstrained speech using hidden Markov models. IEEE Trans. Acoust. Speech Signal Process. **38**(11), 1870–1878 (1990)
9. Teh, Y.W., Jordan, M., Beal, M., Blei, D.: Hierarchical Dirichlet process, J. Am. Stat. Assoc. **101**(47) (2006)
10. Teh, Y.W.: Bayesian Nonparametrics: Dirichlet Process. Machine Learning Summer School Tutorials, Cambridge (2009)
11. Fox, E., Sudderth, E., Jordan, M., Willsky, A.: An HDP-HMM for systems with state-persistence. In: International Conference on Machine Learning, July 2008
12. Sudderth, E.: Graphical Models for Visual Object Recognition and Tracking. Ph.D. Dissertation, Massachusetts Institute of Technology, May 2006
13. Pitman, J., Yor, M.: The two parameter Poisson-Dirichlet distribution derived from a stable subordinator. Ann. Probab. **25**(2), 855–900 (1997)
14. Ishwaran, H., James, L.F.: Gibbs sampling methods for stick-breaking priors. J. Am. Stat. Assoc. **96**(453), 161–173 (2001)
15. Sawyer, S.: Wishart Distributions and Inverse-Wishart Sampling. Washington University, St. Louis (2007)
16. Neal, R.M.: Markov chain sampling methods for Dirichlet process mixture models. J. Comput. Graph. Stat. **9**(2), 249–265 (2000)
17. Rasmussen, C.E., Williams, C.: Gaussian Processes for Machine Learning. MIT Press, Cambridge (2006)
18. Gelman, A., Carlin, J.B., Stern, H.S., Dunson, D.B., Vehtari, A., Rubin, D.B.: Bayesian Data Analysis, 3rd edn. CRC Press, London (2014)
19. Rasmussen, C.E.: The infinite Gaussian mixture model. In: Advances in Neural Information Processing Systems (2000)
20. Görür, D., Rasmussen, C.E.: Dirichlet process Gaussian mixture models: choice of the base distribution. J. Comput. Sci. Technol. **25**(2), 653–664 (2010)
21. Fox, E., Dunson, D.: Bayesian Nonparametric Covariance Regression. Duke University, Durham (2011)
22. Sudderth, E., Jordan, M.I.: Shared segmentation of natural scenes using dependent Pitman-Yor processes, In: NIPS (2008)
23. Shamaie, A.: Rejecting Out-of-Vocabulary Words, U.S. Patent No. 8,565,535, October 2013
24. Johnson, M., Willsky, A.: Bayesian nonparametric hidden semi-Markov models. J. Mach. Learn. Res. **14**, 673–701 (2013)

25. Bargi, A., Xu, R., Piccardi, M.: An online HDP-HMM for joint action segmentation and classification in motion capture data. In: CVPR 2012, Providence, June 2012
26. Torbati, A., Picone, J., Sobel, M.: A left-to-right HDP-HMM with HDPM emissions. In: 48th Annual Conference on Information Sciences and Systems, Princeton, March 2014

Classifying Mutants with Decomposition Kernel

Joanna Strug[1] and Barbara Strug[2]([⊠])

[1] Faculty of Electrical and Computer Engineering, Cracow University of Technology,
ul. Warszawska 24, 31-155 Krakow, Poland
pestrug@cyf-kr.edu.pl
[2] Department of Physics, Astronomy and Applied Computer Science,
Jagiellonian University, Lojasiewicza 11, 30-059 Krakow, Poland
barbara.strug@uj.edu.pl

Abstract. The paper deals with the problem of reducing the cost of mutation testing using artificial intelligence methods. The presented approach is based on the similarity of mutants. The mutants are coded as control flow diagrams representing the programs structure, variables and conditions. The similarity is then calculated with the use of a new graph kernel and used to predict if a given test case detects a mutant or not. The prediction process is performed by a classification algorithm. Experimental results are also presented in this paper on the basis of two systems.

Keywords: Mutation testing · Machine learning · Graph distance · Classification · Test evaluation

1 Introduction

Testing plays a vital role in developing high quality software systems. Testing aims at detecting faults in a system. It involves the execution of the system by providing it with specific inputs and comparing the outputs produced by the system in response to the inputs with expected outputs. The input, expected output and conditions that should hold for a given input are called a test case [25,28]. Selection of an adequate suite of such test cases, being able to detect faults with a high accuracy, is one of the most important activities concerning testing, as the testing results are used for establishing the degree to which a system being developed satisfies certain requirements. This in turn is one of the most important criterion for assessing the system quality and to deciding if it is ready for release.

Thus, adequate assessment and measurement of the quality of a suite of test cases is essential in order to gain confidence in testing results. Over the years a number of different approaches for evaluating test suites were proposed [25,28]. Mutation testing [10] is considered to be the most effective of them [4,18]. The main idea behind the approach is to generate a number of so called mutants by replicating the original system, introducing into each copy one syntactic modification and then executing the mutants with test cases from the suite being assessed. The quality of the suite is determined basing on the value of so called

L. Rutkowski et al. (Eds.): ICAISC 2016, Part I, LNAI 9692, pp. 644–654, 2016.
DOI: 10.1007/978-3-319-39378-0_55

mutation score that is calculated as a ratio of the number of mutants killed (detected) by test cases belonging to the suite over the number of all generated, non-equivalent [18] mutants. The higher the value of mutation score is the higher is the quality of the suite. The mutants are generated using so called mutation operators that define how to modify particular items of the system. Use of such operators ensures that mutants are generated in a systematic and human unbiased way. Although the modification making mutants usually do not reflect real faults, it was shown by several studies that a mutation score calculated for a given suite of test cases is an accurate measurement of the suite ability to detect the real faults (detailed references can be found in [18]).

Mutation testing is a powerful technique supporting various testing activities at different stages of developing systems [1,8,22,27,32,33]. However it is also time consuming due to the necessity to generate and execute a large number of mutants [18]. Intensive research on reducing the costs of applying mutation testing has provided a number of various approaches. Offut and Untch [26] classified the approaches accordingly to strategy they follow into three groups: do fewer, do faster, do smarter. The "do fewer" approaches aim at decreasing the number of mutants to be generated (e.g. selective mutation [23]) or executed (e.g. mutant sampling [2], mutant clustering [7,16]), the "do faster" approaches try to generate and run mutants as fast as possible (e.g. mutant schemata [36]) and the "do smarter" ones usually take advantage of the environment (e.g. parallel computation [24]) or internal information (e.g. week mutation [15]). A survey of the costs reduction approaches can be found in [18]. Nevertheless, the growing size of modern systems requires even more efficient ways of cutting the costs be search for.

The approach to reducing the costs presented in this paper is based on using the similarity between mutants which allows to reduce the number of mutants that have to be executed. The similarity is calculated on the basis of the structure of a mutant. As mutants are programs their structure can be represented as control flow diagrams. Hence each mutant is converted into a specific hierarchical control flow graph, which represents the program's flow, variables and conditions. The calculated similarity is then used within a classification algorithm for predicting if a test would detect a mutant or not. This approach helps to decrease the number of mutants which have to be executed and at the same time helps to assess quality of test suits without the need of running them.

The approach falls into the "do fewer" category, as it aims at reducing the number of mutants to be executed, but it uses the mutants similarity in a given problem instead of basing the assessment only on results obtained for a randomly selected subset of all mutants. It shows some proximity with mutants clustering approaches, such as the ones presented by Hussain [16] or Ji et al. [7] that also attempt to measure similarity between mutants to decide which mutants are likely to be killed by given test cases. Hussain [16] used clustering algorithms to divide all mutants into clusters basing on information gained from execution of mutants to reduce the size of the suite of test cases. Ji et al. [7] proposed to weight the mutants basing on domain analysis. They applied static methods to analyze the domain, hence they were able to avoid the execution of all mutants before their clustering.

The use of graphs to represent different objects is gaining in popularity with growing acceptance in many domains like system modeling and testing, bioinformatics, chemistry and others. In this paper the representation is used to calculate the similarity between mutants. The need to analyze and compare graph data is not new and hence has been a lot of research in this direction and there can be noticed three different, partially overlapping, approaches. The first one uses standard graph algorithms, like finding a maximal subgraph or mining for frequently occurring subgraphs to compare or classify graphs [3,13,17,31,37,38]. The second approach is based on transforming graphs into vectors by finding some descriptive features. Having a graph encoded in a vector a standard statistical learning algorithms can be applied. The main problem is in finding appropriate features/substructures and in enumerating them in each graph. This approach has successfully been applied in many domains like image recognition [6], and especially the recognition of handwritten texts [20,21]. The third method uses the theory of positive defined kernels and kernel methods [29,30]. The research on different kernels for structured data included tree and graph kernels [5,9,11,12,19]. For graph kernels there is a number of different ones proposed so far, for example the all subgraph kernel [11], kernels on computing random walks on graphs, product graph kernel [11] and the marginalized kernels [19]. Such kernels are computable in polynomial time, ($O(n^6)$ [12]).

Currently the main research focuses on finding faster algorithms to compute kernels for simple graphs, mainly for use in bioinformatics. To author's best knowledge, there is no research in the area of defining and testing kernels for different types of graphs, such as hierarchical control flow graphs proposed in this paper.

2   Graph Representation of Programs

In order to be able to classify programs in mutation testing some way of representing the structure of the code has to be decided upon. Representing such a structure of a program by a diagram is a well known approach. It allows us to show the components of the program and the flow of its execution. Such a diagram is called a control flow diagram (CFD) and can be represented by a simple graph. A simple graph G is defined as a non-empty set of nodes (called also vertices) V and a set of edges E, where $E \subset V^2$. Each node and edge can be labeled by a function ξ assigning labels to nodes and edges.

Such a representation is unfortunately insufficient and cannot be directly used to compare programs, as we need to compare each element of any expression or condition separately and a traditional CFD usually labels its elements by whole expressions. So in this paper a combination of CFD and hierarchical graphs is used. Such an approach adds a hierarchy to the traditional flow diagram enabling us to represent each element of a program in a single node and thus making the graphs more adequate to comparison.

Let for the rest of this paper R_V and R_E be the sets of node and edge labels, respectively. Let ϵ be a special symbol used for unlabelled edges. The set R_V

contains all possible keywords, names of variables, operators, numbers and some additional grouping labels (like for example *declare* or *array* shown in Fig. 1. The set $R_E = \{T, F, \epsilon\}$, where ϵ represents the empty edge label. Then the hierarchical control flow graph is defined formally in the following way:

Definition 1. *A labelled hierarchical control flow graph HCFG is defined as a 5-tuple (V, E, ξ_V, ξ_E, ch) where:*

1. *V is a non-empty set of nodes,*
2. *E is a set of edges, $E \subset V \times V$,*
3. *$\xi_V : V \to R_V$ is a labelling function, which assigns labels to nodes,*
4. *$\xi_E : E \to R_E$ is an edge labelling function,*
5. *$ch : V \to 2^V$ is a function assigning to each node a set of its children, i.e. nodes directly nested in v.*

Let, for the rest of this paper, $ch(v)$ denotes the set of children of v, and $|ch(v)|$ be the size of this set. Let *anc* be a function assigning to each node its ancestor and let λ be a special empty symbol (different from ϵ), $anc : V \to V \cup \{\lambda\}$, such that $anc(v) = w$ if $v \in ch(w)$ and λ otherwise (i.e. anc(v) = λ denotes the fact that node v does not have an ancestor).

An example of such a hierarchical control flow graph (HCFG) is depicted in Fig. 1a and b. It represents a method *Search(...)* and its mutant depicted in Fig. 2a and b, respectively. It can be noticed that the insertion of $++$ into variable v in an *if* statement results in replacing a simple node v by an appropriate expression tree inside node labelled *if*.

3   Graph Classification

A well known approach to use traditional classification algorithms for non-vector data is based on the so called kernel trick, which consists in mapping elements from a given set A into an inner product space S (having a natural norm), without having to compute the mapping, i.e. graphs do not have to be mapped into some objects in space S, only the way of calculation the inner product in that space has to be well defined. Linear classifications in target space are then equivalent to classifications in source space A. Using the trick and avoiding the actual mapping relies on using the learning algorithms needing only inner products between the elements (vectors) in target space. Moreover the mapping has to be defined in such a way that these inner products can be computed on the objects in the source (original) space by means of a kernel function.

For the classifiers a kernel matrix K must be positive semi-definite (PSD), although there are empirical results showing that some kernels not satisfying this requirement may still do reasonably well, if a kernel well approximates the intuitive idea of similarity among given objects. Formally a positive semi-definite kernel on a space X is a symmetric function $K : X^2 \to \mathbf{R}$, which satisfies $\sum_{i,j=1}^{n} a_i a_j K(x_i, x_j) \geq 0$, for any points $x_1, \ldots, x_n \in X$ and coefficients $a_1, \ldots, a_n \in \mathbf{R}$.

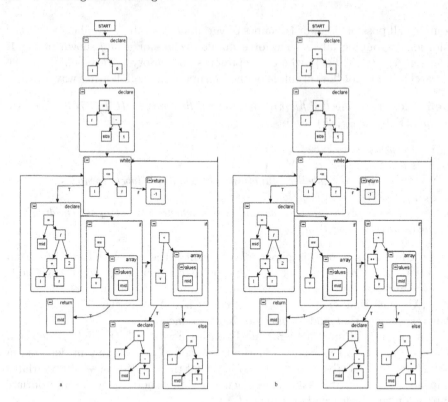

Fig. 1. Examples of flow graphs (a) a graph for program from Fig. 2a, (b) a flow graph for one of AOIS mutants (from Fig. 2b)

The approach that has been successfully used for many types of data is based on convolution kernels [14], which are a general method for structured data (and thus very useful for graphs). Convolution kernels are based on the assumption that structured object can be decomposed into components, then kernels are defined for those components and the final kernel is calculated over all possible decompositions.

To incorporate the information represented in the hierarchical form of the control flow diagram a hierarchical substructure kernel K_H is proposed in this paper. This kernel takes into account the label of a given node, number of its children (hence incorporating the internal complexity), the label of its hierarchical ancestor (and thus its position within the structure of the program), and the number and labels of edges connecting this node with its neighbourhood nodes (both incoming and outgoing edges are taken into account) as well as the labels of the neighbouring nodes. Such a kernel uses two different node kernels, an edge and a tree kernels as base kernels. The node and edge kernels are defined below. The tree kernel, used within the node one to compare expression trees, is a standard one [9].

Definition 2. *A binary node kernel, denoted $k_n(v, w)$, where v, and w are nodes of a hierarchical control flow graph, is defined in the following way:*

$$k_n(v, w) = \begin{cases} 1 : \xi_V(v) = \xi_V(w) \\ 0 : \xi_V(v) \neq \xi_V(w). \end{cases}$$

Definition 3. *A node kernel, denoted $k_v(v, w)$, where v, and w are nodes of a hierarchical control flow graph, is defined in the following way:*

$$k_v(v, w) = \begin{cases} 0 & : \xi_V(v) \neq \xi_V(w) \\ k_n(ch(v), ch(w)) : \xi_V(v) = \xi_V(w) \wedge |ch(v)| = |ch(w)| = 1 \\ k_t(ch(v), ch(w)) : \xi_V(v) = \xi_V(w) \wedge (|ch(v)| > 1 \vee |ch(w)| > 1) \end{cases}$$

It can be observed that for the nodes which have more than one child, i.e. containing an expression tree, a tree kernel K_t is used to compute the actual similarity. For nodes having different labels the kernel returns 0, while for nodes containing one children the binary node kernel is computed on the labels of the child nodes.

Definition 4. *An edge kernel, denoted $k_e(e, f)$, where e, and f are edges of a hierarchical flow graph, is defined in the following way:*

$$k_e(e, f) = \begin{cases} 1 : \xi_E(e) = \xi_E(f) \\ 0 : \xi_V(e) \neq \xi_V(f). \end{cases}$$

On the basis of the above base kernel a hierarchical kernel for HCFG is defined. Let G_i, G_j be two hierarchical control flow diagrams. Moreover let S_i be a substructure of G_i consisting of a node v_i, its direct ancestor $anc(v_i)$, all its children $ch(v_i)$ and its neighbourhood $Nb(v_i)$. Let C_n is the number of children of a given node and $c_n(v_i)$ - the $n - th$ child of v_i.

Definition 5.

$$K_H(G_i, G_j) = \sum_{i=1}^{m} \sum_{j=1}^{n} K_S(S_i, S_j), \tag{1}$$

where m and n, is the number of hierarchical nodes in each graph and

$$K_S(S_i, S_j) = k_n(v_i, v_j) + k_n(anc(v_i), anc(v_j)) + \sum_{r=1}^{C_n} \sum_{t=1}^{C_m} k_n(c_r(v_i), c_t(v_j))$$

$$+ \sum_{w_i \in Nb(v_i)} \sum_{w_j \in Nb(v_j)} k_e((v_i, w_i), (v_j, w_j)) k_n(w_i, w_j), \tag{2}$$

This kernel is based on the decomposition of a graph into substructures according to the concept of $R - convolution$ kernels [14], and so acceptable as a kernel function [29].

It has to be noted that graph kernels are known to have a high computational cost, but in case of HCFG we have some additional knowledge i.e. as each graph represents a first order mutant, two graphs can differ in at most two places and we also know a priori the places where the change happened. Apart from these two places all other elements of both graphs are identical. Hence the actual computation of HCFG kernel can be done much more efficiently than in general case of two random graphs.

4   Experimental Results

The experiment were carried out for two different programs and mutants for them were generated using Mujava tool [22]. One of the examples was a simple search, for which Mujava generated 38 mutants. The second one was binary search, presented in Fig. 2a. For the example there were 87 mutants. The mutants were then converted into graph form described above and depicted in Fig. 1a and b.

```
public int search(int v){          public int search(int v){
  int l=0;                           int l=0;
  int r=size-1;                      int r=size-1;
  while(l<=r){                       while(l<=r){
    int mid = (l+r)/2;                 int mid = (l+r)/2;
    if(v == values[mid]) return mid;   if(v == values[mid]) return mid;
    if(v  < values[mid]) r = mid-1;    if(++v  < values[mid]) r = mid-1;
    else l=mid+1;                      else l=mid+1;
  }                                  }
  return -1;                         return -1;
}                                  }
            a                                   b
```

Fig. 2. (a) A binary search method, and (b) one of its AOIS (Arithmetic Operator Insertion [22]) mutants

For each set of mutants a k-NN classification algorithm (k was set to 5 after a number of experiments) was run using two different distance measures. The first one was based on standard graph edit distance (GED, used in [34,35]), while the second was obtained from the K_H kernel introduced in this paper. In each case the set of mutants was randomly divided into three sets of roughly equal size: a training set and two control sets.

For the first example three test suites were used and for the second one - five test suites. Tables 1 and 2 present the results obtained for the respective examples. The results for mutants classified incorrectly are presented separately for those classified as detectable, while actually they are not (column labelled "incorrect killed") and for those classified as not detected, while they actually are detected by a given test suite (column labelled "incorrect not killed"). This distinction results from the fact that the meaning of these misclassifications in context of testing is different. Classifying a mutant as not detected leads to overtesting, while the misclassification of the second type can result in missing real errors in code and thus is more dangerous as it may lead to undetected errors in code.

Table 1. The classification of mutants for the example 1 with the use of GED and K_H

	Method	Correct	Incorrect killed	Incorrect not killed
		(True positive/negative)	(False positive)	(False negative)
TS 1	GED	65.2 %	13.06 %	21.74 %
TS 1	K_H	70.2 %	11.10 %	20.70 %
TS 2	GED	78.25 %	8.7 %	13.5 %
TS 2	K_H	83.35 %	9.4 %	7.25 %
TS 3	GED	82.6 %	8.7 %	8.7 %
TS 3	K_H	83.8 %	7.7 %	8.5 %

Table 2. The classification of mutants for the example 2 with the use of GED and K_H

	Method	Correct	Incorrect killed	Incorrect not killed
		(True positive/negative)	(False positive)	(False negative)
TS 1	GED	75.7 %	12.1 %	12.2 %
TS 1	K_H	76.8 %	11.3 %	11.9 %
TS 2	GED	73.4 %	6.5 %	20.1 %
TS 2	K_H	86.5 %	5.9 %	7.9 %
TS 3	GED	60.5 %	26.2 %	16.3 %
TS 3	K_H	72.4 %	10.7 %	16.9 %
TS 4	GED	78.2 %	10.3 %	11.5 %
TS 4	K_H	88.4 %	6.4 %	6.2 %
TS 5	GED	76.4 %	11.3 %	12.3 %
TS 5	K_H	84.9 %	5.4 %	11.7 %

The results depicted in tables show that the classification worked well for all test suits. Especially it can be noticed that using GED for TS1 in the first example and for TS3 in the second one performs significantly worse then the graph kernel introduced in this paper. The analysis of this case seems to suggest that it results from the random partition of the set of mutants in which the training set contained unproportionally large number of undetectable mutants. It can also be noticed that results obtained with the use of K_H kernel are slightly better in general, especially the classification for the two tests with the worse results with the use of GED improved significantly, although it may be due to better choice of training sets. It can be also noticed that, in nearly all cases the number of the mutants misclassified to the "incorrect not killed" class is lower thus resulting in better program testing.

It has to be also mentioned that the classification performed for a given program and test suite can be used to evaluate the quality of the test suite itself thus allowing for the improvement of test suites.

5 Conclusions

The paper deals with a dynamic approach to the reduction of costs of mutation testing. A classification approach was proposed in this paper allowing to reduce the number of mutants to be executed. A novelty of this approach consists in the fact that the number of mutants to be executed depends on the program for which they are generated rather than on using some statical method based on the operators or programming language. The approach needs still more experiments to fully confirm its validity, but the results obtained so far are encouraging.

The further research is planned to be focused on two main areas. As mentioned in the description of the results some classification problems result from the way the set of mutants is partitioned into training set and control sets. It seems that performing the partition of mutants in a smarter way instead of random could lead to some improvements. The first idea of how to deal with it could be based on selecting proportional number of mutants of each type (generated by a given type of mutation operators) but this idea needs further development.

The second issue we plan to follow is to do further research related to kernels. On one side we plan to investigate if replacing the $k - NN$ algorithm by more sophisticated methods like for example support vector machines, could lead to better results. On the other hand also new kernels could be developed for the structured data used to represent programs. The node kernel proposed in this paper is based on the label of the node and its direct ancestor but does not take into account higher level ancestors so including this type of information about the node is also planned to be analyzed.

References

1. Aichernig, B.K., Auer, J., Jöbstl, E., Korošec, R., Krenn, W., Schlick, R., Schmidt, B.V.: Model-based mutation testing of an industrial measurement device. In: Seidl, M., Tillmann, N. (eds.) TAP 2014. LNCS, vol. 8570, pp. 1–19. Springer, Heidelberg (2014)
2. Acree, A.T.: On mutation, PhD Thesis, Georgia Institute of Technology, Atlanta, Georgia (1980)
3. Agrawal, R., Imielinski, T., Swami, A.: Mining association rules between sets of items in large databases. In: Proceedings of SIGMOD 1993, pp. 207–216 (1993)
4. Andrews, J.H., Briand, L.C., Labiche, Y.: Is mutation an appropriate tool for testing experiments? In: Proceedings of ICSE, pp. 402–411 (2005)
5. Borgwardt, K.M., Kriegel, H.P.: Shortest-path kernels on graphs. In: Proceedings of ICDM 2005, pp. 74–81 (2005)
6. Bunke, H., Riesen, K.: Recent advances in graph-based pattern recognition with applications in document analysis. Pattern Recognit. 44(5), 1057–1067 (2011)
7. Ji, C., Chen, Z., Xu, B., Zhao, Z.: A novel method of mutation clustering based on domain analysis. In: Proceedings of the 21st International Conference on Software Engineering and Knowledge Engineering (2009)
8. Chevalley, P., Thévenod-Fosse, P.: A mutation analysis tool for Java programs. Int. J. Softw. Tools Technol. Transf. 5(1), 90–103 (2002)

9. Collins, M., Duffy, N.: New ranking algorithms for parsing and tagging, kernels over discrete structures, and the voted perceptron. In: Proceedings of ACL 2002 (2002)
10. DeMillo, R.A., Lipton, R.J., Sayward, F.G.: Hints on test data selection: help for the practicing programmer. Computer **11**(4), 34–41 (1978)
11. Gartner, T.: A survey of kernels for structured data. SIGKDD Explor. **5**(1), 49–58 (2003)
12. Gartner, T.: Kernels for Structured Data. Machine Perception and Artificial Intelligence, vol. 72. World Scientific, London (2009)
13. Han, J., Pei, J., Yin, Y., Mao, R.: Mining frequent patterns without candidate generation: a frequent-pattern tree approach. Data Min. Knowl. Discov. Int. J. **8**(1), 53–87 (2004)
14. Haussler, D.: Convolutional kernels on discrete structures, Technical report UCSC-CRL-99-10. Computer Science Department, UC Santa Cruz (1999)
15. Howden, W.E.: Weak mutation testing and completeness of test sets. IEEE Trans. Softw. Eng. **8**, 371–379 (1982)
16. Hussain, S.: Mutation clustering, Masters thesis, Kings College London, Strand, London (2008)
17. Inokuchi, A., Washio, T., Motoda, H.: An apriori-based algorithm for mining frequent substructures from graph data. In: Zighed, D.A., Komorowski, J., Żytkow, J.M. (eds.) PKDD 2000. LNCS (LNAI), vol. 1910, pp. 13–23. Springer, Heidelberg (2000)
18. Jia, Y., Harman, M.: An analysis and survey of the development of mutation testing. IEEE Trans. Softw. Eng. **37**(5), 649–678 (2011)
19. Kashima, H., Tsuda, K., Inokuchi, A.: Marginalized kernels between labeled graphs. In: ICML 2003, pp. 321–328 (2003)
20. Liwicki, M., Bunke, H., Pittman, J.A., Knerr, S.: Combining diverse systems for handwritten text line recognition. Mach. Vis. Appl. **22**(1), 39–51 (2011)
21. Liwicki, M., Schlapbach, A., Bunke, H.: Automatic gender detection using on-line and off-line information. Pattern Anal. Appl. **14**(1), 87–92 (2011)
22. Ma, Y., Offutt, J., Kwon, Y.R.: MuJava: a mutation system for Java. In: Proceedings of ICSE 2006, pp. 827–830 (2006)
23. Mathur, A.P.: Performance, effectiveness, and reliability issues in software testing. In: Proceedings of COMPSAC 1991, pp. 604–605 (1991)
24. Mathur, A.P., Krauser, E.W.: Mutant unification for improved vectorization, Purdue University, West Lafayette, IN, Technique report SERC-TR-14-P (1988)
25. Myers, G., Sandler, C., Badgett, T.: The Art of Software Testing. Wiley, Hoboken (2011)
26. Offutt, J., Untch, R.H.: Mutation 2000: uniting the orthogonal. In: Proceedings of Mutation Testing in the Twentieth and the Twenty First Centuries, pp 45–55 (2000)
27. Radu, V.: Application. In: Radu, V. (ed.) Stochastic Modeling of Thermal Fatigue Crack Growth. ACM, vol. 1, pp. 63–70. Springer, Heidelberg (2015)
28. Roman, A.: Testing and software quality. In: PWN (2015) (in Polish)
29. Schlkopf, B.: A Short Introduction to Learning with Kernels. LNAI, vol. 2600, pp. 41–64. Springer, Heidelberg (2003)
30. Schlkopf, B., Smola, A.J.: Learning with Kernels. MIT Press, Cambridge (2002)
31. Strug, B., Slusarczyk, G.: Frequent pattern mining in a design supporting system. Key Eng. Mater. **450**, 1–4 (2011)
32. Strug, J.: Classification of mutation operators applied to design models. Key Eng. Mater. **572**, 539–542 (2014)

33. Strug, J.: Mutation testing approach to evaluation of design models. Key Eng. Mater. **572**, 543–546 (2014)
34. Strug, J., Strug, B.: Machine learning approach in mutation testing. In: Nielsen, B., Weise, C. (eds.) ICTSS 2012. LNCS, vol. 7641, pp. 200–214. Springer, Heidelberg (2012)
35. Strug, J., Strug, B.: Using structural similarity to classify tests in mutation testing. Appl. Mech. Mater. **378**, 546–551 (2013)
36. Untch, R.H.: Mutation-based software testing using program schemata. In: Proceedings of the 30th Annual Southeast Regional Conference, pp. 285–291 (1992)
37. Yan, X., Yu, P.S., Han, J.: Substructure similarity search in graph databases. In: Proceedings of International Conference on Management of Data (2005)
38. Yan, X., Yu, P.S., Han, J.: Graph indexing, a frequent structure-based approach. In: Proceedings of International Conference on Management of Data (2004)

On Optimal Wavelet Bases
for Classification of Melanoma Images
Through Ensemble Learning

Grzegorz Surówka[✉] and Maciej Ogorzałek

Faculty of Physics, Astronomy and Applied Computer Science,
Jagiellonian University, 30-151 Kraków, Poland
{grzegorz.surowka,maciej.ogorzalek}@uj.edu.pl

Abstract. This article addresses the medical problem of early detection of the malignant melanoma skin cancer. We present ensemble classification of dermoscopic skin lesion images into two classes: malignant melanoma and dysplastic nevus. The features used for classification are derived from wavelet decomposition coefficients of the image. Our research purpose is to select the best wavelet bases in terms of AUC classification performance of the ensemble. The ensemble learning is optimized by some common quality measures: accuracy, precision, F1-score, FP- rate, specificity, BER and recall. Within the statistics of our machine learning experiments the best model of melanoma uses reverse bi-orthogonal wavelet pair (3.1) and is optimized by FP-rate. This wavelet base performs very well with downscaled image resolutions which matters future small ARM-based devices for computer aided diagnosis of melanoma.

Keywords: Melanoma detection · Wavelets · Ensembling

1 Introduction

1.1 Medical Problem

Pigment cells of the skin (melanocytes) can undergo transformations to benign (melanocytic nevus), atypical (dysplastic nevus) or malignant stages (malignant melanoma) [1]. Medical doctors examine the moles with bare eyes and with help of dermatoscopy (ELM-Epiluminescence Microscopy). The latter is a non-invasive technique that consists in optical enlarging and illumination of the skin by halogen light. The magnified lesion can be displayed on a computer screen or stored for further comparative analysis [2]. The most common are the cheapest, handy dermatoscopes. There are also advanced, dedicated instruments that allow for trans-illumination at an angle of 45° or for a set of wavelengths to penetrate deeper layers of the skin to reveal its spatial structure. Their coverage is however limited.

G. Surówka—This work is supported by the Polish NCBR grant TANGO1/266877/ NCBR/2015.

L. Rutkowski et al. (Eds.): ICAISC 2016, Part I, LNAI 9692, pp. 655–666, 2016.
DOI: 10.1007/978-3-319-39378-0_56

Dermatoscopy images of the same mole recorded and stored on a computer can be compared for how the lesion develops in time or can be transmitted to a clinic/remote specialist for a (tele)consultation [3,4,11].

The most dangerous aspect of cutaneous melanoma is its high mortality rate even in people at an early age. This problem refers to all of the countries but particularly these where melanoma morbidity rate is elevated [5]. Melanoma is a fatal disease due to early metastases. Its prognosis is based on the histologic criterium which is the micrometer measurement of the lesion depth (<0.75 mm, 0.75–1.5 mm, 1.5–4.0 mm and >4.0 mm). Early biopsy of the malignant mole can be a life-saving factor [6] and is the only fully reliable method to identify nevi and melanoma lesions. Unfortunately due to medical (surgical complications, ANS-Atypical Nevus Syndrome) and economic reasons the excision is not always feasible. The key role of the effective treatment is the precise detection of the tumor.

1.2   Computer Aided Melanoma Diagnosis

Stages of pigment cells atypia are recognized by medical doctors with help of the well known descriptive measures: ABCD(E), the 7-Point Checklist, Menzies and other less common [7]. The earliest and still important approaches to the melanoma detection have been based on segmentation techniques of the mole border and inner structures ([9] and references therein). Similar, but synthesis-based approach to the melanoma characteristic structures has been carried out by Hippe and Grzymala-Busse over several years (see [10,11] for references). Although very comprehensive, the segmentation-like approaches seem to suffer from two kinds of problems:

1. Discrimination between benign (dysplastic nevus) and malignant mole (melanoma) at the earliest stages of malignancy is extremely difficult due to the lack of the classic differential structures [8]. The same applies to the clinical descriptive measures which are not sensitive enough even for experienced specialists.
2. Quality/resolution of dermoscopic images may be an extra bias.

For those deficiencies some methods for wavelet based decomposition of the skin lesion images have been proposed [14]. They assume analysis of frequency and scale information of the skin texture for the search of probes of the skin atypia and the melanoma progression. Discrete wavelet transforms are closely related to the theory of digital filtering so the properties of the decomposition filters play an important role in the skin texture characteristics [15,16]. The important factors are [17]:

- decomposition path: recursive decomposition of the low-frequency (averaged) signal (=the pyramidal algorithm) or a selective tree-structured analysis where the consecutive decomposition is applied to the output of any channel (=wavelet packets/trees),
- wavelet base: this choice has a diverse impact on the texture classification,
- wavelet order: decomposition over an optimal finite range of resolutions,

- model constraints: orthogonality (the wavelet transform is energy preserving and non-redundant) versus bi-orthogonality (separate filters for decomposition and synthesis are present, wavelets are more compact and symmetric at the cost of orthogonality),
- sampling of 2D signals: the Mallat algorithm [18].

Pioneering contributions on wavelet based decomposition of melanoma dermatoscopy images belong to Patwardhan et al. [15,16]. This group successfully studied binary classification models for benign nevus and melanoma by decomposing different frequency scales of the skin texture (wavelet packets). This approach corresponds to the observations that the significant sub-bands of the pigmented skin texture belong to the middle frequency range and the standard (recursive) analysis of the low-frequency sub-band only, is less optimal than the wavelet packets (also called selective wavelet trees). Since that time the wavelet-based features have also been successfully studied by other groups [19–27].

1.3 Motivations and Objectives

Beyond the pure scientific interest recently some research groups have been working over handy dermatoscope-like devices with optics and ARM-based processors for computer supported melanoma diagnosis. Such decision supporting devices would help medical doctors in diagnosis of early melanoma. Since the developed algorithms for image recognition and interpretation may demonstrate high complexity and small handheld devices have limited processing power and memory, it is of great importance to use features that preserve high efficiency also in downgraded image resolutions. Our working hypothesis is that wavelet features, as contrasted to segmentation-like methods, can fulfil this requirement.

Melanoma binary classifiers from Patwardhan [15,16] and following contributions [19–21], were using only one wavelet base (Daubechies 3) to build classification models. In this work we study different wavelet bases and analyze how they affect the quality of the classification models. As a framework to test wavelet features we use an ensemble of six different model types. We don't aim at optimization (fine-tuning) of any single model or an ensemble of models beyond the standard machine learning procedure i.e. cross-validation (e.g. through feature selection), but use the ensembling technique as a 'blind' learning environment to find one (a few) optimal wavelet base (bases) in terms of the OOT technique based on the optimization of the well known quality measures: accuracy, precision, recall, specificity, FP-rate, F-score and BER (Balanced Error Rate). This work does not focus or contribute to the methodology of the ensembling, but the standard ensemble technique is used to test how different wavelet bases act (in terms of classification performance) on a collection of different weak learners and to select the best wavelet base.

Melanoma incidence rate may fluctuate over countries, but clinical statistics show an average of about 5 % melanoma images as a fraction of all the dermoscopic images of the melanocytic naevi. This means that the melanoma class is under-represented compared to the benign class. Learning classifiers from such cases would require special rules to properly treat the imbalanced class i.e. to draw equal attention to the minority class [12,13]. In this experiment we build classifiers for almost equal classes (102 malignant melanoma versus 83 dysplastic nevus cases) and we do not take into account the (clinical) class imbalance problem.

Our objectives are:

- to select the best wavelet bases in terms of absolute classification performance
- to analyze how the latter perform in the downgraded image resolutions in terms of absolute classification performance and its variance

In the following sections we show methodology of our machine learning experiments and present and discus the results.

2   Data Analysis

2.1   Signal Processing

The 185 anonymous images of the moles (JPEG pixel resolution: 2272 × 1704, RGB color depth: 24-bit) were collected from patients after separate examinations with Minolta Z5 digital camera with an extra dermatoscopy extension. The resection and hist-pat examination of the moles allowed to assign labels to 102 malignant melanoma and 83 dysplastic nevus cases. In the analysis there were three sets of images: the original set 2272 × 1704 and the two downscaled sets (by averaging neighbor values in 2 × 2 elements) of 1136 × 852 and 568 × 426 pixels respectively. The dermatoscopy images of all three sets were transformed to indexed images with linear, monotonic color maps of double precision numbers to support wavelet transformations. Since each iteration of the wavelet decomposition downscales the input image by a factor of 2 both in rows and columns, to allow for three wavelet iterations the 568 × 426 set was padded with zeros (two rows 427 and 428). To eliminate any bias on the final wavelet base selection no preprocessing tasks to the images were done i.e. no removal of any artefacts (hairs, droplets of immersion fluid, etc.) took place. Our classification setup was coded in Matlab R2015a [28] with Image processing Toolbox, Wavelet toolbox and Entool [29].

Wavelet analysis of signals is well established in theory after works of Gabor, Morlet, Daubechies, Mallat and the others [17,20]. It is also widely used especially for discrete signals in the form of DDWT-Discrete Dyadic Wavelet Transform to analyze the signal structure, signal de-noising and compression capabilities. Images are two-dimensional signals so one iteration of the Mallat filtering algorithm produces 4 sub-images which can be considered as LL, LH, HL and HH filters (L-low-pass, H-high-pass filter) after one-dimensional wavelet transform on the rows and then on the columns. In our analysis we used the wavelet packets so each of the four filters was subject to further wavelet decompositions (not only LL). Altogether in three iterations $1 + 4 + 16 = 21$ different transformation branches were produced. In one branch the following 12 features were calculated: $(e_i, i = 1, 2, 3, 4)$ - energies of the sub-images, $(e_i/e_{max}, i = 1, 2, 3, 4)$ - maximum energy ratios and $(e_i/\Sigma e_k, k \neq i, i = 1, 2, 3, 4)$ - fractional energy ratios [15,16,19]. Energy was defined as a sum of absolute values of the pixels. This procedure was repeated for each wavelet base for the three sets of different image resolutions yielding $21 \times 12 = 252$ attributes in each single set. For the skin pattern analysis we took orthogonal wavelets:

- Haar (wavelet number = 1)
- Daubechies db1-db10 (wavelet numbers = 2 – 11),
- Symlets: sym2-sym8 (wavelet numbers = 12 – 18),
- Coiflets: coifN (wavelet numbers = 19 – 23)

and bi-orthogonal/reverse bi-orthogonal wavelets:

- BiorNr.Nd (wavelet numbers = 24 – 38),
- RbioNr.Nd (wavelet numbers = 39 – 53).

(Reverse) Bi-orthogonal wavelets (wavelet pairs) have the property of perfect reconstruction i.e. X = A+D, where: X-image, A-reconstructed image of approximation and D-reconstructed image of details. This property is possible due to two separate filter sets, one for decomposition and another one for image reconstruction. Those wavelets are not orthogonal. Orthogonal wavelets, on the other hand, fulfil the formula $X^2 = A^2 + D^2$. Symlets, coiflets and (reverse) bi-orthogonal wavelets are symmetric functions, whereas Daubechies - asymmetric [17].

The wavelet features mentioned above were used in the classification procedure by ensembling.

2.2 Machine Learning

Ensembling is a machine learning paradigm to combine predictions of separate classification models by voting or weighted averaging [30]. The generalization error of the ensemble can be decomposed into an average error of the individual models and average ambiguity of the ensemble. The ensemble generalization error is always smaller than the mean of the generalization error of the single ensemble members, which makes this technique a good tool to maximize the classification performance. In order to increase the ensemble ambiguity it should consist of well trained but diverse models (no assumptions are made about the constituent models). To build an ensemble of models starting from an empty ensemble we were selecting step-by-step the best models by a cross-validation scheme for model training (the OOT-Out-of-Train procedure) [31]. The cross-validation was done in several training rounds on different training sets, because this increases the ambiguity of the ensemble and leads to better generalization. The advantages of such approach are as follows:

- Training on slightly different data sets leads to different models so this helps introduce diversity of models,
- An unbiased estimator of the ensemble generalization error can be estimated out of hand.

Our ensembling procedure consisted of the following steps:

1. Data are divided into (A) a training/testing set (80 %) and (B) a validation set (20 %); there are five cross-validation partitions, the final quality of the trained ensemble by means of AUC is calculated as the mean of the five samples.
2. The training/testing data (A) are divided into (A1) a training set (90 %) and (A2) a testing set (10 %) - there are ten cross-validation partitions.
3. Several models are trained on the training set (A1).
4. These models are compared by evaluating the prediction errors on the testing set (A2).
5. The best models are picked up and become ensemble members.
6. Data are divided again in a way that the new testing set has minimal overlap with the former ones.
7. The procedure stops if the ensemble has the desired size.

Training in step (2) was performed with the following six model families:

- Penalized Fishers Linear Discriminant Analysis: classical LDA classifier with spatial constraints on many highly correlated predictors (a model for pixels in an image) [32],
- Kernel Ridge Regression: a model with the Tikhonov-Phillips regularization capable of controlling bias-variance trade-off, with a polynomial kernel $k(x, x') = (a + x.x')^b$, where a and b are the coefficients [33],
- Multi Layer Perceptron: trained with the first order weight update mechanisms (RPROP descent), with the changeable number of nodes [34],
- Perceptron: trained with a second order gradient decent [34],
- Decision Trees: based on the C4.5 algorithm, with pruning procedures based on the cross-validation scheme [35],
- Matlab data trees (dtree) [28].

In binary classification a confusion matrix presents instances of predicted and actual classes [36]. This visualizes performance of the model on validation data. The four statistical entities: t_p = true positive, t_n = true negative (they both are the desired results) and f_p = false positive (type I error) and f_n = false negative (type II error) form a set of values out of which numerous quality measures are derived. The choice for a measure and its application in the classification scheme depends on the research purpose. In our machine learning experiments we used (one by one) seven different quality measures to control how the ensembles of primary models are constructed. The following measures were optimization factors when accumulating best constituent models [36]:

- Accuracy: an overall measure of all desired outcomes in the test $(t_p + t_n)/(t_p + t_n + f_p + f_n)$; this is a common quality measure when no particular requirements are imposed,
- Precision (PPA-positive predictive value) is a fraction of retrieved instances that are relevant, $t_p/(t_p + f_p)$; this is a quality measure of exactness/quality,

- Recall (sensitivity) is a fraction of relevant instances that are retrieved, $t_p/(t_p + f_n)$; this is a quality measure of completeness/quantity.
  Absence of type I and type II errors corresponds respectively to maximum precision (no false positive) and maximum recall (no false negatives).
- F-score (F1) is a harmonic mean of precision and recall: 2*(precision)*(recall)/(precision+recall) = $2 * t_p/(2 * t_p + f_n + f_p)$,
- Fp-rate is a false positive rate $f_p/(t_p + f_p)$,
- Specificity is a fraction of true negatives, $t_n/(t_n + f_p)$; a high specificity has a low type I error rate
- Ber: balanced error rate is an average of the errors on each class $0.5 * (f_n/(t_p + f_n) + f_p/(f_p + t_n))$.

The ensembles trained according to the above mentioned quality measures were finally tested on validation data (B). For the quality measure at this step we chose AUC - the area under the ROC curve (Receiver Operating Characteristic) [37] obtained by plotting sensitivity against (1-specificity), for each confidence value. We selected the ROC curve as the ensemble quality measure as it is better in presenting the quality of the classification system than any single quality measure. With ROC one can show sensitivity and specificity as a function of the confidence level (thresholds between single values of calculations from the model). The values of AUC presented in all the figures were calculated from the ROC curve using the trapezoid method.

3   Results and Discussion

In Sect. 2.1 we explained how wavelet bases were used to decompose a set of dermoscopic images and to calculate corresponding feature sets. These wavelet features were learnt (set A) by an ensemble of models in this way, that the ensemble optimized (one by one) seven different quality measures: accuracy, precision, F1-score, Fp-rate, specificity, Ber and recall. The final model was every time validated on a separate unseen set of data (B). Figure 1 presents the absolute AUC values for different dermatoscopy image resolution for the best wavelet bases. The wavelet bases that produce the highest AUC are:

- Rbio 3.1 (Reverse biorthogonal wavelet pair: (3,1))
- Rbio 2.2
- Rbio 1.5
- Rbio 4.4
- Bior 1.5 (Biorthogonal wavelet pair: (1,5))
- Bior 1.1
- Coif 1 (Coiflet 1)

The AUC values have error bars that reflect standard deviation of the AUC value over different validating rounds.

For most of the quality measures the magnitudes of the error bars are bigger than the fluctuations of AUC over the shown (best) wavelet bases. This confirms

Table 1. Numerical results (value ± standard deviation) for the ensembles.

Wavelet base	Image resolution	AUC for different ensemble optimization factors:						
		accuracy	precision	fscore	fp_rate	specificity	ber	recall
Rbio 3.1	2272 × 1704	0.9379	0.8855	0.7329	0.9234	0.5590	0.9117	0.9165
		±0.0440	±0.0448	±0.2156	±0.0252	±0.0957	±0.0304	±0.0451
	1136 × 852	0.9211	0.8631	0.8187	0.9364	0.6690	0.8982	0.9336
		±0.0148	±0.0445	±0.1889	±0.0271	±0.0857	±0.1126	±0.0424
	568 × 426	0.8699	0.8578	0.8187	0.8967	0.7192	0.8342	0.8668
		±0.0829	±0.0733	±0.1782	±0.0420	±0.1334	±0.0423	±0.0670
Rbio 2.2	2272 × 1704	0.8304	0.8400	0.6666	0.8541	0.7072	0.8079	0.8331
		±0.0794	±0.0894	±0.1627	±0.0262	±0.1257	±0.0427	±0.0539
	1136 × 852	0.8928	0.8581	0.8232	0.8858	0.6409	0.8307	0.8782
		±0.0326	±0.0742	±0.0813	±0.0465	±0.1824	±0.0824	±0.0525
	568 × 426	0.9178	0.7730	0.8151	0.8624	0.8114	0.8297	0.8871
		±0.0447	±0.0883	±0.0610	±0.0147	±0.0618	±0.1232	±0.0327
Rbio 1.5	2272 × 1704	0.8580	0.8804	0.8500	0.8730	0.7749	0.8594	0.9306
		±0.0554	±0.0421	±0.0467	±0.0459	±0.1282	±0.0697	±0.0728
	1136 × 852	0.8237	0.8247	0.6830	0.7886	0.5785	0.7814	0.8128
		±0.0681	±0.0910	±0.1059	±0.0956	±0.1115	±0.0367	±0.0524
	568 × 426	0.8661	0.7311	0.7218	0.8605	0.7031	0.7246	0.8270
		±0.0460	±0.0898	±0.1057	±0.1081	±0.1675	±0.1433	±0.0557
Rbio 4.4	2272 × 1704	0.8641	0.8557	0.7741	0.8740	0.7234	0.8375	0.8019
		±0.0820	±0.0762	±0.0885	±0.0306	±0.0997	±0.0498	±0.0661
	1136 × 852	0.8236	0.8401	0.7165	0.8379	0.6091	0.7917	0.8281
		±0.0293	±0.0938	±0.0779	±0.0391	±0.1398	±0.0573	±0.0485
	568 × 426	0.8764	0.8834	0.8113	0.8876	0.7123	0.7961	0.9092
		±0.0353	±0.0707	±0.0676	±0.0215	±0.1676	±0.0855	±0.0586
Bior 1.5	2272 × 1704	0.8858	0.8758	0.8390	0.8758	0.7045	0.8764	0.9049
		±0.0350	±0.0704	±0.0913	±0.0396	±0.1583	±0.0621	±0.0819
	1136 × 852	0.8737	0.8531	0.7453	0.9048	0.6376	0.8472	0.9130
		±0.0516	±0.0683	±0.1544	±0.0514	±0.1890	±0.0775	±0.0285
	568 × 426	0.8729	0.9027	0.8777	0.9019	0.6881	0.8318	0.9045
		±0.0442	±0.0575	±0.0932	±0.0341	±0.1183	±0.0697	±0.0520
Bior 1.1	2272 × 1704	0.8587	0.8829	0.8323	0.8078	0.7607	0.8675	0.8454
		±0.0568	±0.0434	±0.0497	±0.1054	±0.0985	±0.0857	±0.0625
	1136 × 852	0.8976	0.8582	0.7056	0.8605	0.7890	0.8176	0.9120
		±0.0629	±0.0761	±0.1155	±0.0825	±0.1123	±0.0735	±0.0670
	568 × 426	0.8960	0.7993	0.8245	0.8873	0.7551	0.8008	0.8569
		±0.0310	±0.0434	±0.0980	±0.0543	±0.1599	±0.0577	±0.0549
Coif 1	2272 × 1704	0.8713	0.8507	0.8031	0.8564	0.7513	0.8763	0.8550
		±0.0976	±0.0494	±0.1443	±0.0604	±0.0450	±0.0664	±0.0972
	1136 × 852	0.8495	0.8522	0.7175	0.8692	0.7441	0.8512	0.8745
		±0.0557	±0.0734	±0.1829	±0.0757	±0.1409	±0.0691	±0.0216
	568 × 426	0.9104	0.7820	0.8171	0.8794	0.7313	0.8447	0.9110
		±0.0308	±0.0932	±0.0425	±0.0548	±0.1567	±0.0803	±0.0511

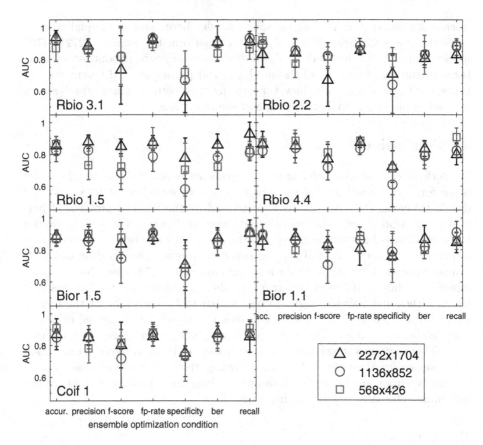

Fig. 1. Results for AUC for three resolutions of the Melanoma dermoscopic images as a function of the ensemble optimization factors: Accuracy, Precision, F-score, FP-rate, Specificity, BER and Recall.

that the learning environment plays an important role in the stability of the models and this factor may screen the impact of a wavelet base. As we can see in Fig. 1 the best wavelet base is Reverse Biorthogonal pair (3,1) which outperforms the following best wavelet bases by 5–10 %. It is clear that careful selection of the wavelet base is a good starting point to fine tune the final classifier model(s). For all the shown wavelet bases the best measure is Fp-rate, accuracy and recall (i.e. sensitivity). All the quality measures show apparent correlations between different wavelet bases which proves stability of the ensemble learning process. Regardless of the particular wavelet base (except Rbio 1.5 and Bior 1.1) the best measure, Fp-rate, shows stable performance between different pixel resolutions and show the least error bars. This is a very encouraging result especially for the downgraded image resolutions which, due to apparent deficiencies in the computing power of the contemporary ARM-based hand-held devices, may be successfully used for an on-site dermatoscopy-based melanoma classification. An interesting observation is that for some wavelet bases and some quality measures the 568×426 and 1136×852 may outperform the genuine 2272×1704 image resolution. In this work we don't draw any conclusions about associations between the skin texture and the mathematical properties of different wavelet bases, the latter observation, however may manifest certain symmetries between the melanoma differential structures and the raster size.

4   Conclusions

We performed some machine learning experiments to search for optimal wavelet bases for decomposition of dermoscopic images of melanoma (102 cases) and dysplastic nevus (83 cases). This is motivated by the medical problem of pattern recognition of early stages of the cutaneous melanoma. We studied wavelet bases of all possible types and selected those maximizing the classification performance. In order to diversify the learning environment, we used an ensemble composed of models with different learning paradigms. This ensemble was optimized according to different (arbitrary) quality measures. Our work shows that the bi-orthogonal wavelet pairs are best suited to be the probe of the human skin when it undergoes transformations to atypical (dysplastic nevus) or malignant (melanoma) stages. The best wavelet base is the reverse bi-orthogonal pair (3,1). This work also shows how the studied wavelet bases preserve classification performance for the case of $2\times$ and $4\times$ image resolution degradation. This is extremely important for projects aiming at designing small, hand-help devices for online automatic melanoma diagnosis.

References

1. Odom, R.B., James, W.H., Berger, T.G.: Melanocytic nevi and neoplasms. Andrews Diseases of the Skin, 9th edn. WB Saunders, Philadelphia (2000)
2. Żabińska-Płazak, E., Wojas-Pelc, A., Dyduch, G.: Videodermatoscopy in the diagnosis of melanocytic skin lesions. Bio-Algorithms Med-Syst. 1, 333–338 (2005)
3. Robinson, J.K., Nickoloff, B.J.: Digital epiluminescence microscopy monitoring of high-risk patients. Arch. dermatol. 140, 49–56 (2004)
4. Jaworek-Korjakowska, J., Tadeusiewicz, R.: Design of a teledermatology system to support the consultation of dermoscopic cases using mobile technologies and cloud platform. Bio-Algorithms Med-Syst. 11(1), 53–58 (2015)
5. Marks, R.: Epidemiology of melanoma. Clin. Exp. Dermatol. 25, 459–463 (2000)
6. Carli, P., De Giorgi, V., Gianotti, B., et al.: Dermatoscopy and early diagnosis of melanoma. Arch. Dermatol. 137, 1641 (2001)
7. Johr, R.H.: Dermatoscopy: alternative melanocytic algorithms - the ABCD rule of dermatoscopy, menzies scoring method, and 7-point checklist. Clin. Dermatol. 20, 240–247 (2002)
8. Roesch, A., et al.: Dermatoscopy of 'Dysplastic Nevi': a beacon in the diagnostic darkness. Eur. J. Dermatol. 16(5), 479–493 (2006)
9. Jaworek-Korjakowska, J.: Novel method for border irregularity assessment in dermoscopic color images. Comput. Math. Methods in Med. 2015, 11 (2015). Article ID: 496202

10. Cudek, P., Grzymaa-Busse, J.W., Hippe, Z.S.: Further research on automatic estimation of asymmetry of melanocytic skin lesons, human-computer systems interaction: backgrounds and application. In: Hippe, Z.S., Kulikowski, J.L., Mroczek, T. (eds.) Human-Computer Systems Interaction: Backgrounds and Application 2. Advances in Intelligent and Soft Computing, vol. 99, pp. 125–129. Springer, Heidelberg (2012)
11. Hippe, Z.S.: e-melanoma diagnosing and learning system. current status, information technologies in biomedicine. In: Piętka, E., Kawa, J., Wieclawek, W. (eds.) Information Technologies in Biomedicine, Vol. 4. Advances in Intelligent and Soft Computing, vol. 284, pp. 95–99. Springer, Switzerland (2014)
12. He, H., Garcia, E.A.: Learning from imbalanced data. IEEE Trans. Knowl. Data Eng. **21**, 1263–1284 (2009)
13. Wang, S., Minku, L.L., Yao, X.: Resampling-based ensemble methods for online class imbalance learning. IEEE Trans. Knowl. Data Eng. **26**, 405–425 (2014)
14. Chang, T., Kuo, C.C.J.: Texture analysis and classification with tree-structured wavelet transform. IEEE Trans. Image Process. **2**, 429–441 (1993)
15. Patwardhan, S.V., Dhawan, A.P., Relue, P.A.: Classification of melanoma using tree structured wavelet transforms. Comput. Methods Programs Biomed. **72**, 223–239 (2003)
16. Patwardhan, S.V., Dai, S., Dhawan, A.P.: Multi-spectral image analysis and classification of melanoma using fuzzy membership based partitions. Comput. Med. Imaging Graph. **29**, 287–296 (2005)
17. Daubechies, I.: Ten lectures on wavelets. CBMS, SIAM **61**, 198–202 (1994)
18. Mallat, S.G.: A theory for multiresolution signal decomposition: the wavelet representation. IEEE Trans. Pattern Anal. Mach. Intell. **11**, 674–693 (1989)
19. Surówka, G., Merkwirth, C., Żabińska-Płazak, E., Graca, A.: Wavelet based pattern recognition analysis of skin lesion images. Bio Algorithm Med Syst. **2**(4), 43 (2006)
20. Surówka, G., Grzesiak-Kopeć, K.: Different learning paradigms for the classification of melanoid skin lesions using wavelets. In: Proceedings of EMBC 2007, Lyon (2007)
21. Surówka, G.: Supervised learning of melanocytic skin lesion images. In: Proceedings of HSI Kraków (2008)
22. Indira, D.N.V.S.L.S., Wieclawek Supriya, P.: Detection & analysis of skin cancer using wavelet techniques. IJCSIT **2**(5), 1927–1932 (2011)
23. Fassihi, N., Shanbehzadeh, J., Sarafzadeh, A., Ghasemi, E.: Melanoma diagnosis by the use of wavelet analysis based on morphological operators. In: Proceedings of International Multiconference Engineering Computer Science, Hong-Kong (2011)
24. Castillejos, H., Ponomaryov, V., Nino-de-Rivera, L., Golikov, V.: Wavelet transform fuzzy algorithms for dermoscopic image segmentation. Comput. Math. Methods Med. **2012**, 11 (2012). Article ID: 578721
25. Ramteke, N.S., Jain, S.V.: Analysis of Skin cancer using fuzzy and wavelet technique review & proposed new algorithm. IJETT **4**(6), 2555–2566 (2013)
26. Sugin, S.V., Jegadeesh, A.: Segmentation of skin images using fixed grid wavelet networks. IJERT **3**(4), 838–841 (2014)
27. Rajarathinam, A., Arivazhagan, A.: Timely efficient automated system by segmentation using wavelet transform. IJSETR **4**(8), 2730–2735 (2015)
28. MATLAB: The MathWorks Inc., Natick (1994–2013)
29. Merkwirth, C., Wichard, J.D., Ogorzałek, M.: A software toolbox for constructing ensembles of heterogenous linear and nonlinear models. In: Proceedings of the 2005 European Conference on Circuit Theory and Design, vol. 3, Ireland (2005)
30. Kuncheva, L.I.: Combining Pattern Classifiers. Wiley, New York (2004)

31. Breiman, L.: Bagging predictors. Mach. Learn. **24**, 123–140 (1996)
32. Hastie, T., Buja, A., Tibshirani, R.: Penalized discriminant analysis. Ann. Stat. **23**, 73–102 (1995)
33. An, S., Liu, W., Venkatesh, S.: Fast cross-validation algorithms for least square support vector machine and kernel ridge regression. Patt. Recognit. **40**, 2154–2162 (2007)
34. Haykin, S.: Neural Networks: A Comprehensive Foundation, 2nd edn. Prentice Hall, Upper Saddle River (1998). ISBN:0-13-273350-1
35. Quinlan, J.R.: Induction of decision trees. Mach. Learn. **1**, 81–106 (1986). Kluwer Academic Publishers
36. http://en.wikipedia.org/wiki/Binary_classification (2015). Accessed Nov 2015
37. Van Erkel, A.R., Pattynama, P.M.: Receiver Operating Characteristic (ROC) analysis. Eur. J. Radiol. **27**, 88–94 (1998)

Comparison of SVM and Ontology-Based Text Classification Methods

Krzysztof Wróbel[3(✉)], Maciej Wielgosz[1], Aleksander Smywiński-Pohl[1,3],
and Marcin Pietron[2]

[1] AGH University of Science and Technology,
al. Mickiewicza 30, 30-059 Krakow, Poland
wielgosz@agh.edu.pl
[2] ACK Cyfronet AGH, ul. Nawojki 11, 30-950 Krakow, Poland
pietron@agh.edu.pl
[3] Jagiellonian University, ul. Golebia 24, 31-007 Krakow, Poland
k.wrobel@epi.uj.edu.pl, apohllo@o2.pl

Abstract. This work addresses the challenging task of text categorization. The main goal is the comparison of two different approaches, i.e. Vector Space Model and ontology-based solutions. The authors compare and contrast them with respect to accuracy and processing flow, which affect the classification results. The ontology-based method outperforms its counter-part when it comes to category resolution, i.e. the number of categories which can be processed. On the other hand, the SVM-based module is much faster and performs well when trained on an appropriately-structured learning set. The authors performed a series of tests to compare the methods and, as expected, the ontology-based solution outperformed the SVM classifier. It reached a micro averaged F1-score of 0.90 with 2.8 million Wikipedia articles, whereas the SVM-based module did not exceed 0.86 with the same data set. The macro averaged F1-score of both solutions was inferior to the micro one and reached values of 0.75 and 0.57, for ontology and SVM-based solutions respectively.

Keywords: Text classification · Vector space model · Ontology-based methods · Support vector machine · Wikipedia

1 Introduction

A broad range of classification methods have been developed over the course of the past years for text processing and analysis [1]. This paper compares two commonly-used techniques: statistical and ontology-based classification.

Most of the statistical classification methods are taken from the field of machine learning (ML), where classified objects are treated as feature vectors and there are multiple ways to transform documents into such vectors [2,3]. On the other hand, the ontology-based solutions assume a set of interrelated concepts (an ontology) that are mapped to the terms that appear in the text.

© Springer International Publishing Switzerland 2016
L. Rutkowski et al. (Eds.): ICAISC 2016, Part I, LNAI 9692, pp. 667–680, 2016.
DOI: 10.1007/978-3-319-39378-0_57

The number of concepts is much smaller than the number of terms, allowing for a dimensionality reduction [4].

The most common way to transform text documents into feature vectors adopts a "bag-of-words" approach [5], which essentially, is a representation where each feature is a single token. However, there is no single definition of a feature and a token, which can either be local or global depending on the scope of the comparison. Consequently, a feature can be either as simple as a single word or phrase, or a much more complicated structure.

The features extracted from the texts are fed into a classifier which decides to which topic group the given document belongs to. Different classification methods were used in text document classification, but the Support Vector Machine (SVM) is considered to be the dominant algorithm in terms of performance [6]. Thus, it was employed in the experiments of the vector space model and ontology-based classification method comparison [7,8].

The ontology-based approach, on the other hand, performs a sophisticated transformation of the analyzed text and, as a result, is computationally much more demanding. Its basic idea is the identification of concepts defined in the ontology that appear in the analyzed text. Then, the classification is performed in a smaller space defined by the concepts. Since the concepts form a hierarchy or a heterarchy, post-processing is employed, in which concepts that are too specific and too general are eliminated, yielding a desired level of generalization.

The mapping of terms into concepts might be performed in many ways. The most basic approach assumes that each concept can be represented by a set of terms in the text. The appearance of a given term is equated with the presence of the concept, and ambiguous terms are not resolved [4]. In more sophisticated approaches, the ambiguity is resolved and the concepts are not represented by a small set of terms, but Named Entity Recognition (NER) is performed in order to represent the underlying semantics of proper names [9].

The aim of this paper is the comparison of performance between vector space model and ontology-based text classification. This general goal is restricted by the application of both methods into the problem of the classification of Wikipedia articles into the Cyc ontology [10]. In our previous research [11], we have developed a set of ontology-based classification methods that were used to classify the articles of the English Wikipedia into OpenCyc. However, these methods have the following limitations: they are quite slow and they require substantial implementation effort. Thus, we wanted to find out whether they can be substituted with fast and generic text classification methods such as SVM.

The text is structured as follows: First, we discuss the idea of the vector space model with special attention to SVM. Then, we briefly discuss the ontology-based methods used to classify the articles. We test both methods on two data sets based on the English Wikipedia. We conclude our paper with the comparison of the results and our future research ideas.

2   Vector Space Model

A text categorization task requires that all symbols (words or n-grams) are converted into a numerical representation, i.e. vectors. In the case of this implementation, single words are used as terms. The vector space model has been successfully used as a conventional method for text representation. This model represents a document as a vector of features [5].

2.1   TF-IDF Representation

The most common algorithm for weighing words in vector space model is the computation of the so-called *Term Frequency* (TF) and *Inverted Document Frequency* (IDF) coefficients. TF-IDF is a numerical statistic that is intended to reflect how important a word is to the document in the context of the whole collection. The TF-IDF value increases proportionally to the number of times a word appears in the document, but it is scaled down by the frequency of the word in the corpus, which helps mitigate the fact that some words are generally more common than others. Therefore, common words which appear in many documents, will be almost ignored. Words that appear frequently in a single document will be scaled up.

2.2   Support Vector Machines

Support vector machines were originally devised and described by Vapnik [12]. They are used for binary classification, which means that there are exactly two classes of objects and the classification formula is found in the training process of the classifier.

The SVM algorithm can be envisioned as a process of creating a hyperplane which separates data in an n-dimensional space. It is conducted in an iterative manner, in which a selected plane is gradually adjusted to provide the optimal so-called generalization margin [13].

3   Ontology-Based Solution

An alternative solution used to classify the documents leverages an ontology – a structured schema that explicitly lists concepts used to classify entities and relations that hold between these concepts. WordNet [14,15] is a quite popular classification scheme, since the number of measures can be defined to compute the semantic relatedness between the concepts that occur in the given text and the target classification scheme, allowing for selecting a type that is closest to the meaning of the document.

However, in our case we have selected OpenCyc [10] as our target classification system. This ontology has a number of interesting features that make it particularly useful for the classification task. Namely, its *structure* is well defined, its *coverage* is broad, especially compared to other general purpose ontologies such as DBpedia [16,17], its server implements a number of *algorithms* for querying and effectively traversing the taxonomy, it has a *modular structure* (thanks to *microtheories*), allowing for encoding alternative perspectives on the organization of entities, the *definitions* of types and relations are strict, leaving little room for misinterpretation, the ontology embraces *meta-modelling* (cf. [18]) that greatly simplifies the encoding of some of the types of meta-properties, the *compound types* are, to a large extent, avoided thanks to type functions, *roles*, as a special type of entity, are also available, and, last but not least, there is a built-in *inconsistency* detection mechanism based on predicate constraints and relation of disjointness.

On the other hand, classifying articles into Cyc types is not as easy, since there is not any publicly available large set of documents classified into Cyc, that could serve as a training set for the machine learning algorithms.

For that reason, we have selected articles found in the English Wikipedia to compare both approaches. First of all, each Wikipedia article usually describes a particular concept or entity, thus, the classification task can be determined as the selection of the generalization of the concept or the selection of the semantic type of the entity. Moreover, these documents have many semi-structural features that can be leveraged to heuristically classify them into Cyc:

- The first sentence of the articles can be treated as the definition – recognizing the types of objects mentioned in the definition and automatically mapping them to Cyc can be a method of article classification,
- They usually include *infoboxes* – pieces of structured data, that can be used to infer the semantic categories of the documents; the most popular infoboxes were manually mapped to Cyc types, providing classification for the articles including them,
- They are organized into a broad set of categories – these categories can be automatically mapped to Cyc concepts, providing classification for the articles included in the mapped categories.

For example the article for *Madagascar* starts with the following text[1]:

Madagascar (...), officially the Republic of Madagascar (...), and previously known as the Malagasy Republic, is an *island country* in the Indian Ocean, off the coast of Southeast Africa,

indicating the semantic type of the entity, namely *island country*. The article includes a `Country` `infobox` which indicates that it is a country. The article is also included in categories such as: *Island countries, East African countries, Countries in Africa,...* which provide similar classification hints.

It should be noted, that the availability of these semi-structured data is varying between articles. Not all of them include infoboxes; some of the specified categories do not indicate the semantic type of the entities; sometimes it is hard to determine the phrase in the first sentence that indicates the semantic type. On the other hand, the types assigned by different methods might be in conflict.

---

[1] cf. http://en.wikipedia.org/wiki/Madagascar.

As a result, a voting mechanism has to be implemented. In our case, we have implemented a simple voting strategy: the number of times a given article was assigned a particular semantic type was counted and the type with the highest count was assigned to the article. In the case of a tie, both types were assigned to the article, allowing for multi-type classification.

4   Experimental Setups Overview

There were two separate series of experiments conduced, separately for the vector-based and ontology-based solutions. Both of them required different experimental setups.

4.1   Vector-Based Solution

The system is composed of several stages which constitute the document processing flow presented in Fig. 1. In the first step, the files are read from external folders in order to train the SVM classifier. All of the files are fed into *text cleaner* and *stoplist* modules which remove all non-alphabetic characters. This happens regardless of the working mode, i.e. for both train and test modes. Then, preprocessed files are used to create the dictionary as well as TF-IDF model which is a core structure for mapping from text to vector space. It is worth noting that the dictionary and model can be either loaded from an external file or generated.

The size of both the dictionary and the model has a significant impact on the processing results since they determine the dimensionality of the vector space. Once the documents are converted to vectors, they may be used to train the classifier, or for classification. In the final step, the classification results are passed on to the *quality evaluator*, which measures the performance of the algorithm in terms of precision, recall, and F1-score.

4.2   Ontology-Based Solution

The processing of documents in the case of the ontology-based solution was much more sophisticated, primarily due to the fact that it tried to extract structured data from semi-structural Wikipedia articles. The second important problem that had to be taken care of was a problem that is characteristic for any Natural Language Processing approach which explicitly models language semantics, namely ambiguity. There were also differences in the processing pipeline, dependent on the source of the classification data.

The first implemented method of extracting the types from the first sentences implemented the following processing approach. It started by detecting the first sentence in the document, that sentence was parsed by the Stanford parser [19], and the phrases linked to the subject of the sentence were extracted as the potential names of the entity described in the document. In the case of *Madagascar*, this stage would extract the *island country* phrase as its type. In the last stage, that phrase was mapped to one concept in Cyc using contextual

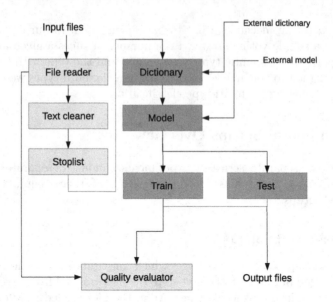

Fig. 1. Algorithm processing flow in the case of vector-based classification.

data (e.g. the categories of the article) to disambiguate the phrase against the available Cyc concepts.

The second implemented method, using *infoboxes*, was the easiest to implement, since in our earlier research [11], we have manually built mapping from infoboxes to Cyc types. As a result, this method was quite straight-forward and relied on Wikipedia infobox data extracted by the DBpedia extraction framework [20]. The documents were assigned Cyc types that corresponded with the infoboxes. Since this dataset included data of relatively high accuracy (relying on manual mapping), they were used as input for the vector-based method.

The last method relied on the automatic mapping of Wikipedia categories to Cyc types. This method was the most sophisticated, since its core problem was very similar to the problem of ontology mapping (Wikipedia categories do not form a taxonomy, but rather a folksonomy). It started with cleaning up the categories (removal of administrative categories), continued with parsing the categories (with help from the Stanford parser), the identification of categories whose syntactic heads were plural (since they usually correspond to classification types) and mapping these categories to Cyc types. The last stage was crucial due to ambiguity. To overcome the problem, we have implemented a disambiguation strategy similar to the first method. We have used the *local* context of the mapped category (i.e. its parent and child categories together with articles in that category) to select the most probable mapping. When the correspondence between categories and types was established, all articles included in the mapped category received its corresponding type. For instance, the *Madagascar* article would receive the Cyc #$Country type, since the *Countries in Africa* category would be mapped to that type.

The final step of the classification involved the selection of one or more types that would best capture the semantics of the given Wikipedia article. Since there were several classification methods implemented, each capable of producing zero, one, or more types, a voting procedure was applied. In the first stage, all types produced by the methods were substituted with a small set of general, but meaningful concepts by following the generalization relation that is well defined in Cyc (the list of types is present in Table 1). Then, the type or types that appeared the most frequently in the classification were selected as the final classification for the article.

5   Experiments

The primary question we wanted to answer during the experiments with both of the approaches was: **is it possible to achieve classification results relying on one relatively simple method (SVM) that would be as good as the results obtained with a combination of several ontology-based methods?**

The problem of Wikipedia article classification is quite popular in literature and there are reports showing that ML methods can achieve very good results (cf. [21]). Usually the training and evaluation of ML methods are performed with classification that is automatically generated from Wikipedia based on the mapping between Wikipedia infoboxes and DBpedia ontology classes [17]. The reason for that is the requirement for a large number of examples needed to train ML classifiers and the belief that the DBpedia classification is almost perfect.

However, as our earlier study shows [11], this classification is not always perfect. Thus, our second question regarding the classification was: **how much will the reported quality of the results change if we substitute the (automatically generated) DBpedia evaluation dataset with a manually validated dataset?** This is why we have manually validated 3,500 examples taken from the English Wikipedia. Each example was independently evaluated by two annotators and disagreements were jointly solved.

5.1   Performance Comparison for Automatic and Manual Validation

We started our experiments trying to answer the second question first, since that result would shed light on the proper way of comparing the implemented methods. Thus for every class in Table 1 we have collected a set of 5,000 Wikipedia articles relying on the mapping between Wikipedia infoboxes and Cyc concepts. For some of the classes the number of examples was smaller than 5,000 – in such cases, all of them were taken. In each case, the set of examples was split, and 80 % of them were used for training and 20 % for evaluation. Each example was described in a file which contained a single (the top) paragraph of the original Wikipedia text extended with the names of its Wikipedia categories. The tokens in the category names were prefixed, thus they formed a different set of features in the feature vectors.

The results of this experiment are presented in Table 1. All scores are provided using standard information retrieval metrics: precision, recall, and F1-score. Due to skewed class distribution, we also report the micro and macro averaged results.

It is apparent that the manually validated dataset poses a much harder challenge for the classification algorithms than the second one. For each and every class, the F1-score is worse for the manually evaluated dataset. The same holds for micro and macro averaged results and is especially apparent for the macro averaged F1-score, where the results are 35% points worse. For that reason, when comparing the results of SVM and ontology-based classification, we only relied on the manually validated dataset.

5.2   Performance Comparison for SVM and Ontology-Based Methods

In the second series of experiments we directly addressed the first question regarding the main topic of this article. To make the most out of SVM when building classification models for the defined ontology classes we have used the full Wikipedia dataset (2.8 million articles with infoboxes). Since the class distribution is very skewed (with #$Person class dominating), some of the models contained hundreds of thousands of examples, while the others contained only several thousand. To process such a big dataset, we have used the Vowpal Wabbit SVM implementation.

Regarding the ontology-based solution we have employed a much more sophisticated pipeline of tools named cycloped.io. They are available as an open source project at github.com/cycloped-io. The processing of the entire English Wikipedia took several days and its details are out of the scope of this article.

The results of the comparison are given in Table 2. It is apparent that for most of the individual classes the results are better for the ontology-based methods. The micro averaged F1-score is 4% points better for these methods, while the macro averaged F1-score is 18% points better. We can conclude that although the SVM-based classification gives relatively good classification results, the ontology-based methods still perform much better.

5.3   Discussion of the Results

The SVM-based classifier requires high quality training data. Unfortunately, the articles acquired from infobox mapping are not perfect, which may, to some extent, affect the performance of the classifier. However, even if it was competently accurate, it would not change the fact that the SVM-based classifier is blind in regards to articles belonging to classes which it was not exposed to during training. In other words, all of the documents belonging to classes which did not exist in the training set are classified with zero accuracy.

The processing speed was not the focus of this paper, but it is worth noting that the Vowpal Wabbit [22] linear SVM performed much better than the Python sklearn module [23].

Table 1. SVM performance on automatically and manually created validation datasets.

Class	Automatically annotated testing set			Manually annotated testing set		
	Precision	Recall	F1-score	Precision	Recall	F1-score
Action	0.75	0.63	**0.68**	0.85	0.17	0.29
Animal	1.0	1.0	**1.0**	0.96	0.92	0.94
Artifact-Generic	0.77	0.87	**0.81**	0.64	0.14	0.23
AspatialInformationStore	0.84	0.84	**0.84**	1.0	0.34	0.51
BiologicalLivingObject	1.0	1.0	**1.0**	0.55	0.75	0.63
ChemicalObject	0.43	0.23	**0.3**	0.0	0.0	0.0
CommercialOrganization	0.99	1.0	**0.99**	0.97	0.74	0.84
ConceptualWork	0.98	0.87	**0.92**	0.99	0.67	0.8
ConstructionArtifact	0.42	0.25	**0.32**	0.38	0.22	0.28
Drink	1.0	1.0	**1.0**	1.0	0.67	0.8
EdibleStuff	0.4	0.24	**0.3**	1.0	0.11	0.19
Event	0.71	0.69	**0.7**	0.55	0.57	0.56
FictionalThing	1.0	1.0	**1.0**	0.93	0.72	0.81
Food	1.0	1.0	**1.0**	0.56	0.83	0.67
GeographicalRegion	0.53	0.35	**0.42**	0.9	0.14	0.25
GeopoliticalEntity	1.0	1.0	**1.0**	0.85	0.91	0.88
Group	0.67	0.4	**0.5**	0.84	0.18	0.3
InanimateObject-Natural	0.68	0.73	**0.71**	0.6	0.64	0.62
InformationBearingThing	1.0	1.0	**1.0**	0.2	0.06	0.1
InorganicMaterial	1.0	1.0	**1.0**	1.0	0.4	0.57
IntelligentAgent	1.0	1.0	**1.0**	0.5	0.04	0.08
MathematicalOr-ComputationalThing	1.0	1.0	**1.0**	0.25	0.39	0.3
Microorganism	1.0	1.0	**1.0**	1.0	0.06	0.11
NonProfitOrganization	1.0	1.0	**1.0**	0.0	0.0	0.0
OrganicMaterial	0.4	0.16	**0.23**	0.0	0.0	0.0
OrganismPart	1.0	1.0	**1.0**	1.0	0.8	0.89
Organization	0.98	0.98	**0.98**	0.92	0.7	0.8
Person	0.99	1.0	**1.0**	0.99	0.97	0.98
PhysicalDevice	0.3	0.1	**0.15**	0.89	0.07	0.14
Place-NonAgent	0.31	0.07	**0.11**	0.71	0.04	0.07
Plant	1.0	1.0	**1.0**	0.92	0.95	0.93
Product	0.98	1.0	**0.99**	0.5	0.1	0.17
Technology-Artifact	0.77	0.92	**0.84**	0.74	0.64	0.69
Thing	0.9	0.88	**0.89**	0.0	0.0	0.0
TimeInterval	1.0	1.0	**1.0**	0.0	0.0	0.0
Weapon	1.0	1.0	**1.0**	0.6	0.67	0.63
Micro averaged	0.85	0.74	**0.79**	0.89	0.63	0.74
Macro averaged	0.82	0.78	**0.79**	0.66	0.4	0.44

Table 2. Classification performance for SVM and ontology-based implementations.

Class	SVM			Ontology-based		
	Precision	Recall	F1-score	Precision	Recall	F1-score
Action	0.66	0.52	0.58	0.64	0.76	**0.69**
Animal	0.97	0.95	0.96	0.95	0.99	**0.97**
Artifact-Generic	0.88	0.17	0.28	0.83	0.53	**0.65**
AspatialInformationStore	0.98	0.76	0.86	0.89	0.87	**0.88**
BiologicalLivingObject	0.5	0.62	0.56	0.75	0.75	**0.75**
ChemicalObject	0.33	0.2	0.25	0.54	0.47	**0.5**
ColoredThing	0	0	0	1	0.5	**0.67**
CommercialOrganization	0.89	0.89	0.89	0.88	0.97	**0.92**
ConceptualWork	0.95	0.91	0.93	0.97	0.97	**0.97**
ConstructionArtifact	0.92	0.91	**0.92**	0.92	0.9	0.91
Drink	1	0.67	0.8	1	0.67	0.8
EdibleStuff	1	0.47	0.64	1	0.7	**0.82**
Event	0.29	0.71	0.41	0.78	0.64	**0.7**
FictionalThing	0.94	0.89	**0.91**	1	0.5	0.67
Food	0.67	1	0.8	1	1	**1**
GeographicalRegion	0.97	0.49	0.65	0.94	0.7	**0.8**
GeometricFigure	0	0	0	1	1	**1**
GeopoliticalEntity	0.82	0.99	0.9	0.86	0.97	**0.91**
Group	0.64	0.28	0.39	0.79	0.64	**0.71**
InanimateObject-Natural	0.89	0.82	0.86	0.93	0.98	**0.95**
InformationBearingThing	0.33	0.06	0.1	0.76	0.76	**0.76**
InorganicMaterial	1	0.4	0.57	1	0.4	0.57
IntelligentAgent	0.57	0.08	0.14	0.75	0.24	**0.36**
MathematicalOrComputationalThing	0.21	0.39	0.27	0.38	0.57	**0.45**
Microorganism	1	0.06	0.11	0.93	0.72	**0.81**
NonProfitOrganization	0.67	0.2	**0.31**	0	0	0
OrganicMaterial	1	0.36	0.53	0.92	0.88	**0.9**
OrganismPart	0.83	1	0.91	1	0.9	**0.95**
Organization	0.9	0.86	0.88	0.89	0.89	**0.89**
Person	0.99	0.98	0.99	0.97	1	**0.99**
PhysicalDevice	0.86	0.85	0.85	0.88	0.93	**0.9**
Place-NonAgent	0.91	0.83	0.87	0.92	0.9	**0.91**
Plant	0.95	0.98	0.97	0.95	1	**0.98**
Product	0	0	0	1	0.67	**0.8**
Technology-Artifact	0.83	0.83	0.83	0.84	0.89	**0.87**
Thing	0	0	0	0	0	0
TimeInterval	0	0	0	0.75	0.75	**0.75**
Weapon	1	0.64	0.78	1	0.82	**0.9**
Micro averaged	0.89	0.82	0.86	0.91	0.90	**0.90**
Macro averaged	0.69	0.55	0.57	0.81	0.71	**0.75**

The ontology-based solution delivers much more detailed results and allows for inference. It is reflected in the module's capability of yielding proper results for categories which it was not trained for. On the other hand, the superior performance of the ontology-based module (Table 2) is achieved at the expense of longer processing time when compared to the SVM-based solution.

6 Original Contribution

The presented research and the results of the experiments should be considered as a step towards building an ensemble of classifiers capable of both fast and accurate document classification. The system is to be composed of a set of modules, as presented in Fig. 2.

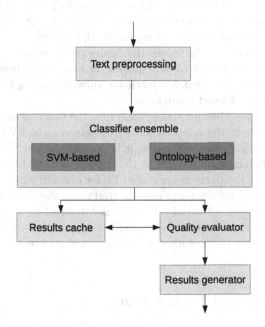

Fig. 2. Architecture of the classifier ensemble

Incoming text documents are to be preprocessed by and fed into the classifier ensemble to be concurrently processed by both SVM and Ontology-based classifiers. If, in the past, the results of both modules more or less matched, the user is instantly presented with the results of the SVM-based classifier, which significantly reduces the system response time.

The results from both modules are cached in the cache module and evaluated by the quality evaluator in terms of any discrepancy in their quality according to the adopted quality assessment measures for all of the covered document categories. If the difference in quality between the results yielded by the SVM and ontology-based solutions according to past statistics is high, the ontology-based result is preferred, and the user has to wait for the module to produce the result. In the opposite scenario (i.e. when the discrepancy in the result quality between the SVM and ontology-based classifiers is low), the result generated by the SVM-based classifier is chosen and sent as the classification result. In the latter case, the classification result is available much faster and with insignificantly worse quality than the one produced by the ontology-based classifier. It is worth noting that the difference in result generation between the SVM and ontology-based classifiers is huge, i.e. minutes vs days in the case of processing the entire Wikipedia corpus.

The decision of which result to choose is made based on past statistics collected by the result cache module for all of the categories the ensemble is supposed to recognize. The statistics are updated for every classification instance. This means that even when the SVM-based result is preferred in a given case, the classification result of the ontology-based module is not wasted and is used to update the global statistics. Consequently, the module progressively builds classification statistics. This improves the future performance of the ensemble.

The main contribution of the paper is the experimental proof of the feasibility of the concept for performance boosting by using hybrid SVM and ontology-based solutions.

Tables 1 and 2 show that for some categories, the differences in the classification quality in terms of the adopted measures between the SVM and ontology-based classifiers are low. In those cases, it is possible to use SVM-based results to speed up the classification process at the expense of very little degradation of quality. On the other hand, there are cases (Tables 1 and 2) where the SVM-based classifier yields results significantly inferior to its ontology-based counterpart or does not produce anything at all (if it was not trained to recognize instances of this particular category). In those cases, it takes much longer for the ensemble to generate results, but eventually they are produced by the ontology-based module.

7   Conclusions and Future Work

In this paper, we have presented two solutions to the problem of the classification of Wikipedia articles. The first one uses an SVM classifier and accomplishes the training in 21 min. This approach needs a large set of annotated data. The second solution applies ontology knowledge and relies on structural information already present in Wikipedia. The micro averaged scores of the classification are similar (the ontology-based methods are 4 % points better), however the ontology-based solution performs much better in terms of macro averaged measures (18 % points difference).

The ontology-based solution outperformed the statistical approach in evaluation metrics. However, the amount of time necessary to develop the system and run the classification is significantly longer. An interesting idea is to use a statistical classifier to limit or extend the category candidates in ontology-based methods. This limitation can lead to a shorter running time. The extension of candidates is more challenging as the classification is performed using more specific classes, but can potentially gain a better score. Another option is to treat the SVM results as equal with the results from ontology-based methods, and treat them as yet another method that participates in the voting for the most reliable classification.

In our future research, we want to further investigate the problem of turning Wikipedia into a computable knowledge base. We plan to particularly focus our efforts on the problem of processing multilingual data. SVM seems to be a good choice for this, since, to a great extent, it is language-agnostic.

References

1. Ng, V., Dasgupta, S., Arifin, S.: Examining the role of linguistic knowledge sources in the automatic identification and classification of reviews. In: Proceedings of the COLING/ACL on Main Conference Poster Sessions, Association for Computational Linguistics, pp. 611–618 (2006)
2. Durant, K.T., Smith, M.D.: Predicting the political sentiment of web log posts using supervised machine learning techniques coupled with feature selection. In: Nasraoui, O., Spiliopoulou, M., Srivastava, J., Mobasher, B., Masand, B. (eds.) WebKDD 2006. LNCS (LNAI), vol. 4811, pp. 187–206. Springer, Heidelberg (2007)
3. Joachims, T.: Text categorization with support vector machines: learning with many relevant features. In: Nédellec, C., Rouveirol, C. (eds.) ECML 1998. LNCS, vol. 1398. Springer, Heidelberg (1998)
4. Hotho, A., Maedche, A., Staab, S.: Ontology-based text document clustering. KI 16(4), 48–54 (2002)
5. Salton, G., Wong, A., Yang, C.S.: A vector space model for automatic indexing. Commun. ACM 18(11), 613–620 (1975)
6. Liu, Z., Lv, X., Liu, K., Shi, S.: Study on SVM compared with the other text classification methods. In: 2010 Second International Workshop on Education Technology and Computer Science (ETCS), vol. 1, pp. 219–222. IEEE (2010)
7. Polpinij, J., Ghose, A.K.: An ontology-based sentiment classification methodology for online consumer reviews. In: Proceedings of the 2008 IEEE/WIC/ACM International Conference on Web Intelligence and Intelligent Agent Technology, vol. 01, pp. 518–524. IEEE Computer Society (2008)
8. Zhao, L., Li, C.: Ontology based opinion mining for movie reviews. In: Karagiannis, D., Jin, Z. (eds.) KSEM 2009. LNCS, vol. 5914, pp. 204–214. Springer, Heidelberg (2009)
9. Muller, H.M., Kenny, E.E., Sternberg, W.: Textpresso: an ontology-based information retrieval and extraction system for biological literature. PLoS Biol. 2(11), e309 (2004)
10. Lenat, D.B.: CYC: a large-scale investment in knowledge infrastructure. Commun. ACM 38(11), 33–38 (1995)
11. Pohl, A.: Classifying the wikipedia articles into the OpenCyc taxonomy. In: Rizzo, G., Mendes, P., Charton, E., Hellmann, S., Kalyanpur, A., (eds.) Proceedings of the Web of Linked Entities Workshop in Conjuction with the 11th International Semantic Web Conference, pp. 5–16 (2012)
12. Cortes, C., Vapnik, V.: Support-vector networks. Mach. Learn. 20(3), 273–297 (1995)

13. Ben-Hur, A., Horn, D., Siegelmann, H.T., Vapnik, V.: Support vector clustering. J. Mach. Learn. Res. **2**, 125–137 (2002)
14. Fellbaum, C.: WordNet: An Electronic Lexical Database. MIT Press, Cambridge (1998)
15. Piasecki, M., Szpakowicz, S., Broda, B.: A WordNet from the ground up. Oficyna Wydawnicza Politechniki Wrocawskiej, Wrocaw (2009)
16. Auer, S., Bizer, C., Kobilarov, G., Lehmann, J., Cyganiak, R., Ives, Z.G.: DBpedia: a nucleus for a web of open data. In: Aberer, K., et al. (eds.) ASWC 2007 and ISWC 2007. LNCS, vol. 4825, pp. 722–735. Springer, Heidelberg (2007)
17. Lehmann, J., Isele, R., Jakob, M., Jentzsch, A., Kontokostas, D., Mendes, P.N., Hellmann, S., Morsey, M., van Kleef, P., Auer, S., et al.: DBpedia-a large-scale, multilingual knowledge base extracted from wikipedia. Semant. Web J. **5**, 1–29 (2014)
18. Motik, B.: On the properties of metamodeling in owl. J. Logic Comput. **17**(4), 617–637 (2007)
19. Manning, C.D., Surdeanu, M., Bauer, J., Finkel, J., Bethard, S.J., McClosky, D.: The Stanford CoreNLP natural language processing toolkit. In: Proceedings of 52nd Annual Meeting of the Association for Computational Linguistics: System Demonstrations, pp. 55–60 (2014)
20. Mendes, P., Jakob, M., Bizer, C.: DBpedia for NLP: A Multilingual Cross-domain Knowledge Base. In: LREC (to appear, 2012)
21. Zhang, X., LeCun, Y.: Text understanding from scratch (2015). arXiv preprint arXiv:1502.01710
22. Agarwal, A., Chapelle, O., Dudík, M., Langford, J.: A reliable effective terascale linear learning system. J. Mach. Learn. Res. **15**(1), 1111–1133 (2014)
23. Pedregosa, F., Varoquaux, G., Gramfort, A., Michel, V., Thirion, B., Grisel, O., Blondel, M., Prettenhofer, P., Weiss, R., Dubourg, V., et al.: Scikit-learn: machine learning in Python. J. Mach. Learn. Res. **12**, 2825–2830 (2011)

Agent Systems, Robotics and Control

Mapping Population and Mobile Pervasive Datasets into Individual Behaviours for Urban Ecosystems

Radosław Klimek[✉]

AGH University of Science and Technology,
Al. Mickiewicza 30, 30-059 Kraków, Poland
rklimek@agh.edu.pl

Abstract. Mobile phone network data routinely collected by providers possess very valuable and encoded information about human behaviours. In order to obtain the information it is necessary to carry out an arduous extraction process. Nevertheless, this information would be of fundamental importance for a successfully building and operating smart urban ecosystem understood as a self-organized and open system gathering and using knowledge about smart city environment. Intensive tourist activities in urban spaces bring smartness via mobile phone fingerprints into urban ecosystems and municipal services. This paper provides a unified approach comprising both informal (use cases) and formal (algorithms) elements to obtain a common framework which after ignoring redundant information maps pervasive datasets into a collection of individual patterns and anonymized tourist behaviours in urban spaces. They strongly influence municipal services to understand urban context and operate more effectively to support tourist activities to become more safe and comfortable.

Keywords: Pervasive dataset · Mobile phone network · Base Transceiver Station · Urban ecosystem · Individual behavior recognition · Multi-agent system · Tourist movement.

1 Introduction

Data ubiquitously generated during the plain interaction between mobile phone and the serving telecommunication network are a rich source of information. These pervasive datasets are recorded and stored in *Base Transceiver Station* BTS which are basic devices providing wireless communication between mobile phones and a telecommunication network. General availability of mobile phones accompanying us in everyday life in most of the time creates a great potential towards identifying people activities. (Anonymized) *Call Detail Records* CDRs produced during the above-mentioned interactions allows to estimate locations of important places as well as other behavioural aspects of user/tourist activities especially when some other open and available technologies are applied

© Springer International Publishing Switzerland 2016
L. Rutkowski et al. (Eds.): ICAISC 2016, Part I, LNAI 9692, pp. 683–694, 2016.
DOI: 10.1007/978-3-319-39378-0_58

supportively. Thus, the purpose of this paper is to map population datasets into a collection of individual behaviours to support urban ecosystem which produce context-aware and pro-active decisions. Activities and use cases for municipal services that support urban management, as well as refer to tourist movement in a destination, are considered.

Quality is always crucial for a successful tourism industry. Thus, the evaluation of effectiveness in achieving the goals of the assumed and expected sustainable tourism development is fundamental. Tourist trajectories and patter behaviours might be extracted from mobile phone datasets, and thus replace inefficient/traditional destination questionnaires, no matter manual/paper or web-based, within leisure, recreation and tourism settings. Since manual surveys are so expensive to conduct in terms of time and money, the automatic surveys based on the analysis of pervasive datasets from mobile networks seems to be an excellent alternative the benefits of which is hard to overestimate. Another advantage of this approach is impartiality as well as the generation in real-time reliable information covering tourist activities.

The aim of this paper is to show how to use information about tourist activity in urban spaces obtained from CDRs for context-aware smart decisions in urban ecosystem. The contribution of the paper is an unified approach consisting of sample use cases for an urban context-aware system and algorithms for software agents which are evidence and an argument validating the proposed system. Another contribution is a novel method of mapping filtered pervasive streams of datasets into a collection of individual and anonymized tourist activities located in a tourist destination. To the best of our knowledge, this early research paper presents the first study for mentioned area as well as the tourist movement case. This research opens some new directions especially related to implementation and experiments in particular.

There are works considering behavior recognition in ubiquitous computing; however, their relevant subset which focuses on pervasive datasets stored in BTS stations is a subject of these research interests. On the other hand, most of works focus on the entire streams of behaviors rather not considering individual one. For example, in work [12] mobile phone data are analyzed as data that create holistic and dynamic city system. It allows to build a dynamic and real-time representation that goes city-wide. Work [6] provides a method of identifying inhabitants' important locations by clustering and regression. Based on some simple rules, algorithms for selecting home and work locations are described, and both individual and population behavior is considered. Work [2] describes mobile phones in a real-time urban monitoring system based on fixed sensors and GPS receivers. These combined approaches allow to prepare a monitoring platform to visualize a vehicular traffic and movements of pedestrians. Behavioral patterns are discussed in work [4]. Summarizing these works, there is a lack of a strong focusing limited only to the individual behaviors within mobile phone datasets. However, the works influence this research showing challenging research direction as well as considering some patterns of behaviors. In work [13] not only current research trends for leisure, recreation and tourist are surveyed but there are also numerous questionnaires included.

2   Mobile Phone Infrastructure

Systems for mobile communications (e.g. GSM or UMTS) are well established. There are many works introducing the world of data communication procedures, e.g. work [5].

Fig. 1. A sample BTS network (source: **btsearch.pl**)

The most obvious part of the mobile phone network is a base station. A *base transceiver station* (BTS) is a piece of equipment that enables wireless communication between a user and the network. Nowadays, cities and regions are covered with a relatively dense network of BTSs, see for example Fig. 1. Although outside the cities networks are less dense, in each case they gather and store important and interesting information about different types of users' activities.

A *call detail record* (CDR) contains data recorded and produced by telecommunications equipment. CDRs, as collections of information, have a special format [3]. Below is a sample fragment of a CDR text decoded from the binary format. The first row must contain a header row which includes the field names:

```
Call Type,Call Cause,Customer Identifier,Telephone Num Dialled,Call Date,
Call Time,Duration,Bytes Transmitted,Bytes Received,Descript,Chargecode,
Time Band,Salesprice,Salesprice (pre-bundle),Extension,DDI,Grouping ID,
Call Class,Carrier,Recording,VAT,Country of Origin,Network,Tariff code,
Remote Network,APN,Diverted Number,Ring time,RecordID,Currency
```

The meaning of the columns is not analysed here since they are intuitive and the detailed discussion is outside the scope of the paper. Location information is extracted as part of the interaction data. These location observations, i.e. the moment of the phone's/object's entry into the area of a station (*log in*), and the moment they leave that area (*log out*), are of fundamental importance to the considerations given in the following sections of the paper.

3   Smart Urban Ecosystem

Ecosystem is a distributed, self-organized and open system gathering knowledge about (selected aspect of) smart city environment. It constitutes a community of digital devices and their environment functioning as a whole (hardware, software, services). This system might be extended considering other aspects of smart city, for example urban pollutions, fire and emergency systems, water and sanitation, energy, etc.

A sample urban system is shown in Fig. 2. Some users (actors) for a smart ecosystem that is context-aware are identified: Emergency services, Municipal police, and Public transportation management. *Emergency services* are organizations ensuring public safety and deal with emergencies when they occur (ambulance service, the police, the fire brigade, and others). *Municipal police*

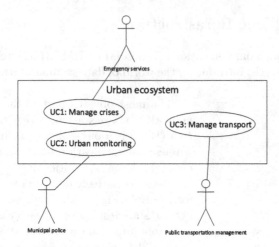

Fig. 2. A use case diagram for a smart urban ecosystem (fragment)

are law enforcement agencies that are under the control of a town, city, or borough or its local government. *Public transportation management* are systematic processes collecting and analyzing information on the condition and needs as inputs to the urban planning processes to support decision-makers for appropriate strategies.

The above actors operate in the context-aware urban system which consist of the following sample use cases: Manage crisis, Urban surveillance (UC2), and Manage transport (UC3). Brief descriptions of use case features are provided instead of a formal scenario.

Manage crisis (UC1) means process dealing with events that threaten for general public. When tourist activities in selected areas increased, responses might comprise: launching/establishing the special emergency call number, increasing the number of open/active, and night shifts, pharmacies in selected areas, increasing the number of hospital emergency rooms, improved security and enforcement of regulations, etc.

Urban monitoring (UC2) means checking processes or tracking in a systematic way, supervising activities in progress. When tourist activities in selected areas increased, responses might comprise: intensification of monitoring in selected areas, increased energy consumption/production, increased waste and pollution issues, additional patrols, sending drones, etc.

Manage transport (UC3) means to supply chain management for transportation operations in the public area. When tourist activities in selected areas increased, responses might comprise: increasing the frequency of buses/trams courses, shuttle services if necessary, activating additional bicycle rental systems, etc.

4   Tourist Destination Questionnaires

A *questionnaire* is a form containing a set of questions usually addressed to statistically important tourist activities. A tourist questionnaire is a typical way of gathering information which can be used for managing context-aware urban ecosystem. A questionnaire for tourist movement in destinations is discussed now to clarify how smart systems basing on recognising tourist activities work.

Fig. 3. Lisbon and close/distance surroundings.

Lisbon, the capital city of Portugal, as well as its surroundings are considered and used as an example.

Tourists/visitors stay in Lisbon and, probably day by day, visit its monuments and various tourist attractions. However, some tourists during their whole stay in the city may wish to visit its surroundings, e.g. Fátima (religious reasons) or Cascais (recreational reasons), as well as Sintra which is known for historical and architectural monuments and is classified as a UNESCO World Heritage Site, see Fig. 3. All these places/sub-destinations, except Fátima, are located in the *Grande Lisboa* subregion[1].

Sample and common questions for visitors are shown in Table 1. There are also available many other tourist questionnaires, for example [1,14]. These questionnaires are distributed to visitors during their stay at a destination. They refer to many details of visitors' trip and stay. Forms are usually designed by tourism organizations for people who are going to spent at least one night at the destination. Questionnaires are conducted anonymously.

---

[1] See http://en.wikipedia.org/wiki/Grande_Lisboa.

Table 1. A sample tourist questionnaire (a sketch).

Questions	Answers
1. When did you come to Lisbon and what day of your stay is it today?	. . .
2. Did you come to Lisbon directly from your residence?	Y/N
3. How long are you going to stay in Lisbon?	. . .
4. Are you accommodate in Lisbon?	Y/N
5. In what type of accommodation in Lisbon do you stay, if any?	hotel, hostel, etc.
6. What were your main aims when selecting this destination?	business, culture, religion, etc.
7. What means of transport did you use to arrive to Lisbon?	train, car, airplane, etc.
8. Do you travel in a group?	Y/N
9. Do you use local guides?	Y/N
10. How many times have you been in Lisbon before?	. . .
11. How much money do you spend per person?	. . .
12. Which places outside Lisbon do you want to visit during your stay?	. . .
13. How do you find selected aspects of your visit (from 1 to 5)?	[aspects to evaluate]
14. How do you find selected services in Lisbon (from 1 to 5)?	[services to evaluate]
15. What are the most attractive places in Lisbon?	. . .
16. What sources of information did you consult before arrival?	[options to select]
17. How would you like to spend your time during your next stay in Lisbon	. . .
18. Are you going to recommend Lisbon to your friends?	Y/N
19. Are you going to come to Lisbon again?	Y/N
20. Personal information about a respondent	. . .

One of the main objectives of the questionnaires is to know more about visitor characteristics for marketing purposes, as well as to identify the size of the tourism activity. Other characteristics cover types of visitors (foreign or home, business or leisure, overnight or day trip). They also allow to identify where visitors, if any, go outside the examined basic destination and what is the scale of sub-destination visits.

The purpose of this paper is also to provide methods of gathering automatically information about tourist movements, that is to replace manual surveys by a fully automatic process, and then use this information for smart urban ecosystem. It should be noted that the typical granulation for the BTS station is about 500 m in a city (urban areas) and about 1,000 m outside a city. On the other hand, there are some advanced algorithms and models [2] enabling an estimation of a phone position between stations with an accuracy of about 150 m in urban areas. Let us also note that *Home Location Register* HLR is maintained in mobile networks in order to provide information about subscribers who are registered in a core/local network. The opposite meaning has the *Visitor Location Register* VLR which provides information about network visitors (outside/country or foreign). These two records are important for the approach since they allow finding who is a visitor and who is not. Although there are some exceptions, the probability of correct verification based on VLRs/HLRs is very high. In the case of any difficulties or doubts, the billing databases of mobile providers might additionally be examined.

5   Towards Algorithm

The analysis of points/questions in Table 1 leads to the following taxonomy based on the information expected to be obtained from the BTS datasets, which constitute an informally expressed algorithm:

1. answers that are obviously easy to obtain, e.g. point 1 or 3;
2. some answers are available through digging deeper but still direct analysis of the BTS data is needed, e.g. point 2 and the VLR/HLR records;
3. a certain number of answers need a pattern analysis for individuals, e.g. the comparison of the locations during day and night for point 4, or less/limited mobility (business) and greater mobility (an active city exploration typical for tourists) for point 6;
4. some answers require a pattern analysis for a group, if any, of visitors, in other words, it is examined whether a group of objects are moving together, e.g. the city exploration with a group of mobile phones/visitors for point 8, or with a one local (c.f. VLR/HLR records) mobile phone of a local guide for point 9;
5. some points need additional (open) technologies to answer questions, e.g. *OpenStreetMap* OSM[2] to locate/identify selected objects like airports or railway stations for point 7, hotels/hostels for point 5, museums/churches for point 6, or suburban areas (close or distant) for point 12;
6. there are some answers that require the historical data analysis, e.g. previous presence in a destination for point 10;
7. some answers require accesses to commercial/bank data, e.g. credit/debit cards used in the destination for point 11;
8. several answers could be obtained while analyzing, for example, social networks, reservation systems or web vendors, e.g. sources of information for point 16;

---

[2] See: http://en.wikipedia.org/wiki/OpenStreetMap.

9. some answers could be obtained when web forms are sent directly to mobile phones, after the visit in the destination is over, e.g. sources of information for points 13–15, 20;

10. some points for which obtaining answers basing on BTS datasets are impossible or problematic, e.g. points 17–19;

11. last but not least, there is some information that could be extracted from the BTS data, and which usually is not a subject of any questionnaire (thus, no points in Table 1 are indicated here) but it could be used to analyze other parameters of tourist activities, e.g. intensity of call/sms/mms/web transmissions during the entire visit or in particular places, and thou numerous valuable conclusions that follow.

The above classification is crucial and gives an idea of the foundations for solutions and methods proposed in the paper, that is how use information gathered in CDRs treated as a base for pro-active decisions of an urban ecosystem. In other words, the above classification constitute a base for methods of building knowledge about tourist activities, c.f. line 2 in Algorithm 2.

6 A Multi-agent System

A multi-agent system and its architecture is proposed in this Section. The system is used to solve the problem of surveying the tourist movement in a destination in the way as described in the previous Section.

The following taxonomy of agent is proposed:

A – *Angel-the-guard agent*, that is an agent created for a new object that appears in the entire destination network when this object is classified as a visitor. From this moment the agent exist in a system until the object leaves the entire network; the agent stores all events that refer to the object. After the object leaves a destination then the gathered information are passed to the agent **Q** and the agent **A** is removed from the system;

E – *Event agent*, that is an agent that exist in a system permanently the purpose of which is to process new events that appear. It is assumed that a list of basic events is pre-defined and only these events are handled;

Q – *Questionnaire agent*, that is an agent that exists in a system and its purpose is to update a questionnaire which is build in this destination. The questionnaire is updated when an object leaves the entire destination and its agent **A** is to be removed. There is one questionnaire agent for one type of questionnaire;

M – *Managing agent*, that is an agent that exists in a system permanently, and the purpose of this agent is to initiate system variables, and to handle two (selected) events as well as to manage questionnaire agents in this destination.

Summing up, the number of agents **A** in a system is equal to the number of visitors in a given destination; there is only one agent **E** in a destination; the number of agents **Q** in a system is equal to the number of questionnaire types built in the system, and there is only one agent **M** in the system.

7   Methods and Algorithms

Several algorithms for handling the entire system are proposed in this Section. They refer to the classification of the agents defined in the previous Section, that is agents that operate in a system.

Some assumptions related to the algorithms are made. There is a pre-defined set/list of BTSs *BTSlist* that belong to a considered destination. This set/area is closed, and only these BTSs constitute the destination. (A "BTS corridor", for surroundings, see Fig. 3, must be built from a destination to a sub-destination.) An event loop (message dispatcher) *EventList* is the primary method of processing. There is also predefined set of events *PredefEvent* which are registered and inserted into loop *EventList*. Every event *e* defines an event type/name and the associate/coupled object *o* (mobile phone). In other words, an event always means a pair of an event's name and an object. The events describe different aspects of objects' activities registered in BTSs and are not widely discussed here. There are two special cases of events *objCome* and *objLeave* which mean that an object enters or exits a destination defined by *BTSlist*, respectively. The "nil" means empty event. The "others" stands for events that are outside the scope of (tourist) interest. Loop *EventList* as well as *PredefEvent* are placed in a basic/native mobile network system, and the system inserts every registered event to the loop which is processed by Algorithms 1–4.

The entire system is initiated by agent **M** whose operations are shown as Algorithm 1. Firstly, the agent initiates system/global variables and questionnaires. Secondly, agent **M** processes in the loop two (special) events that appear in the system. The global variables are *V is* (all active visitors observed/registered in a destination), *Res* (all active residents observed/registered in a destination), *PredefEvent* (list of legal and predefined events that are handled), and list of events *EventList* that are currently being processed in a system. Two of these events are handled directly in the main loop, that is only the agent **M** processes these events.

The agent **Q**, shown as Algorithm 2, processes data gathered by the agents **A**. Data are (temporary) stored in the system. Questionnaire *Que* is updated using data of agent *a* in the way it is required by this questionnaire. The agent **A** gathers data for object *o* and event *e* and is shown as Algorithm 3. Object *o* is a visitor and event *e* belongs to the list of legal events *PredefEvent*. The agent **E** performs events as defined in *EventList* and is shown as Algorithm 4. Events are processed in the (main) loop similar to the loop in the agent **M**'s operations, however, the right to process two events from *EventList* is reserved for the agent **M**.

Call "**call process** *M–operations*" (see also line 8 in Algorithm 1) starts the system. The system does not need a synchronization because of disjoint subsets of events processed in two separate loops (see, line 12 in Algorithm 1 and line 4 in Algorithm 4). If more agents **E** are introduced to speed up the entire system, e.g. call "**call process** (1..p) *E–operations*" (line 8 in Algorithm 1), the synchronization is mandatory.

Algorithm 1. The **M** agent operations (**M-operations**)

1: $BTSlist = ...;$ ▷ destination covered by BTSs
2: $PredefEvent = (objCome, objLeave, ..., others);$
3: $Vis := \emptyset; Res := \emptyset;$ ▷ lists of Visitors and Residents
4: $EventList := \emptyset;$ ▷ events to handle, dispatcher, FIFO
5: **for** $i = 1, .., n$ **do**   ▷ many questionnaires, if $i > 1$
6:     $InitQuestionnaire(Que_i)$ ▷ initialize every Que
7: **end for**
8: **call process** $E\text{--}operations;$ ▷ concurrently
9: **loop**
10:     $e := Get(EventList);$ ▷ read
11:     **if** $e \neq nil$ **then**
12:         **if** $(e \in \{objCome, objLeave\})$ **then**
13:             $v := VerifyVisitor(o);$ ▷ using VLR/HLR
14:             **if** $v \wedge (e = objCome)$ **then**
15:                 $NewAngel(a, o);$ ▷ agent a for object o
16:                 $A\text{--}operations(e);$
17:                 $Vis := Vis \cup \{o\}$
18:             **end if**
19:             **if** $v \wedge (e = objLeave)$ **then**
20:                 $A\text{--}operations(e);$
21:                 **for** $i = 1, .., n$ **do**
22:                     $Q\text{--}operations(Que_i, a);$
23:                 **end for**
24:                 $DisposseAngel(a);$ ▷ remove agent
25:                 $Vis := Vis \setminus \{o\}$
26:             **end if**
27:             $Delete(e)$ ▷ remove from $EventList$
28:         **end if**
29:     **end if**
30: **end loop**

Algorithm 2. The **Q** agent operations (**Q-operations**)

Input: $Que, a;$ ▷ a questionnaire and one agent **A**
Output: Que
1: Store data of $a;$ ▷ in a global repository
2: Update Que using data gathered by agent $a;$

Finding *time complexity*, which signifies the total time required by the algorithm to run to completion, for Algorithms 1–4 begins with Algorithms 2 and 3 which are elementary and called from other algorithms. Time complexity for Algorithm 2 depends on the length of a particular questionnaire $\mathcal{O}(q_n)$, where q_n is a total number of questions in a questionnaire, c.f. Table 1.

Algorithm 3. The **A** agent operations (**A**-operations)

Input: e ▷ event, $e \in PredefEvent$
Output: a ▷ agent **A** for object o
1: Search agent a for event e of object o;
2: Update a using data of event e;

Algorithm 4. The **E** agent operations (**E**-operations)

 1: **loop**
 2:     $e := Get(EventList)$;   ▷ read
 3:     **if** $e \neq nil$ **then**
 4:         **if** $(e \notin \{objCome, objLeave\})$ **then**
 5:             **if** $(e \neq others) \wedge (o \in Vis)$ **then**   ▷ o in e
 6:                 A–$operations(e)$;
 7:             **end if**
 8:             $Delete(e)$ ▷ remove from $EventList$
 9:         **end if**
10:     **end if**
11: **end loop**

Time complexity for Algorithm 3 depends on the number of predefined and considered events $\mathcal{O}(e_p)$ for an agent. Line 6 in Algorithm 4 contains its dominant operation, hence, time complexity for Algorithm 4 is $\mathcal{O}(p')$, where $p' = (PredefEvents \setminus \{others\}) \setminus \{objCome, objLeave\}$, that is all predefined events minus other ones, which are omitted and not considered for questionnaires, and minus two events processed separately in Algorithm 1. Most instructions of Algorithm 1 are fixed cost instructions, even the loop instruction in line 8 has fixed cost. The main purpose of the Algorithm is to pre-handle two special events $objCome$ and $objLeave$, as well as to create/delete the angel for an object. Moreover, Algorithm 3 is always called, as well as Algorithm 2 is called in one case. Thus, worst case time complexity for Algorithm 1 is $\mathcal{O}(e_l + n \cdot q_{i=1,...,n})$, where e_l is a number of predefined events, and n is a number of considered questionnaires, see lines 16, 20, and 22.

8   Conclusion

The paper presents a novel method for mining individual behaviours of visitors in a destination from pervasive BTS datasets. The questionnaire behaviour, see Table 1, is expressed informally in an introduced classification giving an idea how it works, and then authenticated through an architecture of a multi-agent system and more formally through Algorithms 1–4. The gathered information constitute a base for the context-aware urban ecosystem shown in Fig. 2.

Future works should cover more detailed algorithms as well as an architecture for a multi-agent system. Formal logic is an appropriate background, when considering workflows for software models [7,8], applications of formal reasoning processes, e.g. [10,11], or mining behaviours from datasets [9]. More theoretical and especially experimental evaluations are also required for future work.

References

1. Arillas Business association: Tourism questionnaire for arillas and surrounding area (2015). http://arillas.de/arillas_questionaire.pdf. Accesed 21 Feb 2015
2. Calabrese, F., Colonna, M., Lovisolo, P., Parata, D., Ratti, C.: Real-time urban monitoring using cell phones: a case study in rome. IEEE Trans. Intell. Transp. Syst. **12**(1), 141–151 (2011)
3. Federation of Communication Services: UK Standard for CDRs. Standard CDR Format, January 2014
4. Gonzalez, M.C., Hidalgo, C.A., Barabasi, A.L.: Understanding individual human mobility patterns. Nature **453**(7196), 779–782 (2008)
5. Horak, R.: Telecommunications and Data Communications Handbook. Wiley-Interscience, Hoboken (2007)
6. Isaacman, S., Becker, R., Cáceres, R., Kobourov, S., Martonosi, M., Rowland, J., Varshavsky, A.: Identifying important places in people's lives from cellular network data. In: Lyons, K., Hightower, J., Huang, E.M. (eds.) Pervasive 2011. LNCS, vol. 6696, pp. 133–151. Springer, Heidelberg (2011)
7. Klimek, R.: Towards formal and deduction-based analysis of business models for soa processes. In: Filipe, J., Fred, A. (eds.) Proceedings of 4th International Conference on Agents and Artificial Intelligence (ICAART 2012), Vilamoura, Algarve, Portugal, 6–8 February, vol. 2, pp. 325–330. SciTePress (2012)
8. Klimek, R.: A system for deduction-based formal verification of workflow-oriented software models. Int. J. Appl. Math. Comput. Sci. **24**(4), 941–956 (2014)
9. Klimek, R.: Behaviour recognition and analysis in smart environments for context-aware applications. In: Proceedings of the IEEE International Conference on Systems, Man, and Cybernetics (SMC 2015), City University of Hong Kong, Hong Kong, 9–12 October, pp. 1949–1955. IEEE Computer Society (2015)
10. Klimek, R., Kotulski, L.: Proposal of a multiagent-based smart environment for the iot. In: Augusto, J.C., Zhang, T. (eds.) Workshop Proceedings of the 10th International Conference on Intelligent Environments. Ambient Intelligence and Smart Environments, Shanghai, China, 30 June–1 July, vol. 18, pp. 37–44. IOS Press (2014)
11. Klimek, R., Rogus, G.: Modeling context-aware and agent-ready systems for the outdoor smart lighting. In: Rutkowski, L., Korytkowski, M., Scherer, R., Tadeusiewicz, R., Zadeh, L.A., Zurada, J.M. (eds.) ICAISC 2014, Part II. LNCS(LNAI), vol. 8468, pp. 257–268. Springer, Heidelberg (2014)
12. Reades, J., Calabrese, F., Sevtsuk, A., Ratti, C.: Cellular census: explorations in urban data collection. IEEE Pervasive Comput. **6**(3), 30–38 (2007)
13. Sirakaya-Turk, E., Uysal, M., Hammitt, W., Vaske, J. (eds.): Research Methods for Leisure, Recreation and Tourism. CABI Publishing (2011). http://www.worldcat.org/isbn/9781845937638
14. Tourism and Cultural Affairs Bureau, City of Sapporo: Questionnaire for tourists from foreign countries (2015). http://www.city.sapporo.jp/keizai/kanko/program/documents/h21_eigo.pdf. Accesed on 21 Feb 2015

A Decision Support System Based on Hybrid Metaheuristic for Solving the Constrained Capacitated Vehicle Routing Problem: The Tunisian Case

Marwa Harzi[1]([⊠]) and Saoussen Krichen[2]

[1] VPNC Laboratory, Higher Institute of Management,
University of Tunis, Tunis, Tunisia
harzimarwa@yahoo.fr
[2] LARODEC Laboratory, Higher Institute of Management,
University of Tunis, Tunis, Tunisia

Abstract. Various metaheuristic approaches have emerged in recent years to solve the capacitated vehicle routing problem (CVRP), a well-known $\mathcal{NP}-hard$ problem in routing. In CVRP, the objective is to design the route set at a lower cost for a homogenous fleet of vehicles, starting from and going back to the depot, to meet the needs and expectations of all the customers. In this paper, we propose an ILS-VND approach which is a hybrid of Iterated Local Search (ILS) and Variable Neighborhood Descent (VND) approaches. Although both ILS and VND approaches, independently provide good solutions, we found that the hybrid approach gives better solutions than either approach independently. We demonstrate the effectiveness of our approach through experiments carried out on widely used benchmark instances. Numerical experiments show that the proposed method outperforms other local searches and metaheuristics. We also, propose a Decision Support System (DSS) that integrates a Geographical Information System (GIS) to solve the problem under scrutiny. In order to demonstrate the performance of the proposed DSS in terms of solution quality, we apply it for a real case on the city of Jendouba in the north west of Tunisia. The results are then highlighted in a cartographic format using Google Maps.

Keywords: CVRP · Hybrid ILS-VND metaheuristic · ILS · VND · Decision support systems · Geographical information system

1 Introduction

Supply chain involves many activities like supply and production. For a long time, research on logistics has focused on optimizing these activities since this optimization has eliminated the waste of time. The transport activity is one of the most important activities in logistics. A better organization of this activity mainly vehicle routing presents an economic challenge. Because of this economic importance and priority, researchers have paid great interest to the vehicle

© Springer International Publishing Switzerland 2016
L. Rutkowski et al. (Eds.): ICAISC 2016, Part I, LNAI 9692, pp. 695–704, 2016.
DOI: 10.1007/978-3-319-39378-0_59

routing problem VRP. The Vehicle Routing Problem (VRP) is considered as an $\mathcal{NP}-hard$ combinatorial optimization problem, which was proposed, by Dantzig and Ramser in [1]. VRP is identified as a plan to follow for serving a number of customers by a number of vehicles, knowing that the cost of allocating vehicles to customers must be reduced. There are many variations of VRP, such as the Capacitated Vehicle Routing Problem (CVRP), Vehicle Routing Problem with Pickup and Delivery (VRPPD), Dynamic Vehicle Routing Problem (SVRP) and the Vehicle Routing Problem with Time Windows (VRPTW).

The Capacitated Vehicle Routing Problem (CVRP) was first introduced by Dantzig and Ramser (1959) [1]. It consists, in its basic version, of designing a set of minimum cost-routes for a number of identical vehicles having a fixed capacity to serve a set of customers with known demands.

From a theoretical point of view, CVRP is known to be $\mathcal{NP}-hard$ [2], and hence is not expected to be solved by any exact algorithm in a polynomial time in the general case. The computational difficulty of solving CVRP is also confirmed in practice. Indeed, the best existing exact algorithms are limited to moderate only small instances [3–5]. For these reasons, intensive research has been devoted to developing heuristic and metaheuristic methods. Representative heuristic methods include [6,7]. Among the metaheuristic methods, neighborhood search approaches are popular, e.g., tabu search [8,9], variable neighborhood search [10], Iterated local search [11]. As another class of popular metaheuristics for tackling CVRP, population-based algorithms generally achieve better performances, such as the memetic algorithm [12] and the ant colony algorithm [13].

Contributions and Paper Outline: The main contributions of this paper are (i) to solve an important VRP variant named CVRP using a hybrid metaheuristic ILS-VND. (ii) to model mathematically the CVRP. (iii) to propose a DSS based on GIS to aid decision makers on solving the CVRP. And ($iiii$) to to validate the designed DSS using a Tunisia real case study.

The remainder of this paper is structured as follows. The CVRP is stated mathematically in Sect. 2. In Sect. 3 the main steps of the proposed DSS are outlined. Section 4 provides a description of the resolution methodology ILS-VND. Section 5 describes the computational results. Section 6 details the case study. And in the final section, we close with some concluding remarks.

2   Mathematical Model

For more clarity, we define the CVRP on a connected graph G. Let $G = (V, A)$, where $V = \{v_0, v_1, ..., v_{n+1}\}$ is a vertex set and $A = \{(v_i, v_j) \mid v_i, v_j \in V; v_i \neq v_j\}$ is an arc set. Vertices v_0 and v_{n+1} correspond to the depot at which K homogeneous vehicles are based, and the remaining vertices denote the customers. Each arc (v_i, v_j) is associated with a non-negative weight $c_{v_i v_j}$, which represents the travel distance from v_i to v_j. Each customer has a delivery demand q_i. The CVRP consists of determining a set of least cost vehicle routes such as: Each route starts and ends at the depot. Each customer is visited exactly once by

Table 1. List of used parameters

Route	Distance
n	Set of customers
m	Set of vehicles
Q	Capacity of vehicle
D_i	Demand of customer i
d_{ij}	Distance between customer i and customer j
c_{ij}	Total cost

exactly one vehicle. And the total demand of the customers assigned to any vehicle must not exceed the vehicle capacity Q.

The previous description of the VRPTW can be stated mathematically. We enumerate in what follows (Table 1) the main symbols used in the mathematical model (1)–(8):

$$\text{Min } z = \sum_{i=1}^{n} \sum_{j=1}^{n} \sum_{k=1}^{m} d_{ij} x_{ij}^k \tag{1}$$

$$\text{S.t } \sum_{k=1} \sum_{i=0} x_{ij}^k = 1; \quad \forall j = 0, ..., n \tag{2}$$

$$\sum_{k=1} \sum_{j=0} x_{ij}^k = 1; \quad \forall i = 0, ..., n \tag{3}$$

$$\sum_{i=0}^{n} x_{it}^k - \sum_{j=0}^{n} x_{tj}^k = 0; \quad \forall k = 1, ..., m \quad t = 0, ..., n \tag{4}$$

$$\sum_{j=0}^{n} q_j (\sum_{i=0}^{n} x_{ij}^k) \leq Q; \quad \forall k = 1, ..., m \tag{5}$$

$$\sum_{j=0}^{n} x_{0j}^k \leq 1; \quad \forall k = 1, ..., m \tag{6}$$

$$\sum_{i=0}^{n} x_{i0}^k \leq 1; \quad \forall k = 1, ..., m \tag{7}$$

$$x_{ij}^k \in \{0, 1\}; \quad \forall i, j = 0, ..., n \quad k = 1, ..., n \tag{8}$$

- Objective function: Eq. (1) expresses the total distance traveled by all vehicles that must be minimized in accordance with the set of system constraints.
- System constraints: Constraints (2) and (3) impose that each node is visited only once by one vehicle. Constraints (4) ensure the continuity of vehicles pathways. Constraints (5) enforce the capacity constraint of the vehicles. Constraints (6) and (7) ensure that each used vehicle starts and ends at the depot. Constraints (8) are of a binary type.

Table 2. Main steps of the DSS.

Data Inputs	Optimization Tools	Numerical and Geographical solution

3   Decision Support System Architecture

Our DSS (Table 2) is based on a ILS-VND that responds to all customer requests trying to optimally generate vehicles paths. The DSS starts by inputting problem parameters, namely the number of customers to be served, the number of available vehicles and the vehicles capacity. Once these data were provided, customer demands and geographical coordinates are to be set. The VND approach proceeds iteratively by an alternative use of the Local Search in order to diversify the search. Once the numerical solution is generated, the DSS moves to the design of the cartographical solution that well illustrates the real itinerary. Vehicles pathways are then highlighted.

4   Resolution Methodology: Hybrid ILS-VND

4.1   Variable Neighborhood Descent

The Variable Neighborhood Descent (VND) was proposed by Hansen and Mladenovic (2003). VND is a relatively young metaheuristic concept that has successfully been applied to several combinatorial optimization problems. It performs as follows:

Let $N_1, ..., N_n$ be the set of predefined neighborhood structures, and $N_k(s)$ be the set of solutions using the kth neighborhood of s. The local optimum s' of f regarding to $N_k(s)$, is a feasible solution, where no solution $s \in N_k(s')$ such that $f(s) < f(s')$. The VND is a metaheuristic that switches between neighborhoods $N_1, ..., N_n$ according to a predefined order.

Starting with the first neighborhood N_1, VND performs a local search until no further improvements are available. Then, from local optimum, it continues the local search with neighborhood N_2. If there is improvement in the current solution, VND restarts with N_1 again; otherwise, it continues with N_3, and so forth. If the last structure N_n has been performed and no additional improvements are feasible, the solution corresponds to a local optimum with respect to all neighborhoods. The performance of the VND depends significantly on the choice of the neighborhoods at each iteration.

4.2   Iterated Local Search

Local search methods can get stuck in a local minimum, where no improving neighbors are available. A simple modification consists of iterating the local search and each time starting from a different initial configuration, this is called Iterated Local Search (ILS) methods. The main components that need to be tackled to operate an ILS algorithm in order to achieve high performance [14] are: *Generate Initial Solution*, *Local Search*, *Perturbation*, and *Acceptance Criterion*.

- *Generate Initial Solution*: a random solution or a returned solution by some greedy construction heuristic;
- *Local Search*: replaces the current solution by an improvement neighbor solution.
- *Perturbation*: a scheme of how to perturb a solution.
- *Acceptance Criterion*: decide from which solution the search is continued.

An initial solution S_0 is generated and improved by a local search (LS) procedure. The local optimum that is obtained is indicated by S. The following steps are repeated, until predetermined termination criteria are not met. The solution S is perturbed (modified) and a new current solution S^* is obtained. The LS is appliedto S^* and a solution S^{**} is obtained. If S^{**} is accepted (for example, based on its quality) it becomes the new current local optimum.

4.3   ILS-VND Approach for VRPTW

Due to the NP hardness of the addressed problem, we propose to solve it with a hybrid VND-based ILS metaheuristic (Algorithm 1). The main steps of the proposed method are as follows:

Step 1 - Initial Solution: The proposed algorithm starts off by generating an initial feasible solution as the starting point of search by the VND procedure. We applied the saving algorithm by Clarke and Wright (1964) [15] to rapidly obtain a solution, which is based on the notion of savings: firstly, dispatch a vehicle to each customer; then merge two routes into a single one which can generate the maximum distance savings. This heuristic method terminates when there are no more two routes can feasibly be merged, i.e., be merged without violating the route duration or capacity constraints.

Step 2 - Variable Neighborhood Descent: The VND procedure is to search for better solutions in the neighborhood defined by different operators, which is described by Algorithm 3. The operators used in the VND procedure are four operators commonly used for standard VRP, i.e., insert, swap, 2-opt* and 2-opt.

700 M. Harzi and S. Krichen

Algorithm 1. *Hybrid ILS-VND for the CVRP*

    Initialize parameters
2: $S_0 \leftarrow$ Generate Initial Solution S_0
    $S_0^* \leftarrow$ VND (S_0)
4: $S^* \leftarrow S_0^*$
    Let the best solution found $S^{**} \leftarrow S^*$
6: **repeat**
        $S' \leftarrow$ Perturbations (S^*)
8:     $S'^* \leftarrow$ VND S'
        if $f(S'^* < f(S^{**}$ **then**
10:       $S^{**} = S'^*$
        end if
12: **until** terminational rule is met
    return S^{**}

The aim of using multi-operator is to explore the solution space more extensively. When no further improvement can be obtained, the VND procedure stops. The VND procedure is described by Algorithm 1, where LocalSearch(s, N_k) refers to the local search in the neighborhood of solution s defined by the operator N_k. In our VND we used the following operators:

- The relocation consists of removing a customer from its current place and reinserting it into another position in the same route or in an alternative one.
- A swap move consists of exchanging the places of two customers belonging to different routes.
- The 2-opt* operates on two different routes. Firstly, each route is divided into two parts by removing an arc; then, the first part of one route and the second part of the other are combined to generate a new route by introducing a new arc. The remaining two parts build another new route analogously.
- The 2-opt operator is used for intra-route improvement. In a 2-opt move, two non-adjacent arcs are replaced by another two new ones, and the visited order of the customers between the two arcs is reversed.

Step 3 - Perturbation: Once the VND procedure is stopped, a perturbation is started. The perturbation should neither be too strong nor too weak. If the perturbation is too strong, the algorithm may reduce to a random restart method; otherwise, the possibility of escaping from the current local optimum is quite low. In the proposed method, the perturbation move is realized by applying the method in Fig. 1, in which a customer segment of customers on the upper route is exchanged with another on the lower one, while solution feasibility is guaranteed.

Step 4 - Acceptance Criterion: After perturbation and local search phases have been completed, the resulting solution should be compared with the current one. Deciding whether it will be selected or not we adopted an acceptance criterion. In our ILS-VND method only solutions that improve the cost and respect the time windows will be considered.

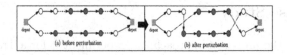

Fig. 1. Illustration of perturbation process

5   Experimentations

In this section, we report the experimental results generated by the proposed ILS-VND to handle the CVRP. The experimentations were conducted on the CVRP benchmarking problems known as Li et al. benchmark instances (2005) [16]. The implementation of the ILS-VND was coded in JAVA language and executed on a computer with a 8.00 GB RAM and an Intel Core $i5$, 2.50 GHz CPU. In order to evaluate the ILS-VND, its performance is compared to previous best known solutions and to some other approaches that were tested on the same set of instances.

The results for the 12 benchmark instances of Li et al. (2005) [16] are presented in Table 3. In Table 3, the best results reported in three recently published papers [16–18] for comparison. For this set of instances, the proposed algorithm found new best solution (numbers in bold font). The average deviation of our best solutions found from the previous best known is 2.12 %. According to this measurement, our results give new best results by the ILS-VND. We can note from these results that the hybridization of the ILS with the VND algorithm has a significant importance since it provides better results in term of solution quality for corresponding problem.

Table 3. Comparison of the results on the benchmark instances

Problem	Previous best known	[16] 2005	[17] 2007	[18] 2011	ILS-VND
21(560)	16212.74	16602.99	16224.81	16212.83	16212.74
22(600)	14584.42	14651.27	14631.08	14631.73	**14433.32**
23(640)	18801.12	18838.62	18837.49	18801.13	18837.49
24(720)	21389.33	21616.25	21522.48	21390.63	21390.63
25(760)	16763.72	17146.41	16902.16	17089.62	**16663.62**
26(800)	23971.74	24009.74	24014.09	23977.73	23971.74
27(840)	17433.69	17823.40	17613.22	17589.05	17433.69
28(880)	26565.92	26606.11	26791.72	26567.23	26606.11
29(960)	29154.34	29181.21	29405.60	29155.54	29154.34
30(1040)	31742.51	31976.73	31968.33	31743.84	31976.73
31(1120)	34330.84	35369.17	34770.34	34333.37	**34240.56**
32(1200)	36919.24	37421.44	37377.35	37285.90	37377.35

6   Real Case Study

In order to test the proposed approach, we experiment it for a Transport Company named SRTJ in the region of Jendouba in the north west of Tunisia. The SRTJ made seven routes of different directions and distances available to its customers as illustrated in Table 4. This Table proves that the costs of the existing routes exceed their incomes, which requires the minimization of these costs, that's why we must also minimize the covered distance.

Table 4. Characteristics of the existing routes

	Route	Distance	Cost	Income
1	Jendouba → Bousselem → Fahs → Kairouane	218	507	448
2	Jendouba → Ain drahem → Tabarka	68	158	140
3	Jendouba → Bousselem → Beja	52	121	107
4	Jendouba → Bousselem → Tborsok → Siliana	125	291	257
5	Jendouba → Essaada → Kef	49	113	101
6	Jendouba → Beja → Ghazela → Bizerte	167	388	343
7	Jendouba → Wed mliz → Ghardimaou	35	81	72

6.1   Distance Minimization

Let us consider an example of 1 depot and 4 customers dispersed around the city of Jendouba as shown in Fig. 2. Different setting parameters of the problem are presented in Table 5 and customers demands are as follows: Kef = 35, Sers = 15, Siliana = 30 and Kairouan = 23.

Table 5. Description of example parameters

Parameters	Distance
Vehicle capacity (kg)	120
Number of vehicles for each depot	1
Number of customers to be served	4

In order to pick out the shortest path between each couple of customers, we need an additional parameter called the distance matrix that calculates the shortest paths between each pair of customers and depots. It consists of distances in meter.

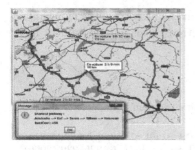

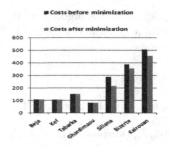

Fig. 2. Geographical solution using the DSS

Fig. 3. Evolution of costs

$$
\begin{pmatrix}
 & Jendouba & Kef & Sers & Siliana & Kairouan \\
Jendouba & 0 & 56 & 76 & 120 & 196 \\
Kef & 56 & 0 & 30 & 60 & 175 \\
Sers & 76 & 30 & 0 & 30 & 100 \\
Siliana & 120 & 60 & 30 & 0 & 80 \\
Kairouan & 196 & 175 & 100 & 80 & 0
\end{pmatrix}
$$

Figure 2 presents a geographical view of the obtained results after solving the example. It illustrates the best traveling path for each vehicle, while taking into account the capacity and the cost constraint. This map is used to guide vehicles drivers to serve customers through the shortest itinerary presented in blue color. In this example, the vehicles leave the depot Jendouba to serve Kef, Seres, Siliana then Kairouan orderly at a cost of 456.

6.2   Cost Minimization

After the minimization of the total traversed distances, we applied the proposed DSS to minimize the costs of these routes. The improvements of the costs before and after minimization are as follows: before minimization (Ghardimaou = 81, Siliana = 291, Bizerte = 388 and Kairouan = 507), after minimization (Ghardimaou = 81, Siliana = 218, Bizerte = 358 and Kairouan = 456) (Fig. 3).

7   Summary and Conclusions

In this paper the Capacitated Vehicle Routing Problem (CVRP) is evoked and solved using hybrid meta-heuristic which gathers the Iterated Local Search approach (ILS) and Variable Neighborhood Descent approach (VND). In order to better visualize the obtained results and make it more intuitive, we proposed a GIS to design a Decision Support System (DSS). The proposed DSS provides assistance to operating managers in transportation logistics. To assess the efficiency of our framework, we proposed to solve an application of a Tunisian case.

And by applying the algorithms to benchmarkS in the literature, the experimental results also showed that the ILS-VND algorithm consistently produces high performance.

References

1. Dantzig, G.B., Ramser, J.H.: The truck dispatching problem. Manage. Sci. **6**, 80–91 (1959)
2. Alba, E., Dorronsoro, B.: Computing nine new best-so-far solutions for capacitated VRP with a cellular genetic algorithm. Inform. Process. Lett. **6**, 225–230 (2006)
3. Roberto, B., Aristide, M., Roberto, R.: Recent exact algorithms for solving the vehicle routing problem under capacity and time window constraints. Eur. J. Oper. Res. **218**, 1–6 (2012)
4. Claudio, C., Rafael, M.: A new exact algorithm for the multi-depot vehicle routing problem under capacity and route length constraints. Discrete Optim. **12**, 129–146 (2014)
5. Juan, C.R., Afsar, H.M., Christian, P.: Mathematical formulations and exact algorithm for the multitrip cumulative capacitated single-vehicle routing problem. Eur. J. Oper. Res. **249**, 93–104 (2016)
6. Leonardo, J., Reinaldo, M.: Heuristic algorithms for a three-dimensional loading capacitated vehicle routing problem in a carrier. Comput. Indus. Eng. **88**, 110–130 (2015)
7. Thibaut, V., Teodor, G.C., Michel, G., Christian, P.: Heuristics for multi-attribute vehicle routing problems: a survey and synthesis. Eur. J. Oper. Res. **231**, 1–21 (2013)
8. Augerat, P., Belenguer, J.M., Benavent, E., Corbern, A., Naddef, D.: Separating capacity constraints in the CVRP using tabu search. Eur. J. Oper. Res. **106**, 546–557 (1998)
9. Yi, T., Fan, W.: An effective tabu search approach with improved loading algorithms for the 3L-CVRP. Comput. Oper. Res. **55**, 127–140 (2015)
10. Lijun, W., Zhenzhen, Z., Defu, Z., Andrew, L.: A variable neighborhood search for the capacitated vehicle routing problem with two-dimensional loading constraints. Eur. J. Oper. Res. **243**, 798–814 (2015)
11. Diego, C., Nabil, A., Dominique, F., Daniele, V.: An iterated local search for the multi-commodity multi-trip vehicle routing problem with time windows. Comput. Oper. Res. **51**, 257–267 (2014)
12. Sandra, U.N., Christian, P., Roberto, W.C.: An effective memetic algorithm for the cumulative capacitated vehicle routing problem. Comput. Oper. Res. **37**, 1877–1885 (2010)
13. Silvia, M., Irene, L.: An ant colony algorithm for the capacitated vehicle routing. Electron. Disc. Math. **18**, 181–186 (2014)
14. Lourenco, H.R., Martin, O., Stutzle, T.: Iterated Local Search. Kluwer Academic Publishers, Norwell, pp. 321–353 (2002)
15. Clarke, G., Wright, J.W.: Scheduling of vehicles from a central depot to a number of delivery points. Oper. Res. **12**, 568–581 (1964)
16. Li, F., Golden, B.L., Wasil, E.A.: Very large-scale vehicle routing: new test problems. Comput. Oper. Res. **32**, 1165–1179 (2005)
17. Pisinger, D., Ropke, S.: A general heuristic for vehicle routing problems. Comput. Oper. Res. **34**, 2403–2435 (2007)
18. Groer, C., Golden, B.L., Wasil, E.A.: A parallel algorithm for the vehicle routing problems. INFORMS J. Comput. **23**, 315–330 (2011)

Iterative Learning in Repetitive Optimal Control of Linear Dynamic Processes

Ewaryst Rafajłowicz[(✉)] and Wojciech Rafajłowicz

Faculty of Electronics, Wrocław University of Technology, Wrocław, Poland
ewaryst.rafajlowicz@pwr.wroc.pl

Abstract. Learning of stochastically independent decisions is a well developed theory, the main of its part being pattern recognition algorithms. Learning of dependent decisions for discrete time sequences, e.g., for patterns forming a Markov chain and decision support systems, is also developed, but many classes of problems still remain open. Learning sequences of decisions for systems with continuously running time is still under development. In this paper we provide an approach that is based on the idea of iterative learning for repetitive control systems. A new ingredient is that our system learns to find the optimal control that minimizes a quality criterion and attempts to find it even if there are uncertainties in the system parameters. Such approach requires to record and store full sequences of the system state, which can be done using a camera for monitoring of the system states. The theory is illustrated by an example of a laser cladding process.

Keywords: Iterative learning · Repetitive optimal control · LTI systems · Camera in the loop

1 Introduction

The idea of learning algorithms can be traced back to the early 1960s. The main stream of research then was (and ut still is) learning classifiers or more generally, learning the Bayes decision rules when underlying probability distributions are unknown and the learning is based on a sequence of examples – called the learning sequence. At the first stage of development of this theory the learning was reduced to estimating unknown parameters of unknown distributions. Then, the so called nonparametric approach emerged, which is based on estimating completely unknown probability density functions (p.d.f.'s) either by Parzen-Rosenblatt kernel methods (see [9]) or by expanding it into a complete and orthonormal bases with estimated coefficients (see [12]). Up to now, these kinds of classifiers have been further developed [17, 28], the support vector machines being the most popular. All these approaches have a common feature, namely, after the learning phase they are applied as follows: when a new vector of features appears, then *it is classified without taking into account neither earlier nor future decisions.* Furthermore, *the result of a classification does not depend*

© Springer International Publishing Switzerland 2016
L. Rutkowski et al. (Eds.): ICAISC 2016, Part I, LNAI 9692, pp. 705–717, 2016.
DOI: 10.1007/978-3-319-39378-0_60

on time, i.e., a vector of features is classified in the same way independently of a time instant when it appears. Rutkowski [25,26] developed the theory of learning when an environment is non-stationary. Recently, such approaches are called: learning when a concept drift is present.

A parallel stream of research (see [15,16]) extended the bayesian decision theory by considering that the next decision should take into account our previous decisions as a local context, as it happens in recognizing letters in a word. In [21,22] an outer context approach in learning decisions is proposed.

However, none of the above sketched approaches to learning do not takes into account future consequences of earlier decisions. In the framework of learning, an approach that explicitly incorporates a system dynamics into a decision process has been proposed by Feldbaum (see [2,3] and the bibliography cited therein). His theory, although pleasing from the methodological point of view, occurred to be too demanding for data, which are necessary for learning. Therefore, many approaches, known under a common name *adaptive control*, have been proposed [3]. Their common feature is gaining information about unknown parameters of a system (or its model) during a decision process, which is split into consecutive steps. In adaptive control approaches usually *only one, but sufficiently long, decision process is considered* and the emphasis of researchers is on the stability of the adaptation process [27].

However, a large number of control processes in industry and in robotics is repetitive in the sense that they are repeated many times in similar circumstances. Repetitions of passes of a process provide additional opportunities for learning and they are in the main focus of this paper. This class contains strictly periodic processes (see [29]), which are not discussed here. We shall also leave outside the scope of this paper the so called run-to-run control approach, since it concentrates mainly on statistical, but static models of processes.

As a motivating example consider a laser cladding process. The laser head moves back and forth, pouring and melting a metal powder. The temperature of the melting lake is observed by an infrared camera. This temperature has to be precisely controlled by changing the power emitted by the laser. The main difficulty is at the end points, in which the laser head changes its direction it stays longer than at other points. This results in an unwanted additional dropping of a material. One can design a desirable trajectory of changing (decreasing) the lake temperature near end points. However, the optimal control signal cannot be calculated once and repeated without changes because of changes of the powder properties when different parts are produced. These changes are rather slow and we can improve the control signal, using information gained from earlier passes. Almost the same general pattern arises in a 3D printing process. Similar control problems arise also in the chemical industry when a batch type chemical reactors are used. Later on we shall call a pass: one run of the laser or a robot arm movement from place to place, or one full batch reaction etc.

In this paper we put an emphasis on learning from pass-to-pass, which is called an iterative learning control (ILC). ILC is a common name for a large number of algorithms (see [31] for a recent survey paper). ILC theory puts emphasis on designing control systems for repetitive processes – see [5,20]. They should be designed in such a way that the stability of the control process is ensured. The stability notions for repetitive processes and ILC are nontrivial (see [7]). A number of approaches to the control problems for such systems has been proposed (see [11,13,14]). In a number of papers the authors optimized ILC procedures (see [1,24]). ILC for optimal control of processes is much less developed, although some results in this direction have been obtained – see [10,19,23] – as close to the problem statement considered in this paper. However, our approach is different, namely, we propose an iterative learning of optimal control that is based on functional analog of the gradient search procedure. We shall provide theorems on its convergence and robustness to small changes of unknown parameters, but the proofs are omitted due to page limitations. They will be published elsewhere.

The paper is organized as follows. In Sect. 2 we state the problem of iterative learning of optimal control (ILOC). Then, in Sect. 3 we provide the algorithm of learning for nominal system parameters. Finally, its on-line version is presented, which is able to work when parameters are uncertain, since it collects information from pass-to-pass behavior of the system. Notice that there is no explicit parameters estimation in our approach. Finally, we provide an example of how the laser power control behaves under the proposed ILOC algorithm.

2   Problem Statement

As the first step toward the problem statement we consider the well known problem of minimization of a quadratic cost function for finding the optimal control of the linear, time-invariant (LTI) dynamic system (LQ problem), but with uncertain parameters. Assumptions concerning their uncertainty will be imposed later.

Generic LQ Optimal Control Problem. The dependence of the system state $x(t) \in R^d$ at time $t \in [0, T]$ on a scalar input signal $u(t)$ is given by

$$\dot{x}(t) = A(\theta^0) x(t) + b u(t), \quad x(0) = x_0, \tag{1}$$

where $A(\theta)$ is a $d \times d$ matrix that depends on a vector of uncertain parameters $\theta \in R^m$, while $\theta = \theta^0$ are their nominal values. In (1) $b \in R^d$ is a vector of known[1] amplifications. In the above, $\dot{x}(t)$ stands for $\frac{d\,x(t)}{dt}$, x_0 is the initial state and T is the control horizon, which is finite and this assumption is important. We confine ourselves to scalar input signals to keep the notation simple. It will be clear that the results can be generalized to the multi-input case.

In the standard setting (see, e.g., [4,18]) the problem is to find a control signal $u^* \in L_2(0, T)$ for which the following cost functional $J(u)$ attains its minimal value:

$$J(u) = \int_0^T \left[(x_{ref}(t) - x(t))^{tr} (x_{ref}(t) - x(t)) + r u^2(t) \right] dt, \tag{2}$$

---

[1] For simplicity of the exposition we omit an easy generalization to the case when also b contains uncertain parameters.

subject to (1) as constraints, where x_{ref} is the known reference signal to follow, but with not too excessive use of the control signal energy, which is tuned by selecting a weighting factor $r > 0$.

One can consider also a more general criterion

$$J(u) = \int_0^T \left[(x_{ref}(t) - x(t))^{tr} Q (x_{ref}(t) - x(t)) + r u^2(t) \right] dt, \qquad (3)$$

where Q is a $d \times d$ symmetric and positive definite matrix of known weights, but it can be reduced to (2) by transforming the state variables using $Q^{1/2}$.

Assuming that there is no uncertainty in parameters, i.e., θ assumes nominal value θ^0 that are known, then also the solution of this problem is well known (see, e.g., [4]), but we summarize it for further references. Define the Hamiltonian

$$H(x(t), u(t), \psi(t)) = (x_{ref}(t) - x(t))^{tr} (x_{ref}(t) - x(t)) + r u^2(t) + \qquad (4)$$
$$+ \psi^{tr}(t) \left[A \left(\theta^0 \right) x(t) + b u(t) \right],$$

where $\psi(t) \in R^d$ is a vector of the adjoint variables, for which the following ordinary differential equations (ODE) hold

$$\dot{\psi}(t) = -A^{tr}(\theta^0) \psi(t) + 2 (x_{ref}(t) - x(t)), \quad \psi(T) = 0. \qquad (5)$$

According to the Pontriagin's minimum principle, if $u^*(.)$ and $x^*(.)$ solves the problem (2) and (1), then there exists $\psi^*(.)$ for which the following equations hold:

$$\dot{\psi}^*(t) = -A^{tr}(\theta^0) \psi^*(t) + 2 (x_{ref}(t) - x^*(t)), \quad \psi(T) = 0, \qquad (6)$$
$$\dot{x}^*(t) = A \left(\theta^0 \right) x^*(t) + b u^*(t), \quad x^*(0) = x_0 \qquad (7)$$

and for each $t \in [0, T]$ the following condition holds

$$\left. \frac{d}{dv} H(x^*(t), v, \psi^*(t)) \right|_{v=u^*(t)} = 0. \qquad (8)$$

For LTI systems with criterion (2) it can be proved that condition (8) is also sufficient for the optimality of $u^*(.)$. Furthermore, $u^*(.)$ is the unique solution of this problem and (8) yields

$$2 r u^*(t) + b^{tr} \psi^*(t) = 0, \quad t \in [0, T]. \qquad (9)$$

Thus, $u^*(t) = P(t) (x_{ref}(t) - x(t))$ where $P(t)$ is a $d \times d$ matrix that solves the well known matrix Riccati quadratic differential equations. Notice that both $P(t)$ and $\psi^*(t)$ in (9) depend on θ^0. When d is large, then finding a numerical solution of the Riccati equations is not easy task and one can consider the approach proposed in this paper as an alternative to the classic approach based on solving these equations. We shall not develop this idea here in order to concentrate on the main topic.

The following facts are crucial for further considerations.

Fact 1. The Gateaux differential (see, e.g., [18]) of J at $u \in L_2(0, T)$ in the direction $\underline{U} \in L_2(0, T)$ has the following form:

$$\frac{d\,J(u + \epsilon\,\underline{U})}{d\,\epsilon}\bigg|_{\epsilon=0} = \int_0^T F(x(t),\, u(t),\, \psi(t))\,\underline{U}(t)\,dt. \tag{10}$$

If the Frechet derivative of J exists (see, e.g., [18]) then F is equal to it and – in our case – it is given by

$$F(x(t),\, u(t),\, \psi(t)) = \frac{d}{d\,v}\,H(x(t),\, v, \psi(t))\bigg|_{v=u(t)} = \tag{11}$$

$$= 2\,r\,u(t) + b^{tr}\,\psi(t),$$

where $\psi(.)$ solves (5).

Fact 2. Direction $\underline{U}(t) = -F(x(t),\, u(t),\, \psi(t))$ is locally the steepest descent direction oh J at $u(.)$. Furthermore, $F(x^*(t),\, u^*(t),\, \psi^*(t)) \equiv 0$. As one can notice, when searching the minimum of J the Frechet derivative F can play the same role as the gradient in searching for the minimum of a multivariate function.

The problem of iterative learning of the optimal control for repetitive processes. When θ in (1) is the uncertain vector of parameters, then it is customary to invoke one of the following two approaches:

Plug-in approach – firstly estimate (identify) unknown parameters, then plug them into (1) instead of θ^0 and consider it as certain,

Adaptive control approach – estimate θ on-line and substitute it into the control law.

Both approaches have been historically developed without taking into account that a large number of processes to be controlled are repetitive (see the Introduction section for examples). In the proposed approach we consider repetitive processes and uncertainty of parameters is taken into account by feedback between the passes of a repetitive process that bears information about the uncertain parameters, which is then used for **iterative learning approach**, without explicitly estimating them.

For n-th pass the system is described by

$$\dot{x}_n(t) = A(\theta^0)\,x_n(t) + b\,u_n(t), \quad x_n(0) = x_0, \quad n = 1, 2, \ldots, \tag{12}$$

where $x_n(t) \in R^d$ and $u_n(t)$, $t \in [0, T]$ are the system state vector and the control signal along n-th pass, respectively. Equation (12) are seemingly unrelated between passes, but our aim is to design a learning procedure that improves $u_n(.)$, taking into account $u_{n-1}(.)$ and $x_{n-1}(.)$ and introduces links between passes. In other words, we are looking for an operator Ψ

$$u_n(.) = \Psi(x_{n-1}(.),\, u_{n-1}(.)), \quad n = 1, 2, \ldots \tag{13}$$

such that
(a) $\lim_{n\to\infty} J(u_n) = J(u^*)$, when $\theta = \theta^0$,
(b) $\lim_{n\to\infty} J(u_n)$ convergent to a value not far from $J(u^*)$, when $\theta = \theta^1$ and $\delta\theta \stackrel{def}{=} ||\theta^1 - \theta^1||_m$ is sufficiently small, where $||.||_m$ is the Euclidean norm in R^m. Our reference point is the solution of the generic problem described in the previous subsection.

3   Iterative Learning Algorithm

In this section we derive an iterative learning algorithm for a repetitive process, assuming that its parameters take nominal values θ^0. Then, we shall prove its convergence and local robustness against uncertainty of parameters.

Derivation of the Learning Algorithm. According to Facts 1, 2, one can expect that the following updates of $u_n(.)$ will lead to improvements of J

$$u_{n+1}(t) = u_n(t) - \gamma F_n(t), \quad t \in [0, T], \tag{14}$$

where $\gamma > 0$ is the step size,

$$F_n(t) \stackrel{def}{=} F(x_n(t), u_{(t)}, \psi_n(t)) = \left(2r\, u_n(t) + b^{tr}\, \psi_n(t)\right) \tag{15}$$

while $\psi_n(.)$ is defined as a solution of the following adjoint equations:

$$\dot{\psi}_n(t) = -A^{tr}(\theta^0)\, \psi_n(t) + 2\, (x_{ref}(t) - x_n(t)), \quad \psi_n(T) = 0. \tag{16}$$

Their solution can be expressed as

$$\psi_n(t) = \exp(-A^{tr}(\theta^0)\, t)\psi_n^0 + \int_0^t \exp(-A^{tr}(\theta^0)\, (t - \tau))\, e_n(\tau)\, d\tau, \tag{17}$$

where $e_n(\tau) \stackrel{def}{=} 2\, (x_{ref}(\tau) - x_n(\tau))$ and ψ_n^0 is selected so as to ensure $\psi_n(T) = 0$. After finding such ψ_n^0 and substituting it into (17), we obtain

$$\psi_n(t) = -\int_t^T \exp\left[-A^{tr}(\theta^0)\, (t - \tau)\right]\, e_n(\tau)\, d\tau. \tag{18}$$

Substitution of this expression into (14) leads to the following learning procedure: for $t \in [0, T]$ and $n = 0, 1, \ldots$ iterate

$$u_{n+1}(t) = (1 - \gamma\, 2\, r)\, u_n(t) + \gamma\, b^{tr} \int_t^T \exp\left[-A^{tr}(\theta^0)\, (t - \tau)\right]\, e_n(\tau)\, d\tau. \tag{19}$$

At this stage, it is worth comparing (19) with the structure of a typical ILC algorithm that for LTI systems has (in our notation) the following form

$$u_{n+1}(t) = \alpha\, u_n(t) + \bar{\beta}^1\, e_n(t) + \bar{\beta}^2\, (x_n(t) - x_{n-1}(t)), \quad t \in [0, T], \tag{20}$$

where $\alpha \in R$, $\bar{\beta}^1$, $\bar{\beta}^2 \in R^d$ are selected in such a way that the repetitive system with such a control law is asymptotically stable.

The similarities between (20) and (19) are apparent, but there are also important differences: (1) the term $(x_n(t) - x_{n-1}(t))$ is not present in (19) and it seems that its presence may slow down the rate of convergence of learning algorithms, but – on the other hand – it may stabilize them, (2) the main updating component $e_n(t)$ is present in the both cases, but in (19) it is integrated (with the weighting matrix) from t to T, which can be interpreted as the integrated prediction error from now to the end of n-th pass, (3) the structure of (19) has been derived as the descent direction of J at $u_n(.)$ and all the weights, except γ, are specified by the system description and J.

Convergence of the Learning Process. In order to select $\gamma > 0$ that locally speeds up the learning process let us $J(u_n - \gamma F_n)$ into the Taylor series, which is exact in this case,

$$J(u_{n+1}) = J(u_n - \gamma F_n) = J(u_n) - \gamma \|F_n(.)\|^2 + (2r)\frac{\gamma^2}{2}\|F_n(.)\|^2. \tag{21}$$

A proper selection of $\gamma > 0$ requires $(1 - r\gamma) < 0$, i.e., $\gamma < 1/r$ in order to ensure $J(u_{n+1}) < J(u_n)$. Indeed, then we have

$$J(u_{n+1}) = J(u_n) - \frac{1}{(r+\nu)}\|F_n(.)\|^2 \tag{22}$$

for arbitrary $\nu > 0$.

Theorem 1. *The learning process*

$$u_{n+1}(t) = u_n(t) - \frac{1}{r+\nu}\left(2r\,u_n(t) + b^{tr}\,\psi_n(t)\right), \quad t \in [0, T], \tag{23}$$

where $\nu > 0$ and $\psi_n(.)$ solves

$$\dot{\psi}_n(t) = -A^{tr}(\theta^0)\,\psi_n(t) + 2\,(x_{ref}(t) - x_n(t)), \quad \psi_n(T) = 0. \tag{24}$$

designed for the following repetitive process

$$\dot{x}_n(t) = A(\theta^0)\,x_n(t) + b\,u_n(t), \quad x_n(0) = x_0, \quad n = 1, 2, \ldots, \tag{25}$$

is convergent to the solution of the optimal control problem for one pass in the following sense: (a) $\lim_{n\to\infty} J(u_n) = J(u^*)$, (b) $\lim_{n\to\infty}\|u_n(.) - u^*(.)\| = 0$, (c) $\lim_{n\to\infty}\|x_n(.) - x^*(.)\| = 0$.

Pass-to-pass on-line Learning. In Theorem 1 it was assumed that θ^0 is known, hence we can calculate $x_n(.)$ as a solution of (25). In this section we present an on-line version of the learning process that uses observations of the system state instead in order to cope with possible inaccuracies in knowledge of θ^0 and/or with from pass to pass fluctuations of these parameters, assuming that they are not too far from θ^0.

Algorithm 1. (Pass-to-pass Learning (PPL))

Step 0. *Select $\hat{u}_0(.) \in L_2(0, T)$ (preferably obtained by running off-line several iterations of (23), (24) and (25)). Set $n = 0$. Select $\varepsilon > 0$ as the level when a desired accuracy is obtained.*

Step 1. *Apply $\hat{u}_n(.)$ along the pass to a real system, then <u>observe</u> and <u>store</u> $\hat{x}_n(.)$.*

Step 2. <u>*Calculate*</u> *the adjoint states $\hat{\psi}_n(.)$ along the pass by solving the following equations:*

$$\dot{\hat{\psi}}_n(t) = -A^{tr}(\theta^0)\,\hat{\psi}_n(t) + 2\,(x_{ref}(t) - \hat{x}_n(t)), \quad \hat{\psi}_n(T) = 0. \tag{26}$$

Adjoint states contain information on the system behavior in the future and therefore they cannot be observed. Hence, we are forced to calculate them using the nominal parameter values θ^0 as the only available.

Step 3. *Calculate $\hat{F}_n(t) \overset{def}{=} (2\,r\,\hat{u}_n(t) + b^{tr}\,\hat{\psi}_n(t), t \in [0, T]$. If*

$$\max_{t \in [0, T]} |\hat{F}_n(t)| > \varepsilon, \tag{27}$$

then skip updating $\hat{u}_n(.)$ and use it in the next iteration. Set $n := n + 1$ and go to Step 1. Otherwise, go to Step 4

Step 4. *Update $\hat{u}_n(.)$ as follows:*

$$\hat{u}_{n+1}(t) = \hat{u}_n(t) - \gamma\,\hat{F}_n(t), \quad t \in [0, T], \tag{28}$$

where $\gamma \leq 1/(r + \nu)$, $\nu > 0$. Set $n := n + 1$ and go to Step 1.

When uncertainties in parameters are allowed, we can not be sure that the step length in (28) is properly selected to ensure the monotonicity of the criterion. If it does not decrease, than one should decrease γ.

Condition (27) is usually used as the stopping condition. Here, it is used to temporarily skip updating $u_n(.)$, but the algorithm is not halted, since we allow small fluctuations of the parameters between passes. In this version the PPL algorithm is able to detect them and reduce their influence by updating $u_n(.)$ again.

A Limiting Point of the PPL Algorithm. For theoretical considerations we assume that:

(a) the parameters can change to a certain $\theta^1 \neq \theta^0$ and these values are kept for a long (infinite) time,

(b) θ^1 is not too far from θ^0 in the following sense: $||\theta^1 - \theta^0||_d \leq C\gamma$, where $\gamma > 0$ is the step size of the PPL algorithm, while $C > 0$ is a certain constant,

(c) Step 3 is omitted in order to have an infinite sequence of passes with updates.

When assumptions (a), (b), (c) hold, then the PPL algorithm can stop updating $\hat{u}_n$ only when there exists a triple $\hat{x}(.)$, $\hat{u}(.)$, $\hat{\psi}(.)$) such that

$$\left(2\,r\,\hat{u}(t) + b^{tr}\,\hat{\psi}(t)\right) = 0, \quad t \in [0, T], \tag{29}$$

$$\dot{\hat{\psi}}(t) = -A^{tr}(\theta^0)\,\hat{\psi}(t) + 2\,(x_{ref}(t) - \hat{x}(t)), \quad \hat{\psi}(T) = 0, \tag{30}$$

$$\dot{\hat{x}}(t) = A(\theta^1)\,\hat{x}(t) + b\,\hat{u}(t), \quad \hat{x}(0) = x_0. \tag{31}$$

Existence of such a triple is further assumed. Notice that in (31) we have θ^1 instead of θ^0. Thus, we cannot check these conditions, but we can do it in a certain vicinity of θ^0.

Theorem 2. *If $\|\theta^1 - \theta^0\| \leq \gamma$, then for the PPL algorithm we have*

$$\lim_{n \to \infty} J(\hat{u}_n) = J(\hat{u}),$$

where $\hat{u}$ is defined through (29), (30) and (31). Furthermore,

$$\lim_{n \to 0} \|\hat{F}_n(.)\| = \|\hat{F}(.)\| = 0. \tag{32}$$

In order to prove the convergence of $\hat{u}_n$ to $\hat{u}$ we have to specify more precisely the dependence of $\mathcal{A}(\theta)$ on perturbations of θ.

Assumption 1. *We shall assume that a perturbation from θ^0 to θ^1 for sufficiently small $\|\theta^1 - \theta^0\| \leq C_0\,\gamma$ invokes the following change*

$$\mathcal{A}(\theta^1) = (1 + \varsigma)\,\mathcal{A}(\theta^0) \tag{33}$$

where $\varsigma \in R$ is a parameter dependent on θ^1 and θ^0.

We sketch the rational arguments in favor of the above assumption. Let us suppose that a perturbation can be expressed as follows: $A(\theta^1) = A(\theta^0) + \Delta A$. Notice that $\mathcal{A}(\theta^1)\Delta u_n(t) = \int_0^T \exp(\mathcal{A}(\theta^1)\tau)\,\Delta u_n(t-\tau)\,d\tau$. It is well known that $\|\exp(\mathcal{A}(\theta^0 t))\|_{d\times d} \leq \exp(\omega\,t)$ for a certain ω, where $\|.\|_{d\times d}$ is the matrix norm. Furthermore, from the theory of perturbations of semigroups (see, e.g., [6,8]) it is also known that

$$\|\exp(\mathcal{A}(\theta^0\,t + \Delta A\,t))\|_{d\times d} \leq \exp((\omega + \|\Delta A\|_{d\times d})\,t) \tag{34}$$
$$\approx 1 + \omega\,t + \|\Delta A\|_{d\times d})\,t.$$

Convergence of Learning under Perturbations. If Assumption 1 holds and a perturbation is such that $(2\,r + (1 + \varsigma)\,\lambda_{min}) > 0$, then for the sequence generated by Algorithm PPL we have: $\lim_{n \to \infty} \|\hat{u}(.) - \hat{u}_n(.)\| = 0$.

4   ILOC for Laser Cladding Process

In this section we summarize simulation experiments of ILOC applied to the laser cladding process described in the Introduction.

Lake Temperature – Laser Power Model. Our starting point is a model that links the laser power $U(t)$ [W], which is our input signal and the temperature of the lake induced by the laser, which is simultaneously our state and output

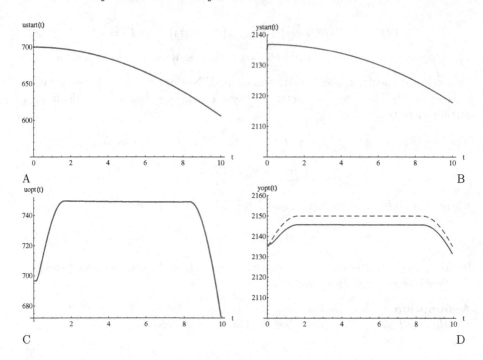

Fig. 1. The starting point $U_{start}(.)$ (panel A) and $y_{start}(.)$ (panel B). Approximately optimal input signal (panel C) and the resulting approximately optimal system state (panel D).

variable and therefore it is denoted as $y(t)$ [K] Using [30] as a guideline, assume the following model:

$$\tau \, \dot{y}(t) + y(t) = K \, (U(t))^{\beta}, \quad y(0) = \tilde{y} \tag{35}$$

where $\tilde{y}$ - given initial temperature. The parameters are explained below, following [30] with small changes. Overall system gain (amplification) $K = K_1 \, (V^{\alpha}) \, (M^{\vartheta}) = 1418.9$, where $K_1 = 1.42 * 10^3$ is the system amplification, $\alpha = -7.1 \, 10^{-3}$, $\beta = 6.25 \, 10^{-2}$, $\vartheta = 3.0 \, 10^{-3}$, where $V = 2$ [mm/sec] is the laser traverse speed. $M = 4.0$ [g/min] is the cladding powder supply rate, while $\tau = 2 \, 10^{-2}$ [sec.] is the system time constant.

Results of simulations. We have developed ILOC procedures for linear systems, while (35) is a nonlinear system, but a simple substitution $u(t) = U^{\beta}(t)$ converts it into the following linear system:

$$\tau \, \dot{x}(t) + y(t) = K \, u(t), \quad x(0) = x_0. \tag{36}$$

It suffices to run ILOC algorithms for (36), since rising to a positive power is the invertible transformation and at each iteration we can calculate $U_n(t) = u_n^{1/\beta}(t)$ and apply it to the real system.

Notice that the adjoint equation for n-th pass has the form

$$\dot{\psi}_n(t) = 2\left(x_{ref}(t) - x_n(t)\right) + \tau^{-1}\psi_n(t), \quad \psi_n(T) = 0., \qquad (37)$$

while the Frechet derivative of J is given by

$$F(x_n(.), u_n(.), \psi_n(.))(t) = (K\,\tau^{-1})\,\psi_n(t) + 2\,r\,u_n(t). \qquad (38)$$

In the simulations reported below $\gamma = 152$ has been used. As a starting point a signal that is shown in Fig. 1 (upper left panel) has been selected. The response of the system (35) to this signal is shown in Fig. 1 (upper right panel).

Our aim is to simulate the learning process, which provides the temperature shape that is close to the profile shown in Fig. 1 by the dashed line. The learning process converges quickly at the first several passes. Then, it slows down, which is typical for gradient improvement procedures. It is however crucial that the learning process provides quick improvements at the first phase and it is sufficiently simple to be learnt from pass-to-pass observations. The shape of the approximately optimal input signal is shown in Fig. 1 (lower left panel), while the system response is sketched in Fig. 1 (lower right panel) by the solid line. As one can notice, the lake temperature differs from the desired one by no more than 5 [K], which is sufficient in practice. It can be further reduced by setting less penalty for the usage of the laser energy.

Acknowledgements. This work has been supported by the National Science Center under grant: 2012/07/B/ST7/01216, internal code 350914 of the Wrocław University of Technology.

References

1. Aschemann, H., Rauh, A.: An integro-differential approach to control-oriented modelling and multivariable norm-optimal iterative learning control for a heated rod. In: 20th International Conference on Methods and Models in Automation and Robotics, pp. 447–452. IEEE (2015)
2. Astrom, K.J.: Dual control theory. i. Avtomat. i Telemekh. **21**(9), 1240–1249 (1960)
3. Åström, K.J., Wittenmark, B.: Adaptive Control. Courier Corporation, Chelmsford (2013)
4. Boltyanski, V.G., Poznyak, A.: The Robust Maximum Principle: Theory and Applications. Systems & Control: Foundations & Applications. Springer, Heidelberg (2011)
5. Cichy, B., Galkowski, K., Rauh, A., Aschemann, H.: Iterative learning control of the electrostatic microbridge actuator. In: 2013 European Control Conference (ECC), pp. 1192–1197. IEEE (2013)
6. Curtain, R.F., Pritchard, A.J.: Functional analysis in modern applied mathematics, vol. 132. Academic Press, London (1977). IMA
7. Dabkowski, P., Galkowski, K., Bachelier, O., Rogers, E., Kummert, A., Lam, J.: Strong practical stability and stabilization of uncertain discrete linear repetitive processes. Numer. Linear Algebra Appl. **20**(2), 220–233 (2013)

8. Debnath, L., Mikusiński, P.: Hilbert Spaces with Applications. Academic press, Boston (2005)
9. Devroye, L., Györfi, L., Lugosi, G.: A Probabilistic Theory of Pattern Recognition. Stochastic Modelling and Applied Probability. Springer, Heidelberg (2013)
10. Dymkov, M., Rogers, E., Dymkou, S., Galkowski, K.: Constrained optimal control theory for differential linear repetitive processes. SIAM J. Control Optim. **47**(1), 396–420 (2008)
11. Galkowski, K., Paszke, W., Rogers, E., Xu, S., Lam, J., Owens, D.: Stability and control of differential linear repetitive processes using an lmi setting. IEEE Trans. Circ. Syst. II: Analog Digit. Signal Process. **50**(9), 662–666 (2003)
12. Greblicki, W., Pawlak, M.: A classification procedure using the multiple fourier series. Inf. Sci. **26**(2), 115–126 (1982)
13. Hladowski, L., Galkowski, K., Cai, Z., Rogers, E., Freeman, C.T., Lewin, P.L.: A 2d systems approach to iterative learning control with experimental validation. In: Proceedings of the 17th IFAC World Congress, Soeul, Korea, pp. 2832–2837 (2008)
14. Hladowski, L., Galkowski, K., Cai, Z., Rogers, E., Freeman, C.T., Lewin, P.L.: Experimentally supported 2d systems based iterative learning control law design for error convergence and performance. Control Eng. Pract. **18**(4), 339–348 (2010)
15. Kulikowski, J.L.: Hidden context influence on pattern recognition. J. Telecommun. Inf. Technol. **20**, 72–78 (2013)
16. Kurzyński, M.W.: On the multistage bayes classifier. Pattern Recogn. **21**(4), 355–365 (1988)
17. Libal, U., Hasiewicz, Z.: Wavelet algorithm for hierarchical pattern recognition. In: Steland, A., Rafajłowicz, E., Szajowski, K. (eds.) Stochastic Models, Statistics and Their Applications. SPMS, vol. 122, pp. 391–398. Springer, Heidelberg (2015)
18. Luenberger, D.G.: Optimization by Vector Space Methods. Wiley, New York (1997)
19. Mandra, S., Gałkowski, K., Aschemann, H., Rauh, A.: On equivalence classes in iterative learning control. In: Proceedings of 2015 IEEE 9th International Workshop on MultiDimensional (nD) Systems - nDS 2015, Vila Real, Portugal, vol. 1, pp. 45–50 (2015)
20. Paszke, W., Aschemann, H., Rauh, A., Galkowski, K., Rogers, E.: Two-dimensional systems based iterative learning control for high-speed rack feeder systems. In: Proceedings of 8th International Workshop on Multidimensional Systems (nDS), VDE, pp. 1–6 (2013)
21. Rafajłowicz, E.: Classifiers sensitive to external context-theory and applications to video sequences. Expert Syst. **29**(1), 84–104 (2012)
22. Rafajłowicz, E., Krzyżak, A.: Pattern recognition with ordered labels. Nonlinear Anal. Theor. Meth. Appl. **71**(12), e1437–e1441 (2009)
23. Roberts, P.: Two-dimensional analysis of an iterative nonlinear optimal control algorithm. IEEE Trans. Circ. Syst. I Fundam. Theor. Appl. **49**(6), 872–878 (2002)
24. Rogers, E., Owens, D.H., Werner, H., Freeman, C.T., Lewin, P.L., Kichhoff, S., Schmidt, C., Lichtenberg, G.: Norm-optimal iterative learning control with application to problems in accelerator-based free electron lasers and rehabilitation robotics. Eur. J. Control **16**(5), 497–522 (2010)
25. Rutkowski, L.: On bayes risk consistent pattern recognition procedures in a quasi-stationary environment. IEEE Trans. Pattern Anal. Mach. Intell. **1**, 84–87 (1982)
26. Rutkowski, L.: Adaptive probabilistic neural networks for pattern classification in time-varying environment. IEEE Trans. Neural Netw. **15**(4), 811–827 (2004)
27. Sastry, S., Bodson, M.: Adaptive Control: Stability, Convergence And Robustness. Courier Corporation, Englewood Cliffs (2011)

28. Skubalska-Rafajłowicz, E.: Pattern recognition algorithms based on space-filling curves and orthogonal expansions. IEEE Trans. Inf. Theor. **47**(5), 1915–1927 (2001)
29. Styczeń, K., Nitka-Styczeń, K.: Generalized trigonometric approximation of optimal periodic control problems. Int. J. Control **47**(2), 445–458 (1988)
30. Tang, L., Landers, R.G.: Melt pool temperature control for laser metal deposition processes part i: online temperature control. J. Manufact. Sci. Eng. **132**(1), 11010 (2010)
31. Xu, J.X.: A survey on iterative learning control for nonlinear systems. Int. J. Control **84**(7), 1275–1294 (2011)

Toward a Knowledge Based Multi-agent Architecture for the Reactive Container Stacking in Seaport Terminals

Ines Rekik[1(✉)], Sabeur Elkosantini[2], and Habib Chabchoub[3]

[1] LOGIQ Research Unit, University of Sfax, Sfax, Tunisia
ines.rekik.86@gmail.com
[2] Industrial Engineering Department, King Saud University, Riyadh, Saudi Arabia
selkosantini@ksu.edu.sa
[3] International school of Business, Sfax, Tunisia
Habib.chabchoub@gmail.com

Abstract. In container seaport terminals, one of the most important problems is the one related to the storage of containers. Seaport authorities have invested in means and decision support systems to solve such problems, referred to in this paper as the Container Storage Problem (CSP). Moreover, many unexpected events may occur during the container storage process and, consequently, scheduled position of containers must be modified. Although the number of developed Decision Support System (DSS) for the management of container storage, there is still a need for DSS able to deal different type of disturbance simultaneously. In this paper, we suggest a set of knowledge based DSS for the distributed control of container storage process in an uncertain and disturbed environment. The suggested system is based on a set of knowledge models and learning mechanisms which are integrated in a multi-agent system. Numerical experiments show that knowledge based systems combined with Multi-Agent Systems seems be effective for the real time Container Storage in seaport terminals.

Keywords: Multi-agent system · Knowledge models · Learning mechanism · CSP

1 Introduction

Nowadays, container terminal management becomes a difficult task due to the increasing number of containers, the different types of incoming containers and the treatment of dangerous containers. It involves a large number of problems. One of these problems is related to the storage of containers in the storage yard (a storage yard is a surface in which containers are temporary stacked in order to be imported or exported). A storage yard is divided into several blocks perpendicular or parallel to the berth. Each block is composed by a number of bays and each bay consists of a certain number of rows (called also stacks) which are characterized by a number of tiers representing its height (see Fig. 1).

© Springer International Publishing Switzerland 2016
L. Rutkowski et al. (Eds.): ICAISC 2016, Part I, LNAI 9692, pp. 718–728, 2016.
DOI: 10.1007/978-3-319-39378-0_61

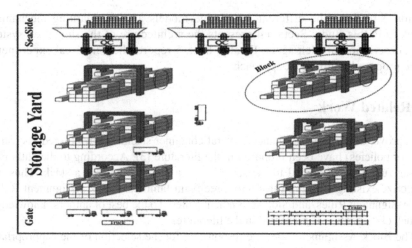

Fig. 1. A container terminal

In this context, the CSP consists of deciding, at the arrival of an imported or exported container, the exact location of the container from the empty slots in order to make efficient its loading onto a ship, truck or train. The CSP is modeled as a complex system consisting of several components in dynamic and continuous interaction not only with each other but also with other elements in the outside world, including ships and cranes [1].

As it will be discussed in Sect. 2, many DSS for container storage have been developed in the literature but these systems suffer from limitations with regards to the knowledge management, the distributed control of containers allocations, the efficiency of used real-time storage strategies particularly in presence of dangerous containers and the disturbances management [2].

This paper presents a Multi Agent System for the real time control of the stacking operations. The allocation decision consists on determining in a first way the allocation strategy adopted and then the application of this strategy to determine the allocation position. The main contribution of the paper concerns the development of a set of knowledge models, learning mechanisms and reactive decision making. The knowledge models allow the structuring and representation of knowledge related to both seaport environment and disturbances such as the arrival of damaging containers with flammable or toxic substances. The learning mechanisms allow the system to use and reuse knowledge related to disturbances and decision in order to be able to learn from past encountered experiences and adjust their decision accordingly. The new suggested reactive and distributed decision making approach combining agents and Artificial Neural System paradigms allowing the system to deal with disturbances and select of the most appropriate block, bay and slot for inbound containers. To the best of authors' knowledge, this paper is the first to suggest an explicit and generic knowledge models to model disturbance and terminal environment.

The remainder of this paper is organized as follows: Sect. 2 introduces a classification of the different stacking rules and the existing studies related to the CSP.

Section 3 presents the different knowledge models and the learning mechanism proposed in this study. Section 4 presents the architecture of the suggested system and a description of each agent. Finally, Sect. 5 reports the numerical experiments of the proposed multi-agent approach.

2   Related Work

To improve terminals performance, several container stacking rules (noted also strategies or policies) have been proposed in the literature [3]. According to the authors, a staking rule may be related to the selection of a block, a bay, or a stack. Thus, we categorize existing stacking rules into three main families: Block Assignment Rules, Bay Assignment Rules, and Slot Assignment Rules. To the best of authors' knowledge, no such classification is presented in the literature.

The Block Assignment rules are responsible for the selection of the "appropriate" block for stacking incoming containers. Several container storage strategies related to the block allocation have been proposed in the literature including *Dedicated areas*, *Role Separation of Blocks*, *Role Separation of Rows* and many others. The Bay Assignment rules are related to the choice of a bay from the pre-selected block. Strategies dealing with bays include: *Concentrated Location Principle*, *Nearest Location Principle*, and *Sequence rule. Finally*, the Stack Assignment rules include strategies adopted to determine the exact storage location in the assigned bays of the assigned block. Several assignment rules have been studied in the literature, such as the *Random rule*, *Levelling rule*, *Closest Position rule*, *Maximum Remaining Stack height rule*. In a previous paper [2], we have detailed these classification.

Many DSS were developed for the CSP using different artificial intelligence approaches Artificial Neural Network (ANN), fuzzy logic or expert systems. However, face to the complexity of real-world applications as well as the continuous changes in the environment, centralized and optimization approaches may become insufficient. For this reason, decentralized approaches, especially, agent technology has attracted a wide attention in various fields. Some container storage management systems were developed using multi-agent systems as the system developed by [6] and denoted COSAH (COntainer Stacking via multi-Agent approach and Heuristic method) that allows to simulate, solve and optimize the amount of storage space for the loading/unloading of incoming containers within a fluvial or maritime port. [9] proposed also a Multi-Agent System for the automatic planning of the operations of a container terminal via market-based allocation of resources. [8] have developed hybrid architecture, using a Cellular Automaton and a Multi-Agent System to handle dangerous containers so as to minimize the safety distance between two dangerous containers. In this context, [11] developed a decentralized and reactive system that determines, for each new ship, the appropriate allocation depending on the assigned ship, its destination port, dimensions, weight, availability, and bay allocation.

The literature review conducted and briefly presented in this paper revealed that there are still limitations of exiting DSS with regards of different aspects. First, most of existing stacking systems are based on pre-defined stacking rules for the determination of exact locations. They use the same storage rule for all containers (even for dangerous containers) and for all situations without taking into account the real-time change in the terminal [4, 5]. Secondly, we noted that there are no generic approaches dealing simultaneously with a variety of disturbances. Indeed, most of the studies so far performed have treated a restricted number of disturbances (dynamic arrival and departure of containers in most studies) but did not take into account the interaction between the different containers stacked in the yard and all disturbances which may occur. Therefore, further studies that take unexpected events and uncertain environments into consideration through suitable reactive assignment strategies remain a relevant global research direction. Finally, we have noted that MAS are not widely used for the real time container staking in port terminals and especially when dangerous containers are considered. There is also no work, as far as we know, using neither Multi Agent System nor knowledge based systems for the disturbances management in seaports terminals.

This paper presents the architecture of an agent-based architecture for a real-time container stacking system. This proposal approach introduces two novel aspects that are not addressed in previous works. Firstly, this approach is conceived as a distributed system for determining in a first way the allocation strategy of an incoming container and in a second way the exact allocation position of this container in the yard by applying this selected strategy. Secondly, knowledge models and learning mechanisms are provided for the system to perform autonomous control of the different disturbances that may occur at any time. This aspect is included in response to the need for an approach for managing disruptive events by taking into account the distributed nature of the container stacking problem.

3   Knowledge Representation and Management

The suggested system has to deal with different types of knowledge, capture, store, use and reuse them. In this section, we introduce a set of knowledge models to be used by the system as well as learning mechanisms allowing the allocation decisions and the disturbances management in order to learn from past encountered good and bad decisions.

3.1   Knowledge Models

Regarding knowledge related to decisions, we suggest a knowledge model with two parts: the first is for knowledge related to the allocation strategy and the second for the exact position of containers in blocks, bays and stacks. The final decision of the system can be represented by the following vector (see Eq. (1)):

$$Decision: <allocation\ strategies,\ container\ position> \qquad (1)$$

Where *Allocation strategies* represents the rules or strategies used for determining how candidates blocks, bays and stacks are selected for the storage of a container. The objective of such rules is not to determine the exact position of containers but how the position will be determined.

The attribute *Allocation strategies* is represented by the following vector (see Eq. (2)):

$$Allocation\ strategies:\ < Block\ assignment\ rules, Bay\ assignment\ rules,$$
$$Stack\ assignment\ rules > \tag{2}$$

Container position is also represented by the following vector (see Eq. (3)):

$$Container\ position:\ <Block\ no,\ Bay\ no,\ Stack\ no> \tag{3}$$

Where

- *Block no*: represents the block where the container must be allocated,
- *Bay no*: represents the bay where the container must be allocated,
- *Stack no:* represents the stack where the container must be allocated

The system should also capture all knowledge related to events. Knowledge related to containers to be stored which should be captured are structured as represented in the following vector (see Eq. (4)):

$$Knowledge = <Container,\ Terminal,\ Event,\ [disturbance]> \tag{4}$$

The container knowledge are represented by the following vector (see Eq. (5)):

$$Container\ knowledge:\ < Container\ ID,\ Origin,\ Destination,\ Date\ in,$$
$$Date\ out,\ Container\ out,\ Container\ Type,\ [Dangerous\ goods\ class] > \tag{5}$$

In addition to the ID, the origin and the destination of the container, the type of container is also collected. Indeed, a container can be: a regular container, an open top container, an empty container, a tank containers, a reefer container or a container with dangerous goods. In case of dangerous goods, the class of goods are also collected (represented by the attribute *Dangerous goods class*).

The system should also have a detailed representation of the actual configuration of the storage space and available positions in all blocs. This knowledge is formalized by the Eq. (6):

$$Terminal\ Knowledge:\ <N_{i,j}^k,\ T_{i,j}^k> \tag{6}$$

Where $N_{i,j}^k$ represents the number of containers in the ith stack of the jth bay of the kth block and $T_{i,j}^k$ is its type.

The system has also to identify the type of the events and the type of the disturbance. An event is characterized by the type of the event and its cause (see Eq. (7)):

$$Event\ Knowledge:\ <Event\ Type,\ Cause> \tag{7}$$

Three types of events are identified: Allocation request, Re-allocation request, Retrieval request and Disturbance events. Such events can be generated by the detection of a disturbance, the need to retrieve a container or a request from another agent.

Finally, the system should also collect data and knowledge related to disturbance if it is detected. A disturbance is characterized by its type and the degree of gravity of the disturbance (which should be indicated by the decision maker. Thus, a disturbance is represented by the following vector (see Eq. 8):

$$Disturbance\ Knowledge: <Disturbance\ Type,\ gravity> \tag{8}$$

Three types of disturbances exists: resources disturbances (yard crane breakage), equipment disturbances (blocks breakdown etc.) and containers disturbances (fault in container placing, container breakdown, container's date out change etc.).

3.2   Knowledge Based System

The proposed system should be able to handle a big number of knowledge. Indeed, learning mechanisms is required in order to allow the envisaged DSS to learn from past encountered experience. Accordingly, we suggest two types of mechanisms: the memorization and the reuse of decisions. These two types of mechanisms are based on an IF… THEN rule based system. The first consists on the memorization of any "good" decisions in order to be used directly by the system in similar situations. In such a case, the system will check its knowledge base for similar situations and select the corresponding allocation strategy to be applied without having to simulate its efficiency. The association between the decision (see Eq. 1) and the knowledge related to a given situation (see Eq. 4) is represented by a rule having this form:

```
IF (Container Knowledge is … AND Terminal Knowledge is …
AND Event Knowledge is AND Disturbance Knowledge is …  )
THEN (Decision is …)
```

The second mechanism is related to the storage of "bad" decisions encountered in the past. Such decisions were not appropriate and have not improved the performance of the port. However, some conflicts between these two mechanisms. Indeed, a given decision for a given situation can be recommended by the first mechanism and considered as bad by the second mechanism. To deal with such conflicts, we introduce a function named *Bad_Impact(Decision)* which will quantify how much the impact of the a decision was bad for the associated situation. It can have one of the three linguistic values presented above (Low, Medium and high).

Two types of rules are used in this second mechanism. The first is used to update the state of this function and have the following form:

```
IF (Container Knowledge is … AND Terminal Knowledge is …
AND Event Knowledge is AND Disturbance Knowledge is …
AND Decision is …AND Bad_Impact(Decision) is Low)
THEN (Bad_Impact(Decision) is Medium)
```

The second type of rules allows the system to update its decision if a bad decision is determine using the memorization mechanisms. In such a case, the system will take into consideration this new knowledge to build its final allocation strategy. Such rules have the following form:

```
IF (Container Knowledge is … AND Terminal Knowledge is …
AND Event Knowledge is AND Disturbance Knowledge is …
AND Bad_Impact(Decision 1) is High)
THEN (select Decision 2)
```

As it will be discussed in next subsections, the knowledge models and learning mechanisms presented in this section will be integrated in a multi-agent system for the use and reuse of knowledge and for the reactive and decentralized decision making.

4   The Multi Agent System

The suggested Multi Agent System architecture is based on a three steps methodology according to the assignment rules classification presented in Sect. 2 for the determination of the exact position of containers: block allocation, bay allocation and stack allocation. Each step is constituted by two phases: the first is the determination of the allocation strategy and the second is the determination of the exact position of containers in blocks, bays and stacks. In general, the determination of a location must be made to minimize the completion time of the loading operation. The final decision of the system is represented by the vector of the Eq. 1 (see Sect. 3.1).

The analysis and the design of our proposed system led us to define five types of agents distributed into three modules including the Decision Support System module, the evaluation module and the interface agent. The Decision support system module contains three agents which cooperate together to generate an allocation decision: the Block Agent which determines the block where the container will be allocated and monitor the state of blocks, the Bay Agent which determines the Bay where the container will be allocated and monitor the state of bays, and the Stack Agent which determines the Stack where the container will be allocated and monitor the state of stacks. The evaluation module is composed of the evaluation agent which evaluates the efficiency of the proposed allocation decision. This agent is solicited particularly by Stack agent. Finally the Interface Agent detects and analyses, in a real time manner, the different requests of containers allocation/retrieval and also the unexpected events and disturbances from the common environment (see Fig. 2).

We present in next sub-sections the goals and behaviors of the different agents constituting our system.

4.1   Interface Agent

The Interface agent plays two main roles. The main objective of this agent is to detect and analyze the different events received from the common environment. These events are of three types: allocation event, retrieval event and disturbances. This agent captures all knowledge corresponding to the terminal configuration, the container in question and the detected disturbances. This agent corresponds also to the HMI (Human Machine

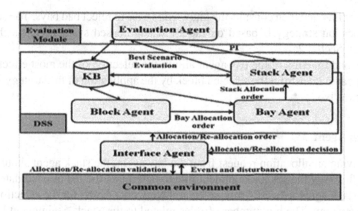

Fig. 2. Multi agent system architecture

Interface) where the final allocation decision is represented in order to inform the managers about this decision.

4.2 Block Agent

The block agent is a cognitive agent as it is able to reason before acting. It performs two functions. The first function consists on determining the allocation strategy of the yard blocks by using the knowledge based system presented in Sect. 3.2. The strategy to be selected varies dynamically according to the knowledge captured by the Interface agent. Each time the adopted strategy is changed; the block agent must update its new strategy. Thus, this agent uses a set of rules having the following form to select the block assignment rule.

```
IF (Container Type= Dangerous) AND (Dangerous goods class
= 3) AND (Dwell time is high)
THEN (Block Strategy = DA)
```

After the determination of the allocation strategy, the block agent consults the knowledge based system in order to check selected block assignment rule (to be rejected to approved) that have been applied to a state similar to the current state of the system and that did not give good results.

The second goal of the agent consists then on the selection of the block that is most favorable by a simple application of the allocation strategy selected. After selecting a block, this agent sends to the bay agent a bay allocation or re-allocation order to select a bay of this block to store the incoming container in question.

4.3 Bay Agent

As the Block agent, the Bay agent is also intelligent. It performs also two functions. It allows firstly determining in a real time manner the allocation strategy adopted for the allocation of Bay and then consults the knowledge base to reject bad bays. The selection of the allocation strategy is based on the knowledge based system and mechanisms presented in Sect. 3.2.

The second function of the bay agent allows the selection of the most effective bay among the candidates from the selected block by the application of the strategy selected to allocate the bay.

4.4 Stack Agent

After receiving an allocation request from the bay agent, the stack agent should determine in a first way the stack assignment rule to determine the list of candidate stacks. Then, the stack agent uses an Artificial Neural Network (ANN) for the selection of the allocation strategy. The big number of rules related to the Stack Assignment led us to use ANN instead of a rule base system.

As the Block and Bay agents, this agent uses the knowledge base for the selection of candidate stacks and neglect bad ones. After the identification of the stack assignment strategy and the list of candidate stacks, the stack agent apply this strategy to these candidate stacks in order to select the most appropriate stack.

4.5 Evaluation Agent

The main task of this agent is the calculation of the performance indicator of the allocation solution constructed by the Block, Bay and Stack agents. The agent evaluates the suggested position with regards to the performance indicator evaluation using the Eq. 9.

$$P(d_1, q, d_2, h) = \alpha d_1 + \beta q + \gamma d_2 + \delta h \tag{9}$$

$P(d_1, q, d_2, h)$ represents the weighted sum of four criteria: d_1 which represents the distance separating the given block to the gate; q represents the waiting queue in front of the given block; d_2 represents the distance separating the given stack to the gate; and h represents the remaining stack height. α, β, γ, and δ represent the related weights.

If P is greater than a predefined threshold, then a request is sent to the Stack agent to change the stack (or bay or block) and another stacking solution will be generated by the block, bay and stack agents. In such case the Evaluation agent will register this ineffective allocation solution to the knowledge base as new IF...THEN rule in order to avoid the reallocation of such containers in future allocation requests with the same situation of the terminal. Otherwise this solution will be accepted and sent to the interface agent to be applied.

5   Implementation and Assessment

The proposed approach has been evaluated based on data collected from the certified ISO Tunisia Sfax seaport in Tunisia. The port has a capacity of 83 000 TEUs and a storage area of 28 hectares. The presented port contains 30 non homogeneous blocks.

Each block is constituted of 5 bays and each bay contains 4 stacks (the maximum stack height is 4). In this work, we simulate the arrival of three kinds of containers: regular, dangerous (with different class of goods) and open top. We assume that only one container is entering to the yard for being stored in each time.

For the assessment of our system, we have defined three scenarios with different initial configurations and different arrival and departure rates of containers: scenario 1 with an empty yard at the beginning of the planning horizon; scenario 2 with a 50 % utilization of the yard; and scenario 3 with an 80 % utilization of the yard. We have also implemented the DSS implemented in [10] using a combined strategy. The Table 1, presents the detailed performance for each type of container with regards the performance indicator of the Eq. 9.

Table 1. Experimental results

	Empty yard			50% congestion			80% congestion		
	Regular	Open top	Danger-ous	Regular	Open top	Danger-ous	Regular	Open top	Danger-ous
Combined strategy	1004.320	1377.500	621.033	1534.125	1633.914	1337.320	1833.066	1763.374	1336.632
The developed system	1020.497	1152.362	625.762	1462.153	1515.558	803.996	1607.380	1689.880	899.148

As shown in Table 1, the agent system combined with knowledge based system and the learning mechanisms can be efficient for the real time container storage co paring with combined system and in presence of dangerous containers. The performance of the system is assessed with different scenario and seems to be promising.

6   Conclusion

In this paper, we presented the prototype of a multi-agent based decision support system for the real-time container stacking management system. The main objective of the system is to monitor terminals, supervise container allocation and react to unexpected events, change and disturbances, as handling of dangerous materials, in an intelligent, self-organizing and real-time manner. The system is based on a set of knowledge models and learning mechanisms allowing it to capture, store, use and reuse knowledge related to disturbances and the agents' environment. The performance of the system is compared to another combined system taken from the literature and the obtained results seem to be promising. The system presented in this paper can be improved in future works by integrating problems related to berthing and quay crane assignment.

References

1. Saurí, S., Martín, E.: Space allocating strategies for improving import yard performance at marine terminals. Transp. Res. Part E **47**, 1038–1057 (2011)

2. Rekik I., Elkosantini S., Chabchoub H.: Container stacking problem: a literature review. In: International Conference on Computers and Industrial Engineering (2015)
3. Ma, Y., Kim, K.H.: A comparative analysis: various storage rules in container yards and their performances. Ind. Eng. Manage. Syst. **11**(3), 276–287 (2012)
4. Woo, Y.J., Kim, K.H.: Estimating the space requirement for outbound container inventories in port container terminals. Int. J. Prod. Econ. **133**, 293–301 (2011)
5. Saanen, Y.A., Dekker, R.: Intelligent stacking as way out of congested yards. Port Technol. **31**, 87–92 (2006)
6. Gazdar, M.K., Korbaa, O., Ghedira, K., Yim, P.: Container handling using multi-agent architecture. Int. J. Inf. Database Syst. **3**(3), 685–693 (2007)
7. Güven, C., Eliiyi, D.T.: Trip allocation and stacking policies at a container terminal. Transp. Res. Procedia **3**, 565–573 (2014)
8. Hamidou, M., Fournier, D., Sanlaville, E., Serin, F.: Management of dangerous goods in container terminal with MAS model. Computer Science (2014)
9. Henesey, L., Wernstedt, F., Davidsson, P.: Market-driven control in container terminal management. In: 2nd International Conference on Computer Applications and Information Technology in the Maritime Industries, pp. 377–386 (2003)
10. Duinkerken, M., Evers, J.: A simulation model for automated containers terminals. In: Business and Industry Simulation Symposium, pp. 134–139 (2000)
11. Rebollo, M., Julian V., Carrascosa C., Botti V.: A multi-agent system for the automation of a port container terminal. In: Workshop in Agents in Industry (2000)

Agents Retaining and Reusing of Experience Applied to Control of Semi-continuous Production Process

Gabriel Rojek[✉]

AGH University of Science and Technology, al. A. Mickiewicza 30,
30-059 Krakow, Poland
rojek@agh.edu.pl
http://www.isim.agh.edu.pl/

Abstract. The model of human decision making involves reusing of earlier gathered experience together with retaining of knowledge related to currently undertaken decisions and its results. Presented here research focuses on the retaining of experience that should enable learning on the basis of results following currently undertaken actions. Such model of human decision making can be used as the basis by construction of a reasoning system in various application areas, one of which can be the control of a semi-continuous production process. Solutions in this application domain are presented, designed and implemented taking into account the paradigm of agent approach to design computer systems and the paradigm of case-base reasoning (CBR) as the methodology of solving present problems with the use of past made solutions.

Keywords: The model of human decision making · Case-base reasoning · Semi-continuous production process · Multi-agent systems

1 Introduction

The main motivation of the research presented here is an attempt to explore and formalize a methodology of resolving problems that relate to situations characterized by an a-priori unknown relationship between an undertaken action and its result. Such type of problems is well resolved by humans using experience which enables to make decisions in a nondescript environment. According to the mentioned motivation, the general scope of the article is an analysis of processes occurring in a human mind. Those processes relate to using and retaining of knowledge being experience gained by resolving of problems that humans are facing at work or everyday life. The analysis of mentioned processes leads to presentation of a methodology that is possible to implement as a problem solver in computer systems in many domains of application areas where proper rules of decision making are difficult to descript in the time of the computer system design and implementation. The control of the oxidizing roasting process of sulphide zinc concentrates [1] is one of exemplary application areas. The nature of

© Springer International Publishing Switzerland 2016
L. Rutkowski et al. (Eds.): ICAISC 2016, Part I, LNAI 9692, pp. 729–738, 2016.
DOI: 10.1007/978-3-319-39378-0_62

this industrial process prevents obtaining proper values of control parameters by computing it with the use of determined dependences in the form of mathematical equations. Proper rules of its control are also difficult to formalize, which handicaps the construction of a knowledge base of an expert system. Due to the problems related to the control of the oxidizing roasting process of sulphide zinc concentrates, this control is still performed by human operators, who use their experience in order to control the mentioned process.

The research presented here focuses on the retaining of experience as the part of processes related to the general use of knowledge. Observation of made decision and its result can be a basis for expanding of experience, which is a form of a knowledge base of a reasoning system. In order to study the impact of the retaining of experience on the overall decision making a simulation is used that results are presented in the article.

2   Human Decision Making and Case-Based Reasoning

The main point of human decision making is the conception of experience as a collection of distributed and autonomous episodes. An individual episode refers to a specific problem that was resolved in the past, an action that was undertaken in order to solve the specific problem, and an observed result. A human making decision according a present problem chooses an episode, which refers to a problem similar to the present one and refers to a result being desired according principal goals. The chosen episode is the basis for final deciding according an action, which has to be presently undertaken. After the present action is undertaken, the human can observe its results. Those results are the basis for creation of a new episode and its adding to experience. The process of creation of episodes relates to the retaining of experience, which enables learning together with and due to human decision making.

Presented view on human decision making is consistent with case-based reasoning (CBR) methodology. Case-based reasoning uses past made experience during solving of a problem associated with the present situation [2]. Such reasoning requires knowledge according made in the past solutions related to specific past problems. This knowledge is organized as a collection of past made experience items, which are called past cases, or cases in CBR conception.

2.1   Cases as Experience Episodes

A case represents an experience item that is referred as an episode by presentation of the general view of human decision making. A case c_i is defined as a triple:

$$c_i = (p_i, s_i, e_i) \tag{1}$$

where p_i is the solved problem, s_i is the solution resolved in order to solve the problem p_i, and e_i is the effect of applying the solution s_i to the situation described by the problem p_i. Definition of a case as a triple corresponds to the concept of a case that is proposed in [3]. This concept is suitable for situations in which an action can result with an a-priori unknown effect.

A single case represents one episode that is an item of human experience. A reasoning system should use knowledge related to many episodes registered in the past (as similar to processes of human decision making). This knowledge is organized as a finite set of cases called a case base Δ:

$$\Delta = \{c_1, c_2, ..., c_N\} \tag{2}$$

where c_i is a case and N is the number of cases in the case base.

2.2 The CBR Cycle

The CBR cycle is the template of four processes that are invoked sequentially in the time of emergence of a new problem that has to be solved. Those processes, called also phases, are invoked in the following order: (1) retrieve phase, (2) reuse phase, (3) revise phase, and (4) retain phase [2].

The retrieve phase starts when a new problem p_n has to be solved. The goal of the retrieve phase is to select one past case from the case base Δ that is relevant to the current situation characterized by the new problem p_n. The retrieve phase is proposed to consist of two steps:

1. choose a number of cases from the case base with the highest similarity rate,
2. select among chosen cases only one that is associated with the effect that represents the highest quality (the most desirable result) of applied solution. The selected case becomes the relevant case c_r.

The notion of similarity plays an important role in CBR, however is highly subordinated to the area of application of the reasoning system. Similarity is usually formalized as a function $sim : P \times P \rightarrow [0, 1]$ that compares two problems from P and returns a similarity assessment as a real value from $[0, 1]$ (as presented in [4]). In many CBR applications a similarity measure is inverse Euclidean or Hamming distance. The quality of the solution should indicate how much is desired result of this solution being applied in order to solve the new problem p_n. The notion of a quality is related to the domain of system application. In the case of control of industrial process, the quality of solution can be equal to the measured quality of made products. In many application areas the quality of the made products is not possible to compute. Measurement of the quality is performed often manually by workers and is not part of the reasoning system.

The reuse phase starts when the relevant case $c_r = (p_r, s_r, e_r)$ is selected. The solution s_r is reused in order to solve the current problem p_n. The reuse phase can be different in various application areas of the reasoning system – in some domains the solution s_r can be returned unchanged as the solution for the problem p_n, but some application areas require an adaption of the solution s_r to the problem p_n [2]. The result of the reuse phase is the solution s_n that should solve the problem p_n.

The revise phase is related to an evaluation of the solution s_n. In many application areas of the discussed reasoning system the evaluation of the solution s_n is possible only by the application of this solution to the real environment, what is performed outside the CBR system. The outcome of the evaluation phase is the effect e_n of the solution s_n applied to the problem p_n.

The retain phase enables learning due to the retaining of the current experience. This experience relates to the application of the solution s_n to the problem p_n that results with the effect e_n. This retaining usually occurs by creation of the case $c_n = (p_n, s_n, e_n)$ and addition this case to the case base Δ [4].

3   The Multi-Agent System Modeling Experience

The basis for human decision making is experience that is a set of episodes. This assumption is consistent with CBR methodology, which relates to a case base as the source for decision making. The case base Δ consists of various past cases that are independent each other and that are autonomous items of the general experience. The perceived autonomy of episodes is the ground for implementation of agent technology at the formalization of the human decision model. As presented in [5], the autonomy is the main characteristic of an agent, what indicates usefulness of agent approach at the design of the human decision model consisting of distributed and autonomous episodes.

The case base Δ is modeled as a set of agents. An agent belonging to this set is named a Past Episode Agent (PEA) and should contain all data related to an episode (a past case) that represents. Past Episode Agents are aimed to communicate with a Control Agent that goal is to solve the current problem p_n and retain the experience related to application of the proposed solution to the current situation. Taking into consideration presented remarks, the set of agents acting in the whole system contains:

$$Ag = \{PEA_1, PEA_2, ..., PEA_N, CA\} \tag{3}$$

where each Past Episode Agent PEA_i represents one case c_i ($1 \leq i \leq N$, N is the number of cases in the current case base Δ) and the Control Agent CA performs all phases of the CBR cycle.

3.1   Interactions in the Multi-Agent System

The Control Agent (CA) starts its functioning when a new problem p_n has to be solved. Next it begins to perform the CBR cycle that involves interactions between agents existing in the system:

1. The CA sends a request of problem statement to all Past Episode Agents.
2. Every PEA_i ($1 \leq i \leq N$, N is the number of PEAs) replays by sending back description of the problem p_i, which is related to the case $c_i = (p_i, s_i, e_i)$.
3. The CA chooses Past Episode Agents, which represent cases that are most similar to the present problem p_n. Next it sends a request of effect statement to all agents chosen in this step.

4. A PEA_i replays by sending back description of the effect e_i.
5. The CA selects PEA_r, which is associated with the effect that represents the highest quality. The PEA_r represents the retrieved case $c_r = (p_r, s_r, e_r)$.
6. The CA adopts the solution s_r to the current problem p_n. The adopted solution is returned as the solution s_n.
7. The solution s_n is applied in order to resolve the problem p_n.
8. The CA obtains e_n – the information concerning the effect of applying the solution s_n to the problem p_n.
9. The CA creates a new Past Episode Agent PEA_n that represents the case $c_n = (p_n, s_n, e_n)$.

4   Semi-Continuous Production Process

Semi-continuous production process is the term that refers to production organized into batches [6]. It is assumed that every batch is continuously controlled, but some circumstances can have influence on the control for a batch, which remain unchanged during an individual batch. This assumption results in distinction of several signals (parameters), which may have influence on production:

- Independent signals I are signals that do not change during a batch and are independent of other process parameters (e.g. chemical characteristics of raw materials). It is assumed that independent signals are measured once at the beginning of a batch.
- Dependent signals X are signals that change during a batch and can be dependent on other production parameters. It is assumed that this dependency is unknown, but can be a hypothetical function of other measured or unmeasured signals and a possible time delay. Dependent signals are measured frequently during a batch period.
- Controllable signals U are signals that can be directly controlled. Controllable signals U are set (adjusted) with the same frequency as the measurement of dependent signals X.

The aim of a production process control is to achieve products characterized by the optimal quality Q. The influence on the quality can have all signals: $Q = f(U, I, X)$. Assuming the quality Q is measured once per a batch, the control of a hypothetical process should be adjusted to specific values of independent signals I, which are measured only once for a whole batch of production. Because dependent signals X can not be directly changed, the only one possibility is to set values of controllable signals U. Summarizing presented reflections on a semi-continuous production process control, it can be noticed that:

- the optimal quality for products made in an individual batch can differ according to values of independent signals I (e.g. the quality of final products depends on chemical characteristics of raw materials),
- the way of control of a hypothetical process can be different for specific values of independent signals I (e.g. characteristics of raw materials influence the way of control),

– controllable signals U should be set in order to obtain desirable values of dependent signals X taking into consideration the characteristic of a current batch, which relates to values of independent signals I.

The oxidizing roasting process of sulphide zinc concentrates [1, 7] is one of industrial processes that is consistent with above presented characteristic.

5   Simulation of a Semi-Continuous Production Process

The research presented in [7] concerns the application of the human decision model to a real world production process. Because the real control of that process is not linked to results obtained by the reasoning system, it is impossible to implement the revise and the retain phases of the CBR cycle performed by the Control Agent. These phases require estimation of quality, what can be obtained only by application of the solutions returned by the reasoning system to the environment, which is the production process. Only one way, which may allow to bypass this handicap, is to use a simulation that enables to compute quality of hypothetical products. This is very important for the research presented here, which focuses on the retaining of experience and its later reuse.

5.1   Input Data

According to the remarks on a semi-continuous production process, a simulation is developed that enables to compute quality of hypothetical products. The input data for one batch of production is specified in the form of values of the signals that are stated as (according to the signals featured in the Sect. 4):

– independent signal $I = [i]$ is one-dimensional value in the range $(0, 20)$ measured once before the start of every hypothetical batch,
– dependent signals $X = [x_1, x_2, ..., x_{20}]$ are one-dimensional values in the range $(0, 20)$ measured 20 times during every batch,
– controllable signals $U = [u_1, u_2, ..., u_{20}]$ are one-dimensional values in the range $(0, 20)$ set (adjusted) 20 times during every batch.

The simulation does not assume any dependencies among values of the specified signals. All initial data (the initial case base Δ) of the multi-agent system are generated randomly. During the functioning of the multi-agent system (for all simulated batches) also independent signals I and dependent signals X are generated randomly, but controllable signals U are set by the Control Agent CA in order to obtain the best possible quality.

5.2   Output Data

The goal of the simulation is to compute the quality Q of hypothetical products made during one batch of production. The batch is specified by values of the signals that are presented as the input data. The quality Q of hypothetical products is obtained according to dependency:

$$Q = \sum_{n=1}^{20}(x_n + u_n - i)^2 \qquad (4)$$

where x_n $(1 \leq n \leq 20)$ are 20 individual measures of dependent signal X, u_n $(1 \leq n \leq 20)$ are 20 individual settings of controllable signal U, and i is the value of independent signal I measured once for every hypothetical batch. It is assumed that the goal of the simulated production is to obtain products characterized by the minimal value of the quality criterion Q – the lower is the value of Q, the better is the quality.

6   Implementation of the Multi-Agent System

Design of the multi-agent system modeling human decision making is adjusted to the control of the production process, which simulation is presented in the previous section.

6.1   Construction of a Case

A case c_i is defined by the Eq. (1) and is represented by a Past Episode Agent PEA_i in the multi-agent system. Adopting this definition to the specific of the presented simulation, the case c_i represents one batch of production:

$$c_i = (I, (X, U), Q) \qquad (5)$$

The problem p_i is described by the value of independent signal I. The solution s_i relates to values of X and U. The effect e_i of the solution s_i applied to the problem p_i relates to the quality Q, which is computed by the simulation presented in the previous section. It should be emphasized that the dependence given by the Eq. (4) is known only by the simulation. The Eq. (4) is unknown by the multi-agent system, which performs reasoning according controllable signals U of the present batch.

6.2   Implementation of Interactions

Interactions in the multi-agent system are shown in the Sect. 3.1. Those interactions are adopted to the specific of the presented construction of a case. All adaptations do not disturb the interactions specified in the Sect. 3.1, however the 6. step of the interactions needs explanation. The Control Agent CA adopts the solution of the retrieved case to the present problem with the use of a multilayer perceptron. The goal of the use of a neural network is related to the necessity of approximation of the way, how values of controllable signals U are adjusted to values of dependent signals X. The multilayer perceptron is trained with the data referring the solution s_r represented by the PEA_r. After this neural net is trained, it is used for setting of the present value of controllable signal U according to the presently measured value of dependent signal X. In the 8. step of the interactions, the presented simulation is used as the source for obtaining the effect e_n that is equal to the computed quality Q.

6.3 Initial Case Base

Before the first start of the multi-agent system 30 initial batches of production are generated by setting random values of signals I, X and U (as presented in the Sect. 5.1). The simulation is used in order to compute the quality Q for the initial batches (as presented in the Sect. 5.2). Those batches are basis for construction of the initial case base of the system. It means that at the start of the multi-agent system 30 Past Episode Agents exist, which represent earlier retained experience related to the 30 initial batches. The average quality for those initial batches is equal to $Q_{initial} = 49.45$.

6.4 Obtained Results

The first run of the multi-agent system concerns the model of human decision making that does not allow the retaining of experience. The Control Agent CA does not perform the retain phase – the 9. step of the interactions presented in the Sect. 3.1 is not performed. It means that the initial case base is used for all batches of production and the case base Δ does not change during the functioning of the system. The multi-agent system is run for 300 batches. The diagram onto Fig. 1 presents the quality obtained during every batch of production. The average quality for this run of the system is equal to $Q_{no\_retaining} = 41.65$.

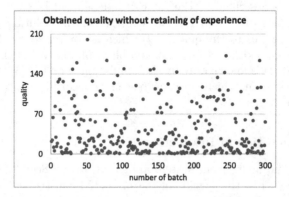

Fig. 1. The system modeling human decision making without the retaining of experience.

The second run of the multi-agent system concerns the model of human decision making that allows the retaining of experience. The Control Agent performs the retain phase – all interactions presented in the Sect. 3.1 are performed. At the end of every batch the case base Δ is enlarged by adding one Past Episode Agent related to the experience that is retained by the control of this batch period. All others parameters of this run of the system are the same as the parameters of the first run of the multi-agent system. The diagram onto Fig. 2 presents the quality obtained during every batch of production. The average quality for this run is equal to $Q_{retaining} = 38.94$.

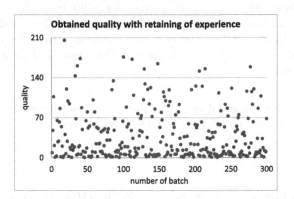

Fig. 2. The system modeling human decision making with the retaining of experience.

Obtained results show that application of the multi-agent system modeling human decision making even without the retaining of experience enables to get the quality, which is better than the quality of the initial batches. It is evident that $Q_{initial} > Q_{no\_retaining}$ and the goal of the simulated production is to obtain the minimal value of the quality criterion Q. Addition of the retaining mechanisms allows the reasoning system to gain new experience due to and together with regular problem solving of current problems. It means that after the end of every batch, the knowledge according its characteristic (including the control and obtained quality) is retained. This enables to get even better quality than the quality obtained by the run of the system without the mechanisms of experience retaining – $Q_{no\_retaining} > Q_{retaining}$.

7   Conclusions

The analysis of humans making decisions in an uncertain and indeterminate environment enables to present the model that central notion is experience. Experience is used to contemplate how to solve problems, and is retained due to observations of effects, which are consequences of deployed solutions. The model of retaining and reusing of experience can be applied as a reasoning engine to various fields of problems, especially to these ones, for which it is impossible to specify any a-priori rules of proper decision making. The discussed design of the multi-agent system modeling human decision making can be a pattern for the design of computer systems resolving problems to which other known computational techniques do not bring desired effects.

In order to determine the effectiveness of the discussed model an exemplary problem is chosen as the application area of the multi-agent system. This problem is related to the control of a hypothetical industrial process that production is organized into individual batches. Each batch is characterized by a constant parameter, but the control of a batch is continuous. Obtained results show that the presented model of human decision making enables to resolve problems without stating any a-priori rules according proper reasoning. The addition of mechanisms related to the retaining of experience increases the effectiveness of the researched model as compared to the model, which enables to use only initially gathered knowledge.

Acknowledgments. Financial support of the Ministry of Science and Higher Education (AGH UST, project no. 11.11.110.300) is acknowledged.

References

1. Sztangret, Ł., Rauch, Ł., Kusiak, J., Jarosz, P., Małecki, S.: Modeling of the oxidizing roasting process of zinc sulphide concentrates using the artificial neural networks. Comput. Methods Mater. Sci. **11**, 122–127 (2011)
2. Aamodt, A., Plaza, E.: Case-based reasoning: foundational issues, methodological variations and system approaches. AI Commun. **7**, 39–59 (1994)
3. Richter, Michael M.: Introduction. In: Lenz, Mario, Burkhard, Hans-Dieter, Wess, Stefan, Bartsch-Spörl, Brigitte (eds.) Case-Based Reasoning Technology. LNCS (LNAI), vol. 1400, p. 1. Springer, Heidelberg (1998)
4. Bergmann, R., Althoff, K.D., Minor, M., Reichle, M., Bach, K.: Case-based reasoning - introduction and recent developments. Künstliche Intelligenz, German J. Artif. Intell. **23**, 5–11 (2009)
5. Wooldridge, M.: An Introduction to MultiAgent Systems. Wiley, New York (2001)
6. Bequette, B.W.: Process Control: Modeling, Design and Simulation. Prentice Hall Press, Upper Saddle River (2003)
7. Rojek, G.: Agents modeling experience applied to control of semi-continuous production process. Comput. Sci. **15**, 411–439 (2014)

Constraint Solving-Based Automatic Generation of Mobile Agent Itineraries

Ichiro Satoh[✉]

National Institute of Informatics, 2-1-2 Hitotsubashi, Chiyoda-ku,
Tokyo 101-8430, Japan
ichiro@nii.ac.jp

Abstract. Mobile agents can migrate among multiple nodes to perform their tasks at each of the visited nodes. The itineraries of agents seriously affect the availability and performance of mobile agent-based processing. However, they tend to be complicated, for example, the order of the nodes that agents should visit may be alternative or commutable. This paper proposes a framework for specifying constraints on the itineraries of agents and generating the itineraries that can satisfy the constraints. The contribution of this framework is to automatically generate the itineraries of mobile agents among computers from application-specific constraints. A prototype implementation of this framework and its application were built on a Java-based mobile agent system.

1 Introduction

Mobile agents are autonomous programs that can travel from computer to computer in a network under their control [4]. The state of the running program is saved, by being transmitted to the destination. The program is resumed at the destination continuing its processing with the saved state. Mobile agent technology is still a convenient, efficient, and robust framework for implementing distributed applications, because of reducing the latency of communications between clients and servers and vulnerability to network disconnection.

Mobile agents visit multiple computers through their own itineraries, so that their itineraries greatly affect their achievements and efficiencies. Most existing mobile agent platforms have no mechanisms to migrate agents among two or more destinations, because they assume that each agent executes their application programming interface (API) for agent migration with at most one destination, e.g., go(*host-address*). Since such APIs are directly embedded in their agent programs, it is almost impossible to modify the itineraries of agents after developing the agents. Furthermore, agent itineraries depend on the structures of networks, which may change due to the connection or disconnection of networks and the addition or removal of nodes. Therefore, mobile agents tend to depend on their target networks and cannot be adapted to changes in the structure of networks.

Therefore, we need an approach to dynamically generating the itineraries of mobile agents according to the structures of the target networks and the

© Springer International Publishing Switzerland 2016
L. Rutkowski et al. (Eds.): ICAISC 2016, Part I, LNAI 9692, pp. 739–748, 2016.
DOI: 10.1007/978-3-319-39378-0_63

requirements of applications after developing the agents. On the other hand, mobile agents do not need to observe their itineraries as long as agents can satisfy the requirements of their applications. Suppose a remote information retrieval, which is one of the most typical applications of mobile agents. Agents can migrate among multiple servers in an arbitrary order if the agents read data sets from these servers. If agents write data sets dependent on the data that they read at other servers beforehand, their itineraries must keep the causality of reading and writing the data. The key idea behind the framework proposed in this paper is to introduce the notion of a constraint satisfaction problem (CSP) into the itineraries of mobile agents. Our framework enables the application-specific requirements of agent itineraries to be specified as constraints and our constraint solver generates agent itineraries that can satisfy constraints corresponding to their agents' requirements. Although our CSP for agent itineraries are evaluated in our original mobile agent platforms, they can be almost directly used in other platforms.

2   Basic Approach

This section presents the requirements of our proposed framework with an example scenario: mobile agent-based information retrieval.

- If a mobile agent can travel among multiple database servers to query and aggregate interesting data from the servers without writing on any of them, the order of its movement is independent of its achievement and the servers (the upper of Fig. 1).
- If a mobile agent queries and carries data from a database server and reflects the data on other database servers, the order of its movement affect the content of the servers (the lower of Fig 1).

The framework specify application-specific requirements imposed on the itinerary of such an agent as a constraint. Note that our approach does not intend to find the shortest path among nodes, because the performance of migrating agents between nodes tends of depend on the workload of their visiting nodes in addition to the latency of transmitting agents through networks.

Since our goal is to present a mechanism that would generate agent itineraries that can satisfy the constraints imposed on their agents. Some readers may think that simple executable languages, such as Lisp and Prolog, should be used to specify itineraries, but it is not easy to exactly verify whether or not itineraries written in such languages satisfy the itinerary required by a request. Note that the order relation selects a better itinerary from a finite set of given itineraries, but is not intended to generate the most efficient itinerary. Thus, the computational complexity for this relation is not large.

3   Constraint-Based Agent Itinerary Generation

This section defines two languages for specifying agent itineraries and constraints, called C and E. To accurately express such itineraries, we need to define a specification language based on a process calculus such as CCS [3].

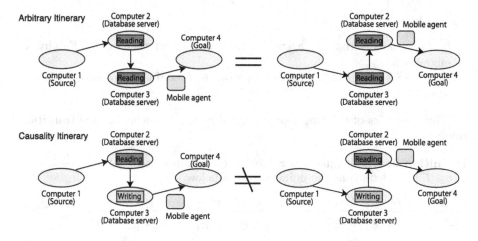

Fig. 1. Agent itineraries and constraints

Definition 1. The set $\mathcal{E}$ of expressions of the language, ranged over by $E, E_1, E_2, \ldots$ is defined recursively by the following abstract syntax:

$$E ::= 0 \mid \ell \mid E_1 ; E_2 \mid E_1 + E_2 \mid$$

where $\mathcal{L}$ is the set of location names, ranged over by $\ell, \ell_1, \ell_2, \ldots$. We often omit 0. □

Intuitively, the meaning of the terms is as follows:

- 0 represents a terminated itinerary.
- ℓ represents agent migration to a node whose name or network address is ℓ.
- $E_1; E_2$ denotes the sequential composition of two constraints E_1 and E_2. If the migration of constraint E_1 terminates, then the migration of E_2 follows that of E_1.
- $E_1 + E_2$ represents an agent moving according to either E_1 or E_2, where the selection can be explicitly performed by the processing of the agent.

Figure 2 shows basic agent itineraries specified in the $\mathcal{E}$ language.

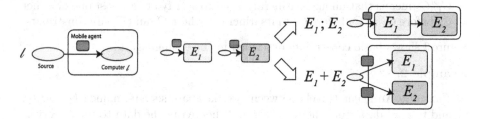

Fig. 2. Agent itinerary language

Example 1.

- $\ell_1 ; \ell_2 ; \ell_3$ means that an agent migrates to ℓ_1 and then to ℓ_2. Finally, it migrates to ℓ_3
- $\ell_1 ; (\ell_2 + \ell_3)$ means that an agent migrates to ℓ_1 and then to one of either ℓ_2 or ℓ_3.

The semantics of the language is defined by the following labeled transition rules:

Definition 2. The language is a labeled transition system $\langle\ \mathcal{E},\ \mathcal{L}\{\ \stackrel{\ell}{\longrightarrow}\subseteq\mathcal{E}\times\mathcal{E}\ |\ \ell\in\mathcal{L}\}\rangle$ is defined as the induction rules below:

$$\frac{-}{\ell \stackrel{\ell}{\longrightarrow} 0} \qquad \frac{E_1 \stackrel{\ell}{\longrightarrow} E_1'}{E_1 ; E_2 \stackrel{\ell}{\longrightarrow} E_1' ; E_2} \qquad \frac{E_1 \stackrel{\ell}{\longrightarrow} E_1'}{E_1 + E_2 \stackrel{\ell}{\longrightarrow} E_1'} \qquad \frac{E_2 \stackrel{\ell}{\longrightarrow} E_2'}{E_1 + E_2 \stackrel{\ell}{\longrightarrow} E_2'}$$

where $0 ; E$ is treated as being syntactically equal to E.   □

The framework provides a library for interpreting the itineraries of agents and migrating the agents to their itineraries. Next, we define a language for specifying constraints on agent itineraries.

Definition 3. The set $\mathcal{C}$ of expressions of the language, ranged over by $C, C_1, C_2, \ldots$ is defined recursively by the following abstract syntax:

$$C ::= 0\ \mid\ \ell\ \mid\ C_1 \succ C_2\ \mid\ C_1 \# C_2\ \mid\ C_1 \& C_2\ \mid\ C_1 \% C_2$$

□

Intuitively, the meaning of the terms is as follows:

- ℓ means that an agent itinerary need to contain a node whose name or network address is ℓ, as one of its destinations.
- $C_1 \succ C_2$ denotes that agent itinerary must satisfy C_2 after satisfying C_1, where C_1 and C_2 are constraints.
- $C_1 \# C_2$ means that an agent itinerary has to satisfy at the least one of either C_1 or C_2, where C_1 and C_2 are constraints.
- $C_1 \& C_2$ means that an agent itinerary has to satisfy two constraints specified as C_1 and C_2, although iterates for C_1 and C_2 constraints can be interleaved.
- $C_1 \% C_2$ means that an agent itinerary need to satisfy at the least one of either C_1 before C_2 or C_2 before C_1 in its itinerary, where C_1 and C_2 are constraints.

Figure 3 shows basic constraints described in the $\mathcal{C}$ language.

Example 2.

- *Causality* An agent travels between two database servers, named ℓ_1 and ℓ_2, and to read data from the ℓ_1 server and then write the data to the ℓ_2 server. The agent has to migrate to ℓ_1 before ℓ_2 as follows:

$$\ell_1 \succ \ell_2$$

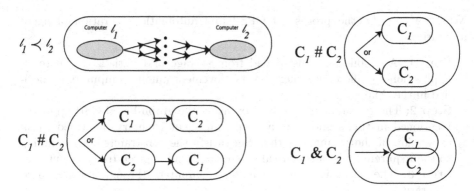

Fig. 3. Constraints for agent itineraries

- *Data Aggregation* An agent travels between two database servers, named ℓ_1 and ℓ_2, to aggregate data from the servers and then reflects the data to another server, named ℓ_3

$$(\ell_1 \% \ell_2) \succ \ell_3$$

- *Independent causality* An agent has to do two independent tasks, where the first task is to read data from the ℓ_1 database server and then write the data to the ℓ_2 database server and the second task is to read data from the ℓ_3 database server and then write the data to the ℓ_4 database server.

$$(\ell_1 \succ \ell_2) \,\&\, (\ell_3 \succ \ell_4)$$

Expressions in the $\mathcal{C}$ language can be transformed into the structures of directed graphs according to the rules proposed in this paper, where each directed graph is defined by a set of operations (vertices) and dependencies (edges). The operation is an equation with the left side consisting of a dependency (acting as a short-term name for the result of the operation), and the right side being the application of an operator to zero or more dependencies. An operation is a source for the dependency on the left side of the equation and a sink for dependencies listed on the right side. A dependency has exactly one source but can have many sinks. Our rules map constraints into graphs. The itinerary of each agent is generated as a path on the graph from at most one source node to destination nodes.

Example 3.

- The first constraint of Example of 2 is transformed into agent itinerary: $\ell_1 \,;\ell_2$.
- The second constraint of Example of 2 is transformed into two agent itineraries: $\ell_1 \,;\ell_2 \,;\ell_3$ or $\ell_2 \,;\ell_1 \,;\ell_3$.
- The third constraint of Example of 2 is transformed into an agent itinerary: $(\ell_1 \,;\ell_2 \,;\ell_3 \,;\ell_4)$ + $(\ell_1 \,;\ell_3 \,;\ell_2 \,;\ell_4)$ + $(\ell_1 \,;\ell_3 \,;\ell_4 \,;\ell_2)$ + $(\ell_3 \,;\ell_1 \,;\ell_2 \,;\ell_4)$ + $(\ell_3 \,;\ell_1 \,;\ell_4 \,;\ell_2)$ + $(\ell_3 \,;\ell_4 \,;\ell_2 \,;\ell_3)$

Next, we describe the process of CPS-based automatic generation of agent itineraries.

- **Step 1:** A mobile agent is loaded from storage and initialized, where its application-specific requirement on its movement among computers is specified in the $\mathcal{C}$ language.
- **Step 2:** The requirement is solved by using the graph-based CSP approach mentioned in this section. As a result, an agent itinerary described as an expression of the $\mathcal{E}$ language that can satisfy the constraints corresponding to the requirement is automatically generated and is given to the agent.
- **Step 3:** The agent is migrated among computers through its generated itinerary.

4   Design and Implementation

There have been many mobile agent platforms so far. Although the framework itself is independent of any platforms, the current implementation is constructed as our original mobile agent platform. As shown in Fig. 4, the platform consists of three parts: runtime system, agent itinerary interpreter, and constraint solver. The first is responsible for migrating mobile agents and executing their application-specific tasks defined as Java programs, the second for interpreting the itinerary of each agent, and third for solving constraints on agent itineraries.

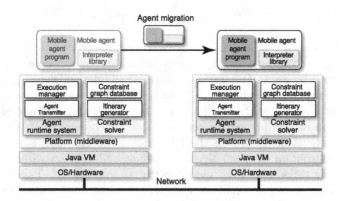

Fig. 4. System structure

4.1   Runtime System

Runtime systems are executed on computers for executing and migrating agents to other runtime systems. Each runtime system is built on the Java virtual machine (Java VM), which conceals differences between the platform architectures of the source and destination computers. Each runtime system governs all the agents inside it and maintains the life-cycle state of each agent. When the life-cycle state of an agent changes, e.g., when it is created, terminates, or migrates to another computer, the runtime system issues specific events to the agent. Each runtime system can exchange agents with another system through a TCP channel using mobile-agent technology. When an agent is transferred over the network, not only the code of the agent but also its state is transformed into a bitstream and then the bit stream is transferred to the destination. Therefore, the arriving agents can continue to execute its processing at the destination. The runtime system on the receiving side receives and unmarshals the bit stream.

Our system uses the Java object serialization package for marshaling agents. The package does not support the capturing of stack frames of threads. Consequently, our system cannot serialize the execution states of any thread objects. Instead, when an agent is serialized, the core system propagates certain events to its descendent agents in order to instruct the agent to stop its active threads, and then automatically stops and serializes them after a given time period.

4.2   Agent Itinerary Interpreter

The framework provides a Java-library for interpreting expressions in $\mathcal{E}$ based on the semantics of Definition 2. Each agent is equipped with the library to evaluate the expressions. The library invokes API for agent migration with the next destination to migrate the agent to there. Each runtime system periodically monitor connection to neighboring runtime systems and the availability of the systems by using a peer-to-peer manner through multicasting UDP. The $+$ operator is evaluated as one of either sub-itineraries by this current runtime system according to the connectivity and availability of the destinations of the sub-itineraries. When there are two or more possible sub-itineraries, one of the sub-itineraries is selected by the runtime systems. Since the size of the library is smaller than 10 KB, the cost of migrating the library can be ignored in most practical applications.

4.3   Constraint Solver for Agent Itinerary

Each constraint is specified on a dependency graph. Constrained path problems have to do with finding paths in graphs subject to constraints. One way of constraining the graph is by enforcing reachability between nodes. For instance, it may be required that a node reaches a particular set of nodes by respecting some restrictions like visiting a particular set of nodes or edges in a given order specified in our constraint language. Our constrain solving system is responsible for generating agent itineraries as paths that can satisfy constraints. Our framework has three arguments for solving constraints: (1) a directed graph, i.e., a directed graph with a source node; (2) the relation graph on nodes and edges of one or more directed graphs; and (3) the transitive closure of the directed graphs. The second represents operators in $\mathcal{C}$ and the third is to find paths that can satisfy multiple constraints connected with the relations in the second. Agent itineraries are generated through the reachability on the transitive closure of the directed graphs by finding a simple path in a directed graph containing a set of mandatory nodes. A simple path is a path where each node is visited once, i.e., given a directed graph, a source node, a destination node, and a set of mandatory nodes mandnodes, we want to find a path in the graph from the source to the destination, going through mandnodes and visiting each node only once.

Remarks. Security is essential in deployable software. The current implementation can directly use the security mechanisms provided in the Java language environment. The Java VM explicitly restricts agents so that they can only access specified resources to protect hosts from malicious agents. To protect against malicious agents being passed between agent hosts, each runtime system supports a Kerberos-based authentication mechanism for agent migration. It authenticates users without exposing their passwords on the network and generates secret encryption keys that can be shared selectively between parties that are mutually suspicious parties.

5   Evaluation

The framework is constructed and available on Java version 7 or later. Its current implementation was not built for performance, but a basic agent migration experiment was done using eight computers (Xeon E5 3.5 GHz), named $\ell_1, \ldots, \ell_8$, connected through a giga-ethernet network. We measured the cost of migrating a null agent (a 5-KB agent, zip-compressed) between two computers to be 28 ms. The cost of agent migration included that of opening TCP transmission, marshaling the agents, migrating the agents from their source computers to their destination computers, unmarshaling the agents, and verifying security. The costs of solving three kinds of constraints were 7 ms, 8 ms, and 10 ms, where the first was specified as $(\ell_0 \succ \ell_1) \& (\ell_1 \succ \ell_2) \& \cdots \& (\ell_7 \succ \ell_8)$, the second as $(\ell_0 \succ \ell_8) \# (\ell_1 \succ \ell_8) \# \cdots \& (\ell_7 \% \ell_8)$, and the third as $(\ell_0 \succ \ell_8) \& \cdots \& (\ell_7 \succ \ell_8)$. We already implemented typical applications of mobile agents with the proposed framework.

5.1   Remote Information Retrieval

As we mentioned in the first section, this is one of the most traditional applications of mobile agents. A mobile agent migrates to four database servers and queries about certain data from the servers, named ℓ_1, ℓ_2, and ℓ_3, and then carries the results of their queries to a specified computer, e.g., its client, named ℓ_4. The order of visiting the servers are arbitrary if their queries have no side effect to the servers. Therefore, a constraint on such an agent is described as follows:

$$(\ell_1 \% \ell_2 \% \ell_3) \succ \ell_4$$

The framework generated the following itinerary that could satisfy the constraint.

$$(\ell_1 ; (\ell_2 ; \ell_3 + \ell_2 ; \ell_1) + \ell_2 ; (\ell_1 ; \ell_3 + \ell_3 ; \ell_1) + \ell_3 ; (\ell_1 ; \ell_2 + \ell_2 ; \ell_1)) ; \ell_4$$

The generated itinerary consisted of six alternative paths. One of them was selected according to the reachability of ℓ_1, ℓ_2, and ℓ_3. In fact, the mobile agent migrates among nodes through the itinerary with keeping its constraints.

5.2   Sensor Network Management

Sensor networks for monitoring nature environments and factories are often used to detect abnormal data to find omens. On the other hand, while the environments are stable, such sensor networks continue to measure steady state. Mobile agents can locally observe and control equipment at each node by migrating among nodes with their program codes to detect abnormal data. As code is very often smaller than the data it processes, the transmission of mobile agents to sources of data creates less traffic than transferring the data itself. Sensor networks may lack routing mechanisms for communications, because their network management systems tend to be poor. Since mobile agents are autonomous entities, they may be able to detect proper destinations or routings on such networks.

$$(\ell_1 \,;\ell_h)\,\&\,(\ell_2\,;\ell_h)\,\&\,\cdots\,\&\,(\ell_8\,;\ell_h)$$

The framework generated multiple paths for the above constrains. For example, one of them is described as:

$$\ell_1\,;\ell_2\,;\ell_3\,;\ell_4\,;\ell_5\,;\ell_6\,;\ell_7\,;\ell_8\,;\ell_h$$

The selection of multiple paths depends on the availability and connectivity of the destinations of the paths. This proved that our framework could generate agent itineraries that can satisfy the requirement of the agent.

6   Related Work

Many mobile agent systems have been developed over the last twenty years. Most of these studies explicitly or implicitly assume that the itineraries of mobile agents were defined in the development phases of their agents. Like our framework, there have been several attempts to introduce theoretical foundations into mobile agents. The ambient calculus [1] allows mobile agents (called ambients in the calculus) to contain other agents and to move as a whole with all its subcomponents. The Seal calculus [5] is similar to the mobile ambients and ours in its expressiveness of hierarchical structure of mobile agents, but its main purpose is to reason about the security mechanism of mobile agents. The Polis language [2] is a theoretical framework for specifying and analyzing mobile entities, including mobile codes and mobile agents, which can contain other entities inside them. However, it is not executable and needs a kind of shared memory over remote nodes, whereas our framework can operate reusable mobile agents for network management in a decentralized manner. Unlike software agents, which are not mobile, there have been a few attempts to merge CSP and mobile agents. They used mobile agent technology as just a solution to distributed constraint problems [6]. As long as our knowledge, there have been no attempts to introduce the notion of CSP into the multiple hop itineraries of mobile agents.

7 Conclusion

We presented a framework for enabling the itineraries of mobile agents to be specified as constraints and the agents to be migrated through paths that could satisfy the constraints. As a result, mobile agents could migrate among multiple nodes to perform their task tasks at each of the visited nodes. The contribution of this framework is to automatically generate the itineraries of mobile agents among computers from application-specific constraints. In fact, it is useful in operating mobile agent-based applications, because the itineraries of agents seriously affect the availability and performance of their processing. This paper presented a framework for specifying constraints on the itineraries of mobile agents and solving the itineraries that could satisfy the constraints. Since the framework is independent of the underlying mobile agent platforms, it is useful to other platforms.

References

1. Cardelli, L., Gordon, A.D.: Mobile ambients. In: Nivat, M. (ed.) FOSSACS 1998. LNCS, vol. 1378, pp. 140–155. Springer, Heidelberg (1998)
2. Ciancarini, P., Franze, F., Mascolo, C.: Using a coordination language to specify and analyze systems containing mobile components. ACM Trans.Softw. Eng. Methodol. 9(2), 167–198 (2000)
3. Milner, R.: Functions as processes. Math. Struct. Comput. Sci. 2(2), 119–141 (1992)
4. Satoh, I.: Mobile agents. In: Nakashima, H., Aghajan, H., Augusto, J.C. (eds.) Handbook of Ambient Intelligence and Smart Environments, pp. 771–791. Springer, Heidelberg (2010)
5. Vitek, J., Castagna, G.: Seal: a framework for secure mobile computations. In: Bal, H.E., Cardelli, L., Belkhouche, B. (eds.) ICCL-WS 1998. LNCS, vol. 1686, pp. 47–77. Springer, Heidelberg (1999)
6. Yokoo, M., Hirayama, K.: Algorithms for distributed constraint satisfaction: a review. Auton. Agent. Multi Agent Syst. 3(2), 185–207 (2000)

Control Planning for Autonomous Off-Grid Outdoor Lighting Systems Based on Energy Consumption Preferences

Igor Wojnicki[✉]

Department of Applied Computer Science,
AGH University of Science and Technology, Al. Mickiewicza 30,
30-059 Krakow, Poland
wojnicki@agh.edu.pl

Abstract. The paper focuses on establishing plans for autonomous off-grid lighting devices. Such a device is equipped with photo-voltaic panels, an energy storage and light points. The plan enables the device to take actions depending on energy availability to ensure compliance with user preferences. The preferences define how the device has to (hard requirements) or should (soft requirements) illuminate a given area. The hard requirements have to be met, while the soft requirements are optional. Having the preferences and the plan enables the device to conserve harvested energy simultaneously meeting all hard requirements and, when possible, fulfilling the soft ones, optimizing energy consumption.

Keywords: Rules · Planning · Multi-variant planning · Energy usage optimization · Power management · Off-grid device

1 Introduction to Autonomous Off-Grid Lighting

The main goal of the research described here is to provide a smart battery management system for off-grid applications such as outdoor lighting systems. An autonomous off-grid lighting system optimizes its actions by fulfilling user preferences, and improves its capabilities by extending battery life and their health. It has to be intelligently managed to deliver it. This paper focuses on user preferences which model energy usage patterns and serve as a basis for its operations planning. The main goal of such planning is to fulfill the preferences under fluctuating energy constraints.

The lighting system under consideration consists of two distinctive components: an instance and a control center. An instance is an autonomous device consisting of a photo-voltaic panel (PV), energy storage and light points. PV generates energy which is stored locally using Lithium-Ion cells. Depending on particular application the light points are of different forms ranging from street luminaires to LED strips. In addition, an instance is also equipped with a control and communication modules which allows to manage charging,

© Springer International Publishing Switzerland 2016
L. Rutkowski et al. (Eds.): ICAISC 2016, Part I, LNAI 9692, pp. 749–757, 2016.
DOI: 10.1007/978-3-319-39378-0_64

discharging, light intensity, collecting diagnostic data and to communicate with the control center.

An instance is autonomous, and self-sustainable. It harvests energy which in turn is used to power light points. To do so it uses a plan, which is a sequence of control commands, telling when and how to discharge the batteries, turn on and off or dim the light points. Thus it is to optimize energy flow increasing battery health and obeying user preferences.

The plans are distributed to each of the instances by the control center. Each plan depends on particular instance's features, parameters, and user preferences as well as weather forecasts. The control center is also responsible for gathering diagnostic data from the instances.

2   Motivation

There are multiple competitive solutions for energy storage available on the market in up to 10 kWh segment which are gathered in Table 1. It needs to be pointed out that no storage solution currently offered is designed to work with renewable energy sources. While each of them optimizes battery health they are not aware of characteristic of the energy generation used for charging. And in case of renewable energy sources their power output, thus the generation, fluctuates directly affecting both battery health and performance of the system. Similarly they are not aware of energy consumption patterns. Thus they do not tackle energy usage optimization at all.

Table 1. Energy storage, competition

	Name	Capacity	Technology
1	Hoppecke Sun.Systemizer	11.6 kWh	Lead-gel
2	EnerSys home energy storage	9.2 kWh	Thin plate pure lead
3	Varta engion	6.9/13.8 kWh	Lithium iron phosphate
4	Victron energy	4.75 kWh	Lithium iron phosphate
5	Samsung SDI	3.6 kWh	Lithium-ion
6	Panasonic SESS	1.35–1.6 kWh / module	Lithium-ion
7	Sony IJ1001M	1.2 kWh / module	Lithium iron phosphate

A key differentiator of the proposed system comparing with the competition is to enable it to be aware of both energy generation and consumption characteristics. Such awareness could increase battery life and allows to fulfill consumption requirements.

The generation is planned based on predictions, such as weather forecast, and generation-storage interaction simulations. Consumption is planned based on user preferences. Generation prediction uses PV simulation [1] employing GridLab-D [2].

The paper focuses on the consumption planning. The planning is enabled by a two-way communication between the actual storage and the control center. It allows the instance to obtain energy usage plans based on current and forecasted environmental conditions such as: temperature, capacity, battery health or weather, and user preferences. What is more, it also enables advanced diagnostics which is performed by the control center. Simultaneously it stays economically viable making an instance to be relatively inexpensive in terms of electronic components.

This paper focuses on establishing a viable plan for an instance. The plan is parametrized by available power gathered by storage and bound by user preferences. The preferences define hard and soft requirements. The hard requirements have to be met, while the soft requirements are optional and they should be met. The plan is robust, being multi-variant, which means that, depending on available charge, the instance is able to make decisions regarding control which maximize fulfillment of the preferences. It is guaranteed that the hard requirements are met at all times while the soft ones if there is enough charge left.

3   General Architecture

The proposed system is physically subdivided into multiple instances and a single control centre. The instances employ energy storage, control and communication hardware. The control centre is responsible for storing and processing control and diagnostic information for the instances and establishing communication with them. It synthesizes energy consumption plans based on user preferences and sends them to the instances. The *plan* is synthesized by the *planning* software module which takes into considerations *preferences* and *sunrise/sunset* times for given *instance*. Timestamps of *sunrise/sunset* events are sent by every *instance* to the *control centre* (Fig. 1) which enables calculations of time-based plans in relation with actual sunrise or sunset times.

4   User Preferences

Initial user preferences are modeled with use of the following features:

- a time stamp, in relation with sunrise or sunset,
- a light point power level, being a percentage of the nominal value.

The proposed model is open for incorporating other features such as: presence, movement, ambient light etc., which can be easily added. Similarly, the power level can be replaced with lighting profile if meeting certain formal requirements, such as lighting norms, is needed [3]. In such a case the lighting profile for particular physical area can be subsequently resolved into power levels for each of the light points involved in illuminating the area.

The preferences are categorized as:

- required (hard requirements), which must be met, or
- preferred (soft requirements), which should be met.

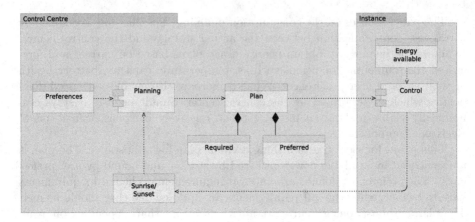

Fig. 1. Planning and control

The preferences are formally expressed as logic rules and processed, together with *Sunrise/Sunset* data, by a rule-based system (part of *Planning* module see Fig. 1) to synthesize a plan. For logic representation predicate logic [4] and especially horn clauses are used which are directly processed by a Prolog based rule engine [5].

```
r(0)  :- time(sunset,0,T),
         then,
         set(pref,100,T).
r(1)  :- time(sunset,+120,T),
         then,
         set(pref,30,T).
r(2)  :- time(sunrise,-60,T),
         then,
         set(pref,30,T).
```

Fig. 2. User preferences rules, preferred behavior (soft requirements).

Example rules for soft requirements in Prolog language are given in Fig. 2. Predicate time/3 indicates time in relation to its first argument in minutes (e.g. time(sunset, +120, T) provides T being 120 min after sunset), Predicate set/3 represents a control action setting power outputs (e.g. set(pref, 30, T) means preferred 30 % power output of the light point at time T), then serves structural identification of conditions and actions. Hard requirements are represented in a similar way (see Fig. 3). As it can be seen number of preferred and required preferences does not have to match. It is assumed that time stamps have a single minute resolution.

```
r(3) :- time(sunset,0,T),
        then,
        set(req,90,T).
r(4) :- time(sunset,+120,T),
        then,
        set(req,20,T).
r(5) :- time(sunrise,-60,T),
        then,
        set(req,20,T).
r(6) :- time(sunrise,0,T),
        then,
        set(req,0,T).
```

Fig. 3. User preferences rules, required behavior (hard requirements).

4.1   Prediction of Load Characteristics and Power Consumption

Based on the user preferences a state-space is built. A state is considered as a point in time at which a decision about changing light intensity is performed according to the preferences. A transition regards the decision, thus there might be multiple transitions between states depending on particular light intensities to be enabled.

The state-space for the example preferences in Figs. 2 and 3 is given in Fig. 4 as a graph. Vertices 1, 2, 3, 4 correspond to: sunset time, 120 min past sunset, 60 min before sunrise, and sunrise time, respectively. The actual values come directly from the time stamps defined by time/3 predicate.

Fig. 4. State-space.

The plan is established based on arbitrarily chosen point in time for 24 h period prior to it. The point defines an instance's time horizon. It is a time to which the instance is assumed to function. Usually it is a sunrise time for outdoor lighting. This point in time becomes a goal for the search algorithm.

Table 2. Example instance's parameters.

Parameter	Value
Power	30 W
Sunrise time	8:00
Sunset time	18:00

The purpose of the plan is to verify if there is enough energy stored if particular decisions regarding energy consumption are made according to the preferences. Thus it enables making such decisions. The hard requirements have to be met at all times, while the soft requirements should be met. It enables planing and optimization since not meeting the soft requirements leads to energy savings. On the other hand meeting the soft requirements has to be maximized.

While power consumption depends on physical characteristic of the instance, in this case light point power rating, the sunrise and sunset times are constantly updated which is reported on a daily basis back to the control centre. Example instance's parameters are given in Table 2.

Starting with the goal, being state 4 (sunrise), a backward breadth-first search is performed resulting in a complete search tree given in Fig. 5. Each node represents a state, starting with 4 which is labeled 4a. Then there are edges to 3a and 3b indicating that there are two distinct path to reach state 3 depending on chosen power level being either 30 % or 20 %, which are indicated as edge labels. Suffixes "a" and "b" are arbitrary to keep vertex labels unique, similarly for other vertices and subsequent letters. At each edge additional information regarding energy being used is given in a form: watts used by the transition / watts used by all the transitions to the goal. For example, if the instance is in state 1 and storage reports 160 Wh capacity then plans starting at vertices: 1c, 1d, 1g, 1h, including all their predecessors, should be considered as viable ones. For example, picking 1c means that there is enough energy to turn lights at 100 % from 1 to 2, than 20 % from 2 to 3 and finally 30 % from 3 to 4. Picking 1 h would follow a plan with enough energy to complete it which turns lights at 90 % from 1 to 2, 20 % from 2 to 3 and 20 % from 3 to 4. Plans starting at other vertices do not meet the energy requirements.

Such a complete tree is not practical. The instance has to choose arbitrarily which plan to follow, either: 1c, 1d, 1g, or 1 h in the example above. Instead of building a complete search tree the following heuristic algorithm based on backward search is proposed:

1. if there are no more transitions from a given state then stop,
2. calculate energy usage for all transitions from a given state,
3. follow to the state with the least energy usage, go to 1.

Applying the above algorithm results in a search tree indicated by dashed vertices in Fig. 5. It is still a multi-variant plan however it becomes more viable for the instance, reducing number of choices. At each state the instance decides which transition to follow, assuming that subsequent transition would use the least energy. For example starting at state 1 and transiting to 2 while storage reports 130 Wh, gives a clear choice of turning lights at 90 % – turning lights at 100 % would require at least 132 Wh which is not available. Thus it enables energy usage optimization at each instance simultaneously maximizing meeting the soft requirements.

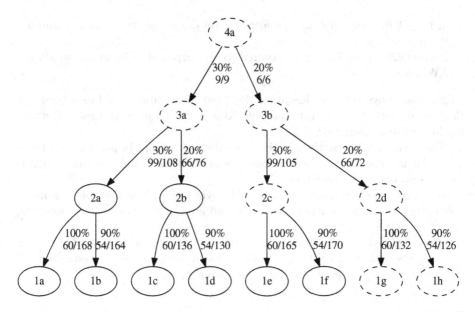

Fig. 5. Example search tree.

The search tree is transformed into a time-based plan. It is calculated by the control center, based on the instance's parameters regarding sunrise and sunset times, in a form of set of tuples given in Fig. 6. Each tuple consists of three entries: time (in minutes), preference or requirement indication, power level (%), energy needed to execute the rest of the plan.

```
[
    [ 420,pref, 30,   9],
    [ 420,req,  20,   6],
    [ 480,req,   0,   0],
    [1080,pref,100,132],
    [1080,req,  90,126],
    [1200,pref, 30,105],
    [1200,req,  20, 72]
]
```

Fig. 6. Example plan.

The plan is sent to the instance and executed by its control module. The instance is able to set light point output depending on current time and energy available, assuming that it is less than or equal to the one needed to execute the plan. For example, considering the first entry which is read as:

1. at time 420, being 7:00, it is preferred to set output at 30 % which, would use 9 Wh, if followed,
2. at time 420, being 7:00, it is required to set output at 20 % which, would use 6 Wh, if followed.

Taking the above into consideration the *Control* module should execute #1 if there is at least 9 Wh energy available. But it must follow at least #2 which would lead to consuming 6 Wh.

There are two alternatives in the example above than. In general case there might be more of them offering energy-wise choices. Number of alternatives depends on particular preferences.

In general case alternative plans may be synthesized based not only on available energy but also other factors represented as sensory data such as: presence, movement, ambient light etc.

The proposed plan generation is based on domain-independent planning. It has been researched since the 1980s [6], it is still being actively investigated [7]. In case of state-space explosion heuristic search methods can be used [8].

5   Conclusions

The paper outlines interactions in an autonomous outdoor lighting system. The system consists of a central control center and multiple instances. The instances are autonomous equipped with photo voltaic panels, an energy storage and light points.

The paper focuses on an issue of synthesizing a plan for controlling energy consumption based on user preferences and energy availability. User preferences are expressed with predicate logic and serve a purpose of generating a state-space. The planning is based on a backward breadth-first search through the state-space. As a result a robust, multi-variant plan is delivered to each instance. Thanks to the plan the instance can control power output of the light points, depending on energy availability. Utilizing the plan allows to ensure fulfillment of user preferences regarding instance operations, thus meeting all hard requirements. Simultaneously, meeting the soft requirements is maximized. The proposed algorithm has been tested and confirmed in a simulated environment.

Further work regards employing different heuristics for calculating energy usage based on actual user experience and different domain-specific goals for other applications. If the state-space size becomes considerably large using other search algorithms is also considered including A-star [9] with proper heuristics [2]. If robustness or number of states grows even more advanced heuristic algorithms for establishing such plans [10] are also considered.

References

1. Tuffner, F., Hammerstrom, J.L., Singh, R.: Incorporation of NREL Solar Advisor Model Photovoltaic Capabilities with GridLAB-D. Technical report
2. Dechter, R., Pearl, J.: Generalized best-first search strategies and the optimality of A*. J. ACM **32**(3), 505–536 (1985)
3. Wojnicki, I., Ernst, S., Kotulski, L., Sędziwy, A.: Advanced street lighting control. Expert Syst. Appl. **41**(1), 999–1005 (2013)
4. Aho, A., Ullman, J.: Foundations of Computer Science: C Edition. Principles of computer science series. W.H. Freeman, New York (1994)
5. Nilsson, U., Małuszyński, J.: Logic, Programming and Prolog. Wiley, New York (1990)
6. Wilkins, D.E.: Domain-independent planning: representation and plan generation. Artif. Intell. **22**(3), 269–301 (1984)
7. Gerevini, A., Kuter, U., Nau, D.S., Saetti, A., Waisbrot, N.: Combining domain-independent planning and HTN planning: the duet planner. In: ECAI, pp. 573–577 (2008)
8. Bonet, B.: Planning as heuristic search. Artif. Intell. **129**(1–2), 5–33 (2001)
9. Hart, P., Nilsson, N., Raphael, B.: A formal basis for the heuristic determination of minimum cost paths. IEEE Trans. Syst. Sci. Cybern. **4**(2), 100–107 (1968)
10. Wojnicki, I., Ernst, S., Turek, W.: A robust planning algorithm for groups of entities in discrete spaces. Entropy **17**(8), 5422 (2015)

Control of the Compass Gait Biped Robot

Ao Xi[1,2(✉)]

[1] School of Electrical and Electronic Engineering, The University of Manchester, Manchester,
M13 9PL, UK
[2] School of Automation, Northwestern Polytechnical University, Xi'an, Shaanxi 710072,
People's Republic of China
xiao6454@outlook.com

Abstract. In this paper, two different controllers have been designed to follow
the desired trajectory. The robot, known as Compass Gait Biped Robot (or Underactuated Biped Robot), is assumed to have 2 legs known as the stance leg and the
swing leg. Both legs have the same mass, with each center of mass located at the
midpoint of the leg. The hip's mass is assumed to represent the weight of the
entire upper body. The locomotion of this kind of robot is constrained in the
sagittal plane, where the friction between links and the energy lost at the impact
are ignored. The dynamic model of the system (i.e. the equation of motion) is
obtained, and is validated by analyzing the kinetic and potential energy. Trajectory is generated by Cubic Spline Method, and the desired joint velocity and
acceleration are obtained by inverse kinematics. Controller design involves the
comparison between the Proportional Integral and Derivative (PID) controller
and the Computed Torque Control (CTC), which indicate that the CTC method
is better for tracking the generated trajectory.

Keywords: Compass gait · Underactuated robot · Trajectory planning · PID ·
Computed torque control

1 Introduction

The compass gait biped robot, known as a kind of passive dynamic system with multiple
input and multiple output, nonlinear characteristics, variable structure and strong
coupling, has become a popular research and experimental platform for control engineering [1–3]. It is also a complex mechanical system with multi-degree of freedom, of
which the walking dynamics is underactuated and unstable. Compared with other types
of robot (tracked and wheeled), the biped robot has better environmental adaptability
and mobility, allowing it to operate under hazardous conditions [4]. The bipedal walking
technology can also provide a theoretical and technical foundation for Exoskeleton
device and any other auxiliary motion mechanisms. It also plays an important role in
the field of rehabilitation therapy, biomedical engineering and even military. The passive
gait biped robot, known as underactuated or passive gait biped robot, was first designed
by McGeer [2]. The simple structure developed in his research, known as the compass-
like biped robot contains two legs with high energy efficiency, which can walk at the
slope steadily under the force of gravity without additional actuated joint forces. He

© Springer International Publishing Switzerland 2016
L. Rutkowski et al. (Eds.): ICAISC 2016, Part I, LNAI 9692, pp. 758–769, 2016.
DOI: 10.1007/978-3-319-39378-0_65

introduced the basic principle about the passive gait, and obtained the dynamic model of the single support and the double support phase. A periodical walking for biped robot consists of the Double Support Phase (DSP) and Single Support Phase (SSP) [5], and the focus of this paper is on SSP only.

In this paper, the mathematical model of the 2 links biped robot is calculated using Lagrange equation in accordance with several assumptions. Then both PID controller and CTC are designed for performance and robustness comparison purposes. Finally, the trajectory is generated using cubic spline approach. Detailed simulation result has shown is each section.

2 Dynamic Modeling

The compass gait biped robot is defined as a mechanical system with 2 degree of freedom (DOF) that consists of two legs (stance and swing leg) and three joints (one ankle on each leg, and the hip).

As shown in Fig. 1, the parameter of the above robot are as follows:

m: mass of each leg
M: mass of hip
a: distance between the lower joint of leg and the center of mass
b: distance between the hip joint and the center of mass
q_1: angle of stance leg with respect to horizontal axis
q_2: angle of swing leg with respect to stance leg (relative angle)
l_1: length of the stance leg
l_2: length of the swing leg

Several assumptions has been made for the analysis of the dynamics of the compass robot [6]:

1. The dynamics of the biped robot is assumed at the sagittal plane
2. The model can be presents in $N - 1$ coordinates with N rigid links
3. The mass of each link is distributed evenly
4. The periodic walking phase can be divided into three parts, which are single support, double support and impact
5. The swing leg and the stance leg are at the same position at the start of walking, and is placed in front of the stance leg at the end of swing phase
6. The double support phase is an instant state after impact, where the impact phase is instantaneous too
7. No friction or sliding at the instant of impact
8. The relative angle α is defined as the angle between the stance leg and the swing leg.

Given $m = 10$ kg, M $= 30$ kg, $l_1 = l_2 = 1$ m, $a = b = 0.5$ m. The dynamic equation of biped robot can be obtained by Lagrange equation of motion, which is the most used method in calculating the dynamics of robot manipulators [7]. This paper only considers SSP for dynamic modeling, where the stance leg is in contact with the ground as shown in Fig. 1. Define the Lagrange of 2-DOF robot manipulator as

$$L(q, \dot{q}) = Ke(q, \dot{q}) - Kp(q) \tag{1}$$

where $Ke(q, \dot{q})$ and $Kp(q)$ are kinetic energy and potential energy respectively. Also notice that $q = [q_1 \quad q_2]^T$ and $\dot{q} = [q_1 \quad q_2]^T$ are the column vector that represent the angle and angular velocity for each point of mass. In accordance with function (1), the dynamic model of the 2-links compass gait biped robot can be derived by applying Euler-Lagrange equation

$$\frac{d}{dt}\left[\frac{\partial}{\partial q_i}L(q, \dot{q})\right] - \frac{\partial}{\partial q_i}L(q, \dot{q}) = \tau_i, \quad i = 1, 2 \tag{2}$$

where τ_i is the torque applied on each joint. According to Eqs. (1) and (2), the Lagrange equation can be presented more detailed as

$$\frac{d}{dt}\left[\frac{\partial}{\partial q_i}K_e(q, \dot{q})\right] - \frac{\partial}{\partial q_i}K_e(q, \dot{q}) + \frac{\partial}{\partial q_i}K_p(q, \dot{q}) = \tau_i \tag{3}$$

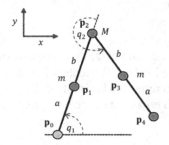

Fig. 1. Compass gait biped robot.

The energy lost during impact phase and the friction is ignored, the energy of biped robot only contains kinetic and potential energy. The potential energy can be calculated as:

$$Kp = \sum_{i=1}^{3} Kp_i = \sum_{i=1}^{3} m_i g Y_i \tag{4}$$

At the same time, the kinetic energy can be represented as

$$Ke = \sum_{i=1}^{3} Ke_i = \frac{1}{2}\sum_{i=1}^{3} m_i \left[\begin{matrix} \frac{d}{dx}X_i \\ \frac{d}{dx}Y_i \end{matrix}\right]^2 \tag{5}$$

where Kp_i and Ke_i represent the potential and kinetic energy of each point of mass, and X_i, Y_i are the horizontal and vertical coordinate respectively. By referencing the position of each point mass (P_1, P_2, P_3) shown on Fig. 1, the velocity (P_1, P_2, P_3) can be easily calculated (i.e. the derivative of the position). As a result, the kinetic energy for each point mass can be obtained respectively for each joint. Applying the energy of each joint into Eqs. (4) and (5), the equation of motion can be written as:

$$M\ddot{q} + C\dot{q} + g = \tau \tag{6}$$

where $M = \begin{bmatrix} M_{ij} \end{bmatrix} \in R^{2\times2}$ is the inertial matrix, $C = \begin{bmatrix} C_{ij} \end{bmatrix} \in R^{2\times2}$ is the centripetal vector of rotational forces, $g = \begin{bmatrix} g_i \end{bmatrix} \in R^2$ is the gravity vector and $\tau = \begin{bmatrix} \tau_i \end{bmatrix} \in R^2$ is the vector of applied torque. Assuming the input signal τ, known as the given torque, equals to zero ($u = \tau = 0$). The nonlinear equation of motion for the swing phase can be re-written in state space form

$$\begin{bmatrix} \dot{q} \\ \ddot{q} \end{bmatrix} = \begin{bmatrix} \dot{q} \\ M(q)^{-1}(\tau - C(q,\dot{q})\dot{q} - g(q)) \end{bmatrix}, x = \begin{bmatrix} q \\ \dot{q} \end{bmatrix} \tag{7}$$

The initial condition is set to $[q_1 = \frac{\pi}{2}, q_2 = \pi]$, which lead to the initial potential energy $K_p = 180.3$ J. Validation of the above nonlinear mathematical model can be simulated in Matlab platform.

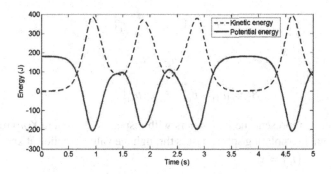

Fig. 2. Kinetic and potential energy (Color figure online).

As shown in Fig. 2, the potential energy (the red curve), decreases from 180.3 after 0.5 s due as a result of gravity. The lost potential energy is transferred into the kinetic energy, which triggers the increase of the kinetic energy (the blue dash). Figure 3 shows the total energy remains constant (approximate 180.3 J) during the simulation period,

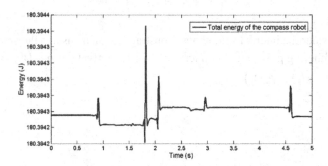

Fig. 3. Total energy of the compass robot (Color figure online).

which equals to the initial potential energy value. Both simulation results validate the correctness of the dynamic model from Lagrange equation.

3   Trajectory Planning

Suppose the robot's swing foot pass through the following sets of points represented in Cartesian Space:

The problem can be separated into two parts: $T \sim X$ and $T \sim Y$.

Considering the relationship between $T(s)$ and $X(m)$, a cubic polynomial $p(t)$ is used to describe the position with time t as the independent variable

$$p_k(t_k) = a_{k1} + a_{k2}t_k + a_{k3}t_k^2 + a_{k4}t_k^3 \tag{8}$$

where $k = 1, 2, 3, 4$ respectively.

Furthermore, define T_k and A_k as:

$$T_k = \begin{bmatrix} 1 & t_k & t_k^2 & t_k^3 \end{bmatrix}$$

$$A_k = \begin{bmatrix} a_{k1} & a_{k2} & a_{k3} & a_{k4} \end{bmatrix}^T$$

$$B_k = \begin{bmatrix} b_{k1} & b_{k2} & b_{k3} & b_{k4} \end{bmatrix}^T \tag{9}$$

where A_k and B_k represent the parameters with respect to $X(m)$ and $Y(m)$ respectively. Considering an interpolating spline passes through the value supplied at knots, Exterior: $p_1(t_1) = x_1$, $p_{k-1}(t_k) = x_k$

Interior: $p_{k-1}(t_k) = x_k = p_k(t_k)$. The trajectory can be easily represented as

$$\begin{cases} T_1 * A_1 = x_1 \\ T_2 * A_1 = x_2 \\ T_2 * A_2 = x_2 \\ T_3 * A_2 = x_3 \\ T_3 * A_3 = x_3 \\ T_4 * A_3 = x_4 \end{cases} \tag{10}$$

Also consider the internal smoothness constrains, which ensures the smoothness of the two neighboring polynomial at interior knots, 1st derivative: $\dot{p}_{k-1}(t_k) = \dot{p}_k(t_k)$ 2nd derivative: $\ddot{p}_{k-1}(t_k) = \ddot{p}_k(t_k)$

$$\begin{cases} (T_2 * A_1) = (T_2 * A_2) \\ \left(T_2 * A_1\right) = \left(T_2 * A_2\right) \\ (T_3 * A_2) = (T_3 * A_3) \\ (T_3 * A_2) = (T_3 * A_3) \end{cases} \tag{11}$$

The boundary conditions required the derivatives at the two exterior knots t_1 and t_4 to be zero:

$$\begin{cases} (T_1 * A_1) = 0 \\ (T_4 * A_3) = 0 \end{cases} \tag{12}$$

The parameters can be obtained by solving the above functions, which yields the trajectory function about movement in horizontal direction and vertical direction. Each function represents the trajectory of the swing leg during the specific period that given in Table 1.

Table 1. Two sets of via points

T(s)	X(m)	Y(m)
0	0.05	0
0.3	0.15	0.2
0.7	0.4	0.2
1	0.5	0

$$\begin{cases} x_1 = 0.05 + 1.4461t^2 - 1.1166t^3 \\ x_2 = 0.0397 + 0.1029t + 1.1029t^2 - 0.7353t^3 \\ x_3 = 0.1705 - 0.4575t + 1.9036t^2 - 1.1166t^3 \\ \\ y_1 = 4.2424t^2 - 6.7340t^3 \\ y_2 = -0.1818 + 1.8182t - 1.8182t^2 \\ y_3 = -2.4916 + 11.7172t - 15.9596t^2 + 6.7340t^3 \end{cases} \tag{13}$$

As shown in Fig. 4, the swing leg moved one step in one second after being picked up and then put down. The next step is to obtain the desired joint velocity and acceleration using inverse kinematics approach. Given the forwards kinematic map is

$$X = f(q) = \begin{bmatrix} l_1 \cos\left(q_1\right) + l_2 \cos\left(q_1 + q_2\right) \\ l_1 \sin\left(q_1\right) + l_2 \sin\left(q_1 + q_2\right) \end{bmatrix} \tag{14}$$

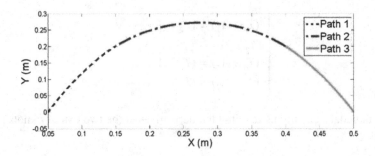

Fig. 4. Trajectory of swing leg in Cartesian space (Color figure online).

By referencing the triangular relationship, the relative joint angle can be obtained by

$$q_1 = \arctan(y/x) - \arcsin(\frac{l_2\sin(q_2)}{X})$$

$$q_2 = \arccos\left(\frac{X^2 - l_1^2 - l_2^2}{2l_1 l_2}\right) \tag{15}$$

The velocity kinematics are found by differentiating the forwards kinematic map

$$\frac{dX}{dt} = \frac{df(q)}{dq}\frac{dq}{dt}$$

$$\dot{X} = J(q)\dot{q} \tag{16}$$

where

$$J(q) = \left[\left[\begin{array}{cc} \dfrac{df_1(q)}{dq_1} & \dfrac{df_1(q)}{dq_2} \\ \dfrac{df_2(q)}{dq_1} & \dfrac{df_2(q)}{dq_2} \end{array}\right]\right] \tag{17}$$

known as Jacobian matrix. As a result, the demanded joint velocity can be calculated by

$$\dot{q} = J(q)^{-1}\dot{X} \tag{18}$$

Similarly, the acceleration kinematics are obtained

$$\ddot{q} = J(q)^{-1}\ddot{X} + J(q)^{-1}J(q) \tag{19}$$

4   Controller Design

4.1   PID Controller Design

The nonlinear dynamic model obtained in Sect. 2 is inherently unstable. Thus control scheme is needed to track the desired trajectory. There are many approaches to control the biped robot. The most common and simple way is the PID controller, which converts the problem into the design of controller for swing leg and the design of controller for stance leg. PID controller is designed for the stance leg and swing leg respectively in accordance with the non-linear compass gait dynamics that has been described in Sect. 2. Considering the swing leg first, the non-linear model can be represented as

$$mb^2\ddot{q} - mgbsin(q) = \tau \tag{20}$$

The 2nd order ordinary differential equation (ODE) can be written as

$$mb^2\Delta\ddot{q} - mgbcos(q^*)\Delta q = \Delta\tau \tag{21}$$

This can be linearized about the vertical downwards for the swing leg $(q^* = [\pi, 0], \ \tau^* = 0)$ to produce a linear ODE of the form

$$\Delta\ddot{q} - \frac{mgbcos(q^*)}{mb^2}\Delta q = \frac{1}{mb^2}\Delta\tau \tag{22}$$

Using a PID controller for the swing leg

$$\ddot{q} + \frac{g}{b}q = \frac{1}{mb^2}\left(k_p e + k_I \int e + k_D \dot{e}\right) \tag{23}$$

where $e = r - y$ and r is the reference trajectory, the close loop ODE can be written as

$$\dddot{q} + \frac{k_D}{mb^2}\ddot{q} + \left(\frac{g}{b} + \frac{k_p}{mb^2}\right)\dot{q} + \frac{k_I}{mb^2}q = \frac{1}{mb^2}\left(k_I r + k_p \dot{r}\right) \tag{24}$$

For stability, k_p must bigger than mgb although the system is not expected to operate outside the design region. The relatively short time constant requires distinct poles so that parameters variation does not introduce oscillations in the response. Three poles are chosen at $s = -20$, $s = -25$, $s = -30$ (time constant $T = 0.05, 0.04, 0.033$). This produces a desired equation of the form $s^3 + 75s^2 + 1850s + 15000$. Comparing the close loop ODE, the PID gains for swing leg can be calculated as: $k_p = 4575$, $k_I = 37500$, $k_D = 187.5$.

PID controller gains for the stance leg can be calculated using the same method above. The generated path from Sect. 3 can be implemented into the system as the input signal. Simulation results have shown below (Fig. 5)

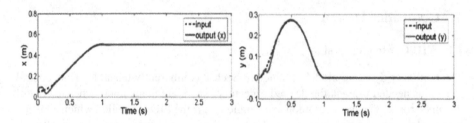

Fig. 5. System response in and axis x and y axis (Color figure online)

Simulation results shows that the maximum error at the beginning is approximate 0.04 m and the settling time is 0.25 s, which basically fulfills the demand. However, that the error can be found in the whole walking period in Cartesian space and drop to zero after 1.5 s, which means the controller is not perfect. Improvements need to be made to eliminate the tracking error.

4.2 Computed Torque Control

Although many advanced control scheme like Sliding Model Robust Control [8] or Neural Network [9] have been proposes, the Computed Torque Control (CTC) is still an effective and widely used approach to control robotic systems, which provides a feed forward compensator to offset the nonlinear part of the system. CTC is also an application of feedback linearization of non-linear systems, which calculate how much torque is needed for each joint to track the reference signal. Considering the dynamic Eq. (6) on Sect. 2, the joint vector $q \in R^2$ is a column vector contains two angles for four joints respectively. The input signal $\tau \in R^2$ is also a column vector, which stores the energy needed for each joint to follow the given trajectory. Suppose that the desired trajectory $q_d(t)$ has been obtained by inverse kinematics, where $q_d(t)$ is the function of time. The tracking error can be defined as

$$e(t) = q_d(t) - q(t) \qquad (25)$$

where $q(t)$ is the feedback signal from the robotic system. Substituting the angular acceleration into Eq. (6) yields

$$\ddot{e} = u = q_d + M^{-1}(C\dot{q} + g - \tau) \qquad (26)$$

where $u \in R^2$ is defined as a column vector that represents the feedback signal for each joints i.e. the input signal. Now, defining the state, x, as

$$x = \begin{bmatrix} e \\ \dot{e} \end{bmatrix} \qquad (27)$$

The tracking error dynamics can be written as

$$\frac{d}{dt}\begin{bmatrix} e \\ \dot{e} \end{bmatrix} = \begin{bmatrix} 0 & I \\ 0 & 0 \end{bmatrix}\begin{bmatrix} e \\ \dot{e} \end{bmatrix} + \begin{bmatrix} 0 \\ I \end{bmatrix}u \qquad (28)$$

It is clear that Eq. (28) is a linear error system, where u is the control input. The error $e \in R^2$ is a column vector. According to the feedback linearizing Eq. (26), the control torque can be derived by

$$\tau = M(q_d - u) + (C\dot{q} + g) \qquad (29)$$

Figure 6 shows the basic structure of CTC. The complex nonlinear control problem is transformed to a simple linear system problem. The input signal for nonlinear part is $q_d - u$, where $u(t)$ is the "error control" that control the error dynamics determined by the error of joint angle $q_e(t)$ and joint angular velocity $q_e(t)$, and q_d is the reference signal with respect to angular acceleration. The error of angle and angular velocity is defined as

$$q_e(t) = q_d(t) - q(t)$$

$$q_e(t) = q_d(t) - \dot{q}(t) \qquad (30)$$

where $q_d(t)$ and $q_d(t)$ are the reference signal obtained by the joint position in 2-D space to calculate the corresponding angle and angular velocity in Cartesian space. This method is called Inverse Kinematics Approach. The outer loop feedback control can be realized by adding a proportional and derivative (PD) controller into the system, where the input signal can be expressed as

$$u = -K_P e - K_D \dot{e} \qquad (31)$$

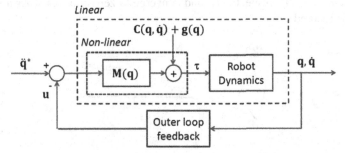

Fig. 6. Computed torque control structure

As a result, the close loop error dynamics are

$$\ddot{e} + K_P e + K_D \dot{e} = 0 \qquad (32)$$

where $K_D = diag[K_{Di}]$ and $K_P = diag[K_{Pj}]$. In order to make the error system stable, the controller gains K_P and K_D must be positive (i.e. $K_{Di} > 0$ *and* $K_{Pj} > 0$), which guarantees that the poles are at left half plane. Normally, the PD gains are chosen to guarantee that the system has no oscillation and overshoot with fast response, which requires a critical damping system ($\zeta = 1$). This gives the final representation of K_D and K_P

$$K_D = diag\left[2\omega_n\right]$$

$$K_P = diag\left[\omega_n^2\right]$$

The natural frequency is supposed to be reasonably large to get a fast response, however it cannot be too large due to the high frequency disturbance. Here, selecting repeated poles to ensure the required properties that $P_1 = P_2 = -25$.

This guarantees that the system response is relatively fast with no oscillation. The PD gain K_D and K_P can be calculated as $K_P = 625$ and $K_D = 50$ (Fig. 7).

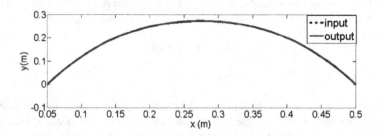

Fig. 7. Trajectory tracking for CTC (Color figure online)

When applied to the system, CTC gives an almost non-error response in Cartesian Space. Indicated in Fig. 8 that the absolute value of the maximum error of x and y are $2 * 10^{-4}$ and $2 * 10^{-3}$ respectively, and converge to zero after 0.4 s. As a result, the error can be ignored.

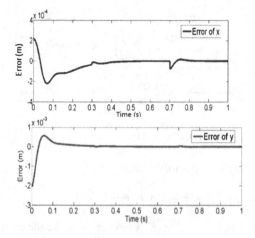

Fig. 8. Tracking error

5 Conclusion

In this paper a compass gait biped robot dynamic system is developed. The proposed mathematical model is obtained using Lagrange equation in Cartesian space. Both PID and CTC controller have their own characteristics in information obtaining, designing and performance. While designing a PID controller, the number of parameters need to be calculated depends on how much legs the system has, which means the more legs the robot has the more PID controller are needed. Two independent PID controller need to be designed in this case for stance leg and swing leg collecting less information. However, this complex procedure can be simplified by CTC controller. CTC controller can be applied in any circumstance for any number of legs, which means one CTC controller can be used for amount of legs. In this case, only one set of parameters are needed for both stance and swing leg collecting more information. Compared to PID controller, CTC respond faster and produces negligible error. Another advantage is that CTC is designed globally while PID controller is designed locally. As a result, CTC performed better than PID control. However, the control gains for both PID and CTC are very high and lead to an extremely high needed-torque, which is consequently unrealistic in real robot. Thus, and alternative control method should be considered in future works which involve an impulsive toe-off or leg extension at the beginning of swing phase.

References

1. Goswami, A., Espiau, B., Keramane, A.: Limit cycle and their stability in a passive bipedal gait. In: IEEE International Conference on Robotics and Automation, pp. 246–251. IEEE Press, Norway (1996)
2. McGeer, Tad: Passive dynamic walking. Int. J. Robot. Res. **9**(2), 62–82 (1990)
3. HC, Steven, Ruina, A., Tedrake, R., Wisse, M.: Effectient bipedal robots based on passive dynamic walkers. J. Sci. **307**, 1082–1085 (2005)
4. Manchester, I.R., Mettin, U., Iida, F., Tedrake, R.: Stable dynamic walking over uneven terrain. Int. J. Robot. Res. **30**(3), 265–279 (2011)
5. Dehghani, R., Fattah, A., Abedi, E.: Cyclic gait planning and control of a five-link biped robot with four actuators during single support and double support phase. Multibody Syst. Dyn. **33**, 389–411 (2015)
6. Westervelt, E.R., Grizzle, J.W., Chevallereau, C., Choi, J.H., Morris, B.: Feedback Control of Dynamic Bipedal Robot Locomotion. Tayler & Francis/CRC, Boca Raton (2007)
7. Dingguo, Zhang: The lagrange dynamic equation of multi-rigidbody systems with external shocks. J. Appl. Math. Mech. **17**, 589–595 (1996)
8. Tzafestas, S., Raibert, M., Tzafestas, C.: Robust sliding-mode control applied to a 5-link biped robot. J. Intell. Robot. Syst. **15**, 67–133 (1996)
9. Manoopong, P., Geng, T., Kulvicius, T., Porr, B., Worgotter, F.: Adaptive, fast walking in a biped robot under neuronal control and learning. Publ. Libr. Sci. Comput. Biol. **3**(9), e191 (2007)

H_∞ Optimal Actuator and Sensor Placement for Linear Systems

Yijin Zhao$^{(\boxtimes)}$

Department of Aeronautics, Imperial College London, London, UK
Yijin.zhao@hotmail.com

Abstract. Optimizing the placement of actuators and sensors for the control and monitoring tasks is one of the most important and challenging research topics in the comprehensive aircraft control systems. This paper proposes a new way to address this issue, in which Heat and Wave Equation discretized by the Finite Differential Method (FDM) were used to describe the inputs/outputs propagation mode for control systems. By utilizing a robust controller design to the models, the complicated optimal actuator and sensor placement problem can be transformed to a judgement on specific characteristics. The feedback controller was designed based on the H_∞ Optimal Control Principles, where the external input w is considered to be the perturbation. The optimal placement is able to be obtained at the place with the best performed controller. The simulation results show that it is reasonable to solve the actuator and sensor placement optimization problem using the proposed method and the results for the two models shared an agreeable trend. Therefore, the process of optimizing the placement of sensors and actuators for control and monitoring system could serve as a natural extension to other structures.

Keywords: Optimal placement · Sensor and actuator · H_∞ optimal control · H_∞ norm · Finite Differential Method (FDM)

1 Introduction

Finding the best position of sensors and actuators to obtain a better control result with the least numbers is one of the most important parts in the field of the modern control. The unsuitable placement of sensors may lead to an accuracy reduction of sensing, while the unsuitable placement of actuators may generate less efficient control. Tremendous work has been done by the researches of the optimal sensor and actuator placement since 1970s. Yu and Seinfeld determined the observability to optimal sensor placement [1]. After that, researchers such as Kumar and Seinfeld [2] and Morari and O'Dowd in 1980 [3] paid more attention on how to minimize estimated error and find the optimal location for sensors. The Optimal Actuator Placement was first proposed by Arbel [4], who measured the controllability of Partial Differential Equation (PDE) models with linear controllers. In order to minimize the cost on system, S. S. Rao introduced the Genetic Algorithms to the research of the optimal controller gain and actuator location [5].

As the control system design of aircraft is becoming a challenge, some researches about optimal sensor and actuator placement problem started to focus on aircraft systems

© Springer International Publishing Switzerland 2016
L. Rutkowski et al. (Eds.): ICAISC 2016, Part I, LNAI 9692, pp. 770–781, 2016.
DOI: 10.1007/978-3-319-39378-0_66

especially. Researchers from Vienna University of Technology minimized the sensor positioning based on the actuator and considered the different mass in the controller design for BWB passenger aircraft with respect to the size of actuators, which indicated that the wingtip is a suited place to put actuator and sensor [6]. K. B. Lim from NASA Langley Research Center used controllability and observability of the system as an appropriate indicator to measure the number and optimal locations of actuators and sensors for large flexible structures [7].

With the development of modern control theory, Robust Control is involved in this area. K. Chen and C. W. Rowley implemented linear Ginzburg-Landau model and designed an H_2 optimal controller to find the optimal actuator and sensor placement by minimizing H_2 norm [8]. They found that adding the number of sensors and actuators may not significantly increase the performance of the controller, while a suitable place-ment of actuators or sensors may greatly improve the result. Afterwards, they also used the eigenvalue sensitivity analysis to predict the performance of controllers when actu-ators and sensors are collocated [9]. M. Pfister, and P. Wolfrum presented two algorithms to solve the sensor and actuator placement problem in linear systems using both H_∞ and H_2 optimization and then relaxed the ℓ_0 norm to a weighted ℓ_1 norm [10]. S. Pequito and S. Kar addressed minimizing the number of required inputs to make sure the character-istics of a Linear Time Invariant (LTI) system satisfied the control principles [11]. The aim of optimizing actuator location is to find the best position where the system could provide the best attenuation in the case with the worst disturbance. D. Kasinathan and K. Morris also carried out a future topic on how to approximate the convergence in a linear quadratic case when calculating the optimal actuator location [12].

In this paper, the author proposed a new methodology to solve the placement optimization problem. Heat Equation and Wave Equation were used to simplify the model and the Linear PDE could be derived from physical principles [13]. The Finite Differential Method (FDM) [14] was used to discretize the PDEs. When designing the robust controllers, H_∞ optimal control theory was used, which combines the advan-tages of classical control theory and balances the trade-off between its performance and robustness. Compared to the H_2 optimization method used before, H_∞ optimal control gives less limitation. The aim of H_∞ optimal control was to minimize the closed-loop norm γ_∞ of the system between external inputs w and outputs z.

2 The Proposed Methodologies

2.1 Partial Differential Equation (PDE)

Considering the propagation mode satisfied the Heat Equation for an Lm long rod or beam with a temperature gradient at the end [15].

$$\frac{\partial x(s,t)}{\partial t} = \alpha \frac{\partial^2 x(s,t)}{\partial s^2}, 0 \leq s \leq L, t \geq 0 \tag{1}$$

where x is the vector of temperature, s is the vector of position, α is a constant coefficient. The Initial Condition (IC) is the initial temperature of the rod. The Boundary Condition (BC) is the affected temperature of the rod. Assuming there is a step input at the end of the rod, then the IC and BC is

$$IC : x(s,0) = 0, \ BC : \begin{cases} x(0,t) = 0 \\ x(L,t) = u(t) = \begin{cases} 0, t < 0 \\ u_L, t \geq 0 \end{cases} \end{cases} \tag{2}$$

The one Dimensional Wave Equation with damping in PDE form [16] is

$$\frac{\partial^2 x(s,t)}{\partial t^2} = c^2 \frac{\partial^2 x(s,t)}{\partial s^2} - 2\lambda \frac{\partial x(s,t)}{\partial t}, 0 \leq s \leq L, t \geq 0 \tag{3}$$

where x is the vector of wave, s is the vector of position, c is the propagation speed of the wave and λ is the damping coefficient. The damping term make sure the system is stable. Assuming that there is an impulse input at the end of the rope, then the IC and BC is

$$IC : \begin{cases} x(s,0) = 0 \\ \frac{\partial x(s,0)}{\partial t} = 0 \end{cases}, \ BC : \begin{cases} x(0,t) = 0 \\ x(L,t) = u(t) = \begin{cases} 0, t \neq 0 \\ u_L, t = 0 \end{cases} \end{cases} \tag{4}$$

2.2 Finite Differential Method (FDM)

The Finite Difference Method involves using discrete approximations [17]. Here are two way to discretize.

Fully-Discretized Method. Discretized the Heat Equation both in time and space by using the Forward Time Central Space (FTCS) method and discretized the Wave Equation by the Second Order Central Difference.

$$\frac{x_i^{j+1} - x_i^j}{\Delta t} = \alpha \frac{x_{i+1}^j - 2x_i^j + x_{i-1}^j}{\Delta s^2} \tag{5}$$

$$\frac{x_i^{j+1} - 2x_i^j + x_i^{j-1}}{\Delta t^2} = c^2 \frac{x_{i+1}^j - 2x_i^j + x_{i-1}^j}{\Delta s^2} - 2\lambda \frac{x_i^j - x_i^{j-1}}{\Delta t} \tag{6}$$

where i is the mesh point in space and j is the mesh point in time. Letting $r = \frac{\alpha \Delta t}{\Delta s^2}$ for Heat Equation, while $r = \frac{c^2 \Delta t^2}{\Delta s^2}$ for Wave Equation, and rearranging formulas (5) and (6) could get the iteration formulas (7) and (8) respectively.

$$x_i^{j+1} = rx_{i+1}^j + (1 - 2r)x_i^j + rx_{i-1}^j \tag{7}$$

$$x_i^{j+1} = r\left(x_{i+1}^j + x_{i-1}^j\right) + 2(1 - r)x_i^j + x_i^{j-1} - 2\lambda\Delta t(x_i^j + x_i^{j-1}) \tag{8}$$

Therefore the discretized equations could be written in a matrix form

$$x^{j+1} = Ax^j \tag{9}$$

Semi-Discretized Method. Discretized the whole rod into N points, $\Delta s = L/(N-1)$, so $n = 0, 1 \cdots N - 1$.

Rewrite the open-loop system in state space form by using Semi-discretized Method

$$\begin{cases} \frac{dx}{dt} = Ax + Bu \\ y = Cx + Du \end{cases} \tag{10}$$

Assuming the external input and control input are at the first and the last node separately, $u = [x((N-1)\Delta s, t) \quad x(0, t)]^T = [w(t) \quad u(t)]^T$.

For Heat Equation, $x = [\hat{x}^T]^T = [x(\Delta s, t) \quad \cdots \quad x((N-2)\Delta s, t)]^T \in R^{N-2}$, while for Wave Equation, the state vector $x = [\hat{x}^T \quad \dot{\hat{x}}^T]^T \in R^{(N-2)*2}$.

Used the Second Order Central Difference method as the formula (11) to discretized the PDEs, we could write all the A, B, C, D matrices.

$$\left.\frac{\partial^2 x}{\partial s^2}\right|_{s=n\Delta s} = \frac{x((n+1)\Delta s, t) - 2x(n\Delta s, t) + x((n-1)\Delta s, t)}{\Delta s^2} \tag{11}$$

2.3 H_∞ Optimal Control Theory

A general H_∞ feedback control system, shown as Fig. 1 [18], could be rearranged as a lower Linear Fractional Transformation (LFT): u is control inputs, y is measured outputs, w is all external inputs including disturbances or noise and z is outputs or error signals.

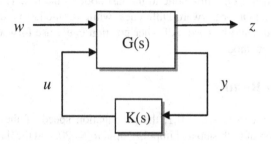

Fig. 1. The configuration of a general H_∞ control problem

The system could be written as the equations below

$$\left\{ \begin{bmatrix} z \\ y \end{bmatrix} = \begin{bmatrix} G_{11} & G_{12} \\ G_{21} & G_{22} \end{bmatrix} \begin{bmatrix} w \\ u \end{bmatrix} \right. \\ u = Ky \tag{12}$$

The transfer function $F(G, K)$ from external inputs w to error signals z shown as formula (13) could be derived [19].

$$F(G, K) = G_{11} + G_{12}K(I - G_{22}K)^{-1}G_{21} \tag{13}$$

The H_∞ norm of the system represents the worst case or the largest possible gain. It is defined as [18, 19]

$$\gamma = \|F(G, K)\|_\infty = sup\bar{\sigma}(F(G, K)(jw)) \tag{14}$$

where $\bar{\sigma}$ is the maximum singular value of the matrix $F(G, K)(j\omega)$ at each frequency.

The H_∞ Optimal Control is to find the stabilizing controller $K(s)$ to minimize the H_∞ norm of the closed-loop system.

2.4 H_∞ Optimal Feedback System

Using H_∞ optimal theory to create a closed-loop system as formula (15).

$$\begin{cases} \dot{x}(t) = Ax(t) + B_1w(t) + B_2u(t) \\ z(t) = C_1x(t) + D_{11}w(t) + D_{12}u(t) \\ y(t) = C_2x(t) + D_{21}w(t) + D_{22}u(t) \end{cases} \tag{15}$$

First, setting $z = \begin{bmatrix} \hat{x}^T & r \cdot u \end{bmatrix}^T$ and $y = [\hat{x}^T]$ to create an H_∞ optimal controller $K(s)$. Then, changing error signals to $z = [\hat{x}^T]$ to get a new closed-loop system.

Optimal Sensor Placement. Fixing the control input and external input at different nodes of the rod. Then changing the measured outputs from the state of all points to just one point on the rod, that means $y = [x(i \cdot \Delta s, t)]$ and $i = 1, 2, \cdots, N - 2$. It needs to be noted that the outputs cannot be at the same position as the inputs.

Optimal Actuator Placement. Fixing the measured outputs $y = [\hat{x}^T]$. Then, changing the control input u from the first node to the last node of the rod. The first node could only use the Second Order Forward Difference, while for the last node, only Backward Difference method could be used. All other position could use forward, backward and central difference method.

3   Simulation Results

Assuming that the constant $\alpha = 0.1$, the propagation speed of the wave $c = 1$, the boundary condition of both step and impulse input $u_L = 20$, and the damping coefficient is $\lambda = 1$.

3.1   FDM

The differential results of the open-loop system by using Fully-discretized method is shown in Fig. 2. The result of Fully-discretized method includes the position of inputs, while the results by using Semi-discretized method excludes.

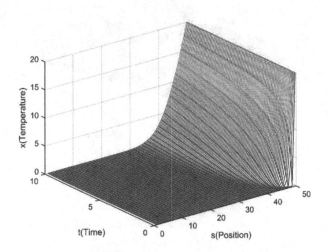

Fig. 2. The result of Fully-discretized Heat Equation

3.2 H_∞ Optimal Control System

After adding the H_∞ Controller, the relationship of r and the norm of the closed-loop system is showed in Fig. 3. Comparing the results with the open-loop system, it is clear that the closed-loop norm γ_{closed} converges to the open-loop norm γ_{open} when r is big

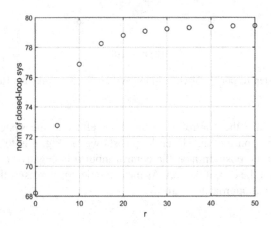

Fig. 3. The closed-loop norm γ_{closed} when r increases for Heat Equation

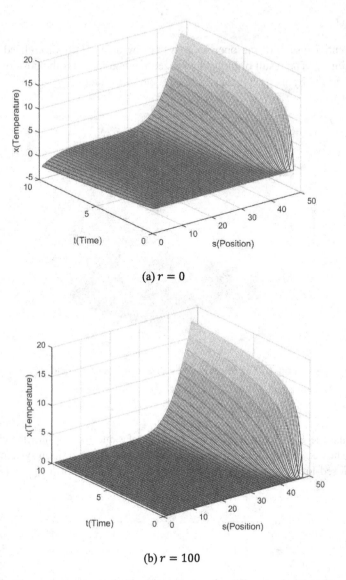

(a) $r = 0$

(b) $r = 100$

Fig. 4. The step responses of closed-loop system for different r for Heat Equation

enough, which means the controller makes little effect to the system. For different
r values, the step response of the closed-loop is showed in Fig. 4(a) to (b). When $r = 0$,
the temperature at the position near the control input u is negative in order to control
the external noise at the end of the rod. As the coefficient r increases, the absolute value
becomes smaller and approaches zero.

3.3   Optimal Placement of Sensor or Actuator

In order to find the optimal sensor placement, the norm of closed-loop system γ_{closed} with fixed control input and changing measured output is represented in Fig. 5. The gain of the controller improves a little as the sensor moving towards the external noise.

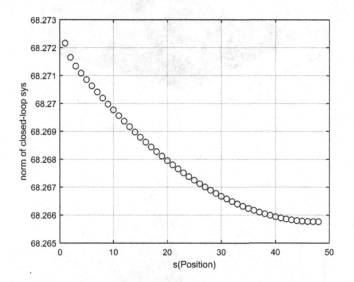

Fig. 5. The norm of closed-loop system as i moving for Heat Equation

This is also proved in Fig. 6, the step responses when i is changing. As i moves, the temperature at the position near the control input increases in negative amount, because when output y moves towards w with positive temperature, it needs to increase in negative amount for the purpose of controlling the positive noise and minimizing the errors.

For the Wave Equation, compared the results shown in Fig. 7, the impulse responses at the beginning part of the rope reacts faster when i is larger, which also proved the conclusion got from the Heat Equation as well.

In order to find the optimal actuator placement, fixed the measured outputs $y = [\hat{x}^T]$ and moved the control input u from the first node to the end of the rod. Placing the actuator at the beginning of the rope may generate a better result because of its smaller γ_{closed}.

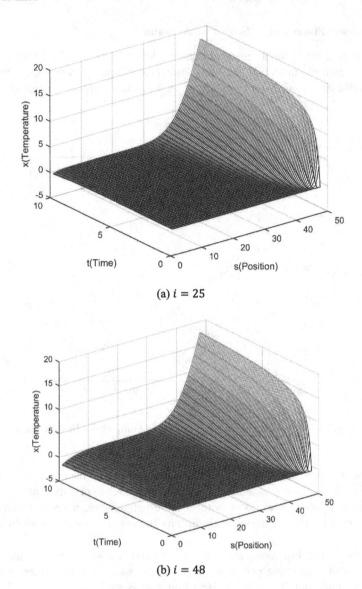

(a) $i = 25$

(b) $i = 48$

Fig. 6. The step responses of closed-loop system as i moving for Heat Equation

3.4 Multiple Actuator or Sensors Problem

For one sensor problem, it may lose its detectability at some position. Thus, the situation with two sensors could be considered. On the other hand, because it is not stabilizable in some cases by only using one actuator, which means it's not stable by using only one actuator, the cases with two actuators could be also discussed.

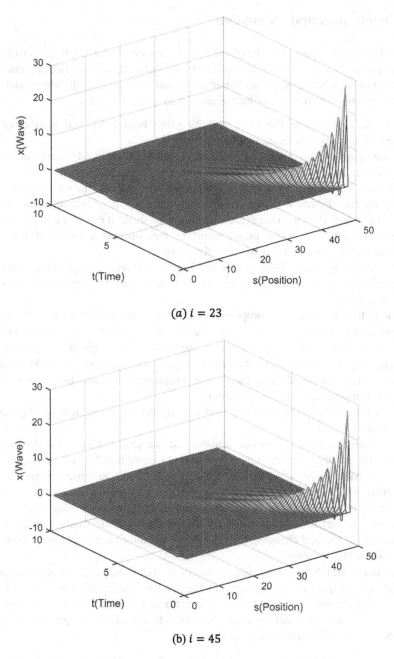

(a) $i = 23$

(b) $i = 45$

Fig. 7. The impulse responses as i moving for Wave Equation with Damping

4 Conclusions and Discussion

On the issue about optimizing the placement of sensor and actuator, there is still a long way to go. In this paper, the author started from the one dimension Heat Equation and Wave Equation which gave an accordant result and received the following conclusions and discussions which may produce extension to other structures.

- It could approximate the PDE well by using both Fully and Semi-discretized method, although there are numerical errors.

    When using the derivation of Finite Differential Method (FDM) to approximate the numerical solutions of PDE, the existing of numerical errors makes the result different. The error term is proportional to the time step and the square of the space step for Heat Equation, while proportional to the square of both the time step and the space step. Although the error is already very small, it can't be ignored. There is another limitation that it might result in the unstable solution of the Fully-discretized method causing by large time step.

- The results by using Heat and Wave Equation shared an agreeable trend. The consequence of H_∞ optimal control, which measured by H_∞ norm, declines when r is increasing.

    One of the most important properties to measure in the performance of H_∞ optimal closed-loop system is its H_∞ norm. The closed-loop norm γ_{closed} is approximating the open-loop norm γ_{open} when r is approaching the infinite. Because as r is increasing, which will make the control input u become very small, the controller could produce little effect on the system. Therefore, the closed-loop system is very much similar to an open-loop system.

- The optimal placement for sensor and actuator can be determined by H_∞ Optimal Control.

    Assuming that there is only one actuator and one sensor. Fixing u at the first node and changing the position of measured output y could find the optimal placement of sensor. As y moves towards w at the end of the rod, the norm becomes slightly smaller, which means the sensor could have a better performance on detecting the external inputs. The state of each position gives a more obvious reaction when output y moves towards the external disturbance w. Then, fixing u at the second node of the rod and changing the position of y could find the optimal placement of sensor in this situation.

    In order to find the optimal actuator placement, fixing the measured outputs $y = [\hat{x}^T]$ and then changing the control input u. The result is smaller when the control input u is at the first node than in other cases, which gives a better location of the actuator.

- More sensors and actuators could be added to overcome the problem of losing detectability and stabilizability in some cases.

Acknowledgement. I would like to express my great appreciation to my supervisor, Dr. Eric Kerrigan from Department of Aeronautics, Imperial College London, for his guidance and constructive advice throughout the project.

References

1. Yu, T.K., Seinfeld, J.H.: Observability and optimal measurement location in linear distributed parameter systems. Int. J. Control **18**(4), 785–799 (1973)
2. Kumar, S., Seinfeld, J.H.: Optimal location of measurements for distributed parameter estimation. IEEE Trans. Autom. Control **AC-23**, 690–698 (1978)
3. Morari, M., O'Dowd, M.J.: Optimal sensor location in the presence of nonstationary noise. Automatica **16**, 463–480 (1980)
4. Arbel, A.: Controllability measures and actuator placement in oscillatory systems. Int. J. Control **33**(3), 565–574 (1981)
5. Rao, S.S., Pan, T.S., Venkayya, V.B.: Optimal placement of actuators in actively controlled structures using genetic algorithms. Am. Inst. Aeronaut. Astronaut. J. **29**(6), 942–943 (1991)
6. Schirrer, A., Westermayer, C., Hemedi, M., Kozek, M.: Actuator and sensor positioning optimization in control design for a large BWB passenger aircraft. ISRN Mech. Eng., Article ID 635815 (2011)
7. Lim, K.B.: Method for optimal actuator and sensor placement for large flexible structures. J. Guidance, Control Dyn. **15**, 49–57 (1992)
8. Chen, K.K., Rowley, C.W.: H_2 Optimal actuator and sensor placement in the linearised complex Ginzburg-Landau system, J. Fluid Mech. **681**, 241–260 (2011)
9. Chen, K.K., Rowley, C.W.: Fluid flow control applications of H_2 optimal actuator and sensor placement. In: American Control Conference, pp. 4044–4049 (2014)
10. Munz, U., Pfister, M., Wolfrum, P.: Sensor and actuator placement for linear systems based on H_2 and H_∞ optimization. IEEE Trans. Autom. Control, **59**(11), 2984–2989 (2014)
11. Pequito, S., Kar, S., Aguiar, A.P.: A structured systems approach for optimal actuator-sensor placement in linear time-invariant systems. In: American Control Conference, pp. 6108–6113 (2013)
12. Kasinathan, D. Morris, K.: H_∞-optimal actuator location. IEEE Trans. Autom. Control, **58**(10), 2522–2535 (2013)
13. Ce, S.: The achievement of heat conduction equation finite difference method by MATLAB. J. Xianyang Normal Univ. **24**(4), 27–29 (2009)
14. Bensoussan, A., Prato, G.D., Delfour, M.C., Mitter, S.K.: Representation and Control Of Infinite Dimensional Systems, vol. 1. Birkhauser Boston Inc., Boston (1992)
15. Stephen, B.: Matrices, polynomials, and linear time-invariant systems. IEEE Trans. Autom. Control **18**, 1–10 (1973)
16. Carcione, J.M.: The wave equation in generalized coordinates. Geophysics **59**, 1911–1919 (1994)
17. Morton, K.W., Mayers, D.F.: Numerical Solution of Partial Differential Equation. Combridge University Press, Cambridge (1994)
18. Barmish, B.R.: New Tools for Robustness of Linear Systems. Macmillan Publishing Company, New York (1992)
19. Skogestad, S., Postlethwaite, I.: Multivariable Feedback Control: Theory and Design, 2nd edn. Wiley, Chichester (2005)

Author Index